Tome of Terror

Horror Films of the Silent Era

Tome of Terror Horror Films of the Silent Era

(1895-1929)

by Christopher Workman and Troy Howarth

Midnight Marquee Press, Inc.
Baltimore, Maryland, USA; London, UK

Acknowledgments

The authors would like to thank the following people for their contributions to and/or support of *Tome of Terror*: Gary Svehla, whose acceptance and support of the project has made its publication a reality; Mark Ege, whose tireless editorial efforts helped shape the individual reviews as well as the book as a whole; the Workman and Howarth families, without whose support the series could not have been written; Steve Fenton, for graciously donating many images from his archive; August Ragone, author of *Eiji Tsuburaya: Master of Monsters*; Jonathan Rigby, author of *English Gothic: A Century of Horror Films*; Matthew E. Banks, Misty Sizemore Beeson, Simon Bousfield, Bryan Brassfield, Diana Sue Brassfield, Rod Burch, Keith A. Burrows, Sandy Crabtree Brogdon, Tony Caldwell, James K. Chambliss, Samantha Clark, Horace Cordier, Luigi Cozzi, Harvey Click, Bruce Crelin, Paul Willetts Crowley, Patrick DeBlasi, Simon Frisby, Jennifer Gantner, Angel Haggerty, Lori Slusher Herriman, Salem Kapsaski, Mike Kenny, Steve Kirkham, Rick Lamb, Brian Lawson, Sasha Levine, Debra Nelson Little, Samantha Little, Scott MacDonald, Steve McCormick, Richard Martin, Lisa Szoyka McCarthy, Melinda York-McCord, Eric McNaughton, Steve and Rosetta Molden, Joseph Parra, Indraneel Potnis, Pedro De Queiroz, Ian Regan, Sarah Angela Regan, Amanda Walls Roberts, Matt Gemmell Robertson, Ellen Vass Sanderson, Martha Schwartz, Steven Smith, Seth T. Smolinske, Joyce Timmons Spangler, David Steigman, Brent Sweeting, Christine Thurow, Jared Upchurch, Marc Vinci, Tim Wickens, Don and Angel Workman, and Mary Coffman Zick, who were kind enough to help spread the word.

Copyright © 2016 Christopher Workman and Troy Howarth
Interior Layout by Gary J. Svehla
Cover Design by Aurelia Susan Svehla
Copy Editing by Linda J. Walter

Without limiting the rights under copyright reserved above, no part of this publication may be reproduced, stored in or introduced into a retrieval system, or transmitted, in any form, or by any means (electronic, mechanical, photocopying, recording or otherwise), without the prior written permission of the copyright owner or the publishers of the book.

ISBN 978-1936168-68-2
Library of Congress Catalog Card Number 2016916582
Manufactured in the United States of America
First Printing December 2016

In loving remembrance of

Diane Howarth
August 16, 1947 - December 20, 2015

Donnie Workman
April 1, 1946 - March 5, 2012

Table of Contents

8	A Note on the Entries
9	Introduction
11	1895
12	1896
14	1897
16	1898
19	1899
22	1900
24	1901
27	1902
28	1903
32	1904
33	1905
35	1906
37	1907
41	1908
50	1909
64	1910
81	1911
91	1912
105	1913
124	1914
143	1915
168	1916
181	1917
196	1918
203	1919
212	1920
231	1921
244	1922
257	1923
273	1924
283	1925
295	1926
309	1927
321	1928
336	1929
350	Bibliography
351	Film Title Index

A Note on the Entries

The entries in this volume are arranged in alphabetical order within the year of each film's production (to the best of our knowledge). Because many were released under different titles in different places, we have listed each under the title most often used in the United States. Alternate titles, if any, are noted beneath the primary title. There is also an Index of Film Titles in the back of this volume to help with cross-referencing purposes. Articles such as *A*, *An* or *The* have been excluded during the alphabetization process. For example, Rowland V. Lee's *The Mysterious Dr. Fu Manchu* is listed in the year 1929 under the letter *M*. Hence, the entry for that title begins like this:

The Mysterious Dr. Fu Manchu

The next line contains the name of the production company, whether the film is in b/w or color, its running time and its country of origin. Because running times sometimes vary from place to place, we have tried to include alternate running times (when known) in parentheses. As pertains to countries of origin, we have spelled them out in full except in the case of the United States, which we abbreviate as U.S. Hence, for *The Mysterious Dr. Fu Manchu*:

Paramount; b/w; 82 min; U.S.

We have also included standard credit information. To conserve space, we generally list only the first letter of each position on the crew, and we have limited ourselves to only the most important credits. These break down as Director (*D*), Scenarist (*S*), Producer (*P*), Cinematographer (*C*), Music (*M*) and Special Effects (*FX*). For **The Mysterious Dr. Fu Manchu**, then, the credit line appears as:

D: Rowland V. Lee *S*: Florence Ryerson, Lloyd Corrigan *P*: Jesse L. Lasky, Adolph Zukor *C*: Harry Fischbeck *M*: Oscar Potoker [Note: the credits do not list a person responsible for FX; therefore, neither do we]

The last line of each entry's credit segment lists the cast members. We include the primary stars of each film first, followed by those whose names might be of interest to genre aficionados. Unless the cast of a film is very small or the film is very important to the genre, we do not provide a complete cast list. (To do so would have grown the size of the volume, which is already lengthy, by a considerable amount and made it an untenable publishing endeavor.) For *The Mysterious Dr. Fu Manchu*, we have the cast listed as:

Cast: Warner Oland, Neil Hamilton, Jean Arthur, O.P. Heggie, William Austin, Claude King, Charles A. Stevenson, Evelyn Selbie, Noble Johnson, Laska Winters, Chappell Dossett, William J. O'Brien

Finally, each review ends with the initials of the person who wrote it: CW for Christopher Workman and TH for Troy Howarth.

Warner Oland stars as the villainous Asian madman in *The Mysterious Dr. Fu Manchu.*

Introduction

Horror was not born, as is commonly believed, with Universal's twin successes of 1931, *Dracula* and *Frankenstein*. While these films may have brought overt supernatural spectacle to homegrown American productions for the first time, the genre had existed in one form or another almost since the beginning of cinema. The first intimations of horror as we know it appeared in the form of stage plays, adapted from classic horror literature, shot on film in brief snippets for later consumption. Outside of that, horror iconography was a visual element rather than a dramatic one. More often than not, it was used as a springboard for fantastic imagery and groundbreaking special effects, designed not to scare but to impress audience members. No one was better at this task than French director Georges Méliès, who almost singlehandedly defined the genre for the first decade of the 20th century. But while Méliès' films may have contained the incidents and certainly the traps of the genre (Gothic castles, demonic manifestations, horrifying transformations, and so on), they were generally self-contained and almost always presented with such short running times that characterization and dramatic tension were all but impossible.

While Méliès may have been oft imitated in the early 1900s, his visions of the macabre had a more lasting impact on comedy than it did on horror. And although the birth of the horror film occurred in the mid-1890s, the genre didn't come into its own until 1919, when Robert Wiene began production on *The Cabinet of Dr. Caligari*. By that time, there had already been film adaptations of Mary Shelley's *Frankenstein*, George Du Maurier's *Trilby*, Robert Louis Stevenson's *Dr. Jekyll and Mr. Hyde*, Arthur Conan Doyle's *The Hound of the Baskervilles*, Victor Hugo's *The Hunchback of Notre Dame* and H. Rider Haggard's *She*, among others. But most of these were short trick films aimed at impressing audiences with cinematic sleight of hand. It wasn't until Wiene tried his hand at something more overtly horrifying and evocative that the true dramatic potential for filmic fright—through a heady combination of shock effects and emotional resonance—was fully realized.

Cabinet's bizarre approach, wherein reality is seen through the distorted lens of an asylum patient, set the tone for the genre in Europe for the next decade. German Expressionism, as the movement came to be called, often featured painted backdrops, bent and twisted set props, stylized lighting and distinctive cinematography to portray the world in surrealist terms, a reaction to the destruction wrought by the Great War, which had come to an end in 1918. The point was to use the medium of cinema as a therapeutic exercise; reflecting Freudian psychoanalysis, filmmakers sought to access the darkest recesses of the human mind and, perhaps, to exorcise them. Thus, the nightmare world of Dr. Caligari and his somnambulistic pawn is an insane view of an even more insane existence, setting up a clash between the real and the unreal that reverberated throughout Europe until shortly after the beginning of the next decade, when the political machinations of Adolf Hitler all but put an end to the innovative German school of filmmaking. What audiences were left with, however, was a rich legacy of exploration, a study in new techniques, effects and concepts that redefined storytelling on the big screen as the silent era was quickly displaced by talking pictures.

As pioneering and inventive as the German school was, however, it had little influence on American cinema at the time, at least not immediately. Instead, U.S. filmmakers—removed from the most overt horrors of World War I—focused on physical deformity. After the war had ended, many soldiers had returned home with grievous wounds to their faces and bodies. When these wounds healed, they left behind scars that would never go away and were horrifying to those people who couldn't possibly understand life in the trenches. As a means of escaping this new, real-life horror, Americans sought to exorcize their fears by flocking to movie screens, where the Man of a Thousand Faces, Lon Chaney, showed them visages that were just as terrible, often sported by men who, like those in real life, had heart despite being driven to despair and crime by their status as outcasts. Quasimodo in *The Hunchback of Notre Dame* (1923) and Erik in *The Phantom of the Opera* (1925) were two of Chaney's famous creations, thanks to their significance as major productions from Universal. But it was the smaller films Chaney made with director Tod Browning that ultimately defined American horror in the 1920s. It would seem that the more deformed a villain was, the more sympathetic he became. Alternately, the more human-

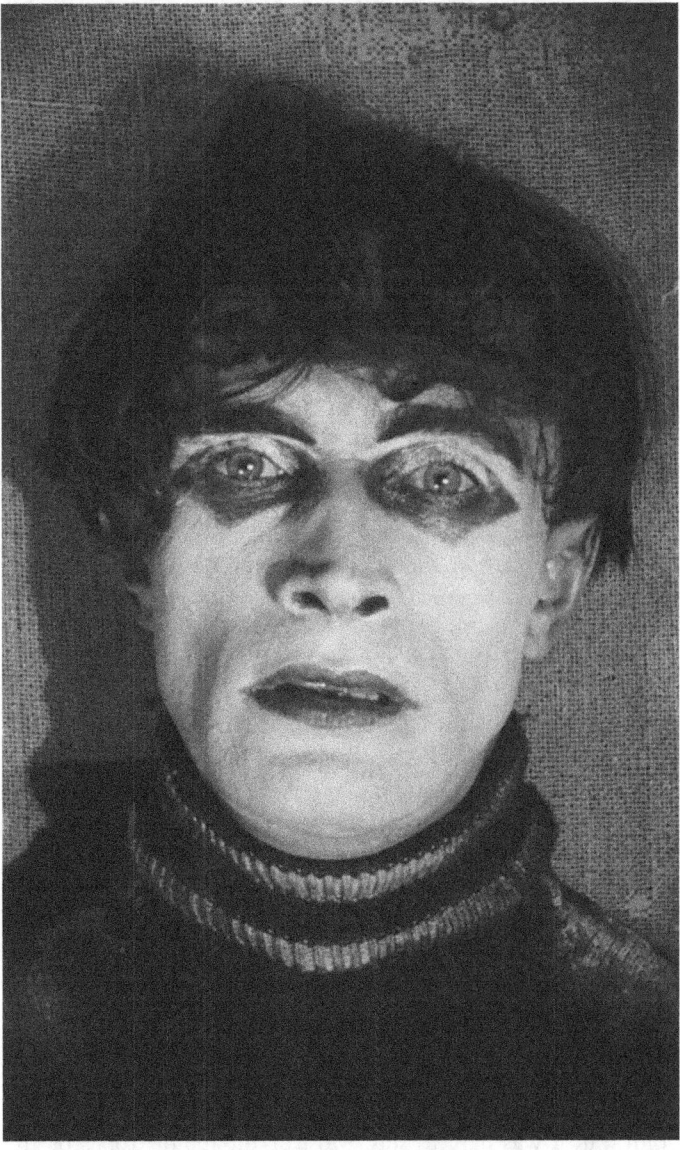

Conrad Veidt as Cesare from *The Cabinet of Dr. Caligari*

Max Schreck as the infamous king of the vampires, Graf Orlok, in F.W. Murnau's *Nosferatu*

looking a villain was, the more brutal and less sympathetic he was. In many ways, then, normality was indicative of the most unnatural of mental inclinations.

Yet, such films were the minority. Most of what passed as horror in the United States wasn't horror at all; it was comedy. Old dark house movies, though they had been around almost since the beginning of cinema in one form or another, were made even more popular by D.W. Griffith's *One Exciting Night* (1923) and remained all the rage into the 1930s. Focused as they were on murder rather than preternatural monsters, they provided a safe haven for audiences looking for a thrill, so long as that thrill wasn't too harsh and was accompanied by a convenient outlet: laughter. The supernatural had no place on American screens.

Outside of the United States, however, it was a different story. Japan continued a tradition that had begun before the turn of the twentieth century. Not afraid to shy away from ghostly manifestations, the nation's filmmakers adapted numerous myths and plays about murdered women seeking vengeance from beyond the grave against their adulterous husbands. Often, the wife would take on the appearance of her husband's new wife or mistress, or she would possess the lithe body of a favored pet, usually a cat.

The horror genre in film might have been young at this point, but it was here to stay. Most of the major tropes of the genre—dark or haunted houses, vampires, werewolves, serial killers, and so on—were well established by the end of the 1920s. All that was left was for the United States to follow Europe and Japan's example, which it most definitely did in 1931 with the release of *Dracula* and *Frankenstein*. The success of these two films would define the genre—which you can read more about in the 1930s volume of this on-going series—but it would be unfair to give short shrift to the groundwork laid by the experimentation-happy filmmakers of the silent era. Unencumbered by clunky sound recording equipment, the directors and cinematographers of the period explored the potential of the moving camera and used the naturally dramatic effect of monochromatic film stock to create images that were indelible in their impact. The shock effects of F.W. Murnau's *Nosferatu* (1922) or Tod Browning's *The Unknown* (1927) may seem old hat today, but if we approach these films with an eye toward the context in which they were made, there's no denying the impact they had on then-contemporary viewers; more to the point, these images and effects remain etched in the cinematic landscape and continue to inspire new generations of filmmakers and artists.

The period 1895 to 1929 is one of the most exciting eras in film history. Viewers able to get past the perceived handicap of the silent format will likely agree that many films of the period hold up remarkably well today. Many works from the era have been routinely overlooked in studies of the genre, but we hope to correct that problem by focusing on everything from the most iconic to the most obscure in *Tome of Terror: Horror Films of the Silent Era*.

Christopher Workman
Troy Howarth

Lon Chaney in *The Unknown*

1895

Trilby Hypnotic Scene
Edison; b/w; 1 min; U.S.
D/C: William Heise *P:* Thomas Edison
Cast: David Henderson

George Du Maurier originally published his best-selling and influential novel *Trilby* as a serial in the magazine *Harper's Monthly* in 1894. During the following half-century, the tale inspired everything from hats to dances. Today, however, it is largely forgotten, eclipsed by nostalgic fondness for various incarnations of the same author's *Peter Ibbetson* (1891). For its own part, however, *Trilby* presents a colorful cast of characters; along with the beautiful title character, there are also the men who love her: Little Billee, the Laird, Taffy and, most significantly, the evil hypnotist Svengali, who uses mesmerism to make Trilby a singing sensation.

Along with Bram Stoker's classic novel *Dracula* (1897), *Trilby* established many of the Gothic horror conventions that remain in place today. There have been numerous screen adaptations of Du Maurier's romantic horror tale, the first being an 1895 series of short pieces by Thomas Edison's film production company. It would seem that someone at Edison had an interest in the David Henderson Burlesque Company's staging of the novel; various scenes from that production were shot as individual productions, two of which were arguably the first horror films ever released.

Scottish-born Henderson (1853-1908) was credited with revitalizing the theater scene in Chicago at the turn of the last century, overseeing adaptations of *Bluebeard*, *The Arabian Nights* and *Sinbad the Sailor*, among others. Whether he approached someone at Edison, or whether someone at Edison simply loved his adaptation of *Trilby* enough to film parts of it, is unknown. But whatever the case, the filmed excerpts included *Trilby Death Scene* and *Trilby Dance* (both 1895). A few years later, Edison's production company would also film *Ella Lola, à la Trilby* (1898), which was merely a dance number "inspired" by the story and starring the then-famous Ella Lola; it was a copycat of Robert W. Paul's 1896 *Trilby Burlesque*, which was another short film featuring a dance based on Du Maurier's novel. Of these earliest *Trilby* adaptations—which would also include American Mutoscope's *Trilby and Little Billee* (1896)—only *Trilby Hypnotic Scene* and *Trilby Death Scene* record darker, more horror-oriented portions of the story. The others explore more innocuous aspects of the tale.

William Heise photographed the Edison contributions, and he is listed as director even though no real direction was necessary. Heise was the house cinematographer at Edison and also shot many films for other directors, most notably James White and William Dickson.

In *Trilby Hypnotic Scene*, which lasts less than a minute, the eponymous heroine comes under the influence of the evil Svengali (probably played by Henderson), a mesmerist planning on turning her into one of the world's great singers. CW

Trilby Death Scene
Edison; b/w; 1 min; U.S.
D/C: William Heise *P:* Thomas Edison
Cast: David Henderson

> **WHERE CELLULOID IS MADE.**
>
> **NEW INDUSTRIES THAT HAVE SPRUNG UP IN JERSEY.**
>
> TRENTON, N. J., Jan. 31.—A number of important new industries have been established in New-Jersey lately. One of these consists of a combination of establishments, the original plants of which were already here. Jersey is the home of celluloid. The invention of that article and its first production belong to Newark. Andrew Albright, once an eager aspirant for Gubernatorial and Congressional honors at the hands of the Democracy, can fairly be called the father of the celluloid industry. He made most of his big fortune out of that article.
>
> The new celluloid company, which includes all but one of the manufacturing interests in celluloid and kindred material, practically came into full-fledged existence with the new year. For the past few weeks the officers of the consolidated company have been exceedingly busy getting everything in readiness, and a vast deal still remains to be done before all the different departments are running smoothly. The new company represents a capital of $8,000,000, which, previous to the amalgamation, was controlled by half a dozen companies. The combined net earnings of all these companies last year was close upon $600,000, so that the stockholders of the new company feel assured of at least a 10 per cent. dividend the first year.

The birth of the movie (or celluloid) industry in New Jersey, as reported in the *New York Times*, Sunday February 1, 1891

Most likely the first death scene ever shot on moving film, *Trilby Death Scene* is an installment of the Edison Studios series of *Trilby* adaptations that also includes *Trilby Hypnotic Scene* and *Trilby Dance* (both 1895), as well as *Ella Lola, à la Trilby* (1898). The play on which the film series was based (itself based on George Du Maurier's novel of the same name) was produced by David Henderson, the Chicago theater maven responsible for building the Chicago Opera House in 1887. It is highly probable that Henderson, who sometimes acted in his productions, played Svengali in the series.

In this installment, Svengali, while attempting to hypnotize Trilby and the Laird, collapses, falls over a table and dies. The film lasts less than a minute, but its focus on hypnotism and death—and its origin in one of the great novels of Gothic literature—argue for *Trilby Death Scene*, together with its predecessor *Trilby Hypnotic Scene*, being the first horror film ever made, beating the sometimes-cited *The Devil's Castle* (1896) by French director Georges Méliès to the punch by a full year.

Strangely enough, Edison Studios' catalog entry for *Death Scene* describes the film as "very funny," despite the fact that it was a scene from a drama and nothing in the film suggests that it was intended to have a humorous bent.

Edison's competitor American Mutoscope (which was established by former Edison employee William Dickson) shot materials for American Mutoscope describe the two as "smoking, kissing and laughing." CW

1896

The Devil's Castle
aka **Le Manoir du diable**; **The House of the Devil**; **The Haunted Castle**; **The Devil's Manor**; **The Manor of the Devil**
Star Film; b/w; 2 min; France
D/S/P/FX: Georges Méliès
Cast: Legris, Georges Méliès, Jeanne d'Alcy

Considered by some to be the first horror film ever made, Georges Méliès' *The Devil's Castle* would probably warrant the claim had Edison Studios not already dabbled in the genre with *Trilby Hypnotic Scene* and *Trilby Death Scene* (both 1895). Moreover, Méliès had already produced *A Terrible Night*, in which an overly large beetle threatens a man attempting to sleep. Here, however, Méliès takes the creepiness several steps further. In fact, several characters associated with evil and horror make their first screen appearances ever in this short film.

It all begins when a bat flies through the window of an ancient castle and transforms into Mephistopheles (Legris). The Father of Lies then conjures up a one-dimensional cauldron, and from the cauldron pops a pretty young woman (Méliès' future wife, actress Jeanne d'Alcy). The devil disappears, and two cavaliers enter the castle. A devilish old hermit with a pitchfork terrorizes them, and one of them flees in horror. Next appears—though not from the cauldron, as so many sources claim—a skeleton, which becomes a bat and then the devil, a bevy of sheeted ghosts and finally the beautiful young woman who transforms into a witch and summons her witch friends. Tired of the castle's horrors, the remaining cavalier (played by Méliès) rips a crucifix from the wall, and the devil vanishes in a column of infernal smoke.

Méliès' films rarely relied on verisimilitude to achieve their thrills. Rather, the intent is to shock audiences jaded by live-action magic through the magical possibilities of the film medium, which Méliès was quickly mastering in ways other filmmakers could only dream of. The longer the director made films, the more technically adept his films became, as he discovered and/or mastered dissolves, stop motion, multiple exposures, masking, fade-ins, slow and fast motion and so on.

A portrait of Georges Méliès

He was, in short, a magician not only of the stage but of the screen as well, and in between his stage shows at the Theatre Robert-Houdin, he would often show off his latest celluloid achievements to a bedazzled audience. His short

its own scene from a play based on *Trilby*, titled *Trilby and Little Billee*, the following year. That piece presents an excerpt in which Trilby eats a piece of cake while talking to Little Billee, who sits next to her with an arm resting on the table. The promotional films quickly became famous worldwide and within the decade were being shown in Nickelodeons—after their introduction in 1905—all over North America and Europe. As demand for more and more short films increased, Méliès was happy to comply, churning them out until the year 1913, when more creative directors and bigger studios with greater resources finally beat him at his own game and forced him to close shop.

Amazingly, the only known copy of *The Devil's Castle* was found in a junkshop in Christchurch, New Zealand, in 1988. It is unfortunate that such a fascinating and historical subject was lost for so many years, during which time a great deal of misinformation about it entered the mainstream, where it remains to this day.

Since a bat in the film takes on humanoid form, many film historians consider *The Devil's Castle* the first vampire movie. While then-contemporary descriptions claim the devil vanishes in a wisp of smoke at the end, this portion of the film is unfortunately missing from the sole existing print. CW

A Nightmare
aka Le Cauchemar
Star Film; b/w; 1 min; France
D/P/S/FX: Georges Méliès
Cast: Georges Méliès

Starting out in silly terrain where a sleeping man (Méliès) dreams that a beautiful woman is teasing him from the foot of his bed, *A Nightmare* abruptly morphs into bizarre fantasy when that same woman transforms into a minstrel playing a banjo and dances about on that very same bed. When the hero tries to grab the minstrel, the musician becomes a clown and disappears through a Gothic door where, just a moment before, there had been a wall. A full moon shines brightly down on the proceedings, and as the nightmare continues, the orb grows larger and develops a smiling face. Its eyes roll from side to side and its mouth opens in an apparent attempt to devour the sleeper, who swiftly punches it back down to size, after which the woman, the minstrel and the clown menace him once again. When he finally awakens, he realizes that it was all a bad dream.

A sequel of sorts to *A Terrible Night* (1896), *A Nightmare* utilizes the same central character, a bearded male sleeper, only this time he's threatened by dreams rather than a living creature.

Here was a milieu Méliès would return to often throughout the remainder of his career, one that allowed him the opportunity to perfect his growing interest in the possibilities of elaborate jump cuts, a process also known as stop-substitution. A static camera was aimed toward the small set and would begin filming. Then the actors were told to freeze. The camera would then be turned off and one or more of the participants removed or replaced, after which the camera would resume filming. The result was the apparent disappearance or change of one character into another right before the eyes of the disbelieving audience.

While such cuts seem inefficient and somewhat obvious in *A Nightmare*, the director would go on to master them. When combined with other types of special effects in later films, the results would often be striking.

It should be noted that during the last few seconds of the film, there is a strange dappling effect over the crotch of the sleeper's pajamas. At first glance, this appears an example of unintentional print damage, but close examination leaves no doubt that the infliction of these scratches was intentional. Without written records to explain why this was done, viewers are left to speculate on the reasons for themselves. CW

A Terrible Night
aka Une Nuit terrible; One Terrible Night
Star Film; b/w; 1 min; France
D/P/S/FX: Georges Méliès
Cast: Georges Méliès

Having been born only a couple of years prior, filmmaking in 1896 was a documentarian pastime. But one man wasn't satisfied with making one-minute films about everyday life as so many others were doing. That man, magician and artist Marie Georges Jean Méliès (1861-1938), single-handedly advanced cinema by tapping into the collective consciousness of an ever-progressing world.

Owner of the Theatre Robert-Houdin in Paris, Méliès understood the interests of a *Belle Époque* audience hungry for the phantasmagorical. Having learned his craft in London and Paris, he knew that a restless public in a time of unprecedented peace had quickly become disinterested in watching films of things they could see by looking out their drawing room windows. Middle-class Parisians—like Europeans in general or, for that matter, Americans—attended magic shows to experience the unreal, to escape the familiarity of their own ordinary existences and to feel the rush that comes with experiencing the hysterical and the horrific.

Understanding this, Méliès in 1896 began a long flirtation with whimsical fantasy tinged at times by horrific imagery. Establishing—and tearing down—film conventions, the director created a new type of cinema that quickly grew in distinction and influenced filmmakers worldwide. His work operated within multiple genres, both inside and outside of what was then the mainstream. As a result, films such as *A Trip to the Moon* (1902), *The Kingdom of Fairies* (1903), and *The Conquest of the Pole* (1912) can be viewed as templates for modern Hollywood's big-budget exercises in special effects-driven banality.

Aiming, as was his wont, to provide his audience with a look at something they couldn't see anywhere else, Méliès concocted this story of a man (played by the director) who, hoping to get a good night's sleep, settles into bed, only to be terrorized by a giant beetle. Finally, after beating the coleopteran to death, he disposes of it in his chamber pot. Unfortunately, he's now paranoid and cannot go back to sleep, both fearing and imagining that there are more bugs in his bed.

As with so many Méliès films to follow, the product he created here shows an interest not only in the extraordinary (a giant beetle attacking a person, more than a half-century before the irradiated bugs of the 1950s and the killer insect hordes of the 1970s) but also in menacing and terrifying imagery. While the approach is humorous, there's little doubt that audiences viewing it at the time would have watched nervously, sympathizing with the threatened hero and breathing a sigh of relief when the man knocks the creature from his bed sheet one final time, stomps on it and discards it in a container of his own waste.

Sadly, horror film historians have largely ignored Méliès' contributions to the genre he arguably created. Phil Hardy's

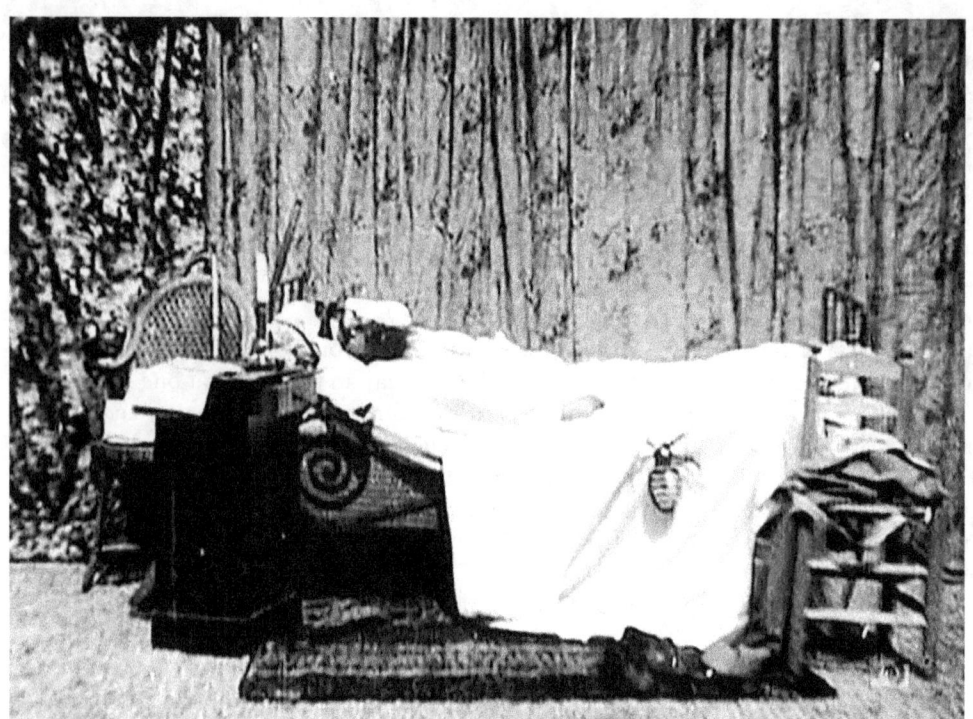

In *A Terrible Night*, Georges Méliès plays a man trying to get a good night's sleep, only to be terrorized by a giant beetle.

groundbreaking and generally inclusive *The Overlook Film Encyclopedia: Horror*, for example, makes the mistake of not merely downplaying Méliès' importance to the genre but going so far as to claim that he had no influence at all. "He was too steeped in the pantomime tradition of amusing fantasy to figure in the history of horror," it states emphatically, and in doing so ignores the terrifying sight of Bluebeard's murdered wives hanging with ropes about their necks in *Blue Beard* (1901) or the gruesome decapitations of political prisoners at the hands of *The Terrible Turkish Executioner* (1904). While Méliès' films may have included elements of amusing fancy, and while they were indeed steeped in the pantomime tradition of the stage, neither of these facts nullifies the nightmarish excess inherent in so many of his productions. That Georges Méliès was the first master of horror simply cannot be denied with any degree of plausibility. CW

1897

The Bewitched Inn
aka **L'Auberge ensorcelé**; **The Bewitch Inn**
Star Film; b/w; 2 min; France
D/P/S/FX: Georges Méliès
Cast: Georges Méliès

Méliès' darker films can be grouped into three broad categories: nightmares (e.g., *A Nightmare*, 1896; *The Astronomer's Dream* and *The Temptation of Saint Anthony*, both 1898); haunted rooms, usually located in inns (*Going to Bed Under Difficulties*, 1900; *The Inn Where No Man Rests*, 1903); and portrayals of demon manifestation (*The Devil's Castle*, 1896; *The Treasures of Satan*, 1902; *The Infernal Cake-Walk*, 1903). *The Bewitched Inn* falls into the second of these categories. A tired man (Méliès), visiting an inn for the evening, hopes to get some rest but instead finds himself bedeviled as he attempts to undress. His bags and other items disappear and reappear, his hat and coat move on their own and unseen forces stack his chair and dresser on top of his bed. Realizing that all is not right with the room, he flees in terror.

While the film is an attempt at light fantasy, the subject matter is most assuredly the stuff of horror, sharing an obvious commonality with the religious horror films of the 1970s. As usual, Méliès proves adept at handling the abrupt cuts needed to make the film's special effects work.

Going to Bed Under Difficulties essentially tells the same story, though to even more humorous effect. A man (Méliès again), attempting to get a good night's sleep, has difficulty removing his attire, and by the end of his struggle finds himself wearing multiple sets of clothes. Unlike *The Bewitched Inn*, however, there is no steady build-up of tension that erupts when the protagonist finally makes his exit in haste. Rather, it ends abruptly and is obviously missing footage. CW

The Cabinet of Mephistopheles
aka **Le cabinet de Mephistopheles**; **The Devil's Laboratory**; **The Laboratory of Mephistopheles**
Star Film; b/w; 3 min; France
D/P/S/FX: Georges Méliès
Cast: Georges Méliès

What little information there is about this lost film can be found in the 1901 Warwick Film Catalog and in reviews written at the time. From such descriptions, one can conclude that it was typical Méliès fare, with the devil making his usual appearance and working his evil deeds, to both the merriment and horror of the audience. While Mephistopheles fans a fire, two cavaliers appear. The devil disappears and is replaced by a ghost whose head leaves his body and floats around the room. Then a chair levitates and flies up the chimney. A cannon appears and spits smoke. A cage materializes in the middle of the room, and the devil reappears. He moves through the bars of the cage, as does one of the cavaliers. (What has happened to the other one is a mystery.)

One can conclude that Méliès played the devil, as he tended to do in so many of his productions. The reviewer for the Warwick Film Catalog clearly liked the film, pointing out that it was "weird and fantastic," two compliments that have been frequently visited upon the French director's movies in the century since he first presented them.

This may have been Méliès' first film to utilize superimposition (an effect in which one frame of film is layered upon another, darker frame, allowing two images to exist simultaneously within a central framing device), though it's difficult to know for certain without the original product at hand. Certainly, the director's subsequent films would frequently use this technique to good effect. CW

Faust and Marguerite
aka **Faust et Marguerite**
Star Film; b/w; 1 min; France
D/P/S/FX: Georges Méliès
Cast: Georges Méliès, Jeanne d'Alcy

This is Méliès' first attempt at filming the legend of Faust, and it is unfortunately lost. Given Méliès' interest in trick photography, with which he had become obsessed the year before in *The Devil's Castle* (1896), one can assume that *Faust and Marguerite* was mostly an excuse to practice jump cuts. It's likely that Méliès starred as Faust or Mephistopheles (probably the latter) and that his favorite actress, Jeanne d'Alcy, starred as Marguerite.

This wouldn't be the only time Méliès would center a film on the fictional character who sells his soul to the devil in exchange for youth and an attempt at love with a beautiful young woman (an act that would eventually damn him to everlasting torment). Méliès would revisit the character the very next year with *The Damnation of Faust* (1898). He would tackle the subject again a couple of years later, this time with two films sharing the same names (at least, in the United States) as his previous pictures—*The Damnation of Faust* in 1903 and *Faust and Marguerite* in 1904.

It has been written that American director Edwin S. Porter was so taken with this film that he made his own *Faust and Marguerite* in 1900, believing that he could best Méliès' special effects. The film's effects, however, are nowhere near on par with what the French director was doing at the time. CW

The Haunted Castle
aka **Le Château hanté**
Star Film; color; 1 min; France
D/P/S/FX: Georges Méliès
Cast: Georges Méliès

In an old chateau, a man directs a cavalier's gaze toward a black box and then the mysterious man disappears. When the cavalier (Méliès) goes to sit in a chair in front of the box, both chair and box disappear ... then reappear, the box now in the chair on the other side of the room. When the man attempts to remove the box from the chair, a sheeted specter appears, holding the box in its arms. Drawing his sword, the cavalier runs the specter through, only to have it become a skeleton. (The box is now completely gone, having vanished as the ghost transformed.) Grabbing the skeleton, the man is surprised to find that he's instead holding an armored knight, who promptly disappears as another man appears on the other side of the screen. This man points, possibly directing the hero to where the box has gone, and the hero moves off in that direction. The specter then reappears without the box, and ... unfortunately, the only existing print of the film ends abruptly at this point. No record of how it originally concluded has survived, leaving today's viewers to guess.

In Georges Méliès' *The Haunted Castle*, a cavalier (Méliès) uses his sword to stab a sheeted specter that suddenly becomes a skeleton.

One thing is certain, however: Méliès was returning to the ground he'd sown so successfully in *The Devil's Castle* (1896). Because what little of it remains is presided over by ghostly apparitions, it's hard to deny the film a place in the horror genre. Some critics have suggested that it tells the tale of a man warned not to spend the night in a haunted castle but who does so regardless, only to be haunted by the castle's spirits. Upon closer inspection, however, this description does not appear to be accurate. Clearly, the two men at the beginning are interested in the contents of what appears to be a locked box, leading one to surmise that the conclusion of the film would have revealed its contents (and why they're of such importance that the hero would challenge the spirits to retrieve them).

The Haunted Castle is one of the oldest surviving Méliès films to have been hand-painted. This is an example of the interest in experimentation that led to Méliès crafting some of the most original and daring cinematic work of the period. The limitations of monochromatic celluloid were obviously taken as a challenge by the director, and he resolved them with surprising ease. Clearly wanting at least some of his films to inhabit a world of vibrant color, he proceeded to hand-paint selected works frame by individual frame, climaxing in the bold hues of *Joan of Arc* (1900), *The Kingdom of Fairies* (1903) and *The Impossible Voyage* (1904). *The Haunted Castle*, then, is the first color horror film, beating the film usually credited with that achievement, *Doctor X* (1932, shot in an early two-color Technicolor process), to the punch by over 30 years. CW

The Haunted Castle
G.A.S. Films; b/w; 1 min; Great Britain
D/S/P/C/FX: George Albert Smith
Cast unknown

The drawing of a moon on a chalkboard becomes an actual moon-faced vampire, replete with extended canines, and attempts to eat everything in sight, from *The Astronomer's Dream*.

George Albert Smith (1864-1959) was an extraordinarily gifted and persuasive man. Having passed himself off as a psychic, magic lanternist and mesmerist, he ingratiated himself with Edmund Gurney, prominent member of the Society for Psychical Research, eventually becoming Gurney's secretary. It has been suggested that Smith hoodwinked Gurney by proficiency with magician's tricks and that he may have had something to do with Gurney's death by drug overdose in 1888 (once Gurney, according to the theory, discovered Smith's trickery). It's difficult to know how much of this is true, but it's indisputable that Smith put some variety of expertise to use when, in 1896, he invented his own movie camera; a little over a decade later he would help develop Kinemacolor, the first color-film process that didn't involve hand stenciling.

After procuring a lease to St. Ann's Well and Wild Garden in Brighton, Smith constructed his own film studio at the location and transformed the gardens into an unprecedented attraction offering amusement-show programs, including his own films. Oddly, despite his obsession with the occult, Smith's films rarely evoked horror, and the few that did seemed more concerned with outdoing French director Georges Méliès than in breaking original ground. Smith did, however, become a pioneer in filmmaking, one of the first to realize that intelligent editing could introduce dramatic impact. And while it was Méliès who discovered the jump cut (and put it to its first good use in *The Devil's Castle* in 1896) and Edwin S. Porter who would make a splash with cross-cutting (*The Life of an American Fireman* in 1903), it was Smith who, in addition to realizing editing's potential, first mastered close shots and inserts.

Though reportedly based on a story entitled *The Haunted Hotel*, *The Haunted Castle* has a title stolen from Georges Méliès (even though the narrative more closely resembles the French director's 1897 film *The Bewitched Inn*). In Smith's film, it is an inn—not a castle—that is haunted by the spirits of the dead. The effects are achieved by wire manipulation, a common trick utilized by the stage magicians with whom Smith was doubtless well acquainted.

The film is apparently lost, with little information about it having survived. From contemporary descriptions, it seems doubtful that Smith had yet discovered the process of double exposure—which he would patent the very next year and use in *The Mesmerist* (1898). Given Smith's heavy interest in humorous films during this period, it is likely that *The Haunted Castle* was a comedy with horror elements thrown in to amaze the audience. That same year also saw the release of Smith's *The X-Ray Fiend*, which is often cited as a horror film but is in fact a comedy. In it, a handheld x-ray device is pointed at two young lovers, revealing their skeletons (which are portrayed by people in costumes). CW

A Twentieth Century Surgeon
aka **Chirurgien Américain**; **Twentieth-Century Surgeon**
Star Film; b/w; 2 min; France
D/S/P/FX: Georges Méliès
Cast: George Méliès

Though the original title literally translates as *American Surgeon*, this film's U.S. release title betrays the film's probable semi-futuristic tone. (It seems that it may well have been the very first mad scientist movie ever made!) The story concerns a tramp awakening to discover that his body has been "replaced" (though by what, existing sources don't say) at the hands of a surgeon whose experiments apparently fly in the face of nature.

Given the nature of Méliès' films at this early stage in his career, it's safe to assume that *Surgeon* was a comedy. Unfortunately, since it's considered lost, it's impossible to assess its virtues or shortcomings. CW

1898

The Astronomer's Dream
aka **La Lune à une mètre**; **A Moon to the Metre**
Star Film; b/w; 3 min; France
D/P/S/FX: Georges Méliès
Cast: Georges Méliès

Another of Méliès' nightmare films, *The Astronomer's Dream* is a return to the same territory the director visited two years before with *A Nightmare* (1896) and would visit again, albeit to express in more fantastic and less terrifying terms a fear of female sexuality, in *The Rajah's Dream* (1900). A more appropriate English-language title might have been *The Astrologer's Dream*, since the title character appears in magician's robe and cap and sits before a book containing what appears to be occult rather than scientific drawings.

The setting is an observatory. After being menaced by a demon (who is vanquished by a caped woman wearing a crescent-shaped tiara), the astronomer/astrologer, unaware of what has just happened, gets up and draws a globe and moon on a chalkboard. To his horror, the drawing comes to life; the moon becomes a head and attaches itself to the globe, which is now a body. The man removes the chalkboard from sight and pulls from his robe a small telescope with which to observe the moon (a strange thing to do given that he has a much larger telescope already set up right in front of him), but the telescope in his hands turns into a rolling pin. After a couple more bizarre events, the moon descends as a round-faced vampire, replete with extended canines. It eats the small telescope and then tries to eat the protagonist as he removes various objects from its mouth. Two demonic children suddenly exit the monster's maw, but the magician throws one of them back in. (The other runs off-screen.) Finally, the vampire face shrinks to a crescent moon in the background—with a woman in white sitting atop it—then disappears. The moon then reappears in its full-blown vampiric form, this time eating the magician and gruesomely spitting out various parts of his body. The demon that had been vanquished by the caped woman reappears and is again banished by that same woman, who then throws the astrologer's body parts back into the moon's mouth. The astrologer then reappears and awakens, realizing that it was all a terrible dream.

While conjuring nightmarish images for his film, Méliès seems to be stating something about female sexuality, which is much less threateningly presented than in *The Rajah's Dream*. Here, the beautiful goddess of the moon is the protagonist's savior, unlike in *Rajah*, where women are portrayed as a threat to the very men who find them attractive. CW

The Cavalier's Dream
Vitagraph; b/w; 1 min; U.S.
D/P/S/C/FX: Edwin S. Porter
Cast unknown

Though he would become most strongly associated with Thomas Edison's film production company, Edwin Stanton (or, depending on the source, "Stratton") Porter began his filmmaking career as a jack-of-all-trades. On his first film, *The Cavalier's Dream*, he seems to have done pretty much everything, from producing chores to orchestrating the special effects.

If French director Georges Méliès is credited for creating the cinematic jump cut, and British director George Albert Smith for pioneering the use of double exposure, then Porter completes their "language of film" *menage-a-trois* by his introduction of cross cutting. Cross cutting is a type of editing in which the camera cuts abruptly from one location to another, or from one person or object to another. Once chanced upon, it quickly became a mainstream filmmaking technique, one that Méliès, oddly, neither caught the significance of nor bothered adapting.

Porter first began to pursue an interest in the cinema in 1896, for a time operating as a projectionist. It's likely that some of the films he projected were those of Méliès. *The Cavalier's Dream* borrows obviously and heavily from the French director's *A Nightmare* (1896) in the ways in which it details the nightmarish dreams of its protagonist. It's also clear that Porter lifted material from both Méliès' aforementioned *The Devil's Castle* and his *The Haunted Castle* (1897), throwing both a witch and Mephistopheles into the mix.

The Cavalier's Dream begins with said cavalier sleeping at a table. An old witch enters the room and then disappears. Mephistopheles appears and the witch reappears, then suddenly transforms into a beautiful young woman. In keeping with the conventions of the trick films of the period, that's pretty much it.

The effects were achieved in much the same way as those in Méliès' films. The camera would start shooting; the actors would move and then freeze; the camera would stop; the actors would shift positions or be replaced and then the camera would resume filming. Porter was nowhere near as adept at this sort of editing as Méliès, a drawback no doubt indicative of the reasons his films never gained the audience, recognition or lasting fame of his (deservedly) more famous contemporary. CW

The Cave of the Demons
aka **La caverne maudite**; **The Cave Demons**; **The Accursed Cave**
Star Film; b/w; 1 min; France
D/P/S/FX: Georges Méliès
Cast: Georges Méliès

While some sources cite the lost *The Cave of the Demons* as the first Méliès film to make use of double exposures, others claim the equally lost *The Cabinet of Mephistopheles* (1897) was the first. Unless and until every Méliès film ever made can be found, the truth won't be known for certain. Many of the director's films were burned during the First World War to provide rubber for boots, and later, in the 1920s, Méliès destroyed many to clear space for his family in his tiny apartment. It's probably pointless to hope that all of his lost films will someday resurface, though the discovery of *The Devil's Castle* (1896) in 1988 and *Cleopatra* (1899) in 2005 does offer hope that there might be at least one or two pleasant surprises yet in store for fans.

The plot of *The Cave of the Demons* reportedly concerned a young woman who stumbles upon a cavern wherein lay the bodies of people who have died under mysterious circumstances. Their spirits and skeletons draw her into a lurid dance of death. CW

The Damnation of Faust
aka **Le damnation de Faust**
Star Film; b/w; 2 min; France
D/P/S/FX: Georges Méliès
Cast: Georges Méliès

This is one of Méliès' lost films; it is not known with any degree of certainty whether the director played Faust or Mephistopheles, but given his penchant for characters from the infernal region, it was likely the latter.

It's too bad that so little is known about *The Damnation of Faust*, as it, along with its precursor *Faust and Marguerite* (1897), was likely an influence on British director George Albert Smith (*Faust and Mephistopheles*, 1898), American director Edwin S. Porter (*Faust and Marguerite*, 1900) and French director Alice Guy (*Faust and Mephistopheles*, 1903). Unfortunately, Smith's film appears lost as well. It is, therefore, impossible to know for certain who borrowed what from whom, though it does seem safe to give Méliès credit for kick-starting the subgenre in 1897.

Méliès revisited the famous character in *The Damnation of Faust* (1903) and *Faust and Marguerite* (1904). The latter film's French release title was *Le damnation de docteur Faust*, leaving one to wonder whether his first effort had already been lost by that time, leaving Méliès free to use an almost identical title. On the other hand, it's also possible that the first film was one burned by Méliès in the 1920s, when his anger at society for having neglected him and his desperation for living space drove him to destroy some of his own films in a bonfire in his backyard. CW

Don Juan Tenorio
Toscano; b/w; length unknown; Mexico
D/P: Salvador Toscano
Cast: Paco Gavilanes

Fantasy has always had a place in Mexican cinema, beginning with the very first fictional film shot in the nation, 1898's *Don Juan Tenorio*. Influenced by French films of the period, some of which had been exhibited in Mexico City by Auguste Lumiére in 1896, *Tenorio* is based on an 1844 play of the same name by José Zorillo. It concerns Don Juan and Don Luis, two rakes who've just had a competition to see who could bed the most women and murder the most men. Don Juan won, and though he's engaged to be wed, he proposes an additional competition with Don Luis over the conquest of two more women. His soon-to-be father-in-law overhears the conversation and vows that Don Juan will never marry his daughter. A rampage of sexual conquest and bloodshed ensues, during which everyone Don Juan loves winds up dead (after which they visit him as ghosts).

The play was an affirmation of Zorillo's Catholic faith, with spirits good and bad playing an extensive part. Considered by many to be the most successful play in Spanish history, it is today generally performed on either All Hallows Eve or All Saints' Day (usually the latter).

This first film adaptation of the play was directed by Salvador Toscano Barragán, better known as Salvador Toscano, who developed an interest in film through exposure to the works of Thomas Edison and the Lumiére Brothers. Born in 1872, he studied mining before switching tracks and opening a theater in Mexico City in 1897. At first his programs consisted solely of foreign movies, but before long he was shooting and screening his own actuality films, short programs about such things as police officers riding horses and men gathering in Mexico City's public square. Emboldened by the success of his short works, he turned to *Don Juan Tenorio* for fresh inspiration.

After the outbreak of the Mexican Revolution in 1910, Toscano hit the front lines with his camera, creating the footage that his daughter later shaped into one of Mexico's most famous historical documentaries, *Memoirs of a Mexican* (1950). Toscano's last film was shot in 1921, and he died in 1947. Today the Mexican film industry's most prestigious cinematography award is named in honor of him.

The next film version of *Don Juan Tenorio* was shot in Spain in 1908. CW

Faust and Mephistopheles
G.A.S. Films; b/w; length unknown; Great Britain
D/S/P/C/FX: George Albert Smith
Cast unknown

Perhaps the earliest film to adhere closely to Goethe's tale, *Faust and Mephistopheles* details Satan's attempt at corrupting the soul of an alleged incorruptible. Refusing at first to sell his soul to the devil, the aging Faust is shown a vision of a beautiful young woman named Marguerite. Hoping to possess her, he gives in and becomes young again. It seems likely that the vision was achieved by superimposition, while Faust's transmutation from old to young was done with a jump cut.

Smith was not the first to toy with Goethe's tale; Georges Méliès had done so with *Faust and Marguerite* in 1897, and Edwin S. Porter would soon do the same with the risible *Faust and Marguerite* (1900). Méliès went on to make several more attempts with varying degrees of success. (The world's first known female director, Alice Guy, would make her own version, *Faust and Mephistopheles*, in 1903.)

Some critics cite Smith's *The Haunted Picture Gallery* (1899) as a horror film, but it is in fact a mild trick film in which a Gainsborough painting comes to life and dances. In his groundbreaking anthology *Dorothy's Dream* (1903), Smith directs a section about Bluebeard, with the rest being mild fantasies. Smith's wife and star of many of his films, Laura Bayley, played Dorothy. Smith also appeared in some of his own films, and he and his wife costarred in *A Kiss in the Tunnel* (1899). CW

Jizo the Spook
aka **Bake-jizo**; **Bake Jizo**; **Bakejizo**
Konishi; b/w; length unknown; Japan
D/C: Asana Shiro S: Hatta Eijiro
Cast: Ishii Soshichi, Sugiura Sojiro

Along the Daiya River of Japan, in an area known as Kanmangafuchi Abyss, sits the popular tourist destination of Jiunji Temple. Sitting below the temple is a series of mysterious and sinister statues known as Bake-Jizou (also known as 100-Jizou, though many of the "hundred" statues were washed away in a flood in 1902). At the time the temple was built in 1654, Jizou was believed to be a god who watched over the souls of dead children as they passed into the afterlife. In fact, the word *bake* (pronounced: bah-kay) means "ghost" or "spook." Hence the name of one of Japan's earliest films: *Jizo the Spook*.

Though often cited as one of the first horror films ever made, little is known about *Jizo the Spook* apart from the fact that it was shot in 1898 by director Asano Shiro. Up until that time, most films in Japan had been produced to show the beauty of the country or incidental daily occurrences (such as a family eating dinner or people passing by). Konishi, a store that sold photographic equipment, produced many of these films. Konishi never intended to get into the filmmaking business; the company merely wanted to know how to use its equipment before selling it to customers. A young store employee by the name of Asano Shiro was assigned the task of learning to operate a new "black on white" camera, and Japanese cinema was born.

Interested in doing more than just filming street scenes or dances, Shiro became obsessed with trick photography, and his first two short films, *Jizo the Spook* and *Resurrection of a Corpse*, both shot in 1898, showcased this interest. While it's difficult to know today whether *Jizo* was truly a horror film, it most likely *was* dark, given the myths behind the god Jizou and the sinister stories surrounding the statues. It should also be noted that both films starred Ishii Soshichi and Sugiura Sojiro, who were Konishi employees. After shooting these two films, Shiro departed the company in 1899 and became a noted cinematographer in his own right. CW

The Mesmerist
aka **The Mesmerist, or Body and Soul**
G.A.S. Films; b/w; 1 min; Great Britain
D/S/P/C/FX: George Albert Smith
Cast unknown

Professor Fluence is an expert on mesmerism. As such, an old woman wishing to learn more about the occult science visits him. To demonstrate the validity of his work, he draws the spirit of a little girl from her body and sends it walking over and through the furniture. After the little girl's spirit returns to her body, the professor wakes her. The old woman is both impressed and relieved to see that the child is fine.

In 1898 Smith patented the first-ever process for double exposure, an amazing discovery that would bode well for cinematic special effects. Obviously Smith employed the effect here, perhaps in an attempt to best Méliès, who had found commercial success with films utilizing jump cuts. Méliès would return Smith's challenge that very same year by putting to use the process of superimposition in *The Cave of Demons* (1898). CW

Photographing a Ghost
G.A.S. Films; b/w; 1 min; Great Britain
D/S/P/C/FX: George Albert Smith
Cast unknown

A photographer is set to film a real ghost, which has been captured in a trunk by two men. They bring the trunk into the room and open it, allowing the ghost to rise into the air and float around. But just as the photographer is about to shoot it, it disappears. The ghost then reappears and floats back into the trunk, which the photographer quickly shuts. Believing he has the spirit trapped, he sits atop the trunk and locks it. However, after he gets up, the ghost appears again and, now angry, throws chairs around the room. As a result, the photographer abandons his plan to film it.

Containing a brew of jump cuts and superimpositions, *Photographing a Ghost* is a classic example of a trick film. Like most films from the period, it was likely intended to make the audience both laugh and shiver. CW

Resurrection of a Corpse
aka **Shinen no sosei**
Konishi; b/w; length unknown; Japan
D/C: Asana Shiro *S:* Hatta Eijiro
Cast: Ishii Soshichi, Sugiura Sojiro

The second of Shiro's short films from 1898 (after *Jizo the Spook*), *Resurrection of a Corpse* is part comedy, part horror and all trick photography. It tells the story of a man who dies and is placed in his coffin. While the coffin is being carried to the cemetery, its bottom drops out and its occupant returns miraculously to life, possibly as a result of prayers said over his corpse.

Not long after his two most famous films for Konishi were completed, Shiro departed the company. Konishi abandoned the simple "black on white" camera and upgraded to a Gaumont, and Shibata Tsunekichi became Konishi's new house director. His first production, *Momijigari* (1899), used an all-male cast even for the female roles, a tradition which lasted in Japanese cinema until 1911, when dancer Tokuko Nagai Takagi starred in her first film, quickly became a sensation and went on to star in four Thanhouser films in the United States. CW

1899

Cagliostro's Mirror
aka **Le miroir de Cagliostro**; **The Mirror of Cagliostro**
Star Film; b/w; 1 min; France
D/P/S/FX: Georges Méliès
Cast: Georges Méliès

The first film to reference Count Alessandro di Cagliostro (the occultist alias of one Giuseppe Balsamo) was George Méliès' 1899 *Cagliostro's Mirror*. But the one-minute work has nothing to do with the infamous figure, being instead a rather dull special effects short with no apparent plot. A basket of flowers appears in a picture frame on a wall, only to be replaced by a portrait of a lady, which in turn comes to life and begs to be set free. A man (Méliès) observes and approaches, but as he nears the woman, she becomes a skeleton, then transforms into Mephistopheles.

The film employs the stop-substitution technique for which its director is famed and offers little of interest to anyone who has already seen a Méliès film. CW

Cleopatra
aka **Cléopâtre**; **Cleopatra's Tomb**; **Robbing Cleopatra's Tomb**
Star Film; b/w; 2 min; France
D/P/S/FX: Georges Méliès
Cast: Georges Méliès, Jeanne d'Alcy

This is, without a doubt, the first mummy movie. Long thought lost, a copy of *Cleopatra* turned up in a storeroom in France in 2005. It had been thought by some historians to detail Cleopatra's death scene from Shakespeare's *Antony and Cleopatra*, but this turns out to most definitely *not* be the case. It is, rather, an outright horror film, originally known in the United States as both *Cleopatra's Tomb* and *Robbing Cleopatra's Tomb*. Méliès stars as the diabolical figure that finds the mummy of Cleopatra and, after apparently cutting it up, uses fire to resurrect it to life. (Méliès' mistress and later his wife, Jeanne d'Alcy, portrays the reborn Cleopatra.)

The trick photography consists entirely of jump cuts, which the director had mastered fairly early on. CW

The Demon Barber
American Mutoscope & Biograph; b/w; 5 min; U.S.
Credits unknown

Though some sources list this early take on *Sweeney Todd: The Demon Barber of Fleet Street* as an Edison production, it was actually produced by American Mutoscope in competition with Edison. American Mutoscope often mimicked Edison's productions. A case in point is the former's lowbrow *Trilby* rip-offs, rushed into the public arena after Edison's success in filming parts of the stage play based upon George Du Maurier's novel.

Very little is known about *The Demon Barber*, and its cast and crew are long since lost to time. It was released in June 1899 and probably had a humorous bent, as so many films of the time did.

The story of Sweeney Todd first appeared in a Victorian Penny Dreadful in 1846 and 1847; the titular character was a barber whose shop was fitted with a trap door through which he dumped the bodies of his murdered and robbed victims into his cellar. There in the cellar Todd's cohort, Mrs. Lovett, stripped them of their flesh and baked the remains into pies to sell in her pie shop.

It's probable that *The Demon Barber* did not follow the Todd story closely but simply touched on its basic theme. Unless and until the film resurfaces, the particulars of the plot will likely remain unknown. CW

The Devil in a Convent
aka **Le Diable au convent**; **The Sign of the Cross**
Star Film; b/w; 3 min; France
D/P/S/FX: Georges Méliès
Cast: Georges Méliès

Disguising himself as a priest, the devil enters a convent, calls a group of nuns to the chapel and preaches from the pulpit. Then, when he transforms back into Mephistopheles before their very eyes, the nuns react in horror and flee. The devil proceeds to corrupt the convent, causing holy paraphernalia to disappear and satanic adornments to replace it. He conjures demons, evil children, a monstrous cat's face and a menacing toad before a nun confronts him with a crucifix. Other nuns—or possibly their spirits; the film isn't quite clear on this—enter the room and join in the confrontation. The sacristan and others appear and do battle as well. The Prince of Darkness seems to be besting them until a statue of Saint Michael the Archangel comes to life, summarily dispatching the devil to the bowels of hell.

Foreshadowing the religious horrors to come 70 years later in the form of *Rosemary's Baby* (1968), *The Exorcist* (1973), *The Omen* (1976) and their many clones, Méliès subdues the horror here with his typical slapstick approach. Even so, it must have been considered quite daring at the time to have the devil emerge from a baptismal font and wreak havoc on a Catholic convent.

Devilish chicanery aside, Méliès achieved some of his most startling effects to date, making flawless transitions as one object becomes another or disappears and then reappears elsewhere. Particularly striking is the moment the devil glides from the font to the floor on the wings of his bat-like cloak. The painted backdrop of the monastery is classic Méliès, who squeezes a great deal of depth from a one-dimensional image.

The Devil in a Convent, like much of Méliès' work, opaquely reflects his Catholic aesthetic. Good triumphs over evil, as it tends to in those Méliès films where demons bedevil people. For whatever reasons, Méliès characters trapped in dreamscapes or haunted rooms tend not to fare so well.

The year 1899 also saw Méliès release *Summoning the Spirits*, which, though containing a devil, lacked even the most basic narrative. An apparent magician (Méliès) hangs a wreath, which turns into a demon, a woman and finally the magician before it is revealed that, nope, it really was just a wreath after all. Despite its title, there are no ghosts, and it is not a horror film. CW

The Haunted House
Lubin; b/w; length unknown; U.S.
Credits unknown

Siegmund Lubin (1851-1923) began his film career in the 1890s by developing an all-in-one camera and working as a distributor for Thomas Alva Edison. He began creating his own pictures in 1897, imitating the work of Edison and French cineaste Georges Méliès. His first film was an actuality film titled *Unveiling of Washington Monument*, where the camera was, à la Andy Warhol, simply set up and allowed to film an actual object or event.

Lubin's career spanned two decades, during which he founded a chain of movie theaters and established studios throughout North America. A Jew of German heritage, he regularly used cinema as a platform against anti-Semitism. But despite a propensity for philanthropic work in general, he wasn't the most honest of businessmen. Not only did he profit from cheaper versions of other people's work, he often stole the films of others outright and sold them as his own, a move that didn't endear him to industry insiders. He faced frequent lawsuits from Edison and others, and at one point even halted production on his films and left the country, allowing the situation an opportunity to cool down. But even after joining the Motion Picture Patents Company in 1908 (thus ending many of his legal troubles), his unscrupulous undercutting of his rivals continued. After a fire at his main studios and the outbreak of World War I in 1914, his company went defunct. What remained of it was sold in 1917 to Vitagraph, at which time Lubin returned to his former career as an optician. He died in his New Jersey home in 1923.

In *The Haunted House*, he exhibits his congenital lack of originality, hopping aboard the special-effects-driven "haunted hotel" comedy/horror bandwagon already mastered by so many more capable filmmakers. The tale is told through the eyes of the cleverly named Silas Hayseed. Silas is a stereotypical country bumpkin who decides to spend the night in a hotel that, unknown to him, is haunted. After he undresses and climbs into bed, a ghost materializes in the middle of the room. When he jumps from his bed and begs the ghost not to hurt him, it vanishes. But as Silas is about to climb back into bed, something even worse than the ghost appears: Satan the Devil. There's some typical stop-substitution, after which a terrified Silas runs outside into the street to escape the terrors of his room.

The "story" is done better in Méliès' *The Bewitched Inn* and George Albert Smith's *The Haunted Castle* (both 1897). CW

A Midnight Episode
aka **Un bon lit**; **A Good Bed**
Star-Film; b/w; 1 min; France
D/P/S/FX: Georges Méliès
Cast: Georges Méliès

Revisiting the theme of his earlier *A Terrible Night* (1896), Méliès here repeats the plot of a man (Méliès) awakened from a deep slumber by a bug crawling across him. He kills it, only to discover several more climbing up his bedroom wall. He lights each of them with his candle, causing them to explode. Then, having dispatched them, he relaxes for a good night's sleep.

The bugs are gigantic, making the film a presentation of the extraordinary. The film was likely intended to be funny, scary and repulsive—all at the same time. CW

The Miser's Doom
Paul; b/w; 3 min; Great Britain
D/S/C/FX: Walter R. Booth *P:* Robert W. Paul
Cast unknown

A former painter and amateur magician, Walter Robert Booth (sometimes credited as W.R. Booth, 1869-1938) devised this, his first film for Robert W. Paul (1869-1943), in 1899.

A self-employed instrument maker and electrician, Paul had been approached by two foreigners to create facsimiles of an Edison-built Kinetoscope (a device that allowed for the exhibition of motion pictures produced with a motion picture camera). After realizing that the machine hadn't been patented in Great Britain (an oversight on Edison's part), Paul made several additional Kinetoscopes and sold them to interested parties around the country. A snag manifested soon, however; those who bought the machines could not display Edison's movies without a license, and Edison wouldn't license to those who had bought the machines from a counterfeiter. This created an instant market for movies produced by companies other than Edison's, and Paul, in association with U.S.-born photographer Birt Acres, quickly developed a motion picture camera of his own. Shortly thereafter Paul and Acres had a falling out that lasted for the rest of their lives. Around the same time, Paul also built his own theater.

Following in the footsteps of French stage magician and director Georges Méliès, Paul's primary focus was on trick films, and to that end he used his own small theater as a film studio, hiring Booth, among others, as technical assistant. While some have claimed that Paul was the person who actually made the films, the existing evidence indicates that Paul was, in fact, the brains behind the business, with Booth doing most of the actual work. It should also be noted that even after production began at his studios, Paul maintained his original business, which won major industry awards in 1904 and 1910. This raises the likelihood that his primary work took up most of his time, leaving the film production chores to Booth. The few films that historians know for certain that Paul directed were mostly simple shorts recording real-life events (or "actuality films" as they became known).

Most of the films the two made together were intended to amuse the audience, not terrify it, but there were occasional forays into darker terrain. In *The Miser's Doom*, for example, the miser of the title inadvertently causes the death of a woman, who then haunts him into an early grave. The effects consisted primarily of stop-substitution rather than the more complicated double exposure, a technique still far from common at the time.

For his next film, *Upside Down, or The Human Flies* (1899), Booth would turn his camera upside down to give the appearance that his actors were walking on the ceiling, hence the title.
CW

Mephistopheles starts and fans the fires of eternal life in this one-minute Georges Méliès short, *Pillar of Fire*.

Pillar of Fire
aka **La danse de feu**; **La Colonne de feu**; **The Dance of Fire**; **The Column of Fire**
Star Film; color; 1 min; France
D/P/S/FX: Georges Méliès
Cast: Georges Méliès, Jeanne d'Alcy

This is the very first film adaptation of H. Rider Haggard's classic and oft-filmed novel *She: A History of Adventure*, first published over two years (1886-1887) in serial form in an illustrated British newspaper (and later in a U.S.-based magazine) before seeing print in novel form. The book proved so successful that Haggard wrote a sequel, *Ayesha: The Return of She* (1905), and two prequels, *She and Allan* (1921) and *Wisdom's Daughter* (1923).

She (which, with 1885's *King Solomon's Mines* a close second, remains Haggard's most famous work) concerns the quest of a handsome young man named Leo Vincey who, with his Neanderthal-like adopted father, Cambridge professor Horace Holly, goes on a quest to find the truth about his ancestry. Along the way, the two men encounter various perils as well as the beautiful murderess and queen, She-Who-Must-Be-Obeyed, Ayesha (pronounced Asha, according to Haggard). Ayesha is convinced that Leo is the reincarnation of her former lover Kallikrates, whom she killed in a jealous rage some two thousand years before. She promises him everlasting life if he pays obeisance to her and bathes with her in the Pillar of Fire.

Haggard's novel, by turns both pulp adventure and horror fantasy, has been filmed numerous times, most often during the silent era but most famously as *She* in 1935 (by the producers of *King Kong*, 1933) and in 1965 (by Hammer Film Productions). A 1985 version transplants the action to a post-apocalyptic world in imitation of the wildly successful *Mad Max* (1979) and presents a milieu in which werewolves and giants are commonplace. This version is straightforward science fiction, however, bearing little resemblance to its source material.

Readers of Haggard's novel will likewise find little similarity between his tale and Méliès' unauthorized adaptation, which is a little over a minute in length. The film pares down the book to a single sequence in which Ayesha (d'Alcy) bathes in the "pillar of fire" referenced in the film's title. The director spells out the source of the fire's power to grant eternal life. None other than Mephistopheles starts and fans the flames; thus, the immortal conflagration is not an agent of a benevolent god but rather the bribe of a malevolent devil.

The film was one of the earliest color productions, each frame having been hand painted. It begins with a mostly brown tint, with the devil colored bright green. As the flames burn brighter and Ayesha, bedecked in a white gown, does her dance, the scene changes to a brilliant and blazing red. It culminates with Ayesha floating up and out of the frame.

Méliès would eventually find himself pushed further in the direction of hand-painted color films by the success of Thomas A. Edison's hand-painted releases, which came to challenge Méliès' success as the leader of the world's film industry. CW

1900

Chinese Magic
aka Yellow Peril
Paul; b/w; 1 min; Great Britain
D/S/C/FX: Walter R. Booth *P:* Robert W. Paul
Cast unknown

Booth's second horror film, made the year after *The Miser's Doom* (1899), concerns a Chinese magician who turns into a very large bat through the sorcery of cinematic jump cutting. If one considers Georges Méliès' *The Devil's Castle* (1896) the first vampire film because it has Mephistopheles transform into a bat, then *Chinese Magic* is the second, achieving as it does the exact same effect in the exact same manner. Booth was, however, never able to match Méliès' delirious sense of editing and effects work and therefore never gained the same fame and renown as his French competitor. CW

Davy Jones' Locker
American Mutoscope and Biograph; b/w; 1 min; U.S.
D: Frederick S. Armitage
Cast unknown

This was the first horror film to reference "Davy Jones' locker," an old nautical euphemism for death by drowning at sea. *Davy Jones' Locker* employed an early and inferior method of superimposition, producing effects that pale in comparison to those employed by Méliès. There's no story to speak of, either, just a creepy image of a skeleton dancing over a shipwreck, probably symbolizing the death of the men who worked the ship.

This wasn't, of course, the only horror film to deal with the terrors of nighttime waters. Méliès dealt with the subject in *The Kingdom of Fairies* (1903), and Pathé shot its own answer to Méliès' production, probably in 1910. The original title of Pathé's film is unknown, but it was re-released in the 1920s under the title *A Trip to Davey Jones' Locker*.

The same year that Frederick Armitage directed *Davy Jones' Locker*, he also combined two pre-existing films to create *Neptune's Daughters*—the first of those films was *Ballet of the Ghosts*, in which a group of women cast aside their garments, perform a ballet and then put their clothes back on; the second was simply an image of a surf. When combined, it appeared that the women were spirits rising out of the sea to do a bizarre and titillating dance. Armitage's third film of 1900, *A Nymph of the Waves*, similarly featured a woman rising up from the waves and performing a seductive dance. It, too, was a combination of two older films, one superimposed over the other.

Davy Jones' Locker was released in December 1900. CW

A Fantastical Meal
aka Le Repas fantastique
Star Film; b/w; 2 min; France
D/P/S/FX: Georges Méliès
Cast: Georges Méliès

For the most part, *A Fantastical Meal* is a silly comedy about a dining room that takes on a life of its own (revisiting Méliès' cherished "haunted room" motif). The film touches upon horror only when a ghastly dancing apparition appears on a dinner table, causing the women to run away and the sole man (Méliès) in the group to fight back. Unfortunately, objects pass through the specter with no effect.

Meal is typical Star Film fare. By this time, Méliès was beginning to run low on creative steam, his films repeatedly playing out in standard fashion with little new to say. The sight of chairs and other objects appearing and disappearing had by now been done too many times by the cinemagician (as well as by others) to be of much interest. It wouldn't be until the fantastic excesses of *Blue Beard* (1901) that the director would succeed, for a time, at making himself relevant again. CW

Faust and Marguerite
Edison; b/w; 1 min; U.S.
D: Edwin S. Porter *P:* Thomas A. Edison
Cast unknown

Often mistakenly cited as a re-release of the (actually lost) 1897 Méliès film *Faust and Marguerite*, the second *Faust and Marguerite* is an Edison production directed by Edwin S. Porter. Méliès would later make *Faust aux enfers*, titled *The Damnation of Faust* (1903) in the United States, and *Damnation du Docteur Faust*, titled *Faust and Marguerite* (1904) in the United States, but both were released after Porter's film. Regardless, Porter's film is, on some level, an attempt to emulate Méliès, particularly in its simplistic (though at the time cutting-edge) special effects. Edison's promotional material described the film thusly: "Marguerite is seated before the fireplace, Faust standing by her side. Mephistopheles enters and offers his sword to Faust, commanding him to behead the fair Marguerite. Faust refuses, whereupon Mephistopheles draws the sword across the throat of the lady and she suddenly disappears and Faust is seated in her place."

Unfortunately, the press materials are not quite accurate, apparently attempting to boil down a complex (i.e., confusing) plot into something more intelligible. While Mephistopheles does rake his blade across Marguerite's throat, what follows makes little sense. Among the things not mentioned in the synopsis is that Faust and Marguerite trade places and continue to do so throughout the film at the prodding of the devil's sword.

Characters appear, disappear and replace each other with reckless abandon. At one point, Faust inexplicably becomes a skeleton. An older gentleman eventually appears and banishes the devil with a prayer, causing the reappearance of Faust and Marguerite, who are now locked hand in hand. The film ends happily enough with the loving couple free of the devil and reciting their wedding vows. Because of the rather abrupt ending in the existing print, one can conclude that the film is missing a couple of seconds, though the primary action appears concluded.

What any of this has to do with the German legend or Goethe's poem is anyone's guess. No information has survived to document just who the participants were, other than the director and producer. The film was released in February 1900. CW

A Jersey Skeeter
American Mutoscope & Biograph; b/w; 2 min; U.S.
C: Arthur Marvin
Cast unknown

This is an early example of a horror/science fiction hybrid. As with George Méliès' *A Terrible Night* (1896) and *A Midnight Episode* (1899), *A Jersey Skeeter* concerns a giant bug attacking a man—in this case, a New Jersey farmer who complains about the size and peskiness of the local mosquitoes. Drinking from a large cask of Jersey applejack as he bitches, he is suddenly beset by a giant "skeeter" flying around his head. He tries to knock it out of the air with a nearby broom but instead falls down himself. The mosquito then swoops down, lifts him off the ground and carries him away. (The effects were achieved in one take using a mechanical contraption for the mosquito.)

Jersey applejack was an alcoholic beverage made from apples and commonly used as a bartering tool or currency in colonial America. It has been alleged that it was made famous by George Washington who, once he had tasted it, paid the family who produced it for their recipe before introducing it to the colony of Virginia. That the farmer drinks it before being apprehended by the skeeter suggests that the entire episode may be an alcoholic delusion. CW

Uncle Josh in a Spooky Hotel
Edison; b/w; 1 min; U.S.
D/S/C/FX: Edwin S. Porter *P:* Thomas A. Edison
Cast: Charles 'Daddy' Manley

A sequel of sorts to *Uncle Josh's Nightmare* (1900; both films were copyrighted on the same day), *Uncle Josh in a Spooky Hotel* has

A portrait of Thomas Alva Edison circa 1922

Uncle Josh (Manley) on a mission to find a ghost, perhaps as a result of his encounter with the supernatural in the previous film. He comes to an inn with a reputedly haunted room and checks it out to ensure that no one plans to deceive him with magicians' tricks. The landlord tells him that the ghost is believed to appear precisely at midnight, and the two take seats in the room and await its arrival. At exactly the witching hour, the ghost indeed appears, but it appears behind them where it cannot be seen and plays a game with them, smacking one, disappearing, reappearing and smacking the other one. As a result, each man believes the other has smacked him, and a scuffle ensues before the ghost

Blue Beard: **The image of Bluebeard's former wives, all hanging in a row, is perhaps the most shocking in Méliès'** *oeuvre.*

is finally seen, sending the landlord scurrying from the room. Uncle Josh turns to speak to the landlord, only to realize that he is seated next to the ghost.

More entertaining than its predecessor, the film's effects are nonetheless primitive when compared to those of George Méliès in France or George Albert Smith in Great Britain. Porter would film Uncle Josh again in *Uncle Josh at the Moving Picture Show* (1902), in which the portly rube, seeing his first movie, becomes so discomfited by the images that he tears down the screen in an attempt to save the distressed heroine.

Porter's greatest contribution to cinema, however, would come with *The Life of an American Fireman* and *The Great Train Robbery* (both 1903), where he would introduce the most innovative, influential, and enduring technique of film editing ever devised: cross cutting. CW

Uncle Josh's Nightmare
Edison; b/w; 2 min; U.S.
D/S/C/FX: Edwin S. Porter *P:* Thomas Edison
Cast: Charles 'Daddy' Manley

Uncle Josh's Nightmare is an early example of a horror comedy, with a title character that carried a short-lived series of films, the first two of which involved demonic manifestation and haunting.

Uncle Josh (Manley), a burly older man who's a bit of a hick, wants to get some sleep. But the moment he gets into bed and closes his eyes, a demon with devil horns and a short black cloak appears and grabs his blanket. When Uncle Josh attempts to retrieve his cover from the demon's clutches, the demon disappears and Uncle Josh falls flat on his derriere. Upset, he gets to his feet and fixes a drink, but the demon reappears and snatches his cup. The two fight, and Uncle Josh knocks the demon out!

Then, after wrapping his supernatural nemesis in a sheet and securing the bundle with rope, Josh places his adversary in a trunk and does a victory dance. But when he opens the trunk to ensure his prisoner is still there, the demon is gone. It appears again, however, and smacks Josh in the face, only to disappear all over again. Josh tries to get back into bed, but the entire bed disappears. After more appearances and disappearances of the demon and various objects in the room, a specter rises from the trunk. Finally, just as Josh seems about ready to give up his room, his bed and other possessions abruptly reappear and the demon vanishes for good.

Charles Manley was a theater actor who made the jump to the big screen with this, his first film. He would return to play Uncle Josh several more times, his final portrayal coming in the daring *How They Do Things on the Bowery* (1902), before he moved on to bigger and better roles. It has been alleged that he was part of the cast of Ford's Theater at the time of President Abraham Lincoln's assassination in April 1865. Manley died in 1916, and his final film, *Her Wayward Parents*, was released posthumously in 1917. Certainly not a terrific actor, Manley lacked the pantomimic approach needed for the humor to work.

The editing effects in *Uncle Josh's Nightmare* are inanely simplistic and come nowhere near to matching the glorious intensity of Méliès' best work from the same period. There are, inevitably, critics who point to this film as an example of pioneering special effects and editing, leaving one to wonder whether they've actually seen much cinema from before this point.

In *Uncle Josh's Nightmare*, one can always tell when an edit is about to occur because Manley assumes the same pose each time: one leg thrown slightly forward, both arms raised in the air with fists clenched and his head raised as if to heaven. CW

1901

Another Job for the Undertaker
Edison; b/w; 2 min; U.S.
D/S/FX: Edwin S. Porter *P:* Thomas Edison
Cast unknown

Edwin Porter was adept at making "rube comedies," or humorous films in which a country bumpkin faces one or more extraordinary aspects of life. Here, what begins as a typical rube comedy ends on a startlingly dark note. *Another Job for the Undertaker* deposits our rube in an apparently haunted hotel room, one obviously influenced by Georges Méliès' *The Bewitched Inn* (1899) and *Going to Bed Under Difficulties* (1900). The bellhop, after showing the protagonist his sleeping quarters, does a somersault and disappears through the closed door. This, for whatever reason, doesn't terrify the man, who sets down the various personal items he's been carrying (which include a satchel and an umbrella), only to have them vanish. The jacket he is wearing likewise disappears, but the man seems determined to stay in the room.

Blue Beard demonstrated the epic filmmaking approach used by Méliès and became his first horror film of sustained length and substance.

When he takes off his boots to prepare for bed, they promptly walk off, and the bed vanishes as well. After a couple of other bizarre things happen, he blows out the gaslight—ignoring the sign on the wall that says "Do Not Blow Out the Gas"—and gets into bed. The scene cuts away to the street below, where passes the horse-drawn wagon of an undertaker. The clear implication is that the rube will be dead before the night is over, a rather grim conclusion to what is, in every other way, a comedy centered on the usual array of disappearing and reappearing items.

Most of Porter's films during this period were shot back-to-back in Edison's Black Maria studio, which had been built in 1892 in West Orange, New Jersey to provide a place for the company's productions. As such, it was the world's first real movie studio, as well as a part of Edison's laboratories. It was closed in early 1901 and destroyed in 1903. CW

Blue Beard
aka Barbe-bleue
Star Film; b/w; 11 min; France
D/P/S/FX: Georges Méliès
Cast: Georges Méliès, Jeanne d'Alcy

Blue Beard followed a return by Méliès to epic filmmaking (begun the year before with the terrific color outing *Joan of Arc*) and is his first horror film of sustained length and substance, a major production complete with multiple sets, period clothing, dissolves and unprecedented violence.

After bribing the father of a beautiful young girl for her hand in marriage, Bluebeard takes his new bride to his chateau. There he shows off his extravagant home and offers her a lavish meal, but he insists that there is one thing she must never do—enter one particular locked room in the house. He then gives her a key to the room as a test of her devotion and departs on the pretext of tending to a business matter. Unable to resist her own natural instincts (which are personified by a demonic imp), she allows her curiosity to get the best of her and, inside the darkened room, finds the hung bodies of Bluebeard's previous wives, all arranged neatly in a row. (This image is arguably the most shocking in Méliès' oeuvre, due mainly to its uncharacteristic realism.)

Literally red-handed upon the return of her husband (she has dropped the key into what appears to be a vat of blood and is desperately trying to clean it off), the wife flees his presence and seeks protection from her brothers, who have come to save her. After a sword fight, Bluebeard is done in when a fairy summons the ghosts of his dead wives to exact vengeance upon their murderer.

Based on French writer Charles Perrault's tale of the same name, Méliès' *Blue Beard* would be the first in a long line of nominal adaptations that include *Bluebeard* (1944, 1972) and *Bluebeard's Ten Honeymoons* (1960). Some of these films combined elements of Perrault's story with the real-life story of Henri Landru, a Parisian swindler who in the early 1900s murdered elderly women after gaining access to their money and assets. Méliès' version is a surprisingly faithful adaptation of the Perrault story, apart from its introduction of supernatural elements.

Perrault is famous for having transmuted folk tales into a new and unique literary genre, the fairy tale. His stories have, among other things, provided subjects for animated Walt Disney films for nearly a century, including *Cinderella* (1950) and *Sleeping Beauty* (1959). Méliès owes Perrault a debt of gratitude for providing the director with fodder for his first attempt at something larger than a short drawing room adventure—Méliès' own version of *Cinderella* in 1899. In fact, Méliès liked the tale so much that he adapted it a second time, as a 24-minute epic in 1912.

Perrault's *Le Barbe bleue* was first published in *Histoires ou Contes du temps passé* in the late 1690s. Many sources have claimed that the story was based on the real-life case of Gilles de Rais, a Breton knight who lived in the first half of the 1400s, but this seems unlikely given that Rais is believed to have been a murderer of children (mostly boys, whom it is claimed he sometimes tore apart with his teeth), not women—and even that is highly doubtful. Many historians believe that Rais signed a confession to murder and witchcraft to outwit the Church. When the Church made the accusation of pederasty and murder—hoping to gain his vast property—it believed he would die insisting upon his innocence, which would cause his property to fall under the Church's provenance. However, by signing his own confession, Rais ensured that the Church would forfeit his property and fortune, which would be consigned to his heirs.

While other figures, both historical and fantastic, have been assigned the role of having influencing Perrault's classic story, it is possible that he simply made it up. He was, after all, a writer. CW

The Devil and the Statue
aka Le Diable géant ou le miracle de la madone
Star Film; b/w; 2 min; France
D/P/S/FX: Georges Méliès
Cast: Georges Méliès

Two young lovers embrace, then the young man departs and the devil (Méliès), growing to monstrous proportions, threatens the maiden. She prays to a statue of the Virgin Mary, who shrinks the devil back down to size and causes him to disappear.

Perhaps the most interesting thing about *The Devil and the Statue* is its imagery of the Madonna coming to life to vanquish evil. In this respect, the film predicts a similar scene in Universal's classic *The Mummy* (1932) in which the heroine calls on the Goddess of Magic, Isis, to save her.

The major trick of the film, the devil's outrageous growth spurt, is a repeat of an effect the director used in *The Man with the Rubber Head* (1901), made just before *The Devil and the Statue*. Interestingly enough, the effect looks better in *Man* than it does in *Devil*, even though the former called for the growth of only a head, not an entire body. Méliès was obviously experimenting in *Devil* to see how far he could push this particular effect. He would continue doing so with his very next film, *The Dwarf and the Giant* (1901), in which two copies of Méliès stand side-by-side. One retains its normal size while the other grows.

Filmmakers created the special effect by placing the object that was to grow on a dolly and pulling the dolly toward the camera. Then that moving image was superimposed over a dark section of a static shot, making the object appear to grow larger while everything else in the shot remained the same size. It was an extraordinary effect, so effective that world-class special-effects experts aped it often, including Ray Harryhausen, who used it in *The Seventh Voyage of Sinbad* (1958). CW

The Drunkard's Conversion
aka **Horrors of Drink**
Paul; b/w; 2 min; Great Britain
D/C/FX: Walter R. Booth *P:* Robert W. Paul
Cast unknown

Influenced by a revival sweeping Great Britain at the time, Walter R. Booth's *The Drunkard's Conversion* reflected a growing religious/political movement that perceived alcohol as a demon needing exorcism. The short trick film concerns a drunkard converted by the Spirit of Temperance after imagining gnomes and snakes are after him. It served as a model for filmmaker William Haggar's *D.T.'s, or the Effects of Drink* (1905), in which a drunken man believes that his furniture has become monsters and decides to give up drinking altogether. It's almost impossible that Haggar was unaware of Booth's film, as both men were prominent filmmakers working in Great Britain at the same time.

In 1904 Booth directed a film entitled *The Haunted Scene Painter*. In the film a painter's art comes to life, but this film was primarily a comedy trading on Booth's interest in animation, which he'd previously indulged in *The Devil in the Studio* (1901) and to which he would return in *The Hand of the Artist* (1906). CW

The Fairy of the Black Rocks
aka **La fée des roches noires**
Pathé; b/w; length unknown; France
Credits unknown

Société Pathé Frères was the brainchild of four brothers—Charles, Théophile, Émile and Jacques Pathé—who founded the company in 1896 to create cinematic material for the French market. Their productions proved successful enough that within their first year they were doing business in the United States. As their popularity grew, they penetrated the British, Belgian, Spanish, Italian, Japanese and Australian markets as well.

One of Pathé's first and most prominent directors was Ferdinand Zecca (1864-1947). Zecca made his first film in 1899 (he and a fellow thespian acted out their own show before a camera), and the following year Charles Pathé hired him to assist in setting up and running a booth at the Paris World Exposition. The two hit it off immediately, and Zecca went on to oversee numerous productions for Pathé.

The Fairy of the Black Rocks has a confused production history. Some sources list the film as being produced in 1901, while others give the date as 1904. Still others claim that the film is a 1905 production from Robert W. Paul, and to confuse matters even more, it seems that Segundo de Chomón (a frequent collaborator of Zecca's) produced a second film with that same title in 1907.

Most likely 1901 is the correct date of Zecca's film, given that it was advertised under its British title as part of a touring program during Christmas of that year. All of this aside, however, a photograph believed to be from the film shows skeletons cavorting in a graveyard, revealing that the film had a dark bent. CW

The Haunted Curiosity Shop
Paul; b/w; 2 min; Great Britain
D/C/FX: Walter R. Booth *P:* Robert W. Paul
Cast unknown

After the entertaining *The Magic Sword* (1901), Booth created this horror comedy in obvious imitation of director George Méliès' "haunted room" movies—derivative, though at least Booth takes a lame stab at originality by changing the locale from an inn to a curio shop.

The owner of said shop opens a large cabinet while a skull floats behind him, wearing what appears to be an Ancient Egyptian headdress. When he turns around and sees it, it instantly becomes the head and torso of a beautiful woman. After retrieving the bottom half of her body, she dances toward the open arms of the excited shop owner; then, in a jarringly racist moment, she becomes a black woman, and he immediately and disgustedly shuts her in the cabinet. Through the closed cabinet doors he spies the spirit of the Caucasian woman and, in a moment of renewed excitement, flings the doors open again. At first the cabinet appears empty, then a woman appears. She transforms into a skeleton, and then a knight, whom the old man takes apart and then disposes. Next, he is bedeviled by bearded elves, which he also quickly bests. Shortly after, the film abruptly ends. Some sources maintain that the curiosity shop deals exclusively in Egyptian antiquities, but a careful examination of the set indicates that it doesn't specialize that neatly.

Little more than an antiquated curio, *The Haunted Curiosity Shop* might hold some interest for those studying racist representations of minorities in century-old films. Otherwise, some so-so effects added to a nonexistent story don't really make for all that interesting a movie. CW

The Magic Sword
aka **The Magic Sword, or A Medieval Mystery**
Paul; b/w; 2 min; Great Britain
D/S/C/FX: Walter R. Booth *P:* Robert W. Paul
Cast unknown

    A witch interrupts a secret rendezvous between a handsome knight and a beautiful lady atop the battlements of a medieval castle. When the knight attempts to apprehend her, she flies off, but not before calling on the spirits of the underworld. A giant ogre reaches over the castle wall and grabs the lady, and as the knight sinks into despair over the loss of his loved one, a fairy appears, gives him a flaming sword and transports him to a cave where he finds his lady. As he prepares to whisk her away to safety, however, the witch once again confronts him. At the last second, the fairy saves the day, intervening before the witch can strike the lovers dead.

    Though heavily influenced by French *fantastique noir* director Georges Méliès (whom producer Paul's catalog at the time referenced), *The Magic Sword* does manage to find a voice of its own, if mostly through decent and varied effects work. The flying witch and the giant ogre are both achieved through double exposures and look fairly realistic (for the time). Certainly, the effects here are much better than the uneven work in Booth's next horror film, the comedic *The Haunted Curiosity Shop* (1901). CW

The Seven Castles of the Devil
aka **Les sept Château du diable**; **The 7 Castles of the Devil**; **Devil's Seven Castles**; **Laboritorio del Diablo**; **Sieben Schlösser Von Teufel**
Pathé; color; 12 min; France
D: Ferdinand Zecca
Cast unknown

    Viewed through modern eyes, *The Seven Castles of the Devil* is entirely pedestrian, and it seems obvious that director Ferdinand Zecca was moving Pathé into the unremarkable direction of Georges Méliès' Star Films (which Pathé would, in fact, later purchase). Given the year in which the film was made, it was a rather long endeavor, foreshadowing Méliès' own move in that direction.

    Seven Castles is hand-painted in a rich tapestry of colors that betrays the spectacular images of Satan's seven castles. The plot has to do with a Faust-like figure who, against his will, navigates a course between Satan's castles (each representing a deadly sin) before being rescued by a beautiful woman. The film is, of course, replete with magic and monsters. But unfortunately, the expertise on display is not up to the standards set by Méliès, who not only mastered sharper and more detailed backdrops but superior editing and effects as well.

    Still, Zecca was a talented individual who refused to be constrained by the filmmaking processes of the period. He experimented constantly with editing techniques and the possibilities of color. And rather than staying within the set boundaries of *fantastique noir*, as so many of his contemporaries (particularly Méliès) did, Zecca made dramas, historical sagas, and even Biblical epics. One such film, *The Life and Passion of Christ* (1903), topped out at 44 minutes in length, making it one of the first feature films, while *Conquering the Skies* (1901) was one of the earliest entries into the science fiction genre. CW

1902

A Fight with Sledge Hammers
Harrison; b/w; 2 min; Great Britain
D/S: Dicky Winslow *P:* George Harrison
Cast: Mr. and Mrs. A.W. Fitzgerald

    Director Dicky Winslow made only three films, but two of them can stake a legitimate claim as early examples of the horror genre. The first, *A Fight with Sledge Hammers*, tells the tale of two burly blacksmiths (one played by A.W. Fitzgerald) in love with the same girl (played by Fitzgerald's wife). Tension between the men leads to an eruption of pent-up sexual frustrations as each wields his sledgehammer against the other.

    While the film appears to be lost, a poster advertising a presentation of it on Berners Street, London, still exists. The ad promises a "Sensational … Melodramatic Film" and proclaims *Sledge Hammers* to be: "The Most Thrilling Film Ever Taken," making clear that the production was designed to create a sense of excitement and horror. A still from the film is the centerpiece of the ad; it shows a woman attempting to halt the violence being perpetrated to gain her romantic attentions. As was usual for the time, the poster makes no mention of the film's true director, leaving producer George Harrison to take full credit for its creation.

    The year 1902 also saw the production of Winslow's most famous film, *Maria Marten: or, The Murder at the Red Barn*, based on an infamous case that had occurred in Suffolk, Great Britain in 1827. The same year Winslow also directed *East Lynne*, based on Mrs. Henry Wood's 1861 novel of the same name. (Mrs. Henry Wood was the pseudonym of Ellen Price Wood.) CW

Maria Marten: or, The Murder at the Red Barn
Harrison; b/w; 5 min; Great Britain
D/S: Dicky Winslow *P:* George Harrison
Cast: Mr. and Mrs. A.W. Fitzgerald

    As with *Fight with Sledge Hammers* (1902), it's likely that Dicky Winslow performed both screenwriting and directing chores on this, his most famous picture.

    Based on the true story of a single mother who falls in love with a farmer's son, *Maria Marten: or, The Murder at the Red Barn* contains an original mix of historical fact, horrific violence and ghostly imagery. Also noteworthy is its reliance on melodrama to entertain, in lieu of the trick photography that was all the rage at the time.

    The actual murder took place in 1827, with the apprehension and trial of the killer in 1828. After impregnating Maria Marten, William Corder had promised to marry her. When the child died soon after birth, Maria nonetheless continued to pursue Corder, possibly even attempting to blackmail him into marriage. Finally, pretending to relent, he asked her to collect some of her things and meet him at "the red barn"—called so because one portion of the roof contained red tiles—outside of town, telling her that from there they would go to Ipswich and wed. For almost a year after Maria left home, her father and stepmother received letters from Corder maintaining that he and Maria had married but that she was either too sick or too busy to write.

    After claiming to have had several terrible dreams in which Maria's ghost visited her, the stepmother insisted to her husband that Maria had been murdered and buried in a corner of the red barn. Maria's father went to the barn with a spade and dug in the very corner his wife had dreamed about; there he found the decomposing corpse of his daughter buried in a grain sack. One of Corder's handkerchiefs was wrapped around her neck, and there was a deep penetration wound to one of her eyes.

After being discovered living with a new wife in London, Corder was quickly apprehended. With much evidence against him (including a witness who saw him with a gun on the day of the murder), the judge in the case found Corder guilty of Maria's murder and sentenced him to death by hanging. In an effort to make himself right with God, Corner admitted that he had indeed shot Maria in the face, but he insisted that it was an accident. (He also suggested that he and Maria had murdered their young child and were arguing over the baby's burial place when the "accident" occurred.)

Following a public execution attended by thousands of people, Corder's body was cut open, and crowds of onlookers were allowed to view the cadaver. The next day the remains were handed over to Cambridge University for dissection. It was later rumored that Maria's stepmother, who wasn't much older than her stepdaughter, had had an affair with William Corder, and that she may have had a role in the murder (hence her knowledge of the body's whereabouts). One version of the story alleges her to have planned Maria's murder with Corder and then, when he ran off afterwards and married another woman, having concocted a story about ghostly dreams as a way to rat him out to the police.

Even before the case was tried, plays casting Corder as a loathsome monster and Maria as a virginal and God-fearing victim were being performed all over Great Britain. It seems only fitting, then, that an incident as famous as this should be one of Great Britain's first contributions to the horror film genre. At five minutes in length, *Maria Marten: or, The Murder at the Red Barn* was the "epic" of Dicky Winslow's three films and one of two to focus on violence and horror. A.W. Fitzgerald starred as Corder, while his real-life wife played Maria. (The two performers had also appeared together in the aforementioned *Fight with Sledge Hammers*.)

Murder at the Red Barn was made up of five scenes, each lasting approximately a minute. The first portrayed Maria and Corder together; the second showed the murder in the red barn; the third presented one of the stepmother's supernatural dreams; the fourth depicted Corder's discovery and arrest and the fifth showed Corder in his cell before his execution. It appears that—like many of the plays based on the incident—the film upped Corder's age and promoted him to village squire and at the same time swapped Maria's sexual past with a more angelic back-story. These particular revisions would continue to persist through many of the subsequent film versions.

The next adaptation of the case would be *The Red Barn Crime* (1908), produced by fairground showman William Haggar. CW

The Prince of Darkness
American Mutoscope & Biograph; b/w; length unknown; U.S.
Credits unknown

Apparently drunk and upset, a man enters a room, takes off his hat, coat and waistcoat and tosses them aside, but they return to him as if by magic. (This was accomplished by reversing the negative.) He throws them to the ground and stomps on them when suddenly the Grim Reaper—or Satan; sources vary as to exactly who—appears in the center of the room, his arms outstretched. The man's clothes again return to his body, and he collapses in a dead faint.

Some sources list the film as having been produced in 1900. CW

The Treasures of Satan
aka **Les Trésors de Satan**; **Mephistopheles' School of Magic**; **The Devil's Money Bags**
Star Film; b/w; 3 min; France
D/P/S/FX: Georges Méliès
Cast: Georges Méliès

A minor relic, *The Treasures of Satan* charts an apparently successful attempt by Satan to keep a miser (Méliès) from retrieving money that Satan has placed within a coffer and over which has cast a spell of protection. As he attempts to gain the money, the old miser is terrorized first by the bags themselves and then by a group of beautiful ladies dressed in skirts and sporting weapons. In the end, he runs off without his loot.

Numerous critics, apparently having neither read the Star Film Catalog's description of the plot nor paid close attention to the film, have assumed that the money belongs to Satan and that the miser is a thief who has broken into Satan's home to steal it. While such an interpretation is possible, it does raise the question of why Satan lives in a chateau—though to be fair, one could also ask, if the miser hordes his money, how can he afford such an ornate and beautiful old home? But, as with so many of the French director's films, questions of storyline are superfluous; *The Treasures of Satan* remains at heart solely an excuse for Méliès to engage in his typical editing and effects trickery. (It must be said, however, that the dance of the moneybags, which recalls something from a bad dream, is striking.)

Méliès' next devil picture would be *The Infernal Cake-Walk* (1903). Despite its title, it is little more than a choreographed dance number (and a dull one at that) set in the bowels of hell, with demons that share heads with the moon men of *A Trip to the Moon* (1902). The two films also share a number of painted backdrops. CW

1903

Apparitions
aka **Le Revenant**
Star Film; b/w; 3 min; France
D/P/S/FX: Georges Méliès
Cast: Georges Méliès, Jeanne d'Alcy

In *Apparitions*, Méliès returns to his world of haunted rooms, last visited in *The Inn Where No Man Rests* (1903). As he retires for the night, a lecherous old man (Méliès) makes a pass at a maid, who rebukes him. Turning from thoughts of sex to the day's newspaper, he sees a candle move mysteriously across the table at which he's sitting. He slides it back, only to have it move again. This comic routine repeats itself too many times before the candle grows to giant proportions and then shrinks back

In *The Treasures of Satan*, Satan attempts to keep a miser (Méliès) from retrieving money placed within a coffer and over which the Devil has cast a spell of protection.

down to size. The games go on, with the candle at last setting the old man's newspaper on fire. A ghostly figure of a woman (d'Alcy) appears in the flames and tempts the old man, but when he engages her taunts, she becomes a ghastly spinster who dances mockingly as she continues to egg him on. When the old man tries to strike her down, she disappears, and he hits the maid who has just entered the room instead.

While credits do not exist for these films, and it's often difficult to know who portrayed whom, the body movements and general size of the dancing ghost woman match those of Méliès, making it likely that he played both this part and that of the old man. When the two appear in the same shot, the dancing woman is obviously superimposed in the darker portion of the frame. And as Méliès proved as far back as *The Dwarf and the Giant* (1901), he could manipulate his images effectively enough to costar alongside himself.

In every other way, the film is strictly routine. CW

Beelzebub's Daughters
aka **La fille du diable**; **The Women of Fire**; **Beelzebub's Daughters, or the Women of Fire**; **The Woman of Fire**; **The Daughters of the Devil**
Star Film; b/w; 3 min; France
D/P/S/FX: Georges Méliès
Cast: Georges Méliès, Jeanne d'Alcy

Claimed by Méliès' own catalog to be the first film of its kind, *Beelzebub's Daughters* concerns a devilish plot to create women in the image of the Dark Lord (Méliès). It begins when Mephistopheles confronts two workers cleaning a hotel room and changes them into dancing demons. The Devil replaces the room with a cavern, conjures what appears to be a fish tank and lies within it. From his fingertips he emits flames and evokes the appearance of three women. Afterward, the cavern transforms back into the hotel room and a hotel manager discovers the reposing figure of the Devil's daughter. The film has cutting-edge special effects, consisting mostly of jump cuts and superimpositions, but in general is a throwback to his films of the late 1800s.

Only a fragment of the film is extant today. CW

The Damnation of Faust
aka **Faust aux enfers**
Star Film; b/w; 7 min; France
D/P/S/FX: Georges Méliès
Cast: Georges Méliès

Not to be confused with Méliès' lost 1898 film of the same title, *The Damnation of Faust* is dull, redundant stuff. While the sets recall the impressive *A Trip to the Moon* (1902), the story is harebrained. Mephistopheles takes Faust down to the infernal regions, where he shows his human hostage the terrifying torments of hell, which include—among other things—female dancers executing a lengthy "brilliant ballet." Faust enjoys the show despite his sadness at the recent death of his beloved Marguerite and his own condemnation to Hell. Then the dancers vanish and the cavern transforms into a waterfall populated by beautiful nymphs. But just when one might conclude that Hell is all ballet and babes, a seven-headed hydra appears. Even here, however, Méliès misses the terror/damnation mark with a rather goofy-looking creation that, had it appeared 65 years later, would have been mistaken for a Yokai monster. This being a Méliès film, however, the hydra quickly vanishes, just as a group of demons appears in the midst of the water and commences frolicking over the rocks and through the falls. The horrible part of Hell, one assumes, has yet to come.

And come it does, sort of. Mephistopheles and Faust sink deeper into the Pit, where more beautiful women are running around in what viewers can assume are flames. Finally, something approximating damnation occurs as Faust is unceremoniously thrown into a furnace. And as the demons and ballerinas continue to shake, rattle and roll, Mephistopheles rises above his subjects and triumphantly spreads his bat-like wings, bringing the events to a merciful conclusion.

At seven minutes, the film is too long, and the direction is stagey and pedestrian. Yet this wouldn't be the end of the director's interest in Faust; he would revisit the character again the very next year in *Faust and Marguerite* (1904). CW

The Enchanted Cup
Paul; b/w; 3 min; Great Britain
D: Walter R. Booth *P:* R.W. Paul
Cast unknown

Dwarves kidnap a peasant girl and plan to burn her as a sacrifice to their god. The girl's sweetheart turns to the Good Fairy for help. The Fairy provides the man with a magic cup, which he uses to rescue the girl in the nick of time.

The Enchanted Cup, it seems, managed to fit some ambitious plotting and effects into its short running time. Its lost status, however, makes it difficult to ascertain just how horror-tinged it really was. It did apparently feature a gorgon, a fearsome creature with snakes for hair that has seldom been convincingly represented on screen in terms of atmospherics (Terence Fisher's poetic *The Gorgon*, 1963, being one of the few exceptions).

British-based Robert W. Paul Productions filmed and distributed over 100 shorts beginning in 1895; many of which vanished sometime before 1909. TH

The Enchanted Well
aka **Le Puits fantastique**
Star Film; b/w; 4 min; France
D/P/S/FX: Georges Méliès
Cast: Georges Méliès

An astounding little film that mixes fantasy and horror with the spectacle of a childhood fairy tale, *The Enchanted Well* is a treat for fans of early special effects, costumes and bizarre monsters. It takes place at a well in the middle of a fort, where a man who is irritated by the begging of an old woman attempts to drive her off by kicking her in the ass. Understandably upset at having her ass kicked, she reveals herself to be a witch and curses the well. After the man draws out water to feed his donkey, an imp appears and turns the water into flames. The well then becomes a gateway to the infernal regions, and out of it comes flames, demons, snakes both large and small, and dinosaur-like frogs. The well then disappears, replaced by the devil, and when the townsfolk unite to banish the Prince of Darkness from their midst, said Prince of Darkness turns into a bat and flies off.

The story appears to be set in pre-modern times. The set consists of the usual painted backdrops and a two-dimensional prop of the well. The two smaller snakes have been described by some film historians as hand puppets, a claim which seems to be true of one but not the other (the second snake is simply too slender and its movement too dexterous to be someone's covered arm). The giant snake is at least partially manipulated by wires, and the donkey and frog-o-saurs are obviously people in costumes. The special effects consist mostly of jump cuts making things appear, disappear or change form altogether.

With the painted, fort-like village and the large fake bat, the film bears a superficial resemblance to parts of Terence Fisher's *The Brides of Dracula* (1960). CW

Faust and Mephistopheles
aka **Faust et Méphistophélès**; **Faust**
Gaumont; b/w; 2 min; France
D: Alice Guy *P:* Léon Gaumont
Cast unknown

Being the talented filmmaker with a knack for complicated storytelling that Alice Guy would become, this version of the Faust legend is a particularly sorry spectacle, with pitiable production values and special effects that were bad even in the context of their time.

Filmed with a static camera on a single set (with jump cuts used to change the poorly illustrated backdrops), *Faust and Mephistopheles* begins with the aging doctor being confronted by an old man who offers him riches in exchange for his soul. Faust at first rejects the intruder, who proves his power by conjuring a demon from a cauldron and turning the imp into a handsome king. The king then strikes the old man, who is revealed (spoiler alert!) to be the devil. Convinced now that that he can indeed be made young through supernatural means, Faust accepts the offer and, after becoming a strikingly handsome cavalier, is shown a vision of the beautiful Marguerite.

From here the narrative crumbles into a nonsensical mélange of appearances and disappearances. A group of specters haunt Faust, but the room changes and the specters vanish. Finally, a woman with a cross appears and banishes the devil, thus inexplicably allowing the younger Faust to ask for the hand of Marguerite in marriage.

The film has little connection with the story upon which it's based, and its happy ending is the mirror-image of the violent and depressing conclusion of the original, in which Faust is forced into hell for his transgressions while Lady Marguerite is consigned to an eternity in heaven without her cherished one.

Guy's *Faust and Mephistopheles* was apparently an attempt to compete with her French contemporary, Georges Méliès. Her attempts at jump cuts were obvious in a way that Méliès' were not, and by 1903 they were indisputably dated. Her trick film is inferior even to W.R. Booth's or Edwin Porter's derived imitations of Méliès and George Albert Smith.

Guy's next horror outing, *Esmeralda* (1905), would move her further in the direction of dramatic storytelling with a feminist bent. She would eventually marry, move to the United States, start her own production company and make some truly astounding films, including *The Pit and the Pendulum* (1913) and *The Vampire* (1915). CW

The Infernal Cauldron
aka **Le Chaudron infernal**
Star Film; color; 2 min; France
D/P/S/FX: Georges Méliès
Cast: Georges Méliès, Jeanne d'Alcy

Following the spectacular success of his epic *The Kingdom of Fairies* (1903), Méliès continued to explore the possibilities of hand-painted images to wow attentive audiences, though in much shorter form. Mephistopheles has a beautiful young lady (d'Alcy) kidnapped, places her in a bag and throws her into a flaming

The spirits of angry females who died in the fiery cauldron become balls of flame that attack the devil, from *The Infernal Cauldron*.

cauldron. He does the same to a second lady and then a third. Almost immediately, their angry spirits escape the pot and turn into balls of flame that attack the devil, driving him into his own cauldron.

The color is particularly striking here. In a creative masterstroke, Méliès portrays the devil and his demon assistant as green (as he had done in *The Pillar of Fire*, 1899) rather than red (though the devil faces adorning Satan's castle are red with yellow horns). There is also a slight greenish tint to the spirits of the roasted women, with colors from the background bleeding through them. When the spirits become fireballs, the deep reds and yellows of the flames are vibrant and realistic.

For his next film, *Apparitions* (1903), Méliès would return to his standard—and much cheaper—use of black and white. CW

The Inn Where No Man Rests
aka **L'Auberge du bon repos**
Star Film; b/w; 5 min; France
D/P/S/FX: Georges Méliès
Cast: Georges Méliès, Jeanne d'Alcy

On the heels of *The Enchanted Well* (1903) and following the pattern of many a previous outing, Méliès shot this weirdly frightening tale about a drunk (Méliès) who holes up for the night in a haunted room. While much of it is typical Méliès (objects moving of their own accord, appearing and disappearing), there are some new elements that keep the proceedings from feeling like total rehash. And despite a zanier-than-usual performance from the director, these new elements add a frightening touch. A picture in the background comes to life and blows out a candle; later its face grows large and its mouth opens to devour that same candle as it glides up a wall. A window in the upper center of the frame develops a moonlike face before being shattered by the boarder; then that same face appears in a grandfather clock before becoming the head of the devil. In a moment that prefigures *The Exorcist* (1973), the boarder's bed shakes and jumps and finally throws him out. Boots walk up walls and a coat rack comes to life. There's even a *Scooby-Doo* moment when the inn's staff chases the boarder through various entrances and exits that can't possibly be connected.

Méliès revisited the character of the drunken boarder three years later in *A Roadside Inn* (1906). This time, the boarder found his room haunted not by genuine spirits but by the inn staff, who use ghostly pranks to rid themselves of unwanted guests. It can reasonably be considered an early example of a film sequel. CW

The Kingdom of Fairies
aka **Le Royaume des fees**; **Wonders of the Deep**; **Fairyland: or, the Kingdom of the Fairies**
Star Film; color; 17 min; France
D/P/S/FX: Georges Méliès
Cast: Georges Méliès, Jeanne d'Alcy

A perfect amalgam of fantasy, horror and adventure, *The Kingdom of Fairies* is one of Méliès' most accomplished films. When the king announces that his daughter, Princess Azurine, is to be married to Prince Bel-Azor, a witch who believes that the king has snubbed her interrupts the proclamation. She curses the princess, kidnaps her and carries her off in a carriage borne by a gigantic, bat-like creature. The king, queen and prince watch the carriage fly across the night sky, surrounded by a coterie of demons and spirits. The prince swears that he will find his princess and avenge her capture. Assisted by a good fairy, the prince goes after his princess.

The Kingdom of Fairies contains some of Méliès' most interesting and varied images, forming a template for future films. Grandiose ideas are set to early celluloid with a refreshing reckless abandon. What seems strange is that the director's most iconic image should come from *A Trip to the Moon* and not this. An extraordinary effort on the parts of all involved, *The Kingdom of Fairies* was followed first by the wonderful if woefully short *The Infernal Cauldron* (1903) and then by a series of repetitious trick films. It would take Méliès' discovery of Grand Guignol with *The Terrible Turkish Executioner* (1904) to revitalize his creativity. CW

The Monster
aka **Le Monstre**
Star Film; b/w; 3 min; France
D/P/S: Georges Méliès
Cast: Georges Méliès

One of the few Méliès films for which the original narration still survives, *The Monster* concerns an Egyptian prince who has lost his beloved wife. He visits a Muslim dervish (Méliès) who lives at the base of the Great Sphinx and who has the power to allow a person one last look at the features of his or her deceased loved one. Having disinterred the remains of the princess, the dervish places her skeleton on the ground and proceeds to draw down the moon, so that it might provide the princess with life. The skeletal remains move, and the dervish places them in a seated position upon hieroglyph-inscribed blocks of sandstone. He covers the skeleton with white linen and places a monstrous mask over its skull. Then, waving his arms toward the figure, he calls upon it to move. As the prince watches in horror, his wife's bones do a bizarre dance of death, sinking into the ground and then growing unnaturally large. When the veil and mask are removed from the dancing figure, the princess is whole and alive. But when the prince embraces her, she returns to her skeletal form and collapses, prompting him to chase the dervish in anger.

Borrowing liberally from Edgar Allan Poe's theme of love overcoming the grave, Méliès' picture makes for a striking production. The painted Egyptian backdrop recalls the one used for *The Oracle of Delphi* (1903), though this time around the image is much deeper and allows for a greater view of the landscape. The Great Sphinx looms; its melancholy eyes gaze over the foreground, perfectly reflecting the distress the prince feels over the loss of his wife. In the background is a tomb, and off in the distance are two of the three great pyramids. Between the foreground, where the action takes place, and the background, where the Egyptian tombs are, flows the River Nile. CW

Faust and Marguerite is a very watchable film by Georges Méliès, with a number of interesting set pieces and a coherent story.

The Oracle of Delphi
aka **L'oracle de Delphes**
Star Film; b/w; 2 min; France
D/P/S/FX: Georges Méliès
Cast unknown

After the charming *The Witch's Revenge* (1903), which is not, despite its title, a horror film, Méliès transposes the site of the Oracle of Delphi from Mount Parnassus in Ancient Greece to the Giza plateau in Ancient Egypt. After a priest places a small treasure chest in the base of the Great Sphinx, a thief comes along, breaks in and steals it. An oracle (Méliès) appears and forces the chest's return, after which he punishes the thief by turning the transgressor's head into that of a donkey.

Running at barely 90 seconds, the film has little time for spectacle; its effects come rapid-fire—ghostly fade-ins and fade-outs of the oracle, the exchange of the villain's head with a donkey's and the transformation of two sphinxes to female guards and back again to sphinxes.

As with many of Méliès' films, the Star Film trademark appears incongruously on the set, in this instance on the base of the Sphinx. The logo had by this time come to replace the one of the Theatre Robert-Houdin Méliès had used in his earliest works. He would go on to find creative ways in all of his films for this personalized brand of product placement to appear.

The donkey head would make a return appearance in *The Enchanted Well* (1903). CW

1904

Faust and Marguerite
aka **Damnation du Docteur Faust**; **Faust et Marguerite**
Star Film; color; 5 min; France
D/P/S/FX: Georges Méliès
Cast: Georges Méliès, Jeanne d'Alcy

It is obvious that Méliès intended *Faust and Marguerite* to be one of his more important films. While the only known existing prints are in black and white, they were clearly struck from a hand-painted master that is apparently lost. This work, a snippet slightly less than five minutes long, is a fragment of a longer film, the remainder of which is also presumed lost. Seemingly intended as a prequel to the previous year's *The Damnation of Faust* (1903), it is far more watchable, with a number of interesting set pieces and a coherent story.

After selling his soul to Satan in exchange for youth and prosperity, Faust is spurned by the beautiful Lady Marguerite, who is put off by his lack of humility. Faust makes a second attempt to woo her, this time with expensive jewels. He is successful, and as they kiss on Marguerite's patio, her brother Valentin interrupts them, having returned home from war and feeling dishonored by what he finds. He and Faust fight it out with swords, but thanks to Satan's intervention, Faust kills Valentin. Marguerite, upset by what has happened, goes to church to beg God's forgiveness, but Satan appears there and prevents her supplications from being heard. As punishment for their sins, Faust and Marguerite both die, but while Faust is taken to the bowels of the underworld to suffer eternal torment, Marguerite is welcomed into Heaven by the angels. CW

A Miracle Under the Inquisition
aka **Une Miracle sous l'Inquisition**
Star Film; b/w; 3 min; France
D/P/S/FX: Georges Méliès
Cast: Georges Méliès

The Inquisition was a tribunal begun by Spanish Catholic leaders in the 1470s with the intent of stomping out heresy within the Christian faith. It enforced its particular brand of Christianity with edicts and violence, marking a brutal period in lower European history that lasted until the early 1800s. Méliès injects a sense of optimism into the despairing atmosphere of this time and place, taking his own Catholic faith to task with his story of a young woman accused by a Grand Inquisitor (Méliès) of returning to her formerly renounced Judaism. She is summarily wrapped in a cloth, tied to a stake and set on fire. His work done, the Inquisitor reclines in his chair and sinks into a pleasant sleep. An Angel of the Lord appears, and by the powers invested in her by God, she transports the Inquisitor to the stake, at the same time resurrecting in his chair the young woman he had just brutally murdered. As the angel leads the young woman away, the Inquisitor bursts into flames—an effect that is dazzling in its realism. Two Catholic assistants then enter the room, only to turn and run in terror at what they see. (Méliès would return to the idea of burning people at the stake with *Justinian's Human Torches 548 A.D.*, 1908, though that film is far less horrific.)

Having tasted the terrors of the Theatre Grand Guignol in *The Terrible Turkish Executioner* (1904), Méliès returns to its macabre and theatrical sense of violence in *Miracle*. This time around, however, there is absolutely no humor to set the audience at ease. Instead, the director transfers his audience from the safety of their theater chairs (or nickelodeon stands) into a sordid past that reveled in brutality and sadism. Yet, not wanting to leave the audience without a sense of hope, he offers an angel whose miraculous hand radiates the power of God and stays—if only briefly—the horrors inflicted by the Inquisition. CW

The Mistletoe Bough
Clarendon; b/w; 6 min; Great Britain
D: Percy Stow
Cast unknown

This short film from Clarendon depicts the legend of the "mistletoe bough"—and the poem by Thomas Haynes Bayley based on it—somewhat faithfully. Percy Stow stars as a bridegroom whose bride vanishes during their wedding celebration. Three decades later, the aging man has a vision that prompts him to look in a chest, and there he finds his former bride's skeletal remains. (In the actual legend the wife's disappearance occurs at the wedding breakfast, during a game of hide and seek.)

Whereas most films from this period were intent on wowing their audiences with cinematic sleight of hand, *The Mistletoe Bough* was a straightforward affair, though with a melancholy ending. Since its initial publication in the early 1800s, Bayley's poem—which takes place at Christmastime—has become a holiday favorite in the United Kingdom. Set to music, it's considered one of the best-known songs in British history. The poem also inspired a play by Charles Somerset and is recited in Alfred Hitchcock's *Rope* (1948).

After leaving Hepworth, lead actor Percy Stow co-founded Clarendon Film Company, for whom he starred in over 250 films between 1904 and 1915. Many of these were trick films, few of which had horror elements, though his turn in Hepworth's *The Glutton's Nightmare* (1901) was one of his more earnestly nightmarish endeavors.

There are three known films based on the "Mistletoe Bough" legend. Clarendon's was the first. The second came in 1923 and starred John Stuart, while the third was an episode in George J. Banfield's *Haunted Houses and Castles of Great Britain* series of two-reel shorts, which was released in 1926. CW

The Terrible Turkish Executioner
aka **Le Bourreau turc**; **Decapitation in Turkey**; **Le terrible bourreau turk**
Star Film; b/w; 3 min; France
D/P/S/FX: Georges Méliès
Cast: Georges Méliès

A surprisingly gory film for its time, *The Terrible Turkish Executioner* may be one of the earliest productions to show a realistic decapitation (or, to be specific, a quadruple decapitation). Four prisoners, hands bound behind their backs, are lined up and their heads placed in stocks. After a joyous session of eating and drinking, the terrible Turkish executioner decapitates them, gathers their heads from the ground and throws them into a barrel. (The beheadings are quite gruesome, and one can't help but wonder what audiences at the time must have thought of them.) The film then transforms into a comic routine as the heads creep out of the barrel, seek out their bodies and reattach themselves. Thus reassembled, the men turn the tables by cutting the Turkish executioner in half; the top portion of his body hits the ground while the lower half stumbles blindly until reunited with the top half. The Turkish executioner then calls for help from policemen and a crowd of onlookers, all of whom chase after the formerly decapitated prisoners.

The backdrop depicts a bazaar on the outskirts of Constantinople and, as usual, displays surprising depth for a one-dimensional painting.

Perhaps in an attempt to grow his already large audience, Méliès here trades his usual *cinema fantastique* for *Grand Guignol*. While Méliès' own Theatre Robert-Houdin emphasized the magical, one of his biggest competitors was the Grand Guignol Theatre in Montmartre, Paris, which, rather than focusing on fantasy, emphasized rape and murder (with copious amounts of blood) for a generally lower class of audience.

While *Turkish Executioner* may have been the first of the director's films to focus on the physically gruesome, it wouldn't be the last. In 1906 he directed *A Desperate Crime*, which reenacted an allegedly true story of a farmer who was brutally butchered and whose property was set afire by a gang of thieves out to steal the earnings from his produce. One of the thieves is caught, tried, convicted and put to death by guillotine. Méliès' camera refuses to flinch as the guillotine's blade comes down and lops off the criminal's head, which plops into a basket. Then, when one of the gendarmes removes the severed head, it sprays blood from its neck. After the head and body have been tossed into a makeshift casket and carted off, a man (Méliès) washes the blood from the guillotine. CW

1905

L'antre infernale
Pathé; b/w; 3 min; France
D: Gaston Velle
Cast unknown

Gaston Velle worked exclusively in the early silent era. His career with Pathé began in 1903; it was over by 1913, despite the fact that he lived until 1948. Most of his films were lame imitations of the work of Georges Méliès, often with a portentous magician doing jump-cut magic for the audience's presumed astonishment. Here, however, Velle rips off a different Méliès motif, that of the Devil dancing around a grotto as he inflicts his black arts upon hapless onlookers.

Several of Velle's films, including *L'ecrin du Raja* and *La peine du Talion* (both 1906), still exist and can be quite easily viewed. CW

The Bobby's Nightmare
Gaumont; b/w; 3 min; Great Britain
D: Alf Collins
Cast: Alf Collins

As its title suggests, *The Bobby's Nightmare* concerns a British police officer's terrible dream. It trots out a barrage of nightmare imagery, after which all is set right when the protagonist wakes up and resumes his daily life. Early cinema utilized a lot of these "it was all a dream" scenarios; the short form was well suited to such fantasies.

Director Alf Collins was a music hall comedian who turned to directing in 1902. He appeared in a number of his own films and possibly essayed the title role in this picture. Known more for action fare, he remained active behind the camera until 1912, after which he appears to have gone back to stage work. He died in 1951. TH

The Conscience
Pathé; b/w; 9 min; France
Credits unknown

Yet another rip-off of a Georges Méliès film, *The Conscience* was shot in France by the fledgling Pathé Brothers and was a short film showcasing, you guessed it, trick photographic effects. There's no indication that it brings anything new to the *fantastique noir* genre with its tale of a mean old miser who stashes his gold away. His servant, knowing where the gold is hidden, murders the miser and buries his body, only to see his victim rise from the grave, pointing a finger of accusation. And as if that isn't enough, the purloined bag of gold becomes a skull, and a portrait of the miser likewise takes to pointing an accusatory finger. The miser's actual spirit then emerges from a cabinet, scaring the servant away from the house and into a nearby park, where he is surrounded by sinister figures.

Some sources relate that the servant is then claimed by the figure of death, decked out in his typical black. Clearly the story was influenced by Edgar Allan Poe's classic short story *The Tell-Tale Heart* (1843). CW

D.T.'s, or the Effect of Drink
aka **The Effects of Too Much Scotch**
William Haggar and Sons; b/w; 2 min; Great Britain
D/S/P/FX: William Haggar
Cast unknown

D.T.'s, or the Effect of Drink was one of two films about alcoholism that director William Haggar shot in 1905 (the other was a short comedy titled *Mary is Dry*). Both imparted an anti-alcohol message stirred by the religious fervor of the day. The model for *D.T.'s* was fellow British director Walter R. Booth's *The Drunkard's Conversion* (1901), but while that film presented a darkly comic look at an alcoholic chased by gnomes and snakes, Haggar's effort was more overtly horrific. Here, after a night of drinking, a man returns home to be menaced by a dog and a monster that form from his coat and bed, respectively. He then sees the light and gives up alcohol.

Booth's emphasis on trick photography (which had in turn been inspired by the *fantastique noir* of French director Georges Méliès) was inarguably a major influence on Haggar. Both hailed from Great Britain, and each was almost certainly aware of the other's work. In any event, both made films designed to scare viewers with the idea that alcohol is a demon, a notion very much in keeping with the claims of temperance societies throughout Great Britain and the United States at the time (and for three decades or so thereafter).

Haggar was a showman who traveled the fairgrounds of South Wales, exhibiting his homemade movies for paying customers. His own children were usually cast in these productions, and while his films were made with limited resources, their subject matter, when he waxed serious, was usually well researched and presented, as *The Life of Charles Peace* (1905) and *The Red Barn Crime* (1908) testify. The plots of those two films concerned the noxious deeds of notorious British criminals: Charles Peace in the former and William Corder in the latter. CW

Esmeralda
aka **La Esméralda**
Gaumont; b/w; 10 min; France
D: Alice Guy *P:* Léon Gaumont
Cast: Henry Vorins, Denise Becker

The first film shot at Gaumont Picture's newly erected La Villette Studios, *Esmeralda* is the earliest known film adaptation of Victor Hugo's classic novel *Notre Dame de Paris*, more famous under its English-language title, *The Hunchback of Notre Dame*. It has been alleged that Guy, who began her directorial career in the mid-1890s for Léon Gaumont and was quite possibly the first female filmmaker anywhere in the world, co-directed the film with Victorin Jasset, but there's no real proof of this. (Jasset would go on to direct *Balaoo*, 1913, the first film version of Gaston Leroux's little-known novel of the same title.) In later years, many of Guy's films had their directorial credits reassigned by future film critics to male colleagues who had little to do with her products (and no involvement in the direction at all).

The notion that Guy and Jasset co-directed *Esmeralda* is rendered more dubious by the blatantly untrue claim that the two were a husband-and-wife team who made films in tandem. In truth, Guy married cinematographer and soon-to-be production manager Herbert Blaché in 1906, after which the two of them moved to the United States. There in the U.S. Guy established her own production company, Solax, before her marriage to Blaché fell apart and she returned to her native country.

An early supporter of the feminist movement, Guy was instrumental in breaking down barriers for women in the silent era. She is credited with having made *La Fée Aux Choux (The Cabbage Fairy)*, which is quite possibly the first scripted feature film. (Some doubt is injected into this claim by the fact that its date of production is reported, depending on the source, as having been anywhere from 1896 to 1900. Guy recollects it as 1896, while Gaumont's catalog places its production in mid 1900.)

After being condemned to the pillory, the misshapen bell-ringer of Notre Dame begs for water, but his pleas go ignored until a beautiful Gypsy girl takes pity on him. Watching over the touching scene, the hunchback's master, the archdeacon who presides over the cathedral, develops an obsessive infatuation with the girl. He commands the hunchback to bring her to him, but a captain with whom she falls in love saves her. After an illicit rendezvous between the two, the evil priest stabs the captain to death and Esmeralda is convicted of his murder and hanged. The melancholy hunchback then hurls the priest to his death from one of the cathedral's towers. With such a short running length, it's hard to know just how Guy fit all this into the final product. The film is now considered lost.

Before filming of *Esmeralda* began, Guy visited the newly completed sets and found them too appallingly futurist. She had them torn down and rebuilt from scratch, pushing the film over budget. While this may have been one of her earliest forays into fantastic filmmaking (with so many of her early films lost, it's hard to tell what came before it, though it's known for certain that she directed a version of *Faust and Mephistopheles* in 1903), she went further into the direction of horror later in her career with *The Pit and the Pendulum* (1913), an adaptation of Edgar Allan Poe's famous tale. It should also be noted that her films *The Monster and the Girl* (1914) and *The Vampire* (1915) are frequently listed as belonging to the horror genre but are in fact romantic melodramas. One of her most notorious films, *Algie the Miner* (1912), was the first American feature to deal openly with the topic of homosexuality, albeit in a humorous way. And Guy frequently appeared in gender-bending roles, either as men or in men's clothes, in many of her films.

Some sources list Jasset as having a role in *Esmeralda*, though they don't make clear whom he would have played. Actor Vorins went on to become a director of little distinction in the French cinema of the 1920s.

The year 1905 was a popular one for the Gypsy girl and her deformed lover. Not only did they make it to the big screen for the first time, but renowned French artist Luc-Olivier Merson also painted his famous *Esmeralda and Quasimodo* that same year. Whether one influenced the other is hard to tell. CW

The Freak Barber
Paul; b/w; 3 min; Great Britain
D: J.H. Martin P: Robert W. Paul
Cast unknown

Very little is known about this obscure film produced by Robert W. Paul. J.H. Martin, Paul's short-lived replacement for Walter R. Booth, who had dissolved his partnership with Paul in favor of the greater freedom afforded by producer Charles Urban's Urban Trading Company, directed the film.

The Freak Barber's narrative reportedly offers a variation on the Sweeney Todd story, one in which the barber cuts the heads off his customers rather than slicing their throats. In the end, he is predictably dismembered. This was all no doubt intended to amuse audiences with the same sort of special effects that made Georges Méliès' films memorable. How successful *The Freak Barber* was is anyone's guess, though the title is certainly intriguing and the plotline sounds like ghoulish fun.

Paul and Martin mined similar territory for *The Fatal Hand* (1907). CW

The Thirteen Club
aka **The 13 Club**
American Mutoscope and Biograph; b/w; 6 min; U.S.
Credits unknown

Little information exists about this apparently lost contribution to the horror genre. A relatively short trick film, *The Thirteen Club* is based on a real-life group of the same name, formed in the 1880s to flout the idea that it was bad luck for 13 people to sit around a table. (The superstition may have grown around Michelangelo's famous painting "The Last Supper," which depicted Jesus and his 12 apostles celebrating Passover at one table. In the actual biblical description of the meal, no table is mentioned.) The monthly meeting of the Thirteen Club always took place on a Friday, believed to be the day of the week on which the Son of God's crucifixion took place. The club also publically encouraged the U.S. government to stop executing people on Fridays, in hopes of halting the widespread notion that the day was unlucky. At various points, the group included numerous people in positions of power, such as presidents, judges, and city leaders. Because it was formed to challenge widely held irrational beliefs and to bring scientific thinking into the mainstream, it enjoyed a relatively high profile.

The Biograph film of 1905 concerns a group called "The Thirteen Club" that mocks superstitions by testing them. On the depicted occasion, as the group's 13 members sit unluckily around a table, a skeleton replaces each one. The clear implication is that ridiculing superstition results in death.

Given the year in which the film was made, the effects seem likely to have been achieved by either jump cuts or superimpositions. CW

1906

The Cabby's Dream
Warwick; b/w; 4 min; Great Britain
D: Charles Raymond
Cast unknown

A cab driver is caught napping by a magician named A. Presto, who then proceeds to conjure up some amazing sights. As the visions turn more horrific, the cabby becomes alarmed … then wakes up.

This obscure short makes extensive use of trick photography as it builds to a horror-tinged crescendo in which ghostly children wearing animal heads frighten the protagonist. Director Charles Raymond also worked extensively as an actor; surviving credits for *The Cabby's Dream* are incomplete, but it seems likely that he played one of the lead characters. Raymond later starred in two versions of *Hamlet*, one in 1910, the other in 1912. He is credited with directing the latter as well. TH

Mephisto's Son
aka **Le fils du diable fait la noce à Paris**; **Son of the Devil**
Pathé; b/w; 19 min; France
D/S: Charles-Lucien Lepine
Cast: Andre Deed

The Devil's son (Deed) is bored with life in Hell, so he ventures to Paris and hooks up with a local girl. He is eventually dispatched via crucifix back to Hell.

Writer/director Charles-Lucien Lepine made over a dozen films in his native France between 1905 and 1907. His filmography mysteriously stops after that point, though he lived until 1941. Long considered lost, *Mephisto's Son* seems to have been Lepine's only foray into horror. Based on surviving data, the film played things fairly light, with an impish Son of the Devil pitching woo in the French countryside.

Andre Deed, a popular music hall entertainer who broke into film in 1905, played the title character. He became his country's first legitimate comedic film star, but his shelf life proved limited. His star faded by the 1920s and he died, broke and forgotten, in 1938.

Though *Mephisto's Son* doesn't seem to have depicted Satan per se, it plays into early cinema's fascination with visualizing him and/or his domain. Literal depictions of Satan can be traced back as far as the work of Georges Méliès (*The Devil's Castle*, 1896). TH

The Merry Frolics of Satan
aka **Les Quatre cents farces du diable**
Star Film; b/w-color; 17 min; France
D/P/S/FX: Georges Méliès
Cast: Georges Méliès, Jeanne d'Alcy

Released just in time for Halloween 1906, *The Merry Frolics of Satan* recalls the delightful excesses of *The Kingdom of Fairies* (1903), though it sorely lacks that film's originality. An alchemist's representative offers to sell a talisman to an engineer. The engineer and his assistant are then taken to the alchemist's laboratory, where everything in the room is alive. (At this point the film kicks into hand-painted color.) After the alchemist introduces himself, the two guests reveal that they are interested in circling the globe at high speed. The alchemist and his helpers create a container of magical pills, one of which produces a beautiful fairy that promptly becomes a hideous monster. The alchemist is revealed to be Satan, and he tells the two men that if they throw one of the pills upon the ground, any wish they make will be granted. All they have to do in return is sign a piece of paper. A series of horror-tinged adventures follow.

In the film's most spectacular scene, the two men escape to a stagecoach whose horse becomes a mythological monster and whose coach transforms into one comprised of stars and comets. It ascends Mt. Vesuvius, reaching its top right at the moment of an eruption, which sends the coach into space where it passes stars, meteors, comets and the ringed planet Saturn. Unfortunately, the film is too mired in Méliès' self-plagiarism to take a fresh artistic risk or two. At the same time that filmmakers in other parts of the world were beginning to move away from the standard static camera to more complicated framing and editing, Méliès, who had for so long been at the cutting edge of global cinema, was being left behind by the very movement he had created and over which he had for so long reigned. CW

The Mysterious Retort
aka **L'alchemiste Parafaragaramus ou la cornue infernale**
Star Film; b/w; 4 min; France
D/P/S/FX: Georges Méliès
Cast: Georges Méliès

Not surprisingly, people disappear and reappear and objects grow and shrink, all for the amusement of a disinterested alchemist. In the film's one striking and quite horrific moment, a face appears, attached to six spider-like legs and sitting on a giant cobweb. The image is similar to one Tod Browning would later use in *The Show* (1927), leading one to wonder if the American director had seen Méliès' film at some point in his youth. The spider creature disappears, replaced by a woman holding a large horn coral containing what appear to be flower petals. A ghost floats up out of a cask, and finally there is an explosion, which causes the alchemist to faint. The film also offers the usual demonic imps and a large, writhing snake (manipulated by strings).

Only ardent devotees of the French director (or those who have seen little of his work) will find much of interest here. CW

In *The Merry Frolics of Satan*, a stagecoach finds its horse transformed into a mythological monster while it is launched into space and passes stars, meteors and comets.

A Spiritualistic Meeting
aka **Le fantôme d'Alger**
Star Film; b/w; 5 min; France
D/P/S/FX: Georges Méliès
Cast: Georges Méliès

An apparently lost film, *A Spiritualistic Meeting* reportedly detailed a gathering for a séance. Méliès no doubt engaged in his usual trick photography, with the result that a spirit (possibly more than one) is raised ... to the hackles of the séance's attendees and the amusement of the film's viewers.

This particular period wasn't the director's most creative, so it's doubtful that the film is astounding stuff in the manner of *A Trip to the Moon* (1902), *The Kingdom of Fairies* (1903) or *The Terrible Turkish Executioner* (1904). Regardless, one can hope that it is someday recovered, as other Méliès productions have been, including *The Devil's Castle* (1896), discovered in New Zealand in 1988, and *Cleopatra* (1899), found in France in 2005.

Different sources cite different running times for *A Spiritualistic Meeting*—one to five minutes, based on various estimates of the number of feet of film used for the work. Given that most Méliès films from this period run, on average, from three to five minutes, a longer running time seems likely.

The larger the number of people in attendance at the séance, the more safely one can conclude that Jeanne d'Alcy was a participant in the proceedings, as, no doubt, was Méliès. CW

The Witch
aka **La Fée Carabosse ou le poignard fatal**
Star Film; color; 12 min; France
D/P/S/FX: Georges Méliès
Cast: Georges Méliès

The Witch contains Méliès' most extraordinary color compositions yet, but they're wasted on a trite tale of a troubadour who, while having his palm read by a witch (Méliès), learns that he is to save an enslaved princess. He then has the nerve to pay the witch with a bag of sand he passes off as gold. Understandably insulted, she conjures the forces of darkness to help her get revenge. She chases him to an old graveyard, where he is haunted by the specters of the dead, only to be saved by the image of the cross.

At the edge of the cemetery he finds a castle but is unable to enter it. A giant frog, a giant owl, a dragon and snakes with humanoid arms and torsos terrorize him. Emissaries of light come to his aid and give him a magic sword. He climbs the battlements, finds the princess and frees her, much to the chagrin of the witch, who rides her broomstick across the sky after them. Atop a mountain, the troubadour asks the princess for her hand in marriage, but the witch attacks before she can accept.

Despite the brilliant colors, The Witch is the usual Méliès hokum. In the United States, Edwin S. Porter had perfected the edit for dramatic effect (rather than mere momentary trickery) as early as Life of an American Fireman (1903), as had George Albert Smith to a lesser degree in Mary Jane's Mishap (1903). Similar edits would have helped The Witch immensely. Méliès, however, had yet to catch on to the possibilities of judicious editing. The French director's "resting on his laurels" had begun by this time to hold him back, even as other filmmakers progressed and prospered. CW

The Witch's Cave
aka **L'Antrere de la Sorciere**; **The Bewitched Shepherd**
Pathé; b/w; 10 (6) min; France
D/S/C: Segundo de Chomon
Cast unknown

A young peasant, stomping through a forest after an argument with his wife, meets up with a witch. She takes him to a cavern and shows him a variety of frightening creatures. Then she displays a collection of beautiful women, one of whom happens to be his wife. The peasant is happy to see her again, and the two make up.

Segundo de Chomon went to work for French Pathé Studios in 1901. By 1902 he was directing, though he also worked for years as a writer, cinematographer, editor, production designer and special effects technician. In the latter category, he contributed to Abel Gance's mammoth production of Napoleon (1927). He quit directing in 1917 after racking up well over a hundred titles in that capacity. One of his last credits was as cinematographer on Guido Brignone's Maciste in Hell (1925).

The Witch's Cave played into de Chomon's interest in camera trickery and lighting effects. (Even scholars occasionally mistake his early films as the work of Méliès.) Cave's slim story served as pretext for a barrage of weird imagery, culminating in the hero's visitation to the creepy cave packed with assorted monsters.

The film is considered lost. TH

1907

Aunt Eliza Recovers Her Pet
b/w; 7 min; France
Credits unknown

In this apparently lost silent French film (even the original French-language title appears to have been forgotten), Aunt Eliza's pet bird is stolen. Understandably upset, she hires a detective to find it. The task isn't too difficult, as the thief has left a trail of feathers for the detective to follow. But alas, when the detective arrives at the thief's home, he finds that the man has cooked the bird and is in the process of eating it. The detective apprehends the fiend, ties him up and whisks him away to his office. There, he hypnotizes the miscreant and cuts him in half, after which the bird flies out of the thief's gut and returns to its thankful owner.

While intended to be comedic, there's obviously a gruesome quality to this nightmarish trick film, which was viewed cheaply in the Nickelodeons that were so prevalent at the time. CW

The Bewildering Cabinet
aka **Le Placard infernal**; **The Closet**
Star; b/w; length unknown; France
D/S/P/FX: Georges Méliès
Cast unknown

This is one of French director Georges Méliès' most obscure films. Almost certainly long lost, it dealt with two girls who step into a magic cabinet and become grotesque monsters. It's likely that the effects were achieved through stop-substitution, with the girls filmed entering the cabinet but replaced by people in costumes once the camera was shut off. Then, with the "monsters" subsequent emergence committed to film, the completed product made it appear as if the girls had transformed into monsters while in the cabinet. While this was amazing stuff in 1897, it had grown rather stale by 1907, particularly with so many other filmmakers following Méliès' lead, even Méliès!

Though many filmmakers employed the use of stop-substitution during the early silent era, at least Georges Méliès mastered it with flawless edits and seamless transitions. CW

The Clock-Maker's Secret
aka **Le secret horlogers**
Pathé; b/w; 15 min; France
Credits unknown

In the year 1648, an old clockmaker sells his soul to the Devil in return for a new clock for the town hall. Before making the exchange, however, the Devil presents the clockmaker with various visions of Heaven and Hell, each consisting mostly of dancing babes. The clockmaker's daughter discovers what's going on, and with the aid of a knight uses a crucifix to drive the Prince of Darkness away. Unfortunately, she banishes her father as well. Still, not all is lost—daughter and knight discover their love for each other and, after receiving a blessing from Heaven, live happily ever after.

At the heart of *The Clock-Maker's Secret* is the idea that it is women, not men, who can best expose the terrors lurking in the dark. Even the sun, shining approvingly down on the happy couple, contains within its center a matriarchal female, her face surrounded by illuminating rays.

The notion of the Devil manifesting himself to tempt and/or torment an innocent individual was popular in early horror cinema. TH/CW

The Doll's Revenge
Hepworth; b/w; 3 min; Great Britain
D: Lewin Fitzhamon *P:* Cecil M. Hepworth
Cast: Gertie Potter, Bertie Potter

Along with George Albert Smith and Walter R. Booth, Cecil M. Hepworth was a progenitor of the British film industry. As a child assisting at his father's magic lantern shows, Hepworth came by his interest in film naturally and early on. His 1897 work *Animated Photography* is generally considered the first filmmaking handbook ever written.

Fascinated by the success of Robert W. Paul (who created a British variant of Edison's Kinetoscope and produced, among other films, 1898's *The Miser's Doom*), and drawing upon his own experience as an assistant to Birt Acres, Hepworth for a time directed movies at the Charles Urban Trading Company. After being terminated there, he and fellow Urbanite Monty Wicks started their own production company (originally titled Hepwix but later rechristened Hepworth). There, assisted by a competent staff of hired professionals, the two produced their own films.

While Hepworth's most famous movie is his 8-minute *Alice in Wonderland* (1903), he did dabble in horror on occasion, most notably as director of *The Basilisk* in 1914. Previous to that piece, however, he produced this relatively unknown little gem about a precocious boy who—much to his sister's horror—breaks her beloved doll. Not to worry, however; the doll supernaturally repairs itself and grows large, then, after a second doll appears in order to assist, tears the boy to pieces and devours him.

The effects were achieved by superimposition and stop-motion via stop-substitution. While the film was doubtless intended to wow the audience with visual trickery, it likely inspired nightmares for many a child who saw it upon its Nickelodeon release.

Real-life siblings Gertie and Bertie Potter portrayed the brother and sister. Director Fitzhamon made numerous films between 1900 and 1914, usually as director but sometimes as writer and actor. Little of his work has withstood the test of time, and his name is largely forgotten today even among film enthusiasts.

This film shouldn't be confused with the comedic trick film *The Doll's Revenge* (1911), which was also shot in Great Britain but by director Percy Stow. CW

The Fatal Hand
Paul; b/w; 5 min; Great Britain
D: J.H. Martin *P:* Robert W. Paul
Cast unknown

Two years after his first serial killer film (1905's *The Freak Barber*), J.H. Martin drew from the same well with *The Fatal Hand*, a short piece distributed to Nickelodeons by the Miles Brothers. But whereas *The Freak Barber* was one of many unoriginal takes on the Sweeney Todd tale (minus the name and with a barber who decapitated his victims rather than slit their throats), this time out the material is somewhat more inventive. A lunatic escapes from authorities, only to murder an innocent woman and a passenger on a train before being caught by a sailor.

Little is known about Martin, other than the fact that he replaced Walter R. Booth as producer Robert W. Paul's primary director after Booth and Paul parted ways, due to creative differences. This same year Martin also made *A Knight Errant* for Paul. CW

The Ghost Holiday
Hepworth; b/w; 6 min; Great Britain
D/S: Lewin Fitzhamon
Cast: Gertie Potter, Thurston Harris

While most of Hepworth's output is long lost, it's known that they produced an astounding number of titles (over 900 in all) between 1898 and 1924. Director Lewin Fitzhamon was one of their most reliable artisans—he directed a number of films for the company between 1904 and 1912 before striking out on his own with his short-lived Fitz Film Company. He continued churning out numerous, mostly forgotten titles until 1914, with his specialty appearing to have been comedic fare.

Based on the scant surviving data on *The Ghost Holiday*, the story dealt with various ghosts and skeletons raising Cain in a graveyard as they celebrate among themselves. Stars Gertie Potter and Thurston Harris were favorites of Fitzhamon; their extant filmographies—though almost certainly incomplete—are comprised of titles that he directed.

This same year Fitzhamon directed the macabre *The Doll's Revenge*, also starring Gertie Potter. TH

The Ghost Story
Vitagraph; b/w; 3 min; U.S.
D/S//Co-P/C/FX: J. Stuart Blackton *Co-P:* Albert E. Smith
Cast unknown

Producer/director J. Stuart Blackton was born in England and immigrated to the United States with his family in 1885. His talent as an illustrator for *New York World* magazine impressed none other than Thomas A. Edison, who photographed some of Blackton's drawings with his new Kinetograph camera. Blackton, fascinated by the new technology, embarked upon a career in the burgeoning motion picture industry. As co-founder of Vitagraph, he worked in a wide variety of genres and brought such literary figures as *Richard III* (1908), Sherlock Holmes (*The Adventures of Sherlock Holmes*, 1905) and *Oliver Twist* (1909) to the screen. Between 1898 and 1933, he directed over 100 titles; among his unique achievements was luring iconic author Mark Twain to make his first of only two film appearances in *A Curious Dream* (1907).

The Ghost Story was something of a follow-up to Blackton's *The Haunted Hotel* (also 1907) and, like that film, seems to have been tempered with an impish sense of humor. The material doubtless allowed Blackton an opportunity to indulge his love of trick photography, functioning, as was his wont, as something of a one-man technical crew.

Images from *The Haunted Hotel*

Both *The Ghost Story* and its predecessor were atypical forays into the horror genre for the filmmaker, though he showed a discernible interest in the fantastic in many other films. TH

The Golden Beetle
aka Le scarabee d'or
Pathé; color; 3 min; France
D: Segundo de Chomón
Cast unknown

While bending to the ground, a turbaned magician perceives a large, golden beetle climbing a wall. He snatches it in his hands, conjures a flaming cauldron and unceremoniously casts the insect into its fires. A fairy appears above the fire and curses the magician for his hateful act, after which she summons a fountain with demonic faces on it. The fountain spouts water and spits fire, at which point this fluffy fantasy becomes absurdist horror as the fairy's two helpers grab the magician and throw him into a large pot, where he burns to death.

This hand-colored film from French director Segundo de Chomón, who built a film career imitating Georges Méliès, is typical of the period, though without Méliès' technical expertise. On a side note, some film historians have mistakenly attributed the film to Ferdinand Zecca. CW

The Haunted Bedroom
Urban/Eclipse; b/w; 5 min; Great Britain/France
D/FX: Walter R. Booth *C:* F. Harold Bastick *P:* Charles Urban
Cast unknown

It's easy for one to speculate that the now-lost *The Haunted Bedroom*, which Walter R. Booth directed the same year as *The Thousand Pound Spook* for Urban Trading, was likely a horror comedy centering on a man staying in a haunted room, a done-to-death theme during this period. Most probably a trick film using wire manipulation, superimpositions and jump cuts to suggest the fantastic, little information survives about the film other than its basic premise, title and relevant crew information. CW

The Haunted Hotel
aka The Haunted Hotel: or, The Strange Adventures of a Traveler
Vitagraph; b/w; 6 min; U.S.
D/S/Co-P/C/FX: J. Stuart Blackton *Co-P:* Albert E. Smith
Cast: Paul Panzer, William V. Ranous

The American Vitagraph Company was the offspring of English émigrés J. Stuart Blackton and Albert E. Smith. The two formed the company in 1897 to compete with Thomas A. Edison (whom Blackton had once interviewed about film production, touring in the process Edison's Black Maria studios). Instead, they made a deal with Edison, whose company included their product in its annual catalog. Rather than shooting the then-common actuality films, Vitagraph was conceived to focus on newsworthy international events, such as the Spanish-American War. In so doing, it both created and fed a public hungry for newsreels, something that would in time adapt to television, first as evening news programs and eventually as 24-hour cable news networks.

It didn't take long, however, for the co-owners to see the additional profit potential in producing short fantasy films with outrageous special effects. To that end producer/director Blackton studied and emulated the short films of French director Georges Méliès. The result was a handful of Vitagraph's own trick films, one of which was *The Haunted Hotel*. (Interestingly, *Hotel* was the first Vitagraph film to do extremely well in France, likely because of its unabashed theft of Méliès' popular style, in addition to its innovative effects.)

Unlike Méliès, however, Blackton refused to confine his work to extraordinary fare, opting instead to "mix it up" by creating films in many different genres. It can be stated that in doing so Vitagraph helped give birth to modern cinema, with Blackton putting particular oomph behind cartoon animation and stop-motion. The studio's groundbreaking eclectic style makes it only fitting that in 1925 it was bought out by one of the studios that became—and remains to this day—a juggernaut of cinema: Warner Bros., who changed its acquisition's name to Vitaphone.

The Haunted Hotel concerns a traveler (Panzer) who spends a night in a hotel room, not suspecting at first that it might be haunted. His clothes disappear, and the room shakes as if caught in an earthquake. A table prepares its own meal, and hooded imps dance around the traveler's bed. Finally, a hideous demon (Ranous) appears and grabs the traveler into its clutches.

While most of the film's special effects were achieved through jump cuts and minor wirework, the segment in which objects on the table prepare themselves was done using stop-motion, an early example of the technique that would later make stars of special effects artists such as Willis O'Brien, Ray Harryhausen and Jim Danforth.

The film's final moment, a close shot of the hideous demon's face, is clearly not meant to be funny and must have terrified audiences in its day. How appropriate, then, that actor William V. Ranous, whose first role was as the hideous demon here, would go on to star in other dark films. These included *Francesca da Rimini: or, The Two Brothers*, *Macbeth*, *Richard III* and *She* (all 1908). He would also, before his death in 1915, become a director in his own right. CW

A Knight Errant
aka **Knight-Errant**; **The Knight Errant**
Paul; b/w; 8 min; Great Britain
D: J.H. Martin S: Langford Reed P: Robert W. Paul
Cast unknown

Producer Robert W. Paul had a fascination with dark subjects, beginning with *Trilby Burlesque* (1896) and continuing through *The Miser's Doom* (1899), *Chinese Magic* (1900), *The Magic Sword*, *The Haunted Curiosity Shop* and *The Drunkard's Conversion* (all 1901), *The Haunted Scene Painter* (1904) and *Is Spiritualism a Fraud* (1906), among others. Products of their time, all of these works were trick films, yet they often contained such perverse imagery that they must have scared many a child who saw them in the Nickelodeons so popular during the period.

A Knight Errant fits firmly in this mold, being fashioned after the aforementioned *The Magic Sword*—which had been directed by Walter R. Booth—with its tale of a knight who turns to the aid of a fairy in order to save a princess from a witch, a dwarf and an ogre. CW

The Madman's Bride
Hepworth; b/w; length unknown; Great Britain
P: Cecil M. Hepworth
Cast unknown

The year 1907 saw producer Cecil M. Hepworth continue to pursue his interest in horror, which had begun as a mild flirtation with the comedic trick film *The Bewitched Traveler* (1904). After *Bride*, he went on to shoot the operatic *Faust* (1911) and *The Basilisk* (1914), while doing production duties on *The Doll's Revenge* and *The Ghost's Holiday* (both 1907), among others.

The Madman's Bride was one of his more gruesome efforts. An insane aristocrat purchases a girl from her itinerant father under the pretext of wanting to marry her, but he murders her instead. CW

Nature Fakirs
aka **Nature's Fakirs**
Kalem; b/w; 8 (6) min; U.S.
Credits unknown

A prehistoric "dingbat," a man-sized creature akin to a chicken, terrorizes a professor and his assistant. The creature is revealed to be a man in a costume, and it turns out to have all been a practical joke played by one of the professor's friends.

This appears to have been the first attempt at a horror film (sort of) by production company Kalem, which went on to make *The Legend of Sleepy Hollow* (1908), *The Mummy and the Cowpuncher* (1912), *The Haunted House* and *In the Grip of a Charlatan* (both 1913), *The Invisible Power* and *The Mystery of the Living Death* (both 1914), *The Black Crook*, *Foiled*, *An Innocent Sinner*, *The Missing Mummy*, *The Secret Room* and *The Vivisectionist* (all 1915) and *Ghost Hounds* (1917). CW

The Red Spectre
aka **Le spectre rouge**
Pathé; b/w; 9 min; France
Co-D/S: Segundo de Chomón Co-D: Ferdinand Zecca
Cast unknown

In a fiery grotto in hell, a casket transforms into a red, devilish figure, complete with horns and a cloak. With a flaming wand, he conjures a group of dancing women who become fiery balls and fly through the air. The apparition next invokes two small cauldrons, out of which appears a pair of beautiful women, whom he levitates before making them disappear. A fairy appears; the red specter banishes her and produces three bottles containing little people (leaving one to wonder if future director James Whale had seen this particular French short before making *Bride of Frankenstein*, 1935). But before the specter can actually do anything with them other than pour liquid over them, the fairy reappears and makes them vanish. A magical contest between fairy and specter ensues, with the fairy emerging victorious as the red specter is turned into a lifeless skeleton.

The film is tinted red to enhance its demonic subject matter, but de Chomón and Zecca seem more interested in their own photographic cleverness than in achieving anything new or interesting. CW

Satan at Play
aka **Satan s'amuse**
Pathé; color; 10 min; France
D/S: Segundo de Chomon
Cast: Julienne Mathieu

Satan (Mathieu), in the form of a skeleton with a long black cape, whiles away his time doing magic tricks.

Satan at Play is a hand-tinted color short that contains some striking visuals, as director Segundo de Chomon presents a parade of bizarre images and trick shots. It opens with the title character emerging from a coffin, after which he performs a series of sleight-of-hand tricks while making his sexy handmaidens disappear and reappear at will. Some of the effects are surprisingly seamless for the period, and the stylized settings create the right mood of dark wonder throughout. TH

The Thousand Pound Spook
aka **The £1000 Pound Spook**
Urban; b/w; 2 min; Great Britain
D/FX: Walter R. Booth C: F. Harold Bastick P: Charles Urban
Cast unknown

In his second horror film for the Charles Urban Trading Company, Booth spins a tale of a magician who conjures a vapor, which then becomes the ghostly figure of a woman.

Given that Booth had an interest in spiritualism (particularly in debunking it), it was probably inevitable that he'd eventually make a film focusing on some sort of ectoplasmic manifestation. The film's ghost effects were achieved through the use of multiple exposures, which Booth had mastered many years before while still working for Robert W. Paul. CW

When the Devil Drives
Urban; b/w; 5 min; Great Britain
D/P/FX: Walter R. Booth *C:* F. Harold Bastick
Cast unknown

When the Devil Drives is a voyage picture, with the twist that the devil is doing the driving.

A family hires a cab to take them to the train station, but the driver turns out to be Mephistopheles. He takes them on a spirited journey from mountaintops to deep sea trenches, and everywhere in between. The effects work is fairly good, though the film as a whole is derivative of Méliès' *The Impossible Journey* (1904), the latter a much slicker film with higher production values, including hand-painted frames.

Established in 1903 by Charles Urban, the Charles Urban Trading Company had up to this point specialized in educational films for public consumption, including shorts by noted British naturalists Percy Smith and F. Martin Duncan, along with programs dedicated to topics as varied as hunting and international conflicts. By 1907, however, the company was losing ground—and revenue—to film houses that offered more explicitly fantastic programming. Deciding that to stay afloat he too needed to make trick films, Urban hired Walter R. Booth, who'd made a successful go of it for Robert W. Paul, to helm a series of fantasy-oriented pictures employing the latest trick photographic effects.

During this time, Booth set up his own studio in his home and hired F. Harold Bastick as his cameraman, reducing the number of hats Booth had to wear during each production. Booth went on to make a number of science fiction films for Urban, many dealing with English invasion by other countries using fantastic ships or submarines. CW

1908

The Bloodstone
Lubin; b/w; length unknown; U.S.
P: Siegmund Lubin
Cast unknown

This lost production from then-mega-player Lubin Manufacturing Company (spearheaded by Siegmund Lubin, who directly oversaw much of the company's output) dealt with a cursed ring trailed by death and destruction everywhere it's taken. Embedded in the ring is a bloodstone, a semi-precious gem of dark green chalcedony and red jasper. Bloodstones are also known under the names Oriental jasper and heliotrope.

The idea of a cursed jewel was popular during the silent era, with most such films being either adaptations or knock-offs of Wilkie Collins' 1868 novel *The Moonstone*. Edison's *The Egyptian Mystery* (1909) was a similar—though likely comedic—film made the year after this particular take on the theme. CW

The Castle Ghosts
aka **Il Fantasma del Castello**
Aquila; b/w; 10 min; Italy
Credits unknown

One of only nine film production companies operating in Italy at the time, Aquila produced mostly short comedies for local consumption. It was based in Turin, the nation's leading exporter of films and well ahead of Rome, Milan and Naples in terms of overall cinematic output. In early 1908, the company made *The Castle Ghosts*, in which said castle is "haunted" by a man impersonating a ghost. More comedic than chilling, it was released in the United States in May 1908.

Aquila did make at least one outright horror film, *The Spectre of Jago* (1913), helping to establish a genre that would not really flourish in the country, thanks to a ban on horror films during Italy's Fascist years, until the release of Ricardo Freda's *I Vampiri* (1956) and Mario Bava's *Black Sunday* (1960). CW

The Cat's Revenge
Lux; b/w; 4 min; France
Credits unknown

This apparently lost short film was produced by Lux Studio—an internationally successful film company based in Gentilly, France—to compete with Georges Méliès' more famous and accomplished trick films. Little is known about the product beyond its basic plot, which borrows an idea from Edgar Allan Poe's 1843 short story *The Black Cat*. The film concerns a man who is haunted by the ghost of a cat, likely because he killed the animal.

Lux would continue to make horror films, including *The Butcher's Dream*, *Her Dolly's Revenge* and *The Mummy of the King Ramsees* (all 1909). CW

Cave of the Spooks
aka **La grotte des esprits**; **Wave of Spooks**
Pathé; b/w; length unknown; France
D/S/C/FX: Segundo de Chomon
Cast unknown

This (probably) short subject by Segundo de Chomon is said to have provided a fanciful glimpse of Hell. Among its reported spectacles was the sight of ghosts turning into skeletons. It was one of many works of the period that attempted a dazzling vision of the nether regions; others include de Chomon's own *The Red Spectre* (1907) and *Satan's Smithy* (1908).

Though forgotten today, de Chomon was one of the first filmmakers to explore the realm of the fantastic. Much of his work is considered lost, but descriptions of the time indicate that he brought a showman's flair and imagination to his macabre subject matter. A native of Spain, he spent the majority of his career working for Pathé in France. He did his last work in Italy, co-directing *The War and the Dream of Momi* (1917) with Giovanni Pastrone, another early cinematic fantasist. TH

The Devil
American Mutoscope & Biograph; b/w; 10 min; U.S.
D/S: D.W. Griffith *C:* G.W. Bitzer
Cast: Harry Solter, Claire McDowell, George Gebhardt, D.W. Griffith, Florence Lawrence, Arthur V. Johnson, Mack Sennett

Harold Thornton (Solter) is a happily married artist. While painting a portrait of a pretty young model (Lawrence), he is tempted for the first time to stray from his wife. His quandary is amplified when the Devil (Gebhardt) pops up, hoping to compel the artist to do the wrong thing.

There is some confusion surrounding this title. Reference materials sometimes credit it as an Edison production, but the

Director and screenwriter D.W. Griffith

official Edison Studios filmography makes no mention of it. Given that its director, cinema pioneer D.W. Griffith, got his start with the American Motoscope & Biograph Company, it seems most likely that AM&B was the film's studio (as many sources list it). In any case, *The Devil* is irrefutably Griffith's work and one of his earliest titles.

The brief running time doubtless prevented a nuanced presentation of the subject matter, but the moralistic tone seems consistent with what is known of Griffith's filmic worldview. His subsequent stab at adapting Edgar Allan Poe's *The Tell Tale Heart* (*The Avenging Conscience, or: 'Thou Shalt Not Kill,'* 1914) adopted a similarly high-handed approach, as did a great deal of his more famous work.

The Devil's supporting cast included legendary producer Mack Sennett, making the briefest of appearances. Sennett later made his name in the comedy genre. Like many of Griffith's early films, *The Devil* is considered lost. TH

Don Juan Tenorio
Hispano; b/w; 15 min; Spain
Co-D/Co-S/C: Ricardo de Baños *Co-D/Co-S:* Alberto Marro
Cast: Cecilio Rodriguez de la Vega

Don Juan Tenorio (de la Vega) competes with another man over which of the two can violate the most women and murder the most men. The debauched contest leads to disaster for all who know Don Juan, including the one woman he actually loves.

A famous Spanish play, written by José Zorillo in 1844, provides the basis for this early horror romance from the nation that later gave the world the brilliant Pedro Almodóvar. Ricardo de Baños, who co-directed and shot this second-ever adaptation of *Don Juan Tenorio*, went on to become one of the most distinguished cinematographers in Spanish history. He began his career as a director in either 1904 or 1905 (sources conflict). His interest in the tale of Don Juan Tenorio was such that he again filmed the play, under the same title, in 1922. Little is really known about the particulars of this first one, however. It may very well be the first film with a horror bent ever shot in Spain. CW

Dr. Jekyll and Mr. Hyde
Selig; b/w; 16 min; U.S.
D: Otis Turner *S:* George F. Fish *P:* William Selig
Cast: Hobart Bosworth, Betty Hart

Formed in 1896, Selig Polyscope was one of the earliest film production companies. Founded by former magician and minstrel performer William N. Selig (1864-1948), SP is probably most noteworthy for its role in relocating the film industry from the East Coast to the West Coast during the second decade of the 20th century.

While Selig is frequently listed in film references as a director, he was in fact a producer who had several often uncredited directors in his employ. He had little interest in fantasy, though he did produce this film in 1908 and *Hugo the Hunchback* and *Mephisto and the Maiden* the following year. Several of his productions from the period appear to be stage adaptations shot on film with a static camera. *Dr. Jekyll and Mr. Hyde* even features a rising and falling curtain between each of its four acts.

As with most stage adaptations, each act consists of a single scene, all of which add up to a complete version of the story. Contemporary reviews praise the actor (Bosworth) who played Jekyll and Hyde and provide clues as to what each act was about. Dr. Jekyll is in love with Alice (Hart), the daughter of a priest. After becoming Mr. Hyde, he attacks Alice and kills the priest. Then, as Jekyll, he visits his lawyer's office and, while there, has visions of his own execution. As Mr. Hyde he visits another doctor and before the man's eyes turns back into Dr. Jekyll. Finally, back in his own laboratory, his lover visits him and, once she leaves, he becomes Hyde again and commits suicide.

This is the first known screen adaptation of Robert Louis Stevenson's famous novella *The Strange Case of Dr. Jekyll and Mr. Hyde* (1886). A screen version produced the following year,

A Modern Dr. Jekyll (1909), also from Selig, updated the story to then-contemporary times. Like this 1908 version, it is now considered lost. CW

Dr. Jekyll and Mr. Hyde
Kalem; b/w; length unknown; U.S.
D: Sidney Olcott
Cast: Frank Oakes Rose, Gene Gauntier

While some sources cite this as the first-ever film adaptation of Robert Louis Stevenson's 1886 novella *The Strange Case of Dr. Jekyll and Mr. Hyde*, it is in fact the second, following Selig's identically titled release of the same year. Little is known about Kalem's picture apart from its central, classic plot—Dr. Jekyll creates a formula by which he liberates his darker side, a fiend named Mr. Hyde. Frank Oakes Rose, who co-directed *Ben Hur* the year before, starred in the lead roles.

In 1907 George Kleine, Samuel Long and Frank J. Marion formed Kalem. Their approach to distinguishing their product in a crowded industry was to adapt classic works of literature (including *The Legend of Sleepy Hollow*, 1908), as well as producing original works. This proved fairly successful for a time, but their fortunes faltered when their main director, Sidney Olcott, left the company to work as a director for hire. After 10 years in the business, Kalem was sold to Vitagraph in 1917.

The next theatrical film adaptation of Stevenson's novella came the very next year with Selig's updated, comical take on the tale, *A Modern Dr. Jekyll*. CW

Dream of an Opium Fiend
aka **Le Rêve d'un fumeur d'opium**
Star Film; b/w; 6 min; France
D/P/S/FX: Georges Méliès
Cast: Georges Méliès

Opium dens were once found throughout large cities in the Western United States, as well as in Europe and China. They were famous for allowing visitors to lie back while holding the bowls of long, opium-filled pipes over oil lamps, which turned the opium to vapor and allowed it to be inhaled. Deep sleep haunted by dreams was often the result. Into this milieu Méliès interjects his usual silliness, playing the Chinaman who runs a den.

A rather sedate entry in the director's nightmare subgenre of films, *Dream of an Opium Fiend* only really enters horror terrain in its last minute, when the goddess of the moon, a beautiful woman after whom the hero lusts, becomes a troll when he attempts to seduce her. The film exhibits a fear of female sexuality, as typified by Méliès' earlier *The Rajah's Dream* (1900). Otherwise, this story of a man who passes out in an opium den and dreams of a woman sitting atop a crescent moon, then drinking a beer on a full moon, is rehashed and largely uncreative stuff.

This film should not be confused with the similarly titled *Les Rêves du fumeur d'opium* from director Victorin-Hippolyte Jasset, which was made two years prior. CW

The Flower of Youth
aka **Fleur de Jeunesse**
Pathé; color-b/w; length unknown; France
Credits unknown

Precious little information survives about this lost Pathé title. The story concerned a fairy that brings some flowers to sentient life in an idyllic garden. One of the flowers is sent to a sort of "Horticultural Hell" for committing a sin. A demon then appears and tries to tempt the other flowers into following suit. Ultimately, the virtuous fairy defeats the evil demon and order is restored.

Official Pathé filmographies are inevitably incomplete, and detailed information on this title is impossible to come by. But the film did apparently make extensive use of trick photography and utilized hand-tinted coloring for the more dramatic moments. Some sources list it as a 1907 title. While that may have been its year of production, it was definitely released in 1908. TH

The Gambler and the Devil
aka **The Devil and the Gambler**
Vitagraph; b/w; 8 min; U.S.
D/S/P/C/FX: J. Stuart Blackton
Cast unknown

While some sources suggest that this horror melodrama anticipates Edgar G. Ulmer's masterpiece *The Black Cat* (1934) with its portrayal of a man wagering the devil for the soul of a woman, this appears to be incorrect. Rather, the film seems to have dealt with a gambler gaming with his own soul until his wife shows up and banishes the Evil One with a crucifix.

The film followed *The Haunted Hotel* and *The Ghost Story* (both 1907) as forays into the horror genre by multi-talented innovator J. Stuart Blackton. Blackton's first love was more fantasy-oriented fare, but on occasion he allowed darker elements to creep into his work. Despite his innovations in stop-motion photography, he is a forgotten figure today. And indeed, his decision to devote less time to filmmaking than to running the Vitagraph studio ensured that he was less prolific than he might have been.

He died in a road accident in 1941, having made his last film in 1933. TH

The Hanging Lamp
aka **La Suspension**
Pathé; b/w; 5 min; France
Cast: Max Linder

Pathé produced this short trick film for France's star comedian Max Linder, who'd found immediate fame with his first starring role in 1905. Though it features a demonic imp with a wolf-like appearance, *The Hanging Lamp*'s primary purpose was to make the audience laugh.

Today he's pretty much forgotten except in his native France, but Linder was a major influence on the best of the silent-era American comedians: Harold Lloyd, Charlie Chaplin and Buster Keaton. He also directed as many films as he starred in. At one point the highest-paid actor in the world, he moved to the United States in the 1920s, hoping to compete with the actors who arose to steal his thunder. The ploy failed, and upon his return to France he found his career waning and his new marriage one of anxiety and depression. In 1925 he killed himself.

While all of his films were comedies, a few of them did contain horror motifs, including *Max Hypnotized* (1910) and *Au Secours!* (1924). CW

The Haunted House
aka **The House of Ghosts**; **La maison ensorcelée**
Pathé; b/w; 6 min; France
D/P: Segundo de Chomón
Cast Unknown

Two men and a woman take refuge from a thunderstorm in an old dark house. Once inside, the place comes alive. A ghost does a sinister dance, tables and chairs appear and disappear and a monster stalks the premises. There's even a dinner that's presumably prepared by ghosts (and achieved through director de Chomón's superior use of stop-motion).

Director de Chomón is sometimes credited as having directed a film titled *The Haunted House* in 1906 as well, though it's difficult to know whether it was this film or another, or when either film was officially released. CW

Legend of a Ghost
aka **La légende du Fantôme**
Pathé; b/w; 13 min; France
D/S: Segundo de Chomón
Cast unknown

A beautiful young woman living alone in an ancient castle is confronted by a ghostly figure. She flees to the castle's cemetery, where she again sees the apparition. This time it grants her magical powers and tasks her with a mission to Hell to find a black substance. Once in the bowels of the underworld, she fights demonic beings and successfully executes her assignment. She then learns that her mysterious phantom is in fact a handsome prince, one who whisks her away to Heaven to be his consort.

Discerning that plot takes some work, the images are a string of loosely connected ideas, some realist in design, others completely surreal. Often cited as an early example of a vampire movie, *Legend of a Ghost*, like so many French films of the period, defies rigid categorization. It's one of many shorts made by the prolific Segundo de Chomón, whose films were so derivative of Georges Méliès that a few critics mistook some of these shorts for inferior works from the master. CW

The Legend of Sleepy Hollow
Kalem; b/w; 14 min; U.S.
Credits unknown

This is the first film known to be based on Washington Irving's classic short story of the same title (first published in 1820 in *The Sketch Book of Geoffrey Crayon, Gent*) and appears to be lost. Little is known about it other than its production company, country of origin and source material. Given its length (epic for the time in which it was produced), it was likely a fairly complete and/or faithful adaptation of Irving's story. If so, it would have presented the tale of lanky and superstitious schoolmaster Ichabod Crane, who competes with the town stud, Abraham Van Brunt, for the love of the beautiful and wealthy young Katrina Van Tassel. After leaving a party at Van Tassel's home late one fall night, Crane is pursued by the Headless Horseman, the ghost of a Hessian—a German soldier hired by the British—who'd gotten his head blown off during the Revolutionary War. At story's end, Crane is gone, leaving the reader to ponder whether he left Sleepy Hollow out of fear, was carted off by the ghostly galloping Hessian or was murdered or driven off by a more flesh-and-blood foe. Writer Irving tantalizes the reader with the suggestion that, whatever the particulars concerning Crane, Van Brunt was the culprit rather than some phantom rider.

The next film version, also titled *The Legend of Sleepy Hollow*, was produced in 1912. CW

Lord Feathertop
Edison; b/w; 11 min; U.S.
D: Edwin S. Porter
Cast unknown

Nathaniel Hawthorne's *Feathertop: A Moralized Legend* was first published in serial form in *The International Magazine* in 1852; two years later it was released *in toto* as part of Hawthorne's *Mosses from an Old Manse*, which also contained the classic *Rappaccini's Daughter*. *Feathertop* is the tale of an old witch named Mother Rigby who creates a scarecrow to oversee her garden. She becomes so enamored of it that she brings it to life. She names him Feathertop, giving him a pipe on which he must puff to remain among the living. On a whim she sends him to town to woo the beautiful Polly Gookin, whose father, Judge Gookin, the old witch despises. As Feathertop rides through town toward the Gookin house, the townspeople are taken with his astounding good looks and air of aristocratic magnificence. When the scarecrow-turned-man finally meets Polly, the two instantly hit it off, but when she spies his true form in a mirror, she faints. Feathertop then rides back to Mother Rigby and, in despair, destroys himself. Mother Rigby, saddened that her beloved scarecrow-man is no longer alive, places his remains back in her garden to tend to the crows.

In 1908 Percy MacKaye played up both the horrific and romantic elements of Hawthorne's story in *The Scarecrow*, a four-act play that changed the names of some of the characters and brought the devil onboard as a major participant. The popularity of the play no doubt influenced Edison Manufacturing Company to make *Lord Feathertop*, the first cinematic take on Hawthorne's fable. Sources from the time suggest that the film stuck somewhat closely to the original story, though it perhaps eliminated some of the more romantic elements as it placed the witch's resentment of the village squire front and center. And while director Edwin S. Porter likely used his knowledge of special effects editing to achieve some startling F/X, it's just as likely that he used cross cutting to emphasize the drama, humor and horror. After all, he'd pioneered such filmmaking with *The Life of an American Fireman* in 1903.

Hawthorne's short story next provided the basis for Éclair's *Feathertop* in 1912. CW

The Man and His Bottle
Hepworth; b/w; 5 min; Great Britain
D: Lewin Fitzhamon *P:* Cecil M. Hepworth
Cast: Thurston Harris

Following belatedly on the heels of Walter Booth's *The Drunkard's Conversion* (1901) and Walter Haggar's *D.T.'s, or the Effect of Drink* (1905), Cecil M. Hepworth released his own anti-drinking rant, *The Man and His Bottle*. As with the previous two films, *Bottle* was intended to be funny, though it was—also like the others—threaded with the stuff of nightmares.

Apparently suffering the effects of a hangover, a man gets out of bed and throws an empty whisky bottle to the ground.

But Satan, seeing an opportunity to corrupt a soul, appears and offers him another. The man refuses it, and the Devil disappears. When the man tries to fix a cup of tea, however, it becomes a group of bottles that perform a dance routine in the air. When the man attempts to get some work done in his office, the bottles—including one man-sized bottle with arms and legs—bedevil him there, too. Panicked, he runs into the street, chased by demons and large, ghostly rats. He hides in a cellar, but there's no relief for him there either; more demons taunt him by dancing around a massive booze bottle, wrapping up the number by imprisoning the hapless hero within the bottle and vanishing in a cloud of smoke.

The film was primarily an opportunity to play with the cutting-edge special effects of the time, though its moralistic message does smack one in the head. Its tone was emblematic of the anti-alcohol sentiment that led, in 1919, to a constitutional amendment prohibiting the sale of alcohol in the United States (and a rise in criminal activity as illicit hooch trade skyrocketed).

Director Lewin Fitzhamon had previously been responsible for *The Doll's Revenge* (1907). He shouts his message loud and clear in *The Man and His Bottle*, with one of the demons in the cellar bearing the letters DT (for, one assumes, "delirium tremens") on its costume. CW

The New Lord of the Village
aka Le Nouveau seigneur du village
Star Film; b/w; 8 min; France
D/P/S/FX: Georges Méliès
Cast: Georges Méliès, Jeanne d'Alcy

As the new lord of a village visits the town square, a young woman accosts him and insists that he come and see something. Along with two townsmen, he follows her to a cavern, only to discover that she's a witch from an otherworldly kingdom. She conjures first a cauldron, then flames and finally a king. After she and the king disappear, various monstrosities (including the giant frog from *The Witch*, 1906) besiege the three men. Finally, the disheveled lord makes his way back to the village where he is laughed at and treated like just another villager, until the witch returns to make him the village lord once again.

The most striking of the film's effects, that of transparent ghosts floating about the cavern in which the witch's kingdom exists, was nothing new for Méliès, and the film has little to distinguish it from his other work. CW

Pharmaceutical Hallucinations
aka Hallucinations pharmaceutiques ou le truc du potard
Star Film; b/w; 14 min; France
D/P/S/FX: Georges Méliès
Cast: Georges Méliès, Jeanne d'Alcy

After spending a period of time attempting to imitate the realist approach of Western filmmakers and receiving diminishing returns as a result, Méliès made an audacious return to *fantastique noir* with *Pharmaceutical Hallucinations*. One can divide the film into three sections: the set up, in which we learn that a pharmacist is good to the wealthy but treats the poor with disdain; the vision, in which the pharmacist is punished for his deeds by a rampage of wraiths and the conclusion, in which the pharmacist visits a wizard (Méliès) and learns that he must give up pharmacy in exchange for baking.

At least that's what appears to happen. As usual, Méliès' film doesn't make a whole lot of sense. But it isn't the plot that makes it great … it's the execution. The first section is slow, the third nonsensical, but the second is an example of the director in top form. The vision of the wraiths is a beautifully frightening one, quintessential Méliès with effects work harkening back to his earlier, better days. Unfortunately, he still hadn't adapted to the use of title cards as so many other directors were beginning to do; it was a troublesome reluctance that would eventually help kill the famed director's career.

Méliès followed *Pharmaceutical Hallucinations* with a variation on the Cinderella theme entitled *The Good Shepherdess and the Evil Princess* (1909), which contained a huge alligator, a dragon and giant faces to torment the titular princess. Overall, it was little more than a lengthy (for the time) fairy tale for young girls.

After only a couple more films, the director's debts would hinder him from producing for a couple of years, and it wasn't until a dubious arrangement with Pathé allowed him to return to filmmaking that he would make *Baron Munchausen's Dream* (1911) and *The Conquest of the Pole* (1912). His final film, *The Voyage of the Bourrichon Family* (1913), was taken from him and shelved by Pathé, bringing one of cinema's most influential and industrious careers to a melancholy end. CW

A Poor Knight and the Duke's Daughter
Gaumont; b/w; 9 min; France
Credits unknown

A knight and a duke's daughter fall madly in love, but the knight feels unworthy of the lady's affections because he is neither rich nor famous. So he goes out into the world and tries to make his name known, after which he intends on returning and asking for her hand in marriage. While he's away, another knight comes along and asks her to marry him. When she refuses, he enlists the aid of a witch, who conjures up a vision of the first knight involved in an affair with another woman. Upon seeing this, she agrees to marry the second knight; but as the two walk down the aisle, the first knight, having presumably accomplished something, shows up. Upset that the love of his life is marrying another, he promptly drops dead of a broken heart. She rushes to his side and dies as well, after which the two are buried together in the cathedral's crypt.

A Poor Knight and the Duke's Daughter is a French film from a period in which most filmmakers wanted to emulate the successful films of Georges Méliès, who by 1908 was making longer and more fantastic productions. In search of a new, untapped market, Gaumont—the home of Alice Guy, the world's first female director and considered by many to have shot the first narrative movie—began to produce scripted melodramas, though these films still occasionally employed trick photography (as the vision in this film demonstrates).

Evil witches figure prominently in many French films of the period. Others include *The Witch* (1906) and *The New Lord of the Village* (1908). CW

The Princess in the Vase
American Mutoscope & Biograph; b/w; 11 min; U.S.
D: Wallace McCutcheon *C:* G.W. Bitzer
Cast: D.W. Griffith, Edward Dillon, Linda Arvidson

In Ancient Egypt, a princess' adulterous affair is supernaturally brought to light, and she is put to death and cremated. Three thousand years later, a Boston professor of archaeology comes into possession of a partially shattered vase containing her ashes. When he falls asleep, he dreams that she comes to life and works her magic upon his household.

Though frequently credited to D.W. Griffith, *The Princess in the Vase* was actually directed by Wallace McCutcheon, with Griffith (under the name Lawrence Griffith) in the starring role. And while McCutcheon is forgotten today, Griffith is enshrined as the leading director of the silent era. He joined Biograph in 1908 and made, among others, *The Suicide Club* and *Edgar Allen Poe* (both 1909).

A former stage actor, Griffith realized that good performances could draw viewers into a film more effectively than trick photography. He also was among the first to comprehend that the intelligent use of camera movements and edits could heighten cinema's emotional impact. He made numerous shorts in the second and third decades of the 20th century that moved cinema overall in the direction of melodrama. With the release of the feature-length epic *The Birth of a Nation* in 1915, Griffith's career really took off. But he failed to make the transition to talkies, and after the relative failure of *Abraham Lincoln* (1930) and *The Struggle* (1931), he retired from directing altogether. In 1948 he was discovered unconscious in the hotel room in which he lived alone. He died thereafter in a Los Angeles hospital of a cerebral hemorrhage. He is buried in a graveyard in his home state of Kentucky.

A print of *The Princess in the Vase* exists in the Library of Congress film archive. CW

The Red Barn Crime
aka **Maria Marten**; **The Red Barn Crime, or Maria Martin**; **The Red Barn Crime, or Maria Marten**
William Haggar and Sons; b/w; 10 min; Great Britain
D/S/P/FX: William Haggar
Cast: Walter Haggar, Violet Haggar

Cinema's second stab at presenting the murder of Maria Marten came via South Wales' own William Haggar, a fairground showman who, together with his sons, produced some of the more interesting films to come out of Great Britain in the early 1900s. After his popular *The Life of Charles Peace* (1905), about a cat burglar and murderer who terrorized Sheffield, England during the 1870s, Haggar produced a small number of short, unremarkable comedies and dramas.

Then he turned to the crime that put Polstead in Suffolk County (England) on the map. It was in Polstead that, in 1827, a young single mother named Maria Marten was brutally murdered by her lover William Corder, who then buried her in the dirt floor of a red-tiled barn. The juicy elements of the case (Maria and William had an illegitimate child whom they may have murdered; Maria's murder was allegedly revealed in the nightmares of her stepmother, who may have been having an affair with William) made the story wildly popular in Great Britain for decades, inspiring plays almost immediately and, in due time, movies. Even today the morbid tale infuses work from artists as diverse as Biserko Fercek and Tom Waits.

This particular version, one of several in early cinema, hews more closely than most to historical fact, with Haggar's son Walter (who had played Charles Peace three years earlier) as Corder and his daughter Violet as Maria. After Maria disappears, her stepmother dreams that the young woman has been murdered and buried in the red barn outside of town. This revelation leads to the apprehension, conviction and execution of Corder.

Haggar's picture neither ups Corder's age drastically (Walter was 28 when the film was shot) nor portrays the murderer as a village squire. Both characterizations, though non-factual, appear frequently in stage and screen adaptations, both before and after this version. CW

The Saloon Keeper's Nightmare
aka **Le Tenancier de saloon's cauchemar**
Gaumont; b/w; 7 min; France
Credits unknown

The Gaumont studios in France produced this obscure short about a saloonkeeper who has a nightmare in which Satan torments him. The film was one of many examples of early cinema's fascination with the Devil, letting filmmakers and spectators alike explore their collective neuroses by putting the ultimate embodiment of evil up on the silver screen for them to view. While many of these early depictions were tongue in cheek, often presenting Satan as a buffoon, it's unclear whether that was the approach utilized here.

Extant credits and information on the film are sketchy, and the film is considered lost. As for producing studio Gaumont, inventor Leon Gaumont established it in 1895; the studio made its first films in 1897, and given that it is still a functioning production company, it can lay claim to being the oldest active film studio in the world. TH

Satan Finds Mischief
Pathé; b/w; length unknown; France
Credits unknown

Some sources attribute this bizarre French short to Georges Méliès, but no such title appears in any reputable filmography of his work. Given its description, it's easy to see why it would be mistaken for one of the master's titles. Various people and objects are transformed into other people and objects by an unseen force, which turns out to be Satan, who then appears in his true form and causes further chaos before making everything disappear in a puff of smoke.

It is unknown who exactly was involved with the production, one of many films of the period to depict the Devil and his works. TH

She
Edison; b/w; 10 min; U.S.
D/FX: Edwin S. Porter
Cast: Florence Auer, William V. Ranous

It's unfortunate that this second adaptation—the first in the United States—of H. Rider Haggard's immortal *She: A History of Adventure* is lost. The novel on which it was based was the *Da Vinci*

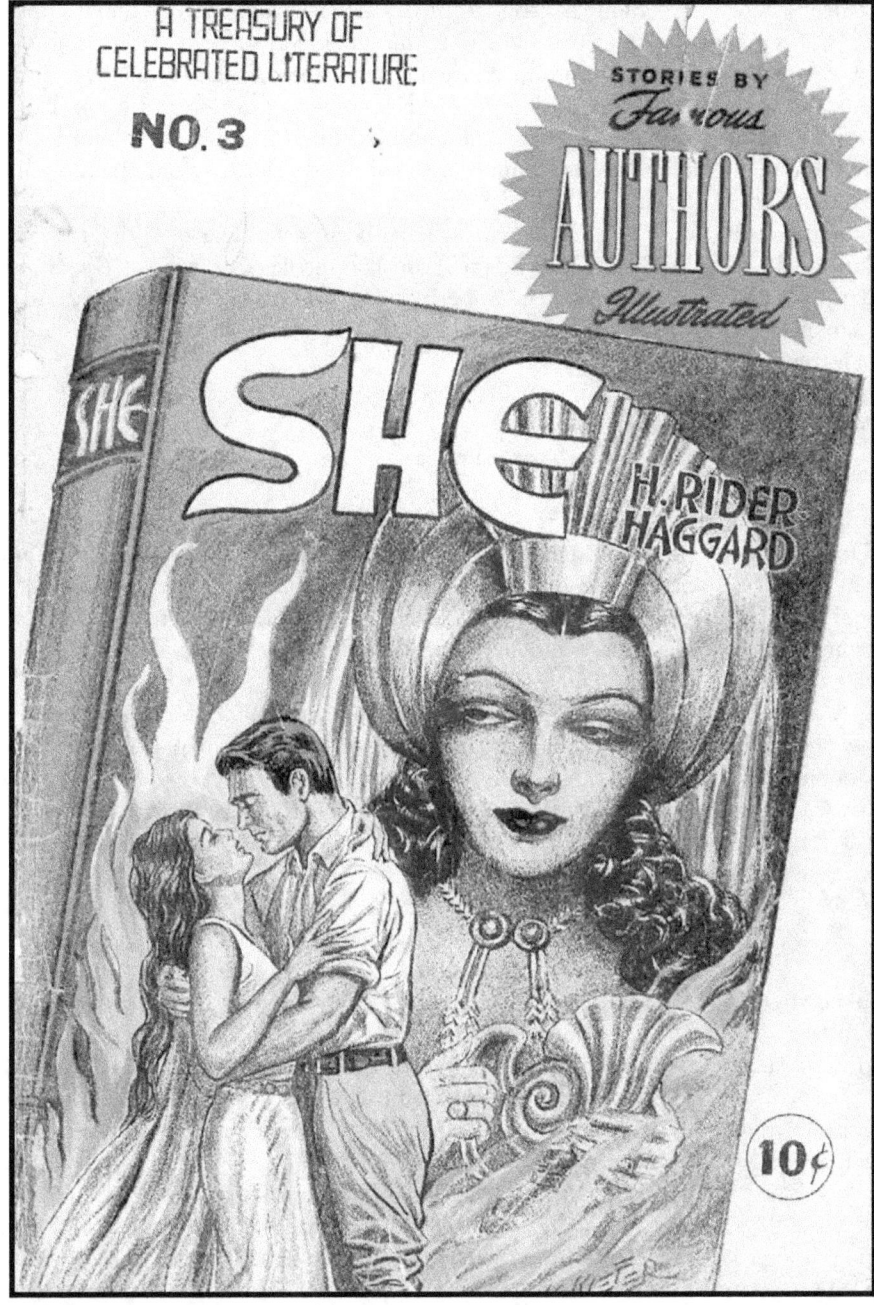

H. Rider Haggard's novel *She* was the *Da Vinci Code* of its day, selling over 80 million print copies.

Vincey, the reincarnation of the queen's lost love Kallikrates.

Transitioning from a fruitful career as a stage actress, Auer entered American cinema at the age of 28, the same year as the production of *She*. Only two months before the release of the Haggard adaptation, she had starred alongside costar Ranous in Vitagraph's adaptation of William Shakespeare's *Richard III* (1908). By the time cinema entered the age of the talkies, she was far enough past her prime to have lost her leading lady status, but her career as a character actor lasted into the 1950s. She died in 1962 at the age of 82.

Actor Ranous (who was also a director) died in 1915, only a few years after his work in *She*. At his age (just over 50 at the time *She* was released), he seems a bit too old for the part of the youthful Leo Vincey. CW

Sherlock Holmes in the Great Murder Mystery
aka **Sherlock Holmes and the Great Murder Mystery**
Crescent; b/w; 10 min; U.S.
Credits unknown

The first cinematic melding of two literary giants, Sir Arthur Conan Doyle and Edgar Allan Poe, combines the former's most famous creation and one of the latter's most famous mysteries. Poe's *The Murders in the Rue Morgue* (1841) introduced literature's first detective of any significance, C. Auguste Dupin, who would return in *The Mystery of Marie Roget* (1842) and *The Purloined Letter* (1844). Dupin, an amateur investigator with an unrivalled intelligence, was a major influence on Doyle when he crafted Sherlock Holmes. The connection is so obvious that Doyle made light of it in *A Study in Scarlet* (1887), in which Dr. Watson tells Holmes that the latter thinks he's Dupin (an assertion to which Holmes takes indignant offense). It's only fitting that for this single-reel adaptation of Poe's classic short story, Holmes replaced Dupin as the case's central investigator.

Code of its day, selling over 80 million print copies and spawning one sequel, two prequels, a host of imitations (one of the most famous of which was Pierre Banoit's *L'Antida*) and numerous film adaptations.

The great French filmmaker Georges Méliès made the first film adaptation, *Pillar of Fire* (1899), a one-minute short based on the novel's final sequence, in which Queen Ayesha bathes in the fires of eternal life and youth, only to perish and disappear. After Porter's version in 1908, numerous other versions would be made, mostly before the advent of sound.

Porter's film was a one-reeler, meaning that it would have run between 10-12 minutes. No known documentation of which aspects of the novel were adapted survived, though we know that Florence Auer played She and William V. Ranous starred as Leo

By all accounts, the film employed several scene changes in its attempt to dramatize the story, and it may have been *the* film that first introduced that staple monster of the heyday of silent horror films, the gorilla. The story reportedly goes as follows: Two young lovers meet in the girl's bedroom to discuss their wedding plans. After the young man, Jim, leaves, a gorilla that has escaped from a ship climbs through the girl's second-story window and kills her. The ship's captain apprehends the gorilla and takes it back to the ship, where they hide. The household butler finds the young woman and tells authorities that her beau was the last person to leave the room. Shortly thereafter, Jim is arrested and brought up on murder charges. Holmes and Watson read about the crime in the paper and insert themselves into the case. After touring the girl's home, Holmes returns to his lodgings and plays his violin. This puts him in a trance, where, incredibly, his brain unravels the mystery.

This is, of course, the part where the director engages in some of the trick photographic effects so popular at the time, with Holmes experiencing visions of both Jim and a burglar committing the crime. Neither rings true to him; but then, having read about a gorilla aboard a local ship, his mind conjures images of the aggressive primate murdering the innocent girl. After a (presumably, it being a 10-minute film, quick) series of dead-ends, Holmes locates the ship and the gorilla. He rushes into the courtroom just as Jim is being sentenced to death. Holmes relates what he has learned, and Jim is freed.

Though largely unfaithful to its source, this is the first known film adaptation of a Poe story. A French version of *The Pit and the Pendulum* (1909) followed in its wake, as would D.W. Griffith's dark, semi-historical *Edgar Allen Poe* (also 1909). The character of Sherlock Holmes, on the other hand, had already appeared in *Sherlock Holmes Baffled*, a short trick film in which Holmes is confronted by a black-clad burglar who vanishes into thin air when the detective tries to apprehend him. That film was shot, directed and edited by Arthur Marvin, and though some sources give its production date as 1900, its title card states the copyright as 1903.

While some film historians claim *Sherlock Holmes in the Great Murder Mystery* was produced in Denmark, others point to the United States as its country of origin. Either way, Crescent Film Manufacturing, the company generally credited as the film's producer, was registered at the time of the film's release as a U.S.-based company. CW

The Snowman
American Mutoscope and Bioscope; b/w; length unknown; U.S.
D: Wallace McCutcheon *S:* Lee Dougherty *C:* G.W. Bitzer
Cast: Edward Dillon, Florence Auer, Robert Harron, Wallace McCutcheon

This obscure, nightmarish fairy tale deals with a snowman that, once brought to life by a fairy, proceeds to frighten an onlooker until angry villagers flog it.

Wallace McCutcheon entered the film industry in 1897 as a cameraman but by 1899 had switched to directing, a logical transition given his background as a stage director. He was active throughout the early silent years, but his filmography stops dead in 1909. His most famous film remains *Dream of a Rarebit Fiend* (1906), while his longest-lasting contribution to film history was his decision to bring D.W. Griffith into the fold of American Mutoscope and Bioscope, a marriage between filmmaker and struggling company that proved fortuitous for all involved. McCutcheon should not be confused with his son Wallace, Jr., who famously committed suicide after a tumultuous, short-lived marriage to silent screen star Pearl White.

Leading man Edward Dillon was successful throughout much of the silent era, but by the dawn of talkies he was reduced to playing unbilled bit parts. TH

The Specter
aka **The Spectre**
Pathé; b/w; 8 min; France
Credits unknown

Some sources list this as a 1910 production. While it's possible that two films with the same (and somewhat generic) title appeared (produced by the same studio Pathé Freres) two years apart, the similarity of their plot synopses makes it more likely that the films are one and the same. The spirit of a murdered man haunts his murderer, but the specter may only be a manifestation of his own guilt.

The film seems to have been something of a dry run for D.W. Griffith's Edgar Allan Poe medley *The Avenging Conscience, or: Thou Shalt Not Kill* (1914) in its lifting of *The Tell Tale Heart*'s theme of a murderer revealed and done in by his own guilty conscience. TH

The Spirit
Gaumont; b/w; 9 min; France
Credits unknown

The Spirit was one of many silent shorts exploring the world of mediums and the supernatural. Gaumont's dabbling in the genre also included such titles as *The Saloon Keeper's Nightmare* (1908) and *Shooting in the Haunted Woods* (1909), though they never delved as deeply into horror as their chief competitor in French cinema, Pathé Freres.

Some sources date *The Spirit* as a 1909 film. That was no doubt the year it was released into foreign markets. TH

Spiritualistic Séance
aka **Séance de spiritisme**
Pathé; b/w; 5 (6, 7) min; France
Credits unknown

The title of this lost trick film indicates its content. A séance is held for a small group of skeptics, and spirits and other supernatural phenomena make appearances. The film was one of many early Pathé efforts with a macabre bent. Given the potential of trick photography, it's no surprise that so many early titles explored the supernatural. While their effects seem crude to modern sensibilities, they made a terrific impact on sensation-hungry audiences of the time.

Surviving information on this title is sparse, though the title and plot indicate that it tapped into a popular market of the time. Interest in the occult was keen at the turn of the 20th century, a trend that continued until World War II, when a new era of conservatism swept in and effectively stifled that craze until the late 1960s.

Some sources list a second film from Pathé having been released under the same title in 1911. The plot describes a disbeliever who scoffs at the supernatural and is haunted by evil spirits. Gaumont is alleged to have made a film with the same title in 1910; that film's plot description suggests that people attending a séance are deceived into believing in spirits by a man hiding under a table. Whether all these films were in actuality the same is unknown at the present, though it seems likely. TH

Spooks Do the Moving
Pathé; b/w; length unknown; France
Credits unknown

This short horror comedy has a group of students pretending to be ghosts in order to scare an elderly couple whose furniture they hope to steal. Unscrupulous people pretending to be ghosts was a common theme in silent cinema, as were haunted rooms, nightmares and Mephistopheles—anything, in short, that provided an excuse to wallow in stop-substitution special effects.

These short films were marketed to the masses in Nickelodeons, where people paid a nickel to view a single film. The first Nickelodeon theater was opened in 1905 in Pittsburgh, Pennsylvania and the notion quickly caught on worldwide. The showplaces were popular until about 1915, when longer films, typified by the pioneering work of D.W. Griffith, forced admission prices up. This in turn sparked the evolution of theaters from small, unimpressive establishments into larger, classier viewing venues. CW

The Thieving Hand
Vitagraph; b/w; 5 min; U.S.
Cast: Paul Panzer

A pathetic, one-armed beggar (Panzer) receives a prosthetic arm via a wealthy philanthropist. But the arm, it turns out, has criminal tendencies, with a habit of picking the pockets of unwary passers-by. When the beggar pawns the arm to be rid of it, it steals jewelry from the pawnshop and makes its way back to him while he sleeps. He is sent to prison for theft and there learns, after the arm has again made its way to him, that there is no escape from it.

This short subject is more comedy than horror, though its theme of a hand with a mind of its own predates Maurice Renard's horror novel *Les mains d'Orlac* (1920). Star Paul Panzer was born in Bavaria but immigrated to the United States. While working as a scenery painter in New York, he developed an interest in acting. He entered films in 1905 and amassed over 300 credits, one of his last being an unbilled bit part in Alfred Hitchcock's classic *Strangers on a Train* (1951). Many of his roles went un-credited, though his filmography includes such major titles as *Casablanca* (1942) and *A Foreign Affair* (1948). He also appeared, likewise unbilled, in *The Vampire Bat* (1933) and *The Black Cat* (1934), with the latter placing him as one of the cultists binding the heroine to a sacrificial altar.

Taken on its own terms, *The Thieving Hand* is an unimposing trifle that aims to tickle the funny bone rather than unnerve the audience, though the spectacle of a disembodied arm moving of its own accord must have caused a shiver or two in its day. It is unknown who directed the picture, but its potential appeal is due more to its quaint trick photography than anything else. TH

Too Much Champagne
Vitagraph; b/w; 4 min; U.S.
Credits unknown

Along with *The Drunkard's Conversion* (1901) and *D.T.'s, or the Effect of Drink* (1905), this is an example of a "cautionary tale" film about the evils of alcohol. As with the others mentioned, *Champagne* gave a showcase to the latest in trick photography while simultaneously preaching to its audience. But here the connection between alcohol and Satanic behavior seems to have been more pronounced, adding a touch of Dante Alighieri's *Inferno* to its surreal and farcical comedy.

This film seems, unlike the others mentioned, to have been a condemnation of mere social drinking, as a well-dressed man who has had a small amount of champagne stumbles home in a

drunken stupor. As he walks, the ground around him waves and rolls like water. When he finally gets home, he flops into bed and sinks into nightmares. Tinted red to reveal their hellish origins, demons dance around the man's bed and, according to some sources, a particularly effeminate imp propositions the drunken man, a clear warning that when you drink, you might—collective gasp—turn gay (or at least be seduced by someone gay).

Another film along the same lines but without the homosexual panic, *The Man and His Bottle*, was also released in 1908. CW

Trilby
aka **Lille Trilby**; **Little Trilby**
Nordisk; b/w; length unknown; Denmark
D/Co-P: Viggo Larsen *S:* Arnold Richard Nielsen *P:* Ole Olsen, *C:* Axel Graatkjaer Sorensen
Cast: Oda Alstrup, Viggo Larsen, Robert Storm Petersen

There are discrepancies among various sources as to who directed, produced and shot this 1908 adaptation of George Du Maurier's classic horror novel *Trilby* (1894), but the bulk of the evidence suggests that Viggo Larsen was the director, despite claims by some that Arnold Richard Nielsen performed that duty. In point of fact, Nielsen wrote the screenplay. And while some sources claim that Ole Olsen was the film's cinematographer, that credit actually goes to Axel Graatkjaer Sorensen. Olsen was the film's producer; he was also the founder of Nordisk

Film Studios, originally (and briefly) called "Ole Olson's Film Factory."

At any rate, *Trilby* was the first Danish adaptation of Du Maurier's tale, though Edison filmed scenes from a stage adaptation as early as 1895. (Two of those short films, *Trilby Hypnotic Scene* and *Trilby Death Scene*, may well have been the very first horror movies ever made.) Nordisk's *Trilby* didn't stray far from either the source material or the previous stage and film adaptations. The beautiful young Trilby unintentionally captures the heart of the Jewish hypnotist Svengali, who uses his powers to subjugate her and make her a great singer. Of the two male leads (Larsen, Petersen), it is unknown which played Svengali and which the hero. A still from the film presents the sight of a man standing over the unconscious figure of Trilby (Alstrup), but his identity is unclear.

Ole Olsen formed Nordisk in 1906, and Jens Viggo Larsen was brought on board as house director. With his handsome features, Larsen usually cast himself as the heroic male lead and often acted as co-producer or writer as well. After he and Olsen had a falling out in 1909, Larsen moved to Germany and there continued his career, making films into the early 1940s. After the defeat of the Nazis in World War II, he returned to his homeland a humiliated figure.

Larsen's next horror film was the Sherlock Holmes thriller *The Grey Lady* (1909), influenced by—though not faithful to—Sir Arthur Conan Doyle's novel *The Hound of the Baskervilles* (1901-1902). CW

The Tyrant Feudal Lord
Gaumont; b/w; 5 min; France
Credits unknown

A variation on Edgar Allan Poe's classic short story *The Masque of the Red Death* (1842), *The Tyrant Feudal Lord* is set in a famine-plagued Europe, where most people are unable to even feed their children. A rich feudal lord ignores the horrors going on around him and flouts his wealth by holding a great feast within the walls of his castle, despite entreaties by local priests that he instead help the peasants who work his land. A group of priests and peasants breaks into the castle and interrupts the proceedings, and the lord orders them put to death. After their executions, their spirits haunt the castle, and the lord kills himself in despair.

The ghostly effects appear to have been achieved through superimpositions. The same year Gaumont made this medieval melodrama, they made another with horror leanings: *A Poor Knight and the Duke's Daughter*. CW

The Wages of Sin, An Italian Tragedy
aka **The Wages of Sin**
Vitagraph; b/w; 10 min; U.S.
Credits unknown

Some sources cite this as an Italian production, but the American Film Institute records that it was made in the United States. The confusion undoubtedly stems from its Italian setting, though it seems the production was shot entirely on North American soil.

The story deals with a cholera victim who comes back to life inside his tomb. It is unclear if the story was explicitly supernatural or if it depicted a case of premature interment; given its popularity in horror productions, the latter seems more likely. The title also suggests that the final denouement was in response to the person entombed alive having committed some transgression against God or man.

The one-reel film was released on September 12, 1908. It should not be confused with any number of other films titled *The Wages of Sin*, released throughout more than a century of popular cinema. TH

Wedding Feast and Ghosts
aka **Nozze in casa Scivoloni**
Cines; b/w; 7 min; Italy
Credits unknown

Ghosts rudely disrupt a wedding celebration.

This is an early example of Italian fantasy cinema. Many sources name Eugenia Testa's *The Monster of Frankenstein* (1921) as the first Italian horror film, but titles such as this and Luigi Maggi's *Satan* (1912) seem worthy challengers to the title. Based on the scant surviving information about *Wedding Feast*, it seems probable that its tone was more impish than spine-chilling—and it's also possible that the supernatural was debunked in its denouement—but it nevertheless flirts with the genre in a way that likely qualifies it for fright flick status.

The film was produced by the remarkably prolific Societa Italiana Cines, which commenced production in 1906. By the time the company stopped making films in 1957 (with Guido Brignone's peplum *The Sword and the Cross*), it had cranked out approximately two thousand titles. TH

The Witch of Seville
aka **Le Strega de Siviglia**
Itala; b/w; 13 min; Italy
Credits unknown

This short subject utilized trick photography in its tale of a witch's enchanted cap and the visions it inspires.

Itala Film was one of the country's busiest motion picture producers in the early days of silent cinema and remained active until the mid-1950s. It was also responsible for another early horror-tinged title, *The Mystery of Souls* (1912). There is some confusion over the long-lost *Witch of Seville*'s year of production, with some sources listing it as late as 1911. Because it is predominantly cited as being produced in 1908 (and because it appears that the film was released in France in early 1909), it is included under that year here.

Witches, along with various and sundry other species of "wicked women," came to dominate Italian horror films when those films were produced *en masse* in the late 1950s and early 1960s, as evidenced by *I Vampiri* (1956) and *Black Sunday* (1960), among scores of others. TH

1909

The Ancient Roman
aka Il Romano Antico
Cines; b/w; 11 min; Italy
Credits unknown

A team of scientists discovers an ancient tomb and makes an amazing discovery—there's a Roman gladiator inside, and he's still alive!

Little information survives about this incredibly obscure Italian film, which is a pity given how interesting it sounds. It seems to have foreshadowed the mummy subgenre, in particular *The Curse of the Faceless Man* (1958), which is about a fossilized inhabitant of Pompeii coming to life.

Production company Societa Italiana Cines churned out nearly two thousand titles between 1906 and 1956. Many of their early offerings focused on Roman spectacle, albeit on very low budgets. This film also appears to have been very similar to a Pathé production titled *The Roman's Awakening* (1910), which had a Roman wake up in his tomb and exit in the modern world. There is no indication, however, that Pathé's film was even remotely horror. TH

The Ballad of a Witch
aka **La Ballata di una Strega**; **The Witch's Ballad**
Ambrosio; b/w; 9 min; Italy
D: Luigi Maggi *P:* Arturo Ambrosio *C:* Giovanni Vitrotti
Cast: Paolo Azzurri, Oresti Grandi, Umberto Mozzato, Mirra Principi, Mary Cleo Tarlarini, Ercolo Vaser

While some credit Eugenia Testa's *Il mostro di Frankenstein* (1921) as the first Italian horror film, that claim is belied by this 1909 title. This long-lost film—sometimes credited to cinematographer Giovanni Vitrotti—took its inspiration from a German fable of a poor fisherman driven to suicide by a malevolent witch, who then sings a ballad celebrating her victim's ill fortune.

While the film is known to have definitely existed, particulars are hazy. Luigi Maggi most likely directed it, but that assumption is an educated guess. There's also confusion as to the film's nation of origin, with some sources listing it as a British co-production. But while international co-financing later became the life's blood of the cash-strapped Italian film industry, it is very unlikely that backing from the U.K. was sought or secured at this stage of the industry's history.

Luigi Maggi directed films between 1907 and 1925. He also had a side career as an actor. He disappeared from film with the arrival of sound and died in 1946. Cinematographer Giovanni Vitrotti shot over 200 films between 1906 and 1953, with one of his last titles, *Against The Law* (1950), being notable for an early screen appearance by the legendary Marcello Mastroianni (*8 ½*, 1963). Vitrotti was also very active as a director, amassing over 100 such credits between 1906 and 1912, but it's impossible to confirm or disprove whether he directed or co-directed *The Ballad of a Witch*.

The film secured a brief release in the United States in 1910. TH

The Bewitched Manor House
aka **Le manoir ensorcelé**; **The Bewitched Manor**
Pathé; b/w; 7 min; France
Credits unknown

A haunted castle yields a variety of frightening sights, including a closet full of dangerous animals, demons and Satan. Thankfully, there's a good fairy to temper the horror for two lonely wanderers who take refuge in the castle late one night.

Yet another entry in the haunted house subgenre, *The Bewitched Manor House* is sometimes mistaken for a Georges Méliès film (an understandable mistake, given that the French director made a film titled *The Bewitched Inn* in 1897). While it's almost definitely not from Méliès, its actual paternity is unclear. It emerged from the depths of the prolific Pathé Freres Company, a major Méliès competitor (and the one that took over the filmmaker's Star production company when he was forced out of independent business in 1913). TH

Bluebeard
Edison; b/w; 3 min; U.S.
D/S: J. Searle Dawley *P:* Thomas A. Edison
Cast: Charles Ogle, Mary Fuller

This is the third film version of Charles Perrault's fairy tale, first published as *Le Barbe bleue* in *Histoires ou Contes du temps passé* in 1697. Originally part of a one-reel production with two other shorts, *Bluebeard* follows Perrault's story fairly closely. After being forbidden by her husband (Ogle) to enter a locked room in their castle home, Bluebeard's wife (Fuller) does so anyway. Inside the room she finds the severed heads of Bluebeard's previous wives. When her husband catches her in the act, he consigns her to the same fate as his former wives, but her brothers show up and rescue her.

With its short running time, the film appears to have been no competition for Georges Méliès' gory epic *Blue Beard* (1901). In fact, the probability that Dawley's adaptation was innocuous is borne out by then-contemporary reviews, which don't mention much about decapitated heads but frequently describe the fight scene between the two brothers and Bluebeard, pronouncing it an exciting climax.

Dawley, Ogle and Fuller reteamed the next year for *Frankenstein*, the first film adaptation of Mary Shelley's *Frankenstein, or The Modern Prometheus* (1818). Fuller's other horror credits include *The House of the Seven Gables* (1910), *The Ghost's Warning* (1911) and *A Witch of Salem Town* (1915), among others. For a time her career was on fire, as she starred in one film after another; at one point, she was as popular as D.W. Griffith's star discovery, Mary Pickford. But both Fuller's burst of success and an attempted comeback were truncated by nervous breakdowns. CW

The Bogey Woman
aka **La femme bogey**
Pathé; color; 7 min; France
Credits unknown

This lost short film had an irresistible draw—a Bogey Woman who, for whatever reason, transforms children into vegetables.

Pathé Freres produced a number of macabre shorts during the early 1900s, making the studio one of the first specialists in the fright genre. *The Bogey Woman* seems to have been a dark fairy tale, designed to frighten children visiting neighborhood Nickelodeons into upstanding behavior. The notion of putting young ones in peril was unusual for the time; it was a number of years before this taboo was breached in more graphic terms in such offerings as Lucio Fulci's *Don't Torture a Duckling* (1972).

Some sources indicate that *Bogey Woman* was hand-colored. It was released on April 27, 1909. TH

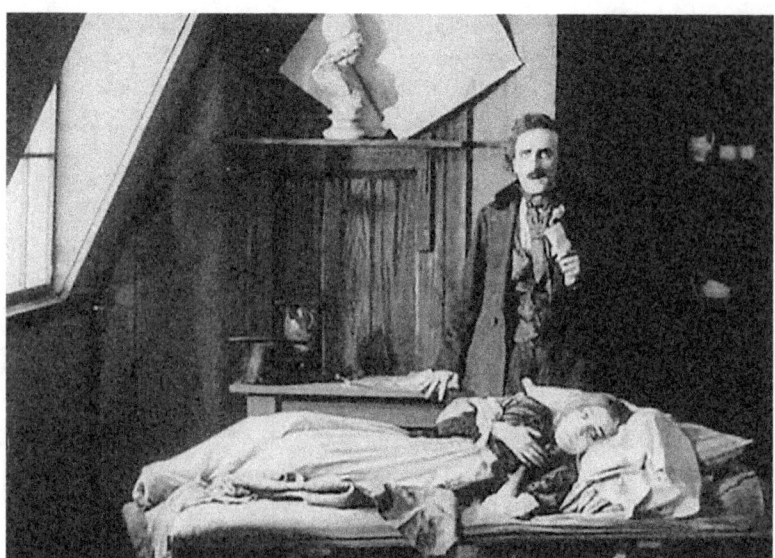

Edgar Allen Poe (middle name misspelled by the producers), directed by D.W. Griffith, features Herbert Yost as Poe and Linda Arvidson as Virginia Poe.

The Butcher's Dream
Lux; b/w; 9 min; France
Credits unknown

This short subject dealt with a butcher who goes to sleep after a long day's work and dreams that his animals are slaughtering him.

Almost no information survives about this title, and what little remains is contradictory. Some sources cite it as an American production, while others list it as being from Lux Studios in France. The latter seems the best guess; if so, that would make this one of their earlier efforts, since they began operation in 1908. Given the time of the creation of *The Butcher's Dream*, it's likely that the titular nightmare was played as much for laughs as it was for shocks. TH

The Cat That Was Changed into a Woman
aka **La Chatte metamorphose en femme**
Gaumont; b/w; 10 min; France
D: Louis Feuillade
Cast: Christiane Mandelys, Alice Tissot, Maurice Vinot

A cat is transformed into a woman, who then seduces a man.

This was the first of two French film versions of the Aesop fable *Venus and the Cat*. In the story, a cat falls in love with a handsome young man. It begs the goddess Venus to change it into a woman, and the goddess complies. The man falls in love with the woman, and they are married. After years of marital bliss, however, Venus lets a mouse loose in the couple's house to see if the woman has truly changed her feline ways. The woman springs after it like a cat, and a disappointed Venus changes her back into one.

It's unclear how closely this short subject followed the story on which it was based, but it certainly provided director Louis Feuillade an opportunity to experiment with trick photography. Feuillade entered films in 1905 as a scenarist and made his debut as a director the following year. He went on to establish himself as France's king of serials with *Fantomas* (1913) and *Les Vampires* (1915).

The next version of *Venus and the Cat*, also titled *The Cat That Was Changed into a Woman*, was released in 1910. TH

The Convict Guardian's Nightmare
Pathé; b/w; 8 min; France
Credits unknown

While some sources list *The Convict Guardian's Nightmare* as a 1906 film, the British Film Institute gives the year as 1909. Since it was shot in France, it's possible that it was produced in 1906 but not released in Great Britain until 1909. At any rate, it's the story of a prison warder who falls asleep and dreams about a convict whose portrait he had just seen. In the dream, the convict escapes from prison but comes to a terrifying end when he is turned into a skeleton (likely via the process of stop-substitution).

This film should not be confused with Cricks and Martin's *The Convict's Dream*, likewise released in 1909, in which a convict dreams of a life of luxury outside his prison's walls. CW

Don Juan Tenorio
Rosas; b/w; length unknown; Mexico
D/P/C: Enrique Rosas
Cast: Enrique Rosas

This is the second known Mexican film adaptation of José Zorillo's play *Don Juan Tenorio* and the third known adaptation overall. It was the brainchild of Enrique Rosas, whose career encompassed every aspect of cinema; he produced, directed, wrote, acted, edited and shot an amazing number of films given that his career began in 1903 and lasted only until 1919. He died in 1920 in his native Mexico at the fairly youthful age of 42.

According to some sources, his twist to *Don Juan Tenorio* was to interpret the tale (of two men in a competition to see which can sexually violate the most women and murder the most men) through a comedic lens. If so, it must've been a hoot. CW

Doomed
Pathé; b/w; 14 min; France
Credits unknown

Doomed was one of many early horror titles exploiting the gimmick of hypnosis. It deals with an evil mesmerist whose gift, it seems, was given to him by Satan; of course, he uses it for nefarious purposes.

Precious little info has survived about this obscurity, which was obviously influenced by the usual suspect, George Du Maurier's Gothic 1894 horror novel *Trilby*. TH/CW

Edgar Allen Poe
aka **Edgar Allan Poe**; **The Raven**
American Mutoscope & Biograph; b/w; 7(9) min; U.S.
D/Co-S: D.W. Griffith *Co-S:* Frank E. Woods *C:* G.W. Blitzer
Cast: Herbert Yost, Linda Arvidson, Anita Hendrie, Arthur V. Johnson, David Miles, Charles Perley

There's an awful lot of handwringing going on in this early example of a biopic from silent film pioneer D.W. Griffith, and

Edgar Allan Poe finds rejection for his poems at yet another editor's office, from *Edgar Allen Poe* (the title misspelled by the film's producers).

while it isn't strictly horror, it should be of interest to horror aficionados for its portrayal of the most famous writer in the history of the genre.

Pity poor Virginia Poe (Arvidson, who was Griffith's wife at the time); she's ill. One can tell this from her overwrought mannerisms, her frequent sorrowful gazing toward Heaven and the time she spends in bed with a deathly look on her face. Worse, she and husband Edgar Allan Poe (his name was misspelled by the film's producers) cannot afford the medicine she needs, a situation that leaves Poe (Yost) understandably distraught. But just when all seems lost, he sees a bust of Pallas with a particularly ominous raven perched upon it, and inspiration strikes. The poem "The Raven" results, and with it the hope of a sale and thus the means to procure the medicine his wife so desperately needs. But alas, every editor/publisher rejects the poem, and Poe can manage only to scrape together enough to purchase a blanket for his wife's comfort and some food to fill her hollow stomach. By the time he gets said supplies home to his wife, however, she has passed away.

The intertitles for *Poe* are long lost, but the proceedings remain easy enough to follow. Running at a long seven minutes, it takes place in three rooms (the Poes' lodgings and the offices of two editors) with few characters. It's typical Griffith, evoking a melancholic mood with a sad but true story. The major problem with it (apart from the leads' overacting) is that little of it is true. Not only did the famous writer not meet rejection at every turn, "The Raven" proved to be one of his most commercially successful and critically acclaimed works. Nor, incidentally, did his wife die before its publication; she lived for a good two years after it first saw print.

In 1909 alone, Griffith turned out almost 150 films (many of which are lost today); thus, it's easy to understand why *Edgar Allen Poe* feels rushed. Yet the acting on display in the minor roles is somewhat prophetic of the naturalistic style that in time came to dominate Hollywood product. Griffith's reactionary mindset results in a portrayal of Poe as a God-fearing family man, which might easily ruin the dramatic punch of the movie for anyone not like-minded. Yet the success of the film sparked other silent-era presentations of the author's life, which include two films titled *The Raven* (1912, 1915).

Griffith's film was released on a split reel with *A Wreath in Time* in February 1909, the bicentennial year celebrating Poe's birthday. CW

The Egyptian Mystery
Edison; b/w; 10 min; U.S.
Credits unknown

A typical trick photographic film, *The Egyptian Mystery* was produced at a time when cinema was beginning to move away from such fare. It's about a pendant found in an Egyptian tomb that causes any object the wearers touch to disappear. Likely intended for laughs as much as for chills, it doubtless employed the by then snooze-inducing effect of stop-substitution to achieve its "frights."

Unable to keep up with public demand for lengthier and more dramatic features, Edison ceased film production within the decade following this movie, leaving newer companies—and filmmakers such as D.W. Griffith and Cecil B. DeMille—to take up the slack.

Other horror films containing a magical or cursed stone or piece of jewelry include *The Bloodstone* (1908), *The Moonstone* (1909), *The Wonderful Pearl* (1909), *The Fairy Jewel* (1911), *The Moonstone* (1911) and *The Devil-Stone* (1917), among many, many others. CW

The Evil Philter
aka **Le Philtre Maudit**
Pathé; b/w; 7 min; France
Credits unknown

A lovesick man turns to an old crone for help. The hag gives him a love potion, promising that it will cure his problems. The potion, however, attracts not love but phantoms and demons to torment him.

A philter (the noun is derived from the French word philtre) is a potion or magic charm. This short subject apparently garnered a release in some English-speaking countries; a surviving newspaper item from *The Evening Post* of Wellington, New Zealand mentions it as being among the latest attractions at a local cinema. Beyond that, little is known about it; the film is believed to be lost. TH

Faust
Edison; b/w; 22 min; U.S.
D/FX: J. Searle Dawley, Edwin S. Porter
Cast: William Sorelle, Laura Sawyer

Based less on Goethe's play than on Charles Gounod's 1859 opera, *Faust* was obviously intended to be a larger-than-usual offering from Edison. It adheres somewhat closely to Méliès' *Faust and Marguerite* (1904), with Faust selling his soul to Mephistopheles (Sorelle) for the love of Lady Marguerite (Sawyer). Equipped with new, dashing looks, the cavalier Faust woos Marguerite successfully, only to desert her after she becomes pregnant. Her brother Valentin then challenges Faust to a duel to avenge her honor. Faust wins, Valentin dies and Lady Marguerite kills her own child rather than be reminded of her former lover. She is thrown into prison for her crime, and there she dies after confessing her love for Faust. Mephistopheles attempts to steal her soul, but angels head him off and bear her spirit to Heaven. Faust, on the other hand, is damned to Hell.

Despite the plot description, the film is less supernaturally inclined than Méliès' version, exploring instead the story's dramatic possibilities. Sources disagree on whether Dawley or Porter directed. Given that the two men had often worked together, it is possible that each had a hand in molding the film's direction.

Interestingly, some sources name stage actor Alfred de Manby as Faust; this is difficult to establish or disprove, given that there are no known prints of the film in existence and reviews written over the decades are muddied with incorrect references to other film versions of the legend. (In the two-year period from 1909 to 1911 there were no fewer than 11 film adaptations of the Faust tale, and considering that most of them are today long lost, the confusion is understandable.) CW

The Grey Lady
aka **Den Graa Dame**; **The Grey Dame**
Nordisk; b/w; 14 min; Denmark
D/S: Viggo Larsen *P:* Ole Olsen *C:* Axel Sorensen
Cast: Viggo Larsen, Forest Holger-Madsen, Gustav Lund, Elith Pio

Sherlock Holmes (Larsen) is called upon to examine a seemingly supernatural phenomenon involving a ghostly woman in gray. Said to appear to individuals who are about to die, she's the spectral suspect in several recent deaths of members of a wealthy family. The skeptical Holmes investigates and does indeed expose the guilty party.

Sir Arthur Conan Doyle dabbled in numerous genres during his writing career, but far and away his most significant creation was super-sleuth Sherlock Holmes. Doyle introduced Holmes in the 1887 novel *A Study in Scarlet*, and an enthusiastic reception led to a total of 4 novels and 56 short stories built around the character.

With his keen sense of observation and arrogant demeanor, Holmes captivated readers the world over. Doyle formed a complicated relationship with his literary progeny, at one point even killing him off (in the 1893 short story *The Adventure of the Final Problem*). Public outrage, and the author's realization that he'd killed the goose that laid golden eggs, prompted him to explain that the details of Holmes' demise had, in fact, been greatly exaggerated.

The character first made his theatrical rounds in Charles Brookfield's play *Under the Clock* (1893), though it would fall to American actor and playwright William Gillette to create the first truly successful stage vehicle for the character. Beginning with his own 1894 play *Sherlock Holmes*, Gillette portrayed the detective more than 1,300 times, his final turn being a radio performance two years before his death in 1937.

As the new medium of cinema caught on, it didn't take long for filmmakers to explore the potential of Doyle's stories. The Danish production company Nordisk began a series of Sherlock Holmes adventures in 1908 with the aptly titled *Sherlock Holmes*. Starring actor/writer/producer/director Viggo Larsen in the title role, its popularity generated a series of Holmes adventures. *The Grey Lady* was the sixth film in the series and Larsen's final portrayal of the character for Nordisk. He also wrote the script and directed. (The following year saw him transfer his Holmes addiction to Germany, where he wrote, directed and starred in a five-part serial called *Arsène Lupin contra Sherlock Holmes*.)

Loosely based on *The Hound of the Baskervilles*, *Grey Lady* has long been considered lost. It seems by all indications to have embraced the moody atmosphere of Doyle's story, with material inevitably compressed and reinterpreted to accommodate the brief running time.

In subsequent Nordisk Holmes films, Otto Lagoni, Alwin Neuss and Holger Rasmusen portrayed the title character. *The Hound of the Baskervilles* was officially adapted in both France and Germany in 1914. TH

The Haunted Hotel
aka **L'hotel hanté**; **L'hotel enchanté**
Pathé; b/w; 6 min; France
D/S: Segundo de Chomon
Cast unknown

Yet another movie about a guest being threatened by a barrage of supernatural events at a ghostly inn (mostly perpetrated by two demonic beings after the protagonist has drunk a potion and fallen asleep), *The Haunted Hotel* is the usual hokum perpetrated by director de Chomon, who made much better films both before and after this. Sources are divided as to whether it was a Pathé Freres production or a Star Film production. Whichever the case, it should not be confused with *The Mystery of the Haunted Hotel*, which was filmed in 1913 by Thanhouser and starred William Russell, Florence La Badie and Harry Benham. In that film, which seems to have been a melodrama, a doctor cures a young woman of her sleepwalking ailment. CW

The Haunted Man
aka **Der Frequentierte Mann**
Duskes; b/w; length unknown; Germany
Credits unknown

This obscure German production is noteworthy for presenting what is likely the earliest exploration of the concept of the *doppelganger* in German cinema. The term "doppelganger," meaning "ghostly double," can be traced to Jean Paul's 1796 book *Siebenkas*, though it was popularized in such works as Fyodor Dostoyevsky's *The Double: A Petersburg Poem* (1846) and Edgar Allan Poe's *William Wilson* (1839).

While little information survives on this film, there seems a thematic connection to Charles Dickens' *The Haunted Man and the Ghost's Bargain*. Published in 1848, Dickens' book told of a chemistry teacher haunted by a spirit representing his grief and bitterness over his past; it's not a conventional ghost but rather a phantom twin who offers the teacher a chance to let go of the past.

The concept of the doppelganger loomed large in German fantasy cinema throughout the great Expressionist period of the 1920s. It's possible to interpret *The Cabinet of Dr. Caligari* (1919) in a similar light, while the theme is even more pronounced in the various film versions of Hanns Heinz Ewers' *The Student of Prague*. TH

Her Dolly's Revenge
Lux; b/w; 5 min; France
Credits unknown

French production company Lux dipped into horror during the middle of the silent era. These efforts included *The Cat's Revenge* (1908), *The Butcher's Dream* and *The Mummy of the King Ramsees* (both 1909), *The American Suicide Club*, *The Buddha's Curse*, *The Secret of the Hand* and *The Snake Man* (all 1910), *Baby's Ghost*, *Bill Taken for a Ghost* and *The Skivvy's Ghost* (all 1911) and *The Vengeance of Poe* (1912).

Her Dolly's Revenge, one of the company's creepier offerings, was also among these. A typically short film focusing on special effects, it showcases a dream sequence in which her own doll stabs a little girl to death. It bears some resemblance to Cecil M. Hepworth's similarly themed *The Doll's Revenge* (1907), which featured a doll tearing apart the boy who broke it. CW

The Hunchback
Vitagraph; b/w; length unknown; U.S.
D: Van Dyke Brooke
Cast: Frank Keenan

This lost short feature joins French director Alice Guy's *Esmeralda* (1905) as one of the earliest film adaptations—though this time unauthorized—of Victor Hugo's *The Hunchback of Notre Dame*. As little information has survived regarding the film, not much can be surmised about it beyond what little can be gleaned from contemporary reviews.

It appears that character actor Frank Keenan—who passed away in 1929, just before the silent era finally gave way to talkies for good—portrays a hunchback in the manner of Hugo's deformed bell-ringer Quasimodo. A young woman named Gertrude (an apparent replacement for Esmeralda) takes pity on the deformed felon, who is being punished for attacking a nobleman, by providing him with water. Once he is released from the stocks, she takes him to her home where he becomes her personal gardener and handyman. When would-be rapists attack Gertrude, the hunchback saves her and kills her attackers, but he is fatally felled as well.

In 1910 William N. Selig would produce another unauthorized version of the Hugo novel entitled *Hugo the Hunchback*, while the French would take another authorized crack at the story in 1911 with *The Hunchback of Notre Dame*. Universal mounted its own epic production—among the most famous screen versions of the novel—starring Lon Chaney in 1923. TH

The Imp of the Bottle
Edison; b/w; 8 min; U.S.
Credits unknown

The November 1909 issue of *Variety* reported the copyright procurement for this obscure Edison production, based on Scottish author Robert Louis Stevenson's short story *The Bottle Imp* (first published in the *New York Herald* in 1891). The tale concerns a Hawaiian named Keawe, who, planning to become rich, purchases a bottle containing a wish-granting imp. There's a catch, however. The bottle must be sold at a loss before the owner dies or said owner goes straight to Hell for all eternity. Keawe takes the risk, certain that he can get rich and sell the bottle in plenty of time. And things do go great at first; he does indeed wish for riches (and a beautiful house) and gets the bottle sold off without a hitch. In a twist used to greater effect by W.W. Jacobs in his 1902 short story *The Monkey's Paw*, Keawe's uncle and cousins are killed, bequeathing him the money for his dream house, with enough extra to provide him—in theory—lifelong security. He gets the house built and marries a beautiful woman, only to develop leprosy, the only cure for which is to track down the bottle and repurchase it for two pennies. This he does, and the treatment duly takes, but his despondency at being doomed to Hell doesn't go unnoticed by his wife. She demands an explanation, he gives it to her and the two embark on a series of failed attempts to resell the bottle. Eventually, they pawn it off on a sailor who has lived a debauched life and expects to go to Hell anyway. And the no-doubt-relieved Mr. and Mrs. Keawe live happily ever after.

Edison's film was apparently faithful to the gist of Stevenson's tale but not the particulars. The official film synopsis describes a sailor who, unable to win a princess' heart in the usual way, purchases cheaply a magic bottle and wishes that she fall in love with him. It works fine at first, but when disaster strikes, the sailor comes to believe that the bottle is responsible. His attempts to sell it, however, fall flat.

The replacement of the original story's Hawaiian leads with a white sailor and a princess was doubtless a ploy to broaden the movie's potential audience. Given that the adaptation shared a "split reel" with *A Winter's Tale* (1909) and was eight minutes long at most, it probably didn't stand much of a chance of being done too faithfully. Considering the period in which the film was made, it's also entirely possible that, synopsis aside, it was a typical special effects short with minimal dramatic narrative to keep it moving. In any case, it was the first film adaptation of Stevenson's tale, which was next adapted as *The Bottle Imp* in 1917 by Famous Players-Lasky. The most famous theatrical version is probably *Love, Death and the Devil*, a 1934 German film starring Brigitte Horney, though even that one is largely forgotten. CW

The Invisible Thief
aka **Le Voleur Invisible**; **L'Homme invisible**
Pathé; b/w; 6 min; France
D: Ferdinand Zecca, Segundo do Chomón
Cast unknown

H.G. Wells' classic science fiction novel *The Invisible Man* was first serialized in *Pearson's Magazine* in 1897. The plot concerns a scientist who creates a serum that blocks the body's ability to reflect light. The scientist takes a dose of the serum (stupidly, since he has yet to develop an antidote) and his inability to be seen sparks a mad, diabolical plan to terrorize the world.

Setting the more malevolent elements of the story aside, *The Invisible Thief* centers on a young man who, obsessed with Wells' novel, develops an invisibility serum. After his body disappears (through the magic of slow dissolve), he takes his clothes off and robs a house. When he returns home, he puts on his clothes and a mask. Soon he's again up to no good, this time robbing people on the street while fully clothed and masked. When the police give chase, he discards his clothing and attacks the authorities who, frightened, scatter and flee.

Though obviously using Wells' book as inspiration, Pathé steered clear of the story's particulars to avoid a copyright in-

Stacia Napierkowska as the libidinous Lucrezia from *Lucrèce Borgia*

fringement lawsuit. Some film historians have credited the film's direction to Albert Cappellani and Louis Garnier, but neither appears to have had anything to do with it. It was, rather, directed by Segundo de Chomón with an assist from Ferdinand Zecca (at a time when he generally did little more than guide the production of Pathé's films).

Some of the film's effects were achieved by a combination of stop-substitution and stop-motion. CW

The Last Look
Pathé; b/w; 7 min; France
Credits unknown

Shot in late 1909 and released in January 1910, *The Last Look* is a mystery film (though most probably one with a humorous bent) in which a murder is solved through an application of the impossible: the retrieval of the killer's image from the eyes of the dead victim.

The idea of a deceased person's eyes holding the last image he or she saw while alive had been around for years. It was famously pursued in 1888, when the police investigating the Jack the Ripper murders photographed the eyes of one of the Ripper's victims expecting to see Jack's unmistakable image imprinted there. Needless to say, the idea is scientifically unsound and had been disproven long before 1909, though some believe the notion even today. CW

The Little Princes in the Tower
Pathé; b/w; length unknown; France
Credits unknown

In 1933 an urn was disinterred from Westminster Abbey for study. It supposedly contained the bones of two children found buried beneath a Tower of London stairwell in 1674, remains that were seen by many as confirmation of what English scholar Sir Thomas More (1478-1535) had written about the 1483 deaths of a child king and his brother. According to More, the young King Edward V and the younger Richard, Duke of York, were taken from the Tower (where they'd been confined by their conniving uncle, the deformed Richard III, who had gained the Crown of England by declaring their births illegitimate) and smothered with pillows. Afterward, they were buried "at the stair-foot."

In all fairness, it should be noted that More was a counselor to the Tudors—the family to which King Richard's rival and successor King Henry VII belonged—who stood to gain by declaring Richard to be the murderer of the boys. Modern historians note that there's no proof Richard murdered the princes and that he had securely taken the throne before they disappeared. Rather, some of these historians suggest that it was Henry Tudor who saw them as a threat and snuffed them out after Richard's death.

Though little final evidence exists for either scenario, William Shakespeare (1564-1616) expanded the historical hearsay into one of his greatest tragedies, *Richard III*. A 1908 film adaptation of the play by William V. Ranous illustrates the world's enduring fascination with More's tale of regicidal intrigue. But, unlike Ranous' film, *Princes* focuses on the horrific fate of the two boys rather than the doings of the man who is alleged to have brought that fate about. The film should not be confused with the also-lost *The Princes in the Tower* (1913), which seems to have had nothing to do with Shakespeare or King Edward V or anyone else under discussion here.

The very next year saw the release of *The Children of Edward IV*, which focused on the murders of the two young royals. CW

Lucrèce Borgia
Pathé; b/w; length unknown; France
D: Albert Capellani
Cast: Stacia Napierkowska, Paul Capellani

The Borgias were a notorious family who, in the late 15th century, rose to political power when Rodrigo Borgia became Pope Alexander VI. He was father to at least four illegitimate children who bore his non-Papal surname nonetheless. These included Cesare and Lucrezia, whose names have long been bywords in the annals of history's darker pathways. It has been suggested that the brothers, sister and father were involved in a web of incestuous relationships, with Cesare leading an effort to consolidate the family's control over the southern part of Europe by systematically murdering enemies and marrying off his sister and youngest brother to influential families. Though never really proved, it has also been claimed that Lucrezia was fond of murder, which she allegedly committed with a hollow signet ring containing a vial of poison. She is said to have invited those with whom she was displeased to extravagant parties, where she poured the poison from her ring into their drinks.

It's only logical that this sort of delicious gossip would become the stuff of nightmare cinema, and indeed the Borgia family has been well represented on film. *Lucrèce Borgia* was the first such effort, with director Albert Capellani casting his younger brother Paul as the bloodthirsty Cesare and Stacia Napierkowska as the libidinous Lucrezia. Long lost, it's impossible to ascertain how well it followed historical accounts, but given that feature-length films were still a few years off, it's doubtful that *Lucrèce* was anything other than a short focusing on a prurient aspect or two of the Borgia persona.

The life of Lucrezia Borgia has been the basis for not only numerous films but for many a book and play as well, including an 1833 fictional novel by Victor Hugo and an 1834 opera by Donetti. German auteur Richard Oswald directed a silent biopic in 1922 with Conrad Veidt as Cesare and Liane Haide as Lucrezia, while Abel Gance made the definitive cinematic take in 1935. Both of those films were titled *Lucrezia Borgia*.

Albert Capellani's most famous film may be *The Hunchback of Notre Dame* (1911), which also starred his brother Paul. CW

Lunatics in Power
Edison; b/w; length unknown; U.S.
Credits unknown

Edgar Allan Poe wrote *The System of Dr. Tarr and Professor Fether* in 1845 as a statement about the treatment of inmates in mental institutions. In it, a young man visits a French asylum to learn about "soothing," an experimental therapy that allows patient freedom of movement within the institution. The visitor finds, that the treatment has been suspended in favor of one created by Dr. Tarr and Professor Fether, two men with whom he is unfamiliar. Soothing's originator, one Monsieur Maillard, invites the man to a feast for the hospital staff where everyone wears ill-fitting clothes and a band plays unfamiliar instruments. Maillard explains that soothing was abandoned because of an incident in which the patients had taken over the hospital and locked the staff away. It turns out that this has indeed happened, but it is Maillard and the current "staff" who are the patients.

The story's controversial nature caused *Graham's Magazine* to delay its publication by several months. And though it's unquestionably intended as satire, its basic premise is securely within the bounds of the horror genre. This, the first of many adaptations sprinkled throughout cinema history, was meant to be comedic, but the concept's dark overtones are inescapable. The film consisted of three scenes, beginning with the dinner table sequence and culminating in the escape of the hospital staff and the restoration of order.

Edison produced *Lunatics* during the centennial celebration of Edgar Allan Poe's birth. The same year saw the release of D.W. Griffith's *Edgar Allen Poe* (one of the first biopics ever made, though it was grounded more in fantasy than reality). *Tarr and Fether* was adapted again three years later, under its original title, by Maurice Tourneur. That version is the more frankly horrific of the two.

Interestingly, the system of Dr. Tarr and Professor Fether refers to the process of tarring and feathering, in which a person is stripped, smeared with burning-hot tar and has feathers poured over him or her. At one time it was a fairly common form of harassment in the United States, frequently aimed at political dissenters. What few people realize is that, more often than not, it resulted in its victim's death. CW

The Man Who Laughs
aka **L'Homme qui rit**
Pathé; b/w; length unknown; France
P: Albert Capellani
Cast unknown

Victor Hugo's 1869 novel *L'Homme qui rit* is one of his most obscure. Existing in the twin shadows of *Notre-Dame de Paris* (1831) and *Les Miserables* (1862), *L'Homme* has the distinction of being a Hugo work that has not been in continuous print in the United States since its original publication. This may be due to its unwieldy length, or to the fact that only one of its four film adaptations (a silent picture, at that) hails from the United States (*The Man Who Laughs*, 1928). The average horror buff, then, might be forgiven for not realizing that the novel is less horror oriented than any of its film versions (all of which focus on the grotesquerie of Gwynplaine's facial features).

The novel's plot, nonetheless, is quite involving. After arranging the murder of an enemy, an evil king has the man's son given to the *Comprachicos*, a roving band of criminals who mutilate children to force them into begging or working in carnivals. This they do to the child, whom they name Gwynplaine, but years later they tire of him and cast him out. While traipsing through the snow in search of food and shelter, he comes across a dead man hanging from a gibbet and below him a frozen woman. In the folds of her clothes is a baby, still alive. Gwynplaine takes the child, a girl whose eyes are clouded by blindness, and the two come upon a small caravan headed by Ursus and his pet wolf Homo. Ursus takes in Gwynplaine and the girl, now named Dea. Over time, Gwynplaine becomes the chief breadwinner for the group, traveling to villages throughout Europe and revealing his features in exchange for money. After a series of adventures, Queen Anne summons and tells him of his privileged heritage, which Gwynplaine rejects in favor of his adopted family. They then board a ship to the continent, but Dea dies, and when Ursus awakes, Gwynplaine is nowhere to be found, probably having jumped overboard in despair.

Given that this, the first film adaptation of Hugo's story, is lost and very little information about it has survived, it's impossible to know just how faithful it was to its source material. Films of this period tended to exclude or condense so much information into their short running times that often only a story's highlights made it to the screen. By 1909, however, films were beginning the shift away from comedic and special effects exercises toward epic drama, a move facilitated by the likes of Alice Guy and D.W. Griffith. *The Man Who Laughs* was likely one of the films that marked a transition between the two extremes.

The next adaptation of Hugo's epic tale was a 1921 German-Austrian co-production. CW

Mephisto and the Maiden
Selig; b/w; 15 min; U.S.
D: Frank (Francis) Boggs *P:* William Selig
Cast: James L. McGee, Tom Santschi, Harry Todd, Jean Ward

After producing the first adaptation of *Dr. Jekyll and Mr. Hyde* (1908), Selig's next horror effort was this tale, in which one Friar

Hugo sells his soul to Mephistopheles for two hours with a beautiful young woman. It seems to have been a variation of Goethe's tragic play *Faust* (1808), with dashes of Matthew Lewis' novel *The Monk* (1796) thrown in. Given the film's year of production and subject matter, it's not a stretch to assume that there was a bevy of special effects on display—jump cuts, multiple exposures, and the like.

Actor Tom Santschi starred in over 300 films before his death in 1931, while Harry Todd starred in about 400, including *Unknown Valley* (1933), before his death in 1935. Actress Jean Ward, on the other hand, starred in only a few films, of which this appears to have been the first.

Though director Francis Boggs (1870-1911) made numerous films in his short career, this was one of only a few horror outings. (Another was *An Evil Power*, 1911.) His life was cut short at age 41 when a disgruntled Selig employee, janitor and gardener Frank Minimatsu, murdered him in an attack that also wounded the company's founder, William Selig (who was shot in the arm as he attempted to wrestle the gun from Minimatsu). A mounted patrolman who was passing the studio at the time of the incident heard the gunshots, ran inside and, with the aid of several actors, subdued Minimatsu before he could shoot anyone else. Because Minimatsu was from Japan, the attack fed the xenophobia of the time. For example, the *Oakland Tribune* stated on October 27, 1911: "MADDENED JAPANESE SLAYS … Niponese Gardener Runs Amuck in Los Angeles Kinetescope Studio." CW

Miss Faust
Pathé; color; 7 min; France
Credits unknown

In an effort to wring something new out of an oft-told story, Pathé Frères took Goethe's *Faust* over the gender barrier, making the title character female in a hand-painted color adaptation of the tale. *Miss Faust* seems an obvious attempt to ride the popularity of George Méliès' *Faust* pictures (at least one of which was hand painted). Apart from the twist, the story was business-as-usual. An aging woman yearns to be young again; Mephistopheles appears and grants her wish in exchange for her soul.

One can reasonably presume that it all ends in tragedy, but very little additional information is available about the film, which is presumed lost. How successful it was, artistically or commercially, is likewise unknown, but the next two years witnessed a slew of *Faust* adaptations, roughly half of which were produced in France.

Pathé's next film based on the tale, *Faust* (1910), restored the eponymous character to his original gender, clocked in at approximately 35 minutes and was also hand-painted. CW

A Modern Dr. Jekyll
Selig; b/w; 7 min; U.S.
D: Kenyon *P:* William Selig
Cast: Barrows (?)

Selig's second attempt at filming Robert Louis Stevenson's classic Victorian novella *The Strange Case of Dr. Jekyll and Mr. Hyde* (1886) is, like its predecessor *Dr. Jekyll and Mr. Hyde* (1908), a lost film. Often cited by film historians as a reissue of the previous film, it was actually an original work in which Dr. Jekyll (credited to "Barrows," quite possibly silent-era actor Henry A. Barrows) uses his formula to evade an inquisitive police officer. The twist is that the formula is more mystical than scientific, apparently allowing Jekyll to transform into anyone he wants, clothes and all. As such, he becomes both a woman and a little girl at various points during the short running time. In this way, the film prefigures Hammer's gender-bending period slasher *Dr. Jekyll and Sister Hyde* (1971) by some 60 years, though with a humorous bent missing in the later production. Reviews at the time found the film "ingenious" and "pure fun."

The next film adaptation of Stevenson's short novel, entitled *The Duality of Man*, was made in Great Britain the very next year. All available evidence indicates that Stevenson's tale was the most filmed horror story of the silent era, with Sir Arthur Conan Doyle's *The Hound of the Baskervilles* far behind. CW

The Moonstone
Selig; b/w; 10 (17) min; U.S.
P: William Selig
Cast unknown

This is the first known film adaptation of Wilkie Collins' 1869 Gothic novel *The Moonstone*, a seamless combination of horror and mystery that met with rousing commercial success. (Uniquely among pop literature of its time—and in a turn that presaged Bram Stoker's 1897 *Dracula*—the tale is told from several angles by several different characters.)

During a siege in India, a British colonel steals a diamond known as "the moonstone" from the forehead of a statue of the Hindu god of the moon. He brings the gem home to Great Britain, dies and leaves it to his niece Rachel, much to the chagrin of a local group of Hindus, who see the diamond as the arbiter of the moon-god's will. When the jewel disappears from Rachel's room mere hours after she wears it to her birthday party, everyone is suspect—from the sinister Hindus to a maidservant who commits suicide in the marshes. Finally, Rachel's boyfriend Franklin Blake sets out to solve the mystery and (by submitting to hypnosis) discovers that on the night of the birthday party he had been surreptitiously drugged. This, combined with his anxiety at Rachel's wearing of the moonstone, caused him to give the diamond to Rachel's cousin Godfrey Ablewhite for safekeeping while sleepwalking. But it turns out that Rachel once refused Godfrey's offer of marriage and, motivated by sour grapes and greed, he decides to keep the diamond to pay off his debts. He's murdered before he can do so, however; Rachel and Franklin marry, and the moonstone makes its way back to the forehead from which it was purloined.

This film has been credited with effectively condensing the elaborate plot of Collins' book into a fast-moving single reel. (There may have been more than one version in circulation; some sources describe the film as 17 minutes long, while others claim 10 minutes.) It does appear that the filmic heroine, instead of the novel's hero, is the one placed in the revelatory trance.

The film was released in June 1909. The next adaptation hailed from British producer Charles Urban in 1911. CW

The Mummy of the King Ramsees
aka **La Momie du roi**; **The Mummy of the King of Ramses**; **The Mummy of the King Rameses**; **The Mummy and the King Rameses**; **The Mummy and the King of Ramsee**
Lux; b/w; 11 min; France
D: Gerard Bourgeois
Cast unknown

Egyptian mythology has inspired countless horror films since the invention of cinema in the late 19th century, beginning with Georges Méliès' *Cleopatra* (1899). The period from 1908 to 1912 saw a surfeit of such films, with France's *The Mummy of the King Ramsees* generally considered the first to contain a mummy of the classic horror sort (a dead person mummified through ancient means is brought back to life). Its title reflects the public's longstanding interest in Ancient Egypt's King Ramses II (also known in classical Greek history as Ozymandias). Ramses was son to Seti and married to Nefertiti; he appears to have lived to the remarkable age of 90 and is believed to have ruled Egypt for over 66 years. His dedication to monument building and historical documentation has provided modern archaeologists with an astounding source of information on Egypt's ancient past.

Swiss-born Gerard Bourgeois directed numerous films in France between 1908 and 1925, including such horror efforts as *The Vengeance of Poe* (1912) and *Faust* (1922). He died in Paris in 1944, just four months after the Nazi withdrawal. Here, he has a professor resurrect the mummy of the King Ramsees (an obvious take on the name Rameses).

The next entry in the mummy subgenre to come out of France was *Romance of the Mummy* (1910). Neither a horror film nor a comedy, it was a straightforward romance in which an Egyptologist investigating the tomb of an ancient queen falls asleep and dreams that he is in a relationship with her while she rules Egypt. When he awakens, he meets a beautiful girl who bears a striking resemblance to the queen. The film was based on the story *Le Roman de la Momie*, written by Theophile Gautier and first published in 1857. CW

The Mystery of Edwin Drood
Gaumont; b/w; length unknown; Great Britain
D: Arthur Gilbert
Cast: Cooper Willis, Nancy Bevington, James Annand

Very little is known about this, the very first cinematic adaptation of Charles Dickens' final novel, *The Mystery of Edwin Drood*. The tale (or at least a chunk of it) was published in magazine format between April and September 1870. Each issue was illustrated by Samuel Luke Fildes and published under Great Britain's famed Chapman and Hall imprint. It was intended to have 12 installments, but only six were completed and published; Dickens died in June 1870 without having completed the story, which deals with the young Edwin Drood, who has been betrothed to Rosa Bud since birth. His choirmaster uncle, John Jasper, who is likewise young, is obsessed with Miss Bud, as is an orphan named Neville Landless. Jasper, an opium user, plays the jealous Neville against Edwin. When Edwin vanishes, Neville becomes the prime suspect in the disappearance.

No fewer than three witnesses, including the serial's illustrator and Dickens' own son, claimed that the author told them directly that the killer was John Jasper, whom, it was to have been revealed, strangled Edwin Drood with a necktie. There's also much evidence within the book as to what the solution to the mystery would have been. How closely the 1909 film adaptation from Gaumont followed the source material isn't known. The cast list does lack mention of John Jasper, though Edwin (Willis), Rosa (Bevington) and Neville (Annand) are listed.

While not nearly as popular as other works by Dickens, *The Mystery of Edwin Drood* was filmed at least four times (1909, 1914, 1935 and 1993). It has also provided the basis for numerous stage adaptations, musicals and television programs. CW

The Mystery of the Lama Convent
aka **Doktor Nikola III**; **Dr. Nicola in Tibet**; **Lamaklostrets Hemmelighed**
Nordisk; b/w; 20 min; Denmark
D: Viggo Larsen *C:* Axel Graatkjaer Sorensen
Cast: August Blom, Axel Boesen, Franz Skondrup, Aage Brandt

This long-lost Danish dark fantasy dealt with a sect of monks who restore life to the dead.

Viggo Larsen was prolific during the silent era, directing nearly 70 features between 1906 and 1921. He was even busier as an actor, appearing in close to a hundred films between 1906 and 1942. He directed a number of the films in which he appeared, though it's unclear whether he did that particular double-duty on this one. It is known that he portrayed Sir Arthur Conan Doyle's immortal sleuth Sherlock Holmes in several films he directed, including *The Grey Dame* (1909).

August Blom, who starred as Dr. Nikola, crossed paths with Larsen on numerous occasions. To judge from available filmographies, Blom acted only sporadically, spending far more time behind the camera than in front of it. Among his many directorial credits is an adaptation of *Dr. Jekyll and Mr. Hyde* (1910) in which Larsen had a supporting role.

Released in November 1909, *The Mystery of the Lama Convent* was the third and final silent film to feature writer Guy Boothby's Dr. Nikola. The first two were *Dr. Nikola I: The Phantom Tax* and *Doctor Nikola II*. The series was abandoned after its initial release due to poor box-office. By then, however, Larson had turned to the life of Napoleon for fresh inspiration (*Et Budskab til Napoleon à Elba*, 1909). TH/CW

The New Jonah
Pathé; b/w; 7 min; France
Credits unknown

The Old Testament's Book of Jonah tells the story of the prophet Jonah, who is commanded by Jehovah to go to the city of Nineveh and preach that its end is at hand. Fearing the inhabitants of the city, Jonah instead flees to Tarshish via ship, but a massive storm arises. The ship's crew, getting wind that Jonah has angered God Almighty and is to blame for the maelstrom, tosses him overboard, where a large fish promptly devours him. The hapless prophet spends three days and nights in the fish's gut, begging for forgiveness and the chance to execute his assignment. Jehovah relents; Jonah is vomited onto dry land and travels to Nineveh to warn its inhabitants of their impending demise.

This short Pathé production apparently retells the tale, only this time it's no ordinary large fish that Jonah encounters. Rather, it's a scaly sea monster with webbed feet. Though only the briefest outline of the film's plot exists and all credit information appears lost, *The New Jonah* probably wasn't a cautionary tale but rather a trick film designed to thrill (and amuse) its audience. CW

The Nymph's Bath
aka **La Nymph de Bain**
Gaumont; b/w; 6 min; France
Credits unknown

This very obscure fantasy film warrants inclusion for its reported depiction of ghostly manifestations. Virtually no other information survives for the presumably lost title. It was an early offering from Gaumont, a successful production company still active as of the early 21st century.

The film's title is a possible reference to 17th-century French sculptor François Girardon's The Nymphs' Bath, a sculpture created to catch the overflow water from the Pyramid Fountain at the Palace of Versailles. TH

The Old Shoemaker
aka **Le vieux cordonnier**
Gaumont; b/w; 6 min; France
Credits unknown

After committing a murder, a man is driven insane by his guilty conscience.

This appears to have been a variation on Edgar Allan Poe's *The Tell Tale Heart*, later brought to the screen by D.W. Griffith as *The Avenging Conscience, or: Thou Shalt Not Kill* (1914), with the difference being that the ghosts in *The Old Shoemaker* are real. Little information survives about the title beyond its plot outline, which was definitely macabre. The theme of a murderer haunted by visions of his victim was popular in the cinema of the time, given the ease with which it played into audience fascination with trick photography and rudimentary special effects.

The film is not to be confused with a dramatic American-made 1915 film of the same name. TH

The Oriental Mystic
Vitagraph; b/w; 5 min; U.S.
Credits unknown

This short feature was heavily influenced by French releases of the period. Though often listed as a drama, *The Oriental Mystic* appears to have been an amusing—if typically dark—production about a woman who becomes frightened by a Turkish magician as he appears, disappears and reappears in a set of mirrors. What makes the film interesting is that it was made six years after Edwin S. Porter established the edit as a tool for dramatic effect rather than mere whimsy. Instead of building on what Porter had established (as filmmakers such as D.W. Griffith began to do this very same year), *Mystic* recycles already passé trick photography methods to relate its tale to audiences.

The film was released on June 4, 1909. CW

The Phantom Sirens
Urban/Eclipse; b/w; 8 min; Great Britain/France
P: Charles Urban
Cast unknown

A silly picture, *The Phantom Sirens* presents the eponymous sirens as progeny of the Devil. A group of fishermen far out to sea encounters a bevy of beautiful, scantily clad nymphs hanging out on the rocks of a deserted island. The water babes call repeatedly to them, but each time the fishermen draw near, the temptresses vanish. Affronted by the teasing, the men return home to wives they now have no interest in. Alarmed, the frustrated wives seek help from the Virgin Mary. Under her divine guidance, the women go to the island, confront the vixens with a crucifix and defeat them. When the fishermen return to the island for another shot at the sirens, they find their wives waiting for them.

While often cited as a co-production between Great Britain's Urban Trading Company, France's Eclipse and America's Kleine, the film was in fact a co-production between Urban Trading and Eclipse, with film producer George Kleine merely picking the film up for U.S. distribution. Nor are the fisherman actually lured to their deaths, as many horror film resources claim. CW

The Pit and the Pendulum
aka **Le Puits et le pendule**
Continental/Warwick; b/w; 11 min; France/Great Britain
D: Henri Desfontaines
Cast unknown

Parisian Henri Desfontaines worked almost exclusively in the silent era. Though primarily a director, he also starred in and wrote several pictures. His acting/directing debut came in 1908 with a French version of *Hamlet*, though he may be most famous for co-directing *Jesus of Nazareth* with André Calmettes in 1911. Three films based on works by Edgar Allan Poe are among the scores of films he directed. *The Pit and the Pendulum* is the first of them; the other two are *The Golden Beetle* and *Hop-Frog*, both 1910.

This *Pit* is, it seems, the first film adaptation of Poe's 1842 short story. During the Inquisition, a man is placed in a chamber of horrors and tortured by a politico-religious tribunal. He faces the pit and the pendulum before finally being saved. Alice Guy in 1913 and Roger Corman in 1961 filmed the story to greater effect, both times under the same title. CW

The Princess and the Fisherman
aka **Le Princesse et le Pecheur**
Gaumont; color; 15 min; France
D/S: Louis Feuillade
Cast unknown

A beggar woman curses a princess who is mean to her. Later, at a local seashore, the Princess tests her suitors by throwing an ornate cup into the sea, with the promise that whoever retrieves the object will gain her hand in marriage. The beggar woman appears in the guise of a beautiful maiden, lures a naïve fisherman into the sea and offers him the princess' cup with the stipulation that he return to the beggar woman whenever she blows a trumpet. The fisherman agrees and delivers the cup to the princess. The princess and fisherman are married, but on the wedding night the trumpet sounds. The princess is abandoned, and her husband drowns in his attempt to join his "fair maiden."

Louis Feuillade, the king of silent French serials, directed the tragic fairytale. Much of Feuillade's work is considered lost today, but portions of this picture have survived. One of the surviving prints, housed in the Joye Collection, is hand-stenciled in color. TH

Satan's Smithy
aka **La Forge du Diable**; **The Devil's Forge**
Pathé; b/w; 8 min; France
D/S/C/FX: Segundo de Chomon
Cast unknown

This short feature dealt with a naïve blacksmith who is lured into hell by Satan. The Prince of Darkness is defeated when a good fairy that has been watching over the blacksmith intervenes.

Pathé Frères dabbled a good deal in horror and fantasy subjects during the early silent era. This film reportedly featured hand-colored sequences, presumably those set in hell. Writer/Director Segundo de Chomon was no stranger to the horror genre, having already directed such works as *The Witch's Cave* and *The Haunted House* (both 1906). Like those earlier efforts, *Satan's Smithy* is believed to be a lost film.

Some sources list *Smithy* as a 1908 production, but the more reliable ones beg to differ. TH

The Sealed Room
aka **The Sealed Door**
American Mutoscope and Biograph; b/w; 11 min; U.S.
D/P: D.W. Griffith *S:* Frank E. Woods *C:* G.W. Bitzer
Cast: Arthur V. Johnson, Marion Leonard, Henry B. Walthall, William J. Butler, Mary Pickford, Owen Moore

A minor historical horror film from soon-to-be world-famous director D.W. Griffith, *The Sealed Room* concerns a king (Johnson) so in love with his wife (Leonard) that he builds a dovecote (a small brick room usually constructed to hold doves or other birds) as a special place for the two of them to rendezvous. After noticing the attention she gives an Italian troubadour (Walthall), however, the king suspects that all is not right between him and his "favored one." Curious to catch her in an act of betrayal, he pretends to be called away. Immediately upon his departure, his wife falls into the arms of her handsome lover, whom she pulls into the dovecote. As they wax romantic, the husband returns, calls a mason and has the unsuspecting couple walled up alive within the dovecote. When the horror of their situation dawns on them, they break into hysterics, suffocating while the king taunts them from outside their makeshift tomb.

At the time of the film's release, producer Biograph attempted to sell it on the claim that it was based on a true story in which an old European castle had been torn down, exposing a formerly sealed room containing the entwined skeletons of two lovers. The idea for this extravagant though untrue ad campaign may have come from the fact that two skeletons *had* been found buried beneath the stairwell in the Tower of London in 1674. They weren't the remains of two lovers, however, but rather those of a pair of children, suspected of being fraternal princes who had disappeared without a trace in 1483. (Such a subject certainly made for a good horror film 30 years later when Universal filmed the events surrounding the boys' disappearance as *The Tower of London*, 1939, starring Basil Rathbone, Boris Karloff and Vincent Price.)

In D.W. Griffith's *The Sealed Room*, the king's wife is alone with her Italian troubadour in the private dovecote.

Frequently cited as being based on (or at least suggested by) Edgar Allan Poe's short story *The Cask of Amontillado*, which has a similar theme of revenge by interment, *The Sealed Room* is in fact based on an Honoré de Balzac collection, *La Grande Bretêche*. The work consists of several interlocking stories surrounded by a framing device in which a doctor investigates why an elderly woman refuses to allow her castle home to be altered until 50 years after her death. The collection's final story, which the doctor has to procure by seducing and making love to a young girl who knows the truth, provides the solution to the mystery. Years earlier, the mistress of the house had carried on an affair with a young lover while, she thought, her husband was away. When her husband caught her in the act, he had a mason wall up the closet in which the young man was hiding. Nor should the film be confused with a short story of the same title by Sherlock Holmes creator Arthur Conan Doyle. While Balzac's story influenced Doyle's most likely, the particulars were much different. In it, a lawyer who helps a wounded man home becomes fascinated by a sealed door, which the wounded man is forbidden to open until his 21st birthday. On that day, he invites the lawyer to his house as a witness to the opening of the door. Within the room, they find the young man's long-dead father, who had disappeared years earlier amid massive debt and the anger of solicitors.

Director Griffith's fourth attempt at horror after *The Devil* (1908), *Edgar Allen Poe* and *The Suicide Club* (both 1909) plays with some of the same themes as his feature-length horror film, *The Avenging Conscience, or: 'Thou Shalt Not Kill'* (1914). After watching *The Sealed Room*, it's easy to see what set Griffith apart from other filmmakers of his time. Less interested in trick photography and silly antics, Griffith focuses not so much on spectacle as on human melodrama. To this end, he shoots on a set comprised of two rooms that realistically intimate the interiors of a Gothic castle, and his actors are bedecked in period clothing. The film obviously had a script, and the acting—particularly that of Johnson, Leonard and Walthall—realistically conveys the emotions inherent in the situation. Distraught by his wife's adultery, the

King becomes angry and verbose, his mannerisms exaggerated. Not knowing what's coming, the two lovers are idyllic, so lost in their passion that they're unaware of the brickwork going on just a few feet from them. Although the camera remains motionless (as was usually the case in films of this period), Griffith's eye is nonetheless a powerful one, finding meaning in the movement of actors and the placement of props.

America's future sweetheart, Mary Pickford, had a small part as one of the Queen's ladies-in-waiting. After being discovered by Griffith, Pickford went on to not only become the biggest star in the world, but also to marry her *Sealed Room* costar Owen Moore (who played a nobleman of the court). However, after several years of physical violence due to Moore's alcoholism, Pickford filed for divorce and married superstar Douglas Fairbanks, with whom she had carried on an affair during her estrangement from her husband. Fairbanks and Pickford co-founded United Artists, which for years was a major player in the Hollywood studio system. Pickford's next and last horror film was *Sparrows* in 1926.

Perhaps because of the negative racial politics of *Birth of a Nation* (1915), some critics have charged *The Sealed Room* with being a racist rant as well, but nothing in the film bears this out. It should also be noted that the film displays little of the Christian iconography that saturated so many of Griffith's later, bigger films. His next flirtation with horror came in 1910's *Rose O'Salem Town*. *The Golden Supper* (1910) is often listed as horror, but though it dealt with a young girl buried alive while in a catatonic trance, it was melodrama through and through. CW

Shooting in the Haunted Woods
aka **La chasse au Bois hanté**; **Hunting in the Haunted Woods**
Gaumont; b/w; 7 min; France
D/S: Louis Feuillade
Cast: Alice Tissot, Maurice Vinot

Remembered best for his serials *Fantomas* (1913) and *Les Vampires* (1915), writer/director Louis Feuillade was remarkably prolific—responsible, in fact, for close to 700 films. He began directing in 1906, with his association with the Gaumont organization in France proving repeatedly and mutually beneficial. Most of his films, this one included, were short subjects. *Shooting in the Haunted Woods* came a mere three years after the beginning of his directorial career. In the film, a hunter enters a copse hoping to shoot some game but is haunted at every turn by the specters of the dead. Released in France as *La chasse au Bois hanté* in 1909 and in the United States in early 1910 under the title *Shooting in the Haunted Woods*, it took up a mere half reel, with the other half occupied by a Gaumont comedy titled *Towser's New Job*.

Shooting in the Haunted Woods cast members Alice Tissot and Maurice Vinot both worked with Feuillade on numerous occasions. Tissot's career lasted into the 1960s, while Vinot's was cut short by his death in 1918. As for Feuillade, while his films often flirted with the macabre, his light touch and impish sense of humor prevents all but a few of his works from being firmly classified as horror. TH/CW

The Suicide Club
American Mutoscope & Bioscope; b/w; 4 min; U.S.
D: D.W. Griffith *S:* Frank E. Woods *C:* G.W. Bitzer, Arthur Marvin
Cast: Herbert Yost, Charles Avery, Charles Craig, John R. Cumpson, Edward Dillon, Arthur V. Johnson, Owen Moore, Mack Sennett

D.W. Griffith's third stab at the horror genre—after *The Devil* (1908) and his take on the life of *Edgar Allen Poe* (1909)—was based on a then-popular (but today mostly forgotten) short story by Scottish writer Robert Louis Stevenson, author of such immortal fare as *The Strange Case of Dr. Jekyll and Mr. Hyde* and *Kidnapped* (both 1886). Relative obscurity aside, there has been a fairly steady stream of film, radio, stage and television adaptations of *The Suicide Club* running through the greater part of the 1900s and into the 2000s. Griffith's take on the material was the very first film adaptation; the rights to the story had been acquired the year before by American Mutoscope & Bioscope who, intending at the time to make a feature-length film, wound up instead offering the material to fledgling director Griffith as one part of a split reel (fleshed out with another of Griffith's 1909 dramas, *The Eavesdropper*). The dual work was released in May, just three months after the aforementioned *Edgar Allen Poe*.

First published in 1878, *The Suicide Club* is a romantic mystery with touches of horror. It consists of three sections: "The Story of the Young Man with the Cream Tarts," "Story of the Physician and the Saratoga Trunk" and "The Adventure of the Hansom Cab." The first section (on which virtually every film adaptation of *The Suicide Club* is based) tells how two characters, Prince Florizel and Colonel Geraldine, learn of, then infiltrate, The Suicide Club, a secret association where people play cards—with losers obliged to kill themselves (or be killed by another if they refuse). At segment's end, Florizel and Geraldine bring the club down.

With a running time of not quite four minutes, Griffith's now-lost film couldn't possibly have done justice to even the first portion of Stevenson's tale. But contemporary reviews indicate that Griffith's film did indeed concern a suicide club wherein those who draw the wrong card die. A young man (Yost) seeking death attends the card games in hopes of drawing the winning (or, rather, losing) card. Just before his last play, however, he learns that he has inherited a fortune. Naturally, he ends up drawing the fatal card.

Mary Pickford's first husband Owen Moore has a small part in *The Suicide Club* as one of the club's members, as do producer/director Mack Sennett and silent film star Charles Avery. Victorin Jasset, working for the French company Éclair, made another version of the story the same year.

The same year Griffith made this short horror feature, he also directed *The Sealed Room*. Griffith's next stab at the horror genre, *Rose O'Salem Town*, was released the following year and would focus on an innocent woman's trial for witchcraft. His first feature-length horror film, *The Avenging Conscience, or: 'Thou Shalt Not Kill'*, returned him to familiar territory, the works of Edgar Allan Poe. CW

The Suicide Club
aka **Nick Carter—Le club des suicides**; **Le Club des suicides**
Éclair; b/w; length unknown; France
D/S: Victorin-Hippolyte Jasset
Cast: Pierre Brassol

Victorin Jasset's film, suggested by—rather than an adaptation of—Robert Louis Stevenson's lengthy short story of the same name, is the second cinematic version of the tale. None other than D.W. Griffith, the preeminent visionary of the silent era, directed the first version earlier the same year.

Here, Stevenson's idea is integrated into a larger series; namely, French production company Éclair's series of mystery thrillers starring detective Nick Carter (most often played by Pierre Brassol). Carter goes up against a suicide club, an organization in which members gather to play sinister games of cards, with the person drawing a specified unlucky card (often a queen or an ace of spades) offering to kill himself. If he refuses, another player who has drawn another specified card must kill him.

Only some of the films in the series were released in the United States. Chaumianne revisited the series in the 1960s, cast as a low-rent James Bond knock-off for a couple of features starring Eddie Constantine. CW

The Sword and the King
Vitagraph; b/w; 11 min; U.S.
Credits unknown

This short film from Vitagraph concerns a king's rudeness to an old woman who, wouldn't you know it, turns out to be a witch. She curses him, and he finds himself bedeviled by a ghost in typical fashion.

If that sounds like a description of Georges Méliès' *The Enchanted Well* (1903), it's because *The Sword and the King* bears more than a little resemblance to the earlier film. Both releases were intended to wow audiences with their trick photography, though Vitagraph's production appears to have included at least some melodramatic elements. *Sword* was copyrighted on July 24, 1909, six years after Méliès' film, though in both movies the moral is the same: You shouldn't mistreat your elders. CW

A Timely Apparition
Urban/Éclipse; b/w; 7 min; Great Britain/France
P: Charles Urban
Cast unknown

This forgotten slice of obscurity concerns a sexually attractive young woman suspected of witchcraft. Her Bible-toting "victims" tie her to a tree, planning to set her ablaze and dispatch her soul to the Devil. But when her dead father's spirit shows up to offer his daughter emotional support, her tormentors die of fright.

Apart from the producer, the names of the film's cast and crew are long forgotten. The film was a co-production between Great Britain's Urban Productions, which was headed by producer Charles Urban, and France's Éclipse. It was one of several collaborations between the two; others include *The Haunted Bedroom* (1907), *The Phantom Sirens* (1909), *Beneath the Tower Ruins* (1911) and *The Curse of the Scarabee Ruby* and *Peter's Evil Spirit* (both 1914). CW

'Tis Now the Very Witching Time of Night
Edison; b/w; 8 min; U.S.
Credits unknown

A young man boasts to friends that he can spend the night in a haunted house. The friends bet him that he can't, and he takes their bet. Unknown to him, however, a magician is hired to rig the house with all manner of ghostly horrors. During the overnighter, both friends and magician sneak into the old dark house and use fake bats, skeletons and witches to scare the braggart, who quickly figures out what's going on and turns the tables.

The film's title is taken from a line in William Shakespeare's classic play *Hamlet*, in which Hamlet says, "Tis now the very witching time of night/When churchyards yawn, and hell breathes out/Contagion to this world: Now I could drink hot blood/And do such bitter business as the day/Would quake to look on …" But the film has nothing to do with Shakespeare, serving up instead the usual mixture of comedic thrills and chills for undiscerning audiences of the time. CW

The Village Scare
Gaumont; b/w; 4 min; France
Credits unknown

A small French village is the scene of a terrible disturbance. A small creature that appears to be half wolf and half bird stalks the streets and alleys, terrorizing the locals. In the end, however, the beast turns out to be a dog in a feather costume.

The film, an example of the comedy-cum-horror that was so popular at the time, was released on a split reel with the comedy short *The Mix-Up at Court*. The two films hit theaters (such as they were at the time) on November 27, 1909. CW

Viy
aka **Buu, The Vij**; **The Wij**; **Vii**
Pathé; b/w; length unknown; Russia
D: Vasilii Goncharov
Credits unknown

Nikolai Gogol (1809-1852) first published his short story *The Vij* in an 1835 collection called *Mirgorod*, after the name of an ancient Ukrainian city. This film, the tale's first cinematic adaptation, is considered lost. Its director Vasilii Goncharov made over a dozen features between 1909 and 1914; he died in 1915, before the next version of *The Vij* (1916) was released.

Gogol's story concerns a philosopher, Khoma Brut, who is called to read psalms over a young woman's corpse for three days. Seeing the body, he realizes it's the remains of a witch he once encountered. He dutifully performs his task nonetheless, and as the nights unfold, he's assailed by progressively more grotesque visions. On the third and final night, the witch rises from the dead and brings the dreadful Vij with her. The Vij is a monstrous, all-seeing creature with eyelids that droop to the floor (and when peeled back reveal a horrifying metallic visage). The Vij attacks Brut, who dies of fright.

This nightmarish tale has had lasting cinematic appeal, beginning with this obscure production. While it's unlikely this film replicated the horrors of Gogol's tale, it pays to remember that the most celebrated cinematic adaptation—Mario Bava's chilling directorial debut, *Black Sunday* (1960)—was a masterpiece despite bearing little resemblance to its source material. TH

The Wild Ass's Skin
aka **La Peau de chagrin**
Pathé; b/w; 16 min; France
D: Albert Capellani *S:* Michel Carré
Cast: Henri Desfontaines, Paul Capellani, Gilberte Sergy, René Leprince, Stacia Napierkowska, Louise Fusier

This was the first cinematic adaptation of Honoré de Balzac's 1831 novel *La Peau de chagrin* (English title: *The Wild Ass's Skin*). In the first of the film's three sections, "Le Talisman," a suicidal young man named Raphael de Valentin enters a curiosity shop and buys a shagreen (a sheet of leather made from the hide of a wild ass). An Arabic inscription on the skin suggests that it will fulfill its owner's every wish, while shrinking a bit (and taking a bit of the user's soul) each time it does so. In the second part, "Le Femme sans Coeur" ("The Heartless Woman"), Raphael tells a friend, Pauline, about the time he sought the hand of one Lady Foedora who, thinking herself far better than he, refused him. The final segment, "L'Agonie," depicts Valentin several years later when he has used the shagreen to become rich and secure. His health is failing, however, and the magic skin has gotten quite small. Worried that he'll die if he makes more wishes, he puts his affairs in order to avoid ever needing the shagreen again. Yet he dies anyway, while at last consummating his passion for his confidante Pauline.

It's fitting that the first filmed version of Balzac's story should come from his native France, albeit 59 years after his death. Director Albert Capellani (*The Hunchback of Notre Dame*, 1911) often cast his younger brother Paul, as well as Stacia Napierkowska, in his films, as is the case here. Screenwriter Michel Carré (*Faust*, 1922) was better known as a director; he retired from directing and acting in 1922 and died in Paris in 1945.

The next adaptation of Balzac's story came in 1914 and was titled *The Magic Skin*. CW

The Witch
The Lion; b/w; 10 min; Belgium
Credits Unknown

Little is known about this short piece, other than it concerned an evil witch who imprisons a virtuous girl's soul in a dummy. The film's parentage is a tad unclear. Some sources list it as a French production, although production company Le Lion was based in Belgium. If anything produced by Le Lion turns out to have survived into the 21st century, it will be something of a miracle. The company was a minor player and very short-lived, and filmographies of the day (though almost certainly incomplete) indicate that its sparse output consisted mainly of travelogues and documentaries. It seems safe to assume, therefore, that *The Witch* was an atypical (for them) foray into the macabre. In addition to a wicked witch, the film reportedly sprinkled in some phantoms and imps, no doubt in an attempt to compete with the *fantastique noir* so popular in French cinema at the time. TH

The Witch's Cavern
aka **The Witches' Cavern**
Selig; b/w; 12 min; U.S.
Credits Unknown

A half-man, half-monster is believed to be a son of a … witch.

Selig Polyscope produced this short subject, but beyond plot description, virtually nothing is known about it. A number of major stars, including Tom Mix and Roscoe "Fatty" Arbuckle, got their start with William Selig, but the company ceased production in 1918. Even so, it was remarkably prolific, churning out 2,000 pictures, many of which are believed lost. Much of its output consisted of melodrama and comedic short subjects, but the company also dabbled in the horror genre with *The Witch's Cavern*, *An Evil Power* (1911) and a couple of minor entries. TH

The Wonderful Pearl
aka **La perla meravigliosa**; **The Marvellous Pearl**
Cines; b/w; 12 min; Italy
Credits unknown

Released in Great Britain as *The Marvellous Pearl* on September 30, 1909, this Italian production was re-titled *The Wonderful Pearl* in the United States when it was released on Christmas Day of that same year. The titular pearl's marvelous qualities are debatable, given that it casts a spell over the man who finds it, prompting him to walk into the sea and drown.

The film appears to have been an amalgam of literary influences, drawing from both an 1811 novella by Friedrich de la Motte Fouqué (about a water nymph who curses the man who abandons her) and Wilkie Collins' 1868 novel *The Moonstone*, about a cursed gem stolen from a Hindu statue in India. How successful it was at melding these elements is unknown; it is believed to be lost, and few reviews of it exist.

This film should not be confused with *The Fatal Pearl*, a 1912 knock-off produced by Italian company Aquila. CW

1910

The American Suicide Club
Lux; b/w; 10 min; France/U.S.
Credits unknown

This French/U.S. coproduction appears to have been shot in the United States with an American cast and crew. It was the third film (after D.W. Griffith's *The Suicide Club* and Éclair's Nick Carter vehicle, also titled *The Suicide Club*, both released in 1909) to draw from author Robert Louis Stevenson's once-influential mystery tale of the same title. Stevenson's story concerns good friends Prince Florizel and Colonel Geraldine and their attempt to shut down a club whose members play a dangerous game of cards, one that results in suicide or murder. To do so they must apprehend the people behind the club, a sinister group who will stop at nothing to prevent themselves from being discovered.

Lux's take on the tale moved the action from continental Europe to the United States. This may have been done to avoid legal issues, as the story was still under copyright and the film rights belonged to American Mutoscope & Bioscope. CW

Another's Ghost
aka **Le Spectre de L'autre**
Pathé; b/w; 9 min; France
Cast: Mevisto, Henri Etievant, Jeanne Grumbach, Henry Krauss

An innkeeper murders an artist, only to be haunted by his victim's ghost. This short from Pathé Frères dealt with the Poe-like notion of a guilty conscience taking sensory form. Murdered people often haunted their killers in Poe-inspired silent fare, the most famous example being D.W. Griffith's hodgepodge *The Avenging Conscience, or: Thou Salt Not Kill* (1914).

Co-star Henry Krauss went on to play Quasimodo in one of the earliest cinematic versions of Victor Hugo's *The Hunchback of Notre Dame* (1911). TH

The Beechwood Ghost
Powers; b/w; length unknown; U.S.
Credits unknown

A local ghost frightens people, until it is revealed that the spirit is a fake.

This is an early example of the "ghost debunking" subgenre, which found popular expression in the old dark house melodramas of the 1920s and '30s. The production company here was the obscure Power Picture Plays, which produced about 800 titles between 1907 and 1923, many of which—including this one—are now believed lost. The company was created by Irish-born Patrick Anthony Powers and was one of several smaller companies that later merged with Carl Laemmle's Independent Moving Pictures (IMP) before becoming Universal Pictures. TH

The Bewitched Messenger
Bat/Brockliss; b/w; 11 min; Great Britain
Credits unknown

If you guessed that *The Bewitched Messenger* was about a messenger cursed by an old hag fond of silent-era special effects trickery, then you'd be correct. The film was a co-production of studios Bat and Brockliss, with Brockliss handling the distribution chores. Neither company appears to have done much beyond this picture, and both petered out within a couple of years of *Messenger*'s release.

While there's some debate about whether the film was American or British, the fact that Brockliss released the British film *Getting Even* in the isles in 1914 suggests that it was indeed produced across the pond. CW

The Bride of the Haunted Castle
Artistic/Pathé; b/w; 10 min; U.S./France
Credits unknown

With titles like *The Bride of the Haunted Castle*, it's impossible to take seriously the notion that the horror genre began in earnest with Tod Browning's 1931 classic *Dracula*.

No, *Bride* isn't about a woman married to a haunted castle. Rather, said bride resides (or, rather, is trapped) in said structure, though she isn't there alone. She has a terrifying castle-mate, a living skeleton, courtesy of the sort of special effects trickery to which producer Pathé was no stranger.

While some sources cite the film as 15 minutes in length, it appears to have topped out at 10. Newspapers from the time show that the film garnered a release in the United States and England, as well as in France. CW

The Budda's Curse
aka **The Buddha's Curse**
Lux; b/w; length unknown; France
Credits unknown

This obscure French horror film from the early silent era exemplifies that era's penchant for presenting foreigners—non-Christian foreigners in particular—as Satanic figures bent on destroying with their lethal magic all that is good. In this case, the evil figure is a Buddhist priest who places a terrible curse on a "proper" family.

The notion might have been palatable had *The Budda's Curse* been produced in Great Britain, where the story could have passed as some sort of anti-colonial analogy. In this case, however, it comes across as simply racist, a common trait in films of the period. CW

Cagliostro
aka **Cagliostro, aventurier, chimiste et magicien**
Pathé; b/w; 20 min; France
Co-D/S: Camille de Morlhon *Co-D:* Gaston Velle
Cast: Jean Jacquinet, Helene du Montel, Jacque Normad, Stacia Napierkowska

The first film to refer to Count Alessandro di Cagliostro, the alias for infamous Italian occultist Giuseppe Balsamo, was French director George Méliès' *Cagliostro's Mirror* (1899). It was a short feature (approximately a minute) with no similarity to this, the next film about the infamous historical figure. Actually, 1910's *Cagliostro* owes less to either the real Cagliostro or Méliès than it does to George Du Maurier's late 19th-century horror novel *Trilby*. The character of Cagliostro is a thinly disguised Svengali, perhaps given the name Cagliostro because of the real man's reputed penchant for mesmerism. This time out, Cagliostro (Jacquinet) becomes obsessed with a beautiful young girl (du Montel) and uses hypnotism to control her.

Cagliostro director Camille de Morlhon was born Louis Camille de la Valette de Morlhon to an aristocratic family in 1869. In 1901, while serving as secretary general of an automobile club, he met French film pioneer Leon Gaumont. Gaumont suggested de Morlhon go into filmmaking, then turned down de Morlhon's first script. Undaunted, de Morlhon approached Pathé, and a long and fruitful partnership was born resulting in de Morlhon forming his own production company and having his films distributed by Pathé. Unfortunately, his success didn't last, and by the time of his death in 1952, he was a forgotten figure. CW

The Castle Ghost
Pathé; b/w; 9 min; France
Credits unknown

Pathé Frères produced this obscure short about a man who is terrorized by a ghost. He takes a shot at the specter, but it turns out that it is really a girl playing a joke on him.

The film is one of many early short subjects that utilized trick photography in order to create apparently supernatural apparitions. And like so many of them, it offers up a rational explanation at the end. Audiences of the period ate this type of material up, and an argument could be made that—even with all the changes in technology and tastes—the same basically holds true to this day, as the various incarnations of *Scooby Doo* attest. TH

The Cat That Was Changed into a Woman
aka **La chatte métamorphosée en femme**
Pathé; b/w; length unknown; France
D: Michel Carré
Cast: Amelie Dieterle, Albert Barre, Rene Hervil, Alice Clairville, Emile Mayo, Georgette Debry

A cat falls in love with a man and beseeches the goddess Venus to be turned into a human so that she may marry him.

This was the second screen version of the Aesop fable *Venus and the Cat*. Like Louis Feuillade's 1909 short on the same subject, it is believed to be lost. Director Michel Carré should not be confused with his famous, likewise-named librettist father. The younger Carré also dabbled in writing lyrics but was far more active in film. His career in cinema began around 1907 and lasted until 1922. One of his last credits was on Gerard Bourgeois' *Faust* (1922), for which he wrote the adaptation. TH

Chibusa no enoki
Yokata Shokai; b/w; length unknown; Japan
Crew unknown
Cast: Matsunosuke Onoe

This is the first adaptation of Sanyutei Encho's story *Kaidan chibusa no enoki*, in which a painter's assistant develops a terrible affliction after murdering his master and taking the man's wife for himself.

The film was released in Japan on August 10, 1910. *Kaidan chibusa enoki*, the next adaptation, saw release in 1917 by the Nikkatsu Kyoto Studios; *Ghost Story of the Mother Tree* in 1939 and *The Mother Tree* in 1958 followed.

Chibusa no enoki means "breast-nettle tree." CW

The Children of Edward IV
aka **Les Enfants d'Edouard**; **The Children of Edward**
Film d'Art/Pathé; b/w; 11 min; France
D: Henri Andréani *S:* Paul d'Ivoi
Cast: René Alexandre, Albert Bras, Jeanne Delvair, Jean Jacquinet, Maiapolska, Rolla Norman

This should not be confused with the 1914 French Cosmograph film of the same name, about which even less is known. What sets this film apart from numerous adaptations of Shakespeare's *Richard III* (c. 1591) is that, as the title suggests, it focuses on the two young sons of Edward IV rather than their alleged murderer, the Duke of Gloucester, Richard III.

After the death of his father, the child Prince Edward (1470-c.1483) becomes King of Great Britain. However, his uncle, the evil hunchback/clubfoot Richard III, wants the throne for himself and has his late brother's marriage annulled and the children of that marriage—Edward V, who held the throne for only two months, and Edward's younger brother Richard of Shrewsbury—declared illegitimate. Thus is Edward dethroned in favor of his evil uncle Richard, who has the two boys confined in the Tower of London and later murdered (at least as far as the film is concerned). The film ends on a moralistic note, however; when the elder Richard goes into battle, haunting visions of his murdered nephews distract him, and he is killed on the battlefield.

The film saw release in the United States in June 1910. CW

Countess Ankarstrom
aka **Gräfin Ankarström**
Deutsche Bioscop; b/w; 20 min; Germany
D: Gebhard Schätzler-Perasini *C:* Guido Seeber
Cast: Paul Bildt, Ludwig Colani

Gebhard Schätzler-Perasini directed three films in his very brief career, all of them in 1910, and all for Deutsche Bioscop. Not much is known about any of them, but sources indicate that *Countess Ankarstrom* was a dark little film about a Gypsy's prediction that the first hand a duke shakes will go on to cause his death. One is left to wonder whether the duke was cursed for something he'd done to the Gypsy. Either way, the plot resembles that of 1996's *Thinner*, among those of other works.

Lead actor Paul Bildt (1885-1957) had quite the career in Europe from 1910 (*Countess* appears to have been his second film) to 1956, the year before his death. He starred in Richard Oswald's lost horror film *Nachtgestalten* (1920) and in F.W. Murnau's *The Haunted Castle* (1921). Little is known about Ludwig Colani, who starred in about 10 films between 1910 and 1919, and in 1915 produced, directed and starred in *Brandung*.

From what can be pieced together, it seems that *Countess Ankarstrom* anticipated the fatalistic tone that would later define Fritz Lang's German work. CW/TH

The Curse of the Wandering Minstrel
aka **Des Sängers Fluch**; **The Singer's Curse**
Messter; b/w; 10 min; Germany
Credits unknown

A feudal lord suspects a minstrel of flirting with his wife. When he has the minstrel put to death, the minstrel's partner curses him, predicting that calamity will strike both master and castle. The forecast comes true when invaders destroy the castle and the lord is crushed in its collapsing gateway.

The film's source material was the ballad "Des Sängers Fluch" ("The Singer's Curse"), written by Ludwig Uhland while Napoleon's army humiliated Germany. Uhland claimed in a letter to a friend to have gotten the idea for the song from an older ballad, "The Bonny Earl of Murray," published by Johann Gottfried Herder in his collection *Volkslieder* (1778-1779). CW

Death
aka **Doden**
Regia Kunstfilms; b/w; 5 min; Denmark
D/S: Holger Holm
Cast: Emilie Sannom, Robert Schmidt

This short pantomime depicted the Grim Reaper as he wanders the streets looking for his next victim. There is some confusion surrounding the paternity of the long-lost title. Some sources list it as being a production of Australia's short-lived Biorama Company, while others credit it—correctly—to Denmark's Regia Kunstfilms. (It has also been referred to erroneously as an American film.) And despite some claims that it was released in 1911, it actually premiered in its native Denmark on January 10, 1910.

Surviving credits attribute the work to director Holger Holm, whose only film this was. Holm was a ballet dancer with the Royal Theatre, which hints that the Reaper's movements through the streets were fantastic and fluid.

Valdemar Psilander plays Dorian Gray (center) in *Dorian Grays Portraet*. Psilander later committed suicide at age 32.

It would be interesting to see how the film compares to later Scandinavian depictions of the Grim Reaper, the most famous being Victor Sjostrom's *The Phantom Carriage* (1921) and Ingmar Bergman's *The Seventh Seal* (1957). TH

The Defeat of Satan
aka **La Défaite de Satan**
Pathé; b/w; 14 min; France
D: Georges Denola
Cast: Madeleine Celiat, Georges Laumonier, Jacques Vandenne

In this short French film, Satan masquerades as a sorcerer and is bested by a mere mortal. Parisian Georges Denola, a prolific filmmaker of the early silent era, directed this film. The bulk of his work is lost and mostly forgotten, but judging from his surviving filmography, it must have found some degree of favor with cineastes of the time, though it stops cold in 1919 despite the director having lived until 1941. He seems to have produced mostly historical melodramas, making *The Defeat of Satan* something of a bastard child.

Defeat's small ensemble consisted of actors common to Pathé films of the period. Given the title, one can safely assume that Satan was presented as something of a buffoon. TH

The Demon of Dunkirque
Ambrosio/Warwick; b/w; 14 min; Italy/Great Britain
Credits unknown

This intriguing short dealt with a devilish creature imprisoned in an alchemist's laboratory. A man frees the demon in exchange for being granted a series of wishes.

Sources from the time indicate that this was a co-production between Italy's Societa Anonima Ambrosia and the British-based Warwick Company. Ambrosio produced over a thousand titles between 1906 and 1922, many of which (including this one) are considered lost today. There have been over a dozen film production companies with the fairly generic moniker Warwick, but it seems likely that Warwick Trading Company is the correct one here. Like Ambrosio, they went under during the silent era, but before that they were very productive, responsible for over 200 titles between 1898 and 1912.

The Demon of Dunkirque, then, is a very early example of the type of international financing that would dominate Italian cinema from the 1950s onward. TH

The Devil's Mother-in-Law
aka **Sogra enviado ao Diabo**
Pathé; b/w; 14 min; France
Credits unknown

A young man attempts to woo his girlfriend but is hindered by her nosy mother. He becomes frustrated and departs, leaving behind a note expressing a wish that the Devil be burdened with them both. Lo and behold, the Devil takes him up on the offer. Donning a mortal disguise and calling himself Lucifer Beelzebub (how's that for subtlety!), the Prince of Darkness courts the young girl and eventually marries her. Marital bliss proves elusive, however, as the Devil becomes increasingly annoyed by the mother-in-law's meddling ways. At first he retaliates by playing cruel jokes on her—for example, he gives her a beard—but eventually he tires of the situation, changes back to his true form and carries the mother-in-law off to eternal damnation.

Strange stuff for a comedy short, perhaps, but viewers at the time no doubt ate up the barrage of visual trickery and lowbrow, slapstick humor. Some sources credit the short as an American production, though it appears to have been made by Pathé in France. TH

Dorian Grays Portraet
aka **Dorian Gray Portrait**; **Dorian Gray's Portrait**; **The Picture of Dorian Gray**
Regia Kunstfilms; b/w; length unknown; Denmark
D: Axel Strom *C:* Mads Anton Madsen
Cast: Valdemar Psilander, Weith, Adam Poulsen, Henrik Malberg

The first appearance of Oscar Wilde's only published novel *The Picture of Dorian Gray* was in *Lippincott's Monthly Magazine* in 1890. It proved controversial enough that the author bowdlerized it before its re-release in standard book form, and while the redone version downplays the story's more homoerotic elements, the forbidden allure of the young Dorian Gray still comes through loud and clear. Beautiful, bisexual and narcissistic, he captivates everyone he meets, including Basil Hallward, an artist who resolves to capture Dorian's essence in portraiture. While sitting for his portrait, Dorian meets Hallward's friend, the corruptive Lord Henry Wotton, who convinces him that beauty is the only important thing in life. Once the portrait is finished and Dorian realizes how attractive he really is, he wishes his picture to grow old in his stead while he remains young. He meets a young singer named Sybil Vane, with whom he develops a brief relationship; after he rejects her, she kills herself. From there, Dorian tumbles into a downward spiral of blackmail, drug abuse and murder—remaining young and attractive, while the painting not only ages but reflects the debauchery to which he's committed his life.

The first film adaptation of Wilde's tale came in 1910 from Axel Strom for Regia, a short-lived Danish production company that made most of its films within the span of a year. Not much is known about Strom, though it seems he was more successful as an actor than as a director. On the other hand, there's a great deal of information available about actor Valdemar Psilander, who portrayed Dorian Gray. He was born in Copenhagen in 1884 and died there in 1917. He took up screen acting in 1910. Immediately after his debut in *Dorian Grays Portraet*, he was picked up by northern Europe's biggest film studio, Nordisk, who proceeded to make him an Eastern European superstar as he enhanced the box office revenue of their pictures. It all came to an end when he committed suicide at the age of 32.

Clara Weith, who likely played Sybil Vane or her dramatic equivalent, was another popular actor of the silent period; she is better known by the name Clara Pontoppidan. CW

Dr. Jekyll and Mr. Hyde
aka **Den Skaebnesvangre Opfindelse**; **Dr. Jekyll and Mr. Hyde; or, a Strange Case**; **The Fatal Invention**
Nordisk; b/w; 17 min; Denmark
D/S: August Blom *P:* Ole Olsen *C:* Axel Graatkjaer
Cast: Alwin Neuss, Oda Alstrup, August Blom, Victor Fabian, Julie Henriksen, Rigmor Jerichau, Ella La Cour, Viggo Larsen, Holger Pedersen, Emilie Sannom, Einar Zangenberg

After telling the attendees of a party that he has created a serum to separate the various aspects of man through both mental and physical change, young Dr. Jekyll (Neuss) settles down for the evening and falls asleep in his chair. He dreams that he takes his own serum and becomes the violent Mr. Hyde.

The film foreshadowed *Life Without Soul* (1915), an unauthorized version of Mary Shelley's novel *Frankenstein, or The Modern Prometheus*, in that most of its action is posited through Jekyll's nightmare, which convinces him not to tamper in God's domain. It's unclear whether Jekyll creates the serum through scientific or occult means, or perhaps by both. The film goes through the usual motions, with Jekyll committing his uninhibited desires through Hyde, until the risk becomes too great. But even after discontinuing the serum, Jekyll finds himself reverting to Hyde and threatening his fiancée. It's at this point that Dr. Jekyll awakens.

Scottish author Robert Louis Stevenson (1850-1894) dabbled in many genres, but there is little doubt that his most enduring contribution to English literature (more so than even 1883's novel *Treasure Island*) is his novella *The Strange Case of Dr. Jekyll and Mr. Hyde*. Since its publication in 1886, *Jekyll* has fascinated readers with its pointed examination of the duality of man. Contemporary readers familiar with the various film and television versions may be surprised by a couple of things. For one, the story is constructed as a mystery—upon its debut, audiences could hardly have been expected to anticipate that the title characters were two manifestations of the same tragic person. It's also noteworthy that no great pains are taken in the book to describe Mr. Hyde's appearance. The many stage and film versions of the story have taken full advantage of this fact, presenting a series of Hydes ranging from the simian-like Fredric March in Rouben Mamoulian's celebrated *Dr. Jekyll and Mr. Hyde* (1931) to the handsome cad-about-town of Hammer's ambitious *Two Faces of Dr. Jekyll* (1960). Sadly, not so much as a still from the lost 1910 version seems to exist, so it's not known just what approach was taken with this particular interpretation of the character.

Den Skaebnesvangre Opfindelse, (the original release title) was the fourth cinematic adaptation of Stevenson's novella, arriving after William Selig's filming of a stage version and Kalem's adaptation—both titled *Dr. Jekyll and Mr. Hyde*—in 1908 and Selig's comical take, *A Modern Doctor Jekyll*, in 1909. The next version, also titled *Dr. Jekyll and Mr. Hyde* and featuring James Cruz in the title role(s), was mounted in the United States in 1912; an identically titled Universal version starring King Baggot followed in 1913.

Alwin Neuss, who executes the title roles here, also starred as Sherlock Holmes in several now-lost mystery thrillers of the silent era. Director August Blom cranked out a number of forgotten features throughout the teens and 1920s. His filmography stops cold in 1925, though he lived until 1947. On a final note, critics at the time were overwhelmingly positive in their view that this was a superior version of Stevenson's novella. TH

Dr. Mesner's Fatal Prescription
aka **Dr. Mesner's Fatal Prediction**
Warwick; b/w; 12 min; Great Britain
Credits unknown

Some sources list the title of this obscure silent horror film as *Dr. Mesner's Fatal Prediction*, but this seems unlikely as there's nary a prediction to be found. Rather, the plot concerns a husband using hypnosis to compel his wife to poison herself. The storyline foreshadows such popular suspense titles as *Gaslight* (1940 and 1944) and *Suspicion* (1941), while the hypnosis angle is a conventional horror/suspense touch for the period.

The Warwick Trading Company produced the short subject. Formed in 1898, it was for a time the leading film production house in Great Britain. Much of its output consisted of travelogues and the like, but titles such as this indicate that the company was attempting to diversify in its later years. Such diversity doesn't seem to have helped much, as the company went bust in 1915. TH

The Duality of Man
Wrench; b/w; 9(5) min; England
Credits unknown

This is the fifth known adaptation of Robert Louis Stevenson's novella *The Strange Case of Dr. Jekyll and Mr. Hyde* (1886) and the first to be filmed in Great Britain. Previous versions include three from the United States and one from Denmark.

Less a direct lift of Stevenson's novella than a filming of the stage play, *The Duality of Man* dishes up a helping of what was already becoming familiar and redundant. Dr. Jekyll creates an elixir to separate the good and evil natures of man, changing himself into the villainous Mr. Hyde. He goes to a gambling den in a nearby park and steals money, only to be chased by an angry mob. He returns to his lab (stopping along the way to assault an old man) and drinks the potion that turns him back into the kindly and upstanding Dr. Jekyll. When his fiancée visits, he reverts to Mr. Hyde and murders her father. Even though his betrothed promises to keep his secret, Dr. Jekyll, upset at what he's done, commits suicide by drinking poison.

Some sources credit prominent stage actor Harry Brodribb Irving (1870-1919)—who played Jekyll and Hyde on stage—as the director of *Duality*, but there's no proof of this. The son of a successful actor with the same name, Harry went by "H.B. Irving" to differentiate himself from his father. He attended Oxford University, originally intending to become a lawyer, but after participating in several school plays, he decided instead to follow in his father's footsteps. He spent a few years recreating roles made famous by his father before distinguishing himself in 1904 with his portrayal of Hamlet in a production staged at the Adelphi Theatre in London.

Irving was married to Dorothea Baird, one of England's most famous actresses, having played the part of Trilby in the stage adaptation of George Du Maurier's famous novel of the same name. Obsessed with real-life crime, Irving founded Our Society, a group that met regularly for dinner to discuss notorious murders; members included Sir Arthur Conan Doyle, creator of the world's most famous detective Sherlock Holmes, and famed coroner Ingleby Oddie.

After he retired from acting, Irving returned to law. He may be best remembered for writing *A Book of Remarkable Criminals*, which outlined the misdeeds of notable figures in the history of crime. CW

L'emmuree des Balkans
Gaumont; b/w; 10 min; France
D/S: Leonce Perret
Cast unknown

Almost nothing is known about this short subject, though its few brief listings all claim that it belonged to the horror genre. It apparently had something to do with an old European superstition that states that a woman must be immured alive during the construction of a bridge or castle in order for the structure's walls to remain stable. It is claimed of numerous bridges and castles in Europe that the spirits of such victims haunt their corridors and their skeletons remain entombed within cemented foundations.

Writer/director Leonce Perret later made *In the Grip of the Vampire* (1913), also produced for Gaumont. Perret's legacy is damaged by the fact that so few of his films survive, but in recent years there have been efforts to secure his reputation as a major innovator of the silent period. TH/CW

The Enchanted Wreath
Warwick; b/w; 8 min; Great Britain
Credits unknown

This morbid fantasy serves up some creepy imagery as an imp makes a girl vanish into thin air, and when she returns, she's been transformed into a frightening witch.

The story has no connection to the Scandinavian folk tale of the same name, which was later adapted by Andrew Lang for his book of fairy tales titled *The Orange Fairy Book*. Great Britain's Warwick Trading Company specialized in musical short subjects, but they occasionally dipped into the horror and fantasy genres. They showed a particular interest in such subject matter in 1910; in addition to this title, they also produced *The Demon of Dunkirque*, *Dr. Mesner's Fatal Prescription*, *The Freak of Ferndale Forest*, *The Golden Beetle*, *Hop-Frog* and *The Witch of the Glen*. TH

Faust
Cines; b/w; 16 min; Italy
D: Enrico Guazzoni
Cast: Fernanda Negri-Pouget, Ugo Bazzini, Alfredo Bracci, Giuseppe Gambardella

Desperate to know the touch of a woman, the aging Faust (Bracci) calls upon the netherworld for assistance. Mephistopheles (Bazzini) appears and, with an eye toward snagging Faust's soul, shows the old man a vision of the young and beautiful Marguerite (Negri-Pouget). Faust agrees to exchange his salvation for youth and virility, hoping thereby to gain Marguerite's hand in marriage. When they meet, however, she wants nothing to do with him, and again Faust invokes Mephistopheles, who uses his powers to assist Faust in a successful seduction. Afterwards, Marguerite's brother Valentin tries to avenge her honor, which proves a bad move when Faust kills him in a duel. Blaming herself, Marguerite goes to church and prays for mercy, but Mephistopheles, who's apparently allowed into churches, appears and distracts her from her entreaties to the Almighty. Somehow she ends up in prison, where Faust, clued in to her whereabouts by Mephistopheles, rushes to her. She dies in his arms, but not before forgiving him for what he's done to her.

The film's *raison d'être* was to show off a series of trick photographic effects that had been done to death by this time and been particularly done to death in *Faust* adaptations. Mephistopheles employs the standard barrage of malevolent superimpositions and jump cuts to turn wood into wine and wine into fire, reveal visions of Marguerite and turn the elderly Faust into a 20-something stud muffin.

The one known existing print of the film appears to be missing a single scene; there was reportedly a prologue that had Mephistopheles challenging Heaven. CW

Faust
Éclair; b/w; length unknown; France
Credits unknown

One of four film adaptations of Goethe's classic play produced in the year 1910 (two were from France, and one was an opera shot with synchronized sound), this *Faust* doesn't stray far from the very (by now *very*) familiar. Aging scientist Faust, who has spent his life shuttered away in his laboratory, decides that asking the Prince of Darkness is his best bet for finding a mate. Upon hearing the old man's prayer, Mephistopheles appears and offers him youth in exchange for, you guessed it, his soul. Faust agrees and becomes young again, after which he meets—thanks to the Devil's machinations—the beautiful Marguerite. One thing leads to another, she becomes pregnant, and when her brother Valentin attempts to avenge her honor, Faust kills him. The death causes her to go mad, and the authorities imprison her. When Faust visits her, she dies in his arms ... though not, of course, before forgiving him for what he's done.

Reference books and websites often confuse cast and credit information among Éclair's *Faust* and two other 1910 productions: a Pathé version directed by Henri Andréani and an Italian version from Enrico Guazzoni. CW

J. Searle Dawley directed Thomas A. Edison's production of *Frankenstein*. Charles Ogle played the grotesque, misshapen monster that flees when Dr. Frankenstein rejects him.

Faust
Pathé; color; 35 min; France
D: Henri Andréani
Cast unknown

Having spent his life in a laboratory looking for disease cures, bitter old Faust prays to Satan to help ease his loneliness. The devil appears and gives Faust back his youth in exchange for the old man's soul. Shortly thereafter, the now-young Faust meets the virginal Marguerite, but after seducing and impregnating her, he loses interest. Unable to cope with the abandonment, Marguerite murders their baby and goes mad. Once she's locked away in prison, Faust despairs at what he's done. He rushes to be with her, but she dies in his arms.

Director Andréani added elements not original to Goethe's story. The film was three reels long and entirely hand-painted. Some sources claim that Georges Fagot directed a 1904 version of *Faust*, while others suggest that he co-directed this version. Either or both of these claims could be true, though it seems unlikely, and neither can be readily confirmed. Still others confuse this film with a British version from director David Barnett. That film was a record of scenes from Charles Gounod's opera, with a libretto written by Jules Barbier and Michel Carré. It was shot in the Animatophone sound-on-disc system, which resulted in synchronized sound but that, because of the complicated setup required to show the product, never really caught on. CW

The Forbidden Fruit
aka **Le fruit défendu**
Pathé; b/w; 10 min; France
D/S: Gaston Velle
Cast unknown

A magician takes pity on a homeless peasant couple and conjures up an imposing castle for them to live in. Though the two are overjoyed, there's a caveat: neither of them may under any circumstances look beneath the lid of a large pot stored in the kitchen. When the wife yields to curiosity, a giant frog jumps out and chases the couple from the castle.

This comic short offered (as the title implies) a fantastical take on the story of the Garden of Eden. Little is known about the film apart from its plot, but the sight of a gigantic frog terrorizing the protagonists must have been impressive for the time.

Writer/director Gaston Velle specialized in trick photographic shorts such as this, though he never had the impact or influence of Georges Méliès. He was prolific, though, racking up over 70 film credits between 1904 and 1913. Velle also helmed an early version of *Cagliostro* the same year he made this picture. TH

Frankenstein
Edison; b/w; 16 min; U.S.
D/S: J. Searle Dawley *P:* Thomas A. Edison
Cast: Augustus Phillips, Charles Ogle, Mary Fuller

Victor Frankenstein (Phillips) aspires to create the perfect human being. He succeeds in creating life, but the result is a grotesque, misshapen monster (Ogle) that flees when Frankenstein rejects him. Later, having become jealous of the happy life his creator enjoys, the monster seeks out Frankenstein on the latter's wedding night.

The story of the creation of *Frankenstein; or, The Modern Prometheus* has become the stuff of legend. During the wet, dreary summer of 1816, 18-year-old Mary Wollstonecraft Godwin conceived the story while vacationing with her lover, the poet Percy

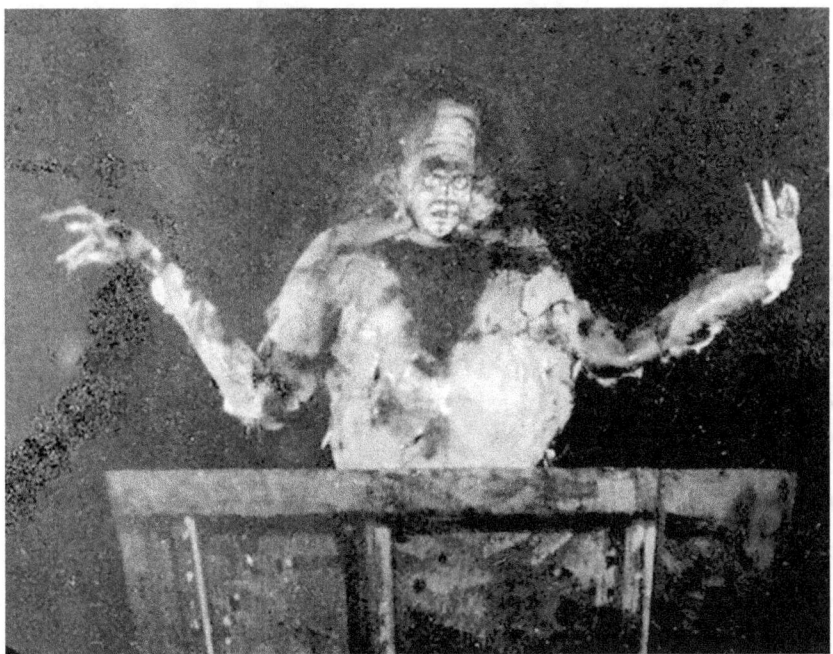

Frankenstein's creation sequence creates the impression of a creature being born out of fire and brimstone.

Bysshe Shelley (whom the young woman would marry later the same year), and their friends at Lord Byron's villa in Geneva. The first edition of the novel was published anonymously in 1818; in 1831 it was reissued with Mary Shelley's name attached. Given its iconic status in the horror genre, first-time readers are often surprised to find that Shelley's book is as much a philosophical tract as a straight-on novel. Yet it contains enough story, and was so immediately successful, that theatrical adaptations were staged early on. It fell to J. Searle Dawley to launch the first film adaptation, which was considered lost until its re-emergence in the 1960s. Producer Thomas A. Edison's role in the production has often been exaggerated; this version of *Frankenstein* was merely one of many quickly lensed films shot by the famed inventor's production company. No reliable evidence exists to suggest that he had any major input into it.

Dawley sensibly delivers an impression of the story rather than a straightforward adaptation. Given the short amount of screen time he had to work with, it's amazing that he was able to convey much of the story at all. Like so many films of its vintage, *Frankenstein* is awfully creaky stuff by contemporary standards. The acting is broad, the camera remains still throughout and there are no good close shots of the monster. Surviving photos grant a far better glimpse of the creature's make-up—reportedly designed by the actor who plays the role, Charles Ogle—than viewers get in the film. Still, the creation sequence is imaginatively handled. By giving the viewer reverse footage of a mannequin burning up, the impression is created of a creature being born out of fire and brimstone. It may seem crude and antiquated to modern eyes, but it undoubtedly impressed theatergoers in 1910.

Dawley's adaptation avoids the ponderous moral analysis found in Shelley's work, but it does convey the message of the dangers of tampering with the natural order of things. The finale gives us the monster disappearing into oblivion, as if by magic, defeated by the love between Victor and his bride. The film doesn't compare to later, more definitive versions of the story (notably James Whale's 1931 masterpiece, *Frankenstein*), but it does retain a special place in cinema history for being the first to tackle Shelley's classic on celluloid. TH

The Freak of Ferndale Forest
Warwick; b/w; 9 min; Great Britain
Credits unknown

A beggar with supernatural powers transforms a child into a monster.

While contemporary filmographies are spotty, the film appears to have been one of the last produced by Great Britain's Warwick Trading Company. Warwick's forays into horror were few; they included the same year's *The Demon of Dunkirque* and a couple of international co-productions, all of which are believed to be lost.

It was a long time before the British film industry embraced the horror film genre. In fact, Great Britain's ban on them had a chilling effect on such production in the late 1930s. Yet, by the late 1950s, the British film industry became synonymous with fright films, thanks to the success of the low-budget (and highly profitable) Hammer Film Productions and its contemporaries. TH

The Ghost in the Oven
aka **The Ghost of the Oven**
Selig; b/w; 6 min; U.S.
P: William Selig
Cast unknown

A pesky ghost interferes with a household's domestic routine.

In foreign markets this bizarre, typically trick-laden horror-comedy was released as *The Ghost of the Oven*. Under either title, it contained plenty of stop-substitution edits for the edification of the Nickelodeon crowd.

Ghost was short enough that producer William Selig sent it out co-featured with another mix of laughs and chills, *Oh, You Skeleton*, which he also produced. The single-reel double feature was released in the United States on October 24, 1910, just in time for Halloween. TH

The Ghost of Mudtown
Pathé; b/w; 9 min; France
Credits unknown

Pathé Frères produced this short about a village under the influence of a ghost. Virtually no information about it, apart from its central conceit, survives. It seems representative of early cinema's love affair with the supernatural. Given Pathé's fondness for trick photography and slapstick, it's likely that this film fell squarely into the horror/comedy camp, aping a myriad of French work from the same period.

That so little is known about *The Ghost of Mudtown* indicates just how unremarkable it was, unable to hold a candle to the work of Georges Méliès, Ferdinand Zecca or Sigundo de Chomon. TH/CW

The Golden Beetle
aka Le scarabée d'or
Continental/Warwick; b/w; length unknown; France/England
D: Henri Desfontaines
Cast: Henri Desfontaines, Denis d'Inès

The Golden Beetle is one of three films that Frenchman Henri Desfontaines directed based on Edgar Allan Poe stories. All three were co-productions between French company Continental and British company Warwick. None appear to have survived.

Beetle was based on Poe's *The Gold-Bug*, first published in the *Philadelphia Dollar Newspaper* in 1843. It tells the story of William Legrand, whose servant believes his master is going insane after having been bitten by a gold bug, likely a beetle. (In fact, in some places the story was published as *The Golden Beetle*.) The story's focus is on cryptography and treasure hunting rather than outright horror, and it remains less famous than many of Poe's other stories.

The next major film to be adapted from this particular Poe story (though far less faithful to its source material) was *Manfish* (1956), which starred Lon Chaney, Jr. in one of his later roles. Billy Wilder's much less successful—and far less talented—older brother W. Lee Wilder directed. The story has also been staged for television on several occasions, including adaptations by Robert Florey and Robert Fuest, and later served as the inspiration for Spanish maverick Jess Franco's very loose adaptation *En busca del dragon dorado* (1983). CW/TH

Haunted by Conscience
Kalem; b/w; 17 min; U.S.
Credits unknown

Ghostly apparitions appear in this long-lost melodrama that was very much in the mold of Edgar Allan Poe's classic short story *The Tell-Tale Heart*. The Kalem Company, a New York-based organization that entered the film industry in 1907, produced. The studio made over 1,500 titles, almost all of which are now considered lost. Among their other productions of note were the first screen versions of *The Legend of Sleepy Hollow* (1908) and *Ben Hur* (1907).

Kalem also made the history books by filming *A Lad from Ireland* (1910) on location in the Emerald Isle, making it most likely the first American-produced motion picture to be shot on location overseas. The company was later sold to the powerful Vitagraph Studios in 1918, which was in turn sold to Warner Bros. in 1925. TH

Hop-Frog
aka The Jester; Hop Frog
Continental/Warwick; b/w; length unknown; France/England
D: Henri Desfontaines
Cast: Colanna Romano

First published in 1849 in *The Flag of Our Union* newspaper under the title *Hop-Frog; or, The Eight Chained Ourang-outangs*, Edgar Allan Poe's *Hop-Frog* concerns a crippled dwarf of the same name who is forced into service as a jester for a despicable king in love with practical jokes. Thinking it funny, the king forces Hop-Frog to consume several goblets of alcohol, despite the fact that Hop-Frog cannot tolerate it. When fellow dwarf and servant Trippetta pleads with the king to stop, he smacks her in the face and douses her with drink. Hop-Frog gets his revenge when the king and his cohorts (who laughed at the incident involving Trippetta) ask for his advice as to what to wear to a masquerade ball. Hop-Frog suggests they dress as orangutans in order to scare the other guests, and they gleefully take his suggestion. The attendees of the ball believe the "apes" to be real, and Hop-Frog, who has arranged that all the doors be locked, sets them all on fire, leaving them to burn while he and Trippetta escape.

From all accounts, this film followed the story closely. CW

The House of the Seven Gables
Edison; b/w; 16 min; U.S.
D/S: J. Searle Dawley
Cast: Mary Fuller

Nathaniel Hawthorne wrote his masterpiece, *The House of the Seven Gables*, in 1851. The house of the title was based on the Turner House, built by Captain John Turner in 1668 and owned in Hawthorne's time by the writer's cousins. Hawthorne was often entertained there while growing up and was much influenced by its atmosphere. Itself a character in the novel, the house was reputed to have been touched by witchcraft and murder. Indeed, one of Hawthorne's own distant relatives was John Hathorne, a judge in the Salem Witch Trials of 1692; in fact, Nathaniel added the "w" to his surname to distance himself from that part of his ancestral past. The novel's central characters, the Pyncheons, were similarly based on real people (ancestors of author Thomas Pynchon).

Hawthorne's story deals with Hepzibah Pyncheon, whose brother Clifford returns home from incarceration for a murder he claims he didn't commit. After an enigmatic visit by an organ grinder, Clifford begins to lose his grip on sanity. His cousin Judge Pyncheon attempts to use Clifford's instability as an excuse to lock him up again, hoping to gain access to the house for diabolical purposes of his own. The judge dies there, however, and Hepzibah and Clifford flee. In due course, they return and learn the truth about the murder for which Clifford was convicted.

Not much is known about James Searle Dawley's film adaptation for Edison, other than the fact that Mary Fuller starred as Hepzibah. It was Dawley's second horror movie of the year, after *Frankenstein* (1910), which was copyrighted in March while *House* was copyrighted in October. No stranger to literary adaptations, Dawley also directed screen versions of *The Prince and the Pauper*, *Hansel and Gretel* and *Bluebeard* (all 1909), *A Christmas Carol* (1910), *The Three Musketeers: Part I* and *The Three Musketeers: Part II* (both 1911), *Treasure Island* and *Mr. Pickwick's Predicament* (both 1912), *Tess of the D'Urbervilles* (1913), *Four Feathers* (1915) and *Snow White* (1916), among others.

In the public domain and long considered classic, Hawthorne's novel has rarely been adapted for the big screen. The next version was Universal's 1940 classic *The House of the Seven Gables*, which starred Vincent Price. The last segment of the anthology horror entry *Twice Told Tales* (1963) was also based on the novel (and starred Vincent Price, this time in an obvious attempt to emulate the success of Roger Corman's treatise on Edgar Allan Poe, *Tales of Terror*, 1962). Then there was an adaptation from Jack Glenn in 1967, but it never saw a proper theatrical release.

Caroline O. Emmerton in 1908 purchased the real House of the Seven Gables; it was refurbished into a museum and settlement house in 1910, the same year Dawley's film was released. CW

Hugo the Hunchback
aka **Hugo, the Hunchback**
Selig; b/w; 16 min; U.S.
D/P: William Selig
Cast: Iva Shepard

Film adaptations inspired by Victor Hugo's novel *Notre Dame de Paris* (1831) were rife during the silent era, beginning with Alice Guy's *Esmeralda* (1905), which shifted the emphasis from the hunchbacked bell ringer to the beautiful Gypsy girl. Van Dyke Brook's *The Hunchback* (1909), a notably dull imitation of Hugo's tale, came next.

Producer/director William Selig's adaptation, then, is the third version, though far from official and apparently not very faithful to Hugo's story. Given that the only performer credit is Iva Shepard, one might conclude that it, like Guy's film, focused on the female love interest. But little solid information exists about the film, and no print is known to exist. It has also been accused of stealing footage from the 1909 adaptation, but such a claim seems spurious at best, given that the sole performer named in Selig's film does not appear in the Brook production.

The year 1910 also saw the release of *The Love of a Hunchback*, which was influenced by—but not directly based on—Hugo's novel. Other silent-era versions include A.E. Coleby's *The Hunchback* and the relatively more faithful Albert Capellani adaptation *The Hunchback of Notre Dame* (both 1911). *The Darling of Paris* followed in 1917 and *Esmeralda* in 1922; Japan entered the fray with *The Hunchback of Enmei-in* in 1924. But the most famous version of the silent era is, without a doubt, Universal's epic *The Hunchback of Notre Dame* (1923), starring Lon Chaney as the deformed Quasimodo and Patsy Ruth Miller as Esmeralda. CW

Inferno
aka **L'Inferno**
Helios; b/w; 22 min; Italy
Credits unknown

Often mistaken for the identically titled Milano Films production, which was released the following year, *Inferno* was a two-reel short following Dante's journey through the nine circles of Hell (actually, a deserted quarry along the Appian Way). There, he encounters various figures, including Francesca da Rimini and Count Ugolino. Finally, in the deepest recess of Hades, he finds an imprisoned Satan.

The film suffered poor reviews, and some then-contemporary sources report legal action by Monopol Film Company against Helios when the film was released in the United States. (Monopol was the American distributor for Milano's feature-length adaptation of the story.)

In any case, Helios released a sequel, *Purgatory*, the very next year, while a third film often confused as being part of the series, *Paradise*, was produced by Psiche and released in 1912. In many areas the latter two films were released together under the title *Purgatory and Paradise*, leading film scholars to conclude that the disparate productions were, in fact, edited into a single film.

At the time of *Inferno*'s production, Helios insisted that it was largely faithful to its source material. In France, the head of the company even sent copies of the published work to theater owners who booked the film so that they could judge its faithfulness for themselves. CW

Jane Eyre
Thanhouser; b/w; 11 min; U.S.
D/S: Theodore Marston *P:* Edwin Thanhouser
Cast: Marie Eline, Gloria Gallop, Frank Hall Crane, Martin Faust, Charles Compton, Amelia Barleon

Originally credited to pseudonym Currer Bell, Charlotte Brontë's *Jane Eyre: An Autobiography* was first published in England in 1847 and in the United States the following year. The book is a highly fictionalized account of Charlotte's own life, cast as a Gothic romance and divided into three parts: the first dealing with Jane's time in Lowood, a school for orphans; the second covering her experience as a governess for the Byronic Mr. Rochester at Thornfield Manor; and the third exploring her stay with the Rivers family. Most film adaptations of the work devote a short, introductory period of time to the first section and a great deal of screen time to the second, with the third given short shrift or done away with altogether.

It's the Thornfield Manor section that takes the book and its adaptations into the realm of the horrific. When the young governess goes to take care of Mr. Rochester's ward Adele in his dark, foreboding and lonely mansion, she is subjected to mysterious sounds and occurrences, including disembodied laughs and weird visitations. When Jane falls in love with Mr. Rochester and agrees to marry him, a terrifying woman sneaks into her room at night and rips apart her wedding veil. Mr. Rochester insists that it's one of his servants under the influence of a few too many, but it turns out that his "former" wife is alive, insane and locked away in the attic!

This very first film adaptation of Brontë's novel was one of two released in 1910 (this one came out in May, the other in June). It set the pattern for future adaptations, with most of the action based on the first and second acts of the book. Interestingly, Frank Crane Hall, who was so fascinated by the story that he shot his own film version of it four years later for IMP/Universal, played Rochester. Amelia Barleon played his insane wife.

Production company Thanhouser was noted for its adaptations of famous novels, including *She* (1911), *Dr. Jekyll and Mr. Hyde* (1912), *The Woman in White* (1912 and 1917) and *The Picture of Dorian Gray* (1915), among others. CW

Jane Eyre
aka **The Mad Lady of Chester**
Cines; b/w; length unknown; Italy
D: Mario Caserini
Cast unknown

This second adaptation of Charlotte Brontë's *Jane Eyre: An Autobiography* (1847), made by Cines in Italy, was released only a month after the first, which had been produced in the United States by New Jersey production company Thanhouser. Neither film appears to have survived, with this Italian production being one of the most obscure adaptations of the novel to date (some sources list it as having been produced in 1909). It was directed by Mario Caserini, a noted Italian director who made numerous features during the silent era, many of which starred his wife Maria Caserini. Some sources assert that she played the character of Jane Eyre in this film, though too little is known to either support or refute the claim. It does appear that the film was released in the United States under the title of *The Mad Lady of Chester*.

The story dealt with a young governess who moves into the house of a rich man, only to find it haunted by his supposedly dead wife, who is in fact insane and locked away in the attic. CW

The Key of Life
Edison; b/w; 11 min; U.S.
Credits unknown

Released on the first day of November 1910, *The Key of Life* was a trick photographic film from the usually more highbrow Edison Studios. In this horror outing from the company, a Hindu priest uses evil magic to turn a harmless kitten into a cat woman with a penchant for killing. It was likely not as gruesome as it might have been, with the stress almost certainly more on the transformation than any murder or mayhem. CW

King Philip the Fair and the Templars
aka **Le roi Philippe le Bel et les templiers**
Éclair; b/w; length unknown; France
D: Victorin-Hyppolyte Jasset
Cast: Georges Saillard, Raoul d'Auchy, Renée Bailly, Germaine Dermoz

After the Crusades claimed much of the Middle East from the Muslims, the Order of the Knights Templar was established to protect wealthy travelers in the Holy Land. Over the next two centuries, the knights are believed to have amassed a fortune in protection money, enhanced by their administration of an early, crude form of a savings-and-loan association. When the group refused a loan to the King of France, Philip IV, in 1302, the King, joined by his good friend Pope Clement V, accused the Knights of homosexuality, denying Christ, urinating on the cross and worshipping the pagan deity Baphomet. On Friday the 13th October 1307, hundreds of Knights were rounded up and tortured into confessing to these crimes, after which three of their leaders, including the Grand Master Jacques de Molay, were slowly roasted over a fire for heresy. (There is a school of thought holding that these arrests mark the origin of the unlucky Friday the 13th" superstition.) Before he died, de Molay is said to have cursed Philip and Clement with the following words: "Within one year, God will summon both Clement and Philip to His Judgment for these actions." And indeed, within a year of Molay's death, both men had died. Philip was felled by a stroke that occurred while hunting. Clement's demise, on the other hand, is shrouded in mystery; it is written that while his body was lying in state, the church that housed it was struck by lightning, with his body destroyed by the ensuing flames.

Jasset's film may be the very first to deal with the subject of the Knights Templar, which later provided fodder for such Spanish horror classics as *The Tombs of the Blind Dead* (1971) and *Return of the Evil Dead* (1973). It appears to have been a fairly accurate telling of the legend, with a supernatural twist to validate the trick photography so common in films of the time.

The plotline of the film is roughly this: King Philip (Saillard), after the vast fortune of the Knights Templar, induces Pope Clement to condemn them. Jacques de Molay is taken into custody and tortured into confessing heresy. As he dies, he curses the King. Then, when the King goes on a hunting trip, de Molay's ghost appears and frightens his horse. The King falls to his death, and his spirit is drawn to Hell. CW

The Legend of the Undines
aka **La Légend des Ondines**
Pathé; b/w; 8 min; France
Credits unknown

In European folklore an undine, or ondine as they're sometimes called, was a female water elemental cursed to remain celibate, with the penalty for sex being a loss of her youth and immortality. In one popular story, an undine fell in love with a handsome knight, married him willingly and bore his child. But as she aged, her husband lost interest in her. One day she heard his familiar snoring coming from a nearby barn, where she found him sleeping in the arms of another woman. When he awoke, she cursed him never to sleep again under pain of losing his breath and dying.

In 1811 that story was adapted to novel form by a German romance author, Friedrich de la Motte Fouqué. Its success sparked its adaption into many languages as well as into an opera by E.T.A. Hoffman in 1814 (for which Fouqué wrote the libretto). In 1909 an English version of the book, with accompanying art by Arthur Rackham, hit the market. This particular edition was an immediate hit, and it inspired numerous short silent films from production companies all over Europe. While most of these adaptations were straight-up works of fantasy, a few of them drifted into the horror realm. Pathé's *The Legend of the Undines* is one such film, diverging from the original plotline by having the knight meet his end by drowning, lured into the ocean by the beautiful undine.

The same year that Pathé made its version of the story, Cines in Italy released its own, titled *The Spirit of the Lake*. Both of these films proved successful enough that both Pathé and Cines followed them up with minor variations (*The Fisherman's Nightmare* and *The Legend of the Lake*, respectively, both 1911). Other romantic silent-era adaptations included Thanhouser's *Undine* (1912), starring Florence La Badie in the title role, and Universal's *Undine* (1916), with Ida Schnall as the titular water nymph. The latest adaptation, shot in Ireland in 2009, stars Colin Farrell as a fisherman who catches an undine (Alicja Bachleda) in his net. This version was directed by Neil Jordan (*Interview with the Vampire*, 1994) and was entirely a work of romance. CW

The Love of a Hunchback
Empire; b/w; 6 min; Great Britain
Credits unknown

Often described as an unauthorized remake of Alice Guy's *Esmeralda* (1905), it would seem that this 1910 British version of Victor Hugo's novel *Notre Dame de Paris* (1831) likewise focused on Esmeralda's love for deformed bell ringer Quasimodo, probably depicting the scene in which the Gypsy girl gives water to the chained hunchback.

Hunchbacked men were apparently seen as sex symbols in the early 1900s. Numerous films dealt with their romantic/horrific exploits, including *The Hunchback* (1909), *Francesca da Rimini* (two versions in 1910, another in 1911, and a fourth in 1922), *Hugo the Hunchback* (1910), *The Hunchback* and *The Hunchback of Notre Dame* (both 1911), *Esmeralda* (1922), Lon Chaney's silent-era classic *The Hunchback of Notre Dame* (1923) and Japan's sole entry, *The Hunchback of Enmei-in* (1924).

In 1914, two additional films titled *The Hunchback* were released, but both appear to have been romantic crime melodramas. Another film, *The Humpback of Cedar Lodge* (1914), seems to have been more horror oriented, though it too had nothing to do with Hugo. CW

Lucrezia Borgia
Cines; b/w; length unknown; Italy
D: Mario Caserini
Cast: Francesca Bertini, Maria Gasperini, Maria Jacobini

This is one of two 1910 Italian films based on the lives of Lucrezia and Cesare Brogia, a notorious brother and sister who slept and murdered their way to political success after their father Rodrigo was elected Pope Alexander VI. In Cines' take on the tale, Francesca Bertini appears as Lucrezia. Though Cesare appears to have orchestrated most of their power plays, Lucrezia has emerged as the more famous of the two, perhaps because, after her brother's death, she reportedly turned her life around and worked to increase recognition of, and interest in, the arts. Whether this change of heart was true or apocryphal, she's best known for possessing a hollow ring that she allegedly loaded with poison and used to kill her enemies.

Without a *Lucrezia Borgia* cast list in existence, it is unknown which historical figure (or fictionalized character) the director's wife Maria portrayed. Having begun her career as a stage actress, Maria jumped to the big screen in 1906 in a production of *Othello*, the first-known adaptation of Shakespeare's play, also directed by her husband. The two went on to make numerous films together, including versions of *Romeo and Juliet* and *Hamlet* (both 1908) and *Macbeth* (1909), among many others. Her career ended in 1927, seven years after the death of her husband, though she lived until 1969.

Giuseppe de Liguoro directed the other 1910 film based on the Borgias, alternately titled *The Feud of the Borgias* and *Dinner With the Borgias* (*Le cena del Borgia* in Italy), released in early 1911. From published descriptions, it appears to have been a short film depicting a family argument at the Borgias' dinner table.

The assistant director on Caserini's picture was none other than Gerolamo Lo Savio, who was so fascinated by the Borgias that he went on to film his own take on Lucrezia's life. CW

Lured by a Phantom
aka **Le Roi de Thule; The King of Thule; Lured by a Phantom, or, The King of Thule**
Gaumont; b/w; 6 min; France
D: Étienne Arnaud, Louis Feuillade
Cast: Rénee Carl, Alice Tissot

Based on the poem *Der König in Thule* (aka *The King in Thule*) written by Johann Wolfgang von Goethe in the mid-1770s (and later grafted by the author onto his famous play *Faust*), *Lured by a Phantom* follows the demise of the King of Thule. Depressed over the death of his wife, the king sees a vision of her—the phantom of the film's U.S. title—which he follows into the sea and drowns.

In the United States George Kleine, whose distribution company dealt almost exclusively with foreign product, picked up the film for release. The film was released in its native France in September 1910, and Kleine released it in the U.S. in December on a split reel with Gaumont's comedic short *Nancy's Wedding Trip*. The two films were most likely an odd combo, with *Lured by a Phantom* being far darker in mood than its sprightly companion.

Phantom was co-directed by two of France's most famous filmmakers of the silent era, Étienne Arnaud and Louis Feuillade. Arnaud also helmed *Robert the Devil* (1909) and *The Legend of Sleepy Hollow* (1912), while Feuillade oversaw *The Princess and the Fisherman* and *Shooting in the Haunted Woods* (both 1909), as well as the original *Fantomas* film series in the teens. CW

Max Hypnotized
aka **Max Hypnotisé; Max 1st Hypnotisiert**
Pathé; b/w; 9 min; France
D: Lucien Nonguet
Cast: Max Linder

This middle-period film featuring Max Linder (France's answer to Charlie Chaplin) takes a leaf from George Du Maurier's hypno-*Trilby* playbook. A comedy, it features Linder as a man named Max (!), who is repeatedly hypnotized by a couple of servants with a mere gesture of their hands. Sometimes the servants change places with him, impelling him to perform their duties, and sometimes they command him to commit frenzied, humorous acts of destruction against random pieces of furniture. When they place a knife in his hands and order him to commit murder, he instead stabs some cheese, awakens and resumes his daily routine.

Max Hypnotized was first released on December 1, 1910, and went into heavy circulation in January 1911. It was one of several films in which popular comedian Linder was placed in horror-tinged situations; other examples include *The Hanging Lamp* (1908) and Abel Gance's *Au Secours* (1924). After finding massive success in his native France, he moved to the United States in the hopes of wowing a much bigger audience. But he failed to score in *les États-Unis* and returned to his homeland with his tail between his legs to resume a career he soon found was out of steam. In October 1925, depressed at flopping on both sides of the pond, he and his much younger wife committed suicide, leaving behind a young daughter.

Lucien Nonguet started as a filmmaker in 1901, co-directing the short feature *Quo Vadis?* with Ferdinand Zecca for the Pathé Brothers. He quickly graduated to making his own films and struck gold in 1910 when he hooked up with Linder for a series of slapstick comedies. He is believed to have been born in France in 1868. There is no record of his death, though his last film was shot in 1919 and released in January 1920. CW

The Minotaur
aka **Theseus and the Minotaur; Thesus and the Minotaur; Theseus and the Minotaurus**
Vitagraph; b/w; 11 min; U.S.
D/S/C/FX: J. Stuart Blackton
Cast unknown

In Greek mythology, Minos hoped to become King of Crete. He prayed to Poseidon for assistance, and the god of the sea sent

Minos a white bull as a symbol of his support. When Minos was duly crowned, he was expected to sacrifice the bull in gratitude but instead decided to keep it for himself. As punishment, his wife was cursed to copulate with it. The resulting child was part bull and part man, and when it grew into a beast that fed upon human flesh, it was placed in a labyrinth where it could do no harm. Around this same time, Crete conquered Athens, after which Minos decreed that a specific number of children be fed to the Minotaur at regular intervals. Angered by this, the demigod Theseus of Athens entered the labyrinth and, marking his path with a ball of string, found the Minotaur and decapitated it with his sword.

Vitagraph's *The Minotaur* is one of the earliest known films to portray Greek mythology. With its emphasis on monster over man, it was something of a horror/fantasy hybrid and a very early example of the peplum subgenre. In 1910 the sight of such a monster, even if it was likely a man in costume, must have sent shivers down many a viewer's spine.

There is some question as to whether *The Minotaur* was a one- or two-reel film, but the preponderance of available evidence suggests that it was comprised of a single reel. CW

A German and Russian version of *The Queen of Spades* appeared in 1910; here is a sequence from the Russian version.

The Mystery of Temple Court
Vitagraph; b/w; 11 min; U.S.
Credits unknown

Likely shot in early 1910 and released in March of that same year, *The Mystery of Temple Court* was one of many short horror films helmed by Vitagraph. In it a woman is murdered and, unknown to those close to her, interred in a closet in her home. When someone else comes to live in the home after her disappearance, he has a dream in which the woman's spirit appears to him and points to the closet. He investigates and discovers her remains.

While most suspense films from this period were special-effects-driven comedies, *The Mystery of Temple Court* was a rather grim affair. It utilized low-key lighting and didn't flinch at depicting murder. With its amalgam of horror and mystery and its utilization of light and shadow, one could say that it foreshadowed *film noir*. CW

Necklace of the Dead
aka **Den Dodes Halsband**; **Den Doddet Halsband**; **Den Skindode**
Nordisk; b/w; 17 min; Denmark
D: August Blom *C:* Axel Graatkjaer Sorensen
Cast: Ingeborg Middleboe Larsen, Thorkild Roose, Nicolai Neiiendam, Rasmus Ottesen, Adam Poulsen, Petrine Sonne, Otto Lagoni, Julie Henriksen, Ingeborg Larsen

A girl (Larsen) is nearly buried alive in this morbid melodrama from director August Blom. Blom was prolific in the Danish film industry throughout the silent era, but his career died off as sound movies caught on. In addition to writing, directing and producing, he also gathered a handful of acting credits. As a director, his work included literary adaptations of *Hamlet* (1910) and *Dr. Jekyll and Mr. Hyde* (1910), but usually ordinary, commercial melodramas comprised most of his output.

It would appear that Blom derived inspiration for this film from Edgar Allan Poe's *The Oblong Box*, though the film was not billed as an actual adaptation. Premature interment, of course, was a fixation of Poe's, and his explorations of the theme eventually provided the basis for numerous horror films.

Cinematographer Axel Graatkjaer Sorensen later photographed F.W. Murnau's *The Phantom* (1922), which, despite its eerie moniker, was not a horror movie. TH

Oh, You Skeleton
aka **Oh! You Skeleton**; **Oh You Skeleton**
Selig; b/w; 6 min; U.S.
Credits unknown

An eccentric professor purchases a skeleton but loses it on the way back to his university. It turns out that he has left it sitting in a streetcar, where it frightens a young woman who is mourning a lost love. She runs off in horror, only to imagine seeing the skeleton at every turn. Meanwhile, the skeleton continues to frighten others who come across it.

This comedic short from Selig was released on the same reel with another horror-comedy, *The Ghost in the Oven* (1910). Films of this type sought to confront death—and then laugh at it. And they are not confined to the simpler past; horror spoofs remain popular today. TH

The Phantom
aka **Le Fantome**
Pathé/Le Film Russe; b/w; 12 min; France
Credits unknown

The evil God of Phantoms places a curse on a young girl, transforming her into an old witch. To regain her youth and beauty, she must place a curse on another young girl.

While still fairly fresh at this point, the plot device of one person escaping a curse by transferring it to another person became hackneyed by the dawn of the sound era. The concept had a heyday during the late 1960s and all through the 1970s, when a more pessimistic worldview came into vogue.

This obscure short was a co-production between Pathé Frères and Le Film Russe, but surviving details are sketchy. It should not be confused with F.W. Murnau's *The Phantom* (1922), which, despite its title, is not a horror movie. TH/CW

The Queen of Spades
aka **Pikovaya dama**

Khanzhonkov; b/w; 15 min; Russia
D/S: Pyotr Chardynin *P:* Aleksandr Khanzhonkov *C:* Louis Forestier
Cast: Pavel Biryukav, Aleksandra Goncharova, Antonina Pozharskaya, Andrej Gromov

Aleksandr Sergeyevich Pushkin, better known as Alexander Pushkin, was the premier Russian writer of his day, credited by many with formulating modern Russian literature. He was a playwright, poet and novelist who clashed at times with governmental bureaucracies and was at one point exiled to Southern Russia. He ended his life in deep debt, a circumstance he attributed to an alleged affair on the part of his wife. Wounded in a duel with her purported lover, he died two days later, leaving behind a rich and enduring body of work.

In 1833 he wrote *Pikovaya dama* (aka *Queen of Spades*), which was published in a Russian magazine the following year. The story in time formed the basis of an opera by Tchaikovsky and an operetta by Franz von Suppé. In all three incarnations, the central character is a man named Hermann who, after learning about a Countess with a supernatural ability to win card games, becomes obsessed with knowing her secret.

Khanzhonkov's film version of *The Queen of Spades* is the earliest known adaptation of the tale for the big screen. Drawing upon Tchaikovsky's 1890 opera at least as much as Pushkin's work, director Pyotr Chardynin follows the original story fairly closely, though Hermann's name is translated as German, and Liza has gone from being the Countess' ward to being her granddaughter.

Miserly young soldier German (Biryukav) has never played cards, fearing the loss of all his money. One day while he watches a group of his friends play, a Countess (Pozharskaya) walks by with her entourage. One of the men mentions that the old woman knows "the secret of the three winning cards." Intrigued, German goes to the Countess' house, where her granddaughter Liza (Goncharova) has just turned down a suitor's offer of marriage. German woos the young woman and, when she rejects him, threatens suicide. And that, it turns out, is the way to her heart! The two kiss, part and meet later at a ball, where she gives him a key to her bedroom. Instead of visiting Liza, however, he sneaks into the old woman's room and confronts her with a gun, demanding to know her secret. The old woman dies of fright, and Liza, alarmed by the commotion, bursts into the room. German attempts to talk his way out of things, but Liza, sobbing over her grandmother's body, insists that he leave.

Back in his barracks, German receives a letter from Liza demanding that he meet her and explain things after all. But before he can leave, the spirit of the Countess appears and shows him a vision of the three cards he must play to win. He goes to Liza and shares with her what he's learned and how he's learned it. Her horror does nothing to dampen his enthusiasm, and after he leaves, she throws herself over the side of a bridge. He makes a beeline directly to the nearest gaming house, where he plays—and loses. This unhinges him; he imagines the ghost of the Countess tormenting him while his fellow gamers look on, and he collapses, dead.

Chardynin's direction is entirely static and the sets thoroughly threadbare, though the costumes are decent. The same year saw a second motion picture adaptation of Pushkin's tale, that one from Germany. But the greatest silent-era version, also from Russia, came in 1916. CW

The Queen of Spades

Deutsche Bioscop; b/w; 15 min; Germany
Credits Unknown

Russian writer Alexander Pushkin's most filmed literary work is doubtless *Pikovaya dama* (*The Queen of Spades*), first published in *Biblioteka dlya chteniya* magazine in 1834, though it had been written the year before. There are nine known silent versions, with several others from the period following the advent of talkies in the late 1920s. Deutsche Bioscop's was the second version, shot on the heels of a Russian adaptation done the same year. So little is known about the German film that it can only be conjectured how closely it followed Pushkin's tale.

Said tale concerns an army engineer named Hermann who learns from his friend Tomski that Tomski's grandmother, a countess, once settled all her debts by winning at cards. She had, her grandson claims, learned the secret of card playing from infamous alchemist/occultist Compte de Saint-Germain. Hermann, a miser who squirrels away every penny he can, becomes obsessed with the old lady, eventually confronting her and threatening to shoot her if she doesn't reveal her secret. Her response is to die on the spot of a heart attack. After attending the Countess' funeral (where she opens her eyes and looks at him), Hermann is visited by her ghost, who tells him that he'll win a bundle if he plays three specific cards (the three, the seven and the ace of spades), one each day over three consecutive days. He is expected to give up gambling thereafter, however, and also to marry the Countess' ward Lizaveta Ivanovna (whom he earlier wooed, then abandoned). Hermann does as instructed, but on the third day the queen of spades is somehow played in place of the ace. He loses all his savings, goes insane and is placed in an asylum, where he endlessly repeats, "The three, the seven, and the ace! The three, the seven, and the queen!" CW

The Red Inn
aka **L'Auberge rouge**

Pathé; b/w; length unknown; France
D: Camille de Morlhon *S:* Abel Gance
Cast: Jeanne Cheirel, Julien Clément, Georges Saillard, Jean Worms

This is one of two horror films directed by Camille de Morlhon in 1910, the other being *Cagliostro*. What makes *The Red Inn* noteworthy is that it was written by cinematic newbie Abel Gance, destined to become one of France's most important filmmakers. Two years later Gance wrote and directed *The Mask of Horror* for his own company, Le Film Francais; that film was the beginning of Gance's long flirtation with the horror genre.

Rose O'Salem Town expressed director D.W. Griffith's views that individuals should be left alone to live their lives as they see fit, told in a tale of the Salem witch trials.

The Red Inn was based on Honoré de Balzac's novella *L'Auberge rouge*, which was inspired by rumored doings at a hostel in the French region of Ardeche. The isolated inn was said to have been the site of more than 50 murders between 1805 and 1831. The inn's owners, a farming couple struggling to make ends meet, were allegedly the perpetrators, robbing and killing their guests and destroying the bodies in the inn's large oven. The couple, Peter and Mary Martin, along with their servant Rochette, was convicted of one murder. An itinerant who snuck into the inn's barn to sleep allegedly witnessed the crime. In 1833 the couple and their servant were guillotined, though today there is some doubt as to the veracity of the itinerant's claims.

Though the case had not yet been resolved in 1831, rumors about it reached the ears of a young Balzac, who regurgitated the gossip as *L'Auberge rouge* and got the work published in the *Revue de Paris*. Balzac's narrative concerns a German banker named Hermann who, while dining with members of Parisian high society, tells a story he once heard about two surgeons spending the night in a hostel. They share a room with a businessman who has fled the Napoleonic Wars and who confesses to them that he has a great deal of wealth on his person. In the middle of the night the man is murdered and his wealth stolen, and afterwards an innocent man is put to death for the crime. As the banker relates his tale to the astonished diners around him, he comes to realize that the real murderer is at the table with them.

The next film adaptation of Balzac's story came in 1923 and was released under the same title. CW

Robert, The Devil: or, Freed from Satan's Power
aka **Robert le diable**
Gaumont; b/w; 11 min; France
D: Etienne Arnaud
Cast: Leonce Perret, Maurice Vinot

A famed libretto by Eugene Scribe and Casimir Delavigne was the basis for this long-lost short, the production of which premiered in 1831 at the Paris Opera House. Scribe and Delavigne took inspiration from the legend of Robert the Devil, in which a woman turns to Satan for solace and ends up bearing the Evil One's child. The original tale has Duke Robert the Magnificent of Normandy discovering who his father is and, despite his heritage, being redeemed by a chaste love for Princess Isabelle.

Just how much of the original concept made its way into this short subject is open to conjecture. Director Etienne Arnaud made his first films in France but later moved to the United States, where he directed an early version of *The Legend of Sleepy Hollow* (1912). *Fra Diavolo*, another libretto by Scribe, became the basis for several movies (most famously the 1933 Laurel and Hardy vehicle *The Devil's Brother*) but, title aside, did not dip into the supernatural or horrific. TH

Rose O'Salem Town
aka **Rose of O'Salem Town**
American Mutoscope and Biograph; b/w; 13 min; U.S.
D: D.W. Griffith *S:* Emmett C. Hall *C:* G.W. Bitzer
Cast: Dorothy West, Clara T. Bracy, Henry B. Walthall, George Nichols, Arthur V. Johnson, Alfred Paget, Guy Hedlund, William Chyristie Miller

The Salem Witchcraft Trials began in the small village of Salem, Massachusetts (a long-gone community not to be confused with the still-extant city of Salem) in 1692 when a group of young girls claimed that a household slave woman had persuaded them to worship the Devil. That and further accusations led to numerous arrests, convictions and executions—mostly of women—for the crime of witchcraft. And even though the Massachusetts government later recognized its error and attempted to atone for its part in the hysteria, the incident has passed into historical infamy.

Set against the backdrop of the trials, *Rose O'Salem Town* opens with a declaration:

> Reliable authority states that nine million human lives were sacrificed through the zeal of fanatical reformers during the Christian epoch. Religious fanaticism was in most cases the cause, still there were many victimized to satisfy a personal grudge.

The narrative that follows stars Dorothy West as "the sea child," an innocent young woman who refuses the sexual advances of a Puritan elder. Angered by the rebuff, the old man accuses the girl and her mother of witchcraft and demands that they be burned at the stake. Though the mother is indeed executed, the girl escapes when a trapper (Walthall) with whom she's in love, along with his Native American cohorts, comes to her rescue.

Though *Rose* isn't strictly a horror film, it contains enough of the genre's convictions and historical connections to warrant inclusion here. The point Griffith seems to be making—that individuals, no matter how different they might be, should be left alone to live their lives as they see fit—contradicts the view he expressed only five years later with the racist *Birth of a Nation*, which helped spur a Ku Klux Klan resurgence throughout the United States.

Griffith flirted more overtly with the horror genre in *The Avenging Conscience, or: 'Thou Shalt Not Kill'* (1914). CW

Satan's Rival
aka **Rival de Satan**; **Satan's Rival**; **A Rival to Satan**
Pathé; b/w; 10 min; France
D: Gerard Bourgeois
Cast: Stacia Napierkowska, Georges Wague, E. Prefonds

Bored with his life in Hell, Satan visits Earth to choose a wife. A woman named Beryl (Napierkowska) strikes his fancy, but she's betrothed to Oliver the Knight. Undeterred by her romantic status, Satan dons the guise of a Hindu prince and asks for the maiden's hand in marriage. A good fairy tips off Oliver to the situation, and he and Satan battle. With the assistance of both the fairy and a Holy Hermit, Oliver vanquishes the Evil One and solidifies his claim to Beryl.

Swiss-born Gerard Bourgeois directed this melodramatic fantasy. The film was one of many of the period that humanized Satan, though it seems that it was less comedic than others of its ilk. Leading lady Stacia Napierkowska was a former dancer who found some success in silent films. Her career, however, waned as her once-petite figure began to swell. She also appeared in the Honore de Balzac adaptation *The Wild Ass's Skin* (1909).

Satan's Rival was released in the United States in 1911. TH

The Secret of the Hand
Lux; b/w; 17 min; France
Credits unknown

This may be the first horror film to concern itself with the subject of Tong murders, presaging Hammer's classic *The Terror of the Tongs* (1960) by 50 years. Like that later film, *The Secret of the Hand* deals with a Chinese gang that severs appendages and sends them to people as warnings. *Hand*'s plot centers on the severed hand of a man, sent by the evil cult to the victim's friends.

French studio Lux produced; the production house made several horror films in the early 1900s, most of which are now lost. CW

The Skeleton
Vitagraph; b/w; 7 min; U.S.
Credits unknown

An accident-prone professor tries to impress his students by purchasing a skeleton to use as a teaching aid. He wraps his purchase and carries it with him, then grows weary on the way home and takes a break on a park bench. He absentmindedly leaves the skeleton on the bench, and some kids steal it. Delighted at their find, they dress the skeleton in a full suit and take it back to the park, where they prop it up on another bench. A policeman notices the figure and, mistaking it for a man sleeping off a drunk, attempts to haul it off to jail; when he realizes that it's a skeleton, he runs off in terror.

This comedic short subject used trick photography to make its "protagonist" appear to move on its own. The premise is similar to Selig's *Oh, You Skeleton*, which was released the same year.

The Skeleton was released as part of a split reel with *Caught in His Own Trap* (1910), which had no actual horror film connection. TH

The Soap Bubbles of Truth
Pathé; b/w; 7 (5) min; France
Credits unknown

This should not be confused with George Méliès' *Les Bulles de savon animees* (1906), titled *Soap Bubbles* in the United States and Great Britain. In that film, the great director stars as a magician who blows soap bubbles with women's heads in them. In this Pathé short, an old well produces strange bubbles that rise and foretell the murder of a miser at the hands of a thief. CW

The Snake Man
aka **The Serpent Man**
Lux; b/w; length unknown; France
Credits unknown

This obscure short foreshadows such later horror titles as *The Reptile* (1966), *The Snake Woman* (1961) and *Ssssss* (1973). As its title suggests, *The Snake Man* concerns a man who can transform into a snake. Given that serpents have gotten thousands of years' worth of bad, even Satanic, press, it is no surprise that the creatures have a secure place in horror iconography, slithering through everything from "snake on the loose" thrillers such as *Venom* (1982) to the over-the-top giant monster schlock of *Anaconda* (1997). TH

The Sorceress of the Strand
aka **La Sorcière de la Grève**
Éclair; b/w; 7 min; France
D/S: Victorin-Hippolyte Jasset *C:* Raymond Agnel
Cast: Eugenie Nau, Emile Keppens, Marie Barthe, Gilbert Dalleu

As with so many silent films of its ilk, *The Sorceress of the Strand* gives a humorous bent to its tale of a fisherman who mistreats an old crone. By way of revenge, the crone disguises herself as a beautiful maiden and lures the fisherman to his death in the sea. The film was one of several horror-oriented trick films directed by Victorin Jasset. The others include *The Suicide Club* (1909), *King Philip the Fair and the Templars* (1910) and *Balaoo* (1913). CW

The Spirit of the Lake
aka **Il Genio del Lago**
Cines; b/w; 10 min; Italy
Credits unknown

A knight and his beautiful lover die when a spirit that inhabits a lake curses them. Though the film is lost, reviews from the time indicate that the jealous spirit was an actual apparition and that sea nymphs were somehow involved in the proceedings.

The Spirit of the Lake is the British title; it's unknown whether the film ever received a release in the United States, though it seems likely given the vast circulation of European films in American Nickelodeons. *Spirit* was created by production house Cines, which is known for certain to have done business as early as 1905 and as recently as 1959. The company was one of three that heralded the birth of Italian cinema after the turn of the 20th century; the other two were Ambrosio and Itala.

Other horror films produced by Cines included *Wedding Feast and Ghosts* (1908), *The Wonderful Pearl* (1909) and *The Love of a Siren* (1911). Cines also tried in 1911 to emulate the success of *The Spirit of the Lake* with *The Legend of the Lake*, in which a sea nymph avenges a murder by killing the people responsible. CW

The Spirit of the Sword
Pathé; b/w; 8 min; France
Credits unknown

In this gimmick-laden short subject, a master orders his servant to fetch a favorite sword. When he attempts to retrieve the weapon, it moves on its own. Naturally the servant is frightened since the implication is that an evil spirit possesses the sword.

Some confusion surrounds the origin of this title. It is generally listed as a French film made by Pathé Frères, but some sources list it as an American film (distributed by the short-lived Empire Film Company). Surviving filmographies for Empire are incomplete, but the studio appears to have folded around the time of the film's debut. It is possible that there were two films produced the same year and bearing the same title, but given that this is not a particularly generic title, this seems unlikely. A more probable conclusion is that it was produced by Pathé in France and distributed by Empire in the United States. TH

Testing a Soldier's Courage
Gaumont; b/w; 8 min; France
Credits unknown

Little information survives about this obscure trick film from France. It dealt with a French lieutenant whose room is apparently haunted. At length he shoots the ghost, only to learn that he's been hoodwinked; the ghost never existed at all. The whole affair was staged to test the soldier's courage. (One can assume that he acquitted himself with his actions.) CW

A Trip to Davey Jones' Locker
aka **A Trip to Davy Jones' Locker**
Pathé; b/w; 8 min; France
Credits unknown

In this film, a prince and a queen of a tribe of women travel through the bowels of Hell and into the deepest recesses of the ocean, with the Devil making mischievous appearances along the way (accompanied by all kinds of ghoulish spirits).

While the original title of this film is unknown, as is its original release date (it was re-released in the 1920s under the title *A Trip to Davey Jones' Locker*), it was probably shot sometime during 1910. It bears a striking resemblance to Georges Méliès' fantastical *The Kingdom of Fairies* (1903) and seems to have been influenced by it. And like the Méliès film, *Locker* was epic in scope, designed to showcase the varied sets and special effects available to the director (whoever that might have been) at the time.

"Davy Jones' locker" is an old nautical euphemism for death by drowning in the ocean. This wasn't the first horror film to play with the concept; that would have been *Davy Jones' Locker*, released in 1900. CW

Vengeance of the Dead
Pathé; b/w; 11 min; France
Credits unknown

This lost short subject told the tale of a haunted portrait of a murdered woman. Things get creepy when the woman's murderer visits the home wherein the portrait hangs. The image comes to life and points an accusing finger at the killer. The panic-stricken culprit then watches in horror as the subject steps out of the portrait to claim vengeance.

This is an early example of the "cursed portrait" subgenre, which arguably found its most popular realization in the various adaptations of Oscar Wilde's novel *The Picture of Dorian Gray* (1890). TH

Wanted—A Mummy
aka **Wanted, a Mummy**; **Mumien Gesucht**
Cricks and Martin; b/w; 4 min; Great Britain
D: A.E. Coleby
Cast unknown

This, one of the earliest films to explore the notion of a living mummy, is something of a cheat. It begins with two men, Bill and Tom, reading a newspaper ad in which a professor offers to pay a fair amount of money for a real mummy. Bill convinces Tom to wrap himself in linen and pretend to be one, after which he's nailed into a coffin. After a few screwball attempts at getting the mummified Tom to the professor's house, Bill finally does so. The professor opens the casket, planning to dissect the mummy inside. Fearing he's about to be killed, Tom as the "mummy," along with Bill, makes a run for it, and once the two are outside, they get into a fight.

Director Coleby made another film along these same lines in 1912. Titled *The Mummy*, it concerned a man dressing up as a mummy to fool his girlfriend's father. Coleby's main claim to fame came in the 1920s, when he directed a series of Fu Manchu shorts for Stoll, beginning with *The Scented Envelopes* (1923). CW

The Witch of the Glen
Warwick; b/w; 9 min; Great Britain
Credits unknown

A witch controls two spirits and uses them to terrorize various men.

Warwick was one of the earliest producers to become involved with international co-financing, mostly with independent producers in other European nations. As pertaining to the horror genre, these cooperative productions included *The Pit and the Pendulum* (1909), *The Golden Beetle* (1910) and *Hop-Frog* (1910), all done jointly with French company Continental, and *The Demon of Dunkirque* (1910), which was co-produced with Italian company Ambrosio. Solo Warwick horror efforts apart from *The Witch of the Glen* included *The Enchanted Wreath*, *The Freak of Ferndale Forest* and *Dr. Mesner's Fatal Prescription* (all 1910).

The Witch of the Glen has no connection to Sally Watson's book *The Witch of the Glens* (1962), which was part of her popular *Family Tree* series. TH/CW

The Witch of the Ruins
aka **La Sorcière des décombres**
Pathé; b/w; 7 min; France
Credits unknown

A man explores a supposedly deserted ruin and encounters an old hag, who beats the crap out of him with a stick.

Yet another work about witches and witchcraft, this apparently lost title was one of many horror entries from the prolific Pathé Frères Company. Little is known about the film beyond its basic outline, but improbably it is said to have been of a more serious tone than most of the goofy horror shorts of the period. Either way, one detects the influence of Georges Méliès, even from the scant information available. TH

The Witches' Spell
aka **The Witch's Spell**
Urban Trading; b/w; length unknown; Great Britain
P: Charles Urban
Cast unknown

This is one of countless horror films produced by Charles Urban during the first decade of the 20th century. Others include *The Haunted Bedroom, The Thousand Pound Spook* and *When the Devil Drives* (all 1907). Urban also produced the first horror films that utilized an actual color process (Kinemacolor), as opposed to hand stenciling; *Faust* and *Mephisto* (both 1912) and *Dr. Jekyll and Mr. Hyde* (1913) were among these works.

The Witches' Spell is a cautionary tale—though, adhering to the manner of the time, a humorous one—warning viewers against curiosity concerning the occult. Its plot concerns a peasant who spies on a black mass, is caught by a coven of witches and gets himself turned into a monster. CW

1911

Baby's Ghost
aka **The Baby's Ghost**
Lux; b/w; 7 min; France
Credits unknown

A ghost frightens burglars!

Records indicate that *Baby's Ghost* received a U.S. release in February 1912, double-billed with another Lux short, *Bill Tunes His Piano* (1912). Lux remained active until the 1960s, though the studio generally worked in conjunction with other companies. Among the final films with which they were associated were Piero Francisci's *Hercules Unchained* (1959), Jacques Tourneur and Mario Bava's *The Giant of Marathon* (1959) and Pier Paolo Passolini's *The Gospel According to St. Matthew* (1964), the latter of which would prove to be their last feature.

Despite the supernatural theme, *Baby's Ghost* was comic in nature and used the ghost angle as a device for producing pratfalls. While most sources list this as a 1912 production, it was likely shot and released in its native France in late 1911. TH

The Bells
Amalgamated; b/w; 45 min; Australia
D/S: W.J. Lincoln *C:* Orne Perry
Cast: Arthur Styan, Nellie Bramley, Miss Grist, J. Ennis, Ward Lyons, Charles Lawrence, Mr. Johns, Mr. Ebbsmith, George Kensington, Mr. Devon, Mr. Devine, Mr. Cullenane, Mr. Colleridge, Mr. Sinclair, Marion Willis

Published posthumously in 1849, Edgar Allan Poe's famous poem "The Bells" is the author's contemplation of love and loss. It was written in May 1848—a little over a year after the death of his wife Virginia—and sold for $15 to *Sartrain's Union Magazine* (Poe died a mere month before its publication). The work has four parts, each examining both a season of the year and a stage of life, with the sound of bells evoked throughout.

In 1867 two French writers, Émile Erckmann and Alexandre Chatrian, grafted Poe's poem onto the same author's *The Tell-Tale Heart* to create the play *Le Juif Polonaise* ("The Polish Jew"). Typical of the duo's work, *Le Juif Polonaise* was a morality play set within a horror milieu. The narrative concerns an innkeeper named Mathias who is reminded at his daughter's wedding—by the sound of bells—of the murder of a Jew he had committed years before. The play was an overnight sensation, adopted within a year by Camille Erlanger into a three-act opera. In 1871 the work was translated into English by Leopold Lewis and re-titled *The Bells*, providing British thespian Henry Irving with his signature role.

This *Bells* appears to have been the first film adaptation of the play. It opened at Taits Glaciarium in Melbourne, Australia on October 7, 1911. Arthur Styan portrayed the murderous Mathias, while a Mr. Cullenane played the part of the Polish Jew. One Mr. Johns took on the role of the mesmerist, a part Boris Karloff assumed for the most famous screen version of the play, which was released in 1926.

Writer/director W.J. Lincoln was also responsible for the earliest film adaptation of *It Is Never Too Late to Mend* (also 1911), making his earliest efforts some of the most sought after Australian silent horror films.

The year 1913 saw the next two film adaptations of Poe's poem, one a second take on the Erckmann-Chatrian play, the other an (un)original screen story done by Edison Studios. CW

Beneath the Tower Ruins
Urban/Eclipse; b/w; 8 min; Great Britain/France
P: Charles Urban
Cast unknown

British film producer Charles Urban was one of the earliest filmmakers to understand the potential of international financing. He brokered many co-production deals in various parts of the world, but it was in France that he was most successful. He made deals with at least two French companies (Eclipse and Gaumont) and was also active with other filmmakers from his native England. He also helped invent the world's first known two-color process with George Albert Smith.

Beneath the Tower Ruins was typical of many of Urban's productions in that it was a trick photographic film, this time out involving a ghost that haunts the ruins of an old tower. George Kleine, who distributed many of Urban's films during this period, released the film in the United States. (These movies are often incorrectly cited as co-productions with Kleine's company.) It was released on a split reel with Urban's short documentary subject *The Abbey of Pavia* (1910) in April 1911.

Though some sources cite *Beneath the Tower Ruins* as being 14 minutes long, the fact that it shared a reel with another film is evidence against such a claim. CW

The Bewitched Window
Pathé; b/w; 11 min; France
Credits unknown

Director Thomas H. Ince died under mysterious circumstancs aboard the yacht of William Randolph Hearst in 1924.

Pathé produced this short subject about a painter who is tormented by visions of a spirit and the Devil. It's not certain who exactly was responsible for the production, but the titular window surely lent itself to the kind of trick photography that audiences ate up during the early silent era. Just how horrific the film was is open to speculation, but given that the Devil factors into the protagonist's visions, creepiness of some sort was almost certainly in there somewhere. TH

Bill Taken for a Ghost
aka **Patouillard fantôme**
Lux; b/w; 8 min; France
D: Romeo Bosetti
Cast: Paul Bertho

Patouillard (Bertho) is an inveterate prankster. While visiting the aptly named Chateau of Spookeybrook, he disguises himself as a ghost in order to frighten the other guests.

Director Romeo Bosetti was active throughout the early silent era. Born in Italy, Bosetti made his way to France, where he directed over 300 short subjects between 1906 and 1916. He is best remembered, however, as the producer of Louis Feuillade's *Fantomas* serial of 1913 and 1914. He also had a hand in the wildly successful Onésime series, producing *Onésime, Clockmaker* (1912). The Onésime character was Anglicized for export (as Simple Simon), and he, like Patouillard, did some time in the horror spoof genre (*Simple Simon and the Devil*, 1912; *Simple Simon and the Haunted House* and *Simple Simon and the Suicide Club*, both 1913).

Bill Taken for a Ghost is part of a long-running series of comic shorts built around Paul Bertho's Patouillard character. The films were successful enough to garner some exposure in the United States, where the character's name was changed to Bill. There were about 60 Patouillard adventures, commencing with *Les patouillard chez le photographe* (1909). TH

Blood Vengeance
aka **Fiaccola sotto il moggio**
Ambrosio; b/w; length unknown; Italy
D: Luigi Maggi *P:* Arturo Ambrosio
Cast: Antonietta Calderari, Norina Rasero, Mary Cleo Tarlarini

A young woman is compelled by her murdered mother's ghost to exact revenge, which the daughter does with the aid of a bag filled with poisonous snakes.

A story by Gabriele D'Anunzio forms the basis for *Blood Vengeance*. D'Anunzio's actual movie work included on-screen title cards for the epic *Cabiria* (1914), but his first-hand activity with the motion picture industry was very limited. He was, however, a prolific writer, arguably best known for his novel *The Innocent* (1892), which provided the basis for Luchino Visconti's elegant cinematic swansong in 1976. The charismatic D'Anunzio is remembered almost as much as a figure in Italian politics as he is a writer and intellectual. An activist, he was so popular with the public that Mussolini wound up bribing him to keep out of the political limelight (though this didn't stop D'Anunzio from attempting to stop Italy from joining Hitler as one of the Axis Powers by disrupting a meeting between the two dictators).

Director Luigi Maggi also directed *Satan* (1911), making him one of the few Italian directors of the silent era to dabble in the horror genre before Mussolini's strict censorship made horror and fantasy taboo subjects. TH

By the House That Jack Built
Universal/IMP; b/w; 11 min; U.S.
D: Thomas H. Ince
Cast: Mary Pickford, Ethel Grandin

A naïve young girl (Pickford) comes under the influence of a wicked witch (Grandin) in this, a tale more inspired by the Grimm brothers than by the nursery rhyme alluded to in the title.

Though many of his films are forgotten today, in his time Thomas H. Ince was a respected and very productive director. He came to directing after a stint as an actor and during his career helped establish numerous production houses, including his own Thomas H. Ince Studios. More interesting to contemporary readers, however, would probably be the sordidness surrounding his untimely death. In 1924, after a cruise on the yacht of newspaper tycoon William Randolph Hearst, Ince was rushed to a hospital, where he died. According to Hearst (and Hearst's newspapers), Ince had had a heart ailment, but others insist that he was accidentally shot. Gossip-turned-legend has it that Hearst caught fellow passenger Charlie Chaplin in a compromising position with Hearst's mistress, the actress Marion Davies and, in a jealous fit, chased the comic while firing shots at him, one of which fatally wounded Ince.

By the House That Jack Built's cast included Mary Pickford, a silent-era icon of idealized femininity of the "nice" variety—she was the type of girl one could take home to mother—in such films as *The Poor Little Rich Girl* (1917) and *Pollyanna* (1920). While "America's Sweetheart" made her name in wholesome fare, she also appeared in the mildly horrific *Sparrows* (1926). TH

Dandy Dick of Bishopgate
Natural Color Kinematograph; color; 19 min; Great Britain
D: Theo Frenkel
Cast unknown

A man is driven to despair by the death of his fiancée. In her memory, he locks her room and forbids anybody to enter it. Forty years pass, during which he succumbs to insanity. Then he sees a vision of the dead girl, and it frightens him to death.

This short subject was shot in the two-color Kinemacolor process. Developed by Englishman George Albert Smith in 1906, Kinemacolor found some popularity between 1908 and 1914, but it flopped in the long run, due to the expense of equipping theaters with the special projectors the process required.

Director Theo Frenkel was born in the Netherlands and helmed over 200 titles in a variety of countries, including Great Britain, where this film was produced. TH

The Demon
aka **Demonio**
Ambrosio; b/w; 17 min; Italy/Russia
D/C: Giovanni Vitrotti
Cast: Mikhail Tamarov, Mme. Cemesnova, M. Navatzi

Satan tempts a young woman, who tries to retain her virtue.

This obscure short was based on a poem by Mikhail Lermontov, regarded as one of the most significant writers in all of Russian literature. His poetry covered the same metaphysical ground as did the Russian Romantic writers of the first half of the 1800s. Though his name is virtually unknown in the United States, his work remains etched into Russian culture. *The Demon* was one of his most ambitious poems, and its celebration of atheism ensured it a stormy reception. It remained a hotly debated item for years, even as its haunting imagery influenced a generation of authors.

Director/cinematographer Giovanni Vitrotti was a prolific talent. As a director, he churned out over 100 titles between 1906 and 1912. After that, he focused exclusively on cinematography until he retired from film in the early 1950s; among the many titles he photographed is the film *Satan* (1912), a precursor of sorts to Fritz Lang's *Destiny* (1921). He died in 1966.

It is unclear whether *The Demon* really was an Italian/Russian co-production, as is often reported, or whether it was Italian alone. Given the source material and the presence of Russian actors, it seems safe to assume that some type of Russian input, creative and likely financial, was involved. TH

The Devil as a Lawyer
aka **Der Teufel als Rechstanwalt**
Messter; b/w; 10 min; German
Credits unknown

This long-lost German short anticipated *The Devil's Advocate* (1997) by over 80 years. It depicted the Devil, assuming human form as—wait till you hear—a sly, villainous attorney. Lawyers have long been the butt of jokes, so the idea of having Old Scratch favor such a disguise must have been a natural.

Production company Messter Film was one of the first to emerge in Germany; entrepreneur Oskar Messter started the fledgling studio in 1897, though it was subsequently sold to the country's "super studio" UFA in 1918. TH

The Devil's Sonata
Scandinavian; b/w; 14 min; Denmark
Credits unknown

A violinist with evil powers controls the girl he loves via hypnosis.

The title of this long lost short suggests that its makers may have drawn a spark of inspiration from Giuseppe Tarantini (1692-1770), an Italian violinist and composer of a famous piece entitled "The Devil's Sonata." There's a peculiar, if possibly apocryphal, story associated with the musical work. Tarantini is said to have told friends that he had struggled desperately to finish the "Sonata," unable to do so until the Devil appeared in a dream and played the conclusion of the piece on a violin. In every other way, it sounds like yet another knock-off of *Trilby*. TH

An Evil Power
Selig; b/w; 17 min; U.S.
D/S: Francis Boggs *P:* William Selig
Cast: Sydney Ayres, Frank Clark, Frank Richardson, Al E. Garcia, Fred Huntley, Roy Watson, Edward H. Philbrook, Phyllis Gordon, Eugenie Besserer, Betty Harte, Bessie Eyton, Genevieve Davis

An Evil Power is yet another entry in the "evil hypnotist" subgenre that flourished in the early days of silent melodrama, with the typical innocent young girl on the receiving end of a hypnotist's typically impure advances.

The film was one of many written and directed by silent film pioneer Francis Boggs. A forgotten figure today, he was incredibly prolific in his time. He entered show business as a stage actor while still in his teens. While visiting Chicago, he made the acquaintance of producer William Selig of Selig Polyscope. It was Boggs who persuaded Selig to move camp to Los Angeles, and the two were among the first filmmakers to work in what would become the movie capital of the United States: Hollywood. Between 1907 and 1911, Boggs directed nearly 200 short subjects, though today most of these, including *An Evil Power*, are considered lost. Boggs' career was cut tragically short on October 27, 1911, when a studio groundskeeper went berserk and shot the filmmaker to death, wounding Selig in the process. TH

The Fairy Jewel
aka **La gemma solitaria**
Milano; b/w; 7 min; Italy
D: Giuseppe de Liguoro
Cast unknown

Often cited in film resource books as a 1910 release, *The Fairy Jewel* was released in Great Britain in February 1911. (It is possible that the film was produced in its native Italy in late 1910, but there's not enough information to confirm or deny this.)

The film's plot concerns a hunter who seeks a rare gem and will stop at nothing to get it. In the end, however, the fairy that guards it drowns the hunter. The plot was similar to Cines' *The*

Wonderful Pearl (itself a take on Wilkie Collins' novel *The Moonstone*, via the legend of the undines); that film was shot in Italy two years before.

Director Giuseppe de Liguoro (1869-1944) also shot the non-horror Borgia picture *La Cena del Borgia* as well as *Inferno* (1911), in which he is known to have had an acting part. Though he didn't outlast the silent era, his son went on to a career in Italian cinema as a director, actor and cinematographer. CW

Faust and Marguerite
aka Faust et Marguerite
Gaumont; b/w; length unknown; France
D: Jean Durand
Cast: Gaston Modot

For this 1911 version of Goethe's famous two-part play, director Jean Durand follows the story closely *but* for one major change. This time it's Marguerite who kicks Faust to the curb.

Grieving over his advanced age and intense loneliness, Faust is confronted by Mephistopheles, who promises to make him young again in exchange for his soul. Faust agrees, is transformed into an attractive young man and meets and fawns over the beautiful Marguerite. She quickly grows tired of his neediness, however. At length, as punishment for the pact Faust made with the devil, she's borne to Heaven while Faust remains on Earth to grieve her absence.

Other than the brief description and few credits given above, little is known about this apparently lost film. The same year it was released, Cecil M. Hepworth made his own version in Great Britain. That film starred Hay Plumb as Faust, Claire Pridelle as Marguerite and Jack Hulcup as Mephistopheles. It was a live recording of an opera performance, with synchronized sound, much like the 1910 version from David Barnett. Neither film is strictly a horror film, and as such neither warrants extensive mention here.

Director Durand made well over 200 films in his native France, including one of the earliest film versions of Edmond Rostand's play *Cyrano de Bergerac* (1909). His career doesn't appear to have lasted beyond the silent film era, nor should he be confused with the actor of the same name. Durand's next horror film was the comedic *Simple Simon and the Devil* (1912). CW

The Fisherman's Nightmare
Pathé; b/w; 10 min; France
Credits unknown

This obscure movie portrays a typical silent-era fisherman lured to his typical death by a typical undine—a water nymph of European folklore—for his crimes against humanity. The twist here, such as it is, is that rather than the man drowning, he is buried alive.

Little else is known about the picture, which apparently used stop-substitution to relate the fisherman's confrontation with the nymph and his subsequent execution. It was one of many supernatural-themed films released by Pathé in the early years of the silent era, and like so many of the others, it was probably played as much for humor as for horror. CW

From Death to Life
Rex; b/w; 11 min; U.S.
Credits unknown

Like so many films from the early 1900s, the only thing known about *From Death to Life* is its overall plot, which concerns a mad scientist—who believes he can resurrect the dead—turning his unsuspecting bride to stone. It was released on June 11, 1911 by Rex (a production house that later became part of Universal Pictures) and appears to have been a single reel in length.

Other horror films from Rex include *The Evil Power* (1913) and *A Night of Thrills* (1914). CW

The Ghost's Warning
Edison; b/w; 11(17) min; U.S.
D: Ashley Miller
Cast: Mary Fuller, Marc McDermott, Miriam Nesbitt, William Wadsworth, Ethel Browning, Darwin Kerr

The story of Mary Claire Fuller (1888-1973) is something of a true-life melodrama. One of cinema's first scream queens, she starred in over 200 silent movies between 1907 and 1917, including *Bluebeard* (1910), *Frankenstein* and *The House of the Seven Gables* (both 1910), *It Is Never Too Late to Mend* (1913) and *A Witch of Salem Town* (1915). She began her career with Vitagraph and moved on to Edison, where she worked frequently with director James Searle Dawley and fellow actor Charles Ogle. Her career took a major turn when fledgling company Universal hired her for heroine roles in their widely distributed films, but she retired from acting after suffering a nervous breakdown related to an affair she was having with a married man. She moved to Washington, D.C. and lived with her mother, whose death in the mid-1940s left Mary depressed and alone; she suffered a second breakdown in 1947 and remained in an institution until her death in 1973. She was buried in an unmarked grave in the city's famed Congressional Cemetery.

The Ghost's Warning was a one-reel thriller about a castle haunted by the spirit of a girl. Fuller played the daughter of a millionaire (Wadsworth), while Darwin Karr played an artist. This was one of Karr's earliest films. He went on to become the star of numerous films for Alice Guy's U.S.-based film company Solax. He also starred in Guy's *The Pit and the Pendulum* (1913). CW

Haunted Café
aka Das Verzauberte Café; Bewitched Restaurant
Messter; b/w; 7 min; Germany
P: Oskar Messter
Cast: Henny Porten

A man nods off while waiting for his food in a restaurant and dreams that the place is haunted. Various disturbing things assail him before he wakes up—just in time to eat his meal.

Oskar Messter's production company was responsible for this short film shot in Berlin. *Haunted Café* is packed with Méliès-style imagery and trick shots. People appear and disappear, furniture moves on its own, etc. It probably all seemed a bit hackneyed, even in 1911, with its it-was-all-a-dream twist-ending showing signs of wear even then. TH

A montage of four stills from *The Hunchback of Notre Dame*

The Haunted House
aka **La maison hantée**
Gaumont; b/w; 13 min; France
Credits unknown

A house, reputed to be haunted, is actually just a cover-up for a gang of criminals who have made the place their hideout.

Not to be confused with the same year's *The Haunted House* produced by IMP, this was more of a crime melodrama than an actual horror film. Gaumont later produced another film titled *The Haunted House* (1913), which was by all accounts far darker in nature than this film. TH

The Haunted House
IMP; b/w; 17 min; U.S.
D: William F. Haddock
Cast: King Baggot

Carl Laemmle's Independent Moving Pictures Company of America (IMP) was responsible for this short subject. Like so many so-called haunted house films of the period, the film utilizes the standard "the house isn't really haunted" sting in the tail. A man (Baggot) makes people believe that the spirits of the dead possess the house, though it's unclear exactly what his motivation is for this.

King Baggot went on to top-line IMP's *Dr. Jekyll and Mr. Hyde* two years later. He found some success as a writer and director before problems with alcohol prematurely derailed his career.

Director William F. Haddock was active until 1919, after which he apparently left pictures for good; he died in 1969. TH

The Hunchback
Cricks and Martin; b/w; 9 min; Great Britain
D: A.E. Coleby
Cast: Edwin J. Collins

A.E. Coleby's 1911 film *The Hunchback* bears only a fleeting resemblance to Victor Hugo's 1831 novel *Notre Dame de Paris*, which deals with the deformed bellringer of Notre Dame Cathedral and the Gypsy girl he attempts to rescue from a lecherous archdeacon named Frollo. This entry eschews the classic narrative, piggybacking instead on the then trendy idea of having an innocent hunchback (Collins) accused of a crime he didn't commit (a scenario that served as a minor subplot in Hugo's book). In revenge, the hunchback sets alight the home of the crime's real perpetrator, a local farmhand. The nature of the central crime may forever be unknown, as the film appears to be lost.

Coleby was a prolific actor, writer and director in the silent era. Though his film career began in 1907, he is best known for the series *The Mystery of Dr. Fu-Manchu* (1923), which began with *The Scented Envelopes* and ended with *The Shrine of the Seven Lamps*. He made his last film in 1929 and died the following year.

Edwin J. Collins starred as the hunchback, but he spent more of his career directing movies than he did acting in them. He took his own directorial dip into Hugo's novel with *Esmeralda* in 1922. CW

The Hunchback of Notre Dame
aka **Notre-Dame de Paris**; **Notre Dame de Paris**
Pathé; b/w; 26 min; France
D: Albert Capellani
Cast: Henri Krauss, Stacia Napierkowska, Claude Garry, René Alexandre, Jean Angelo, Paul Capellani, Jean Dax

One day while dancing for change in the atrium of Notre Dame Cathedral, a poor Gypsy girl named Esmeralda (Napierkowska) catches the attention of sexually frustrated archdeacon Claudio Frollo (Garry). Dedicated to the archdeacon is a lonely, deformed bellringer (Krauss)—looking remarkably like Charles Ogle in Edison's 1910 *Frankenstein*—who lives in the cathedral's towers. Under orders from his master, the wretch tries to kidnap Esmeralda, but he fails and is taken into custody by the handsome Phoebus (Alexandre), captain of the guards. The hunchback is sentenced to public humiliation in the stocks, where Esmeralda takes pity on him and gives him water. She falls in love with Phoebus, and as they rendezvous one evening, the archdeacon murders him and frames her for the crime. She's found guilty and sentenced to death, but the hunchback—who has fallen pitifully in love with her—comes to her aid and hides her in the castle tower. There Frollo makes a play for her, and when she rejects him, he leads authorities to her hideout. Again she's arrested, but this time there's no escape; she is hanged, and the hunchback takes revenge on Frollo by throwing him over the side of the cathedral to his death.

This adaptation of Victor Hugo's classic novel is remarkably faithful to its source material (minus a missing subplot or three, doubtless in deference to the film's compressed running length). It contains no discernable humor—unlike most other

Henri Krauss (as the hunchback bellringer) and Stacia Napierkowska (as the Gypsy Esmeralda) from *The Hunchback of Notre Dame*

horror films of the period—and this shift from the whimsical represents a bellwether of sorts for the genre. The film's production values also reflect this shift. While earlier scenes evoke the "fantastical" look of Georges Méliès' films, most of the film shows a marked trend toward a naturalism similar to that of filmmaker D.W. Griffith's future productions.

Like the novel on which it's based (which sat for years on the Catholic Church's Index of Banned Books), the film has an axe to grind with organized Christianity. Not only does it take place in and around the famous Notre Dame Cathedral in Paris, France, but also the Church's clergy is depicted as duplicitous and sadistic. The archdeacon lusts, commits murder and then tortures the woman he cannot have for a crime that he committed (in a chamber where the violence plays out beneath the holiest symbol in Christendom, the cross).

The Hunchback of Notre Dame was released in the United States in December 1911, just in time for Christmas! CW

Hypnotism

Lux; b/w; 11 min; France
Crew unknown
Cast: James Mapelli

This short French production from Lux is sometimes confused with Cesare Gani Carini's Italian production of 1912, *Ipnosi*, which starred James Mapelli and Brice Valerian (mother of filmmaker Sergio Leone).

An obscure film, *Hypnotism* is likely lost, as are most of Lux's early films. It trots out that popular theme of silent horror cinema: the evil hypnotist who captures a beautiful young girl in his mesmeric web (in this case compelling her to commit robbery). If this sounds like an abbreviated rip-off of George Du Maurier's *Trilby* (1894), that's because it is. CW

Inferno
aka **Dante's Inferno**; **L'Inferno**

Milano; b/w; 67 min; Italy
D: Francesco Bertolini, Adolfo Padovan, Giuseppe De Liguoro
C/FX: Emilio Roncarolo
Cast: Salvatore Anzelmo Papa, Arturo Pirovano, Giuseppe De Liguoro, Atilio Motta, Augusto Milla, Emilise Beretta

Among the best known of the many silent film adaptations of Dante Alighieri's *The Divine Comedy* (first penned between 1308 and 1321), *Inferno* is an example of pomp and circumstance without story. As it opens, the viewer is informed that Dante was so inspired by the beauty of a nine-year-old girl that he immortalized her with a poem. Thus did young Beatrice, who died at the age of 24, become a major character in one of the most famous literary works of all time.

The film begins with Dante ascending the hill of salvation, but the way is barred by three beasts representing Avarice, Pride and Lust; thankfully, the descending Beatrice asks the poet Virgil to rescue Dante and guide him through the Nine Circles of Hell (though the reason for her wanting him to do this isn't stated). Virgil obligingly takes over, and he and Dante enter a cave wherein they find the River Acheron, over which Charon ferries the dead to the depths of despair. The two visitors cross and on the other side meet those whom both Heaven and Hell deny, a group which includes Homer, Horace, Ovid and Lucanus. On their voyage, they also see Cleopatra, Dido, the Queen of Carthage, Helen of Troy and the traitor Caiphus, as well as a group of spendthrifts who are doomed to eternally roll their bags of gold around a narrow circle. They keep walking, and at times the film takes on an anthology feel as various people whom Dante meets—including Francesca Da Rimini and her lover Paulo, Count Ugalino and Peter of Vigna—tell their stories in flashback form. And while most of the film is realistic in its approach, the flashback segments are generally shot with a single painted backdrop, recalling the oddness of a Georges Méliès production.

Watching one vision of Hell after another, as striking as some of them are, gets repetitious in *Inferno*.

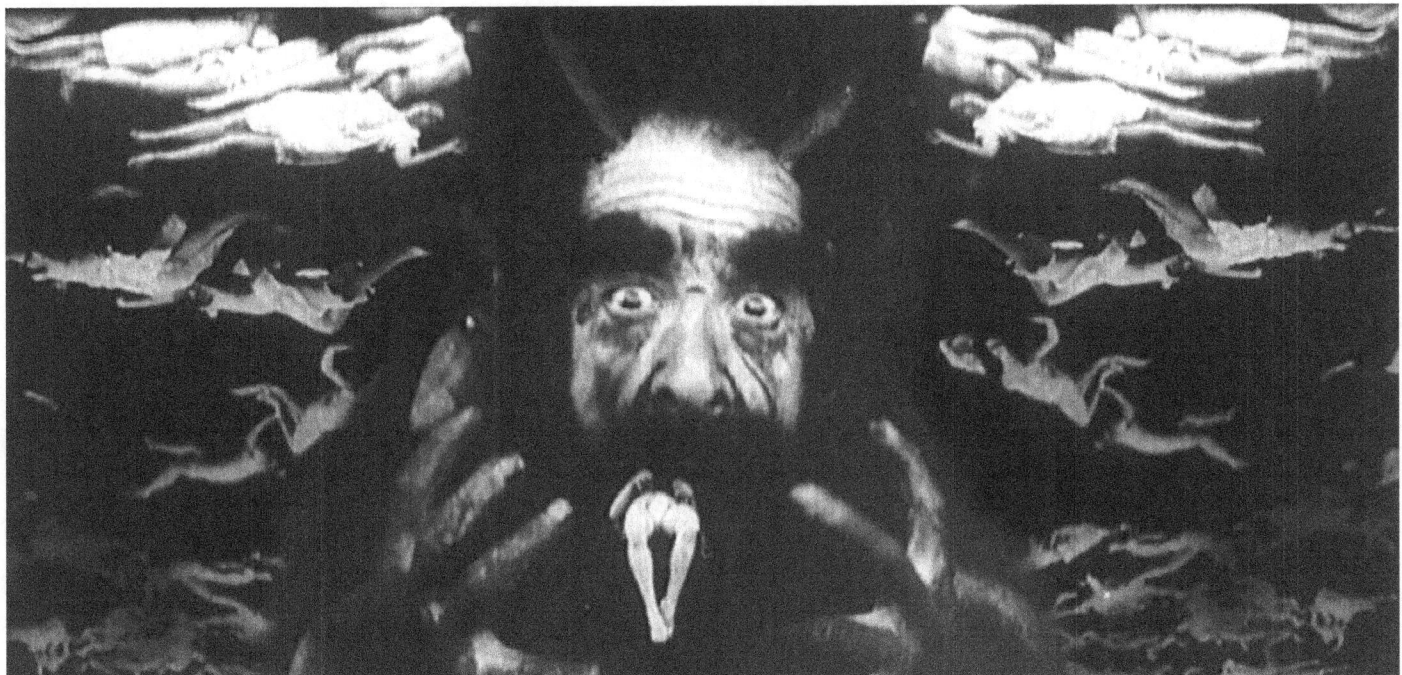
Inferno **features startling imagery, including the Devil eating a soul.**

The set designs by Francesco Bertolini and Sandro Properzi provide the film with its only possible reason for existence. There are some striking images to be found—flatterers half-buried upside-down in flaming muck; a giant, winged Lucifer feasting on the bodies of Brutus and Cassius while traitors frozen in ice look on, and the souls of suicides trapped in trees on which harpies feast are just a few of the more interesting ones. If it sounds like the film is a gruesome exercise in indulgence, that's because it is. Mohammed's chest and stomach are torn open and his entrails hang out; a wicked man carries his severed head in his hands and winged demons brutally whip a number of the damned. Others are forced to lie in rain they cannot drink, still others must bear the eternal heat of flames on their bodies. The brutal images have an obvious dual purpose—to scare people into belief while titillating them with what it pretends to condemn. To those ends, the film contains a then unprecedented amount of violence and nudity, with a long running time unusual for the period.

The special effects from cinematographer Emilio Roncarolo range from the mediocre (the animals representing Avarice, Pride and Lust; the three-headed Cerberus) to the magnificent (Dante and Virgil riding Geryon, a flying serpent with reptilian wings and the face of a man; an image of souls flying in great circles around the night sky). Yet even the best of the imagery cannot save the film as a whole. Watching one vision of Hell after another, as striking as some of them are, gets repetitious, and without a story (as opposed to a premise) or characters (as opposed to figures), the film plays like a big-budget spectacle meant to communicate the vastness of … not much. CW

It Is Never Too Late to Mend
Tait; b/w; 45 min; Australia
D/S: W.J. Lincoln *C:* Johnson and Gibson
Cast: Stanley Walpole

W.J. Lincoln's first feature film is also the first known adaptation of Charles Reade's once-popular novel *It Is Never Too Late to Mend: A Matter-of-Fact Romance*, initially published in 1856. The book, which tells the story of a squire who has a romantic rival thrown into prison, caused a furor in its day with its indictment of Great Britain's corrupt, abusive penal system. Primarily a melodrama, the tale is remarkably frank in its depiction of the darker aspects of prison life.

Lincoln's career was brief, beginning with this film and ending in 1916 with the release of the drama *La revanche* (*The Revenge*). He died in 1917 at about 47 years of age in Sydney, New South Wales, Australia. The film had its premiere on January 7, 1911 at the Olympia Theatre in Sydney, and with a release date so early in the year, one can conclude that it was actually shot sometime the year before.

The next adaptation of the novel was shot in the United States in 1913, though the most famous version didn't come until 1937. That adaptation starred Tod Slaughter as the evil squire. CW

Jones' Nightmare; or, The Lobster Still Pursued Him
aka **Jones' Nightmare**
Acme; b/w; 5 min; Great Britain
D: Fred Rains
Cast: Fred Rains

This was a more ambitious knock-off of Walterdaw's *The Lobster Nightmare*, which was produced the same year. A man named Mr. Jones (Rains) falls asleep and dreams that impish demons and a giant lobster chase him before he is shot to the moon. The special effects are typical of the period, utilizing trick photography—mostly of the stop and start variety—to achieve visual thrills.

The film was directed by and starred Fred (Frederick Williams) Rains, father of future Oscar-winner Claude Rains. Acme was Rains' own short-lived production company, which made films in 1910 and 1911. When the venture proved unsuccessful, the elder Rains left directing to focus entirely on his acting career, which ended in 1936, just three years after his son found major success in James Whale's classic *The Invisible Man*. Fred Rains died in London, England almost a decade afterward, in late 1945. CW

The Legend of the Lake
aka **La leggenda del lago**
Cines; b/w; 10 min; Italy
Credits unknown

Shot in 1911 and released in 1912, *The Legend of the Lake* is Cines' second take on the legend of the undines, the first being 1910's *The Spirit of the Lake*. This time around, however, adultery is replaced by murder. The water elemental that presides over a lake in Italy witnesses said crime and avenges the victim by summoning the murderers to their own deaths.

If the plot sounds stale and clichéd, that's because it is. Silent-era filmmakers hacked up numerous variations on the "vengeful water spirit" theme, most of them shot between 1909 and 1912. These included *The Princess and the Fisherman* (1909), *The Sorceress of the Strand* (1910), *The Fairy Jewel* (1911) and *An Indian Legend* (1912), among many others. CW

The Life of a Nun
aka **Nonnen fra Asminderod**; **The Nun**
Nordisk; b/w; 13 min; Denmark
Crew unknown
Cast: Edith Buemann Psilander, Lauritz Olsen, Otto Lagoni, Axel Mattson, Petrine Sonne, Carl Alstrup

This may very well be the first nunsploitation horror film ever made. It certainly clings to the conventions of that subgenre, which came into full lurid flower in trashy European cheapies during the 1970s and '80s. *The Life of a Nun* offers up an evil monk who lusts after a beautiful young virgin. When she refuses his advances, he persuades her father to place her in his monastery. The night before she is to be betrothed to Christ, however, she is discovered cavorting with a handsome lover. The boy is imprisoned and the girl taken to the monk's room, where he tries unsuccessfully to have his way with her, then accuses her of blaspheming the Holy Spirit and decrees that she be interred alive. In the end, a prince who had gotten the lowdown on her plight from her lover rescues her. The boy and girl marry, and the monk is taken into captivity.

As if to establish its horror credentials, the virginal heroine resists the monk's attack by brandishing a crucifix. The object stops him cold, effectively establishing him as a vampire. (This may have influenced comic book legend Bob Kane to create the Monk, a Batman foe who was very much a vampire; Kane freely acknowledged that silent films were a major influence on his work.) One must, of course, overlook the question of why the monk here is repelled by holy imagery yet lives in an active Christian monastery. CW

The Lobster Nightmare
Walturdaw; b/w; 6 min; Great Britain
Credits unknown

This was the first of two horror movies shot in 1911 that dealt with a man having a dream in which he is attacked by a giant lobster. It is likely that *The Lobster Nightmare* influenced the second such film, *Jones' Nightmare; or, The Lobster Still Pursued Him*. Both films are representative of an earlier, more innocent period in film history that focused on trick photography rather than the dramatic implications of cinema. In *The Lobster Nightmare*, a man falls asleep and has a dream in which he is pursued by imps and a monstrous lobster. If the film's plot sounds at all original, it becomes far less so when compared to a number of other films from the period, including the many nightmare productions of French *fantastique noir* pioneer Georges Méliès.

The film was one of the last produced by British studio Walturdaw, which, shortly after its release, decided to focus entirely on distribution. The company's last film in that capacity was Walter West's 1928 adaptation of *Sweeney Todd*, starring Moore Marriott as the villainous, throat-slitting barber.

The Lobster Nightmare should not be confused with Herbert M. Dawley's animated short of 1923, which bore the same name. CW

The Love of a Siren
aka **Amore di sirena**
Cines; b/w; 7 min; Italy
Credits unknown

After their success with 1909's *The Wonderful Pearl* (in which a pearl casts a spell over a man and lures him into the sea to drown) and 1910's *The Spirit of the Lake* (which dealt with the legend of the undines), Cines followed up with two very similar features in 1911. *The Legend of the Lake* was a return to the myth of the undines, while *The Love of a Siren* dealt with a boy who falls under the spell of a beautiful water spirit and is drawn to his death at her hands. The idea of gorgeous water-women casting spells over men—sometimes guilty of murder, sometimes innocent—was popular in the second decade of the 20th century. CW

The Masque of the Red Death
Ambrosio; b/w; length unknown; Italy
Credits unknown

Edgar Allan Poe's *The Masque of the Red Death: A Fantasy* was first published in *Graham's Magazine* in May 1842. The tale is set in an ancient abbey-turned-castle where Prince Prospero gathers his rich and noble friends to revel and feast, while outside the fortress walls a plague rages. Indifferent to the poor who suffer in the disease-infested countryside, Prospero throws a masquerade ball for his guests. The shindig takes place in seven rooms in the abbey, each painted a different color. As one of the guests—dressed like a plague victim—stalks through the ball, Prospero grows angry. He chases the specter into the final room, where it reveals itself to be the Red Death and curses Prospero and his companions to suffer the same fate as the neglected peasants.

This particular film version, which apparently didn't acknowledge Poe in its credits, was set in Naples, where a king lives in fear of a plague that is ravaging the countryside. He orders his court to accompany him to a castle in the country, taking along a poor woman and her two children, whom he hopes to corrupt. Inside the castle walls, he and his followers revel in adultery and sadism as the peasant woman prays to God for escape. Her prayers are answered when the Spirit of Death, brandishing a scythe, shows up and strikes down everyone—except for the peasant woman and her children.

***Purgatory* is the first and only sequel to *Inferno*, tracing Dante and Virgil's journey through Purgatory after they have exited Hell.**

According to Kevin J. Harty, author of the *The Reel Middle Ages* (McFarland Press, 2006), the film was "noteworthy for its chilling special effects." Unfortunately, little additional information about the film exists, though it seems to have influenced Charles Beaumont when he wrote the classic version of the tale, Roger Corman's *The Masque of the Red Death* (1964). CW

The Moonstone
Urban; b/w; 22 min; Great Britain
P: Charles Urban
Cast unknown

Like so many of Charles Urban's films, this—the second adaptation of Wilkie Collins' popular horror mystery *The Moonstone* (1868)—is considered lost. The plot followed the basic structure of Collins' story, though with an added focus on the supernatural. In the novel, a "cursed" diamond is stolen from its resting place on a Hindu idol's forehead. The gem is taken to Great Britain, where it falls into the hands of a beautiful young woman and is stolen from her on the night of her birthday. A series of narratives follow in which various suspects and amateur sleuths give their accounts of what happened on the night of the jewel's disappearance (and over the days and months that follow). *The Moonstone* was a two-reel feature, roughly twice as long as the first known adaptation, a 1909 U.S. production.

Writer Wilkie Collins (1824-1889) hit it big in 1850 with *Antonina*. A string of successes followed, including *The Woman in White* in 1860. (*Woman* provided the basis for several horror/mystery films, including five official silent adaptations). He was a good friend of author Charles Dickens, with whom he frequently traveled; and Dickens produced and starred in two of Collins' stage plays. Collins was a controversial figure in his day, as his analyses of social ills of the time frequently stepped on toes. And, perhaps even more daring, he refused to marry—opting instead to live with one mistress while keeping another ... and fathering several children in the process.

The next film with a cursed moonstone theme, *The Mystic Moonstone*, was produced in 1913, while the next official adaptation of *The Moonstone* was released in 1915. CW

The Mummy
Urban; b/w; 16 min; Great Britain
P: Charles Urban
Cast unknown

There were two films produced in 1911 with the title *The Mummy*, both of which were apparently more romantic than horrific. The first, made by the Thanhouser Company, starred William Garwood and Harry Benham. At 17 minutes long, it concerned a beautiful female mummy brought to life when electricity is accidentally sent through her body. The handsome Egyptologist overseeing the mummy becomes the object of her romantic inclinations, and the Egyptologist's fiancée becomes upset by the situation. (The idea of electricity bringing a mummy to life was an old one, first used in Jane Webb's 1827 novel *The Mummy! A Tale of the Twenty-Second Century*.)

Urban's film, then, was the second of the two. At 16 minutes, it concerned a professor who falls asleep in an Egyptian tomb and dreams that the mummy therein returns to life. Some sources have suggested that it was another version of *Le Roman de la Momie* by Theophile Gautier, which was first published 1857 and provided the basis for the 1910 film *The Romance of the Mummy*. CW

An Old Time Nightmare
Powers; b/w; length unknown; U.S.
Credits unknown

Giant birds threaten a youngster.

One can conclude from the title that the kid involved was threatened in a dream, only to wake up safe and sound at the film's conclusion. Too little information has survived about *An Old-Time Nightmare* to know whether the giant birds were modern flighted avians or the grounded terror birds of the prehistoric past. Five years after this film was made, the extinct terror bird Diatryma became the subject of its own science fiction comedy, *Prehistoric Poultry* (1916), with special effects by none other than a young Willis O'Brien!

Nightmare was released in September 1911 on a split reel with the humorous *Lost in a Hotel* (1911). Just as little is known about that film as is known about this one. CW

Purgatory
aka **Purgatorio**; **Purgatory and Paradise**; **Dante's Purgatorio**; **Paradise and Purgatory**
Helios; b/w; 22 min; Italy
D: Giuseppi Berardi, Arturo Busnego
Cast: Giuseppi Berardi, Armando Novi

In its first and only sequel to *Inferno* (1910), Helios Films continued the story of Dante who, with the poet Virgil as his guide, leaves Hell and embarks on a trip through Purgatory. There he meets the spirits so well known to the readers of Dante's *La Divina Commedia*. As each spirit tells its tale, the film flashes back to a scene in the Earthly realm, adhering closely to the structure of the previous film.

Purgatory was likely shot in the same deserted Appian Way quarry as the first film. It was followed the next year by Psiche's production of *Paradise*, which is often mistaken for a third film in the series. That misconception isn't helped by the fact that the latter two films, *Purgatory and Paradise*, were released together as a single feature in the U.S.A. All three films are considered lost.

One of the first film companies in Italy, Helios began making movies in 1900 with a documentary about the Pontine Marshes. That film was purchased and distributed by an ardent lover of cinema and proved quite successful throughout Europe, leading the fledgling Helios to pursue bigger and more lavish productions. The company's last film appears to have been produced in either 1915 or 1916 (sources don't agree). It's been alleged that a lawsuit brought by the American distributors of Milano's competing version of *Inferno* (1911) resulted in the company's quick departure from the Italian film scene. It made only a few horror-oriented titles, including *The Spell of the Hypnotist* (1912).

According to critics of the time, both the look and direction of *Purgatory* were superior to Milano's more famous adaptation of Dante's tale. CW

Queen of Spades
aka **La dama di picche**; **Pique Dame**; **La reina de espadas**
Cines; b/w; 8 min; Italy
Credits unknown

This is the first of two silent Italian versions of Russian writer Alexander Pushkin's *Pikovaya dama*, a short story written in 1833 and published the following year. Director Baldassarre Negroni made the second of these versions two years later. Some film historians maintain that the two adaptations are actually one and the same, but reliable documentation from the time indicates that this is not the case.

The cast and crew of this 1911 version are, however, unknown, and the film is lost. Even the British Film Institute, which has copies of both the 1910 and 1916 Russian versions, reveals little about this particular adaptation; it's therefore impossible to identify how closely it followed Pushkin's tale of a young Russian soldier who develops an unhealthy obsession with a fellow soldier's grandmother. Pushkin's original story tells how, after attending a game of cards, the soldier (named Hermann) learns that a countess once won a lot of money in three consecutive card games after learning the "secret of the cards" from a notorious occultist. Hermann develops a relationship with the old woman's ward, Lizaveta, but his designs to reap a reward from the old woman's knowledge don't go as planned . CW

Satan Defeated
aka **Satan Vaincu**
Pathé; b/w; 7 min; France
Credits unknown

This short film is believed lost, with no complete synopsis in existence. It is known to have contained a sequence in which Satan's face transforms into a series of ever more grotesque visages. One can conclude from the title that the Prince of Darkness is vanquished by the end, but how this comes about is anyone's guess. *Satan Defeated* was released on March 3, 1911, on a split reel with the documentary *Around Constantina, Algeria*. Pathé produced both films. TH/CW

Satan on Mischief Bent
Urban; b/w; length unknown; Great Britain
P: Charles Urban
Credits unknown

The Charles Urban Trading Company was behind this short feature, which details Satan's adventures in the city of Paris. Urban specialized in documentaries and travelogues. Given that he was fond of exotic locales (and that France is just across the English Channel from Great Britain), it's entirely possible that *Satan On Mischief Bent* made use of actual Paris settings. It is doubtful that Charles Urban directed this title, though he definitely produced it. Born in the United States, he moved to England in the early 1900s and established his eponymous production company. He also had a hand in the French-based Eclipse Company. He returned to the United States for a while during the early 1920s, where he continued to produce educational features, but then he moved back to the United Kingdom in the hopes of finding still greater success. Such success was not forthcoming, however, and his career met an untimely death before the coming of sound. TH

The Saving of Faust
aka **Faust sauvé des enfers**
Pathé; b/w; 11 min; France
Credits unknown

Very little is known about this minor French production from the Pathé Brothers, apart from its basic plot. Faust is freed from Purgatory to visit the city of Paris (presumably in contemporary times), where he does a good deed. As a result, he is forgiven for past misdeeds and, as per the title, given a deferment from Hell.

This was one of two *Faust* films made the same year—both of them in France, where the story appears to have been wildly popular. This one, it seems, had little to do with Goethe's actual story, instead serving as a sort of cinematic sequel. The other was Jean Durand's *Faust and Marguerite*, made for Gaumont. CW

She
Thanhouser; b/w; 25 min; U.S.
D: George Nichols *S:* Theodore Marston *P:* Edwin Thanhouser
Cast: Marguerite Snow, James Cruze, Viola Alberti, William C. Cooper, Irma Taylor, Harry Benham

In 350 B.C. Egypt, the Pharaoh's daughter Amenartes (Alberti) convinces Kallikrates (Cruze), a priest in the order of Isis, to elope with her. The two travel for two years, during which time they produce a male child. While on the coast of Africa, they come upon a giant stone bust known as Negro's Head. Little do they know that, watching them by sinister and magical means, a woman (Snow) called She-Who-Must-Be-Obeyed (by the superstitious natives who worship her) sees their approach and falls in love with Kallikrates. She summons them to her throne and bids Kallikrates to bathe in the fires of life, by which he will gain immortality. When he refuses, She strikes him dead. (Or so the intertitles tell the audience; the scene doesn't actually show his murder, instead displaying Kallikrates' prostrate body.) Amenartes takes her son and flees, vowing revenge.

Three thousand years later, Kallikrates' young male descendant Leo (played by actress Marie Eline) is orphaned. Raised by guardian Horace Holly (Cooper), Leo grows into a "fair and handsome" man (also Cruze, who is, frankly, neither fair nor handsome). Holly, on the other hand, is nicknamed "The Monster" due to his ugliness (despite the fact that he's far better looking than Leo, even with the ridiculous fake beard he sports). On his 25th birthday, Leo is entrusted with the contents of a chest, which include a letter spelling out his life's mission—find and destroy the evil She-Who-Must-Be-Obeyed—along with a map that shows the way. Leo and Holly embark upon the quest, and when they reach Negro's Head, She spies and summons them, believing Leo to be the reincarnation of her deceased love, Kallikrates. Leo attempts to strangle her, but She stays his hand, then gives him a dagger to finish the job. When he tries to follow through on the job, she makes the knife disappear. She then shows him the body of his former self before destroying it and revealing to Leo and Holly the source of her eternal youth. She begs Leo to join her as she bathes in the flames that have kept her young for three millennia. When he refuses, she jumps in anyway, but the flames have the opposite effect. It takes away the youth it had given, and She dies.

Thanhouser's take on H. Rider's Haggard's novel *She: A History of Adventure* (first serialized in *The Graphic* between October 1886 and January 1887) manages to be relentlessly dull despite its brief running time, and an obviously threadbare budget does nothing to convince audiences that the setting is anything other than an East Coast beach. Much of the film's action plays out in drab medium shots (with costumes apparently borrowed from a local repertory theater group), and its special effects are inane for the period, though the destruction of Kallikrates' body and She's subsequent death in the flames are admittedly well done.

This was the third film adaptation of Haggard's novel, after Georges Méliès' *Pillar of Fire* (1899) and Edison's *She* (1908). The next version, also titled *She*, saw release by Barker in 1916. Meanwhile, Thanhouser ripped off the story's plotline for the much less horrific *Hidden Valley*, also done in 1916. CW

Trilby and Svengali
Kinematograph; color; 17(15) min; Great Britain
D: Theo Frankel *P:* Charles Urban
Cast: Theo Frankel, Julie Meijer

Natural Colour Kinematograph produced an imposing 100 films between 1908 and 1914 that utilized an early two-color process. Films so shot were difficult to screen, requiring that theater owners upgrade to more expensive equipment, an idea few of them relished. Still, Kinemacolour was moderately successful in Europe. It was a different story in the United States, where it was held at bay by a Patent Office tasked with reducing competition against North American corporations by ostensibly "outsiders," namely European companies.

Trilby and Svengali is the very first color film adaptation of George Du Maurier's 1894 novel of the same title. Theo Frankel directed and also starred as Svengali, the mad hypnotist so obsessed with the gorgeous Trilby (Meijer) that he uses mesmerism to make her a famous singer, taking over her will in the process.

Like so many of Charles Urban's and George Albert Smith's early color films, this one appears to be lost. After losing a patent suit in 1914, Natural Colour Kinematograph folded. In the resulting confusion surrounding their titles, some sources erroneously list *Trilby and Svengali* as having been produced and released in 1912. CW

Willy the Ghost
aka **Willy Fantome**
Éclair; b/w; 7 min; France
D: Joseph Faivre
Cast: Willy Sanders

A ghost (Sanders) wreaks havoc. This horror spoof was part of a series of films built around young star Willy Sanders, who seems to have been a one trick pony. Between 1910 and 1916, he appeared in almost 70 titles—always as the same character, cleverly named "Willy." Born in England in 1906, Sanders entered films at the age of four; by the time he was 10, he had amassed more credits than many performers do in a lifetime. Curiously, he made his mark in France rather than in his native country. All of the Willy films were produced by Éclair, and few, if any, secured distribution elsewhere. Sanders passed away in 1990, having long been forgotten by his once-adoring public.

Director Joseph Faivre apparently helmed the majority of the Willy films, which may have been as much a curse as a boon. He doesn't seem to have achieved much outside of the franchise. His last known credit was in 1915. TH

The Witch of Abruzzi
Le Lion; b/w; 8 min; Belgium
Credits unknown

A witch curses a girl. This short came from Belgium-based studio Le Lion and appears to have been partly shot in France. (Abruzzi, by the way, was once located in what is now Italy and is today better known as Abruzzo.) Le Lion had previously produced *The Witch* (1909), but it's unclear whether there were any thematic connections between that title and this one. Both are believed to be lost, with little information available about either. TH

1912

Andalusian Superstition
aka **Superstition andalouse**; **Rêver réveille**
Iberico; color; 13 min; France
D/S/C/FX: Segundo de Chomon
Credits unknown

Segundo de Chomon directed this surreal short film, set in the world of the imagination. A young girl daydreams of exacting revenge on her hurtful boyfriend; the more she muses, the more elaborate and morbid her plans become.

Relying on imagery rather than intertitles (which were not commonly used in 1912), de Chomon creates a progressively uneasy atmosphere as sinister images escalate, culminating in visions of monsters inside a mysterious cavern. The film is hand-tinted with color, containing some striking visual effects. Though somewhat difficult to locate and screen, it does exist. TH

Baron Munchausen's Dream
aka **Le Hallucinations du Baron de Münchausen**; **Le aventures de baron de Münchausen**
Star Film/Pathé; b/w; 11 min; France
D/P/S/FX: Georges Méliès
Cast: Georges Méliès, Jeanne d'Alcy

Not so much based on Rudolf Erich Raspe's *The Surprising Adventures of Baron Münchausen* as an outright theft of the novel's lead character, *Baron Munchausen's Dream* is situated firmly in the Méliès tradition of nightmares and dreamscapes. After overindulging in food and spirits, Baron Munchausen is taken to a large sofa bed where he passes out. He immediately falls into a dreamful state, at first benign but later terrifying. In some of the best special effects shots of the director's career, Munchausen interacts with his dreams as they occur in the large mirror over his bed. The worst of his nightmares involve strange worlds wherein monstrous lizard men and humanoid insects live, water streams from living fountains comprised of the bodies of beautiful women, fire-breathing dragons populate caverns housing beast men and spider women and, in a scene most reminiscent of the director's previous work, a moon with a lolling tongue, prehensile snout, broken teeth and lopsided eyes terrorizes a horrified Baron. Munchausen awakens to an upset stomach and sore muscles, suggesting that his dreams might not have been dreams after all …

Many directors of the silent era adapted the stories of Baron Munchausen; a few even did so successfully. Méliès' version, while nowhere near the best and certainly not the most faithful, belongs not merely to a world of fantasy but to one of nightmarish horror. The director's next film was the epic science fiction fantasy, *The Conquest of the Pole* (1912). CW

Bébé and Spiritualism
aka **Bébé fait du spiritisme**
Gaumont; b/w; length unknown; France
D/S: Louis Feuillade
Cast: Rene Dary, Paul Manson

Bébé (Dary) and his father (Manson) are confronted with the supernatural in this comedic short tale. The Bébé (French for "baby") series, about the farcical adventures of a precocious child, got its start with *Bébé apache* (1910), which was an immediate hit with the public and made an overnight star of child actor Rene Dary. Given that Dary was only five when the franchise began, he would have been a comparatively over-ripe seven years old by the time this title arrived. Louis Feuillade directed all 64 installments in the series, and Dary was able to parlay his early success into a film career that lasted until his death in 1974. TH

Bertie's Book of Magic
Hepworth; b/w; 6 min; Great Britain
D: Frank Wilson
Cast unknown

A woman is transformed into a black cat in this comic short subject, which comes to a surprisingly grisly end when she is transformed back into human form … after a butcher has slit the cat's throat. There are a number of silent comedies that contain the character name Bertie in the title, but given that some of these were made in France (*Bertie and His Rivals*, 1911, for instance) while others, including this title, hailed from England, it is unclear whether they formed an actual series, or if any of them were connected at all.

Director Frank Wilson started off as an actor but found his true calling behind the camera. He directed over 200 titles between 1907 and 1922, with a specialty in slapstick comedy. TH

Billy's Séance
IMP/Universal; b/w; 13 min; U.S.
Crew unknown
Cast: John R. Cumpson, Charles Arling

This was a spoof of the mystically themed films so popular at the time. Billy (Cumpson) holds a séance, where things backfire in an amusing manner. John R. Cumpson specialized in comedic characterizations. His greatest success came from playing the role of Bumptious in a short series of comedies (e.g., *How Bumptious Papered the Parlor* and *The Joke They Played on Bumptious*, both 1910). His career was cut short when he died from complications related to diabetes and pneumonia in 1913. TH

Bob's Nightmare
Monofilm; b/w; 9 min; France
Credits unknown

French production company Monofilm was quite prolific during the early silent era, operating from 1911 to 1914. But unlike its competitors in the European market (which included Star Films, Pathé and Gaumont), Monofilm produced relatively few horror films. Indeed, *Bob's Nightmare* may have been the only one. (If there were others, any information about them is apparently long lost.) In *Nightmare*, the eponymous Bob has, yes, a nightmare in which he sees a ghostly couple dressed in white, along with a person being decapitated by a large knife. The plot device of presenting nightmarish incidents only to reveal that they were all part of a dream was introduced by Méliès and quickly became a cliché of the silent era. CW

The Brute
Champion; b/w; 11 min; U.S.
D: Ulysses Davis *P:* Mark M. Dintenfass
Cast unknown

In cinema's earliest days, filmmakers realized the moralizing potential of celluloid. A reactionary subgenre of horror film arose where alcohol was depicted as a demon corrupting otherwise respectable men, destroying their lives and driving them to despair. Such films included *The Drunkard's Conversion* (1901), *D.T.'s, or the Effect of Drink* (1905) and *The Man and His Bottle* and *Too Much Champagne* (both 1908). Released on January 22, 1912, *The Brute* was of the same stripe, with the Grim Reaper stalking an alcoholic in anticipation of snatching the man's soul.

Another film of a similar nature, *Distilled Spirits*, followed in 1915. CW

Conscience
aka **The Chamber of Horrors**
Vitagraph; b/w; 10 min; U.S.
D: Maurice Costello *P:* Albert E. Smith
Cast: Rose Tapley, Maurice Costello, Robert Gaillard, Julia Swayne Gordon, Mary Maurice, Van Dyke Brooke

Eleanor (Tapley) elopes to New York with her lover Eric (Costello), but after marriage and the arrival of a baby, he abandons her. When Eleanor attempts to steal milk for her infant, a policeman pursues her. She takes refuge in a chamber of horrors, where her fate—and that of her errant husband—is sealed.

Born in Pittsburgh, Pennsylvania, Maurice Costello had a lengthy career as a character actor, amassing over 250 credits in that capacity, though many of his sound-era appearances went unbilled. As a director, he racked up 79 credits between 1910 and 1915, though many of his films, including this macabre melodrama, were short subjects made before feature-length products were common. Costello is credited with discovering Moe Howard of The Three Stooges. He was also the grandfather of John Drew Barrymore (the product of the marriage between his daughter, actress Dolores Costello, and John Barrymore; Costello was dead-set against the marriage, which did indeed end disastrously) and the great-grandfather of Drew Barrymore.

The plot synopsis of *Conscience* sounds intriguing enough, but one can only guess whether much was made of the "chamber of horrors" locale. The film has long been considered lost, making an informed evaluation of its merits impossible. Some sources credit co-star Van Dyke Brooke with co-directing the picture. TH

Convicted by Hypnotism
aka **A Double Life**; **Double vie**
Éclair; b/w; 30 min; France
D: Victorin-Hippolyte Jasset *S:* Robert Boudrioz *C:* Lucien N. Andriot
Cast: Cecile Guyon, Charles Krauss, Josette Andriot, A. Bahier

The old "hypnotism used to accomplish evil" bit, already stale in 1912, is beaten still deeper into the ground in this French production. This time out, an unscrupulous husband (Krauss) uses hypnosis to compel his wife (Guyon) to murder her father (Bahier).

Victorin-Hippolyte Jasset was a multi-talented artist, racking up credits as a director, writer, production designer and costume designer before his untimely death in 1913. *Convicted by Hypnotism* was one of his later films. Star Cecile Guyon was popular with French audiences of the period, but her career, too, ended early when she died in 1927 at the age of 36. Some sources mistakenly credit another actress with a similar name (Lucille Guyon) as *Convicted by Hypnotism*'s lead. TH

The Curse of the Hindoo Pearl
aka **The Curse of the Hindu Pearl**
American Standard; b/w; 37 min; U.S.
Credits unknown

Though some sources credit *The Curse of the Hindoo Pearl* to D.W. Griffith at American Mutoscope and Biograph, there is little evidence to support this assertion. Rather, it appears to have been made and released by American Standard, with the director's name lost to time. Regardless of who worked behind the camera, it's obvious that the film was yet another in a long line of knock-offs of Wilkie Collins' classic novel *The Moonstone* (1868), with a plot concerning an accursed pearl that brings death to those who possess it. CW

The Diabolical Box
Urbanora; b/w; 6 min; Great Britain
Credits unknown

This obscure, long-lost British short depicted an imp who transforms into an animal and goes on a rampage.

Production company Urbanora was an offshoot of Charles Urban's Urban Trading Company. While Urban tended to focus on documentaries and educational subjects, Urbanora appears to have been developed for less sophisticated fare. (By the same token, Urban's Kinematograph was set up to release bigger-budgeted, color fare.)

Some sources list the date of production for *The Diabolical Box* as 1911. TH

Dr. Jekyll and Mr. Hyde
Thanhouser; b/w; 12 min; U.S.
D: Lucius Henderson *S:* Thomas Sullivan *P:* Edwin Thanhouser
Cast: James Cruze, Florence La Badie, Marie Elnie, Jane Gail, Marguerite Snow, Harry Benham

Respected scientist Dr. Jekyll (Cruze) uses drugs to separate the two sides of the human personality. His experiments climax when he uses the drugs on himself, unleashing a vicious, animalistic alter ego who calls himself Mr. Hyde. Jekyll is mortified when Hyde commits crimes in the town, but his efforts to keep his other self in check prove futile. All the while, he continues to romance the local minister's daughter (La Badie). Things take a tragic turn when Hyde murders the woman's father, forcing him into a life or death struggle with the police.

Given its obvious potential for dramatic realization, it's not surprising that a stage adaptation first hit theaters a scant year after the book's original publication. Richard Mansfield made a major impression in Thomas Russell Sullivan's popular play, which reportedly ran for 20 years! So vivid was his performance that one impressionable theatergoer accused the actor of being the sought-after Jack the Ripper. (Apparently the well-meaning but presumably naïve Londoner felt that no actor could so convincingly play a psychotic without actually being unbalanced!)

It didn't take long for early filmmakers to tap into the material's potential, either, with the first cinematic version on record emerging from producer William N. Selig in 1908. Though a lost film today, it is of historical importance as the one that got the ball rolling. In the four years between that film and Henderson's, no fewer than three other film versions were made, not all of them authorized. Here, the filmmakers opted to go to the Sullivan stage adaptation for inspiration rather than adapt Stevenson's book. The obvious advantage was that, within the framework of a 12-minute narrative, the play offered a basic compendium of potted highlights from which to draw inspiration. By the same token, it would have been unreasonable to expect such a short subject to fully explore the rich vein of material offered by Stevenson's template.

Seen today, Henderson's film is little more than a curio, but it's easy to imagine the impression it made at the time. James Cruze portrays Jekyll as a well-meaning, middle-aged, bourgeois scientist. Nothing is really shown of his practice or his conflict with his stuffy superiors and colleagues; the film instead cuts immediately to the chase by introducing Jekyll as he experiments on himself. Cruze doesn't make much of an impression early on,

James Cruze portrays the tormented Dr. Jekyll (top) and the hideous Mr. Hyde (bottom), from *Dr. Jekyll and Mr. Hyde*.

but upon his transformation into Hyde, he cuts loose and delivers a memorable bit of pantomime acting.

The first transformation is surprisingly striking. It unfolds in a single take and makes use of a seamless lap dissolve as he morphs into an impish and violent sociopath. Alas, the film fails to capitalize on the character's baser elements, limiting his reign of terror to a briefly glimpsed shot of Hyde knocking over a small child and then strangling Jekyll's prospective father-in-law—changed per the stage play from a pompous aristocrat to a pious minister—in a fit of rage. As such, Hyde is never allowed to develop into a genuine menace. Instead, he comes across like an unrestrained child who is allowed to run amok by a distracted parent.

The make-up is crude but mildly effective, halfway between the grotesquerie of Fredric March and the more recognizably human boogeyman portrayed by John Barrymore in the famed 1920 version. The film ends rather limply as Hyde holes up in the lab and poisons himself while the police pound at his door.

Henderson's direction is simple and efficient, with plenty of static shots and anonymous shot compositions, but it gets the job done. Production values are slim as well, with the closet-like set standing in for Jekyll's laboratory being the worst offender.

On the whole, the film doesn't rank among the most memorable takes on Stevenson's story, but it is reasonably diverting for genre completists. TH

The Fatal Pact
aka Le pacte fatal
Pathé; b/w; 7 min; France
Credits unknown

This supernatural-themed comedic short dealt with an inveterate gambler who promises a genie that he will give up his hobby. However, the temptation is too strong, he breaks his vow and the genie retaliates by making the gambler disappear. The film almost certainly utilized trick photography as it sought to capitalize on the public's interest in gambling and table games. TH

The Fatal Pearl
aka La perla sanguinosa
Aquila; b/w; 8 min; Italy
Credits unknown

This is something of a knock-off of Cines' 1909 horror entry *The Wonderful Pearl*. As its title suggests, it concerns a cursed pearl with the mysterious power to cause the untimely deaths of its possessors.

Considering the fact that *The Fatal Pearl* received its first known theatrical release in January 1912, it was likely shot in late 1911. It bears no relation to the 1914 horror film *The Mystery of the Fatal Pearl*, which was produced in the United States and was a feature-length film. CW

Faust
Natural Color Kinematograph; color; length unknown; Great Britain
P: Charles Urban
Cast unknown

A companion piece to Charles Urban's *Mephisto* (also 1912), *Faust* was shot in color in obvious response to similarly enhanced versions from French film companies Star and Pathé. But unlike the colorizing methods of those companies, Kinemacolor involved neither hand-painting nor stenciling. Rather, a mechanical two-color process was used that resulted in a slightly more natural look than that obtained from handwork, though with some fringing of individual images within a frame.

Little is known about this particular lost version of *Faust*, but there's no reason to suppose it was much different from the many other silent versions of Goethe's tragic tale. The story dealt with an old man, regretful that he's spent his life in study and quiet solitude, who sells his soul to the Devil in exchange for youth, vitality and a chance at love with the beautiful Marguerite. But deals with the Devil never go as planned, and after a series of disasters, Faust's spirit is borne to Hell.

Urban's next color horror film was a version of *Dr. Jekyll and Mr. Hyde* (1913). CW

Feathertop

Éclair/American Standard; b/w; 15 min; France/U.S.
Crew unknown
Cast: Muriel Ostriche, Julia Stuart

This is the second film adaptation of Nathaniel Hawthorne's story *Feathertop: A Moralized Legend* (1852). It stars Murial Ostriche as Polly Gookin, the virtuous daughter of a squire against whom an old witch (Julia Stuart) bears a grudge. The crone creates a scarecrow, imbues it with life and sends it into the Gookin household to destroy it from within. But the scarecrow-turned-man falls in love with Polly and destroys himself to save her.

Ostriche (1896-1989) had already established her horror credentials with *The Raven* (1912), and she and Stuart went on to star in Éclair/American Standard's *The Legend of Sleepy Hollow* (1912), which was based on a short story by Washington Irving. Ostriche starred in numerous films through 1921, but her involvement in horror seems to have waned after 1912, when she ditched her home studio Éclair for the much-bigger and more successful Thanhouser.

The next adaptation of Hawthorne's story came the very next year and is the most obscure: Charles Urban's color treatment, also known as *Feathertop*. CW

Gavroche and the Spirits

aka **Gavroche et les spirits**; **Funnicus' Ghost**; **Funnicus and the Ghost**
Éclair; b/w; length unknown; France
D: Romeo Bosetti
Cast: Paul Bertho

A bumbling character known as Gavroche (Bertho) has a run-in with some ghosts. In addition to helming the Patouilliard series (which includes *Bill Taken For a Ghost*, 1911), Italian-born Romeo Bosetti was also responsible for the comedic short films of the Gavroche franchise. Gavroche was introduced to audiences with *Les débuts amoureux de Gavroche* in 1912, and he appeared on screen frequently until *Gavroche cul-de-jatte* in 1914. All told, the Gavroche character made his way through more than 40 short subjects in the course of only a couple of years.

Interestingly, star Paul Bertho also played Patoulliard. A popular comic performer in his day, Bethro has since fallen into complete obscurity. Very few of his films were shown outside of their native France, which may help explain his lack of fame. TH

The Ghost of Sulphur Mountain

Star Film/American Wild West; b/w; 11 min; U.S.
Co-D: Robert Goodman *Co-D/P:* Gaston Méliès
Cast: Francis Ford

While some sources cite this film as being co-directed by brothers Gaston and Georges Méliès, it's more likely that it was produced by Gaston, who lived in the United States at the time, and directed by Robert Goodman (though Gaston was not above taking directorial credit for other people's work, as he attempted to do with some of his brother's pictures).

The Ghost of Sulphur Mountain was shot in and around Ventura County, California in early 1912. It has been alleged that, just two days before the sinking of the *Titanic*, the film's stars got into a fight at the Glen Tavern Inn, where Gaston supposedly spent much of his time during the film's shooting (possibly because of the brothel on the second floor). Though he returned to his native France soon afterward, it's said that Gaston's spirit still roams the Inn's corridors in search of women and alcohol. Though highly doubtful, it's fun to contemplate, given that *Sulphur Mountain* was—as one might guess from the title—about the ghost of a man who haunts an old mine.

The film was copyrighted and released on April 18, 1912, less than a week after production officially wrapped. CW

Ghosts

Essanay; b/w; 11 min; U.S.
Crew unknown
Cast: Norman MacDonald, Joseph Allen, Sr., Frank Dayton, Charles Huntington, Eleanor Blanchard, E.H. Calvert

This apparently lost title depicts a haunted house. While cast credits have survived, there is no record of who worked behind the scenes on the film. It was produced by the Essanay Film Manufacturing Company, which was founded in Chicago, Illinois in 1907 by George K. Spoor and Gilbert M. Anderson. They found their greatest commercial success with Westerns and Charlie Chaplin comedies, including the classic *The Tramp* (1915). Chaplin was reportedly unhappy at Essanay, however, and when he left to work for other companies, the studio responded by creating their own Chaplin films out of outtakes and cut footage from the previous films he had made for them. The ruse didn't fool audiences; those "films" were by and large unsuccessful, and Warner Bros. bought the studio in 1925.

This film was one of two films bearing the title *Ghosts* that appeared in 1912. Cecil M. Hepworth produced the other. TH

Ghosts

Hepworth; b/w; 7 min; Great Britain
D: Hay Plumb *P:* Cecil M. Hepworth
Cast: Harry Buss, Ivy Close, Austin Melford

Not to be confused with an Essanay production of the same name from the same year, *Ghosts* was a depiction of supernatural visions. It is unclear what the tone of the film was, but director Hay Plumb was an old hand at melodrama and action.

Leading lady Ivy Close—who won a "most beautiful woman in the world" contest held by Great Britain's *The Daily Mirror*—later married Elwin Neame, with whom she had two children. One of those children, Ronald Neame, became a major cinematographer (*Blithe Spirit*, 1945) and director (*The Horse's Mouth*, 1958) in his own right. TH

The Herncrake Witch

Heron; b/w; length unknown; Great Britain
D/S: Mark Melford *P:* Andrew Heron
Cast: Jakidawdra Melford, Mark Melford

This obscure short dealt with a witch named Jakidawdra (Melford). That the witch's name is the same as that of the actress who played her suggests that director Mark Melford was having a bit of fun with the material. It seems likely that Mark was the father or uncle of Jakidawdra, whose film career seems to have begun and ended with this title.

Mark Melford racked up a few credits as a writer, director and actor and indeed he wore all three hats for this production.

A forgotten figure from the silent era, he died in 1914, but film and theater appears to have been in his family's bloodline. His nephews Austin and Jack went on to successful careers in their own right; Austin worked primarily as a writer (though he also dabbled in acting and directing), while Jack was a familiar face in many British films and television shows produced between 1931 and his death in 1972 (his last horror credit was as the Bishop in famed horror production company Hammer's *Lust for a Vampire*, 1970). TH

The Hindoo Charm
Lubin; b/w; 18 min; U.S.
D: Maurice Costello *S:* Eugene Mullin
Cast: Maurice Costello, Clara Kimball Young, James Young, William V. Ranous, Helene Costello, Dolores Costello

Clara Kimball Young

A wife (Young) sticks a pin in a voodoo doll, and her husband (Costello) experiences pain. This early voodoo-themed film (though voodoo is in fact a West African, not Hindu, tradition) is something of a family affair. Director/star Maurice Costello cast his daughters, Dolores and Helene Costello, in key supporting roles. Co-star Clara Kimball Young plays Costello's wife, with her real-life spouse, James Young, in a supporting role. Both appeared in other horror-tinged titles at various stages in their careers. Maurice Costello appeared in *Conscience* (1912) and *The Man Who Couldn't Beat God* (1915), both of which he also directed, and he later made an un-credited appearance in the Boris Karloff vehicle *The Climax* (1944). Kimball Young later played lead roles in *Lola* (1914, directed by husband James) and Maurice Tourneur's *Trilby* (1915). Her later years were marred by bad publicity—stemming from a well-publicized affair that resulted in the dissolution of her first marriage—and unworthy vehicles such as *The Return of Chandu* (1934), with Bela Lugosi. TH

In the Shadow of the Sea
aka **Der Schatten des Meeres**; **The Sea's Shadow**
Messters Projektion; b/w; 20 (38) min; Germany
D: Curt A. Stark *P:* Oskar Messter *C:* Carl Froehlich
Cast: Lizzy Krueger, Henry Porten, Frau Retzlag, Curt A. Stark

An unhappy painter (Krueger) whose married lover has committed suicide is compelled to commit suicide by the shadowy specter of Death, which she accomplishes by hurling herself into the sea.

This lost subject boasts an intriguing concept. It would seem an ideal candidate for the Expressionist school of cinema—its time, country of origin and the idea of a shadowy image of Death suggest such—but nothing exists to indicate with certainty that it was in any way influenced by the movement. So while it's tantalizing to think that it may have been a forerunner of sorts to Fritz Lang's *Destiny* (1921), in lieu of any surviving materials, it is impossible to get a feel for either the film or its merits.

Shadow was produced by Oskar Messter, who is generally considered to be Germany's first cinema pioneer, thanks to his invention of a film projector and the creation of the first production company in the country. Between 1896 and 1917 he produced (and frequently directed) hundreds of films before selling his film holdings to UFA, a government-run company that specialized in war propaganda. UFA would, in due course, be privatized and become a major producer of genre films. TH

An Indian Legend
Broncho; b/w; 11 min; U.S.
D: Francis Ford *S:* E. Kershaw *P:* Thomas H. Ince
Cast: Ethel Grandin Anna (Ann) Little, Robert Stanton, Grace Cunard, Sherman Bainbridge

Two films titled *An Indian Legend* (one released in 1911, the other in 1912) were shot approximately one year apart, and information on them has become intertwined in film history references. Neither appears to exist today, and sources differ on who directed which, with some stating that this version was directed by Charles Giblyn and written by Harry G. Stafford. Either way, it focused on an old Native American legend wherein the spirit of a murdered Indian girl haunts the lake in which she drowned. CW

The Knight of the Snows
aka **Le Chevalier des neiges**
Star Film/Pathé; b/w; 16 min; France
D/P/S/FX: Georges Méliès
Cast: Georges Méliès, Jeanne d'Alcy

For his last Devil-themed picture, Méliès tells the story of an evil knight (though not the knight of the title) who, wishing to betroth a beautiful princess, makes a pact with Satan (Méliès) and his minions. In exchange for the knight's soul, the Devil agrees to kidnap the princess and take her to the knight's castle. This he does in a carriage led by a dragon that looks conspicuously like a winged ankylosaur (making a return engagement after its star turn in *Baron Munchausen's Dream*, 1911). The princess' beau, the good knight of the title, follows in a ship helmed by an angel and surrounded by the powers of light. After the princess' rescue, the evil knight is captured and taken to the gallows, but before he can be put to death, the Devil takes him to an even worse fate in Hell.

In *Knight*, Méliès betrays a rudimentary sense of editing and pacing, but it's too little, too late. The cinema he helped create had passed him by, and it was simply too late in the game to experiment further with processes that others had long ago perfected. For this reason, many of Méliès' native contemporaries, such as Alice Guy, went on to make some of the most ingenious horror films of the period (*The Pit and the Pendulum*, 1913, for example), while Méliès lagged behind and finally fell to the wayside. Fortunately, he lived to see a revival of interest in his work throughout the 1920s and 1930s, and in 1931 was awarded the French Legion of Honor.

His last actual film, *The Voyage of the Bourrichon Family* (1913), though a comedy, does contain some of his classical horror elements, including a haunted inn; but such scenes are simply too insignificant to the film for it to be considered an entry into the horror genre. And it was doubtless too old-fashioned to have any sort of impact on audience of its day, though some of the scenes of moving furniture, like those in *The Inn Where No Man Rests* (1903), prefigure *The Exorcist* (1973).

Méliès died of cancer in 1938 and is buried in Père Lachaise Cemetery alongside such notables as writer Oscar Wilde and rock musician Jim Morrison. CW

The Legend of Sleepy Hollow
aka **Sleepy Hollow**
Éclair/American Standard; b/w; 11 min; France/U.S.
D: Étienne Arnaud
Cast: Alec B. Francis, John G. Adolfi, Louis R. Grisel, Lamar Johnstone, Isabel Lamon, George Larkin, Murial Ostriche

The second known film adaptation of Washington Irving's classic tale, set in Sleepy Hollow near Tarry Town, New York, was a single-reel, somewhat truncated, effort. Fear-ridden schoolmaster Ichabod Crane is in love with Katrina Van Tassel, but he has a rival—the brutish prankster Abraham Van Brunt, known as "Brom Bones" amongst the townspeople. After leaving a party at the estate of Katrina's father late one autumn night, Crane is pursued by the apparent horse-riding spirit of a headless Hessian mercenary killed during the Revolutionary War. (Well, not *exactly* headless; the specter appears to have his displaced head fixed on the saddle's knob.) Believing that evil cannot cross running water and that a church is nearby, Crane races toward a bridge on the outskirts of town .... The next day Crane's still-saddled horse Gunpowder is found munching grass near the schoolmaster's front gate. Dusty foot tracks from the late-night flight are also discovered, along with Crane's hat in the brook, near the remnants of a shattered pumpkin. From that point on, the mention of Crane's name causes Van Brunt to snap to attention. Thus does writer Irving suggest that it was Van Brunt who took after Crane, either running him out of town or murdering him to remove competition for Katrina's hand in marriage.

By all accounts, Étienne Arnaud's film, like the 1980 made-for-American-television version (starring Jeff Goldblum as Crane and Dick Butkus as Van Brunt), focused on the comedic aspects of the tale—though the fact that it deals with a possible ghost with a jack-o'-lantern for a head is enough to warrant its inclusion here.

Other film versions of the story include *The Headless Horseman* (1922), a silent adaptation starring Will Rogers, and *The Adventures of Ichabod and Mr. Toad* (1949), an animated Walt Disney film that melded the tale with Kenneth Grahame's 1908 children's book *The Wind in the Willows*. But the most straightforwardly horrific version to date remains Tim Burton's Hammer-influenced Gothic, *Sleepy Hollow* (1999). CW

Lucrezia Borgia
Film d'Art; b/w; length unknown; Italy
D: Gerolamo Lo Savio *S:* Ugo Falena
Cast: Vittorio Lepanto, Achille Vitti, Gustavo Serena, Giovanni Pezzinga

There is so much conflicting information about films on the life of Lucrezia Borgia that it's difficult to definitively sort it all out. The spotty cinematic record keeping of the early 1900s and the number of countries and languages involved further complicate such a project. Still, the weight of evidence suggests that while three films about the Borgias are credited to Gerolamo Lo Savio and one to Ugo Falena, Falena's film is actually this production from Lo Savio.

After the success of Mario Caserini's *Lucrezia Borgia* for Cines in 1910, production studio Film d'Arte Italiana hired that film's assistant director, Gerolamo Lo Savio, to make his own film about the Borgias, a sexually amoral family of murderers who rose to Italian prominence after father Rodrigo's appointment as Pope Alexander VI.

This 1912 film seems subject to confusion with two French productions made by Pathé the same year. Those films, *Cesare Borgia* and *Lucrezia Borgia*, each focused on one of two apparently incestuous siblings (it has been suggested that Lucrezia may have borne Cesare a child between her first two marriages), the first of which may have been sparked by the publication of Rafael Sabatini's nonfiction book *The Life of Cesare Borgia*, released earlier in the year.

Director Lo Savio's version was written by Falena, himself a director who had something of a fascination with seductive women of history and/or literature, including *Beatrice Cenci* and *Salomé* (1910), *Francesca da Rimini* (1911), Isolda of *Tristan and Isolda* and Juliet of *Romeo and Juliet* (both 1912), *Beatrice d'Este* (1912) and *Lilly Pussy* and *Anna Karinene* (both 1917), among others.

For this film, Lo Savio cast Vittorio Lepanto as the murderous Lucrezia, who hides poison in a hollow ring and slips it to her enemies, with Achille Vitti as her violent brother Cesare, who will stop at nothing to attain greater power for the Borgia family. Giovanni Pezzinga portrayed Lucrezia's third and final husband, Alfonso d'Este. CW

A Magnetic Influence
Urbanora; b/w; 8 min; Great Britain
P: Charles Urban
Cast unknown

Prolific silent-era producer Charles Urban founded several production companies during his career. Urbanora was one of these. Under the Urbanora banner, the man made numerous films, including this one, which served up the then-popular *Trilby* motif: An evil hypnotist exerts control over a beautiful young girl.

The title comes from the fact that some people once considered hypnotism to be based on a scientific principle similar to magnetism. CW

The Mask of Horror
aka **Le Masque of d'horreur**; **La maschera dell'orror**
Le Film Francais; b/w; length unknown; France
D/S: Abel Gance
Cast: Édouard de Max, Charles de Rochefort, Florelle, Mathilde Thizeau, Jean Toulout

Abel Gance was a premier talent during the early years of French cinema, following closely on the heels of Alice Guy, the world's first major female director. Like Guy, Gance started out making trick-photography films and graduated to serious dramas. *The Mask of Horror* straddles the line between the two with its depiction of an insane sculptor who, to provide a model for a bust, turns his face into a mask of horror. Standing before a mirror, he smears himself with blood, then swallows poison to induce painful facial contortions for his own observation and study.

While the most famous film of his career is doubtless the silent *Napoléon* (1927), Gance had a soft spot for horror. His next work as director in the genre was the bizarre short *A Drama of the Castle, or Do the Dead Return?* (1915), followed by the anti-war film *J'Accuse* (1919) and in later years by the comedy-tinged *Au Scours* (1924), the melodramatic *Lucrezia Borgia* (1935) and a second and even more overtly horrific version of *J'Accuse* (1938).

Actress Ruth Roland was a major star in silent era Westerns and comedies.

Gance began his film career as an actor and screenwriter. In 1911 he started Le Film Francais, his own production company, and in 1912 he married *The Mask of Horror* star Mathilde Thizeau, who retired from acting shortly thereafter. (She was the first of three wives Gance would eventually have.) Gance's talent was such that when he traveled to the United States in the early 1920s and met D.W. Griffith, he was immediately offered a Hollywood job. He declined, preferring instead to return to his native country to continue working autonomously. CW

Mephisto
Natural Color Kinematograph; color; length unknown; Great Britain
P: Charles Urban
Cast unknown

With the debut of George Albert Smith and Charles Urban's two-color Kinemacolor process in 1909, a series of short "actuality films" were released to exploit it. These included *Representatives of the British Isles, View of the Brighton Front, Carnival Scenes at Nice and Cannes, Riviera Coast Scenes* and *Swans*, among many others. Believing that audiences were equally interested in seeing high drama shot in color, Charles Urban stepped down as president of Urban Trading Company and formed Natural Color Kinematograph, producing a series of fictional films based on great works of literature or opera. Most were shot and released in 1912, including *Faust, The Scarlet Letter* and *Robin Hood*, while *Dr. Jekyll and Mr. Hyde* followed in 1913. Also included was a version of *Mephisto*, which was likely a precursor to the aforementioned *Faust*. It, along with the rest of the company's output, is lost. There were probably few prints to begin with, given the difficulty and expense of producing them. By 1916, Kinemacolor had fallen to the wayside, squeezed out by constant improvements in color technology. It certainly didn't help any that many viewers of Kinemacolor programs complained of headaches as a result of color fringing on the images. CW

The Mummy
Britannia; b/w; 6 min; Great Britain
D: A.E. Coleby
Cast unknown

A mix of science fiction, horror and comedy, *The Mummy* gives viewers one Professor Darnett, who has invented an elixir that can bring the dead back to life. What he doesn't know is that his assistant is in love with his daughter. When the assistant learns what the professor has done, he fixes upon an idea to take advantage of the doctor's newfound discovery to marry the man's daughter. But in order to succeed, the assistant must pretend to be a living mummy.

This wasn't Coleby's first flirtation with the world's fascination with Egyptian mummies. Two years before he'd made *Wanted—A Mummy*, in which two penniless men devise a scam in which one pretends to be a living mummy to procure money from a desperate professor. CW

The Mummy and the Cowpuncher
Kalem; b/w; 5 min; U.S.
Crew unknown
Cast: Ruth Roland, John E. Brennan, Otto Lederer, Robert Barry, Vincente Howard

Actress Ruth Roland was a major star in silent-era Westerns and comedies. Born to artistic parents in 1892, her mother died in the year 1900 and an aunt raised her. After establishing herself as a vaudeville act, she was "discovered" in 1909 by a director at Kalem and became the studio's major draw until 1915, when she moved to Balboa for four years before forming her own production company. She took a break from film in 1923, focusing instead on stage work until her return to the screen in the 1930s. She made two talkies, neither of which was successful, and then retired for good. In 1937 she died of cancer.

The Mummy and the Cowpuncher apparently combines two of her pet genres, Western and comedy, with the added attraction of a mummy. It should be noted that the term "cowpuncher" was parlance at the time for "cowboy" (though in this case it appears that cows do indeed get punched). The film was released on a split reel with the documentary *Strange Places and Quaint People in New York* (1912). Some sources cite Roland as *Mummy*'s director, but this is difficult to verify.

The year 1912 also brought the release of *When Soul Meets Soul*, an Essanay production from director Farrell MacDonald and starring Francis X. Bushman as the reincarnation of an Ancient Egyptian prince, whose lover had committed suicide. That film was reportedly more romance than horror.

The year 1913 saw yet another comedic stab from Kalem, *The Egyptian Mummy*. It too starred Ruth Roland. In it, a young man poses as the mummy of Rameses III to convince his girlfriend's archaeologist father to allow him to marry her. In 1914 Vitagraph released a second film bearing that title and plot. CW

The Mystery of Souls
aka **I misteri della psiche**; **The Mysteries of Souls**
Itala; b/w; 50 min; Italy
D: Vincenzo Denizot
Cast: Alessandro Bernard, Lydia Quaranta, Luciano Daleza, Edoardo Davesnes, Giovanni Casaleggio, Evangelina Vitaliani

This Italian-made outing dealt with an evil hypnotist who uses an innocent girl to carry out his crimes. From the sounds of it, Du Maurier's *Trilby* influenced the story, but little else is known about it.

Director Vincenzo Denizot was active in the silent era; contemporary filmographies are almost certainly incomplete, but among his other titles are several early entries in the *pepla* (sword-and-sandal) genre: *Maciste* (1915) as well as *Maciste atleta* and *Maciste medium* (both 1918).

Some sources list this film's date of production as 1911. TH

The Myth of Jamasha Pass
aka **The Mystical Maid of Jamasha Pass**
American; b/w; 16 min; U.S.
D: Allan Dwan
Cast: J. Warren Kerrigan, Jack Richardson, Jessalyn Van Trump

This appears to have been the first horror film directed by Allan Dwan, who followed it up the next year with *The Occult* and later with *The Forbidden Room* (1914) and *The Gorilla* (1939).

The Myth of Jamasha Pass concerns three miners who stop for the night in rocky Jamasha Pass, where the eldest member of the group insists that a mystical maiden sometimes appears and lures men to their doom. The two younger men laugh at him, and he exits the camp in haste, leaving the younger men to their fate. The two fall asleep, but one, Dick (Richardson), is awakened by the sound of a falling stone. Looking up into the mountains, he spies a beautiful girl (Van Trump) in tattered clothing, waving at him from a rocky promenade. He makes his way up a lonely path, but when he meets the girl at a solitary tree and reaches out to her, she disappears. Meanwhile down below, someone touches his arm and awakens the other miner, Jim (Kerrigan). Next to him he sees the same beautiful young girl and proceeds to follow her up the same path, only to meet his fellow miner. Again the girl disappears, and the two men part ways, promising not to search for her. However, the moment their backs are turned to each other, they each try to find her. Dick finds her first, but then Jim appears to stake his claim. The two men fight over the girl, and Dick falls to his death. Jim, horror-stricken at what has happened, nonetheless follows the specter over the rocks. He slips and falls, and the last thing he sees before death claims him is the smiling girl waving at him to follow her. CW

One Too Exciting Night
Hepworth; b/w; 15 min; Great Britain
Credits unknown

A man buys a house that turns out to be haunted. *One Too Exciting Night* doesn't seem to have been distinguishable from other haunted house films of its time. Cecil M. Hepworth, whose eponymously named production company cranked out about a thousand titles between 1896 and 1923, produced. He directed many of his own productions, but it's uncertain whether that was the case here.

While Hepworth was key in the establishment of the British film industry, bad financial management put him out of business prematurely. He wound up so deeply in debt that he resorted to melting down all of the original film materials he possessed for their silver content. Prints of a few titles survive, but it's unknown whether this is one of them.

The film shouldn't be confused with the later haunted house comedy *One Exciting Night* (1922). TH

Queen of Spades
Eclipse; b/w; 15 min; France
Credits unknown

Less an adaptation of Russian author Alexander Pushkin's *Pikovaya dama* (1833) than a take on Scottish author Robert Louis Stevenson's *The Suicide Club* (1878), this 1912 French film from Eclipse concerns a young reporter investigating the death of an acquaintance who had joined a mysterious club. The club, he learns, is one wherein the members play cards, with the person who draws the queen of spades obliged to commit suicide (or, if he refuses, a member who draws a different unlucky card must murder him). After joining the club, the reporter draws the queen of spades, thus sealing his own fate.

During the silent era, there were numerous versions of both Pushkin's and Stevenson's famed stories. This may be the only film to draw overtly from both. With the coming of sound, both stories fell out of favor as common studio fare. CW

Paradise
aka **Paradiso**; **Purgatory and Paradise**
Psiche; b/w; 22 min; Italy
Credits unknown

Often mistakenly considered a sequel to Helios Film's *Inferno* (1910) and *Purgatory* (1911), *Paradise* was in fact produced by Psiche Studios. It was based on the third act in Dante Allighieri's *La Divina Commedia* (first written and published as *Commedia* in the early 1300s). Dante's work contains three parts, *Inferno*, *Purgatorio* and *Paradiso*, each one focusing on a different aspect of Dante's travels through the afterlife, guided by the spirit of the poet Virgil.

As the title implies, *Paradise* focused on the last section, in which Dante is finally reunited with his lover Beatrice. The two-reel film was released in some parts of the world with Helios' *Purgatory* under the title *Purgatory and Paradise*, leading some scholars to erroneously maintain that it was shot as the second half of the former film. It wasn't as dark as the first two productions, and critics who observed and wrote about the film in the early 1900s noticed even then the difference in quality between the first and last halves of *Purgatory and Paradise*, leading them to con-

clude that either whoever made the first part was not responsible for the second, or it was much more difficult to shoot visions of Heaven as opposed to visions of Hell. Reviewers of both schools praised the images of Heaven that were presented.

That same year, Italian film company Ambrosio made its own romance based on Allighieri's original source material. It was titled *Dante and Beatrice*. CW

The Plague-Stricken City
Gaumont; b/w; length unknown; France
Credits unknown

Heavily influenced by the Italian version of *The Masque of the Red Death*, which was filmed the year before by Ambrosio, Gaumont's *The Plague-Stricken City* explores the same premise, that of a prince who escapes a plague by holing up in his castle in the country. He invites wealthy nobles to join him but refuses to concern himself with the plight of the disease-ravaged poor. Encased within the castle walls with little to do but eat and be merry, the prince develops a lust for a captain's wife and two daughters. He kills the captain, but the woman and her daughters escape to the plague-ridden city, where they contract the disease themselves. They then return to the castle to infect its vile and selfish inhabitants, including, of course, the murderous prince. CW

Polidor at the Death Club
aka **Polidor al Club della Morte**; **Polidor, a Member of the Death Club**
Pasquali; b/w; 11 min; Italy
Crew unknown
Cast: Ferdinando Guillaume

Actor Ferdinando Guillaume began his film career playing a character named Tontolini, whose slapstick graced more than a hundred silent shorts between 1910 and 1913. When Tontolini waned in popularity, Guillaume introduced a second character named Polidor, whose success was so great that Guillaume took the name as his own. The first of hundreds of Polidor films (many directed by the star) appeared in 1912. Guillaume retired the character in 1918, and his career lost steam shortly thereafter. In the ensuing decades he made only a handful of minor appearances, his last role being an unbilled bit part in 1968's *Spirits of the Dead*.

Polidor at the Death Club is a spoof of Robert Louis Stevenson's classic short story *The Suicide Club*. Polidor joins a club whose members draw cards, with the winner expected to commit suicide. When he shows up at the club's door, he is admitted by a servant and draws his card—which, it turns out, is the fatal one. He is locked in a room filled with implements of death, including guns, poison and rope. Taunted by a floating skull, he tries unsuccessfully to escape. At length, members of the club enter the room and demand that he kill himself.

Only portions of *Death Club* are known to exist. CW

The Raven
Éclair/American Standard; b/w; 22 min; France/American
Crew unknown
Cast: Guy Oliver, Muriel Otriche

The Raven told the "true story" of Edgar Allan Poe, one of the world's most important writers. (It followed in the footsteps of D.W. Griffith's *Edgar Allen Poe*, 1909, which was also presented as an accurate biopic.) This version reportedly fabricated a happy ending in which Poe (Oliver) finds enough monetary success by writing his most famous poem, *The Raven*, to sustain him and his wife. The narrative also incorporated elements from other Poe stories, including *The Black Cat* (1843), *A Decent into the Maelstrom* (1841), *The Gold-Bug* (1843), *The Murders in the Rue Morgue* (1841), *The Pit and the Pendulum* (1842) and *The Premature Burial* (1844), among others.

Muriel Ostriche portrayed Poe's wife Lenore, who in reality was named Virginia, was Poe's cousin and was a child bride at 14 years of age. (To be fair, the film does stick fairly close to the truth in one respect: Ostriche was approximately 16 years old when she played the part.) The film was shot in Fort Lee, Texas, where French studio Éclair had set up shop. Though numerous sources claim that it was three reels long, press releases at the time indicate that it was made up of two. The first reel detailed Poe's life and the events leading up to his writing of *The Raven*. It's the sad tale of Poe's difficult life exacerbated by his wife's deteriorating physical condition ... and, needless to say, the loving couple is deeply in debt. In the second reel, Poe struggles with depression as he tries to write something that will pay enough to get him and his wife out of the red. Things work out when he passes out at his desk and has visions that will later comprise the bulk of his stories. He's transported from his poor surroundings to an affluent home, where he wants for nothing but the presence of his lost Lenore. Here the director flashes between Poe writing the words of his poem and a raven perched upon a bust of Pallas. When Poe awakens from his dreams, he finds that he has written his most famous work. He rushes it to his publisher, who gives him—in the words of *Moving Picture World* (April 27, 1912)—"a niggardly $10 for his masterpiece." Poe then returns to his wife with flowers and the provisions they need to survive. (It should be noted that while the critic at *Moving Picture World* loved the film, its description convinces this reviewer that it was most probably a melodramatic mess passing itself off as historical fact.)

Though the film is long lost, the original advertising poster for it still exists. It shows Poe sitting at a desk in a dark room, one hand in his hair, the other writing with a quill upon a tablet of paper. In the background is a radiant vision of a beautiful woman looking over him.

The next major movie to focus on the life of Edgar Allan Poe, also titled *The Raven*, was released in 1915. It was the first feature-length treatment of the subject matter. CW

The Reincarnation of Karma
aka The Reincarnation of Komar
Vitagraph; b/w; 30 min; U.S.
D: Van Dyke Brooke *S:* Eugene Mullin
Cast: Courtenay Foote, Rosemary Theby, Lillian Walker, Charles Eldridge, Edith Storey

Van Dyke Brooke was one of Vitagraph's most prolific directors. Having made *The Hunchback* in 1909, his next attempt at horror, *The Reincarnation of Karma*, was even more overt. In an ancient temple, a high priest named Karma (Foote) finds himself the object of a priestess named Qunitreea (Theby), who attempts to seduce him. When he rejects and curses her, she becomes a huge snake. While exploring that same temple two thousand years later, the priest's reincarnation, Leslie Adams (also Foote), encounters and captures a suspiciously similar serpent, which becomes a woman (Theby again) and offers Adams' fiancée, Lillian White (Walker), a beautiful amulet. Lillian accepts it and falls into a permanent slumber. Thus does Qunitreea have her revenge on the reincarnation of Karma.

Rosemary Theby was a popular actor during the silent era, but when talkies came, she was reduced to un-credited bit parts. One of her last roles was as a shell person in the original *One Million B.C.* (1940). English actor Courtenay Foote also found great success in the age of silent cinema, but he died in 1925 while visiting Italy. CW

Satan
aka Satana; Satan: or, The Drama of Humanity
Ambrosio; b/w; 40 min; Italy
D: Luigi Maggi *S:* Guido Volante *C:* Giovanni Vitrotti
Cast: Rina Alby, Mary Cleo Tarlarina, Mario Bonnard, Antonio Grisanti, Rina Albri, Arrigo Amerio

Satan

John Milton's *Paradise Lost* (1667) and Friedrich Gottlieb Klopstock's *The Messiah*, a series of cantos written between 1745 and 1773, reportedly inspired this early Italian silent fantasy. The film explores Satan's influence through the ages; in that respect, it can be viewed as a precursor to D.W. Griffith's far more renowned *Intolerance* (1916).

Mario Bonnard, who was at the time one of Italy's top matinee idols, portrayed Satan. He began directing in 1916, though he continued to dabble in acting until 1924; as a director, he worked until three years before his death in 1964. One of his last directing credits was for *The Last Days of Pompeii* (1959), a relatively classy *pepla* starring Steve Reeves. (Interestingly, Bonnard fell ill early in the shoot, leaving much of the directing work to his assistant, a young Sergio Leone.) TH

The Secrets of House No. 5
Pathé; b/w; length unknown; Russia/France
Credits unknown

This obscure horror melodrama reportedly featured a detective who went up against ghosts and goblins. What makes the film especially noteworthy is that it also apparently featured vampires, a cinematic rarity at the time and predating Murnau's *Nosferatu* by a decade. This is fitting given that Russia, the nation from which it sprang, was long steeped in vampire lore (famously exemplified by Alexai Tolstoy's classic 1839 tale *The Family of the Vourdalak*, which formed the basis for a segment in Mario Bava's 1963 trilogy of terror, *Black Sabbath*).

Though shot in Russia, *The Secrets of House No. 5* was produced by the Moscow arm of Pathé, which had been established by the French studio Pathé Brothers in 1910.

Some sources erroneously cite *The Secrets of House No. 5* as a British picture. CW

Simple Simon and the Devil
aka Onésime aux enfers; Simple Simon in Hell; Onésime et la Diable
Gaumont; b/w; 8 min; France
D: Jean Durand
Cast: Ernest Bourbon, Gaston Modot

Director Jean Durand (1882-1946) had an unexceptional career in silent cinema, working predominantly in comedy series. These included the *Simple Simon*, *Zigoto* and *Calino* films, none of which are remembered much today, and with good reason. Made mostly in the second and third decades of the 20th century, they offered absolutely nothing new, wallowing instead in the slapstick goofiness typical of the time. There were, all told, no less than 60 Simple Simon films (the character was called Onésime in his native country of France). All were shorts focusing on the zany antics of the brainless title character, including his harrowing encounters with trick photographic effects. Durand was not, to be kind, the most innovative of filmmakers. Most often, his direction consisted of pointing a stationary camera at a single, cheap-looking set and letting the action unfold. Editing afterwards was minimal, though he did embrace a then-innovative novelty called title cards (not that they were needed with such simplistic stories). In *Simple Simon and the Devil*, Simple Simon has a dream where he goes to Hell and meets the Devil. The film was a spoof of the *fantastique noir* of Georges Méliès, who concocted numerous productions featuring Mephistopheles. In 1911 Durand made his own entry in that subgenre with *Faust and Marguerite*, which starred frequent *Simple Simon* co-star Gaston Modot.

Simon's next brush with horror came when he joined a killer club in *Simple Simon and the Suicide Club*. CW

The Skivvy's Ghost
Lux; b/w; length unknown; France
Credits unknown

This comedy from Lux offers yet another tongue-in-cheek variation on the haunted house theme. A couple moves into a house, not realizing that it is haunted by a whimsical specter.

Ghost stories have been a film staple since the dawn of cinema (*The Devil's Castle*, for one, was shot in 1896). The frequency with which such subject matter has been presented can no doubt be partially explained by the fact that film technology has made it easy to depict supernatural phenomena on celluloid in a surprisingly believable manner. In the early days, clever editing and other simple tricks accomplished this; today, of course, there's CGI. The subject matter also lends itself to slapstick, and by the end of the silent era, the haunted house comedy was already something of its own genre.

Such films aren't limited to the silent era, of course. Countless horror comedies have featured comedians as varied as Bud Abbott and Lou Costello (*Hold That Ghost*, 1942), Bob Hope (*The Ghost Breakers*, 1940), Dean Martin and Jerry Lewis (*Scared Stiff*, 1953) and Bill Murray (*Ghostbusters*, 1984). TH

A Son-in-Law's Nightmare
aka **Le beau-fils du cauchemar**
Pathé; black and white; 6 min; France
Credits unknown

A young man dreams that he murders his mother-in-law, only to have his relief shattered when her severed head begins to follow him around.

Jokes about mothers-in-law are as old as time itself, so it's no great surprise that an early feature would utilize one for comic—and gruesome—ends. Judging by the surviving synopsis, the film likely utilized then-striking trick photography to create the illusion of an avenging disembodied head. Nightmares were a perfect framework for early fantastic films; they leant themselves to brevity but also provided a device for filmmakers whose dark visions would be too upsetting if depicted realistically. TH

The Speckled Band
aka **Le mystère de Val Boscombe**
Éclair; b/w; 19 min; France/England
D: Georges Treville
Cast: Georges Treville, Mr. Moyse

A young woman dies, and her last words are "speckled … band." Sherlock Holmes (Treville) is called in to investigate.

First published in 1892, *The Adventure of the Speckled Band* is one of the more macabre Sherlock Holmes stories. Its author, Sir Arthur Conan Doyle, penned a stage adaptation of the tale and produced it for London's Adelphi Theatre in 1910. The first (and long-lost) film adaptation of *The Speckled Band* followed in 1912.

Director/star Georges Treville—who played the part of Holmes in the film—acted for the screen during the silent era and through the 1930s, working mostly in his native France. He played Holmes in only three films, all of them for Éclair and produced in 1912. His directorial career was apparently limited—he is known for certain to have directed just seven films, between 1912 and 1930. Some film historians have suggested that Adrian Caillard directed *The Speckled Band*, which is possible given that Caillard directed the other two in the series. It does appear that the film was shot in Bexhill-on-Sea, Great Britain, which partially accounts for its status as a French-British coproduction.

Doyle's story was next filmed in 1923 as part of the Holmes series starring Eille Norwood. TH

The Spell of the Hypnotist
Helios; b/w; 8 min; Italy
Credits unknown

Italian production company Helios made only a few films during its short lifetime, beginning with the documentary *Pontine Marshes, Italy* in 1909. The bulk of its product was produced during 1910 and 1911, some of it horror themed, including the supernatural epics *Inferno* (1910) and *Purgatory* (1911). *The Spell of the Hypnotist*, likewise horror, came along in 1912. The film concerned a man with the ability to place people under his control, with murder the result. The company did little after this unremarkable outing, coming to an official end in 1916.

Italy's Helios does not appear related to the German film production company of the same name, which produced *Dance of Death* (1919) and *The Hunchback and the Dancer* (1920). CW

Spooks
Pathé; b/w; 15 min; France
Credits unknown

This is yet another obscure short from French company Pathé that utilized trick photography to establish a tone of comedic horror. The plot concerned a man confronted by the ghost of his dead brother. Little beyond that is known, and credit information has long since fallen to the wayside.

Other Pathé horror films of the same year include several co-productions with Georges Méliès' Star Films, such as *Baron Munchausen's Dream* and *The Knight of the Snows*, as well as solo efforts such as *The Fatal Pact*, *A Son-in-Law's Nightmare* and *Les terreurs de Rigadin*, among others. CW

Supernatural Power
Pathé; b/w; 7 min; France
Credits unknown

A fake medium conducts a séance and is surprised when real ghosts come a-calling from the nether realm. This extremely short film, intended for show in Nickelodeons, was the usual ho-hum fare, intended to spark laughs but probably also garnering a shiver or two from younger or more naïve viewers. The supernatural aspect capitalized on the still-youthful cinematic medium's ability to present crude optical effects through skillful, judicious edits and superimposition. CW

The System of Dr. Tarr and Professor Fether
aka **Le systeme du Docteur Goudron et du Professeur Plume**; **The Lunatics**
Éclair; b/w; 15 min; France
D: Maurice Tourneur *S:* Andre de Lord
Cast: Henri Gouget, Henri Roussell, Renee Sylvaire

Edgar Allan Poe's *The System of Dr. Tarr and Professor Fether* was first published in 1845, meeting with some controversy over its comedic treatment of the insane. The tale's anonymous narrator visits an asylum with a companion, Monsieur Maillard, who, it so happens, has developed a new system of caring for lunatics, a "therapy" that allows patients to indulge their delusions without fear of consequence. As events progress, however, it becomes clear that the inmates have in fact taken over.

Tarr got its first cinematic treatment in the 1909 Thomas Edison production *Lunatics in Power*, with the story's more disturbing content watered down. Maurice Tourneur, who began his career in his native France, directed the second version. A later period of success in the United States ended with his removal from MGM's troubled Jules Verne science-fiction epic *Mysterious Island* (1929), after which he retreated back to France and there worked until the late 1940s. These days, he's best known as the father of Jacques Tourneur, director of such genre-straddling hits as *I Walked With a Zombie* (1943) and *Out of the Past* (1947).

The System of Dr. Tarr and Professor Fether apparently made an impression on Tourneur's son, who later reused a memorable image from it—that of a pool of blood oozing from under a closed door—in his own horror/noir hybrid, *The Leopard Man* (1943).

Tarr's screenplay was written by Andre de Lord, who had previously adapted the story for the stage. TH

Trilby

Les terreurs de Rigadin
Pathé; b/w; length unknown; France
D: Georges Monca
Cast: Charles Prince

A comic figure named Rigadin (Prince) contends with a variety of seemingly supernatural happenings. Introduced to audiences worldwide by Pathé in 1909, the Rigadin character was an instant hit. Played by French comedian Charles Prince, he was the central figure in well over a hundred films. His popularity became so widespread as to leave competing franchises such as Gavroche (*Gavroche et le spirits*, 1912) and Patoulliard (*Bill Taken for a Ghost*, 1911) in the pop-culture dust. Prince became so identified with the character that he seldom played anything else. At his career peak, it is said that he provided the only real native competition to France's comedic superstar Max Linder.

That aside, the humor in his surviving adventures hasn't aged well. Unlike fellow Frenchman Linder or, for that matter, Charlie Chaplin in United States, the Rigadin character was all pratfalls and no heart. TH

Trilby
aka **Three Tales of Terror**; **Trilogy of Terror**
Osterreichisch; b/w; 50 min; Austria/Hungary
Co-D/P: Luise Kolm, Anton Kolm, Claudius Veltee *Co-D/Co-P/C:* Jakob Fleck
Cast: Frau Galafres Hubermann, Paul Askonas

Austrian husband and wife team Luise and Anton Kolm co-directed *Trilby*, the first of two features Luise produced based on George Du Maurier's classic 1894 novel. Also helping out with the directing chores were Luise's brother Claudius Veltee and cameraman Jakob Fleck (whom Luise married after the death of Anton). Her second film to focus on the novel was *Svengali* (1914).

Little is known about either film; they were both made in Austria, and both were feature-length productions running nearly an hour in length. It's possible that the 1912 version of *Trilby* focused on the beautiful young singer (Hubermann) while the 1914 film focused on the evil hypnotist (played in 1912 by Askonas and in 1914 by Ferdinand Bonn), who takes her under his wing and makes her a great singer. Given the various alternate titles, it would appear that the 1912 film adhered closely to the format of Du Maurier's novel, which was told in three parts, only one of which focused on the sinister Svengali.

The four filmmakers responsible for *Trilby*—the two Kolms, Veltee and Fleck—started the first Austrian film production company in 1910. Originally known as Erste Osterreichische, then Osterreichische and finally Wiener, it fell apart in 1919 and was re-structured as Vita-Film. Shortly thereafter, the original producers dropped out, Anton died and Luise and Jakob moved to Germany, where they continued to make films. For a while Jakob was interned at the notorious concentration camp Dachau before being freed and moving with his wife to Shanghai.

Kolm returned to the idea of a Svengali-like hypnotist subverting the will of a beautiful woman in *Trance* (1920). CW

Trilby
Standard; b/w; length unknown; Great Britain
Credits unknown

Though not much is known about this obscure romantic thriller, it was released in Great Britain in April 1912, having been produced by Standard. It was based on one-third of George Du Maurier's 1894 novel of the same title, which focuses on the possession of the eponymous Trilby, a beautiful but talentless young woman who becomes a famous singer after falling under the spell of evil hypnotist Svengali. When he dies, her will is so intertwined with his that she dies as well.

Just how closely Standard followed Du Maurier's tale is anyone's guess and will most likely remain so; the film now appears to be lost. Great Britain's next stab at the story came a scant two years later, with London's *Trilby* (1914). CW

The Vengeance of Edgar Poe
aka **Une vengeance d'Edgar Poe**; **The Vengeance of Edgard Poe**
Lux; b/w; 30 min; France
D/Co-S: Gerard Bourgeois *Co-S:* Abel Gance
Cast: Édouard de Max, Jean Worms, Pierre Pradier, Louis Tunc

The same year he shot *The Mask of Horror*, French filmmaker Abel Gance co-wrote this melodrama about the great horror author Edgar Allan Poe, specifically, his descent into insanity thanks to drug addiction. It was here that Gance first evidenced his preoccupation with historical figures and their (generally dark) obsessions—a fascination that found greater expression in *Napoléon* (1927) and *Lucrezia Borgia* (1935). Other horror films produced by the filmmaker include two versions of *J'Accuse* (one made in 1919, the other in 1938), as well as the horror comedy *Au Secours* (1924), which served as homage to the great French film pioneer Georges Méliès.

Interestingly, Poe's life had already been cinematically examined twice before, none too successfully either time; first in 1909 as *Edgar Allen Poe* (by D.W. Griffith) and again in 1912 as *The Raven*. In 1915, it would be filmed yet again as a feature-length drama, also titled *The Raven*. CW

The Vengeance of Egypt
aka L'anneau fatal
Gaumont; b/w; 45 min; France
Credits unknown

In 1912, an archaeological team led by Ludwig Borchardt made a startling discovery in Amarna, Egypt. A bust of Nefertiti, the wife of Egyptian Pharaoh Arkhenaten, was found among the ruins of a workshop belonging to a sculptor named Thutmose. Thutmose is believed to have crafted the bust circa 1345 B.C. Some film historians have suggested that this startling event and the worldwide media coverage it received led to a short-lived craze for big-screen mummies and Egyptian curses. Yet a look at the timeline refutes this; the bust was discovered in December 1912, whereas the spate of mummy films had begun in 1911, with most of the 1912 releases occurring before the Amarna discovery. If anything, the fascination with the Nefertiti find was likely stoked by mummy movies rather than vice-versa.

The Vengeance of Egypt is one of said movies. Its plot goes something like this: Napoleon Bonaparte oversees the excavation of an Egyptian tomb. The mummy found therein contains a scarab ring on its finger, and a soldier steals it and sends it to his sweetheart in France. After receiving it, the girl has a nightmare about the mummy and is then promptly murdered by a burglar. The ring then falls into the hands of an antiques dealer, who develops horrible skin blotches and also dies. Another man buys the ring and is shot to death. Finally, an Egyptologist recovers the ring and replaces it on the mummy's hand, which causes the thing's eyes to glow in appreciation.

What makes *The Vengeance of Egypt* unique among its contemporaries is that its main character is not a person but rather the prop ring. There is also evidence that it was one of the earliest feature films to be advertised and sold on the basis of its horror aspects. CW

Whiffle's Nightmare
aka Le cauchemar de Rigadin
CGPC/Pathé; b/w; 8 min; France
D: Georges Monca *S:* Louise Foreau
Cast: Charles Prince

Rigadin (Prince) has a nightmare about a haunted house.

Mistakenly cited by some sources as a 1914 production, *Whiffle's Nightmare* is an early entry in France's Rigadin series of shorts. The fact that the film debuted in America (where the character Rigadin was unknown, hence the title change) two years after its production and initial release in France only added to the confusion concerning its release date. Charles Prince first brought Rigadin to the screen in *Rigadin* (1909). The comedic character's exploits were amazingly popular with the French public, so much so that Rigadin returned well over a hundred times.

The character had at least one other encounter with the mildly horrific—*Les terreurs de Rigadin* (also 1912). TH

The Woman in White
Thanhouser; b/w; length unknown; U.S.
S: Lloyd Lonergan
Cast: Marguerite Snow, James Cruze, William Garwood

This is the first known film adaptation of Wilkie Collins' serialized novel *The Woman in White* (1859-1860). The production company founded by Edwin Thanhouser in 1909 (though he parted ways with the business for a time beginning in early 1912) produced. Partners included his wife Gertrude and brother-in-law Lloyd Lonergan, who also wrote many of the company's films (including this one and a second adaptation of the tale in 1917).

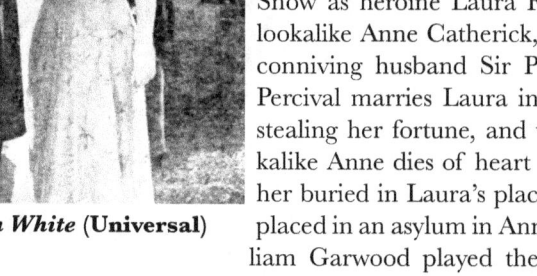

The Woman in White **(Universal)**

Regular Thanhouser players Marguerite Snow and James Cruze starred: Snow as heroine Laura Fairlie and her lookalike Anne Catherick, and Cruze as conniving husband Sir Percival Glyde. Percival marries Laura in the hopes of stealing her fortune, and when her lookalike Anne dies of heart failure, he has her buried in Laura's place—and Laura placed in an asylum in Anne's place. William Garwood played the hero, Walter Hartwright, who sorts it all out and rescues Laura in the end.

Both Snow and Cruze were reteamed from the earlier Thanhouser hit *Dr. Jekyll and Mr. Hyde*, which had been released early in 1912. Both, along with Garwood, retired from acting not long after Thanhouser's liquidation in 1918.

This particular adaptation of *The Woman in White* was the first of two that were released in 1912; it beat the second, produced by Gem, into theaters by two days. CW

The Woman in White
aka Woman in White
Gem/Universal; b/w; 35 min; U.S.
Crew unknown
Cast: Janet Salisbury (Salzberg), Alexander F. Frank, Viola Alberti, Charles Perley, Charles Craig, Lyman R. Abbe

There were no less than five official silent adaptations of British novelist Wilkie Collins' Gothic romance *The Woman in White*, which first saw light in serialized form in the Victorian periodical *All the Year Round* in 1859 and 1860. It proved a huge success and solidified the author's growing reputation among the masses. An epistolary novel, it consisted of letters, personal accounts, journal entries and so on, pieced into a single, coherent narrative. (The format was most famously used by Bram Stoker in his 1897 novel *Dracula*.)

In the novel, Laura Fairlie is engaged to Sir Percival Glyde but in love with her art tutor Walter Hartright. After Laura marries Glyde, her half-sister Marian Halcombe—who is her constant companion—comes to suspect that Glyde has married Laura for her fortune. While standing in the rain and eavesdropping on a conversation between Glyde and his crony, the sinister Count Fosco, Marian becomes soaked and as a result grows sick. When she awakens, she learns that Laura has died; around the same time, a white-clad woman bearing a striking resemblance to Laura is seen wandering the estate grounds. It turns out that the mysterious woman, Anne Catherick (who may be Laura's illegitimate half-sister), was an escapee from a nearby asylum and that it was she, not Laura, who died of heart failure. Glyde substituted her remains for the still-alive Laura, burying Anne in Laura's stead and placing Laura in the asylum as Anne. But during an attempt to destroy evidence that proves him illegitimate and therefore not a legal heir to his own title, Glyde is killed in a fire and Laura rescued.

Given that this film's cast list does not provide a credit for the novel's Marian Halcombe, it's possible that this character was omitted from the film to tighten the story. Salisbury played Laura Fairlie, Charles Perley played Walter Hartright, Charles Craig played Sir Percival Glyde and Alexander F. Frank played Count Fosco. CW

Yotsuya kaidan
Nikkatsu; b/w; length unknown; Japan
D: Shozo Makino
Cast: Matsunosuke Onoe

Nikkatsu is Japan's oldest existing film studio, created in 1912 by a merger of four smaller silent-era studios and still producing films today. It may be best known for its string of commercially successful and critically admired softcore "Roman Porno" films (including, notably, its 21-installment *Apartment Wife* series), filmed during the 1970s and '80s.

It's fitting that such a venerable company should have been the first to produce a film adaptation of Tsuruya Nanboku IV's classic 1825 Kabuki piece *Yotsuya kaidan*. A horror tale set in feudal Japan, the play concerns a woman driven to her death by her philandering husband, only to return from the grave for ghostly retribution against him and his lover.

Born in 1878, Shozo Makino got his start in cinema in 1908, proving so prolific and popular that he is today known as the "godfather" of Japanese film. Not content with mere directing, Makino also wrote screenplays and, in 1923, started his own production company, the better to maintain creative control over his films. He is also credited with plucking silent-film superstar Matsunosuke Onoe from a traveling theater troupe. Makino died in the late 1920s, right around the advent of sound, and his last film was released posthumously.

Some sources cite a 1913 adaptation of Nanboku's five-act play, but it's not known whether that film was a separate production or merely a re-release of the original. The fact that it also starred Matsunosuke Onoe lends weight to the latter possibility. CW

1913

The Adventures of Three Knights
aka **The Adventures of the Three Knights**; **Adventure of Three Knights**
Eiko; b/w; 48 min; U.S.
Credits unknown

Some sources cite this obscure film as an Eiko production, but that studio is not the same Eiko as the modern Japanese studio of the same name. *The Adventures of Three Knights* was a five-reel film released in 1913—a year before D.W. Griffith's groundbreaking *Birth of a Nation*—making it something of an aberration, as most films of that period were minor shorts utilizing film trickery, usually for comedic effect.

Knights tells of three soldiers who, in their travels, have a series of adventures, one of which includes a visit to an old castle haunted by the ghost of a Countess. CW

After the Welsh Rarebit
aka **After the Welsh Rabbit**
Edison; b/w; 10 min; U.S.
D: C.J. Williams *S:* William W. Hanson *P:* Thomas Edison
Cast: William Wadsworth, Ida Williams, Edward Boulden, Arthur Housman, Julian Reed, Yale Benner

The bulk of this short comedy depicted a dream sequence in which the protagonist (Wadsworth), snoozing after a meal, sees himself being tortured in hell. Director C.J. Williams specialized in comedic subjects, spending most of his career with Edison (who produced this picture) and Vitagraph. He often cast his wife, Ida Williams (then billed as Mrs. C.J. Williams) in his pictures, as he did here.

The Welsh rarebit, incidentally, is a dish made of toast covered in a cheese sauce, along with various other ingredients such as ale, mustard and Worcestershire sauce. It is sometimes referred to as Welsh rabbit, though it contains neither rabbit nor any other type of meat. TH

The Alchemist
Kinematograph; color; 30 min; Great Britain
P: Charles Urban
Cast unknown

A girl's doom is predicted by an evil alchemist's astrology. This is one of several silent horror films shot between 1911 and 1913 by producer Charles Urban that utilized an early color format developed by Urban and fellow filmmaker George Albert Smith. The film should not be confused with a Russian film of the same title, which appears to have been produced around the same time. CW

Balaoo
aka **Balaoo the Demon Baboon**; **Balaoo ou Des pas au plafond**
Éclair; b/w; 24 min; France
D/S: Victorin-Hyppolite Jasset
Cast: Lucien Bataille, Camille Bardou, Henry Gouget, Madeleine Grandjean, Josette Andriot, Gilbert Dalleu

French writer Gaston Leroux's *Balaoo* was first published in serial form in the magazine *Le Matin* in 1911, the same year his famed novel *Le Fantôme de l'Opéra* made its debut. *Balaoo* eventually saw print in English as *The Mysterious Mr. Noel*, but Balaoo the baboon never achieved the same level of superstardom as did Erik the Phantom, a discrepancy most likely due to *Balaoo*'s lack of a Lon Chaney portrayal, as *Fantôme* got with Universal's massively successful *The Phantom of the Opera* (1925). Still, *Balaoo* was successful enough to eventually warrant three film versions—this eponymous one, another entitled *The Wizard* in 1927 and a third, *Dr. Renault's Secret*, in 1942. Today only the 1942 adaptation is available for viewing in its complete form. While parts of the 1913 *Balaoo* are known to exist in various North American archives, much of the film is believed lost.

In the film, Dr. Coriolis (Gouget) succeeds in giving a baboon, which he names Balaoo (Bataille), human qualities. But while the ape has the intelligence of a man (indeed, he falls in love with the doctor's pretty young niece, Madeleine), he nonetheless retains the strength of a primitive primate. After being reprimanded by his creator for committing mischief around town, Balaoo runs away and is caught in a poacher's trap. The poacher (Bardou) offers to free him under the condition that Balaoo become his slave. Balaoo agrees, and it isn't long before the poacher has him committing murder. When the poacher takes a liking to Coriolis' niece (Grandjean), he orders the creature to kidnap her. Balaoo does so but then rebels and is shot by the poacher. Though mortally wounded, he manages to both lay a trap for his tormentor and rescue Madeleine. He lives just long enough to see the poacher arrested and carted away for murder. (It should be noted that some sources cite the doctor's name as Coriolia, and Madeleine—sometimes listed as Madeline—as his daughter.)

Despite having a law degree and a large inheritance, author Leroux (1868-1927) nearly bankrupted himself in the late 1800s, after which he turned to writing for a living. It was a smart move; he had one success after another and lived to see several of his novels made into feature films, including *Balaoo*, *Le Fantôme de l'Opéra*, *Le mystère de la chambre jaune* and *Chéri-bibi*.

Director/scenarist Jasset began his career at Gaumont, France's largest film studio, in 1905, working with the likes of the legendary Alice Guy. Though he is sometimes credited with having co-directed *Esmeralda* (1905) with her, evidence for this is scant. *Balaoo* proved one of the last of the nearly 200 films he either directed or co-directed in a short, work-intensive career. He died in 1913, the same year the film was released. CW

The Bells
Reliance; b/w; 30 min; U.S.
D: Oscar Apfel *S:* Forrest Halsey
Cast: Edward P. Sullivan, Sue Balfour, Irving Cummings, Gertrude Robinson, Irene Howley, Oscar Apfel

Erckmann-Chatrian was the collective name employed by writing team Émile Erckmann and Alexandre Chatrian. While they composed many novels and plays about military life and adventure, most of their work was inspired by ghost stories and folk tales of the region of France in which they were born and raised. Famous British writer M.R. James (author of *Casting the Runes*, which provided the basis for the classic 1957 film *Night of*

***Balaoo* features a baboon that is given human qualities and intelligence, but ultimately it becomes a murderous slave.**

the Demon) claimed the two as an inspiration for his own short horror stories. While one author tended to write the majority of their plays and the other wrote most of their novels, they were far more collaborative at the conceptualization stage. But after a quarrel in the 1880s, they never produced another work together. Erckmann died in 1899 and Chatrian followed the next year.

Their best-known work outside of France is the play *Le Juif Polonaise* ("The Polish Jew"). Popular in Europe, Leopold Lewis adapted it (re-titling it *The Bells*) for English-speaking audiences. Given the popularity of the fledgling cinematic art form, it was inevitable that the work would jump to the big screen. W.J. Lincoln filmed a version in 1911 in his native Australia, while this, the first of two 1913 films to bear the title *The Bells*, was shot by Oscar Apfel for Reliance in the United States. It was released in February, five months before the next film titled *The Bells*—apparently an adaptation of Poe's poem—was released.

The story concerns the murderer of a Jew who becomes haunted by the spirit of his victim. CW

The Bells
Edison; b/w; length unknown; U.S.
D: George Lessey *S:* Henry Irving
Cast: May Abbey, Robert Brower, Frank McGlynn, Augustus Phillips

Lucy (Abbey) is convinced by her father (Brower) to marry Leo (McGlynn) rather than her true love, Donald (Phillips). But when a fire breaks out during church services, Donald's failed attempt to save Leo makes Lucy available to him. It's likely that the bells of the title are a reference to church bells, which often signify death in Poe's stories.

While this film is often assumed to be a third screen version of Leopold Lewis' adaptation of Erckmann-Chatrian's play *Le Juif Polonaise* ("The Polish Jew"), it was apparently a love story loosely inspired by the Edgar Allan Poe poem of the same title. It does not seem to have borne any resemblance to the already twice-filmed tale of a man haunted by visions of the Jew he murdered years before. The next true film adaptation of Lewis' Anglicized take on Erckmann-Chatrian's play was produced and released by Sawyer's Features the following year. CW

The Bewitched Matches
Éclair; b/w; 8 min; France
D: Emile Cohl
Cast unknown

This short feature mixes live action, animation, humor and horror. It is about a group of women who summon forth an old witch, whom they ask to read their palms. An older gentleman interrupts them and insults the witch. Enraged, the hag places a curse on his box of matches, which come alive and turn him into a skeleton.

Director Emile Cohl was a pioneer in the mixing of live action with animation. He created over 200 short subjects in his native France but appears to have stopped making films in the early 1920s. He died at age 71 from pneumonia in 1938. TH

The Black Opal
Ramo; b/w; 11 min; U.S.
Credits unknown

This apparently lost short film had a typical horror plot taken directly from Wilkie Collins' 1868 novel *The Moonstone*. A gemstone made of hydrated silica, opal is known for its beautiful iridescence, which makes it understandable that a black ring made of such a mineral would be used as a prop in a horror film. In this case, the ring is cursed and brings the usual calamity down upon its possessors' heads.

Despite some claims that it was a reel and a half long, *The Black Opal* was contained on a single reel, making it no more than 11 minutes in duration. It was released on September 3, 1913. CW

The Brand of Evil
aka **Brand of Evil**
Essanay; b/w; 30 min; U.S.
D: Harry McRae Webster S: Edward T. Lowe
Cast: Thomas Commerford, Ruth Stonehouse, Richard C. Travers, E.H. Calvert

Influenced to a degree by Wilkie Collins' classic horror-mystery novel *The Moonstone* (1868), *The Brand of Evil* concerns a thief who steals the jeweled eye of a religious idol, only to find that the hand with which he committed the crime is withering away.

Though Harry McRae Webster sometimes wrote his own screenplays, Edward T. Lowe, his literary superior in every way, furnished him a script. Lowe was born in Nashville, Tennessee in 1890, and he broke into filmmaking in 1912 as a screenwriter of short subjects. By the 1920s he was commanding a respectable salary and working in the big leagues, with his most famous film of the silent era, *The Hunchback of Notre Dame* starring Lon Chaney, coming in 1923. Though he worked in several genres, he is most remembered today for his many horror and mystery scripts, including those for *The Vampire Bat* (1933), *House of Frankenstein* (1944) and *House of Dracula* (1945). He also worked on various entries in the Fox *Charlie Chan*, Universal *Sherlock Holmes* and RKO *Tarzan* series. His film credits date to 1947, though he lived until 1973, when he died at the ripe old age of 82.

The Brand of Evil was released on November 28, 1913. CW

The Clown Hero
IMP; b/w; 13 min; U.S.
S: Richard Goodall
Cast unknown

A young boy goes to sleep and dreams of being saved by a circus clown from strange creatures and animals. He awakens to find himself safe in his bed.

Not much is known about this short from IMP, a small studio later rolled into Universal Pictures. Scenarist Richard Goodall contributed to a handful of mostly now-forgotten titles between 1913 and 1924. *The Clown Hero* appears to have been his only horror-tinged film, with a tentative connection to fright at best. TH

Le cottage hantée
Pathé/Nizza; b/w; 5 min; France
D/S/C/FX: Segundo de Chomon
Cast unknown

Le Cottage Hante evidences writer/director Segundo de Chomon's ongoing fascination with the morbid. Like so many of his films, it apparently went for as many chuckles as scares with its tale of a haunted cottage certainly making use of the trick photography for which he was known.

Sadly, de Chomon made only a handful of films after this one. After *The War and the Dream of Momi* (1917, co-directed with Giovanni Pastrone), he turned his focus exclusively to cinematography and special effects work; one of his last credits was the fantastical *Maciste in Hell* (1925) for Guido Brignone. He died in 1929, leaving behind a legacy of engaging short films. TH

The Dead Secret
Monopol; b/w; 50 min; U.S.
D: Stanner E.V. Taylor C: H. Lyman Broening
Cast: Marion Leonard

Wilkie Collins is best remembered for *The Woman in White* (1860), but the British author wrote many stories grounded in the morbid. One of his lesser-known tales, *The Dead Secret* (1857), provided the basis for this obscure silent film in which a naïve girl falls under the influence of an evil hypnotist.

This appears to have been director Stanner E.V. Taylor's only foray into the horror genre. The prolific St. Louis-born filmmaker entered the movies as a scenarist in 1908, but his career died with the coming of sound. Beautiful leading lady Marion Leonard was a favorite with audiences of the time; she played the leads in many Biograph productions, including a few of D.W. Griffith's early works. TH

The Death Stone of India
Bison; b/w; 45 min; U.S.
D: Milton J. Fahrney S: James Dayton
Cast: William Clifford, Paul Machette, Belle Bennett, Edna Maison, Louis Fitzroy, Harry Schumm, Bud Osborne

This is one of several movies influenced by Wilkie Collins' *The Moonstone*, an 1868 novel about a cursed jewel stolen from an idol in India. U.S.-based production company Bison doesn't seem to have diverged much from that basic plot—Hindi laborers who steal the jeweled eye from an idol die mysteriously before the jewel makes its way into the hands of a British colonialist.

King Baggot plays Dr. Jekyll (top) and Mr. Hyde (bottom) in the IMP/Universal production of *Dr. Jekyll and Mr. Hyde*.

Born in Dayton, Ohio in 1872, Milton J. Fahrney made a career filming comedy shorts based on the slapstick character Jerry, who was portrayed by George Ovey. *Death Stone*'s lead, Cincinnati-born William Clifford, made his film debut in 1910 in a Western titled *The Blazed Trail*. Although he appeared in between 150 and 200 films, he never really did anything of repute, and his career ended with the coming of sound. Of *Death Stone*'s other actors, only Belle Bennett (who died in 1932) and Bud Osborne (whose career lasted into the 1960s) did anything on screen after the silent era.

Universal (which absorbed Bison) released *The Jewel of Death* in 1917, a film Fahrney directed and James Dayton wrote; given its title and the exact duplication of the cast and crew, it appears to be a renamed re-release of *The Death Stone of India*. CW

The Devil and Tom Walker
Selig; b/w; 15 min; U.S.
D: Hardee Kirkland S: Edward McWade
Cast: Harry Lonsdale, William Stowell, Lafayette McKee, Tom Nelson, Rose Evans, Winifred Greenwood

Tom Walker (Lonsdale) is a miser ever in search of greater wealth. While walking home one day, he meets a stranger (Stowell) who reveals himself as the Devil. Ever on his toes, Satan recognizes Tom's greedy nature and offers to make him rich in exchange for his immortal soul. Tom agrees and, sure enough, finds himself very wealthy. But Old Scratch gets the final laugh.

The Devil and Tom Walker is based on the Washington Irving short story of the same name, first published in an 1824 anthology titled *Tales of a Traveler*. An obvious take on the legend of Faust, the tale has always been tinged with controversy due to its presentation of Satan as a black man. Nonetheless, it was a hit both in its day and long afterward (Stephen Vincent Benet acknowledged a debt to it when he wrote *The Devil and Daniel Webster* in 1937).

The film was directed by Hardee Kirkland, whose career behind the camera came to an end a year after this film's release. He fared better (and longer) as an actor; among his performances was a role in Maurice Tourneur's lost Lon Chaney vehicle, *While Paris Sleeps* (1923). TH

Dr. Jekyll and Mr. Hyde
Natural Color Kinematograph; color; 33 min; Great Britain
P: Charles Urban
Cast unknown

Not only is this the first color version of Robert Louis Stevenson's tale, it is one of the first color horror films produced in Great Britain (after Urban's *Trilby and Svengali*, 1911, and *Mephisto* and *Faust*, both 1912), although hand-painted horror films had been done in France by Georges Méliès as early as 1897. And though it was a commercial bust, the Kinemacolor process *was* aesthetically successful, so much so that it was at one point demonstrated for the Pope in Vatican City.

It's too bad the film played in so few theaters. Even trade magazines of the time dedicated to motion pictures seem to have missed it, and as such modern film historians know little about either its approach to the material or its credits. CW

Dr. Jekyll and Mr. Hyde
IMP/Universal; b/w; 27 min; U.S.
D/S: Herbert Brenon P: Carl Laemmle
Cast: King Baggot, Jane Gail, William Sorelle, Howard Crampton, Matt Snyder, Herbert Brenon

Dr. Henry Jekyll (Baggot) divides his time between running a successful practice and tending to the poor. His investigations into the duality of man lead him to develop an elixir that unleashes the dark side of human nature. He drinks it and is taken over by an evil alter ego, Mr. Hyde, who attracts notoriety for terrorizing Londoners. Jekyll is sporadically able to repress Hyde, and during those periods he pursues a normal life with his fiancée, Alice (Gail). In the end, however, Hyde's influence proves stronger and disaster ensues.

German émigré Carl Laemmle saw great potential in the fledgling motion picture industry and in 1909 formed Yankee Film Company with associates Abe and Julius Stern. The company changed its moniker to Independent Moving Pictures Company (IMP) not long thereafter and in 1912 joined forces with eight other small studios to become Universal Film Manufacturing Company. By 1925 the name evolved into Universal Pictures, and the rest, as they say, is history.

Long before Universal dominated the horror genre with such box-office triumphs as *The Phantom of the Opera* (1925) and *Dracula* (1931), the still-new company dabbled in the macabre with this adaptation of Robert Louis Stevenson's venerable novella, *The Strange Case of Dr. Jekyll and Mr. Hyde*. The film was an ideal vehicle for the company's resident star, King Baggot. Baggot is a forgotten figure today; his star waned as he descended into alcoholism, though he continued to work until the mid-1940s (often in un-credited bit parts). He died in 1948. To a contemporary audience, it's difficult to understand what made him a popular actor. He certainly wasn't handsome in any conventional sense of the term, and his style of performing seems artificial to the modern eye. His name in the credits, however, ensured success for scores of early Universal (and IMP) productions.

Dr. Jekyll and Mr. Hyde gives Baggot a chance to carry a film, taking on a difficult dual characterization. But his performance—like the film—has not aged well. Baggot's Jekyll is a prig, callous toward his fiancée and displaying little charm or humor in his less intense moments. And his portrayal of Hyde is worse still; he can't really be faulted for evoking comparisons with Jerry Lewis' much later performance as *The Nutty Professor* (1963), but with his unruly hair and prominent buckteeth, it's hard to picture anything else. The actor also employs a severe, hunched-over walk that, while doubtless meant to evoke the crab-like visage in Stevenson's book, nonetheless comes across as forced and ridiculous. At least this version—as compared to some of the earlier cracks at the tale—allows Hyde a chance to indulge in some real violence, but even that isn't really significant when it's all said and done.

Herbert Brenon's direction is functional at best. The transformations are achieved with a dissolve effect that pales in comparison to the comparatively sophisticated transformation scene in the earlier 1912 version starring James Cruze. TH

Dr. Trimball's Verdict
aka Dr. Trimball's Secret
Hepworth; b/w; 18 min; Great Britain
D: Frank Wilson *P:* Cecil M. Hepworth
Cast: Alec Worcester, Chrissie White

Dr. Trimball (Worcester) doesn't like the fact that he has a rival, so he kills the man in cold blood and disposes of the body. Sometime later, he purchases a skeleton for use in his medical practice. What he doesn't realize is that the bones are those of his victim. When the victim's ghost appears (via the process of superimposition) over the bones, Dr. Trimball has a heart attack and dies.

What's interesting about *Dr. Trimball's Verdict* is that, although it's a horror film, it focuses more on melodrama than camera tricks, saving its major effect—the appearance of the ghost—for the final scene. This is in contrast to most films of its ilk and period, which sought to dazzle the audience with a constant bombardment of photographic effects. But unlike filmmakers such as Georges Méliès and George Albert Smith, Hepworth understood that film audiences were growing more sophisticated. The novelty value of moving pictures was quickly diminishing and eye candy was simply not enough to keep patrons coming back to cinemas. People wanted engaging stories, appealing plot devices and identifiable characters. To this end, Hepworth hired talented people who could deliver the goods in terms of story construction and pacing.

One such person was Frank Wilson, whom Hepworth hired in 1908 to direct comedy shorts. He proved successful enough that Hepworth kept him on and gave him increasingly challenging material. Wilson was also an actor frequently cast in Hepworth's films, including some that he directed. He portrayed Marguerite's brother Valentin in Hepworth's version of *Faust* (1911) and was on hand for Stoll's *The Mystery of Fu Manchu* series that began with *The Scented Envelopes* (1923). His last known film performance came in 1924, his last script was shot in 1926 and he directed his final film, *Saddle King*, in 1929. CW

L'effroi
Gaumont; b/w; 12 min; France
D: Louis Feuillade, Georges-Andre Lacroix
Cast: Marthe Vinot, Jeanne Marie-Laurent

Some sources cite *L'effroi* (the title translates as *The Terror*) as a horror film, but specifics of the storyline seem to have fallen by the wayside. It's known to be an obscure short co-directed by Louis Feuillade and Georges-Andre Lacroix. Feuillade may have been the most prolific filmmaker in history—he amassed over 700 cinematic credits, most of them as director. He dabbled in the horror genre on occasion but is best remembered for such escapist fare as the *Fantomas* (1913-1914), *Les Vampires* (1915) and *Judex* (1916) serials. His co-director, Georges-Andre Lacroix, was far less prolific and is a forgotten figure today. A look at his filmography reveals a predisposition toward costume drama, but it is unclear whether this particular title made use of a period setting.

L'effroi co-star Jeanne Marie-Laurent also had a featured role in *Les Vampires*, which, despite its title, offers nary a bloodsucker. TH

The Evil Power
Rex; b/w; 30 min; U.S.
D/S: Otis Turner
Cast: Margarita Fischer

Director Otis Turner is credited with having directed the very first film adaptation of Robert Louis Stevenson's *Dr. Jekyll and Mr. Hyde* in 1908, though it appears to have been merely a play shot on film—complete with rising and falling curtains between acts. Here, however, he crafts an original work; too bad its "original" plot is a knock-off of so many other short films, novels and plays that came before it: A young woman (Fischer) is hypnotized by an evil doctor who has become obsessed with her.

Margarita Fischer, who was born Margarita Ficher in Missouri Valley, Iowa in 1886, was a popular performer during the silent era, though fear of a backlash against her German-sounding last name led her to insert an *s* into it as World War I approached. Shortly after launching her film career in 1910, she married actor/director Harry Pollard. The two worked closely together until she retired after her last role as the slave girl Eliza in 1927's *Uncle Tom's Cabin* (which Pollard directed). Though her husband died in 1934, Fischer never remarried. She succumbed to heart disease in Encinitas, California in 1975. CW

Feathertop
Natural Color Kinematograph; color; length unknown; Great Britain
P: Charles Urban
Cast unknown

Of the films that were produced with the Kinemcolor process, several can be considered horror, including *Faust* and *Me-*

phisto (both 1912), as well as *Dr. Jekyll and Mr. Hyde* and *Feathertop* (both 1913). The latter was based on Nathaniel Hawthorne's once-popular short story about a witch who endows a scarecrow with life and sends it to destroy the house of her enemy, a village judge. The living scarecrow, transformed into a handsome young man named Feathertop, falls in love with the judge's daughter, but when she sees what he really is, she faints from shock. Feathertop then kills himself in despair.

Feathertop is one of many Natural Color Kinematograph films that is now considered lost. The next version of Hawthorne's tale came in 1916 and was also titled *Feathertop*. CW

From the Beyond
Éclair/American Standard; b/w; 35 min; France/U.S.
D/S: O.A.C. Lund
Cast: Alec B. Francis, Barbara Tennant, O.A.C. Lund, Julia Stewart, Will E. Sheer, J.W. Johnston

Though some sources maintain that *From the Beyond* deals with the ghost of a jilted lover returned from the grave to haunt a former rival, it appears to have actually been about a professor (Francis) who, with the help of a fellow scientist (Sheerer), invents a camera that allows him to record images of the spirits of the dead. If so, the film qualifies as a horror/science fiction hybrid. The film was released on October 15, 1913, two weeks before Halloween, and was produced by the U.S. branch of French company Éclair.

Swedish-born Oscar Alarik Lund (1886-1963) was not only a prolific writer and director, but he was also an actor. His career began in 1912, but he barely made it into the talkie era, directing his last picture in 1933. Most of his early films were done for Éclair, and he often used the same repertory theater of actors. CW

The Ghost
Victor; b/w; length unknown; U.S.
D: James Kirkwood
Cast: James Kirkwood, Gertrude Robinson

Released in August 1913, *The Ghost* was directed by and starred James Kirkwood. He and Gertrude Robinson apparently played a couple that move into a country estate, unaware it may be haunted. The spooky sounds and sinister sights they experience turn out to be caused by—surprise—crooks trying to scare them away from their stash, the famous Remington diamonds.

Since the film is lost, it's difficult to verify specifics about its plot, cast and crew. The idea of criminals holing up in a dilapidated mansion and either pretending to be ghosts or being haunted by real ghosts was a standard of silent cinema. Variations on the theme include *Spooks Do the Moving* (1908), *Baby's Ghost* and *Bill Taken for a Ghost* (both 1911), *Gavroche and the Spirits* (1912), *Ghost of the Hacienda*, *The Haunted House* and *The Tenderfoot's Ghost* (all 1913), *The Haunting of Silas P. Gould* (1915), *Ghost Hounds* and *The Ghost House* (both 1917) and *The Haunted House* (1921), among many others. CW

The Ghost of Sea View Manor
aka **The Ghost of Seaview Manor**
Dragon; b/w; 17 min; U.S.
Credits unknown

A ghost reputedly haunts a manor, but the film's hero unmasks a human culprit.

This obscure short was an entry in the "fake ghost" subgenre. Dragon Film Company is today as obscure as *The Ghost of Sea View Manor*. Filmographies from the time credit the company with only a handful of titles, all of them made in 1913. They almost certainly produced more pictures than what is known, but the particulars are likely lost to time. TH

Ghost of the Hacienda
American/Flying A; b/w; 22 min; U.S.
D: Thomas (Tom) Ricketts
Cast: Edward Coxen, Jean Durrell, George Field, Winifred Greenwood, William Tedmarsh, Chester Withey

Enid (Durrell) and her father take possession of a hacienda they've inherited from a deceased relative. They meet Billy, for whom Enid falls head over heels, and the two get engaged. They also meet Pedro, who tells them of Enid's aunt Ysolda, who was murdered nearby by a Mexican bandit and whose spirit is still alleged to haunt the place. Things get as lively when Billy receives a shipment of gold and hides it as notorious robber Tocquinado looks on. Tocquinado and his men attack the hacienda, but Enid and Billy see them approaching and prepare themselves. When the bad guys break down the door, the ghost of Ysolda confronts them. After they scatter, it turns out that Ysolda is none other than Enid, dressed as her aunt's ghost in order to frighten off the attackers.

Ghost of the Hacienda is an early example of a weird Western, prefiguring a spate of horror-tinged oaters that glutted the market in the 1930s. CW

The Ghost of the White Lady
aka **The White Ghost**
Nordisk; b/w; 45 min; Denmark
Crew unknown
Cast: Rita Sacchetto

A woman (Sacchetto) uses a local legend to frighten a man who has offended her.

The "white lady" ghost archetype turns up in virtually every culture. Typically the female ghost, whose life was ended by traumatic violence, stalks various roads at night. This Danish production isn't really about said ghost, but it uses the archetype as the starting point for a revenge melodrama.

Star Rita Sacchetto was born in Germany to Italian parents; she had a brief silent-era career starring in films in Denmark. She died in Italy in 1959.

Great Northern, Nordisk's usual distributor in North America, released *The Ghost of the White Lady*. TH

The Ghosts
aka **Ghosts; or Who's Afraid?**
Vitagraph; b/w; length unknown; U.S.
D: William J. Bauman *S:* Mary H. O'Connor
Cast: Myrtle Gonzalez, George Cooper, Patricia Palmer, Charles Bennett, Dolores Brown, Thomas Colmensil

The Ghosts is a short about a mansion bedeviled by the spirit of a dead soldier. One of a couple of films with the same title released in 1914, it doesn't appear to have taken its eerie subject matter particularly seriously. Director William J. Bauman (sometimes billed as W.J. Bauman) helmed several films with horrific-sounding titles, including *The Face of Fear* (1913) and *The Terror of the Fold* (1915). But of these, only *The Ghosts* had a degree of horror content. His filmography stops cold in 1915.

George Cooper was something of a favorite of Bauman. The actor's career had the same trajectory as that of many other silent screen stars: The size and quality of his roles diminished with the coming of sound. He did make a brief appearance in *The Return of the Terror* (1934), however. TH

The Green Eye of the Yellow God
Edison; b/w; 10 min; U.S.
D: Richard Ridgely
Cast: Charles Ogle

English poet J. Milton Hayes wrote *The Green Eye of the Little Yellow God* in 1911. It has gone down as the author's best-known work, often read and even spoofed by such luminaries as Harry Secombe, Spike Milligan, Peter Sellers (on *The Goon Show*), Tony Randall and Miss Piggy (on *The Muppet Show*). The poem concerns a British soldier who, to impress his girlfriend, steals the emerald eye from the golden idol of a Hindu goddess. A native murders him and then returns the "eye" to its rightful location.

This sole cinematic adaptation simplifies the title a bit but still offers a faithful interpretation. In it, Carew (Ogle) asks a beautiful girl what she wants for her birthday; she jokes that she would like the green eye from the golden statue worshiped by the locals. Carew takes the joke to heart and in doing so seals his fate.

Lead actor Charles Ogle is best remembered for playing Frankenstein's monster in Edison's *Frankenstein* (1910), though he played a variety of roles throughout his career. Director Richard Ridgely was likewise active in the silents; among his most notable efforts was a version of Balzac's *La Peau de chagrin*, titled *The Magic Skin* (1915). TH

The Haunted Bedroom
Edison; b/w; 10 min; U.S.
Cast: Harry Beaumont, Jack Strong, Mabel Trunnelle, Harry Linson, Harry Eytinge, Carlton S. King

Various characters grasp at a hidden stash of money, but a protective ghost gets in the way.

Edison produced this short variation of the haunted house formula. Rather than make mischief, the spirits here guard against a villainous collection of people who are trying to get rich quick. Surviving credits are sparse, but given that star Harry Beaumont was beginning to dabble in directing around this time, it's possible that he helmed this title. Beaumont was later nominated for an Oscar for directing *The Broadway Melody* (1929). He gave up acting in 1918 and remained active behind the camera until the late 1940s. TH

The Haunted Chamber
Anderson; b/w; 45 min; U.S.
Credits unknown

This obscure silent film may have been influenced by Henry Wadsworth Longfellow's poem of the same title, from his 1873 collection *Birds of Passage*. In it, the poet describes memories of the past as demons, haunting the house of the heart.

Anderson was a short-lived production and distribution house, active during the early part of the 20th century. None of its work has withstood the test of time and is as little known today as *The Haunted Chamber*. Though information for this particular film is sparse, sources do cite it as a horror film, though one likely tempered by humor. CW

The Haunted House
American; b/w; length unknown; U.S.
S: Maie B. Havey
Cast: Vivian Rich, Julius Frankenberg, Jack Richardson, Harry Van Meter

A girl (Rich) has more beaus than she can handle. In an effort to narrow the field to "the one," she appeals to their sense of machismo—whoever is able to spend the night in a local haunted house will have her hand in marriage. Several men take her up on the challenge, but only one emerges to claim the prize.

Leading lady Vivian Rich was a popular ingénue between 1912 and 1931, after which she retired from cinema. She died in a car crash in 1957. Her co-star, Jack Richardson, made a career of unbilled bit parts; some of his later credits include Frank Capra's *Mr. Smith Goes to Washington* (1939) and horror titles *The Son of Kong* (1933) and *The Climax* (1944).

Screenwriter Maie B. Havey (sometimes credited as M.B. Havey or Maybelle Harvey) was also a part-time actress. Her credits are confined to the early silent era, and it appears that melodrama was her specialty. TH

The Haunted House
Kalem; b/w; 15 min; U.S.
Credits unknown
Cast: Edgar L. Davenport, Olive Temple, Adelaide Lawrence, Stephen Purdee

A burglar known as "Spider Pete" (Purdee) sets his eyes on a swanky house, not realizing that it's haunted. The home's resident ghost thwarts Spider Pete's attempts at robbery.

One of several films released in 1913 under the same title, this *Haunted House* plays things straight without the standard "ha, no ghosts after all" ending. It also offers a benevolent spirit instead of the usual malefic force. Stephen Purdee plays the colorfully named Spider Pete, whose surviving filmography reflects that he was typecast as various knaves, villains and slippery types. The presence of child actress Adelaide Lawrence may yield some clue as to who was responsible for the film. Her father, Edmund Lawrence, directed the bulk of the films in which she appeared, so it's probable that he called the shots here. Edmund finished his career with *The House of Secrets* (1929) and died in 1931. Adelaide made her last appearance (at age 13) in her father's *The Queen of Hearts* (1918), though she lived until 1989.

The Kalem Company, whose flirtations with the horror genre also yielded *The Legend of Sleepy Hollow* (1908) and *Haunted by Conscience* (1910), produced *The Haunted House*. TH

The Haunted House
Pathé; b/w; 8 min; France
Credits unknown

Pathé produced this obscure short, set near rather than within a haunted house. Little is known about the film—no information has survived naming its participants—but it appears to have utilized a full arsenal of photographic trickery. Set in a Spanish inn, *The Haunted House* concerned a group of peasants who observe some weird, possibly supernatural goings-on. A haunted house is observed in the distance, with strange faces and other oddities appearing in its windows.

The film was one of at least four in 1913 bearing the same title. Some sources say this particular one dates from 1912, but the actual evidence suggests that it was released in July 1913. TH

The Haunted House
aka La maison abandonée
Pathéplay; b/w; 17 min; U.S.
Crew unknown
Cast: Charles E. Bunnell, Julia Walcott, Morris W. McGee, Octavia Handworth, Crane Wilbur

In this short feature, a little girl fears a haunted house near which she is forced to walk one creepy night.

The Haunted House's supporting cast included Crane Wilbur (1886-1973), who was then in the midst of a reasonably successful career as a young lead. Soon after its release, he expanded his efforts from acting to writing and directing, logging his first off-screen credits in 1915. By the mid-1940s, he had given up acting completely, working behind the scenes on Broadway as he continued writing and directing motion pictures. His most significant horror credits are the Vincent Price vehicles *House of Wax* (1953) and *The Mad Magician* (1954).

Production company Pathéplay was the American arm of the French company Pathé, though the company later adopted the name of its parent company. It was one of a group of studios absorbed into RKO in the late 1920s. French Pathé, on the other hand, is still in operation today. Pathéplay made a number of short features between 1913 and 1915. Redundantly, the company's French parent also produced a film titled *The Haunted House* in 1913. TH

In the Grip of a Charlatan
Kalem; b/w; 17 min; U.S.
Crew unknown
Cast: Alice Joyce, Tom Moore, Robert Paton Gibbs, Richard Purdon

Young heiress Anne Sinclair (Joyce) comes to believe that occultism can cure society's ills. She falls in with Swami Baroudi (Gibbs), a charlatan who uses trickery to fake amazing displays of occult power (though he *does* possess the power of hypnotism). Baroudi places Anne in a trance and sends her to steal a bejeweled necklace. She returns with the item, but a disturbance in the house awakens her from her stupor. She tries to leave, and Baroudi, fearing the law, restrains her. Anne's father (Purdon) and her fiancé Robert (Moore) worry over the girl's absence. After hiring detectives to find her, to no avail, Robert finds the Swami's business card, connects the dots and leads police to the charlatan's residence. Sure enough, they find Anne, who has gotten her hands on a knife and is planning Baroudi's murder. The girl is freed, and Baroudi is taken into custody.

Alice Joyce was born in Kansas City, Missouri in 1890; after the dissolution of her parents' marriage in 1900, her father took her and her brother to Falls Church, Virginia. By 1910 the kids were back with their mother (and her new husband) in the Bronx. That same year Sidney Olcott, an up-and-coming director who had been lured away from Biograph by the Kalem Company, discovered Alice. It was for Kalem and Olcott that Joyce made her first film, *The Deacon's Daughter*, in 1910. Joyce proved popular with audiences, and she had a successful career until the advent of sound. During her early film years, she often starred beside her first husband, Tom Moore, with whom she had a daughter.

In the Grip of a Charlatan was released on April 7, 1913. CW

In the Grip of the Vampire
Gaumont; b/w; length unknown; France
D/S: Leonce Perret
Cast unknown

An evil guardian drains the life out of his female ward. After tiring of her, he uses a drug to drive her insane. A kindly scientist intervenes, using hypnosis.

Details for *In the Grip of the Vampire* are scant. Some sources, including Raymond T. McNally and Radu Florescu's groundbreaking *In Search of Dracula* (1972), mistakenly cite it as an American film. The story doesn't seem to have actually had anything to do with a supernatural vampire, though it did reportedly contain some ghoulish flourishes. It is commonly acknowledged that Leonce Perret wrote the film. Perret was a silent-era, avant-garde filmmaker, and his innovations in the areas of lighting, camerawork and editing have long been overlooked. He began his entertainment career in the theater, and after making some small films in Germany, he returned to his native France and worked for Gaumont. His ambition eventually took him to Hollywood where, despite the success of his anti-war drama *Lest We Forget* (1918), he was unable to comfortably settle. In time he returned to France and there finished out his career.

Perhaps owing to the lukewarm reception of his final films, Perret's work was forgotten for many years. In the new millennium, however, his value and importance in the development of cinematic techniques have been recognized. Many of his films are considered lost, including this title (which is not listed on many of his filmographies). TH

In the Power of the Hypnotist
Warner; b/w; 45 min; U.S.
D: Sidney Olcott, T. Hayes Hunter
Cast: Sidney Olcott, Gene Gauntier, Jack J. Clark

This is one of many silent-era melodramas dealing with an evil hypnotist.

Co-director T. Hayes Hunter was at the beginning of his none-too-distinguished career here. He continued to work into the mid-1930s, helming his only well-remembered feature, *The Ghoul*, in 1933. Shortly after that his career came to an end, with the films he left behind generally proving him to be a pedestrian journeyman. He died in 1944.

Hunter's collaborator, Sidney Olcott, revisited the genre with *The Ghost of Twisted Oak* in 1915. TH

In the Toils of the Devil
Milano; b/w; 40 min; Italy
Credits unknown

This short feature was typical of Italian cinema at the time in that it was yet another rip-off of *Faust*. In it, a man makes a pact with Mephistopheles, only to have that pact come back and bite him. It is unknown whether a print of this feature-length (for the time) film still exists, though its original Italian title is apparently lost. It was released in the U.S. in 1913, but it's likely that it reached Italian audiences earlier. Production company Milano also released *The Fairy Jewel* and *Inferno* (both 1911), *The Thief and the Porter's Head* (1913) and *The Mechanical Man* (1921). CW

The Island of Terror
aka **L'île d'epouvante**
Eclipse; b/w; length unknown; France
D: Joë Hamman
Cast: Joë Hamman

Prolific British author Herbert George (H.G.) Wells (1866-1946) may have been one of the major political commentators of his time, but he is best known today for his provocative science fiction novels, most of which were written between 1895 and 1910. These include *The Time Machine* (1895), *The Invisible Man* (1897), *War of the Worlds* (1898), *First Men in the Moon* (1901), *The Food of the Gods* (1904), *In the Days of the Comet* (1906) and *The Sleeper Wakes* (1910).

Among these works was *The Island of Dr. Moreau* (1896), a thinly veiled diatribe against animal vivisection. The story concerns a shipwreck victim named Edward Prendick who, after being rescued, is taken to a tropical island. There he's introduced to Dr. Moreau, who lives on the island and is conducting unspecified experiments. A short time later, Prendick spies mysterious, manlike creatures that have the heads of hogs, and it's revealed that Moreau is creating new types of "men" by vivisecting animals and splicing their parts to one another. It's also explained that in order for the "beast men" to behave like humans (and to protect Moreau), a body of laws has been put in place that prohibits tasting blood or eating flesh. In the end, however, the beast men cannot be controlled. Moreau and Montgomery are killed, and Prendick accidentally sets Moreau's enclosure alight. Months later, Prendick is still living on the island with the increasingly wild creatures; he escapes when a ship occupied by two dead men washes ashore.

The first unofficial adaptation of Wells' novel came from France in 1913 (some sources maintain that 1911 was the year of production and 1913 the year of release). Titled *The Island of Terror*, it was a short by Eclipse which pared Wells' story down to the basics. And since Wells was known to ferociously protect his copyrights, names and incidents were changed to avoid legal action. Edward Prendick became George Ramsey, who is washed ashore on a remote island in the Pacific after a shipping accident. There he meets Moreau substitute Dr. Wagner, who is conducting weird experiments in his private rooms. Not long afterward, Ramsey spies blood flowing from beneath Wagner's door and bursts in to find the doctor experimenting on a native. The experiment is a failure, leaving Ramsey to be Wagner's next victim. But the lab catches fire, Ramsey escapes on a raft and three of Wagner's more successful "experiments" trap and kill the doctor.

Wells' novel has been adapted legitimately no less than three times, as *Island of Lost Souls* in 1932 and *The Island of Dr. Moreau* in 1977 and 1996. It also provides the unofficial basis for *The Island of the Lost* (1921), *Terror Is a Man* (1959), *The Twilight People* (1973) and the shot-on-video *Dr. Moreau's House of Pain* (2004). Yet *The Island of Terror*, forgotten though it is, can lay claim to being the first film adaptation of *Moreau* ever produced.

Joe Hamman directed several films during the silent era, but he is better known as an actor. He appeared in approximately 100 films between 1907 and 1967, though his last credited role was in *Face of Destiny* in 1940. CW

The Isle of the Dead
Gluckstadt; b/w; length unknown; Denmark
D/P: Wilhelm Gluckstadt
Cast unknown

This Danish fantasy included some ghostly set pieces.

Director Wilhelm (or Vilhelm) Gluckstadt was active in Denmark during the early days of cinema, but most of his filmography appears to have vanished. It is unclear whether Gluckstadt derived inspiration here from Arnold Bocklin's painting *Isle of the Dead* (aka *Der Toteninsel*), which later provided a major influence for a 1945 film of the same name starring Boris Karloff.

As a point of trivia, the Karloff film, which is part of the now-legendary series of suggestive horror films produced by Val Lewton, was set during the Balkan War, which was winding down around the time this picture was released. TH

It Is Never Too Late to Mend
Edison; b/w; 23 min; U.S.
D/S: Charles M. Seay
Cast: Walter Edwin, Wyatt Burns, Mary Fuller, John Sturgeon, William Bechtel, Charles Ogle

British author Charles Reade was a popular playwright who, in the mid-1800s, dealt with England's then-horrendous prison system in his first major novel, *It Is Never Too Late to Mend: A Matter-of-Fact Romance* (1856). Though the political leaders of the day challenged the book's veracity, the Queen took stock of the situation and ordered major penal reforms. (It was only the beginning for Reade, who went on to write a series of novels pressing for change in such disparate arenas as private asylums and trade unions.) Reade's novel proved successful and was eventually adapted into play form. It's also the source of this Edison film, the story's second cinematic adaptation. What's strange here is that neither of these early adaptations came from Great Britain, where the book made its biggest splash.

The story concerns one Tom Robinson, who is in love with Susan Merton. Village squire John Meadows also has his heart set on the young woman, and he falsely accuses Tom of a crime. Tom is thrown in the slammer, where he experiences the system's violence and corruption first-hand. But in the end, everything works out: the Squire's plan is revealed, Robinson's name is cleared and Susan is reunited with her lover once and for all.

Mary Fuller and Charles Ogle, who had costarred in *Bluebeard* (1909) and *Frankenstein* (1910), are teamed here as well. Throughout their careers, the two starred in approximately 80 films together.

A third adaptation, *It's Never Too Late to Mend*, was made in Great Britain in 1917. CW

Love from Out of the Grave
Film d'Art; b/w; 25 min; France
Credits unknown

A tortured artist murders his wife's lover, only to be haunted by the adulterer's ghost.

This extremely obscure, probably lost French short film was made by Film d'Art, which had once been associated with Pathé. Film d'Art also had a studio in Italy, Film d'Art Italiana. The company's most ambitious feature may have been *The Life and Death of Richard III*, the very first feature-length adaptation of William Shakespeare's tragedy *Richard III* (c. 1591), which was co-produced with U.S. production companies. CW

The Man in the White Cloak
Nordisk; b/w; 33 (45) min; Denmark
Credits unknown

This minor film from producer Nordisk dealt with a doctor who is trapped in a terrible snowstorm and led to an old castle (and a treasure) by a pointing apparition. Whether the film's tone was one of horror or melodrama is difficult to know for certain, but newspapers of the day declared it:

> Absolutely the Most Sensational and Exciting Photo-Play every [sic] produced by the Famous Nordisk Company … IT IS WONDERFUL! Be Sure and See this Masterpiece!

The same paper also stated that the film was filled with "weird scenes," suggesting at least some horror content.

Nordisk's usual North American distributor, Great Northern, released *The Man in the White Cloak* in the United States. Other horror films produced by the Danish company include *Trilby* (1908), *The Grey Lady* and *The Mystery of the Lama Convent* (both 1909), *Dr. Jekyll and Mr. Hyde* and *Necklace of the Dead* (both 1910), *The Life of a Nun* (1911), *Atlantis* (1913) and *Leaves from Satan's Book* (1921). CW

Maria Marten, or The Murder in the Red Barn
aka **Maria Marten: a Murder in the Red Barn**
Motograph; b/w; Great Britain
D/S: Maurice Elvey
Cast: Elizabeth Risdon, Nessie Blackford, Maurice Elvey, Fred Groves, Mary McKenzie, A.G. Ogden, Douglas Payne

Perhaps the most influential of the silent versions of the grisly true story, *Maria Marten, or The Murder in the Red Barn* tells the tale of young Maria, who was murdered by her lover, William Corder, in a red-tiled barn in Polstead, Suffolk, Great Britain in 1827. Director/screenwriter Maurice Elvey (1887-1967) lifts from various stage adaptations a depiction of Corder as a mature, wealthy landowner. When his affair with Maria (Risdon) threatens to be made public by her pregnancy, Corder (Groves) arranges to meet her in a red barn on the outskirts of Polstead where he murders and buries her there. Her mother begins to have dreams in which her daughter's ghost visits her and claims that her body is buried in the red barn. (Some sources claim, incorrectly, that in this version it is Corder's mother who experiences the ghostly visitations while sleeping.) Corder is apprehended and put to death.

This is one of Elvey's earliest films; he went on to a lengthy career marked by notable successes in several genres, though he is best remembered for his horror films, including *The Suicide Club* (1914), *Flames* (1917), *At the Villa Rose* (1920), *The Hound of the Baskervilles* (1921), *The Phantom Fiend* (1932) and *The Clairvoyant* (1934), as well as his science fiction entry, *Transatlantic Tunnel* (1935). He directed his last film, *Second Fiddle*, in 1957, 10 years before his death at age 79.

Elvey, who also has a part in the picture as Captain Matthews, shot *Maria Marten* on location in the county of Suffolk, along the eastern coast of Great Britain. It was there that the original red barn stood and the murder of Maria Marten took place, though the county may today be as famous for having housed British mystery writer Ruth Rendell as it is for a murder committed almost two centuries ago.

The next screen version would be *Maria Marten* (1928), though the most famous would be the film that made Tod Slaughter a household name in Great Britain, *Maria Marten, or The Murder in the Red Barn* (1935). CW

The Medium's Nemesis
Thanhauser; b/w; 17 min; U.S.
Crew unknown
Cast: Mrs. Lawrence Marston, Marie Eline, Harry Benham, Sidney Bracey

A phony medium (Marston) is unmasked by a client (Eline), but not before the medium has frightened a man into believing that he has come face to face with the ghost of the person he murdered.

Spirits and ersatz spiritualists populate this long-lost melodrama from Thanhauser. Mrs. Lawrence Marston was, as one might guess, the wife of actor and scenarist Lawrence Marston. Little is known about either of them, though they occasionally turned up together in the odd melodrama. Among the actors, Sidney Bracey had the longest career, though most of it was comprised of unbilled bit appearances. Among his later credits are roles in such classics as *Duck Soup* (1933), *The Mystery of the Wax Museum* (1933), *The Black Room* (1935), *Les Miserables* (1935) and *Meet John Doe* (1941). TH

The Mysterious Stranger
Essanay; b/w; 11 min; U.S.
Credits unknown
Cast: Bryant Washburn, E.H. Calvert

This one-reel comedy from Essanay appears to have been a typical attempt at mining an oft-repeated theme: A buffoon is haunted by visions. It starred prolific Chicago-born actor Bryant Washburn, who entered films in 1911. After an initial period in which he had large parts in many minor films, he became a noted character actor in well over 300 films before retiring in the late 1940s. Virginia-born E.H. Calvert was not quite as active, but his career was also a long one, lasting from 1912 to 1939. In addition to acting, he directed well over 60 films, all of them during the silent era.

The Mysterious Stranger should not be confused with the many other silent films bearing the same title, which were produced in 1908, 1911, 1921 and 1925. CW

The Mystic Moonstone
aka **Mystic Moonstone**
Lion's Head/Cricks and Martin; b/w; length unknown; Great Britain
D: David Aylott
Cast unknown

Not to be confused with the various adaptations of Wilkie Collins' horror mystery *The Moonstone* (1868), which had previously been filmed in 1909 and 1911, *The Mystic Moonstone* is yet another trick-photography picture. It seems that David Aylott was oblivious to how stale these films were becoming, what with melodramas quickly overtaking special effects extravaganzas in popularity. This tale of a farmer who discovers a magic moonstone and learns that he can use it to make objects disappear is decidedly old hat even by the standards of its day. CW

The Occult
American/Flying A; b/w; length unknown; U.S.
D: Allan Dwan
Cast: Sydney Ayres, Jacques Jaccard, Violet Knights, Louise Lester, Jack Richardson, Vivian Rich

Little is known about this short subject containing hypnotism and séances. It was a relatively early directorial effort by Allan Dwan (1885-1981). Born in Canada, Dwan entered the U.S. film industry in 1911. Though he had only been making movies for two years at the time of *The Occult*, he had established himself as a reliable craftsman by then, with a string of solid short subjects under his belt. He later proved to be particularly adept at action and adventure; his work includes the classics *Robin Hood* (1922) with Douglas Fairbanks, Sr., and *The Sands of Iwo Jima* (1949) with John Wayne. He revisited the horror genre with *The Forbidden Room* (1914) and *The Gorilla* (1939), though the latter's chills were smothered in the crib by the nauseating comedy of the ever-mugging Ritz Brothers.

Leading man Sydney Ayres was popular with audiences, thanks largely to his good looks and easy charm. He died in 1916 due to complications from multiple sclerosis. TH

The Other
aka **Der Andere**
Vitaskop; b/w; 65 min; Germany
D/S: Max Mack *P:* Jules Greenbaum *C:* Hermann Boettger
Cast: Albert Basserman, Hanni Weisse, Emerich Hanus, Rely Ridon, Otto Collot, Paul Passarge

Dr. Hallers (Basserman) professes skepticism at the concept of dual personality disorder, even as he suffers from blackouts. It is eventually revealed that during these episodes, his baser instinct takes over and runs amok.

A stage play by Paul Lindau formed the basis of *The Other*; the play took its inspiration from Robert Louis Stevenson's classic novella *The Strange Case of Dr. Jekyll and Mr. Hyde*. The play changes many of the particulars, including the occupation of the protagonist; instead of being an overzealous scientist working to better mankind, Dr. Hallers is a lawyer well known in Berlin society. Nor does Hallers concoct a potion that unleashes his evil side. He merely suffers from a split personality (even as he smugly denies the existence of such a disorder).

The film is notable as one of the first screen appearances of the great Albert Basserman. Born in Germany in 1867, Basserman devoted much of his career to the stage, though he took occasional film roles. The rise of Hitler forced him to leave his homeland; his wife was Jewish, and Hitler, who admired the actor, said he would only be permitted to keep working if he divorced her. Basserman made his way to the United States, where he was nominated for an Oscar for his performance in Alfred Hitchcock's *Foreign Correspondent* (1940). In addition to Hitchcock, he also worked with such giants as Ernst Lubitsch (*Pharaoh's Wife*, 1922), George Cukor (*A Woman's Face*, 1941), Leo McCarey (*Once Upon a Honeymoon*, 1942), Michael Powell and Emeric Pressburger (*The Red Shoes*, 1948). The latter proved to be his last film; he died in 1952. Director Max Mack also fled Germany in the 1930s, finishing out his career in the United Kingdom. He was remarkably prolific in the early days of German cinema, but his output dwindled considerably with the coming of sound. TH

Owana, The Devil Woman
Nestor; b/w; 11 min; U.S.
P: David Horseley
Cast unknown

This short subject tells the tale of a Native American prince who runs afoul of an evil witch named Owana. The witch transforms the man into a horse on his wedding day, but he is restored to his normal form when a benevolent spirit intercedes.

No cast information has survived on this short subject, which has long been considered lost. Production company Nestor Film churned out almost 1,000 titles between 1909 and 1919, several of which had horrific aspects (*Poisoned Waters*, 1913; *The White Wolf*, 1914; *His Egyptian Affinity* and *When the Spirits Moved*, both 1915 and *Mingling Spirits*, 1916). By 1920, the studio had quietly folded up shop.

Owana, The Devil Woman was released on June 6, 1913. TH

The Phantom Signal
Edison; b/w; 20 min; U.S.
D: George Lessey *S:* John H. Collins
Cast: Charles Ogle, Mary Abbey, Bessie Learn, Ben Wilson, Edna Hamel, Bigelow Cooper

Railway disasters are foretold by the appearance of a skeleton. This obscure short from Edison is believed to be lost, but it's safe to assume that the skeleton was intended to be eerie and that trick photography abounded.

George Lessey had an undistinguished career during the silent era. His last film as a director was probably *The Evil Dead* (1922), which, despite its title, wasn't a horror film. (It was a re-titled, presumably re-edited, segment of a 1920 serial originally called *The $1,000,000 Reward*.) Lessey also directed several mystery thrillers, but *The Phantom Signal* (along with *The Bells* and *It Is Never Too Late to Mend*, both also released in 1913) was one of the few that were horror-themed. After hanging up his megaphone, Lessey focused on an acting career. In that capacity he remained active until his death in 1947, finishing out his career in unbilled bits in everything from *Now, Voyager* (1942) to *Charlie Chan in the Secret Service* (1944).

The Phantom Signal's cast included Charles Ogle, best remembered for portraying the monster in Edison's *Frankenstein* (1910). TH

The Picture of Dorian Gray
New York Motion Picture; b/w; length unknown; U.S.
D: Phillips Smalley *S:* Lois Weber
Cast: Wallace Reid, Lois Weber, Phillips Smalley

Based on the famed novel by Oscar Wilde, this adaptation is one of the lesser-known silent film versions, and, like the others, appears to be lost. The movie covered the basics of Wilde's story, with Reid playing the handsome young man whose image in a portrait ages and rots while he remains young and indulgent of his carnal appetites. Weber likely played the role of Sybil Vane, the lover Dorian spurns and drives to suicide. Director Phillips Smalley may have played a variation on Lord Henry Wotton, the corruptive influence who teaches Dorian how to trade on his youth and beauty.

Phillips was a popular director during the silent era, amassing over 300 credits. He launched his career in 1911, co-directing short features with film pioneer Edwin S. Porter. He was married at the time of this production to frequent collaborator Lois Weber, who later became a director as well (she is often mistakenly referred to as the first woman to have directed a feature-length film, an honor that most likely goes to France's Alice Guy). CW

The Pit and the Pendulum
aka **Rivals**
Solax; b/w; 36(50) min; U.S.
D/S/Co-P: Alice Guy-Blaché *Co-P:* Herbert Blaché
Cast: Darwin Karr

By 1913, Alice Guy-Blaché's production company Solax was headed in the direction of bona fide feature-length films. Guy-Blaché examined the technical innovations of her contemporaries, particularly those of Edison director Edwin S. Porter, and tweaked the advances into a style wholly her own, similar to the way D.W. Griffith later became famous for introducing his own hybrid aesthetic into the mainstream. Guy-Blaché's unique cinematic voice infuses works such as *La vie du Christ* (1906) and *The Pit and the Pendulum*, the latter the first English-language adaptation of Edgar Allan Poe's short story and one set toward the end of the Spanish Inquisition. (The tale was previously filmed in 1909 in Guy-Blaché's native France by Henri Desfontaines.)

The film begins with a romantic outing during which Pedro forces his affections on a beautiful young woman. Pedro's heroic rival Alonzo (Karr), who appears from nowhere and physically separates the two, defends her honor. As Alonzo and the young woman walk away, Pedro gives chase and attempts to stab them; this time Alonzo throws him down a hillside. The spurned would-be lover then comes upon a monastery of excommunicated monks who live by a creed of violence. He applies for admission and is accepted. Eventually, after years of pondering his revenge, he gets the opportunity to frame Alonzo—who is now a physician tending the poor—for theft and sorcery. Alonzo is brought before the Grand Inquisitor, found guilty and sentenced to death by pit or by pendulum. At the film's climax, Alonzo is tied to a rack while the pendulum's blade swings ever closer. But at the last possible moment, hungry rats gnaw through his ropes, setting him free to escape and reunite with his lover.

The film illustrates the director's ongoing obsession with rats, which had begun with *The Sewer* and *Dublin Dan* (both 1912) and skittered its way through *Dick Whittington and His Cat* (1913) on its way to *The Ocean Waif* (1916). Certainly, lead actor Karr had a difficult time on set with the small but dangerous rodents, who insisted on biting *him* rather than the ropes. It's not surpris-

A beautiful young woman becomes the cause of the conflict that leads to injustice, from *The Pit and the Pendulum*.

ing, then, that the climactic scene in the final release is reputed to have consisted entirely of first-take material. Not only did Karr refuse to do any retakes involving the rats, but also the vermin reportedly got so aggressively out of control that the crew took it upon themselves to destroy them!

It's unfortunate that only a portion of the film (from its first reel) is known to exist; even that much is enough to suggest that *The Pit and the Pendulum* is an important film in the Poe canon, with a fairly large budget and, according to some contemporary reviewers, a major finale set piece, one that today would seem to rival that of Roger Corman's classic 1961 version.

Guy-Blaché's film was a big moneymaker with movie audiences across North America, leaving one to wonder why she so rarely tackled horrific subject matter in the years that followed. Without, apparently, an ounce of comic relief, her film stands as a major horror effort years before the genre was honed by the German Expressionist movement of the 1920s.

In an apparent attempt to head off religious objections over its depiction of the Roman Catholic Church, the film strains to portray the Inquisition as a group of renegade monks living outside the sway and working against the will of the Church. Of course, nothing could have been further from the truth. The Inquisition was instituted in the 1470s by Spanish Catholic leaders in an effort to prevent converted Jews from returning to their traditions, since doing so threatened to deny the Church access to the converts' wealth and property.

Though some sources claim that the film contained four or five reels, Guy-Blaché, in her autobiography, puts the number at three. CW

Poisoned Waters
Nestor; b/w; length unknown; U.S.
D: Milton J. Fahrney *P:* David Horsley
Cast: Valleria Alison, Louis Fitzroy, Paul Machette, Miss Miller, Lindley Phipps, Hugh Vernon

A witch places an unusual curse on a fountain. Anybody who bathes in its water will become beautiful … but anybody who drinks from it will die!

Producer David Horsley ensured his place in film history by being the first to film a motion picture in Hollywood, California. Born in Great Britain, Horsley made his way to the United States and established the Centaur Film Company. This became the Nestor Motion Picture Company, which opened the first studio in Hollywood in 1911. Horsley then struck a deal with Carl Laemmle, whereby Nestor merged with a number of other smaller studios to form an early incarnation of Universal Pictures. But after a falling out with Laemmle in 1913, Horsley sold off his share of the company and left the industry for a brief period. He returned toward the end of the teens under a new production banner (David Horsley Productions), which he ran until 1926. He died in 1933.

Director Milton J. Fahrney was a favorite of Horsley's. A quick, efficient journeyman, he never created a lasting name even though he helmed over 150 (mostly slapstick) titles. A look at the two men's filmographies reveals that *Poisoned Waters* was a fairly atypical choice of subject matter for both of them. TH

The Queen of Spades
aka **La Dama di Picche**; **La dame de pique**; **Le reina de Bastos**; **Queen of Spades**
Cines/Acquila; b/w; 23 min; Italy
D: Baldassarre Negroni
Cast: Leda Gys, Hesperia, Ignazio Lupi, Adele Bianchi Azzarili, Alberto Collo

This 1913 adaptation of Alexander Pushkin's *Pikovaya dama* (*The Queen of Spades*) is best known for the casting of Hesperia, otherwise known as Olga Mambelli. Mambelli was an Italian actress who'd gained fame as a diva, performing in operas around Europe. She was married to producer and director Baldassarre Negroni, who directed the picture. The two wound up working on a couple of dozen films or so.

The plotline of the film (and of Pushkin's story) concerns a soldier who attempts to steal the secret of winning at cards from an old dame. His pushiness causes her death, but her ghost appears to him several days later and reveals the secret while setting up several additional conditions for victory. Unfortunately it all goes bad, and he forfeits the final game, after which he goes insane.

Negroni's film is notable for being based less on Pushkin's story than on Tchaikovsky's 1890 three-act opera adaptation, hence the casting of notable opera performers Hesperia, Ignazio Lupi (her frequent male co-star) and Leda Gys (pseudonym for Giselda Lombardo, wife of producer Gustavo Lombardo).

This was one of two film adaptations of the story made in 1913; the other, *Queen of Spades*, was done by U.S. studio Fidelity. CW

Queen of Spades
Fidelity; b/w; length unknown; U.S.
Credits unknown

This is one of the more obscure film adaptations of Alexander Pushkin's 1833 short story *Pikovaya dama*. The story deals with Hermann, a young Germanic-Russian soldier who attempts to learn the secret of winning at cards from an old countess (who in turn learned it from the infamous Compte de Saint-Germain). After Hermann seduces her young female ward and causes the old woman's death, the Countess' spirit visits him and reveals the secret he seeks; the results, however, are not what he expects.

Very little is known about the particulars of this film or its production, other than the fact that it was made by Fidelity Pictures Company, a U.S.-based distributor with a small amount of product to their name, all of it released in the second and third decades of the 20th century.

The next version, *The Queen of Spades* from Russian director Yakov Protazanov, came in 1916 and remains one of the best known of the silent era. CW

Simple Simon and the Haunted House
aka **Onésime et la maison hanté**; **Simple Simon Has a Fright**
Gaumont; b/w; 11 min; France
D: Jean Durand
Cast: Ernest Bourbon, Gaston Modot

Simple Simon becomes smitten with a beautiful young woman. After stalking her to her home, he breaks in and leaves a note expressing his undying devotion. Her father (a doctor) finds the note and, apparently not of a romantic bent, becomes angry and decides to teach Simon a lesson. He has a patient in need of a new pair of legs, so he ties Simon to a table and amputates both his legs, causing the love-struck young man consternation but no apparent pain.

Though the bent is entirely humorous, the film's interest in severed (though bloodless) appendages foreshadows the darkly comical *Grand Guignol* of the films of H.G. Lewis (*Blood Feast*, 1963), and, later, the torture porn subgenre (*Saw*, 2004).

Despite the title, there's no haunted house. And as usual, uninspired Jean Durand handled the film's directing chores. Ernest Bourbon portrayed Simple Simon. The film was part of a long-running series centered on the character of Onésime, or Simple Simon, as the name translates into English. Onésime was a fairly typical stock character, the simpleton with a heart of gold. The character got his start in *Onésime garçon costumier* (1912), and he proved popular enough with French audiences to spawn an entire series. All told there were at least 63 Onésime short subjects, only a few of which ever made it to the United States. CW/TH

Simple Simon and the Suicide Club
Gaumont; b/w; 7 min; France
D: Jean Durand
Cast: Ernest Bourbon, Gaston Modot

Simple Simon, known as Onésime in his native France, starred in a series of films corresponding to the United States' "hayseed" comedies, in which a moronic character inadvertently escapes danger through his own bumbling stupidity. After facing down the Devil in the previous year's *Simple Simon and the Devil* (1912), he finds himself here tangled up with a suicide club.

The idea of suicide clubs was first unleashed upon the world through Robert Louis Stevenson's 1878 short story *The Suicide Club*. Cinema expressed its interest early on when D.W. Griffith filmed the first adaptation in 1909, also titled *The Suicide Club*. Imitations followed immediately, most produced by French companies, including Éclair's Nick Carter vehicle *The Suicide Club* (1909) and Lux's *The American Suicide Club* (1910). (One must assume that these latter two films varied the material enough to avoid copyright infringement.) By 1913, the story and subsequent film versions were popular enough that a comedic take was inevitable. Director Jean Durand and actor Ernest Bourbon took the leap. CW

The Spectre of Jago
aka **Lo Spettro di Jago**; **Iago's Inheritance**; **Heir of Jago**; **L'erede di Jago**
Savoia; b/w; 32 min; Italy
D: Alberto Carlo Lolli
Cast: Ubaldo Maria Del Colle, Adriana Costamagna, Giovanni Spano, Arturo Garzes, Ettore Mazzanti

Director Alberto Carlo Lolli was active from 1909 until the early 1920s. It is unclear whether this film (considered, like the bulk of the Lolli's work, to be lost) can legitimately be called horror, but the scant information available on it makes it seem likely.

Based on a novel by Charles Darlington (whose work was the basis of the same year's *By Power of Attorney*), *The Spectre of Jago* was probably similar in plot to Pierre Caron's 1921 film *The Man Who Sold His Soul to the Devil*, in which a banker uses supernatural means to replenish his dwindling fortune.

Jago is unusual in its reported length, indicating that it took up at least three reels. Most movies of the time were less than a single reel, clocking in at between 5 and 9 minutes. TH/CW

The Spell
Power Picture Plays; b/w; 35 min; U.S.
Credits unknown

An evil hypnotist places an innocent young girl under his spell. When the girl's dashing fiancé gets wind of what is going on, he uses his own mental abilities to defeat the villain.

Power Picture Plays began making films in 1909, but by the early 1920s they had gone under. They didn't dabble much in horror, though in addition to this title they also produced *The Beechwood Ghost* (1910) and *An Old Time Nightmare* (1911). *The Spell* should not be confused with another film with the same title released in 1913; in that production, hypnosis is used purely for comedic purposes. TH

The Star of India
aka **Star of India**
Blaché; b/w; 40 min; U.S.
D/Co-P: Herbert Blaché *Co-P:* Alice Guy-Blaché
Cast: Fraunie Fraunholz, Claire Whitney, Andrew Rogers, Joseph Levering, Fred English, William Boyd

Some sources wrongly identify this as a Blanche production. Others, equally mistakenly, list the film as a Blacke production directed by R. Prieur. In truth, *The Star of India* was the work of husband-and-wife team Herbert and Alice Guy-Blaché. Alice had already been a filmmaker for some years. Her husband entered cinema in her wake. *The Star of India* was an unremarkable take on a long-worn theme. A British diplomat steals a precious jewel from an Indian statue of Buddha, and the purloined gem brings death to all who possess it. It falls into the hands of Captain Kenneth (Frauholz) and his wife (Whitney), who are determined to return the jewel and set matters right.

This clichéd knock-off of Wilkie Collins' 1868 novel *The Moonstone* was the first film to star Claire Whitney (1890-1961), who had found success on stage in her native New York City. She went on from here to a long and varied career, first as a leading actor in the silent era, and then as a capable character actor in the talkies. Her most famous role was as Catherine in *The Great Gatsby* (1926), though she may be best remembered to horror aficionados for her small parts in Universal's *Tower of London* (1939), *The House of the Seven Gables* (1940) and *The Mummy's Ghost* (1944). Her last role, in the 1949 film *Dancing in the Dark*, went un-credited.

The Star of India was released on November 17, 1913 and should not be confused with the 1916 film bearing the same title. CW

Strangers from Nowhere
aka **Two Strangers from Nowhere**
Solax; b/w; 11 min; U.S.
P: Herbert Blaché
Cast unknown

Balduin (Paul Wegener) sits front and center in *The Student of Prague*.

This short feature concerns a man selling his soul to the devil.

Faustian pacts were a staple of silent horror, with F.W. Murnau's *Faust* (1926) being one of the best-known examples. What little information exists on *Strangers from Nowhere* hints that the production was equal parts melodrama and horror. The film was released on June 20, 1913. TH

The Student of Prague
aka **Der Student von Prag**; **A Bargain with Satan**
Deutsche Bioscop/ PAGU; b/w; 41 min; Germany/Denmark
D: Stellan Rye, Paul Wegener *S:* Alfred de Musset, Hanns Heinz Ewers *C:* Guido Seeber
Cast: Paul Wegener, John Gottowt, Grete Berger, Lyda Salmonova, Lothar Korner, Fritz Weidemann

Balduin (Wegener) is a university student and a renowned fencer. However, he runs into financial difficulties and is lured into a strange agreement by the mysterious Scapinelli (Gottowt). The older man promises to give Balduin a small fortune in gold if he agrees to hand over any one possession that strikes Scapinelli's interest. Knowing that he doesn't own anything of value, Balduin readily agrees. The agreement is signed, and Scapinelli hands over the gold—then takes Balduin's reflection from a mirror and departs.

Drawing its inspiration from Edgar Allan Poe's short story *William Wilson* (1839), *The Student of Prague* explores the concept of the doppelganger in literal terms. The film is an early effort from actor/director Paul Wegener (1874-1948), best known today for his Expressionist classic *The Golem: How He Came into the World* (1920). Though far too old to be credibly cast as a starving young student, Wegener's intensity is the key to the film's effectiveness. The film doesn't impress on a technical level—the camerawork is static, the settings often look impoverished—but the concept is an interesting one, and Wegener's impassioned performance helps to sustain just the right air of hysteria.

The split-screen effects are surprisingly effective given the film's vintage. The spectacle of two Balduins duking it out in the same frame must have been quite a sight in 1913! The popular German actor, poet, philosopher and author Hanns Heinz Ewers, who also wrote the novel *Alraune* in 1911 (a variation on the Frankenstein theme that would be made into a 1928 film also starring Wegener), crafted the screenplay. Ewers is a forgotten name today (perhaps owing to his later affiliation with the Nazi party), but during his heyday, he was a prolific, creative talent in the horror genre.

On the whole, *The Student of Prague* as it exists today is hard to appreciate properly. For one thing, surviving video editions are of a poor, murky quality, apparently with some of the intertitles missing. It's still possible to follow the plot, but a great deal of subtlety is muddled or lost altogether. Also unfortunate, the running time is known to have been 85 minutes (the original film consisted of at least five reels), but the only surviving copies run a mere 41 minutes. Even factoring in discrepancies caused by a transfer at anything other than the proper 20 to 24-frames-per-

Paul Wegener and Grete Berger in *The Student of Prague*

second projection speed, it's obvious that there is a good deal of material not present. As it stands, the film retains some interest as a curiosity, but it inevitably fades in comparison to Henrik Galeen's superior 1926 version.

The story was remade twice after Galeen tackled it, both versions using the same title, in 1935 and 2004. TH

The Suicide Club
aka **Der Geheimnisvolle Klub**; **The Mysterious Club**; **The Secret Club**
Eichberg; b/w; 31(40) min; Germany
D: Joseph Delmont *P:* Franz Vogel
Cast: Fred Sauer, Ilse Bois, Joseph Delmont

Rotterdam is the setting for this German version of Scottish author Robert Louis Stevenson's 1878 short story *The Suicide Club*, a mystery with touches of horror. The story deals with a club in which members play dangerous games of cards, with the loser expected to commit suicide. If he refuses, another unlucky player must murder him. While the film retains some of Stevenson's original ideas, it changes the names of important characters, condenses much of the action and introduces some entirely new elements. In short, director Joseph Delmont and producer Franz Vogel did what almost all filmmakers aspire to do ... recast another's work into something both interesting and wholly their own.

Delmont has been credited with trailblazing the dark obsessions of Joe May and Fritz Lang in silent German cinema. His career didn't last nearly as long as theirs, though, nor did he manage to escape Nazi occupation to the United States. He did produce and act in several films; *The Suicide Club* was one in which he got to flex his thespian muscles. His film career ended in the mid-1920s, after which he was relatively successful as a novelist. CW

The Tempter
Natural Colour Kinematograph; color; 28 min; Great Britain
D: F. Martin Thornton, R.H. Callum *S:* Leedham Bantock, Alfred de Manby *P:* Charles Urban
Cast: Harry Agar Lyons, Alfred de Manby, F. Martin Thornton, Leedham Bantock

This early horror anthology foreshadows the later work of Amicus Productions, which makes it fitting that it was produced in Great Britain. In it, Satan (de Manby) relates three stories illustrating, respectively, the perils of drink, deceit and gambling.

In the first tale, a drunkard (Thornton) takes his wife's hard-earned money to the local tavern. His wife follows and through the window spies Satan seated next to him, encouraging him to drink. When she goes in and tries to convince her husband to leave, he physically attacks her and is thrown out by his fellow drinkers. Once the two are back home, the man again tries to take his wife's money and leave. She manages to prevent him but is viciously attacked in the process. A fire pops up, and a laughing Satan appears and engulfs the unhappy couple in his wings.

The second story concerns a handsome man (Lyons) who receives a mysterious letter. As he reads it, his wife appears and he conceals the message. The maid brings the couple their child, after which the husband leaves, obliviously dropping the missive in the process. The wife picks it up, reads it and learns of a planned rendezvous between her husband and his mistress. Understandably upset, she puts the baby to bed and goes to the café where the meeting is to take place. Sure enough, she discovers her husband in the arms of his lover. She makes a scene, and when the other guests mock her, she goes home, grabs the baby and heads off to the nearest bridge. Satan then appears and coaxes her to fling herself and her baby into the water below. This she does as the Prince of Darkness laughs.

In the final story, a bank manager (Bantock) gambles away his fortune in Monte Carlo, then he writes his fiancée to confess and assure her that he plans on winning the money back. She locates and confronts him, begging him not to gamble any further, but he does so anyway as Satan spurs him on. He loses more money, of course, and as the two lovers argue, the man tries to kill himself. Instead, he accidentally shoots his fiancée. Satan again appears, and the man shoots himself as the Father of Lies laughs and exits.

The Tempter was one of many films shot in an early color process by Charles Urban's Natural Colour Kinematograph. Interestingly, the film's crew also served as its primary stars, with the co-director portraying the drunkard and the screenwriters taking on the parts of the Devil and bank manager. The story was far from original, even in the silent era, when the propensity to engage in overt Christian preaching was often indulged in cinema. *The Tempter* was one of many films to use the Devil to preach against drinking, gambling and adultery. It was no better than the majority of them, though it at least eschewed the slapstick humor that marred so many films of its ilk. CW

The Tenderfoot's Ghost
Frontier/St. Louis; b/w; 17 min; U.S.
Credits unknown

A bumbling robber taking refuge from authorities matches wits with a ghost—and loses.

A "tenderfoot" is a city-bred person who tries to acclimate to rural life. The term was popular in the 19th and early 20th centuries but faded from use as technology infiltrated into even the remotest, least developed areas of the country. There were numerous comedies in the late silent and early sound days of cinema that dealt with tenderfoots—depicted as urbane, overeducated buffoons, usually from the eastern U.S. who moved westward and discovered that all their fancy book learnin' couldn't hold a candle to the good common sense of simple folk. These tenderfoot comedies largely replaced the "rube comedies" of the cinema's earliest days, with the dandified tenderfoot standing in for the noble hick. But whereas the rube invariably achieved success through his own inherent worthiness, the tenderfoot was always a ludicrous failure, a clueless know-it-all unable to cope with the simplest of everyday situations. Films such as *The Tenderfoot's Ghost* are, in fact, early examples of a long tradition in American cinema, movies that cater to mass distrust of (if not disdain for) intelligence and education. More recent examples include *City Slickers* (1991) and, of course, the apex of the "Dumb people are smarter than smart people" subgenre, 1994's reactionary and ridiculous *Forrest Gump*.

The Tenderfoot's Ghost was one of over 170 films produced by Frontier, a company formed solely to make Western-themed short subjects. They were in business from 1912 to 1915, often co-producing films with the St. Louis Motion Picture Company, which had a similar run of titles. In 1915 distributor Universal Pictures absorbed both companies. CW

The Thief and the Porter's Head
aka **Il ladro e la testa del portinaio**
Milano; b/w; 7 min; Italy
Credits unknown

A doctor uses electricity to revive a decapitated head.

This Italian short subject utilized trick photography and seems to have been played more for laughs than chills. It apparently received some exposure in cinemas in the United Kingdom, but there's no evidence that it was ever released in the United States. TH

The Treasure of Buddha
Gerrard; b/w; 30 min; U.S.
Credits unknown

As if Wilkie Collins' horror/mystery hybrid *The Moonstone* (1868) hadn't already been done to death by 1913, along came *The Treasure of Buddha*, about some jewels belonging to the goddess Kali getting stolen by a non-native type who then suffers a just reward. There's also the requisite sinister Hindu with the mandatory supernatural powers on hand to scare the bejesus out of people and to show why one doesn't mess with the Mother of Tears.

This mess might have worked better if someone had informed the filmmakers (whoever they were) that the figures of Buddha and Kali spring from separate religious traditions, with any mythological connection between them both tenuous and belated. This sort of slipshod approach may partially explain why Gerrard Studios lasted for such a short time. CW

Trilby
Vitascope; b/w; 22 min; U.S.
Credits unknown

Yet another minor take on George Du Maurier's famous novel *Trilby*, which was originally serialized in *Harper's* from January to August 1894 and was filmed numerous times during the silent era. Vitascope's obscure version doesn't seem to have diverged much from other adaptations in its tale of a beautiful young woman named Trilby O'Farrell who comes under the spell of an evil hypnotist named Svengali. He makes her a star, but when he dies, she expires as well.

Since the novel's original publication, much has been made of its effeminate, Jewish villain, who represents the anti-Semitic views of the period in which the book was written. In said view, Jews were a destructive force with an almost supernatural power to subjugate others while simultaneously having the ability to take something (in this case Trilby) that amounts to little and turn it into a cash cow. This view, advanced by so much entertainment and media of the time, became the justification for the mass genocide of Jewish people after Adolph Hitler's rise to power in Germany in the early 1930s. CW

The Vampire
Searchlight; b/w; 11 min; Great Britain
Credits unknown

Virtually nothing is known about this lost early horror film apart from its basic plot. In it, a Hindu woman in India kills a hunter who is trespassing on sacred land. In turn, the hunter's friend shoots and kills her. Her spirit then materializes in the form of a snake and gets the final word by killing him as well.

The theme of British colonialism harming the native populace in occupied foreign territory pops up fairly often in British cinema; such horror films include *The Fakir's Spell* (1914), *The Stranglers of Bombay* (1959) and *The Oblong Box* (1969).

The Vampire's plot was 'borrowed' by another British horror film two years later, *Heba the Snake Woman*, leading one to suspect that whoever made that film had seen this one first. Unlike the much shorter *Heba*, however, *Vampire*'s running time presumably allowed for some semblance of story development. Both films were forerunners of Hammer's *The Reptile* (1966), which remains to this day the definitive example of the snake woman subgenre.

This *Vampire* should not be confused with Robert G. Vignola's *The Vampire*, which was produced in the U.S. by Kalem Studios the same year. Vignola's film dealt with an older woman (the vamp of the title, portrayed by Alice Hollister) chasing after a much younger man (Harry F. Millard). CW

The Vampire of the Desert
Vitagraph; b/w; 26 min; U.S.
D: Charles Gaskill
Cast: Helen Gardner, Tefft Johnson, Harry T. Morey, James Morrison, Leah Baird, Flora Finch

It's unclear just how horrific this film actually was, since it appears that the vampire of the title was nothing more than a

> **DON'T MISS THIS FOR YOUR LIFE!**
>
> **AT THE ROYAL**
>
> Tonight and Tomorrow, June 17-18
>
> The Vitagraph Big Special Feature
>
> # THE VAMPIRE OF THE DESERT
>
> Story of a beautiful and bewitching sorceress. Her insatiable desire proves to be her own undoing. A powerful and marvelous drama.
>
> **CAST:**
>
> Lispeth, the Vampire ..... MISS HELEN GARDNER | Mrs. Corday, his wife ..... MISS LEAH BAIRD
> Ishmael ..... MR. T. HARRY MOREY | Derrick Corday, his son ..... MR. JAMES MORRISON
> Hagar ..... MISS FLORA FINCH | Ethel, Derrick's fiancé ..... MISS NORMA TALMADGE
> William Corday ..... MR. TEFFT JOHNSON

woman, Lispeth (Gardner), using her innate seductiveness to cast hypnotic spells over men. Tefft Johnson starred as William Cordray, "the vampire's victim," James Morrison as his son and Leah Baird as his wife. This title is frequently listed in vampire filmographies, despite the fact that it was based on the very non-vampiric poem "The Vampire" by Rudyard Kipling. Vitagraph's promotional material, for its part, doesn't elucidate the film's plot.

> This powerful photo-drama forms a two-part feature. Featuring the world's moving picture star, Miss Helen Gardner. This story shows, above all else, the actual nature of the coquette, and, although the case taken is an extreme one, teaches the danger of playing with fire.

In other words, the evil seductress gets her well-deserved comeuppance while the victim learns from the negative experience of falling in love with a *bad* woman. CW

Voodoo Fires
Tampa; b/w; length unknown; U.S.
D: Frank Whitman *S:* Joe Brandt
Cast unknown

Little information survives about this lost title. Regardless, *Voodoo Fires* rates a mention as possibly the earliest cinematic exploration of voodoo. Generally believed to have hailed from the Caribbean, voodoo melds African superstitions with aspects of Roman Catholicism (though the Church, it must be said, does not endorse it). The cross-pollination came about when Africans, brought to Haiti as slaves, had Catholicism forced upon them. Eventually, the hybrid belief system made its way to the continental Americas, taking particular hold in New Orleans and its environs. Often erroneously associated with Satanism, some of voodoo's better-known conventions (chicken blood, voodoo dolls) are entrenched in the iconography of the horror genre. Just how far this film went in detailing the more exotic aspects of the religion is open to speculation, but it's known that it did break ground by depicting voodoo ceremonies on film, the likely first step on the eventual path to the classic *White Zombie* (1932).

This film should not be confused with *Voodoo Fires* (1939), a straightforward documentary that also dealt with voodoo. TH

The Werewolf
Bison; b/w; 18 min; Canada/U.S.
D: Henry McRae *S:* Ruth Ann Baldwin
Cast: Clarence Barton, Marie Walcamp, Phyllis Gordon, Lule Warrenton, Sherman Bainbridge, William Clifford

Cinema's first-ever werewolf movie transplanted the superstitions of Eastern Europe to the western United States, where a Navajo woman (played by both Walcamp and Warrenton), who is also a witch, believes that her Caucasian husband (Burton) has deserted her, when in actuality he's been killed. Embittered at being alone, she raises their daughter (Gordon) to hate all white men. When the girl grows up, she turns into a wolf, exacting vengeance for her mother by attacking and/or killing white settlers and prospectors. Along the way, her lover is shot and killed by one such man. 100 years after her own death, she returns to take revenge on the reincarnation of her lover's killer.

Ruth Ann Baldwin's script was based on a story titled *The Werewolves* by Honoré (Henry) Beaugrand, first published in the magazine *The Century* in 1898. A dull tale with little to recommend it, it concerns a Christmas Eve celebration at Fort Richelieu, in the heart of Iroquois country, in 1706. A group of soldiers, hunters and traders sit around a fire telling tales of the "red devils" and their uncanny ability to escape the rifle fire of the fort's inhabitants. One trapper claims that he and a companion had once come upon a group of men-wolves known as *loups-garous*, carving up a human body to satisfy their unnatural cravings. As he continues his story, he relates that he and his friend carved crosses into their bullets and fired into the crowd of beasts but didn't know whether any of them had been killed. (The idea that crosses repel werewolves was also embraced in the film version, a notion that—along with Native Americans using magic to transform into wolves—is one of the few of the story's particulars to make it into the big-screen adaptation.)

According to then-contemporary sources, a real wolf was used for the film's werewolf sequences, and simple camera dissolves affected the transformation from woman to wolf. Henry McRae, who directed well over a hundred films in the silent and early sound eras guided the film. He became famous as a producer of serials in the 1930s and '40s, including Universal's *Flash Gordon* (1936) and *The Phantom Creeps* (1939). He shot *The Werewolf* on location in Canada for Bison, who partnered with Universal to get the film released.

The Werewolf wasn't Bison's only horror film dealing with Native Americans; the company also produced *Legion of the Phantom Tribe* and *The Phantom Light* (both 1914), in addition to being responsible for *The Death Stone of India* (1913). *The Werewolf* is presumed lost after the destruction of the only known print in a fire in 1924. CW

"The Werewolf"
"101 BISON" TWO-REEL DRAMA

THOUGH CLIFFORD OBJECTS, THE FRIARS DRIVE WATUMA AWAY.
A beautiful story, based on an Indian legend. Watuma, daughter of a wronged Indian squaw, is turned into a wolf. She returns, years later, as a "wolf-woman" to wreak vengeance on Clifford, reincarnated as a prospector. Distinctly novel.

What the Gods Decree
aka Le collier de Kali

Éclair; b/w; 75 min; France
D: Victorin-Hippolyte Jasset *S:* Robert Boudrioz *C:* Lucien N. Andriot
Cast: Charles Krauss, Josette Andriot, Maryse Dauvray, Camille Bardou, Simone Genevois

It's difficult to know whether this long-lost melodrama qualifies as a horror film, but it would appear to warrant that classification due to a key plot point—a statue of the Hindu goddess Kali comes magically to life. Worshipers of Kali—a ferocious, energetic, feminine entity—later provided inspiration for such realist horror as Hammer Film Productions' *The Stranglers of Bombay* (1959) and Merchant Ivory's *The Deceivers* (1988). While such fare has been criticized as racist in some circles, the Thuggee cult's habit of strangling victims as a sacrifice to their goddess has a well-documented basis in fact.

Director Victorin-Hippolyte Jasset had earlier directed an adaptation of Gaston Leroux's *Balaoo* (1913) and allegedly co-directed—with Alice Guy—an adaptation of Victor Hugo's *The Hunchback of Notre Dame*, titled *Esmeralda* (1905). *What the Gods Decree* was his last picture; he died shortly after its release. TH

When Spirits Walk
aka The Spirits Walk; When Spirits Walked

St. Louis/Frontier; b/w; 17 min; U.S.
Cast: Lloyd Hamilton, Eva Thatcher, Joseph Franz, Buck Connors

This comedic short subject made use of such macabre tropes as a haunted house and—prefiguring *The Cabinet of Dr. Caligari* (1919)—a somnambulist crook. Not much else is known about the film, which was a vehicle for then-popular comic actor Lloyd Hamilton. Hamilton is a forgotten talent today, but some film historians claim that in his heyday he was envied by no less than Charlie Chaplin. Like so many comedians, Hamilton had something of a tragic life off-screen; he was an unpleasant drunk, and his inability to control his drinking damaged both his family life and his career. He died at the age of 43 in 1935, and his reputation hasn't sustained to the same degree as such contemporaries as Chaplin or Buster Keaton.

Some sources list this as a 1914 release, but it made its theatrical bow in October 1913. TH

While John Bolt Slept

Edison; b/w; 10 min; U.S.
Crew unknown
Cast: Charles Ogle

A wandering spirit travels through the nether regions. But, as the title suggests, the entire enterprise is nothing more than a dream by the titular John Bolt (Ogle).

This short was one of many produced by Thomas Edison's film company starring Charles Ogle in a major role. Many were horror films, including *Bluebeard* (1909), *Frankenstein* and *The House of the Seven Gables* (both 1910) among many others. The film has been mistakenly listed as a 1914 release under the erroneous title *White John Bolt Slept*. The film was in fact released on June 7, 1913. CW

The Witch of Salem

New York; b/w; 20 min; U.S.
D: Raymond B. West *S:* C. Gardner Sullivan *P:* Thomas H. Ince
Cast: Charles Ray, Clara Williams

The Witch of Salem is a rip-off of D.W. Griffith's *Rose O'Salem Town* (1910). It concerns a young girl (Williams) named Prudence who is spiritually betrothed to the handsome son (Ray) of a Puritan. She's accused of witchcraft and sentenced to burn at the stake (a common mistake in these old films; historically speaking, no convicted "witch" was ever burned at the stake during the Salem Witchcraft Trials of 1692. They were hanged), after which a hysterical fear of Satanism sweeps the town. As was the case in the Griffith film, her lover's Native American friends rescued the protagonist. This motif was later used in the execrable *The Scarlet Letter* (1995).

West's film, released on November 20, 1913, is primarily a historical drama with horror asides. The next film centering on the Salem Witchcraft Trials was Lucius Henderson's *A Witch of Salem Town* (1915), starring Mary Fuller, though it would take *Maid of Salem* in 1937 for a depiction of the Trials to merit lasting, classic film status. Another picture to deal with the subject was *Witchcraft* (1916). CW

1914

The lovely Blanche Sweet from *The Avenging Conscience*

Yoshiwara kaidan: Kozakura choji
Nikkatsu Kyoto; b/w; length unknown; Japan
D: Shozo Makino
Cast: Matsunosuke Onoe

This is one of many short horror films directed by Shozo Makino for Nikkatsu Studios' Kyoto branch and starring Matsunosuke Onoe in the lead. It's uncertain just who Onoe played, but the film dealt with a ghost that haunts the Yoshiwara district of Japan, an area noted for its geisha prostitutes. During Japan's silent-film era, Nikkatsu was the preeminent producer of horror movies. Unfortunately, virtually the company's entire catalog from this time is lost, leaving it impossible to properly assess their importance to either Japanese cinema or to the horror genre as a whole.

By the early 1940s, the Kyoto production house folded up shop, and Nikkatsu ceased film production. However, in the early 1950s, a rebranded Nikkatsu once again began to produce and distribute film and is today known for its popular line of S&M films known as Roman Porno. CW

Alone With the Devil
aka **Ekspressens Mysterium**; **Alone With a Devil**; **Eksprestogets Mysterium**
Nordisk; b/w; 52 (39) min; Denmark
D: Hjalmar Davidsen C: Louis Larsen
Cast: Christel Holch, Valdemar Psilander, Carl Lauritzen, Svend Aggerholm, Birger von Cotta-Schonberg, Oluf Billesborg

Hjamlar Davidsen, one of Denmark's earliest directors, helmed this feature-length thriller about a manufacturer (Psilander) and his wife (Holch) who get mixed up with hypnosis. Carl Lauritzen played the man's best friend and lawyer, while Svend Aggerholm portrayed a co-worker. The actors who played these four roles are considered to be among the greats of silent Danish cinema.

While few of his films survive today, Davidsen appears to have worked almost exclusively for Nordisk, though he ended his career with the lesser-known Palladium Films. Existing stills from *Alone With the Devil* suggest that Davidsen and cinematographer Louis Larsen dressed the Gothic sets in deep shadows and chiaroscuro lighting to affect a gloomy atmosphere befitting the story. CW

An Ancestor's Legacy
aka **L'eredità di Rodolfi**
Ambrosio; b/w; 18 min; Italy
D/S: Eleuterio Rodolfi P: Arturo Ambrosio
Cast: Gigetta Morano, Eleuterio Rodolfi

Eleuterio Rodolfi was a popular and multi-talented presence in the early days of Italian cinema, appearing in everything from Shakespeare to lowbrow comedy. *An Ancestor's Legacy* appears to have been his only flirtation with the horror genre, though the film was likely more comedic than horrific. Regardless, its tale of a creepy castle's visitors being menaced by nightmares doubtlessly lent itself to macabre imagery.

Rodolfi's most important credit was as co-director (with Mario Caserini) of the epic *The Last Days of Pompeii* (1913). He committed suicide in 1933, 10 years after his career had petered out. TH

The Avenging Conscience, or: 'Thou Shalt Not Kill'
Mutual; b/w; 56 min; U.S.
D/S/P: D.W. Griffith C: G.W. Bitzer
Cast: Henry B. Walthal, Blanche Sweet, Spottiswoode Aitken, Ralph Lewis, George Siegmann, Mae Marsh

A young man (Walthal) is frustrated by his uncle's (Aitken) opposition to the girl he loves (Sweet). He murders the old man and hides the corpse in their home, but his conscience gets the better of him and he gives himself away to the police, at which point it's revealed that the whole thing was only a dream.

Edgar Allan Poe is as remembered today for his short, tragic life as he is for his extraordinary literary output. He was the epitome of the suffering artist. A gifted poet, author and literary critic, he was nevertheless plagued by personal demons (notably an addiction to alcohol). He died, virtually penniless, at the age of 40 after hours of wandering in a confused state up and down the streets of his beloved Baltimore. His death has been attribut-

The earliest surviving Poe adaptation of note is *The Avenging Conscience, or: Thou Shalt Not Kill*. The film is of historical importance not least because it marked one of writer/producer/director D.W. Griffith's few feature-length forays into the horror genre. It was also, among other things, a follow-up to Griffith's own short, dark adaptation of Poe's life, *Edgar Allen Poe* (1909).

Contemporary audiences often have a hard time relating to Griffith (1875-1948), due to his racist politics (his 1915 epic *The Birth of a Nation*, for example, climaxes with the unlikely spectacle of a heroic band of Ku Klux Klan members swarming in and saving the day). But he is an indisputable pioneer of the cinema, arguably the first American filmmaker to display a true understanding of the medium's potential to tell stories in a complicated and sometimes fragmented manner. He helped invent the mechanics of cinematic storytelling, and giants such as Alfred Hitchcock and Orson Welles have admitted his importance.

So one might come to *The Avenging Conscience* with reasonably high hopes. Unfortunately, the film takes too many ill-advised liberties with a clumsy amalgam of Poe's poem "Annabel Lee" (posthumously published in 1849) and his famous short-story *The Tell-Tale Heart* (1843). The concept of a protagonist haunted by a horrid crime he has committed is rife with dramatic potential, but Griffith fails to dramatize it compellingly. The first half of the film, leading into the central murder, is reasonably engaging. Griffith's use of camera and lighting may seem conventional today, but for its time it displayed genuine creativity and sensitivity. The film goes off the rails quite badly after the crime, however, with an air of preachy Christianity permeating the rest of the proceedings. The hero's Biblical visions

ed to causes ranging from heart disease (brought on by excessive drinking), to syphilis, to having been a victim of "cooping"—a term for the coercion of citizens into voting repeatedly for a particular politician, by means of prolonged, extreme ill-treatment at the hands of political thugs. With the number of juicy possibilities that are part and parcel of Poe's mystique, it's no surprise that he continues to arouse the curiosity of new generations of fans. It helps too that he was a legitimately talented writer. And while his name conjures images of horror and the grotesque, he actually dabbled in many genres—from a difficult-to-pigeonhole novel (*The Narrative of Arthur Gordon Pym of Nantucket*) to an early example of what would become known as the detective story (*Murders in the Rue Morgue*). Equally renowned is his poetry, including such remarkable work as "The Raven," "Lenore" and "Annabel Lee."

Filmmakers began mining Poe's legacy early on, with such French adaptations of *The Pit and the Pendulum* (1909) and *The Golden Beetle* (1910), both of which are now considered lost films.

are particularly out of place, having no foundation in (and in no way enhancing) the film's classic narrative. Worse yet, Griffith undermines the entire film by trotting out a lame "it was all just a dream" ending. In so doing, he transforms Poe's somber, chilling vision of life into a shaggy-dog story. Along the way, we're treated to a preachy diatribe on the value of the Ten Commandments—hardly the sort of thing Poe would have had in mind! Yet Griffith's talent remains such that, despite his flaws, an effective moment does break through here and there.

Henry B. Walthall (who went on to develop into a capable character actor; his next-to-last film was Tod Browning's bizarre *The Devil Doll*, 1936) carries the film. His performance is, typically for the era, overripe. But it would be misguided to criticize him too strongly; he does make a better impression than much of the supporting cast, especially the aptly named Blanche Sweet, who takes a decidedly saccharine turn as his love interest.

It is to be regretted that this pioneering filmmaker's few forays into the genre should prove so uneven, but ultimately *The*

The nightmarish visions of horror in *The Avenging Conscience* turn out to be only a dream.

Avenging Conscience and his next horror film, *One Exciting Night* (1922), are mere footnotes in his career; genre scholars will want to see *The Avenging Conscience* out of curiosity, but casual movie fans will likely want to give it a miss. TH

Banchō sarayashika

Nikkatsu Kyoto; b/w; length unknown; Japan
D: Shozo Makino
Cast: Matsunosuke Onoe

In Japanese folklore, Okiku is a poor but beautiful servant girl who's forever fending off the advances of her samurai master, Aoyama. One day Aoyama hits upon the idea of shaming Okiku into submission by telling her that she's responsible for the breakage of one in a set of 10 valuable plates. Unwilling to believe that she's caused the destruction of such a family heirloom, Okiku counts the remaining nine plates, then counts them again, and again, and again … After a time, Aoyama grows angry at her response to his ploy and murders her by throwing her down a well. In some of the earliest versions of the tale, she returns from the grave and counts and recounts the plates, ad infinitum.

Sometime around 1741, the story became the basis of a theatrical piece. Less than a century later, Segawa Joko III turned the tale into a famous Kabuki play, *Minoriyoshi Kogane no Kikizuki*. Then, in 1916, Japanese playwright Okamoto Kido wrote the two-act *Banchō sarayashika* for the stage; in Kido's version, samurai Aoyama is recast as a shogun's vassal, and he and Okiku are madly in love. But when Okiku gets wind of another woman's marriage offer to Aoyama, she breaks one of his family's 10 precious dinner plates in a jealous fit. Aoyama responds with a rage of his own, breaking the remaining plates, murdering Okiku and throwing her body down a well.

This 1914 film adaptation—completed two years before Kido's reimagining and therefore almost certainly a traditional take on the tale—may have been Nikkatsu Studio's first production of the story, but it appears that an earlier version was shot, by persons unknown, sometime between 1909 and 1912. Nikkatsu's adaptation was released in June 1914, with a second version, also starring Matsunosuke Onoe, possibly following in 1918, although that film could just as likely have been a re-release of this one. CW

The Basilisk

Hepworth; b/w; 28 min; Great Britain
D/P/S/C: Cecil M. Hepworth
Cast: William Felton, Alma Taylor, Tom Powers, Chrissie White, Cyril Morton

Yet another take on George Du Maurier's classic literary characters, first introduced in his 1894 serialized novel *Trilby*. William Felton plays the Svengali-like villain, a mesmerist obsessed with possessing a beautiful young woman named Freda (Taylor). Her fiancé (Powers) stands in the way, however, and the mesmerist commands her to stab him to death. But before she can do so, a serpent attacks and kills the mesmerist, releasing her from his control.

In ancient mythology, a basilisk was a lizard-like creature hatched from the egg of a cock. Its gaze had the power to kill, hence the word's use as a title for a film about an evil mesmerist. Another level of meaning emerges when one considers that his demise comes by way of a snake, an evolutionary descendent of lizards.

Much has been made of the fact that original prints of *The Basilisk* were tinted green in anticipation of Universal's use of the color for the 1931 release of *Frankenstein*, for which they had sent out some early prints with a green tint. Considering that fellow Brit Charles Urban had already made several films, including *Dr. Jekyll and Mr. Hyde* (1913), using a two-color process, green tinting seems a minor accomplishment. CW

Batty Bill and the Suicide Club

Georges Méliès; b/w; length unknown; U.S.
Credits unknown

The year 1914 saw the release of at least 10 Batty Bill comedies, most on split reels with other short films. This suggests that each film averaged out to six minutes or so in length. They were rube comedies aimed at Middle America, with the eponymous dull-witted character caught in crazy situations and having to use resourcefulness—as in "dumb luck"—to get out of them. He seems related to France's Simple Simon, several of whose films had been released in the United States. In fact, the Batty Bill movies (among many others) were produced by the Georges Méliès Company, a U.S. production house founded not by French director Georges Méliès but by his disreputable brother Gaston without Georges' knowledge or consent and with no money going to the company's namesake.

This appears to be the only Batty Bill film to spoof the horror genre. In it, Batty Bill finds himself in a suicide club, from which he has to escape using his, um, wits. CW

The Bells
Sawyer's Features; b/w; 40 min; U.S.
Credits unknown

This is by far the most obscure of the many film adaptations of Leopold David Lewis' English adaptation of French writers Émile Erckmann and Alexandre Chatrian's horror play *Le Juif Polonaise* ("The Polish Jew"), itself based on Edgar Allan Poe's poem "The Bells" (1849) via his short story *The Tell-Tale Heart* (1843). (There are some indications that another part of its base was formed by a French legend from the region in which the authors wrote.) It's anyone's guess just how faithful this film was to the tale of a murderer whose conscience hounds him to his grave; even cast and crew names are lost to time. It was most definitely the third straightforward adaptation of the Erckmann/Chatrian/Lewis story and is often confused with the 1918 release, which starred Frank Keenan as the mad and penniless innkeeper Mathias, who kills a Jew he believes is rich.

This same year, Gaumont announced intentions to film a *Bells* adaptation starring H.B. Irving (son of the famous actor Sir Henry Irving, who made the play famous in 1871). There is some confusion, however, as to whether it was actually shot. CW

Botan dōrō
Nikkatsu Kyoto; b/w; length unknown; Japan
D: Shozo Makino
Cast: Matsunosuke Onoe

The first horror films shot in Japan, *Jizo the Spook* and *Resurrection of a Corpse* (both 1898), were short affairs made to cash in on the nation's interest in a new art form called cinema. It wasn't until around 1910 that Japanese filmmakers began in earnest to explore the horror genre, dramatizing legends of beautiful, mysterious women who sucked the lifeblood from their male victims, or retelling folktales of morose ghosts seeking revenge. One of the earliest such pictures, *Botan dōrō*, was made in 1910. Here is what is known about that lost film. Based on a story by Sanyutei Encho (1839-1900), which in turn was based on a Chinese legend, it concerns a samurai's daughter who falls in love with a handsome warrior. After using her, deserting her and leaving her to die, he launches an affair with a second woman who visits him nightly, sometimes preceded by a nursemaid who carries a lantern festooned with peonies. A priest alerts the warrior to the fact that the new lover is the ghost of his former lover, but the news comes too late.

Like the perennial favorite *Yotsuya kaidan*, the *Botan dōrō* tale became a silent-film staple. Even the popular team of director Shozo Makino and actor Matsunosuke Onoe got in on the act, producing this short feature in 1914. It too is lost, as are all of the *Botan dōrō* adaptations made during the silent era. CW

The Chimes
Hepworth; b/w; 28 min; Great Britain
D/S: Thomas Bentley *P:* Cecil M. Hepworth
Cast: Warwick Buckland, Stewart Rome, Violet Hopson, Harry Gilbey, Johnny Butt, John MacAndrews

Trotty (Buckland), who is down on his luck, is further fed up by newspaper reports of crime running rampant. He attempts to hide his disgust from his daughter Meg (Hopson), who is riding a wave of delight at the prospect of marrying Richard (Rome). As Trotty's spirits continue to sink, he goes to bed. He is later awakened by the sound of chimes coming from the local church. He leaves his bed and is met by a goblin that proceeds to show him just how bad his life really could be. The visions convince him that he really doesn't have it so bad, and he awakens in the morning to the joyous sounds of church bells.

If the story sounds familiar, there's good reason for it. Charles Dickens penned *The Chimes: A Goblin Story of Some Bells that Rang an Old Year Out and a New Year In* in 1844, a year after his massive success with *A Christmas Carol*. The writer intended the story to embellish the themes of his earlier novel, but it comes off as something of a carbon copy. It was met with mixed reactions at the time of its publication and has since fallen into comparative obscurity. Still, 1914 saw two cinematic adaptations of the story, and a direct-to-video remake emerged in 1999.

This version from Hepworth was directed by Thomas Bentley, who had already been responsible for adaptations of Dickens' *Oliver Twist* (1912) and *David Copperfield* (1913) and would later direct *Hard Times* (1915) and *The Old Curiosity Shop* (1921). Bentley remained active until the early 1940s; one of his last credits was the horror-in-name-only *Murder at the Baskervilles* (1937). TH

The Chimes
U.S. Amusement Corp.; b/w; length unknown; U.S.
D/S: Herbert Blaché
Cast: Tom Terriss, Faye Cusick, Alfred Hemming, Clarence Harvey, Harry Hitchcock, Robert Vivian

Trotty Veck (Terriss) is spending a particularly miserable New Year's Eve bemoaning the sorry state of humanity. Rather than waste his time observing people enjoying themselves—including his young daughter Meg (Cusick) and her suitor Richard (Hitchcock)—Trotty goes to bed. He is awakened by the sound of chimes, whereupon he encounters a goblin that shows him how bad his life *could* be.

Charles Dickens' *The Chimes: A Goblin Story of Some Bells that Rang an Old Year Out and a New Year In* hasn't inspired many cinematic adaptations, but it did yield two competing versions in 1914. The story is a heavy-handed treatise about the need for man to love his fellow man, and both versions hewed closely to its basic structure and tone. Given that the tale incorporates imagery that makes Ebenezer Scrooge's visions in *A Christmas Carol* look quaint, there's little doubt that the two versions of *Chimes* can be classified as horror films.

Actor Tom Terriss also top-lined *The Mystery of Edwin Drood* (1914) for Blaché, and he racked up a number of directorial credits of his own. The supporting cast of *Chimes* includes his real-life brother William and daughter Milly. TH

The Crimson Moth
Biograph; b/w; 20 min; U.S.
D: Travis Vale
Cast: Jack Drumier, Louise Vale, George Morgan, Franklin Ritchie

This take on the banshee theme has members of a cursed family doomed to die whenever one of them sees the Crimson Moth.

Far more interesting than the film was the life of its leading lady, Louise Vale, who was married to director Travis Vale at the time *The Crimson Moth* was produced. She starred in numerous movies between the years 1912 and 1915, most of them directed by her husband. Among the classics in which she starred were silent versions of *Jane Eyre* and *East Lynne* (both 1915), but her career was cut short when, in 1918, she fatally contracted either the Spanish influenza or pneumonia (sources conflict; given the times, the former seems most likely) while doing volunteer work.

Some sources attribute *The Crimson Moth* to 1915, but it was in fact released on December 29, 1914. CW

The Crown of Richard III
Pathé; b/w; length unknown; France
Credits unknown

The infamous historical figure the Duke of Gloucester is known to millions from William Shakespeare's famous tragedy *Richard III* (c. 1591), first filmed in 1908 by William V. Ranous and starring Ranous and Florence Auer. The play was shot again in 1911 by Will Barker and a third time as a five-reel epic by James Keane in 1912. This short film, presented as a more overtly horrific approach to the story, followed.

Richard III was a member of the House of Plantagenet and brother to King Edward IV. Historians once disputed the existence of Richard's deformities (which included a hunched back and a club foot), believing that they were fabricated after his death to provide evidence of his evil character. (At the time, physical disabilities were often considered evidence of witchcraft or evil, and accusing someone of having a birth defect was a sure-fire way of impugning that person's moral fiber.) The recent discovery of his skeleton, however, has confirmed that the longheld views on his physical state, as codified by Shakespeare, were in fact true. It also remains irrefutable that Richard was desperate for the throne and would have done anything to get it. After the death of Edward IV, Richard declared his brother's two young sons to be illegitimate, executed their guardians and locked them away in the notorious Tower of London, from which they disappeared not long after. Whispers at the time suggested that Richard had them murdered and buried within the Tower, a claim seemingly confirmed in 1674 when the bones of two children were reportedly recovered from beneath a Tower stairwell. Since that time, at least some of those bones have been determined to be those of animals, thus deepening the mystery.

Two years after his coronation, Richard III was defeated in battle. The throne went to rival Henry Tudor, who became King Henry VII.

Though little information about *The Crown of Richard III* is available today, what is known suggests that it was darker than its more straightforward counterparts. Then contemporary descriptions of the film indicate something more along the lines of Universal's classic *Tower of London* (1939) than Shakespeare's tragic play. In *The Crown of Richard III*, the Duke of Gloucester seeks out a sorceress named Rachel who tells him that he is destined to possess the Crown of England. Taking this pronouncement as assent from God, the Duke murders his way to the throne, disposing of his nephews along the way. His further attempts to dominate his opposition, particularly the Duke of Buckingham, result in his death on the battlefield. CW

The Curse of the Crimson Idol
Phoebus; b/w; 37 min; country unknown
Credits unknown

This film is one of dozens of silent-era offerings about a Hindu cult's attempt to retrieve a treasure (in this case a jeweled idol) after it is stolen from an Indian temple.

Films such as this, lifting their central concept from Wilkie Collins' 1868 horror-mystery *The Moonstone*, were as common as dirt during the silent era. However cinematically appealing they were in their time, the idea behind them proved a nonstarter in the sound era—when, no doubt, the saturation point was at last reached.

Though *The Curse of the Crimson Idol*'s country of origin is unknown, film scholars suspect it to be of U.S. or British derivation. CW

The Curse of the Scarabee Ruby
Gaumont/Eclipse/Urban; b/w; 42 min; France/Great Britain
Credits unknown

Mixing elements of Wilkie Collins' novel *The Moonstone* (1868) and George Du Maurier's novel *Trilby* (1894), *The Curse of the Scarabee Ruby* deals with an evil spirit's possession of a young girl. It was a coproduction of three different studios, one British (Urban), one French (Eclipse) and one both British and French (Gaumont). It's likely that the actual producer was Charles Urban, who around this time also started a separate production entity to make and release films in an early two-color process.

The film's running time betrays the then-current trend toward feature-length films. This coincided with a shift in focus from special effects to drama, though *Curse* appears to have had a healthy dose of both. CW

A Deal with the Devil
aka **Den Mystiske Fremmede**
Nordisk; b/w; 37 min; Denmark
D: Holger-Madsen *C:* Marius Clausen
Cast: Olaf Fonss, Ebba Thomsen, Alf Blutecher, Ingeborg Bruun-Berthelsen, Philip Bech, Johannes Ring

This Danish melodrama offers a variation on the story of Faust. A man swaps 10 years of his life to the devil (Fonss) in exchange for fame and fortune. Director Holger-Madsen was a specialist in melodrama, though he also made the early space opera *400 Million Miles from Earth* (1918), while actor Olaf Fonss later played the lead role in the serial *Homunculus* (1916).

A Deal with the Devil is believed to be lost. It should not be confused with the Cecil M. Hepworth film bearing the same plot and title. TH

A Death in Real Estate
Lubin; b/w; 11 min; U.S.
P: Siegmund Lubin
Cast: Louise Huff, Edgar Jones

This one-reel comedy was released in March 1914 and concerned a mansion reputed to be haunted. Said haunting turns out to be a scam to lower the mansion's sale price.

Though she was born in 1895 and lived until 1973, Louise Huff's filmography begins in 1913 and ends in 1922, indicating a short but fruitful career in silent cinema. Most of her films were comedies aimed at the family crowd; *A Death in Real Estate* came fairly early in her career, before she jumped the Lubin ship to star in films for up-and-coming producers such as Jesse L. Lasky.

Edgar Jones' career began only a year before Huff's and ended the same year as hers, though he made considerably more films than she did. Jones was also a director and producer. He was born in the 1870s in London, England and, considering that his various film careers all came to an end at the same time, it's possible that he died sometime around 1922.

Other than these two principal players, information about the remaining cast and crew of *A Death in Real Estate* is lost. CW

The Diamond of Disaster
aka **Diamond of Disaster**
Thanhouser; b/w; 22 min; U.S.
D: Carroll Fleming *S:* Phil Lonergan
Cast: J.S. Murray, Ernest Warde, Morgan Jones, Irving Cummings, Carey L. Hastings, Muriel Ostriche

India was the exotic locale, at least in part, of this adventure/horror film that featured Ernest C. Warde, J.S. Murray, Morgan Jones, John Richards and Muriel Ostriche as East Indian types obsessed with a stolen diamond. That diamond, and its obligatory death curse, has fallen into the hands of an Englishman (Cummings) and his wife (Hastings).

Kentucky-born Carroll Fleming's directorial career was short-lived, spanning a mere two years; all of his films were shot for Thanhouser, most of them written by siblings Philip or Lloyd Lonergan.

In an early example of conscious film marketing, Thanhouser released *The Diamond of Disaster* on October 14, 1914, just two weeks before Halloween. CW

Doctor Polly
Vitagraph; b/w; 30 min; U.S.
D: Wilfred North, Wally Van *S:* Mrs. H.M. Hodson
Cast: Lillian Walker, Wally Van, Josie Sadler, William Shea, Arthur Ashley

This silent-era comedy placed its titular heroine (Walker) in a haunted mansion, where she is terrified by trick photographic effects.

Co-director Wilfred North was active throughout the silent era, after which he turned to acting, generally in unbilled bit parts; in that capacity, he made two of his last appearances in *The Man Who Reclaimed His Head* (1934) and *The Black Room* (1935) before his death in 1935. North was assisted in directing *Doctor Polly* by one of the film's costars, Wally Van. New York-born Van was a prolific writer, actor and director during the silent era, but his career ended with the coming of sound; he died, long forgotten, in 1974. TH

Dr. Jekyll and Mr. Hyde, Done To a Frazzle
Crystal-Superba/Warner; b/w; 10 min; U.S.
Crew unknown
Cast: Charles De Forrest

This short subject featuring actor Charles De Forrest was a satiric variation on Robert Louis Stevenson's novella. Beating the likes of Jerry Lewis' *The Nutty Professor* (1963) to the punch by about 50 years, *Frazzle* offered a humorous slant on the oft-told tale. Unfortunately, not much else in the way of information exists about this long-forgotten relic. Reviewers at the time had little to say about it other than that it was "fun."

Charles De Forrest, who played both Dr. Jekyll and Mr. Hyde, was a prolific presence in the comedy scene at the time, playing the lead characters in then popular titles as *Binks Did It* (1913), which yielded 13 sequels, and *Charlie's Little Joke* (1913), which spawned over 20. The actor fell into obscurity even before the silent era ended, however, and his legacy remains buried by the work of such contemporaries as Harold Lloyd (who appeared in his own horror spoof, *Haunted Spooks*, in 1920) and Charlie Chaplin. De Forrest's last film, *Damaged Hearts* (1924), was a rare dramatic role. He passed away in Los Angeles in 1944.

The title of *Frazzle* betrays a certain ironic disenchantment with the number of *Dr. Jekyll and Mr. Hyde* variations already on the market by 1914. Indeed, Stevenson's novella is considered the most filmed work of literature in the silent era. TH

The Dream Woman
Blaché; b/w; 44 min; U.S.
D/S: Alice Guy
Cast: Fraunie Fraunholz, Claire Whitney

Stable boy Francis Raven (Fraunholz) suffers through the same horrific dream—an unknown woman brandishing a knife attempts to kill him—each year on the eve of his birthday. Finally his macabre vision comes true. Based on a story by Wilkie Collins (best known as the author of *The Woman in White*, 1859), *The Dream Woman* is a parable about the inevitability of fate. Collins' tale made its debut in the collection *The Frozen Deep and Other Stories* (1874) but never attracted the same attention as some of his other works. Given Alice Guy's previous forays into the genre, it seems likely that the film embraced its morbid subject matter whole-heartedly. But alas, the film has apparently disappeared. TH

The Fakir's Spell
aka **The Fakier's Spell**
Dreadnought; b/w; 28 min; Great Britain
D/C: Frank Newman *S:* Idleton Newman
Cast: Idleton Newman

The Fakir's Spell provides an early example of a classic movie monster, the gorilla, which entered the horror lexicon with the publication of Edgar Allan Poe's famous short story *The Murders in the Rue Morgue*, first printed in *Graham's Magazine* in 1841. Here, the action is moved from Paris to British-controlled India. But while some sources claim that the film is about a murderous ape, there's more evidence that the narrative actually concerns an illicit romance between a British gentleman and an Indian princess. Unhappy about the affair, a Hindu fakir casts a spell on the Englishman, turning him into an ancestral, ape-like creature. The creature is locked in a cage, but when the cage catches fire, the beast escapes and transforms back into a human being.

Director Frank Newman worked mostly in educational filmmaking, often shooting scripts he'd written himself. Much of his work centered on animals and their habits, though he occasionally explored and documented the ill effects of war.

It does not appear that *The Fakir's Spell* has survived, and what information there is about the film is decidedly second-

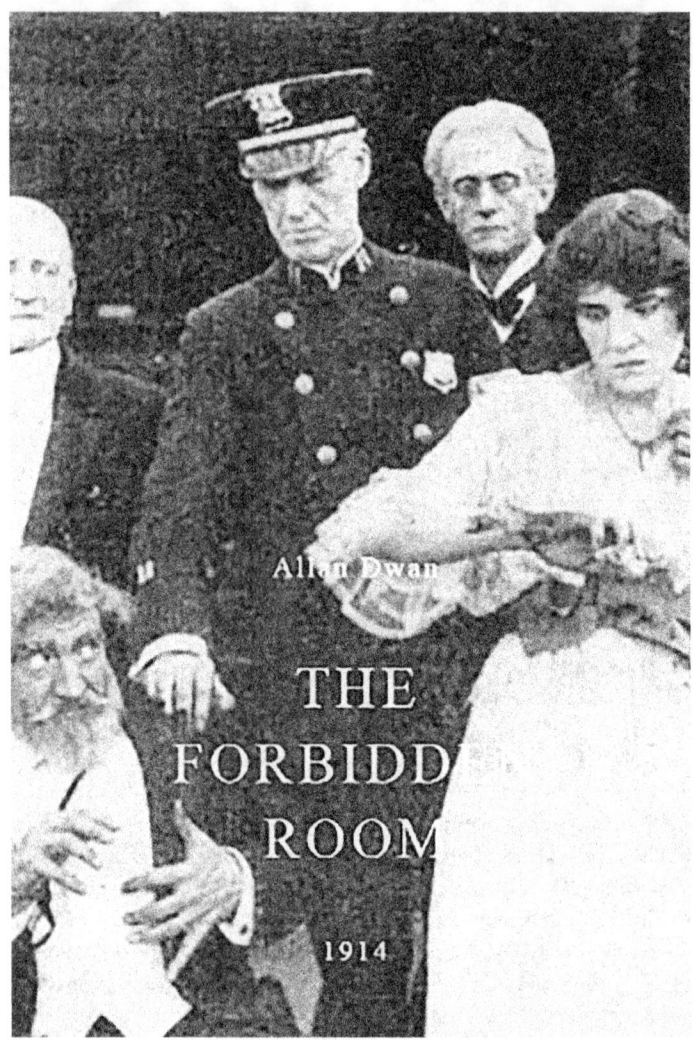

hand. The plot, however, indicates the filmmakers' disapproval of Great Britain's policy of colonialism, which for centuries was used to justify the British government's invasion and control of other nations, the taking of their resources and the transfer of that wealth to the mother country. While large British corporations (such as the British East India Company) got rich this way, native populations rarely benefited and in most cases suffered horrible deprivations. Numerous British horror films have touched on the effects of colonialism, albeit in more condemnatory terms than those dealt with here. They include John Gilling's *The Reptile* (1965) and Gordon Hessler's *The Oblong Box* (1969), though the masterpiece of the genre may be Terence Fisher's *The Stranglers of Bombay* (1959). CW

The Fiends of Hell
aka **Guarding Britain's Secrets**
Walturdaw; b/w; 37 (20) min; Great Britain
D: Charles Calvert *S:* Nikola Hamilton
Cast: Douglas Payne, Nikola Hamilton, Norman Howard

A detective with psychic powers does battle with an evil medium. The story combined such tried-and-true genre staples as hypnosis and the occult, and surprisingly was played more for suspense than for comedy. Leading man Douglas Payne was active from about 1912 to 1933; his filmography stops short at that point, though he lived until 1965. *The Fiends of Hell*'s screenplay was credited to one Dr. Nikola Hamilton, who also played one of the key supporting roles; this appears to have been his only credit in either capacity. Director Charles Calvert helmed a number of Anglo-themed melodramas between 1912 and 1926, many of which were geared toward bucking up his nation's image, with such stirring titles as *A Soldier's Honour* and *His Country's Honour* (both 1914). He delved into the horror genre one more time with *The Avenging Hand* (1915), which also featured Payne. TH

The Forbidden Room
aka **The Web of Circumstance**
Bison/Universal; b/w; 45 min; U.S.
D: Allan Dwan *S:* Bess Meredyth *C:* Lee Bartholomew
Cast: Murdock MacQuarrie, Pauline Bush, William C. Dowlan, Lon Chaney, John Burton

After his sister gives birth to an illegitimate daughter and runs away, Dr. James Gibson (MacQuarrie) promises his dying mother that he will find the two and bring them home. The mom dies, and the doctor does indeed find his sister (Bush) and niece (also Bush). But unfortunately, the sister has gone insane. The doctor locks her away in his vast home and cares for her daughter as he would his own. Time passes, and one night, during a discussion of mesmerism with his friend John Morris (Chaney), Dr. Gibson places his niece under hypnosis. When Morris leaves, the mother sees him from her window and realizes that he is the father of her daughter. In a frenzy, she escapes and stabs him to death. Her daughter is blamed, and authorities come to believe she may have committed the crime while under hypnosis.

Released by Universal in June 1914, this lurid Bison-produced melodrama continued its distributing company's trend toward horror, though the *Moving Picture World*'s review at the time opined that the movie depended "upon the powerful, thoroughly human situations involved rather than on any sensational, hair-raising incidents." That same review called the film "distinctly original, with powerful situations and strong climaxes" and praised Pauline Bush in her dual roles as a mother and daughter caught up in a sinister web of events. (In fact, the film's original working title was *The Web of Circumstance*.) The review continued its praise by saying that the film was "horrible, in the same way that Poe's stories are horrible, and audiences that enjoy a strong admixture of the weird and terrible will find this greatly to their liking."

Canadian émigré Allan Dwan directed numerous classics, including the Shirley Temple vehicles *Heidi* and *Rebecca of Sunnybrook Farm*, during a lengthy career that lasted from 1911 to 1961. He worked in many genres, though his only other horror films appear to have been the believed-lost *The Occult* (1913) and the terrible Ritz Brothers comedy *The Gorilla* (1939). In addition to directing, he also wrote and produced many pictures and appeared at least twice as himself on NBC's *Screen Director's Playhouse*. In all, he made well over 400 films. The year after *The Forbidden Room* was released, he married his leading lady, Pauline Bush, though the marriage lasted only a few years. He died of heart failure in 1981.

If the film is at all remembered today, it's because of Lon Chaney's appearance in a small role as the murder victim. Chaney, of course, went on to become one of the biggest names in the history of horror cinema. As is the case with so many of the actor's films from this period, *The Forbidden Room* is considered lost. CW

The Forces of Evil; or, The Dominant Will
aka **The Forces of Evil; The Dominant Will**
Leading Players/Éclair; b/w; 33 min; U.S.

A beautiful woman unintentionally entices an evil hypnotist, who attempts to subvert her will to his own. Yawn.

The Forces of Evil is yet another rip-off of George Du Maurier's 1894 serialized novel *Trilby*. While some sources contend that it was an early co-production between film companies located in the United States and France, it was actually produced in the U.S. by Éclair American and released by Leading Players. Beyond that, very little is known about the production. CW

Fune yurei
Nikkatsu; b/w; 18 min; Japan
D: Shozo Makino
Cast: Matsunosuke Onoe

This was one of many horror films produced by Nikkatsu Studio during the silent years and perhaps one of the most original as well. Rather than trotting out the typical Japanese folklore—ghostly cats or the murderous spirits of scorned women—*Fune yurei* dealt with a haunted ship. Little is known about the film apart from its central idea, which is suggested by a literal translation of its title, though the film has been included in Japanese lists of domestic horror films. CW

The Ghost Breaker
Lasky/Paramount; b/w; 60 min; U.S.
Co-D/Co-P: Cecil B. DeMille *Co-D:* Oscar C. Apfel *Co-P:* Jesse L. Lasky
Cast: H.B. Warner, Rita Stanwood, Theordore Roberts, Betty Johnson, Jode Mullally, Horace B. Carpenter

Warren Jarvis (Warner) is persuaded by Princess Maria Theresa (Stanwood) to help her rid her familial castle of ghosts. It turns out that unscrupulous characters, as part of a scheme to scare the Princess out of her home and loot the place of its gold, fabricated the "ghosts."

Cecil B. DeMille remains something of an enigma to contemporary viewers. His garish spectacles made millions, reaped prestigious awards (DeMille won an Oscar for directing 1952's Best Picture winner *The Greatest Show on Earth*, and today a special award is given annually in his honor) and established him in the public mind as one of cinema's foremost talents. Seen today, however, the bulk of his films look creaky, contrived and laughably kitschy. That said, however, it's indisputable that he knew how to appeal to the masses with a formula blending sex, exoticism and heroics into crowd-pleasing extravaganzas. He got his start as an actor on Broadway before donning a film director's hat in 1913. By 1919, with the release of *Don't Change Your Husband*, he was on his way to becoming a major name. His reputation was cemented with his 1923 version of *The Ten Commandments*, which he remade as an even gaudier all-star epic in 1956. He occasionally made cameos in his own films, usually as an off-screen narrator (as an onscreen performer, his best known credit is his portrayal of—who else—*himself* in Billy Wilder's acerbic masterpiece *Sunset Blvd.*, 1950).

The Ghost Breaker, co-directed with Oscar C. Apfel, is one of DeMille's earliest credits. Adapted from a stageplay by Paul Dickey and Charles W. Goddard, it anticipates the "old dark house" horror/comedy subgenre by several years; the formula reached its peak in the late 1920s and early 1930s with such classics as Roland West's *The Bat* (1926), Paul Leni's *The Cat and the Canary* (1927) and James Whale's *The Old Dark House* (1932).

The cast here includes all-purpose leading man H.B. Warner, then a favorite of Griffith, who would become an equally reliable character actor in the 1930s. Director Alfred E. Green again filmed the story in 1922, but its most famous incarnation was as a vehicle for Bob Hope in 1940's *The Ghost Breakers*. The 1914 film is considered lost. TH

The Ghost of the Mine
Éclair; b/w; 20 (15) min; U.S.
Crew unknown
Cast: Robert Frazer, Edna Payne, Norbert A. Myles, Lottye Fowler

This early entry in the "weird Western" subgenre has the spirit of a girl helping to solve her own murder.

23-year-old Robert Frazer (born Robert William Browne in Worcester, Massachusetts in 1891) got his start in films in 1912 and became a star of the silent screen. He was one of the few silent-era actors to successfully make a long-term transition to the talkies, working right up until his death in 1944. Among his horror credits are *White Zombie* and *The Crooked Circle* (both 1932), *The Vampire Bat* (1933), *Circumstantial Evidence*, *Condemned to Live* and *Death from a Distance* (all 1935), *The Amazing Exploits of the Clutching Hand* (1936), *Daughter of the Tong* (1939) and *Black Dragons* (1942).

The Ghost of the Mine was filmed in Tuscon, Arizona by Texas-based Éclair American, a U.S.-based arm of the French company Éclair. Released on November 29, 1914, Universal Pictures distributed the film. CW

A Ghostly Affair
Hepworth; b/w; 5 min; Great Britain
D: Hay Plumb *S:* Harry Buss *P:* Cecil M. Hepworth
Cast unknown

This long-lost short involved a haunted castle and supernatural apparitions. Whether the material was played for laughs is unknown, but sources indicate that the ghosts proved bogus, and the film's brevity hints that it was a throwback to the earlier, trick-laden work of Georges Méliès.

Director Hay Plumb (sometimes billed as E. Hay Plumb) was born in England. He broke into films as an actor in 1910 and by 1911 was writing scenarios and directing. A competent journeyman, he worked in a wide array of genres until 1920, at which point he appears to have retired from cinema. He died in 1960.

Harry Buss is credited in some sources as writing *Ghostly Affair*'s scenario; his official (though incomplete) filmography lists only his work as actor and director. If indeed he did write the script for this film, there remains another facet to his career remaining to be explored. Both Plumb and Buss were regulars at Hepworth, which produced this picture. TH

Ghosts

Close; b/w; 19 min; Great Britain
D/Co-P/S: Elwin Neame *Co-P:* Ivy Close
Cast: Ivy Close

Mischievous spirits haunt a house. *Ghosts* was one of numerous collaborations between writer/director Elwin Neame and star Ivy Close, preceding their creation of another horror subject, *The Haunting of Silas P. Gould*, by a single year. In addition to being frequent collaborators onscreen, the two were also married in real life.

As if there weren't enough films bearing the generic moniker of *Ghosts*, including another from 1914 titled *The Ghosts*, added confusion is caused by the fact that Close also appeared in an earlier film entitled *Ghosts*, produced by Cecil M. Hepworth and dating from 1912. TH

Hands Invisible

Powers; b/w; 15 min; U.S.
D/S: Edwin August
Cast: Edwin August, Ethel Davis, Hal August

A man (August) is horrified to find that his hands have an impulse to strangle his wife (Davis).

The story of *Hands Invisible* anticipates elements of Maurice Renard's classic horror story *Les mains d'Orlac* (1920), about a concert pianist who loses his hands in a crash and receives in exchange a homicidal pair from an executed murderer. While it's unknown whether the surgical angle was utilized in *Hands Invisible*—the film is considered lost—it seems more likely that the film was simply about a man's unconscious desire to do in his nagging wife.

Actor/writer/director Edwin August was responsible for this strange little melodrama. August directed a number of titles between 1912 and 1919, though his acting career had greater longevity. He did a number of mostly un-credited bit parts over the decades, albeit in such distinguished fare as Frank Capra's *Mr. Smith Goes to Washington* (1939) and Orson Welles' *The Magnificent Ambersons* (1942). He died in 1964. TH

Henpeck's Nightmare

Cosmograph; b/w; 5 min; U.S.
Cast and crew unknown

This is one of a loosely connected series of comedic shorts featuring a goofball character named Henpeck. The films appear to have been created randomly and independently of each other, made by various production companies—including Lux and Nordisk—in different parts of the world. This one features that old standby from the earliest days of horror cinema, the drunken nightmare. When the titular character passes out after a night of sophomoric binge drinking, he has visions of being pursued by horrible monstrosities.

These films were designed to teach the viewer a moral about the sinfulness of drink. Other films from the same subgenre include *A Jersey Skeeter* (1900), *The Drunkard's Conversion* (1901), *D.T.'s, or the Effect of Drink* (1905), *The Man and His Bottle* and *Too Much Champagne* (both 1908), *The Brute* (1912), *The Tempter* (1913), *Distilled Spirits*, *The Raven* and *The Warning* (all 1915) and *The Craving* (1918). CW

The Hound of the Baskervilles
aka Le chien des Baskerville

Pathé; b/w; 45 min; France
Credits unknown

The Hound of the Baskervilles is the most famous (and most frequently filmed) story in Sir Arthur Conan Doyle's Sherlock Holmes canon. First published in serial form in 1901, the novel depicts an archetypal conflict between cold reason (represented by the tale's detective hero) and the power of superstition. Reason and logic emerge victorious when the ghostly hound haunting Dartmoor, Devon County, Great Britain is exposed as something all too earthbound.

The story was previously brought to the screen in Denmark as *The Grey Lady*, with alterations that included the substitution of the tale's "supernatural" hound for a "supernatural" woman in a gray shroud. But this obscure French production is probably the first credited adaptation. Some sources mistakenly apply the film's French title to a completely unconnected German production from the same year.

Virtually no useful information is available about this particular rendering of the tale, not even a list of cast or crewmembers. It is generally considered the first official feature-length adaptation of Doyle's classic tale. TH

The Hound of the Baskervilles
aka Der Hund von Baskerville

Vitascope; b/w; Germany
Part 1: 65 min; Part 2, *The Solitary House*: 55 min
D: Rudolph Meinert *S:* Richard Oswald *P:* Josef Greenbaum *C:* Karl Freund, Werner Brandes
Cast: Alwin Neuss, Friedrich Kuehne, Erwin Fichtner, Hanni Weisse, Andreas Van Horn

Part One: Sherlock Holmes (Neuss) is called upon to protect Lord Henry (Fichtner) and his fiancée Laura Lyons (Weisse) from a supernatural force. The detective learns the legend of the Hound of the Baskervilles, a phantom-like creature blamed for the deaths of Sir Hugo Baskerville and many of his male descendants. Holmes discovers that the true villain is the chameleon-like Stapleton (Kuehne), who is apprehended and taken to prison. Part Two: Stapleton escapes from prison and, in disguise, gains entry to the Baskerville estate, where he abducts Lord Henry and Laura. The detective tracks Stapleton to his lair, rescues the young couple and consigns his nemesis to a well-deserved demise.

This two-part adaptation of Arthur Conan Doyle's novel *The Hound of the Baskervilles* (1901) was re-released as a slightly shortened single feature in 1921. Despite the existence of a print in the Gosfilmofond film archive, the work remains virtually impossible to see. Alwin Neuss first played Holmes in 1911's *The Stolen Legacy* in his native Denmark, where he had also essayed the lead role(s) in an early version of *Dr. Jekyll and Mr. Hyde* (1910). He proved popular in the role of the great detective and revisited it several times, including here.

The script by Richard Oswald (*Weird Tales*, 1919) took many liberties with Doyle's text, not least of which was the complete omission of Holmes' friend and confidante, Dr. Watson. The depiction of Stapleton as a criminal mastermind suggests that Oswald drew inspiration from the most infamous of the detective's enemies, Professor Moriarty, the so-called "Napoleon of Crime."

The first part of the series is noteworthy for its photography by the great Karl Freund, whose name came to be connected to many seminal works in the genre, both as a cinematographer (*Dracula*, 1931) and as a director (*The Mummy*, 1932). Part Two, subtitled *The Solitary House*, seems to have been more outlandish, with Stapleton assembling a submersible house that enables him to hide his victims in a lake.

Director Rudolf Meinert is a figure of marginal interest in early German cinema, directing his last film in 1935. *Hound* remains his best-known title. The success of the two installments led to complications that today induce headaches in anyone trying to create a chronology of adaptations. It seems that after the release of these chapters, producer Josef Greenbaum left Vitascope to form his own company. Greenbaum released a third installment, *The Hound of the Baskervilles* (subtitled *The Uncanny Room*), in 1915. The brass at Vitascope (newly rechristened PAGU) responded by releasing their own Part Three (having lost to Greenbaum major cast members from the first two installments) under the title *The Hound of the Baskervilles: The Dark Castle*. Undaunted, Greenbaum oversaw yet another episode subtitled *The Legend of the Hound*, also released in 1915. Vitascope/PAGU regarded Greenbaum's follow-up as unauthorized and sought to have it suppressed. TH

The House of Fear
Lubin; b/w; 22 min; U.S.
P: Siegmund Lubin
Cast: Rosetta Brice

Based on a story by Emmett C. Hall, *The House of Fear* dealt with a typical heiress encountering typical ghosts in a typical haunted house. Pennsylvania-born leading lady Rosetta (or Betty) Brice made one of her earliest appearances in the lead role. She debuted in 1913 and was active through the mid-1920s. She passed away at the age of 42 in 1935.

This film should not be confused with any number of other films having the same title, including two non-horror works from 1915, a 1939 horror film from director Joe May and a later (1945) horror-tinged entry in the Basil Rathbone Sherlock Holmes series.

Some sources list *House* as being 35 minutes long, but it fit on a mere two reels, making such a length impossible. TH

The Humpback of Cedar Lodge
aka **The Hunchback of Cedar Lodge**
Balboa; b/w; 45 min; U.S.
Credits unknown

U.S.-based Balboa Amusement Producing Company made over 100 films between 1913 and 1918, most of them shorts. This was one of their few feature-length dramas. In it a rich man has two sons, one "normal," the other a hunchback. The father showers his healthy son with love and attention, creating a climate wherein it's acceptable for others to abuse the physically challenged son. As the years go by, the "humpback" grows to hate others, not the least of which is his family. When his father makes it clear that his beloved son will inherit his fortune, the hunchback murders the old man and frames the brother for the crime. Then, in a twist ending, the hunchback accidentally seals himself permanently in the vault that contains his father's gold.

In a surprisingly liberal move for the time, the film offers up condemnation against the societal behaviors that lead to the hunchback's angry and violent tendencies. In the end, however, the title character does get his just reward for bad behavior.

Some sources erroneously describe the plot for this film, often under the title *The Hunchback of Cedar Lodge*, as being about the spirit of a girl who haunts a library! CW

The Hypnotic Violinist
aka **Zigo**
Filmfabrikken; b/w; 33 (45) min; Denmark
Crew unknown
Cast: Emilie Sannom, Rasmus Ottesen, Hakon Ahnfelt-Ronne, Soren Fjelstrup, Charles Lowaas, Valdemar Moller

A mysterious musician wields hypnotic influence over a young woman (Sannom) as her husband (Ottesen) tries to find a way of breaking through to her.

Little information survives about this Danish picture. A clip from it was utilized in *Daredevil of the Movies* (1923), a promo film about starlet Emilie Sannom, but it failed to generate much interest in the original film. Sannom appears to have been the only performer in the film who established much of a name in the industry, though she pretty much disappeared from view by 1923. She died in 1931, just short of her 45th birthday. The film almost certainly focused on melodramatics rather than the usual comedic aspects that were often the focus of such a vehicle in the silent era, with the evil hypnotist a genre staple by this point. TH

The Imp Abroad
Victor; b/w; 15 min; U.S.
D: Harry Revier *P:* Louis Burns, Harry Revier
Cast: Rupert Julian, Elsie Jane Wilson, Iva Shepard, James W. Horne, Mildred Bracken, Allen Froelich

An heiress (Wilson) falls in love with an imp, unaware of his satanic nature.

This comedic short is chiefly notable for the appearance of future director Rupert Julian in its cast. Surviving data leaves it unclear whether he played the title character, but if the testimonials of those who later worked for him are any indication, it would have been an appropriate piece of casting. Julian acted until 1928, often in bit parts, but his definitive performance was in real life as the ultimate in martinet directors—a Von Stroheim without talent. He did have a (heavy) hand in the classic Lon Chaney version of *The Phantom of the Opera* (1925).

This appears to have been the first film directed by Harry Revier, who remained active until the 1930s; his last credit was as a writer on the Buster Crabbe sci-fi cheapie *Planet Outlaws* (1953), which was cobbled together from the *Buck Rogers* 1939 serial. TH

The Invisible Power
Kalem; b/w; 40 min; U.S.
D: George Melford
Cast: Paul Hurst, William H. West, Cleo Ridgely, Frank Jonasson, Jane Wolfe, Thomas Gillette

Beautiful young Mabel Whitney (Ridgely) is seduced by the supernatural charms of Lorenzo (Hurst), who takes her back to his dance hall and gambling den and makes her his love slave. Years pass and an army doctor, Major Dean (West), discovers her while doing research on mental telepathy. Adept of the black arts, Dean clears Mabel of Lorenzo's influence, but the girl gets shot in the process and her memory erased as she attempts to flee her situation. Dean, likewise obsessed with the girl, gets her home and dishonestly tells her that she is his daughter, but Lorenzo, not to be robbed of her, follows. In a head-to-head mystical match-up between Dean and Lorenzo, the latter loses. Simultaneously, another army enlistee, Sergeant Whitney (Jonasson), recognizes the girl as his own long-lost daughter. He and Lorenzo fight to their mutual deaths as the girl escapes.

Yet another knock-off of George Du Maurier's *Trilby*, *The Invisible Power* was one of director George Melford's few stabs at horror. He was later cheated out of the directorial chores on Universal's talkie hit *Dracula* (1931), exiled instead to the Spanish-language version, shot at night on the same sets and with many of the same crew. CW

Jane Eyre
IMP/Universal; b/w; 20 min; U.S.
D: Frank Hall Crane
Cast: Ethel Grandin, Irving Cummings, John McCabe, Miss Burke, Mrs. Hempstone, Lois Alexander

Having starred in the very first film adaptation of Charlotte Brontë's *Jane Eyre: An Autobiography* (1847), Frank Hall Crane stepped behind the camera to direct the third one for German émigré Carl Laemmle's film production company IMP, which later morphed into Universal.

Like the book, the film concerns the eponymous Jane Eyre, a young teacher who takes the position of governess over the ward of the strange but handsome Mr. Rochester, who is 20 years her senior. Jane falls in love with Mr. Rochester, but after she agrees to marry him, she finds herself tormented by mysterious goings-on. Rochester's insane wife, whom he has locked away in the attic, perpetrated such strange occurrences.

The film was one of two adaptations of Brontë's novel made in 1914. It was released in February, with the second, produced by Whitman, released in June. Both were shot in the United States. CW

Jane Eyre
Whitman; b/w; 50 min; U.S.
D: Martin Faust
Cast: Lisbeth Blackstone, John Charles, Mary Fry Clements, Irving Cummings, Viola Allen Frayne

This is the second film adaptation of Charlotte Brontë's novel *Jane Eyre: An Autobiography* (1847) to be released in 1914; it arrived four months after the first. This one was also the longer of the two, clocking in at approximately 50 minutes.

Whitman Features Company was an independent studio that produced all of its output within the span of a single year, 1914, and then dissolved. Little is known about most of these films, although actor Martin Faust directed at least two of them (the other was *The Toll of Love*). As a thespian, he starred in well over 100 films, beginning with this version of *Jane Eyre*. Roughly half of his roles went un-credited, all of them in the sound era. Faust died in 1943 with several of his films yet to be released.

Lisbeth Blackstone starred as Jane Eyre, who falls in love with the mysterious Mr. Rochester (Charles), unaware that his previous "deceased" wife is still both very much alive and insane, locked away in the attic. CW

Kaidan Asamagatake
aka **Asamagatake**
Nikkatsu Kyoto; b/w; length unknown; Japan
D: Shozo Makino
Cast: Matsunosuke Onoe

Released in December 1914, this horror short was one of many produced by Nikkatsu's Kyoto branch. Though little is known about it today, Asamagatake is the name of a mountain in Japan that, at 555 feet, is the highest in Ise-Shima National Park; it's also home to a famous Shinto temple. The film's title translates as *Ghost Story of Mt. Asamagatake*. Just what that ghost story might have been is anyone's guess, given that the area plays host to more than its share of spooky legends.

As is typical of films from Nikkatsu's Kyoto branch during this time and vintage, *Kaidan Asamagatake* was directed by Shozo Makino and starred Matsunosuke Onoe. CW

The Last Egyptian
Oz; b/w; 55 min; U.S.
D: Joseph Farrell MacDonald *S/P:* L. Frank Baum
Cast: Joseph Farrell MacDonald, Howard Davies, Jefferson Osborne, Mai Wells, J. Charles Haydon, Jane Urban

Best known as the author of one of the most famous novels in children's literature (*The Wonderful Wizard of Oz*, 1890), Lyman Frank Baum (1856-1919) was greatly intrigued by the potential of cinema. In 1914 he started his own production company, which he called The Oz Film Manufacturing Company. His aim was to produce family entertainment and in so doing shift children's tastes away from the violent Westerns that had grown so popular after Edwin S. Porter's *The Great Train Robbery* (1903). The company made a few feature films, most of them based on the Oz stories, along with a small number of shorts. The first of these was picked up by Paramount; after it flopped, Alliance picked up the remainder.

Without the sort of market for juvenile fare that exists today, none of Oz's other family films did very well either, so Baum (under some pressure from his investors) changed the company's name to Dramatic Feature Films and focused on material of interest to adults. This led to the company's only non-Oz feature film, *The Last Egyptian*, an odd brew of action and adventure with a dash of horror that at times prefigures Universal's 1999 "remake" of *The Mummy*. Baum's film was based on the novel *The Last Egyptian: A Romance of the Nile*, which had been published anonymously in 1908 by Edward Stern & Co. The novel's adaptation by a company owned by L. Frank Baum pretty much gave away who'd written it, however, and it was eventually reprinted with Baum credited as author.

As with the novel, the film deals with Kara (MacDonald), the last in a long line of priests descended from those who attended the Egyptian god Amen. He is called to his grandmother Hatacha's (Wells) deathbed where she tells him that British aristocrat Lord Roane (Moore) misused her and left her destitute. Kara promises revenge on Lord Roane. Unfortunately, most of

L. Frank Baum sits in the center of the photo.

the movie's remainder focuses less on his violent machinations than on the romance between Lady Aneth (Reed) and Winston Bey (Davies). In fact, the film's tag line reads, "A Thrilling Oriental Romance Full of Love and Adventure."

A print of the film exists in the Museum of Modern Art in New York City. CW

Legion of the Phantom Tribe
aka **Legend of the Phantom Tribe**
Bison; b/w; 22 min; U.S.
Crew unknown
Cast: William Clifford, Marie Walcamp, Helen Clark, Sherman Bainbridge, William Ellingford, Val Paul

Bison, whose explorations of Native American folklore had begun the previous year with *The Werewolf* (likewise starring William Clifford, Marie Walcamp and Sherman Bainbridge), followed up with this horror Western about an American Indian who is turned into a bear via witchcraft.

The year 1914 also saw Bison produce and release *The Phantom Light*, about an American Indian who is haunted by the ghost of his brother. CW

Lola
aka **Without a Soul**
Schubert; b/w; 50 min; U.S.
D/S: James Young *P:* Lewis J. Selznick
Cast: Clara Kimball Young, Alec B. Francis, Edwin Kimball, James Young, Frank Holland, Olga Humphries, Irene Tams

Dr. Barnhelun (Francis) is devastated when his beloved daughter Lola (Young) is killed in a car crash, but using a new ray he helped discover, he brings her back from the dead. What he doesn't count on, though, is that the resurrected Lola is only a shell of her former self, since her soul has left her body.

This variation on the Frankenstein theme is considered a lost film. It was reissued in 1916 under the more literal title *Without a Soul*, so one can assume that it made some kind of a splash upon its original release. Director/writer/co-star James Young was a popular presence on the silent film scene. He directed close to a 100 films between 1912 and 1928, the best remembered being *The Bells* (1926). As an actor, he had a small role in Maurice Tourneur's 1915 version of *Trilby*. Clara Kimball Young, who was the real-life wife of the director, played *Lola*'s eponymous lead. They worked together on numerous occasions, though most of those collaborations are long lost.

The making of *Lola* sparked a bit of real-life drama. Producer Lewis J. Selznick seduced Clara, which led to a nasty and highly publicized divorce from her director/husband. While Young's screen image before *Lola* had been clean and wholesome, her portrayal here neatly dovetailed with the public perception of her as something of a "vamp." Though she rejoined her estranged husband for a role in the aforementioned *Trilby*, their divorce was finalized in 1916, just in time for *Lola*'s reissue under its second title. TH

The Magic Skin
Victor; b/w; 35 min; U.S.
Crew unknown
Cast: J. Warren Kerrigan, George Periolat, Jessalyn Van Trump, William Wadsworth, Ed Brady

Honoré de Balzac was born in France in 1799. He was immediately placed in the care of a wet nurse and was, when not with her, most often looked after by a governess. Later, in boarding school, he was a poor student who spent much of his time in a solitary room as punishment for alleged disobedience. All of this, of course, belies the fact that he became a successful author, writing some of the most beloved stories in French history. His writing style was realistic, distinguished by a droll sense of humor and symbolism that condemned the societal ills around him. In 1850 he died in Paris, a mere five months after marrying the love of his life, a countess he'd met in 1833 and with whom he'd corresponded for years.

The Magic Skin was the second film adaptation of Balzac's novel *La Peau de chagrin* (known in English as *The Wild Ass's Skin*), the first having been made in France in 1909 under the novel's original title. This version was shot in 1913 but wasn't released until January 1914. It's about a magic skin, processed from the hide of a wild ass, that grants wishes at the cost of its owner's soul.

Kentucky-born J. Warren Kerrigan was a popular leading man during the silent era, starring in approximately 350 films. His career hit a bump during World War I when a chance remark during an interview (he suggested that he'd be happy to join the war effort so long as all the "men who aren't good for anything else" were called up first) damaged his popularity with the masses. He found professional success again in 1923 when James Cruze cast him in *The Covered Wagon*. Afterward, due his studio's discomfort with the fact that he refused to marry, Kerrigan, who was both openly gay and partnered, retired on his substantial lifelong savings. He died of pneumonia in 1967. CW

The Moonstone of Fez
Vitagraph; b/w; length unknown; U.S.
D: Maurice Costello, Robert Gaillard *S:* Robert Welles Ritchie
Cast: Maurice Costello, Constance Talmadge, Eulalie Jensen, Thomas R. Mills, George Stevens, Robert Gaillard

When a relative dies, Winifred Osborne (Talmadge) inherits not only a great fortune but also the "Moonstone of Fez," a Moroccan gem supposedly haunted by the obligatory curse. Afterward, while visiting Paris with her mother, she goes out on her own and returns to find that her mother has disappeared. The mystery deepens as everyone around her, including the hotel staff, refuses to admit that the older woman was there in the first place. Winifred contacts the police, but when they investigate, they too find no trace of her (and according to the hotel records, Winifred checked in alone). Winifred suspects that the curse of the moonstone is to blame for it all, but Schuyler Van Norden (Costello) believes there's a more logical explanation. Through investigation, he learns that the mother is both quite real and quite dead. Bubonic plague, it turns out, has taken her, with both hotel staff and Paris authorities covering up the incident, fearing public riots—and, no doubt, loss of tourism—if word gets out.

Director Maurice Costello's film, while not an adaptation per se, does borrow a major plot point from Wilkie Collins' classic Gothic horror novel *The Moonstone* (1868). In 1949 future horror director Terence Fisher co-directed a far better version of this same (allegedly true) "missing person" story, an overlooked little gem titled *So Long at the Fair*. Fisher, however, forwent the bit concerning the moonstone, giving his film a more mysterious but less horrific tone.

Both Costello and co-director Robert Gaillard had parts in *The Moonstone of Fez*, Costello as the male lead, Gaillard in the much smaller role of French consul. Collins' novel had been filmed at least twice previously, once in 1909 and again in 1911. CW

Murders in the Rue Morgue
Paragon; b/w; length unknown; U.S.
D/Co-S: Robert Goodman *Co-S/P:* Sol A. Rosenberg
Cast unknown

While this second film adaptation of Edgar Allan Poe's short mystery story *The Murders in the Rue Morgue* (1841) is now lost, some information about it has survived. An amateur detective living in then modern-day Paris (the script simply refers to him as "author," leading film historians to suspect that the character is based on Poe) embroils himself in the case of a friend, Dupin, whose sister's fiancé, Le Bon, is suspected of murder. Le Bon maintains his innocence, and the author helps solve the case. Though existing information about the film doesn't identify who the killer was, it's safe to assume that it was a non-human primate of some sort, possibly an orangutan or gorilla.

The next legitimate version of the tale was Universal's 1932 classic *The Murders in the Rue Morgue*, starring Bela Lugosi. CW

The Mysterious Mr. Wu Chung Foo
Feature Photoplay Company; b/w; 4 chapters; U.S.
Credits unknown

Sax Rohmer was a pseudonym used by British novelist Arthur Henry Sarsfield Ward (1883-1959). Though he had a fairly prolific career writing skits for stage comedians and short stories for magazines, it wasn't until he created the evil "Oriental" fiend Fu Manchu that he found lasting fame. The villain first appeared in a series of short stories that in 1913 were collated into a novel, *The Mystery of Fu Manchu* (known as *The Insidious Dr. Fu Manchu* in North America). The book proved successful enough that, a year after it appeared, Feature Photoplay Company appropriated the character (though not by name to avoid paying royalties) for the big screen.

Not only is *The Mysterious Mr. Wu Chung Foo* a clone of Rohmer's criminal mastermind, but the film freely steals other Rohmer characters as well; Sir Nayland Smith can be found under the name Lord Lister and Dr. Petrie under the name Charles Brand. And, in what seems a fair case of turnabout, the film introduces Wu Chung Foo's adopted daughter Hattie ... who changed her name to Fah lo Suee and became Fu Manchu's daughter in the third novel in Rohmer's series, written several years after *The Mysterious Mr. Wu Chung Foo* hit the big screen.

Released in July 1914, *Wu Chung Foo* finds Lord Lister, just after a poker game at the Astor Club, coming across a dollar bill with an inscription written on it. The message is a plea for help from someone claiming to be held by a Chinese gang in Cosia, near Sacramento. Lister enlists the aid of good friend Brand,

and the two travel to Cosia where they meet a sinister Asian merchant named Wu Chung Foo who claims that his employees are disappearing and that he has no idea why. But when Foo realizes that his adopted daughter Hattie has fallen for Brand, he jealously kidnaps the man and takes him to an underground lair. There Brand discovers that the vanished men are doing forced hard labor, with nothing to look forward to but death. When Lister investigates his friend's disappearance, he too is forced into the underground labor camp. Unable to bear having her lover work in the camp, Hattie goes to authorities for help. Wu Chung is arrested and Lister, Brand and the others freed.

This appears to be the only major knock-off of Rohmer's character until the *Dr. Sin Fang Dramas* began with *The Scarred Face* in 1928. In 1920 Oswald Stool officially adapted Sax Rohmer's novel *The Yellow Claw* (featuring another "Oriental" villain, this one named Mr. King). *Claw* had been envisioned as a kickoff for a feature film series based on great works of literature. Tepid response, however, prompted the producers to downsize their offerings to two-reel adaptations (the first of which was based on Sir Arthur Conan Doyle's *The Adventures of Sherlock Holmes*, with Eille Norwood as the famous detective). From this sprung a series called *The Mystery of Dr. Fu-Manchu*, containing the first official movie incarnation of the eponymous character. CW

The Mystery of Edwin Drood
aka **Edwin Drood**
World; b/w; 55 min; U.S.
Co-D: Herbert Blaché *Co-D/S:* Tom Terriss
Cast: Tom Terriss, Rodney Hickok, Vinnie Burns, Paul Sterling, Faye Cusick, Margeret Prussing

Alice Guy's husband Herbert Blaché shot this second adaptation of Charles Dickens' 1870 Gothic novel *The Mystery of Edwin Drood* (which was serialized but never completed due to the author's death). The novel dealt with a jealous rivalry among three men for the affections of the beautiful young Rosa Bud. Two of those men—choirmaster John Jasper and orphaned Neville Landless (twin brother to Helena Landless)—are painted as suspects in the disappearance of Edwin Drood, to whom Rosa Bud has been betrothed since birth. Clues in the novel as well as interviews with those who knew Dickens leave little doubt that the killer was to have been revealed as John Jasper, who, it was claimed by Dickens' illustrator, did Edwin in with a necktie.

Blaché's film provides quite a departure from the accepted solution to the mystery. While Jasper's opium addiction is retained, and he does indeed instigate a feud between Drood and Neville Landless, the novel and the film drastically part ways. Upset that Drood and Landless reconcile after a fight, Jasper knocks his nephew unconscious and throws him into a lake. Landless is arrested and charged with Drood's murder after Jasper arouses the townspeople's suspicions. Eventually, after being hounded by a mysterious man named Datchery, Jasper is revealed to be the true criminal, though in fact Drood isn't dead; it turns out that he was rescued by fishermen and that it's none other than accused murderer Neville Landless' sister Helena (in disguise as Datchery) who has engineered the exposure of the truth.

The next cinematic adaptation, Universal's *The Mystery of Edwin Drood* (1935), starring Claude Rains and David Manners, is the best known. CW

The Mystery of Grayson Hall
Éclair; b/w; 22 min; U.S.
Crew unknown
Cast: Lindsay J. Hall, Fred Hearn, Edna Payne, Hal Wilson

Little is known about this lost short subject. The American arm of Éclair produced, with Universal picking up the distribution rights. The story involved a detective who impersonates a murdered man in the hopes of tricking the killer into revealing himself. The film was almost certainly a thriller, though the set up betrayed its horror potential.

No information has survived as to who worked behind the scenes, and the credited performers all had relatively minor careers confined to the silent era. TH

The Mystery of the Fatal Pearl
American Kineto; b/w; 55 min; U.S.
Credits unknown

In a temple in India, a high priest curses the pearl eye of an idol so that anyone who steals it will die. And wouldn't you know, two British interlopers soon happen by the temple and swipe that very object. Not surprisingly, things get ugly pretty quickly. One of the thieves stays overnight at the home of a jewel dealer, hoping to sell the pearl in the morning. But during the night he has a terrible vision of the vengeful idol, suffers a heart attack and dies. The dealer takes the object, only to quickly get his in a horse riding accident. His son takes possession of it and commits suicide; then the son's wife sells the stone to a moneylender. The original thief, apparently a bit slow on the uptake, seeks and finds employment at the moneylender's home, hoping to get the pearl back. He is tasked with finding entertainment for a party and—damn his luck—unknowingly hires a Hindu who belongs to the cult of the pearl. In fairly short order the thief is "accidentally" killed, the moneylender offs himself and the Hindus get their pearl back, with plenty of action and romance along the way.

The Mystery of the Fatal Pearl was told in five parts, which theaters presented either over successive evenings or in one sitting. It was produced by the American Kineto Corporation and released theatrically by Empress. Reviews at the time found that it strained credulity but was nonetheless entertaining. CW

The Necklace of Rameses
Edison ; b/w; 32 min; U.S.
D: Charles Brabin *S*: Charles Vernon
Cast: William Bechtel, Mrs. William Bechtel, Gertrude Braun, Robert Brower, Marjorie Ellison, Mary Fuller

A thief steals a jewel from the mummy of a daughter of Egyptian King Rameses, but because of a curse on the precious stone, he is unable to part with it.

Shot in Belgium, *The Necklace of Rameses* is an early production from British-born director Charles Brabin (1882-1957). Brabin began his film career in 1910 as an actor for Edison but switched to directing in 1912. Though he made several horror films, including *The Raven* (1915) and *The Mask of Fu Manchu* (1932), his greatest claim to fame comes from his 1921 marriage to silent screen vamp Theda Bara. They remained together until 1955, when she died of cancer.

Another notable figure in the cast is Rex Hitchcock, whose real name was Rex Ingram Montgomery Hitchcock. Two years after this production, Universal gave him his first directing assignment with *The Great Problem*. He later achieved acclaim for such films as *The Prisoner of Zenda* (1922) and *The Magician* (1926).

The year 1914 also saw the release of *Oh! You Mummy* from production company Crystal. Phillips Smalley directed and Pearl White, Charles De Forrest and Vivian Prescott starred. The film doesn't appear to have survived, making analysis of it impossible. A still photo does exist of Pearl White astride a camel with a sphinx in the background, but whether it belongs to this film or some other is difficult to say. It was released on a split reel with *Naughty Nellie* (1914) and probably contained both comedy and adventure elements. CW

A Night in the Chamber of Horrors
Éclair; b/w; 11 min; France
Credits unknown

This extremely obscure silent motion picture is listed variously as an Éclair and A.C.A.D. production; the former seems more likely. Either way, it is said to have lifted its tone from the famed Grand Guignol Theatre in Paris, where violent, gruesome plays were enacted for onlookers in search of voyeuristic thrills.

The plot concerned a man who hides out in a chamber of horrors and winds up as one of its exhibits. CW

A Night of Thrills
Universal/Rex; b/w; 25 min; U.S.
D: Joseph De Grasse
Cast: Lon Chaney, Pauline Bush, William C. Dowlan, Charles Manley

Ostensibly a comedy, *A Night of Thrills* involved a haunted house and may well have been part of the then-current fad of horror/comedy hybrids. Engaged to be married, young Hazel has an argument with her fiancé Jack and flees to a country house given her as a wedding gift by her uncle. Crooks invade the place while she's there, and when she attempts to flee, she runs into her fiancé, screams and faints. The crooks believe the place to be haunted and run off. The real ghost of the house reunites Hazel and Jack.

Director Joseph DeGrasse was prolific during the silent era, but his directorial career came to an abrupt halt with the coming of sound; as an actor, he continued to work until the mid-1930s, mostly in minor roles. More interesting here is the presence of Lon Chaney in one of his earliest roles with a horror connection. Though he'd only entered the film industry the year before (some sources claim his debut came in 1912's *The Honor of the Family*, but this has never been irrefutably confirmed), the versatile character actor had amassed a sizable number of credits by this time. His ability to change his appearance would eventually make him one of the silent screen's biggest stars and a horror icon to boot, but his first star turns wouldn't come until *The Penalty* (1920) and *The Hunchback of Notre Dame* (1923).

Fledgling studio Universal had a hand in this film and would subsequently utilize Chaney for two of the biggest box-office hits of the 1920s: the aforementioned *Hunchback* and *The Phantom of the Opera* (1925). TH

Okazaki no neko
aka **Okazaki no kaibyô-den**
Nikkatsu; b/w; 30 min; Japan
D: Shozo Makino
Cast: Matsunosuke Onoe

While the first film on the subject of the Okazaki ghost cat appears to have been made by Nikkatsu in 1912, little is known about that particular venture. The studio revisited the tale again in 1914, this time with director Shozo Makino at the helm. The title translates as *Ghost Cat of Okazaki*—Okazaki being a city in the Aichi Prefecture on the island of Japan. There, a castle and its surrounding park provides the city with an attractive tourist trap; it was near the walls of the castle (which was originally built around 1455, torn down in 1873 as a vestige of the eradicated feudal system and rebuilt to the original specifications in 1959) in a temple along the Takaido road on which the story takes place.

Unlike most of Japan's ghost cat movies, the story the film was based on was comical in nature. It found its first literary expression as part of Jippensha Ikku's humorous novel *Shank's Mare* in the early 1820s and later as a Kabuki play (1827). The tale concerns a witch who uses the temple at Okazaki for her nefarious conjurations, which include summoning the spirit of a cat. Silent Japanese superstar Matsunosuke Onoe plays the man who hunts the cat down.

Okazaki no neko was released in April 1914. The story got another telling by Nikkatsu's Kyoto branch under the title *Okazaki kaibyô-den* in 1919, with the first sound version, *Yaji and Kita's Cat Trouble*, following in 1937. CW

Out of the Far East
aka **Eyes in the Dark**
IMP/Universal; b/w; 22 min; U.S.
D: Frank H. Crane *S:* Stuart Paton
Cast: Leah Baird, Stuart Paton

This obscure melodrama is built around that staple of silent-era horror cinema, a cursed ruby with supernatural powers. (One can assume that the film's title refers to the origin of the ruby, which came, no doubt, from India as had so many others in the wake of Wilkie Collins' *The Moonstone*, 1868.)

Though originally produced and released in 1914 by IMP, *Out of the Far East* proved an even bigger success when Carl Laemmle reformed IMP as Universal and re-released the company's catalog titles under new names. *Far East* was given the lurid new title *Eyes in the Dark* and re-released in 1917 as an original production. This somewhat dishonest marketing strategy has caused a great deal of confusion, with many sources today giving each of the two titles individual status.

Actor Frank Hall Crane directed, and he immediately followed it up with his own rendition of *Jane Eyre* (also 1914). His career as a director and actor was prolific, to say the least, and finally wound down after a series of un-credited roles in low-budget films during the mid-to-late 1930s.

Stuart Paton began his career as a writer and actor with this film, but he too soon graduated to directing. His work eclipsed that of Frank Hall Crane with such titles as *20,000 Leagues Under the Sea* (1916) and *The Voice on the Wire* (1917). His final horror film was the appalling *Chinatown After Dark* (1931). CW

Peter's Evil Spirit
Urban/Eclipse; b/w; 8 min; Great Britain/France
P: Charles Urban
Credits unknown

A demon-possessed derelict haunts a man named Peter. When he tries to flee, magic flames and furniture that sports a life of its own besieges him.

The only surprising thing about this formulaic hokum is the year in which it was made. By 1914, the public's interest in trick photographic shorts had waned in favor of longer, more realistic melodramas (as envisioned by D.W. Griffith). *Peter's Evil Spirit* was yet another co-production between British producer Charles Urban and French company Eclipse; they had teamed up for *The Haunted Bedroom* in 1907, and earlier in 1914 they'd also made (in conjunction with Gaumont) *The Curse of the Scarabee Ruby*. As with so many of Urban's films, *Peter's Evil Spirit* appears to be lost. CW

The Phantom Light
Bison; b/w; 30 min; U.S.
D: Henry McRae S: Margaret Oswald
Cast: William Clifford, Marie Walcamp, Val Paul, Sherman Bainbridge

Director Henry McRae (sometimes billed as his birth name MacRae) was no stranger to horror films, films about Native Americans or, as in this case, combinations of the two. He was a regular contributor to Bison, a film company focused on Native American-themed Westerns, and he often worked with a repertory of actors—William Clifford, Marie Walcamp, Sherman Bainbridge and others. In *The Phantom Light*, he offers up a tale of a Native American who murders his brother and is haunted by the ensuing ghost.

The Phantom Light was released on October 10, 1914. CW

The Phantom Violin
aka **Phantom of the Violin**
Universal; b/w; 40 min; U.S.
D: Francis Ford S: Grace Cunard
Cast: Grace Cunard, Francis Ford, Harry Schumm, Duke Worne

A wonderfully disturbed little melodrama from Francis Ford, the older brother of filmmaker John Ford, *The Phantom Violin* is set in Paris, where a young woman (Cunard) awakens during a thunderstorm to the haunting strains of a violin being played next door. The next morning she meets Ellis, the handsome musician who played the mournful tune, and the two quickly fall in love and get married. But then she meets one of Ellis' friends while listening to her husband's performance in a nightclub, and she begins an affair with him. When Ellis learns of this, he attempts to kill himself by jumping into the Seine, but a policeman stops him. Disheartened, he wanders back to the nightclub, where he finds a secret door leading into the bowels of a Parisian crypt; there, among the bones of the dead, he marks time and plots revenge. One evening he hears his wife and her lover making fun of his music, and he rushes out and murders his former friend, sets fire to the nightclub in which he'd so often performed and forces his wife back into the crypt with him. There he holds her tight as he jumps into a pit, killing them both.

It has long and often been reported that Ford was married to his frequent screenwriting collaborator Grace Cunard (who starred with him in many of their films, often as his wife or girlfriend). While it is likely true that they had a relationship, they were never married.

Other horror films from Ford include *The Craving* and *The Silent Mystery* (both 1918). CW

The Quest for the Sacred Jewel
aka **Quest of the Sacred Gem**
Pathé; b/w; 40 min; U.S./France
D: George Fitzmaurice C: William H. Edmond
Cast: Charles Arling, Edna Mayo, William Roselle, Ernest Treux

A knockoff of Wilkie Collins' horror mystery *The Moonstone* (1868), *The Quest for the Sacred Jewel* charts a course through familiar terrain. While traveling through the mysterious East, David Harding (Arling) stumbles upon a sacred Hindu temple wherein resides a statue with a priceless gem embedded in its forehead. He steals it and returns to the United States, but the temple's priests have seen what has occurred. They find and kill him in New York City, but it turns out that Harding has willed the gem to his niece, May Rowland (Mayo). May is engaged to Joe Marsden (Rosell), and during a celebration of their engagement, Joe is hypnotized into returning the jewel to a disguised priest. May sees Joe's theft and cancels their engagement. Thankfully a detective and his assistant (Treux) solve the case, the diamond is returned to its natural place in the temple and May learns the truth about Joe's actions and forgives him.

The film diverged little from its source material, despite the fact that the title and character names were changed. CW

San'nô no bakeneko
Nikkatsu Kyoto; b/w; length unknown; Japan
D: Shozo Makino
Cast: Matsunosuke Onoe

The same year Nikkatsu produced *Okazaki no neko*—a comedy/horror hybrid about a ghostly cat that haunts a temple in Okazaki—the studio also produced this outright horror tale, about a ghostly cat haunting San'nô, Japan. *Okazaki no neko* was released in April, and *San'nô no bakeneko* was released in July. Both films were directed by Shozo Makino and starred Matsunosuke Onoe. CW

Ein Seltsamer Fall
Vitascope; b/w; 50 min; Germany
D: Max Mack S: Richard Oswald
Cast: Alwin Neuss, Hanni Weisse, Lotte Neumann, Max Mack

In this unofficial adaptation of Robert Louis Stevenson's 1886 novella *The Strange Case of Dr. Jekyll and Mr. Hyde*, a doctor (Neuss) concocts a potion that unleashes an evil alter ego.

Very little is known about this lost production. It's worthy of note as the first German version of Robert Louis Stevenson's famous novella, beating F.W. Murnau's *Der Januskopf* (1920)—which is also lost—to the punch by six years. Alwin Neuss, popular in his day for his portrayal of Sherlock Holmes in a number of German pictures, played the central role(s). Interestingly, Neuss had already played the roles of Jekyll and Hyde in August Blom's 1910 version, which is yet another lost title.

Director Max Mack was a prolific figure throughout the silent era, though his filmography dries up in the mid-1930s.

Screenwriter Richard Oswald amassed a number of genre-oriented credits, ranging from *Weird Tales* (1919) and its sound remake (1932) to *Cagliostro* (1929) and the first sound version of *Alraune* (1930). Some sources list a young Albert Basserman (*The Red Shoes*, 1948) among the cast, but the title is absent in his official filmography.

In 2005, Stefan Drössler, director of the Filmmuseum Muenchen, oversaw a reconstruction of the *Ein Seltsamer Fall*, which clocked in at 31 minutes. TH

Sinews of the Dead
Méliès; b/w; length unknown; U.S.
D/P: Gaston Méliès
Cast unknown

After receiving a skin graft from a dead murderer, a man slides into madness.

This obscure short is sometimes accredited to Georges Méliès but was, in fact, the work of Méliès' older brother Gaston. A producer, director and sometimes actor in his own right, Gaston's output was overshadowed by that of his younger brother, even in their day. Due largely to this longtime lack of interest, much of the elder Méliès' output is lost. Gaston made his film industry debut playing a role in his brother's film *Une partie de cartes* (1896), but things didn't gel for him until 1903 when he emigrated to the United States. He produced a number of films there, many of which he also directed. Unlike Georges, Gaston didn't display much interest in—or flair for—dark and fantastic subject matter.

Sinews of the Dead was one of only a few exceptions. While surviving credits ascribe Gaston only with producing the film, it is likely that he also directed it. The story anticipates Maurice Renard's classic medical horror novel *The Hands of Orlac* (1920), which was filmed under that name by Robert Weine the same year, and again by Karl Freund in 1935 (as *Mad Love*). TH

The Spiritist
aka **Spiritisten**; **Spiritism**; **The Ghosts**; **A Voice from the Past**; **The Spiritualist**
Nordisk; b/w; length unknown; Denmark
D: Holger Madsen *C:* Marius Clausen
Cast: Marie Dinesen, Vibeke Kroyer, Carl Alstrup, Robert Schyberg, Frederik Jacobsen, Moritz Bielawski

Ghosts and spiritualism were featured in this lost Danish production. Director Holger Madsen was also responsible for *A Deal with the Devil* (1914), though his forays into horror were few. And though he remained active in the Danish film scene until the mid-1930s, his most productive years were pre-sound.

Nordisk was the predominant creator of (mostly minor) horror tales in Denmark during the silent era. It took visionary filmmaker Benjamin Christensen to really push Danish cinema into the *fantastique* with *Häxan* (1922), his stunning essay in black magic.

Some sources cite *The Spiritist* as having been produced and released in 1916. In all probability, it was produced in 1914 and released in some quarters that same year, with additional releases elsewhere spaced over the next few years. TH

Stellar Razeto plays the innocent young girl who comes under the power of an evil hypnotist in *The Strange Case of Princess Khan.*

The Strange Case of Princess Khan
aka **How Love Conquered Hypnotism**
Selig; b/w; 20 min; U.S.
D: Edward J. LeSaint *P:* William G. Selig
Cast: Stella Razeto, Jack McDonald, Guy Oliver, Ada Snyder, Scott Dunlap

This is one of innumerable silent films to borrow liberally from George Du Maurier's classic horror tale *Trilby*, despite being officially based on a story by James Oliver Curwood. In it a typical beautiful young girl (Razeto) becomes the object of attraction for a dirty old hypnotist who uses his powers of mind control to subjugate her.

Leading lady Stella Razeto and director Edward J. LeSaint had married the year before *The Strange Case of Princess Khan* was produced and remained so until his death in 1940. Though she continued to use her maiden name throughout her career, she's best known today as Stella LeSaint. She starred in films from 1912 until around 1917, took a break and then returned during the early sound era, mostly in un-credited bit parts. Her last film, *The Undercover Man* (1949), saw release a year after her death. Her husband had far more parts as an actor than she, though they too went mostly un-credited. His directorial career was less prolific (though still numbering over 100 films). He also wrote several scripts, including his most famous work, *The Three Godfathers* (1916), which was later remade as a classic vehicle for John Wayne. CW

The Suicide Club
Apex/British & Colonial; b/w; length unknown; Great Britain
P: Maurice Elvey
Cast: Elizabeth Risdon, Montagu Love, Fred Groves, M. Gray Murray, A.V. Bramble, Compton Coutts

This is one of the more faithful adaptations of Robert Louis Stevenson's macabre short story *The Suicide Club* (1878), and surprisingly (given that Stevenson was Scottish) the first British version. Montagu Love stars as Prince Florizel, while M. Gray Murray plays his friend and confidant Colonel Geraldine. Together the two attempt to shut down a club of card players where he who draws the wrong card must either commit suicide or be murdered by another member of the club. Elizabeth Risdon plays the love interest.

The Suicide Club was only Maurice Elvey's second horror film (after the 1913 dark historical melodrama *Maria Marten, or: The Murder in the Red Barn*), though he went on to direct many more, including *London's Yellow Peril* (1915), *At the Villa Rose* (1920), *The Hound of the Baskervilles* (1921), *The Tower of London* (1926), *The Phantom Fiend* (1932) and *The Clairvoyant* (1934), among others. By no means a great director (most of his films are justly forgotten), Elvey was a strict professional who brought films in on time and within budget. He worked across genres and for a time was production company Stoll's house director.

This was the last of the silent adaptations of Stevenson's story. Universal announced plans for its own version (in 1932 and again in 1933) to star Boris Karloff and Bela Lugosi, but the project never came to fruition. (Instead, the horror masters' first collaboration came with an adaptation of an Edgar Allan Poe story, *The Black Cat* in 1934). In the end, it was left to MGM to make the first sound version of the tale, *Trouble for Two* (1936), starring Robert Young as Florizel and Frank Morgan as Geraldine. CW

Svengali
aka **Der Hypnotiseur**
Wiener; b/w; 58 min; Austria
D/Co-P: Luise Kolm, Jakob Fleck *Co-P:* Anton Kolm
Cast: Fraulein Nording, Ferdinand Bonn

Louise Kolm's second stab at George Du Maurier's 1894 novel *Trilby* may well be a sequel to her first take on the subject matter, *Trilby* (1912). Here, directing chores were shared with cinematographer Jakob Fleck, her eventual second husband. Given the title, the film appears to have focused on the sinister villain Svengali (Bonn), a man of uncanny mesmeric ability who places the beautiful young Trilby O'Farrell (Nording) under his spell. He makes her a great singer, but in the process she loses all trace of her individuality. When Svengali dies, she dies as well.

Du Maurier's novel told Trilby's story in three parts, only one of which focused on Svengali, and that portion provided the basis for Kolm's reexamination of the infamous character. CW

The Temptations of Satan
U.S. Amusement; b/w; 55 min; U.S.
D: Herbert Blaché
Cast: Joseph Levering, Vinnie Burns, James O'Neill, Fraunie Fraunholz

Satan (O'Neill) and his minions set their sights on the virtuous and innocent Everygirl (Burns), who has aspirations of becoming an actress. Satan approaches her in human form and offers her success in exchange for her soul.

Little information survives on this obscure version of the Faust story. It seems to have been a little on the abstract side, with a female protagonist identified only as "Everygirl." British-born director Blaché made a number of films during the silent era, including *The Mystery of Edwin Drood* (1914). His career fizzled with the coming of sound, with his marriage to fellow director Alice Guy dissolving even sooner—in 1922, possibly due to his envy of his wife's success.

Like so many of the Guy/Blaché pictures, *The Temptations of Satan* is assumed to be lost. TH

The Terrible Two in Luck
Phoenix; b/w; 9 (13) min; Great Britain
D/S: James Read
Cast: Joe Evans, James Read

The Terrible Two series, which began with the film of the same name, was a short-lived string from British production company Phoenix. It starred Joe Evans and James Read as the eponymous duo, who had a knack for blundering into trouble. There were at least 14 of these films, possibly more, all made during the years 1914 and 1915. In *The Terrible Two in Luck*, the hapless heroes go in search of a lost treasure and instead find a ghost. Others in the series included *The Terrible Two on the Warpath*, *The Terrible Two on the Wangle* and *The Terrible Two Abroad*.

The two starring actors, Joe Evans and James Read, were also associated with various other silent film series; each was known just as much for their director's credits as for comedic acting. CW

Through the Centuries
Selig; b/w; 11 min; U.S.
D/P: Fred W. Huntley *S:* L.J. Withers
Cast Harold Lockwood, Mabel Van Buren, Henry W. Otto

Two Egyptologists (Lockwood, Otto) make an unexpected discovery—that of an Ancient Egyptian princess (Van Buren) who has been lying dormant in her tomb for 2,000 years. They revive her and soon realize that both are in love with her. This is actually no great surprise, as they are the reincarnations of two men who were once rivals for her affection.

This one-reel short focuses on romance rather than chills, though its predictable final revelation adds a haunting touch of pathos. The year 1914 also saw the release of *Naidra, The Dream Woman* from Thanhouser. While often described as having an Egyptian theme, *Naidra* in fact deals with a contemporary scientist who toils in his laboratory in the hopes of uncovering the secret of life. One day he stumbles upon an ancient book that tells him how to create a beautiful woman, albeit one without a soul. When he does so and falls in love with her, she refuses to love him in return. He then receives a visit from a handsome young organist with whom she does fall in love. Unable to abide seeing them kiss, he attacks them, only to awaken and learn that it was all a dream. CW

The Tower of the Phantoms
aka **La Torre del Fantasmi**; **The Ghostly Band**
Celio; b/w; 30 min; Italy
D: Ivo Illuminati
Cast: Mary Cleo Tarlarini, Enzo Boccacci, Amedeo Ciaffi, Arnaldo Frassi

Virtually nothing is known about this probably lost and definitely forgotten short subject, apart from the fact that it was a horror offering from Italian production company Celio.

Three men (film director Baldassare Negroni, the company's primary director until he moved to London Films in 1914; lawyer Mecheri Joachim and financier Alberto Del Gallo Roccagiovane) founded Celio in 1912. The studio signed some of

Italy's most famous actors for its earliest productions and Cines purchased the company in 1913; Cines had done some distribution work for them. Celio came to an inglorious end in 1920 when its studio building was foreclosed upon and demolished by local authorities.

Director Ivo Illuminati entered cinema in 1914 and helmed a small number of productions through the 1920s. The 1930s found him working sporadically as an assistant director and screenwriter. His directorial swan song was in 1941, and he died in 1963 having long since faded into obscurity.

The Tower of the Phantoms was released in August 1914 in its native Italy. Beginning in January 1915 it had an additional run in Great Britain, where it was titled *The Ghostly Band*. TH/CW

Trilby

London; b/w; 38 min; Great Britain
D/P: Harold Shaw
Cast: Herbert Tree, Viva Birkett, Philip Merivale, Ian Swinley, Charles Rock, Wyndham Guise

In the first half of the 19th century, a Parisian named Svengali (Tree) meets and falls in love with the beautiful but virginal Trilby (Birkett), who in turn is in love with Little Billee (Swinley). No matter how hard he tries, Svengali cannot make the strong-willed Trilby return his affections. He eventually hypnotizes her and, though he makes her a great singer, still cannot make her love him. Instead, she loses all sense of individuality, becoming little more than a living, breathing puppet. In the end, Svengali dies of a broken heart, and Trilby—whose will he owns—follows him into the grave.

This particular version of George Du Maurier's 1894 novel of the same title owes more to Paul Potter's stage adaptation than it does the original source material. Unfortunately, what remains of the film in the archives of the British Film Institute is incomplete—missing, most significantly, the climax. It does contain a great deal of the original setup, however, in which three art students, Little Billee, Taffy (Merivale) and the Laird (Rock), move into an upstairs apartment where they soon meet Svengali, who rents the apartment below theirs. He plays the piano for them and becomes smitten when the students' friend Trilby, an artist's model, joins them. In due course, he hypnotizes her into posing nude, something he hopes will upset suitor Little Billee so much that he will have nothing more to do with her. The plan backfires, however, and Svengali instead gains control of Trilby's will, making her a great singer but ultimately killing her.

While popular at the time of its release, London Studio's film was eclipsed by Maurice Tourneur's still famous, feature-length adaptation, *Trilby* (1915). CW

Tsuchi gumo

Nikkatsu; b/w; length unknown; Japan
D: Shozo Makino
Cast: Matsunosuke Onoe

There are a myriad of Japanese legends in which animals take on human form, or vice versa, to work mischief or to wreak vengeance. Raccoons and dogs are common characters in these tales, but far more numerous are ghost cats, possessed by human spirits and able to take on human shape. Numerous film versions of these folk stories were made during the silent era, and while many of them—particularly those not involving cats—were fantasies, the scarcity of information available about them makes determining which ones actually contained horror elements a difficult task.

Tsuchi gumo is a rare exception to this sad state of affairs. One of many collaborations between director Shozo Makino and actor Matsunosuke Onoe, it was based on a hoary folktale that had popped up periodically over the centuries in various play forms, including Kabuki and a type of puppetry known as Bunraku. Both film and plays depict a warrior, Yorimitsu, who meets up with an evil priest. And not just any ol' evil priest, either, but a vengeful spider in human form. No worries, though, the phantasm is defeated by the valiant and resourceful Yorimitsu.

Onoe portrays Yorimitsu in this film adaptation, shot in 1913 and released theatrically on January 15, 1914. The term *tsuchi gumo* translates as *ground spider* and should not be confused with the Tsuchigumo, a Japanese people who are believed to have lived during the Asuka period. CW

The Unknown Country

Lubin; b/w; 10 min; U.S.
S: Emmett Campbell Hall *P:* Siegmund Lubin
Cast unknown

Based on a story by Emmett Campbell Hall, who likely also wrote the script, *The Unknown Country* concerns the alleged ability of some people to send their spirits to possess the bodies of others. In this particular case, the spirit of one man takes over the body of another, only to fall in love with the second man's fiancé. When the woman spurns him, he tries to return to his own body but finds it dead. Thankfully, the spirit who was ousted in the first place manages to return to its own body before it too dies.

This short subject from producer Siegmund Lubin was exemplary of the filmmaker's antiquated style, unfortunately maintained at a time when other producers were moving on to larger, longer and more realistic films. This inability to keep up, along with a fire that destroyed numerous yet-to-be-released films, led to the demise of Lubin's studio, which closed its doors for good in September 1917, while the pioneer filmmaker died in 1923. CW

The White Wolf

Nestor/Universal; b/w; length unknown; U.S.
Credits unknown

Long before Stephenie Meyer's *Twilight Saga*, there was *The White Wolf*, an early werewolf film mixing Native American religious beliefs with unbridled romanticism. The film deals with a white wolf that, caught in a trap, transforms into a man. He's a Native American medicine man in love with a woman already engaged to another man. Intrigue presumably ensues.

The Nestor Motion Picture Company, formed by brothers David and William Horsley in 1911, produced *The White Wolf*. Though the company began in New Jersey, the brothers grasped the potential of doing business in California; that same year they opened a branch of Nestor in Hollywood, making them the first filmmakers to ever base themselves there. Universal purchased the studio in either 1912 or 1914 (sources conflict), though it continued to make films under its own auspices until 1919 when it was dissolved by Universal and its assets absorbed. The actual studio lot existed until 1935, when it was purchased by Columbia Broadcasting System and demolished to make room for a newer, more modern radio and television studio.

Other horror films produced by Nestor during its brief run include *Poisoned Waters* (1913), *His Egyptian Affinity* and *When the Spirits Moved* (both 1915) and *Mingling Spirits* (1916). CW

The Woman of Mystery
Blaché; b/w; 40 minutes; U.S.
D/S/P: Alice Guy-Blaché
Cast: Vinnie Burns, Fraunie Fraunholz, Claire Whitney

A mysterious Hindu princess (Burns) threatens Norma's (Whitney) life. Detective Nelson (Fraunholz) attempts to protect her, but he is no match for the princess' psychic powers. Her malevolent spirit compels Nelson to rob a bank and leave clues at the scene. Norma helps clear Nelson, after which the two capture the evil princess. But before justice can be meted out, she commits suicide by swallowing the contents of her poisoned ring.

This highly improbable melodrama evidences writer/producer/director Alice Guy-Blache's interest in the horror genre. Guy is best remembered as a pioneer in the film industry, a woman who, during the early years of cinema, managed to attain real clout in a male-dominated profession. Not only was she arguably the first female director, but also her work holds its own next to any film of the period. In addition to this title, she also directed such horror fare as *Esmeralda* (1905) and *The Pit and the Pendulum* (1913). *The Woman of Mystery* took a decidedly less macabre approach to its material than some of Guy-Blaché's other spooky films, but its emphasis on spiritualism and hypnotism was obviously engineered to create the odd goose bumps. TH

Yoshiwara kaidan: Teburi bozu
Nikkatsu Kyoto; b/w; length unknown; Japan
D: Shozo Makino
Cast: Matsunosuke Onoe

Released five months after *Yoshiwara kaidan: kozakura choji* (1913), this short "benshi" film was one of many adaptations of Tsuruya Nanboku IV's classic 1825 Kabuki play *Yotsuya kaidan*. The title refers to a waving bronze hand of the Ghost of Yotsuya. Unfortunately, most pertinent information about the film is lost.

Silent Japanese films often utilized neither subtitles nor inserts. Instead, performers called benshi would stand to one side of the screen and narrate the action. Because many theaters at the time housed around 1,000 people, Benshi performers had to be able to project their voices across the crowd and to work effectively with musical accompaniment. CW

1915

Adachihara Ubagaike yurei
Nikkatsu; b/w; length unknown; Japan
Crew unknown
Cast: Matsunosuke Onoe

This may be the first film based on the legend of Ubagaike Pond, known alternately as *Adachihara* or *Asajigahara*, depending on the version of the tale in question. The original story had to do with a house near Asakusa (a district in Tokyo) that was owned by a poor couple and their daughter. Unable or unwilling to support themselves by honest means, the couple sent their daughter into society to lure wealthy men back to their home, where they would then murder them and steal whatever valuables they carried.

Over time the legend evolved. The old couple and their daughter were replaced by a lone woman who was, in fact, an *onibaba*, or flesh-eating demon, and survived by luring samurai to her home and devouring them. Whether connected or not, a similar story can be found in the Hokuriku region of Honshū that concerns a woman who so wants to frighten her daughter that she places a terrifying mask on her own face, only to find that it's impossible to remove. She and her daughter adapt to the situation by murdering wandering and hungry samurai to support one another.

The legend of *Adachihara* was immortalized first as a traditional poem, then as a Noh play, then as a Kabuki play and finally as a Bunraku or puppet play. In each incarnation, the story concerns the demon woman going after a group of Buddhist monks holing up in her dilapidated house. Various permutations of these legends were adapted in several Japanese horror films, including *Asajigahara hitsotsuya* and *Nikuzuki no men* (both 1922), as well as the classic *Onibaba* (1964).

In *Adachihara Ubagaike yurei*, it seems likely that Matsunosuke Onoe played one of the demon woman's intended victims. Though definitive proof of the director's identity has not survived, it's probable that it was Shozo Makino, who worked for Nikkatsu at the time and frequently shot movies starring the actor. CW

The Agony of Fear
Selig; b/w; 32 min; U.S.
D: Giles Warren *S:* William E. Wing
Cast unknown

A man is frightened to death. Director Giles R. Warren (elsewhere billed simply as Giles Warren) was at the end of his short and none-too-distinguished career when he helmed *The Agony of Fear*. Surviving filmographies credit him with an underwhelming number of directorial credits, all in 1914 and 1915. He made his cinematic home at Selig Polyscope, which ceased production in 1921. *The Agony of Fear* was apparently Warren's last gasp.

Screenwriter William E. Wing was far more prolific; his career lasted from 1912 until 1927. TH

The Arrow Maiden
Reliance/Mutual; b/w; 15 min; U.S.
D: Francis Powers
Cast: Billie West, Harry Moody, Eagle Eye, Dove Eye, Dan Davis

The silent era displayed an unprecedented degree of interest in Native American legends and beliefs, using them as a basis for numerous films of a fantastic nature. Most were sympathetic to the plight of Native Americans, either portraying them as heroes or, at worst, as villains made so by the white man's oppression. In *The Arrow Maiden*, a medicine woman (Dove Eye) brings a Native American warrior back from the dead, only to frighten to death another brave. Kentucky-born actor Billie West (1891-

1967) played the Arrow Maiden, a character whose exact role in the proceedings is unclear. West achieved short-term celebrity during the silent era, starring in almost 70 films between 1912 and 1917.

The Arrow Maiden is listed erroneously in some film guides under the year 1916, with the direction credited to Leslie Fenton. CW

The Avenging Hand
aka **The Wraith of the Tomb**
Cricks and Martin; b/w; 33 min; Great Britain
D: Charles Calvert S: William J. Elliott P: George H. Cricks
Cast: Dorothy Bellew, Douglas Payne, Syndey Vautier

This is not, as some claim, Great Britain's first feature-length horror film, since its running time is close to those of Charles Urban's *Dr. Jekyll and Mr. Hyde* (1913) and Cecil M. Hepworth's *The Basilisk* (1914), both of which came before it. It does, however, bear more than a superficial resemblance to a much later Hammer production, *Blood from the Mummy's Tomb* (1971), in its story of an Egyptian princess (Bellew) whose tomb is discovered and pillaged by an archaeologist (Payne). One of the items stolen is the princess' severed hand. Her ghost awakens and searches London for it, and when she finally learns her defiler's whereabouts, she places a curse on him.

The script was written by William J. Elliott from his own story, though he may have been influenced by Bram Stoker's novel *The Jewel of Seven Stars*, first published in 1903 and again in 1912 (with a new, less gruesome ending). In the novel, the desecration of a tomb by an archaeologist leads to tragedy, much as it does in *The Avenging Hand*. Stoker's novel was the acknowledged basis for the aforementioned *Blood from the Mummy's Tomb*, lending further credence to the notion that Elliott was probably, consciously or otherwise, influenced by Stoker's work.

Douglas Payne previously starred in Maurice Elvey's 1913 horror entry *Maria Marten; or, The Murder in the Red Barn*. CW

The Blood Seedling
Selig; b/w; 30 min; U.S.
D: Tom Santcschi P: William N. Selig
Cast: Tom Santschi, Leo Pierson, Thomas Bates, George Larkin, Lafe McKee, Marion Warner, Roy Clarke

Allen Golyer (Santschi) is a simple farmer who falls in love with Susie, but their idyll is shattered when Susie runs away with traveling salesman Bertie Leon. The salesmen's friend Colonel Blood visits Allen, who gives him a present: a sapling. Soon after Golyer plants the tree, he gets an even greater gift—Susie returns to him. She explains that Bertie has disappeared and it is assumed that he grew bored with her, dumped her and returned to the city. Allen inexplicably takes her back and 20 years of wedded bliss ensue. Then, one fateful day, Allen visits a psychic. What starts as a lark turns tragic when the psychic discerns that Allen murdered Bertie and buried the corpse beneath the sapling. Allen flees, and when the psychic leads the police to his home, they find him dead, a suicide, beside the now fully-grown sapling that had hidden his crime.

While some of *The Blood Seedling*'s cast is known, who played whom is difficult to peg today. Actor/director Tom Santschi was born in Missouri, though he perpetuated the legend that he hailed from the more exotic Switzerland, which is where his father was born. Rugged and good looking, Santschi was a popular leading man in the silent era, though he is more or less forgotten today. He directed about 50 titles between 1914 and 1916, the majority of which are believed to be lost.

The notion of a murderer being exposed by a psychic has been utilized throughout horror film history, most memorably in Dario Argento's masterpiece, *Deep Red* (1975). TH

The Bribe
Victor/Universal; b/w; 11 min; U.S.
D: Lucius Henderson S: Catherine Carr
Cast: Charles Ogle, Mary Fuller, Harry Spingler, Paul Panzer, Clara Beyers, Johnny Walker

Lucius Henderson, rather than Edison's J. Searle Dawley (who more typically worked with stars Charles Ogle and Mary Fuller), directed *The Bribe*. A Thanhouser favorite, Henderson also oversaw such horror efforts as *Dr. Jekyll and Mr. Hyde* (1912) and *A Witch of Salem Town* (also starring Fuller). Henderson was a musician who entered Repertory Theater in the mid-1880s before making a successful transition to the big screen. His first job was as director with the East Coast-based Thanhouser, though he later moved west to work for Majestic and Universal. He also occasionally acted and worked as a radio announcer.

Apart from its director and cast, *The Bribe* has little to recommend it. Trotting out that blandest of all silent-horror tropes (already overused by 1915), it deals with an evil hypnotist who mesmerizes an innocent girl into stealing for him. CW

Call From the Dead
aka **From the River's Depths**; **To the River's Depths**
Thanhouser; b/w; 15 min; U.S.
D: Clem Easton S: Gertrude Thanhouser P: Edwin Thanhouser
Cast: Ethyle Cooke, Justus D. Barnes, Boyd Marshall, Thomas A. Curran

The Thanhouser Company was co-founded in 1909 by Edwin Thanhouser, and almost immediately his stage-actress wife Gertrude Thanouser (1880-1951) became one of the major creative forces behind the company, operating as writer, actor, editor and general studio executive. The New York-based film production company quickly became one of the biggest grossers in the United States, and in 1912 the Thanhousers retired and sold their shares in the company to Mutual Film Corporation, which was headed by Charles J. Hite. When Hite was killed in an automobile accident, the company failed to maintain its success, and Mutual found itself desperate for assistance in turning things around. To this end, they coaxed the Thanhousers out of retirement with a lucrative offer and a great deal of power within the company. One of Gertrude's primary responsibilities was to again write films that would lure audiences into theaters. Thus was created *Call from the Dead* (originally known as *From the River's Depths* and released in Europe as *To the River's Depths*), a typical silent horror short about a murdered man who returns from the grave to wreak vengeance against his killer. Considering that it concerns a reanimated corpse, the film can reasonably be considered one of the earliest zombie movies.

Despite the renewed involvement of its namesakes, The Thanhouser Company's fortunes failed to turn around completely. Though it did get out of debt, the company couldn't weather the tragic death of its major star Florence LaBadie or the strong competition from the feature-length dramas of other studios. In 1918, the Thanhousers again retired from the film industry, this time permanently. To their credit, The Thanhouser Company continues to exist today as a corporate entity. CW

The Case of Becky
Lasky; b/w; 50 min; U.S.
D: Frank Reicher *S:* Margaret Turnbull *P:* David Belasco, Jesse L. Lasky *C:* Walter Stradling
Cast: Blanche Sweet, Carlyle Blackwell, James Neil, Carlyle Blackwell, Jane Wolfe, Frank Reicher

Dorothy (Sweet) is put under hypnosis, and it's discovered that she has a split personality. She and her alter ego Becky become engaged in violent conflict.

The Case of Becky originated as a stage play by Englishman Edward Locke. Some sources credit American theatrical impresario David Belasco (founder of New York's Belasco Theater) with co-authoring the play, though reviews of the period indicate that he merely staged it. First produced in 1912, it was a hit with audiences and critics alike. Its themes of hypnotism and split personalities evoke such horror standards as *Trilby* and *The Strange Case of Dr. Jekyll and Mr. Hyde*. For this first of two silent film adaptations, Blanche Sweet, a popular actress during the days of silent melodrama, filled the central role.

Director Frank Reicher was born in Germany in 1875 and moved to the United States in 1899. He directed *The Case of Becky* during his first year in the film business, and it was also the first film in which he acted (though his part went unbilled). He did both until the early 1930s, after which he focused solely on acting. In that capacity, he's best remembered for his appearances as Captain Englehorn in *King Kong* and its quickie sequel *The Son of Kong* (both 1933). He racked up a number of other horror credits, ranging from *Life Returns* and *Charlie Chan in Egypt* (both 1935) to *The Mummy's Ghost* (1944). TH

The Castle of Thornfield
aka **Il castello di Thornfield**
Savoia; b/w; length unknown; Italy
Credits unknown

The year 1915 saw two film adaptations, released a mere month apart, of Charlotte Brontë's novel *Jane Eyre: An Autobiography* (1847). The first one, Biograph's *Jane Eyre*, came out in August, while this Italian version, *Il castello di Thornfield*, appeared in September. The Italian film was the sixth silent-era version, following two in 1910, two in 1914 and the aforementioned one in 1915.

Savoia, who produced well over 200 titles between 1911 and 1918 and released an additional 200 titles from other studios during that same period, created this version. Though little is known about the film, the title suggests that it was based on the second section of Brontë's book, which dealt with Jane becoming governess to Adele, the ward of the mysterious and lonely Mr. Rochester. She falls in love with the older man, only to learn that his "former" wife is not dead; she is, however, insane and still wanders the corridors of the estate late at night when everyone has fallen asleep.

The year 1918 also saw an adaptation of the novel, strangely titled *Woman and Wife*, but it eschewed the Gothic horror elements altogether in favor of a straightforward romance. CW

The Cheval Mystery
Victor; b/w; 35 min; U.S.
D: Harry Myers
Cast: Harry Myers, Rosemary Theby

The dangers of hypnotism inform this lost melodrama. Hypnotism was a popular motif for genre fare of the period, and it doesn't appear that *The Cheval Mystery* did anything unusual with the topic. In it a hypnotist (Myers) transforms a young woman (Theby) into a raving lunatic.

Director/star Harry Myers was a strong presence in the silent era, though his popularity waned with the coming of sound. One of his last noteworthy roles was as an eccentric millionaire in Charles Chaplin's *City Lights* (1931); almost all of his appearances thereafter were un-credited bit parts. He directed almost 50 short subjects between 1913 and 1917, one of which, *The Latest in Vampires* (1916), may sound like horror but was in fact a comedy about seductive females. He died in 1938 at the age of 56.

Leading lady Rosemary Theby was married to Myers in real life; they wed in 1915 and remained together until his death. She was a mainstay in his films and afterwards remained a familiar face in comedies starring the likes of Laurel and Hardy (*Our Relations*, 1936), Franklin Pangborn (*Doctor's Orders*, 1932) and W.C. Fields (*Man on the Flying Trapeze*, 1935). Her last role was as a cavewoman in the hopelessly silly *One Million B.C.* (1940). She died in 1973. TH

The Chronicles of Bloom Center
Selig; b/w; 25 min; U.S.
D: Marshall Neilan
Cast: Sidney Smith, William Hutchinson, Irene Wallace, Ralph McCormas, Lillian Leighton, George Hernandez

This short comedy concerns a man who plays a prank on a phony spiritualist by dressing up as a ghost. The tables are turned, however, when real ghosts show up.

This appears to have been the first supernatural-themed film from director Marshall Neilan. It was terrain he revisited in less comedic terms with *The Bottle Imp* (1917), *Go and Get It* (1920), *Black Waters* (1929) and *Chloe, Love Is Calling You* (1934). Though a director of note in the silent era, his career sputtered through the 1930s and stagnated in the early 1940s. He did come out of retirement, however, for a small role as a senator in Elia Kazan's controversial classic, *A Face in the Crowd* (1957). CW

The Circular Staircase
aka **The Bat**
Selig; b/w; 55 min; U.S.
D: Edward J. LeSaint *P:* William N. Selig
Cast: Eugenie Besserer, Stella Razeto, Guy Oliver, Edith Johnson, William Howard, Anna Dodge

In need of fresh air, Aunt Ray (Besserer) leases a beautiful country estate from banker Paul Armstrong (Hernandez). She invites her niece Gertrude (Razeto) and nephew Halsey (Oliver) to stay there with her for the summer, as well as Gertrude's fiancé Jack (Howard). The old, dark house is adorned with a magnificent circular staircase, and on their first night there, Aunt Ray and Gertrude find Armstrong's son Arnold (Benson) dead at the foot of those stairs. Because he had argued with Arnold, and because he was missing during the period in which Arnold was killed, Jack is immediately suspected. Arnold's sister Louis (Johnson), who is supposed to be traveling with their sick father, is discovered in the house in a muddled state and unable to remember much of anything. And the housekeeper (Watson) gets sick from blood poisoning she allegedly received when she cut herself falling down that same suspected staircase. After news arrives that the Armstrong bank has failed due to the theft of a million dollars in securities and that the elder Armstrong is now dead, the housekeeper confesses to having shot and killed the abusive Arnold. Then she dies, and it isn't long before nosey Aunt Ray manages to lock herself in a secret room inhabited by the real villain.

Mary Roberts Rinehart's novel *The Circular Staircase* was the basis for the movie. Rinehart was a prolific writer whose popularity led to her being dubbed the "American Agatha Christie" (despite the fact that her first works predated Christie's by more than a decade). Born in 1876 to a poor family in Pittsburgh, Pennsylvania, Mary went to nursing school and there met her husband, Dr. Stanley Marshall Rinehart. After the couple lost their savings in the stock market crash of 1903, Mary turned to writing to make ends meet. She became a regular contributor to *The Saturday Evening Post* and in 1907 wrote *The Circular Staircase*, her first full-length novel, which was published the following year to instant international acclaim and monetary success.

Hollywood quickly came knocking, and in 1915 the book was translated into a feature-length film. The success of book and film led Rinehart, along with Avery Hopwood, to adapt the story to the stage in 1920 under the title *The Bat*. That adaptation was also successful, so much so that the author took some of the original bits in it and fleshed them out to create a second novel, also titled *The Bat* (after the nefarious murderer who stalked the play). This book was also highly successful, and it became the basis for several film adaptations, including *The Bat* (1926 and 1959) and *The Bat Whispers* (1930). (Comic book writer Bob Kane later admitted that the 1926 film inspired him to create the iconic superhero The Batman.)

Rinehart wrote numerous other bestsellers, as well as short stories, articles and travelogues. In fact, the famous phrase "The butler did it!" comes from her 1930 novel, *The Door*. (Though the phrase is not actually uttered anywhere in the novel, the butler did indeed do it, and that was enough to add the phrase to the American idiom.) After 50 years of literary achievement, she died in New York City in 1958 at the age of 82.

The film adaptation of *The Circular Staircase* was released on September 20, 1915. Edward J. LeSaint, a major force during the silent era, directed. He wrote approximately 10 films, directed over 120 and acted (in mostly un-credited roles) in more than 300 others. CW

The Club Pest
Biograph; b/w; 8 min; U.S.
Credits unknown

Released on February 6, 1915, *The Club Pest* concerns a man who takes a bet to spend the night in a haunted house. That plot device was a common one for decades, persisting all the way through the more horrific genre films of the 1960s and '70s, including *Castle of Blood* (1964) and *Web of the Spider* (1971).

The Club Pest likely included comedic elements, given that it was housed on a single reel with the 1915 comedy *Winning the Old Man Over*. Though produced by Biograph, General Film Company released the two short films. Cast and crew names of the participants are lost, making a more complete description of the film and its background difficult. CW

A Cry in the Night
New Agency; b/w; 20 min; Great Britain
D: Ernest G. Batley
Cast: James Russel

This must have been one bizarre film. A horror drama with science fiction elements, it was reportedly about a mad scientist who creates a winged gorilla (Russel). The creature murders a man, though the victim's daughter is left alive.

The filmmaker behind the movie, Ernest G. Batley, was, in addition to being a director, a writer and actor. He was born in England sometime around 1873 and died there in 1965; his daughter Dorothy entered show business as an actor in 1910 at the age of eight but quit after *The Sins of Youth* in 1919—the same year her father retired—to pursue an education, though she temporarily returned to acting in the late 1940s. CW

Destiny's Skein
Lubin; b/w; 30 min; U.S.
D/S: George Terwilliger
Cast: Earl Metcalfe, Ormi Hawley, Hazel Hubbard, Kempton Greene, George Terwilliger

An upstanding citizen suffers from blackouts, during which he commits crimes.

This silent melodrama evokes Robert Louis Stevenson's *The Strange Case of Dr. Jekyll and Mr. Hyde*, though the protagonist is unaware of his dark side. The notion of a "split personality" was popular in fright films of the period and was especially prevalent in German horror cinema of the time, as evidenced by the country's various versions of *The Student of Prague* (1913, et al.).

George Terwilliger entered films in 1910 as a scenarist. He soon became a director, supplementing his income by taking on the occasional acting gig. He never established himself as anything more than a capable craftsman and ended his career on a particularly sour note with the abysmal voodoo tale *Ouanga* (1936). TH

The Devil
aka **Satan's Pawn**
New York; b/w; 52 (55) min; U.S.
Co-D: Reginald Barker, *Co-S:* Charles Swickard *Co-D/Co-S/P:* Thomas H. Ince
Cast: Bessie Barriscale, Arthur Maude, Rhea Mitchell, Edward Connelly, Clara Williams, J. Barney Sherry

Harry Lang (Maude) is a successful painter dogged by false accusations that he is still carrying on an affair with an old flame, Isabella (Barriscale). Given that Isabella is now married to Alfred

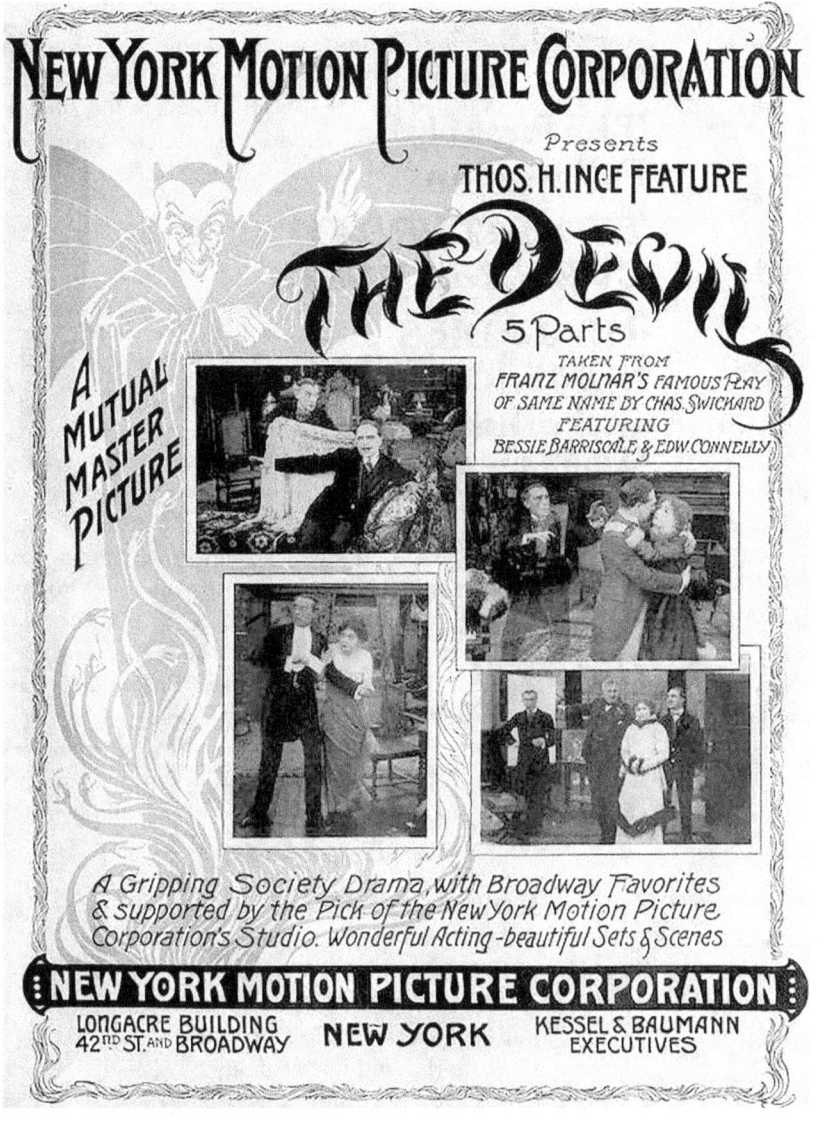

Zanden (Sherry), such gossip could prove ruinous. The situation is worsened when a dapper gentleman who turns out to be the Devil (Connelly) visits Harry. The Evil One prompts Harry and Isabella to meet and reminisce, and the affair reignites for real. Isabelle leaves Alfred, and the Devil watches as the two illicit lovers condemn themselves to eternal hellfire.

This melodramatic supernatural tale was adapted from the play by Ferenc Molnar, best remembered for his 1909 play *Lilliom* (made into a film of the same name by Fritz Lang). *The Devil* was produced and co-written by Thomas H. Ince, who later died under suspicious circumstances while yachting with newspaper magnate William Randolph Hearst. Ince had previously dabbled in horror with *By the House That Jack Built* (1911) and *The Witch of Salem* (1913), and four years after *The Devil* he oversaw *Behind the Door* and *The Haunted Bedroom* (both 1919).

Records from the time indicate that while Ince produced the picture and co-authored its script, he split directorial duties with Reginald Barker. Canadian Barker was an all-purpose journeyman who did much of his work in the silent era; he later directed such horror-tinged fare as *Seven Keys to Baldpate* (1929) and *The Moonstone* (1934). TH

The Devil to Pay
Cricks and Martin; b/w; 7 min; Great Britain
D: Edwin J. Collins
Cast: Jack Jarman

An old alchemist (Jarman) wishes to regain his youth, and the Devil is happy to oblige … for a small price of course. This obscure British short was apparently something of a trick film, which would have made it a bit of a throwback in 1915. The Faustian scenario was also far from novel by that time, but ultimately whatever merits it may have possessed can only be guessed at; little critical information about it has survived and the film is believed to be long lost.

Director Edwin J. Collins was also responsible for the comical *Which is Witch?* (1915) and the romantic *Esmeralda* (1922). *The Devil to Pay* should not be confused with the 1920 horror melodrama of the same name. TH

The Devil's Profession
Arrow; b/w; 33 min; Great Britain
D/S: F.C.S. Tudor
Cast: Alesia Leon, Nancy Roberts, May Lyn, Rohan Clensy, Sidney Strong, Charles Ashwell

An insane asylum is the setting for this morbid silent film from Great Britain's Arrow Productions. The asylum's director (Clensy) keeps his patients doped up with illegal drugs, maintaining in them the appearance of lunacy so that their relatives can steal their fortunes. The tale climaxes with an attack by one of the patients upon the director, at which point the latter stumbles to his death out an upstairs window.

The Devil's Profession seems to have been influenced by Charles Reade's 1856 novel *It Is Never Too Late to Mend: A Matter-of-Fact Romance* (which was, beginning in 1911, the source of many silent-era adaptations). The film also foreshadows Val Lewton and Mark Robson's 1946 horror classic *Bedlam*, starring Boris Karloff and Anna Lee. Purportedly based on either a novel or a poem (depending on which source one believes) by one Mrs. G. Wentworth-James, *Profession* is as forgotten today as its source material. CW

Distilled Spirits
MinA; b/w; 11 min; U.S.
D: Milton J. Fahrney *P:* David Horsley
Cast unknown

Shot in late 1914 and released in January 1915, *Distilled Spirits* is yet another timely message picture of the silent era done up in horror garb, with its drunkard experiencing visions of terrible creatures. The plot bears a striking resemblance to William Haggar's preachy *D.T.'s, or the Effect of Drink* (1905). And, like that film, *Spirits* features a bevy of trick photographic effects.

The idea of a man struggling with alcohol found its most striking presentation in Billy Wilder's *The Lost Weekend* (1945), which featured an Oscar-winning performance by Ray Milland. While it wasn't a horror film, it did contain one horror sequence in which Milland's character experiences the D.T.s. CW

A Drama of the Castle, or Do the Dead Return?
aka **Un drame au chateau d'Acre; ou, les morts revienent-ils?**; **Un drame au chateau d'Acre**; **Les morts revienent-ils?**; **Un Dramma al castello d'Acre**
Film d'Art; b/w; 6 min; France
D/S: Abel Gance P: Louis Nalpas C: Léonce-Henri Burel
Cast: Yvonne Briey, Henry Maillard, Aurele Sydney, Jacques Volnys, Jean Toulout

This appears to have been noted French director Abel Gance's second directorial effort in the horror genre, the first being his 1912 short *The Mask of Horror*. (He also wrote *The Red Inn* in 1910 and co-scripted *The Vengeance of Edgar Poe* the same year as *Mask*.) After writing and selling a war feature to Film d'Art, he was hired by the company to direct this bizarre short about hypnotism, resurrection, jealousy and madness. It was released on the first day of May 1915.

Cinematographer Léonce-Henri Burel, born in November 1892, was an immortal lensman of French cinema. Like Gance, he got his start in the silent era and worked into the 1960s on some of his nation's most prestigious films. Gance died in 1981; Burel in 1977.

The same year as *A Drama of the Castle, or Do the Dead Return?* Gance created one of his most famous short films, the science fiction comedy *The Insanity of Dr. Tube* (1915). Unlike *A Drama of the Castle*, *Dr. Tube* is easily accessible today. CW

The Dream Dance
Lubin; b/w; 30 min; U.S.
D/S: Leon D. Kent P: Siegmund Lubin
Cast: Velma Whitman, Leon C. Shumway, Melvin Mayo, Mary Couglin, George Berrell, Adelaide Bronti

A man (Shumway) suffers from terrible nightmares, which eventually result in his death.

Long before Wes Craven's *A Nightmare on Elm Street* (1984), filmmakers set films within dreamscapes. Many silent short subjects utilized dreams for comedic purposes, but every now and again a more horrific scenario emerged. *The Dream Dance* fits this latter description. Here for once is a disturbing reverie in which the protagonist does not awaken at the end to laugh it all off. In fact, he doesn't get to awaken at all.

Leading man Leon C. Shumway later changed his name to Lee Shumway and became a staple of B-Westerns. He also put in bit appearances in everything from *Mystery of the Wax Museum* (1933) and *Charlie Chan at the Opera* (1936) to *The Grapes of Wrath* (1940) and *Sherlock Holmes in Washington* (1943). Director Leon D. Kent, born as Leon De La Mothe, had a rather prolific although undistinguished career that died with the coming of sound cinema. TH

The Duel in the Dark
Thanhouser; b/w; 22 min; U.S.
S: Philip Lonergan
Cast: Morris Foster, Florence La Badie, Carey L. Hastings, Arthur Bauer, Morgan Jones, Maude Fealy

John Gregory (Bauer) and his wife (Hastings) must rescue their virginal daughter Florence (La Badie) from the clutches of Sardo (Jones), an evil hypnotist whose mind control is effective across great distances.

Regular Thanhouser screenwriter Philip Lonergan wrote this typical silent-era horror outing as a star vehicle for Florence La Badie. (The cutoff age for "virginal daughter" roles was apparently quite a bit higher back then.) True to the fashion of the times, the story is a mix of motifs lifted from popular horror literature, including George Du Maurier's *Trilby* (1894) and Bram Stoker's *Dracula* (1897).

The two-reel film was first released on March 23, 1915. CW

The Dust of Egypt
Vitagraph; b/w; 66 minutes; U.S.
D: George D. Baker S: Alan Campbell C: Joe Shelderfer
Cast: Antonio Moreno, Edith Storey, Hughie Mack, Charles Brown, Jay Dwiggins, William Shea

After stumbling home drunk from an engagement party, Geoffrey Lascelles (Moreno) is asked by his amateur Egyptologist friend Simpson (Brown) to keep an eye on a mummy. Lascelles agrees, but after Simpson leaves, he falls asleep and dreams that the mummy comes to life in the form of Amenset (Storey). The beauteous visage immediately takes a liking to Lascelles and follows him to the home of his girlfriend, where she terrorizes the butler Billings (Mack) and threatens to kill Simpson. But before any real harm can be done, Lascelles awakens.

The film is one of many from the period that prefigures the movie convention of having someone from the past come to the present and find modern trappings (such as telephones and matches) difficult to grasp. CW

The Eleventh Dimension
IMP; b/w; 25 min; U.S.
D: Clem Easton S/P: Raymond L. Shrock
Cast: Howard Crampton, Allen Holubar, Frances Nelson,
Scientists attempt to restore life to the dead.

This long-lost short could just as easily be classified as science fiction. It was the brainchild of Raymond L. Schrock, a jack-of-all-trades who wrote, produced and directed numerous titles from 1915 to 1951. He also served as an un-credited executive production manager on Universal's troubled "super jewel" production, *The Phantom of the Opera* (1925).

Schrock both wrote and produced *The Eleventh Dimension*, leaving directing chores to unremarkable hack Clem Easton. Easton's career had far less longevity than Schrock's, and filmographies credit him with a mere handful of titles shot during 1915 and 1916. Lead player Howard Crampton had earlier played the stuffy Dr. Lanyon in the King Baggott version of *Dr. Jekyll and Mr. Hyde* (1913), which was also produced by IMP. TH

Faust
Lubin; b/w; 22 min; U.S.
D: Edward Sloman P: Siegmund Lubin
Cast: Edward Sloman

Though it follows Goethe's story (and the plot of Charles Gounod's opera) fairly closely, this version of Faust takes one major liberty by setting the film in contemporary times. Apart from that, it's pretty much the same-old same-old: Faust the elderly scientist sits in his study, disheartened at having allowed life to pass him by, until a deceptively pleasant encounter with Mephistopheles (played by Sloman) sets the stage for tragedy. Mephistopheles grants Faust youthfulness in exchange for his soul, and the two go in search of adventure and passion. Faust spots the virginal Marguerite and becomes obsessed with her beauty. With her brother Valentin away at war, Faust is free to court and seduce her, and she becomes pregnant. Upon his return, Valentin attempts to avenge her honor in a duel with Faust, but Faust slays him instead. The rest of the story is likewise rehash; Marguerite dies, and Faust realizes that his regained youth is for naught.

Faust was one of British-born Edward Sloman's earliest films. He had a fruitful career in B-pictures through the 1930s, but his best-known films remain the 1929 adventure *The Lost Zeppelin* and the 1931 horror classic *Murder by the Clock*. CW

Foiled
aka **Foiled!**
Kalem; b/w; 11 min; U.S.
D/S: Rube Miller
Cast: Bud Duncan, Ethel Teare, Harry Griffith, Dave Morris, Charles Simpson

Released on September 22, 1915, this one-reel comedy short featured Bud Duncan as Aloysius Apricot. Ethel Teare co-starred as "village belle" Gwendolyn, Harry Griffith played her father and Dave Morris appeared as Reckless Reginald. There's also a genie named Rubdub Ali Rumney, played by Charles Simpson.

Though comedic in nature, the film offers one grotesque moment when the genie changes a man into a skeleton via the overused effect of stop-substitution.

Foiled should not be confused with the 1909 Lubin film of the same name. CW

The Fox Woman
Majestic/Mutual; b/w; 45 min; U.S.
D: Lloyd Ingraham
Cast: Seena Owen, Elmer Clifton, Teddy Sampson, Bert Hadley

Based on a novel titled *The Fox-Woman* by John Luther Long, *The Fox Woman* concerns a hunchbacked Japanese artist named Marashida (Clifton) who marries his sweetheart, Jewel (Sampson). But their wedded bliss hits the skids when the half-caste daughter (Owen) of an American missionary enters their lives. Named Alice Carroway and known locally as Ali-San, she is in fact a "fox woman," a woman with no soul who must therefore steal someone else's to live. She convinces Marashida to pose for a sculpture of a deformed Japanese god, and as he becomes closer to Ali-San (and loses his soul to her), he becomes less interested in, and increasingly abusive to, his wife. The final humiliation comes when Jewel is forced into slave labor in Ali-San's father's Christian mission, a dishonor to which she reacts by escaping to the tomb of her ancestors to kill herself. Meanwhile, Jewel's father tracks down the fox woman with the aim of destroying her. When she sees him coming for her, she falls from her balcony to her death. Marashida's entrapped soul then leaves Ali-San's body and returns to his own just in time to prevent his wife's suicide. With his spirit back where it belongs and the fox woman gone, husband and wife go on to live happily ever after.

John Luther Long was a lawyer in his native United States but is best known as the author of the classic short story *Madame Butterfly*, which was first published by *Century Magazine* in 1898. *Butterfly* was based on a tale told by Long's sister, the wife of a Methodist missionary who had lived in Japan. It went on to form the basis for a popular 1900 stage play by David Belasco and an even more popular 1904 opera from composer Giacomo Puccini. Long's interest in Japanese culture and beliefs provided the basis for several of his stories, including the one on which *The Fox Woman* is based. His narratives were often sympathetic to Japanese people, presenting them as victims of an imperialist West personified first and foremost by Americans.

Seena Owen, under the name Signe Auen, essayed the role of Ali-San. Owen found fame the following year when she starred in D.W. Griffith's *Intolerance* (1916); her career faded somewhat with the coming of sound, but she did continue to work in the industry as an actress and screenwriter. She is best known today for having been one of the partygoers (with Charlie Chaplin and Marion Davies) aboard William Hearst's yacht when writer/director/producer Thomas H. Ince died under mysterious circumstances.

Elmer Clifton started out as an actor working for the likes of D.W. Griffith before becoming a director. One of his most famous films is the anti-marijuana classic *Assassin of Youth* (1937). He died of a cerebral hemorrhage while shooting his last picture, *Not Wanted*, in 1949. Teddy Sampson (1898-1970) had a decade-long career during the silent era, but she is best remembered as the wife of actor and photographer Ford Sterling. CW

The Ghost Fakirs
Mittenthal/Starlight; b/w; 11 min; U.S.
Crew unknown
Cast: Jimmy Aubrey, Walter Kendig

The *Heinie and Louie* films were a series of shorts shot between 1914 and 1916. Jimmy Aubrey starred as Heinie, while Walter Kendig played Louie. When Kendig died in October 1915, the franchise continued without him. Aubrey's career outlasted the series, thanks to Laurel and Hardy, who cast him in many of their films. After his leading-man heyday, he worked in un-credited bit roles in numerous films. He died in 1983.

In *The Ghost Fakirs*, the two men spend the night in an allegedly haunted house, with the usual mugging and pratfalls. The film was released on May 20, 1915. CW

Ghost of Twisted Oaks
Lubin; b/w; 33 min; U.S.
D: Sidney Olcott *S:* Pearl Gaddis *P:* Siegmund Lubin
Cast: Valentine Grant, Florence Wolcott, James Vincent, Arthur Donaldson

This three-reel melodrama deals with a love triangle in the swamps of Florida. What sets it apart from other romantic melodramas of the period is its depictions of voodoo ceremonies, as well as its ghosts.

Toronto-born Sidney Olcott (1873-1949) directed *The Ghost of Twisted Oaks* and cast his sister Florence in a supporting role. This was a rare acting role for her, though her brother was a major director during the silent era, churning out well over 130 features. (He also acted in many films.) Showing that nepotism was alive and well during the silent era, Olcott cast his wife, Indiana-born actress Valentine Grant, as *Ghost*'s female lead. Grant

The Golem, made from clay and other inanimate materials, protects Jewish people from anti-Semites.

Amid the ruins of a Jewish temple, an antiques dealer (Galeen) discovers an ancient Golem (Wegener), created over four centuries earlier by a well-meaning Rabbi to defend his people from persecution. When the dealer brings the Golem to life for use as a servant, it falls in love with the dealer's daughter (Salmanova—who was, incidentally, Wegener's wife during two of his five marriages). The daughter rejects the Golem and the creature goes on a rampage.

Paul Wegener had already dabbled in horror cinema with his 1913 version of *The Student of Prague*, but his lasting contribution to the genre came with his explorations of the character of the Golem. A long-standing feature of Jewish mythology, a Golem is a creature made from clay and other inanimate materials. The most popular variation of the Golem myth involves 16th century Rabbi Judah Loew ben Bezalel, who created one to protect his people from anti-Semites.

starred in several of her husband's productions before retiring from acting in 1918. She died in March 1949, and her distraught husband followed in December of that same year.

The Ghost of Twisted Oaks was released on November 11, 1915. CW

Ghosts and Flypaper
aka **Ghosts and Fly Paper**; **Ghosts and Flypapers**
Vitagraph; b/w; 10 min; U.S.
D/P: Ulysses Davis *S:* Louis B. Rose
Cast: Anne Schaefer, Marguerite Reid, Otto Lederer, George Kunkel, Gayne Whitman

This comedic short subject about an ersatz haunted house was one of many silent efforts that used trick photography to create ghostly apparitions. Like virtually every other film of its ilk and time period, the spirits in question turn out to be fake and the eerie goings-on a scam perpetrated by bad guys.

Producer/director Ulysses Davis was nearing the end of a not-very-long and not-at-all-distinguished career at the time he made this picture. He dropped off the radar for good not too awfully long after this.

Ghosts and Flypaper was released on November 25, 1915. TH

The Golem
aka **Der Golem**; **Monster of Fate**
Deutsche Bioscop; b/w; 60 min; Germany
D: Paul Wegener, Henrik Galeen *S:* Paul Wegener, Henrik Galeen *P:* Hanns Lippman *C:* Guido Seeber
Cast: Paul Wegener, Rudolf Blumner, Carl Ebert, Henrik Galeen, Lyda Salmanova, Jakob Tiedtke

For this, his first of three cracks at the legend, writer/director/actor Wegner updated the story to then-contemporary Europe. There has been some confusion over the literary source Wegener and his collaborator Henrik Galeen drew upon for their first effort. It's frequently asserted that they were inspired by Gustav Meyrink's 1915 novel *The Golem*, but it's more likely that they simply drew upon European folklore. (Their subsequent—and far more famous—version, *The Golem: How He Came into The World*, 1920, is actually credited by its makers as an adaptation of Meyrink's book, but it too bears little overt resemblance to it.)

In any event, apart from a synopsis and a few surviving sequences, nothing much remains of this first version. The few extant scenes do reveal that Wegener did not modify his make-up and costume for the creature much when he revisited the story in 1920; the surviving clips also show him stumbling around in a manner he would repeat in the later film.

The heavy involvement of Galeen—who plays a key role in addition to co-directing and co-authoring the script—is significant here as it marks his first major contribution to the burgeoning horror genre; he would later lend his hand to such key titles as F.W. Murnau's *Nosferatu—A Symphony of Terror* (1922) and Paul Leni's *Waxworks* (1924).

In addition to the two Wegener "Golems" already mentioned, the director also revisited the character in *The Golem and the Dancing Girl* (1917). TH

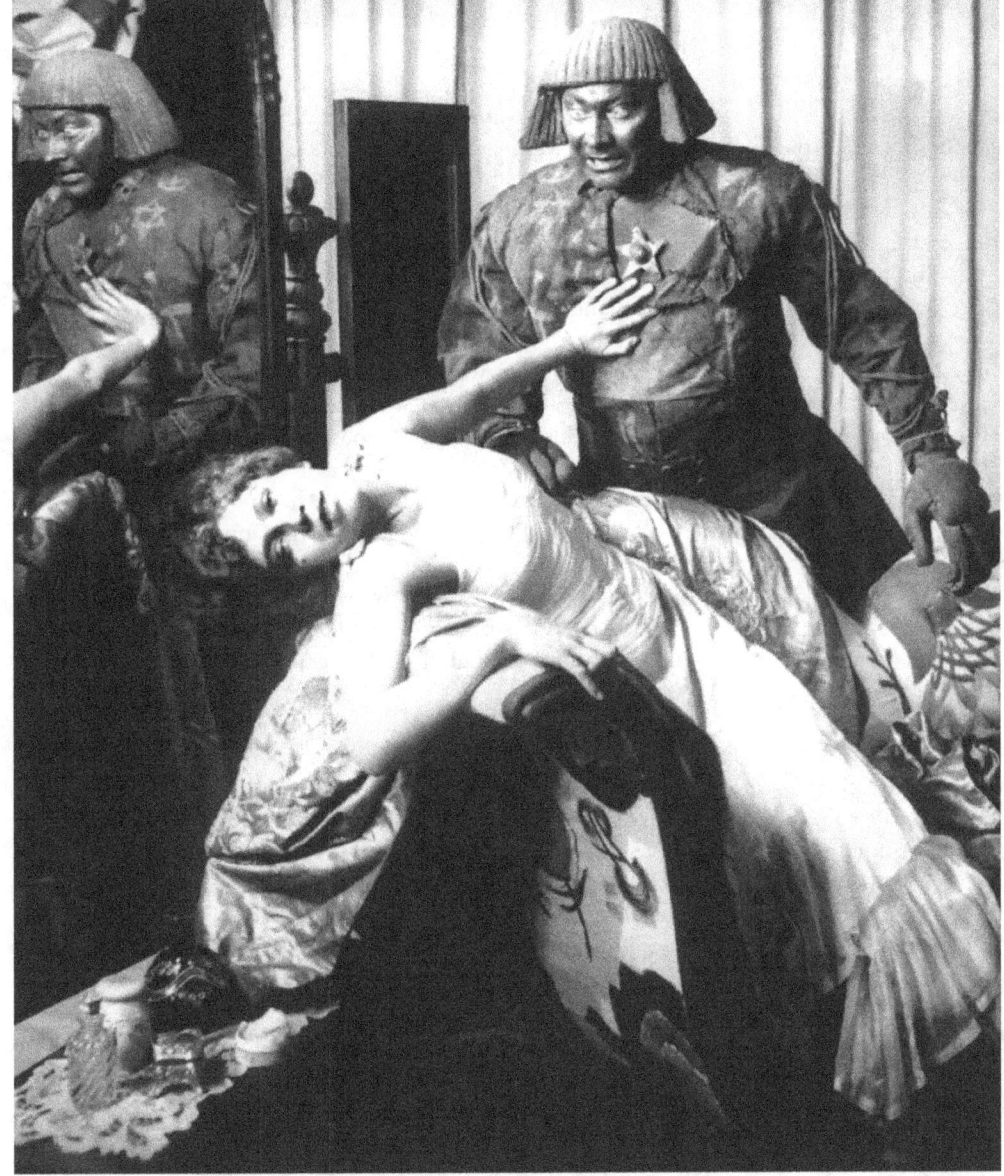

Co-director Paul Wegener plays the Golem, who is given life by an antiques dealer. When the creature falls in love with the dealer's daughter (Lyda Salmanova) and is rejected by her, the Golem goes on a rampage.

The Gray Horror
Lubin; b/w; 33 min; U.S.
D: Joseph W. Smiley *S:* Shannon Fife *P:* Siegmund Lubin
Cast: Joseph W. Smiley, Lilie (Lila) Leslie, John Smiley, James Cassady, Clarence Elmer, Percy Winter

As prolific a director as Massachusetts-born Joseph W. Smiley (1870-1945) was during the silent era, he was an even more prolific actor. Here he stars as a lawyer who, with his ward (Leslie), spends the night in an old mansion, only to be terrified by its resident ghosts. *The Gray Horror* wasn't Smiley's only work in the horror genre; he directed the infamous—and unfortunately lost—*Life Without Soul* (1915), an unauthorized adaptation of Mary Shelley's classic novel *Frankenstein, or The Modern Prometheus* (1818). He also had parts in *The Haunted Bell* (1916) and *Seven Keys to Baldpate* (1917). Though his directorial career ended in 1916, his acting career lasted until 1927, expiring with the advent of the talkies. His Scottish costar and wife Lila Leslie fared no better; though she was popular during the silent era, her career pretty much ended in 1929. She attempted a comeback in 1933, but continued success simply wasn't in the cards. After giving up on the acting game, she died in 1940 at the age of 50. Her husband died five years later. CW

The Greater Will
aka The Antique Dealer
Premo; b/w; 55 min; U.S.
D/S: Harley Knoles
Cast: Cyril Maude, Lois Meredith, Montagu Love, Henry J. Carville, William T. Carleton, Lionel Belmore

This dark melodrama features Cyril Maude as antiques dealer Professor Cornelius Sloane, whose daughter Peggy (Meredith) has been dead for seven years. One evening, while playing chess with a priest (Carville), the dealer tells how his daughter was introduced to a millionaire art collector named Stuart Watson (Love), a Svengali type with the ability to place people under hypnotic spells. Becoming infatuated with the girl, Watson had hypnotized her and forced her into a sham marriage with him. After impregnating her, however, he grew tired of her and sent her on her way and she subsequently died while giving birth to their child. Now the professor has sworn revenge, and with the arrival of Watson from Europe, his plan is set in motion. The two meet, and when the professor confronts Watson with the result of his handiwork, Watson attempts to place the old man under a spell. But instead the professor hypnotizes Watson, commanding the art collector to imagine that the spirit of his deceased wife visits him every evening at 11:00 pm. The mesmeric suggestion takes, and unable to face what he has done, Watson kills himself.

The Greater Will was director Harley Knoles' first attempt at a horror film and a highly unoriginal one at that. He and production company Premo followed it up in 1916 with *The Devil's Toy*, about an artist's Faustian pact with the Devil.

Actor Montagu Love began his career by playing Prince Florizel in Maurice Elvey's horror film *The Suicide Club* (1914). He played his *Greater Will* character again, albeit with a different name, in his very next film, the aforementioned *The Devil's Toy*, and also in *Rasputin, The Black Monk* (1917). His other horror films include *The Case of Becky* (1921), *The Haunted House* (1928), *The Last Warning* (1929), *The Cat Creeps* (1930), *The Mystic Hour* (1933) and *Menace* (1934). CW

The Hand of the Skeleton
aka La main du Squelette
b/w; length unknown; France
D/C: George Schnéevoight
Cast unknown

This bizarre little film is thought to be a French production, though its director was a Danish filmmaker who worked almost exclusively within the borders of his own homeland. Sources state that it offered an appearance by a ghost, though the title suggests a skeleton (or at least a hand thereof). Very little is known about it; it doesn't even appear on most of George Schnéevoight's filmographies.

Schnéevoight (1893-1961) began his cinematic career with 1913's *Skyggedanserinden*, on which he served as writer, director, actor and cinematographer. He worked on many films during a long career, including an uncredited role as cinematographer on Carl Theodor Dreyer's *Leaves from Satan's Book* (1921). He left cinema in 1942. He seems to have specialized in comedy, leaving one to surmise that *The Hand of the Skeleton* was likely a trick photographic film with a humorous bent. CW

Haunted
Superba; b/w; 7 min; U.S.
Credits unknown

This silent-era short depicted a man tormented by visions of the dead. While the subject matter sounds grim, contemporary sources indicate that the film was released as part of a double bill (or split reel, as they used to be called) with the comedy *Novelty in Servants* (1915), hinting that *Haunted* may have also been a comedy. No credit information has survived, but it is known that the short-lived Superba Film Company produced the film. While its surviving filmographies are almost certainly incomplete, the company was apparently only active from 1914 to 1915.

The film should not be confused with E&R Jungle Film's *Haunted* (1916). TH

The Haunted Attic
aka The Haunted House
Lubin; b/w; 5 min; U.S.
D/P: Siegmund Lubin
Cast: John Edwards, Mattie Edwards, David Roseborough

This short feature was a throwback to the earliest days of cinema, when trick photography held sway and making the audience laugh was cinema's *raison d'être*. A barber's ghost haunts an old attic. Though some sources cite *The Haunted Attic* as a 1914 release, it was in fact produced in early 1915 and released on April 24 of that same year on a split reel with another Lubin film, the Billy Bowers comedy *The Fresh Agent* (1915). CW

The Haunting of Silas P. Gould
Ivy Close Films; b/w; 16 min; Great Britain
D: Elwin Neame
Cast: Ivy Close

This is yet another comedic entry in the haunted house subgenre. The story concerns a cash-strapped heiress (Close) who sells her ancestral home to an American millionaire. Once paid, the heiress dresses up in white sheets and pretends to be a ghost in order to scare the new owner off.

Director Elwin Neame and leading lady Ivy Close were married in real life, and together they had two children—scenarist Derek Neame (*The Hideout*, 1948) and cinematographer/director Ronald Neame (*The Poseidon Adventure*, 1972). The elder Neame came to directing after establishing himself as a first-class photographer. His career ended in 1923 when he died at the age of 38 in a motorcycle accident.

Some sources list this as a Hepworth production, but in fact the film was one of a handful of titles produced by Ivy Close Films; as the moniker indicates, the husband-and-wife team of Neame and Close controlled the company. Only a few films are credited to the company, all of them directed by Neame and starring Close. Hepworth was their distributor.

Rowland V. Lee borrowed the plot of *The Haunting of Silas P. Gould* for his 1922 old dark house comedy, *Money to Burn*. TH

Haunting Winds
Powers Picture Plays/Universal; b/w; 11 min; U.S.
D: Carl M. Leviness S: Earl R. Hewitt P: Pat Powers
Cast: Sydney Ayres, Doris Pawn, Frank MacQuarrie

Based on a story by G.E. Jenks, *Haunting Winds* follows a man who has accidentally killed someone; he's taken down by his own guilty conscience as he sees and hears horror everywhere he looks: voices of the dead howling on the midnight wind, tree branches clutching at wary passers-by, doors banging in the middle of the night and so on.

Haunting Winds was released in the United States on August 14, 1915. Directed by small-time character actor Carl M. Leviness (who had bit parts in films right up until a year before his death in 1964), the film starred Frank MacQuarrie in a lead role, though it's unclear whether he portrayed the killer or his victim. MacQuarrie's acting career was brief, lasting from 1915 to 1919, though he lived until 1950. He also had two brothers, Murdock and Albert. They too were actors, both of them more prolific than he. CW

Heba the Snake Woman
Yorkshire/Excelsior; b/w; 2 min; Great Britain
Credits unknown

Much like its British predecessor *The Vampire* (1913), *Heba the Snake Woman* deals with a beautiful woman (this time around an Aztec princess rather than a Hindu) who is shot by a British colonist. Rather than die, however, Heba turns into a poisonous snake to seek revenge on her shooter, which she achieves by biting him. As with *The Fakir's Spell* (1914) before it and numerous films after it (including a host of mummy movies), *Heba* draws on the horrors visited by British forces upon the occupants of foreign territories.

Both *The Vampire* and *Heba the Snake Woman* prefigure Great Britain's cinematic fascination with snake women that would continue with the risible *The Snake Woman* (1961), Hammer's classic example of the subgenre, *The Reptile* (1966) and finally Ken Russell's *The Lair of the White Worm* (1986). In France, Lux Studios entered the subgenre with *The Snake Man* (1910), though, as the title suggests, the company changed the monster's gender to male. In the United States, Universal contributed *Sssssss* (1973), which likewise featured a young male—this time a college athlete—who is the victim of sinister experiments by a mad doctor. At the film's conclusion, the boy transforms into a King Cobra. CW

His Egyptian Affinity
Nestor; b/w; 22 min; U.S.
D/S/P: Al Christie
Cast: Victoria Ford, Eddie Lyons, Lee Moran

After the worldwide success of H. Rider Haggard's *She: A History of Adventure* (published in serial form in 1886 and 1887 and subsequently released as a novel), cinematic adaptations legitimate and otherwise soon followed. First out of the chute was French filmmaker Georges Méliès' one-minute *fantastique noir* short *Pillar of Fire* (1899). Another adaptation (now considered lost) followed in 1908, and a third came from Thanhouser in 1911 (still extant). More were done in the decades that followed. In the midst of these was *His Egyptian Affinity*, an adventurous spoof in which a reawakened 3,000-year-old Egyptian princess (Ford) is united with the reincarnation (Lyons) of her long-deceased paramour. Their love is threatened by another reincarnation (Moran), the son of a sheik who had also loved the princess.

That same year, Nestor reteamed the same director and cast for the comedic *When the Mummy Cried for Help*, wherein a man disguises himself as a mummy to play a trick on someone. Both films were released through Universal and were likely shot on the same sets around the same time. CW

His Phantom Sweetheart
Vitagraph; b/w; 8 min; U.S.
D/P: Ralph W. Ince *S:* Earle Williams
Cast: Earle Williams, Anita Stewart, Thomas Mills

Jack (Williams) goes to the theater where he meets a sexy woman (Stewart), whom he escorts home. Her jailbird husband (Mills) is a lunatic, however, and when he escapes prison, he goes looking for his wife. He finds and strangles her in front of Jack, then attempts to do the same to Jack. Before he can, however, Jack wakes up and realizes that it was all just a dream.

His Phantom Sweetheart was released on April 14, 1915. A horror comedy, it was produced and directed by Ralph Ince, who went on to a prolific career of over 170 films as director and over 100 as actor. Horror, however, was not one of his abiding interests. CW

Horrible Hyde
Lubin; b/w; 5 min; U.S.
D: Howell Hansel *S:* E.W. Sargent *P:* Arthur Hotaling
Cast: Jerold T. Hevener, Eva Bell, Mae Hotely, Billie Reeves

Shot in the internationally-renowned fright-film Mecca of Jacksonville, Florida (not!), *Horrible Hyde* is yet another comic variant on Robert Louis Stevenson's novella *The Strange Case of Dr. Jekyll and Mr. Hyde* (1886). Hevener took on the dual role of Jekyll and Hyde, with the latter doing little more than playing childish pranks on people.

Given that the film was released on a single reel with another, unrelated, feature (Vincent Whitman's *Relentless Dalton*, 1915), *Horrible Hyde* was likely no longer than five minutes long. Different sources credit the film with different directors, including lead actor Hevener and producer Arthur Hotaling, who were both known to direct for Lubin and may have assisted Howell Hansel. Records from this period are spotty, and it's difficult at times to document filmic details with any degree of certainty; the films rarely give directorial credits, and in some cases when they do, the names given are not, for contractual reasons, those of the people who had made them.

Indiana-born Hansel worked entirely within a four-year period, from 1913 until his death in 1917. His most famous film may be *A Dog of Flanders* (1914) for Thanhauser. Jevener starred in approximately 40 films during the silent era, all of which are pretty much forgotten today. His last film was the amusingly titled *The Hash House Mystery* (1917). CW

The Hound of the Baskervilles
aka **Der Hund von Baskerville**
Greenbaum; b/w; Germany
Part 3, The Uncanny Room: 50 min
Part 4, The Legend of the Hound: 50 min
D/S: Richard Oswald *P:* Josef Greenbaum
Cast: Alwin Neuss, Friedrich Kuehne, Erwin Fichtner, Andreas Van Horn, Tatjana Irrah, Hilde Borke

Part 3: The sinister criminal Stapleton (Kuehne) escapes from near death and returns to threaten Lord Henry (Fichtner) and his fiancée (Irrah). Sherlock Holmes (Neuss) attempts to stop Stapleton for good.

Part 4: A flashback explains the curse of the Baskervilles. It seems that one of Lord Henry's none-too-illustrious ancestors murdered his wife and her faithful dog. Since that time, the ghost of the hound is said to haunt the moors and kill the descendants of the man responsible for its death.

Having left Vitascope to form his own production company, producer Josef Greenbaum continues his *Hound of the Baskervilles* saga without the blessing of his erstwhile employers. The resulting two chapters of melodrama utilize most of the cast from the Vitascope *Hound*s, including Danish actor Alwin Neuss as Sherlock Holmes. (And Dr. Watson again is nowhere to be seen.)

Having written the first two installments in 1914, Richard Oswald was here promoted to director. His career also included the early horror anthology *Weird Tales* (1919), which he remade to greater success as *Uncanny Stories* in 1932. Hermann Warm appears to have been *Hound*'s production designer; he subsequently collaborated on the groundbreaking visual design of Robert Weine's *The Cabinet of Dr. Caligari* (1919).

Based on surviving plot descriptions, neither Part Three nor Part Four seems to have adhered much to Doyle's original text. And unlike the 1914 installments, these chapters do not appear to have survived. Greenbaum revisited the story once again with yet another two-part installment in 1920. TH

The Hound of the Baskervilles: The Dark Castle
aka **Der Hund von Baskerville: Das Dunkle Schloss**; **Das Dunkle Schloss**
PAGU; b/w; 50 min; Germany
D: Willy Zeyn
Cast: Eugen Burg, Friedrich Zelnik, Friedrich Kuehne, Hanni Weisse

Sherlock Holmes (Burg) battles the villainous Stapleton (Kuehne) as he continues to harass Lord Henry (Zelnik) and his finacée (Weisse).

Harry Mestayer and Edgar Nelson in *The House of a Thousand Candles*

As rife with plot twists as Sir Arthur Conan Doyle's novel *The Hound of the Baskervilles* (1901) may be, the tale pales in comparison to the drama driving the 1915 onslaught of cinematic adaptations. Vitascope funded the 1914 version, which they released in two parts. Producer Josef Greenbaum thereafter left the studio and irritated company executives by making *The Hound of the Baskervilles*—a follow-up in two parts, one subtitled *The Uncanny Room* and the other *The Legend of the Hound*—in 1915. Between those two releases, Vitascope—by now re-named PAGU—unleashed this, its own follow-up.

Vitascope's film is intended as the *real* third part of the story, following up the apparent demise of bad-guy Stapleton at the end of Part 2 (subtitled *The Solitary House*). Since Greenbaum had lured away most of the 1914 cast—excluding leading lady Hanni Weisse, who remained loyal to Vitascope—PAGU was forced to recast several of the key roles. Eugen Burg replaced Alwin Neuss as Holmes; this is his only known appearance as the character, so it seems safe to assume that he didn't click with audiences as effectively as Neuss had done. (Tragically, Burg later ran afoul of the Nazi regime and died in a concentration camp in 1944.)

Both of the competing sequels (Greenbaum's and PAGU's) cast actor Friedrich Kuehne in the role of Stapleton. *The Dark Castle* marked the end of PAGU's infatuation with the story, though the company re-released its 1914 version as a single, slightly trimmed feature in 1921. Like the unauthorized Josef Greenbaum episodes, PAGU's authorized "Part 3" is considered lost. TH

The House of a Thousand Candles
Selig; b/w; 50 min; U.S.
D: Thomas N. Heffron *S:* Gilson Willets
Cast: Harry Mestayer, Grace Darmond, George Backus, John Charles, Forrest Robinson, Edgar Nelson

Based on the novel by Meredith Nicholson, *The House of a Thousand Candles* is an unremarkable old dark house mystery with the requisite sliding panels and hidden money. Squire John Glenarm (Backus) has developed a crush on Marian (Darmond) and hopes to persuade his son Jack (Mestayer) to marry her. Jack, however, believes himself to be in love with sexy dancer Carmen (Robson). The fun begins when Squire John goes off to Europe and apparently dies in an earthquake, leaving Jack his spooky estate with the stipulation that Jack first live in it for one year. Along with his friend, Larry Donovan (Nelson), Jack moves in; he meets Marian and the two fall deeply in love. But the executor of the will, Arthur Pickering (Charles), has a thing for Marian as well and teams up with Carmen to split up the new couple. When Jack learns that Arthur is skulking about the estate looking for a million dollars that the Squire has reputedly left behind, a fight breaks out between the two, after which it's revealed that the Squire isn't really dead at all. It was all just a plot to get his son to meet and marry Marian.

Meredith Nicholson was a popular author and politician from Crawfordsville, Indiana. He began his career as a journalist for various Indianapolis newspapers in the late 1800s before becoming a bestselling novelist. In 1928 the avowed Democrat entered politics, winning a seat on the city council in Indianapolis; he later became a federal envoy to Paraguay, Venezuela and Nicaragua.

Nicholson's novel was filmed again in 1920 under the title *Haunting Shadows* and in 1936 by Republic Pictures; that particular adaptation starred Mae Clark of *Frankenstein* (1931) fame and transposed the old dark house setting with that of a casino. CW

The House with Nobody in It
Rialto/Gaumont; b/w; 33 min; U.S.
D: Richard Garrick *S:* Clarence J. Harris *C:* Walter Pritchard
Cast: Ivy Troutman, Bradley Barker, Frank Whitson, James Levering, Charles W. Travis

An old house is believed to be haunted due to mysterious lights in its rustic windows. Despite a claim that it was based on a story by screenwriter and Universalist missionary Clarence J. Harris, *The House with Nobody in It* was likely influenced by the poem of the same name by Joyce Kilmer, published in his collection *Trees and Other Poems* in 1914. His verses examine a dilapidated, long-deserted, lonely old house on the road to Suffern along the Erie track. He imagines it as being haunted, concluding that occupying spirits would make the place less melancholy.

The film *The House with Nobody in It* was released on September 22, 1915. CW

The Inner Brute
Essanay; b/w; 21 min; U.S.
Crew unknown
Cast: Warren Waite, Warda Howard, John Lorenz, Peggy Sweeney, Hugh Thompson

Released just before the Fourth of July in 1915, this strange little melodrama tells of a pregnant woman who is frightened by a tiger. As a result, her son's nature after maturity becomes

The inhabitants of the house skulk about searching for the million dollars that the Squire has supposedly left behind, from *The House of a Thousand Candles*.

increasingly bestial. The theme of a pregnant woman giving birth to a monstrosity as a result of interaction with a wild animal was a new one in 1915, but it was revisited decades later by Frank R. Strayer in his otherwise forgettable *Condemned to Live* (1935) and suggested by David Lynch in *The Elephant Man* (1980). There are a handful of further examples, but the notion never really caught on, probably because of its comparative ridiculousness when pitted against the likes of such classic humans-into-monsters as Dr. Jekyll and Mr. Hyde, werewolves and snake women. CW

An Innocent Sinner

Kalem; b/w; 33 min; U.S.
D: Kenean Buel
Cast: Katherine La Salle, Guy Coombs, Robert Walker, Mary Kennedy, James B. Ross, Helen Lindroth

Not be confused with the 1917 Raoul Walsh film of the same name, this *Sinner* was based on a play by Lawrence Marston and concerned a love affair between female orphan Hinda (La Salle) and a young man named Tom Bridges (Coombs). In typical silent-era fashion, a jealous doctor (Ross) threatens their love with—yikes—hypnotic powers. If the plot seems overly familiar, that's because it is.

Kentucky-born Kenean Buel made a second horror film (of sorts) with Fox's supernatural opus *She* in 1917, but most of his efforts were minor romantic melodramas, a category into which even *Sinner* and *She* arguably fall. After a lackluster career that began in 1908 and produced approximately 100 films, Buel retired from filmmaking in 1920. He lived out the last 28 years of his life in relative anonymity.

An Innocent Sinner was released on May 3, 1915. CW

Jane Eyre

Biograph; b/w; 30 min; U.S.
D: Travers Vale
Cast: Franklin Ritchie, Louise Vale, Gretchen Hartman, Herbert Barrington, Kate Bruce, Kenneth Davenport, Alan Hale

Charlotte Brontë was one of six siblings—five girls and one boy—born to a clergyman and his wife in the early 1800s. When their mother died, four of the five girls were sent to a girls' school, the conditions of which Charlotte would later blame for the deaths of her two older sisters. When Charlotte returned home, she and her remaining siblings began to construct elaborate stories about fictional kingdoms, leading to a lifelong interest in writing. Brother Branwell became a poet, while all three surviving sisters wrote novels: Emily, *Wuthering Heights* (1847); Anne, *Agnes Grey* (1847) and Charlotte, *Jane Eyre* (1847), among others. Originally published under a male pseudonym (at the time it was rare for women to publish novels under their own names), *Jane Eyre: An Autobiography* was an immediate success, and it led to three additional novels from Charlotte (the last, published posthumously, was actually written first but had been rejected by publishers during Charlotte's lifetime). To this day, *Jane Eyre* remains Charlotte's most famous book, and it has resulted in more film adaptations than any other Brontë novel. This particular film adaptation was the fifth during the silent era and the first of two made in 1915. (The second, titled *The Castle of Thornfield*, was shot in Italy.)

Traveling in the West Indies, Edward Rochester (Ritchie) meets Bertha Mason (Hartman), falls in love with her and marries her. What he doesn't know, however, is that her mother is insane, a mental condition that Bertha has inherited. Rochester takes his wife back to England where he hires a nurse to care for her and hides her away in the attic. He also hires a governess, Jane Eyre (Vale), to instruct his ward Adele. He soon finds himself in love with Jane, but before they can get married, Jane learns his terrible secret and flees. Bertha escapes, sets fire to the Thornfield Mansion and dies. After learning this, Jane returns to Mr. Rochester and agrees to marry him. CW

The Japanese Mask

Pathé/Aetna; b/w; 30 minutes; France/U.S.
Credits unknown

Some sources describe this extremely obscure French film as being four reels in length; in fact, it was only three. A trick film, it dealt with a mask that carries a terrifying curse: anyone looking upon it will die a horrible death.

While Pathé was a large outfit known for making films in several countries, Aetna was a much smaller company operating mostly out of the United States, making *The Japanese Mask* something of an international co-production. There was also a 1915 production bearing the same title but from the United States, allegedly made by Balboa. CW

The Legend of the Lone Tree
Vitagraph; b/w; 11 min; U.S.
D: Ulysses Davis *S:* Archie R. Lloyd
Cast: Myrtle Gonzalez, Alfred Vosburgh, George Kunkel, Otto Lederer, George Holt

This was one of many silent Westerns that blended an element of the fantastic into its narrative. In it, a medicine man curses a murderer, transforming him into a tree in the middle of an open plain.

Myrtle Gonzalez began her film career in 1913 with Vitagraph, a company with which she worked for the next several years before taking her act to Rex. Her career was brought to a sad close in October 1918 when she died of influenza at the age of 27. Her costar here, Alfred Vosburgh, acted under a variety of screen names in both the silent and sound eras. He starred in over 200 films, mostly in un-credited bit parts.

Though shot in late 1914, *The Legend of the Lone Tree* was not released until January 14, 1915. Like most Westerns ("weird" or otherwise) from this period, it is today presumed to be lost. CW

Life Without Soul
aka **Live Without Soul**; **Life Without a Soul**; **Frankenstein**
Ocean; b/w; 70 min; U.S.
D: Joseph W. Smiley *S:* Jesse J. Goldburg *P:* John I. Dudley
Cast: Percy Standing, William A. Cohill, Jack Hopkins, Pauline Curley, David McCauley, Violet De Biccari

In contemporary Manhattan, Dr. Victor Frawley (Cohill) undertakes a series of experiments to discover the secret of life. His friends and associates warn him that he's intruding on sacred terrain, but he scoffs at their platitudes. Relaxing in his laboratory one evening, he falls asleep while reading Mary Shelley's *Frankenstein, or The Modern Prometheus*. He dreams that he is Victor Frankenstein, and the familiar tale unfolds to its tragic conclusion—albeit in modern times. In the end Frawley awakens and, ashamed of his own ambition, decides to abandon his experiments.

This variation on Mary Shelley's oft-filmed novel is widely considered a lost film today. Done on a very low budget (though allegedly shot on location throughout the United States), it seems to have employed a novel approach to the source material; the birth of the monster, for instance, appears to have been more influenced by Paul Wegener's *The Golem* (1915) than by anything in Shelley's tale. Interestingly, this film was the first feature-length adaptation of the book; the 1910 Thomas A. Edison version, directed by J. Searle Dawley, was a short subject. (One might wonder if the character name Frawley is a referential variation on the name of the previous film's director.)

Reviewers of the period were impressed by English actor Percy Standing's portrayal of the creature. The monster elicited more sympathy than revulsion, which foreshadows Boris Karloff's iconic performance in James Whale's *Frankenstein* (1931). The advertising ballyhoo at the time promised, "A Dramatic Masterpiece, Pulsating With Heart Interest, Interwoven With A Love Tale Of Sacrificial Devotion," but all indications are that the subtext was pretty much limited to warning science against tampering in "God's domain."

An interesting and, at the time, original twist here is that most of the cast members played dual roles—as members in Frawley's inner circle in his "real life" and as characters from Shelley's novel in his dream.

Though some sources cite the original release date as 1916, *Life Without Soul* was actually released on a "states rights" basis in November 1915. The film was retooled for a re-release in 1916, with some footage cut while other footage illustrating reproduction in the natural word was added; since then, all copies of both versions have vanished.

Director Joseph W. Smiley helmed over 60 forgotten features from 1911 to 1916; for one reason or another he opted to focus entirely on acting from 1916 until his retirement in 1927, making *Life Without Soul* one of his last films as a director. TH

The Live Mummy
Brittania; b/w; 15 min; Great Britain
Credits unknown

The Live Mummy is yet another silent film comedy centering on a man who poses as a mummy, an idea already done in *Wanted—A Mummy!* (1910) and *The Mummy* (1912, also from Britannia). Because *The Live Mummy* is now lost, it's difficult to know how closely it resembled the company's previous film, though it does seem to have been twice as long. The same year also saw *The Missing Mummy*, which was made in the United States by Kalem, and *When the Mummy Cried for Help*, both of which had plots almost identical to *The Live Mummy*. CW

London's Yellow Peril
British & Colonial; b/w; 25 min; British
D: Maurice Elvey *S:* Eliot Stannard
Cast: Elisabeth Risdon, Fred Groves, A.V. Brambles, M. Gray Murray

This is an early short built around the very real problem of drug abuse, viewed through the lens of that stereotypical bane of silent cinema, the Yellow Peril.

As fear of Asian, particularly Chinese, immigration grew at the turn of the 20th century, a new type of pop literature developed in which Asians were depicted as cunning masterminds of a new—and very violent—world order, one in which the only place for Caucasians was as slaves. Though the first known use of the disparaging term "Yellow Peril" was in 1895 by Kaiser Wilhelm II, it reared its ugly head as the alternate title for Walter R. Booth's 1900 film *Chinese Magic*. The first major entry in the cinematic version of the subgenre was the four-part serial *The Mysterious Mr. Wu Chung Foo* (1914), a rip-off of Sax Rohmer's literary Oriental villain Dr. Fu Manchu (who would become the basis of numerous future films).

Popular British director Maurice Elvey made his own first foray into the subgenre with *London's Yellow Peril*. Elvey later became the house director for Stoll Picture Productions, which began a series based on Rohmer's infamous character with A.E. Coleby's *The Scented Envelopes* (1923). Elvey is considered the most prolific filmmaker in British history, guiding approximately 200 films into existence between 1913 and 1957.

Screenwriter Eliot Stannard went on to write several movies for Alfred Hitchcock, including *The Lodger: A Story of the London Fog* (1927) and *The Manxman* (1929), while Elisabeth Risdon (*Weird Woman*, 1944) forged herself a healthy acting career during the first three decades of the talkie era. CW

Lord John in New York
Universal; b/w; 44 min; U.S.
D: Edward LeSaint *S:* Harvey Gates, A.M. Williamson, C.N. Williamson
Cast: William Garwood, Stella LeSaint, Ogden Crane, Stella Razetto, Walter Belasco, Jay Belasco

Lord John (Garwood) is a detective novelist. One of his stories rushes toward production on the stage, but he receives word that the play is canceled because the producer, Roger Odell (Crane), has a grudge against him. Lord John joins Odell on a cruise, hoping to talk some sense into him. But then he discovers that Dr. Rameses (MacQuarrie), an evil hypnotist, plans to steal a gold-filled mummy from Odell's sister Maida (Razetto), and he decides that it's up to him to save the day.

This far-fetched melodrama is the first of five films (known collectively as *Lord John's Journal*) showcasing the adventures of William Garwood's intrepid Lord John. The other four are *The Grey Sisterhood*, *Three Fingered Jenny*, *Eye of Horus* and *The League of the Future* (all 1916). A look at their plots reveals them all to be as busy and improbable as the first, though none contain anything as ghoulish as a gold-filled mummy and a hypnotist.

Garwood was a reasonably popular leading man of the silent era who also amassed a few credits as a director. Director Edward LeSaint was prolific in silents but even moreso as an (often unbilled) character actor in the 1930s. Among his many appearances onscreen were roles as judges in James Whale's *Wives Under Suspicion* (1938) and cult favorite *Reefer Madness* (1936). He was married to *Lord John* leading lady Stella LeSaint until his death in 1940. TH

The Magic Skin
aka **The Ass's Skin**
Kleine/Edison; b/w; 50 min; U.S.
D/S: Richard Ridgely *P:* Thomas A. Edison
Cast: Everett Butterfield, Mabel Trunnelle, Bigelow Cooper, Frank A. Lyons, William West, George A. Wright

The Magic Skin is the third cinematic adaptation of Honoré de Balzac's 1831 novel *Le Peau de chagrin*, though this version buries the supernatural portions of Balzac's plot in a dream sequence. Ralph Valentine (Butterfield) is left destitute when his wealthy father (Cooper) dies. Pauline (Trunnelle), the daughter of his landlord (Grant), proves a trustworthy confidante to him as he romances Flora (Crute), a woman he believes to be rich but is actually a prostitute. Ralph falls asleep in an antique shop one night and has a nightmare in which an antiques dealer (Prior) appears as the Devil and offers him, in exchange for his soul, a magic skin that will grant his every wish. He makes the deal and with each wish grows weaker as the skin shrinks. Unwilling to put up with her plaything's deteriorating health, Flora dumps Ralph, and Pauline, who has come to believe that she will never be with him, drowns herself in a river. The magic skin shrinks to nothing while Ralph dies and goes to Hell. Dream over. He awakens, realizes that it's Pauline he loves and marries her.

A copy of Ridgely's film exists in the Library of Congress. The next cinematic adaptation of Balzac's story came in 1920 with George Edwardes-Hall's more overtly horrific *Desire*. CW

The Man Who Couldn't Beat God
Vitagraph; b/w; 55 min; U.S.
D: Maurice Costello, Robert Gaillard *S:* Harold Gilmore Calhoun *C:* William McCoy
Cast: Maurice Costello, Charles Eldridge, Robert Gaillard, Denton Vane, Estelle Mardo, Edwina Robbins

Martin (Costello) accidentally kills the rakish Lord Wexford (Mills). There are no witnesses, but he flees his home in England for a new start as a construction worker in the United States. The guilt of his crime dogs him, and he is haunted by visions of the dead man. Still, he manages to do well for himself, becoming first a vice president of the construction company and then governor of New York. But his success is short-lived; he suffers a nervous breakdown, and his family takes him to England to recuperate. He ends up unexpectedly back at the scene of his crime, where the shock kills him.

The Man Who Couldn't Beat God offers a moralistic variation of the "crime doesn't pay" formula. Just how horrific the protagonist's visions of his victim were is unknown, as the film disappeared years ago.

Co-director/star Maurice Costello was on the downhill side of his career by the time he made this film; the remainder of his movie work consisted of small, often unbilled acting gigs. But as bad as things were for him, his co-director and co-star Robert Gaillard's film career ran out of steam even before Costello's; 1932 saw his last work, also as an actor. TH

The Mesmerist
Neptune/Browne; b/w; 14 min; Great Britain
D: Percy Nash
Cast: Douglas Payne

An unscrupulous mesmerist (Payne) compels his victims to commit robberies. This British item offered one of many explorations of the "evil hypnotist" theme. The notion of hypnosis was, like spiritualism, very trendy in English-speaking countries during the last half of the 19th century and the first three decades or so of the 20th.

Director Percy Nash broke into films in 1912 with *David Garrick*, a biopic of the 18th century performer/playwright who also inspired James Whale's comedy *The Great Garrick* (1937). Nash also directed *The Scorpion's Sting* in 1915, the same year as *The Mesmerist*. He never made much of a name for himself, and his career fizzled out in the early 1920s. He later went blind, reportedly due to excessive exposure to the powerful carbon-based Klieg lamps (limelight) used during the early days of cinema. He died in 1958.

The Mesmerist is believed to be lost. TH

Miss Jekyll and Madame Hyde
Vitagraph; b/w; 33 min; U.S.
D/S: Charles L. Gaskill
Cast: Helen Gardner, Paul Scardon, Edward Elkas, Gladden James, J.H. Lewis, Richard Osborne

Despite the title, this has little connection to Robert Louis Stevenson's classic novella about man's dual nature. It owes far more to the legend of Faust, with Paul Scardon starring as Satan the Devil, who offers Ms. Jekyll (Gardner) youth and beauty in exchange for her soul.

Helen Gardner has been called the first vamp of cinema. She got her start at Vitagraph with the role of Becky Sharp in *Vanity Fair* in 1911. Her success was so quick and dramatic that she struck out on her own the following year and formed her own production company along the New Jersey/New York border. There she produced approximately 10 films before returning to Vitagraph and making *Miss Jekyll and Madame Hyde*, portraying yet another evil, seductive woman. Her only other horror film appears to have been *The Sleep of Cyma Roget* (1920, also written and co-directed by Charles L. Gaskill), which cast her in a rare sympathetic role. Not long after, she retired from cinema altogether.

Miss Jekyll and Madame Hyde is considered a lost film. CW

The Missing Mummy
Kalem; b/w; length unknown; U.S.
D: William Beaudine
Cast: Bud Duncan, Charles Inslee, Ethel Teare, John McDermott, Gus Leonard, Charles Mulgro

The same year that Britannia made *The Live Mummy* in Great Britain, Kalem produced its own comedic short about a man who dresses up like a mummy. It was hardly an original idea even then, having been done in Cricks and Martin's *Wanted— A Mummy!* (1910) and Brittania's *The Mummy* (1912). Nor, sadly, would this be the industry's final take on the hackneyed notion.

The Missing Mummy was directed by William "One-Shot" Beaudine, best remembered for Mary Pickford's sole horror outing *Sparrows* (1926). During the late 1930s he went to work for famed poverty-row outfit Monogram, where he made several cheapies starring Bela Lugosi (*The Ape Man* and *Ghosts on the Loose*, both 1943; *The Voodoo Man*, 1944). His other horror films include *Lucky Ghost* and *The Living Ghost* (both 1942), *The Mystery of the 13th Guest* (1943), *Crazy Knights* (1944), *The Face of Marble* and *Spook Busters* (both 1946), *Bela Lugosi Meets a Brooklyn Gorilla* (1952) and *Jesse James Meets Frankenstein's Daughter* and *Billy the Kid vs. Dracula* (both 1966). CW

The Monkey's Paw
Magnet; b/w; 31 min; England
D: Sidney Northcote
Cast: John Lawson

W.W. Jacob's short horror story *The Monkey's Paw*, first published in Great Britain in 1902, has been adapted for the stage, radio, cinema and television, as well as taking a turn or two as pop song and opera. But despite the tale's popularity, most of the film versions are lost, including this, the very first. The story is one of a husband and wife, Mr. and Mrs. White, who receive a gift of a mummified monkey's paw from a friend in the military. That friend, Sergeant-Major Morris, received the paw from an Indian fakir, and he tells the couple that the paw has the power to grant three wishes. Mr. White's first wish is for 200 pounds, which he promptly gets in the form of an insurance check when his son is killed in an accident at work. Apparently a bit slow on the uptake, Mrs. White nags her husband into wishing their son back from the grave. When Mr. White complies, there's a knock at the door. Realizing that the son may have returned in the same mangled condition in which he died, Mr. White uses the third wish to make the young man dead again and "at peace." The knocking stops and, when Mrs. White opens the door, she cries in despair because no one is there. The moral, of course, is that man should not interfere with fate, which seems a somewhat simplistic and dubious viewpoint given that every decision one makes affects his or her future.

How faithful this film was to the original story is unknown, though it appears to have been based largely on Louis Napoleon Parker's 1907 one-act play (which may explain why only John Lawson's name appears in cast lists for the film; he portrayed Mr. White in the stage version). The next cinematic rendering was done in 1919. CW

The Moonstone
World; b/w; 50 min; U.S.
D: Frank Hall Crane *S:* E. Magnus Ingleton
Cast: Eugene O'Brien, Elaine Hammerstein, Ruth Findlay, William Roselle, Edmund Mortimer

This is perhaps the best-known silent adaptation of Wilkie Collins' 1868 horror-mystery *The Moonstone*. An ambitious effort, it focuses on the darker elements of Collins' story.

John Herncastle (Mortimer) steals the diamond known as "the moonstone" from a stone Buddha at the Temple of the Moon in Delhi, India. But unknown to him, he is followed back to Great Britain by three members of the priesthood who guard the jewel. He then drowns, and the moonstone passes to his niece Rachel (Hammerstein), who entrusts it to the executor of her uncle's estate, Franklin Blake (O'Brien). When the jewel vanishes, everyone comes under suspicion, and while Blake investigates the diamond's whereabouts, he and Rachel are tormented by the three Indians, who will apparently stop at nothing—not drugging people, nor poisoning them, nor murdering them—to

Elaine Hammerstein as she appeared in *The Moonstone*

get the diamond back. Eventually Blake discovers that he took the jewel while sleepwalking and gave it to his rival suitor, Godfrey White (Rosell), thinking that White would protect it. But White, while planning to use the diamond to pay off his debts, is killed by the priests. The gem is eventually returned to its rightful place in the eye of the Buddha statue, and Rachel and Franklin admit their love for each other and marry.

While slow at times, the film is visually striking, thanks to Frank Crane Hall's fluid direction. Hall began his career as a stage actor, but in the early 1900s he jumped to the big screen. Shortly thereafter, he began directing and writing movies. His ability to find nuance in every camera angle, along with some mesmerizing tracking shots inside the Herncastle Estate, make this third adaptation of Collins' tale something to behold. CW

Mortmain

Vitagraph; b/w; 55 min; U.S.
D: Theodore Marston *S:* Marguerite Bertsch *C:* Reginald Lyons, Arthur T. Quinn
Cast: Robert Edeson, Donald Hall, Edward Elkas, Joseph Webber, Muriel Ostriche, Karen Norman

Mortmain (Edeson) is a musician and art collector. His friend, Dr. Pennison Crisp (Frank), has recently performed a miraculous surgery, transplanting a paw from one cat to another. When Mortmain (the word, incidentally, is read in French as "dead hand") injures his hand, he goes to Dr. Crisp for medical attention. Dr. Crisp puts him under anesthesia, and while doped up he hallucinates that his hand is amputated and replaced by that of a suspected murderer.

This long-lost melodrama is of interest for the way it foreshadows Maurice Renard's classic medical horror story *Les Mains d'Orlac* (1920). Renard's story was adapted numerous times—most famously as *The Hands of Orlac* (1924) starring Conrad Veidt and *Mad Love* (1935) starring Peter Lorre and Colin Clive. Documentation of the time indicates that the more macabre elements of *Mortmain* are the result of an ether-induced hallucination, but the concept of an artist losing his hand (in essence, his creative outlet) and having it replaced by the hand of a murderer hints strongly that Renard was likely aware of Vitagraph's film.

Director Theodore Marston was active from 1910 until his death in 1920; his work is long forgotten, though he did helm early versions of *David Copperfield* (1911) and *Robin Hood* (1913). Star Robert Edeson was well-liked by Cecil B. DeMille, who cast him in many films throughout the 1920s (including *The King of Kings*, 1927), but his career was cut short by his death from heart disease in 1931. TH

The Picture of Dorian Gray
aka **Portret Doryana Greya**; **Alt yazisi Portret Doryana Greya**; **Portret Doriana Greja**
Thiemann and Reinhardt; b/w; length unknown; Russia
Co-D/S: Vsevolod Meyerhold *Co-D:* Mikhail Doronin
Cast: Varvara Yanova, Vsevolod Meyerhold, G. Enriton, P. Belova, Mikhail Doronin, Yelizaveta Uvarova

The third film adaptation of Oscar Wilde's 1890 novel *The Picture of Dorian Gray* was made in Russia by popular actor/director Vsevolod Meyerhold, who also starred as Gray's friend and corruptor Lord Henry Wotton. Female actor Varvara Yanova essayed the part of Dorian, a daring move that put the character's androgynous nature front and center. Though the film is lost, stills from it do exist showing Yanova as Gray, dressed in men's clothes and striking an effeminate pose.

Thanhouser's two-reel adaptation of Oscar Wilde's classic 1890 novel *The Picture of Dorian Gray* met with positive critical reception in its day. Harris Gordon starred as Dorian, a young man who comes to believe that his portrait is aging while he remains young. He eventually locks the image away in a secret room, where he visits it often. Meanwhile, he engages in ever more rakish behavior, driving his young lover Evelyn (Fulton) to kill herself over his rejection of her. Angry at the turns his life has taken, Dorian destroys the portrait with a knife, then drops dead.

Though lost, the film seems to have been somewhat faithful to its source, though it does appear that the more homoerotic components of the story were toned down. The next adaptation was made in Great Britain in 1916. CW

The Portrait
aka **Portret**
Skobeliew; b/w; 8 min; Russia
D/S: Wladyslaw Starewicz
Credits unknown

A man buys a portrait of a sinister figure from a local artist. Excited by his purchase, he takes the painting home and hangs it in his bedroom. That night he sleeps uneasily, even as the figure in the painting stirs to life. He awakens the next morning and dismisses his uneasiness as the residue of a bad dream. But when he inspects the painting, the subject turns and looks right at him. He backs away as the figure climbs out of the picture frame and comes for him.

This short subject by Wladyslaw Starewicz explores a motif that came to be visited often in horror-themed films and television shows. The notion of art as an object of menace is a powerful one, perhaps finding its fullest expression in Dario Argento's *The Stendhal Syndrome* (1996), which uses a real-life psychological disorder (a state of confusion and terror brought about by exposure to great works of art) as a narrative lynchpin. Starewicz may be the only person in history who came to filmmaking via a love of entomology. He used his first camera to film insects and in the process discovered the joys of stop-motion animation. *Portrait* doesn't include as many elaborate effects as some of his other pictures, but it does utilize simple tricks to good effect.

Casting Yanova in the part may have allowed Meyerhold to explore the bisexual implications of the character, in accordance with Russia's increasing social openness at the time—something that would be clamped down upon a mere two years later when the Russian Revolution replaced the semi-lenient ruling powers with a new, stringent Communist regime. In any case, the story deals with a beautiful young man who remains young and vibrant while his portrait reflects his true age and decadent nature. Another version of Wilde's story appeared the same year in the United States, produced by Thanhouser. It, too, was titled *The Picture of Dorian Gray*. CW

The Picture of Dorian Gray
Thanhouser; b/w; 20 min; U.S.
D/P: Eugene Moore
Cast: Harris Gordon, Ernest Howard, Helen Fulton, W. Ray Johnston, Morgon Jones, Claude Cooper

Starewicz (who was billed, alternately, as Ladislas Starevitch, Ladislas Starewicz, Ladislaw Starewicz, Ladislas Starewitch and Ladislaw Starewitsch) next dipped into horror with his version of Nicolai Gogol's *The Viy* (1916). TH

The Raven

Essanay; b/w; 45 (57) min; U.S.
D/S: Charles Brabin
Cast: Henry B. Walthall, Warda Howard, Ernest Maupin, Eleanor Thompson, Marian Skinner, Harry Dunkinson

Based on a play by George Cochran Hazelton, Charles Brabin's *The Raven* is the third biopic to cover the life of Edgar Allan Poe. The first two were D.W. Griffith's *Edgar Allen Poe* (1909) and Éclair's *The Raven* (1912).

Like its predecessors, Brabin's film is steeped in high melodrama and riddled with factual errors, all the while ignoring the fact that Poe's wife was also his first cousin and that he married her when she was the ripe old age of 13. *Raven* inexplicably begins in 1745 as the author's great-grandfather, Irish immigrant John Poe, settles in the New World. Then it skips to grandfather David Poe (Hamilton), an alleged hero of the Revolutionary War, and then skips again to his father, David Poe, Jr. (Thompson), who meets and marries fellow thespian Mrs. Hopkins (Meredith) in 1805. They have two children, Edgar (born in 1809) and Rosalie. But when David, Jr. dies, he leaves his wife and children without means of support. The widow duly falls ill, leaving her friend Mrs. Allan (Thompson) to arrange a charity performance for her. But when Mrs. Allan delivers the proceeds to Mrs. Poe's house, she finds that the woman has expired. Enter husband John Allan (Maupin), who is convinced by his wife to adopt the Poe children and raise them as his own.

As an adult, Poe (Walthall) is given to drink and to losing at cards as his brain plays host to the fanciful illusions that provide the fodder for his tales. As he romances his wife-to-be Virginia Clemm (Howard, who has several parts in the film, including Helen Whitman, the lost Lenore and a spirit), he gives up his alcoholic ways and becomes a strong, heroic figure who rescues a black man (Weston in blackface) from his abusive slave master. But when his wife grows sick, he falls into a stupor inhabited by ravens, spirits and skeletons. Afterwards, he writes his most famous poem "The Raven" and takes it to multiple publishers, all of whom refuse to publish it. Thus unable to provide his wife with the most basic care, Poe watches helplessly as she dies. The film ends with Poe at his wife's sepulcher, crying for his lost love.

Brabin's direction is far superior to the material he's given, particularly during the film's more atmospheric moments, which are similar in tone to both his earlier *The Necklace of Rameses* (1914) and his later *The Mask of Fu Manchu* (1932). His only lapse in directorial taste comes when actor Henry B. Walthall is introduced as Poe; his supposed resemblance to the famed author apparently warranted an extreme long-lasting and grating close-up. (This wasn't the actor's first portrayal of Poe; he had played the writer the year before in D.W. Griffith's *The Avenging Conscience, or: 'Thou Shalt Not Kill'*, 1914.) CW

The Return of Maurice Donnelly

Vitagraph/Broadway Star; b/w; 44 min; U.S.
D: William Humphrey *S:* William Addison Lathrop
Cast: Leo Delaney, Leah Bird, Anders Randolph, Mary Maurice, Denton Vane, Garry McGarry

Maurice Donnelly (Delaney) is sent to the electric chair for a crime he did not commit. After a doctor (Randolph) uses science to restore him to life, Donnelly sets out to find the real murderer.

Despite a somewhat macabre central premise, later exploited to more horrific ends in the Boris Karloff vehicle *The Walking Dead* (1936), *The Return of Maurice Donnelly* was primarily conceived as a social fable against the death penalty. Capital punishment was, after all, as controversial a topic then as it is today, and the notion of a wrongly accused man being restored to life certainly lends itself to a horror scenario.

Director William Humphrey was far more prolific as a performer than as a director, amassing over 100 acting credits before he left the business in 1937. He had small roles in the Lon Chaney vehicles *The Unholy Three* and *The Phantom of the Opera* (both 1925); one of his last credits was in the creaky *Tangled Destinies* (1932). TH

The Return of Richard Neal

Essanay; b/w; 30 min; U.S.
S: Edward T. Lowe, Jr.
Cast: Francis X. Bushman, Bryant Washburn, Neil Craig, Ernest Maupin, Harry Dunkinson

The evil Count Nikola (Maupin) mesmerizes the naïve Doris Blake (Craig). It's up to dashing hypnotist Richard Neal (Bushman) to free the girl of such a malevolent influence and save the day.

It is unknown who directed this long-forgotten picture, but its screenwriter, Edward T. Lowe, Jr., entered cinema in 1912 and by this time had established himself as a prolific talent. He later directed at least one feature—*The Losing Game* (1915)—though his first love remained writing. He spread his talents across many genres, even as he crafted such horror-oriented titles as *Tangled Destinies* (1932), *The Vampire Bat* (1933), *House of Frankenstein* (1944) and *House of Dracula* (1945). He retired from the industry in 1947 and passed away in 1973 at the age of 82.

Leading man Francis X. Bushman was a silent-screen superstar, known affectionately at the time as King of the Movies. He later scored a major triumph playing the lead in *Ben Hur: A Tale of the Christ* (1925), but his popularity waned with the coming of sound. He wound down his career playing unbilled bit parts, eventually reduced to collecting paychecks for such drek as *The Ghost in the Invisible Bikini* (1966), which also served up the dispiriting sight of Boris Karloff and Basil Rathbone slumming through Grade-Z drivel. TH

Satanic Rhapsody
aka Rapsodia Satanica

Cines; color-b/w; 40 (45) min; Italy
D: Nino Oxilia *S:* Alberto Fassini *C:* Giorgio Ricci
Cast: Lyda Borelli, Andrea Habay, Ugo Bazzini, Giovanni Cini

An elderly Countess (Borelli), upset that her beauty has faded, wishes to the Devil for a return to her glory days ... and lo and behold, Mephisto (Bazzini) appears in her room late at night and promises her eternal youth on the condition that she never falls in love. She accepts his offer, falls asleep and awakens to find herself young and beautiful. In short order she becomes quite the party girl, with a bevy of beefcake vying for her attentions. A pair of brothers falls in love with her, and she, as is her wont, cruelly selects one over the other. Things get briefly ugly when the rejected one commits suicide. The remorseful Countess, now experiencing love for the first time since sealing her deal with the Devil, makes plans to marry the remaining brother. In retaliation, Mephisto changes her back into an unsightly old hag.

Satanic Rhapsody has little to recommend it. Its supernatural plotline is unoriginal and too much of its running time is dedicated, at the expense of a story, to women in diaphanous outfits fleeing from the clutches of the groping men who desire them. There's also far too much celluloid wasted on the central character sitting or standing around and having conversations with handsome young men (not the most exciting thing to watch in a silent film). The effects are primitive even by 1915 standards, and though only 40-minutes long, the film outstays its welcome.

On the sparse upside, the film, while predominantly black and white, does contain some interesting hand-stenciled color shots. The Devil wears a bright red robe, while the heroine has a fondness for red and green. Other tinted items pop up throughout, providing a degree of visual distraction from the fact that cinematographer Giorgio Ricci had no idea how to shoot the action (or, rather, lack thereof).

While some sources claim (probably because of its posthumous release in 1917) that *Satanic Rhapsody* was director Nino Oxilia's final film, it was actually shot in 1915, and he followed it with several films. Oxilia was a poet and actor who became interested in moving pictures in 1912. After studying under such noted Italian filmmakers as Ubaldo Maria Del Colle (*The Spectre of the Vault*, 1913) and Luigi Maggi (*Blood Vengeance*, 1911), he took to directing. *Satanic Rhapsody* is his best-known film and is based on a poem by Fausto Maria Martini. Oxilia died in combat in 1917 while serving his country during World War I. CW

The Scorpion's Sting
aka **The Devil's Bondman**; **The Devil's Bondsman**
Transatlantic/Victor; b/w; 44 min; Great Britain
D: Percy Nash *S:* Rowland Talbot
Cast: George Bellamy, Fay Temple, George Scott, J. Hastings Batson, Douglas Payne, Daisy Cordell

This is a run-of-the-mill horror-tinged melodrama in which a former criminal makes a deal with the Devil in exchange for his soul. Shot in Great Britain and first released under the title *The Devil's Bondman* in 1915, the film was re-titled *The Scorpion's Sting* for American consumption when it was released here in June 1916. Percy Nash directed, and he followed it up with *The Mesmerist* (1915), also starring Douglas Payne. CW

The Secret Room
Kalem; b/w; 22 min; U.S.
D: Tom Moore
Cast: Tom Moore, Marguerite Courtot, Robert Ellis, Ethel Clifton, Betty K. Peterson, Robert Paton Gibbs

A mad scientist (Moore) hopes to cure his son's mental retardation by transferring the soul of a derelict (Ellis) into the young man's body. Substitute "soul" for "brain" and the film would thematically fit into the horror cinema of the 1930s. As it stands, the film is representative of the silent era from which it comes, during which metaphysical themes ran rampant, with people changing souls (as well as personalities) with reckless abandon.

The Secret Room was directed by and starred Tom Moore, a popular filmmaker of the silent era. Born in Ireland, he and his brothers moved to the United States where, in 1908, Moore made his acting debut for D.W. Griffith at American Mutoscope & Biograph. He directed movies from 1914 until the end of the silent era and continued to act in them and on television until 1954. His career came to an end when he died of cancer on February 12, 1955.

The Secret Room was released on February 22, 1915. CW

Shunen no hebi
Komatsu; b/w; length unknown; Japan *D:* Uichiro Tamura
Cast unknown

Snakes have long loomed large in Chinese and Japanese folklore, often as embodying the spirit of a human who bears a grudge. The title *Shunen no hebi* means "vindictive snake," and this short film from 1915 concerned a snake possessed by the spirit of a murdered person wreaking vengeance on those responsible for his (or her) death.

Like the majority of films from Japan's silent era, *Shunen no hebi* is considered lost, and there is little extant information about it. CW

The Silent Command
Universal; b/w; 44 min; U.S.
D/S: Robert Z. Leonard *P:* Carl Laemmle *C:* Stephen S. Noron
Cast: Robert Z. Leonard, Ella Hall, Harry Carter, Allan Forrest, Mark Fenton

A man (Leonard) is unable to pay for his daughter Ella's (Hall) life-saving operation, and in exchange for the procedure, he agrees to hand over the girl to Dr. Sevani (Carter) on her 18th birthday. After the surgery, however, he learns that the doctor plans to use Ella in hypnotism experiments and, panic stricken, backpedals on his promise. Enraged, Sevani hypnotically forces Ella to murder her father. The police apprehend her, but her lawyer boyfriend clears her name and ensures that the doctor is brought to justice.

Robert Z. Leonard started as a film actor in 1908 before moving on to writing, producing and directing. His name is mostly forgotten today, despite having directed Greta Garbo in her first American screen test and being twice nominated for an Oscar (for directing *The Divorcee*, 1930, and *The Great Ziegfeld*, 1936). He amassed over 30 film credits by the time of *The Silent Command*, though he'd been directing for a mere two years.

The Silent Command was, for Universal, an early and tentative foray into outright horror. The scenario blends melodrama and suspense, with unsavory elements sprinkled in to give it a darker-than-usual edge. Indeed, the idea of a father promising his virginal daughter to a lecherous benefactor foreshadows one of Jess Franco's more notorious shockers, *Lorna the Exorcist* (1974).

The film is no relation to the 1923 film of the same name, which was notable for providing Bela Lugosi with his first role in an American picture. TH

The Soul of Phyra
Domino; b/w; 22 min; U.S.
D: Charles Swickard
Cast: Enid Markey, Herschel Mayall, J. Frank Burke

India certainly provided its share of horror fodder in cinema's early days, from cursed rubies stolen from ancient temples, to mystic swamis foretelling doom and to the reincarnation of souls good and bad to do the bidding of various powers. In *The Soul of Phyra*, horror takes the form of a distant voice calling the virginal Phyra (Markey) to the jungles of India, there to be sacrificed to Kali. When the deed is done, her spirit calls out to her husband, who dies from a broken heart.

One might well ponder precisely what sort of marriage leaves its wife a virgin, though it seems that during the heyday of the silent screen, most women—single or married—never knew the touch of a man (or a woman, for that matter). Sexually active women were labeled "vamps" and invariably met a horrible fate (not that staying pure ultimately helped Phyra much).

From 1911 to 1920, Enid Markey was a silent-era celebrity, though she's best known today for starring as Jane Porter in the earliest screen appearances of Edgar Rice Burroughs' venerable Tarzan: *Tarzan of the Apes* and *The Romance of Tarzan* (both 1918). Afterward, she left cinema for the stage, where, she later claimed, she hoped to learn how to act. She popped up in films now and again over the next few decades before launching a television career in the 1950s. She is remembered by television enthusiasts for her starring role as another virgin, the spinster "Aunt Violet" on the short-lived CBS sitcom *Bringing Up Buddy*. Her last big-screen performance was as Edna in *The Boston Strangler* (1968).

Charles Swickard had a career as an opera singer before switching to acting and then to directing. He crafted more than 40 silent films, including comedies, dramas and Westerns. CW

The Spectre of the Vault
aka Lo Spettro del Sotterraneo
Riviera; b/w; 37 min; Italy
D/S: Ubaldo Maria Del Colle
Cast: Ubaldo Maria Del Colle, Corinna Ristori

As the title suggests, *The Spectre of the Vault* concerned a spirit haunting an old tomb. The film was produced by Riviera, which was formed in 1913 by a group of Italian filmmakers, including Del Colle. The company didn't last long, producing only a few films between 1914 and 1916.

Actor/writer/director Ubaldo Maria Del Colle was active during the silent era, after which he took a break until *Menzogna* (1952); by then, he was pushing 70 years old. His work received scant notice outside Italy at the time, and even in his native country he is an obscure figure today. TH/CW

The Strange Unknown
Lubin; b/w; 33 min; U.S.
D/S: Wilbert Mellville *P:* Siegmund Lubin
Cast: L.C. Shumway, George Routh, Helen Eddy, Dorothy Barrett, Melvin Mayo, Adelaide Bronti

Based on a story by William H. Ratterman, *The Strange Unknown* presents Helen Eddy as a woman who inherits a fortune from her deceased father. The downside is that she also has a disinherited actress half-sister (Barrett) who lives in Paris and not only wants her sister's money but her sister's artist boyfriend (Shumway) as well. When the actress comes to visit the family's sprawling, haunted estate, she drugs her sister and locks her in the garret. She then assumes control of all the assets and makes her move on the struggling artist. But when the real heir escapes, the truth emerges.

The Strange Unknown belongs to the same subgenre of horror as the many adaptations of Charlotte Brontë's *Jane Eyre: An Autobiography* and Wilkie Collins' *The Woman in White*. Melodramatic rather than supernatural, these films are grounded in the horrors of the real world. Director Wilbert Melville's films existed in such a world, though the melodramatics were usually a bit more subdued than they are here. CW

The Three Wishes
Gaumont; b/w; 8 min; France/Great Britain
Credits unknown

This obscure film, thought lost, offered up chills and humor with its tale of an evil imp who grants an aging couple three wishes. Though it sounds similar to both Robert Louis Stevenson's *The Bottle Imp* (1891) and W.W. Jacobs' *The Monkey's Paw* (1902), this short, effects-laden film wasn't based on either. Regardless, the idea of a supernatural being granting three wishes had been around since time immemorial. CW

Togakushi-yama no kijo
Nikkatsu; b/w; length unknown; Japan
Crew unknown
Cast: Matsunosuke Onoe, Enichiro Jitsukawa

Though the director of this (probably short) Japanese horror film is unknown, it seems likely to have been Shozo Makino, who was at the time Nikkatsu Studios' lead filmmaker and who frequently paired himself with actor Matsunosuke Onoe. The title refers to a maple tree, and the story originated as a portion of a Japanese Noh, or musical play. The narrative was later adapted into a Kabuki piece, and it's probable that this latter type of play actually provided the basis for Onoe's adaptation, which was released in March 1915.

A military leader named Koremochi Tairano goes on a hunting trip in the Mt. Togakushi region and comes across a

group of mysterious and beautiful women throwing a banquet. He partakes of their feast, and just as he is about to succumb to their wiles, he discovers that they are *oni*, demons that take on human form to work their evil magic. Tairano appeals to the powers of Heaven to defeat the demons, however, and is saved.

The film is set during the Heian period of Japanese history, which lasted from approximately 794 to 1185. CW

Trilby
Equitable/World; b/w; 60 min; U.S.
D: Maurice Tourneur *S:* E.M. Ingleton
Cast: Clara Kimball Young, Wilton Lackaye, Chester Barnett, Paul McAllister, James Young, Phyllis Neilsson Terry

Following on the heels of Louise Kolm's *Svengali* and Harold Shaw's *Trilby* (both 1914), French émigré Maurice Tourneur took a stab at George Du Maurier's oft-told tale. Silent screen superstar Clara Kimball Young stars as an ingénue named Trilby, who makes ends meet by working as an artist's model. She meets three young Bohemians, Little Billie (Barnett), the Laird and Taffy. Billie and Trilby fall in love, but that love faces an obstacle in the person of Svengali (Lackaye), a musician who takes a deep interest in the girl. Svengali ingratiates himself into the group's good graces with his musical skills, even as his uncanny control over his assistant, Gecko (McAllister), fails to ring any alarm bells. On the night that Trilby and Billie are to announce their engagement, Trilby is lured from her beau by Svengali's hypnotic powers. He takes her to England where, under his preternatural influence, she becomes a great singer. But the stress of maintaining a constant hold on Trilby induces minor heart attacks in Svengali, and when each occurs, Trilby becomes her old self for a short period of time. Finally, during a performance on the continent, Svengali suffers one final heart attack and dies, and Trilby is set free. Unfortunately, her voice returns to its original gruff form, and she is booed off the stage.

Reviews of the film were not flattering. In its September 10, 1915 edition, *Variety* correctly opined that "[t]here are a number of faults to be found with *Trilby*." The most obvious of these is Wilton Lackaye, whose portrayal of Svengali is, as the journal put it, a "distinct disappointment." He is simply too staid in the role, ludicrously underplaying what should have been, as *Variety* stated, a cause for "sensationalism." (It doesn't help that the actor was too overweight for the part, a flaw made more glaring by the producers' apparent insistence on putting him in clothes that are too small for him.) And while the publication reported "Clara Kimball Young gave a most convincing characterization," this is only true if one compares it solely to the others in the film. She is also too old for her part, straining audience credulity even further.

Trilby had its premiere at the 44th Street Theatre in New York City on September 6, 1915, a full week before Equitable Motion Pictures Corporation (on September 13) copyrighted it. It went into national distribution on September 20 and was released again by World Film Corporation in 1917 and Republic in 1920. By that time an opening card had been added describing Du Maurier's illustrious career and giving a brief history of *Trilby* and its director and participants. The redone version also removed the finale, in which Trilby dies after dismissing her friends and Svengali's sinister presence appears in a mirror to remind the audience that even in death he has control over her. As amended, the film ends with the words, "A promise of good old times again," as Trilby shows her friends out the door, a smile playing on her lips. CW

The Unfaithful Wife
Fox; b/w; 55 min; U.S.
D: J. Gordon Edwards *S:* Mary Murillo *C:* Phil Rosen
Cast: Genevieve Hamper, Runa Hodges, Robert B. Mantell, Stuart Holmes, Warner Oland, Lawrence White

A cholera epidemic has swept through Naples, Italy and Count Fabiano Romali (Mantell) is stricken. His faithless Juliet

Genevieve Hamper from a 1919 stage production

(Hamper) uses his incapacitated state as a pretext to bury him alive. But unknown to Juliet and her lover/accomplice Arturo (Holmes), the Count frees himself from his tomb. In disguise, he ingratiates himself with Juliet and proposes marriage. When she accepts, Arturo is furious and challenges Fabiano to a duel. Fabiano kills Arturo and marries Juliet, then leads her to a tomb, promising to show her riches. Once there, he reveals his true identity, locks her in the tomb and leaves her to die.

One need only read the above synopsis to see how patently absurd and unbelievable the film must have been, though its sting in the tail—the Count turning the tables on his wife—must have been quite the crowd pleaser. Despite the Italian setting, the film was shot in the United States with domestic talent (the absence of a dialogue track no doubt made the subterfuge easier to pull off). The cast includes future Charlie Chan Warner Oland in one of his earliest roles; the Swedish-born actor built a career doing "exotic" foreign characterizations, though his life and career ended prematurely due to alcohol abuse. Director J. Gordon Edwards remained prolific until his demise in 1925, at the age of 58, from complications due to pneumonia; his grandson, Blake Edwards, later became a major director of comedies (the *Pink Panther* series starring Peter Sellers) and dramas (*Days of Wine and Roses*, 1962) ... and married Julie Andrews, of course. TH

The Vivisectionist
Kalem; b/w; 18 min; U.S.
D: James W. Horne *S:* Hamilton Smith
Cast: Marin Sais, William H. West, Paul Hurst, Arthur Shirley, Edward Clisbee, Frank Jonasson

Released on June 23, 1915, *The Vivisectionist* deals with the then-topical and controversial idea of vivisection, the act of cutting or injuring living animals for the purpose of scientific research. William H. West plays vivisectionist Dr. Jardine, while Marin Sais stars as Lila, a special investigator looking into his questionable activities. Paul Hurst is cast as the doctor's servant, Arthur Shirley as his neighbor and Edward Clisbee as his brother.

James W. Horne directed well over 200 films, of which he wrote more than 40. He also had parts in several films, mostly during the silent era. He made numerous *Our Gang* and Laurel and Hardy comedies in the 1920s and beyond, and his career lasted well into the sound era. His last film was completed in 1942, the same year he died of a stroke at the age of 62. He was the uncle of famed film director George Stevens (*The Diary of Anne Frank*, 1959).

This *Vivisectionist* is based on a story by Hamilton Smith and should not be confused with another 1915 film of the same name, which was a short romantic drama directed by and starring James Levering. CW

The Warning
aka **The Eternal Penalty**
Triumph/Equitable; b/w; 60 (50) min; U.S.
D: Edmund Lawrence *S:* Julius Steger
Cast: Henry Kolker, Lily Leslie, Christine Mayo, Master Frank Longacre, Edna Mayo, Mayme Kelso

This outing qualifies as horror largely due to its depiction of Hell. In essence a cautionary melodrama against Demon Rum, it concerns a man named Robert (Kolker) and his gradual descent into alcoholism. The tale begins with a fight between an intoxicated Robert and his son Bobbie (Longacre), during which Robert pushes Bobbie into traffic and the boy winds up paraplegic. Though devastated, Robert remains unable to quit drinking. He winds up losing everything that matters to him before he literally dies in the gutter. Then, just as he's about to be engulfed by the flames of Hades, he wakes up and realizes it was all a dream. Duly terrified, he finally swears off strong drink for good.

The Warning has more in common with early anti-drinking diatribes wrapped up in horror clothing, including *The Drunkard's Conversion* (1901) and *D.T.'s, or the Effects of Drink* (1905), than it does with serious and intelligent efforts such as *The Lost Weekend* (1945). Director Edmund Lawrence had a none-too-distinguished career during the silent era; his last film was *The House of Secrets* (1929). Leading man Henry Kolker later appeared in such horror fare as *Rasputin and the Empress* (1932), *Black Moon* (1934) and *Bluebeard* (1944), the latter being one of his last screen appearances before he died in a fall in 1947. *The Warning*'s supporting cast includes Dorothy Gish, the lesser-known sister of the legendary Lillian Gish. TH

When the Spirits Moved
Nestor/Universal; b/w; 11 min; U.S.
D/S: Al Christie
Cast: Lee Moran, Eddie Lyons, Victoria Forde, Harry Rattenberry

This interesting horror-comedy short is one of Universal's earliest forays into dark terrain. Directed by the prolific Al Chris-

Mary Fuller plays Desire in *A Witch of Salem Town*.

tie—who frequently teamed with such silent-era A-listers as Lee Moran, Eddie Lyons and Victoria Forde—it's about a man who is vexed by spirits with an apparent weakness for slapstick humor.

Alfred (Al) Ernest Christie was born in Ontario, Canada in 1881. After a stint in theater, he went to work at New Jersey's Nestor Studios before that company became part of Universal Pictures. There he focused on comedies and Westerns. Six months after the production of *When the Spirits Moved*, Christie's success got him a position as head of Universal's comedy department, but he quickly tired of the job and jumped ship to form his own production house, Christie Film Company, which—to nobody's surprise—focused on two-reel comedies. Between writing, producing and directing, Christie amassed over 1,000 credits and remained in the movie business until the late 1940s. Among his better work was a spoof of H. Rider Haggard's classic novel *She: A History of Adventure* titled *His Egyptian Affinity* (1915), which featured a revived mummy. Christie died in 1951. CW

Which is Witch?
Cricks and Martin; b/w; 6 min; Great Britain
D: Edwin J. Collins
Cast unknown

This British-made short recycles the oft-done premise of a witch's curse on an innocent man. The title *Which is Witch?* was a piece of wordplay several animated shorts later used, none of which had any connection to this film. One was a 1948 Bugs Bunny cartoon directed by Fritz Freleng, another a *Caspar the Friendly Ghost* cartoon from 1958 and the third a 1967 Ralph Bakshi-directed short. TH

A Witch of Salem Town
Victor; b/w; 18 min; U.S.
D: Lucius Henderson
Cast: Mary Fuller, Curtis Benton, Matt Moore, Edna Hunter

Based on a story by Margaret Hovey, *A Witch of Salem Town* was the third film to deal with an innocent woman accused of witchcraft during the Salem Witchcraft Trials of 1692. It was clearly influenced by D.W. Griffith's better-known *Rose O'Salem Town* (1910). Mary Fuller stars as Desire, whose name alone would seem sufficient to get her in trouble in Puritan-controlled America. What separates this film from the previous two is that here the protagonist is unable to escape her violent fate.

Curtis Benton and Matt Moore also starred together in the 1916 science fiction epic *20,000 Leagues Under the Sea*, which was based on the novel by Jules Verne. Moore had a part in Tod Browning's *The Unholy Three* in 1925 as well, though his horror appearances are otherwise sparse. Brother of actress Mary Moore, he was born in Ireland in 1888 and starred in films through the 1950s. He died in Hollywood in 1960.

A Witch of Salem Town was released on May 24, 1915. CW

The Wraith of Haddon Towers
American Film Manufacturing/Clipper; b/w; 33 min; U.S.
D: Arthur Maude
Cast: Constance Crawley, Arthur Maude, Beatrice Van

The wraith of the title is an alleged ghost that dwells in a locked upper room of the likewise-titular Haddon Towers in a set up that recalls E.F. Benson's short story *The Room in the Tower*.

The American Film Manufacturing Company produced *The Wraith of Haddon Towers* with some involvement by Clipper Star Features, which may have been a subsidiary of, or alternate name for, the AFMC; however, Mutual Film released the film. Its male lead was British-born Arthur Maude, also a writer and producer, and he was the director. A veteran of the stage, Maude began his film career in 1913 and remained active in cinematic circles until 1951.

Wraith also starred Maude cohort Constance Crawley. A Shakespearean actress of great range who often shared the stage with Maude, she died of heart failure in 1919, just a few weeks before her 40th birthday.

Shot in 1915, the film's official release was on the very first day of 1916. Though some sources maintain that *Wraith* had a 45-minute running time, the fact that it fit onto three reels makes that impossible. CW

Yurei yashiki
Nikkatsu; b/w; length unknown; Japan
D: Kyomatsu Hosomaya
Cast unknown

Haunted houses have long been a staple of Japanese lore, yet the nation's cinema never fixated on them to quite the same degree that it did ghost cats and vengeful female spirits. Examples of the subgenre did pop up now and then, with *Yurei yashiki* being one of the earliest. (Its title literally translates as "Haunted House.") More atypical than the film's subject matter was the presence of Kyomatsu Hosomaya in the director's chair. At this time in Nikkatsu history, it was usually Shozo Makino who oversaw the studio's horror product. Nor does it appear that studio horror-staple Matsunosuke Onoe played the lead role, no doubt making for a change of pace and possibly style. But with the film now lost, it's impossible to tell for certain. CW

Satanic Rhapsody's running time is dedicated, at the expense of a story, to women in diaphanous outfits fleeing from the clutches of the groping men who desire them.

1916

Arima no neko sodo
Nikkatsu; b/w; length unknown; Japan
Crew unknown
Cast: Matsunosuke Onoe

Though the name of this film's director is unknown, it was likely Shozo Makino, who worked for Nikkatsu Studios at the time and frequently cast his star find, Matsunosuke Onoe, in lead roles. The title translates as *Arima Cat Trouble*. Arima is the town near Mt. Kumuchi in which the story is set. There, within the ruins of a palace built some 1,300 or so years ago for Emperor Kotoku, is said to live a ghostly cat woman.

Arima no neko sodo is the second known film based on the legend. The first, *Arima kaibyô-den*, was produced in 1914, with all but the title lost today. (That said, it seems likely that Nikkatsu produced.) Other silent-era versions of the "Ghost Cat of Arima" folktale were done in 1920 and 1922 (both under the title *Arima no neko*). Nikkatsu's rival Kyokuto remade this 1916 adaptation under the same title in 1936. CW

Bâke ginnan
aka **Kaizaka bâke ginnan**; **Bâke-ichou**
Nikkatsu Kyoto; b/w; 30 min; Japan
D: Shozo Makino
Cast: Matsunosuki Onoe

This long-lost film, released in October 1916 in its native Japan, was directed by Shozo Makino and starred legendary actor Matsunosuki Onoe in the lead role. Though considered a horror film, few details about its plot have survived. It appears to have had something to do with a haunted gingko tree, hence the title, which translates as "Monster Gingko." The film's alternate title includes the word *Kaizaka*, which is a place name (hence the translation "Monster Gingko of Kaizaka." CW

The Black Crook
Kalem; b/w; 60 min; U.S.
D: Robert G. Vignola *S:* Phil Lang
Cast: Edward P. Sullivan, Gladys Coburn, Roland Bottomley, Henry Hallam, Charles De Forrest, Mae Thompson

Count Wolfenstein (Hallam), devastated when Amina (Coburn) rejects him in favor of Rudolph (Bottomley), imprisons his rival in a dungeon. Meanwhile, Hertzog (Sullivan), "The Black Crook," must fulfill a deal with the Devil by providing the Prince of Darkness with a fresh soul each year. When Hertzog hears of Amina and Rudolph's troubles, he decides that they might be easy to lure into the realm of darkness.

Based on Broadway's first musical comedy, this magical melodrama is of note for having the first original choreographed dance numbers created specifically for a motion picture. The story, based on a play by Charles M. Barras, repeats Faustian motifs as its unscrupulous protagonist attempts to lure the young lovers into eternal damnation.

Director Robert G. Vignola was active from 1911 through 1937; he also worked a great deal as an actor, often appearing in the films he directed. He did much work for the Kalem Company, which was a prolific outfit until it disbanded in 1918. TH

The Bogus Ghost
aka **The Bogus Count**
Kalem; b/w; 11 min; U.S.
D: Harry F. Millarde *S:* S.A. Van Patten
Cast: Ethel Teare, Victor Rodman, Merta Sterling, Freddie Fralick

A phony mystic posing as a nobleman (Rodman) uses a woman (Teare), believed to have drowned, as a phony ghost in his act. This is yet another entry in the charlatan fake mindreader/fake ghost subgenre. The plot offers no major innovations to its already-tired formula, and chills were soft-pedaled in favor of slapstick.

Harry F. Millarde (often billed without the middle initial and sometimes without the "e" at the end of his surname) was a prolific actor and director during the silent era. As a director, his specialty was melodrama; this appears to have been his only flirtation with the horror genre. TH

Crime and the Penalty
Cricks and Martin; b/w; 38 min; Great Britain
D: R. Harley West
Cast: Alesia Leon, Jack Lovatt, Louis Nanten

Despite a title that suggests otherwise, *Crime and the Penalty* is an outright horror film that owes a great deal to Edgar Allan Poe's classic short story *The Murders in the Rue Morgue* (1841) and

George Du Maurier's Gothic horror novel *Trilby* (1894). A criminal who has developed an obsession with his cousin's wife enlists the aid of a scientist to kidnap her. To help the scientist, he provides the assistance of his chimpanzee, which he has—through hypnosis—trained to murder. The chimpanzee's *modus operandi* is strangulation!

After starring in a couple of films, R. Harley West turned to directing, which consisted of only a few films made within a two-year span, all of them for Cricks and Martin. This was his last picture. CW

The Crimson Stain Mystery
Erbograph/Consolidated; b/w; 16 chapters; U.S.
D: T. Hayes Hunter *S:* Albert Payson Terhune *C:* Ludwig G.B. Erb
Cast: Maurice Costello, Ethel Grandin, Thomas J. McGrane, Olga Olonova, William Cavanaugh, John Milton

Dr. Montrose (McGrane) attempts to develop a drug to increase human intelligence. Not only do his experiments fail, but also the test subjects turn into monsters (led by a crimson-eyed mutant) that attack the elite of New York City. This gang of creatures proves difficult for the police, led by the daring Layton Parrish (Milton), to apprehend.

The Crimson Stain Mystery was a serialized hybrid of horror, mystery, science fiction and cliff-hanger melodrama divided into 16 separate chapters: 1. *The Brand of Satan*; 2. *In the Demon's Spell*; 3. *The Broken Spell*; 4. *The Mysterious Disappearance*; 5. *The Figure in Black*; 6. *The Phantom Image*; 7. *The Devil's Symphony*; 8. *In the Shadow of Death*; 9. *The Haunting Spectre*; 10. *The Infernal Fiend*; 11. *The Tortured Soul*; 12. *The Restless Spirit*; 13. *Despoiling Brutes*; 14. *The Bloodhound*; 15. *The Human Tiger*; and 16. *The Unmasking*. While prints of some of the episodes are preserved at the Library of Congress—with others known to be in the care of a Canadian archive—a couple of episodes remain missing and are presumed lost.

Director T. Hayes Hunter is a figure of minor note whose best-remembered (though hardly revered) title is the 1933 Boris Karloff vehicle *The Ghoul*. Leading man Maurice Costello, born in Pittsburgh, Pennsylvania, had made his screen debut in one of the earliest film portrayals of Sherlock Holmes, the now-lost *The Adventures of Sherlock Holmes* (1905). He went on to rack up over 200 acting credits over the next 40 years, but after the sound era commenced, he was mostly confined to bit parts; one of his last credits is another less-than-renowned Karloff vehicle, *The Climax* (1944). TH

A Daughter of the Gods
Fox; b/w; 180 min; U.S.
D/S: Herbert Brenon *C:* Andre Baraltier, A. Culp, J. Roy Hunt, Marcel Le Picard, William Marshall, C. Richards, Edward Warren
Cast: Annette Kellerman, William E. Shay, Hal De Forest, Marcelle Hontabat, Violet Horner, Jane Lee

As a sultan (De Forest) grieves the death of his son, a cunning sorceress (Allen) offers to restore the offspring to life. There's a catch, of course. The sultan must assist the sorceress in destroying the beautiful and virtuous Anitia (Kellerman), a daughter of the Gods.

Long considered lost, this fantasy with horror elements has claimed a place in cinema history. It's considered the United States' first million-dollar film production, and the leading lady, Annette Kellerman, reportedly offered American cinemas their first nude scene in a major motion picture.

Writer/director Herbert Brenon had previously directed King Baggott in IMP/Universal's adaptation of *Dr. Jekyll and Mr. Hyde* (1913), but he seems to have bitten off more than he could chew here. Production delays and cost overruns pushed the film wildly over budget, and William Fox, the head of Fox Film Corporation, sought to punish the filmmaker by removing his name from the credits; Brenon fought back, however, and by means of a lawsuit retained directorial credit. The tempest didn't damage Brenon's standing in Hollywood; he went on to be nominated for an Oscar for *Sorrell and Son* in 1927.

As for Kellerman, the actress was no stranger to scandal—she'd been arrested in 1907 in Boston on charges of indecent exposure for wearing a one-piece bathing suit. Taking to the water, it seems, was a means of empowerment for her. She was born with crippled legs and swam routinely to keep them strong. Her regimen encompassed three unsuccessful attempts to traverse the English Channel, with the ensuing publicity enhancing her box-office popularity. Though largely forgotten today, she did inspire a Technicolor extravaganza called *Million Dollar Mermaid* (1952) with Esther Williams as Kellerman; the title refers to the expense of creating *A Daughter of the Gods*, with the production portrayed in typically glamorous, if inaccurate, MGM style. TH

The Dead Alive
aka **His Wife's Double**
Gaumont; b/w; 55 min; U.S.
D/S: Henry J. Vernot
Cast: Marguerite Courtot, James Levering, Sidney Mason, Henry Pemberton

Old Jim (Levering) gambles away all his money and is reduced to working for den operator Doc Ardini (Pemberton). Jim's twin daughters, Jessie (Courtot) and Mary (also Courtot), are at first unaware of their father's situation, but things deteriorate further when Ardini's gambling den is raided, Jim accidentally kills a man and the two are sent to prison. Jessie, who is married to the respectable Stuyvesant (Mason), keeps it from her husband out of fear that the scandal will spoil their union. But when Ardini, who receives a shorter prison term, is released, he uses his hypnotic powers to force Mary into extorting money from Jessie. Jessie instead commits suicide, with Stuyvesant still ignorant of her familial woes. In the end, when Ardini attempts to cash in on the bereaved husband's grief, Mary confesses all.

This film is more melodrama than horror, but its elements of mind control and "twinning" link it to the popular horror potboilers of the day. It's lost, making it impossible to tell how lurid the proceedings were.

Writer/director Henry (sometimes billed as Henri) J. Vernot had previously overseen an adaptation of *Rob Roy* (1913), but his output was far from prolific. He made approximately eight titles between 1912 and 1921 and died in 1928. Leading lady Marguerite Courtot was regarded as a screen beauty in her day, but her career ended before the coming of sound. She died in 1986, with her reputation—and most of her cinematic output—clouded in obscurity. TH

A Deal with the Devil
Hepworth; b/w; 17 min; Great Britain
D: Frank Wilson *P:* Cecil M. Hepworth
Cast Unknown

This is a standard knock-off of the Faust legend, with an old chemist making a deal with the Devil in order to gain eternal youth. Frank Wilson directed the film, and he was quite prolific during the first half of the silent era (a period that also brought his 1913 horror film *Dr. Trimball's Secret*). By the early 1920s, he had shifted his focus to writing and acting. Among his many horror credits are those as co-scenarist for the many episodes of the film series *The Mystery of Dr. Fu-Manchu* (1923). He also starred in that series and its follow-up, *The Further Mysteries of Dr. Fu Manchu* (1924), as Inspector Weymouth. CW

The Devil's Bondwoman
aka **The Devil's Die**
Universal; b/w; 55 min; U.S.
D: Lloyd B. Carleton *S:* Maie B. Havey, Fred Myton
Cast: Dorothy Davenport, Emory Johnson, Richard Morris, Adele Farrington, William Canfield, Miriam Shelby

Mason Van Horton (Johnson) begins an affair with Doria (Farrington), the wife of business associate John Manners (Canfield). But when he falls in love with Beverly Hope (Davenport), an outraged Doria tells her husband, John (Canfield), that Mason seduced her. John sets out to ruin Mason's business empire but comes upon Doria making love to Prince Vandloup (Morris). Getting her number at last, he rejects her, only to learn that Prince Vandloup is the Devil incarnate.

This early horror melodrama from Universal offers an unusual spin on a traditional tale. The final reveal that one of the characters is actually the Devil takes the story into horror terrain, as does a prologue depicting Satan and his minions plotting away in the depths of Hell.

Leading lady Dorothy Davenport was the daughter of character actor Harry Davenport. She was a mid-level star who later turned to directing, though without much real success. Her last directing credit was the borderline horror title *The Woman Condemned* (1934).

Character actor Arthur Hoyt made one of his earliest appearances here in a small role; among his later credits (many of them unbilled, making him one of those familiar faces it's almost impossible to put a name to) was a brief appearance in *The Raven* (1935), in which he shared a scene—as a fellow Poe enthusiast—with Bela Lugosi. TH

The Devil's Toy
Premo/Equitable; b/w; 50 min; U.S.
D: Harley Knoles *S:* Edward Madden, Maurice Marks *C:* Arthur Edison
Cast: Adele Blood, Montagu Love, Edwin Stevens, Jack Halliday, Madge Evans, Arnold Lucy

Based on Edward Madden's poem "The Mill of the Gods," *The Devil's Toy* concerns two struggling artists, Paul La France (Halliday) and Wilfred Barsley (Love). Barsley hates La France, who's in love with a beautiful actress named Helen Danver (Blood). When La France's paintings begin to sell, Barsley makes a deal with the Devil (Stevens) to murder his rich uncle and inherit his fortune. Conveniently for Barsley, La France goes mad and winds up in an insane asylum. Barsley steals his fellow artist's work and passes it off as his own, growing famous and successful as a result. But when she sees these works of art, Helen—who has been away on an acting tour—recognizes them for what they are: her lover's life work. She concocts a plan to ruin Barsley, while at the same time searching for her lover. Eventually La France's mind is restored, he and Adele are reunited, Barsley dies and his soul goes straight to Hell.

This was one of director Harley Knoles' earliest films and only his second attempt at horror (after *The Greater Will*, 1915); the filmmaker worked exclusively in the silent era, making films that few remember today. Though born in England, he began his film career in the United States with Premo before returning to his native country in 1921 to make films there. His film career ended in 1928, and he died in London in 1936. His son later became a pulp novelist, finding about as much fame as his father.

Just the right length, *The Devil's Toy* is an interesting film that owes more to previous works of silent cinema than it does its source material, despite the involvement of the poem's author in writing the script. CW

Doktor Satansohn
Projektions/AG Union; b/w; 44 min; Germany
D/S: Edmund Edel *P:* Paul Davidson *C:* Ernst Krohn
Cast: Ernst Lubitsch, Hans Felix, Marga Kohler, Yo Larte, Erich Schonfelder

Doctor Satansohn (Lubitsch) invents a machine that restores youth and beauty. An older woman with designs on her own son-in-law calls upon him. The doctor uses his machine to make the woman look like her daughter, but things don't go as planned for the frustrated couger.

This dark comedy is chiefly of note for its central performance by Ernst Lubitsch. Lubitsch went on to establish himself as the world's foremost director of sophisticated comedy, including *Ninotchka* (1939) and *To Be Or Not To Be* (1942), but at this stage of his career he dabbled in both directing and acting; his final performance was as a hunchback in *Sumurun* (1920). In *Satansohn*, Lubitsch chews the scenery in a role that's pure Jewish caricature. The evil doctor's Satanic-looking machine gives the film a sci-fi feel, and the scene in which the transformed mother confronts her daughter reflects silent German cinema's fascination with the doppelganger motif. TH

Feathertop
Gaumont; b/w; 55 min; U.S.
D: Henry J. Vernot *S:* Paul M. Bryan
Cast: Mathilde Baring, Marguerite Courtot, Charles Graham, Gerald Griffin, James Levering, Sidney Mason

When self-absorbed young lady Elsie (Courtot) goes to live with her city uncle, she completely forgets about her country boyfriend, instead becoming enamored of prissy urban fop Percy Morleigh (Reinhard). To teach her a lesson in values, the uncle feigns death, pretending to leave her a copy of Nathaniel Hawthorne's *Feathertop*, a short story about a scarecrow that comes to life. She duly reads the tale, then falls asleep and dreams that she is protagonist Polly Gookin, with Percy as humanized scarecrow Feathertop. In the course of her imaginings, she realizes that Percy is as vapid and soulless as the straw-stuffed clothing from which he's made. Awakening, she comprehends why her uncle left her the copy of Hawthorne's story. She comes to her senses, leaves the city and returns to her former beau, having learned the "common sense" truth that a simple life is the happiest. She also finds out that her still-alive uncle has similarly wised up, abandoning the degenerate world for a simple life as a ... sailor?

Famersonly.com commercials don't get any more insulting than this. Paul M. Bryan's script has little to do with Hawthorne's story, deliberately and clumsily misreading the title character (in the story, Feathertop is anything but insipid, which is why he ultimately destroys himself). Director Henry J. Vernot's film is the least horrific of the silent films based on the tale, replacing fright and suspense with straight romantic melodrama and silly ruminations about how superior country folk are to city folk, who may have book learnin' but ain't got no common sense. Vernot also directed *The Dead Alive* (1916), which, though predominantly a drama, still contained more horrific elements than the simple-minded affair that is 1916's *Feathertop*.

Both Marguerite Courtot and John Reinhard played dual roles as the film's "real-life" characters and their literary counterparts in Elsie's dream.

The next horror adaptation of *Feathertop: A Moralized Legend* (1852) came in 1923, was partially based on Percy MacKaye's four-act play *The Scarecrow* (1908) and was given the moniker *Puritan Passions*. CW

The Grasping Hand
aka **La main qui étreint**; **Max and the Clutching Hand**; **Max et la main-qui-étreint**; **Max victime de la Main-qui-étreint**
Pathé; b/w; 13 min; France
D/S: Max Linder
Cast: Max Linder, Henri Collen

This humorous short featured France's number one comedian Max Linder facing off against a ghost. It should not be confused with Jacques de Baroncelli's 1916 *La main qui étreint*. This wasn't Linder's first attempt at a horror comedy (that was *The Hanging Lamp*, 1908), and neither would it be his last. In 1910 he was hypnotized into attempting murder in *Max Hypnotized*, and in 1924 he attempted to revive his career in the haunted house comedy *Au secours!* The talented Abel Gance, who went on to become one of France's most popular filmmakers, directed.

In 1925 Linder killed himself by ingesting Veronal, injecting morphine and slitting his wrists. His wife joined him in the act, and the two left behind a baby girl. CW

The Green-Eyed Monster
Fox; b/w; 50 min; U.S.
D/Co-S: J. Gordon Edwards *Co-S:* Mary Murillo *C:* Phil Rosen, Arthur Ripley
Cast: Robert B. Mantell, Stuart Holmes, Genevieve Hamper, Pauline Barry, Henry Leone, Charles Davidson

Shot in 1915 but not copyrighted or released until 1916, *The Green-Eyed Monster* is a Gothic tale of jealousy, obsession and murder. Brothers Raimond and Louis de Mornay (Mantell and Holmes, respectively) love the same woman, their cousin Claire (Hamper). When Louis wins her affection, the jealous Raimond flees first to Europe and then to India to escape his feelings. Years later, he returns upon the request of his brother's son Paul and, still jealous, murders Louis with cobra venom and places the body in a casket. He tries to court the definitely-not-interested Claire, but when she refuses him, he shows her Raimond's dead body. She dies from shock, whereupon Raimond sinks further into madness. Finally, believing that it will kill Paul—who is the last reminder of Louis' and Claire's love—he decides to show his nephew the body as well. But things don't work out as planned.

J. Gordon Edwards, Mary Murillo and Phil Rosen had worked on *The Unfaithful Wife* (1915) together and went on to share screen credits for *Tangled Lives* (1917). Edwards and Rosen also worked on *The Darling of Paris* (1917) while Murillo helped with the reimagining of H. Rider Haggard's *She* (1917). All of these productions were for Fox.

The Green-Eyed Monster should not be confused with another film of the same title, released in 1919. CW

Haunted
E&R Jungle; b/w; length unknown; U.S.
Crew unknown
Cast: Lillian Leighton, Ralph McComas, Napoleon, Sally

A newlywed couple (Leighton, McComas) honeymoon in a secluded bungalow, but their attempts at *amour* are interrupted by strange happenings. They begin to fear that the bungalow is haunted, but it turns out that the supernatural happenings are the work of a pair of mischievous chimpanzees.

As their moniker indicates, E&R Jungle Film Company specialized in films with a wildlife slant. Napoleon and Sally were the company's prized chimpanzee performers, and they were featured in no less than seven shorts: *From the Jungle to the Stage* (1914), *What D'Ye Think O' That!* (1916), *Uncle's Little Ones* (1916), *The Jungle Cure* (1916), *Some Detective!* (1916), *Napoleon and Sally* (1916) and *Haunted*. The simian stars were popular with audiences, but it appears that the majority of their work is lost in the mists of time. TH

The Haunted Bell

IMP; b/w; 20 min; U.S.
D: Henry Otto *S:* J. Grubb Alexander
Cast: King Baggot, Edna Hunter, Joseph Granby, Sam Crane, Frank Smith, Joseph W. Smiley

Based on the short story by Jacques Futrelle, *The Haunted Bell* stars King Baggot as John Lane, a man who, while writing a book about the wonders of India, acquires a large Indian bell to help set the mood. Because the bell rings for no apparent reason at the top of each hour, Lane's wife (Hunter) fears that it may be haunted. The mystery deepens when, after dinner one evening, their guest Professor Nassaib Haig (Granby) acts strangely around the bell, even bowing before it. He tells them that it is a sacred bell stolen years earlier from the Taj Mahal and offers to buy it (as do, later, a Hindu priest and an antiques dealer). But John refuses to sell, keen to solve its mystery. He eventually realizes that the bell rings only when the living room window is open, and he concludes that the vibrations of a nearby church bell are setting it off. The mystery thus solved, John settles down for the night, but the next day he discovers the murdered body of the antiques dealer in his den. At first the butler is suspected, but the police show up with the Hindu priest in their custody. The priest admits to the murder, after which John and his wife decide that ridding themselves of the bell might be for the best.

Director Henry Otto's best known feature is probably the 1924 Fox horror film *Dante's Inferno*, though he made numerous other pictures in a variety of genres, including the romantic allegory *The Ancient Mariner* (1925) starring Clara Bow. CW

Haunts for Rent
aka **Haunts for Hire**

Bray-Gilbert; b/w; length unknown; U.S.
D/Co-S/P: C. Allan Gilbert *Co-S:* Oliver Herford
Cast unknown

The old trope of spending the night in the haunted house on a wager bit got a go-around in this short subject. The story concerned a woman's promise to marry whichever brave soul manages to spend a night in a creepy mansion that's reputed to be haunted. Out of a small group of contestants, only one man is left standing.

Some sources claim that *Haunts for Hire* combined live action with animation, which would have facilitated the various depictions of supernatural phenomena. It's also said that the film was part of a series of animated shorts from writer/director C. Allan Gilbert, which kicked off with *Inbad the Sailor* (1916). According to these sources, *Haunts for Hire* was the first follow-up in the *Inbad* series and was followed in turn by *The Chess Queen*, *In the Shadows*, *Inbad the Sailor Gets Into Deep Water* and *The Toyland Paper Chase*, all released in 1916. Gilbert did much of the animation himself, and he also served as his own producer; however, given that surviving filmographies credit him more or less only with these titles, all of which have fallen into obscurity, he has not exactly gone down as a pioneer in the field of animation. TH

Her Father's Gold
aka **The Water Devil**

Thanhouser; b/w; 55 min; U.S.
D: Eugene Moore *P:* Edwin Thanhouser *C:* George Webber
Cast: Barbara Gilroy, Harris Gordon, William Burt, Louise Bates, Ed Lawrence, Violet Hite

Based on a story of the same name by Crittenden Marriott, *Her Father's Gold* seems to have been little more than a gangster picture with a ridiculous creature tossed in. It apparently featured a reporter who encounters a sea monster—or is it—while investigating the theft of some gold off the coast of Florida. Although the film is lost, one can take a wild stab and assume the monster is a ruse by criminals to frighten off the gold's rightful owner. (In that respect, it sounds terribly familiar to the much later Roger Corman cheapie *Creature from the Haunted Sea*, 1961.)

Her Father's Gold was one of several productions from producer Edwin Thanhouser. Eugene Moore was a minor actor and director during the second decade of the silent era. He made between 30 and 40 films between 1913 and 1919, though only a few had any horror connection. Those included *The Picture of Dorian Gray* (1915) and *The Image Maker*. CW

Homunculus

Deutsche-Bioscop; b/w; 6 chapters; Germany
D: Otto Rippert *S:* Robert Reinert *P:* Hanns Lippmann *C:* Carl Hoffmann
Cast: Fern Andra, Lia Borre, Josef Bunzl, Maria Carmi, Aud Egede Nissen, Olaf Foenss

A scientist (Kuehne) creates a creature (Foenss) in his laboratory. Intended as the perfect human, it proves instead to be a soulless homunculus (a Latin term meaning "little man"). When the creature discovers its inability to love, it is devastated and goes on a rampage, while the scientist who created it attempts to locate and destroy it.

Reportedly the most successful German-made serial produced during the First World War, *Homunculus* was originally released in six installments throughout 1916. The individual segments all bore the Homunculus title and were distinguished by the following subtitles: 1. *Teil*; 2. *Teil—Das geheimnisvolle Buch*; 3. *Teil—Die Liebestragodie des Homunculus*; 4. *Teil—Die Rache des Homunculus*; 5. *Teil—Die Vernichtung der Menschheit* and 6. *Teil—Das Ende des Homunculus*. The subtitles describe the story arc—the creation of the creature, its quest for love, its attempt at vengeance on mankind and its destruction. The basic story outline bears a similarity to Mary Shelley's *Frankenstein, or The Modern Prometheus*, which had first been filmed in the United States in 1910 by Thomas A. Edison's production company. Similarities can also be noted to the German-lensed Golem films of Paul Wegener, as well as the various silent versions—most notably

Devastated by its inability to love, a soulless homunculus (Olaf Foenss) goes on a rampage, from *Homunculus*.

Henrik Galeen's 1928 version—of *Alraune*. The serial is considered lost. TH

Luke's Double

Rolin/Pathé; b/w; 11 min; France
D/P: Hal Roach
Cast: Harold Lloyd, Bebe Daniels, 'Snub' Pollard, Gaylord Lloyd, Sammy Brooks, Bud Jamison

Stealing an idea from the 1910 Danish version of *Dr. Jekyll and Mr. Hyde*, Hal Roach's whimsical comedy *Luke's Double* has a man known as Lonesome Luke (Harold Lloyd) read Robert Louis Stevenson's 1886 novella *The Strange Case of Dr. Jekyll and Mr. Hyde* and then fall asleep and dream that he has an evil double (played by Harold's older brother Gaylord Lloyd).

Lonesome Luke was one of Harold Lloyd's earliest creations, with numerous silent shorts centered on him. The character was little more than an imitation of Charlie Chaplin, something Lloyd later admitted. Still, as Luke grew in popularity, Lloyd became a household name, allowing him to star in a wider array of comedic material. His other horror comedies include *Haunted Spooks* (1920) and *Hot Water* (1924).

Stan Laurel visited *Double*'s comedic terrain in the interesting *Dr. Pyckle and Mr. Pride* (1925). The idea of someone falling asleep after reading a horror novel, then dreaming about its contents, had also been done with Mary Shelley's *Frankenstein* in *Life Without Soul* (1915). CW

The Man Without a Soul
aka I Believe

London; b/w; 80 min; Great Britain
D/S/P: George Loane Tucker
Cast: Barbara Everest, Milton Rosmer, Edna Flugrath, Edward O'Neill, Kitty Cavendish, Hubert Willis

Influenced by his father (Rock) to enter a seminary, young student Stephen Ferrier (Rosmer) is killed in a tragic accident. A scientist (Willis) who has struck upon a way to bring the dead back to life sets his sights on Stephen's body. But after reviving Stephen, he finds that the young man has no soul and hides a terrible darkness within. The zombie Stephen engages in amoral activities, but after his father and mother (Everest) make supplications and entreaties to God on his behalf, his soul is returned to his body.

Illinois-born Tucker began his career working with Carl Laemmle's Independent Moving Pictures Company. Together the men produced *Traffic in Souls* (1913), a notorious exposé of the white slave trade. (As with most moral "warning" films, *Traffic*, while posing as a call to action, is a voyeuristic exploitation of what it's pretending to condemn.) Tucker eventually emigrated to Britain, where he made pictures for London Film Productions, the studio that later produced such classics as Alexander Korda's *The Private Life of Henry VIII* (1933) and Harold Young's *The Scarlet Pimpernel* (1934). Tucker also met and married London-born actress Elisabeth Risdon, whose second film had been Maurice Elvey's 1913 version of *Maria Marten; or, The Murder in the Red Barn*. When Tucker moved back to the United States to resume work with Universal, he took his bride with him. After her husband's death in 1921, Risdon continued to work in Hollywood, becoming a noted character actor until her retirement in 1956, two years before her death.

Barbara Everest

A decade after the release of *The Man Without a Soul*, actor Rosmer became a director in his own right. His most famous film may be the 1935 version of *Maria Marten, or The Murder in the Red Barn*, which made a star of Tod Slaughter. CW

Mingling Spirits

Nestor/Universal; b/w; 11 min; U.S.
D/P/S: Al Christie
Cast: Lee Moran, Eddie Lyons, Betty Compson, Stella Adams

Born Eleanor Luicime Compson in March 1897 in Beaver, Utah, Betty Compson learned to play the violin at an early age. By her teens she was starring in vaudeville shows, and while on tour she came to the attention of Hollywood producer Al Christie. Christie, who was anchored at Universal, signed Compson to a studio contract with the intention of making her a comedy sensation. Her first role came in late 1914, and she followed it with a string of minor hits, including *Mingling Spirits*, which was shot in late 1915 and copyrighted and released in early 1916. It

dealt with a phony spiritualist whose deceit is revealed by a man posing as the Devil.

Compson's success lasted well into the talkie era. One of her most famous roles was as Mary opposite Erich von Stroheim in the nightmarish *The Great Gabbo* (1929), directed by her first husband, James Cruze (whom she divorced a year later). In 1930 she was nominated for an Academy Award for Best Actress for her work in the melodramatic romance *The Barker*. She made a handful of horror appearances, including a role in the poverty row cheapie *The Invisible Ghost* (1941). She retired from film in 1948 to focus on her own business, Ashtrays Unlimited, until her death from a heart attack in 1974. CW

Mr. Tvardovski
aka Pan Tvardovsky
Skobelev; b/w; length unknown; Russia
D/S/C: Ladislas Starevitch (aka Wladyslaw Starewicz)
Cast: Nicolai Saltykov, Sabina Valovska, Igor Selinsky, Semion Chapelsky

This hard to come by horror film from pre-Revolutionary Russia was directed by leading filmmaker Ladislas Starevitch, who also made a version of Nikolai Gogol's novel *The Vij* the same year. *Mr. Tvardovski* is one of the earliest film adaptations of a then-successful J.I. Kraszevski novel, which in turn draws from a well-known Polish folktale. All concern a young man, hounded by the Devil, who finally sells his soul in exchange for the love of a beautiful woman. The story was popular enough that it became something of a staple of Polish cinema, filmed there at least three times (in 1921, 1936 and 1955), the final version being an animated short.

The idea of Satan tempting people into wrongdoing and stealing their souls is a perennial favorite in literature and cinema, and Russia in the early years of the 20th century was no exception. This motif is on display in the many film adaptations of Alexander Pushkin's *Pikovaya dama*. All of these films bore the implicit message that eternal damnation is the price for violating societal norms.

Like so many of Starevitch's films from the period, it appears that *Mr. Tvardovski* was—at least in part—animated, a type of filmmaking the director was immensely fond of. Some sources cite a probable sequel, made by Starevitch the following year, titled *Mr. Twardosky in Rome*. CW

The Mysteries of Myra
Wharton International; b/w; 15 chapters; U.S.
D/P: Theodore Wharton, Leopold Wharton *S:* Charles W. Goddard
Cast: Jean Sothern, Howard Estabrook, Allen Murname, M.W. Rale, Bessie Wharton, Elsie Baker, Warner Oland

The Grand Master of the Black Order—descended from the Knights Templar—creates a huge, powerful creature known as a "Thought Monster." The monster goes on a rampage but proves easily distracted from its misdeeds.

The titles of several of *Myra*'s installments are unknown, but a list of surviving chapter titles gives an idea of the serial's tone and contents—*Chapter 3: The Mystic Mirrors; Chapter 9: The Invisible Destroyer; Chapter 10: Levitation; Chapter 11: The Fire-Elemental; Chapter 12: The Elixir of Youth; Chapter 13: Witchcraft; Chapter 14: Suspended Animation; Chapter 15: The Thought Monster*. Given that the final chapter is named for the film's oddly described monster figure, it would appear that the opening chapters lead up to its creation, with the mayhem and destruction (at least mostly) saved for the finale. Producer/director team (and brothers) Theodore and Leopold Wharton were prolific purveyors of popular fare in the early silent era, though their careers stalled in the early 1920s. Leopold died in 1927 and Theodore in 1931. Co-star Howard Estabrook proved more successful as a screenwriter than as an actor. Though *Myra* marked his final screen appearance, he went on to co-author such classics as *Cimarron* (1931), for which he netted an Oscar, and *David Copperfield* (1935). *Mysteries of Myra* comes from a novel by Hereward Carrington, who served as a consultant on the picture. He was fascinated by paranormal activity and psychic phenomena and authored a number of books on the subject. Contrary to some ill-informed sources (including several well-known Web sites), famed magician Harry Houdini did not participate in the film. The supporting cast included Warner Oland, later famous for his portrayals of Dr. Fu Manchu and Charlie Chan; he also played the villainous Dr. Yogami in Universal's *Werewolf of London* (1935).

Apart from fragments of three of the chapters, the serial is considered lost. Reliable sources state that there were 31 reels in total, leading one to suspect that either the first or the last episode likely consisted of three reels. TH

Night of Horror
aka **Nächte des Grauens**; **Night of Terror**; **A Night of Horror in the Menagerie**; **Nights of Horror**; **A Night of Horror**; **A Night of Terror**
Lu Synd-Film; b/w; length unknown; Germany
Co-D/S: Richard Oswald Co-D: Arthur Robison P: Lu Synd C: Max Fassbender
Cast: Emil Jannings, Werner Krauss, Laurence Kohler, Hans Mierendorff, Ossi Oswalda, Lupu Pick

This obscure collaboration between Richard Oswald (who went on to direct *Weird Tales* in 1919) and Arthur Robison (who went on to direct *Warning Shadows* in 1923) has been cited as the first vampire film, since it reputedly contains a group of vampiric characters. But even if said creatures were indeed in the film, both *The Devil's Castle* (1896) and *Chinese Magic* (1900) have claims to have broken that particular ground first. Almost no firm conclusions can be drawn about *Night of Horror* in any case, owing to the fact that not only has it apparently disappeared, but virtually no information—not even a plot synopsis—has survived. By sparse account, it was shot in Berlin. Given the interesting group of creative personnel allegedly involved—including such noteworthy actors as Emil Jennings (*Waxworks*, 1924) and Werner Krauss (*The Cabinet of Dr. Caligari*, 1919)—*Night of Horror* remains a title of interest. TH

Only a Room-er
Cricks; b/w; 10 min; Great Britain
D: Toby Cooper S: Ernest Dangerfield
Cast: Jack Jarman, Mrs. Dangerfield

A man (Jarman) finds himself the butt of a tasteless joke after he spends a night in a room rumored to be haunted. This British short offered yet another variation on the "fake haunting" theme. Not much information survives about the film, though its punny title and the presence of comedic-short "names" in the cast and crew indicate that it was humorous in nature. Screenwriter Ernest Dangerfield and co-star Mrs. Dangerfield were married in real life. Their daughter, Winnie Dangerfield, also had a brief career in silent comedies. TH

The Phantom of the Opera
aka **Das Phantom der Oper**
Greenbaum; b/w; 76 min; Germany
D: Ernst Matray S: Greta Schroder P: Julius Greenbaum
Cast: Nils Olaf Chrisander, Aud Egede Nissen

Owners of the Paris Opera House are terrorized by the mysterious "Phantom of the Opera," a presumed ghost who lurks in the cellars. In fact, the specter is flesh and blood—a demented impresario named Erik (Chrissander) who has gone into hiding because of his disfigurement. Erik falls in love with pretty understudy Christine Daae (Nissen), with disastrous consequences.

This seems to have been the first film version of Gaston Leroux's most enduring literary creation, *Le Fantôme de l'Opéra*. The story was an instant success when it first appeared in serial form between November 1909 and January 1910, and it has remained in print ever since. This adaptation remains something of an enigma and has long been considered lost.

Director Ernst Matray worked more often as a choreographer and as an actor, and his directorial output was apparently as sporadic as it was unremarkable. Contemporary sources credit him with a mere five features between 1916 and 1955, though he died in 1978. Swedish actor Nils Olaf Chrisander, who racked up less than two-dozen credits between 1915 and 1921, played the Phantom. Leading lady Aud Egede Nissen was far more prolific, appearing in a number of features and serials (including *Homunculus*, 1916) between 1913 and 1942. But despite the casting of Swedish leads, the film was German in origin; it's unclear whether the film had any kind of international distribution.

The next adaptation of Leroux's book would prove the most iconic: *The Phantom of the Opera* (1925), starring Lon Chaney. TH

The Phantom Witness
Thanhouser; b/w; 33 min; U.S.
D: Frederick Sullivan S: Philip Lonergan P: Edwin Thanhouser
Cast: Kathryn Adams, Edwin Stanley, William P. Burt, Samuel N. Niblack

A beautiful young woman, Lilavan MacLeod (Adams), has inherited a large fortune, and she plans on marrying her fiancé, a district attorney named David Thayer (Stanley) whose reputation is on the rise. But her evil guardian, Jacob Wiener (Burt), knows that he—being her nearest "relative"—will inherit her fortune if she dies, provided it happens before her marriage takes place. When Jacob does bring about her untimely demise and thus inherits everything, David decides to force Jacob to admit his crime. To that end, he uses hypnosis (?) to conjure the dead girl's spirit and force a confession.

To say, as some do, that Kathryn Adams was a silent screen actress who failed to make the transition to talkies isn't quite fair, given that her career as a lead ended in 1925, several years before talkies took hold. All that aside, she was a popular player, particularly during her Thanhouser years (before the company went belly up). Afterward, she meandered for a while before settling down at Vitagraph, but that relationship didn't last long either, and after one final un-credited role in MGM's *The Squaw Man* in 1931, she left the big screen for good.

The Phantom Witness also marked the acting debut of Edwin Stanley, who went on to a lengthy career in Hollywood. He died in 1944 after starring in about 250 films.

This film was released on January 19, 1916. CW

The Picture of Dorian Gray
Barker/Neptune/Browne; b/w; 60 min; Great Britain
D: Fred W. Durant S: Rowland Talbot
Cast: Henry Victor, Pat O'Malley, Jack Jordon, Sydney Bland, A.B. Imeson, Douglas Cox

This is the first British adaptation of Oscar Wilde's infamous 1890 novel *The Picture of Dorian Gray*. Previous versions had been filmed in Denmark, the United States and Russia. Perhaps Great Britain's delay in creating its own version stemmed from the fact that the book none-too-subtly brushed against the taboo subject of homosexuality, for which the country had prosecuted its author. The case had drawn international attention, condemnation … and fascination. It concerned Wilde's homosexual relationship with Lord Alfred Douglas that, when discovered by Douglas' father the Marquis of Queensberry, resulted in harassment of the two men. In response Wilde filed a charge of libel, only to be disgraced by not only losing the suit but also being sentenced

This second Russian version of *The Queen of Spades* concerns a card game, an officer of the Horse Guards and a Countess with the secret of always winning at cards.

to two years in a hard labor camp for "gross indecency." Three years after his release, he died, penniless and depressed, of cerebral meningitis. His last words were said to have been, "Either that wallpaper goes, or I do."

The well-known facts surrounding his "crime" and imprisonment did not hamper the worldwide success of his work, and filmmakers began exploiting its big-screen potential early on. The first film adaptation of *Dorian Gray* was made in 1910, a mere 20 years after the novel's original publication. It was quickly followed by at least three more versions, then by Britain's sole silent-era entry.

The film's eponymous hero is a libertine who remains young while his portrait's image grows older and more decomposed with each sin he commits. Henry Victor starred as Dorian, while Pat O'Malley portrayed Dorian's lover, Sybil Vane. Jack Jordan played the corrupt but influential Lord Henry Wotton, and Sydney Bland was cast as artist Basil Hallward. Douglas Cox portrayed Sybil's brother James. The film reportedly contained the interesting twist of presenting Satan (A.B. Imeson) as Dorian's master, to whom Dorian sells his soul in exchange for youth.

The next cinematic version of the tale to come out of Great Britain was *Dorian Gray* (2009). CW

The Queen of Spades
aka **Pikovaya dama**
PFA; b/w; 63 min; Russia
D: Yakov Protazanov *S:* F. Otsep *P:* Joseph N. Ermolieff *C:* Yevgini Slavkinsky
Cast: Tamara Duvan, Ivan Mozzhukhin, Vera Orlova, Nikolai Panov, Polikarp Pavlov, Yelizaveta Shebueva

This is the second film adaptation of Alexander Pushkin's classic short story *Pikovaya dama* (1833) to come out of Russia in the second decade of the 20th century. While watching a game of cards at the house of Narumov, an officer of the Horse Guards, German (Mozzhukhin), confesses his interest but refuses to play for fear that he will lose all his earnings. Narumov proposes a toast to his grandmother, whose birthday it is, and proceeds to tell how, in her youth, she was an expert card player. The film then flashes back 60 years, when the young Countess (Duvan) was the talk of Paris. She was in desperate financial straits and asked her husband (Pavlov) to pay her debts. He balked at the amount, sending her into the arms of the notorious alchemist the Count Saint-Germain (Panov), who taught her a way to win at cards and never be in debt again. That same night, the Countess played cards at Versailles, won an appreciable sum, and settled her debts.

German becomes obsessed with the story, certain that he can charm the now-aged Countess (Shebueva) into telling him her secret at winning cards. After observing the Countess' young ward Liza (Orlova) in the old woman's window, he decides to romance the maiden. He writes Liza daily, and she at length agrees to meet him. While the Countess is away, German sneaks into the house, but instead of meeting Liza, he hides in the Countess' room to await her return. When the old woman gets home, German confronts her about her secret; unfortunately, she dies from fright. Later that night, the Countess' ghost visits German, who tells him that the secret is to play the three, the seven and the ace in succession. Armed with that knowledge, German visits a wealthy society of gamblers in Moscow. After showing proof of his value, he plays as told by the old woman's ghost, to unexpected results.

Paul Fejos filmed the next version of Pushkin's tale in Hungary in 1922. But this one, from director Yakov Protazanov, remains one of the most faithful adaptations ever filmed and is easily the most interesting version of the silent era. CW

The Real Thing at Last
British Actors; b/w; 30 min; Great Britain
Co-D/S: James M. Barrie, L.C. MacBean *P:* A.E. Matthews
Cast: Ernest Thesiger, Gladys Cooper, Godfrey Tearle, Owen Nares, A.E. Matthews, Nelson Keys

This low-budget British comedy is a satirical take on the American film industry. It updates Shakespeare's *Macbeth* to just after the end of the Edwardian Era, leaving intact much of the play's focus on witches, ghosts and murder. Created to raise funds for the YMCA, *Real Thing* had its debut before the British Royal Family, hosted live by fictional American film producer Robert K. Thunder (played by Edmund Gwenn). It had a European theatrical run afterward and was released to U.S. theaters in April 1922.

What makes the film of interest to film buffs is not so much its satiric approach to Shakespeare's most overtly horrific play, which has been filmed as a straight horror film many times (including by Orson Welles in 1948 and Roman Polanski in 1971); rather, it's the people involved in its production, which include Peter Pan creator James M. Barrie (1860-1937) as writer and co-director. Scottish author Barrie was a gifted playwright and novelist who became interested in the film industry after the first cinematic production based on one of his stories was released in 1913. His first actual screenplay, based on his play *The Little Minister* (1891), was filmed and released in 1915. (And since his death in 1937 from pneumonia, well over 50 film and television productions have been based on his work.) *The Real Thing at Last* appears to have been the only horror-oriented film work in which he was involved as a writer.

Among the film's cast was a (relatively) young Ernest Thesiger as a witch, long before he made film history by starring in James Whale's classic *Bride of Frankenstein* in 1935. CW

The Romantic Journey
Astra; b/w; 50 min; U.S.
D: George Fitzmaurice *S:* Ouida Bergere *C:* Arthur C. Miller, Harold Louis Miller
Cast: William Courtenay, Macey Harlam, Alice Dovey, Norman Thorpe

East Indian mystic Ratoor (Harlam) hypnotizes Cynthia (Dovey) in a plot to get her to marry the millionaire Broadhurst (Thorpe) and provide Ratoor with access to the man's fortune. Peter (Courtenay) suspects that something is amiss with Cynthia, but he's unable to prove anything. The wedding takes place, after which Ratoor kills Broadhurst and orders Cynthia to sign over the fortune to him. But when the evil mystic attempts to bury the millionairess alive, Peter arrives in the nick of time to save the day.

The Romantic Journey is a far-fetched romantic melodrama with elements of the macabre. Ouida Bergere, who married screen star Basil Rathbone in 1926, wrote the screenplay. Bergere's extravagances (she was notorious for her lavish parties) obliged her husband to work well past the age at which he'd have preferred to retire. Even so, theirs was a happy union, and they remained inseparable until Rathbone's death from a heart attack in 1967. *The Romantic Journey* seems a representative example of her work as a silent-era screenwriter.

The film was directed by George Fitzmaurice, an American of French descent who remained prolific until his death in 1940. The cast included then-popular leading man William Courtenay, a stage veteran who made a successful transition to pictures. He died in 1933 from complications arising from a severe cold. TH

Saint, Devil and Woman
Thanhouser; b/w; 60 min; U.S.
D: Frederick Sullivan *S:* Philip Lonergan *P:* Edwin Thanhouser
Cast: Florence La Badie, Wayne Arey, Hector Dion, Claus Bogel, Ethyle Cooke, Ernest Howard

When her uncle dies, Florence Stanton (La Badie) is set to inherit his fortune. Alvarez (Dion), the executor of the estate, makes a show of caring for Florence, a naïve young thing who's spent the better part of her life in a convent. The executor's true nature becomes clear, however, when he hypnotizes Florence and forces her to do his bidding. Her demeanor changes from saintly to demonic, and Dr. Gregory Deane (Arey), a young psychiatrist, is called in to investigate. Deane uncovers Alvarez's dastardly plan and pits his will against that of the evil mesmerist.

Right wins over wrong, Deane defeats Alvarez, and the psychiatrist ends up with the pretty and financially well-off Florence.

Saint, Devil and Woman is a typically overwrought slice of silent-era melodrama. Leading lady Florence La Badie was born in 1888 and made her screen debut in 1909, quickly becoming a major star (though one typecast as militantly virtuous) until her death in a road accident in 1917. Her other genre films include *Dr. Jekyll and Mr. Hyde* (1912) and *The Woman in White* (1917).

On the whole, the film seems to have followed the usual La Badie template. That is, a heroine of an impossibly pure-hearted sort is set upon by a parade of mustache-twirling baddies before finding true love in the arms of a strapping hero. The twist here, such as it is, is the hypnotism, a nod toward such literary models as Du Maurier's *Trilby* and Stoker's *Dracula*. TH

Seven Keys to Baldpate
William; b/w; length unknown; Australia
D: Monte Luke *S:* Alex C. Butler *P:* J.C. William
Cast: Dorothy Brunton, J. Plumpton Wilson, Agnes Keogh, Alex C. Butler, Gerald Harcourt

A writer (Wilson) makes a bet that he can write a mystery thriller in a single night. The needed atmosphere is given to him when he's provided access to the deserted Baldpate Inn. His writing is repeatedly interrupted, however, by a succession of weird visitors and even weirder goings-on.

Earl Derr Biggers (1884-1933) is best remembered for his Charlie Chan novels, but his prolific output included a thriller titled *Seven Keys to Baldpate* (1913). The twist-laden story was a hit with the public, and it was quickly adapted into a hit play by George M. Cohan. The production ran for 320 performances and ultimately inspired no less than a half dozen straightforward film adaptations, along with a couple of re-christened, slightly altered takes on the material. This obscure Australian production was the first filmic crack at the story, though little information about it has survived.

Screenwriter Alex C. Butler did double duty on the picture, also filling one of the supporting roles. Contemporary filmographies for the remainder of the cast yield little in the way of concrete data; it *is* an interesting coincidence that the hero of Hammer's *The Kiss of the Vampire* (1962) is named Gerald Harcourt, the same name as an actor featured here.

Seven Keys was one of the earliest Australian contributions to the horror genre (sandwiched between *It Is Never Too Late to Mend*, 1911, and *The Face at the Window*, 1920). It was another half century before the "land down under" embraced fright films with any degree of enthusiasm with such popular titles as *Patrick* (1978) and *Thirst* (1979).

Biggers' story got its next (and far from last) screen incarnation in 1917 under the same title. TH

She

Barker; b/w; 60 min; Great Britain
Co-D/P: William G.B. Barker *Co-D:* Horace Lisle Lucoque *S:* Nellie E. Lucoque
Cast: Alice Delysia, Henry Victor, Sydney Bland, Blanche Forsythe, Jack Denton, J. Hastings Batson

H. Rider Haggard's best-selling novel *She: A History of Adventure* has been the basis for numerous film adaptations, most of them made during the silent era. The most famous adaptations remain RKO's 1935 version starring Randolph Scott and Hammer's 1964 version starring Ursula Andress. This lost 1916 version was the first to be made in Great Britain, which is a surprise given that author Haggard was British and his novel a major success in the country (as it was elsewhere). It followed the novel fairly closely, with all the major characters making an appearance. French actress Alice Delysia of Moulin Rouge fame took on the role of Ayesha, otherwise known as She-Who-Must-Be-Obeyed, while Henry Victor played Leo Vincey, the reincarnation of her lost lover, Kallikrates. Sydney Bland played Vincey's guardian and confidant, Horace Holly, while Blanche Forsythe starred as the unfortunate Ustane, with whom Vincey falls in love, thus invoking the wrath of She. Jack Denton played Job, while J. Hastings Batson essayed the part of Bilali, Ayesha's high priest.

The production designer on the film was Lancelot Speed, who doubled as an illustrator for Haggard. Haggard claimed to have seen the film; in a journal entry he called the adaptation "fair … though somewhat distressing to an author." CW

The Shielding Shadow
aka **Ravengar**

Pathé/Astra Film; b/w; 15 chapters; U.S.
D: Louis Gasnier, Donald MacKenzie *S:* George B. Seitz
Cast: Grace Darmond, Ralph Kellard, Leon Barry, Madlaine Traverse, Lionel Braham, Frankie Mann

Leontine (Darmond) faces constant danger but is ever protected by a mysterious figure with burning eyes. *The Shielding Shadow*'s emphasis seems to have been on action rather than the macabre, but it's difficult to ascertain how strongly its hypnotism and invisibility angles were developed. The chapter titles were: *Chapter 1: The Treasure Trove*; *Chapter 2: Into the Depths*; *Chapter 3: The Mystic Defender*; *Chapter 4: The Earthquake*; *Chapter 5: Through Bolted Doors*; *Chapter 6: The Disappearing Prisoner*; *Chapter 7: The Awakening*; *Chapter 8: The Haunting Hand*; *Chapter 9: The Incorrigible Captive*; *Chapter 10: The Disappearing Mantle*; *Chapter 11: The Great Sacrifice*; *Chapter 12: The Stolen Shadow*; *Chapter 13: The Hidden Menace*; *Chapter 14: Absolute Black*; *Chapter 15: Who Is the Shielding Shadow?* At least one complete print of the serial exists.

Hypnotism and the use of invisibility pellets factor into this horror-tinged Astar/Pathé co-production. Frenchman Louis Gasnier also directed the famed serial *The Perils of Pauline* (1914), starring Pearl White, though he is today best known for the camp classic *Reefer Madness* (1936), which deals with the "horrors" of marijuana. Donald MacKenzie, a Scottish-born director who also helped out on the aforementioned *Perils*, assisted him on *Shadow*. It should be noted that MacKenzie acted in a couple dozen films, including an un-credited bit part in *The Mysterious Dr. Fu Manchu* (1929).

Leading lady Grace Darmond, a popular silent-screen starlet, acted in the first Technicolor feature, *The Gulf Between* (1917). A confirmed—though twice-married and twice-divorced—lesbian, Darmond met long-time lover Jean Acker in 1918. Acker married Rudolph Valentino in 1919, allegedly running from the matinee idol on their wedding night and finding solace in Darmond's arms, where she remained throughout most of the 1920s. When Valentino married another woman in 1921, Acker brought charges of bigamy against him. Darmond's career died with the coming of sound, though she lived until 1963. TH

The Silent Stranger
aka **The Silent Man**

Universal; b/w; 11 min; U.S.
D: King Baggot *S:* Frank Smith
Cast: King Baggot, Irene Hunt, Frank Smith

A mysterious man (Baggot) moves into town and at first refuses to talk to anyone. When he finally speaks, he relates that he was once a prosperous New England lawyer engaged to a beautiful dance hall girl (Hunt). The girl died on the eve of their wedding, and the lawyer cursed God, calling upon the Devil for assistance. The Devil promised to return the girl to life, with the stipulation that if the lawyer ever again laughed or smiled, she would again die. The lawyer accepted the offer, but then smiled upon seeing his love again. After concluding his tale, the mysterious man declares that Satan has come for him, then falls over dead.

King Baggot was one of Universal's biggest stars at the time. Among the most famous of his 300 films were *Dr. Jekyll and Mr. Hyde* (1913) and *The Corsican Brothers* (1915). *The Silent Stranger*'s screenwriter, Frank Smith, played a doctor in the film. CW

Sold to Satan
Lubin; b/w; 33 min; U.S.
D: Edward Sloman *S:* R.P. Rifenborich, Jr. *P:* Siegmund Lubin
Cast: Edward Sloman, Leon C. Shumway, Adelaide Bronti, May Cruze, Allan Forrest, Ben Hopkins

Sold to Satan was made at Lubin's studios in Coronado, California. The film concerns a man (Shumway) who makes a deal with the Devil (Sloman), exchanging his soul for both wealth and eternal youth.

This wasn't the first time Sloman had taken on Mephistophelean themes; his first film as a director had been *Faust* the year before, and there too he played the part of Satan the Devil. Born in London in 1884, he worked in British theater before moving to the United States. He became first an actor for Universal and then a film director for Lubin. After the success of the independently produced *The Westerners* in 1919, he returned to Universal, this time as a director. With the coming of the sound, he was relegated mostly to B-pictures and for a time was successful. Finding film work harder to come by as the 1930s wore on, he retired from cinema in 1938 and went to work in the burgeoning radio market. He died in 1972 in Woodland Hills, California.

Sold to Satan was released in February 1916. Sloman's next horror film didn't come until the sound era, when he directed the classic *Murder by the Clock* (1931) for Paramount. CW

The Soul's Cycle
Centaur/Mutual; b/w; 55 min; U.S.
D: Ulysses Davis *S:* Theodosia Harris *P:* David Horsley
Cast: Margaret Gibson, John Oaker, Roy Watson, George Claire Jr., George Stanley

In Ancient Greece a powerful senator named Theron (Stanley) is to wed the beautiful young Nadia (Gibson), but she flees him to marry her true love, Lucian (Oaker). Angered, Theron captures the couple and has them thrown into an active volcano. Viewing the event from above, the gods take the side of the murdered lovers and condemn Theron to roam eternity in the form of a lion, with one possible means of escape: His soul can be freed if he makes amends for his crimes. Centuries later Nadia is reincarnated as Agnes (Gibson, again), and Lucian is likewise back as Arthur (Oaker, again). Arthur is a Wall Street broker who, as it happens, is also a big game hunter. While on a recent safari, he has fortuitously captured the very lion that contains Theron's imprisoned soul. And while Agnes and Arthur indeed love each other, another broker, Henry Kimball (Watson), stands between them. Fixated on Agnes, he frees the lion that Arthur has captured in the hope that it will attack and kill Arthur. Instead, the lion turns upon and kills Kimball, removing the obstacle that's keeping the spirits of Agnes and Lucian apart. They again hook up, and Theron's spirit, having set things right, is freed from its potentially eternal damnation.

While hardly remarkable, *The Soul's Cycle* is of interest in that it prefigures Universal's 1932 classic *The Mummy* in its theme of reincarnated love traversing the centuries. (Interestingly enough, in its own pre-release incarnation, *The Mummy* contained scenes showing its heroine's spirit transmigrating through the ages.)

Cycle was released on February 12, 1916. CW

Trilby Frilled
aka **Frilby Frilled**
Lubin; b/w; 10 min; U.S.
D/S: Edwin McKim *P:* Siegmund Lubin
Cast: Davy Don, Patsy De Forest, George Egan, Charles Ebbinger, Bernard Siegel

Film adaptations of George Du Maurier's 1894 novel *Trilby* were wildly popular during the silent era, so it should come as no surprise that by 1916 the story was being spoofed. This particular version was designed to take advantage of the popularity of Maurice Tourneur's 1915 film adaptation starring Wilton Lackaye and Clara Trimball Young. Here, Davy (David) Don stars as Svengalic, an evil mesmerist who turns Patsy De Forrest (De Forest) into a singer. Slapstick hilarity ensues.

De Forest was known for playing herself (though with an additional "r" in her last name) in a series of Lubin comedies from the period, and *Trilby Frilled* was no exception. Her career had begun in earnest in 1914 when she starred in multiple films as the eponymous Patsy Bolivar. Her last role came in Fox's 1920 Western *Sunset Sprague*, which also featured future Universal horror bit player Noble Johnson as a Native American named Crow. Davy Don received his moment of fame by playing a character named Otto in a series of movies that posited him in various workplace roles, including gardener, cobbler, reporter, sleuth and salesman. His career lasted only from 1916 to 1919, though he lived until 1949. The Otto films were also written and directed by *Trilby Frilled* director Edward McKim, who may be most famous for being the father of 1930s and '40s starlet Ann Dvorak.

Some sources list *Trilby Frilled* and *Frilby Frilled* as two separate films, though in fact they are one and the same. CW

Ultus and the Grey Lady
aka **Ultus 3: The Grey Lady**; **Ultus 4: The Traitor's Fate**
Gaumont/Victory; b/w; 50 min; Great Britain
D/S: George Pearson *P:* Leon Gaumont
Cast: Aurele Sydney, Mary Dibley, Jack Leigh, Frank Dane, M. Gouget

The success of *Ultus, The Man from the Dead* (1916) prompted three follow-ups, of which this is the first. (It can be deduced from the alternate titles that *Grey Lady* was distributed as two separate features in some countries.) The Ultus series was made in response to the popularity of Louis Feuillade's *Fantomas* serials; today, each of the four Pearson films is at least partially, if not entirely, lost.

The title of this second film evokes the early Sherlock Holmes thriller *The Grey Lady* (1909)—a disguised version of *The Hound of the Baskervilles*—but whether there's any connection is difficult to ascertain. Such a link is at least plausible, as writer/director George Pearson was certainly no stranger to the character of Holmes; he had, after all, filmed a version of *A Study in Scarlet* in 1914.

Ultus returned the same year in *Ultus and the Secret of the Night*. The series wound down the following year with *Ultus and the Three-Button Mystery* (1917). TH

Ultus and the Secret of the Night
aka **Ultus 5: The Secret of the Night**; **The Secret of the Night**; **Secret de la Nuit**
Gaumont; b/w; length unknown; Great Britain
D/S: George Pearson
Cast: Aurele Sydney, J.L.V. Leigh, Mary Dibney, Lionel D'Aragnon, Mary Forbes

Aurele Sydney—also known as Aurelio Sydney—returns as Ultus in this third installment of the franchise. Like other Ultus films, *Secret of the Night* is difficult to find today. Its plot concerns Ultus—who by now has evolved into a superhero of sorts—rescuing a child from an evil couple, Sir Miles and Lady Fleet.

Writer/director George Pearson earned some critical praise for the *Ultus* series, while star Sydney maintained an impressive film career in Italy, France and England until his death from smallpox in 1920. He also directed a handful of films in Italy, though it's not clear whether he was Italian by birth (as the alternate spelling of his first name seems to imply). TH

Ultus, the Man from the Dead
aka **Ultus 1: The Townsend Mystery**; **Ultus 2: The Ambassador's Diamond**
Gaumont; b/w; 69 min; Great Britain
D/S: George Pearson *P:* Leon Gaumont
Cast: Aurele Sydney, J.L.V. Leigh, A. Caton Woodville, Marjorie Dunbar, M. Goujet

Ultus (Sydney) is robbed and left for dead in the Australian desert by a business partner. Several years later he returns to exact vengeance on the man who has used his ill-gotten gains to buy himself the honorific "Baronet."

Great Britain's answer to the fictional French sociopath Fantômas (who had by 1916 starred in at least five serials), the Ultus franchise was the brainchild of George Pearson, a significant figure in early British cinema though his career went downhill with the coming of sound. (He later directed the interminably creaky *Midnight at Madame Tussaud's*, 1936.)

This first Ultus adventure (which, to judge from its known alternate titles, was probably divided into two parts for distribution outside Britain) was successful enough at the box-office to prompt three follow-ups. Reviews at the time praised *Man from the Dead*'s energetic staging. Today only a few fragments are known to survive, preserved by the British Film Institute and an archive in France.

The name Ultus, incidentally, is Latin for "avenger." TH

The Vij
aka **Wij**
Khanzhonkov; b/w; 82 min; Russia
D/S/C: Ladislas Starevitch (aka Wladyslaw Starewicz)
Cast: Ivan Mosjoukine, Olga Obolenskaya, V. Turzhansky

This second adaptation of Nikolai Gogol's short story (first filmed in 1909 as *Viy*) is an early example of stop-motion animation. The film has long been considered lost and very little material survives in reference to it, but given its length and use of animation, chances are it offered a more literal adaptation of the story than the 1909 short subject.

Director Ladislas Starevitch began his career in 1910, focusing at first on fantasy subjects but eventually moving into the realm of animation. He was indisputably a stop-motion pioneer—indeed, he actually beat his more famous American competitor Walt Disney to the punch by several years (though French director Georges Méliès and some of his American contemporaries had used a rudimentary form of stop-motion over a decade before this). Starevitch was something of a one-man show in the burgeoning Russian film industry, painstakingly animating his own films—and sometimes blending live-action footage into the mix in a way that anticipated the work of Willis O'Brien, Ray Harryhausen, Jim Danforth and others. This seems to have been the case with *The Vij*, which almost certainly employed animation for its climactic revelation of a horrific, heavy-lidded, metallic-faced monster. The director/writer/experimenter eventually relocated to France, where he continued to work with animation, though Disney and O'Brien eclipsed his reputation. He made his last film in 1958 and died in 1965.

Gogol's story would next be filmed in Italy as *Black Sunday* (1960) by cinematographer-turned-director Mario Bava. TH

The Wheel of Death
Davidson; b/w; 33 min; Great Britain
D: A.E. Coleby
Cast: Arthur Rooke, Joan Legge, Frank Robert Cheroka, Charles Vane, Peggy Richards

A dastardly villain (the worst kind) matches wits with a detective and winds up tormenting him in a mad scientist's torture chamber. This British thriller's title refers to an implement of torture, doubtless located in the aforementioned torture chamber. Director A.E. Coleby seems to have specialized in cliffhanger fare such as this; he was also responsible for a series of Sax Rohmer adaptations starring H. Agar Lyons as Dr. Fu Manchu. TH

The Witch of the Mountains
Knickerbocker; b/w; 35 min; U.S.
Crew Unknown
Cast: Marguerite Nichols, Gordon Sackville, Richard Johnson, Frank Erlanger, Bert Francis, Corinne Grant

This minor short film concerns a witch who resides in a cave in the mountains. Short-lived production company Knickerbocker Star Features, which had released its first film the previous year and its final feature the same year as *The Witch of the Mountains*, produced. These films were fairly obscure even in their day, and little is known about most of them. The crew of *Witch* is long forgotten; none of its cast did anything of much cinematic importance.

The Witch of the Mountains was released on March 24 and quickly forgotten. CW

Witchcraft
Feature Player; b/w; 50 min; U.S.
D: Frank Reicher *S:* Margaret Turnbull *P:* Jesse L. Lasky *C:* Dent Gilbert
Cast: Fannie Ward, Jack Dean, Paul Weigel, Lillian Leighton

A New England community is consumed by bigotry, and anybody who fails to conform to its standards of so-called normalcy is labeled a witch and heretic. When Suzette (Ward) turns to an Indian (Leighton) in the hope of saving her infirm mother, the miserly Struble (Weigel) uses the paranoia of the townsfolk to his advantage. He accuses the mother of practicing witchcraft and threatens to "expose" her unless Suzette marries him. Suzette reluctantly complies, but the old woman then dies and Struble becomes increasingly sadistic. In her grief and anger, Suzette wishes her husband dead, and when he is nearly killed during an Indian

1917

uprising, he accuses Suzette of orchestrating the attack via witchcraft. A trial follows, but Richard (Dean), her frustrated suitor, prevents her execution.

Based on a story by Robert Ralston Reed, *Witchcraft* explores the religious fervor and intolerance behind the infamous New England witch-hunts of the late 1600s. Director Frank Reicher was born in Munich, Germany in 1875. He moved to the United States in 1899 to pursue acting on the stage and made his motion picture acting and directing debuts in 1915. Though he gave up directing pictures in 1931, he continued to act until 1951's *Superman and the Mole-Men*.

This 1916 *Witchcraft* has no connection to the British-made *Witchcraft* (1964), which was directed by Don Sharp and featured Lon Chaney, Jr., in one of his last respectable outings. TH

The Witching Hour

Frohman Amusement; b/w; length unknown; U.S.
D: George Irving *S:* Anthony P. Kelly *P:* William Sherrill *C:* William A. Reinhart
Cast: C. Aubrey Smith, Marie Shotwell, Robert Conness, Jack Sherrill, Freeman Barnes, Lewis Sealy

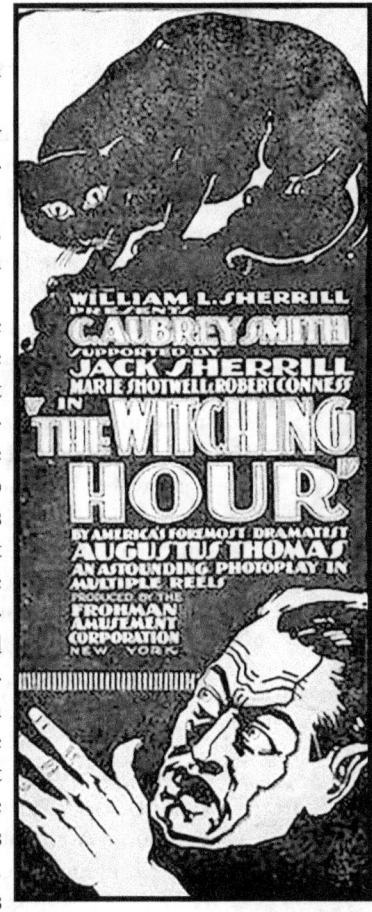

Though Frohman wanted stage actor John Mason to reprise his role as Jack Brookfield for this, the first film adaptation of Augustus Thomas' 1907 play *The Witching Hour*, the part went to C. Aubrey Smith, who afterward had a long and prosperous career in Hollywood. Born in Great Britain in 1863, Smith achieved fame as an athlete in both his native country and South Africa before he turned to stage performance. After conquering Broadway, he set his sights on Hollywood. Eventually he became one of Hollywood's most prominent character actors, usually playing "the crusty old Britainer." *Hour* contains one of his earliest film performances. He died of pneumonia in 1948, his last film, *Little Women*, released posthumously in 1949.

The decidedly unfaithful plot of this particular adaptation of the play concerns gambler Jack Brookfield (Smith) using his psychic abilities for personal gain. After his niece's boyfriend, Clay Whipple (Sherrill), kills a man (Barnes) who taunts him with a cat's eye pin (it is explained that the Whipple family has a fear of cat's eyes after a curse has been placed on them), it's up to Jack to prove that suggestive hypnosis has transferred another person's will to Clay, and that the will to kill was triggered when he saw the cat's eye pin. During Clay's trial, Jack's powers cause the real person behind the killing to confess.

Though director George Irving made many films in his career, he's more famous for his acting roles. He starred in approximately 250 films, including such classics as *Bringing Up Baby* (1938) and *Knute Rockne All American* (1940), as well as in such genre fare as *Charlie Chan in Egypt* and *Dante's Inferno* (both 1935) and *Son of Dracula* (1943). CW

Black Orchids
aka The Fatal Orchid

Universal; b/w; 55 min; U.S.
D/S: Rex Ingram *C:* Duke Hayward
Cast: Cleo Madison, Dick La Reno, Francis McDonald, Wedgwood Nowell, Howard Crampton, Jean Hersholt

Author Emile De Severac (La Reno) is worried that his daughter Marie (Madison) is becoming a tease. In order to "cure" her of her wanton ways, he tells her a horrific tale that illustrates what wanton sexuality can lead to.

Based on a scenario by leading lady Cleo Madison, *Black Orchids* is writer/director Rex Ingram's early flirtation with the horror genre. The Dublin-born Ingram went on to helm the memorable Expressionist horror film *The Magician* (1927), which in turn inspired James Whale's *Frankenstein* (1931). He was responsible for a number of colorful films throughout the silent era, though his career petered out with the coming of sound. His biggest hits include *The Four Horsemen of the Apocalypse* (1921) and *The Prisoner of Zenda* (1922); his larger than life style was particularly well suited to those spectacular tales of derring-do. These days he's perhaps best remembered as the mentor of Michael Powell, one of the most significant figures in the history of British cinema. Powell often credited Ingram with teaching him everything he knew, and he never forgot his debt to the older man.

Black Orchids is a particularly preachy and sordid tale of sexuality gone awry, and the delirious finale—in which the story-within-the-story reaches a Poe-like apotheosis—raised a few eyebrows in its day. As for Cleo Madison, she rose up the ranks of the film industry after this, moving from bit parts to more substantial roles, becoming one of the earliest female directors in the American film industry (though her work is long forgotten). A workaholic, she drove herself to a nervous breakdown in 1922 but recovered well enough to appear in another handful of films; she disappeared from the film scene altogether in 1924 and passed away in 1964.

Among *Black Orchids*' supporting cast is Jean Hersholt in one of his earliest U.S. films; the Danish-born actor later appeared in two MGM horror titles: *The Mask of Fu Manchu* (1932) and *Mark of the Vampire* (1935).

Ingram remade *Orchids* as the decidedly more romantic *Trifling Women* in 1922. TH

The Bottle Imp
aka The Mountain Devil

Famous Players-Lasky/Paramount; b/w; 50 min; U.S.
D: Marshall Neilan *S:* Charles Maigne *P:* Jesse Lasky *C:* Walter Stradling
Cast: Sessue Hayakawa, Lehua Waipahu, H. Komshi, George Kuwa, Guy Oliver, James Neill

This second version of writer Robert Louis Stevenson's *The Bottle Imp* (1891) is closer to the original story than Edison's *The Imp of the Bottle* (1909) had been. Whereas Edison's film changed the ethnicity of the hero and heroine, Lasky's film retains the story's Hawaiian locale and native characters (though the names are inexplicably changed). It begins with Robert Louis Stevenson (Neill) reading his story to two children. Fade to the tale itself, which goes

encounters a dying priest (Neill again) who possesses a magic bottle containing the spirit of the volcano god Kono. Though Kono grants wishes to the bottle's possessor, he also metes out damnation should the owner die before selling the bottle for less than its purchase price. Lopaka is fine with all this; he buys the bottle, and the impish god within makes him rich. But after Lopaka sells the magic container, he contracts leprosy, which prompts him to rebuy the bottle and wish his condition away. His ploy works, but now he's stuck with a bottle that's as cheap as it can get. Kokua, who by this time is his wife, attempts to take the bottle off his hands (thus transferring the damnation onto herself) but a depraved sailor already bound for Hell buys it first. Sailor and bottle are lost at sea, and Lopaka's wealth disappears. But at least he and his wife are safe from everlasting hellfire.

Marshall Neilan was a popular director during the silent era. His decision to cast *The Bottle Imp* with Asian actors and to shoot the film entirely on location in Hawaii (according to the studio's press release) was a smart one, lending the film an authenticity rare in cinema of the time. And while his career path got a bit tentative with the coming of sound, he did (after contributing the story for Howard Hughes' *Hell's Angels*, 1930, and directing several low-budget indies) direct the not-uninteresting *Chloe, Love Is Calling You* (1934), which dealt with a voodoo priestess' revenge on the white plantation owner she believes is responsible for her husband's death. Neilan sensibly cast that movie with African American actors, and it played mostly in black cinemas in the Deep South and in various big cities.

The next adaptation of *The Bottle Imp* was made in Germany as *Life, Death and the Devil* in 1934; the directors of that version also produced a French version, *Le Diable en bouteille*, the same year. CW

Brand of Satan
Peerless/World; b/w; 55 min; U.S.
D: George Archianbaud C: Philip Hatkin
Cast: Montagu Love, Gerda Holmes, Evelyn Greeley, Al Hart, Nat C. Gross, J. Herbert Frank

This silent film is an interesting take on the theme of split personality. The villainous Manuel Le Grange (Hart) rapes Christine (Holmes). The resultant child, Jacques Cordet, grows up to be a successful district attorney (Love). Owing to his half-criminal parentage, however, he is also a violent strangler who runs the Parisian criminal underground. The D.A. and the criminal, each unaware of the other's existence, become involved in a bizarre cat-and-mouse game. Livening things up even more, the D.A. falls in love with Natalia (Greeley), while the criminal falls for a notorious moll named Marie (Johnston). When the D.A. pulls out all the stops to catch the criminal, Marie saves both and then she dies. The truth is revealed about the dual nature of Cordet's personality, whereupon he is cured by Natalie's father Dr. Despard, (Frank), who was once Christine's lover.

something like this: A poor Hawaiian fisherman named Lopaka (Hayakawa)—Keawe in Stevenson's story—falls in love with the beautiful Kokua (Waipahu), but before he can marry her, her father demands two cloaks made from the feathers of a rare bird. Lopaka goes off to the mountains in search of the bird and there

The Son of the Shiek and *Don Juan* (both 1926), *King of Kings* and *Jesse James* (both 1927), *Vanity Fair* (1932), *The Prince and the Pauper* (1937), *The Adventures of Robin Hood* (1938) and *The Man in the Iron Mask* (1939). His horror film appearances include *The Suicide Club* (1914), *Rasputin, the Black Monk* (1917), *The Haunted House* (1928), *The Last Warning* (1929), *The Cat Creeps* (1930) and *Menace* (1932). He died in Beverly Hills, California on May 17, 1943.

Brand of Satan was based on a story by J. F. Looney and was released on July 9, 1917. CW

The Darling of Paris
Fox; b/w; 66 min; U.S.
D: J. Gordon Edwards *S:* Adrian Jackson *C:* Phil Rosen
Cast: Theda Bara, Glen White, Walter Law, Herbert Heyes, Miss Carey Lee, Alice Gale

Embittered scientist Claude Frallo (Law) stalks the beautiful Esmeralda (Bara), who was raised a Gypsy. When Frallo sends his servant Quasimodo (White) to kidnap her, Captain Phoebus (Heyes) rescues her. Phoebus and Esmeralda are smitten with each other, but when they make a rendezvous, Frallo attacks them and kills Phoebus. The Gypsy girl is blamed, placed on trial and tortured into confessing. But luckily Quasimodo, who saw the whole thing, testifies on her behalf and saves her.

No known copies exist of this early adaptation of *The Hunchback of Notre Dame*. A modestly budgeted entry from the recently formed Fox Film Corporation, *The Darling of Paris* ran into trouble with critics for a number of reasons. *Variety* took particular issue with the casting; in a review dated January 26, 1917, the magazine stated:

> Its main weakness is the casting of Theda Bara in the role of an innocent Gypsy girl, with no opportunity to wear modern alluring costumes or give her any opportunity to "vamp." The first portion of the photoplay is merely a series of "high spots" from the famous novel, but culminates in the trial of Esmeralda for

Theda Bara plays Esmeralda, who was raised a Gypsy, from *The Darling of Paris*; Bottom right: A cast list from *The Darling of Paris*

Born in England in 1880, Montagu Love worked as a newspaper cartoonist during the Boer War. His heart was not in his work, however, and he traded in his artist utensils to pursue an acting career. He toured with a U.S. theater troupe before finding work on Broadway, and from there he transitioned to the movies, signing his first contract with World Studios in New Jersey. He perfected a style of screen villainy during the early cinematic years that became an influence on major movie villains for years to come, and by the advent of the talkies he was a popular character actor. Among his most notable screen appearances are

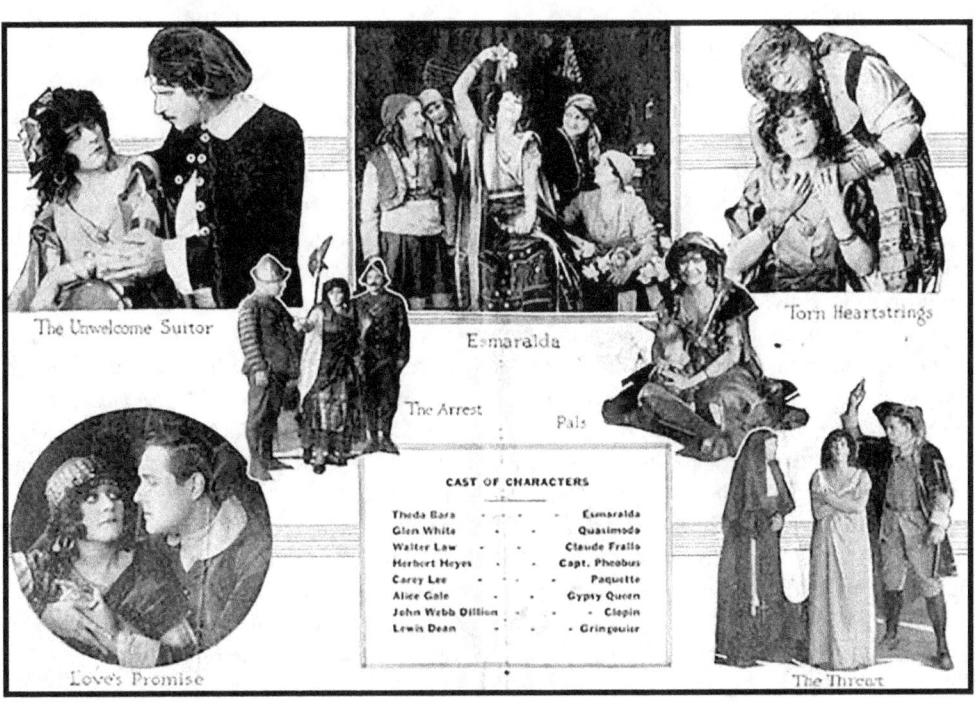

murder, her being tortured until she confesses to a crime she didn't commit, her rescue by the Gypsies, etc.

Bara will forever be enshrined among the pantheon of major screen sirens. Despite her exotic *non de plume*, which is an anagram for "Arab Death," she was born into an average American family in Cincinnati, Ohio. She embodied exotic allure and raw sexuality but failed to make the transition to talkies. Much of her work perished in a fire at Fox's studios in 1937, including, sadly, *The Darling of Paris*, and she passed away in 1955.

The next version of Hunchback, one of several that were titled *Esmeralda*, was released in 1922. TH

The Devil-Stone
aka **The Devil Stone**; **The Devil's Stone**
Artcraft; b/w; 60 min; U.S.
D: Cecil B. DeMille *S:* Jeanie MacPherson *P:* Jesse L. Lasky *C:* Alvin Wyckoff
Cast: Geraldine Farrar, Wallace Reid, Hobart Bosworth, Tully Marshall, James Neill, Gustav von Seyffertitz

On the coast of Brittany, France, a peasant woman named Marcia Manot (Farrar) finds a priceless emerald that once belonged to an ancient Viking queen. Believing it to be "The Devil Stone" and thinking it cursed, Marcia is distracted from an appreciation of its true value. Silas Martin (Marshall) is not, however, and he marries Marcia in hopes of gaining possession of the jewel. In cahoots with his business manager, Guy Sterling (Reid), he hatches a plan to frame Marcia for adultery, divorce her and keep the stone for himself. But oops, Sterling falls in love with Marcia, reneges on his part of the plan and tells her what her husband is up to. Understandably upset, Marcia decides to take her emerald and leave, but in the heat of the moment she and Martin fight and she inadvertently kills him. Though found out by an investigating detective (Bosworth), it's quickly ascertained that the death was an accident. Marcia is now free to marry Sterling and get rid of the accursed—though highly valuable—Devil Stone.

The Devil-Stone was noted director Cecil B. DeMille's second flirtation with horror, after his 1914 comedy/thriller *The Ghost Breaker*. It wasn't a genre he visited often. His affection was for more grandiose fare. Horror films tend to be smaller, more personal affairs—the type of filmmaking with which DeMille was least comfortable.

Massachusetts-born leading lady Geraldine Farrar was an opera singer who made her stage debut in Germany in 1901 and went on to worldwide acclaim with the New York Metropolitan Opera's 1906 production of *Romeo and Juliet*. Such was her fame that a subculture of young female fans, known as Gerry-flappers, took shape in the 1910s and '20s. It wasn't long before cinema came knocking at her door, and she wound up cast as Carmen in Cecil B. DeMille's film of the same name. It was the first of several roles she did for DeMille, including *Temptation* (1915), *Maria Rosa* and *Joan the Woman* (both 1916) and *The Woman That God Forgot* (1917). *The Devil-Stone* was her last picture for the director; Reginald Barker mostly helmed her remaining films. She retired from acting and singing in 1922, her voice on the wane after much overuse. (Most of her movies were shot between opera seasons.)

Jeanie MacPherson wrote *Devil-Stone*, based on an idea by Beatrice DeMille and Leighton Osmun, who co-wrote the 1917 horror film *Unconquered*. Beatrice was Cecil's mother.

Essaying a smaller role in the film was Bavarian actor Gustav von Seyffertitz. CW

The Devil's Assistant
Mutual; b/w; 50 min; U.S.
D/P: Harry A. Pollard *S:* J. Edward Hungerford
Cast: Margarita Fischer, Monroe Salisbury, Jack Mower, Kathleen Kirkham, Joseph Harris

Dr. Lorenz (Salisbury) develops an unhealthy obsession for the beautiful Marta (Fisher). He lures her to a cabin in the mountains, gets her hooked on narcotics and rapes her. *The Devil's Assistant* is an early melodrama so over-the-top and sleazy that it teeters into the horror genre. Dr. Lorenz is a demented scuzzball of a medico whose libido overrides all else, and the frank depiction of drug addiction and sexual mania must have been shocking in its day.

Director Harry A. Pollard specialized in two-hankie weepies and fast-paced serials (though he obviously had a taste for the seedy). He was married to leading lady Margarita Fischer, who often played major roles in his films. Pollard's best-known credit was the first screen version of *Show Boat* (1929), a mostly silent picture that shoehorned some musical numbers in at the last second thanks to the newfound popularity of sound recording. He died of cancer in 1934. TH

The Enchanted Kiss
Vitagraph; b/w; 20 min; U.S.
D: David Smith *S:* Harry Southwell
Cast: Chet Ryan, Frances Parks, Walter Rodgers, Charles Wheelock, Claire Toner, Jack Pierce

This short subject contains a ghoulish dream sequence in which a young man imagines that he can sustain his youth by eating the flesh of a virgin once a year. A story by O. Henry about a young store clerk obsessed with the beautiful, virginal daughter of his landlady formed the basis of the screenplay.

Born William Sydney Porter in North Carolina in 1862, O. Henry was convicted of embezzlement (from a bank in which he was employed) and started writing fiction while doing a three-year stretch in prison. The name change came after his incarceration, when he took up writing full time, earning a steady income by penning a story per week for the *New York World* magazine. His success didn't last as long as he did, however; he died, virtually penniless, in 1910. Filmmakers recognized the filmic potential of his stories early on, though the adaptations seldom did justice to the author's penchant for clever sting-in-the-tail endings.

The Enchanted Kiss' supporting cast includes a young Jack Pierce (1889-1968), who later gave up acting to become a make-up artist. In that capacity, his accomplishments for Universal Studios included the iconic designs for Bela Lugosi in *Dracula* (1931), Boris Karloff in *Frankenstein* (1931) and *The Mummy* (1932) and Lon Chaney, Jr. in *The Wolf Man* (1941). Sadly, the studio he helped put on the map ended up turning its back on Pierce, who finished out his career doing no-budget cheapies and episodes of the popular TV series *Mister Ed*. TH

The renegade monk Grigori Rasputin (Edward Connelly, top left) exerts a strong influence over the Russian Royal Family, from *The Fall of the Romanoffs*.

The Eternal Sin
aka **Lucretia Borgia**; **The Queen Mother**

Selznick/Select/Brenon; b/w; length unknown; U.S.
D/Co-S/Co-P: Herbert Brenon Co-S: George Edwardes-Hall Co-P: Lewis J. Selznick C: J. Roy Hunt, David Calcagni
Cast: Florence Reed, William E. Shay, Stephen Grattan, Richard Barthelmess, Alex Shannon, A.G. Parker

Based nominally on Victor Hugo's novel *Lucrèce Borgia* (aka *Lucretia Borgia*, 1833), *The Eternal Sin* has little to do with the historical figure on which it's based. The film overlooks known history to wallow in the depravity depicted in Hugo's book and rumors surrounding Lucrezia. It casts Florence Reed as the famed female reprobate (here spelled Lucretia) and Richard Barthelmess as fictional hero Gennaro. Stephen Garran plays "Lucretia's brother" Cesare, with William E. Shay as the real villain of the piece, the Duke of Ferrara. Director Brenon's wife was also given a small role.

With character names such as Gubetta, Jeppo, Liverretto, Jester, Negroni and Flametta, it's easy to discern how non-biographical the film was. Gennaro has no idea that he is the son of the hedonistic Lucretia Borgia, who is married to the Duke of Ferrara. Conspirators who also happen to be the fathers of Gennaro's friends murder Cesare, and Lucretia has the men tortured to death. Gennaro and his friends seek her out, and when Lucretia's husband sees Gennaro, he believes the young man to be Lucrezia's lover and administers poison to him. Knowing that Gennaro is her son, Lucretia saves him with an antidote. She later invites his friends to a grand party and poisons them to death, but Gennaro shows up and takes the poison as well. When she tries to administer the antidote once again, he refuses and stabs her. While they both lie dying, he learns the truth about his heritage.

When Victor Hugo learned that his novel had been adapted into an opera in 1834, he objected, and the French government insisted that changes be made to it to lessen the obvious theft. One wonders what Hugo would have thought of this aberrant film adaptation!

The next film to be based on the life of Lucrezia Borgia came along shortly in 1919. CW

Even As You and I
Universal; b/w; 72 min; U.S.
D: Lois Webber S: Maude Grange
Cast: Harry Carter, Ben F. Wilson, Mignon Anderson, Bertram Grassby, Priscilla Dean, Maude George

Satan (Carter) tempts a pair of pious artists, Carillo (Wilson) and Selma (Anderson), dispatching nefarious emissaries to appeal to their weakness. But ultimately goodness prevails, and the two remain unspoiled.

The most interesting aspect of this cinematic morality play is that it was written and directed by women. In the male-dominated film industry of its day, this was quite a novel thing. Director Lois Webber was born in Allegheny, Pennsylvania and is credited by some as being the first woman to direct a feature length motion picture (1914's *The Merchant of Venice*). It's a distinction both difficult to document and more often awarded to French director Alice Guy. Scenarist Maude Grange is an obscure figure; little is known about her, and contemporary sources credit her with only a handful of screenplays written in 1916 and 1917.

Even as You and I is considered a lost film, and the scenario sounds more melodramatic than horrific, but the notion of Satan tempting humanity outside of a Biblical context justifies its inclusion here. TH

The Fall of the Romanoffs
Brenon/Iliodor; b/w; 80 min; U.S.
D/P: Herbert Brenon S: George Edwardes-Hall, Austin Strong
Cast: Edward Connelly, Iliodor, Alfred Hickman, Conway Tearle, Charles Craig, Georges Deneuborg

Renegade monk Grigori Rasputin (Connelly) exerts a strong and mysterious influence over the Russian Royal Family. In response, his enemies orchestrate a plan to assassinate the "mad monk" before he gains control of the country.

The story of Rasputin has been dramatized over 40 times on screen, the character providing such notable performers as Conrad Veidt, Lionel Barrymore, Christopher Lee and Tom Baker with opportunities to shine. 1917 saw the productions of the first three screen versions of his story—*Rasputin*, *Rasputin, The Black Monk* and *The Fall of the Romanoffs*—with the latter often credited as the first attempt to bring the Russian Revolution to the screen. However, it wasn't released until January 1918, making the claim somewhat dubious. The timing was opportunistic,

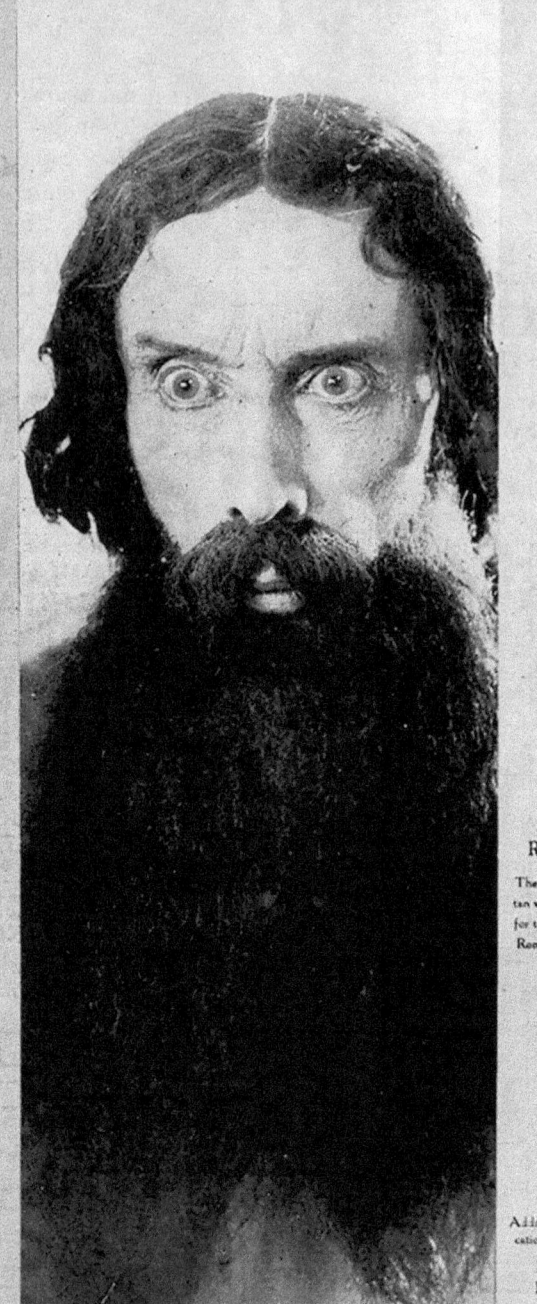

to say the least; Rasputin had been assassinated in 1916, and in 1917 his story still loomed large in the public consciousness.

The Fall of the Romanoffs was adapted from a book nominally written by Rasputin's chief rival, a monk who called himself Iliodor (real name: Sergei Trufanov); indeed, Iliodor also took part in the film's production and played himself. The book had yet to emerge in print—it became widely available later in 1918—but Iliodor clearly recognized early on the potential for the drama it contained and engineered its arrival to the screen.

American actor Edward Connelly played Rasputin; he was a popular performer in the silent era, remaining active until his death in 1928, with his last film being released posthumously in 1929. Stills reveal that he evoked the distinctive, wild-eyed, shaggy-haired visage of Rasputin so popular at the time. As for Iliodor's performance, reviews of the time indicate that his status as a novice was painfully evident. He appears, in other words, to have come up short playing himself. TH

The Fatal Ring
Pathé/Aster; b/w; 20 chapters; U.S.
D: George B. Seitz S: Frederick J. Jackson, George B. Seitz, Bertram Millhauser P: Louis J. Gasnier
Cast: Warner Oland, Pearl White, Earle Foxe, Ruby Hoffman, Henry G. Sell, Floyd Buckley

A lost serial of the silent era, *The Fatal Ring* casts serial queen Pearl White as Pearl Standish. Various sources assert that Pearl possesses a ring rendering its wearer invisible and/or a diamond stolen by her father from a lost Egyptian city. From the episode titles, one can conclude that there is indeed a ring involved. In any case, a high priestess (Hoffman) of an ancient and sacred order wants the object back, and evil foreigner Richard Carlslake (Oland) gives her aid. White teams up with former enemy Nicholas Knox (Fox) in an effort to keep the purloined property.

Episode titles include *The Violet Diamond, Borrowed Identity, The Warning on the Ring, Danger Underground, Rays of Death, The Signal Lantern, The Switch in the Safe, The Dice of Death, The Perilous Plunge, The Short Circuit, A Desperate Chance, A Dash of Arabia, The Painted Safe, The Dagger Duel, The Double Disguise, The Death Weight, The Subterfuge* and *The End of the Trail*. Whether even these 18 known titles are in correct order is unknown, as the series is lost.

Both producer Louis J. Gasnier and co-writer George B. Seitz reportedly had small roles in the serial. CW

Fear
aka **Furcht**
Messter; b/w; 72 min; Germany
D/S: Robert Wiene P: Oskar Messter
Cast: Bruno Decarli, Bernhard Goetzke, Mechthildis Thein, Conrad Veidt

Count Greven (DeCarli) is traveling the world when he comes upon an Indian temple in Java that houses a striking religious idol. He steals the figure and takes it with him to his home in Germany. Once there, he is plagued by a series of increasingly harsh nightmares, for which he begins to suspect that the idol is responsible. In time he grows paranoid, certain that an Indian priest (Veidt) has placed a curse on him. When the priest shows up unexpectedly, he tells the count that he will enjoy seven years of great success and accomplishments, after which he will be

killed at the hands of someone he loves very much. As the seventh year approaches, Greven's paranoia worsens.

Fear was the first collaboration between director Robert Wiene and actor Conrad Veidt. They reteamed two years later for Wiene's masterpiece, *The Cabinet of Dr. Caligari* (1919). The director's distinctive use of Expressionism in *Caligari*'s set design was one of the most influential devices horror cinema would see over the next two decades, not only in Germany but also in the United States where films such as *Frankenstein* (1931) and *Son of Frankenstein* (1939) co-opted the deep shadows and pointed, angular sets to greater and lesser degrees. CW

Flames
Butcher's; b/w; 65 (58) min; Great Britain
D: Maurice Elvey *S:* Eliot Stannard *P:* F.W. Baker
Cast: Owen Nares, Margaret Bannerman, Edward O'Neill, Clifford Cobb, Douglas Munro

Based on the Richard Hichens novel of the same name, prolific British horror director Maurice Elvey's *Flames* concerns a naïve young man (Cobbe) and an aging occultist (Munro) who swap bodies. When the elderly man refuses to trade back, the youth's loved ones get involved and set things right.

In 1917 the idea of souls swapping bodies was a relatively original one, though it became lame through overuse during the following couple of decades. There is some indication that Elvey didn't intend for his film to be taken entirely seriously, though the book on which it was based is thoroughly humorless.

Novelist Hichens began his writing career as a journalist, doing mostly music reviews. But after a chance encounter with Lord Alfred Douglas and Oscar Wilde in Egypt in the winter of 1893-94, he focused almost exclusively on fiction. He became a major success in the 1920s, and his novels have been adapted to the big screen under the auspices of such noteworthy directors as Alfred Hitchcock, Irving Pichel and Rex Ingram. CW

Ghost Hounds
Kalem; b/w; 15 min; U.S.
D: Lloyd Hamilton
Cast: Lloyd Hamilton, Bud Duncan, Ethel Teare, Henry Murdock

This comedy-horror short concerns an attempt by Ham (Hamilton) and Bud (Duncan) to steal some eggs. They get caught and are found guilty by the local judge. The daughter (Teare) of the farmer from whom they stole pleads for mercy, and the judge sentences them to spend the night in a haunted house in lieu of jail time. This they do, taking the girl along, and ghosts and skeletons dancing and writhing in the night duly scare these three. In the end it all turns out to have been orchestrated by—can you guess—criminals, who are using the house as a hideout and fabricating spooks to keep the nosy at bay.

Lloyd Vernon Hamilton was born in Oakland, California in 1891. He entered pictures in the silent era and found success as half of a comedic duo co-featuring Bud Duncan. Duncan was a short, pudgy actor who appeared in well over 150 films, most notably a pair of "Snuffy Smith" adaptations, *Hillbilly Blitzkrieg* and *Private Snuffy Smith* (both 1942). Hamilton broke up the duo in 1917 and went on to solo comedy success. A portly fellow whose routines were admired by the likes of Buster Keaton and Charlie Chaplin, he often played oversized prissy types. He was an alcoholic, and his addiction eventually did him in. He died in 1935 during a failed operation on his booze-damaged stomach. In addition to starring in over 250 films, Hamilton was also a noted producer and director. He also occasionally wrote scripts. CW

The Ghost House
Jesse L. Lasky Feature Players/Paramount; b/w; 55 min
D: William C. DeMille *S:* Beulah Marie Dix *P:* Jesse L. Lasky *C:* Paul P. Perry, Joseph Shelderfer
Cast: Jack Pickford, Louise Huff, Olga Grey, James Neill, Eugene Pallette, Mrs. Lewis McCord

Jeremy Foster (Pickford) is a burglar posing as a gardener at a country estate. In a scheme to relieve the house of its valuables, he spreads rumors that the place is haunted. But his plans are threatened by the arrival of the owner's poor relatives.

The Ghost House is an early example of an "old dark house" spoof. Director William C. DeMille was the older brother of producer/director Cecil B. DeMille. Though he never attained the popularity or critical acclaim of his younger sibling, he helmed a number of titles from the silent era to the early 1930s.

Leading man Jack Pickford was the older brother of popular star Mary Pickford. Mary reportedly used her clout to get him work, and he racked up a respectable number of credits during the silent era. He even directed a couple of films, including *Little Lord Fauntleroy* (1921), but in the end his love for the bottle derailed his career. Despite his sister's devoted efforts to find him employment and help him pull his life together, he died from the effects of alcohol and syphilis in 1933.

Paul Wegener as the Golem

The Ghost House's supporting cast includes cherub-faced character actor Eugene Pallette, best known to contemporary audiences as Friar Tuck in the classic Michael Curtiz/William Keighley version of *The Adventures of Robin Hood* (1938). TH

The Ghost of Old Morro

Edison; b/w; 50 min; U.S.
D: Richard Ridgely *S:* James Oppenheim *C:* George W. Lane
Cast: Mabel Trunnelle, Robert Conness, Helen Strickland, Herbert Prior, Marie La Corio, Dorothy Graham

Thomas A. Edison's film studio was only two years away from the end of its nearly 30-year history when it produced this strange Gothic barnstormer. An old witch named Mother Morro (Strickland), who is also a local innkeeper, inhabits Morro Castle. To keep herself supplied with money, she runs a protection racket with pirates who smuggle goods along the coast. One evening she kidnaps an innocent girl for the pleasure of a notorious ship captain (Conness). The girl's father places a curse on the old woman, and soon her own daughter (Trunnelle), who resides in a nearby convent, betrays her vows by falling in love with that very same captain. The vengeful Mother Morro hires a ruffian (Cooper) to assassinate the captain, but the daughter intervenes and saves her lover's life. The ruffian then throws the girl over a cliff, and in despair the old witch falls to her doom, thus ensuring that her evil spirit will forever reside within the stone walls of Castle Morro.

This appears to have been the last film of director Richard Ridgely, though he lived until 1949. He had begun his film career in 1911 as an actor and soon turned to writing screenplays and directing. He gave up acting in 1913, writing in 1915 and directing in 1917. One of his few notable films was the 1915 adaptation of Honoré de Balzac's *The Magic Skin*, which also starred Bigelow Cooper. CW

The Golem and the Dancing Girl
aka Der Golem und die Tänzerin

Deutsche Bioscop GmbH; b/w; length unknown; Germany
D: Paul Wegener, Rochus Gliese *S:* Paul Wegener *P:* Paul Davidson, Siegmund Jakob, Hanns Lippmann *C:* Mads Anton Madsen
Cast: Paul Wegener, Lyda Salmonova, Rochus Gliese, Wilhelm Diegelmann, Fritz Feld, Emile Kurz

An actor (Wegener) is impressed to see that his screen performance as a monstrous Golem frightens people (here the film utilizes clips from *The Golem*, 1915), so he decides to dress up in the costume while attending a party at the apartment of a dancer (Salmonova) in order to make an even bigger impact.

Not much is known about this, Paul Wegener's self-lampooning return to his iconic role as the Golem. Not only is the film considered lost, it doesn't seem to have generated much notice upon its original release. What's interesting, however, is that it remains one of the earliest filmed examples of a horror spoof. The interesting set-up—an example of the self-reflexive nature of cinema—makes it all the more regrettable that it has vanished so completely.

Wegener revisited the character one final time for his most enduring contribution to cinema, *The Golem: How He Came into the World* (1920). TH

The Haunted House

Triangle; b/w; length unknown; U.S.
D/S: Albert Parker
Cast: Winifred Allen, Richard Rosson, Albert Parker, Albert Day, Mac Barnes, Mabel Wright, Eddie Kelly

This is one of many films from the silent era to bear the title *The Haunted House*. Most are comedies wrapped up in horror trimmings, but this one offers up a romantic story with a touch of horror. The townspeople shun Anne (Allen), whose mother and father are dead, because she believes she can communicate with spirits and fairies—and she does, in fact, hold conversations with the spirit of her dead mother (Wright). When Jimmy (Rosson) is wounded while robbing a bank, he takes refuge in a deserted, old dark house, unaware that it's reputed to be haunted. There he meets Anne and the two fall in love. The authorities discover Jimmy's hideout, but when they attempt to apprehend him, the "ghost" of the mansion—Anne in disguise—scares them away.

The Haunted House is one of the earliest works of director Albert Parker, who went on to make a couple of the most famous films of the 1920s: *Sherlock Holmes* (1922) with John Barrymore and *The Black Pirate* (1926) with Douglas Fairbanks. His career waned as the popularity of talkies outpaced that of silents, and though he made quite a few sound films between 1932 and 1938, most were

The Golem and the Dancing Girl

low-budget affairs for Fox's British quota-quickie arm. Among these was *After Dark* (1932), a combination of old dark house, romance and comedy motifs, and *Blind Man's Bluff* (1936), which featured a young James Mason. Parker also had an acting role in *The Haunted House*. CW

Hilde Warren and Death
aka **Hilde Warren und der Tod**
May-Film; b/w; 80 min; Germany
D/P: Joe May *S:* Fritz Lang *C:* Curt Courant
Cast: Mila May, Bruno Kastner, Georg John, Hans Mierendorff, Ernst Matray, Aud Egede Nissen

The gaunt figure of death (Georg John) stalks the material world, from *Hilde Warren and Death*.

Actress Hilde Warren (May) falls in love with and marries the shifty Hector (Kastner), who impregnates her. When Hector is shot dead while holding up a bank, Hilde learns of his criminal past (which includes murder) and is horrified by the prospect of giving birth to his child. While wrestling with the dilemma of what to do about her pregnancy, the gaunt figure of Death (John) visits her and offers to take her as a means of escape. She rejects the offer, has a son and raises him to adulthood. When the man becomes a wanted murderer just like his father, Hilde is again visited by Death.

An early example of future director Fritz Lang's obsession with sex and death, *Hilde Warren and Death* sounds like a very interesting melodrama. Though the film's survival status is unknown, it marks one of several collaborations between Lang and director Joe May. The two would later clash over the production of *The Indian Tomb* (1921), a colorful slice of exotica that Lang had hoped to direct but lost to May. (Infuriated, Lang bided his time until he could direct his own color remake in 1959.) At this stage in his career, however, Lang was still a relative unknown while May was successful enough to call the shots. Like Lang, May later immigrated to the United States to escape the Nazi regime. Yet, whereas Lang found himself helming A-class pictures, May was consigned to B-movies for the remainder of his career. One of May's most interesting U.S. films was *The Invisible Man Returns* (1940), a stylish follow-up to James Whale's 1933 classic *The Invisible Man*.

May's real-life wife Mia, who appeared in a number of her husband's early works, portrayed the leading lady in *Hilde*. Character actor Georg John, a visible presence in German genre films of the period including Paul Leni's *Waxworks* (1924), as well as Lang's *Dr. Mabuse, the Gambler* (1922) and *The Testament of Dr. Mabuse* (1933), played Death.

Lang recycled the concept of Death visiting a grieving woman to strike a bargain for his film *Destiny* in 1921. TH

The Image Maker
Thanhouser; b/w; 55 min; U.S.
D: Eugene Moore *S:* Emmett Mixx *P:* Edwin Thanhouser *C:* George Webber
Cast: Valda Valkyrien, Harris Gordon, Inda Palmer, Morgan Jones, Arthur Bauer, Boyd Marshall

Less a full-fledged horror film than an outright melodrama, *The Image Maker* is nonetheless of interest to horror fans in that it anticipates elements of Karl Freund's classic *The Mummy* (1932). It deals with an actress (Valkyrien) and a stranger (Gordon) who fall in love at first sight. They are both overcome with a sense of *déjà vu*, however, and they slowly come to realize that they've met in a previous life—specifically, one in ancient Egypt where she was a lowly sculptress (hence the film's title) and he a powerful prince. The prince had tried to save the sculptress from being sacrificed but had failed in doing so. And now their story is poised to repeat itself as a salacious producer who does his best to keep the lovers apart lusts after the actress.

Leading lady Valda Valkyrien (here billed by her surname alone) was the real-life Baroness DeWitz. She parlayed her title and her interest in acting into various roles for production company Thanhouser Films. Later she moved to Fox, but after a falling-out with studio head William Fox, her career never recovered. She made her last film, *Bolshevism on Trial*, in 1919.

Director Eugene Moore (sometimes billed as W. Eugene Moore, or W. Eugene Moore, Jr.) made a number of minor films in the silent era, including *The Picture of Dorian Gray* (1915). His career, like Valkyrien's, petered out in 1919. TH

The Inspirations of Harry Larrabee
Balboa Amusement; b/w; 40 min; U.S.
D: Bertram Bracken *S:* Douglas Bronston, Howard Fielding *P:* E.D. Horkheimer, H.M. Horkheimer *C:* Victor Milner
Cast: Clifford Grey, Margaret Landis, Winfred Greenwood, Frank Brownlee, William Ehfe, Charles Blaisdell

Harry Larrabee (Grey) is a playwright drawn into a mystery involving residents of his apartment building: Carolyn Vaughn's (Landis) precious jewelry has been stolen by a notorious thief known as the Wolf (Brownlee) with the aid of neighbors who were blackmailed into helping carry out the crime. Carolyn is badly wounded, and Larrabee takes her for medical attention. At the film's climax Carolyn's estranged husband is revealed to be the Wolf.

Based on a story by Howard Fielding, *The Inspirations of Harry Larrabee* was as unwieldy and convoluted as its title. The "inspirations" refer to Larrabee's ability to intuit the best time to enter any given situation, a talent that enables him to save the girl and presumably find love in the final fadeout. Clifford Grey, a British-born lyricist turned actor, played Larrabee. His song

"What a Duke Should Be" was included on the soundtrack for Robert Altman's Oscar-nominated *Gosford Park* (2001). Grey's acting career lasted between 1914 and 1922, after which he turned to script writing.

Director Bertram (Bert) Bracken was prolific during the silent era, but he was unable to make the adjustment to talkies; he made his last film in 1932 and died in 1952. TH

It's Never Too Late to Mend
Martin; b/w; 62 min; Great Britain
D/S: Dave Aylott
Cast: George Leyton, Margaret Hope, George Dewhurst, Charles Vane, Franco Fraticelli, Maurice Gerrard

John Meadows (Gerrard) lusts after Susan Merton (Hope), but she's engaged to the handsome Tom Robertson (Leyton). So Meadows accuses Robertson of a crime he didn't commit and has him sent to prison. There Robertson learns how terrible the British penal system is. In the end, however, Meadows' plan is discovered and Robertson is exonerated.

British filmmaker Dave Aylott directed hundreds of shorts during the silent era, almost all of which are forgotten today. (He also frequently wrote and starred in them.) Though his specialty was comedy, in 1917, less than 10 years into his career, he scripted an adaptation of Charles Reade's political novel *It Is Never Too Late to Mend: A Matter-of-Fact Romance* (1856). Far darker than the bulk of his work, it was the first British adaptation of Reade's tale, though Australia had offered up a version in 1911 and the United States in 1913. At just over an hour in length, this particular rendering excised a great deal of the story's drama in favor of the horrors of Britain's penal system.

The next adaptation of Reade's story came in 1922 and starred Dame Sybil Thorndike's less famous brother Russell. CW

Kaidan chibusa enoki
aka **Chibusa enoki: Takeda genpachiro**
Nikkatsu Kyoto; b/w; length unknown; Japan
Crew unknown
Cast: Matsunosuke Onoe, Kakumatsuro Arashi, Kitsuraku Arashi, Utae Nakamura, Hidesaburo Onoe, Kyuzo Ichikawa

Based on a story by noted Japanese writer Sanyutei Encho (who also wrote *Botan dōrō* and *Shinkei Kasane-ga-fuchi*), this 1917 offering deals with a lowly artist's assistant who murders his master in order to steal the man's wife. Some years later a terrible disease strikes him that causes his breast to swell. Finally, he pricks his chest and out flies a group of birds, causing his wife to die. His former master's young son kills him.

The film's title translates as *Ghost Story of the Breast-Nettle Tree*. It was the second adaptation of Encho's tale. An earlier version starring Matsunosuke Onoe and made by Yokata Shokai appears to have been released under the title *Chibusa no enoki* in 1910 but very little is known about it. The tale was shot again more famously in 1958 as *The Mother Tree*, but not before it got a go-around in 1939 under the title *Ghost Story of the Mother Tree*. CW

Magia
Corvin; b/w; length unknown; Hungary
D: Alexander Korda S: Frigyes Karinthy, Kalman Sztrokay C: Gustav Mihaly Kovacs
Cast: Mihaly Varkony, Lucie Labass, Magda Nagy, Antal Nyaray, Várkonyi Mihály

A man meets Baron Munchausen, gazes into his magic mirror and learns that the Baron is, in fact, a malevolent magician who needs human blood to survive. Just why the Baron was transformed into an evil bloodsucker for this picture is anybody's guess, and given that it's lost, it's hard to ascertain just how macabre the end product really was. This obscure, long-lost entry obviously played fast and loose with the life story of the legendary Baron Munchausen. Born Karl Friedrich Hieronymus, Freiherr von Münchhausen was a German nobleman who turned his own humble exploits into imaginative flights of fancy. His stories were collected and published in the late 1700s, making him into a celebrity for the ages. Many filmmakers have translated his colorful fantasies to the screen, with the most successful effort being Terry Gilliam's *The Adventures of Baron Munchausen* (1988), which cast John Neville in the title role.

Magia was an early effort by Hungarian producer/writer/director Alexander Korda. Born in 1893, Korda entered the film industry in his native Hungary in 1914. He immigrated to the United States in the late 1920s and later moved to Great Britain, where he established London Film Productions. He scored a major hit with *The Private Life of Henry VIII* (1933), which netted Charles Laughton a Best Actor Oscar, and he had a major hand in the fantasy classic *The Thief of Bagdad* (1940). As a producer he oversaw such classics as *The Four Feathers* (1939), Carol Reed's *The Fallen Idol* (1948) and *The Third Man* (1949) and Laurence Olivier's *Richard III* (1955). Korda was knighted in 1942 and passed away in 1956. TH

The Memoirs of Satan
aka **Die Memoiren Des Satans**
LUNA; b/w; length unknown; Germany
D/S: Robert Heymann
Cast: Kurt Brenkendorf, Friedrich Kuhne, Kathe Dorsch, Ernst Hofmann, Max Kohler, Ilse Oeser

Satan's misadventures are recounted in this German serial, which is divided into three chapters: *Doktor Mors*, *Fanatiker des Lebens* (*Life's Fanatics*) and *Der Fluchbeladene* (*The Accursed*). The first two installments hit German theaters in 1917, and the last premiered in 1918; it is unclear whether they were distributed outside the country, though it doesn't seem likely.

Writer/director Robert Heymann was something of a specialist in serials during the silent days of German cinema. Friedrich Kuhne also appeared in Fritz Lang's epic serial *Spiders* (1919), as well as the horror serials *Homunculus* (1916) and *The Hound of the Baskervilles* (1914). In the latter he played the villainous Stapleton. TH

Midnight
Universal/IMP; b/w; 11 min; U.S.
D: Allen Holubar S: E.J. Clawson
Cast: Allen Holubar, Zoe Rae

Though shot late in 1916, this short film from IMP was copyrighted by Universal on January 3 and 4 of the following year. It was based on a story by Frank H. Spearman and concerned a dying man who desperately needs a priest; a girl summons one who, it turns out, is actually a ghost. The film's sinister appeal is widened by the inclusion of some Yellow Peril drama.

The fact that its script was written by E.J. Clawson, a four-time Oscar nominee (all for work released in 1928 and 1929), is perhaps most interesting of all. He contributed to nearly 100 films in the silent era, several of which have stood the test of time though none more so than Lon Chaney's *The Phantom of the Opera* (1925), to which he contributed without credit. He also wrote the scripts for the Browning/Chaney collaboration *West of Zanzibar* (1928) and the far less interesting *The Thirteenth Chair* (1929).

Born in 1888 in San Francisco, Allen Holubar starred in slightly more films than he directed, often doing double duty as actor and director in the same film. His most famous role was as Captain Nemo in Stuart Paton's *20,000 Leagues Under the Sea* (1916), which remains readily available today and was something of an influence on Disney's more famous film adaptation. He died in 1923 from complications related to gall bladder surgery. CW

Nabeshima kaibyô
Nikkatsu Kyoto; b/w; 66 min; Japan
Crew unknown
Cast: Matsunosuke Onoe, Suminojo Ichikawa, Kakumatsuro Arashi, Ichitaro Kataoka, Sennosuke Nakamura

Historians today regard Naoshige Nabeshima as a great Japanese general. Connected to the Ryuzoji clan, he distinguished himself in the late 1500s when he and his 5,000 men made a surprise nighttime raid on 60,000 enemy soldiers who were surrounding them at Saga Castle. In 1853, playwright Joko Segawa III wrote the Kabuki play *Hana Saga neko mata zoshi*, a fictionalized account of the incident, complete with a mother and son who return from the dead as ghostly cats seeking vengeance. Segawa's tale became the basis for a handful of silent Japanese horror films, of which this one and several others came from Nikkatsu Studio (including *Saga no yozakura*, 1917, *Nabeshima neko sodo*, 1919 and *Saga neko sodo*, 1921).

Nabeshima kaibyô was released on April 14, 1917. CW

The Picture of Dorian Gray
aka **Das Bildnis des Dorian Gray**
Oswald; b/w; 80 min; Germany
P/S/D: Richard Oswald *C:* Max Fassbender
Cast: Bernd Aldor, Lupu Pick, Ernst Pittaschau, Andreas Van Horn, Lea Lara, Ernst Ludwig

Cinema's first unambiguously gay-themed film was probably Richard Oswald's *Different from the Others* (1919), starring Conrad Veidt as a homosexual pianist blackmailed by a professional criminal. (Other gay films from the silent period include Carl Theodor Dreyer's *Michael*, 1924, and William Dieterle's *Sex in Chains*, 1928.) *Different* took advantage of the thematic ground that Oswald helped break, facilitating Germany's early openness toward the subject. After all, Oswald had spearheaded what was apparently a remarkably homoerotic 1917 film version of Oscar Wilde's controversial 1890 novel *The Picture of Dorian Gray*.

There had already been five official adaptations of Wilde's classic work, but by all indications most of them ignored the bisexuality of the title character. (The only exception may have been the 1915 Russian adaptation, which cast a woman in the role of the effeminate Mr. Gray—but until such time as a print of the film is found, it's difficult to know just how overtly homoerotic it was.) While Oswald's film most likely didn't openly portray Dorian's gayer side, sources suggest that it strongly hinted at such, thus setting the stage for future explorations of the theme. Oswald was attracted to the theme of a double life, so richly explored in Wilde's story. On the surface, Dorian (Aldor) is a vapid but upstanding member of society, while behind the scenes he indulges his many and varied whims, including illicit affairs and murder. It was a theme Oswald would repeatedly revisit as he helped establish a whole new category of film: the horror genre. Among Oswald's other horror entries were *The Hound of the Baskervilles* (1915), *Night of Horror* (1916), *Weird Tales* (1919), *Nachtgestalten* (1920), *Lucretia Borgia* (1922), *Cagliostro* (1929), *The Hound of the Baskervilles* (1929), *Alraune* (1930) and *Uncanny Stories* (1932).

Of Jewish decent, Oswald fled Europe in the late 1930s when the Nazis began dominating many of the continent's more progressive countries. He eventually settled in the United States and there made his final film in 1949, *The Lovable Cheat*, starring Charles Ruggles. CW

Rasputin
Saturn; b/w; length unknown; Germany
D/S: Herr Arno
Cast: Max Hiller, Fritz Hofbauer

Grigori Yefimovich Rasputin rose to fame as a "mystical counselor" to the Tsaritsa Alexandra Romanov, the wife of the Tsar of Russia, who believed that the priest had healing powers and could cure her son's hemophilia. By all accounts, Rasputin had a strange and controlling power over the Tsaritsa. It was also said that, despite his notoriously bad hygiene, he regularly bedded a variety of women, insisting that doing so was good for his soul. A Russian prince named Yusupov, fearing Rasputin's power, organized the priest's assassination in December 1916. Though evidence casts doubt on parts of Yusupov's account, the prince maintained that he and his associates fed Rasputin poisoned cakes and wine, shot him four times, beat him, castrated him and finally drowned him in the River Neva. When the priest's body was later disinterred and burned, witnesses claimed that it sat up and moved in the fire; if true, the phenomenon was likely caused by the fire's heat constricting the joints, a not uncommon occurrence when bodies are burned without first slicing their joints and tendons.

Given his larger-than-life status, one can't be surprised that in the very first year after Rasputin's death he was the subject of at least three fictionalized biopics. It's difficult to establish which came first, though this German *Rasputin* seems the most likely candidate, followed by *Rasputin, The Black Monk* and *The Fall of the Romanoffs*, the latter shot in 1917 but not released until January 1918. None of these films, incidentally, was made in Russia, where mention of the monk was largely forbidden and Prince Yusupov made it clear that any ill use of his name would result in legal action.

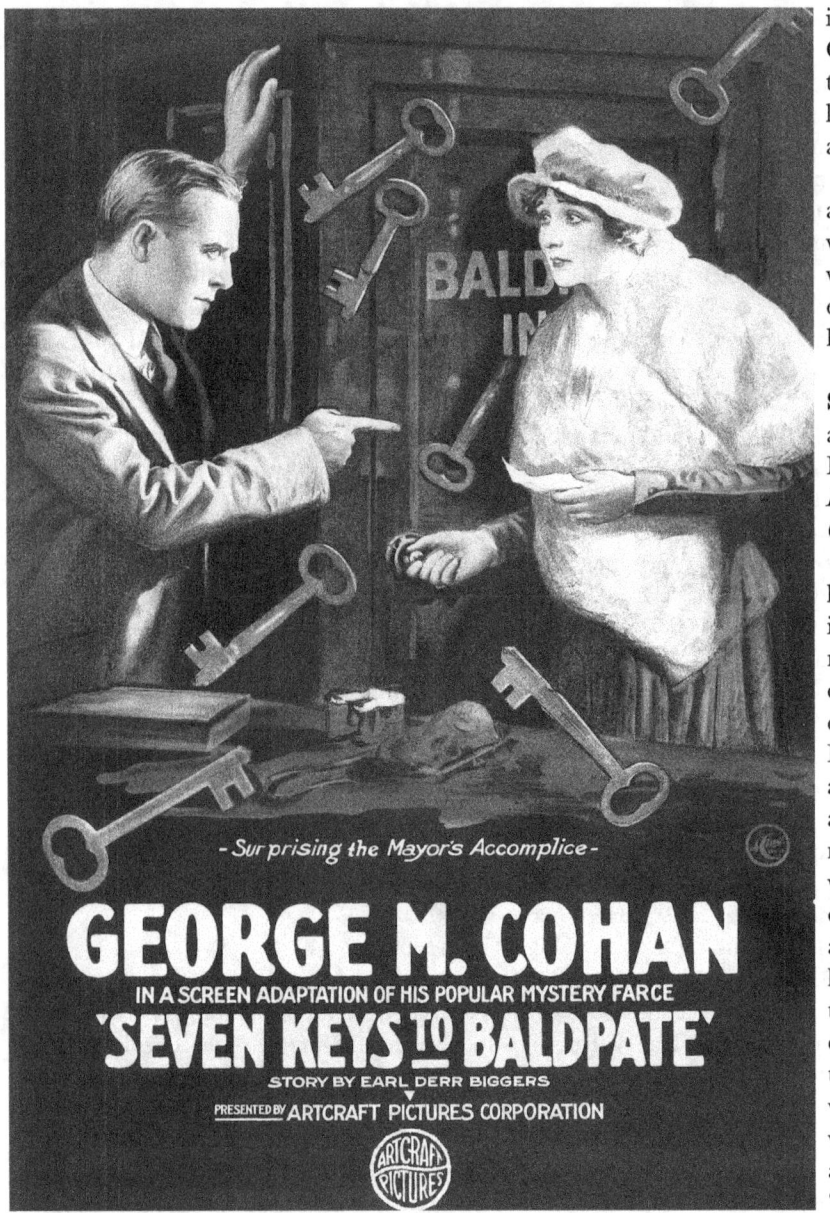

This particular version of *Rasputin* was written and directed by Herr Arno, who has only one other known film credit to his name, *Die Kleptomanin* (1918). CW

Rasputin, The Black Monk
World; b/w; 70 min; U.S.
D: Arthur Ashley
Cast: Montagu Love, Henry Hull, June Elvidge, Arthur Ashley, Violet Axzelle, Lillian Cook

There are conflicting plot descriptions for this highly searched lost film. It's a fictionalized retelling of the life of Grigori Yefimovich Rasputin, the peasant priest who climbed the ranks of Russian power by convincing the Tsarina that he could cure her hemophiliac son. In this account, however, Rasputin (Love) seems to have been a leader of the Russian Revolution who uses his preternatural gifts of hypnosis and subjugation to infiltrate and bring down the House of the Tsar (Wilke). When the young Tsaravitch (Grassby) contracts an illness, Rasputin comes to the boy's rescue, insisting that the child can only survive so long as the priest remains near. Years afterward, during World War I, Rasputin overreaches by aiding the German army's attack on Russia. When he attempts to rape a Russian princess (Nesbit), a revolutionary leader (Ashley), whose wife Rasputin once despoiled, assassinates him.

Director Arthur Ashley also starred in the film as the head of the revolution. It's no surprise that he would have been onscreen; he was primarily an actor who wrote and directed only occasionally. His last cinematic work in any capacity came in 1922, after which he retired from film. CW

Saga no yozakura
aka **Saga yozakura**
Nikkatsu; b/w; length unknown; Japan
D: Shozo Makino
Cast: Matsunosuke Onoe

Ghostly cats have been a staple of Japanese folklore since the early 1600s, when cats were turned loose in cities to dispatch the rats and mice that fed on the nation's silkworms, which were doing great economic damage. Over time, various areas developed their own particular superstitions concerning the creatures. In some quarters, any cat that lived past 13 years of age (or gained too much weight) was said to become a ghost, with such spectral felines often able to summon fireballs or enter the dreams of the living. There were also urban legends in which cats drank the blood of a murdered person, took on that victim's grudge and mounted a vendetta against the killer. It was believed that such creatures could be spotted by the fact that they sometimes walked on their hind legs. They could be tricked, when in human shape, into reverting to their true form. The city of Saga, Japan, located within the Saga prefecture on the island of Kyushu, was one of many areas to develop its own pet story about a ghostly cat. The legend's name translates as "Cherry blossoms by night in Saga" and was encapsulated by Joko Segawa III's 1853 Kabuki play *Hana Saga neko mata zoshi*. Nikkatsu Studio's 1917 film *Saga no yozakura* appears to have been the second cinematic telling of the tale (after a 1910 version that, along with most of the information about it, is lost). Like many films of its genre, time, place and studio, Shozo Makino directed with actor Matsunosuke Onoe in the lead role of the ghost cat.

The story borrowed from what has come to be known as the "Nabeshima Disturbance," an allegedly historical incident in which a military general named Nabeshima executed two people for adultery in or around Saga Castle in the late 1500s. Stories quickly surfaced around town that the adulterous couple's ghosts had been seen out and about, seeking revenge.

Nikkatsu made other versions of the film in 1917 (*Nabeshima kaibyô*), 1919 (*Nabeshima neko sodo*), 1921 (both *Saga neko sodo* and *Nabeshima neko sodo*) and 1938 (*Ghost-Cat Legend*), while rival studios produced versions in 1923 (*Nabeshima no neko*), 1929 (*Legend of the Nabeshima Cat Ghost*), 1936 (*Cat Ghost and Cherry Blossoms at Night in Saga*), 1937 (*Legend of the Saga Cat Monster*) and 1939 (*Silver Cat's Curse*). CW

Satan Triumphant
aka Satana likuyushchiy
b/w; length unknown; Russia
D: Yakov Protazanov *S:* Olga Blazhevich *P:* Iosif Yermolyev Yermoliev *C:* Fyodor Burgasov
Cast: Pavel Pavlov, Ivan Mozhukhin, Aleksander Chabrov, Nathalie Lissenko, Vera Orlova

A minister (Mozhukhin) lives with his hunchbacked brother (Pavlov) and the latter's wife (Lissenko). One stormy night, a stranger (Chabrov) arrives at their home seeking shelter. It turns out that the stranger is Satan in disguise, and he lures the minister into illicit congress with his brother's wife. A child, Sandro, results. As an adult, Sandro (Mozhukhin, again) is also tempted by the Devil.

This moralistic melodrama was directed by Yakov Protazanov, who is recognized as principal in the formation of the Russian film industry. Among his credits is an early version of *The Queen of Spades* (1916). Leading man Ivan Mozhukhin, a veteran of numerous Protazanov films, was briefly pitched as a Russian rival to Rudolf Valentino, though he failed to catch on with audiences. TH

Seven Keys to Baldpate
Artcraft; b/w; 55 min; U.S.
D/S: Hugh Ford *C:* Ned Van Buren, Lewis W. Physioc
Cast: George M. Cohan, Anna Q. Nilsson, Hedda Hopper, Corene Uzzell, Joseph W. Smiley, Armand Cortes

George Washington Magee (Cohan) wagers his friends that he can write a complete thriller in 24 hours. His friends give him the key to the abandoned, spooky Baldpate Inn, where he can work uninterrupted, but his progress is hindered by a variety of weird visitors, all of whom possess their own key to the inn.

This is the first U.S. film version of Earl Derr Biggers' popular 1913 page turner, notable for its casting of George M. Cohan in the lead role. Cohan was a popular actor, singer, lyricist, playwright and overall entertainer; his life story was told in the beloved Michael Curtiz musical *Yankee Doodle Dandee* (1942), with James Cagney turning in an Academy Award-winning performance. Cohan had earlier adapted *Seven Keys to Baldpate* as a popular Broadway play, thus enhancing the material's box office appeal.

The supporting cast includes then-popular Swedish starlet Anna Q. Nilsson and future gossip columnist Hedda Hopper. Director Hugh Ford made a number of unremarkable films between 1917 and 1921; some sources credit him as scripting this film, but it seems likely that Cohan oversaw the writing.

Seven Keys was next brought to the screen in 1925 for nowhere near the final time. TH

She
Fox; b/w; 55 min; U.S.
D: Kenean Buel *S:* Mary Murillo *C:* Frank Krugler
Cast: Valeska Suratt, Ben Taggart, Miriam Fouche, Thomas Wigney Percyval, Tom Burrough, Martin Reagan

A not-very-faithful adaptation of H. Rider Haggard's novel *She: A History of Adventure*, Fox's *She* casts Valeska Suratt as immortal Egyptian Queen Ayesha, who has waited 3,000 years for the reincarnation of her dead lover, Kallikrates. When she finds him in the body of adventuresome Leo Vincey (Taggart), she must compete with his new lover, Ustane (Fouche), his mentor Horace Holly (Burrough) and his best friend Job (Reagan) for his affection. In the end, her obsession with him causes her downfall.

This film has long been considered lost, and sources disagree as to Ayesha's fate at its climax. Some claim that she steps into the flames of eternal life and has her youthfulness replaced by old age (as happens in the novel and in most other film versions), while others state that she is turned into an ape (which is plausible given the primate's prevalence in silent-era horror films). Sources also disagree as to whether the film looked magnificent or low-rent, while others suggest that there was an element of cannibalism in the proceedings.

Indiana-born Valeska Suratt got her start in theater after producer Edward Edelston saw her stride down a staircase wearing that most daring of wardrobe choice in the early years of the 20th century—a backless gown. She starred in several Broadway musicals and in 1915 was signed to an exclusive deal with Fox after the studio won a bidding war with Paramount. Garnering the nickname "The Vampire Woman" for her seductive and villainous roles, she worked with several noted directors, including George Melford and Roland West, before being kicked to the curb by the very company that had brought her stardom. She died in a Washington, D.C. nursing home in 1962, a lonely and forgotten figure. Her ashes are buried in her mother's grave in Terre Haute, Indiana.

In 1937, a fire broke out in Fox's Fort Lee, New Jersey film vaults, and all known copies of Suratt's films went up in flames, much like the character of She. CW

A Sleeping Memory
Metro; b/w; 75 min; U.S.
D: George D. Baker S: Albert S. Le Vino C: Ray C. Smallwood
Cast: Emily Stevens, Frank Mills, Mario Majeroni, Walter Horton, Richard Thornton, Francis Joyner

Eleanor Styles Martin (Stevens), disgraced by the suicide of her father, goes from a comfortable life as a socialite to a job as a clerk in a New York City department store. One day she meets the wealthy Powers Fiske (Mills), who offers to marry her if she'll first submit to an operation that will erase her memory. Eleanor agrees, and the surgery turns her into a cold and soulless woman. Powers, devastated by this unforeseen side effect, enlists the help of a friend, hypnotist Dr. Trow (Majeroni), to uncover her past lives. Eleanor recalls incarnations as a Viking woman, a princess and a Salem woman executed for witchcraft. For some reason, Trow determines that she'd be better off dead and attempts to kill her, but Fiske intervenes and saves her life. He then contacts a renowned brain surgeon, who restores Eleanor's sense of self. The two marry and live happily ever after.

Edward Phillips Oppenheim (1866-1946) was an English novelist who specialized in thrillers. A number of his stories, including *The Great Impersonation* (1920), were adapted to film. His 1902 thriller *A Sleeping Memory* (aka *The Great Awakening*) provided the basis for this melodrama. George B. Baker, who was also responsible for *Slave of Desire* (1923), a loose adaptation of Honoré de Balzac's short story *Le peau de chagrin*, directed. *Memory*'s small cast is riddled with performers whose careers were cut short by the coming of sound; an exception is character actor Francis Joyner, who later appeared in a horror curio titled *Chloe, Love is Calling You* (1934) before retiring from film. TH

The Sorrows of Satan
Samuelson/Walker; b/w; 56 min; Great Britain
D: Alexander Butler S: Harry Engholm P: G.B. Samuelson
Cast: Cecil Humphreys, Gladys Cooper, Owen Nares, Lionel d'Aragon, Winifred Delevanti, Alice de Winton

Marie Corelli lived from 1855 to 1924. Her 1895 novel *The Sorrows of Satan* received a great deal of critical condemnation and—in a not unrelated development—sold very well, to the extent that it's looked upon today as one of the world's first "blockbuster" works of fiction. A fairly uninventive collation of preexisting folk stories, it tells of a penniless writer so frustrated with his miserable existence that he sells his soul to the devil. What doubtless offended people at the time, however, wasn't the notion that someone might give up something as precious as the human soul, but Corelli's presentation of Satan in a sympathetic light. In the book, the Prince of Darkness yearns for God's forgiveness, but God cruelly refuses it. Nor could it have helped much that Corelli's personal religious views were, in the eyes of many, thoroughly suspect. Though ostensibly Catholic, she had a taste for philosophies of a distinctly non-Christian flavor. For her, the divinity of Jesus co-existed comfortably alongside a belief in reincarnation and astral projection. She came by her religious curiosity naturally; the illegitimate daughter of a poet/doctor and his mistress/servant, she was partially the product of a convent education. For years, she shared a home with a woman who may have been her lover or her stepsister; the specifics are unclear. Either way, it's indisputable that her books contributed to the body of ideas that emerged as "new age" thought in the second half of the 20th century. She also encouraged women to question and explore their sexuality and to examine their traditional, passive roles in society. This did not endear her to the establishment of the time.

The 1917 film version of *Sorrows* doesn't follow its source material closely. Here, Satan assumes the form of a handsome Prince (Humphreys), while the rich and beautiful Lady Sybil Elton (Cooper) shoves the poverty-stricken writer to the side. And while its Faustian approach was the stuff of then-contemporary horror films, director Butler took what would today be called a "chick flick" approach to the material. It wasn't until he oversaw the Egyptian thrills and chills of *The Beetle* (1919) that he fully embraced horror, helping forge a subgenre that found its apex with *The Mummy* (1932).

Despite being terribly unoriginal, the film version of *Sorrows* was by all accounts commercially successful. It was remade by Paramount, with D.W. Griffith at the helm, in 1926. CW

Tangled Lives
Fox; b/w; length unknown; U.S.
D: J. Gordon Edwards S: Mary Murillo C: Phil Rosen
Cast: Genevieve Hamper, Stuart Holmes, Robert B. Mantell, Walter Miller, Henry Leone, Claire Whitney

Ignore the misleading title; this is a version of Wilkie Collins' 1859-60 serialized Gothic romance *The Woman in White*. It's probable that Fox changed the name to stave off competition from Thanhauser's version that same year. Nor should this *Tangled Lives* be confused with the Vitagraph film of the same title made the following year. With this particular version—one of at least five silent cinema translations of Wilkie's narrative—Fox toned down the darker elements in favor of a staid approach more apropos to 1950s soap operas than silent-era horror films. For reasons inexplicable, overzealous screenwriter Mary Murillo—apparently and mistakenly thinking she was brilliant enough to effectively re-envision the classic source material—cut some characters, added others and changed the names of still others. (The novel's Count Fosco and his wife, for instance, became the Dassoris.) Enough of the story's original elements remain to qualify the film for inclusion here; Genevieve plays the dual roles of Laura Fairlie and Anne Catherick, one of whom dies and is buried as the other while the other is placed in an asylum so that her husband can steal her inheritance.

Tangled Lives was shot by the always reliable Phil Rosen, who previously completed the photographic chores for a version of Victor Hugo's novel *Notre Dame d'Paris* (1831) titled *The Darling of Paris* (1917). After 1920 Rosen abandoned cinematography to become a director, but despite an A-list career in the silent era, he spent the talkie years shooting B-pictures. These included such horror fare as *The Phantom Broadcast* and *The Sphynx* (both 1933), *Picture Brides* (1934), *Murder by Invitation* and *Spooks Run Wild* (both 1941), *The Man With Two Lives* and *The Mystery of Marie Roget* (both 1942) and *Return of the Ape Man* (1944). He also directed some of the worst Charlie Chan films in history.

Two years after this torpid Fox production, Collins' story provided the unofficial basis for *The Twin Pawns*. CW

Ultus and the Three-Button Mystery
aka **Ultus 6: The Three-Button Mystery**; **Ultus 7**; **Ultus Seven**
Gaumont; b/w; length unknown; Great Britain
D/S: George Pearson P: Leon Gaumont
Cast: Aurele Sydney, Manora Thew, Charles Rock, Alice De Winton, Fred Morgan, Frank Drake

Director George Pearson was a former schoolmaster who entered the film industry in the early silent era. He made his debut as director with a version of the Sherlock Holmes mystery *A Study in Scarlet* (1914), becoming established as a versatile and reliable talent. His pinnacle of success came with the Ultus series, which commenced with *Ultus, The Man from the Dead* (1916). The series starred Aurele Sydney as a man seeking revenge against those who betrayed him, utilizing all manner of disguises and trickery to outwit them. The series came to an end with *Ultus and the Three-Button Mystery* and, given that the first three in the franchise were released in 1916 with this one pulling up the rear a year later, it could be that Pearson cranked them out too fast to retain any inspiration—or that audiences were simply tiring of the character.

The plot of *Three-Button* concerns the kidnapping of several British statesmen who are then rescued by Ultus with the assistance of an hotelier's daughter. As with the first film in the series, this entry appears to have been cut into two parts for audiences in the United States.

Unlike so many other silent screen staples (including Fantomas, who provided the inspiration for this character), Ultus has never been revived for modern audiences. All four Ultus films are considered lost, save for a few archival fragments. TH

Unconquered
Lasky/Paramount; b/w; 55 min; U.S.
D: Frank Reicher S: Beatrice DeMille, Leighton Osmun P: Jesse L. Lasky C: Dent Gilbert
Cast: Mabel Van Buren, Fannie Ward, Hobart Bosworth, Tully Marshall, Jane Wolfe, Jack Dean

British-born Beatrice DeMille was the screenwriting mother of famed director Cecil B. DeMille. She was also the brain behind two horror films made during the silent era, the first being *Unconquered*, which was released in May 1917. The second, *The Devil-Stone*, was released later the same year (and was directed by her son).

Mrs. Jackson (Ward) is trapped in an abusive marriage to husband Henry (Bosworth), with her son Billy (Jacobs) the only source of comfort. When Henry's cruelty reaches the point that he insists his wife invite his mistress, a widow named Mrs. Lenning (Van Buren), to their home, Mrs. Jackson asks for a divorce. Henry refuses to consider it without full custody of his son, something Mrs. Jackson simply won't allow. She turns to handicapped author Richard Darcier (Dean) for emotional support, which prompts Henry to frame the two for adultery and divorce his wife, winning custody of his son and marrying Mrs. Lenning along the way. In the meantime, Richard's African American caretaker Jake (Marshall) falls in with a voodoo queen (Wolfe), who needs a human sacrifice and has her eye on Billy. Jake tries and fails to stab Billy and is carted off to an asylum, but he escapes and kidnaps the boy, prompting Mrs. Jackson to offer herself as a substitute. Richard finds and rescues mother and son, resulting in Henry improbably conceding full custody of Billy to his ex-wife, since she's the better parent.

The very white Tully Marshall—in blackface, today considered a racist convention of the silent era—portrayed Jake. Born William Phillips in California shortly after the gold rush, he took on the name Tully Marshall and starred on the stage in San Francisco before conquering Broadway in 1887. In 1914 he returned to California to take up film work. Though his most famous role is in D.W. Griffith's *Intolerance* (1916), he starred in numerous other films, including *The Devil-Stone* and *The Hunchback of Notre Dame* (1923). He also had smaller roles in *The Cat and the Canary* and *The Gorilla* (both 1927), *Strangers of the Evening* (1932) and *Night of Terror* (1933). He was married to Marion Fairfax, the screenwriter of *Go and Get It* (1920) and *The Lost World* (1925). He died of a heart attack in 1943. CW

The Voice on the Wire
Universal; b/w; 15 chapters; U.S.
D: Stuart Paton S: J. Grubb Alexander
Cast: Ben Wilson, Neva Gerber, Francis McDonald, Joseph W. Girard, Kingsley Benedict, Nigel De Brulier

Based on a 1915 novel by Eustace Hale Ball, *The Voice on the Wire* was an action serial in 15 chapters. The installments were titled thus: *1. The Oriental Death Punch*; *2. The Mysterious Man*; *3. The Spider's Web*; *4. The Next Victim*; *5. The Spectral Hand*; *6. The Death Warrant*; *7. The Marked Room*; *8. High Finance*; *9. A Stern Chase*; *10. The Guarded Heart*; *11. The Thought Machine*; *12. The Sign of the Thumb*; *13. Twixt Death and Dawn*; *14. The Light Dawn* and *15. The Living Death*. Each episode consisted of two reels and was a little over 20 minutes in length. Despite the lurid titles of some chapters, the emphasis was on cliffhanger-style thrills. Still, the serial's incorporation of gimmicks such as mummification and limb transplants seems sufficient reason for its inclusion here. The storyline dealt with a series of murders of rich men, whose deaths are trumpeted by a voice on the telephone (hence the wire of the title). It's up to one man to solve the mystery, but first he has to face a series of perils and smaller mysteries.

The cast included B-Western favorite Hoot Gibson and character actor Nigel De Brulier, who went on to appear in

Chandu the Magician (1932) and *The Hound of the Baskervilles* (1939). TH

The Woman in White
aka **The Unfortunate Marriage**
Thanhouser; b/w; 68 min; U.S.
D: Ernest C. Warde *S:* Lloyd Lonergan *P:* Edwin Thanhouser *C:* William M. Zollinger
Cast: Florence La Badie, Richard Neill, Gertrude Dallas, Arthur Bauer, Wayne Arey, J.H. Gilmour

Thanhouser's second film rendering of Wilkie Collins' serialized novel, *The Woman in White*, was more successful than their first version, perhaps because it wasn't released to theaters directly opposite a competing version (Thanhouser's 1912 version hit screens a scant two days before an adaptation from Gem). But success or no, it didn't save the then-struggling studio; a year later Thanhouser liquidated. They weren't helped by the fact that just one month after *The Woman in White*'s release, Edwin Thanhouser's personal star discovery, Florence La Badie, was involved in a car accident; six weeks later she died from the injuries she sustained.

Lloyd Lonergan wrote the script, as he had for the 1912 version. The film cast La Badie as Laura Fairlie and her mysterious double Anne Catherick, the eponymous woman in white. Richard Neill stars as Sir Percival Glyde, Laura's husband who, along with his crony Count Fosco (Arthur Bauer), hopes to steal her fortune by switching her and Anne after Anne's death. But Wayne Arey as Walter Hartright (Anne's art tutor) saves the day.

The film was re-released in the early 1920s under the title *The Unfortunate Marriage*. A print of this version resides in the Library of Congress' film archive.

1917 also saw the release of Fox's *Tangled Lives*, another adaptation of Collins' venerable novel. CW

1918

Akakabe myojin
aka kaibyô kaidan
Nikkatsu Kyoto; b/w; length unknown; Japan
Crew unknown
Cast: Matsunosuke Onoe

A young woman is falsely accused of an illicit affair with her master's retainer. She is executed and her body sealed within a red wall. A black cat, however, is trapped in this makeshift mausoleum with her. The animal becomes possessed by her spirit and seeks vengeance against those who had framed her.

Though the director of this film is unknown, one can fairly assume that silent Japanese superstar Matsunosuke Onoe played the role of the retainer. It has been alleged that a second version of the tale, starring Shirogoro Sawamura, was filmed and released sometime this same year, but this is not known for certain. Sawamura did star in a version of the story a mere two years later, which bore the same title but was produced by Kokkatsu Studios.

This particular adaptation of the tale was released on December 1, 1918. CW

Alraune
Phoenix; b/w; 80 min; Hungarian
D: Michael Curtiz, Edmund Fritz *S:* Richard Falk
Cast: Geza Erdlvi, Gyula Gal, Kalman Kormendy, Margit Lux, Rozsi Szollosi, Jeno Torzs

A mad scientist forces a woman to copulate with a Mandrake root—a plant reputed to have mystical powers—and the union produces a woman named Alraune (Gal). Though beautiful, she is an evil creature without a soul.

Published in 1911, *Alraune* is Hanns Heinz Ewers' most significant novel. A variation of sorts on the Frankenstein story, it has its origins in a German superstition dating from the Middle Ages, which suggested that if a man executed on the gallows would, at the moment of death, ejaculate onto the human-shaped Mandrake root, the root would absorb his "essence." Witches and warlocks, it was said, could use such ejaculate as an ingredient in a potion to impregnate sterile women desperate to have children. Pretty heady stuff, to be sure, and it's easy to see why Ewers—who, being among the first serious novelists to see the potential for narrative cinema, also wrote the screenplay for *The Student of Prague* (1913)—used the notion as inspiration for a novel.

Unfortunately, this first screen adaptation of the tale is among the many lost films of the silent era. Produced in Hungary, it provided an early credit for co-director Michael Curtiz under the pseudonym Mihaly Kertesz (his birth name was Manó Kertész Kaminer). It's unclear how Curtiz split his duties with collaborator Edmund Fritz, but he would later establish himself as a versatile and talented Hollywood filmmaker, accumulating such genre-spanning credits as *Dr. X* (1931), *The Adventures of Robin Hood* (1938) and *Casablanca* (1942).

A German version of Ewer's novel was shot later the same year under the title *Alraune, die Henkerstochter, genannt die rote Hanne* but would become best known under the title *Alraune*. The tale was subsequently filmed in 1928, 1930 and 1952. TH

Alraune
aka **Alraune, die Henkerstochter, genannt die rote Hanne**; **Sacrifice**

Luna-Film; b/w; 88 min; Germany
Co-D/C: Eugen Illes, *Co-D:* Joseph Klein *S:* Carl Froehlich, Georg Tatzelt
Cast: Max Auzinger, Joseph Klein, Hilde Wotner, Friedrich Kuhne, Ernst Rennspies, Tatjana Sand

A demented scientist uses a dead man's sperm to impregnate a prostitute. The resulting child, Alraune (Wotner), grows into a lovely woman who turns upon her "creator."

The second version of Hanns Heinz Ewers' novel to be filmed in 1918 (the other was Hungarian), this was allegedly the more explicit of the two in its interpretation of the text. Director/cinematographer Eugen Illes had, before moving to Germany, directed a number of features in his native Hungary. He would go on to direct more than a dozen other films; his last known directorial credit is in 1927, and he passed away in 1951 after having moved back to his native country. His work is mostly forgotten today, and *Alraune* is his only known contribution to the horror genre.

Co-director Joseph Klein amassed far more credits as an actor than as a director—his only other directing credits, in fact, are the same "co-director" billing on chapters one and four of the eight-part serial *Die Herrin der Welt* (1919-20). One can safely assume that his duties in *Alraune* were geared more toward working with the actors than with guiding the technical side of the process.

The film was released in the U.S. under the title *Sacrifice*, and an American archive reputedly houses a print; it has yet to emerge on home video, however, and as such remains virtually impossible to see. Given the lurid plot, one can imagine it being a title of some interest, but like its competing Hungarian version, it has slid into obscurity. Subsequent adaptations by Henrik Galeen (*Alraune*, 1928) and Arthur Maria Rabenalt (*Unnatural*, 1952) remain much easier to access and are renowned among film buffs. TH

The Bells
Anderson-Brunton; b/w; 50 min; U.S.
D: Ernest C. Warde *S:* Gilson Willets, Jack Cunningham
Cast: Frank Keenan, Lois Wilson, Edward Coxen, Carl Stockdale, Joseph J. Dowling, Ida Lewis

In desperate need of money, Alsatian innkeeper Mathias (Keenan) murders and robs a Polish Jew, Koveski (Law), who is staying in one of his rooms. Afterward, whenever he hears bells, Mathias flashes to the sleigh bells that signaled Koveski's approach on the night of his death. When Mathias' daughter Annette (Wilson) marries a captain of the guard (Coxen), Mathias throws a celebration in honor of the young couple. One of the party's guests is a mesmerist who has been hired to entertain the other guests, and Mathias, fearing that the man may somehow hypnotize him into confessing his crime, goes to bed and falls asleep. He dreams that the hypnotist has placed him under a spell and coaxed a confession from him. In his delirium, he rushes downstairs shouting, "The bells!" Then he dies.

This is the fourth confirmed adaptation of Leopold Lewis' Anglicized take on Érckmann-Chatrian's *Le Juif Polonaise*, itself a mélange of Edgar Allan Poe's poem "The Bells" (1849) and his short story *The Tell-Tale Heart* (1843).

Anderson-Brunton made only a few films, all of them between March 1918 and May 1919, including the partially lost comedy/drama *Ghost of the Rancho* (1918). While most of their films were directed by either Ernest C. Warde (who oversaw this one), William Worthington or Robert Thornby, there was one (*The Silver Girl*, 1919) directed by here-leading-man Frank Keenan. Keenan, born in 1858 in Dubuque, Iowa, was no stranger to horror films, having starred in 1909's bizarre *The Hunchback*. An alcoholic, he was known for having to hold onto things while performing to keep from falling down; his biggest claim to fame, however, may be as the grandfather of noted actor Keenan Wynn. Frank Keenan died of pneumonia in Hollywood, California in 1929. CW

Cagliostro
aka **Kaliostro**

Torgovy; b/w; length unknown; Russia
D: Wladyslaw Starevich
Cast: M. Yarosh, Arseniy Bibikov, V. Dzenjaevic, Bronislava Rutkovskaya, Olga Tschechowa, V. Satin

Based on the novel *Count Cagliostro* by E. Salias, this 1918 Russian film was apparently more historical melodrama than horror story. It followed the exploits of self-proclaimed occultist and mesmerist Count Alessandro di Cagliostro, aka Italian playboy and criminal Giuseppe Balsamo. The film appears to be lost, but given the nature of the source material and the historical figure on which it's based, it's likely that it focused on Cagliostro's occult claims and criminal behavior (which, in real life, led to his execution).

In the earliest years of cinema, Count Cagliostro was a prime subject, beginning in 1899 with George Méliès' *Cagliostro's Mirror* and continuing with Camille de Morlhorn's 1910 French two-reeler, the *Trilby*-influenced *Cagliostro*. Nor would this 1918 Russian film be the last. At least two more silent films followed, both by the name of *Cagliostro*, in 1920 and 1929. CW

The Craving
aka **Delirium**

Universal; b/w; 50 min; U.S.
D/S: Francis Ford *C:* Edward Gheller
Cast Francis Ford, Peter Gerald, Mae Gaston, Duke Worne, Jean Hathaway, W.A. Hoffman

Carroll Wales (Ford) is a recovering alcoholic who has made a name for himself as a chemist. He develops a formula for a potent explosive, which attracts the interest of sinister Ala Kasarib (Gerald). Using his hypnotic powers on his ward, May (Gaston), Kasarib schemes to steal the formula for his own use. Under Ala's malevolent influence, May tempts Carroll with alcohol. He succumbs, and Kasarib uses his weird talents, assisted by Carroll's overindulgence in drink, to inflict terrible hallucinatory visions upon him.

Critics at the time assailed the filmmakers for not pursuing a stronger anti-alcohol message. In *Variety*'s September 27, 1918 write-up, the reviewer stated:

> There is not much plot, nor is there a lesson tangibly taught. The picture is a fantasy, dealing with the sins of the flesh, and the power of the mind. Tricks and illusions are shown on the screen, but the photography is not particularly extraordinary.

Just how fully the film delved into the horror can only be guessed.

The film should not be confused with the Paul Naschy werewolf film *Night of the Werewolf* (1980), which was re-titled *The Craving* for its U.S. release. TH

The Eyes of the Mummy
aka **Die Augen der Mumie Ma**; **Die Mumie Ma**; **Eyes of the Mummy Ma**
PAGU/UFA; b/w; 58(64) min; Germany
D: Ernst Lubitsch *S:* Hans Kraly, Emil Rameau *C:* Alfred Hansen
Cast: Emil Jannings, Pola Negri, Harry Liedtke, Max Lawrence

While hiking across an arid desert in Egypt, a young painter named Albert Wendland (Liedtke) comes across a beautiful girl (Negri) drawing water from a well. When she sees him, she runs off in fear. Later, at a market square in Cairo, Wendland tries to find someone who will take him to the tomb of Queen Ma, but the locals fear the queen's power and refuse. He winds up going it alone on horseback and once there meets Radu, the strange guardian of the tomb. Radu takes him inside and shows him a stone face with living eyes, set into the wall of the chamber. A fight ensues during which Wendland shoots his opponent. As he delves deeper into the tomb, he comes upon the beautiful woman (also named Ma) who had fled from him earlier. She tells him that she was abducted by Radu and taken to the tomb's chamber of death. There the guardian had attempted to seduce her, threatening her with enslavement if she did not acquiesce. Moved by her story, Wendland whisks her off to Europe and shapes her into the perfect European wife. Meanwhile, Prince Hohenfels (Lawrence) prepares to tour the burial chamber of the queen, though he's warned that doing so might result in the loss of his sanity. When he speaks to a gentleman who's actually been to the tomb, all the man can say is, "The eyes are alive! The eyes are alive!" The Prince nonetheless mounts his expedition, finding the wounded Radu and taking him to a nearby hospital. Radu is nursed back to health and becomes Hohenfels' servant, all the while planning revenge on the Lady Ma.

The protests of some film historians aside, *The Eyes of the Mummy* is an outright horror film wallowing in sexual obsession, madness, hypnotism and astral projection. That isn't to say that the film is entirely successful. Too much is made of Radu's "frightening" appearance, which in truth comes across as a bit comical. Nor is Polish-born Pola Negri all that believable as Ma. At one point she performs a dance that astounds onlookers and results in a job as a professional performer in a local theater, The

Emil Jannings from *The Eyes of the Mummy*

Alahambra. Yet the dance is entirely flat and uninventive, leaving one to wonder what the big deal is. And when attempting to convey emotion, the actress comes across as more sober than nuanced. Still, her performance here and in Lubitsch's later melodrama *Sumurun* (1920) received a great deal of critical acclaim at the time, and when the director departed Germany for Hollywood at the invite of Mary Pickford, Negri was quick to follow. She found work in the U.S. with directors George Fitzmaurice and Herbert Brenon, and in 1924 reunited with Lubitsch for the highly successful *Forbidden Paradise*.

Often portraying licentious ladies onscreen, her offscreen love life was every bit as vampish and public. She carried on affairs with Charlie Chaplin and Rudolph Valentino, among others, but her career took a downturn after she threw herself onto Valentino's casket at his funeral. The public saw it as an ostentatious career move rather than a legitimate expression of grief. This impression was strengthened when Negri then announced that she had been engaged to Valentino, following his funeral procession across the continental United States and posing for newspaper and magazine photographers at every opportunity. The American public turned away from her, and the coming of sound pounded the final nail in her career's coffin (though she did continue to nab small roles here and there). In the 1930s she returned to Germany where—it was rumored with little proof—she and Hitler had an affair. The actress finally left Germany for good in 1938 when it was determined that she had Jewish ancestry. She became a U.S. citizen in 1951 and died in 1987 after refusing treatment for a brain tumor.

Negri wasn't the only *Mummy* star to make a go of it in Hollywood. Swiss actor Emil Jannings also immigrated to the U.S., where he received the very first Academy Award for Best Actor—not for one motion picture but for two: *The Way of All Flesh* and *The Last Command* (both 1929). Due to his thick Eastern European accent, however, he had a difficult time adjusting to talkies and finally moved back to Germany, where he became active in Nazi propaganda films. When World War II ended, his past as a Nazi brought his film career to an end. He died of cancer in 1951, and his Oscar is today housed in a museum in Berlin.

with one leg crossed over the other (the director?) can be plainly seen in the lower left-hand pane. CW

The Ghost of Slumber Mountain
World; b/w; 19 (30; 12) min; U.S.
D/S/FX: Willis O'Brien *P:* Herbert M. Dawley
Cast: Herbert M. Dawley, Willis O'Brien

Two young boys beg their "Unk" Jack Holmes (Dawley), an author and amateur artist, to tell them a true story about the animal world. So Uncle Jack reads them an entry from his diary, which tells of a mountain valley he once explored with his partner Joe and their dog Soxie. This is how it goes: While exploring, they come across a cabin allegedly haunted by the spirit of an old hermit known as Mad Dick (O'Brien). Joe tells Jack that he once saw Mad Dick's spirit leaving the cabin and that he followed it to the top of Slumber Mountain, where it gazed through a strange instrument at the valley below. Later that same night, Uncle Jack sits by the campfire thinking about Mad Dick, and after his friend falls asleep and the campfire dies down, he imagines a voice calling to him. He follows the sound to Mad Dick's cabin, where he comes upon strange bones, books about prehistoric life and other oddities. After examining small models of a ceratopsian and a hadrosaur, he opens a box and finds the instrument Joe told him about. He hears the voice again and follows it to the top of Slumber Mountain, where Mad Dick appears and bids him look through the instrument. When Jack does so, he sees a 100-foot-long grazing "Brontosaurus," followed by a flightless terror bird feasting on a snake. Next he watches as two *Triceratops* eat foliage and fight each other. Then a *Tyrannosaurus rex* appears, kills one of the three-horned herbivores and tears chunks of flesh from its body. The terrifying beast turns, sees Jack watching it and chases after him. Jack shoots to no avail, and just when the beast is poised to pounce and devour him, the amateur artist awakens to find himself next to Joe at their campsite.

Though some sources claim *Slumber Mountain* was 90 minutes in its original form, the evidence suggests that it was likely around half an hour long before being cut down to 12 minutes. For years this shorter print was the only one in circulation, but the film was eventually restored to a 19-minute cut. Given that the original edits were made by producer Dawley (who also starred as Jack), one might wonder what was cut and why. It has been suggested that the missing footage was deemed too homosexual in subtext, an idea borne out by a scene that did get restored: Jack and Joe stop over at Rhododendron Lake so that Jack can paint, and Jack tries "to persuade Joe to remove his clothes and pose as a faun." (Joe refuses, not out of shyness or fear of how it might look, but because there are too many mosquitoes around.)

Reviews for *Slumber Mountain* were generally positive, with *Variety* (on April 18, 1919) stating: "[T]hese dinosaurs that sug-

Despite its career-boosting effect, *The Eyes of the Mummy* never achieved classic status and is mostly forgotten today. With the coming of sound, Lubitsch never again attempted to make a film as dark as *Eyes*, focusing instead on musicals and comedies.

On a humorous note, at the point in the film where Radu breaks out a window to get to Ma, the reflection of a man sitting

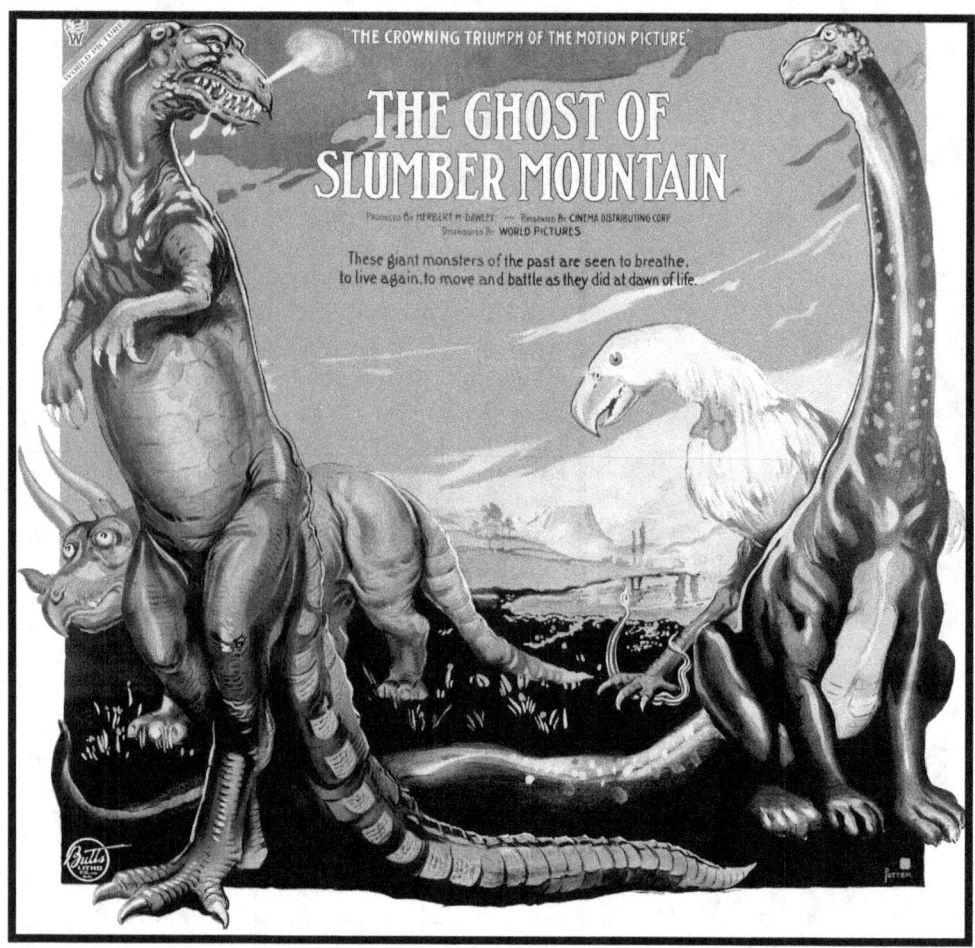

gest impossible lengths and heights, as well as the horned hobgoblins of the period ... walk, twist, gaze and eat, as we might imagine they must have in the long, long, long ago." On November 18, 1919, the *New York Times* called the film's prehistoric animals "remarkably lifelike ..." The effects were achieved by a then-relatively new process of stop-motion animation and presented a far superior sight to some of Willis O'Brien's previous films. O'Brien began his professional life as a cartoonist and sculptor and branched into cinema when he filmed a number of shorts with prehistoric themes. These included *The Dinosaur and the Missing Link: A Prehistoric Tragedy* (1915) and *R.F.D. 10,000 B.C.* and *Prehistoric Poultry* (both 1916). After writing and directing the successful *The Ghost of Slumber Mountain* (which reportedly made over three times its production costs during its original theatrical run), he was approached by First National to provide the special effects for their relatively big-budget adaptation of Sir Arthur Conan Doyle's *The Lost World* (1925). This in time led to O'Brien's special effects masterpiece, *King Kong* (1933).

In 1917 O'Brien married his first wife, Hazel Ruth Collette, who bore him two sons. The couple separated in 1930, and she suffered thereafter from both tuberculosis and cancer. Their older son contracted tuberculosis as well and went blind. In 1933, while O'Brien was filming *The Son of Kong*, Hazel shot and murdered the older son while he lay sleeping in bed, then shot the younger son who died on his way to the hospital. In a truly bizarre twist, Hazel tried to top her filicide by committing suicide, but the bullet passed through her chest, draining her tubercular lung. Due to her cancer, however, she was never tried for her crimes. She died not long after the incident while in custody in a Los Angeles hospital.

One of O'Brien's technical advisors on *Slumber Mountain* was none other than Barnum Brown, the famous dinosaur hunter who discovered T-rex. The dinosaur models used in the stop-motion effects for the film were clearly based on the paintings of paleoartist Charles R. Knight.

Outtakes from *Slumber Mountain* were used, it is believed, for the special effects sequences in Herbert M. Dawley's 1920 straight science fiction film, *Along the Moonboom Trail*. CW

The Ghost of the Rancho
aka **Ghost of the Rancho; Range Rider**
Anderson-Brunton; b/w; 42 min; France
D: William Worthington *S:* Jack Cunningham, Arthur Henry Gooden *C:* Charles Kaufman
Cast: Bryant Washburn, Rhea Mitchell, Joseph J. Dowling

Originally released by distributor Pathé on August 11, 1918, *The Ghost of the Rancho* was an amalgam of genres—comedy, drama, Western, action/adventure and horror. Some sources claim that the film included a ghostly posse stalking the night à la Hammer's *Captain Clegg* (1962), but this does not seem to have been the case. Rather, the ethereal manifestation of the title is the hero, Jeffrey Wall (Worthington), who dresses as a ghost to rescue his would-be girlfriend Mary (Mitchell) from outlaws hiding out at a ranch after killing its owner. As the terrified criminals attempt to flee, the town sheriff arrests them. With the blessing of the elder Wall (Dowling), Jeffrey and Mary marry, thus ending the film on an upbeat note.

William Worthington directed approximately 70 films during the span of his career; he also had well over 100 outings as an actor, most of them un-credited bit parts in the 1930s. He died in 1941, and his last two films were released posthumously.

The Ghost of the Rancho was re-released in 1922 under the title *Range Busters*. Despite rumors to the contrary, it is not a lost film; prints of it are housed at the Library of Congress Film Archive. CW

The Haunted Hotel
aka **Kinekature Komedies: The Haunted Hotel**
Hagan & Double/Kinekature; b/w; 11 min; Great Britain
D: Fred Rains *P:* Julius Hagan
Cast: Will Asher, Marion Peake, Lupino Lane

This is one of only a few silent horror comedies from director Fred (Frederick) Rains, father of actor Claude Rains. This time out, the elder Rains uses distorting lenses to create comedic images of ghostly activity in a haunted hotel (a by then already hackneyed convention, thanks to the likes of Georges Méliès, George Albert Smith and Edwin S. Porter). The film was part of the Kinekature Komedies series, and, like Rains' previous horror outing (*Jones' Nightmare; or, The Lobster Still Pursued Him*, 1911) was predominantly a trick film aimed at making the masses bust a gut rather than scream in fear. There were nine Kinekature Komedies in total, all of them produced by film entrepreneur Julius Hagan. The films were intended as star vehicles for up-and-coming Lupino Lane, who was considered something of a viable competitor to popular British comedienne Billy Merson. Lane's wife, Violet Blythe, also starred in some of the Kinekature films with him. CW

The Haunted House

Frazee; b/w; 22 min; U.S.
P/S: Edwin A. Frazee
Cast unknown

This short silent film is so obscure that it doesn't even appear in most Edwin A. Frazee filmographies. While most of Frazee's works were comedies, this one featured a haunted house and depicted apparently supernatural episodes. The cast names, as well as those of the production crew apart from Frazee, are unknown. In addition to being a producer, Frazee was a writer and actor, though his real love was for directing. His most famous film is *Her Father's Station* (1917), which was shot for the fledgling Fox Film Corporation. He also wrote and shot the Stan Laurel vehicles *Hickory Hiram* and *Phony Photos* (both 1918).

Despite the director's last name and the film's title, *The Haunted House* does not appear to have had anything to do with Cleveland, Ohio's infamous Frazee House, which was built between 1825 and 1827 by Stephen Frazee for his wife Mehitable. That house is today reputed to be haunted by Stephen as well as by one of his children, who is said to have died there at a young age. Some sources state that there may have also been a lynching on the property during a brief period when a portion of the house served as a makeshift jail while a nearby canal was being dug. To this day Frazee House remains without indoor plumbing, running water and electricity and is owned and administered by the National Park Service. Two of its original bricks still bear the hand-carved initials of its first occupants. CW

Izumo kaidan

Nikkatsu Kyoto; b/w; 40 min; Japan
S: Midirikawa Fnabashi
Cast: Matsunosuke Onoe, Kitsuraku Arashi, Kijaku Otani, Suminojo Ichikawa, Sentaro Nakamura, Chosei Kataoka

It's difficult to know what this film was actually about. Its title translates roughly as "Ghost Story of Izumo." The Izumo in question may refer to a province in the Shimane Prefecture—named after the Japanese goddess Izanami, who was said to have given birth to Japan. According to Japanese folklore, Izanami is buried in Mt. Hiba, which overlooks the province. It's also possible that "Izumo" is a reference to author Takeda Izumo, famed for adapting the classic Kabuki play *Chushingura* (based on a Japanese war legend) from an original bunraku (or puppet theater) play. Either way, *Izumo kaidan* appears to have been released, in Japan at least, on May 18, 1918, not sometime in 1917 as some sources claim (though it may well have been shot in 1917). CW

The Other Self
aka **Das Andere Ich**

Sascha; b/w; length unknown; Austria
D: Fritz Freisler *S:* Ladislaus Tuszynski
Cast: Fritz Kortner, Raoul Aslan, Magda Sonja

This German entry melded horror with a touch of science fiction. The story concerns a scientist (Kortner) who develops a technique for separating the human soul from the body it inhabits. He serves as his own guinea pig, with messy results.

Leading man Fritz Kortner was born in Vienna in 1892 and entered film in 1915; his lengthy career saw him working with such luminaries as F.W. Murnau, Robert Weine and G.W. Pabst. He eventually made his way to the United Kingdom and then the United States, where he scored work in such variable fare as *The Strange Death of Adolf Hitler* (1943) and *The Razor's Edge* (1946). He died in 1970.

Director Fritz Freisler was active in the silent era, but his career came to a halt with the arrival of sound; this appears to have been his only flirtation with the horror genre. The notion of isolating the unseen aspects of human beings informed Robert Louis Stevenson's novella *The Strange Case of Dr. Jekyll and Mr. Hyde* and its umpteen screen treatments, but the idea of actually separating body and soul found expression in far fewer films; among these, Terence Fisher's *Frankenstein Created Woman* (1966) is probably the best-known example. TH

The Picture of Dorian Gray
aka **Az Elet kiralya Dorian Gray**; **Az Elet kiralya**; **Dorian Gray Arckepe**

Star; b/w; length unknown; Hungary
D: Alfred Deésy *S:* Jószef Pakots
Cast: Norbert Dán, Bela Lugosi, Lajos Gellért, Annie Góth, Ella Hollán, Richard Kornay, Ila Lóth, Gusztáv Turán

Very little is known about this final silent adaptation of Oscar Wilde's novel *The Picture of Dorian Gray* (1890), which was shot in Hungary in 1918 by Alfred Deésy. Deésy was a popular director whose career lasted into the late 1940s. Unfortunately, most of his films—along with the majority of films from Hungary's silent days—are lost, making it impossible to assess the virtues or flaws of this particular version of Wilde's story. Even the assertion that Bela Lugosi played Lord Henry Wotton is hotly debated. It seems likely, however, given that Lugosi began his acting career in his native Hungary and starred in features there as late as 1920.

The story is simple enough. The handsome Dorian Gray remains young while his picture, which reflects the stain of his sins, continues to age. CW

The Pied Piper of Hamelin
aka **Der Rettenfanger von Hameln**

PAGU; b/w; 64 min; Germany
D/S: Paul Wegener *P:* Paul Davidson *C:* Frederik Fuglsang
Cast: Paul Wegener, Lyda Salmanova, Clemens Kaufung, Wilhelm Diegelmann, Marte Marte, Armin Schweizer

Rats overrun the German town of Hamelin. The creatures terrorize the helpless residents until a strange musician (Wegener) with an enchanted flute brings the beasts to heel. In time, the villagers likewise fall under his spell, especially local beauty Ursula (Salmanova). It turns out that the musician is the victim of a curse, which can only be lifted if a young maiden becomes his wife. But when he proposes to Ursula, she rejects him. The piper is thus doomed to wander aimlessly, and as retaliation for Ursula's rebuff, he lures the local children away from their homes to wander aimlessly with him.

The legend of the Pied Piper of Hamelin is believed to have originated in the 1300s as a means of explaining the odd disappearance of over 100 village children. The story was embroidered upon over time; some accounts cast the Piper as a full-fledged pedophile, and at some point rats were brought on board the narrative. (The strange disappearances have never been rationally explained.) The legend has inspired countless works of art, ranging from operas to children's stories. It found its way into cinema early on, with versions popping up at least as early as 1903. The adaptations before this one, all considered lost, reportedly shied away from the more sinister aspects of the story, which would make this the first version to examine the tale's less savory side.

Writer/director/star Paul Wegener had already made his mark on fantasy cinema with *The Student of Prague* (1913) and *The Golem* (1915), and he would continue to explore morbid themes for years to come. He was often cast in his own films as a character reaching for an unattainable love, and he was frequently cast similarly in films by other filmmakers, making him something of a German counterpart to Lon Chaney. Wegener's propensity for weird make-ups also links him to the legendary silent film icon.

Art director Rochus Gliese had already worked on *The Golem* and co-directed the parody *The Golem and the Dancing Girl* (1917) with Wegener; Gliese's most enduring credit, however, is F.W. Murnau's classic *Sunrise: A Song of Two Humans* (1927), on which he worked as art director. Cinematographer Frederik Fuglsang later photographed Richard Oswald's *The Hound of the Baskervilles* (1929), while leading lady Lyda Salmanova rejoined Wegener for his definitive crack at the Golem legend, *The Golem: How He Came into the World* (1920). TH

The Silent Mystery
Burston; b/w; 15 chapters; U.S.
D: Francis Ford *S:* Elsie Van Name, John B. Clymer *P:* Louis Burston
Cast: Francis Ford, Rosemary Theby, Mae Gaston, Elsie Van Neame, Olive Valerie, Hap Ward

Priestess Kah (Theby) seeks vengeance on those who stole a priceless jewel, The Eye of the World, from a Pharaoh's tomb. It falls upon the valiant Phil Kelly (Ford) to save the day. This 15-chapter serial anticipates the run of Egyptian-themed horror films that commenced with Universal's *The Mummy* in 1932. Rather than an avenging mummy, however, the film presents a vampish Priestess striking down the members of an expedition; in this respect, it may well have been inspired by Bram Stoker's novel *The Jewel of Seven Stars* (1903), later filmed as *Blood from the Mummy's Tomb* (1971), *The Awakening* (1980) and *Legend of the Mummy* (1997).

Francis appeared in a whopping 479 films overall; among his roles is an un-credited turn as one of the monster's victims in *Frankenstein* (1931). As a director, he helmed 174 titles, the majority of them long forgotten. Rumor has it that his younger brother John, who went on to become one of the most famous directors in film history, enjoyed casting him in bit parts as a way of belittling him. (Francis' son John Phillips Ford—under the name Philip Ford—also had a minor career as a stuntman, acting double and assistant director.)

Actress Rosemary Theby was popular in the silent era, where she specialized in vamp roles. She seems a perfect choice, then, as the vindictive Princess Kah.

Like so many serials of the era, *The Silent Mystery* is considered lost; a five-reel condensation was reportedly released in feature form in some areas. TH

The Two-Soul Woman
Universal; b/w; 50 min; U.S.
D/S: Elmer Clifton
Cast: Priscilla Dean, Ashton Dearholt, Joseph W. Girard, Evelyn Selbie

Chester Castle (Dearholt) is in a bad car wreck, after which beautiful heiress Joy Fielding (Dean) tends to him. The two duly fall in love, but there's a sudden and disconcerting change in Joy's personality. Leah (Selbie), the girl's maid, explains that Joy is under the spell of physician, Dr. Chopin (Girard), who hopes to gain access to Joy's family fortune via hypnotism. Chester proposes marriage as a means of undoing Chopin's spell, and the doctor responds by attacking Chester and attempting to kill him. During the ensuing struggle, Chopin is shot to death with his own revolver. Chester and Joy get married.

The Two-Soul Woman used the novel by Gelett Burgess, an American writer most remembered for his poetry, as its basis. (As a point of trivia, he is credited with coining the term "blurb" as a description of a brief synopsis.) *Two-Soul* utilizes the silent horror cliché of hypnotism and may have been influenced by the popular story of *Alraune*, with its image of a predatory woman without a soul.

Elmer Clifton made his debut as a director in 1915 and remained cinematically active until his death in 1949 (his last work was released posthumously in 1950). He spent most of his career helming low-budget fare, including such borderline genre films as *Seven Doors to Death* (1944; not to be confused with Lucio Fulci's *The Beyond*, 1981, which was re-edited and re-titled in the United States as *The Seven Doors to Death*).

Priscilla Dean was one of Universal's most popular starlets in the 1920s, but the coming of sound derailed her career. She retired from the screen in 1932. TH

Yotsuya kaidan jitsuhi kanetani goro
Nikkatsu Kyoto; b/w; length unknown; Japan
Crew unknown
Cast: Matsunosuke Onoe, Sentaro Nakamura, Kijaku Otani, Sennosuke Nakamura, Suminojo Ichikawa, Kitsuraku Arashi

This, the second film to draw upon Tsuruya Nanboku IV's 1825 horror play *Yotsuya kaidan*, is either a remake of or a sequel to Shozo Mikino's 1912 original, also titled *Yotsuya kaidan*. Given that both films are long lost, it's impossible to sort out the matter satisfactorily. Whatever the case, it's near certain that *Yotsuya kaidan jitsuhi kanetani goro*, like Shozo Makino's film, offered up the ghost of a scorned woman, seeking to hound her adulterous lover and his mistress to their deaths.

Both the 1912 adaptation and this film starred Matsunosuke Onoe as said unfaithful husband. Born Tsuruzo Nakamura in September 1875, he left home at age 14 to join a traveling theater troupe. He eventually assumed the moniker Matsunosuke Onoe and was hired to work for a theater owned by Makino. Several of Onoe's performances there were filmed, becoming some of the first Japanese "movies." Onoe went on to star in over 1,000 films, roughly half of which were shot by Makino. His trademark large eyes led him to be cast in both sinister and humorous roles, but it was through a series of historical epics that he became Japan's first true cinematic superstar. Afflicted by heart disease, he preceded Makino into the afterlife by a little over two years, and his funeral became the subject of a short documentary feature. CW

1919

Werner Krauss as Dr. Caligari from *The Cabinet of Dr. Caligari*

L'atleta fantasma
A. De Giglio; b/w; 85 min; Italy
D: Raimondo Scotti *S:* Renee De Liot *P:* Alfonso De Giglio
Cast: Mario Guaita-Ausonia, Elsa Zara, Dino Bonaiuti, Gaetano Rossi

The gentle, humble Harry Audressen (Guaita-Ausonia) is in love with the beautiful, haughty Jenny (Zara), but she's the adventurous type and not interested in marrying a wallflower. She gets her share of said adventure when she and her father visit a museum, where she convinces daddy to buy an ancient gold buckle that the curator has on sale. Two antiques dealers are also interested in the item, and they'll stop at nothing, including theft and murder, to obtain it. Yet, every time they attempt to seize the accursed thing, a mysterious masked phantom shows up and thwarts them. When they kidnap Jenny with the aim of using her to ward off their nemesis, the police apprehend them. That's when the muscular, bare-chested phantom is revealed to be the introverted Harry. Needless to say, Jenny realizes her love for him, and the two live happily ever after.

Primarily an adventure story, *L'atleta fantasma* includes the cursed antique so popular in silent horror cinema. Its tale of a masked superhero with a mild-mannered secret identity is the stuff of comic books—two decades before Superman and Batman became so wildly successful with schoolchildren (and more than a few grownups) everywhere. The wrestler-*cum*-superhero was a beloved pop archetype in Italian silent cinema, with numerous films of the period built around the fictitious exploits of popular grapplers. Another example of the genre is *Maciste in Hell* (1925), which injects the superhero motif into *Dante's Inferno*. After the silent era, however, masked wrestler films ran their course in Italy, leaving Mexican cinema to fill the vacuum with a brand all its own.

Some sources mistakenly refer to *L'atleta fantasma* as *L'atketa fantasma*. The woman who wrote it, Renee De Liot, scripted no fewer than 15 films for Guaita-Ausonia. The title here translates roughly into *The Athlete Phantom* or *The Athletic Ghost*. Prints of the film exist in the National Museum of Cinema in Turin and the Cinémathèque Royale in Brussels. CW

The Beetle
Barker; b/w; 62 min; Great Britain
D: Alexander Butler *S:* Helen Blizzard *P:* Jack Smith
Cast: Leal Douglas, Fred Morgan, Maudie Dunham, Hebden Foster, Frank Reade, Rolf Leslie

Based on the 1897 novel *The Beetle: A Mystery* by Richard Marsh (a pseudonym of Richard Bernard Heldmann), *The Beetle* is a feature-length horror film made in Great Britain after the First World War. It concerns an Egyptian high priestess (Douglas) who, reincarnated as a beetle, wreaks vengeance on a member of the British Parliament (Foster).

From the sounds of it, the film wasn't very faithful to the novel. The book had been a huge success, outselling Bram Stoker's *Dracula*, which beat it into print by only a few months. *Beetle* the book remained available until 1960, after which it fell out of public interest and its publication ceased. (It has since been reprinted.) It may have served as an inspiration for Stoker's *The Jewel of Seven Stars* (1903), about an Egyptian princess reincarnating into the body of an archaeologist's daughter. That novel provided the basis for several films, relegating Marsh's novel to relative obscurity. And indeed, the book isn't very good. It tells the tale, in multiple parts and from various viewpoints, of a member of Parliament, in love with a young woman, whose career and impending marriage are threatened by a deed from his past. Haunted by a mysterious creature that can change form (appearing as male, female and a beetle), he enlists the aid of an unlikely ally, a rival suitor, to thwart his supernatural nemesis.

Director Alexander Butler also made the first film version of Maria Corelli's 1895 Gothic novel *The Sorrows of Satan* in 1917, as well as having an acting part in the 1925 film adaptation of H. Rider Haggard's *She: A History of Adventure*. CW

The Cabinet of Dr. Caligari is, quite simply, the cinema's first horror masterpiece. From left to right: Warner Krauss, Conrad Veight and Lil Dagover

The Cabinet of Dr. Caligari
aka Das Cabinet des Dr. Caligari
Decla-Bioscop AG; b/w; 71 min; Germany
D: Robert Wiene *S:* Hans Janowitz, Carl Mayer *P:* Erich Pommer, Rudolf Meinert *C:* Willy Hameister
Cast: Werner Krauss, Conrad Veidt, Friedrich Feher, Lil Dagover, Hans Heinrich von Twardowski, Rudolf Lettinger

Francis (Feher) and his friend Alan (von Twardowski) visit a carnival sideshow attraction emceed by a man who calls himself Dr. Caligari (Krauss). The doctor displays to the crowd a somnambulist named Cesare (Veidt), whom he claims can foretell the future. When Cesare predicts that Alan will die before dawn, the two men laugh it off. But the next morning, Alan is dead. Francis, convinced that Caligari is up to no good, determines to unmask him.

The Cabinet of Dr. Caligari is, quite simply, the cinema's first horror masterpiece. Its nightmarish exploration of paranoia and madness has influenced generations of filmmakers, and its bizarre imagery remains the touchstone by which the Expressionist movement in German cinema will forever be judged.

Expressionism originated in Germany in the early 20th century as an attempt to articulate the inner psyche in physical (though highly symbolic) terms. In the field of painting, Expressionist artists such as Otto Dix and Erich Heckel drew inspiration from past masters such as Edvard Munch and Vincent Van Gogh. (Heckel's woodcut *Portrait of a Man* is a classic example of the German Expressionist method applied to still art.) Rather than bind themselves to literal representations, Expressionist painters strove to capture the darkly emotional aspects of their subjects. In the theatrical world, celebrated director Max Reinhardt capitalized on the popularity of the movement by incorporating deliberately abstract and exaggerated set designs into his productions. Combined with experimental uses of lighting and careful choreography, these productions helped revolutionize the theatrical scene throughout Europe. It didn't take long for German filmmakers to explore the possibilities of this movement on the newest of visual art forms, with Paul Wegener's 1913 adaptation of *The Student of Prague* often cited as the first Expressionist feature-length motion picture. But it was *Caligari* that set the gold standard for the movement, and to this day it is the picture most often referenced whenever the school is discussed.

It's easy to see why! The story provides a perfect springboard for exploring the fragile psyches of its characters, and the film's extraordinary visual design impresses no less today than

The use of obvious backdrops, with painted shadows and highlights, expresses the concept of a world gone mad, from *The Cabinet of Dr. Caligari*.

it undoubtedly did then. *Caligari* remains one of the most resolutely artificial films ever made. The use of obvious backdrops, with painted shadows and highlights, expresses the concept of a world gone mad—a reflection of Germany following World War I—in clear and jarring visual terms. Director Robert Wiene (1873-1938) was hired to helm the film after it had been rejected by Fritz Lang, though Lang later claimed to have suggested the story that bookends the film. Given Lang's disinterest in the more artificial aspects of the Expressionist movement, it isn't surprising that he'd give it a pass; while he's often grouped with cinematic artists from the school, he considered himself a social realist and wouldn't have been interested in the man-made reality of a project like *Caligari*. The fact that he sought to claim authorship of the bookend material, which serves to bring some level of rationale to the proceedings, further demonstrates his pragmatic leanings. While Lang's visual style at times betrayed an obvious Expressionist influence, the heart of his work was always concerned with the material world and the occurrences therein. In any event, Wiene proved to be the ideal director for *Caligari*. Much of his directorial work is either lost or forgotten today, but his reputation will always be secure based on this one film alone. While much of the film's style is attributable to its art direction and design (the work of Walter Reimann, Walter Rohrig and Hermann Warm), Wiene's judicious use of framing is every bit as compelling.

The film's final revelation has long been criticized as simplistic and forced, but in truth the final fade-out leaves the viewer with more questions than answers. If, as Lang suggested, the finale was meant to bring order to a disordered narrative, it doesn't succeed. Yes, the narrative—told via flashback by Francis in the none-too-idyllic garden of an insane asylum—is indeed the product of a diseased mind, but upon reflection the film avoids triteness by implying that, insane or not, Francis may well be telling the truth. Caligari is revealed to be the director of the asylum, after all, and his sinister final look into the camera isn't that of a benevolent figure. Wiene draws effective performances from his entire cast. The acting reflects the consciously fake aesthetic very effectively, with the central characterizations by Werner Krauss and Conrad Veidt remaining particularly impressive even today. Krauss, hidden behind thick glasses, a top hat and an unruly mess of hair, is convincingly perverse as the demented Caligari who, driven by megalomania, forces Cesare to murder all who displease him. Veidt gives one of his most memorable performances as the somnambulistic Cesare. With his skeletal build, gaunt features and pale make-up, he is the living embodiment of the bogeyman. He uses his body expressively to convey pathos, but he is also effectively macabre when the occasion calls for it. The images of Cesare stalking Francis' girlfriend (Dagover) and carrying her over the rooftops have been mimicked to the point of parody, but they retain an off-kilter poetry through the sheer conviction of Veidt's pantomime.

Ultimately, the film has been the subject of so much in-depth analysis and criticism that one is tempted to write that too little remains to be said about it. Whether or not this is true, *Caligari* indisputably remains one of the key horror titles of any period. TH

Creaking Stairs
aka **Dearie**
Universal; b/w; 66 min; U.S.
D/S: Rupert Julian *C:* Edward A. Kull
Cast: Mary MacLaren, Herbert Prior, Jack Mulhall, Clarissa Selwynne, Lucretia Harris

"Dearie" Lane (MacLaren) was once involved with notorious gangster Fred Millard (Mulhall). She has since gone straight, but when Mark Winfield (Prior) proposes to her, she knows she must confess her past. She does so, Mark forgives her and they are married. But not long afterward, Fred comes back to collect a debt. He dies in the process, and Dearie fears that everyone will believe that she is responsible.

Rupert Julian is best remembered as the main director of the Lon Chaney version of *The Phantom of the Opera* (1925). The tempestuous, immaculately outfitted Julian was something of a taskmaster on that latter film's set, alienating both cast and crew, and when the film tested poorly in preview screenings, Edward Sedgwick was brought in to do key retakes. (Legend has it that Chaney was so put off by the proceedings that he staged many of his own scenes himself.) In any event, Julian's is the only name listed on the film, and its status as a classic has ensured him a measure of immortality. Interestingly, he died during the same year as Universal's lavish Technicolor remake of *Phantom*, starring Claude Rains. Julian's other credits, such as this initial foray into horror, have generated considerably less interest. He penned the melodramatic scenario himself based on a story by Evelyn Campbell. The film mixes romance, gangsters and old dark house tropes, and while not lost, it remains difficult to screen.

Leading lady Mary MacLaren was born in Pittsburgh, Pennsylvania in 1896; she started out as a fashion model and entered films in 1916, becoming a popular actress on the strength of her performance in *Shoes* (1916), which was only her second screen credit. She worked throughout the silent era, but her career became spotty with the advent of sound. She continued to find work until 1949, albeit often in small, unbilled roles (one of her last screen appearances is an un-credited role as a nun in Jacques Tourneur's *The Leopard Man*, 1944). Her final years were the stuff of real-life horror, as she was declared legally incompetent and struggled with poverty. She died in 1985. TH

Dance of Death
aka **Totentanz**
Helios; b/w; 84 min; Germany
D: Otto Rippert *S:* Fritz Lang *P:* Erwin Rosner *C:* Willy Hameister
Cast: Werner Krauss, Sascha Gura, Karl Bernhard, Walter Goebel, Richard Kirsch, Joseph Romer

An embittered cripple (Krauss) uses a beautiful dancer (Gura) to lure men to their deaths. But when the dancer falls in love with one of her intended victims, a bargain is struck that will result in either tragedy or freedom for the prospective couple.

Fritz Lang wrote the screenplay for this kinky melodrama. Like the same year's *The Plague in Florence*, *Dance of Death* was directed by Otto Rippert, who emerges as something of an early specialist in the horror genre. In addition to the two Lang-scripted pictures, Rippert also directed the six-part monster serial *Homunculus* (1916). All of these films appear to be lost, so his talents as a filmmaker are impossible to assess first-hand.

A glance at the synopsis for *Dance* reveals that Lang's propensity for dark, twisted themes is fully on display; the tone, however, seems to have been more somber and elegiac than some of his harder-edged scenarios. The cast includes the wonderful Werner Krauss, most remembered as the demented title character in 1919's *The Cabinet of Dr. Caligari*, though he truly excelled in more low-key character roles, such as that in G.W. Pabst's *Secrets of a Soul* (1926). Cinematographer Willy Hameister and production designer Herrmann Warm were alumni of *Caligari* as well, and surviving stills from *Dance of Death* indicate an overtly Expressionist aesthetic. TH

The Devil's Locksmith
aka **Der Teufelsschlosser**; **The Devil's Locksmiths**
Regent; b/w; length unknown; Austria
D: Franz Ferdinand
Cast: Franz Ferdinand, Herr Ruibar, Eugen Jensen, Armin Seydelmann

A locksmith (Ruibar) makes a pact with Mephistopheles (Jensen). But, as so often happens in these situations, the deal turns sour. To judge from existing stills, this forgotten film was typical of the silent European horror tradition epitomized by *Destiny* (1921) and *Nosferatu—A Symphony of Terror* (1922).

Director Franz Ferdinand made only a few films in his short career, always casting himself in important roles. Eugen Jensen,

A German movie poster from *Dance of Death*

on the other hand, was a prolific actor who starred in approximately 40 films between 1914 and 1950. Few of them found release in English-language markets, having been made primarily for German-speaking audiences. CW

The Face at the Window
D.B. O'Conner; b/w; length unknown; Australia
D: Charles Villiers *S:* Gertrude Lockwood *P:* D.B. O'Conner *C:* Lacey Percival
Cast: D.B. O'Conner, Agnes Dobson, Claude Turton, Gerald Harcourt, Collet Dobson, Charles Villiers

F. Brooke Warren's 1897 play *The Face at the Window*—a gaudy mix of horror, melodrama and police procedural—opened to generally positive reviews and enthusiastic audiences, who made it a hit for three decades. It dealt with Parisian bank robber and serial killer Le Loup ("The Wolf"), who is hunted down by police detective Paul Gouffet and exposed by a (briefly revived) murdered victim. Its smash success led to several film adaptations, the first of which was this relatively unknown (and apparently lost) Aussie film produced by and starring D.B. O'Conner (his only known foray into the world of cinema). O'Conner played Lucio Delgrado, aka Le Loup, while Claude Turton played Gouffet. Agnes Dobson was the requisite love interest. The film's

At its heart *J'Accuse* is an anti-war diatribe.

director Charles Villiers portrayed Lucien Cortier, who is falsely accused of one of Le Loup's murders. Villiers was a popular actor in Australia during the silent period, starring in such disparate films as *Sea Dogs of Australia* (1913), *Satan in Sydney* (1918) and *Daughter of the East* (1924). This appears to have been his only foray into directing.

The next film adaptation of the play was produced in Great Britain and released the following year, though the most famous was made in 1939 and starred Tod Slaughter. CW

The Haunted Bedroom
aka **The Ghost of Whispering Oaks**
Ince; b/w; 60 min; U.S.
D: Fred Niblo *S:* C. Gardner Sullivan *P:* Thomas H. Ince *C:* George Barnes
Cast: Enid Bennett, Dorcas Matthews, Jack Nelson, Lloyd Hughes, William Conklin, Harry Archer

Dolores Arnold (Matthews) and her brother Daniel (Nelson) rent a supposedly haunted house in Virginia, but shortly after moving in, Daniel disappears. A New York City newspaper sends ace reporter Betsy Thorne (Bennett) to investigate. She dons the guise of a housemaid and is admitted onto the estate, where she sees a ghost exiting the chapel in the family graveyard. When she screams, she's locked into her bedroom overnight. The next day, she discovers that Dolores plans to marry a doctor (Conklin) once Daniel is found. She also learns that an investigating detective (Archer) believes the doctor's son (Hughes) murdered Daniel. During her second night at the estate, she escapes from her bedroom and again spies the ghost stalking the graveyard. She chases the specter to the chapel and loses it. Playing around on the chapel organ, she strikes some notes and inadvertently opens a secret passageway. It leads to a hidden tomb, and there she again finds the ghost, who turns out to be Daniel, not dead at all but rather an insane forger wanted by the police.

Born in 1874 in Nebraska, Frederick Leidtke acted under the stage name Fred Niblo. In 1916 he entered the movies and in 1918 married Edith Bennett, whom he cast in several of his films (including this one). He became a major director during the silent era, helming such classics as *The Mark of Zorro* (1920), *The Three Musketeers* (1921), *Blood and Sand* (1922), *Ben-Hur: A Tale of the Christ* (1925) and *Camille* (1926). He also worked with a young Greta Garbo on *The Temptress* (1926) and *The Mysterious Lady* (1928). His last film, *Diamond Cut Woman*, was shot in 1932 and was co-directed by prolific British filmmaker Maurice Elvey. Niblo retired the following year and died in 1948 in New Orleans, Louisiana, leaving a rich legacy of films that, for the most part, remain easily accessible today. CW

J'Accuse
aka **I Accuse**
Pathé; b/w; 166 min; France
D/S: Abel Gance *P:* Charles Pathé *C:* Marc Bujard, Leonce-Henri Burel, Maurice Forster
Cast: Romuald Joube, Severin-Mars, Maryse Dauvray, Maxime Desjardins, Angele Guys, Mancini

When France goes to war against Germany during WWI, Francois Laurin (Severin-Mars) is quick to enlist. He's a man with a hair-trigger temper, and he suspects that his wife, Edith (Dauvray), is having an affair with poet Jean Diaz (Joube). Jean also enlists and winds up in the same regiment as Francois. Though things between the two are tense at first, that tension gradually dissipates and they become good friends. But when they go home on leave, Edith reveals that she's given birth to Jean's child. Jean and Francois understandably fall out again,

Conrad Veidt and Gussy Hole, from *Madness*

this time vowing to settle their differences on the battlefield. Francois, however, is killed in battle. A shell-shocked Jean then succumbs to insanity, plagued by visions of dead soldiers rising from their graves and stalking the countryside.

Abel Gance was born in Paris. After a stint as a clerk, he entered the theater as an actor. He eventually made his way into cinema, first as an actor and then as a screenwriter. His directorial debut came with *La Digue* (1911), and he remained active in that capacity for the next 60 years; *Bonaparte et la revolution* (1971) marked his final work as a director. *J'Accuse* is one of the director's most renowned efforts, and he remade the film in 1938 to comparable acclaim. Like many of his films, this 1919 version went through changes as the director continued to tinker with the film after its initial release. Thankfully, the full-length version has been preserved on home video (with its 166-minute running time dwarfed by the original, uncut version of his follow-up feature *La Roue*, which clocks in a little under nine hours!).

At its heart, *J'Accuse* is an anti-war diatribe. The director often stated that, while he was generally disinterested in politics, he saw war as a futile and senseless act. It's said that he was so fully immersed in the project that he enlisted in the French army's film unit, the Service Cinematographique, to capture real images of horror on the front lines. The finale in which the dead soldiers rise from their muddy graves to bring forth a message of peace caused much consternation in its day and remains impressive still. Gance's 1938 revisitation is not a straightforward remake; it can, however, easily be read as warning of an impending WWII. TH

Lilith and Ly
aka **Lilith und Ly**
Fiat; b/w; length unknown; Austria
D: Erich Kober *S:* Fritz Lang *C:* Willy Hameister
Cast: Elga Beck, Ernst Escherich, Franz Kammauf, Hanns Marschall

An inventor finds a jewel that has the ability to give life to inanimate objects. He tries the precious stone out on a statue of Lilith, a Mesopotamian demon believed to be a bearer of death and disease. When the statue actually does come to life, the inventor falls in love with her, not realizing that she is a psychic vampire who is slowly draining his life energy.

An early but lost film scripted by Fritz Lang, *Lilith and Ly* gives a foretaste of the thematic elements that would come to dominate his work as a director. The supernatural theme makes it of particular interest; the synopsis indicates a far more overtly horrific scenario than was usual for the director. The linkage of sex and death is typical of his work, however, and would later color his many thrillers and noir pictures.

Lang made his first film as a director the same year as *Lilith and Ly* after years of frustration at watching his screenplays be interpreted by directors for whom he had contempt. Director Erich Kober is an obscure figure, a part-time actor and writer who helmed only three films between 1919 and 1932. *Lilith* marks his directorial debut, and from all indications it was likely his most interesting film. He co-directed his final film, *Die Wasserteufel von Hieflau*, with special effects pioneer Eugen Schufftan. TH

Lucrezia Borgia
b/w; length unknown; Italy
D: Augusto Genina
Cast: Diana Karenne

Director Augusto Genina's *Lucrezia Borgia* followed on the heels of the preposterous *The Eternal Sin* (1917). Diana Karenne was cast as the historical figure upon which it's based.

Lucrezia Borgia was an illegitimate daughter of Pope Alexander VI (aka Rodrigo Borgia), who fathered three other known illegitimate children, all of them male. While it has been long rumored that Lucrezia was a murderer whose M.O. was to pour poison from a hollow ring into the drinks of enemies, there is no conclusive evidence of this. Nor is there any proof that she bore a child by her older brother Cesare, whose machinations brought the family greater power but eventually led to his death on the battlefield.

Augusto Genina was a popular Italian director in his day. Though he made most of his films during the silent era, his career lasted until 1955, a couple of years before his death from pneumonia. In 1954 his film *Maddalena* was nominated for the Grand Prize at the Cannes Film Festival. He also won several Venice Film Festival awards throughout the 1940s. CW

Madness
aka **Wahnsinn**
Veidt Film; b/w; 70 min; Germany
D/P: Conrad Veidt *S:* Margarete Lindau-Schulz, Herrmann Fellner *C:* Carl Hoffmann
Cast: Conrad Veidt, Reinhold Schuenzel, Gussy Hole, Grit Hegesa

A Gypsy tells successful banker Lorenzen (Veidt) that an object in a lost trunk (the key to which she gives him) will lead to either his happiness or his death. His obsession over the prediction (and vain search for the trunk) results in his mental breakdown.

Having established himself as one of Germany's leading actors in such masterful films as *The Cabinet of Dr. Caligari* (1919)

and *Waxworks* (1924), Conrad Veidt tried his hand at directing and producing with this psychological thriller under the auspices of his independent (and aptly named) company *Veidtfilme*. Adapted from an obscure novel by Kurt Muenzer, *Madness* allowed Veidt to further explore the Expressionism of *Caligari* and to portray another unbalanced character. The film had little impact at the box office, and both Veidt and his company made only one more—*Die Nacht auf Goldenhall* (1920)—before he returned his focus exclusively to acting. Both of his directorial efforts appear to be lost today. TH

The Monkey's Paw
b/w; length unknown; Great Britain
Credits unknown

Prolific British author W.W. Jacobs wrote numerous stories and novels, mostly humorous ones dealing with life in naval settings. But he may be best remembered for *The Monkey's Paw*, a macabre short story first published in the 1902 collection *The Lady of the Barge*. The story concerns an aging couple who receive a magical monkey's paw that grants its possessor three wishes, none of which go as intended. The first film adaptation of the story came in 1915 and starred John Lawson, who'd also starred in the one-act stage play written by Louis N. Parker in 1907. About this 1919 version there is little information, other than the title and the fact that it was made. While a print of the next version (1923) still exists, the most famous adaptation, done in 1933, is also considered lost. CW

Nabeshima neko sodo
Nikkatsu; b/w; 80 min; Japan
Crew unknown
Cast: Matsunosuke Onoe

Joko Segawa III's fictionalized Kabuki take on the heroic tale of Naoshige Nabeshima gets yet another go-round in this third silent adaptation from Nikkatsu. Like the previous two known film adaptations, *Saga no yozakura* and *Nabeshima kaibyô* (both released in 1917), this one starred Matsunosuke Onoe in the lead.

The tale concerns the ghost cat of Saga Castle, which wants revenge for the murder of its master, Matahichiro Ryuzoji, and Ryuzoji's mother at the hands of a 16th century warlord known as Nabeshima. In reality, there is little evidence that Nabeshima killed Ryuzoji, for whom he had been a retainer, though it is known that Nabeshima took charge of the clan's domain upon the death of his master.

Nabeshima neko sodo was released on June 14, 1919. Nikkatsu also produced the next adaptation of the tale, *Saga neko sodo* (1921). CW

Okazaki kaibyô-den
Nikkatsu Kyoto; b/w; length unknown; Japan
Crew unknown
Cast: Matsunosuke Onoe

This short film from Nikkatsu's Kyoto branch is the third from the studio to deal with a witch who holes up in a temple along Takaido road in Okazaki where she conjures the spirit of a cat to do dirty but humorous deeds. Unlike most ghost cat films of the period, the film, based on a section of an early 1820s novel as well as an 1827 Kabuki play, wasn't so much horror as it was comedy. The next known adaptation of the tale, *Yaji and Kita's Cat Trouble*, came in 1937 and was the first to utilize sound-recording techniques in its production.

Okazaki kaibyô-den was released on October 26, 1919. CW

The Phantom Honeymoon
Dawley; b/w; 60 min; U.S.
D/S/P: J. Searle Dawley
Cast: Leon Dadmun, Marguerite Marsh, Vernon Steele, Henry Guy Carleton, Charles P. Patterson, Grace Bryant

Professor Tidewater (Dadmun) takes his daughters to Ireland. As they tour the supposedly haunted Belmore Castle, Sakes the caretaker (Carlton) tells of his master's involvement in a tragic love triangle. Sakes contends that the ghosts of the people involved still roam the castle, but Tidewater is skeptical. Yet when Sakes shows Tidewater the room where the deaths occurred, the professor's disbelief is challenged—he sees the spirits himself, though he wonders if Sakes, a Hindu, may have hypnotized him.

Rationalism goes toe to toe with the supernatural in *The Phantom Honeymoon*. The story deals with an academic whose fascination with the supernatural leads him to debunk it at every turn. The "Irish" locale is striking, but the film was made in the United States with a budget that likely didn't extend to location shooting. The cast is mostly unknown today. Co-star Vernon Steele went on to appear in a number of major films but always in a minor capacity and often without billing (for example, he makes an un-credited bit appearance as a victim of *Dracula's Daughter*, 1936).

Writer/producer/director J. Searle Dawley is best remembered for making the first version of *Frankenstein* in 1910. He reportedly considered himself to be "the first motion picture director," a claim easily dismissible. After a stint at Thomas Edison's company, he branched off on his own, setting up a production house that gave a start to filmmakers such as Henry King (*Haunting Shadows*, 1919). While his work (apart from *Frankenstein*) is largely forgotten today, he was quite successful in his day. He was a founding member of the ill-fated Motion Pictures Directors Association (MPDA), which sought to give filmmakers a degree of clout in the fledgling film industry and to provide moral vision to films in light of criticism that the new medium was having an adverse affect on the public. The group advocated self-censorship and "good taste." Filmmakers as diverse as John Ford and William Beaudine supported it. TH

The Plague in Florence
aka **Die Pest in Florenz**
Decla; b/w; 96 min; Germany
D: Otto Rippert *S:* Fritz Lang *P:* Erich Pommer *C:* Willy Hameister, Emil Schuenmann
Cast: Otto Mannstaedt, Anders Wikman, Theodor Becker, Marga von Kierska, Julietta Brandt, Karl Bernhard

Cesare (Mannstaedt) rules over the city of Florence, but his power is compromised by the appearance of a mysterious woman (Kierska). He falls madly in love with her, as does his adult son (Wikman). The two vie for her affections, and their subsequent falling out has disastrous consequences, not only for themselves but also for the entire city.

A poster from *The Plague in Florence*

Based on Edgar Allan Poe's *The Masque of the Red Death*, *The Plague in Florence* is among the lost early films scripted by Fritz Lang. Lang's main innovation here was to heighten the original story's sexual tension by transforming the force of evil into a seductive woman. Beyond that, it seems that he was generally faithful to the outline of Poe's tale, including the epic vision of horror that descends upon the populace during the final act. The thematic content of the story—a plague ravages a village as a decadent prince hosts an orgy in his supposedly impenetrable castle—was a perfect fit for Lang's fatalistic sensibility. It can only be regretted that the soon-to-be-director never revisited Poe's work later in his career.

Granted a comparatively lavish budget, director Otto Rippert assembled some of the key creative personnel responsible for that same year's *The Cabinet of Dr. Caligari*, including cinematographer Willy Hameister and production designers Herrmann Warm, Walter Reimann and Walter Roehrig. Rippert is forgotten today, but his name is attached to some reputedly intriguing German genre films of the silent period, all of which appear to be lost. In addition to *Plague*, Rippert also helmed Lang's other horror-tinged scenario of 1919, *Dance of Death*. TH

Satanas
aka Satan
Viktoria-Film; b/w; 54 min; Germany
D: F.W. Murnau *S/P:* Robert Wiene *C:* Karl Freund
Cast: Fritz Kortner, Sadjah Gezza, Ernst Hofmann, Margit Berna, Else Berna, Kurt Ehrle, Conrad Veidt

This is a historical drama in three parts. *Part One, The Tyrant* deals with a love triangle between a Pharaoh (Kortner), the beautiful Nouri (Gezza) and the young man she loves (Hofmann). *Part Two, The Prince* is an adaptation of Victor Hugo's *Lucrezia Borgia* and features Berna in the role of Lucrezia. The third section deals with an idealistic young revolutionary (Wolfgang), prodded into violence by Grodski (Veidt), who may or may not be the Devil in human form.

Satanas is one of F.W. Murnau's earliest efforts as a director. It shares an unfortunate commonality with many of his other early works (including *Der Januskopf* and *The Hunchback and the Dancer*, both 1920) in that it seems, at least for the most part,

***Satanas* is a historical drama in three parts. Here in Part Two Margit Berna plays Lucrezia Borgia.**

lost. A brief fragment does exist in storage at the *Cinematheque Francaise*, leading one to hope that the entire feature may surface one day. Until such a time, one can surmise a few things about the film from materials available. Despite its provocative title, it doesn't seem to have been an absolute horror film, though the final story in which Conrad Veidt may be the Devil suggests that, as with so many Murnau films, it does lurch into genre territory to some degree.

The fact that the film was written and produced by the talented director Robert Wiene (*The Cabinet of Dr. Caligari*, 1919) would seem to suggest that Murnau was less a motivating force than usual, but the colorful mixture of melodrama and spectacle sounds like the sort of thing he loved to tackle. And the casting of Conrad Veidt (who figured into several of the director's early films, including the aforementioned *Der Januskopf*) and the presence of the brilliant Karl Freund as cameraman contribute even more to the film's promise. TH

The Thirteenth Chair
ACME; b/w; length unknown; U.S.
D/S: Leonce Perret *C:* Alfred Ortleib
Cast: Yvonne Delva, Creighton Hale, Marie Shotwell, Christine May, Suzanne Colbert, Georges Deneubourg

Conrad Veidt (far right) in one of the segments from *Weird Tales*

This is the first screen version of the hit 1916 play by Bayard Veiller. Long considered lost, it doesn't seem to have had much impact upon its release. When a man is murdered, medium Madame LeGrange (Shotwell) conducts a séance to discern the responsible party. During the séance, however, a second person is killed. The film's writer/director Leonce Perret began a career in his native France before making his way to America. After U.S. success as writer, director and actor eluded him, he returned to France. His only other English-language brush with the horror genre, 1917's *The Twin Pawns*, is likewise obscure.

This *Thirteenth Chair* starred Creighton Hale, who later toplined such noteworthy horror outings as *Trilby* (1923), *The Cat and the Canary* (1927) and *Seven Footprints to Satan* (1929). The bulk of *Chair*'s cast, however, consists of little-known performers, most of whom seem to have abandoned acting by the dawn of the sound era. The next adaptation of the play, directed by Tod Browning in 1929, is better known. TH

To Let
Harma; b/w; 20 min; Great Britain
D: James Reardon *S:* Reuben Gillmer
Cast: James Reardon, Peggy Patterson, James Prior, Ida Fane

A couple shows interest in an old house, only to be scared off by its resident ghost—which isn't a ghost at all but a retired magician.

To Let was the typical combination of horror and comedy, with any hints of the supernatural explained away in the denouement. The most surprising thing about it is that it got made at all. Neither director James Reardon nor scenarist Reuben Gillmer appear to have been involved in the making of any other horror films, unless one considers the Gillmer-scripted *Inventing Trouble* (1915), a science fiction comedy in which a scientist who invents a machine of some sort winds up getting eaten by a prehistoric creature.

Harma Photoplays produced and distributed films between the years 1917 and 1921 before going the way of the dinosaurs. CW

The Trembling Hour
Universal; b/w; 60 min; U.S.
D: George Siegmann *S:* Doris Schroeder *C:* Alfred Gosden
Cast: Kenneth Harlan, Helen Eddy, Henry Barrows, Willis Marks, Clyde Hopkins, Edna Shipman

This strange little melodrama concerns a man (Harlan) who suffers from blackouts and killer impulses; not surprisingly, he becomes the suspect in a murder case. In a ploy to flush out the real killer, he convinces the victim's twin brother to pretend to be the deceased man's ghost.

Director George Siegmann was better known as an actor. He appeared in well over 100 films, among them *The Sealed Room* (1909), *The Avenging Conscience: or, 'Thou Shalt Not Kill'* (1914), *The Hawk's Trail* (1919) and *The Cat and the Canary* (1927). His last film, Paul Leni's *The Man Who Laughs* (1928), was released five months after his death from anemia.

Part of *The Trembling Hour* was shot at the notorious San Quentin State Prison in California. CW

The Twin Pawns
aka **The Curse of Greed**
ACME; b/w; 80 min; U.S.
D/S/P: Léonce Perret *C:* Harry D. Harde, Alfred Ortlieb
Cast: Mae Murray, Warner Oland, Jack W. Johnston, Henry G. Sell

Violet and Daisy White (both played by Murray) are twins, but neither knows about the existence of the other. Violet has been raised by her father (Johnston) and given everything her heart desires. Daisy, on the other hand, was raised by her penniless mother and has nothing. John Bent (Oland) knows the truth of the situation and hatches a scheme to steal Violet's fortune. He marries Violet, then, when she dies, pretends that Daisy is Violet, has her declared insane and places her in an asylum. In the end, Bob Anderson (Sell), who loves Daisy, discovers the ruse.

A play by Wilkie Collins has long been credited as the source material for the film, but no such play exists. The film does bear a close resemblance to Collins' *The Woman in White*, a Gothic romance first serialized in 1859 and 1860 in the Victorian periodical *All the Year Round*, though character names and locations have been changed. CW

Weird Tales
aka **Unheimliche Geschichten**; **Eerie Tales**; **Five Sinister Stories**; **Tales of Horror**; **Tales of the Uncanny**
Oswald; b/w; 95 min; Germany
D/S/P: Richard Oswald *C:* Carl Hoffmann
Cast: Conrad Veidt, Anita Berber, Reinhold Schunzel, Hugo Doblin, Paul Morgan, Georg John

Three figures emerge from a painting in an antique shop and read five macabre tales for the viewer. In the first, a man (Veidt) and woman (Berber) check into a hotel; the next morning the woman cannot be found and the management denies that she was ever there. In the second, two men (Veidt, Schunzel) vie for the affections of a woman (Berber) before one of them ends up dead. In the third, based on Edgar Allan Poe's *The Black Cat*, an alcoholic (Schunzel) introduces a stranger (Veidt) to his wife (Berber), with disastrous consequences. The fourth, an adaptation of Robert Louis Stevenson's *The Suicide Club*, deals with a card game that results in the death of one of its participants. And in the fifth, a French marquis (Veidt) encourages his wife (Berber) to have an affair with a stranger (Schunzel).

Austrian writer/producer/director Richard Oswald (1880-1963) engineered this macabre anthology, which draws inspiration from a variety of sources. The film sets something of a standard for subsequent German anthologies, including Fritz Lang's *Destiny* (1919) and Paul Leni's *Waxworks* (1924), but overall this is pretty heavy going. Its tone vacillates clumsily between the macabre and the farcical—the segments based on *The Black Cat* and *The Suicide Club* hint at what an effective horror film this might have been, but they sit uncomfortably in a film also containing the mugging comedy of, for example, the final segment.

The first story recounts the same basic tale that would later inspire Alfred Hitchcock in *The Lady Vanishes* (1938) and Terence Fisher in *So Long at the Fair* (1950), but it is far too short to be effective. And this touches upon the film's major problem: its abundance of stories and lack of screentime ultimately work against each other, and the movie wears out its welcome. Each actor in the small ensemble is required to play multiple characters, but only Conrad Veidt makes much of an impression. Whether playing a panic-stricken lover in the first segment or a sardonic Marquis in the last, he consistently rises above the mediocre quality of the rest of the picture.

Oswald remade the film as a talkie in 1932 under the title *The Living Dead*. TH

1920

Akakabe myojin
Kokkatsu; b/w; 70 min; Japan
D: Jiro Yoshino
Cast: Shirogoro Sawamura

Released on November 18, 1920, this appears to have been the second film made bearing the title *Akakabe myojin*. (The first was released in 1918.) Both films concerned a lady-in-waiting who is falsely made to look by rivals as if she's fooling around with her master's retainer. She is executed and interred, along with a black cat, behind a red wall. Her spirit inhabits the animal's body and seeks vengeance against those who wronged her.

This second version was a feature-length film, whereas the previous adaptation had been a short feature. The story was again filmed in 1938 under the title *Ghost Cat and the Red Wall*.

The same year Kokkatsu produced this film, they allegedly produced another ghost cat movie titled *Hida no kaibyô*. It, too, supposedly starred Shirogoro Sawamura (alongside Enjuro Ichikawa). It was allegedly eight reels in length and released in June 1920, five months before Yoshino's film. The director for that film is unknown, and finding irrefutable proof that it existed is difficult.

The Japanese term *Akakabe myojin* roughly translates as "Red Wall God." CW

Arima no neko
aka **Arima kaibyô-den**
Nikkatsu Kyoto; b/w; 75 min; Japan
Crew unknown
Cast: Matsunosuke Onoe, Sentaro Nakamura

This is Nikkatsu's second—or possibly third—movie to center on the ghost cat reputed to haunt the palace ruins in the Japanese town of Arima, near Mt. Kumuchi. As with the company's previous known effort (*Arima no neko sodo*, 1916), the name of the director is lost, though it was likely Shozo Makino. The title, *Arima no neko*, translates as *Cat in Arima*.

Arima isn't the only place in Japan cinematically linked to a ghost cat or cats; others include Enma (*Enmadera no kaibyô*, 1938), Okazaki (*Kaibyô Okazaki sodo*, 1954), Otamaga (*Kaibyô Otamagaike*, 1960) and Saga (*Cat Ghost and Cherry Blossoms at Night in Saga*, 1936).

A star of the silent era, Sentaro Nakamura also had a relatively small part in Shozo Makino's epic silent feature *Chushingura* (1926). *Arima no neko* was released July 30, 1920. CW

At the Villa Rose
Stoll; b/w; 70 (79) min; Great Britain
D: Maurice Elvey *S:* Sinclair Hill *P:* Oswald Stoll
Cast: Manora Thew, Langhorn Burton, Teddy Arundell, Normal Page, Joan Beverly, Eva Westlake

Alfred Edward Woodley Mason (better known as A.E.W. Mason) was a British politician and author who wrote *At the Villa Rose*, his most famous mystery, in 1910 shortly after retiring from Parliament, where he served only a single term. It introduced French detective Inspector Hanaud and was a big hit at the time, though with none of the enduring popularity of Mason's biggest success, *The Four Feathers* (1902). *Villa* was filmed no less than four times, with this 1920 adaptation being the first. The other three adaptations, *Le mystère de la Villa Rose* and *Mystery at the Villa Rose* (both 1930) and *At the Villa Rose* (1940) were products of the sound era.

The story is steeped in the then-in-vogue notion of spiritualism, with a fake spiritualist named Ceila Harland (Thew) kidnapped by a group of crooks during an attempt to rob an old widow (Westlake). When the widow is murdered, Harland is framed for the crime, and it's up to Inspector Hanaud (Arundell) to solve the mystery before she is sent to the gallows.

The film was shot on location in Monaco, as Maurice Elvey's travelogue-like direction makes clear. To the good, however, he livens things up here and there with a focus on the more horror-oriented aspects of the story. In one scene, for example, Thew is bound and gagged and forced to listen to her mistress being strangled. In another, she stages a creepy séance with glowing orbs and mounted alligators. One of the film's more inventive (for the time) twists is its revelation that the murderer is a woman, with actress Kate Gurney providing the film's best performance.

At the Villa Rose was one of the more successful episodes of Stoll's *Eminent British Authors* series. Other Stoll series focused on characters rather than authors, highlighting such literary figures as Sherlock Holmes and Fu Manchu. CW

The Barton Mystery
Stoll; b/w; 72 min; Great Britain
D: Henry Roberts *S:* R. Byron-Webber *P:* Oswald Stoll *C:* E.

Harvey Harrison
Cast: Lyn Harding, Edward O'Neal, Arthur Pusey, Enid Bell, Maud Cressall, Austin Camp

Stoll Picture Productions was the brainchild of Oswald Stoll (1866-1942), an Australian immigrant who first got rich by opening and managing a chain of British movie theaters. While his films are today mostly forgotten, Stoll received a knighthood in 1919 for his philanthropic work. In 1916, he'd taken on the cause of housing military veterans who suffered from disabilities or mental illness, or who simply found themselves homeless after their service. His charitable foundation still exists today.

In 1919 Stoll formed his own film production company with the intent of adapting "great works of literature" (mostly modern novels he personally liked). Audiences, he believed, were growing tired of short features designed only to wow viewers with their spectacular though increasingly redundant special effects. To this end, he hired Maurice Elvey as house director and launched an aggressive production schedule, shooting no less than seven features in 1919. When most of them didn't do well, Stoll gave up on feature-length dramas in favor of action-packed short films (also based on what he considered great works of modern literature). This change of focus included several film series, most notably *The Adventures of Sherlock Holmes*, starring Eille Norwood, and *The Mysteries of Dr. Fu-Manchu*, starring H. Agar Lyons. The formula proved successful, and he stuck with it for years.

Poster art for *Cagliostro*, photo from *Conrad Veidt On Screen*

One of Stoll's earliest forays into the horror genre came in 1920 with *The Barton Mystery*. Billed, as its title implies, as a murder mystery, the sinister shenanigans it portrays are sufficient to warrant inclusion here. After attempting to blackmail one Mrs. Standish (Bayley) with some incriminating letters, Beverly Barton (Harding) is shot to death in his apartment. Mrs. Standish's soon-to-be-brother-in-law Harry Maitland (Pusey) is immediately suspected, having visited the murder victim earlier in the evening in an attempt to retrieve the letters. Finally, thanks to the intervention of a psychic, the real killer, Barton's Japanese servant, is flushed out, though not before there's a séance.

A four-act play by Walter Hackett, which was first staged in October 1917, formed the basis of the film. It was a departure for Hackett, who generally wrote comedies. Elvey was busy, so Stoll went with Harry T. Roberts, who had few films to his directorial credit. (Nor, apparently, did he make much of a splash here, as his career seems to have completely stalled afterward.)

The idea of a Japanese killer is not surprising, given that Stoll's films tended toward xenophobia. The production company had entered the Yellow Peril stakes with *Mr. Wu* in 1919 (though it was an outright crime drama rather than a horror film) and followed it up with an adaptation of Sax Rhomer's *The Yellow Claw* in 1920. Of course, their biggest claim to fame in the subgenre came with their Fu Manchu pictures, of which there were 23. CW

Cagliostro
aka **Der Graf von Cagliostro**; **The Count of Cagliostro**

Micco; b/w; length unknown; Germany
D/Co-S: Reinhold Schuenzel *Co-S:* Robert Liebmann *C:* Carl Hoffmann
Cast: Reinhold Schuenzel, Anita Berber, Conrad Veidt, Carl Gotz, Walter Huber, Heinrich Jensen

The infamous mesmerist and occultist Giuseppe Balsamo, better known as Count Alessandro di Cagliostro, is the subject of this long-lost production.

Sources are conflicted as to whether its country of origin was Austria or Germany. Director/co-scenarist/star Reinhold Schuenzel was an established presence in the German film scene by the time of this production, lending weight to the notion that the film was German-made. Schuenzel's considerable talents eventually landed him roles in such American-made thrillers as Fritz Lang's *Hangmen Also Die!* (1943) and Alfred Hitchcock's *Notorious* (1946), where he gave a scene-stealing performance as a Nazi doctor working in collaboration with a German spy (Claude Rains).

Conrad Veidt is credited with playing a minister in this particular version of *Cagliostro*. He likely would have been ideally cast in the title role, but it seems that Schuenzel, the driving force behind the film, took that role for himself. Cinematographer Carl Hoffmann compiled an impressive resume during his career, photographing films for the likes of Fritz Lang (*Die Nibelungen*, 1924), E.A. Dupont (*Variety*, 1925) and F.W. Murnau (*Faust*, 1926), before becoming a director and making the obscure horror film *The Mystic Mirror* (1928).

Given the impressive roster of talent involved in *Cagliostro*, it is to be lamented that so little is known about the film. TH

The Dark Mirror
aka **Jericho**

Famous Players-Lasky; b/w; 56 min; U.S.
D: Charles Giblyn *S:* E. Magnus Ingleton *C:* John Stumar
Cast: Dorothy Dalton, Huntley Gordon, Walter D. Nealand, Jessie Arnold, Lucille Carney, Pedro de Cordoba

Based on a story by Louis Joseph Vance, *The Dark Mirror* is an obscure blend of horror and melodrama that appears to be long lost, with little known about it beyond its basic premise. In

the film leading lady Dorothy Dalton portrays twins, one poor and one well off, with personalities just as disparate as their economic backgrounds. It seems to bear little similarity to the Robert Siodmak 1946 *film noir* of the same name, though that film is also built around a pair of identical twin sisters.

Director Charles Giblyn was prolific throughout the silent era, with a side career as a character actor and bit-part player. Cinematographer John Stumar was younger brother to cinematographer Charles Stumar, who shot such Universal fare as *The Mummy* (1932) and *Werewolf of London* (1935). Charles Stumar was killed in a plane crash in 1935, but John never achieved the same level of acclaim. One of John's last jobs was on the Columbia B-picture *The Return of the Vampire* (1944), starring Bela Lugosi.

The Dark Mirror's cast includes Pedro de Cordoba, who later appeared in such genre fare as Tod Browning's *The Devil Doll* (1936) and Robert Florey's *The Beast with Five Fingers* (1946). Dorothy Dalton wound up with a star on the Hollywood Walk of Fame, but her career ended in 1924; she died in 1972. TH

Desire
aka **The Magic Skin**; **Magic Skin**
British & Colonial; b/w; 54 min; Great Britain
D/S: George Edwardes-Hall *P:* Edward Godal
Cast: Dennis Neilson-Terry, Yvonne Arnaud, Christine Maitland, George W. Anson, Chris Walker, Pardoe Woodman

This, the fourth adaptation of Honoré de Balzac's novel *Le Peau de chagrin* (1831), was released in January 1920. It turned out to be the first of three adaptations done that same year. (The other two were *The Dream Cheater* and *Narayana*.) Some sources describe *Desire*, under its original British title *The Magic Skin*, as a tale in which the hero dreams that he is the central character in Balzac's story. Whether that is accurate or arises from confusion with the dream-based previous film adaptation, also titled *The Magic Skin* (1915), is unknown. Either way, director Edwardes-Hall's film deals with a man named Valentin (Neilson-Terry) who obtains a magic shagreen (leather hide) made from the skin of a wild ass. The shagreen fulfills its owner's fondest desires, but at the cost of … you guessed it: his soul. All of the story's major characters are here, including Pauline (Arnaud) and Fedora (Maitland).

George Edwardes-Hall was a temporary transplant to the United Kingdom, having been born in Brooklyn, New York in 1872. His career as director was slight, but he maintained a fairly busy schedule as a scriptwriter from 1912 until his death in Los Angeles, California in 1922. He also wrote plays and short stories. The last film to be based on his work, *One of the Best*, was released in 1927. *Desire* was released in January 1920, which makes it likely that it was shot sometime in 1919.

Hall's *Desire* should not be confused with Rowland V. Lee's film of the same title, released three years later. CW

The Devil to Pay
Brunton; b/w; 60 min; U.S.
D: Ernest C. Warde *S:* Jack Cunningham *P:* Robert Brunton *C:* Arthur L. Todd
Cast: Roy Stewart, Robert McKim, Fritzi Brunette, George Fisher, Evelyn Selbie, Joseph J. Dowling

Based on a 1918 morality tale by Alabama-born novelist Francis Nimmo Greene, *The Devil to Pay* foreshadows the 1930s-'40s spate of Boris Karloff "mad scientist" movies (including, but not limited to, *The Walking Dead*, 1936, and *The Man They Could Not Hang*, 1939), though to a far less horrific degree.

In the small town of Hammond, a beloved banker, also a politician (McKim), has a man murdered, and then escapes justice by sending a lackey (Dowling) to the gallows in his place. The district attorney (Stewart) is certain that the banker is the real murderer and has him arrested, but the locals stick by their man (it doesn't help matters that the D.A.'s former lover is the banker's current fiancée). The D.A. is forced to set the banker free. But when the fiancée's brother gets a job for the banker, he does some snooping and uncovers incriminating evidence. The murderer is rearrested and at last stands trial … and there's a lulu of a surprise witness: the banker's wrongly executed former employee, brought back from the dead.

Director Warde's other horror credits include *The Woman in White* (1917), *The Bells* (1918), *The Dream Cheater* and *The House of Whispers* (both 1920), all of which contained heavy doses of crime or melodrama. Prolific screenwriter Jack Cunningham wrote all but one, and in 1939 he suffered a stroke while writing Cecil B. DeMille's *Union Pacific*. Weakened by the attack, he died in Santa Monica, California in 1941. CW

The Devil Worshippers
aka **Die Teufelsanbeter**; **Bei Den Teufelsanbetern**
Ustad/Droop; b/w; length unknown; Germany
D/Co-S: Marie Louise Droop *Co-S:* Karl May
Cast: Carl de Vogt, Meinhart Maur, Tronier Funder, Bela Lugosi, Fred Immler, Ilja Dubrowski

This silent, six-part German serial concerns a cult of Devil worshippers called the Jesidi, whose village is destroyed, under the pretext of religion, by a general (Funder) and his men hoping to make themselves richer. Soon afterward, Kara ben Nemsi (de Vogt) and his attendant Hadschi Halef Omar (Maur) come upon the ravaged village and swear to avenge the Jesidi and rescue their loved ones, who have been taken into captivity by the general. It emerges that the Jesidi is in fact a peace-loving group, despite their affinity for secret rites at the shrine of Sheik Adi, but the general plans to dispose of them, one and all, for his own gain.

The Devil Worshippers was one of the earliest productions to be based on a novel by Karl May, whose work provided film fodder for decades to come. May was a German writer who was heavily influenced by James Fenimore Cooper and is best known for a series of novels set in the old American West. The book on which *The Devil Worshippers* is based, *Die Teufelsanbeter*, contains the characters Kara ben Nemsi and Hadschi Halef Omar, who made regular appearances in a separate series by May set in the Middle East.

Long considered lost, the serial gave an early role to future horror star Bela Lugosi, though it's unknown exactly whom he played. The lead went to Carl de Vogt, who, apart from a decade-long break beginning in World War II, remained a major player in German cinema until the early 1960s. He died in 1970, having finished his career with *krimis* such as *The Invisible Dr. Mabuse* (1962) and *The Strangler of Blackmoor Castle* (1963). CW

Dr. Jekyll and Mr. Hyde
Paramount; b/w; 77 min; US
D: John S. Robertson *S:* Clara Beranger *P:* Adolph Zucker *C:* Roy Overbaugh
Cast: John Barrymore, Martha Mansfield, Charles Lane, Brandon Hurst, Nita Naldi, Cecil Clovelly, George Stevens

Dr. Henry Jekyll (Barrymore) gives so freely of his time doing charity work that he has little opportunity to enjoy himself. While dining one evening with his fiancée, Millicent Carew (Mansfield), as well as her friends and family, Jekyll's soon-to-be-father-in-law Sir George Carew (Hurst) begins to exert a malevolent influence. Sir George encourages Jekyll to indulge in every vice imaginable while he's still young. Jekyll is disturbed by this but sees in it a connection to some of his current attempts to isolate the baser instincts of the human organism. In order to put his theories to the test, Jekyll injects himself with a serum, thus unleashing a grotesque alter ego known as Mr. Hyde. Jekyll is able to regain control of his body with little difficulty but comes to fear that Hyde may be able to escape at will, so he takes steps to ensure that the latter's presence is accepted in the community. Each time Hyde emerges, however, he becomes more perverse and destructive. He dominates and eventually destroys an Italian dancer (Naldi) working in a Soho nightclub and makes life in general miserable for anybody who crosses his path. His sa-

John Barrymore in make-up as the evil half of *Dr. Jekyll and Mr. Hyde*

bit of greasepaint, some false teeth and an elongated skull cap), preferring instead to contort his face to create a monstrous effect. The end result is generally successful, though the broader aspects of his performance at times push the character into the realm of caricature. Compared to the inane posturing of Sheldon Lewis in the competing 1920 version, however, Barrymore is a revelation. It may be a bit hammy by today's standards, but one can easily imagine the profound impression it likely had on audiences of the time.

The supporting cast is generally unremarkable, though Nita Naldi is photogenic as the doomed dancer who runs afoul of Hyde, while Brandon Hurst is properly slimy as Sir George Carew. The introduction of the Sir George character (who shares a surname but little else with a minor character from Stevenson's novel) betrays the influence of Oscar Wilde's *The Picture of Dorian Gray* (published in 1890); the film's Carew is basically a variation on Wilde's Lord Henry Wotten. Both men are sophisticated cads with a cynical point of view, and they both tempt the protagonists to ruin. The inclusion of the Sir George character in Robertson's film suggests that the director and his scenarist, Clara Beranger, were worried that allowing Jekyll to proceed without outside prompting might make him less sympathetic. Turning Jekyll into an easily manipulated pawn, however, lessens the impact of the tale's "freedom of choice" moral by making him less responsible for his own actions and fate.

Robertson's direction is economical and effective, and he manages one legitimately chilling highlight when Jekyll tosses and turns in bed, imagining Hyde as a spider-like creature scut-

dism culminates in the trampling of a small child and, ultimately, the death of Sir George. Jekyll manages to overcome Hyde long enough to hole up in his laboratory to find an antidote that will permanently suppress his alter ego, but in the end Hyde's influence is too strong.

If F.W. Murnau's now-lost *Der Januskopf* is the most intriguing of the Jekyll and Hyde films of 1920, John S. Robertson's version starring stage legend John Barrymore is probably the most famous and celebrated. Seen today, the film is undeniably dated, but its status as a key title in the development of the horror genre cannot be disputed.

Canadian director Robertson (1878-1964) created his only truly enduring work with this film, designed as something of a showcase for Barrymore. Known as "the Great Profile" in his day, Barrymore is as infamous today for his drunken escapades as he is famous for his acting abilities. Truth be told, modern audiences accustomed to more realistic acting styles are likely to wonder what all the fuss was about with regards to the actor, a stage performer who never entirely learned how to restrain himself for the benefit of the motion picture camera.

Barrymore excelled at playing comedy onscreen, but many of his dramatic roles—especially those in the silent era—look a bit florid and overacted today. His take on Jekyll and Hyde is no exception, though his early scenes as the selfless doctor are nicely restrained. Barrymore opted to rely on very little make-up for his transformation into Hyde (some putty to extend his fingers, a

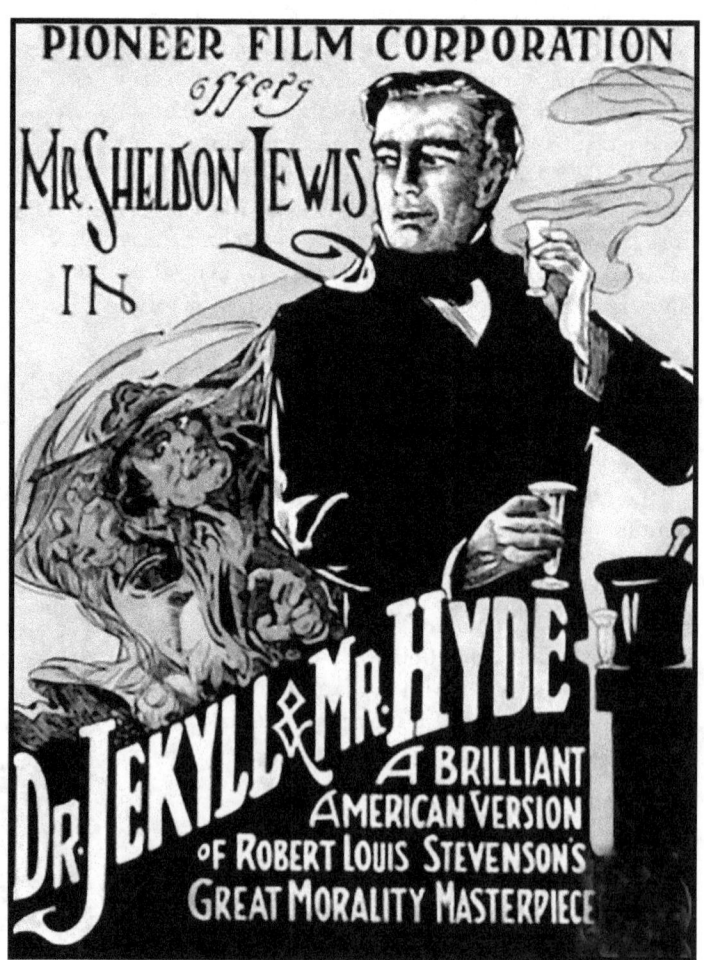

tling across the floor and crouching over him. It's the kind of flourish that could have been totally laughable, but Robertson and his crew pull it off. Production values are excellent on the whole—period detail is nicely rendered, and the sets look impressive and richly dressed. Ultimately, the film pales in comparison to some of the later versions of Stevenson's oft-adapted tale, but its place in the pantheon of significant early horror films is indisputable. TH

Dr. Jekyll and Mr. Hyde
Pioneer; b/w; 40 min; US
D/S: Charles J. Haydon *P:* Louis Meyer
Cast: Sheldon Lewis, Alex Shannon, Dora Mills Adams, Gladys Field, Harold Forshay, Leslie Austin

Dr. Henry Jekyll (Lewis) is a well-respected surgeon venerated for his charity work. He begins a series of experiments designed to disprove the existence of God and the soul. To this end, he determines to segregate the two sides of the human personality using himself as a guinea pig. The strain of his work and experiments proves too great for his fiancée, Bernice (Field), who is the daughter of his old friend Dr. Lanyon (Shannon). The engaged couple separate, and Bernice finds consolation in the arms of Utterson (Forshay). Distraught by this turn of events, Jekyll puts more energy into his experiments, eventually unleashing the baser side of his personality in the form of the impish Mr. Hyde. Hyde goes on a reign of terror, killing several people and causing all manner of problems before being arrested and put in jail. While incarcerated, the transformation reverts and Jekyll returns to his normal self. The police are baffled, but while they question the doctor, they are witnesses as the transformation takes place once again. Mr. Hyde is summarily put to death for his transgressions.

1920 was a busy year for Jekyll and Hyde adaptations. In addition to the now-lost F.W. Murnau version, *Der Januskopf*, and the well-known production starring John Barrymore, this version also made its way into theaters. Of the existing early versions of Robert Louis Stevenson's novella, this is one of the least interesting. The film was clearly made on the cheap and rushed through production, and rumor has it that the director was so displeased with the end result that he had his name removed from the credits. (For the record, the director was Charles J. Haydon, who also adapted the story for the screen.) Rather than explore the moral implications of Stevenson's text, Haydon saw fit to turn the story into a springboard for religious propaganda. Jekyll is an avowed atheist looking to use science to disprove the existence of God; he is eventually punished for this transgression by being plunged into the abyss. To press the point even further, Haydon wheels out a tiresome final twist that reveals the whole thing to have been a nightmare, prompting a contrite Jekyll to announce to his friends and fiancée that he has learned the error of his wicked ways and is now prepared to embrace religion and the Almighty. (In fairness, the whole "it was all just a dream" sting-in-the-tail would have still been fairly fresh in 1920, before years and years of bad horror films made it a difficult pill to swallow.)

Jekyll and Hyde are both played by Sheldon Lewis, a prolific character actor of the silent period whose filmography ends abruptly in 1936, though he lived until 1958. His only other noteworthy genre credit is "The Spider" in Benjamin Christensen's *Seven Footprints to Satan* (1929). As Jekyll, Lewis fares little better than James Cruze in the 1912 adaptation. The script does allow the character more background detail—taking great pains to emphasize his philanthropic work, for example—but Lewis fails to bring him to life. He comes off as a bit of a pompous stiff, one who elicits little interest or empathy. And unfortunately, Lewis' portrayal of Hyde is very much of the Snidely Whiplash school of pantomime—lots of handwringing, rolling of the eyes and the like. The make-up is low-key: some false teeth, matted hair and a cocked hat. Unlike Cruze, Lewis is at least able to indulge in some legitimate mayhem before meeting his just reward, but his frantic overacting makes the character unintentionally humorous. It's hard to believe that even audiences of the period would have found him credibly sinister, and such a dated central performance makes it difficult today to appreciate the film as a whole.

The script updates the action to the contemporary period, but this was likely done more for budgetary reasons than out of artistic consideration. Haydon's direction is functional at best, and even at an abbreviated running time, the pace feels rather slow and deliberate. Ultimately, the film doesn't compare to the Barrymore version of the same year, making one even more rueful that the Murnau adaptation remains a lost production.

As a final point of marginal interest, producer Louis Meyer should not be confused with famed MGM mogul Louis B. Mayer. TH

Dr. Jekyll and Mr. Hyde
Hank Mann Comedies/Arrow; b/w; length unknown; U.S.
P: Morris R. Schlank
Cast: Hank Mann

One of the original Keystone Cops, Hank Mann (1887-1971) was a box-office draw during the silent era, successful enough for Mack Sennett and William Fox that he formed his own production studio in 1919. Distributed to theaters by Arrow, the output of Hank Mann Comedies enjoyed short-lived success before the studio went under in 1920. Mann continued working in movies as a bit player into the sound era, eventually making the jump to television.

Among the films produced by Mann's company was this obscure adaptation of Robert Louis Stevenson's *The Strange Case of Dr. Jekyll and Mr. Hyde* (1886). It was a send-up of the wildly successful John Barrymore adaptation of the same year, also titled *Dr. Jekyll and Mr. Hyde*. It appears that Mann starred in the film as both the kindly Dr. Jekyll and the goofy Mr. Hyde. Given his studio's quick death and the lost status of the film, the film was likely not too successful. Even the bulk of its credit information is difficult to confirm. CW

The Dream Cheater
Brunton; b/w; 55 min; U.S.
D: Ernest C. Warde *S:* Jack Cunningham *P:* Robert Brunton *C:* Arthur L. Todd
Cast: J. Warren Kerrigan, Wedgwood Nowell, Alice Wilson, Joseph J. Dowling, Tom Guise, Fritzi Brunette

When his father dies, a penniless Brandon McShane (Kerrigan) is forced to take a room in a sleazy neighborhood. He briefly becomes involved with Mimi (Wilson), a gold digger who in short order dumps him for a wealthier man. Dejected and disgusted, Brandon acquires a magic skin that allows its owner a certain number of wishes—albeit at the cost of a shortened life.

French novelist and playwright Honoré de Balzac (1799-1850) is best remembered for his epic *La Comedie humaine*, a collection of linked novels and short stories set in post-Napoleonic France. His 1831 short story *Le peau de chagrin* (*The Magic Skin*) provided the inspiration for this obscure title.

Director Ernest C. Warde also made an early version of Henry Irving's *The Bells* (1918). J. Warren Kerrigan, an immensely prolific and popular actor of the silent era, essayed the lead role in *The Dream Cheater*; he retired from the screen after portraying the title character in 1924's *Captain Blood*. TH

The Face at the Window
British Actors; b/w; 63 min; Great Britain
D: Wilfred Noy *S:* Adrian Brunel *P:* Gerald Malvern
Cast: C. Aubrey Smith, Gladys Jennings, Jack Hobbs, Charles Quartermaine, Ben Field, Sir Simeon Stuart

Agnes Ayres played the female lead in *Go and Get It*.

Despite claims to the contrary, this is not the first film adaptation of F. Brooke Warren's once-popular stage play *The Face at the Window*. It is in fact the second—the first was produced in Australia in 1919—though it was the first made in Great Britain. This time around, a respectable gentleman (Quatermaine) prowls the night as a murderous burglar known as Le Loup ("The Wolf") and renders his victims senseless by frightening them with his horrible visage, thus giving the tale its title. But when a banker (Stuart) is murdered, a young man named Lucien Cartwright (Hobbs) is arrested for the crime, much to the chagrin of his lover (Jennings), who is also the dead banker's daughter. A clever detective (Smith) eventually solves the case; with the help of a doctor (Peile), he uses electricity to revive one of Le Loup's victims (Brunel), who is then able to complete the word he had begun to write before his untimely death: the name of his killer!

The Face at the Window was one of C. Aubrey Smith's earliest roles. He went on to a distinguished Hollywood career, starring in such classics as *Tarzan the Ape Man* (1932), *The Prisoner of Zenda* (1937), *Rebecca* (1940), *Madame Curie* (1943), *An Ideal Husband* (1947) and *Little Women* (1949), among many others. His horror titles include *The Witching Hour* (1916), *The Phantom of Paris* (1931), *The Monkey's Paw* (1933), *The Florentine Dagger* (1935), *Dr. Jekyll and Mr. Hyde* (1941), *Flesh and Fantasy* (1943) and *And Then There Were None* (1945).

A German movie poster for *The Golem: How He Came into the World*

It wasn't until the sound era that the next film version of Warren's play was produced, in 1932. CW

Genuine: A Tale of a Vampire
aka **Genuine**; **Genuine, die Tragödie eines seltsamen Hauses**
Decla-Bioscop; b/w; 43 min; Germany
D: Robert Wiene *S:* Carl Mayer *P:* Rudolf Meinert, Erich Pommer *C:* Willy Hameister
Cast: Fern Andra, Albert Bennefeld, Lewis Brody, John Gottowt, Ernst Gronau, Harold Paulsen

Genuine (Andra), the high priestess of a strange religious cult, is kidnapped and sold into white slavery. A weird elderly man buys her and keeps her in a sealed room, watching her as if she were an insect under a microscope and keeping her existence a secret from others. Two young men who nonetheless discover her fall madly in love. Genuine uses her feminine wiles to drive them to the brink of insanity, compelling them to commit acts of murder and suicide to prove their devotion.

With the success of *The Cabinet of Dr. Caligari* (1919), Robert Wiene became a major player in the German film industry. He followed up his financial and artistic triumph with *Genuine: A Tale of a Vampire*.

Despite its title, this is not a standard vampire movie. Genuine is a vamp, not a vampire, a succubus who uses her seductive powers to torment the men who love her. Considering the talent at work here, it also comes as a surprise that the film is something of a mess—though, in fairness, it's difficult to properly appreciate the film when the only edition readily available in the United States is a 43-minute condensation of the original, longer cut.

Still, despite it all, Wiene's hand remains evident in *Genuine*'s bizarre aesthetic. The film reunites the director with the same writer (Carl Mayer) and cinematographer (Willy Hameister) who had worked on *Caligari*, and it boasts a similarly eccentric production design courtesy of Expressionist painter Cesar Klein. Wiene revels in the film's bizarre imagery, which also extends to the make-up, hairstyles and costumes.

The film unfolds in a fairy tale universe, and its book-ended structure makes it clear that it's all a nightmare suffered by a man who falls asleep while reading a fantasy book (a motif previously used in *Dr. Jekyll and Mr. Hyde*, 1910, and *Life Without Soul*, 1915). As such, the film is random in incident and logic. Fern Andra is effective as the sultry Genuine, however, and the film's rich visual tapestry extends to some surprising nudity during a sequence set in a slave market.

Genuine was a critical and commercial flop, compromising for a time Wiene's status in the industry; he returned to form with *The Hands of Orlac* in 1924. TH

Go and Get It
Neilan; b/w; 70 min; U.S.
Co-D/P: Marshall Neilan *Co-D:* Henry Roberts Symonds *S:* Marion Fairfax *C:* David Kesson
Cast: Pat O'Malley, Wesley Barry, Agnes Ayres, J. Barney Sherry, Noah Beery, Bull Montana, Charles Hill Mailes

Helen Allen (Ayres) has inherited a newspaper from her father, but someone is trying to bankrupt it in order to steal it out from under her. She assumes a false identity and gets a job for her own paper to root out the guilty party. Instead, she finds herself pairing with fellow reporter Kirk Connelly (O'Malley) to investigate a series of grisly murders, including that of a famous surgeon named Dr. Ord (Beery). In time, the two uncover the truth: Dr. Ord had transplanted a criminal's brain into the body of a gorilla (Montana), after which the beast had gone on a killing spree, eliminating the criminal's enemies. Oh, and the two also discover just who is trying to ruin the paper.

The simian monstrosity, called Ferry in the film, was portrayed by Bull Montana. Montana was born Luigi Montagna in Voghera, Italy in 1887. Having been a professional wrestler—"Bull" Montana was in fact his wrestling name—the actor's squat, fit body and puggish features were perfect for the part. (Luigi should not be confused with Italian wrestler/actor Lenny "The Bull" Montana, who portrayed mob enforcer Luca Brasi in 1972's *The Godfather*.) Bull repeated his ape shtick in the big-budget blockbuster *The Lost World* (1925), about a plateau in South America still inhabited by prehistoric animals.

Go and Get It and *The Lost World* share more than an ape man, however; they also share a screenwriter, Marion Fairfax. It's been long reported that it was Fairfax who, recalling Montana's performance in the first film, recommended him for the part in the second. Montana went on to work in several films between the years 1917 and 1937, though most of his parts went un-credited. He died of a heart attack in 1950.

Another connection between *Go and Get It* and *The Lost World* is the presence of Noah Beery, whose older brother Wallace

Paul Wegener as the Golem, from *The Golem: How He Came into the World*, is impressive with scenes in which he stalks the countryside and turns on his would-be masters.

starred in *The Lost World*. Noah was a popular actor in his day and became father to Noah Beery, Jr., who likewise became a noted actor with a movie/television career spanning more than six decades. CW

The Golem: How He Came into the World
aka Der Golem: Wie Er in die Welt Kam; Der Golem; The Golem

PAGU; b/w; 85 min; Germany
D/Co-S: Paul Wegener, Carl Boese *Co-S:* Henrik Galeen, Gustav Meyrink *P:* Paul Davidson *C:* Karl Freund
Cast: Paul Wegener, Albert Steinruck, Lyda Salmonova, Ernst Deutsch, Hans Sturm, Max Kronert

In the 16th century, the Jews of Prague—at the time part of the Hapsburg Empire—are under threat by the establishment. Rabbi Loew (Steinruck) turns to magic for protection, creating a monster known as a Golem out of clay to defend the Jews against Rudolph II's anti-Semitic policies. The Golem (Wegener) is effective in this, but eventually goes on a rampage, thus endangering the very people he was created to protect.

Writer/actor/director Paul Wegener clearly had a fixation on the Jewish folktale of the Golem. His first adaptation of the tale, made in 1915 and now thought lost (apart from a few battered fragments), set the tale in modern times. In 1917, he revisited the legend in the short subject *The Golem and the Dancing Girl*, a more comedic spin on the story that is also believed to be lost. While the titles for this version credit Gustav Meyrink's 1914 novel, the film seems to actually borrow little from it. It is definitely both the most accomplished and influential of Wegener's three attempts, however.

The story of the Golem has obvious parallels to Mary Shelley's *Frankenstein*, and there's no doubt that Wegener's picture had an influence on James Whale's classic 1931 adaptation. Stylically *The Golem* is also linked to the German Expressionist movement, most obviously in the stark lighting of Karl Freund and the exaggerated set designs of famed architect Hans Poelzig.

Wegener's direction is fluid and assured. An enchanting fairy tale tone is established from the first shot, a tone the director maintains throughout. There are a number of impressive set pieces, none more striking than the Rabbi's invocation to find the magic word that will bring the Golem to life, a scene amazingly state-of-the-art for its day.

Wegener is physically imposing as the Golem, though his stylized acting is somewhat one-note and fails to engender the degree of empathy that the screenplay obviously desires. Even so, the scenes of the Golem stalking the countryside and turning on his would-be masters are wonderfully executed, and Wegener, with his sheer physical presence, convincingly pulls them off. Albert Steinruck is comparatively nuanced as the well-meaning Rabbi, giving arguably the most convincing performance in the film.

If Wegener's vision fails to create the same sense of wonder as those of Robert Wiene (*The Cabinet of Dr. Caligari*, 1919), Paul Leni (*Waxworks*, 1924), Fritz Lang (*Destiny*, 1919) or F.W. Murnau (*Nosferatu—A Symphony of Terror*, 1922), the fact remains that, taken on its own terms, *The Golem* is an impressive production, well mounted, smoothly paced and loaded with striking imagery. While it doesn't evoke quite the same air of macabre poetry as the other films cited, it must be noted that these are truly difficult films to compare. Perhaps a more sensitive portrayal of the Golem would have elevated Wegener's film to a higher level—the mind certainly toys with the notion of Conrad Veidt or Emil Jannings in the central role. Rather than be too harsh on Wegener, however, let's concede that his genuine interest in the material inspired him to create a template for the many "monster on the loose" pictures yet to come.

Julien Duvivier would direct the next cinematic adaptation of the Golem story, *The Legend of Prague* (1936). TH

The Great London Mystery

T&P; b/w; 12 chapters; Great Britain
D/Co-S: Charles Raymond *Co-S:* Hope Loring
Cast: David Devant, Lady Doris Stapleton, Lester Gard, Lola de Liane, Charles Raymond, Martin Valmour

An illusionist known as The Master Magician (Devant) sets out to thwart an Asian villain (Raymond) who claims to possess supernatural powers. There's also a sacred, cursed jewel stolen from an Indian cult.

This 12-part serial was a showcase for David Devant (1868-1941), who was one of the most famous magicians of

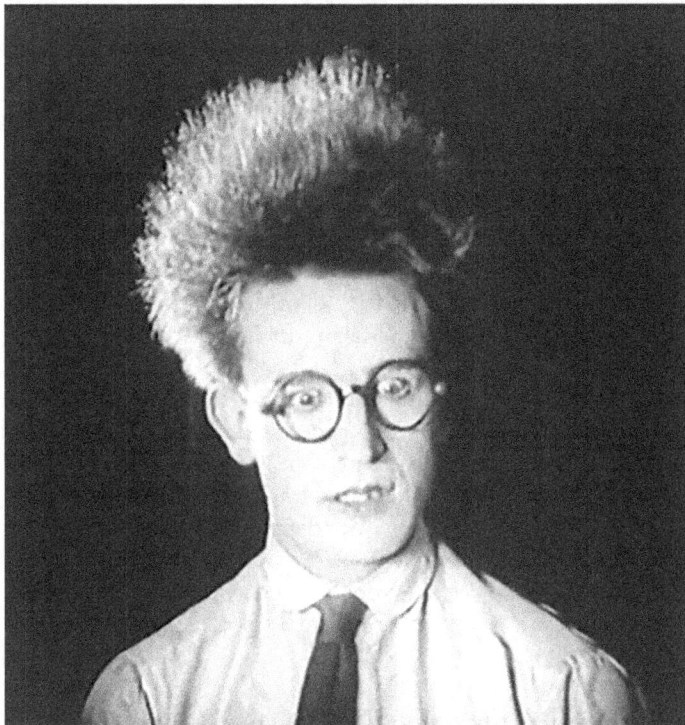

Silent screen superstar Harold Lloyd was the primary force behind *Haunted Spooks*.

his time. His sleight of hand wowed audiences in Victorian England, and he eventually turned his hand toward acting and film exhibition.

The Great London Mystery allowed him to present his routine on celluloid; its plotline seems to have presented him as a two-fisted action hero, up against a Yellow Peril scoundrel with the unfortunate name of Ching Ling Fu. It's unlikely that it was played too seriously, though there seems to have been some borderline horror on display, including a character with the irresistible moniker "Froggie the Vampire" (de Liane, no doubt playing a vamp rather than a vampire)! One chapter was titled *The Living Dead*, though whether it actually involved reanimated corpses is anybody's guess. Some sources indicate that portions of some chapters have survived, but for all intents and purposes the serial remains lost. TH

Haunted Spooks
Hal Roach; b/w; 25 (22) min; U.S.
D: Hal Roach, Alf(red J.) Goulding S: H.M. Walker P: Hal Roach
C: Walter Lundin
Cast: Harold Lloyd, Mildred Davis, Wallace Howe, Blue Washington, Ernest Morrison, Dee Lampton

Along with Charlie Chaplin and Buster Keaton, Harold Clayton Lloyd (1893-1971) was one of the great American comedians of the silent era. Though he began his career with appearances in slapstick comedies produced by his good friend Hal Roach, he was later instrumental in moving big-screen comedy away from the physical and toward the romantic. As a result, he became a cinematic icon and heartthrob, speaking a language that translated well outside of the United States and influenced others worldwide, though in recent years his fame has taken a back seat to his more celebrated contemporaries.

Beating the film usually credited with jump-starting the old dark house subgenre (D.W. Griffith's *One Exciting Night*, 1923) into theaters by three years, *Haunted Spooks* straddles the line between slapstick and romantic comedy, with reveling ghosts and frightened servants thrown in for good measure. Some of the comic routines are funny while others are offensive, but there are a couple of effectively chilling images here and there.

Girl and boy "meet cute." The girl (Davis) has inherited a house from her miserly Confederate grandfather, but she stands to lose it unless she and her husband live in it for one year. Unfortunately, she isn't married and doesn't have any prospects. The boy (Lloyd) has just been spurned by the latest in a series of girls he believed was "the one." After trying and failing at various ways of killing himself, he throws himself in front of an oncoming car. Amazingly, the girl's lawyer is driving the car and she has a proposal for the boy: Marry the girl and inherit a large house and fortune. The two get hitched, and the night the newlyweds arrive at their mansion is a dark and stormy one. Inside, the girl's scheming uncle and a female accomplice have devised a plan to scare them away so that the uncle can profit from the house and grounds. Their plan is to pretend to be ghosts. And to help keep things lively, the uncle tells the African-American servants that the place is haunted and, on this night in particular, spirits roam the halls.

The film may be most famous for the fact that it cost Lloyd two fingers after a prop bomb exploded in his hand (though it's difficult to figure how a prop bomb might have figured into the storyline). The mishap resulted in the actor wearing a glove with prosthetic fingers for the rest of his career, and because it happened a mere couple of weeks into the shoot, production on *Haunted Spooks* was halted for several months while Lloyd recovered. The film, which resumed shooting early the following year, was finally released in March 1920.

Given that there are no ghosts being haunted by other ghosts here, one is left to conclude that the title is a racial slur, and while most of the servants are portrayed by African-American actors, a single, gratuitous shot of a white actor in blackface stands out as particularly tasteless. There's also a predictable abundance of the standard (for the time) scared black shtick, with the unfortunate actors running the gamut of offensive stereotypical behaviors, including wide eyes and shaking knees. A butler becomes so scared that he runs in place, while the young son of another servant provides scares of his own after being accidentally doused with flour, etc.

In only his second screen performance, Blue Washington stars as one of the African-American butlers. He would go on to repeat the same role with minor variations a handful of times, including a portrayal of a scared cowboy in the weird John Wayne Western *Haunted Gold* (1932). He also allegedly had an incidental and un-credited part as a Skull Island native in the classic *King Kong* (1933).

Three years after the film was released, Lloyd and Davis married in real life and remained wed until her death in 1969. Davis was sister to Jack Davis, who was a member of producer Roach's famous child comedy group *Our Gang*. CW

Haunting Shadows
aka House of a Thousand Candles
Hampton; b/w; 55 min; U.S.
D: Henry King S: Eugene B. Lewis P: Jesse D. Hampton C: Victor Milner
Cast: H.B. Warner, Edward Peil, Jr., Charles Hill Mailes, Frank Lanning, Florence Oberle, Margaret Livingston

In order to collect an inheritance left him by his grandfather, John Glenarm must spend an entire year on the old man's haunted estate. But as mysterious happenings pile up, he realizes that there is more to the situation than meets the eye.

Meredith Nicholson's 1906 novel *The House of a Thousand Candles* was a major bestseller. Its blend of mystery and horror, capped off with a sting-in-the-tail ending, made it a natural for film adaptations, the first of which emerged in 1915 under the same title. This, the second version, changed the title but retained the basic structure and content of the book.

Director Henry King began his prolific career in 1915; by the time he retired in 1962, he had racked up over a hundred credits and garnered two Oscar nominations (for *The Song of Bernadette*, 1943, and *Wilson*, 1944). A talented and efficient craftsman who thrived under the studio system, he brought integrity and flair to everything from Westerns (*Jesse James*, 1939) to war films (*Twelve O'Clock High*, 1949). *Haunting Shadows* came relatively early in his career, but he had already amassed over 40 credits as a director by the time of the film's release. He did a lot of acting during the silent era as well, appearing in over a hundred films between 1913 and 1922.

The cast of *Haunting Shadows* is headed by H.B. Warner, best remembered for his Oscar-nominated turn as Chang in Frank Capra's classic *Lost Horizon* (1937). He also played Christ in Cecil B. DeMille's 1927 version of *King of Kings* and ended his long career in the same director's gaudy Technicolor epic *The Ten Commandments* (1956).

The House of a Thousand Candles was filmed again, under its original title, in 1936, though that version stripped most of the horror from the story. TH

The Hound of the Baskervilles
aka Der Hund von Baskerville
Greenbaum; b/w; Germany
Part 1, *Dr. MacDonald's Sanitorium:* 73 min
Part 2, *The House Without Windows:* 84 min
D: Willy Zeyn S: Robert Liebmann P: Josef Greenbaum
Cast: Willy Kayser-Heyl, Lu Juergens, Erwin Fitchner, Ludwig Rex

Willy Kayser-Heyl here takes over from Erwin Neuss and Eugen Berg as Sherlock Holmes. Producer Josef Greenbaum launched the German *Baskervilles* craze with a two-part 1914 production of *The Hound of the Baskervilles*, produced by Vitascope. After leaving the company to form his own, he continued the story's serialization with a 1915 follow-up. Incensed executives at Vitascope responded by making their own installment, *The Hound of the Baskervilles: The Dark Castle* (1915), and attempting to get Greenbaum's independently produced sequel, along with another that Greenbaum produced that same year, suppressed.

Greenbaum visited the story one last time with this 1920 two-parter, which apparently owed less to the Sir Arthur Conan Doyle original than his previous adaptations had. Certainly the subtitles of the two segments—*Dr. MacDonald's Sanitorium* and *The House Without Windows*—don't have any discernable connection to Doyle's novel. Neither segment survives, and very little is known about either. TH

The House of the Tolling Bell
Feature/Blackton; b/w; 65 min; U.S.
D/P: J. Stuart Blackton C: William S. Adams
Cast: May McAvoy, Bruce Gordon, Morgan Thorpe, Edward Elkas, Eulalie Jensen, William R. Dunn

Anthony Cole (Thorpe) disowns his daughter when she marries a man without means. Years later, he dies and leaves behind a will stipulating that his fortune go to anyone able to stay in his spooky manor house for an entire year. Richard Steele (Gordon), a grandson Cole never met, takes up the challenge. Strange goings-on appear to confirm that the house really is haunted, but it turns out that covetous relatives are behind it all.

Yet another entry in the "greedy would-be heirs in a spooky old house" subgenre, *The House of the Tolling Bell* doesn't seem to have brought anything new to the table. The scenario was adapted from a novel by Edith Sessions Tupper, a minor writer who supplied script treatments for a handful of silent era films. Based on surviving credits, some of her script treatments were adapted from short stories she had published.

Producer/Director J. Stuart Blackton was born in England in 1875, and he and his family moved to the United States in 1885. He worked in vaudeville before landing a job with a newspaper, and it's said that one of his assignments led him to interview Thomas Edison about the miracle of the motion picture camera. This, the story goes, interested him in filmmaking.

Blackton worked in a number of genres—creating such literary adaptations as *Richard III* (1908), *Julius Caesar* (1908) and *Oliver Twist* (1909)—and made quite a few pictures, but today he is mostly forgotten. His other horror credits include *The Haunted Hotel* (1907) and *Francesca da Rimini: or, the Two Brothers* (1908). He died in 1941 as the result of a car accident. TH

The House of Whispers
Brunton; b/w; 55 min; U.S.
D: Ernest C. Warde S: Jack Cunningham P: Robert Brunton C: Arthur L. Todd

A German movie poster for *The Hunchback and the Dancer*

Cast: J. Warren Kerrigan, Joseph J. Dowling, Fritzi Brunette, Margery Wilson, Myrtle Rishell, Herbert Prior

Spaulding Nelson (Kerrigan) moves into his uncle's (Dowling) apartment to investigate ghostly cries and whispers—and the sounds of footsteps—said to be coming from the walls. He meets his uncle's neighbors, the sisters Barbara (Brunette) and Clara (Wilson) Bradford, the latter of whom is being terrorized by a voice that sounds like that of her deceased husband Roldo (Jones). It turns out that Roldo is very much alive and in cahoots with the man (Kent) who built the apartment building in which they're all living (which has come to be known as the "house of whispers"). Spaulding soon discovers that the house is riddled with secret passageways, and it isn't long before he's using them to escape from the police after being wrongly accused of an actress' murder. And the passageways, it turns out, lead not only to safety but also to the real criminals.

Based on a novel by William Andrew Johnston (cofounder of Dell Publishing Company), *The House of Whispers* begins as a typical horror film of the period and digresses into a typical mystery of the period (though it thankfully goes easy on the subgenre's usually mandatory comedic interludes). It was released in October 1920, just in time for Halloween.

Ernest C. Warde was born in Liverpool, England in 1874 and went on to star in almost as many films as he directed. His other horror films included *The Woman in White* (1917), Thanhouser's second adaptation of Wilkie Collins' famous novel of the same name, and *The Dream Cheater* (1920), among others. He died of a stomach ailment in Los Angeles, California, in 1923.

That same year actor J. Warren Kerrigan starred in his most famous film, James Cruze's classic *The Covered Wagon* (1923). Though he'd been a fixture in films of the silent era, he retired from acting the following year, shortly after starring in the successful *Captain Blood* (1924). CW

The House Without Windows
aka **Das Haus des Dr. Gaudeamus**; **Haus ohne Tür and Fenster**

Vita; b/w; length unknown; Austria/Germany
D/Co-S: Friedrich Feher *Co-S:* Johannes Brandt
Cast unknown

Friedrich Feher is best remembered for his role as Francis, the hapless hero of Robert Wiene's *The Cabinet of Dr. Caligari* (1919). That film's impact on German horror cinema was enormous, and Feher wasted little time in following it up with this one. *The House Without Windows* is long lost but was, from all indications, a full-blown homage to *Caligari*, with Feher's art directors mimicking that masterpiece's Expressionist set designs. Reports from the time, however, indicate that the attempt at replication fell flat. The story dealt with a young married couple trapped in a windowless house of horrors.

Feher first entered films in 1913, dividing his time between acting and directing. After *Caligari*, his screen appearances became steadily fewer as he focused more on directing and writing.

This *House Without Windows* should not be confused with "Das Haus ohne Fenster," a chapter from the 1914 serialization of *The Hound of the Baskervilles*. Instead, it is based on the novel *Hause ohne Tür and Fenster* by Thea von Harbou.

The film was not released in most foreign territories until 1921. TH

The Hunchback and the Dancer
aka **Der Bucklige und die Tänzerin**

Helios Film; b/w; 50 min; Germany
D: F.W. Murnau *S:* Carl Mayer *C:* Karl Freund
Cast: Sascha Gura, John Gottowt, Paul Biensfeldt, Henri Peters-Arnolds, Bella Polini, Anna Von Palen

James Wilton (Gottowt) discovers a diamond mine in Java. Due to his hunchback, he ordinarily repels women, but his newfound fortune changes his societal standing. He begins a romance with a young woman named Gina (Gura) who is getting over a breakup with another man. Wilton explains to Gina that during his travels he has learned all the secrets of cosmetics and perfumes. When Gina later rejects him to reconcile with her previous lover, Wilton concocts a potion that, while not harming her, kills anybody who kisses her. The potion bumps off two people before Gina realizes that Wilton is responsible. She gets her revenge by allowing Wilton to kiss her, thus poisoning him.

The Hunchback and the Dancer is among the lost early works of the great German director F.W. Murnau. Unlike *Der Januskopf* (1920), however, not much info survives about this film. The synopsis certainly suggests that it warrants inclusion in any book dedicated to the horror genre, though the film might have been played more for melodrama than for shock value. Given Murnau's interest in the occult and the macabre, it does seem safe to assume that the film would have offered more than tepid soap opera dramatics.

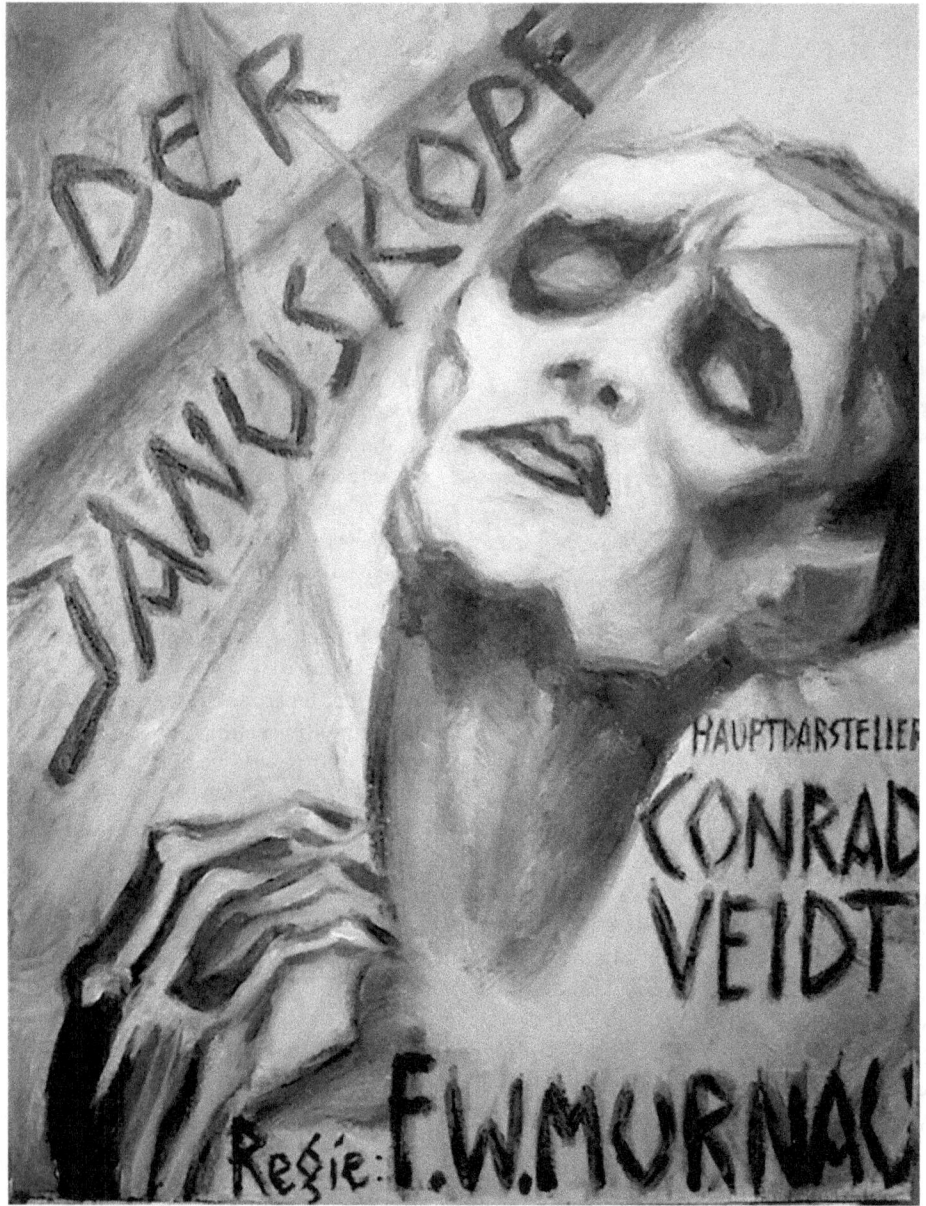

A German poster for *Der Januskopf*, F.W. Murnau's unauthorized take on Robert Louis Stevenson's *The Strange Case of Dr. Jekyll and Mr. Hyde*

Lipow Film/Decla Bioscop; b/w; 107 (77) min; Germany
D: F.W. Murnau *S:* Hans Janowitz *P:* Eric Pommer *C:* Karl Freund, Carl Hoffman, Carl Weiss
Cast: Conrad Veidt, Magnus Stifter, Margarete Schlegel, Willy Kaiser-Heyl, Bela Lugosi, Margaret Kupfel

Dr. Warren (Veidt) is a respected physician in love with Jane Lanyon (Schlegel). In order to impress her, he purchases for her a bust of the Roman god Janus. She rejects the gift, forcing Warren to keep it for himself. The bust yields an unusual influence over the doctor, unleashing a sadistic alter ego named Mr. O'Connor. O'Connor goes on a rampage before turning back into the buttoned-down Warren, who realizes what has happened and attempts to sell the bust. The bizarre influence of the statue proves too strong, however, prompting yet another transformation resulting in more mayhem and violence. When the police attempt to arrest O'Connor, he locks himself in his laboratory and poisons himself.

Renowned today for a handful of surviving films, Friedrich Wilhelm Murnau (1888-1931) was a major innovator during the silent film era of Germany, the most cutting-edge of film industries during that time. Alas, many of his earliest films are now considered lost. These include such titles as *Der Knabe in Blau* (1919), *Satanas* (1920), *The Hunchback and the Dancer* (1920) and, perhaps most tragically, *Der Januskopf*. The literal English translation of the title is "The Janus Head," which was designed to conceal the fact that the film was an unauthorized adaptation of Robert Louis Stevenson's *The Strange Case of Dr. Jekyll and Mr. Hyde*. Cineastes familiar with Murnau's work will recall that a similar ploy nearly sabotaged his later "concealed" adaptation of Bram Stoker's *Dracula* (*Nosferatu—A Symphony of Terror*, 1922). It is unknown whether the subterfuge resulted in the strange disappearance of this Jekyll and Hyde picture, but as of this writing, not one frame from a print is known to exist.

From what can be gathered from the surviving stills and production notes, one can only conclude that it would be a title well worth celebrating were it ever to resurface. The film's mystique is solidified by the collaborative strength of Murnau, ace cinematographer Karl Freund (whose genre credits include *The Golem: How He Came into the World*, 1920, and *Dracula*, 1931), star Conrad Veidt (merely a year removed from *The Cabinet of Dr. Caligari*, 1919, and already an established star in Germany) and supporting player Bela Lugosi, whose casting as Warren's butler foreshadows his red herring appearances in numerous American B-films of the 1930s and '40s. This was Lugosi's first genre credit, though he had been appearing in small roles in films made in Germany or his native Hungary since 1917.

The film's cinematographer, Karl Freund, subsequently shot such significant genre titles as Paul Wegener's *The Golem: How He Came into the World* (1920) and Tod Browning's *Dracula* (1931) before putting on a director's hat and helming two of the most delirious genre titles of the 1930s: *The Mummy* (1932) and *Mad Love* (1935).

Murnau would eventually find notoriety with his unauthorized adaptation of Bram Stoker's *Dracula*, titled *Nosferatu—A Symphony of Terror* (1922), before triumphing in Hollywood with *Sunrise* (1927). Scenarist Carl Mayer was one of the writers of *The Cabinet of Dr. Caligari* (1919), while co-star John Gottowt is best known to horror buffs as a Professor Van Helsing substitute named Professor Bulwer in the aforementioned *Nosferatu*. TH

Der Januskopf
aka **Januskopf, eine Tragödie am Rande der Wirlichkeit; The Two-Faced Man; Dr. Jekyll and Mr. Hyde; Love's Mockery; The Janus Face; The Head of Janus; Schrecken**

Given the occult leanings of Hans Janowitz's adaptation, it is conceivable that many viewers of the time may have not realized the connection to Stevenson's novella. Rather than relying on the usual self-experimentation with a magic formula, Murnau and Janowitz chose to portray the mysterious and inexplicable in the form of a bust of Janus exuding a malevolent influence over Dr. Warren. Conceptually, it's a promising starting point, and given the roster of talent involved, one can only hope that the film, or at least some surviving fragment, will eventually surface. TH

Kurfurstendamm
Oswald; b/w; 89 min; Germany
D/S/P: Richard Oswald *C:* Karl Hoffmann
Cast: Conrad Veidt, Erna Morena, Asta Nielsen, Rudolf Forster, Theodor Loos, Paul Morgan

The Devil (Veidt) notices that a large number of souls are entering Hell from Berlin's seedy Kurfurstendamm district, and he sets out to find out why. Disguising himself as a nobleman, he takes a room at a boarding house. There he meets Dr. Li (Sze), who takes him out and shows him the carnal delights Kurfurstendamm has to offer. Satan revels in the available female flesh, though he does take time along the way to start up a film production company (a move that ends on a disastrous note). After he is beaten up and robbed on the street, he returns to the comfort and solace of the nether regions.

Richard Oswald was responsible for this blend of humor and horror, with Conrad Veidt perfectly cast as a pleasure-seeking Satan. The two men worked together on numerous occasions, with their best-remembered collaboration being the portmanteau *Weird Tales* (1919).

Cinematographer Karl Hoffmann was one of the key cameramen of silent German cinema; he also worked with such major filmmakers as Fritz Lang (*Dr. Mabuse, The Gambler*, 1922) and F.W. Murnau (*Der Januskopf*, 1920).

This story was later remade in Bulgaria as *Satan in Sofia* (1921). TH

Lord Arthur Saville's Crime
aka **Lidércnyomás**; **The Mark of the Phantom**
Phőnix; b/w; length unknown; Hungary
D/S: Paul (Pál) Fejos *S:* György Halász *C:* József Karbán
Cast: Margit Lux, Lajos Gellért, Odon Bardi, Gusztáv Pártos

First published in 1891 in the collection *Lord Arthur Savile's Crime and Other Stories*, Oscar Wilde's tale concerns one Lord Arthur Savile, who is introduced by an acquaintance, Lady Windermere, to a palm reader named Septimus R. Podgers. Podgers reads Savile's palm and divines that Savile is destined to commit murder. Savile, who is engaged, decides that to prevent his marriage from being sullied, he must commit the crime beforehand. His first attempt, slipping poison to his Aunt Clementina as a cure for her heartburn, appears to work; she dies and leaves him a nice inheritance. But then his fiancée, Sybil Merton, finds the poison pill among Clementina's things, revealing to Savile that he was not responsible for the old woman's death. He tries again with another more distant relative, and once again he fails. Worried that he will never marry, the depressed Savile comes across the palm reader while wandering London late one night and, seeing an opportunity, pushes the seer into the Thames. Fortuitously for Savile, Podgers' death is ruled a suicide. Feeling free at long last, Savile marries Sybil but learns years later from Lady Windermere that Podgers was a charlatan, with no gift whatsoever for telling the future.

Like his more famous novel *The Picture of Dorian Gray* (1890), Wilde's *Lord Arthur Savile's Crime* is a black comedy with horror overtones. *Crime*'s denouement leaves it to the reader to decide whether the murder was due to fate or a matter of free will.

With at least seven film adaptations of *Dorian Gray* in the can by 1920, it was inevitable that studios would turn to some of Wilde's lesser-known works for inspiration. This obscure Hungarian film (notice that the English-language credits misspell the last name of the film's eponymous hero) appears to have been the first released (though the second filmed) adaptation of *Lord Arthur Savile's Crime*. Two other versions were shot during the silent years, both in European countries, and many more followed in the sound era.

As with so many Hungarian films of the period, this one is believed lost. It was shot in 1920 and released in its native country in either July 1920 or February 1921, depending on which source one chooses to believe. It was one of director/screenwriter Paul Fejos' earliest films and perhaps his first horror film. In 1922 he shot *Queen of Spades*, based on Pushkin's venerable tale. By 1927 he had moved to the United States, and there he helmed Universal's *The Last Performance*. In 1932 he went to France to direct *Fantômas*, a blatantly horror-oriented take on the fictitious criminal mastermind. CW

Love Without Question
Rolfe Photoplays; b/w; 70 min; U.S.
D/P: B.A. Rolfe *S:* Violet Clark *C:* Arthur A. Thadwell
Cast: Olive Tell, James W. Morrison, Mario Majeroni, Ivo Dawson, Charles Mackay, George S. Stevens

The unlikely title aside, this is very much a horror-tinged murder mystery. In the Gothic mansion of elderly Silas Blackburn (Majeroni), there is a room, believed haunted, in which members of three generations of Blackburns have died. When Silas is found murdered in that room, his grandson Robert (Morrison) falls under suspicion, along with his ladyfriend Katherine (Tell). The two have ample motive—the old man's death gives them access to his fortune—and it doesn't help their cause that Robert suffers from frequent blackouts. During the investigation of the crime, a police detective is also slain and, soon after, the apparent ghost of Silas appears. By the end Silas is revealed to be alive but also the murderer. It had been the old man's twin brother who was killed in the supposedly haunted room to ensure that Silas could keep his wealth. Robert and Katherine are cleared, paving the way for the consummation of their romance.

The novel *The Abandoned Room* by Charles Wadsworth Camp forms the basis for *Love Without Question*. Camp (1879-1936) wrote several novels and at least one screenplay (*The Gray Mask*,

1915) during his lifetime, but he may be most famous for being the father of Madeleine L'Engle, the award-winning author of the children's classic *A Wrinkle in Time* (1962). Camp's novels later became the basis for such Universal horror films as *The Last Warning* (1929) and *The House of Fear* (1939). Producer/director/presenter B.A. Rolfe's production company made approximately 20 films between 1915 and 1920 before its head retired from film to become a musician. *Love Without Question* was released on April 3, 1920 and was one of the last films the company made. CW

Luring Shadows
Catholic Art Association; b/w; 75 min; U.S.
D: Joseph Levering *S:* O.E. Goebel
Cast: Aida Horton

J.H. Waering is found murdered, and a search of his apartment reveals that some valuable items have been stolen. Suspicion falls on the man's butler Jason, though there are other possible culprits. Dr. Barton, a spiritualist, arranges for a séance in order to identify the real murderer. The ploy blows up in Barton's face, however, when the murdered Waering appears to him alone. Barton breaks down and confesses, and the estate is awarded to Waering's virtuous daughter, Florence (Horton).

This is a very obscure and apparently quite macabre little mystery. Surviving information on it is minimal, but the finale involving the unmasking of a killer at a séance would seem to foreshadow such genre fare as the three versions of *The Thirteenth Chair* (1919, 1929, 1937), as well as Dario Argento's *Deep Red* (1975) and *Trauma* (1992). Credit information on the film is largely lost, with the only confirmed player being Aida Horton (1912-1983), whose filmography seems to span the period from 1917 to 1920. *Luring Shadows* is her penultimate credit, if surviving records of her activity are accurate.

The Catholic Art Association produced a handful of films between 1917 and 1920, nearly all of them involving director Levering and/or writer O.E. Goebel. TH

The Monster of Frankenstein
aka **Il Mostro di Frankenstein**; **Il Monstro di Frankenstein**; **Frankenstein's Monster**
Albertini Film; b/w; 39 min; Italy
D: Eugenio Testa *S:* Giovanni Drovetti *P:* Luciano Albertini *C:* Alvaro de Simone
Cast: Luciano Albertini, Umberto Guarracino, Linda Albertini, Aldo Mezzanotte

Frankenstein (Albertini) creates a living man (Guarracino) out of human body parts but is horrified and saddened to discover that his creation is a monster without a soul. When it goes on a rampage, the grief-stricken Frankenstein confronts it in a gloomy cave, after which he is forced to destroy his work.

This early adaptation of Mary Shelley's *Frankenstein, or The Modern Prometheus*—previous versions included *Frankenstein* (1910) and *Life Without Soul* (1915)—is one of a handful of Italian horror films produced during the silent era. Censorship had reared its head in Italy from cinema's very beginnings, and once Benito Mussolini became Prime Minister in 1922, horror and fantasy films were strictly forbidden. *Monster*, then, was Italy's final overt horror film for the following three decades. It would not be until 1956 that Italian filmmakers openly revisited the genre with the release of Riccardo Freda and Mario Bava's *I Vampiri*, though in the interim producers did at times dodge censorship by placing their striking scenes of horror in the context of morality plays.

Not surprisingly, rumor has it that *Monster* suffered greatly at the hands of the censors, who insisted on snipping anything they considered even remotely disturbing. This may partially explain why the film disappeared so soon after its initial release: little of interest to audiences remained.

Producer and actor Luciano Albertini, a popular box-office draw in his native country in his day, executed the role of Frankenstein. He tried to find success in the United States with Universal's *The Iron Man* (1924) but failed, and he returned to Italy where he continued to star in films. After spending his final days in a mental institution, Albertini died in 1945—the very year Mussolini was defeated by the Allies. TH

Les Morts qui parlent
aka **Les Morts parlent**
b/w; 66 min; France
D: Pierre Marodon *C:* Willy Faktorovitch
Cast: Lady Nobody

Though born in 1873, Pierre Marodon doesn't appear to have begun his film career until 1918, the year in which he directed (and starred in) *Mascamor*. Two years later he made his first and apparently only horror film, *Les Morts qui parlent* (literally, "The Dead Who Speak"). His career was comparatively short; his last film was made in 1927, though he lived until 1949.

Whether *Les Morts qui parlent* still exists is anyone's guess; little information about the film is available, though it is frequently listed in horror filmographies. Lead actress Lady Nobody starred in a handful of films in the early-to-mid 1920s, all of them for director Marodon.

Marodon also directed the fantastical 12-chapter (but non-horror) serial *The Haunted Castle* in 1923. CW

The Mystery Mind
Supreme; b/w; 15 chapters; U.S.
D: William S. Davis, Fred Sittenham *S:* John W. Grey, Arthur B. Reeve
Cast: J. Robert Pauline, Violet MacMillan, Peggy Shanor, Paul Panzer, Ed Rogers, Saville De Sacia

This lost serial serves up an heiress, Violet Bronson (MacMillan), pursued by a cult of Satan worshipers from the lost city of Atlantis! The group, led by a disembodied voice known as The Mystery Mind, is intent on both sacrificing her and obtaining her fortune.

Released in September 1920, *The Mystery Mind*'s chapters are *Prologue: The Road to Yesterday*; *1. The Hypnotic Clue*; *2. The Fires of Fury*; *3. The War of Wills*; *4. The Fumes of Fear*; *5. Thought Waves*; *6. A Halo of Help*; *7. The Nether World*; *8. The Mystery Mind*; *9. Dual Personality*; *10. Hounds of Hate*; *11. The Sleepwalker*; *12. The Temple of the Occult*; *13. The Blinding Ray*; *14. The Water Cure* and *15. The Gold of the Gods*. Its plot is known due to Marc Edmund Jones' deplorably written novelization of Grey and Reeve's apparently nonsensical screenplay. The book, also titled *The Mystery Mind*, is an early example of a movie tie-in by a major publisher (in this case, Grosset & Dunlap).

None of the film's cast and crew appears to have achieved any degree of fame. Star Violet MacMillan began her career

Lon Chaney's stark performance dominates *The Penalty* with a portrayal of unbridled ferocity.

with L. Frank Baum's Oz Film Manufacturing Company, which the author formed to adapt his own works to the big screen. Paul Panzer had un-credited bit parts all the way through the early 1950s, while Ed Rogers found steady work as the character Ed Simpson on the daytime soap opera *Days of Our Lives* between 1965 and 1979. CW

Nachtgestalten
aka Eleagable Kuperus; Figures of the Night
Richard Oswald; b/w; 106 min; Germany
D/S/P: Richard Oswald *C:* Carl Hoffmann
Cast: Paul Wegener, Conrad Veidt, Reinhold Schunzel, Erna Morena, Erik Charrell, Anita Berber

Not much is known about this film. It's based on a ghost story written by Austrian-turned-German-nationalist Karl Hans Strobl (1877-1946), a popular horror author in the early 20th century who has since fallen into obscurity. The story itself, 1910's *Eleagable Kuperus*, was by all accounts an anti-materialist, pro-Socialist propagandistic piece of literature. Though the film's plot is unknown, the cast includes Erik Charrell as a gorilla, a common monster in horror films of this vintage. The film was shot at Babelsberg Studio in Berlin.

Nachtgestalten is noteworthy for its casting of both Paul Wegener (as Thomas Bezug) and Conrad Veidt (as Clown). Each at one point had the lead role in a version of *The Student of Prague* (Wegener in 1913; Veidt in 1926), and both left an indelible impression on the horror genre during the silent era.

Writer Strobl was also the editor of *Der Orchideengarten*, a German magazine dedicated to horror, science fiction and fantasy. His most popular work appears to have been *Lemuria*, a collection of short horror stories influenced by Edgar Allan Poe. Strobl's obscurity today may be due to his eventual membership in the Nazi Party, where he was able to freely engage in his anti-Semitic views and behaviors.

Screenwriter/producer/director Richard Oswald also directed the horror anthology *Weird Tales* (1919), which he remade to greater acclaim as *Uncanny Stories* in 1932 (with Wegener in a key role). Cinematographer Carl Hoffmann also collaborated with such luminaries as F.W. Murnau (*Der Januskopf*, 1920) and Fritz Lang (*Dr. Mabuse, The Gambler,* 1922). TH

Narayana
Gaumont; b/w; 62 min; France
D: Léon Poirier *C:* André Lecurieux
Cast: Laurence Myrga, Edmon Van Daële, Charles Norville, Marcelle Souty, Jacques Robert, Marguerite Madys

The word "Narayana" is the Sanskrit term for Vishnu, the name of the supreme god in Hinduism. In this French adaptation of Honoré de Balzac's 1831 novel *Le Peau de chagrin*, the tale's magical wish-granting skin has been swapped for a magical wish-granting statuette of Narayana, thus sprinkling elements of Wilkie Collins' *The Moonstone* into the mix. A man, Jacques Hebert, comes into possession of the statuette (apparently through theft), which has the power to grant five wishes, each costing a portion of the wisher's life force.

While a copy of the film does exist, it's apparently quite difficult to view outside of France. By all accounts, the effects are solid if typical—double exposures and jump cuts—of their period.

The next adaptation of Balzac's story came in 1923 with *Slave of Desire*. CW

One Hour Before Dawn
aka Behind Red Curtains
Hampton; b/w; 53 min; U.S.
D: Henry King *S:* Fred Myton *P:* Jesse D. Hampton *C:* Victor Milner
Cast: Anna Q. Nilsson, H.B. Warner, Augustus Phillips, Frank Leigh, Howard Davies, Adele Farrington

Hypnotist Norman Osgood (Leigh) mesmerizes Harrison Kirke (Davies) without the man's consent. When Kirke awakens, he is enraged by Osgood's stunt and threatens to kill him. Fearful for his life, Osgood hypnotizes George Clayton (Warner), instructing him to kill Kirke "one hour before dawn." Kirke is found dead the following day, and Clayton is troubled by the memory of a dream in which he was compelled to commit the murder. Clayton's suspicious behavior makes him a prime suspect in the crime until the real culprit is unmasked.

Like *Haunting Shadows* (1919), *One Hour Before Dawn* finds director Henry King (*The Gunfighter*, 1950) honing his craft in

Lon Chaney's range as an actor is evident in the touches of pathos and humanity he imbues in his characterization, from *The Penalty*.

the horror genre. The following year, he made one of his best-remembered silent features, *Tol'able David* (1921). He worked consistently throughout the 1920s but didn't really hit his artistic stride until the 1930s.

Swedish-born starlet Anna Q. Nilsson (1888-1974) moved to the United States in 1910 to pursue an acting career. Her talent and good looks made her popular in the silent era, but like so many stars of the period, she was unable to make a successful transition to talkies. The great writer/director Billy Wilder later cast her in a cameo role in *Sunset Blvd.* (1950) as a member of Norma Desmond's (Gloria Grahame) "waxworks." As a further point of trivia, leading man H.B. Warner, who had also played the lead in *Haunting Shadows*, played a member of Desmond's entourage in that same film.

The film was released to theaters on July 11, 1920. TH

The Penalty
Goldwyn/Eminent Authors; b/w; 90 min; U.S.
D: Wallace Worsley S: Charles Kenyon, Philip Lonergan P: Samuel Goldwyn, Rex Beach Goldwyn C: Donovan D. Short
Cast: Lon Chaney, Charles Clary, Claire Adams, Ethel Grey Terry, Doris Pawn, Jim Mason

An inexperienced doctor (Clary) needlessly amputates a teenage boy's legs following a road accident. The boy grows into an embittered criminal mastermind nicknamed Blizzard (Chaney), who seeks revenge on the doctor who maimed him.

Based on a pulp novel by Gouverneur Morris, *The Penalty* is of note for its ferocious central performance by Lon Chaney, who is so convincing in the role of the cynical cripple that he elevates a fairly trite and formulaic crime melodrama into the realm of *Grand Guignol*. (The supporting cast, in fact, can't help but fade into the background whenever Chaney is onscreen.) The actor catapulted himself to superstardom with this film, and it was soon thereafter that he became one of the highest paid actors in Hollywood.

The Penalty also manages to work some surprisingly adult subject matter—including drug addiction and a nude model in an artist's studio—into an engaging if at times implausible narrative. Director Wallace Worsley later re-teamed with Chaney on *A Blind Bargain* (1922), but their biggest commercial triumph came with 1923's *The Hunchback of Notre Dame* (1923).

Given the somewhat inept direction on display in *Hunchback*, Worsley's efficient handling of *The Penalty* is something of a pleasant surprise. It's true, of course, that this film is a far smaller, more intimate affair than the later "super production," leaving one to surmise that the surfeit of extras and elaborate sets on *Hunchback* overwhelmed the director. And while he doesn't display the sort of creativity that made Tod Browning a master of silent cinema, Worsley also doesn't pull any punches, making his film an audacious amalgam of crime and horror.

In the end, however, it's Chaney who dominates *The Penalty* with a performance of unbridled ferocity, and his range as an actor is evident in the touches of pathos and humanity he imbues in his characterization. TH

The Perils of Paul
aka **Perils of Paul or the Duchess at Bay**; **Paul's Peril**
American Lifeograph; b/w; 22 min; U.S.
D: Bob Gray S: William Keefe, Eve Sturtvant C: Hal Mohr
Cast: J. Parks Jones, Clare Morris, Eugenia Gilbert, William Dills, Eugenia Gilbert

This short subject sought to capitalize on the popularity of the Pathé serial *The Perils of Pauline* (1914), with a few supernatural elements tossed into the mix. Given that public interest in the occult was rife at the time, a spooky adornment or two doubtless made the picture more commercial. Still, it's most likely that the film's primary genre was adventure, despite portrayals of Ouija board usage and a depiction of the spirit realm (a brew à la 1981's *Raiders of the Lost Ark*, perhaps).

Director Bob Gray (sometimes billed as Robert Gray) created a string of now-forgotten titles in the decade or so after 1910, achieving marginally greater success as an actor. Cinematographer Hal Mohr entered films in 1915, with this being one of his earliest credits in a long and distinguished career that would see him netting Oscars for work in black and white (*A Midsummer Night's Dream*, 1935) and color (*Phantom of the Opera*, 1943).

The short-lived American Lifeograph Company, which was responsible for a succession of unremarkable short subjects and serials, produced *The Perils of Paul*. Records indicate that the studio was active from 1915 to 1920, though its surviving filmography appears hopelessly incomplete. TH

The Phantom Carriage
aka **Körkarlen**; **The Phantom Chariot**; **The Stroke of Midnight**; **Thy Soul Shall Bear Witness**
Svensk; b/w; 74 min; Sweden
D/S: Victor Sjostrom *P:* Charles Magnusson *C:* Julius Jaenzon
Cast: Victor Sjostrom, Hilda Borgstrom, Tore Svennberg, Astrid Holm, Concordia Selander, Lisa Lundholm

David Holm (Sjostrom) slips into a life of alcoholism, abandoning his job and family along the way. A kindly Salvation Army worker, Edit (Holm), attempts to steer him back to a decent way of life, but he wants no part of it. As the New Year approaches, David tells his friends the old fable of the Phantom Carriage, which states that any person who dies at the stroke of midnight on New Year's Day will be sentenced to drive the ghostly vehicle, collecting the souls of the dead for an entire year. When disagreement breaks out between David and his friends, he is fatally wounded and left to die as the clock strikes midnight.

Ingmar Bergman considered this early Scandinavian fantasy/horror piece "the film of all films," and the influence it had on his own work—notably *Wild Strawberries* (1957) and *The Seventh Seal* (1957)—is obvious. At heart, *The Phantom Carriage* is less a horror film than a melodramatic diatribe on the dangers of alcohol, but its then-innovative narrative structure and atmospheric visuals make it worthwhile viewing for fright fans.

Based on the 1912 novel of the same name by Selma Lagerlof, *Carriage* bears some similarities to Charles Dickens' short story *A Christmas Carol* (1843) in its depiction of a wayward soul given a second chance by ghostly visions. Writer/actor/director Victor Sjostrom (1879-1960) was a major presence in the Swedish film industry of the period, and he was a logical choice to bring the story to the screen. He had previously adapted three of Lagerlof's other novels. He gives a strong performance as the anti-hero David Holm, a man who throws away a successful life and career in favor of aimless debauchery.

The use of superimpositions to create the impression of souls leaving their bodies was standard stuff by 1921, having been done numerous times over the previous two decades by such pioneer filmmakers as Georges Méliès, George Albert Smith, Edwin S. Porter and Walter R. Booth, but they're done by Sjostrom with such a degree of craftsmanship and fidelity that they are nonetheless impressive. The images of the ghostly carriage moving through the deadened landscape are striking, and the visualization of the coach driver as a grim reaper, complete with scythe and rotting cloak, evoke comparisons to many a more recent horror film.

But it is the film's complex structure that commands the most attention. *The Phantom Carriage* unfolds as a string of flashbacks within flashbacks, and the viewer is required to remain attentive in order to keep track of the story. Not surprisingly, the film was radically re-edited for some areas upon its original release, with foreign distributors worried that audiences wouldn't be able to comprehend the complicated composition.

Despite the cloying sentimentality sometimes on display, Sjostrom and his cast manage to milk the scenario for genuine pathos. The pathetic figure of the Salvation Army worker desperately trying to correct David's way of life, for example, is indisputably moving.

The film had a lasting influence on major directors. Bergman, mentioned above, crafted an homage, *The Image Makers*, in 2000. It dealt with the making of the film, while Stanley Kubrick virtually re-staged the scene where David takes an axe to a locked door to get at his terrified family in *The Shining* (1980).

Lagerlof's story was remade in 1939 as *The Phantom Wagon* by Julien Duvivier and again in 1958 as *The Phantom Carriage* by Arne Mattson. TH

The Phantom Foe
Astra/Seitz/Pathé; b/w; 15 chapters; U.S.
D: Bertram Millhauser *Co-S:* Frank Leon Smith *Co-S/P:* George B. Seitz
Cast: Warner Oland, Juanita Hansen, William Norton Baily, Harry Semmels, Wallace McCutcheon, Jr., Nina Cassavant

Despite assertions by some to the contrary, this 15-part serial is not lost, though it remains difficult to view. An adventure with horror overtones, it contains the mesmeric villain (Semmels) and occult paraphernalia typical of serials from the period. The chapter titles are: *Chapter 1: Doom*; *Chapter 2: Disappearance of Janet Dale*; *Chapter 3: Trail of the Wolf*; *Chapter 4: The Open Window*; *Chapter 5: The Tower Room*; *Chapter 6: The Crystal Ball*; *Chapter 7: Gun Fire*; *Chapter 8: The Man Trap*; *Chapter 9: The Mystic Summons*; *Chapter 10: The Foe Unmasked*; *Chapter 11: Through Prison Walls*; *Chapter 12: Behind the Veil*; *Chapter 13: Attack at the Inn*; *Chapter 14: Confession* and *Chapter 15: Retribution*. It was released beginning in October 1920.

Prints of 14 of the serial's chapters exist in the International Museum of Photography and Film at George Eastman House in Rochester, NY, while a copy of the remaining one can be found at the Library of Congress. CW

The Phantom Melody
Universal; b/w; 66 min; U.S.
D: Douglas Gerrard *S:* F. McGrew Willis *C:* Roy H. Klaffki
Cast: Monroe Salisbury, Henry A. Barrows, Ray Gallagher, Charles West, Jean Calhoun, Joe Way

Count Camello (Salisbury) loves Mary Drake (Calhoun), but his like-minded cousin Gregory Baldi (West) disrupts his wooing. The tension among the three is broken when Italy goes to war and Gregory is apparently killed in battle. Camello and Mary become engaged, but Gregory returns on the eve of their wedding. Desperate for money and none too happy about the engagement, he buries Camello alive in the family vault. But Camello manages to free himself and win a deadly duel against his rival.

Irish-born Douglas Gerrard entered films as an actor in 1913; he directed his first film *The Price of Victory* in 1916, although he gave up directing not long after *The Phantom Melody*. Scenarist F. McGrew Willis also wrote such horror-tinged fare as *The Devil's Bondwoman* (1916) and *Even As You and I* (1917).

Carl Laemmle's Universal Film Manufacturing Company was still a long ways from revolutionizing the horror film with mega-hits such as *The Phantom of the Opera* (1925) and *Dracula* and *Frankenstein* (both 1931), though they had dipped an occasional toe into the genre with such titles as *Dr. Jekyll and Mr. Hyde* (1913).

The Phantom Melody is primarily melodrama, but its premature-burial plotline tilts it toward the horror genre. TH

The Power of the Borgias
aka I Borgia; The Borgias
Medusa; b/w; length unknown; Italy
D: Luigi Caramba
Cast: Irene Saffo-Nomo, Enrico Piacentini, Carmen di San Giusto, Eugenio Giraldoni

An absurdist fantasy based on the doings of the Borgia family of Renaissance Italy, *The Power of the Borgias* seems to have been little more than an excuse to craft a film around brutality while exploiting the name of a family famous for its violent nature. The film has vile Cesare attack, rape and blind young Rosa, prompting her friend to take on the persona of a jester and be introduced to the Borgia's court. There he witnesses the various machinations of the family's political machine as Cesare manipulates Lucrezia Borgia into marrying for solely political gain. A revolt, however, sends the jester into exile as part of the Borgias' clan.

The same year Caramba made this feature, Italian director Armando Carbone made *The Last of the Borgias*. Few details exist about the film, making it impossible to tell whether it dealt with Lucrezia or a descendent, or whether it was even a horror film.

It wasn't until 1922 that the greatest silent-era version of the Borgias' sordid lives was produced, Richard Oswald's German classic *Lucrezia Borgia*, starring Conrad Veidt as Cesare and Liane Haid as his sister Lucrezia. CW

The Price of Silence
aka At The Mercy of Tiberius
Samuelson; b/w; 65 min; Great Britain
D: Fred Leroy Granville *S:* Augusta Jane Evans Wilson *P:* G.B. Samuelson *C:* Leland Lancaster
Cast: Peggy Hyland, Campbell Gullan, Tom Chatterton, Van Dycke, Dorothy Gordon

Beryl Brentano (Hyland) obtains money from her estranged grandfather for her ailing mother's (Gordon) operation, and later that night the old man is found dead. Foul play is assumed. Beryl fears that her brother is responsible and draws suspicion toward herself in order to protect him. But, though she is sent to prison, the grandfather's restless spirit leads authorities to the truth—that the grandfather was killed by lightning while arguing with Beryl's brother in the garden.

Also known as *At The Mercy of Tiberius*, *The Price of Silence* was nothing more than a three-hanky melodrama done-up as a ghost story. Its plot comes off as absurdly contrived, which isn't to say that it wouldn't have been popular in its day.

Australian-born Fred Leroy Granville, who as a young man immigrated to the United Kingdom, directed. There he began a career as a cameraman and worked his way up to directing. His filmography is somewhat thin; he is credited with photographing a mere 16 films and directing only 14, the last two of which were produced in France.

Of the cast, only Tom Chatterton seems to have had a lengthy tenure in the movies. He continued to work until 1949, usually in bit parts; his later credits include appearances in John Brahm's *The Locket* (1946) and Frank Capra's masterpiece, *It's a Wonderful Life* (1946). TH

The Screaming Shadow
Hallmark/Wilson; b/w; 15 chapters; U.S.
D: Duke Worne *S:* J. Grubb Alexander, Harvey Gates *C:* King Gray
Cast: Ben Wilson, Neva Gerber, William Dyer, Howard Crampton, William Carroll, Fred Gamble

This long-lost 15-chapter serial seems to have emphasized cliffhanger thrills over horror. Still, its overarching theme of eternal life, not to mention such tantalizing chapter titles as "Entombed Alive," hints at horror amid the mayhem. A gang called The Black Seven looks for the means to eternal life. They'd also like world domination, which they hope to achieve by seizing the throne of Prince Rupert of Burgonia.

Leading man Ben Wilson (also known as Ben Wilson, Sr., and Ben F. Wilson) shared directorial duties for *Shadow* with Duke Worne, an undistinguished veteran of B-features dating from 1919 to 1931. A heart ailment claimed Wilson in 1930 at the age of 54, and though he accumulated voluminous credits during his lifetime as a producer, director and actor, he is today forgotten. Worne later directed Boris Karloff in a small role in the romance *The Devil's Chaplain* (1929). As an actor, Worne appeared in Francis Ford's lost horror-melodrama *The Craving* (1918).

The complete list of chapters are as follows: 1: *A Cry in the Dark*; 2: *The Virgin of Death*; 3: *The Fang of the Beast*; 4: *The Black Seven*; 5: *The Vapor of Death*; 6: *The Hidden Menace*; 7: *Into the Depths*; 8: *The White Terror*; 9: *The Sleeping Death*; 10: *The Prey of Mong* 11: *Liquid Fire*; 12: *Cold Steel*; 13: *The Fourth Symbol*; 14: *Entombed Alive* and 15: *Unmasked*. TH

The Silence
aka Le silence
Le Film D'Art; b/w; 25 min; France
D/S: Louis Delluc *C:* Louis Chaix
Cast: Gabriel Signoret, Eve Francis, Ginette Darnys, Andrew Brunelle

Pierre (Signoret) is hounded by the feeling that his ex-wife's ghost is haunting him. His despair eventually drives him to commit suicide.

Writer/director Louis Delluc may well have been the first film critic to make the transition to directing. Among his writings is the book *Charles Chaplin* (1921), a very early example of a text about the career of an actor. Born in France in 1890, Delluc made his film debut with *The Silence*. Unfortunately, he directed only a handful of titles before his premature death from tuberculosis in 1924.

Delluc was married to leading lady Eve Francis, who starred in all his films. Francis outlived her husband by more than 50 years, and she remained active on screen until 1975. She died at the age of 94 in 1980.

Some sources list the international export title as *The Silence*, but it is not known how widely the film was distributed outside of French-speaking territories. TH

The Sleep of Cyma Roget
aka The Devil's Angel
a'Hiller; b/w; 55 min; U.S.
Co-D/P: Lejaren a'Hiller *Co-D/S:* Charles L. Gaskill

Cast: Helen Gardner, Templar Saxe, Peggy O'Neil, C.D. Williams, Lejaren a'Hiller, Marc Connelly

Cyma Roget (Gardner) falls under the malevolent spell of a Hindu hypnotist named Chandra Dak (Saxe). But as Dak slowly falls in love with Cyma, his power over her becomes less and less. And when Cyma falls for a young artist, an insanely jealous Dak sends her into a hypnotic coma resulting in her premature burial.

Hypnotism was a trope during the silent years of horror cinema, as evidenced by the numerous adaptations of such novels as Bram Stoker's *Dracula* (1897) and George Du Maurier's *Trilby* (1894). The title of this obscure, long lost horror melodrama evokes Poe's *The Mystery of Marie Roget*, an 1842 short story starring the intrepid C. Auguste Dupin, hero of *Murders in the Rue Morgue* (though the two directors don't seem to have attempted a literal adaptation). The finale, in which the heroine was entombed alive, would surely have pleased the American master of the macabre.

Co-director/producer Lejaren a'Hiller was known more for this background in the arts than he is as a filmmaker. Contemporary sources credit him with a mere handful of titles, suggesting either that his tenure in film production was brief or that his other titles have disappeared into oblivion. His major credit as an artist is with American photographic illustration, for which he is considered the originator. He died in 1969, though much of his art today resides at the Art Institute of Chicago.

Writer/co-director Charles L. Gaskill, however, has one other credit of interest to horror fans—he wrote the screenplay for 1915's *Miss Jekyll and Madame Hyde* (in which Helen Gardner, the star of *The Sleep of Cyma Roget*, essayed the title roles), a gender-reversed variation on Robert Louis Stevenson's novella *The Strange Case of Dr. Jekyll and Mr. Hyde* (1886).

The Sleep of Cyma Roget was one of Gaskill's final credits; he retired from films in 1924 and died in 1943. TH

Trance
aka **Anita**
Wiener; b/w; length unknown; Austria
D: Luise Kolm, Jacob Fleck *S:* Fritz Lohner-Beda
Cast: Lola Urban-Kneidinger, Wilhelm Klitsch, Julius Strobl, Nora Herbert

This obscure take on George Du Maurier's *Trilby* concerns a vile hypnotist who exerts control over the virtuous Anita (Urban-Kneidinger).

Though co-directors Luise Kolm and Jacob Fleck married in 1922, Luise was at this point hitched to producer/director Anton Kolm. Jacob made his directorial debut in 1910; Luise, one of the few women to rise to the position of director during the silent era, lensed her first work in 1911. Among their many joint directorial efforts were two earlier versions of Du Maurier's tale: *Trilby* (1912) and *Svengali* (1914). Both retired in 1941. She passed away in 1950; he in 1953. TH

When Dr. Quackel Did Hide
aka **When Quackel Did Hide**;
Aywon; b/w; 24 (40) min; U.S.
D: Charles Gramlich
Cast: Charlie Joy, Edgar Jones

A scientist, Dr. Quackle, creates a potion to bring out the evil in man and takes it. The only cure is a powdery substance. Zaniness ensues.

Like *Dr. Jekyll and Mr. Hyde, Done To a Frazzle* (1914), this is an early parody of the venerable R. L. Stevenson staple, and not a very funny one at that. Florida filmmaker Charles Gramlich (whose entry on the IMDb lists only one film, despite the fact that he made several two-reel comedies) directed. It was clearly made to capitalize on the success of John Barrymore's *Dr. Jekyll and Mr. Hyde* (1920), which had been released by Paramount to strong box-office receipts. In fact, in 1920 alone, there were multiple films based on or spoofing Stevenson's novella, including a serious adaptation starring Sheldon Lewis, a comedy starring Hank Mann and an unauthorized version from F.W. Murnau titled *Der Januskopf*. *Quackel* appears to have been released in July, four months after the release of Barrymore's film.

Gramlich should not be confused with science fiction and horror author Charles Gramlich, who was born in Arkansas in 1958. The former Gramlich was the directorial pseudonym of comedian Charlie Joy, who plays the lead. TH/CW

The Yellow Claw
Stoll; b/w; 68 min; Great Britain
D: Rene Plaisetty *S:* Gerard Fort Buckle *P:* Oswald Stoll *C:* Jack Cox
Cast: A.C. Fotheringham-Lysons, Arthur Cullin, Mary Massart, Miss June, Cyril Percival, Norman Page

After its film adaptation of *The Barton Play* (1920), Stoll's next attempt at horror was this entry into the Yellow Peril subgenre based on a 1915 novel by Sax Rohmer. The story opens with a desperate, frightened woman (June) murdered in the London flat of novelist Henry Leroux (Lysons). Scotland Yard detains Leroux's butler Soames (Page), but he manages to slip away to the lair of mysterious opium dealer Mr. King. Detective Gaston Max (Braban), who has been investigating Mr. King, arrives from Paris to help out. Action and intrigue ensue, and the Asian gang is eventually destroyed, though King escapes with his true identity remaining a secret.

Hot on the heels of his first successful Fu Manchu novels, Rohmer cobbled together this story swapping Mr. King for Fu Manchu and Gaston Max for Nayland Smith. It's difficult to know how successful the film was, but Stoll released a yellow-peril melodrama titled *Mr. Wu* in 1919 (based on the play by Harry Maurice Vernon and Harold Owen and remade by MGM in 1927 with Lon Chaney as Wu). Later, when the studio decided to make short-film adaptations based on great works of literature, one of their productions was 1923's 15-part *The Mystery of Dr. Fu-Manchu*. All this suggests that xenophobic entertainment was at least somewhat profitable at the time, a conclusion further supported by the fact that the following year Stoll released another eight-film series, *The Further Mysteries of Dr. Fu Manchu*. CW

1921

All Souls' Eve
Realart; b/w; length unknown; U.S.
D: Chester Franklin *S:* Elmer Harris *C:* Faxon M. Dean

Bernhard Goetzke as Death from Fritz Lang's *Destiny*

Cast: Mary Miles Minter, Jack Holt, Carmen Phillips, Clarence Geldart, Mickey Moore, Fanny Midgley

Olivia Larkin (Phillips) is so obsessed with sculptor Roger Heath (Holt) that she'll stop at nothing to win his love. She convinces a lunatic that Mrs. Heath (Minter) has been keeping from him a sizeable fortune, with the intended result that the woman is murdered. Larkin's ploy doesn't work. Heath instead falls for his young son's nursemaid (also Minter), an immigrant from Ireland whom he believes to be the reincarnation of his wife.

Based on a play by Anne Crawford Flexner, *All Souls' Eve* is mired in heavy-handed spiritualism. It begins with Norah, at home in Ireland on the titular holiday, being visited by the spirits of her late father and brother. Not long after, she travels to the United States to be with her mother, only to find that the woman has died also, at which time she's forced to take work in the Heath household. The following All Saints' Night, the spirit of Mrs. Heath appears to warn the girl that the Heath child is sick. It would seem that Norah is a receptacle for spirit activity.

Most of this—apart from the sexual obsession angle and the murder of Mrs. Heath—was the stuff of religious nonsense. In some belief systems, All Soul's Eve is the one night of the year that the spirits of the dead may appear to the living, and it's this belief that informs the picture.

More interesting than anything in the film is the real-life scandal surrounding lead actress Minter. In 1919 she starred in *Anne of Green Gables*, her first film for director William Desmond Taylor. She fell in love with him, but after a brief affair, he broke it off due to the difference in their ages. (He was 30 years her senior.) In early 1921, Taylor was murdered. The gruesome crime was never solved, and the press speculated—despite a lack of evidence—that Minter was somehow involved. The resulting scandal tainted her career, and when her contract with Paramount was up, the studio refused to renew it.

All Souls' Eve is considered lost. CW

Bakemono yashiki
Nikkatsu; b/w; length unknown; Japan
Credits unknown

The title of this obscure Japanese film translates as "The Haunted House." Sources suggest it was a horror film, possibly based on a tale of the same name from a collection of short stories put together by James S. De Benneville. But until more information is unearthed, we may never know for sure.

De Benneville's book *Tales of the Tokugawa, Vol. 2* was published in 1921 and was a follow-up to the author's *Yotsuya Kwaidan*. Both volumes consisted of retellings of various supernaturally tinged Japanese folktales. The second story in *Vol. 2* was, like this film, titled *Bakemono Yashiki*. It has to do with a girl, accompanied by her sister's ghost and a friend, who tries to protect her family and their belongings from would-be thieves. CW

Botan dōrō
Shochiku; b/w; length unknown; Japan
D: Kaname Mori
Cast unknown

As is the case with other silent adaptations of Japanese *rakugo* performer Sanyutei Encho's *Botan dōrō*, little information exists about this 1921 adaptation from director Kaname Mori (*Yotsuya kaidan*, 1923). Rakugo is a style of theatrical performance in which a single narrator sits center-stage, a fan in hand to keep him cool as he recites a long, complicated tale.

Encho wrote *Botan dōrō* and performed it many times before his death in 1900, and by 1910 the story had been adapted to the big screen. Encho had lifted the plot from a Chinese ghost story about a woman bearing a peony-adorned lantern, who nightly visits a handsome soldier. Eventually, it is revealed that she is the ghost of the soldier's former lover, whom he had spurned.

In adapting the story, Encho also borrowed liberally from the 1825 Kabuki play *Yotsuya kaidan*, in which a woman, spurned by the man she loves, dies, with her spirit returning afterward to exact revenge. CW

The Case of Becky
Realart; b/w; 60 min; U.S.
D: Chester M. Franklin *S:* J. Clarkson Miller *C:* George Folsey
Cast: Constance Binney, Glenn Hunter, Frank McCormack, Montagu Love, Margaret Seddon, Jane Jennings

Carnival hypnotist Uriah Stone (Love) uses mesmerism on his assistant Dorothy (Binney) as part of his act. While under hypnosis, Dorothy reverts to her evil alter ego, Becky. Despite Stone's attempts to use her personality disorder for his own malicious ends, she runs away and finds love in the arms of another man (Hunter).

This is the second—and to date, last—screen adaptation of the stage play by Edward Locke. As with the first version (which had been produced in 1915), the 1921 adaptation is more melodrama than horror.

Amid a generally forgotten cast, Montagu Love had something of a significant career. He went on to appear in several more horror titles, including *The Haunted House* (1929) and *The Cat Creeps* (1930), and was also active in more mainstream fare, including *The Prisoner of Zenda* (1937), *Kidnapped* (1938) and *The Sea Hawk* (1940).

Director Chester M. Franklin, on the other hand, never made much of a name for himself among cineastes, though he *was* later nominated for an Oscar for the short subject *A Gun in His Hand* (1945), which he produced for a young Joseph Losey. Franklin also did some second unit work on such major productions as *Gone with the Wind* (1939) and *Duel in the Sun* (1946), both without credit. TH

Death
aka **Gevatter Tod**; **Der Gevatter Tod**

Astoria; b/w; length unknown; Austria
D: Heinz Hanus *S:* Hans Berger, L. Gunther *C:* Hans Androschin, Eduard Hoesch
Cast: Armin Seydelmann, Artur Ranzenhofer, Erika Wagner, Fritz Strassny, Louise Nerz, Kurt Erhle

This obscure Austrian picture was reportedly based on the story *Der Pate des Todes* by Rudolf Baumbach. Baumbach (1840-1905) was a German-born poet, successful in his day, who is probably best known for his witty and suggestive drinking songs. He published *Der Pate des Todes* in 1884, and it remains available today (though apparently not in an English translation).

Given that the film's original title, *Gevatter Tod*, evokes the Grimm's Fairy Tale "Godfather Death," it's likely that the film's narrative blended that tale with Baumbach's. In the Grimm story, a poor man struggles to support his 12 children. When a 13th child is born, the father determines to appoint a godfather to help shoulder the new burden. Soon afterward, he happens upon Death and decides that the grim reaper would make an excellent godfather.

Director Heinz Hanus was active throughout the silent era, but his career didn't survive the coming of sound; the same is apparently true of the cast, all of whom have faded into obscurity. Some sources claim Artur Ranzenhofer and Fritz Strassny both played Death, but in actuality it appears that only Ranzenhofer played the part, with Strassny portraying a chancellor. TH

Destiny
aka **Der müde Tod**; **The Weary Death**; **Between Two Worlds**; **Beyond the Wall**; **The Three Lights**

Decla-Bioscop; b/w; 99 min; Germany
D/S: Fritz Lang *S:* Thea Von Harbou *P:* Erich Pommer *C:* Bruno Mondi, Erich Nitzchmann, Herrmann Saalfrank, Bruno Timm, Fritz Arno Wagner
Cast: Lil Dagover, Walter Janssen, Bernhard Goetzke, Hans Sternberg, Rudolf Klein-Rogge, Karl Ruckert, Max Adalbert, Erich Pabst

A young couple (Dagover, Janssen) stops for the night at a village inn. While there, the man is taken by Death (Goetzke), who explains to the grieving widow that the man's time has come. But, touched by her devotion, he offers her a bargain. If she can prevent the deaths of any of three men about to be taken, her lover will be returned to her safe and sound. Death shows her three candles, representing three souls who live, respectively, in Persia, Venice and China. When the woman fails to save any of them, Death nonetheless unites her with her lover, though the realm in which this occurs is not clearly spelled out.

Der müde Tod (literally, *Weary Death* or *The Tired Death*, though it is best known in the United States under the more generic title *Destiny*) is one of the earliest artistic triumphs of legendary writer/director Fritz Lang (1890-1976).

Following the demobilization of Germany after World War I, Lang entered the country's burgeoning film industry as a screenwriter. Quickly tiring of seeing his imaginative sex-and-death plays mishandled by unimaginative hacks, he demanded the opportunity to direct one of his own scripts. *Halbblut* (1919, aka *The Half-Caste*) marks his directorial debut; today considered lost, it was successful enough to compel producer Erich Pommer of Decla-Bioscop to fund further directing projects for Lang. The two-part cliffhanger thriller *Spiders* (1919/20) followed, establishing Lang as a first-class director of mystery and melodrama.

With *Destiny* he shifted gears and attempted something more artistic than anything he'd done before. The film anticipates Paul Leni's *Waxworks* (1924) in its use of the multi-story format. While Lang establishes a melancholy tone in the framing story, he opts for more colorful flights of fancy during the various segments. While this easily could have proven jarring and no doubt would have in lesser hands, it works reasonably well here due to Lang's mastery of the material and the medium—though it must be noted that the jauntier tone of the stories takes the film out of purebred horror fare and makes it a more borderline affair.

The screenplay, by Lang and his collaborator/wife Thea Von Harbou, plainly draws inspiration from fairy tales and *Arabian Nights*–type fantasies as it builds to a memorably bittersweet finale. The individual stories vary in effectiveness, but Lang's imagination ensures that each segment has memorable moments. The special effects work is state-of-the-art stuff for its time, enhancing the already-dreamlike texture. The cast performs admirably, with Bernhard Goetzke making a particularly strong impression as the world-weary figure of Death. His haunted expression and soulful eyes ensure that the character never comes across as a monster—he is a fearful presence, to be sure, but not one who takes pleasure in the job he is obliged to perform. Lil Dagover (*The Cabinet of Dr. Caligari*, 1919) is also quite effective as the resourceful heroine, while Lang favorite Rudolf Klein-Rogge (*Dr. Mabuse, The Gambler*, 1922) appears and does adequate work in two of the three stories.

If *Destiny* lacks the brilliance of Lang's more mature pictures, it is still a worthy inclusion in his towering body of work. His usual fascination with sex and death is vividly on display, and the film's comparatively gentle—though no less fatalistic—tone gives it a unique place in his *oeuvre*. TH

The Devil

Associated Exhibitors/Pathé; b/w; 60 (70) min; U.S.
D: James Young *S:* Edmund Goulding *P:* Andrew J. Callaghan, Harry Leonhardt *C:* Harry Fischbeck
Cast: George Arliss, Sylvia Breamer, Lucy Cotton, Florence Arliss, Edmund Lowe, Roland Bottomley

A horror film done up as satirical Christian allegory, *The Devil* features a beautiful woman named Marie (Cotton) who, upon seeing a Renaissance painting of a martyr, remarks to her fiancé Georges (Bottomley) that evil could never triumph over good. Unknown to them both, Dr. Muller (Arliss), a man they've just met, is the Devil; thus challenged, he immediately sets to work on their downfall. In the end Marie prays to God for help and is rewarded by the appearance of a shining crucifix that causes the Devil to burst into flames.

The Devil was British actor George Arliss' first theatrical film after a successful career on Broadway. It was based on the play *Az ordog* by Ferenc Molnar, which Arliss had essayed on stage. His Dr. Muller was evil personified, the first in a string of successes that powered his career well into the talkie era. The film also starred his wife Florence, billed as Mrs. George Arliss (the two had frequently co-starred on the stage before this and continued to do so occasionally until his death in 1946). George Arliss' last theatrical film was the minor horror classic *Doctor Syn* in 1937, while Mrs. Arliss' last film proved to be *The House of Rothschild* in 1934 (which featured Boris Karloff in a non-horror role).

The film also provided an un-credited bit part to future Oscar-winner Fredric March (*Dr. Jekyll and Mr. Hyde*, 1931). It was directed by James Young (*Trilby*, 1923), former husband to silent screen star and real-life vamp Clara Kimball Young.

Long considered lost, a print of *The Devil* was discovered in the 1990s and restored by the Library of Congress. CW

Drakula halála
aka **Dracula's Death**; **The Death of Dracula**

Corvin; b/w; 60 (55) min; Austria/Hungary
D/Co-S: Károlay Lajthay *Co-S:* Miháley Kertesz (Michael Curtiz) *C:* Eduard Hoesch
Cast: Paul Askonas, Lena Myl, Carl Goetz, Aladár Ihász, Dezsö, Lajos Réthey, Elémer Thury

Alleged to have been shown in Vienna in early 1921, *Drakula halála* was the first film suggested by Bram Stoker's classic 1897 novel *Dracula*. But never fear—its plot bears no resemblance to Stoker's story, thus leaving *Nosferatu—A Symphony of Terror* (1922) in its revered spot as the first actual adaptation. There is some dispute as to where *Drakula* was actually filmed, with the weight of the evidence supporting Hungary and Austria rather than France and Germany, as some film historians contend. Its title translates as *Dracula's Death*, though it appears that the English title at the time of its 1923 re-release was *The Death of Dracula*.

The story concerns an orphan named Mary Land (Lux) who, while in an insane asylum, meets a sinister, Caligari-esque madman who believes he is the undead Count Dracula. Mary is both repulsed by and drawn to the lunatic, and when she sleeps, he haunts her dreams. This continues even after she escapes the psychiatric hospital and gets married, and she remains unsure to the end whether Dracula's existence is real or nightmarishly imagined.

Director Károlay Lajthay had a sparse career, the bulk of it between 1918 and 1923, with an additional film in the 1930s and one more in the 1940s. He acted in nearly as many films as he directed and wrote almost as many as he starred in. His first production was most likely the Hungarian melodrama *I Want to Die* (1918), in which Fate shows an old man what his daughter's life would have been like had she lived rather than died during a riding accident, while his last was a thriller titled *Sárga kaszinó* (1944). While active, he garnered much praise as a unique stylist in Hungarian cinema; this makes it all the more unfortunate that most of his works are, like the majority of Hungarian films made during the silent and early talkie eras, lost. (A print of this film is alleged to exist in a Hungarian archive.)

Actor Paul Askonas was no stranger to horror. He got his start in Louise Kolm's *Trilby* (1912) and followed it through with Michael Curtiz's *Labyrinth of Horror* (1921; which, despite the title and the claims of many historians, is a melodrama rather than a horror film) and Robert Weine's *The Hands of Orlac* (1924). Existing stills from *Drakula halála* reveal striking images of the actor as a leering figure, thin and pale with unkempt black hair coming to a widow's peak high on the forehead, pointy ears and a sinister, sharp-toothed smile; it's an image repeated by the original movie poster, which presents a

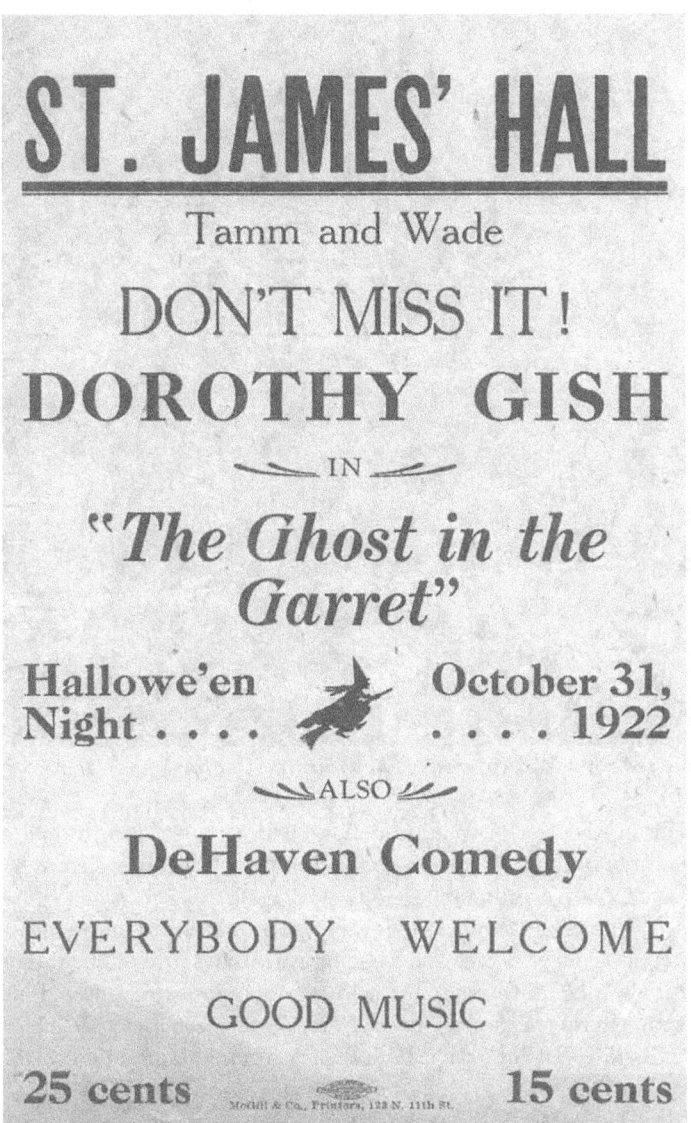

lurid character with green skin, vampire fangs and talon-like fingernails. In at least one still, the actor appears to be wearing a cape with a slightly upturned collar, presaging the classic image of the arch bloodsucker. CW

Faust
Producer unknown; b/w; length unknown; U.S.
D: Frederick A. Todd
Cast unknown

An apparently lost film, little information exists about this 1921 version of the Faust legend, shot in the United States by director Frederick A. Todd. Not only is the cast unknown, but so are the producer and most of the crew. Nor does any information seem to exist shedding light on Todd's career apart from this production.

One can reasonably conclude that this film followed the classic story's basic outline—an aging scientist named Faust regrets that he's wasted his life serving humanity. His dark thoughts conjure up Mephistopheles, who offers him youth and the opportunity to relive his life in exchange for his soul. After Faust seals the deal, he meets the beautiful virgin Marguerite and seduces her, an act that has tragic results for them and others.

This wasn't the only film produced in 1921 to contain the name of Faust in its title. Two others were released, both in Germany. *Die drohende Faust* was produced by Althoff & Company and directed by Bruno Eichgrün. It starred Eichgrün, Fritz Kampers, Ferdinand Robert, Hans Tillo and Erna Weissenberg. The other, *Die eiserne Faust*, was produced by Albertini-Film. It was written and directed by Joseph Delmont and starred Luciano Albertini, Linda Albertini, Ellen Ulrich, Umberto Guarracino, Erner Huebsch and Eva Richter. It was a six-reel film released in September 1921. Neither of these productions were horror films. CW

The Ghost in the Garret
New Art; b/w; 50 min; U.S.
D: F. Richard Jones *S:* Fred Chaston, Wells Hastings
Cast: Dorothy Gish, Downing Clarke, Mrs. David Landau, William Parke, Jr., Ray Grey, Walter P. Lewis

During a visit by Delsie O'Dell (Gish) to the home of her aunt (Landau) and uncle (Clarke), her aunt's necklace, valued at $75,000, is stolen. Determined to find the culprit, Delsie trails the necklace to an abandoned house that is rumored to be haunted. She then pretends to be a ghost to frighten the thieves into giving up their ill-gotten gains.

Prolific silent film director F. Richard Jones was responsible for this stale old dark house comedy-thriller. Though a forgotten figure today, Jones made some popular films in his day. A comedy specialist, he seemed a good fit for what here is basically a lighthearted affair. Leading lady Dorothy Gish was the younger sister of screen legend Lillian Gish. She never became as popular as her sister and retired from films in 1928, after which she went on to a respected career on stage before passing away in 1968 from pneumonia.

The Ghost in the Garret brought nothing new to the genre and seemed awfully clichéd to even 1921's critics. Jones ended his career with *Bulldog Drummond* (1929), his only sound film. TH

The Golem's Last Adventure
aka **Der DorfsGolem**; **The Village Golem**; **Des Golems Letzte Abenteuer**
Sascha-Verleih; b/w; length unknown; Austria
D: Julius Szomogyi
Cast unknown

In a small European village, a schoolmaster discovers the infamous scroll containing the magical word used by Prague's Jews to bring a Golem, a clay figure that does the bidding of its master, to life. Sensing an opportunity to help locals too lazy to reap their own harvests, the schoolmaster creates a Golem to do the grunt work. The creature comes to life as planned, but it isn't very bright and doesn't complete tasks assigned to it. The villagers become angry at its ineptitude and run it out of town, where it is caught in a thunderstorm and melts.

This obscure send-up of Paul Wegener's classic *The Golem: How He Came into the World* (1920) is—like 1917's *The Golem and the Dancing Girl*—an early example of a horror spoof (apparently something about the creature inspired good-natured humor). Surviving publicity materials make no mention of the involvement of anyone beyond director Julius Szomogyi, and he doesn't appear to have ever done much of anything apart from this. The film was apparently very low budget and its special effects primitive. Sources from the time also note poor performances. Despite the definitive nature of the title, more was in store for the eponymous character. Director Julien Duvivier would revisit the tale of the Golem in 1936 with the somber *The Legend of Prague*. TH

The Haunted Castle
aka **Schloß Vogeloed**; **Schloß Vogeloed—Die Enthüllung eines Geheimnisses**; **Vogelod Castle**
Uco-Film; b/w; 81 min; Germany
D: F.W. Murnau *S:* Carl Mayer *P:* Erich Pommer *C:* Fritz Arno Wagner
Cast: Arnold Korff, Lulu Keyser-Korff, Lothar Mehnert, Paul Bildt, Olga Tschechowa, Paul Hartmann

Lord Vogelod (Korff) invites friends to his castle in the country for some weekend hunting. A thunderstorm forces the group to stay inside, and things grow complicated when the uninvited Count Oetsch (Mehnert) shows up on the doorstep. Oetsch, as it happens, has long been implicated in the murder of a fellow nobleman whose wife (Tschechowa) is among the stranded guests. As bad weather and mysterious disappearances build a mood of distrust, new facts emerge about the long-unsolved murder case.

Despite its title, *The Haunted Castle* is less a horror film than a moody psychodrama. One of the earliest surviving works from the oeuvre of the great F.W. Murnau, the film blends complex structure, including multiple flashbacks and dream sequences, with an appropriately gloomy atmosphere. The claustrophobic tone is maintained throughout; most of the action unfolds indoors, and Murnau stages things in ways that stress the growing tension and unease among the characters.

Compared to his subsequent films, *Castle* comes off as a bit stagy and primitive, though it isn't without interest. The screenplay by Carl Mayer (*The Cabinet of Dr. Caligari*, 1919) is a hotbed of psychological tension. The characters almost invariably know more than they're letting on, and Murnau does a capable job of juggling their various motivations. The film's mystery angle is actually less interesting by comparison, though its resolution is reasonably satisfying.

A competent cast aids the director. Though none of the performances stand out, the ensemble as a whole does a fine job. Murnau's Expressionist leanings are only sporadically evident. Apart from a few stylized set-ups and a memorably garish dream sequence—a sleeping character imagines a gigantic claw coming through his bedroom window to steal him into the night—most of the action unfolds in realistic terms.

Fritz Arno Wagner shot the film and he was, along with Karl Freund, one of the director's key cameramen, and the film certainly looks polished enough. The restless camera style typical of the director's later films is not on display here, while the

A German poster for F.W. Murnau's *The Haunted Castle*

editing displays sensitivity to both performance and dramatic content (though the exterior model shots of the castle, it must be noted, are hit and miss).

The film overall is enjoyable and interesting, although it lacks the sheer power and imaginative visual sense of the director's subsequent work. Best seen as a stepping-stone toward his genre masterpiece *Nosferatu—A Symphony of Terror* (1922), *Castle* is definitely of interest to both fans and general film buffs. TH

The Haunted House
Schenck; b/w; 22 (21, 19) min; U.S.
Co-D/Co-S: Buster Keaton *Co-D/Co-S:* Eddie Kline *P:* Joseph M. Schenck *C:* Elgin Lessley
Cast: Buster Keaton, Virginia Fox, Joe Roberts, Edward Kline, Natalie Talmadge

Buster Keaton stars as a teller whose bank funds are being embezzled and replaced by counterfeit loot. After a comical event in which he clumsily spills glue over numerous counterfeit bills—resulting in various people getting stuck to each other or the fake money—the bank is robbed, but the teller and the bank president's daughter escape to a nearby house that's reputedly haunted. It is haunted—by sundry ghostly figures, walking skeletons and a headless man, all of whom are actually counterfeiters hoping to hide their operation from the police by scaring the neighbors away from their base of operations.

Among the overused sight gags is a stairwell that becomes a slide with the flick of a switch, a motif reused at the film's climax when Keaton is knocked unconscious and dreams that he's climbing the Stairway to Heaven. When he gets to the top, he finds himself rejected by Heaven, at which time the stairwell becomes a slide and sends him to the depths of Hell. Luckily for him, he awakens to find that his death was merely hallucinatory.

The Haunted House belongs to a different, more simplistic era of comedic storytelling. As such it doesn't work too well today, though some viewers might find that it has a certain amount of naïve charm. Even in its day there wasn't much original about it, given that haunted houses occupied by criminals had been a staple of the genre for nearly two decades already. CW

His Brother's Keeper
American Cinema; b/w; 60 min; U.S.
D: Wilfrid North *S:* Brewster Morse *C:* William Crolly, Arthur T. Quinn
Cast: Albert L. Barrett, Martha Mansfield, L. Rogers Lytton, Fraser Coalter, Gretchen Hartman, Gladden James

Rex Radcliffe (Lytton) is the vice president of a railroad company. He also has a flair for hypnotism and thought transference, which he uses to compel the company's secretary (James) to murder its president (Coulter). Radcliffe's plan is to replace the murdered executive, but his baser instincts get the better of him, and his guilt is exposed.

His Brother's Keeper is yet another early horror title trading on the theme of hypnotism. Unlike most films of its ilk, however, it is set in the present and also throws in a bit of social commentary. Its story of greed and avarice in corporate America, with its Svengali-like protagonist wielding his sinister influence, certainly sounds interesting. But the film is considered lost, so not much is known about it apart from the basics.

Director Wilfrid North made over a hundred films between 1910 and 1922; he also worked a good deal as a character actor until his death in 1935. *His Brother's Keeper* was one of his last titles as a director. As an actor, he made one of his last appearances in an unbilled bit part in the stylish Boris Karloff vehicle *The Black Room* (1935). TH

The Hound of the Baskervilles
Stoll; b/w; 64 min; Great Britain
D: Maurice Elvey *S:* William J. Elliott, Dorothy Westlake
Cast: Eille Norwood, Hubert Willis, Catina Campbell, Rex McDougall, Lewis Gilbert, Allan Jeayes

Sherlock Holmes (Norwood) and Dr. Watson (Willis) are called upon to guard Sir Henry Baskerville (McDougall), who is due to become the latest in his family line to be felled by a ghostly hound. Holmes sends Watson to the Baskerville estate alone, claiming to be occupied with another case but in truth working to unmask the flesh-and-blood culprit who is really responsible for the threat to Sir Henry's life.

This is the first British adaptation of Sir Arthur Conan Doyle's much-filmed Sherlock Holmes adventure. Eille Norwood (1861-1948) is a forgotten performer today, but his portrayal of Holmes was admired by no less than Doyle himself, and with 47 silent film appearances as the character, he holds the record for playing the role on the silver screen. (Hubert Willis also holds the record for on-screen Dr. Watson portrayals.) But despite Norwood's claim as the silent screen's pre-eminent Holmes, stills indicate that the fit was odd; he looks far too old and short to fill the part, at least in terms of Doyle's description of the character. Even so, his public identification with the role was so complete that his film career effectively ended with his final appearance as Holmes in 1923's *His Final Bow*.

Most of the entries in this particular Holmes series are lost, and even though this version of *Hound* isn't—a print exists in the British Film Institute's archives—it remains virtually impossible to see in the United States. Those who have managed a viewing of this rare feature report that the adaptation is generally faithful, right down to the phosphorous paint on the hound. Upon the film's initial release, theatrical prints featured the hound in hand-painted color.

Director Maurice Elvey amassed almost 200 film credits. He made minor features well into the 1950s, though he didn't pass away until 1967. After a glut of adaptations, Arthur Conan Doyle's story disappeared from the screen until the end of the decade, returning with Richard Oswald's *The Hound of the Baskervilles* (1929). TH

The Island of the Lost
aka Die Insel der Verschollenen
Corona; b/w; 90 min; Germany
D: Urban Gad *S:* Bobby E. Lüthge, Hans Behrendt *C:* Willy Hameister
Cast: Erich Kaiser-Titz, Alf Blutecher, Tronier Funder, Hans Behrendt, Hanni Weisse, Ludmilla Hell

A group led by Dr. Robert Marston (Blutecher) stumbles upon a secret research facility on a deserted South Seas island. There, they find Professor McClelland (Kaiser-Titz) hard at work fusing animal genes to human genes, with horrific results.

The Island of the Lost is an unauthorized adaptation of H.G. Wells' 1896 novel *The Island of Dr. Moreau*. The film was the book's second adaptation after 1913's *The Island of Terror*.

The novel's plot is more science fiction than horror but filmmakers have always seen fit to exploit its more sensational aspects. The first American crack at the story, *Island of Lost Souls* (1932), was no exception. Wells was reportedly incensed by that adaptation, though he likely would have been even more upset had he had been aware of *Lost*'s existence. The practice of creating royalty-free adaptations of copyrighted source material by changing character names and other particulars was not uncommon in the silent German film industry. F.W. Murnau employed this tactic with *Der Januskopf* (1920, a variation on Robert Louis Stevenson's *The Strange Case of Dr. Jekyll and Mr. Hyde*), and it landed him in hot water with *Nosferatu—A Symphony of Terror* (1922, based on Bram Stoker's *Dracula*). *Nosferatu*, in fact, was nearly obliterated; as a result of a lawsuit by Stoker's widow, all copies were ordered destroyed. Thankfully, a few survived, and the film is readily available today.

The Island of the Lost has disappeared from public view, though a print does exist in the Bundesarchiv in Berlin, Germany; the film was screened for the first time in the United States at Monster Bash in 2014. Reviews of the period as well as from attendees of the Monster Bash event noted that the film was short on logic and long on comedy and romance, but offering memorable glimpses of animal-human hybrids.

Director Urban Gad started his career in his native Denmark, where he met and eventually married actress Asta Nielsen, a woman he saw as his muse. They both went to work in the German film industry and found some success in doing so. They divorced in 1918, and by 1927 Gad's film career had all but dried up. He died in 1947. TH

Jane Eyre
Ballin; b/w; 70 min; U.S.
D/S/P: Hugo Ballin *C:* James Diamond
Cast: Norman Trevor, Mabel Ballin, Crauford Kent, Emily Fitzroy, John Webb Dillon, Louis R. Grisel

This is one of many silent adaptations of Charlotte Brontë's Gothic romance *Jane Eyre: An Autobiography* (1847). Orphaned Jane (Ballin) is sent to a girls' school where she's mistreated by her instructors but manages to get an education nonetheless. As a young woman, she goes to work for Mr. Rochester (Trevor) as the governess for his ward, Adele. Jane and Mr. Rochester fall in love, he proposes, and she accepts. But on their wedding day, Jane learns that Mr. Rochester is already married and that his wife (Arians) is insane and locked away in the attic. She flees to the home of John Rivers (Crauford Kent), a clergyman who also falls for her. However, after Mrs. Rochester escapes from her attic, starts a fire that destroys much of the Rochester estate and dies—leaving Rochester blinded—Jane quickly leaves Rivers to return to Rochester. After Jane prays for Mr. Rochester's sight to return, it does so, and the two marry.

Ditching many of the more disturbing aspects of the book's semi-horror-oriented second section, *Jane Eyre*, in the style of the time, goes straight for sappy romance aimed squarely at young Christian women.

Director and screenwriter Hugo Ballin entered the film industry after his career as a muralist failed. Producing his own films, he often hired his wife Mabel as the female lead. A popular actress in her day, she starred in versions of *East Lynne* (1921) and *Vanity Fair* (1923) before retiring in 1925.

Orphan of Lowood, the next film adaptation of Brontë's book, came from Germany in 1926 and was much, much darker. CW

Leaves from Satan's Book
aka Blade af Satans Bog; Leaves Out of The Book of Satan
Nordisk; b/w; 121 min; Sweden
D/Co-S: Carl Theodor Dreyer *Co-S:* Edgar Hoyer *C:* George Schneevoigt
Cast: Helge Nissen, Halvard Hoff, Jacob Texiere, Hallander Helleman, Ebon Strandin, Johannes Meyer

After being condemned by God, fallen angel Satan (Nissen) is left to roam the Earth. Four anecdotes illustrate his malevolent influence: first, he tempts Judas (Texiere) into betraying Jesus (Hoff); then he oversees the Spanish Inquisition; he goes on to incite the French Revolution, and finally he sows the discontent that sparks the Russo-Finnish war of 1918.

Carl Theodor Dreyer made his directorial debut with *The President* in 1919, though it was his second film, *The Parson's Wife* (1920), that heralded his arrival as an innovative cinematic artist. *Leaves from Satan's Book* was his third picture. It remains one of his more obscure titles, largely because he later outclassed it with such towering achievements as *The Passion of Joan of Arc* (1928) and *Vampyr* (1931).

That's not to say that *Leaves* is an unambitious undertaking. Indeed, the success of his previous picture gave Dreyer the means to do the project on a fairly large scale. Structurally, the film is reminiscent of D.W. Griffith's *Intolerance* (1916), though it also evokes F.W. Murnau's long-lost tale of Satan through the ages, *Satanas* (1920).

The problem with *Leaves* isn't an absence of inspiration; it's that Dreyer becomes so taken with composing artful tableaux that he allows nuance to get away from him. The end result is frequently painterly—his recreation of The Last Supper is almost a parody in this context—but without emotional depth. Dreyer and his star, Helge Nissen, allow Satan dignity and pathos, but nothing else about the fallen angel's character is sufficiently developed. On the one hand, he clearly despises the fact that he's condemned to spread evil in the world; on the other, he seems too passive and low-key to truly defy God.

The historical framework likewise lacks shading. It's fine to insert Satan into famous historical incidents, provided that one avoids portraying humans as mere playthings with no volition of their own; Dreyer does not. He also fails to control his actors; apart from the too-understated Nissen, the cast emotes to a degree too theatrical for even silent cinema. The end result is visually striking but the film lacks the uncanny allure of Dreyer's later, more mature work.

Were it not for the presence of Satan, *Leaves* wouldn't warrant inclusion in a study of the horror genre; in truth, it's more a quaint pageant play than a horror film. It would take more than a decade after this film for the director to demonstrate a true feel for the genre and its mechanics with the release of *Vampyr* (1932). TH

Lord Arthur Savile's Crime
aka Le crime de Lord Arthur Savile
Pathé/Legrand; b/w; 69 (89) min; France
D: René Hervil *C:* Amedee Morrin
Cast: Monique Chrysés, André Dubosc, Catherine Fonteney, Andé Nox, Olive Sloane, Violette Jyl

This appears to have been the second cinematic stab at Oscar Wilde's 1891 tale of the same name after Paul Fejos' likewise-named *Lord Arthur Saville's Crime* (1920). That film had been shot in Hungary and is considered lost. This one is a French production from Pathé. A third effort, *Lord Saviles brott* (1921), was filmed in Denmark in 1919 (before either of the other two) but was the last to be released theatrically.

This time out, the tone appears to have been a mix of comedy and drama, though the story's inherent darkness remains unsullied. Lord Arthur Savile meets a palm reader who predicts that he will commit murder. What ensues is a comedy of manners in which Savile attempts to murder various people just to get it out of the way. He fails miserably and repeatedly, until the perfect opportunity arises.

From 1912 until 1936, René Hervil was one of France's most popular directors. He began his career with a series of short comedies starring Aimée Campton as Maud. His only other horror film appears to have been *Le mystère de la Villa Rose* (1930). CW

Lord Saviles brott
Palladium; b/w; 35 min; Denmark/Sweden
D: Gunnar Klintberg
Cast: Carl Alstrup, Ernst Eklund, Ivar Kåge, Astri Torsell

This Swedish production was the last of the silent adaptations of Oscar Wilde's 1891 tale *Lord Arthur Savile's Crime* to be released, though it was the first one made. Shot in 1919 by Denmark's Palladium films, it followed *Lord Arthur Saville's Crime* (1920) and *Lord Arthur Savile's Crime* (1921) into theaters, premiering in Hellerup, Demark and in Sweden on September 16, 1921. Sources indicate that it was a loose adaptation of Wilde's story, with Carl Alstrup as Lord Arthur Savile, whose fortune as told by Septimus R. Podger (Eklund) convinces him that he is destined to murder someone. Rather than be a slave to fate, Savile sets out to commit the crime before his marriage to Sybil Merton (Torsell) and thus ensure that his marriage vows remain unsullied.

Danish star Carl Alstrup was both an actor and director; he appeared in over 20 films between 1908 and 1942 and directed four during the years 1909 and 1910. His performance in *Lord Saviles brott* came during his middle period, a time when he was relatively inactive. He had a bit of resurgence with the coming of sound and in 1941 appeared in one of his most popular films, *Peter Anderson*. His death in 1942 brought his career to a close.

The next and most famous film adaptation of Wilde's story came in 1943, when it appeared as the second episode in the Universal anthology horror film *Flesh and Fantasy*; Edward G. Robinson starred as the Savile character, renamed Marshall Tyler for American consumption. CW

The Lost Shadow
aka Der Verlorene Schatten
UFA/Film Union; b/w; 63 min; Germany
D: Rochus Gliese *S:* Paul Wegener *C:* Karl Freund
Cast: Paul Wegener, Hannes Sturm, Lyda Salmonova, Wilhelm Bendow, Adele Sandrock, Hedwig Gutzeit

Unattractive but brilliant violinist Sebaldus (Wegener) makes a deal with a mysterious visitor (Sturm) wherein he trades his shadow for both the affection of a beautiful woman (Salmanova) and a magic violin. What Sebaldus doesn't anticipate is the overall reaction to his shadowless state; the woman becomes so terrified that she enters a convent, and the locals, believing him possessed, run him out of town. All ends well, though, when Sebaldus plays a wonderful tune on the charmed violin and so wins the woman's heart.

Paul Wegener wrote and starred in this variation on *The Student of Prague* (1913), a film in which he had played the title role. He seems beholden here to the legend that surrounded violinist Nicolo Paganini (1782-1840), who was said by some to have murdered his wife and imprisoned her soul in his violin, thus creating his mournful playing style.

Director Rochus Gliese's only other fantastical directorial credit is the spoof *The Golem and the Dancing Girl* (1917), which also starred Wegener. Gliese did helm a few non-horror productions during the silent era, but his career as a director petered out with the advent of sound, at which time he returned to his former field of production design. (In fact, he had designed the sets for Wegener's first crack at *The Golem*, 1915.) He continued working in an artistic capacity until the 1940s. He was also an accomplished costume designer who turned in work for another famous Golem film, Wegener's *The Golem: How He Came into the World* (1920), thus making him the only person to collaborate on all three of the actor/writer/director's *Golem* adventures.

The cinematographer on *The Lost Shadow* was Karl Freund, no stranger to horror films of the silent era (*Der Januskopf*, 1920)

or thereafter (*Dracula*, 1931). The supporting cast included Greta Schroder, the heroine of F.W. Murnau's masterpiece *Nosferatu—A Symphony of Terror* (1922).

For some reason, the American release of *Shadow* was delayed until 1928. The film has since disappeared. TH

The Man Who Laughs
aka **Das Grinsende Gesicht**; **The Grinning Face**
Olympia; b/w; 87 min; Germany/Austria
D: Julius Herzka *S:* Louis Nerz *C:* Eduard Hosch
Cast: Franz Hobling, Nora Gregor, Lucienne Delacroix, Anna Kallina, Eugen Jensen, A. Seydelmann

In the late 1600s, the widowed Lord Fermain is abducted by the *Comprachicos*, who murder him and mutilate his son. The boy, a hideous grin forever carved onto his face, falls in love with the blind Dea (Delacroix) and joins a touring company headed by the gruff Ursus (Weismuller). Renamed Gwynplaine (Hobling), the young man supports his adopted family by revealing his face to those who are willing to pay. Later, when he learns the truth of his moneyed heritage, he chooses his adopted family over his newfound fortune.

Though obviously made on a low budget, this German adaptation has much to recommend it. It sticks fairly close to its source material, French novelist Victor Hugo's underappreciated novel *L'Homme qui rit* (1869). The film is also beautifully rendered and atmospheric—condensing the lengthy story into a tight 87-minute timeframe—and the acting is decent overall. Particularly effective is Nora Gregor, who gives the film's best performance as the sexually perverse, seductive Josiane, a woman who lusts after the disfigured Gwynplaine.

While it really does offer more melodrama than horror, the film's focus on the twisted features of the eponymous character and the sinister Josiane's peculiar attraction to him portends Germany's pop-culture obsession with kink, violence and shadowy spectacle.

The next film adaptation of Hugo's novel is also the most famous, Universal's *The Man Who Laughs* (1928). A fourth version was made in 1966. CW

The Man Who Sold His Soul to the Devil
aka **L'Homme qui vendit son ame au diable**
b/w; length unknown; France
D: Pierre Caron *C:* Andre A. Dantan
Cast: Charles Dullin, Jean-David Évremond, Yvonne Fursey, Gladys Rolland

Shot in 1920 and released in France in 1921, *The Man Who Sold His Soul to the Devil* was not distributed in the United States until 1926. In keeping with the silent era's obsession with Mephistopheles, the film concerns a banker who, depressed by a series of business failures, decides to commit suicide. But before he can do so, the Devil appears and makes a Faustian pact with him. After the agreed-upon deed is done, however, the banker meets a beautiful shop employee. Luckily, love proves a powerful force, and the girl is able to drive Satan away.

The film was remade in France in 1943. CW

The Mechanical Man
aka **L'uomo meccanico**; **O homem mechanico**

Milano; b/w; 80 (60, 26) min; Italy
D/S: André Deed *C:* Alberto Chentrens
Cast: André Deed, Giulia Costa, Valentina Frascaroli, Mathilde Lambert, Gabriel Moreau, Ferdinando Vivas-May

A scientist invents a giant mechanical man controlled by electrical waves. A gang of thieves led by female mastermind Mado (Frascaroli) wants such a beast to aid in the commission of crimes. They murder the scientist, not thinking to first procure the instructions for building their own machine, after which they're captured and sentenced to lengthy prison terms. Mado cleverly escapes from the slammer by getting herself sent to the hospital, then catching her bed on fire, causing a ruckus during which she exits unnoticed. She resumes her criminal ways, taunting the police with letters that brag about her exploits. She also kidnaps the scientist's daughter, from whom she finally obtains the instructions for making her very own mechanical man. The electrical monster, once built, is sent out via remote control to steal valuable objects from wealthy homes, and there's nothing anyone can do as it rips safes out of walls and walks off with them. But when the monstrosity goes on a rampage during a ball at a local opera house, one Professor D'Ara (Moreau) sends his own mechanical man to destroy it. The two colossi fight to the death, taking down the opera house in the process. Mado is killed when her remote control apparatus short-circuits.

So maintains a plot synopsis written around the time the film was made. Today, less than half of *The Mechanical Man*, sections of a Portuguese print discovered in a Brazilian archive, survives. The footage comes mostly from the middle and end of the film and showcases the evil robot, including what must have been a shiver-inducing scene for audiences of the early 1920s. As a car attempts to get away from the mechanical man, the robotic creature moves faster and faster until it overtakes its quarry. Another jarring moment occurs when the thing throws a helpless young woman over an opera house balcony to her death below.

It's too bad that this otherwise entertaining footage is infected by the presence of director André Deed, portraying a comedic character named Saltarello. With so much footage missing, his purpose within the narrative isn't entirely clear, but he manages to stink it up nonetheless, repeating routines from his early 1900s work when he was a famous actor in French comedies.

By 1921 Deed's slapstick career in Georges Méliès-style productions had waned, and he moved to Italy to recapture his popularity by doing his same shtick in a new country. It didn't work, and shortly after *The Mechanical Man*'s release, he returned to France, where he took on a series of small roles in other peoples' films. In all, he directed approximately 40 films and starred in over 200 before his death in October 1940.

The Mechanical Man was produced six years before Fritz Lang's groundbreaking *Metropolis* (1927), which it surely must have influenced. CW

A Midnight Bell
First National; b/w; 66 min; U.S.
D: Charles Ray *S:* Richard Andres *C:* George Rizard
Cast: Charles Ray, Donald MacDonald, Van Dyke Brooke, Doris Pawn, Clyde McCoy, Jess Herring

Martin Tripp (Ray), a salesman from the big city, uses his expertise to turn a struggling small-town store into a local success. He also becomes involved in a local mystery surrounding a deserted church that is believed to be haunted. After some investigation, he discovers that the supernatural happenings have a logical explanation.

Based on a play by Charles Hale Hoyt, *A Midnight Bell* was one of a handful of films directed by silent screen star Charles Ray. Ray rose to popularity playing amiable, naïve sorts, but like so many stars of the silent screen, he was unable to maintain his popularity into the talkie era. Ray was also responsible for the notorious flop *The Courtship of Myles Standish* (1923), a vanity project that cost him his fortune. He remained active in bit parts until his death in 1943 from a severe tooth infection.

A Midnight Bell appeared to have been more comedy and down home melodrama than horror, but its haunted-church subplot—in which Ray's character is inevitably challenged to spend the night in the building—moves it toward fright-film terrain. TH

Missing Husbands
aka **L'Atlantide**; **Queen of Atlantis**; **Lost Atlantis**; **A Woman of Atlantis**
International et Commercial de la Cinématographie; b/w; 136 (212) min; France/Belgium
D/S: Jacques Feyder *P:* Louis Aubert *C:* Victor Morin, Georges Specht, Amédée Morein
Cast: Jean Angelo, Stacia Napierkowska, George Melchior, Marie-Louise Iribe, Abd-el-Kader Ben Ali, Mohamed Ben Noui

Pierre Benoit was born in 1886. His father was a member of the French Army, and he spent most of his early years in Northern Africa. As a young adult, he joined the military and, in 1918, published his first novel, *Koenigsmark*, which proved popular with French audiences. He quickly followed it up in 1919 with *L'Atlantide*, his most successful book and one that inspired numerous film adaptations beginning in the silent era.

L'Atlantide's story concerns an officer named André de Saint-Avit, who is working in the French Sahara of 1896 to uncover the mystery surrounding the disappearances of several fellow officers. When he and a friend save the life of a native tribesman, they are drugged for their troubles and taken to an underground city, the last remnants of the fabled Atlantis. There they meet the beautiful Queen Antinéa, great-granddaughter not only of an ancient Atlantean king but of Egyptian Queen Cleopatra as well. Antinéa's secret palace turns out to contain a chamber filled with the bodies of her victims, including those of the missing officers. De Saint-Avit proceeds to fall under the queen's spell, though his friend—who also happens to be a monk—does not. At the behest of the queen, the mesmerized officer bludgeons his chum to death with a hammer. When he realizes what he has done, the spell over him is broken and he escapes the temple. The queen follows but dies in the desert.

In October 1919, eight months after *L'Atlantide* first appeared in print, a French literary magazine published an article by Henry Magden that noted the similarities between Benoit's tale and H. Rider Haggard's massively successful novel *She: A History of Adventure* (1886-1887), going so far as to accuse Benoit of plagiarism. (In point of fact, Benoit's book bears a greater resemblance to Haggard's novel *The Yellow God: An Idol of Africa* than it does to *She*, though that book had not yet been translated into French and Benoit could not read English.) Upset, Benoit sued Magden and the magazine for libel—and not only lost but also had to reimburse the court for expenses.

The controversy didn't hurt sales of Benoit's book, however; it wound up selling over two million copies. Nor did the dust-up discourage filmmakers from knocking on the writer's door. The first cinematic adaptation was made in 1921 by Belgian filmmaker Jacques Feyder (1885-1948), who borrowed money from a cousin to purchase the rights to the story and finance the production. Silent European superstar Stacia Napierkowska was cast as the cold-blooded queen who, once she tires of her lovers, has their remains sealed in gold and stored in glass cases. The film follows the novel closely, though the ending is altered and much of the action is presented as a series of flashbacks, each set within the framework of a larger flashback. What does set the film apart from other epics of its period is that much of it was actually shot on location in Saharan Algeria (at a cost of over two million francs!).

Despite a running length of over three hours, the film met with critical and box-office success and was reissued, albeit with several cuts, in 1928. In the United States, it was saddled with the unfortunately exploitative moniker *Missing Husbands*. A mere four years later, a second film adaptation—this one with sound—was released under the title *Mistress of Atlantis*. It is this latter version that is best known today. CW

Nabeshima neko sodo
Nikkatsu; b/w; length unknown; Japan
D: Kaname Mori
Cast unknown

This is the second adaptation of Joko Segawa III's 1853 Kabuki play *Hana Saga neko mata zoshi* to be produced by Nikkatsu

Studios in 1921. It appears to have been the first horror film from director Kaname Mori, who went on to direct *Botan dōrō* (1921) and *Yotsuya kaidan* (1923). Mori did most of his work for Nikkatsu's rival in the horror business, Shochiku. By this time, Nikkatsu's usual horror director, Shozo Makino, had gone off to start his own production studio.

The story has a war general named Nabeshima haunted by the spirit of the man he murdered, who takes the form of a ghost cat.

Nikkatsu is alleged to have produced yet another version of the story the following year under the title *Nabeshima no neko*. It is believed to have starred Matsunosuke Onoe, who took the lead in many ghost cat movies, but so little is known about Japanese films of this period that it's possible the film in question was a re-release of some previous adaptation. CW

The Other Person
aka Onder spiritistischen dwang
Granger/Binger; b/w; 74 (66) min; Great Britain/Netherlands
D: Maurits Binger, B.E. Doxat-Pratt *S:* Benedict James *C:* Feiko Boersma, Jan Smit
Cast: Zoe Palmer, Adelqui Migliar, Arthur Pusey, Ivo Dawson, Nora Hayden, Willem Hunsche

During a séance, a spiritualist's dark secret is revealed.

This co-production between Great Britain and the Netherlands is based on Fergus Hume's novel of the same name. Hume's books were successful in his day—he wrote mysteries and thrillers until 1932—but his main claim to lasting fame is incidental. His novel *The Mystery of the Hansom Cab* (1886) inspired Sir Arthur Conan Doyle to write *A Study in Scarlet* (1887), which marked the debut of Sherlock Holmes. *The Other Person* was published in 1920, and its leap to the screen one year after its publication is an indication of the author's popularity at the time. The storyline presages a key plot point in Dario Argento's masterpiece *Deep Red* (1974)—the unmasking of a murderer during a séance—but the similarity is undoubtedly accidental.

This obscure thriller is difficult to screen, and the absence of major names in both its cast and crew likely ensures that it will continue to be elusive. Leading lady Zoe Palmer also appeared in *Sweeney Todd* (1928), but co-directors Maurits Binger and B.E. Doxat-Pratt seem to have dropped off the map sometime between this film and the advent of talking pictures. TH

Pan Twardowski
Polfilma; b/w; 59 min; Poland
D/Co-S: Wiktor Bieganski *Co-S:* Mieczyslaw Szerer, Adam Zagorski *P:* Jozef Szwajcer *C:* Stanislaw Sebel
Cast: Bronislaw Oranowski, Wanda Jarszewska, Antoni Nowara-Piekarski, Maria Krzyzanowska, Mila Kaminski

After Ladislas Starevitch's Russian-made *Mr. Tvardovski* (1916), Poland served up its own version of the popular legend about a 16th-century Krakow occultist who sold his soul to the Devil in exchange for magical powers and then tried to renege on the deal. There were many variations on the folktale, and it's difficult to know which was used as the basis for this particular film adaptation; it was likely most similar to the 1936 version, which is considered a remake by many historians.

It's possible that the central character in these films (as well as the novel and legends on which they are based) was a real 16th-century German nobleman (hence the word *Pan*, which in the Polish language is a title often given to diplomats or members of the noble class) about whom little is today known except that he lived, variously, in Nuremberg, Wittenberg and Krakow.

Though shot mostly in late 1920, the film was released in its native Poland in February 1921. CW

Saga neko sodo
Nikkatsu; b/w; length unknown; Japan
Crew and crew unknown

This is the fourth but not the final version of Joko Segawa's classic Kabuki play *Hana Saga neko mata zoshi* (1853) from Nikkatsu Studios. The story concerns a ghost cat out for vengeance against the man who killed both its master and its master's mother.

The play was a highly fictionalized account (obviously) of the true story of Naoshige Nabeshima, a 16th century warlord who took over the Ryuzoji clan when its leader died. He later led 5,000 men, all holed up in Saga Castle, in a successful battle against a surrounding army of 60,000.

Short-lived production company Teikine produced the next adaptation of the tale, *Legend of the Nabeshima Cat Ghost* (1929). CW

Satan in Sofia
aka Dyavolat v Sofia
Gendov; b/w; length unknown; Bulgaria
D/S/P: Vassil Gendov
Cast: Vassil Gendov, Zhana Gendova, Ivan Popov, Meri Mihaylova, Georgi Sotirov, Elena Snezhina

This lost Bulgarian film was based on the also-lost Richard Oswald film *Kurfürstendamm* (1920). The story concerns the Devil (Gendov) who, tired of life in Hell and looking for excitement, poses as a gentleman and wreaks havoc upon an unsuspecting neighborhood in the Bulgarian capital. When the debauchery he witnesses above ground is too much even for him, he heads back to the comfort and solace of his kingdom.

Bulgaria came to filmmaking relatively late, around 1915. Writer/producer/director/actor Vassil Gendov was one of the country's cinematic pioneers, making his first films in 1915 and working sporadically until 1937. Long forgotten, he died in 1970. TH

Soul of the Cypress
Murphy; b/w; 9 (7) min; U.S.
D/S/P: Dudley Murphy
Cast: Chase Harringdine

Somewhere along the California coast, a handsome young musician plays his composition while staring longingly at the sea. A dryad (in Greek mythology a tree nymph) living in a nearby cypress tree hears the music and, charmed by it, appears as a beautiful young woman. The man pursues her back to her tree, where her voice calls to him, telling him that he must throw himself into the ocean so that their spirits might join each other in eternity. Unable to live without her, the man drowns himself.

Soul of the Cypress is a belated entry in a subgenre that had flourished over a decade previously, when films about water spirits casting spells over men and luring them to their deaths were

prevalent. It was the first film from director Dudley Murphy, an erstwhile journalist with an obsession for music. After the success of this debut, he formed his own production company, Visual Symphony, and made a series of pictures in which ballet dancers acted out the plots of classical compositions. Of the over 20 films made by Visual Symphony, few survive today, the horror-oriented *avant-garde* classic *Danse Macabre* (1922) being one of them. Murphy's most famous films remain *Ballet Mécanique* (1924) and *The Emperor Jones* (1933).

Murphy's real-life wife at the time, Chase Harringdine, played the role of the dryad in *Soul of the Cypress*. CW

Torgus, the Coffin Maker
aka **Verlogene Moral**; **Brandherd**; **Torgus; or, The Coffin Maker**; **Torgus**
Union/UFA; b/w; 70 min; Germany
D: Hanns Kobe *S:* Carl Mayer *C:* Karl Freund
Cast: Gerd Fricke, Eugen Klopfer, Maria Leiko, Ferdinand Gregori, Kaethe Richter, Adele Sandrock

John (Fricke) impregnates Anna (Leiko), a poor servant girl. Though he intends to marry her, his furious aunt insists that he hold out for a local rich woman. The aunt sends the young man to a school in another town and arranges for Anna to live with the sinister Torgus (Klopfer), the local coffin maker. Torgus takes a fancy to Anna, who pines for John's return. But when her baby is stillborn and John never arrives, Anna too passes away—on the same day that John is scheduled to marry her rival. Upset, Torgus places the girl's body in a coffin and sends it to John as a wedding gift. When the gift is opened before the wedding assemblage, John snaps and strangles his aunt to death.

Not much more info has survived about this Expressionist melodrama by obscure filmmaker Hanns Kobe. The film is allegedly available in truncated form, though it is difficult to procure. However, the involvement of screenwriter Carl Mayer and cinematographer Karl Freund lead one to believe that it's of at least marginal interest. Mayer—co-writer of *The Cabinet of Dr. Caligari* (1919)—was one of the more prominent scenarists of silent German cinema, while Freund's moody lighting and dazzling camerawork graced the films of F.W. Murnau (*The Last Laugh*, 1924), Fritz Lang (*Metropolis*, 1927) and many others. Freund eventually became a talented director in his own right, helming two standout horror films of the 1930s: *The Mummy* (1932) and *Mad Love* (1935).

Eugen Klopfer's portrayal as Torgus is described by sources of the time as "Golem-like," and his profession as a coffin-maker, along with the film's macabre overtones and gruesome ending, clearly justify its inclusion in a book dedicated to the horror genre.

Torgus has also been compared to *Warning Shadows* (1922), *Waxworks* (1924) and *The Student of Prague* (1926) in its Expressionist approach to its subject matter. TH

Whispering Shadows
Peerless/Peacock; b/w; 72 min; U.S.
D: Emile Chautard *S:* Walter Hackett, William B. Loeb, Harry Chandlee *C:* Jacques Bizeul
Cast: Lucy Cotton, Charles A. Stevenson, Robert Barrat, Celestine Saunders, Philip Merivale, George Cowl

During a séance, a weird presence—apparently the spirit of the recipient's deceased father—warns a young woman that her former beau is in peril just as she is about to marry an unscrupulous criminal. Or something similar to that. The plot as revealed by contemporary sources is a bit confusing, and given *Whispering Shadow*'s status as a virtually impossible film to view (some sources list it as lost; others claim that a single print exists in the Library of Congress but that it may not be viewed), it isn't likely to be cleared up anytime soon.

Whispering Shadows should not be confused with the Bela Lugosi cliffhanger *The Whispering Shadow* (1933). Rather, it was a silent 1921 mystery/horror fusion from director Emile Chautard, who had begun his career in France in 1910 shooting staid melodramas. In 1919 he made his most famous film, *The Mystery of the Yellow Room*, based on a novel by Gaston Leroux, author of *Le Fantôme de l'Opéra* (1909-1910). By 1924 Chautard's career as a director was over, though he popped up onscreen now and then in small parts until his death in 1934.

Few of the film's actors did anything that is thought noteworthy today, but it should be mentioned that Charles A. Stevenson's last role was as General Petrie in Rowland V. Lee's 1929 production of *The Mysterious Dr. Fu Manchu*, while Philip Merivale had a part in Alfred Hitchcock's comedy classic *Mr. and Mrs. Smith* (1941). Robert Barrat did go on to a distinguished career in Hollywood, starring in numerous films and television shows between 1915 and 1964. His other horror/suspense credits include *Secret of the Blue Room* (1933), *Return of the Terror* (1934), *The Florentine Dagger* (1935) and *Strangler of the Swamp* (1946). CW

The Witching Hour

Paramount/Famous Players-Lasky; b/w; 82 min; U.S.
D: William Desmond Tayler *S:* Julia Crawford Ivers *P:* Jesse Lasky *C:* James Van Trees
Cast: Elliott Dexter, Winter Hall, Ruth Renick, Robert Cain, Edward Sutherland, Mary Alden

Probably the least interesting of the three film adaptations of Augustus Thomas' 1907 stage play, *The Witching Hour* focuses on the murder of a governor by Clay Whipple (Sutherland) after an incident involving a cat's eye pin. Whipple is convicted and sentenced to death. Psychic Jack (Dexter) believes that Clay is innocent because he was hypnotically controlled at the time of the murder; he convinces a judge that a retrial is in order, hoping to use his abilities to ferret out the real murderer (and thwart a second murder attempt in the bargain).

After a decade as an actor in silent cinema, British-born Edward Sutherland (1895-1973) became a director, making such horror thrillers as *The Secrets of the French Police* and *Murders in the Zoo* (both 1932), as well as fantasies (*Beyond Tomorrow*, 1940) and science fiction films (*The Invisible Woman*, 1940).

The Witching Hour was released on April 10, 1921. A print of the film currently exists in the Library of Congress. CW

Yotsuya kaidan

Kokkatsu; b/w; length unknown; Japan
D: Yoshino Jiro
Cast: Shirogoro Sawamura

Oume, a rich landowner's beautiful daughter, lusts after a studly samurai named Iemon. The attraction is mutual, but Iemon is married to the semi-impoverished Oiwa. So he sorts things out by administering a poison that disfigures, then kills, his longtime wife. Marriage to Oume follows in short order, but on their wedding night, Owia's ghost besets the two newlyweds. In a determined but klutzy attempt to destroy the spirit, Iemon decapitates his new bride, which causes him to go insane.

Yotsuya kaidan literally translates as *Ghost of Yotsuya* (or, as some film historians prefer, *Yotsuya Ghost Story*), and an 1825 Kabuki play of the same title by Tsuruya Nanboku IV (1755-1829) becomes the basis for the movie. Reportedly an amalgam of two actual events—one involving two servants who murdered their employers, the other involving a samurai who slaughtered his mistress after discovering her infidelity—Nanboku's famous play has been filmed more times than any other Japanese horror story. Shozo Makino directed the first adaptation of the tale, starring Matsunosuke Onoe, and produced by the Nikkatsu Studio in 1912. A follow-up production (a possible sequel) called *Yotsuya kaidan jitsuhi kanetani goro* appeared in 1918.

The adaptation following this 1921 version, produced by Shochiku, came along in July 1923 and also starred Shirogoro Sawamura. CW

1922

Arima no neko

Shochiku; b/w; length unknown; Japan
D: Jiro Yoshino
Cast: Shirogoro Sawamura

This version of the "Ghost Cat of Arima" legend was released on May 1, 1922. It was produced by Shochiku Studios, silent-era juggernaut Nikkatsu's biggest competitor in the horror market at the time, and was directed by Jiro Yoshino, who produced numerous films for Shochiku, including the dark fantasies *Bancho Sarayashiki*, *Hachisuka no neko*, *Nabeshimo no neko* and *Osaka-jou tenshu no kai* (all 1922), as well as *Nabeshimo no neko* (1923). Many of these films starred Shirogoro Sawamura in the lead role.

In Japanese tradition, it was believed that if a cat drank the blood of a dead person, it would be imbued with said person's spirit. And if the person/soul in question had been murdered, the ghostly cat would seek vengeance on whoever had wronged the original owner. CW

Asajigahara hitsotsuya

Shochiku; b/w; length unknown; Japan
D: Kaname Mori
Cast unknown

This is the only film (known for certain) to be based on the legend of the Horror House of Asajigahara. There, near what is now Asakusa (a district in Toyko, Japan), sat an isolated and dilapidated house wherein lived an old couple and their daughter. In order to support the family, the couple sent their daughter out to snare wealthy men, luring them back to the crumbling home with the promise of sex. The men, once inside, were butchered and their belongings stolen. Things hit a snag when one evening the couple mistook their daughter for an intruder and murdered her too, after which the mother, grief-stricken at what she had done, jumped into a pond and killed herself.

The tale is a gruesome one, making it surprising that more films weren't based on its grisly premise. The pond into which the woman allegedly jumped was called Ubagaike, which may have provided the setting for the very similar story of *Adachihara*, filmed in 1915 as *Adachihara Ubagaike yurei*. CW

At the Sign of the Jack O' Lantern
Renco/Hodkinson; b/w; 58 min; U.S.
D/Co-S: Lloyd Ingraham *Co-S:* David Kirkland *P:* H.H. Reynolds
Cast: Betty Ross Clarke, Earl Schenck, Wade Boteler, Victor Potel, Frances Hatton, Monte Collins

This silent old dark house comedy stars Earl Schenck as Harlan Carr and Betsy Ross Clark as his wife. They've inherited from Harlan's uncle a country estate—known as the Jack O'Lantern—as well as a small sum of money. There's more cash to come, but with a catch: The Carrs must live on the estate for six months to collect it. Ghostly manifestations fail to drive them out, and their patience is further tested when a group of disinherited relatives shows up and tries to take over. In the end, they evict the scroungers, and the late uncle's lawyer informs them that they've done exactly as the uncle had wished. They are summarily awarded the remainder of the inheritance.

Myrtle Reed's (1874-1911) novel *At the Sign of the Jack O'Lantern* formed the basis of the movie's screenplay. Chicago-born Reed was a popular novelist in her day and also wrote numerous cookbooks under the name Olivia Green. Her most famous work is undoubtedly *Lavender and Old Lace*, which was published in 1902; typical stuff for the period, it dealt with women in search of love.

Reed was not so lucky at love herself. In 1906 she married a Canadian pen pal, Sydney McCullough, who came to be considered a "Model Husband" by Chicago's elite. But all was not as it seemed; on August 17, 1911, Reed wrote a note to her maid that read, "If my husband had been as good and kind to me and as considerate as you, I would not be going where I am." That same day, she took an overdose of drugs and ended her life. CW

Banchō sarayashiki
aka **Banshū Sarayashiki**
Shochiku; b/w; length unknown; Japan
D: Jiro Yoshino
Cast unknown

The title of the Japanese folktale *Banchō sarayashiki* translates as "Dish House of Banchō." The story concerns servant girl Okiku, who rejects the advances of either a samurai or a shogun's vassal (depending on the version), only to be murdered by him and thrown into a well after she allegedly breaks one of 10 valuable plates belonging to her murderer's family. Understandably upset by the incident, Okiku's ghost returns from the grave and haunts her former place of employment, repeatedly counting to nine, then letting out a terrifying shriek if a living person doesn't shout "10" quickly enough.

The *Banchō sarayashiki* legend's origins are lost to antiquity, but by the 1700s a widespread belief existed that when a type of worm with a body making it appear to be bound began to infest old wells in Japan, superstitious peasants thought them to be manifestations of Okiku's waterlogged spirit. This idea was codified when famous Japanese artist Katsushika Hokusai (1760-1849) painted Okiku as a worm with the head of a woman, rising from an old well. CW

A Blind Bargain
aka **The Octave of Claudius**
Goldwyn; b/w-color; 57 min; U.S.
D: Wallace Worlsey *S:* J.G. Hawks *P:* Samuel Goldwyn *C:* Norbert Brodin
Cast: Lon Chaney, Raymond McKee, Jacqueline Logan, Fontaine La Rue, Virginia True Boardman, Aggie Herring, Wallace Beery

Dr. Anthony Lamb (Chaney) carries out unorthodox experiments in the hopes of learning how to prolong human life. His work produces some unfortunate misfires, including a half-man/half-ape creature (Chaney, again) that stalks his home. As he buries himself in his work, a man named Robert Sandell (McKee), who lacks the money to secure his ailing mother (Boardman) the medical attention she requires, decides to rob Lamb, apparently oblivious to the doctor's macabre reputation. But the robbery attempt fails, and Lamb emerges with the upper hand. After listening to the young man's pleas, the doctor offers to tend to Robert's mother if the young man will willingly serve as the doctor's guinea pig.

Lon Chaney's skill at evoking the monstrous quickly transformed him into a genre icon. A look at his memorable gallery of misfits and outcasts reveals that not only were they often good guys at heart, but that many of the actor's horror films were something closer to dramatic morality plays. With this in mind, it is all the more regrettable that *A Blind Bargain* is believed to be lost. There's no question that it was—along with a handful of other titles including *The Monster* and *The Phantom of the Opera* (both 1925)—indisputably part of the horror/melodrama genre.

The film gave Chaney an opportunity to play two roles: a mad scientist and one of his pitiful, distorted victims. The supporting cast included future Oscar-winner Wallace Beery (*The Lost World*, 1925; *The Champ*, 1931), unbilled as a monstrous "Beast Man" who wreaks vengeance on Chaney's character.

The screenplay is based on the novel *The Octave of Claudius* by Barry Pain. The production reteamed Chaney with Wallace Worsley, who had directed him in his star-making turn in *The Penalty* (1920); the two men would reteam again for their biggest box-office triumph, *The Hunchback of Notre Dame*, the following year.

Reviews of *A Blind Bargain* were generally positive, with Chaney yet again being commended for excellent mime and make-up work. A party sequence was reportedly done in the

Original advertisement for the Spanish chiller *Don Juan Tenorio*

early Prizmacolor process (also known as Handschiegle Color), which entailed etching each frame in color by hand.

The synopsis and surviving stills give weight to this film—moreso than Tod Browning's *London After Midnight* (1927)—being the true Holy Grail of lost Chaney films. TH

Danse Macabre
Visual Symphony; b/w; 6 (8) min; U.S.
D: Dudley Murphy S: Adolph Bolm P: Claude H. Macgowan
Cast: Adolph Bolm, Olin Howland, Ruth Page

A visualization-through-dance of Camille Saint-Saëns' composition of the same title, *Danse Macabre* opens with an animated sequence depicting skeletons that move to form the main title. The film then takes a moment to provide background information about composer Saint-Saëns before delving into its story of Youth (Bolm) and Love (Page) becoming a sweet young couple fleeing from envious Death (Howland) as he attempts to cut them down. The lovers seek refuge in an old castle and there attempt to ward off the Grim Reaper with a series of balletic dances. Death, his ghostly violin in hand, finds them and claims Love, but a last minute prayer to the Virgin Mary brings God's intervention; Love breathes, the cock crows and Death is banished to the nether realms. Youth and Love are reunited and live happily ever after or until, one assumes, Death returns to claim them in old age.

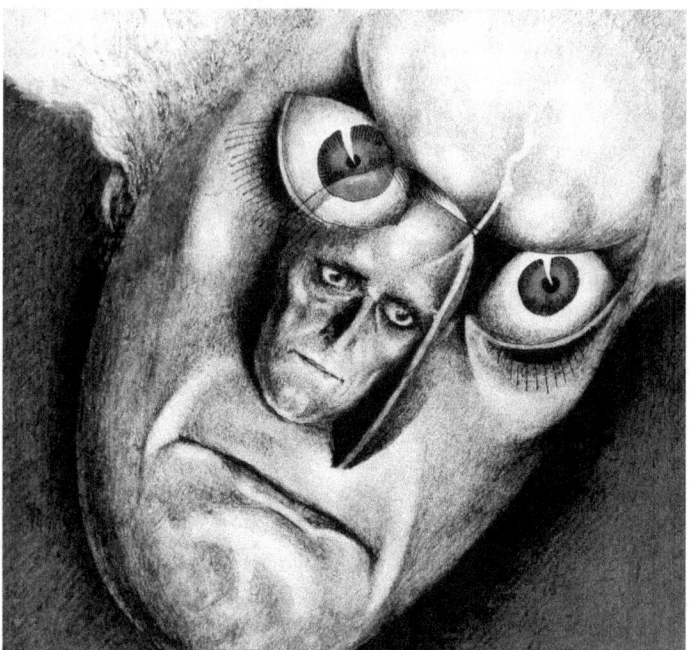

Original art from the German poster for *Dr. Mabuse the Gambler*

Director Dudley Murphy's own production company Visual Symphony produced the film, which as its name suggests, aimed to interpret music through visual imagery. It was of the *avant-garde* style of filmmaking, much more so than Murphy's previous horror outing, *Soul of the Cypress* (1921). *Avant-garde* was a relatively new thing in the 1920s, but it proved popular enough with film students that it's still around today, albeit mostly in academic circles. Other silent examples of the style within the horror genre include *Johann the Coffinmaker* (1927), *The Tell-Tale Heart* and *The Fall of the House of Usher* (both 1928).

Russian-born Adolph Bolm was about as famous as a dancer could be in the early 1900s. He began his work in his native country with the Russian Imperial Ballet School, moving from there to the Mariinsky Ballet. After collaborating with Diaghilev in Paris, he relocated to the United States, where he became a choreographer. He worked in both New York City and Chicago, where he likely met costar Ruth Page, a darling of that city's ballet scene. In addition to starring, Bolm also choreographed the dance routines for *Danse Macabre*.

The simplistic but interesting animation was the work of noted artist F.A.A. Dahme. CW

Don Juan and Faust
aka **Don Juan et Faust**
Gaumont; b/w; 73 min; France
D: Marcel L'Herbier S: Christian Dietrich Grabbe, Nikolaus Lenau C: Georges Lucas
Cast: Philippe Heriat, Vanni Marcoux, Marcelle Pradot, Jacques Catelain

Written and first published circa 1829, Christian Dietrich Grabbe's *Don Juan und Faust* was a four-act play that combined elements from Mozart's "Don Giovanni" with Goethe's two-part *Faust*. Aided by a knight who stands in for fallen archangel Mephistopheles, Faust prevents Don Juan from seducing the beauti-

Rudolf Klein-Rogge as the evil *Dr. Mabuse, the Gambler*

was in 1975, three years before his death. In *Don Juan and Faust*, L'Herbier employed a curious mixture of Expressionistic and Impressionistic styles to create a somewhat unique tableau, one with a staunchly conservative bent. CW

Don Juan Tenorio
Royal; b/w; length unknown; Spain
D/S/C: Ricardo de Baños
Cast: Fortunio Bonanova, Inocencia Alcubeirre, Jaime Planas, Ramón Quadreny, Ramón Bañeras, Julio López de Castilla

This is Ricardo de Baños' second stab at the tale of Don Juan as told by Spanish playwright José Zorillo. As with the other adaptation, this one dealt with the titular anti-hero who has made a bet with the equally vile Don Luis concerning which of them can destroy the most lives. Their exploits result in the deaths of many, including that of the one woman Don Juan truly loves.

Spanish production company Royal was a short-lived one, producing films between around 1916 and 1922, with *Don Juan Tenorio* being one of its last. De Baños' directorial career lasted into the 1930s before coming to an end with his death in 1939.

Like most other adaptations (both theatrical and cinematic) of Zorillo's play, this version of *Don Juan Tenorio* was released in October (the original play is culturally attached to the holidays of All Hallow's Eve and All Saints' Day). While some sources list the film as having a running time of over two hours, others cite it as a short. CW

ful Donna Anna on her wedding day—though Don Juan does slay both her bridegroom and her father. Faust magically whisks Anna off to a fortified castle, but once there, she refuses *his* advances, and he kills her. Then, mortified at what he's done, he submits himself to the Devil, while Don Juan refuses to do the same for his own evil acts.

In L'Herbier's film, Faust is an alchemist in need of four tears from a virgin of aristocratic birth, Donna Anna, for his alchemy. Convinced that she has eloped with Faust, Anna's boyfriend Don Juan drowns his sorrow by bedding other women. Anna stabs Faust to death and goes in search of her beau, only to find him engaged in an orgy. He doesn't recognize her and is chased by the men whose wives he has conquered. He takes refuge in the tomb of Anna's father and later repents, along with Anna, offering his soul to Christ.

Despite claims from some quarters that it was a short, *Don Juan and Faust* was a feature-length film. It was shot at the Studios La Villete in Paris, France—though parts of it were allegedly filmed in Spain—in early-to-mid 1922 and released in October of that same year.

Marcel L'Herbier (1890-1979) was a jack-of-all-trades in the French film industry, working variously as a writer, director, art director, producer, editor and actor. He wrote and directed his first film, *Phantasmes*, in 1917 and remained a popular director and screenwriter through the 1950s. Even after retirement, he made the occasional foray into film production. His last project

Dr. Mabuse the Gambler
aka **Dr. Mabuse, der Spieler—Ein Bild der Zeit**; **Dr. Mabuse, der Spieler**; **Dr. Mabuse, King of Crime**
Uco-Film; b/w; Part 1: 155 min, Part 2: 115 min; Germany
D: Fritz Lang *S:* Thea von Harbou *P:* Erich Pommer *C:* Carl Hoffmann
Cast: Rudolf Klein-Rogge, Aud Egede Nissen, Gertrude Welcker, Bernhard Goetzke, Alfred Abel, Paul Richter

Part One: Dr. Mabuse, The Great Gambler, A Picture of Our Time: Criminal mastermind Dr. Mabuse (Klein-Rogge) oversees a massive crime wave, outwitting in the process State Prosecutor Von Wenk (Goetzke). But things become complicated when Mabuse falls for Countess Told (Nissen), wife of the weak-willed Count Told (Abel). Using his hypnotic powers, Mabuse humiliates the Count by forcing him to cheat at cards. Then he has his men abduct the Countess and imprison her in his lair.

Part Two: Dr. Mabuse, Inferno, A Play of People of Our Time: Von Wenk continues his obsessive search for Mabuse, who holds the Countess Told hostage. The Count attempts to help, but Mabuse forces him to commit suicide. The doctor then underestimates Von Wenk, leading to a confrontation that threatens to destroy Mabuse's criminal empire.

The brainchild of popular German novelist Norbert Jacques, the Dr. Mabuse character here attracts the attention of the great German director Fritz Lang. Having established himself as a major talent with such films as *Spiders* (1919) and *Destiny* (1921), Lang embraces Mabuse as an epic study of the

Lobby card for the old dark house thriller *The Ghost Breaker*

criminal mind. With his own obsessive attention to detail, Lang was the perfect director to bring the story to the screen. Obviously fascinated by both the character's meticulous persona and his ability to remain anonymous, Lang crafts a compelling melding of melodrama and detective fiction.

Working with his wife and regular screenwriting collaborator, Thea von Harbou, the director transforms Jacques' pulp-fiction villain into someone far grander and more psychologically resonant. The end result was so sweeping, in fact, that it had to be split into two parts. The first part—*The Great Gambler*—establishes Mabuse as a shadowy figure who can move among the populace with the aid of a series of elaborate disguises. He is easily the most interesting character in the piece, though the heroic Von Wenk establishes himself as a worthy adversary.

The director's ongoing ambivalence toward Expressionism is on display in the sequence in which Count Told, who is an avid art collector, asks the doctor his opinion on that school of art. "Expressionism is just playing about," Mabuse replies curtly. Yet the Count has an interest in Expressionist art that allows Lang & Co. to create a fabulously exaggerated milieu in which to house him. The Count's drawing room, scattered with Expressionist artifacts, is truly a wonder to behold.

Elsewhere, Lang employs his typical, far more realistic, style. The cinematography by Carl Hoffmann (*Faust*, 1926) is top-notch. Lang's use of camerawork isn't as elaborate as that of, say, Paul Leni (*The Cat and the Canary*, 1927), but his control of images is consistently masterful. He doesn't shy away from the seedier aspects of the criminal scene either. Overt references to cocaine addiction (one of Mabuse's henchman has a bad drug habit) help ground the film in a sense of social realism, removing it from the more romanticized portrait of criminality typical in many films of this vintage. Lang also indulges in a discreet view of female nudity during a visit to a clandestine casino as a dancer wearing a sheer dress is put on display.

The director's obsessive attention to detail is most evident in the way he lovingly portrays Mabuse's various criminal exploits. The end result is almost documentary-like in tone as the director lingers on the mechanics of how the doctor plans and executes each crime.

Things take on a darker tone in the second part—the aptly titled *Inferno*—as Mabuse's plans begin to fall apart. Various key characters are disposed of, sometimes quite alarmingly (as with the suicide of the well-meaning if ineffectual Count Told), and the tale moves inexorably to a finale that is less triumphant than melancholy.

Ultimately, the film serves as something of a template for any number of crime films; the shadow of Mabuse looms large over the megalomaniacal antics of the various villains of the James Bond franchise. Its inclusion in the pantheon of horror films has less to do with its plot than its almost supernatural depiction of the character of Dr. Mabuse, a man whose capacity for evil is equaled only by his ability to "magically" disappear in a crowd.

Rudolf Klein-Rogge is perfect in the lead. His acting is generally subtle and low-key, making Mabuse all the more sinister and powerful. He is well matched by Bernhard Goetzke, so memorable as "the weary death" in Lang's *Destiny*, here giving a fine performance as Von Wenk. Goetzke certainly had his work cut out for him, playing an avenging authority figure against so charismatic a villain, but he admirably acquits himself.

The box-office success of the film's two parts would cement Lang's reputation as one of the major talents in the German film industry, paving the way for such ambitious flights of fancy as *Die Niebelungen* (1924) and *Metropolis* (1927), the latter being the most expensive German film of its time.

Lang would revisit the Mabuse mythos two more times: in 1933's *The Testament of Dr. Mabuse* (arguably the most horror-oriented of the films) and with his last film, 1960's *The Thousand Eyes of Dr. Mabuse*. TH

The Dungeon
Micheaux; b/w; 71 min; U.S.
D/S/P: Oscar Micheaux
Cast: William E. Fountaine, Shingzie Howard, J. Kenneth Goodman, William Crowell, Earle Browne Cook, Blanche Thompson

Oscar Micheaux has been referred to as the African American Cecil B. DeMille, due to his prolific work behind the camera during cinema's silent era. Born outside Metropolis, Illinois, the sense of ambition instilled in him by his parents, both former slaves, led to Micheaux forming his own publishing and film production companies. Though many of his films are considered lost today, those that survive are cult classics, with several of them, such as *Body and Soul* (1924), being easily obtainable.

His first horror effort appears to have been *The Dungeon*, an early blaxploitation take on the Bluebeard story. Myrtle Downing (Howard) is forced to marry Gyp Lassiter (Goodman), despite the fact that she's in love with a lawyer named Stephen Cameron (Fountaine). Even worse, she discovers after the wedding that her new husband, a politician, is as corrupt as they come, selling out his own people by supporting segregationist policies so as to remain financially successful and powerful. When she objects to his bigoted backroom deals, her husband has her thrown into the basement torture dungeon where he murdered his previous wives.

Micheaux was criticized by African American leaders of the time because, in an effort to make his films more palatable to the masses, he mostly cast light-skinned actors who could pass for white. Since *Dungeon* is lost, it's impossible to know how apt the criticism was in this instance, though such casting was a common practice at the time. If true, it was arguably a lesser evil than those other extremes of early cinema: the filling of African American roles by Caucasians in blackface (*The Lost World*, 1925) or by Caucasians whom the audience was expected to believe were light-skinned blacks (*Pinky*, 1949). CW

Esmeralda
aka The Hunchback of Notre Dame
Master; b/w; 13 min; Great Britain
D: Edwin J. Collins *S:* Frank Miller
Cast: Sybil Thorndike, Booth Conway, Arthur Kingsley, Annesley Healy

As the title suggests, this is yet another adaptation of Victor Hugo's 1831 novel *Notre Dame de Paris*. Here again the focus is squarely on the Gypsy dancer Esmeralda rather than the hunchbacked bell ringer Quasimodo.

Part of the *Tense Moments from Great Plays* series, *Esmeralda* nixed the horrific elements in favor of romance and melodrama. The film featured Dame Sybil Thorndike (sibling to actor/novelist Russell Thorndike) as Esmeralda and Booth Conway as Quasimodo. Arthur Kingsley played Phoebus and Annesley Healy a priest who is a proxy for the novel's villain, Claude Frollo. Edwin J. Collins, a former actor who had played a hunchback in A.E. Coleby's wildly divergent take on the tale, *The Hunchback* (1911), handled the directing chores. Given that she was approximately 40 years of age when the film was shot, Thorndike was much too old for the role of the young and virginal Esmeralda, as images for the film attest.

Esmeralda has long been considered lost. The next version of Hugo's novel was Universal's massively successful *The Hunchback of Notre Dame* (1923), starring Lon Chaney. CW

Faust
Master; b/w; 14 min; Great Britain
D: Challis Sanderson *S:* Frank Miller
Cast: Dick Webb, Sylvia Caine, Lawford Davidson, Gordon Hopkirck, Minnie Rayner

In yet another British variation on Johann Wolfgang von Goethe's tale, Webb stars as Faust, who sells his soul to the Devil (Davidson) in exchange for youth and virility. With Satan's help, he pursues and seduces the beautiful Marguerite (Caine), and when her brother Valentin (Hopkirk) tries to defend her honor in a duel with Faust, he is killed. Marguerite is imprisoned and dies, her soul flies off to Heaven and Faust must live out his days with the torment of what has happened.

The very next year, Great Britain would again produce a version of the play, this one directed by Bertram Phillips. The definitive take on the story wouldn't come until 1926, however, when F.W. Murnau (*Nosferatu—A Symphony of Terror*, 1922) would try his hand at the tale. CW

Faust
Azur; b/w; length unknown; France
D: Gerard Bourgeois *S:* Michel Carré *P/C:* Cesar Parolini
Cast: Maurice Varny, Christine Kerf, George Wague, Jeanne Leduc

This is one of two film adaptations in 1922 of Goethe's tragedy, first published in 1808. Like most of the others, it tells the story of an aging scientist who sells his soul to the Devil in exchange for youth, then seduces the beautiful Marguerite, kills her brother and thus drives her mad. What sets this one apart is not its approach to the material, which is strictly routine and derivative, but an unusual approach in the direction. Often credited as the first 3D movie, it called for its filmed images to be projected on transparent material, behind which was a set with props. The purpose was the simulation of a live-action stage performance. It apparently either didn't work or didn't catch on, since the process was abandoned not long after its invention.

Both 1922 adaptations of *Faust* were released in the same month, July, in their native countries. CW

The Ghost Breaker
Paramount/Famous Players-Lasky; b/w; 57 min; U.S.
D: Alfred Green *S:* Jack Cunningham, Walter de Leon *P:* Jesse L. Lasky *C:* William Marshall
Cast: Wallace Reid, Lilla Lee, Walter Hiers, Arthur Edmund Carewe, J. Farrell McDonald, Snitz Edwards

Walter Jarvis (Reid) and his servant Rusty (Hiers) assist a beautiful heiress (Lee) in ridding her father's estate of ghosts. After a lot of false scares, it turns out that Duke D'Alba (Carewe) fabricated the ghosts in an attempt to scare the heiress away from a hidden cache of gold.

Adapted from a stage play by Paul Dickey and Charles W. Goddard (previously filmed by Cecil B. DeMille in 1914), *The Ghost Breaker* is an early stab at combining horror with humor. The film incorporated a grabbag of elements that were already cliché in 1922: a stoic hero and his cowardly servant, a beautiful heiress, a spooky old house and a secret plot to make off with someone else's fortune. DeMille's version hadn't done much to advance his career, and it doesn't seem as if this remake generated a lot of interest either.

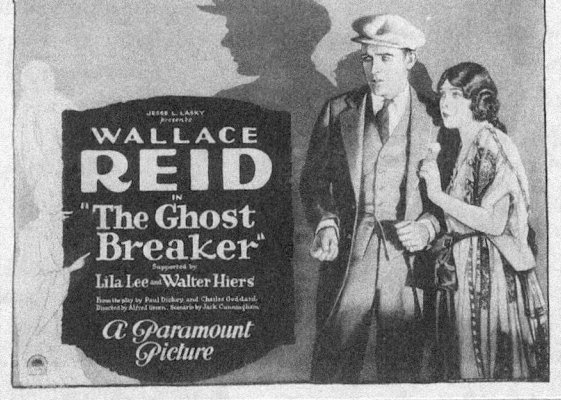

Reviews of the time took issue with Alfred Green's direction. The reviewer for the *New York Times*, for example, opined in his September 11, 1922 write-up:

A spooky image of the Devil manifest in *Häxan*

A Scandinavian poster for *Häxan*

The main fault seems to be in the direction. Alfred Green has not enlivened the film … Instead, he has made many meaningless scenes that let the spectator's imagination go to sleep … When the picture finally does get to the business of the ghosts and the treasure, it picks up a little, and although it never has the pictorial vitality one is always expecting of it, it takes on a certain intensity of life that makes it fairly interesting and amusing.

The supporting cast includes two actors later reunited for Universal's lavish *The Phantom of the Opera* (1925), Arthur Edmund Carewe and Snitz Edwards. Contemporary sources cite future leading man Richard Arlen (*Island of Lost Souls*, 1933) and future Oscar-nominated director Mervyn LeRoy (*The Bad Seed*, 1956) as un-credited ghosts.

The story got another go-around in the 1940's Bob Hope vehicle *The Ghost Breakers*; the Dean Martin/Jerry Lewis comedy *Scared Stiff* (1953) changed the title but retained the same scenario. Both the 1914 and the 1922 versions are considered lost. TH

Hachisuka no neko
Shochiku; b/w; length unknown; Japan
D: Jiro Yoshino
Cast: Shirogoro Sawamura

This is one of an apparently inexhaustible number of silent-era Japanese "ghost cat" movies, Japan being the one Asian nation that reveled in such feline horror fare.

Little is known about *Hachisuka no neko*. The title translates as "Cat of Hachisuka," Hachisuka being a venerable Japanese clan dating from the mid-800s. The film starred Shochiku Studios' primary leading man Shirogoro Sawamura and was helmed by the company's leading director, Jiro Yoshino.

Sawamura and Yoshino were strangers neither to each other nor to horror cinema. The supernatural thrillers on which they worked in tandem include *Akakabe myojin* (1920), *Yotsuya Kaidan* (1921), *Arima no neko* (1922) and *Nabeshima no neko* (1923).

Hachisuka no neko was released in Japan on September 20, 1922. CW

The Haunted House
Fox; b/w; 20 min; U.S.
D: Erle C. Kenton *P:* William Fox
Cast unknown

Erle C. Kenton directed this lost Sunshine Comedy for William Fox. It was a black and white two-reeler that, to judge from surviving images, was typical fluff for its time. Unsuspecting people spend a night in a haunted house along with their African American servants (obviously men in blackface), who perform the endlessly unentertaining "scared black" routine. It was released on October 29, 1922, just in time for Halloween.

Former actor Kenton was still a relative unknown at this point in his career, though he'd already directed over 20 short features. He went on to make some of the more distinguished and/or famous horror films of the 1930s and '40s, including *Island of Lost Souls* (1932), *The Ghost of Frankenstein* (1942), *House of Frankenstein* (1944) and *House of Dracula* (1945), before shifting his efforts to television. CW

Häxan
aka **Häxan: Witchcraft Through the Ages**; **The Witches**; **Witchcraft Through the Ages**; **The Witch**
Svenska; b/w; 104 min; SW
D/S: Benjamin Christensen *C:* Johan Ankerstjerne
Cast: Benjamin Christensen, Astrid Holm, Maren Pedersen, Clara Pontoppidan, Elith Pio, Orcar Stribolt

Filmmaker Benjamin Christensen examines the history of witchcraft and its connection to mass hysteria in Häxan, one of the horror genre's all-time unique achievements. Part pseudo-documentary, part social document and part dark comedy, the film explores the history of witchcraft from a psychoanalytical perspective. But unlike so many other psychology-themed films of the period (G.W. Pabst's 1926 work *Secrets of a Soul*, for example), *Häxan* is never dry or academic.

It's easily the best work of its writer/director. Danish-born Christensen (1879-1959) began his career as a stage actor and opera singer, but his intense stage fright got the better of him. He managed to act sporadically in films—he portrays both Satan and Jesus Christ in *Häxan*, though he's probably best remembered as the jilted homosexual in Carl Theodor Dreyer's *Michael* (1924). With 1914's *Sealed Orders*, his filmmaking career began in earnest. Yet, while Christensen had great faith in cinema's potential, he was seldom given the opportunity to express his vision as he saw fit. Finally, disgusted by studio politics and front-office interference, he retired in 1942 after the release of his mystery *Lady with the Light Gloves*.

It is generally accepted that *Häxan* represents the pinnacle of his career, and for good reason. It moves smoothly from academic treatise on the history of witchcraft to stunning costume horror-melodrama as it ghoulishly charts the horrific treatment of innocent women put to trial for being witches. Christensen was clearly influenced by the German Expressionist movement, but his vision goes beyond mere imitation. *Häxan* is at its best during its imaginative fantasia sequences, with their perverse presentations of a leering Satan holding sway. The marvelous use of framing, lighting, and cutting creates a hallucinatory sense of delirium in the fire-lit tableaux of satanic orgies, with surprising glimpses of female nudity amid the pernicious goings-on (such as the famed sequence in which a line of frenzied women stoop, one by one, to kiss a demon on its bared backside).

The final section of the film, which pursues the psychoanalytic angle in a contemporary setting, came under fire from some critics, and the director later came to regard it as ill advised. But mistake or no, *Häxan* remains fascinating from beginning to end. It retains its visual and narrative power, even if facets of it seem dated from a modern point of view. Christensen pulls out all the stops, employing eye-popping production designs, grotesque make-up and then-elaborate special effects work. The director's condemnation of the church and its role in the persecution of innocent women landed the film in hot water in some quarters at the time of its release, and his condemnation still comes off as strong today.

The film was re-released in Denmark in 1941 with an on-screen introduction by Christensen that outlines the film for those who may not be able to grasp it. In 1968 a heavily cut, 77-minute version was released in the United States under the title *Witchcraft Through the Ages*, with narration by none other than beat writer William S. Burroughs, author of the controversial *Naked Lunch*. TH

The Headless Horseman
Sleepy Hollow; b/w; 71 (68, 51) U.S.
D: Edward D. Venturini *S/P:* Clarence Stearns Clancy *C:* Ned Van Buren
Cast: Will Rogers, Lois Meredith, Ben Hendricks, Jr., Charles Graham, Mary Foy, Bernard Reinold

Set in "the little Dutch village of Sleepy Hollow" in 1790, *The Headless Horseman* is the longest of the three silent adaptations of Washington Irving's classic short story *The Legend of Sleepy Hollow*, first published in 1820 in *The Sketch Book of Geoffrey Crayon, Gent*. This 1922 version is also the only one of the three known to exist today.

When a new schoolmaster, Ichabod Crane (Rogers), arrives in town, many of the local townsfolk see him as aloof and uppity; his insistence that children learn in class rather than goof off may win over a few of the locals but it alienates most of them. He courts Katrina Van Tassel (Meredith), the beautiful daughter of a wealthy local farmer, hoping to gain access to her father's money in a move that incites the jealousy of Van Tassel's former beau, Brom Bones (Hendricks, Jr.). One day, while traipsing with his students through the graveyard, Crane shudders as he hears the story of the Headless Horseman, the ghost of a Hessian mercenary who allegedly haunts the little town in search of his battle-severed head. Bones gets wind of the incident and hatches a plan to use Crane's fear of the supernatural to discredit him. First he trashes the schoolhouse and makes it appear as if the act were committed by witches, then he plants the idea in the schoolchildren's heads that they've been bewitched by their schoolmaster. When the townspeople attempt to tar and feather Crane, the school committee prevents them from doing so, and Bones' plot is revealed. The subsequent apology Bones is forced to make only strengthens his resolve to destroy his rival using the story of the Headless Horseman.

The Headless Horseman gives the viewer many reasons to dislike it, not the least of which is its snarky, disdainful portrayal of those who are well educated. Ichabod Crane, there to "impart knowledge" to "rural people," is presented as a gold digger and a know-it-all (though one who disingenuously shares the locals' belief in the supernatural). When Brom Bones destroys the schoolhouse, the audience is expected to cheer his action, since it's directed at an institution that disregards the down-home wisdom of common folk. The school committee that ultimately saves Crane from being tarred and feathered is likewise presented as a pack of buffoons, drunk on its own power. And when Crane finally meets his fate at the hands of the neighborhood specter, the audience is meant to sigh with relief that his highfalutin attitude will no longer vex the uneducated but much wiser townspeople.

Conrad Veidt (center) as Cesare Borgia had another opportunity to tear up the screen, from *Lucrezia Borgia*.

The film is also marred by a couple of way-too-long sequences celebrating the religiosity of the villagers, such as Crane teaching the young men and women of the village to sing the Psalms and the townspeople listening to the minister's Sunday sermon. The costumes look like they were swiped from a touring theater group, while the obvious day-for-night shooting foreshadows the work of Edward D. Wood, Jr. Worst of all for monster fans, the Headless Horseman shows up exactly twice: briefly toward the film's beginning and again at the story's climax. The cumulative result of all this is a motion picture that wavers between irritating and flat-out dull.

While many film historians claim that the role of Ichabod Crane was a departure for vaudeville comedian Will Rogers, it was anything but, given the almost slapstick style with which he animates the character (an approach later borrowed by Johnny Depp for Tim Burton's now-classic 1999 adaptation, *Sleepy Hollow*). CW

It's Never Too Late to Mend

Master; b/w; 12 min; Great Britain
D: George Wynn *S:* Frank Miller
Cast: Russell Thorndike, Ward McAllister, Alec Alexander

Born in Rocester, Kent, England and taught at Windsor Castle, Arthur Russell Thorndike (1885-1972) was younger brother to famous British thespian Dame Sybil Thorndike. The two acted together in stage tours throughout the United States, but when Great Britain went to war with Germany in 1914, Russell enlisted in the military. His brother Frank, also an actor, was killed in action, and Russell was discharged after being severely wounded in Gallipoli, Turkey. Back in Great Britain, he published his first novel, *Doctor Syn: A Tale of the Romney Marsh*, to a resounding success that ensured a continuing series of Syn adventures.

At the same time, he resumed his stage work, and in 1922 he starred in this silent film adaptation of Charles Reade's 1856 novel *It Is Never Too Late to Mend: A Matter-of-Fact Romance*. The book deals with a man named Tom Robertson who, incarcerated for a crime he didn't commit, experiences the brutality rife in Britain's penal system at the time. The film, part of the *Tense Moments from Great Plays* series, was simply filmed footage of a portion of the stage version of Reade's story.

Thorndike played the villain, Squire Meadows, who trumps up the charge that removing Tom as a romantic rival. Thorndike's movie career was sporadic, but his film work was often playing characters from great novels or plays. His only other horror films appear to have been *Lucrezia Borgia: Or, Plaything of Power* and *The Bells* (both 1923) and *A Shot in the Dark* (1933).

The year 1925 saw the release of another film, *It Is Never Too late to Mend*, but it had nothing to do with Reade's story. The next adaptation of Reade's novel didn't come until 1937, when George King released *Never Too Late to Mend*, a barnstormer starring Great Britain's own horror star, Tod Slaughter. CW

Lucrezia Borgia
aka **Lucretia Borgia**
Oswald; b/w; 96 (120, 75) min; German
D/S/P: Richard Oswald *C:* Karl Freund, Karl Vass, Carl Drews
Cast: Liane Haid, Conrad Veidt, Albert Bassermann, Paul Wegener, Henrich George, Adolf E. Licho, William Dieterle

Cesare Borgia (Veidt) will stop at nothing—not even the seduction of his own sister Lucrezia (Haid) or the murder of his own male siblings—in his quest for pleasure and power.

Richard Oswald's take on the infamous Borgia family—remembered for their corruption in the late 1400s under the rule of family patriarch Rodrigo (aka Pope Alexander VI)—was something of a super production. The impressive cast list alone is evidence that no expense was spared in the film's creation. Given the macabre circumstances surrounding the family's notable history and Oswald's own preoccupation with perverse subject matter, it seems only fair to cover this precursor to Rowland V. Lee's *Tower of London* (1939) in a book dedicated to horror films. After all, Oswald found his greatest success with the morbid omnibus thriller *Weird Tales* (1919) and its 1932 remake, *Uncanny Stories*. His version of the Borgias' story was controversial in its day; it was seen as an attack on the Catholic Church and was suppressed in the United States until 1928, when it was released in heavily truncated form.

Lucrezia provided yet another opportunity for Conrad Veidt to tear up the screen; by this time he was already entrenched as a major acting talent in German cinema. The cast also includes such luminaries as Albert Bassermann (*The Red Shoes*, 1948) as Rodrigo, Paul Wegener (*The Golem: How He Came into the World*, 1920) as Michelatto and Wilhelm Dieterle as Lucrezia's impotent first husband, Giovanni Sforza. Dieterle later changed his first name to William and directed such classics as *The Hunchback of Notre Dame* (1939) and *The Devil and Daniel Webster* (1941).

The title role was taken by leading lady Liane Haid, a prima ballerina and stage actress who found success on the silver screen during the silent era; she more or less disappeared from filmdom in the late 1930s, making only a handful of cinema appearances thereafter. Her interpretation of Lucrezia Borgia was a sympathetic one that blamed the machinations of her brother Cesare for her indiscretions.

Renowned auteur Abel Gance (*Napoleon*, 1927) took his own crack at the Borgia saga with *Lucrezia Borgia* (1935). But the most famous theatrical incarnation remains Donetti's opera of 1834, *Lucrezia Borgia*, which was based on Victor Hugo's novel of the same name. TH

The Marriage Chance
Del Ruth; b/w; 65 min; U.S.
D/S/P: Hampton Del Ruth *C:* Dal Clawson
Cast: Alta Allen, Milton Sills, Henry B. Walthall, Tully Marshall, Irene Rich, Milton Lewis

Eleanor Douglas (Allen) and William Bradley (Sills) are engaged. On the eve of their wedding, Eleanor drinks some water given to her by Dr. Graydon (Warner). She falls unconscious, and Dr. Graydon pronounces her dead. Sometime later a cat drinks from the same water and appears to drop dead, only to revive shortly before it is to be buried. Suspicions are aroused, and the authorities break into Graydon's home. There they find Eleanor on an operating table and the good doctor dead on the floor, the victim of a gunshot. The dazed Eleanor is at first suspected of killing Graydon, but her sister (Rich) confesses.

Then-contemporary reviews describe *The Marriage Chance* as a broad comedy that takes a serious turn in its final act. This mixture of farce and the macabre certainly sounds interesting, but since it's a lost film, one can only speculate as to its merits.

Hampton Del Ruth, older brother of producer/director Roy Del Ruth (*Phantom of the Rue Morgue*, 1954), wore a number of hats in his cinematic career. In addition to directing, he produced, acted, wrote and worked as a production manager, even providing "mechanical special effects" work (on the Douglas Fairbanks version of *The Thief of Bagdad*, 1924). *The Marriage Chance* appears to be his only directorial work within the horror genre.

Leading man Milton Sills was popular during the silent era and even made a successful transition to talkies, but stress in his personal life led him to an early grave. He succumbed to a heart attack in 1930 at the age of 48.

The supporting cast includes Henry B. Walthall, already seen as Edgar Allan Poe in Charles Brabin's *The Raven* (1915) and later to appear in Tod Browning's *The Devil Doll* (1936). TH

Money to Burn
Fox; b/w; 55 min; U.S.
D: Rowland V. Lee *S:* Jack Strumwasser *C:* David Abel
Cast: William Russell, Sylvia Breamer, Otto Matieson, Hallam Cooley, Harvey Clark

After making a fortune on Wall Street, Lucky (Russell) buys a country estate where he goes to relax. The problem is that the house is still occupied by its previous tenant, a married Countess who tries to trick Lucky into leaving by making it seem as if the place is haunted. After a few escapades, romance kicks into high gear, and the two fall in love.

This romantic comedy with ghostly overtones was an early effort by director Rowland V. Lee (1891-1975). The Ohio native entered the film industry in 1917, writing *Wild Winship's Widow* starring Alice Terry. He directed his first film, *What Ho, The Cook*, in 1921. *Money to Burn* was his first horror-oriented film, and he later teamed with star Basil Rathbone on three stand-out horrors of the late 1930s: *Love from a Stranger* (1937), *Son of Frankenstein* (1939) and *Tower of London* (1939). By that time he had established himself as a major talent, and at Universal—where he directed *Son* and *Tower*—he was able to command respectable budgets and a high degree of autonomy, producing as well as directing his own pictures. He even gave a young Vincent Price his start in the business, headlining the stage actor in the frothy comedy *Service De Luxe* (1938).

Money to Burn only marginally belongs in the subgenre of old dark house comedy/horrors, thanks to its emphasis being more on laughs and romance than chills.

The film is considered lost. TH

Nikuzuki no men
Makino; b/w; 8 min; Japan
P: Shozo Makino
Cast unknown

The Japanese term *Nikuzuki no men* translates roughly as "mask stuck to face" and refers to a legend that arose during feudal times in the Hokuriku region of Honshū, the country's main island. The tale concerns a domineering mother who wanted to frighten her daughter-in-law; to accomplish this, she placed a terrifying mask on her own face. The mask became a permanent part of her countenance, resulting in the old woman terrorizing not only her intended victim but also everyone else who saw her as well.

The first film adaptation of the tale came sometime between 1910 and 1912 and is often credited to Yokota Shokai Studios. That film is considered lost, and only the name of its central player—Matsunosuke Onoe—is known. Given that at the time Onoe worked predominantly with director Shozo Makino for Nikkatsu Studios, it's likely that version was actually a Nikkatsu production shot by Makino. This idea is lent even more weight when one considers that Makino remade the film for his own production company in 1922, something he did with many of the properties he and Onoe had developed at Nikkatsu.

Though Onoe played the part of the mother in the original movie (it was commonplace at the time for men to take on female parts both on stage and in the movies), it is unknown who took on the role in this 1922 film. Either way, the story was pretty much abandoned by Japanese filmmakers until the definitive screen adaptation, *Onibaba*, was made in 1964. It has since become a staple of Japanese animation. CW

Nosferatu—A Symphony of Terror
aka **Nosferatu—eine Symphonie des Grauens**; **Nosferatu—A Symphony of Horrors**; **Nosferatu**
Prana Film; b/w; 94 min; Germany
D: F.W. Murnau *S:* Henrik Galeen *P:* Enrico Diekmann, Albin Grau *C:* Fritz Arno Wagner, Gunther Krampf
Cast: Max Schreck, Gustav Von Wagenheim, Greta Schroder, Alexander Granach, Georg H. Schnell, Ruth Landshoff

Max Schreck as Count Orlof from *Nosferatu*

German cover for a book about *Nosferatu*

Thomas Hutter (Von Wagenheim) is a young and happily married clerk at the law office of the mysterious Mr. Knock (Granach) in the fictional German port city of Wisborg. Knock sends Hutter to the Carpathian Mountains to deliver legal documents to Count Orlok (Schreck) and thus help facilitate the Count's move to a secluded house close to the city. Upon meeting the Count, Hutter is alarmed by his bizarre, rodent-like appearance but reluctantly stays on to perform his duty. The following night, he dreams that the Count enters his room and feeds on his blood, and at daybreak he awakens to find two marks on his throat. While exploring the castle in the daylight, he discovers a crypt containing a large coffin. His curiosity aroused, he opens the coffin and finds the sleeping Count within. He flees in panic and is knocked unconscious when he jumps from a high castle window. Orlok awakens at dusk and continues with his plans to relocate, loading his coffins onto a vessel bound for Wisborg. The journey is a horrific one, with the Count decimating the crew one by one. When the ship arrives at port, the Count slips off before his arrival can be noticed. While Hutter struggles to cross the Carpathians, desperately hoping to arrive in time to prevent the vampire from infecting his hometown, Orlok settles into the house Hutter helped procure for him and exerts his malevolent influence over Knock. Knock's behavior becomes progressively stranger, and he is eventually committed to an insane asylum from which he foretells the coming of a plague. This comes to pass, and rats from the abandoned ship are blamed. Meanwhile, Hutter's wife, Ellen (Schroder), falls under Orlock's sway and, upon Hutter's belated return, occult expert Professor Bulwer (Gottwot) is called upon for assistance. Ellen fears, however, that her beloved husband is next on Orlok's list of victims, and she sacrifices herself to ensure the creature's final destruction.

Written by Irish novelist and stage manager Bram Stoker, the novel *Dracula* was released to generally positive reviews in 1897; it was not, however, an immediate hit with the public. Yet, over time the book's impact has far exceeded anything else written by Stoker. It is said to have been adapted for the screen more times than any other literary work except The Bible (with the latter most always being merely excerpted).

Nosferatu, the first cinematic adaptation of *Dracula* of any significance (though *Drakula halála*, 1921, referred to the character), reached the screen in an unusual way—its makers sought to avoid paying for the film rights by changing the names of the characters and altering elements of the plot. But it didn't take long for word of the ruse to reach Stoker's widow Florence, who sued the production company and sought to have all prints of the film destroyed. The production company, Prana Film, filed for bankruptcy, and while judgment was indeed rendered requiring all prints to be destroyed, many copies had already "escaped" into general release. Were it not for this fortuitous turn of events, *Nosferatu* would have joined the ranks of most of director F.W. Murnau's early works, lost to the ravages of time. (Interestingly, one of these lost films was *Der Januskopf*, 1920, a similarly unauthorized adaptation of Robert Louis Stevenson's novella *The Strange Case of Dr. Jekyll and Mr. Hyde*.)

The genesis for *Nosferatu* came not from Murnau but from producer/set designer Albin Grau. A lifelong devotee of the occult, Grau saw Stoker's novel as a perfect vehicle to translate his interests to the screen. His choice of Murnau to direct was an inspired one; while Murnau had yet to be established as one of the major artists in German cinema, his early films had been well received and showed him to be an original director with a distinctive style. He respected Grau's screenplay and camera suggestions, but his use of light, shadow and composition transformed virtually every set-up into something visually remarkable.

Murnau's alteration of the original finale would have a major impact on nearly a century of vampire films to follow. The defeat of the vampire by the rays of the sun does not appear in Stoker's original novel. (In fact, in Stoker's book, Dracula is actually able to walk about in the sunlight, though with greatly diminished powers.) In addition, Murnau's invention of the heroine who sacrifices herself for the sake of her beloved provides an early example of an empowered female. She's not exactly a template for feminism, true, but neither is she the usual shrinking violet so typical of films of the period.

Murnau's homosexuality has long been seen as a major influence over the film's use of phallic imagery, which is of course debatable. There's little doubt, however, that Murnau's personality, including his sexuality, had a significant influence on the film (though the argument presented in some critiques that the image of Orlok was intended to evoke that of an erect penis may be stretching the point too far). In any case, an aura of perverse eroticism energizes much of the film, most noticeably during the final confrontation between the Count and Ellen.

Max Schreck's portrayal of Orlok is impressive even today. With his pointy ears, rat-like teeth and bald dome, he is truly a terrifying visage. Unlike subsequent adaptations that would attempt to humanize or even romanticize the image of Dracula, Murnau and Grau depict him as evil and pestilence incarnate. There is nothing remotely sympathetic in the character; he is as despicable as he looks.

Murnau and cinematographer Fritz Arno Wagner create some unforgettable images of the character, including the oft-imitated low-angle shot of the vampire creeping side-to-side across the deck of the ship he uses to escape from his homeland. The supporting cast may be guilty of over-emoting from time to time, but Schreck's performance is a model of restraint in comparison. He doesn't have to do much to assert his power, and as movie monsters go, he remains as fascinating and legitimately creepy today as ever.

Murnau's mastery of the medium is evident throughout. The pacing is tight, the imagery is consistently hypnotic and the weird atmosphere is maintained from beginning to end. Despite some minor handicaps with regards to the supporting performances (Von Wagenheim and Schroder are not exactly the most inspiring of juvenile leads, for example), the film has aged beautifully and remains one of the most successful and compelling adaptations of Stoker's story. A handful of sped-up shots are an unfortunate miscalculation, but it is important to realize that Murnau was doing his best to experiment with every available technique (one shot is even presented in negative) to highlight the unusual nature of the material. Similarly, the film has been criticized for some unconvincing day-for-night shots, but now that it has been properly restored on video with the original, intended use of blue filters for nighttime sequences, it's easier to understand Murnau's intention. With its grim tone and admirable absence of clumsily inserted comic relief, *Nosferatu* is one of the first cinematic masterpieces of the macabre.

In 1930, the film was given a brief re-release under the title *The Twelfth Hour* (aka *Die Zwoelfte Stunde*). This version was the result of a brief trend in re-releasing silent films with added sound and dialogue effects. It has since disappeared.

A German advertisement for *Nosferatu*

Maverick filmmaker Werner Herzog remade the film as *Nosferatu The Vampyre* (1979), starring Klaus Kinski in the lead role, a rare example of a remake of a great film that is on a par with the original. TH

One Exciting Night
aka **The Haunted Grande**
Griffith; b/w; 107 (128) min; U.S.
D/S/P: D.W. Griffith *C:* Irving B. Ruby, Hendrik Sartov
Cast: Carol Dempster, Henry Hull, Morgan Wallace, Porter Strong, Margaret Dale, Charles Kroker-King

Although she doesn't know it, Agnes Harrington (Dempster) is the daughter of a rich man; 16 years earlier, in Africa, her uncle separated her from the family for fear of losing his brother's inheritance. But now that her uncle has fallen deathly ill, he's written a letter requesting that Agatha be restored to her rightful status—this despite him having a son and heir of his own, the handsome John Fairfax (Hull). At the same time, Agnes' bitchy stepmother Mrs. Harrington is planning to sell Agnes into marriage with a wealthy older man (Wallace). Things start to congeal when John meets Agnes at a party and invites her and Mrs. Harrington to his home for some late-night socializing with the "in" crowd. What nobody knows, however, is that the place, the famous Fairfax Estate, is a base for bootleggers. There's also a scarecrow-like madman stalking the grounds and an alleged treasure hidden somewhere nearby. As the after-party gets going, a storm rolls in, and the bodies begin to pile up.

Inspired by the success of such Broadway hits as *The Bat* (which had opened in August 1920) and *The Cat and the Canary* (which had opened in February 1922), D.W. Griffith here brings his own old dark house mystery-comedy to the big screen. He wrote the script for *One Exciting Night* under the pseudonym Irene Sinclair. The film was released in October 1922, just in time for Halloween, ensuring massive office box-office receipts that an additional 20 years of stormy nights, sliding panels and clutching hands were guaranteed.

Success aside, *Exciting Night* brings absolutely nothing new to the subgenre. Griffith does manage a couple of startling shots within this otherwise typical melange; there's a terrific image of the shadow of a hand gliding over the Fairfax Estate, as well as a handful of spooky shots of the madman decked out in a creepy outfit that makes the modern viewer flash on either Fred Kruger, the *Batman* comic book villain The Scarecrow or both.

On the much-larger downside, however, the film doesn't seem to know whether it wants to evoke suspense or laughter, and in the end it does neither. The surfeit of Caucasian actors in blackface pantomiming the not-so-classic "scared black" act doesn't help things. Nor does much tension occur when, apropos of nothing, a massive hurricane blows in, downing trees and ripping homes apart (though the effects are admittedly top notch). On top of it all, this overlong opus crams so many subplots into the narrative that it becomes difficult to keep it all straight, nor is there much of a payoff for those who can do so.

While it's clear that Carol Dempster—who portrays the young heroine—is intended to be the show's star, it is relative newcomer and Broadway star Henry Hull who steals the proceedings. He brings conviction and integrity to the part of John Fairfax, displaying the traits that won him strong supporting roles in classics to follow, including *Great Expectations* (1934), *Jesse James* (1939) and *The Fountainhead* (1949). His horror resume includes *Rasputin, The Black Monk* (1917), *The Last Moment* (1923) and *Werewolf of London* (1935). Born in Louisville, Kentucky, he died in 1977 from a massive stroke while traveling in Cornwall, England.

On the other hand, Dempster (1901-1991), despite being groomed by Griffith to become America's next big star, never really caught on, perhaps because—by this time—audiences had begun to tire of innocent heroines and were opting instead to watch the latest vamp strut her stuff across the screen. Dempster did manage one major role outside of a Griffith film, as Alice Faulkner in John Barrymore's *Sherlock Holmes* (1922). Her last screen performance was in Griffith's *The Sorrows of Satan* (1926), which was also the director's final attempt at horror. CW

One Glorious Day
aka **Souls Before Birth**; **The Melancholy Spirit**; **Ek, a Fighting Soul**
Famous Players-Lasky/Paramount; b/w; 56 (50) min; U.S.
D: James Cruze S: A.B. Baringer, Walter Woods C: Karl Brown
Cast: Lila Lee, Will Rogers, Alan Hale, John Fox, George Nichols, Emily Rait

On Labor Day weekend in 1921 actor Roscoe "Fatty" Arbuckle, along with two friends (director Lowell Sherman and cinematographer Fred Fischbach), threw a party in a room at the St. Francis Hotel in San Francisco. During the course of the evening, Virginia Rappe was found ill in an adjoining room that was also being rented by Arbuckle. A couple of days later the starlet was hospitalized, at which time one of her friends informed a doctor that the young woman had been raped by Arbuckle. Rappe died from her injuries shortly thereafter, at which time the doctor passed on the information about her and Arbuckle to the police. The police deduced that Arbuckle's extreme weight (reportedly well over 300 pounds) had ruptured Rappe's bladder during forced intercourse, thus bringing about her death. The actor was arrested, and it didn't take long for the scandal to hit the newspapers. Arbuckle was eventually acquitted of rape and manslaughter, but his career, while not completely destroyed, never completely recovered.

Famous Players-Lasky yanked the shamed actor from an upcoming comedy vehicle titled *The Melancholy Spirit*, changed the project's name to *Ek, a Fighting Soul*, and cast up-and-coming actor Will Rogers in Arbuckle's role. The film was released to theaters in early 1922 as *One Glorious Day*.

While hardly an outright horror movie, the film presages Jerry Lewis' *Dr. Jekyll and Mr. Hyde* spoof *The Nutty Professor* (1963) with its tale of Ek (Fox), a spirit who has missed his turn to be born into the world and is impatient for another opportunity. He sneaks off to Earth where he tries and fails to possess various human forms. Then he comes upon a psychic researcher, Professor Ezra Botts (Rogers), who can leave his body during self-induced traces. One day, as Botts' spirit flies off to spy on a meeting involving his mayoral-candidate girlfriend (Lee), Ek takes up residence in the available body. The people who know Botts see a changed man, more interesting and alive than he's ever been. Meanwhile, Botts' real spirit becomes anxious that the being inhabiting his form might destroy it through too much action. When the body faints from exhaustion, Botts seizes what is rightfully his. He awakens a man much changed for the positive.

The special effects were achieved via double exposures. The film's comical study of the fantastic left a deep impression on a young Forrest J Ackerman, who later credited it as the film that created his lifelong interest in science fiction and horror. CW

Osaka-jo tenshu no kai
Shochiku; b/w; length unknown; Japan
D: Jiro Yoshino
Cast: Shirogoro Sawamura

Osaka Castle is located in Japan's Osaka Prefecture. The structure was begun in 1583 and completed in 1597. The moat and main tower were added in the 1600s to provide protection from invading armies, but the castle nonetheless sustained a great deal of damage due to fires and bombings in 1660, 1665, 1868 and 1945. In the 1990s it went through a major restoration effort and today is something of a tourist trap.

Osaka-jo tenshu no kai was apparently an original story set within the confines of the castle's central tower. Predominantly a mystery, it likely worked in horror overtones to give it appeal to audiences in search of the dark and frightening. CW

Queen of Spades
aka **Szenzáció**; **Pique Dame**; **Sensation**
Studio unknown; b/w; length unknown; Hungary
D: Paul (Pál) Fejos *S:* Louis Valentine, Bard Odon
Cast: Mara Jankovszky, Léona Károlyi, Antal Matány, Pál Zilahi, Bard Odon

This film should not be confused with the 1936 Hungarian film *Szenzáció*, which was based on a novel by Ferenc Herczeg and Gyula K. Halász. Rather, *Queen of Spades* is one of many adaptations of Alexander Pushkin's short story *Pikovaya dama* (1833).

Fejos' film tells the story of a young army officer who attempts to extricate the supernatural secret of winning at cards from an old lady, first by seducing her ward, then by threatening her directly. She dies, but her ghost visits the young man and offers him the secret … with a string or three attached.

According to European press reviews at the time of the film's initial release, Fejos successfully built tension to a thrilling, special effects-laden climax. The sets, costumes and lighting also garnered positive praise. The film was, in more than one critic's estimation, an "artistic achievement," which makes it all the sadder that it's currently unavailable.

Fejos was Hungary's premier director. Born in Budapest in 1897 as Pál Fajos, he got his start in the Hungarian film industry in 1919. After several notable successes there, he moved to the United States in 1924 and became a short-lived talent in Hollywood under the name Paul Fejos. He landed a directorial deal with Universal and directed the Conrad Veidt vehicle *The Last Performance* (1927). A restless spirit, he went on to become a director for Nordisk in Denmark, and made his last film, a documentary titled *Yagua*, in Peru in 1941. He died in New York City in 1963. In addition to being a filmmaker, he was also a noted scientist, publishing several papers on chemistry.

The next known film to be titled *Queen of Spades* came in 1925. It was a Western having nothing to do with Pushkin's story, which would next be adapted for the big screen in Germany in 1927. CW

A Spectre Haunts Europe
aka **Prizrak brodit po Yevrope**
VUFKY; b/w; 94 min; Russia
D: Vladimir R. Gardin *S:* Georgi Tasin *C:* Boris Zavelev
Cast: Zoya Barantsevich, Oleg Frelikh, Yevgenii Gryaznov, Lidiya Iskritskaya-Gardina, Ivan Kapralov, Vasili Kovrigin

Though Russian filmmakers made hundreds of films during the silent era, this is one of the few horror movies to be produced there—along with two versions of *The Queen of Spades* (1910 and 1916) and two of *The Vij* (1908 and 1916).

Spectre was tenuously based on Edgar Allan Poe's 1842 short story *The Masque of the Red Death*, about an apparition that reveals itself during a costumed ball in an old European castle. The spirit strikes down Prince Prospero and his guests, a group that has holed up inside the castle's walls to escape a plague raging outside. As Poe makes clear, the sadistic Prospero, having refused to help his suffering subjects, is deserving of his fate.

Here, the egocentric leader of a fictional European nation goes for a walk and comes across a lonely shepherdess. He falls in love with her, but fate dictates that he be tormented by the people he has subjugated and tyrannized. There's little of Poe's story here and even less horror, with much of the emphasis on adultery and court intrigue. The film was shot on location in Crimea by noted Russian cinematographer Boris Zavelev. Though often cited as a 1921 release, Russian sources indicate that it was actually released in 1922. CW

Spooks
Hamilton-White; b/w; 22 min; U.S.
D/P: Jack White
Cast: Lige Conley

This short horror comedy from European-born director/producer Jack White was released on April 16, 1922. It presents White regular Lige Conley as a man who spends the night in a wax museum with the aim of winning a prize. There he faces the obligatory spooks of the film's title.

Even in 1922, this scenario was far from original, with a chamber of horrors providing the backdrop for terror as far back as Maurice Costello's *Conscience* in 1912. The idea really caught on in the early 1930s, however, with such efforts as *The Secrets of the French Police* (1932) and *The Mystery of the Wax Museum* (1933).

White wrote, produced and directed numerous short films between 1917 and 1959. Lige Conley's acting career, on the other hand, ended with the coming of sound, and he died in 1937 after being hit by an automobile.

Some sources list Robert Kerr as a co-director on this picture. CW

Trilby
aka **Tense Moments with Great Authors: Trilby**
Master; b/w; 15 min; Great Britain
D: Harry B. Parkinson *S:* Walter Courtenay Rowden
Cast: Phyllis Nelson-Terry, Charles Garry, Hilda Moore

This was the first film in Master's *Tense Moments with Great Authors* series, which contained a total of 12 films, all produced in 1922. *Les Miserables*, *Sappho*, *Nancy*, *Fagin*, *La Tosca*, *Scrooge*, *Vanity Fair*, *East Lynne*, *A Tale of Two Cities*, *Moths* and *David Garrick* were the others in the series; and the works of Alphonso Daudet, Charles Dickens, Victor Hugo, William Makepeace Thackeray and Mrs. Henry Wood formed the basis of these entries. All were directed by Harry B. Parkinson and written by Walter Courtenay Rowden (who is sometimes listed as co-director). Parkinson also produced and directed *Tense Moments from Great Plays*, as well as produced *Tense Moments from Opera* (both 1922).

Trilby is based on George Du Maurier's blockbuster novel of the same title, first published as a serial in *Harper's* in 1894. It concerns the beautiful young Trilby O'Farrell (Nelson-Terry) who falls under the spell of the vile Svengali (Garry). Svengali hopes to not only make Trilby a great opera singer (which he does), but force her to love him (which he doesn't). CW

1923

Aaron's Rod
Stoll; b/w; 21 min; Great Britain
D/Co-S: A.E. Coleby *Co-S:* Frank Wilson *P:* Oswald Stoll *C:* D.P. Cooper, Phil Ross

Cast: Harry Agar Lyons, Fred Paul, Joan Clarkson, H. Humberston Wright, Frank Wilson, Percy Standing

In Biblical mythology, Moses' brother Aaron carried a wooden staff with miraculous powers. The Book of Exodus tells how the rod was cast to the ground before Pharaoh and became a serpent that devoured those conjured by the court's magicians. In the Book of Numbers, the stick blossomed with life, even bearing ripe almonds. Judaic tradition maintains that the rod was passed down along generations, going through a number of important hands, including those of a young David around the time he slew the giant Goliath. After being concealed, along with the Ark of the Covenant, by King Josiah, the rod's whereabouts are said to have become and remain lost.

With one of its two reels missing, it's difficult to know the complete plot of this, the ninth film in the Fu Manchu series launched by *The Scented Envelopes* (1923). What is known is that it concerns Fu Manchu's attempt to obtain Aaron's rod in hopes of using its occult powers for his own evil purposes. A man who owns the artifact, Abel Slattin (Standing), is killed and Fu Manchu (Lyons) sends his servant to Slattin's home to steal the relic. But Dr. Petrie (Wright) knocks the man out by striking him with a rod that bears the head of a snake. The rod turns out to be, yes, the staff of Aaron, with a living, moving, venomous serpent's head—the bite of which, it is revealed, is what killed Slattin.

Despite the loss of half of the film, *Aaron's Rod* appears to have been the most overtly supernatural entry in the series. Shortly thereafter, Smith and Petrie would find themselves threatened by a new horror, *The Fiery Hand* (1923). CW

The Bells
aka **Gems of Literature #6: The Bells**
British & Colonial; b/w; 20 min; Great Britain
D: Edwin Greenwood *S:* Elliot Stannard *P:* Edward Godal
Cast: Russell Thorndike, Arthur Walcott, Daisy Agnew

Background information is sparse about this obscure adaptation of Leopold Lewis' adaptation of Émile Erckmann and Alexandre Chatrian's play *Le Juif Polonaise* ("The Polish Jew"), first performed in 1867. It *is* known, however, that the film featured actor/writer Russell Thorndike as Mathias, an indebted innkeeper who kills a wealthy Jew but is driven to remorse when visions of the man's ghost are evoked by a mesmerist (played by Arthur Walcott).

Lewis' play achieved fame with English actor Sir Henry Irving in 1871 and again in the early 1900s by Irving's son H.B. *The Bells* wasn't Lewis' only theatrical flirtation with Judaism; he also wrote *The Wandering Jew*, which was first presented at the Adelphi Theater on April 14, 1873, just two years after *The Bells* debuted at the Lyceum Theater in London.

The film was released on May 1, 1923. CW

The Bishop of the Ozarks
Cosmopolitan; b/w; 54 min; U.S.
D/S: Finis Fox *C:* Sol Polito
Cast: Milford W. Howard, Derelys Perdue, Cecil Holland, Fred Kelsey, William Kenton, R.D. MacLean

A bizarre mix of religious melodrama and subdued horror, the latter reminiscent of George Du Maurier's bestselling 1894 novel *Trilby*, this film proffers escaped criminal Tom Sullivan (Howard) stealing the identity of recently deceased minister Roger Chapman, to whom he bears an uncanny resemblance. Taking over Chapman's work, Sullivan becomes beloved by the mountain folk to whom he ministers, resulting in his change of heart and acceptance of Jesus Christ (as well as the commutation of his sentence by the governor). When Chapman's daughter Margery (Perdue) is wooed by two suitors—a doctor (Kenton) who truly loves her and another (Holland) who seeks control of her via supernatural powers—Sullivan invokes the Holy Ghost to surmount the evil of beau #2.

In addition to a séance and telepathy, there is "a definite instance in which occult powers are demonstrated," according to the magazine *Moving Picture World*, dated March 10, 1923. Director Finis Fox's script came from a story by Milford W. Howard, who starred in the dual roles of Tom Sullivan and Roger Chapman. A two-term congressman from Alabama, Howard was born near Rome, Georgia in 1862. Interested in writing, he moved to Los Angeles in 1918 and embarked on a career as a novelist and editor. *The Bishop of the Ozarks* was the only film adaptation of his work and the only time he ever acted on the screen. He died in 1937 and is interred in the Sallie Howard Chapel near Mentone, Alabama.

The film was released in February 1923 to decent reviews. CW

Blood and Soul
aka **Chi to rei**
Nikkatsu; b/w; length unknown; Japan
D/Co-S: Kenji Mizoguchi *Co-S:* Kokuseki Oizuimi *C:* Junichiro Aoshima
Cast: Yutaka Mimasu, Yoneko Sakai, Ryotaro Mizushima

This was the first horror film from acclaimed director Kenji Mizoguchi, who went on to direct *Passion of a Woman Teacher* (1926) and *The 47 Ronin* (two parts, both 1941). Based on a novel by E.T.A. Hoffman, *Blood and Soul*'s look and style were seemingly informed by silent German Expressionism in general and *The Cabinet of Dr. Caligari* (1919) in particular. The film concerns a Chinese jeweler, disfigured by a hereditary disease, who is driven to rob and murder with reckless abandon.

Blood was released on November 9, 1923, a little over two months after the Great Kanto earthquake. Japanese critics at the time panned the film as a vapid exercise in European style. When screened in Europe, however, it met with a more positive reception, making lamentable the fact that it, like the aforementioned *Passion of a Woman Teacher*, is today considered lost. CW

The Call of Siva
Stoll; b/w; 21 min; Great Britain
D/Co-S: A.E. Coleby *Co-S:* Frank Wilson *P:* Oswald Stoll *C:* D.P. Cooper, Phil Ross
Cast: Harry Agar Lyons, Fred Paul, Joan Clarkson, H. Humberston Wright, Frank Wilson, Harry J. Worth

After its popular series of Sherlock Holmes shorts (directed by Maurice Elvey and starring Eille Norwood), Stoll set its sights on Sax Rohmer's famous Oriental villain Fu Manchu, who'd been introduced to the public in a short-story-collection-turned-novel called *The Mystery of Fu Manchu* in 1912-13. Stoll's series, collectively titled *The Mystery of Dr. Fu-Manchu*, contained 15 films, each a self-contained narrative, all released the same day (though in different venues) throughout Britain. The first three films (in terms of series chronology) were *The Scented Envelopes*, *The West Case* and *The Case of the Pigtail*. While these entries flirt with Fu Manchu's uncanny abilities—he demonstrates hypnotic powers and is unscathed when shot point blank—the fourth film in the series, *The Call of Siva*, is more frankly horrific.

On their way to warn expatriated British citizen Graham Guthrie (Worth) that his return to his home in Bhutan may be complicated by an attempt on his life, Nayland Smith (Paul) and Dr. Petrie (Wright) are kidnapped by their arch nemesis, Fu Manchu (Lyons). They are taken to the villain's obligatory evil lair and there tortured by snakes, scorpions and spiders, among other things. In the process, Fu mentions that Guthrie will die when he hears the call of Siva at 12:30 that night. Fortunately, Fu Manchu's disloyal slave/agent Karamenah is nearby, and she helps the two men escape to the River Thames. From there, with a scant two hours before Siva demands that Guthrie throw himself from atop a building, Smith and Petrie rush to Guthrie's apartment. As they save the day, Smith is attacked by one of Fu Manchu's men, whom he shoots and kills. The film concludes with the spirit of Fu Manchu passing between the heroes, another in a string of hints that the Asian villain has unspecified supernatural powers.

The next two-reel tale in the series is *The Miracle* (1923). CW

The Clue of the Pigtail
Stoll; b/w; 22 min; Great Britain
D/Co-S: A.E. Coleby *Co-S:* Frank Wilson *P:* Oswald Stoll *C:* D.P. Cooper, Phil Ross
Cast: Harry Agar Lyons, Fred Paul, Joan Clarkson, H. Humberston Wright, Frank Wilson, Ernest Spalding

The Clue of the Pigtail is the third film in Stoll's 1923 series of two-reelers, *The Mystery of Dr. Fu-Manchu*. It puts Karamenah (Clarkson), Fu Manchu's sexy slave/agent, front and center.

When Nayland Smith (Paul) and Dr. Petrie (Wright) find a pigtail attached to the body of a murdered detective, Petrie goes to the victim's home to investigate. There he finds the sultry Karamenah, who begs him to save her from her evil boss. Further investigation leads Smith and Petrie to an opium den, where their cover is blown and they wind up confronting none other than Fu Manchu (Lyons) himself. In the end Karamenah saves them, while Fu (in what was to become a standard outcome in these films) eludes capture.

Pigtail continues the progressive dehumanization of Fu Manchu, here imbuing him with an aura of supernatural invulnerability as Smith and Petrie fire their revolvers directly into him and he escapes unharmed. His next appearance is in the more overtly horrific *The Call of Siva* (1923), which showcases his penchant for torture.

Actress Joan Clarkson, who portrayed Karamenah in this first series of Fu Manchu pictures, never starred in another film after the series ended. Little else is known about her, and Dorinea Shirley replaced her in the second series. CW

The Cry of the Nighthawk
Stoll; b/w; 25 min; Great Britain
D/Co-S: A.E. Coleby *Co-S:* Frank Wilson *P:* Oswald Stoll *C:* D.P. Cooper, Phil Ross
Cast: Harry Agar Lyons, Fred Paul, Joan Clarkson, H. Humberston Wright, Frank Wilson, Harold Cundell

The 1923 Stoll series *The Mystery of Dr. Fu-Manchu* followed *The Knocking on the Door* (the seventh of its 15 two-reelers) with a notably silly eighth installment titled *The Cry of the Nighthawk*. Here, a tree outside Dr. Petrie's office shines mysteriously in the night. When Petrie (Wright) and a patient named Forsyth (Cundell) investigate, a nighthawk's cry draws Forsyth's attention upward onto the tree's branches. A cat falls onto his head, its poison-dipped claws scratching his face and he falls dead instantly—the victim of an attack intended for Nayland Smith (Paul). The next day, Petrie catches sight of a mysterious old woman and follows her into a field. She proves to be none other than Karamenah (Clarkson), the ex-assistant of Fu Manchu (Lyons) who has again fallen under the Asian villain's sway. She escapes with Petrie, and when he next sees Smith, he learns that Smith has caught—and apparently killed—a cat with poisoned claws. As night returns, the tree outside Petrie's practice once again glows with a foreboding light. This time it's Smith who joins Petrie in checking it out, and they discover (and kill) the henchman who, the night before, had pretended to be a nighthawk so as to drop the toxic-toed cat onto its victim's face. As Smith and Petrie leave the scene, Fu Manchu appears and disappears via a trick photographic effect. The shot is striking in its implication of Fu Manchu's preternatural powers.

Nighthawk was based on Chapter 4 of Sax Rohmer's 1916 novel *The Return of Dr. Fu-Manchu* (aka *The Devil Doctor*).

Fu Manchu next menaced Smith and Petrie with *Aaron's Rod (1923)*. CW

The Drums of Jeopardy
Tru-art/Hoffman; b/w; 70 min; U.S.
D: Edward Dillon *S:* Arthur Hoerl, Alfred A. Cohn, A. Carle Palm *P:* M.H. Hoffman *C:* James Diamond
Cast: Elaine Hammerstein, Jack Mulhall, Wallace Beery, David Torrence, Maude George, Eric Mayne

Journalist Harold MacGrath was a successful screenwriter and novelist during the early 20th century. His first novel, *Arms and the Woman*, was published in 1899, with his most successful novel, *The Drums of Jeopardy*, first appearing as a serial in *The Saturday Evening Post* beginning in January 1920. The latter story's villain was a mad Russian scientist named Boris Karlov, a character whose popularity is commonly believed to have inspired an English émigré actor named William Henry Pratt to dub himself Boris Karloff. (In fact, Karloff adopted the name long before McGrath's novel was published.) MacGrath's episodic novel was soon adapted for Broadway, and in 1923 it became the basis for this cinematic treatment. However, with Boris Karloff beginning to make the Hollywood rounds, the villain's name was changed to Gregor Karlov.

Drums concerns Jerome Hawksley (Mulhall), who has been bequeathed two diamonds by Grand Duke Alexis of Russia. The gems bestow a mysterious power upon their owner, and when Gregor Karlov (Beery) learns of them, he immediately sets out to steal them, even if it means killing anyone who gets in his way.

Starring as the vile Gregor Karlov is none other than Wallace Beery, who went on to even greater success in the sound era in such classic films as *The Champ* (1931), *Grand Hotel* (1932), *Din-

films as producer, and its success catapulted him into the big leagues. In 1927 he became president of Tiffany Pictures, and in 1931 he founded Allied Pictures. He died in 1944.

The story was filmed again in 1931 with Warner Oland in the role of Karlov, whose Christian name of Boris was finally returned to him. CW

Faust

Butcher; b/w; 22 min; Great Britain
D: Bertram Phillips S: Frank Miller
Cast: Jeff Barlow, Queenie Thomas, Frank Stanmore, Adeline Hayden Coffin, Fatty Phillips, Peter Upcher

While some sources list this as a comedy, the assertion seems dubious given that it was part of the *Syncopated Picture Plays 2-Reel* series, and that the play on which it was based was a famous tragedy. The film concerns Faust, an aging doctor who regrets having grown old without knowing the passionate embrace of a woman. He calls upon the Devil, who offers him youth and vitality in exchange for his soul. Faust agrees, grows young, and is introduced to the beautiful Marguerite, whom he seduces … Needless to say, it doesn't end well.

Virtually everyone involved in this particular version of Goethe's play were frequent collaborators. The same year they also made *Tut-Tut and His Terrible Tomb* and *The School for Scandal*, the latter noteworthy for having given an early role to future star Basil Rathbone.

The same year that *Faust* was produced, Ernst Lubitsch (*Eyes of the Mummy*, 1918) did some work on a version titled *Faust and Marguerite*, but it was never completed. All that exists of that property today are its screen tests. CW

The Fiery Hand

Stoll; b/w; 29 min; Great Britain
D/Co-S: A.E. Coleby Co-S: Frank Wilson P: Oswald Stoll C: D.P. Cooper, Phil Ross
Cast: Harry Agar Lyons, Fred Paul, Joan Clarkson, H. Humberston Wright, Frank Wilson, Pat Royale

The Gables is a house with a haunted history, a situation most recently underscored by the discovery of two occupants—both apparently frightened to death! Nayland Smith (Paul) and Dr. Petrie (Wright) disguise themselves as practitioners of the occult and spend the night there to investigate. Once darkness falls, they experience tinkling bells, doors that open and shut by themselves and a ghostly, flaming hand holding a dagger. While these things frighten Petrie, Smith believes them to be the work of arch criminal Fu Manchu for the purpose of scaring people away from one of his lairs. After Smith and Petrie return to London, Karamenah's (Clarkson) brother Aziz (Royale) approaches them and begs them to (again) save his sister from Manchu, her former master. When the two attempt to do so, they are captured

ner at Eight (1933) and *Treasure Island* (1934). The heroic Jerome Hawksley is played by Jack Mulhall, who worked in films from 1910 to 1959; his final appearance was in the sublimely ridiculous *The Atomic Submarine*. Elaine Hammerstein played love interest Dorothy Burrows, and she got her start portraying Rachel Verinder in the 1915 adaptation of Wilkie Collins' *The Moonstone*. The granddaughter of Oscar Hammerstein and daughter of Arthur Hammerstein, her career never made it out of the silent era. She was killed in an automobile accident in Mexico in 1948 that also claimed the life of her husband, a prominent member of the California Democratic Party.

M.H. Hoffman, who had worked as a manager at Universal, produced *The Drums of Jeopardy*. It was one of his earliest and tortured in a cellar until an escaped Karamenah appears. She shoots Fu Manchu, and the cellar collapses. The Asian mastermind's body can't be found in the ruins, leading Smith to believe that the evildoer has escaped yet again.

The Fiery Hand is the 10th in Stoll's first Fu Manchu two-reeler series; its title was taken from Chapter 26 of Sax Rohmer's 1916 novel *The Return of Dr. Fu Manchu* (aka *The Devil Doctor*). Though not as supernatural as the series' previous outing (*Aaron's Rod*, 1923), *Hand*'s haunted house and torture dungeon settings (courtesy of art director Walter H. Murton) make it clear to which genre the film belongs.

The next film in the series is the decidedly less horrific *The Man with the Limp* (also 1923). CW

The Fungi Cellars
Stoll; b/w; 21 min; Great Britain
D/Co-S: A.E. Coleby *Co-S:* Frank Wilson *P:* Oswald Stoll *C:* D.P. Cooper, Phil Ross
Cast: Harry Agar Lyons, Fred Paul, Joan Clarkson, H. Humberston Wright, Frank Wilson, Pat Royale

Fu Manchu's ex-assistant Karamenah (Clarkson) tells Nayland Smith (Paul) and Dr. Petrie (Wright) that she will take them to Fu Manchu if they will rescue her younger brother Aziz (Royale) from the evil mastermind's clutches. They agree, and she takes Smith, Petrie and Scotland Yard Inspector Weymouth (Wilson) to Fu's lair, where they are promptly captured and tied up. They watch helplessly as several police officers arrive, become trapped in a cellar with fungal growths on the walls and are killed by the poisonous spores. Knowing that, with his location revealed, there isn't much time before more officers arrive, Fu Manchu shuffles his remaining prisoners aboard a boat in which he plans to escape (wired with a ticking bomb in case he needs to dispose of his trussed enemies early). But when the criminal mastermind tries to kill Karamenah, Weymouth wiggles free and takes on Fu Manchu. The two struggle and disappear into the water while the rest of the party goes free. Weymouth winds up rescued while Fu escapes to shore.

Cellars is the sixth film in the series *The Mystery of Dr. Fu-Manchu*. Along with the rest of them, cinematographers D.P. Cooper and Phil Ross shot the film partially on location, this time along the River Thames (possibly near Windsor, where parts of *The Call of Siva*, 1923, had been filmed). Cooper went on to shoot *The Greed of William Hart* in 1948, which is one of Tod Slaughter's last theatrical horror films. CW

The Hunchback of Notre Dame
Universal; b/w; 122 min; U.S.
D: Wallace Worsley *S:* Edward T. Lowe, Jr., Perley Poore Sheehan *P:* Carl Laemmle, Irving Thalberg *C:* Robert Newhard, Tony Kornman, Virgil Miller, Stephen S. Norton, Charles J. Stumar
Cast: Lon Chaney, Patsy Ruth Miller, Norman Kerry, Ernest Torrence, Brandon Hurst, Kate Lester

Paris, 1482; the city is sharply divided between the rich and the poor, and a mass rebellion led by Clopin (Torrence) is imminent. In the midst of this, Quasimodo (Chaney), an unsightly hunchback, falls in love with a beautiful Gypsy named Esmeralda (Miller). Esmeralda, however, is in love with a dashing nobleman named Phoebus (Kerry). When the corrupt Jehan Frollo (Hurst) stabs Phoebus, the Gypsy is accused and put on trial. Esmeralda had earlier rejected the lovelorn Frollo, and this is his revenge. The trial culminates with the girl being condemned to death, but Quasimodo comes to the rescue, dramatically saving her from the scaffold and closeting her in the sanctuary of the Notre Dame cathedral.

Lon Chaney as Quasimodo with Patsy Ruth Miller as Esmeralda from *The Hunchback of Notre Dame*

Novelist, poet, playwright and political activist Victor Hugo (1802-1885) created one of his most enduring works with the 1831 publication of *The Hunchback of Notre Dame*. Despite its grotesque central character, the book was not really intended to be frightening. Hugo's intent was, rather, to construct a sociopolitical allegory to explore the political and religious mindset of a particular culture and period. The hunchback is a misunderstood misfit, not a bloodthirsty monster. Even so, the character has entered the pantheon of movie monsters due almost entirely to the unforgettable impression made by Lon Chaney in this 1923 film adaptation.

This was not the first time the story had made its way to the screen. As far back as 1905, the 10-minute short *Esmeralda* (original French title: *La esméralda*) sought to bring the tale's cutting political commentary and lush visual pageantry to life. Other early versions included a 1911 French film titled *Notre-Dame de Paris*, an American feature titled *The Darling of Paris* (1917) starring silent screen vamp Theda Bara and a 1922 adaptation also titled *Esmeralda*, among others. (F.W. Murnau's *The Hunchback and the Dancer*, 1920, is assumed by many to be an adaptation, but a look at the lost film's synopsis reveals that the story has nothing to do with Hugo's novel.)

It is the 1923 version that is most deeply etched into the consciousness of the public. The reasons for this have less to do with its merits as a film than they do with the central performance—and make-up—of silent screen legend Lon Chaney.

Surviving documents from the files of Chaney's business manager Alfred Grasso establish that it was Chaney who pushed for the film to be made. The actor had read Hugo's novel and was immediately captivated by the description of the hunchbacked bell ringer of the Notre Dame Cathedral. Having established himself as a bankable star with 1920's *The Penalty*, Chaney commanded a high salary ($2,500 a week) and plenty of clout. It took a great deal of persistence, however, to find a studio willing to put up the money for such a grand production. Eventually Universal optioned the project, but Chaney was frequently exasperated with the selective penny-pinching antics of the studio.

While no expense was spared in the creation of the massive Notre Dame set, Universal managed to find ways of cutting corners in other areas, notably in the hiring of a suitable director. According to the commentary by Chaney scholar Michael F. Blake for the 2007 Image Entertainment DVD release of *Hunchback*, the actor campaigned for the services of an A-level director like Frank Borzage or Raoul Walsh, but Universal held fast in its insistence upon a less extravagant choice. (No doubt the studio's woes in dealing with the notorious Erich Von Stroeheim on *Blind Husbands* (1919) and *Foolish Wives* (1922) were somehow connected to their reluctance.) In any event, Chaney reluctantly accepted Universal's choice of Wallace Worsley, a journeyman whose credits reveal little of lasting interest. (Worsley had, however, directed Chaney in *The Penalty* and, as a result, there was enough familiarity between the two to ensure a smooth collaboration.)

Rumors have long circulated that Chaney directed much of the film himself, but little evidence has ever emerged to prove this. In any case, it is the film's thoroughly uninspired direction that proves to be its downfall. Worsley displays little affinity for his performers, many of whom shamelessly overact. His blocking and staging are usually competent but never inspired. The massive sets, while impressive, are seldom utilized to their full potential. Ultimately, the film emerges as something of a missed opportunity—interesting enough on its own merits, but with little advantage taken of the potential that could have made it a bona fide classic.

While much of the acting appears stilted or hammy by today's standards, the high regard for Chaney's performance remains justifiably undiminished. The legendary "Man of 1,000 Faces" inarguably rose to the challenge of bringing Quasimodo to life—his make-up reflects careful consideration of the physical description of the character in Hugo's novel, and his acting is often striking in its nuance and detail. He does not play the character as a monster but instead as a lonely misfit, too grotesque to fit in with polite society, yet possessing a sensitivity that far exceeds that of the people around him. Especially when compared to the posturing Phoebus (a dreadfully dated performance from Norman Kerry), Chaney comes across as sweet and lovable. The vivid impression made by his physical appearance has

made the character a staple in horror film iconography, but there is nothing horrific in his realization of the character's psyche and emotions.

Of the supporting players, only Patsy Ruth Miller and Ernest Torrence make much of an impression. Miller is pretty and vivacious in her portrayal of Esmeralda, while Torrence does a capable job of playing her foster father, the Parisian "King of the Underworld."

All things considered, William Dieterle's 1939 version starring Charles Laughton is a far more satisfactory dramatization of Hugo's novel. TH

Itching Palms
FBO/Robertson-Cole; b/w; 66 min; U.S.
D: James W. Horne
Cast: Tom Gallery, Virgina Fox, Tom Wilson, Victor Potel, Herschell Mayall, Joseph Harrington

Based on the play "When Jerry Comes Home" by Roy Briant, *Itching Palms* concerns two crooks (Mayall, Walker) in a dispute over a bag of stolen cash. One hides the cash in a reputedly haunted house before being murdered by the other. The surviving crook then assumes the identity of the sinister Doctor Peak and is forced to match wits with his former partner's mother (Claire), who knows the approximate whereabouts of the money. When her grandson Jerry (Gallery) appears, he and "Doctor Peak" battle it out, only to discover the stolen loot hidden in a well. Their bout causes the house to catch fire, though not before the money is saved. Unfortunately, it turns out to be counterfeit.

In addition to directing numerous films, James W. Horne also took on bit parts in various productions, including such horror features as *The Imp Abroad* and *The Invisible Power* (both 1914). His horror-related directorial efforts included *The Vivisectionist* (1915) and *Scared Stiff* (1926).

Itching Palms was released on July 22, 1923. CW

The Knocking on the Door
Stoll; b/w; 29 min; Great Britain
D/Co-S: A.E. Coleby *Co-S:* Frank Wilson *P:* Oswald Stoll
C: D.P. Cooper, Phil Ross
Cast: Harry Agar Lyons, Fred Paul, Joan Clarkson, H. Humberston Wright, Frank Wilson, W.G. Saunders, Pat Royale

Each consecutive film in Stoll's 1923 series of two-reelers, titled *The Mystery of Dr. Fu-Manchu*, tended to up the ante on fantastic and horrific elements. In this, the seventh entry, Inspector Weymouth (Wilson) has gone crazy and run off after being poisoned by Fu Manchu during their climactic battle in *The Fungi Cellars* (the sixth film). Weymouth's brother James (Saunders) is looking after Weymouth's wife, who's being awakened nightly by a knocking on her front door. The story proper kicks in when, following a tour of Madame Tussauds' waxworks in London, Nayland Smith (Paul), Dr. Petrie (Wright), Manchu's sultry ex-assistant Karamenah (Clarkson) and her brother Aziz (Royale) spot a mysterious figure whom Aziz insists is Fu Manchu (Lyons). In due course, Smith and Petrie discover that yes, it was indeed Fu, and also that it's the hopelessly insane Weymouth who's been knocking on his wife's door. After Fu Manchu's men kidnap Karamenah, Smith and Petrie learn that Scotland Yard has captured the master criminal. Agreeing to cure Weymouth of his insanity, but only in a spot of

Henry Hull, Louis Calhern and Doris Kenyon play the kidnapped victims of *The Last Moment*.

his own choosing, Fu Manchu leads the group to a peculiar cottage outside town. There he does indeed cure Weymouth, but he is also apparently killed in an explosion he has orchestrated.

Actor W.G. Saunders, who plays James Weymouth, starred in relatively few films during his 20-year career. After the first of Stoll's two Fu Manchu series ended, Saunders starred in director Coleby's *The Prehistoric Man* (1924), a send-up of the idea that man evolved from more primitive primates. (Its comedic plot involved prehistoric cars, football cups and slave auctions.)

With late-night rappings at the door, Smith's visions of Fu Manchu and the isolated setting of the country cottage (courtesy of art director Walter H. Murton), *Knocking* posits its characters in an eerie setting that is most definitely the stuff of nightmares, though the horror elements are balanced by a fast-paced sense of adventure.

The next film in the series is *The Cry of the Nighthawk* (1923). CW

The Last Moment
Goldwyn; b/w; 62 min; U.S.
D/P: J. Parker Read, Jr. S: J. Clarkson Miller C: J.O. Taylor
Cast: Henry Hull, Doris Kenyon, Louis Walheim, Louis Calhern, William Nally, Mickey Bennett

Hercules Napoleon Cameron (Hull) has an imposing name … and little else. He attempts to woo Alice Winthrop (Kenyon), but he has a rival in the handsome and manly Harry Gaines (Calhern). The three are kidnapped when they visit a shady saloon, and Alice finds herself being menaced by a monster.

This obscure picture is a typical (for the time) melodrama melding horror with humor. The eventful scenario, based on a story by Jack Doyle, trades on humorous stereotypes in its depiction of a love triangle between a bland heroine and two contrasting beaus, the simpering and cowardly Napoleon and the macho Harry.

Director J. Parker Read, Jr. was involved in a small number of films in the silent era. He helmed only four between 1913 and 1923, of which *The Last Moment* was the last.

The cast includes two actors who went on to bigger and better things. Henry Hull makes one of his earliest film appearances, having been in only one other comedy/horror film, *One Exciting Night* (1922), just before headlining this picture. Universal Studios later attempted to transform him into a horror star with *Werewolf of London* (1935), but the actor balked at being typecast and resisted involvement with further films of the horror ilk. Born in 1890 in Louisville, Kentucky, Hull established himself as a serious stage performer before trying his hand as a gold prospector and mining engineer. When he didn't make a go of either, he returned to acting. And while he never became a major star—critics and audiences found him too mannered—he did appear in a steady stream of films of various types through the mid-60s before retiring to his farm in Connecticut. He died in 1977.

The Last Moment also marks an early appearance by smooth-as-silk character actor Louis Calhern. Later nominated for an Oscar for his portrayal of Oliver Wendell Holmes in *The Magnificent Yankee* (1950), Calhern worked for such auteurs as John Huston (*The Asphalt Jungle*, 1950), Alfred Hitchcock (*Notorious*, 1946) and Joseph L. Mankiewicz (*Julius Caesar*, 1953).

The remainder of the cast failed to find lasting success, though leading lady Doris Kenyon played a minor role in James Whale's last respectable picture, *The Man in the Iron Mask* (1939). TH

The Lost Soul, or: The Dangers of Hypnosis
aka **Das Verlorene Ich**; **Gefahren der Hypnose**; **The Dangers of Hypnosis**; **The Lost Soul**
Astra; b/w; length unknown; Austria
D: Hugo Werner-Kahle S: L. Thomas, J. Malina C: Rudolf Maté, Hans Pebal
Cast: Hugo Werner-Kahle, Paul Kronegg, Annemarie Steinsieck

This should not be confused with Richard Eichberg's *Hypnosis* (1920), which despite containing an early Bela Lugosi appearance was not a horror film. Little information has survived about *The Lost Soul*, but to judge from its alternate titles, it was likely a cautionary tale against the then-popular pseudoscience of hypnotism. Hypnotism, also called mesmerism, had informed such seminal written works of horror and melodrama as Bram Stoker's *Dracula* (1897) and George Du Maurier's *Trilby* (1894). As such, it also inevitably reared its head in early horror films.

The Lost Soul starred and was directed by Hugo Werner-Kahle, a stage performer who made a successful transition to silent and then to talking pictures. He was active between 1913 and 1944, amassing a number of credits as an actor in both leading and supporting roles. His work as a director was, by comparison, sporadic.

The film also featured early cinematography by Rudolf Mate, who later became one of the industry's most sought-after directors of photography; he is renowned for his work on Carl Theodor Dreyer's *The Passion of Joan of Arc* (1928) and *Vampyr* (1932), and he went on to be nominated for five Oscars for such films as Alfred Hitchcock's *Foreign Correspondent* (1940) and Alexander Korda's *That Hamilton Woman* (1941). Mate also directed the noir classic *D.O.A.* (1950), though he never attained the same renown as a director that he did as a cinematographer. TH

Lucrezia Borgia; Or, Playing of Power
British and Colonial Kinematograph; b/w; length unknown; Great Britain
D: Edwin Greenwood S: Eliot Stannard P: Edward Godal
Cast: Nina Vana, Russell Thorndike

Yet another big-screen version of the Borgia family's foibles, this time starring Dame Sybil Thorndike's younger brother Russell, who was not only a star of the silent screen but found fame in 1915 as the novelist of *Dr. Syn: A Tale of the Romney Marsh* (itself adapted to the big screen in 1937, 1962 and 1964). Here he plays the violent Cesare Borgia, who lusts after his illegitimate sister, Lucrezia (Vana). Given the film's title, it's likely that it took the same position as so many films before and after it, that Lucrezia was the innocent pawn of her older brother who used her to gain power by marrying her into wealthy, powerful Italian families.

Thorndike also starred in two films from the *Tense Moments from Great Plays* series, which includes *Macbeth* and *It's Never Too Late to Mend* (both 1922), as well as in the 1923 version of *The Bells*, in which he played murderer Mathias.

The next film appearance of the Borgia family came in Warner's big budget *Don Juan* (1926). That film starred silent film superstar John Barrymore as Don Juan, who, after rejecting the advances of Lucrezia Borgia (Estelle Taylor), finds the entire Borgia family coming down on his head. Future definitive Charlie Chan actor Warner Oland starred as Cesare Borgia, while Myrna Loy had a part as a Lady in Waiting. CW

The Man with the Limp
Stoll; b/w; 26 min; Great Britain
D/Co-S: A.E. Coleby *Co-S:* Frank Wilson *P:* Oswald Stoll *C:* D.P. Cooper, Phil Ross
Cast: Harry Agar Lyons, Fred Paul, Joan Clarkson, H. Humberston Wright, Frank Wilson, Julie Suedo, Roy Raymond

The 11th and perhaps least horrific entry in *The Mystery of Dr. Fu-Manchu*, a series of 15 two-reel features that begins with *The Scented Envelopes* and ends with *The Shrine of the Seven Lamps* (both—and the 13 between them, for that matter—released on the same day in 1923), *The Man with the Limp* concerns an attempt on the life of Sir John Trevor, a former ambassador, by a mysterious man with a limp. Although Fu Manchu (Lyons) is apparently dead (shot at the end of the previous film and buried beneath the rubble of a collapsed cellar), Nayland Smith (Paul) suspects that he might somehow have survived and may be plotting his next nefarious move against the British government. While investigating, Smith discovers that a man with a limp runs an Asian club known as the Joy-Shop Club. The hero is taken captive but rescued by his comrades—Dr. Petrie (Wright), Inspector Weymouth (Wilson) and Sergeant Fletcher (Raymond)—while the man with the limp is indeed revealed to be none other than Fu Manchu.

The idea for the film was lifted from Sax Rohmer's 1917 novel *The Hand of Fu Manchu* (aka *The Si-Fan Mysteries*).

This entry introduces newcomer Julie Suedo as Zarmi, a despicable female agent of Fu Manchu. She returned in the very next film, *The Queen of Hearts*, before disappearing until *The Golden Pomegranates* (1924), the sixth film of the second Stoll series, *The Further Mysteries of Dr. Fu Manchu*. She later played an un-credited part as Orloff's secretary in *The Human Monster* (1939), a classic British horror film that offered Bela Lugosi a rare opportunity to shine in a double role (despite being partially dubbed). CW

The Miracle
Stoll; b/w; 27 min; Great Britain
D/Co-S: A.E. Coleby *Co-S:* Frank Wilson *P:* Oswald Stoll *C:* D.P. Cooper, Phil Ross
Cast: Harry Agar Lyons, Fred Paul, Joan Clarkson, H. Humberston Wright, Frank Wilson, Stacey Gaunt, Austin Leigh

Oswald Stoll's production company released a series of two-reel Fu Manchu films, all on the same spring day in 1923, under the banner of *The Mystery of Dr. Fu-Manchu*. Each is a self-contained narrative (as opposed to a chapter in a serial) beginning with *The Scented Envelopes* and continuing (chronologically) with *The West Case*, *The Clue of the Pigtail*, *The Call of Siva* and this one, *The Miracle*, followed by 10 others. At 27 minutes *Miracle* is a longer-than-average entry, allowing for a little "action-padding" in a program already starting to suffer from redundancy.

Lord Southery (Gaunt) is found dead, and Nayland Smith (Paul) and Dr. Petrie (Wright) conclude that their persistent antagonist, Dr. Fu Manchu (Lyons), is to blame. Fu's traitorous ex-assistant Karamenah (Clarkson) shows up and begs for help for her younger brother Aziz (Royale) who, she maintains, is dying. Smith and Petrie follow her to Fu Manchu's hideout, where they find that Aziz is in fact already dead. Fu enters, and the three watch in hiding as the insidious Chinese villain revives the boy with a mysterious liquid. The two men escape with the elixir, which Petrie uses to revive Southery. The resurrected lord informs them that he'd been poisoned by his own valet (Leigh), himself in the service of the dastardly Manchu. Before Smith and Petrie can apprehend the disloyal servant, he kills himself with the same poisoned port he'd slipped to Southery. (Nobody bothers to revive him.)

Smith, Petrie and Karamenah were next terrorized in *The Fungi Cellars* (1923). CW

The Mistletoe Bough
British & Colonial; b/w; 20 min; Great Britain
D: Edwin J. Collins *S:* Eliot Stannard *P:* Edward Godal
Cast: John Stuart, Flora le Breton, Lionel d'Aragon, William Lugg

The second (and to date most horrific) film to be based on Great Britain's legend of the "mistletoe bough"—the first cinematic take was in 1904—British and Colonial's *The Mistletoe Bough* stars John Stuart and Flora le Breton as newlyweds whose bliss is shattered by tragedy. Adapted from Thomas Haynes Bayley's poem (later set to traditional music) and the 1834 play by Charles Somerset, Stuart plays Lord Lovell, whose beautiful bride Lady Agnes de Clifford goes missing during a Christmas party. Her father, the Baron de Clifford (Lugg), assists in trying to find her but to no avail. Her body is eventually found in a chest, and it's revealed that jilted lover Sir Reginald de Courcey (d'Aragon) placed her there before stabbing her to death and closing the lid. Sir Reginald is subsequently driven to suicide by the young lady's vengeful spirit.

Somerset's two-act play, titled *The Mistletoe Bough; or, The Fatal Chest*, threw a ghastly, mischievous imp into the mix. The play made enough of an impression on writer Henry James that he turned to it as a source of inspiration for his ghostly tale "The Romance of Certain Old Clothes," first published in *The Atlantic Monthly* in February 1868.

The year before this film's release, Edwin J. Collins directed another horror film, *Esmeralda*, based on the famous literary work *Notre Dame de Paris* by Victor Hugo. Strangely enough, he had starred as the lead in a peculiar film version of that same tale, simply titled *The Hunchback*, in 1911.

Three years after the Walterdaw Company released British & Colonial's *The Mistletoe Bough* to theaters, screenwriter George J. Banfield produced his own version of the tale as part of his *Haunted Houses and Castles of Great Britain* series of pseudo-documentaries. CW

The Monkey's Paw
Artistic; b/w; 64 (55) min; Great Britain
D: Manning Haynes *S:* Lydia Hayward *P:* George Redman
Cast: Moore Marriott, Marie Ault, Charles Ashton, Johnny Butt, A.B. Imeson, George Wynn

Based on W.W. Jacob's 1902 short story of the same title, *The Monkey's Paw* is an early feature-length horror film from Great Britain. British mainstay Moore Marriott (*Sweeney Todd*, 1928) stars as Mr. White, who has received from a friend (Butt) a monkey's paw with the power to grant three wishes. His first wish results in the death of his son (Ashton). His wife (Ault) makes the next wish, which is to bring her dead son back to life. But when the boy comes back as a zombie, the father wishes him back into his grave to rest peacefully.

As with the 1910 version of the tale, this film incorporated elements from Louis N. Parker's 1907 one-act play and, while relatively faithful to the original source, emphasized the sinister aspects of the story. CW

Nabeshima no neko
Shochiku; b/w; length unknown; Japan
D: Jiro Yoshino
Cast: Shirogoro Yoshino

It was inevitable that Nikkatsu's biggest rival in the horror genre would create its own adaptation of Joko Segawa III's classic 1853 Kabuki play *Hana Saga neko mata zoshi*. Directed by Shochiku's lead filmmaker Jiro Yoshino, it starred the company's lead actor Shirogoro Yoshino. Though no plot synopsis exists, one can assume that it followed, at least loosely, the play's narrative of a retainer (medieval soldier) named Nabeshima, who murders his master to steal his clan, after which the murdered master's spirit passes into a cat and exacts revenge. CW

Puritan Passions
Film Guild; b/w; 70 min; U.S.
D/Co-S: Frank Tuttle *Co-S:* James Ashmore Creelman
C: Fred Waller
Cast: Glenn Hunter, Mary Astor, Osgood Perkins, Maude Hill, Frank Tweed, Dwight Wiman

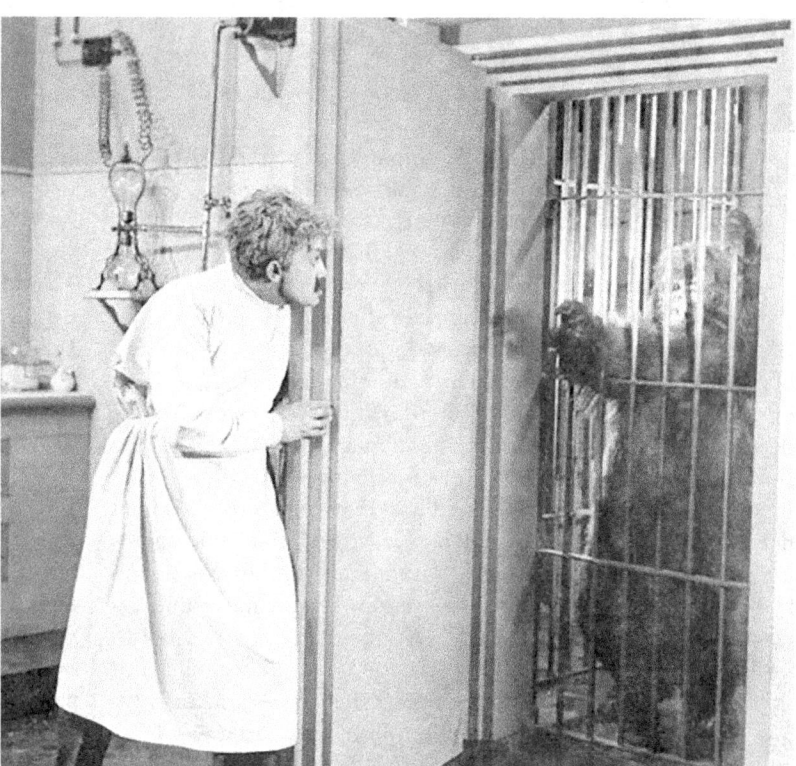

***Red Lights* offers mystery, science fiction, comedy, drama and horror in equal measure.**

Gillead Wingate (Tweed) impregnates Goody Rickby (Hill) but refuses to accept responsibility for their child. The devastated Goody turns to black magic in search of revenge. Years pass, and she becomes adept enough at the dark arts to summon Satan. The two concoct a scheme to destroy Wingate, who has become a respected elder in the community. Satan breathes life into a scarecrow and introduces it to the community as Lord Ravensbane (Hunter). The plan is for Ravensbane to seduce Wingate's niece Rachel (Astor) and convince the villagers that the Wingates practice black magic. But things go south when Ravensbane acquires a soul and falls in love with Rachel.

Director Frank W. Tuttle was born in 1892 in New York. He entered the film industry as a screenwriter in 1921 and made his directorial debut the following year with *The Cradle Buster*. His long and prolific career lasted until 1959's *Island of Lost Women*; he died in 1963.

Puritan Passions was one of Tuttle's earliest films as a director, and it appears to have been one of his most unusual. The story was heavily influenced by a play titled *The Scarecrow* (1908), which was in turn based on a short story by Nathaniel Hawthorne titled *Feathertop: A Moralized Legend*, published in two installments in 1852.

The original tale was much changed by playwright Percy MacKaye and further altered by Tuttle (and co-writer James Ashmore Creelman) on its way to the screen. In Hawthorne's story, a lonely witch called Mother Rigby makes a scarecrow to protect her garden, and then wishes it to life. She sends the creature, which she names Feathertop, to woo Polly Gookin, the daughter of a judge Rigby detests. But in time Polly discovers the true nature of her beau and faints. Feathertop returns to Mother Rigby and, anguished by what has happened, "dies." Mother Rigby realizes the error of her ways and returns Feathertop to the field, where he can be just a scarecrow.

In adapting the story to the stage, MacKaye punched it up by including the Devil as an actual character; the story made a successful Broadway debut in 1911. It would seem that Tuttle's filmic adaptation kept the basics of the play, so why it was retitled as the more generic *Puritan Passions* is anybody's guess.

Leading lady Mary Astor went on to a long and successful career in the cinema. *Puritan Passions* was one of her earliest substantial roles following two years of bit parts. She later weathered a storm of public scandal—a messy divorce in 1936 in which she was romantically linked to numerous prominent names—and continued to secure roles in noteworthy pictures. She is best remembered today as the double-crossing Brigid O'Shaughnessy in John Huston's celebrated directorial debut, *The Maltese Falcon* (1941); she was also a member of the all-star cast of Robert Aldrich's southern gothic *Hush … Hush, Sweet Charlotte* (1964), which proved to be her last film.

The cast of *Passions* includes Osgood Perkins, a busy character actor of the period. He later fathered a son who followed in his footsteps: Anthony Perkins, the star of *Psycho* (1960). TH

The Queen of Hearts
Stoll; b/w; 25 min; Great Britain
D/Co-S: A.E. Coleby *Co-S:* Frank Wilson *P:* Oswald Stoll *C:* D.P. Cooper, Phil Ross
Cast: Harry Agar Lyons, Fred Paul, Joan Clarkson, H. Humberston Wright, Frank Wilson, D. Bland, Julie Suedo, Fred Raynham

Another less than stellar entry in *The Mystery of Dr. Fu-Manchu*, which cast Henry Agar Lyons as cinema's first-ever

Fu Manchu, *The Queen of Hearts* continues the series' move away from outright horror toward adventurous melodrama. The idea for the story was lifted from Chapter 18 of Sax Rohmer's 1917 novel *The Hand of Fu Manchu* (aka *The Si-Fan Mysteries*) and features Julie Suedo's second stint as Fu Manchu's murderous henchwoman, Zarmi. (In 1936 she starred in another film titled *Queen of Hearts*, a stand-alone comedy with no relation to this picture.)

The plot of this—the 12th of 15 two-reelers—concerns the disappearance of famous surgeon Baldwin Frazer (Raynham). Nayland Smith (Paul) and Dr. Petrie (Wright) investigate, interviewing Frazer's secretary Logan (Bland), who reveals that Frazer was last seen in the company of a beautiful woman claiming to have a sick mother. While Smith and Inspector Weymouth (Wilson) search for Frazer and the lady, Petrie does a bit of sleuthing on his own. He comes across Zarmi (Suedo) but, while following her, is captured by Fu Manchu's armed robbers. When he later returns, he at first seems out of his wits but, after coming to his senses, reveals what transpired. Fu Manchu, shot at the end of *The Fiery Hand* (1923), suffered a debilitating paralysis of his leg and face and kidnapped Frazer and Petrie to operate on him. When the operation was finished and Manchu had recovered, the two captives were set free, though not before a game of cards.

The next film in the series, *The Silver Buddha* (1923), continues the series' move away from horrific elements toward the typical xenophobia of the Yellow Peril subgenre. CW

Red Lights concerns a scientist who uses telepathic messages to scare the heroine.

The Red Inn
aka L'auberge rouge
Pathe; b/w; 66 min; France
D/S: Jean Epstein *C:* Raoul Aubourdier, Roger Hubert
Cast: Leon Mathot, Gina Manes, Jean-David Evremond, Pierre Hot, Jacques Christiany, Robert Tourneur

Two young men, stranded at an inn during a violent storm, are not thrilled at having to room with a diamond merchant (Bourdelle). During the night, the merchant is killed and one of the young men, Prosper (Mathot), disappears. Prosper's traveling companion is accused of the crime, and he is executed on flimsy evidence. Years later, a traveler uses the story to regale some of the Inn's guests at a dinner party. Unknown to the traveler, one of those guests is Prosper himself.

Jean Epstein (1897-1953) is renowned today for his innovative approach to cinema, which sought to combine the everyday with the *avant-garde*. *The Red Inn* followed closely on the heels of his debut feature *Pasteur* (1922), but it wasn't until his loose adaptation of Edgar Allan Poe's *The Fall of the House of Usher* (1928) that his reputation was made.

The Red Inn was an adaptation of a Honoré de Balzac story and appears to have been Epstein's first true attempt at horror. Balzac's story *L'auberge rouge* had already been adapted by Abel Gance and directed by Camile de Morlhon in 1910. Balzac is best remembered for his ambitious *La Comedie humaine*. He made an additional mark in the horror genre with *Le Peau du chagrin* (1831, also known as *The Wild Ass's Skin* and *The Magic Skin*), which was filmed a number of times during the silent film era.

The Red Inn explores the theme of crime and punishment, with its protagonist haunted by reminders of his ghastly misdeeds; in this respect, it's comparable to some of Poe's best work, most notably *The Tell-Tale Heart* (1843).

Balzac's story was adapted again in 1951, also as *The Red Inn*, though that version made some heavy alterations to the original tale. TH

Red Lights
Goldwyn; b/w; 70 min; U.S.
D: Clarence Badger *S:* Alice D.G. Miller, Carey Wilson *C:* Rudolph J. Bergquist
Cast: Marie Prevost, Raymond Griffith, Johnnie Walker, Alice Lake, Dagmar Godowsky, William Worthington

Based on the play *The Rear Car* by Edward E. Rose, *Red Lights* offers mystery, science fiction, comedy, drama and horror in equal measure. Taking place almost entirely on a moving train, it concerns Ruth Carson (Prevost), a railroad magnate's (Worthington) daughter who was kidnapped years ago. Now found, she is being looked after by a "crime deflector" (Griffith), a man with the psychic ability to foresee and forestall criminal activity. While the deflector doesn't really work his mojo much here, he does solve the mystery of why the red lights flashing over Ruth's head signal death. And he does unmask a man who's hatching a plot to kill Ruth.

Two faces familiar to classic horror fans appear in small roles here: Lionel Belmore and Jean Hersholt. Belmore went on to appear in *Stark Mad* and *The Unholy Night* (both 1929), *Le Spectre vert* (1930), *Frankenstein* (1931), *The Vampire Bat* (1933), *Jane Eyre* (1934), *Maid of Salem* (1937), *Son of Frankenstein*, *The Hunchback of Notre Dame*, and *Tower of London* (all 1939) and *The Ghost of Frankenstein* (1942). Jean Hersholt's horror work included performances in *The Cat Creeps* (1930), *The Phantom of Paris* (1931), *The Mask of Fu Manchu* (1932) and *Mark of the Vampire* (1935).

Red Lights isn't very faithful to its source material—a scientist who uses telepathic messages to scare the heroine is strictly a filmic addition, and the villain is Ruth's half brother rather than the believed-dead uncle of the play (very much alive and orchestrating events to steal her inheritance). But it's a moderately enjoyable ride regardless.

Rose's play was adapted again in 1934 as *Murder in the Private Car*, starring comedian Charles Ruggles as the deflector, with his psychic power diluted even further—reduced, in fact, to mere deductive ability. And though it contains an occasional disembodied voice to frighten the heroine (Mary Carlisle), it's a romantic comedy/mystery all the way. CW

The Sacred Order
Stoll; b/w; 24 min; Great Britain
D/Co-S: A.E. Coleby *Co-S:* Frank Wilson *P:* Oswald Stoll *C:* D.P. Cooper, Phil Ross
Cast: Harry Agar Lyons, Fred Paul, Joan Clarkson, H. Humberston Wright, Frank Wilson, Percy Clarbour, Laurie Lesie, H. Manning

After the aggressively uninteresting *The Silver Buddha* (1923), which showcased Dr. Petrie (Wright) over Nayland Smith (Paul), the two again team up against Fu Manchu (Lyons) in *The Sacred Order*, the penultimate entry of Stoll's 15-film series. Here, one of Fu Manchu's dacoits offers to lead one of them—but *only* one of them—to his master. Failing to see through the obvious ruse, Smith volunteers, departs with the Chinaman and disappears without a trace, leaving Petrie and Scotland Yard Inspector Weymouth (Wilson) to fear the worst. When Petrie goes in search of his housemate and friend, he's captured and imprisoned alongside Smith. Improbably, they negotiate their release offering Fu Manchu (Lyons) a document he desperately wants (and over which he has been threatened by an unseen presence who considers the original's loss an insult to their religion).

This two-reel film was suggested by Chapter 13 of Sax Rohmer's 1916 novel *The Return of Dr. Fu Manchu* (aka *The Devil Doctor*). The last film in the series, *The Shrine of the Seven Lamps* (1923) featured the return of Roy Raymond as Sergeant Fletcher, last seen in *The Man with the Limp* (also 1923). It was also a reversion to the more supernatural thrills of some of the series' previous outings. CW

The Scented Envelopes
Stoll; b/w; 27 min; Great Britain
D/Co-S: A.E. Coleby *Co-S:* Frank Wilson *P:* Oswald Stoll *C:* D.P. Cooper, Phil Ross
Cast: Harry Agar Lyons, Fred Paul, Joan Clarkson, H. Humberston Wright, Frank Wilson, Charles Vane, Booth Conway, Robert English

Often incorrectly categorized as a serial (a single narrative made up of multiple, separately titled chapters), *The Mystery of Dr. Fu-Manchu* is, rather, a film series—separate, self-contained narratives—revolving around Sax Rohmer's literary criminal mastermind. Or, to be even more precise, it's the first such series, produced in 1923 and consisting of 15 films. (A second one, *The Further Mysteries of Dr. Fu-Manchu*, came the following year and contained eight films.) All 23 films—which were surprisingly faithful to their literary sources—starred Harry Agar Lyons as Rohmer's dastardly Fu Manchu, an Asian villain intent on subjugating Occidental cultures, doing battle with his nemeses, Sir Nayland Smith and Dr. Petrie.

Fu Manchu first appeared in a series of short stories eventually collated (in 1913) into a novel titled *The Mystery of Fu Manchu*, known as *The Insidious Fu Manchu* in North America. The character proved popular, becoming the baddie in a series of novels that catered to xenophobia in Europe and North America. Writer Rohmer addressed the controversy by claiming that his books were a realistic portrayal of the Chinese, among whom "criminality" was "rampant." Writers such as Harry Stephen Keeler also dabbled in the genre, and it was inevitable that some of their work would make it to the big screen. Yellow Peril films reached their zenith in the 1930s with such entries as *The Mask of Fu Manchu* (1932) and *The Mysterious Mr. Wong* (1934) and got a minor resurrection in the 1960s with Hammer's *The Terror of the Tongs* (1961) and Harry Alan Towers' *The Face of Fu Manchu* (1965). Peter Sellers posthumously sounded the death knell of the subgenre, lampooning it in the cobbled together and rush-released *The Fiendish Plot of Dr. Fu Manchu* (1980).

Though Stoll had already flirted with Yellow Peril in 1920 with an adaptation of Rohmer's *The Yellow Claw* (a 1915 novel with another villainous Asian named Mr. King), Fu Manchu's first official big-screen appearance came in *The Scented Envelopes*. This, film #1 of the first series, has Nayland Smith (Paul) and Dr. Petrie (Wright) attempting to solve the murder of Sir Crichton Davey (Vane), whom they believe to have been targeted by the evil Fu Manchu (Lyons). After an attempt is made on Smith's life via a poisonous insect attracted to the smell in a set of envelopes, Smith and Petrie learn the truth about Davey's demise.

Despite Fu Manchu's obvious Asian heritage, Irish-born actor Harry Agar Lyons put forth little effort to make himself seem anything other than Caucasian. The role of Oriental heavy was one he'd revisit repeatedly over the following 15 years. Not only did he portray Rohmer's literary villain 23 times, he also starred as Dr. Sin Fang, an obvious variation on the part, in a series of Z-grade films released in 1928. His last role was in the 1938 cheapie *Chinatown Nights*, playing Mr. Fang one final time.

Fred Paul, who starred as Nayland Smith, went on to direct and co-star in both the second series of Fu films and the Dr. Sin Fang shorts. He retired shortly after the end of the silent era and so had nothing to do with the final two Sin Fang features, *Dr. Sin Fang* (1937) and the aforementioned *Chinatown Nights*.

Envelopes is the only film in Stoll's original series considered lost (the British Film Institute holds copies of the remaining films, though *Aaron's Rod* is missing a reel). The other films in the series include *The West Case, The Clue of the Pigtail, The Call of Siva, The Miracle, The Fungi Cellars, The Knocking on the Door, The Cry of the Nighthawk, Aaron's Rod* (see above), *The Fiery Hand, The Man with the Lamp, The Queen of Hearts, The Silver Buddha, The Sacred Order* and *The Shrine of the Seven Lamps* (all 1923). CW

The Shrine of the Seven Lamps
Stoll; b/w; 22 min; Great Britain
D/Co-S: A.E. Coleby *Co-S:* Frank Wilson *P:* Oswald Stoll *C:* D.P. Cooper, Phil Ross
Cast: Harry Agar Lyons, Fred Paul, Joan Clarkson, H. Humberston Wright, Frank Wilson, Roy Raymond

Following the sublimely ridiculous *The Sacred Order* (1923), *The Shrine of the Seven Lamps* returns the series *The Mystery of Dr. Fu-Manchu* to more horror-oriented ground. The final two-reeler of 15, its plot was lifted from Chapter 32 of Sax Rohmer's 1917 novel *The Hand of Fu Manchu* (aka *The Si-Fan Mysteries*).

On a train to London, Dr. Petrie (Wright) encounters a strange woman in his compartment and later has nightmares about his arch nemesis, Fu Manchu (Lyons). As he departs the train, he sees a monkey he recognizes as belonging to the criminal mastermind. Following it, he comes to a house where Fu's organization is in the midst of a sinister ceremony, with one of the participants being a disguised Nayland Smith (Paul). The gathering ends in a police raid; the aforementioned criminal mastermind imprisons Petrie and Karamenah but is shot dead by Smith. The film and series ends with Smith being rewarded and Petrie asking for Karamenah's hand in marriage.

The series proved successful enough that Stoll followed the next year with another: *The Further Mysteries of Dr. Fu Manchu*, which was only eight films long. Director A.E. Coleby was replaced by actor Fred Paul, who would also assume the writing chores. Actress Dorinea Shirley took over for Joan Clarkson as Karamenah. The first film in the second series was titled *The Midnight Summons* (1924) and opened on a horrific note, with the stolen body of Fu Manchu brought back to life. CW

The Silver Buddha
Stoll; b/w; 21 min; Great Britain
D/Co-S: A.E. Coleby *Co-S:* Frank Wilson *P:* Oswald Stoll *C:* D.P. Cooper, Phil Ross
Cast: Harry Agar Lyons, Fred Paul, Joan Clarkson, H. Humberston Wright, Frank Wilson, E. Lewis Waller

Probably the least interesting film in Stoll's 15-film *The Mystery of Dr. Fu-Manchu* series, *The Silver Buddha* (entry number 13) directly follows *The Queen of Hearts* (1923). While Nayland Smith (Paul) visits the British Museum, Dr. Petrie (Wright) explores the antiques shops that line the nearby streets and stumbles upon one of Fu Manchu's (Lyons) dens of operation. There, he spies Fu Manchu's sometimes-assistant Karamenah (Clarkson) and, after a few mini-adventures within the shop, finds Smith and tells him what he has seen and experienced. But when the shop is raided, Fu Manchu and his lackeys are nowhere to be found.

This two-reeler is based on Chapter 18 of Sax Rohmer's 1916 novel *The Return of Dr. Fu Manchu* (aka *The Devil Doctor*). Smith and Petrie next encounter the Asian criminal in *The Sacred Order* (1923). CW

Slave of Desire
Goldwyn; b/w; 70 min; U.S.
D: George D. Baker *S:* Charles E. Whittaker, Alice D.G. Miller *C:* John Boyle
Cast: George Walsh, Bessie Love, Carmel Myers, Wally Van, Edward Connelly, Eulalie Jensen

Raphael Valentin is a struggling poet whose luck changes for the better with the support of the provocative Countess Fedora. When he falls in love with her, however, she rejects him. Falling into a deep, resentful despair, he comes across an antiquarian with a piece of leather that has the ability to grant wishes; this he buys and uses to destroy Fedora.

Honoré de Balzac's short story *Le peau de chagrin* (literally "The Skin of Sorrow," but renamed in English as *The Magic Skin*) was first published in 1831. The first of its many silent-era adaptations was 1909's *The Wild Ass's Skin*. Baker's film takes great liberties with its literary source, but it retains the story's basic theme of would-be lovers using an enchanted object to strike back at those who have rejected them.

George D. Baker was active in cinema between 1908 and 1924. *Slave of Desire* was one of his last films; he died in 1933. Leading lady Bessie Love, who'd had a small role in D.W. Griffith's *Intolerance* (1916), went from *Slave* to a period of steady success in more lightweight fare; her star waned in the 1930s, but she continued to pop up now and then, notably in a supporting role in José Larraz's sexy and sadistic *Vampyres* (1974). She had a very good 1981, appearing in two of that year's most prestigious films: Milos Foreman's *Ragtime* and Warren Beatty's *Reds*. Her final appearance was in Tony Scott's stylish lesbian vampire film *The Hunger* (1983). She died in 1988. TH

The Speckled Band
Stoll; b/w; 20 min; Great Britain
D: George Ridgwell *S:* George H. Malins, P.L. Mannock *P:* Oswald Stoll *C:* Alfred H. Moise
Cast: Eille Norwood, Hubert Willis, Lewis Gilbert, Cynthia Murtagh, Henry Wilson, Mme. d'Esterre

When a woman dies mysteriously, Sherlock Holmes (Norwood) suspects the brutish Dr. Grimsby Roylott (Gilbert) of being the one responsible. Intrigued by the oblique nature of the woman's dying words—"speckled band"—he and Dr. Watson (Willis) tackle the mystery.

This, the second screen version of Sir Arthur Conan Doyle's short story *The Adventure of the Speckled Band*, was part of Stoll's two-reel mystery series *The Last Adventures of Sherlock Holmes*, which starred Eille Norwood as the great detective. Norwood portrayed Holmes on screen more times than any actor in history—47, all told—though his work is almost completely forgotten today. Doyle liked Norwood's Holmes, though, and audiences of the day were apparently taken with him as well. Indeed, the role kept him sufficiently busy that he found little time (or reason, apparently) to do much else. His final picture, a Holmes outing entitled *His Final Bow*, was part of this same series and was released the same year. The actor lived until 1948.

Director George Ridgwell helmed the majority of the Norwood Holmes films, but—like Norwood—his career didn't last into the talkie era.

The Speckled Band was translated to film for a third time and with the same title in 1931, featuring the great Raymond Massey as Holmes. TH

MOVIES BEAT BOOKS, EDISON DECLARES

Children Can Learn Better From Them, He Testifies at Famous Players Hearing.

SEES VAST POWER IN FILM

Sustains Government's Contention That a Trust Would Exert Enormous Influence.

Thomas A. Edison gave his opinions of the movies as an influence on public opinion and as a medium of education for children yesterday when called as an expert witness for the Government at a hearing in the Federal Trade Commission's investigation of charges that the Famous Players-Lasky Corporation was trying to monopolize the moving picture industry.

Mr. Edison was called as a Government expert at the hearing to testify in support of the contention that control of the motion picture industry would give tremendous power to anybody or any company that controlled it.

Asked whether he thought moving pictures were very powerful in influencing people, Mr. Edison replied:

"There is nothing so powerful as motion pictures in influencing people. They are the most powerful means of influencing people at the present time and will increase in power from year to year. Whoever controls the motion picture industry controls the most powerful medium of influence over the people."

Calls Pictures Better Than Books.

"I think motion pictures have just started," he said in answer to a question about the future of the industry. "It is my opinion that in twenty years children will be taught through pictures and not through books."

Mr. Edison said that he regarded moving pictures as 100 per cent. perfect for teaching. They could influence people mightily for good or bad in the moral sense. They were the best means for the dissemination of knowledge, especially among children. He said he believed that children were more susceptible to education through the screen than persons over twenty years of age—more susceptible to good and bad influences alike.

Wednesday May 16, 1923, from the New York Times

Trilby

Richard Walton Tully/First National; b/w; 82 (80) min; U.S. *D:* James Young *S/P:* Richard Walton Tully *C:* George Benoit *Cast:* Andree Lafayette, Arthur Edmund Carewe, Creighton Hale, Philo McCullough, Wilfred Lucas, Francis McDonald

In a laundry, a young artist's model named Trilby (Lafayette) meets Little Billee (Hale) and falls in love. Unfortunately, she also crosses paths with the sinister Svengali (Carewe), who develops an obsession with her. On the night of her engagement to Little Billee, Svengali abducts Trilby and turns his supernatural powers of mesmerism on her. Though he is unable to make her love him (instead erasing her will entirely), he does turn her into a talented singer. After Trilby becomes the sensation of Europe, Svengali dies of a heart attack; Trilby loses her ability to sing and shortly thereafter dies as well.

In its review of July 26, 1923, *Variety* praised Tully's production and the film's two central performances, calling the picture "especially satisfying" and Andree Lafayette "an ideal Trilby in face and figure." This was French actress Lafayette's first major role, which she followed up with a single Canadian picture before returning to her native country and continuing to star in films there. She pretty much retired in the mid-1930s, though she did return to French cinema for a couple of films in the early 1950s.

Arthur Edmund Carewe, on the other hand, had a healthy career in Hollywood, portraying shady characters right up until his death in 1937. His other horror credits include *The Ghost Breaker* (1922), *The Phantom of the Opera* (1925), *The Cat and the Canary* (1927), *Doctor X* (1932), *The Mystery of the Wax Museum* (1933) and *Charlie Chan's Secret* (1936).

The same year that *Trilby* was shot, Creighton Hale made an appearance in a "stag" film titled *On the Beach*, or *Getting his Goat*, the plot of which involved three nude women, a hole in a fence and a goat. Such controversial fare doesn't appear to have hurt his career any, as he went on to star in innumerable films, including such genre entries as *The Cat and the Canary* (1927) and *Seven Footprints to Satan* (1929). His later career was spent doing un-credited bit work in countless films of the 1930s and '40s.

Tully's *Trilby* was yet another silent adaptation of George Du Maurier's novel of the same name, first published in *Harper's* in 1894. It was a best-selling sensation, with the eponymous character lending her name to everything from hats to alcoholic drinks. It had been filmed numerous times before, first in 1895 as a series of shorts taken from a stage adaptation and later by the likes of Maurice Tourneur (whose 1915 version is often compared unfavorably to this one).

Director James Young shot two versions of the ending: a traditional one in which Trilby dies and a non-traditional one in which she lives. The studio opted for the traditional ending upon release, perhaps because it was so familiar to movie audiences of the time. Interestingly, Young had a small part in Tourneur's adaptation, which starred Young's wife at the time, Clara Kimball Young, as Trilby.

The next version, simply titled *Svengali*, came in 1927, but it is the 1931 version that is considered the definitive adaptation today. CW

Warning Shadows explores the very nature of cinema itself as Alexander Granach's leering illusionist entertains the guests with a puppet play.

Tut-Tut and His Terrible Tomb

Butcher; b/w; 23 min; Great Britain
D: Bertram Phillips *S:* Frank Miller
Cast: Queenie Thomas, Frank Stanmore

Discovered in 1922 by British archaeologist Howard Carter, King Tutankhamun's tomb was an instant public sensation. It wasn't long before cinema responded, and among its many Tut-themed offerings was *Tut-Tut and His Terrible Tomb*, in which revived mummies stalk the discoverers of an Egyptian tomb. The film was the second in the *Syncopated Picture Plays* series, and, as per the times, its focus was on comedy rather than chills.

The same team of director Bertram Phillips and writer Frank Miller made Butcher's *Faust* the same year. That film likewise starred Queenie Thomas and Frank Stanmore. CW

The Veil of Happiness
aka La voile du bonheur

Establissements Louis Aubert; b/w; 65 (75) min; France
D: Edouard-Emile Violet
Cast: Susie Wata, Shu Hou, Liao Szi-Yen, Chen Pao-Tan, Jean Bradin

In China a blind man's sight is restored by a witch doctor. The man is initially elated, but his happiness sours as his regained sight allows him to see the contempt with which his wife and so-called friends view him. Eventually, tired of the inhumanity to which he bears witness, he gouges out his eyes.

The Veil of Happiness was adapted from a story by French politician and author Georges Clemenceau. The written tale was more a philosophical treatise than an out-and-out horror story, while the film version plays up the story's more morbid aspects. (The story had also been adapted in 1910 under the same title, but that version was played for comedy rather than horror.)

Veil's director, Edouard-Emile Violet, was active throughout the silent era, also amassing a number of credits as an actor and screenwriter. His film career apparently ended with the coming of sound, and he committed suicide in his native France in 1955.

Typically for the era, the Chinese characters were actually Caucasian performers done up to look Oriental. TH

Warning Shadows
aka Schatten—Eine nächtliche Halluzination; Shadows—a Nocturnal Hallucination

PAN Film; b/w; 85 min; Germany
D: Arthur Robison *S:* Albin Grau *P:* Enrico Dieckmann, Willy Seibold *C:* Fritz Arno Wagner
Cast: Fritz Kortner, Ruth Weyher, Gustav Von Wagenheim, Alexander Granach, Eugen Rex, Fritz Rasp

A Count (Kortner) invites some people to his mansion for a gathering. As the evening unfolds, a mysterious magician (Granach) intrudes and begins to weave a spell over the guests. The Count becomes convinced that his beautiful wife (Weyher) is being unfaithful, and he challenges his perceived rival (Von Wagenheim) to a duel. Things take a tragic turn, but could it all just be an illusion conjured up by the magician?

Born in Chicago, Illinois in 1883, Arthur Robison was brought up in Germany and there established a career as a writer and director. His debut was the Expressionist horror film *A Night of Horror* (1916), but his most celebrated work by far is *Warning Shadows*.

The film is fascinating primarily on a visual level. As an exercise in Expressionism, it fully deserves inclusion in the canon of great German horror films. The visuals and technique are every bit as bold and imaginative as those found in the best of F.W. Murnau, Paul Leni, Robert Weine and Fritz Lang. So confident is the direction, in fact, that Robison tells the story in purely visual terms, without benefit of dialogue cards or intertitles. Even the three-act structure is punctuated with close-ups of a hand displaying the appropriate number of digits instead of the usual title cards.

The film explores the very nature of cinema itself as Granach's leering illusionist entertains the guests with a puppet play that looks very much like someone's old home movie. The use of shadows as an expressive element—restating a scene's implicit emotion in visual terms—cuts to the heart of what the Expressionist form was all about. Working with the brilliant cinematographer Fritz Arno Wagner (*Destiny*, 1921), Robison turns *Shadows* into a literal celebration of shadow play and mood.

Unfortunately, the film loses momentum toward the end, with the arbitrary happy ending feeling particularly discordant. Overall, in fact, the screenplay is the movie's weakest aspect. No doubt the gifted screenwriter Albin Grau—whose deep interest in mysticism and the occult would have a huge impact on the development of Murnau's *Nosferatu—A Symphony of Terror* (1922)—believed that a generic storyline would better enable the director to tell his story visually, without undue distraction by questions of motivation or back-story. Put simply, viewed for content rather than style, the film comes up short. The characters are stereotypes that generate little audience interest or empathy. The actors do a respectable job with what they're given, and genre buffs will particularly enjoy the presence of Gustav Von Wagenheim and Alexander Granach, reteamed here after playing major roles in *Nosferatu*.

With its seductive technique and vivid imagery, *Warning Shadows* remains one of the most visually fascinating contributions to the German horror cinema of the 1920s. Robison would later return to the genre for his last film, a sound remake of *The Student of Prague* (1935). TH

The West Case
Stoll; b/w; 22 min; Great Britain
D/Co-S: A.E. Coleby *Co-S:* Frank Wilson *P:* Oswald Stoll *C:* D.P. Cooper, Phil Ross
Cast: Harry Agar Lyons, Fred Paul, Joan Clarkson, H. Humberston Wright, Frank Wilson, Wyngold Lawrence

The Mystery of Dr. Fu-Manchu was a series of two-reel films built around writer Sax Rohmer's criminal mastermind. The first in the series was *The Scented Envelopes* (1923); *The West Case* was the second. Fred Paul starred here and throughout the series as Nayland Smith, while Harry Agar Lyons portrayed Smith's arch-nemesis, the conniving Dr. Fu Manchu. H. Humberston Wright played the aging Dr. Petrie, and Joan Clarkson was Fu Manchu's seductive agent, Karamenah (called Kâramanèh in the novels and sometimes—mistakenly—Zaramenah in some film resources).

In this outing, an inventor named Frank West (Lawrence) is targeted by Fu Manchu, who wants the blueprints for a new aerial torpedo. While visiting an Asian club, West meets a beautiful woman who, unknown to him, is in the dastardly villain's employ. She slips him intoxicating drugs, he winds up semi-unconscious in his apartment and Chinamen break in and steal the missile plans from his wall safe. Still in a drugged-out haze, he calls Scotland Yard. Inspector Weymouth (Wilson) is put on the case and, along with Smith and Petrie, interviews West. The three conclude that Fu Manchu is behind the documents theft.

This film introduced Fu Manchu's penchant for mind control through hypnosis, though he's aided this time out by drugs. Its notion of flying torpedoes, at the time the stuff of science fiction, has long since proved prescient.

Frank Wilson, who starred as Weymouth, was also—along with director A.E. Coleby—the film's co-scenarist. Coleby (1876-1930) worked exclusively in the silent era, making his first stab at fantastic cinema in 1908 with *The Somnambulist's Crime*. In that film, a cashier is wrongly accused of a bank robbery committed by a sleepwalking bank manager. But despite the premise, the film is too subdued and focused on the crime's aftermath to qualify as horror. Coleby also directed two other films of interest to horror aficionados: *A Case for Sherlock Holmes* and *The Hunchback* (both 1911). Despite his directorial work on almost 250 films, he is today known almost exclusively for this first, relatively obscure Fu Manchu series.

The next film in the series is *The Clue of the Pigtail* (1923). CW

While Paris Sleeps
aka **The Glory of Love**
Tourneur; b/w; 54 min; U.S.
D/P: Maurice Tourneur *S:* Wyndham Gittens *C:* René Guissart
Cast: Lon Chaney, Mildred Manning, John Gilbert, J. Farrell MacDonald, Hardee Kirkland

Based on a novel by Pan (a pseudonym for author Leslie Beresford), *The Glory of Love* was shot in 1920 by Maurice Tourneur. Due possibly to its gruesome nature, popular director Tourneur (*The System of Dr. Tarr and Professor Fether*, 1912; *Trilby*, 1915) was at first unable to get it released. The film remained unseen for three years before it was picked up by the W.W. Hodkinson Corporation, its title changed to *While Paris Sleeps* and finally shown in theaters nationwide. Reviews at the time picked up on the delay, with *Variety* stating that the film looked:

> As though it was an old boy that had been lying around for some little time, finally patched up and released to salvage whatever could be got from it. It has all the appearances of a picture that might have been made three or four years ago …

The impetus to finally take it public might have come from the fact that star Lon Chaney had achieved a level of success by then, with a series of dark, melodramatic endeavors (*The Penalty* and *Outside the Law*, both 1920; *Oliver Twist* and *A Blind Bargain*, both 1922), though his star-making turn in *The Hunchback of Notre Dame* (1923) was still several months away.

At any rate, *While Paris Sleeps* offers one Henri Santados (Chaney), a mad sculptor who lives in Paris' famed Latin Quarter. He meets and falls in love with the young and beautiful Bebe Larvache (Manning), but she has no romantic interest in him, falling instead for dashing American Dennis O'Keefe (Gilbert). Dennis' father (Kirkland) objects to their relationship and convinces Bebe to cut it off, although not before they share one final night together at a Mardi Gras celebration. What she doesn't realize, however, is that Santados, along with Father Marionette (MacDonald)—the owner of the wax chamber of horrors at which Santados works—plans to force Bebe into a compromising position, after which he and Marionette will abduct and torture Dennis.

Actors Lon Chaney and John Gilbert reunited the very next year for *He Who Gets Slapped*, and frequent Chaney collaborator Tod Browning later cast Gilbert in a role more fitting for Chaney in *The Show* (1927). But while Chaney made a career out of horror films, Gilbert drifted off to portrayals of male love interests in big-budget romantic dramas, often opposite MGM superstar Greta Garbo (to whom he was at one point engaged). Gilbert's acting career ended in 1934 with the comedic *The Captain Hates the Sea*, just two years before his death from heart failure.

As a point of interest, Lon Chaney's actual Christian name was Leonidas and not, as is commonly reported, Alonzo. CW

Yotsuya kaidan
Shochiku; b/w; length unknown; Japan
D: Kaname Mori *C:* Gakusui Ego
Cast: Shirogoro Sawamura, Taro Nakamura

This version of the famed Kabuki play *Yotsuya kaidan* (literally: *Ghost of Yotsuya* or *Yotsuya Ghost Story*—Yotsuya being the village in central Japan that serves as the story's location) was the second of two to star Shirogoro Sawamura, one of Japan's most famous silent-era actors. Born in 1877, Sawamura's career followed a similar trajectory to that of fellow Japanese superstar Matsunosuke Onoe. Both entered Kabuki Theater while relatively young, and both moved from stage to screen in the early 1900s. Yoshino Jiro directed many of Sawamura's early films, while several of his later ones were helmed by Kaname Mori.

Though little information exists about any of these silent adaptations of Tsuruya Nanboku IV's tale, one can assume that Sawamura played Iemon, the samurai who does away with his faithful wife in favor of a much younger, richer and more beautiful woman. The end result is that his former wife's ghost drives both him and his mistress to their own deaths.

Another version of the story, *Yotsuya kaidan Oiwa*, appeared the same year from director Shozo Makino's production company. CW

Yotsuya kaidan Oiwa
Makino; b/w; length unknown; Japan
P: Shozo Makino
Cast: Ichitaro Kataoka, Shinso Arashi

The year 1923 saw at least two adaptations of Tsuruya Nanboku IV's Kabuki play *Yotsuya kaidan*. This time out, however, the emphasis was placed squarely on the wife's plight, hence the appearance of her name in the title. Director Shozo Makino's own production company produced, a production company he had formed to give himself greater autonomy. (Coincidentally, Makino had directed what may have been the first legitimate film adaptation of the play in 1912, though some sources cite a 1911 version as having been produced.)

Due largely to the Great Kanto earthquake of 1923 and the destruction wrought by World War II, the overwhelming majority of Japan's silent films, along with most information about them, are lost. That is unfortunately the case here. CW

1924

Au secours!
aka The Haunted House; Help!
Gance; b/w; 23 min; France
D/Co-S/P: Abel Gance *Co-S:* Max Linder *C:* Émile Pierre, André-Wladimir Reybas, Georges Specht
Cast: Max Linder, Jean Toulout, Gina Palerme, Gaston Modot

Allegedly made on a dare, *Au Secours!* was completed by producer, director and co-scenarist Abel Gance in less than three days. It starred his good friend Max Linder, who had returned to his homeland after spending several years attempting to rev up a comedy career in the United States.

The tale begins in a private club, where Count Maulette (Toulout) regales guests with a tale about himself and nine friends, all armed to the teeth, spending time in a haunted castle he owns. Within 10 minutes, he claims, six members of the group had fainted. He mentions that he would "give a lot" to any man who spends an hour within the castle's walls. Enter newlywed Max (Linder), who has recently proved his manliness by taking on an attacker who was armed with a knife. He accepts the Count's challenge, provided that there's a thousand francs in it for him. Count Maulette agrees and the two set the bet for that very night, during the hour between 11:00 pm and midnight. A bell will be provided for Max to summon help, but if he uses it he forfeits the cash.

The castle is indeed a large and foreboding place, and when Max arrives, the front door opens of its own accord. Inside, a mannequin comes to life and then freezes again, and when Max attempts to melt its finger with a lighter, it attacks him. A series of comedic/horrific incidents follows, none of it particularly funny or scary, employing props, techniques and effects that were already old hat in 1924—fast motion, slow motion, stunt doubles on trampolines, stock footage spliced with new footage, wire work, superimpositions, men in ghost and skeleton costumes, a man on stilts, live animals and prop animals, etc.

The film's most successful moment comes at the end. When it becomes apparent that he's actually going to win the bet, Max receives a call from his wife Edith (Palerme) claiming that a monstrous intruder is threatening her. He rings the bell to summon help, and it turns out that the "threat" was engineered by the Count to prevent Max from winning his francs.

A little over a year after the release of *Au Secours!*, and with only one more credit to his name, Max Linder, who'd been battling chronic depression since his service in World War I (he was a dispatch driver) and who was unhappy with his waning career, entered into a suicide pact with his much younger wife, whom he'd married in 1923. Their first attempt in 1924 failed and was hushed up. But in October 1925, they ingested Veronal, injected morphine and sliced their wrists, successfully ending it all. They left behind a young daughter who became the subject of a custody battle between their two families, her parents having left conflicting instructions concerning her care and custody.

Linder's greatest fame, however, may have come almost a century later, when Quentin Tarantino referred to him in *Inglourious Basterds* (2009). There, a young Jewish woman passing for a French cinema owner holds a Max Linder festival and enters into a conversation about the actor's merits with a German soldier who is obsessed with her. CW

Behind the Curtain
aka Souls Which Pass in the Night
Universal; b/w; 55 min; U.S.
D: Chester M. Franklin *S:* Emil Forest, Harvey Gates *C:* Jackson Rose
Cast: Lucille Rickson, Johnny Harron, George Cooper, Winifred Bryson, Charles Clary, Eric Mayne

Sandwiched between Universal's two biggest horror hits of the silent era (*The Hunchback of Notre Dame*, 1923, and *The Phantom of the Opera*, 1925) were several minor Universal films with horror elements. These included short subjects (*What an Eye*, 1924) and weird Westerns (*Spook Ranch*, 1925).

Behind the Curtain was a part of that group. A lurid melodrama based on a story by William J. Flynn—former director of the (Federal) Bureau of Investigation—it concerns George Belmont (Clary), a wealthy man whose mistress, Laura (Bryson), is told by a psychic (Mayne) that her world is filled with death. When

Laura's sister (Rickson) elopes with Belmont's son (Harron), Belmont decides that Laura is to blame and offers her money to bring about an end to the affair. Shortly afterward he's brutally murdered. Innocent people are subsequently suspected and even convicted of the crime, but the real killer is eventually revealed.

Behind the Curtain was one of two horror films directed by Chester M. Franklin. The other, *The Thirteenth Hour* (1927), was the more atmospheric of the two. This *Curtain* should not be confused with the first Charlie Chan adaptation of the talkie era, *Behind That Curtain*, which was released in 1929. CW

Botan dōrō

Shochiku; b/w; length unknown; Japan
D: Yoshiro Edamasa S: Hideo Nagata
Cast: Kotaro Ichikawa, Aiko Azuma, Midori Komatsu

Though it borrows heavily from Sanyutei Encho's *rakugo* (a type of monologue) play *Botan dōrō*, this film appears to actually have been based on a novelization by poet and playwright Hideo Nagata. Both play and novel tell the tale of a beautiful girl named Otsuyu, who falls in love with a handsome young samurai named Shinzaburo. He claims to love her as well, but he tires of her and deserts her, leaving her to grow sick and die. She returns from the grave, disguises herself and seduces, then kills, her former lover. CW

The Café L'Egypte

Stoll; b/w; 25 min; Great Britain
D/S: Fred Paul C: Frank Canham P: Oswald Stoll
Cast: Harry Agar Lyons, Fred Paul, H. Humberston Wright, Frank Wilson, Dorinea Shirley

After the successful series *The Mystery of Dr. Fu-Manchu*, which contained 15 two-reel films, Stoll produced an eight-film follow-up, *The Further Mysteries of Dr. Fu Manchu*. The first four films in the second series were *The Midnight Summons, The Coughing Horror, Cragmire Tower* and *The Green Mist* (all 1924) and were among the most horrific of Stoll's productions.

The Café L'Egypte is the fifth in the series. Little information exists about the film, though it seems likely that it was based on Chapter 24 of Sax Rohmer's popular 1917 novel *The Hand of Fu Manchu* (aka *The Si-Fan Mysteries*). In Rohmer's tale, Smith and Petrie discover that the Café de l'Egypte, in London's Soho district, is a meeting place for Fu Manchu's operatives.

The next film in the series is *The Golden Pomegranates* (1924). CW

The Coughing Horror

Stoll; b/w; 21 min; Great Britain
D/S: Fred Paul C: Frank Canham P: Oswald Stoll
Cast: Harry Agar Lyons, Fred Paul, H. Humberston Wright, Frank Wilson, Dorinea Shirley, Johnny Butt, Fred Morgan, Harry Rignold

Apart from *The Midnight Summons* (1924), Stoll's second entry in their *The Further Mysteries of Dr. Fu Manchu* series is the most horrific of the eight-film bunch. The plot revolves around that staple of silent horror cinema, the killer ape (Rignold), known this time around as the Coughing Horror.

While held captive by Fu Manchu's men, Nayland Smith (Paul) and Dr. Petrie (Wright) befriend Antonio Strozza (Morgan). Once they're all rescued, Strozza heads out to a relative's (Butt) farm to rest. There he's awakened at night by an ape-man trying to strangle him. After fending off the beast, he sends for Smith and Petrie. When they arrive, they find the ape again trying to strangle Strozza. A fight ensues during which the creature's arm is torn off, though not before Strozza has died. Its hand left behind (still, in fact, clutching the victim's throat), the beast escapes and returns to its master, Fu Manchu (Lyons).

Fred Morgan, who portrayed Antonio Strozza, previously starred in the 1919 horror film *The Beetle* for producer/director Alexander Butler. *The Coughing Horror* seems to have been his last film. It was suggested by Chapter 14 of Sax Rohmer's 1916 novel *The Return of Dr. Fu Manchu* (aka *The Devil Doctor*).

The next film in the series moves the action to *Cragmire Tower* (1924). CW

Cragmire Tower

Stoll; b/w; 23 min; Great Britain
D/S: Fred Paul C: Frank Canham P: Oswald Stoll
Cast: Harry Agar Lyons, Fred Paul, H. Humberston Wright, Frank Wilson, Dorinea Shirley, George Foley, Rolfe Leslie

Cragmire Tower made its first hardcover appearance (after a debut in the July 17, 1915 issue of *Collier's Magazine*) at the end of Chapter 21 of Sax Rohmer's 1916 novel *The Return of Dr. Fu Manchu* (aka *The Devil Doctor*) and is the place where Rohmer protagonists Nayland Smith and Dr. Petrie meet with retired American explorer Kegan Van Roon. In Chapter 22, the two warn the crippled Van Roon that his life is in danger from Fu Manchu's minions. In turn, Van Roon relates the haunted history of Cragmire Tower and the moors surrounding it. After the explorer leaves the room, Smith and Petrie spot witch-lights dancing on the moors. Smith charges in hot pursuit, and a few chapters later learns that the real Van Roon has been dead all along, with one of Fu Manchu's cronies impersonating him.

Heavily influenced by Sir Arthur Conan Doyle's *The Hound of the Baskervilles* (1901-02), this portion of *The Return of Dr. Fu Manchu* appears to have been faithfully brought to the big screen by producer Stoll and director Paul. *Cragmire Tower* is the third of eight in Stoll's two-reeler series *The Further Mysteries of Dr. Fu Manchu*. Rolfe Leslie filled the dual roles of Kegan Van Loon and his Asian impersonator Ki Ming, while George Foley played Van Loon's mulatto servant, Hagar.

Smith and Petrie's next adventure would put them in contact with *The Green Mist* (1924). CW

Dante's Inferno

Fox; b/w; 57 (60, 53) min; U.S.
D: Henry Otto S: Edmund Goulding, Cyrus Wood P: William Fox C: Joseph H. August
Cast: Ralph Lewis, Winifred Landis, William Scott, Pauline Starke, Josef Swickard, Gloria Grey, Lorimer Johnston, Lawson Butt, Howard Gaye, Noble Johnson

Charles Dickens' famous short story *A Christmas Carol* (1843) meets Dante Alighieri's famous cantica *Inferno* (1308-1321) in this modern parable of sin and redemption.

Greedy businessman and slumlord Mortimer Judd (Lewis) has climbed to the top using every nasty means available to him. Now that he's rich, he finds himself pestered by charities seek-

Despite some massive, striking sets and a few truly magnificent moments—a flying angel, sword raised, parting a sea of demons so that Dante may pass; naked sinners doused in burning pitch by a horned demon and a forest of trees inhabited by suicides, eternally fed upon by monstrous birdmen—the repeated red-tinted shots of bodies writhing in flames get old quick; without much story to shore it up, the film falls flat well before its conclusion. Director Henry Otto did at least understand the need to break the underworld action on occasion for the slightly less dull real-world storyline, where Judd is bedeviled for his misdeeds by one of Satan's minions until he redeems himself by preventing Craig from committing suicide. He does still die and go to Hell, but things, it turns out, aren't what they seem.

Fox remade the picture under the same title in 1935 with Spencer Tracy in the lead. That version was even less interesting, with the vision of Hell compressed into a single 10-minute segment. CW

The Golden Pomegranates

Stoll; b/w; 23 min; Great Britain
D/S: Fred Paul C: Frank Canham P: Oswald Stoll
Cast: Harry Agar Lyons, Fred Paul, H. Humberston Wright, Frank Wilson, Dorinea Shirley, Julie Suedo, Fred Hearn

Stoll's second series of Fu Manchu films followed its fifth entry, *The Café L'Egypte* (1924), with this sixth film, about which a great deal more is known. *The Golden Pomegranates* features the return of Julie Suedo as Zarmi, last seen (as far as is known) in *The Queen of Hearts* (1923), the 12th episode of Stoll's first Fu Manchu series (*The Mystery of Dr. Fu-Manchu*).

Pomegranates owes as much to Edgar Allan Poe as it does to Sax Rohmer. Nayland Smith (Paul) and Dr. Petrie (Wright) steal a chest owned by Fu Manchu (Lyons) and take it to their hotel. A waiter (Heard) attempts to break into it and is killed, though not before shouting the words, "Golden pomegranates!" A typical action-film plot then kicks in, with Fu's erstwhile assistant, Karamenah (Shirley), saved from Fu's current assistant, Zarmi (Suedo), by Scotland Yard Inspector Weymouth (Wilson), while Smith and Petrie are kept busy discovering what's inside the chest. Karamenah reveals Fu Manchu's hideout to authorities, but Smith insists on disguising himself and doing recon before the place is raided. Petrie, Karamenah and the police wait for Smith outside Fu's lair and, when Smith fails to emerge, everyone but Karamenah goes in. Left alone, she's kidnapped by Fu Manchu's men (who have, it turns out, already captured Smith). Smith and Karamenah are taken to yet another of Fu's hideaways where Karamenah is placed in a mummy case and snakes

ing help for the downtrodden. He dismisses such pleas on the grounds that no one ever gave *him* a handout. He falls equally short in the fatherly compassion department, destroying a radio bought for his ailing wife by their loving son, insisting that she needs no such diversion despite being housebound. After refusing to help a neighbor (Swickard) whom he has thrust into bankruptcy, he receives a copy of Dante's epic poem *Inferno* in the mail. He reads it, and his imagination whisks him off to the nine circles of Hell to be scared straight about the importance of self-sacrifice and humility.

Dante's Inferno was one of many big-budget spectacles shot by Fox during the latter part of the silent era (others include *A Daughter of the Gods*, 1916, and *She*, 1917) and appears to have been influenced by Italian studio Milano's highly successful 1911 film adaptation of Dante's tale, *Inferno*. Its heavy doses of both male and female nudity caused a stir in its day, resulting in the film being shortened by as much as 20 percent in some territories. The skin quotient is minimal in the version available today, in part due to the poor nature of extant prints.

A pianist (Conrad Veidt) is given hands that kill in *The Hands of Orlac*.

"Greywater Park stood upon a well-wooded slope, and, to the southwest, starting above the trees almost like a giant Spanish priest, showed a solitary tower." Thus Sax Rohmer describes Greywater Park—"a fortress, a monastery and a manor-house"—in Chapter 32 of his 1917 novel *The Hand of Fu Manchu* (aka *The Si-Fan Mysteries*). It is there that Sir Lionel Barton is struck with a mysterious ailment, leading Smith and Petrie to conclude that Fu Manchu may be using as a weapon the mysterious creatures Barton has brought back from abroad.

Given that most of Stoll's Fu Manchu two-reelers are adapted chapters from Rohmer novels, it's safe to assume that this one probably is too. It's also likely that whoever played the role of Sir Lionel Barton in *The Green Mist* (1924) did so here as well.

At any rate, *Greywater Park* is the eighth and final film of Stoll's second Fu Manchu two-reeler series *The Further Mysteries of Dr. Fu Manchu*. The first seven were *The Midnight Summons, The Coughing Horror, Cragmire Tower, The Green Mist, The Café L'Egypte, The Golden Pomegranates* and *Karamaneh* (all 1924).

While Stoll's first series based on Rohmer's character proved tremendously successful, there's no indication that the same was true of the second. What is known is that, following *Greywater Park*, Stoll abandoned the character altogether to focus on its *Thrilling Stories from the Strand Magazine* series.

The character of Fu Manchu was, however, revisited by Paramount in 1929 in *The Mysterious Dr. Fu Manchu*, the first of three such films (the other two being 1930's *The Return of Dr. Fu Manchu* and 1931's *Daughter of the Dragon*) starring Warner Oland. Oland also appeared in character for a short section in *Paramount on Parade* in 1930. The actor thereafter became famous as good-guy Asian detective Charlie Chan in a series of Fox productions in the 1930s. As for bad-guy Fu, well, he migrated to MGM, where he took up residence in Boris Karloff in *The Mask of Fu Manchu* (1932). CW

Hands of Orlac
aka **Orlacs Hande**; **Die unheimlichen Hände des Doktor Orlac**
Pan Film; b/w; 112 min; Germany
D: Robert Wiene *S:* Louis Nerz *C:* Gunther Krampf, Hans Androschin
Cast: Conrad Veidt, Alexandra Sorina, Fritz Kortner, Carmen Cartellieri, Fritz Strassny, Paul Askonas

Successful pianist Paul Orlac (Veidt) survives a devastating train wreck, but his hands are crushed. His wife (Sorina) begs a renowned surgeon to help her husband, whom she insists will die if he does not regain the ability to play. The surgeon capitalizes

and rats are loosed upon Smith. Thankfully, Petrie and the police show up in the nick of time.

The film recalls such Poe shorts as *The Premature Burial* and *The Pit and the Pendulum*. Its title was taken from Chapter 14 of Sax Rohmer's 1917 novel *The Hand of Fu Manchu* (aka *The Si-Fan Mysteries*). The next installment in the series is titled *Karamaneh* (1924). CW

The Green Mist
Stoll; b/w; 20 min; Great Britain
D/S: Fred Paul *C:* Frank Canham *P:* Oswald Stoll
Cast: Harry Agar Lyons, Fred Paul, H. Humberston Wright, Frank Wilson, Dorinea Shirley

This, the fourth film in Stoll's *The Further Mysteries of Dr. Fu Manchu* series, finds Nayland Smith (Paul) and Dr. Petrie (Wright) taking up the case of a clergyman being tormented by the nefarious Fu Manchu (Lyons). This time the arch mastermind uses poison gas to dispatch his victims, unsuccessfully in the cases of both the Reverend and an Egyptologist named Sir Lionel Barton.

The title and plot appear to have been lifted from Sax Rohmer's *The Mystery of Fu Manchu* (1913)—also known as *The Insidious Dr. Fu Manchu*—itself a collation of previously published short stories, one of which involves a "living" green mist that wafts from a mummy case and suffocates a man everyone assumes is Sir Lionel (but who is, in fact, his secretary Strozza).

The next entry in the Stoll series places the action in *The Café L'Egypt* (1924). CW

Greywater Park
Stoll; b/w; 27 min; Great Britain
D/S: Fred Paul *C:* Frank Canham *P:* Oswald Stoll
Cast: Harry Agar Lyons, Fred Paul, H. Humberston Wright, Frank Wilson, Dorinea Shirley

on the execution of a murderer, Vasseur, by transplanting the killer's hands onto Orlac. The operation is a success, but when Orlac learns that he has the hands of a murderer, he begins to fear that they will compel him to do horrible things.

Maurice Renard (1875-1939), a once-popular French author of science fiction-tinged thrillers, today is somewhat obscure. While his output was once prolific, his most famous title remains the 1920 *Les Mains d'Orlac*. A skillful mixture of drama, suspense and science fiction, it tells of a concert pianist who ends up with a murderer's hands after a freak accident. The notion of hands possessing an individual is far-fetched, of course, but it made for a good piece of pulp fiction, and readers responded with enthusiasm. The story first reached the screen in 1924, though it has been filmed (officially and otherwise) numerous times since.

Hands of Orlac reunited director Robert Wiene and star Conrad Veidt, who had teamed up for the 1919 masterpiece *The Cabinet of Dr. Caligari*. *Orlac* doesn't have the same towering reputation as that earlier collaboration, but it is, in many respects, equally satisfying. Wiene tackles the material with style and gusto—the psychosexual implications of Renard's text are brought into sharp focus, and the gradual build-up of paranoia is mesmerizing to behold.

The film is far less stylized than *Caligari*, but it is still recognizable as a product of the Expressionist movement. Some have theorized that the film's mixture of Expressionist and Realist imagery is a result of its low budget and rushed shooting schedule. The film never looks impoverished, however. Perhaps the move away from *Caligari*'s deliberate visual exaggeration put off fans that would have liked to see more of the same here. All that aside, the look of *Orlac* is, in its own way, equally striking, with its large looming shadows, long desolate corridors and general air of gloom.

The film's effectiveness is enhanced in no small measure by Veidt's sensitive performance. His surreal acting style manages to evoke audience sympathy for his character, whose growing panic over his state of mind provides ample opportunity to overact. Yet Veidt refrains from doing so. It's a stylized performance, not a barnstorming one. The actor is well supported by Alexandra Sorina, as his loving wife, and especially by Fritz Kortner, impressive as a sleazy con artist who tries to blackmail Orlac.

The finale has been criticized for imposing logic where none belongs (a claim to which there is some validity), but it works well enough on a purely dramatic level and doesn't detract significantly from the picture's overall impact.

Well-paced and confidently told, the film marked Wiene's final foray into the horror genre. He would complete only four more features before his death during the production of his final film, the spy thriller *Ultimatum* (1938). Karl Freund would remake the Orlac story as *Mad Love* (1935) for MGM; and later, lower-budgeted versions emerged from Britain/France (*The Hands of Orlac*, 1960) and the United States (*Hands of a Stranger*, 1962). While it's not officially credited as a remake, *Body Parts* (1991) also draws heavily on Renard's text. Of the versions that followed Wiene's, only Freund's provides serious competition. TH

Hot Water
Pathé; b/w; 59 min; U.S.
Co-D/Co-S: Sam Taylor *Co-D:* Fred Newmeyer *Co-S:* John Grey, Tommy Gray, Tim Whelan *P:* Harold Lloyd *C:* Walter Lundin
Cast: Harold Lloyd, Jobyna Ralston, Charles Stevenson, Josephine Crowell, Mickey McBan, Andy De Villa

Some sources cite this as a spoof of D.W. Griffith's (itself comedic) take on horror movies, *One Exciting Night* (1922), despite there being little similarity between the two films.

Hot Water stars Harold Lloyd in three barely connected skits examining the perils of domestic life. In the first, Lloyd's character, aptly named Hubby, wins a turkey in a raffle and has to battle both it and the unruly passengers of a streetcar while on his way home. In the second, he takes his family on a *laff*-filled outing in a brand new automobile. And in the third, he comes to believe that he has accidentally killed his wife. She's very much alive, however, and when she begins to sleepwalk, he becomes certain that her spirit is haunting him.

At a way, way too long 59 minutes, *Hot Water* relies on a seemingly endless succession of pratfalls for its yuks. The only horror-tinged segment is the third, with the other two thoroughly pedestrian. Still and all, the film was a huge success, grossing over two million dollars in its initial box-office run. CW

The Hunchback of Enmei-in
aka **Enmeiin no semushi-otoko**; **Enmeiin no semushi**
Kokkatsu; b/w; length unknown; Japan
D: Tomu Uchida *C:* Eiji Tsuburaya
Cast: Chieko Matsui, Shoshichii Shimada, Kyoko Matsunami

Little is known about this effort from Japan, other than the fact that the cinematographer was the great Eiji Tsuburaya, who went on to become the country's leading special effects man with *Gojira* (1954; it was heavily re-edited and re-titled *Godzilla, King of the Monsters!* for release in the United States). From that film on, Tsuburaya was the head of Toho's effects unit and founder of his own, working on virtually all the studio's Godzilla films until his death on January 25, 1970.

The Hunchback of Enmei-in appears to have begun production in 1920 but not completed until 1924, the year after Tsuburaya had left Kokkatsu (later to become part of Nikkatsu) and joined Ogasaware Productions. (This explains why sources list its year of production variously as 1920, 1924 and 1925.) Some sources also assert that the film was an adaptation of Victor Hugo's much-filmed 1831 novel *Notre Dame de Paris*. That claim seems dubious; if anything, the film may have been suggested by the novel, with its action likely transplanted to feudal Japan.

Director Tomu Uchida began his career in the silent era, but most of his early efforts—which often concerned the relationships between gangsters and police officers—are lost (only one, 1933's *Policeman*, is known to survive). His 1924 effort *Tale of Crab Temple* was an early example of Japanese anime.

It wasn't until the 1950s—when Japanese cinema made a major leap forward after the country was opened to the West—that Uchida's career really took off. Coincidentally, Uchida died the same year as Tsubuyara, on August 7, 1970. His last film was released posthumously in 1971. CW

Karamaneh
aka **Karamenah**
Stoll; b/w; 26 min; Great Britain
D/S: Fred Paul *C:* Frank Canham *P:* Oswald Stoll
Cast: Harry Agar Lyons, Fred Paul, H. Humberston Wright, Frank Wilson, Dorinea Shirley

After the Poe-like *The Golden Pomegranates* (1924), which was the sixth film in Stoll's *The Further Mysteries of Dr. Fu Manchu* series, director/scenarist Fred Paul turned to the character of Karamenah for fresh inspiration. Though little is known about this seventh film, it can be concluded from the title that it centers on Karamenah (Shirley), a former slave of Fu Manchu's who, in the 1923 series *The Mystery of Dr. Fu Manchu*, betrayed her master to the authorities in favor of marriage to Dr. Petrie (Wright). Between that point and this, she's mostly gone back and forth between being Fu's captive and leading police to his various lairs.

Dorinea Shirley plays the character here and throughout the second series, replacing the first series' Joan Clarkson. Clarkson's only known films are those in which she played Karamenah, whereas Shirley made a couple more films after this series ended. (Her last performance was in Jack Raymond's *Zero* in 1928.)

The eighth and final film of Stoll's second Fu Manchu series (and Stoll's final presentation of the Asian villain, period) was *Greywater Park* (1924). CW

Kasane-ga-fuchi
Teikine; b/w; length unknown; Japan
D: Shiroku Nagao
Cast: Monjuro Onoe, Tsuruko Matsuda

Written sometime around 1860 by playwright and novelist Sanyutei Encho—who was also responsible for the oft-filmed one-man play *Botan dōrō*—the novel *Shinkei Kasane-ga-fuchi* concerns a female schoolteacher who falls in love with a blind masseur. Unknown to her, her lover is simultaneously carrying on an affair with one of her much-younger students. When she discovers the truth, the teacher kills herself and then returns from the dead for revenge.

This 1924 cinematic adaptation appears to have been the first. It was not the most popular of the silent era versions, however; that distinction goes to director Kenji Mizoguchi's *Passion of a Woman Teacher*, which was produced in 1926 by Nikkatsu Kyoto. Nor would Shiroku Nagao's film be the only one based on the subject to be produced by Teikine; the studio apparently found it profitable enough to remake, with the same title, in 1928. CW

The Midnight Summons
Stoll; b/w; 20 min; Great Britain
D/S: Fred Paul *C:* Frank Canham *P:* Oswald Stoll
Cast: Harry Agar Lyons, Fred Paul, H. Humberston Wright, Frank Wilson, Dorinea Shirley

Following on the heels of their successful 1923 film series *The Mystery of Dr. Fu-Manchu* (which began with *The Scented Envelopes* and ended with *The Shrine of the Seven Lamps*), Stoll continued the criminal mastermind's adventures in 1924 with *The Further Mysteries of Dr. Fu Manchu*. Originally called *The Mystery of Dr. Fu Manchu (Second Series)*, *Further Mysteries* consists of eight films as opposed to the first series' 15, possibly to compensate for larger individual budgets this time out. Actor Frank Paul took over directing and writing chores from A.E. Coleby and Frank Wilson, respectively, though Wilson continued on as Scotland Yard Inspector Weymouth. Actress Dorinea Shirley replaced Joan Clarkson in the role of Karamenah. The second series retained the two-reel format, with a mixture of location and studio footage.

Embracing the supernatural motif often suggested in the original series, this outing has Fu Manchu's (Lyons) body stolen from the morgue and brought back to life (perhaps with the reanimating libation introduced in *The Miracle*, 1923). Fu then kidnaps the recently married Karanmenah (Shirley) and takes her to Burma, where a traveling Nayland Smith (Paul) spots her.

The film was based on the first chapter of Sax Rohmer's 1916 novel *The Return of Dr. Fu Manchu* (aka *The Devil Doctor*). The other films in this second series include *The Coughing Horror*, *Cragmire Tower*, *The Green Mist*, *The Café L'Egypte*, *The Golden Pomegranates*, *Karamaneh* and *Greywater Park* (all 1924). CW

Moken no himitsu
Nikkatsu Kyoto; b/w; length unknown; Japan
D: Minoru Murata *S:* Shuichi Hatamoto *C:* Junichiro Aoshma
Cast: Ryotaro Mizushima, Haruko Sawamura

This little-known Japanese horror-mystery was a take on Arthur Conan Doyle's *The Hound of the Baskervilles*, which was originally presented as a serial in *The Strand Magazine* from August 1901 through April 1902. European adaptations of Conan Doyle's classic novel, beginning with those of Germany and France in 1904, were extremely popular. Several found their way to Japan, where it was inevitable that Japanese filmmakers would try their hand at adapting the tale to a Nipponese setting with Asian sensibilities. Thus *Moken no himitsu* was born.

Minoru Murata was born in Tokyo in 1894 and began acting on stage before moving to films. In 1920 he became a contract player for Shochiku Studios and, by the following year, was directing his own movies (one of them, *Souls on the Road*, has actually survived). He moved to Nikkatsu Studios for a time before starting up his own magazine and helping to form the Directors Guild of Japan, for which he acted as the first president. He died in 1937. Most of his films were domestic dramas (many of which he wrote), with this production apparently his only flirtation with horror.

Moken no himitsu was released on March 24, 1924, in Japan. CW

On Time
Carlos; b/w; 67 min; U.S.
D: Henry Lehrman *S:* Garrett Fort *P:* Richard Talmadge *C:* William Marshall
Cast: Richard Talmadge, Billie Dove, Charles Clary, Stuart Holmes, Tom Wilson, Fred Kirby

Produced by and starring Richard Talmadge, who had been a stunt double for both Douglas Fairbanks and comedian Harold Lloyd, *On Time* is a dire comedy with horror asides. It offers Talmadge as Harry Willis, a man who leaves his bride-to-be with the promise that he will return in six months a wealthy man. When that doesn't happen, fiancée Helen (Dove) gives him a Chinese good luck talisman, after which a Chinaman (Siegmann) immediately offers him a $10,000 job. All Harry has to do is follow a set of "simple" directions that turns out to be anything but. He surmounts various obstacles on the way to his goal, the most notable being a mad scientist who wants to transplant a gorilla's brain into his head. He also attends a bizarre costume ball and dukes it out in a temple with a group of Asians who want his good luck charm. In the end, he learns that it was all a test designed to discern his ability for movie acting. He winds up with both a film contract and a marriage license.

The most notable thing about the film may be that Garrett Fort was its writer. Fort went on to pen the final script for Universal's masterful *Dracula's Daughter* (1936). Other horror films on which he worked include *The Devil Doll* (1936), *Among the Living* (1941) and *The Man in Half Moon Street* (1945). CW

One Spooky Night

Sennett; b/w; 20 min; U.S.
D: Del Lord *S:* John A. Waldron *P:* Mack Sennett *C:* Ernie Crockett, George Unholz
Cast: Billy Bevan, Harry Gribbon, Andy Clyde, Madeline Hurlock, Billy Armstrong, Sid Smith

Shot in late 1923 and released in January 1924, *One Spooky Night* was a spoof of D.W. Griffith's hugely successful *One Exciting Night* (1922), which was itself a send-up of old dark house films. Like that film, *One Spooky Night* deals with a young man (Bevan) who finds himself in a supposedly haunted house.

After being discovered by producer Mack Sennett while touring the United States with a repertory theater group, Australian-born comic Billy Bevan starred in over 250 films between 1916 and 1950, with many of his appearances un-credited from the 1940s on. Though he made few outright horror films, he did have parts in *A Study in Scarlet* (1933) and *Dracula's Daughter* (1936). He retired from acting in 1950 and died in Escondido, California in 1957. CW

The Phantom of the Moulin-Rouge
aka Le fantôme du Moulin-Rouge

Fernand; b/w; 70 min; France
D/S: Rene Clair *P:* Rene Fernand *C:* Jimmy Berliet, Louis Chaix
Cast: Georges Vaultier, Albert Prejean, Sandra Milovanoff, Paul Ollivier, Madeleine Rodrigue, Maurice Schutz

Julien Boissel (Vaultier) is in love with Yvonne (Milovanoff), but his dreams of marrying her are dashed by her father (Schutz), a minister of state who is being blackmailed by a corrupt newspaper publisher. That publisher, Jean Degland (Prejean), has access to some incriminating documents and, as part of his extortion scheme, insists on marrying Yvonne himself. A despair-wracked Boissel visits the famed Moulin Rouge nightclub, where one Dr. Renault (Ollivier) promises to make him forget his worries. Intrigued, Boissel promptly disappears and, not long afterward, a series of odd but innocuous crimes strikes Paris.

This early effort from writer/director Rene Clair blends comedy and science fiction with touches of the macabre. It's a bit too subtle and jokey to be properly considered horror, but it has enough elements of such to interest fright film aficionados.

Clair (1898-1981) worked as a journalist before entering the film industry as an actor. He directed his first film, *The Crazy Ray*,

In *The Phantom of the Moulin-Rouge*, Julien Boissel (Georges Vaultier) submits to mesmerist Dr. Renault (Paul Ollivier) and finds his soul leaving his body.

in 1924, followed by *Entr'acte* the same year. His career eventually took him from his native Paris to Hollywood, where he directed such well-regarded titles as *I Married a Witch* (1942) and *And Then There Were None* (1945), the latter routinely cited as the best screen version of Agatha Christie's oft-filmed murder mystery. His last film, *The Lace Wars*, was released in 1965. He remains renowned for his delicate touch; he excelled at quirky subject matter, often with a comedic or fantastical tone.

This early effort shows a novice director in the process of refining his skills. The story of a man who falls under the influence of a mesmerist of sort bears some similarity to Robert Weine's *The Cabinet of Dr. Caligari* (1919), but *Phantom*'s tone is far lighter and more upbeat. When Boissel submits to Renault's experiments, he finds a form of joyful release; his spirit literally leaves his body without him dying. And the disembodied spirit's subsequent rampage is a good-humored one, a series of harmless, humorous pranks.

Clair effectively uses rapid editing to build tension, and his knack for light and shadow gives the film an appropriately moody look. Viewers expecting a downbeat adventure, however, are likely to be disappointed, while those attuned to Clair's appealing, understated style should be properly entertained. TH

The Shadow of the East
aka Shadow of the Desert

Fox; b/w; 60 min; U.S.
D: George Archainbaud *S:* Fanny Hatton, Frederic Hatton *C:* Jules Cronjager
Cast: Frank Mayo, Mildred Harris, Norman Kerry, Bertram Grassby, Evelyn Brent, Edythe Chapman

Barry Craven (Mayo) runs into former lover Gillian Locke (Harris) while she's traveling near his home in India. The two decide to rekindle their relationship, even though Barry is married to a native girl named Lolaire (Brent). When Lolaire discovers her husband's infidelity and commits suicide, Barry and Gillian return to their native England and marry. But they are followed by former Craven servant Kunwar Singh (Grassby), who casts a spell—known as "the shadow of the east"—on Barry in retribution for his treatment of Lolaire. The enchantment compels him to leave his new wife and go into the Algerian desert, and there he has a chance encounter with old school chum Said (Kerry), the son of an Algerian sheik. Gillian and Singh both follow Barry to the desert, the vindictive ex-servant is killed, the spell is lifted and Barry resumes his happy new life with Gillian.

While none of this sounds terribly horrific, the film made use of narrative tropes (hypnotism, infidelity and murder) typical of early horror fare. Husband-and-wife screenwriting team Frederic and Fanny Hatton based their script on Edith Maude Hull's 1924 novel of the same name. It appears to be the only cinematic adaptation of the book.

Director George Archainbaud went on to direct the obscure *Easy Pickings* (1927) and ended his career directing episodes of such popular TV series as *The Lone Ranger* and *Lassie*. Star Frank Mayo was most popular during the silent era but continued to work into the 1940s. He made bit appearances in *The Phantom Creeps* (1939), starring Bela Lugosi and *The Return of Dr. X* (1939), Humphrey Bogart's only stab at the horror genre.

Co-star Norman Kerry was typical of the wax-mustached, marionette-style leading men of the period; a well liked if none-too-versatile performer, he's best remembered for his three pairings with the legendary Lon Chaney: *The Hunchback of Notre Dame* (1923), *The Phantom of the Opera* (1925) and *The Unknown* (1927). TH

Shin sarayashiki
Shochiku; b/w; 50 min; Japan
D: Zanmu Kako *S:* Atsushi Suzuki *C:* Kyō Ego
Cast: Shirogoro Sawamura

Director Zanmu Kako was a minor success between the years 1921 and 1926, with 1924 being his most prolific. Here he took a stab at the story of Okiku, more often told under the name *Banchō sarayashiki*. The title *Shin sarayashiki* translates as "New Story of the Dish House" and tells the tale of servant woman Okiku, who works for a shogun's vassal named Aoyama. The two fall in love and marry, but after a spat, Okiku deliberately breaks one of her husband's prized dishes. Aoyama initially forgives what is, in fact, a capital offense warranting execution, but later, after discovering a dark reason for her anger, murders her and dumps her body down a well. Okiku gets the last word, however, by returning from the grave to loudly and repeatedly (and, one assumes, maddeningly) count off the remaining nine dishes in the set.

Teikine Studios, with Shuichi Yamashita at the helm, remade *Shin Sarayashiki* in 1926. CW

A Son of Satan
aka **The Ghost of Tolson Manor**; **The Ghost of Tolston's Manor**; **Son of Satan**
Micheaux; b/w; 65 min; U.S.
D/S/P: Oscar Micheaux
Cast: Andrew Bishop, Ida Anderson, Lawrence Chenault, Shingzie Howard, Edna Morton, E.G. Tatum

Among African American director Oscar Mischeaux's most obscure films is this interesting horror melodrama (his second after *The Dungeon*, 1922), which caused quite a stir upon its original stateside release. Shot in Virginia and New York, it concerns a black man who, after an argument, accepts a bet that he will spend an entire night in an allegedly haunted house. Records of the time state that the picture was "filled with scenes of drinking, carousing and shows masked men becoming intoxicated. It shows the playing of crap money, a man killing his wife by choking her …" and so on. It was widely banned due to its presentation of domestic violence and murder, showing the killing of both a cat and a Ku Klux Klan leader, and its presentation of miscegenation was deemed offensive to "Southern ladies." In at least one state the film was banned because of its title alone, likely due to both religious concerns and racial politics.

Though he made films in many genres, Micheaux can be rightly called the father of blaxploitation horror, a new subgenre in the 1920s that proved so popular with audiences that it has never really gone away (though modern examples tend to be shot-on-video affairs). The subgenre includes such *classic* films as *Ingagi* (1930), *Son of Ingagi* (1940), *Naked Evil* (1966) and *Blacula* (1972), among many, many others. CW

That's the Spirit
Warner; b/w; 11 min; U.S.
D: Roy Mack *C:* E.B. DuPar
Cast: Noble Sissle, Cora La Redd, The Washboard Serenaders, F.E. Miller, Mantan Moreland, Buster Bailey

A pair of night watchmen (Moreland, Miller) are frightened as they work their shift at a haunted pawn shop; fortunately for them, not only are the spirits friendly—they've got rhythm!

This short subject is a showcase for the then-popular Noble Sissle and his orchestra. The setup is spooky enough, but the emphasis is more on music and mirth than on thrills and chills. Indeed, the ghosts in question materialize for the sole purpose of playing some tunes!

African American comic Mantan Moreland does his renowned "scareda dem spooks" routine, which he reprised in such Poverty Row fare as *King of the Zombies* (1941) and *Revenge of the Zombies* (1943). Director Roy Mack spent the better part of his career making short subjects like this. TH

Those Who Dare
Creative; b/w; 66 (70) min; U.S.
D: John B. O'Brien *S:* I.W. Irving, Frank S. Beresford *C:* Deveraux Jenkins
Cast: John Bowers, Marguerite De La Motte, Joseph J. Dowling, Claire McDowell, Martha Marshall, Edmund Burns

Captain Manning (Bowers) is ordered to remove his ship, *The Swallow*, from a town's harbor because the vessel is a center of superstition and rumor. He tells how, years earlier, he first found the ship—adrift at sea with a mutinous crew aboard. He brought the boat safely back to land and in the process discovered that the crew was under the sway of a voodoo practitioner.

Little information has survived on this long-lost movie. The director, John B. O'Brien, made films from 1914 until 1926; after that, he focused on acting, appearing in bit parts until his death in 1936. *Those Who Dare*'s supporting cast includes some familiar faces, including Sheldon Lewis (*Dr. Jekyll and Mr. Hyde*, 1920) and Cesare Gravina (*The Man Who Laughs*, 1928). The synopsis suggests that the film flirted with horror, though without a print in

Waxworks belongs to the silent German Expressionist school of filmmaking.

existence, it's impossible to know how overt the voodoo element was. TH

Unseen Hands

Encore; b/w; 65 min; U.S.
D: Jacques Jaccard *S/P:* Walker Coleman Graves, Jr.
Cast: Wallace Beery, Joseph J. Dowling, Fontaine La Rue, Jack Rollens, Cleo Madison, Jim Corey

Jean Scholast (Beery) impresses the wife (La Rue) of Le Quintrec (Dowling), a wealthy businessman. The wife insists that Le Quintrec hire Jean as a reward, and the husband grudgingly complies. After some time, Jean kills Le Quintrec and gains control of both wife and fortune. In the end, however, the scoundrel is frightened to death when he sees his victim's spirit in the desert.

Producer Walker Coleman Graves, Jr. developed *Unseen Hands*' hackneyed scenario; contemporary reference materials list this as both his only writing and sole production credit. Director Jacques Jaccard hailed from New York and made over 80 features between 1914 and 1936. He seems to have specialized in B-Westerns and action fare, making *Unseen Hands* something of a one-off for him. Wallace Beery went on to become a popular character actor, netting an Oscar for *The Champ* (1931) in the process. TH

Waxworks
aka **Das Wachsfigurenkabinett**; **The Three Wax Works**; **Three Wax Men**

Neptune-Film A.G.; b/w; 83 min; Germany
D: Paul Leni *S:* Henrik Galeen *P:* Leo Birinsky, Alexander Kwartiroff *C:* Helmar Lerski
Cast: Emil Jannings, Conrad Veidt, Werner Krauss, Wilhelm Dieterle, Olga Belajeff, John Gottowt

A poet (Dieterle) visits a waxworks museum at the invitation of its mysterious proprietor (Gottowt), who asks his guest to write a tale for each of three prized exhibits: the dread Harun Al-Rashid (Jannings), Ivan the Terrible (Veidt) and Jack the Ripper (Krauss). The poet takes up the offer, leading the viewer into three tales of adventure, intrigue and horror. The story of Harun al-Rashid takes place in a distant Arabian fantasy world where al-Rashid takes a fancy to the wife (Belajeff) of a local baker (Dieterle). The Ivan the Terrible segment shows us the despot as he disrupts the wedding of a young couple (Dieterle and Belajeff), while battling a paranoid fear of assassination. And in the final tale, the poet, exhausted by his labors, dreams of being terrorized by Jack the Ripper.

Paul Leni is seldom grouped with the great German innovators of the silent cinema—Fritz Lang and F.W. Murnau chief among them—but a look at his surviving work should spark deep and serious consideration of doing so. He began painting while still in his teens and eventually became a successful theatrical set designer, doing in this latter capacity some startling work with famed theater director Max Reinhardt. Given that Reinhardt was a key pioneer in the development of German Expressionism, it's no surprise that Leni's directorial work was heavily influenced by that style. Much of Leni's early work as director—*Das Tagebuch des Dr. Hart* (1916), *Prinz Kuckuck* (1919), *Patience* (1920) and *Backstairs* (1921)—appears to have been lost, but most of his pictures from 1924 on, including *Waxworks*, still survive.

Waxworks is a striking contribution to the German horror film. As a *portmanteau* of three tales, it—like Lang's *Destiny* (1919)—anticipates such popular fare as Ealing Studios' *Dead of Night* (1945) and Mario Bava's *Black Sabbath* (1963). Of all the later horror anthologies, it seems to have had the most direct influence on Amicus' *Torture Garden* (1967), which reuses the waxwork motif.

Among anthologies, Leni's work is remarkable in its fluidity and coherence. The three tales are rendered in different styles and have different moods. The linking segment involving the waxworks exhibit is done with ample attention to atmosphere. Just the right tone of spookiness is established in the opening shots, which are sensibly kept to a minimum as the director opts instead to focus on the three tales themselves. He starts the film proper on a jocular note with the tale of Harun Al-Rashid. This fanciful, imaginative visual evocation of a fairy tale land is said to have impressed Douglas Fairbanks, Sr. so strongly that it prompted him to make *The Thief of Bagdad* (1924).

Because the tone is light, the segment provides great silent film star Emil Jannings (best remembered for his heartbreaking turn in Murnau's *The Last Laugh*, 1924) a rare opportunity to play broad comedy. Jannings is wonderful as the lecherous, childlike Caliph. Though he doesn't make for a credible menace, he is

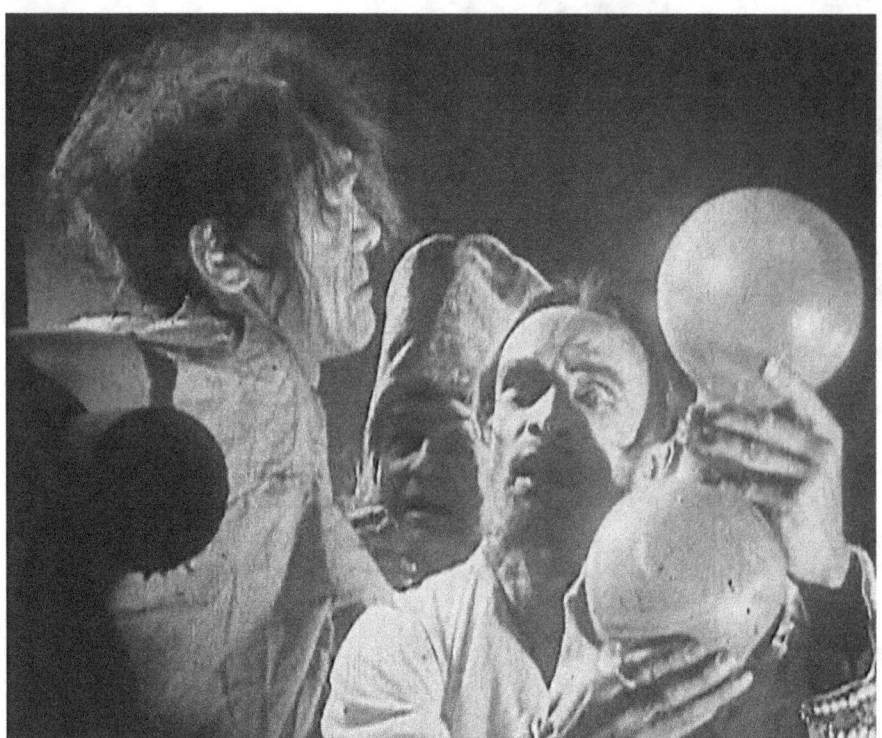

A waxworks exhibit provides the backdrop for horror in Paul Leni's *Waxworks*.

capricious and prone to throwing fits, with the implication being that he's very much a naughty schoolboy at heart.

The second episode, which focuses on Conrad Veidt's monstrous Ivan the Terrible, is a more recognizable genre piece. The dank, dingy atmosphere is beautifully rendered. Leni creates some memorable tableaux as Ivan lords over his kingdom, poisoning for his own sick amusement the people who displease him. And as usual, Veidt steals every scene in which he appears. With his long beard and matted hair, he oozes giddy sadism up until the episode's finale, when he goes completely berserk.

The final segment is the least developed of the three, but it is also the most overtly Expressionistic and experimental. Left to his writing in the waxworks, the poet falls asleep and dreams that the figure of Jack the Ripper—referred to as Spring Heeled Jack—has come to life and is trying to kill him. Leni makes inspired use of tilted angles, shadowy lighting and all kinds of trick photography to create the right mood of terror. Alas, it's the shortest segment, too much so to deliver on its full potential—though Werner Krauss (who played the demented title character in Robert Weine's masterpiece, *The Cabinet of Dr. Caligari*, 1919) is effectively creepy as the world's most famous serial killer.

Wilhelm Dieterle, later to become a director in Hollywood, and Olga Belajeff perform the lead roles. Neither come close to matching the intensity of the film's great character actors, but they're at least credible in their performances.

The fantastic cinematography by Helmar Lerski, along with Leni's imaginative production design, ensures that every frame is interesting to view, making *Waxworks* one of the key genre films to have emerged from Germany in the 1920s. (The 1988 American film *Waxwork* arguably recycles the central conceit of Leni's film, but any similarity between the two ends there.)

As a result of going over budget, an intended fourth segment based on an infamous robber from a series of German novels by Christian August Vulpius was never shot. Leni subsequently relocated to the United States, where he directed several more films of note before his tragic demise from blood poisoning at the age of 44. TH

What an Eye
Universal; b/w; 22 min; U.S.
D/S: Edward I. Luddy
Cast: Buddy Messinger, Hilliard Karr

A mostly run-of-the-mill haunted house comedy, *What an Eye* does have the distinction of presenting a purported monster with an extremely large eye. The film was directed by Edward I. Luddy, one of several pseudonyms for Russian-born Edward Ludwig, who came to the United States when still a child. He got his start in the industry as a silent-era writer before moving up to shooting live-action shorts. By the 1930s he was directing mostly second-rate features, though he did squeeze in some distinguished work now and again, most notably the Claude Rains-starrer *The Man Who Reclaimed His Head* (1934) and the John Wayne classic *Wake of the Red Witch* (1948). Luddy eventually shifted his efforts exclusively to the hot new medium of television, wrapping up his career in the mid-1960s. He died in Santa Monica, California in 1982.

Neither of *Eye*'s leads, Buddy Messinger and Hilliard Karr, did much after the silent era other than un-credited bit roles. As for the film itself, it was released on October 8, just in time for Halloween 1924. CW

Wild Oranges
Goldwyn; b/w; 88 (76) min; U.S.
D/Co-S: King Vidor *Co-S:* Tom Miranda *C:* John W. Boyle
Cast: Frank Mayo, Virginia Valli, Ford Sterling, Nigel De Brulier, Charles A. Post

John Woolfolk (Mayo) sets sail after his wife is killed in a freak accident. At sea, the aroma of wild orange trees lure second mate Paul Halvard (Sterling) and him to a remote desert island. There they meet Litchfield Stope (De Brulier) and his granddaughter Millie (Valli), along with the slow-witted Iscah Nicholas (Post). Woolfolk falls in love with Millie, but it turns out that Iscah is an escaped convict who has been keeping the Stopes hostage. In fact, Woolfolk's romantic interest in Millie pushes the convict over the edge.

King Vidor (1894-1982) was born in Galveston, Texas and entered the film industry as a clerk for Universal studios. He made his directorial debut with *Hurricane in Galveston* (1913), which dealt with a major disaster that befell his hometown in 1900. His first big splash came with the war drama *The Big Parade* (1925). Though well regarded in his time—he earned five Oscar nominations—and being the recipient of an Honorary Academy Award in 1979, Vidor's name hasn't sustained his reputation as well as some of his contemporaries. He worked consistently until 1959, retired, then reemerged in 1980 with a documentary on painting titled *The Metaphor*. (A career bookended by work in 1913 and 1980 garnered him a place in the *Guinness Book of World Records* as the filmmaker with the longest career.)

Wild Oranges came just before Vidor's major breakout success. The film's depiction of people at the mercy of a psychopath in an isolated locale set the stage for many horror films and thrillers to follow. In terms of performances, obscure character actor Charles A. Post steals the film as escaped convict Iscah Nicholas. Post's imposing height dwarfs the rest of the cast, and he provides a convincing portrait of homicidal mania.

Leading man Frank Mayo was a popular lead in the silent era but drifted into un-credited bit parts after the coming of sound; among these later roles were turns in *The Phantom Creeps* (1939), starring Bela Lugosi, and *The Return of Dr. X* (1939), starring Humphrey Bogart (in his only horror film appearance). Virginia Valli likewise transitioned to talkies, but her star soon waned and she left films in 1931. Nigel De Brulier appeared in *The Hound of the Baskervilles* (1939), which inaugurated the long-running series of Sherlock Holmes adventures starring Basil Rathbone and Nigel Bruce. TH

1925

The Bear's Wedding
aka **Medvezhya svadba**; **The Legend of the Bear's Wedding**; **The Bear's Marriage**
Mezhrabpom-Rus; b/w; Russia
D: Konstantin Eggert, Vladimir Gardin S: Georgiy Grebner C: Eduard Tisse, Pyotr Yermolov
Cast: Vera Malinovskaya, Natalya Rozenel, Yuri Zavadsky, Konstantin Eggert

A bear frightens a pregnant Countess. She later gives birth to a child with animalistic tendencies. When the boy reaches adulthood, he marries a woman and, on their wedding night, transforms into a bear, attacks his wife and drinks her blood.

Prosper Mérimé, best remembered as the author of *Carmen* (1845), also demonstrated a flair for the macabre in stories such as *La Venus d'Ille* (1837), which told of a statue of Venus that comes to life and crushes a man in her metallic embrace and *Lokis* (1869), which can be seen as an early variation on the werewolf theme. *Carmen* would be transformed into a very popular opera of the same name by Georges Bizet, while *Venus* would serve as the inspiration for Italian horror maestro Mario Bava's swansong, the made-for-television *La Venere d'Ille* (1978). As for *Lokis*, it served as the uncredited inspiration for this Russian production. The title is a corruption of the Lithuanian word "lokys," which means "bear." The story has its roots in such popular fairy tales as *Beauty and the Beast*, and its fatalistic tone and theme of love not conquering all anticipates such lycanthropic efforts as Guy Endore's *The Werewolf of Paris* (1933, later adapted as *The Curse of the Werewolf*,

1961), as well as ground-breaking genre films such as *Werewolf of London* (1935) and *The Wolf Man* (1941).

In his book *Tod Browning's Dracula*, author Gary D. Rhodes points to *The Bear's Wedding* as one of several European productions of the period that helped lay the groundwork for Browning's seminal horror classic. Critics of the time considered it to be pretty gruesome, which would seem to have worked against its chances of getting much of a theatrical showing, but it nevertheless managed to secure an American theatrical release in 1927. Extant reviews are contradictory, with some making it sound as though the groom literally changes into a bear—thus making it possibly the first depiction of a man-into-beast scenario—and some indicating that the condition is more psychological, with the groom donning a bearskin to commit his crime. In more recent years, unfortunately, the film has become obscure, never securing a home video release, though prints are reportedly stored in a couple of archives.

Directors Konstantin Eggert and Vladimir Gardin enjoyed some success in the early days of Russian cinema. They both worked as screenwriters and actors in addition to directing. Gardin's career extended into the early 1950s and saw him bestowed with a number of honors from his peers, while the comparatively obscure Eggert seems to have petered out in the late 1930s. He died in 1955; Gardin followed 10 years later.

Lokis was filmed under its original title in 1970 by Polish filmmaker Janusz Majewski. The film won Grand Prix prize at the 1971 Stiges Film Festival. The most famous adaptation came several years later, however, when eccentric Polish auteur Walerian Borowczyk used the story as the inspiration for what would become his most notorious film, *The Beast* (1975). TH

The Bells
aka **Le Juif Polonais**; **The Polish Jew**
Belga; b/w; length unknown; Australia/Great Britain/Belgium
D: Harry Southwell S: Fernand Crommelynck P: Paul Dallemagne C: Henri Barreyre, Charles Lengnich
Cast: Harry Southwell, Myra Bertsini, Berthe Charmal, Fernand Crommelynck, Micky Damremont, Charles Schauten

After a five-year stint with Vitagraph in the United States, Cardiff-born actor, writer and director Harry Southwell moved to Australia and set up his own production company. It was an unmitigated disaster, and in the early 1920s he returned to Europe. There he shot several pictures, including this British-Belgian co-production based on Leopold Lewis' famed stage play, itself an Anglicized adaptation of Émile Erckmann and Alexandre Chatrian's French horror production *Le Juif Polonaise* ("The Polish Jew").

It reportedly took over five months to shoot this version of *The Bells*, with Southwell starring as Mathias, an innkeeper who murders a Jew for his money and is thereafter haunted by the sound of the bells he associates with his victim.

After the film was completed, Southwell went back to Sydney, Australia and worked for Australian Players. Several of his films were based on the infamous Kelly Gang, including *The Kelly Gang* (1920), *When the Kellys Were Out* (1923) and *When the Kellys Rode* (1934). One of his last features was a 1935 remake of *The Bells* titled *The Burgomeister*.

The next film adaptation of the Erkmann-Chatrian-Lewis work is also the most famous: *The Bells* (1926), starring Lionel Barrymore and Boris Karloff. CW

Dr. Pyckle and Mr. Pride, Stan Laurel's comedic take on *Dr. Jekyll and Mr. Hyde*

Dr. Pyckle and Mr. Pride
aka **Dr. Pyckle and Mr. Pryde**; **Doctor Pyckle and Mister Pride**
Rock/Pathé; b/w; 20 min; U.S.
D: Scott Pembroke, Joe Rock *P:* Joe Rock *S:* Tay Garnett *C:* Edgar Lyons
Cast: Stan Laurel, Julie Leonard

Dr. Pyckle (Laurel) believes he can divide the human personality into good and evil aspects. To that end, he shutters himself in his castle laboratory and sets about concocting a formula. After a series of failures (and explosions), he hits upon the right combination of ingredients, drinks it and becomes the sinister Mr. Pride, who steals into the city to do mischief. Rather than the usual Hyde-like antics, however—stomping little children on street corners and the like—this monster steals and eats their ice cream and blows spit wads in their faces. But even these relatively innocuous actions don't sit well with the city folk who witness them, and they chase Mr. Pride to the residence of Dr. Pyckle. When they bang on the castle door, the kindly doctor greets them. The game is almost given away when his pet dog consumes the formula, grows a mane of curly black hair and bites the doctor's behind, but the doctor manages for the moment to avoid discovery. Once the angry townspeople leave, however, Dr. Pyckle again becomes Mr. Pride and progresses to terrorizing lonely old widows and rube police officers. Again, the townspeople chase him, and again he safely makes his way home. Once holed up in his laboratory, he vows to never again take his formula, but after his assistant (Leonard) shows up, he finds himself changing spontaneously into the vile Mr. Pride one final time.

Dr. Pyckle and Mr. Pride is a spoof not so much of Robert Louis Stevenson's classic novella *The Strange Case of Dr. Jekyll and Mr. Hyde* (1886) as it is of John Barrymore's popular film adaptation of 1920, *Dr. Jekyll and Mr. Hyde*. Laurel's Mr. Pride make-up is a comical dead ringer for Barrymore's, complete with long, straightened black hair and extended fingers. In his guise as Dr. Pyckle, Laurel resembles a bespectacled Harold Lloyd.

The production is slick, and much of the comedy is actually funny. Part of its success can be attributed to the fact that it never strays too far from the film or genre it's spoofing, unlike genre comedies such as *Young Frankenstein* (1974) or the later entries in the *Scary Movie* series, which throw in so many unrelated references that they seem to lose sight of what they're lampooning.

Stan Laurel (1890-1965) hit upon prolonged and massive success the very next year as one half of the comedy duo Laurel and Hardy. (Both men had starred together in *The Lucky Dog* in 1921, but they did not play off each other as they were to do in later films.) Their relationship would last until the early 1950s and would include well over 100 films.

Pete the Dog, who actually gets a screen credit, later starred in a series of Buster Brown silent films as Buster's dog Tige. The animal is immediately recognizable by the ring around his eye, which was painted onto him by a make-up artist. CW

The Green Archer
Pathé; b/w; 10 chapters; U.S.
D: Spencer Gordon Bennet *S:* Frank Leon Smith
Cast: Allene Ray, Walter Miller, Frank Lackteen, Burr McIntosh, Dorothy King, Stephen Grattan

Dissolute millionaire Abel Bellamy (McIntosh) has amassed his fortune by means not altogether honest. He arranges for an English castle to be dismantled and transported to the United States, where it is reassembled so that he can live there in gaudy splendor. But the building is haunted by a mysterious figure armed with a crossbow, known only as "the green archer." Several people in turn are suspected of being the green archer as various murders are committed.

The prolific British mystery author Edgar Wallace unleashed his novel *The Green Archer* on the public in 1923. The story was a hit, and this serialization by Pathé followed soon thereafter. The filmmakers took some liberties with the material, including devising a clever (if impractical) way of relocating the action from the English countryside to the United States. Alas, of the 10 chapters, only the third, fourth and fifth are known to still exist, preserved in UCLA's film and television library. (Columbia Studios' 15-part 1940 *The Green Archer* serialization, to the contrary, is easily seen.)

The Lost World **tells of the discovery of a plateau where prehistoric beasts have survived extinction.**

Leading lady Allene Ray was something of a rival to serial queen Pearl White (*The Perils of Pauline*, 1914); in addition to *The Green Archer*, she also top-lined such then-popular serials as *The Terrible People* (1928; it was another Wallace serialization), *Hawk of the Hills* (1929) and *The Indians Are Coming* (1930). *Archer* director Spencer Gordon Bennett also made a mark in B-serials, helming everything from the aforementioned *Terrible People* to *G-Men vs. The Black Dragon* (1943).

Wallace adaptations continued to hit screens throughout the early 1930s but really took off with a series of British-lensed, low-budget adaptations in the latter half of that decade. For many viewers, however, Wallace's legacy is inextricably linked to the German made *krimi* films of the late 1950s through the early 1970s, the majority of which were produced by Rialto and directed by the likes of Harald Reinl and Alfred Vohrer. TH

The Haunted Honeymoon
aka **Billy Gets Married**
Roach; b/w; 22 min; U.S.
Co-D/S: Fred Guiol *Co-D:* Ted Wilde *P:* Hal Roach
Cast: Glenn Tryon, Blanche Mehaffy, James Finlayson, George Rowe, Yorke Sherwood, Helen Gilmore

This is a typical Hal Roach comedy short about two honeymooners (Tryon, Mehaffy) in a haunted house. Apart from the atmospheric sets (which are impressive), the only other things of note are the film's tentative connections to later greatness. There's an un-credited appearance by Janet Gaynor, who went on to win the Best Actress Academy Award in 1928 (for her work in three 1927 films, before Oscar's rules were modified to recognize individual performances only). She remained the youngest woman to ever receive the award until Marlee Matlin (at the same age, 21) won for *Children of a Lesser God* in 1986.

Gaynor wasn't the only one here to later hit the big time. Writer/director Fred Guiol received an Oscar nomination for Best Adapted Screenplay for his 1956 big-screen adaptation of Edna Ferber's novel *Giant*.

The slight similarities between this 1925 film and 1986's *Haunted Honeymoon*, a horror spoof starring Gene Wilder and Gilda Radner, aren't striking enough to indicate a significant relationship between the two. CW

The Hidden Menace
Steiner; b/w; 55 min; U.S.
D: Charles Hutchison *S:* Jack Natteford
Cast: Charles Hutchison, Frank Leigh

Very little information has survived about this obscure film. Based on a then-contemporary synopsis, it appears to have anticipated such popular horror titles as *The Mystery of the Wax Museum* (1933) and its various imitators (*Secrets of the French Police*, 1932, for instance) and remakes (*House of Wax*, 1953) in its tale of a woman menaced by a crazed sculptor. The sculptor comes to believe that the heroine is the perfect inspiration for his masterpiece, and it's up to an intrepid reporter to save her before she perishes for the sake of art.

Director/star Charles Hutchison was born in Pittsburgh, Pennsylvania in 1880; his directorial career lasted from 1915 to 1938 and his acting career from 1914 to 1944. His final work was an unbilled bit part in the 1944 serial *Captain America*. He presumably played the hero in *The Hidden Menace*, but there's as little solid info about the cast as there is concerning anything else connected to the film. TH

Living Buddhas
aka **Lebende Buddhas**
Wegener; b/w; 139 min; Germany
D/Co-S: Paul Wegener *Co-S:* Hans Sturm *P:* Berthold Held *C:* Guido Seeber, Reimar Kuntze, Joseph Rona
Cast: Paul Wegener, Asta Nielsen, Hans Sturm, Kathe Haack, Gregori Chmara, Carl Ebert

Professor Campbell (Sturm) and his young wife (Haack) are members of an expedition to Tibet, the mission of which is to investigate the rituals of a cruel and primitive cult. Once there

Bull Montana as the Ape Man in *The Lost World*

they run afoul of the High Llama (Wegener), who wishes to use Mrs. Campbell in one of their sacrifices. Campbell extricates the team from imminent danger and in so doing comes into possession of a sacred document belonging to the cult. Once back to civilization (i.e., Europe), he works to decipher the document, but there's still the cult to contend with …

This five-chapter fantasy by Paul Wegener mixes equal parts hokum and horror. Some sources indicate that the parts were rationed out between 1923 and 1925; others simply list the film as dating from 1925. In any event, all but five minutes of its epic running time are believed to be lost. This is regrettable, as Wegener's contributions to the cinema of fantasy and the macabre hold up reasonably well. Typically, he cast himself as the villain of the piece, though one could argue that the meddling archaeologist played by Hans Sturm (who co-wrote the script with Wegener) also comes off in a less than sympathetic light.

Danish actress Asta Nielsen plays the archetypal damsel-in-distress; she climbed to superstardom in the 1920s German film industry. At first she coasted by on her good looks and shapely figure, but the coming of sound revealed that her speaking gifts were less than ideal; her career went into decline thereafter.

The surviving fragments of the film indicate a strong visual style and atmosphere galore, which should come as no surprise to those familiar with Wegener's signature contribution to the genre, *The Golem: How He Came into the World* (1920). *Living Buddhas*' ambitious vision reportedly extended to some elaborate FX and animation work, which helped to make the Llama into a credibly mystical figure. TH

The Lost World
First National; b/w; 75 (64, 100) min; U.S.
D: Harry O. Hoyt S: Marion Fairfax P: Earl Hudson C: Arthur Edeson FX: Willis O'Brien, Marcel Delgado
Cast: Bessie Love, Lewis Stone, Wallace Beery, Lloyd Hughes, Alma Bennett, Arthur Hoyt, Bull Montana, Jocko the Monkey, Arthur Conan Doyle

Edward Malone (Hughes) wants to marry Gladys (Bennett), but she will only "marry a man of great deeds and strange experiences—a man who can look death in the face without flinching!" When he tries to change her mind, she insists, "Not until all London rings with your name!" Edward, a reporter for the London Record Journal, takes up her challenge when his boss sends him to the Zoological Hall to cover a lecture from Professor Challenger (Beery). Challenger, a scientist who has "nearly killed" three reporters sent to interview him, insists that living dinosaurs still exist. During the lecture, college students attempt to shout the Professor down, but he somehow manages to goad famous hunter and explorer Sir John Roxton (Stone), as well as Edward, into joining an expedition to the so-called Lost World, a plateau where prehistoric beasts allegedly still roam. Challenger also introduces Edward to Paula White, the daughter of an explorer who went missing in the Lost World. Only the elder

White's notebook was ever found, and its detailed drawings of dinosaurs are the reason Challenger is convinced of the reality of living dinosaurs. Also on the expedition is the skeptical Professor Summerlee (played by the director's older brother, actor Arthur Hoyt). After encountering several perils, the group does indeed find the Lost World, replete with dinosaurs galore.

In 1902 fossil hunter Barnum Brown made an astounding discovery in the Hell Creek Formation of Montana—the remains of one of the largest predatory dinosaurs ever discovered. Three years later Harry F. Osbourne, the curator of New York's American Museum of Natural History, named the find *Tyrannosarurs rex* ("Tyrant Lizard King"). News of the discovery and its impact on paleontology spread around the globe, and Scottish writer Sir Arthur Conan Doyle was so inspired by it and other recent dinosaur discoveries that he wrote a novel about prehistoric animals existing in the modern world. 1912's *The Lost World* told of a trek through the South American jungles and the discovery of a plateau where prehistoric beasts have survived extinction.

The book was a sensation, and it didn't take Hollywood long to come knocking on Doyle's door. After all, the author's *The Hound of the Baskervilles* had been filmed numerous times already, and the writer was pretty much a household name. First National Pictures ponied up the money for the rights to *Lost World* and assigned playwright Marion Fairfax, the wife of actor Tully Marshall, to write the script. Virtual unknown Harry O. Hoyt was chosen to direct.

Fairfax followed Doyle's story fairly closely, though she added a love interest to give the movie some crossover gender appeal. The opening credits call the film "Sir Arthur Conan Doyle's Stupendous Story of Adventure and Romance," the "romance" angle further underscored by giving Bessie Love top billing despite her playing a character created just for the film. But while Fairfax's script is serviceable, Hoyt's direction is insipid. Believing that the audience would be more interested in Bessie Love than in the denizens of the antediluvian past, Hoyt never misses an opportunity to show the heroine's face in close shot, her eyes wide with wonder, fear, excitement or romance (her mood is at times hard to pin down, as she uses the same expression for every emotion).

The lame creative decision is admittedly understandable; Love had begun her acting career in 1915 and was a big star by the mid-1920s. She maintained a respectable career even after she peaked, working until three years before her death in 1986; her last role was in Tony Scott's *The Hunger* (1983). Here, however, she pales in comparison to Wallace Beery as the curmudgeonly Professor Challenger, though she's the perfect foil for the dull Lloyd Hughes as Edward. Rounding out the cast is the top-notch Lewis Stone, who made a career out of playing strong older men (he also portrayed famous literary character Nayland Smith in *The Mask of Fu Manchu*, 1932).

But let's be honest: The actors aren't the stars here. It's all about the dinosaurs. The man behind them, special effects technician Willis Harold O'Brien (1886-1962), had worked with stop motion since at least 1915, when he animated *The Dinosaur and the Missing Link: A Prehistoric Tragedy* for Edison. He followed that up with the poorly reviewed but monetarily successful *The Ghost of Slumber Mountain* (1918), and it was on the strength of *Ghost*'s box-office receipts that he landed the job of effects technician on *The Lost World*. This, in turn, led to his work on one of the most famous and beloved films of all time, the original 1933 version of *King Kong*. By 1925, the process of stop motion had been around for two and a half decades. Here it entailed getting a brief shot of a dinosaur model or models, repositioning them slightly, taking another shot, and so on, so that when played consecutively, the film frames gave the impression that the beasts were moving. The end result was somewhat jerky, but because silent cinema tended to look jerky to begin with, the dinosaurs didn't seem anywhere near as unreal to audiences at that time as they do today.

This then is what qualifies the movie as horror. The stop-motion technique had, quite simply, never been used to such great effect. One can only imagine how terrifyingly awesome it was to see a giant *Allosaurus* attacking a massive but defenseless "Brontosaurus," a "Trachodon" or a *Brachiosaurus*. Then there's the herd of what most people today would recognize as *Triceratops*—in fact, it was based on a Charles R. Knight painting based on a dubious ceratopsian known at the time as Agathaumas—fleeing an erupting volcano while a group of *Allosaurus* gorily feed on a kill. And there are also fleeting shots of a *Diplodicus*, a *Styracosaurus* and a *Tyrannosaurus rex*. When the visitors to the prehistoric plateau first arrive, they spy a *Pteranodon*, though Professor Challenger mistakenly refers to it as a *Pterodactyl*.

Given the year in which the movie was made and what was known about dinosaurs at the time, the film is amazingly accurate in its depictions. It wasn't yet known that the "Brontosaurus" in the New York Museum of Natural History (the specimen on which this film's primary creature was based) was a chimera reconstructed from the (skeletal) body of *Apatosaurus*, the skull of *Camarasaurus* and the feet of *Diplodicus*. (The corrected animal

Lon Chaney, wearing less make-up than usual, in *The Monster*

is now simply referred to as *Apatosaurus*.) Similarly amiss is the film's representation of the long-necked sauropods, which are depicted with snakelike necks when in fact their neck vertebrae were generally locked in place, limiting their mobility. *Brachiosaurus* is correctly shown as having longer arms than legs, though its hind-end is too small, and *Diplodicus* has a suitably long neck and long, whip-like tail, moreso than the diplodicid *Apatosaurus*. "Trachodon" (a wastebasket taxon first named from the teeth of both duckbilled and ceratopsian dinosaurs) is today called *Edmontosaurus* and should have had a more rounded snout than the flat bill with which it is presented.

The film's climax, in which the heroes bring a "Brontosaurus" back to London (in the novel it's a flying reptile), only to have it escape into the city, was so shocking to audiences at the time that some people allegedly left theaters believing that what they'd seen was real. And indeed, the final moments are so effective and powerful that they ensured cinema would be doomed to repeat them over and over again for decades to come in such films as *King Kong*, *The Beast from 20,000 Fathoms* (1953) and *The Valley of Gwangi* (1969). CW

Maciste in Hell
aka Maciste all'inferno
Excelsior/Olympia; b/w; 66 (95, 97); Italy
D: Guido Brignone S: Riccardo Artuffo C: Ubaldo Arata, Massimo Terzano FX: Segundo de Chomon
Cast: Bartolomeo Pagano, Franz Sala, Elena Sangro, Lucia Zanussi, Umberto Guarracino, Domenico Serra

Muscleman superhero Maciste made his big-screen debut in Giovanni Pastrone's *Cabiria* in 1914. So enduringly popular was the mythical he-man (many of the 1960s films in which he appeared were rendered as Hercules movies when anglicized) that he wound up appearing in approximately 60 films. About half of these were made during the silent era, with the character a sort of one-man propaganda machine, popping up in different periods to save Italy from her enemies. He was especially active during World War I, often incarnating as a soldier defending his comrades from enemy fire.

Bartolomeo Pagano, who played the part during the silent era, was no actor, a fact that didn't hurt his career and may have actually added to his popularity. He was discovered in 1914 while working the docks of Genoa as a longshoreman (though he appears to have had a small part in *The Last Days of Pompeii* in 1908). His buff physique immediately caught the eye of director Brignone, who cast him as the muscular hero of *Cabiria*. Pagano went on to legally change his name to Maciste, though he retired from acting in the late 1920s to marry and raise a family.

While many of the Maciste films had darker or fantastical elements, *Maciste in Hell* appears to have been the only one of the original series that's an outright horror film. Influenced by *Inferno*, the first portion of Dante Alighieri's 14th century poem *La Divina Commedia*, the movie begins by quoting Longfellow's description of the Powers of Evil as they plan a visit to Earth.

Then it's on to the story. Pluto's minions assume human form in an attempt to conquer man. They arrive at twilight and the Devil, sensing that the farmer Maciste is too strong for the infernal usurpers, offers him anything his heart desires to join the evil army. Maciste reacts by threatening to throw the Devil out a window, and the Devil vanishes. Shortly thereafter the Infernal One strikes upon a plan to force Maciste's hand. This leads to Maciste being trapped in Hell, where he's tricked into becoming a demon by kissing a beautiful woman who is in reality a hideous fiend. A war ensues, during which heads are torn off and thrown about with abandon. Maciste is forced to remain in the underworld until the prayer of a child on Christmas Eve frees his soul and enables him to return to the physical realm.

While the film's theological/metaphysical underpinnings are more than a tad bit confused and its storyline is, to be kind, convoluted, its visuals more than make up for these problems—demons fly in great circles through the sulfuric air; a wilting flower loses petals one by one; a satyr reattaches his head to his body; a ceiling of naked, intertwined bodies reach out to grab Maciste as he passes; the giant bat-winged Lucifer feasts on the bodies of those frozen in the lake around him and a fire-breathing dragon is ridden by Maciste and Luciferina (Zanussi) through the skies of Hell. The arresting images that comprise the bulk of the movie are based on the art of Gustav Doré, a 19th-century French artist known for illustrating many famous works of literature, including the Bible.

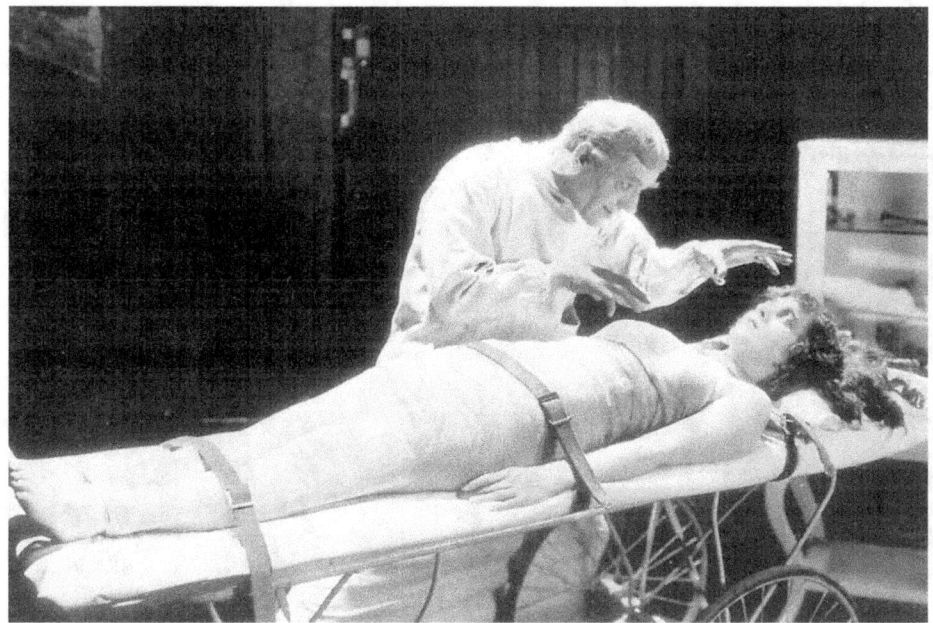
Lon Chaney plays the mad scientist Dr. Ziska in *The Monster*.

Guido Brignone (1886-1959), who began his career as a director in 1913, quickly graduated to major productions and by 1934 had won the Venice Film Festival's top award, the Mussolini Cup, for Best Italian Film for *Teresa Confalonieri* (known as *Loyalty of Love* in the United States). He continued directing until the year of his death, when he completed the sophomoric *Nel Segno di Roma* (*The Sign of Rome*); when it was released in the United States, American International Pictures felt that the title wasn't interesting enough and changed it to *Sign of the Gladiator*, despite the fact that there were no gladiators in it. CW

The Monster
MGM; b/w; 95 min; U.S.
D/Co-S/P: Roland West *Co-S:* Willard Mack, Albert G. Kenyon
C: Hal Mohr
Cast: Lon Chaney, Johnny Arthur, Gertrude Olmstead, Hallam Cooley, Charles Sellon, Walter James, Knute Erickson, George Austin, Edward McWade, Ethel Wales, Matthew Betz

A series of disappearances baffle the police in a small town. Johnny Goodlittle (Arthur), an aspiring detective employed as a grocery clerk, determines to get to the bottom of the matter. To this end, he reluctantly teams with his boss, Amos Rugg (Cooley), who is also his rival for the hand of lovely Betty Watson (Olmstead). The inept duo manages to link the disappearances to a deserted sanitarium. During a violent thunderstorm, Johnny, Amos and Betty decide to investigate the dilapidated building. Much to their surprise, they find that the place isn't deserted at all. The strange Dr. Ziska (Chaney) has been left in charge, and there's every reason to believe that the lunatics are running the asylum.

New York-born playwright Crane Wilbur (1886-1973) is best remembered for having written the 3D horror hit *House of Wax* (1953), but his prolific career touched upon the horror genre fairly frequently. His 1924 play *The Monster* was a huge hit, and its melding of humor, horror and suspense was a major influence on many an old dark house film to follow. Metro Goldwyn Mayer saw the show as a perfect fit for top star Lon Chaney and hired innovative director Roland West to direct its transition to the screen.

West is something of a forgotten figure today, but genre buffs remember him for his work on *The Bat* (1926) and its elaborate sound remake, *The Bat Whispers* (1930). Those with a taste for scandal, though, may also know his name for a very different reason. He was the long-time lover of actress Thelma Todd, who died of carbon monoxide poisoning under mysterious circumstances in 1935. West, who was married to another woman during his affair with Todd, has long been considered one of the leading suspects in the case. Still, before his career was derailed by public scandal and humiliation, he proved himself to be an imaginative and original talent.

Sadly, it's difficult to really appreciate *The Monster* today. The reasons for this are many. Viewers expecting a typical Lon Chaney vehicle are in for a major disappointment; the actor doesn't show up until well into the picture. And while he admittedly makes for an alarming presence—an interesting combination of the suave and the decayed—it's not much of a role and doesn't allow him to evoke the kind of audience empathy one normally associates with the great actor.

To be fair, the finale is undeniably exciting. To get there, however, the viewer is required to sit through, among other sour notes, a lot of not-very-funny comedy courtesy of Johnny Arthur's would-be detective. And though West and cinematographer Hal Mohr (*The Walking Dead*, 1936) manage some atmospheric set-ups, the film's overall pace is mostly slow. The supporting cast is generally forgettable as well, adding to the blandness.

That's not to say that the film is without its pleasures. West manages a wonderful beginning detailing the abduction of "the monster's" latest victim. And when *The Monster* finally gets down to business in the above-referenced final reel, it's actually rather stirring. Had the film been played a little straighter—or, at the very least, had Arthur's excessive mugging been toned down in favor of more Chaney—*The Monster* might warrant more serious consideration than it receives. As it is, the film is an elaborate, well-made but ultimately frustrating horror/comedy hybrid. TH

The Mystic
MGM; b/w; 70 min; U.S.
D/P: Tod Browning *S:* Waldemar Young *C:* Ira H. Morgan
Cast: Aileen Pringle, Conway Tearle, Mitchell Lewis, Robert Ober, Stanton Heck, David Torrence

Michael Nash (Tearle) convinces a fortune-teller (Pringle) to help him rob a young heiress. To that end, the fortune-teller dupes the heiress into believing that her dead father is instructing her to turn over all her possessions to the unscrupulous duo.

Director Tod Browning continues his fascination with hucksters and carnival types with this dark melodrama. If the story sounds familiar, there's a good reason. Browning pretty much pillaged his own *The Unholy Three* (1925)—his biggest hit to that

Lon Chaney poses—as the Phantom—with his famous make-up kit.

date—for inspiration. The screenplay by Waldemar Young alters some of the earlier film's plot elements, but the basic set-up of carnival hucksters using their ingenuity to pursue ignoble ends is pretty much the same.

Alas, Browning was unable to secure the services of his favorite star, Lon Chaney, so the cast is comprised of now-forgotten names. The fact that the film failed to make much of an impact at the box-office and remains almost impossible to see today seems to confirm that the director was at something of a loss without his famous star.

According to David Skal and Elias Savada's *Dark Carnival*, an excellent biography about Browning, the film was "especially distinguished by the costumes of the famous French designer Romain de Tirtoff—otherwise known, internationally, as Erte." The presence of such an illustrious designer on the production indicates that Browning was sitting comfortably atop the success of *The Unholy Three*.

Browning and Chaney continued their series of collaborations the following year with the crime melodrama *The Black Bird* (1926). TH

The Phantom of the Opera
Universal; b/w, color sequence; 106 (94) min; U.S.
D: Rupert Julian *S:* Elliot J. Clawson, Raymond L. Schrock, Bernard McConville, Jasper Spearing, Richard Wallace, Walter Anthony, Tony Reed, Frank M. McCormack *P:* Carl Laemmle *C:* Charles Van Enger
Cast: Lon Chaney, Mary Philbin, Norman Kerry, Arthur Edmund Carewe, Gibson Gowland, John St. Polis

In 1880s Paris, the city's famed Opera House is beset by a run of bad luck attributed to a mysterious masked phantom (Chaney) who lives in the maze of catacombs beneath the building. A seat is reserved for him in Box Number Five in hopes of placating him, and he soon becomes smitten by a beautiful young understudy named Christine Daee (Philbin). He takes advantage of the ingénue's naïveté by convincing her that he is the Spirit of Music, eventually leading her to his underground lair to seduce her. Once there he holds her captive. When a curious Christine removes his mask, the hideously disfigured Phantom lashes out in fury. Christine's fiancé Raoul De Chagny (Kerry) and a police inspector named Ledoux (Carewe) rescue her. An angry mob

Lon Chaney makes for a frightening but sympathetic "monster" in Universal's *The Phantom of the Opera*.

follows the two men into the Phantom's lair and drives him into the Seine, where he apparently drowns.

Gaston Leroux was a French author who is often compared to Edgar Allan Poe. Like his American counterpart, Leroux was a pioneer in the field of detective fiction, one whose novels had a devoted following in Europe. Most of his books are long forgotten, but his 1910 novel *The Phantom of the Opera* ensures his immortality. Essentially a mystery with heavy doses of horror and romanticism, it tells of a disfigured musical genius that haunts the opulent Paris Opera House. Set amid the splendor of France's *Belle Epoque*, it is in large part a variation on the *Beauty and the Beast* fairy tale.

With its elements of rich pageantry, romance, horror and mystery, the novel became, early on, a source of inspiration for filmmakers. The first film version was the Scandinavian *Das Phantom der Oper* (1916), now believed to be lost. But it was the second adaptation that would prove the most famous, despite its many deficiencies. As with *The Hunchback of Notre Dame* (1923), Universal conceived *Phantom* as one of their select "super jewel" productions—films that were designed for prestige engagements and thus granted far larger budgets than the studio's usual B-picture fare.

Producer Carl Laemmle sought to duplicate the success of *Hunchback* by again securing the services of Lon Chaney. Chaney approached the role as diligently as always, devising truly horrific make-up that again ensures his character's place in the pantheon of iconic movie monsters. But alas, Laemmle also repeated the same mistake that plagued *Hunchback*—he went cheap with his choice of director.

While *Hunchback* director Wallace Worsley had proven to be an amiable colleague for Chaney, the same could not be said of Rupert Julian, the director of *Phantom*. A hack with little to recommend him, he was likely selected by Laemmle on the strength of finishing 1923's *Merry-Go-Round* after the original director, Erich Von Stroeheim, was fired for going drastically over budget. By all accounts, Julian was something of a dictator on the set. Impeccably groomed, he played the role of big-time director without possessing the technical prowess to bolster it. He and Chaney clashed early on, and cinematographer Charles Van Enger later claimed in interviews to have acted as their go-between. Julian, it's said, attempted to direct his star, but Chaney would have none of it—he pretty much did as he wanted, and the director took his frustration out on the rest of the cast and crew. Great films have, of course, been crafted out of adversity—it's not necessary for creative talents to get along—but *Phantom* isn't one of them.

Julian's temperament and posturing aside, it's his obvious lack of imagination that works most strongly against the picture. Much of the film plays out in static wide and medium shots, and the one truly remarkable set piece, the unmasking scene, is rumored that Chaney staged it himself. Given the unremarkable quality of the surrounding material, it's easy to believe such an allegation; for the only time in the film, the set-ups are selected with feeling and the cutting displays some flourish and panache.

The initial cut of the film was presented in early 1925, but a panic-stricken Laemmle ordered retooling when it didn't go over well. A second director, Edward Sedgwick, was brought in to stage a dynamic finale, but the result looks more like an out-take from a Universal B-Western serial of the period and doesn't provide anything approaching satisfactory closure.

After some drastic reediting, the film was finally put into general release later that same year and became a box-office sensation, which can be attributed virtually to Chaney alone. The master character actor created one of his most memorable portrayals in *Phantom*. A more menacing and vindictive personage than Quasimodo had been, the Phantom still displays the pathos and humanity that nearly always elevated Chaney's performances above mere melodrama. The make-up is so vivid and memorable that it's easy to forget how good Chaney really is in the part; forced to wear a mask for much of the film's running time, he uses his body language to suggest emotion. In doing so, he rises above Rupert Julian's sea of mediocrity to create one of the most enduring characterizations in cinema history.

The remainder of the cast is generally ill supported by Julian's insensitive direction. Mary Philbin is particularly stagy as Christine, though one needs only to see her work in something such as *The Man Who Laughs* (1929) to understand that, given the guidance of a good director, she was a capable performer. Norman Kerry is his usual stiff, marionette-like self as Raoul. Arthur Edmund Carewe skulks about as the mysterious Parisian, a police inspector on the Phantom's trail, and as he does so manages to make a better impression than most of the supporting cast.

Julian's amateurish direction is probably most apparent in his staging of the chandelier sequence—a terrific opportunity for suspense is squandered, and the jerky stop-motion of the chandelier's fall fails to convince. Thanks to the opulent art direction and some nice touches in Van Enger's cinematography (especially the use of looming shadows in the catacombs), the film retains some interest on a visual level. If only a capable director had been assigned to the project!

The film was re-released in 1929 with added sound and dialogue effects, but Chaney was not brought in to dub any of the Phantom's dialogue. TH

Rasputin, The Love Life of a Strange Holy Man
aka **Rasputin, Das Liebesleben des Sonderbaren Heiligen**; **Rasputin**
Gersik; b/w; length unknown; Austria
D: R. Gersik.
Cast: Paul Askonas, Rolf Meinau, Milena Pavlovna, Nini Schulz-Forstner

Rasputin (Askonas) rises from poverty to a position as spiritual advisor for the Russian royal family. Using the royal son's hemophilia as leverage, he eases himself into the Tsarina's good graces. But his mysterious powers incite fear among the people, and a plot is hatched to assassinate him.

Yet another variation on the story of Russian monk Grigori Rasputin, this film appears to have vanished long ago. Little information about it has survived, but reviewers at the time noted that it aimed for a more true-to-life approach than other, more lurid depictions of the historical figure.

Paul Askonas played Rasputin, and he appears to have specialized in villains with hypnotic powers—he played Svengali in *Trilby* (1912) and a lunatic who claims to be Dracula in *Drakula halála* (1921).

The film's director, listed as "R. Gersik," doesn't appear to have made any other films; if the name is a pseudonym, there are no known records suggesting who actually may have crafted the film. TH

Seven Keys to Baldpate
Paramount; b/w; 66 min; U.S.
D: Fred C. Newmeyer *S:* Wade Boteler, Frank Griffin *P:* Douglas MacLean *C:* Jack MacKenzie
Cast: Douglas MacLean, Edith Roberts, Anders Randolf, Crauford Kent, Ned Sparks, William Orlamond

William Magee (MacLean) bets his friends that he can write a mystery-thriller in 24 hours. He sequesters himself in the secluded, dilapidated Baldpate Inn to do so, but as he works, he's interrupted by a succession of strangers, each with a key to the place.

Seven Keys star (and producer) Douglas MacLean divided his time between producing, writing and acting. As an actor, he flourished during the silent era, often playing well-meaning romantics in popular commercial fare. *Seven Keys to Baldpate* seems to have been his attempt at something a bit (but only a bit) heavier.

The emphasis in this third film version of the Earl Derr Biggers novel is as much on comedy as it is on chills and suspense (director Fred C. Newmeyer went on to work on the *Our Gang* series), and it seems likely that most viewers were familiar with the story's convoluted plot by this time. Still, the story was further adapted in 1929, 1935, 1946 (an early TV production) and 1947. In 1983 it was redone yet again by British director Pete Walker under the title *House of the Long Shadows* as a "last hurrah" for genre icons Vincent Price, Christopher Lee, Peter Cushing and John Carradine. TH

She
aka **Mirakel der Liebe**
Lee-Bradford; b/w; 95 (64, 74, 69) min; Great Britain/Germany
Co-D: Leander Cordova *S:* Walter Summers, H. Rider Haggard *Co-D/Co-P:* G.B. Samuelson *Co-P:* Arthur A. Lee *C:* Sidney Blythe
Cast: Betty Blythe, Carlyle Blackwell, Marjorie Statler, Mary Odette, Tom Reynolds, Heinrich George, Alexander Butler

This is the last of the many silent film adaptations of H. Rider Haggard's novel *She: A History of Adventure* (1886-1887). It is also the most faithful, thanks to the fact that writer Walter Summers worked closely with Haggard, with the famous author creating the title cards. (Unfortunately, H. Rider Haggard died before the film was completed and never saw the finished product.) There was also a much larger budget allocated this time out, allowing for a more authentic recreation of the book's locales and incidents. All of the novel's major characters make an appearance this time around, with Betty Blythe taking on the role of Ayesha, She-Who-Must-Be-Obeyed; Carlyle Blackwell playing both Leo Vincey and his ancient Egyptian counterpart Kallikrates; Mary Odette as Vincey's doomed lover Ustane; Heinrich George as Vincey's guardian, the apish Horace Holly; Tom Reynolds as third-wheel Job and Jerrold Robertshaw as She's high priest, Billali. Alexander Butler, who had directed *The Sorrows of Satan* (1917) and *The Beetle* (1919), had a small role as Mahomet.

The film follows Leo, Horace and Job as they set out to find the mysterious Pillar of Fire and the immortal queen who guards it. Along the way, Leo marries the gorgeous Ustane, a member of a cannibalistic tribe threatening the group. Ayesha watches their progress in her mystical pool of water as she rules her subjects with an iron hand. When the group finally reaches the lost city hidden deep within the volcanic caves of Ethiopia, it is revealed that Leo is in fact the reincarnation of an Ancient Egyptian named Kallikrates, who was murdered by Ayesha because of his love for Amenartes (Statler). Convincing Leo to join her in the immortality-giving flames of Kor, She is done in by bathing a second time in those selfsame flames.

Made by a British film company but shot in Berlin, Germany, *She* wasn't released in the United States until 1926. Part of its success on a visual level can be attributed to the art direction of Heinrich Richter, whose impressive set designs include the Ethiopian Head that overlooks seafarers along the African Coast, the ornate inner rooms of the temples of Ancient Egypt, the Caves of Kor and the mountains of Africa.

Unfortunately, the film's performances aren't on a par with its sets and direction, with the women (Blythe, Odette) faring particularly poorly as they ham it up to a degree outlandish even for the silent era. Blythe was a Hollywood actress imported to England for the role. The producers obviously hoped to cash in

A French movie poster for *The Unholy Three*

his first major success as director, *The Lodger: A Story of the London Fog* (1927). The actor's only other notable turn in a horror film came in 1929's *The Hound of the Baskervilles*, in which he played Sherlock Holmes for famed German director Richard Oswald. CW

Spook Ranch
Universal; b/w; 60 min; U.S.
D: Edward Laemmle *S:* Raymond L. Schrock, Edward Sedgwick
C: Harry Neumann
Cast: Hoot Gibson, Tote DuCrow, Ed Cowles, Helen Ferguson, Robert McKim, Frank Rice

The sheriff (Rice) of a small mining town orders itinerant cowboy Bill Bangs (Gibson) and his remarkably unfunny African American sidekick, George Washington Black (Cowles in blackface), to investigate a purportedly haunted ranch. The two discover not spirits but rather a gang of criminals headed by Don Ramies (McKim), who has kidnapped the daughter (Ferguson) of the ranch owner with an eye toward getting the man's gold. In the end, Bangs and Black thwart the dastardly plan, and Bangs wins the girl.

Edward Laemmle, nephew of Universal founder Carl Laemmle, entered the family business in 1915 at the behest of his uncle. In 1920 he produced his first film, *Shipwrecked Among Cannibals*, which became the studio's biggest hit to date, and he made his directorial debut with the film *Cinders* the same year. The bulk of his output consisted of Westerns, with *Spook Ranch*, a comedic horror oater, among them. Laemmle continued directing films into the sound era, but his career hit the skids when the Laemmle family lost controlling interest in Universal. His last film, *A Notorious Gentleman*, was shot in 1934 and released in early 1935, and he died in 1937.

Actor Hoot Gibson was a major Western star during the silent era, having found fame in John Ford's *Action* in 1921. By the late 1930s, however, his career had pretty much run its course. He did experience a bit of a comeback in the early- and -mid 1940s, working for Monogram alongside other has-been Western stars, including Ken Maynard and Bob Steele. He attempted a second comeback, this one in television, during the 1950s but failed to make much of a mark and died penniless, of cancer, in 1962.

Leading lady Helen Ferguson retired from acting in 1930 (the same year Gibson lost his contract with Universal) to become a movie-star publicist. Her clients included Henry Fonda and Barbara Stanwyck. CW

The Unholy Three
MGM; b/w; 77 min.; U.S.
D: Tod Browning *S:* Waldemar Young *P:* Tod Browning, Irving G. Thalberg *C:* David Kesson
Cast: Lon Chaney, Mae Busch, Harry Earles, Victor McLaglen, Matt Moore, Matthew Betz

Three sideshow workers—the ventriloquist Professor Echo (Chaney), the midget Tweedledee (Earles) and the strongman Hercules (McLaglen)—abandon the circus to pursue a life of crime. They create a seemingly ideal front as owners of a bird shop, with Professor Echo taking on the guise of a kindly old woman named Mrs. O'Grady and Tweedledee posing as a baby.

on her vamp appeal, even placing her in a daring see-through negligee, but it all seems very dated today.

Still, despite her tendency to overact during the silent era, Blythe managed to tone down her style and become a major supporting and bit player in the talkies. Her career lasted right up until 1964, her last performance an un-credited part in George Cukor's *My Fair Lady*. She died in Woodland Hills, California in 1972. She may be best known today for her famous quote, "A director is the only man besides your husband who can tell you how much of your clothes to take off" than she is for her movie roles.

French actress Mary Odette (real name: Odette Goimbault), on the other hand, never escaped the silent era. Though she starred in over 30 films (most of them British) in a career that spanned a decade; her last production was the romantic adventure *The Emerald of the East* (1928), based on the novel by Jerbanu Kothawala.

This isn't to say that the ladies are the only ones turning in bad performances. Lead actor Carlyle Blackwell was much too old for the part of the youthful Leo Vincey, and the pasty-faced make-up and ludicrous blond wig he is forced to sport only make his age more obvious. Perhaps understandably, he walks through the part without showing the least bit of interest in any of it. Though he starred in approximately 200 films in his two-decade-long career, Blackwell is noted for providing Hitchcock

The Unholy Three are a little person (Harry Earles), a strongman (Victor McLaglen) and a professor (Lon Chaney), from a 1925 lobby card.

Their plans go off the rails when their first heist brings about the death of the person they're robbing. They determine to pin the crime on the innocent Hector MacDonald (Moore), whom they have hired to assist in the shop, but Rosie (Busch), with whom Echo is in love, objects.

It's become almost fashionable to deride Tod Browning, but his position as a key architect of the horror genre is hard to dispute. Born in Louisville, Kentucky to an affluent family, he ran away from home at the age of 16 and embarked on a career in the circus. He did everything from serving as carnival barker to performing a routine of his own ("The Living Corpse") that entailed his being buried alive. Given this colorful background, it's no surprise that his imagination was so fertile—and lurid.

A chance meeting with D.W. Griffith led Browning into the burgeoning motion picture industry. He appeared in several of Griffith's early films, including in a bit part in *Intolerance* (1916), before making his directorial debut with a one-reel short subject titled *The Lucky Transfer* (1915). His early work achieved some measure of success, but his career was handicapped by a scandalous car wreck in 1915 that severely injured the director and resulted in the death of one of his passengers, an actor named Elmer Booth. A contributing factor to the crash, Browning's alcoholism would prove to be a life-long issue, and over time he fell out of favor with many of the major studios.

Despite this, he remained a favorite collaborator of silent screen legend Lon Chaney, the so-called "Man of a Thousand Faces." They first worked together on a melodrama titled *The Wicked Darling* (1919) and ended up re-teaming for a grand total of 10 pictures. There's little doubt that the two men brought out the best in each other: Browning was the kind of forceful, intelligent director Chaney needed to rein in his tendency to overact, while Chaney's willingness to portray the most unsavory of characters fueled the director's imagination.

1925's *The Unholy Three* came at a key point for Browning, and its success reignited the director's fading career. Having fallen out of favor with the major studios, he nonetheless approached Irving G. Thalberg of MGM to back the film, based on a novel by Tod Robbins. Thalberg recognized the story's potential and agreed to allow Browning to direct. The film reunited the director with his favorite star and gave Chaney an opportunity to deliver yet another *tour de force* performance.

The story is ingenious and gives ample evidence of Browning's fixation on everything connected to the circus. He hired his favorite screenwriting partner, Waldemar Young, to adapt Robbins' story, resulting in one of his most tightly plotted pictures. Even as the proceedings teeter on the ridiculous, the director and cast sell it convincingly.

Chaney's performance is a variation on his "lovelorn misfit" theme. Professor Echo is tough as nails but vulnerable in that the girl of his dreams doesn't view him in amorous terms. Echo masterminds the robbery scheme and rules the roost with an iron fist, even as his plans are undone by the treachery of his less-than-brilliant collaborators.

Tweedledee is played by diminutive German performer Harry Earles, best remembered today for his lead role in Browning's notorious *Freaks* (1932). *Unholy* was Earles' film debut, and he proved so convincing in the part that he would be reunited with Chaney for a sound remake of the film five years later. In his early 20s when he played the role for the first time, his condition made him perfectly believable as he masqueraded as a tantrum-throwing baby.

Victor McLaglen, later to become a favorite of director John Ford, plays the strongman. It was one of McLaglen's first substantial screen appearances, although he had already made about two-dozen appearances since his debut in 1920, and he acquits himself well as the slow-witted brute.

Browning paces the film beautifully—there's never a dull moment, and his camera setups are judiciously chosen. Never the most visually dynamic of filmmakers, he nevertheless conjures a few striking images, most notably the silhouette of the titular trio plotting their first major job. Browning's other strengths—an ability to coax effective performances from his actors, an attention to realistic details and an ability to spin the most lurid of scenarios into an engaging story—all come together to make *The Unholy Three* one of his best pictures.

As mentioned above, director Jack Conway remade the film in 1930, but despite the addition of sound, it failed to capture the edgy brilliance of Browning's original. TH

The Vampires of Warsaw
aka **Wampiry Warszawa**; **Wampiry Warszawy, Tajemnica taksówki nr 1051**; **Les vampires de Varsovie**
Merkurfilm; b/w; 36 min; Poland
D/S: Wiktor Bieganski *C:* Antoni Wawrzyniak, Ferdynand Vlassak
Cast: Oktawian Kaczanowski, Halina Labedzka, Maria Balcerkiewiczowna, Lech Owron, Igo Sym, Marian Kiernicki

Sources alternately classify this obscure Polish film as a crime film, a horror film and a drama. It possibly combined elements of all three, but its lost status makes any direct verification impossible. The original Polish title, *Wampiry Warszawy, Tajemnica taksówki nr 1051*, translates as *Warsaw Vampires, Mystery Taxi no. 1051*, though what that refers to is hard to say. The plot apparently concerned a plan by a Russian Duchess (Balcerkiewiczowna) to arrange the wedding of her consort to the daughter (Labedska) of a wealthy industrialist (Kaczanowski). An apparent murder occurs, and various people are suspected, but in the end it turns out to have been an accident caused by the butler (Pogorzanka). The film does not appear to have contained literal vampires.

The Vampires of Warsaw marked the debut of Igo Sym, who went on to become a popular actor of the period thanks to his good looks, cinematic charm and appearances opposite Marlene Dietrich and Lilian Harvey. His greatest—though most dubious—claim to fame came after the Nazis invaded Poland in 1939. Sym allied himself with the Gestapo and rooted out fellow actors and theater owners suspected of organizing resistances. (Some were arrested for little more than refusing to star in a Nazi propaganda film produced by Sym.) Because Germany presented Sym as a person whom Poles should emulate, he was assassinated in 1941 by Polish resistance forces. In retaliation, the Gestapo took 118 hostages and killed 21 of them by firing squad. Others were placed in the infamous concentration camp at Auschwitz. CW

Wolf Blood: A Tale of the Forest
aka **Wolf Blood**
Ryan Brothers; b/w; 68 min; U.S.
D: George Chesebro, Bruce M. Mitchell *S:* C.A. Hill, Bennett Cohen *P:* Ryan Brothers *C:* R. Leslie Selander
Cast: George Chesebro, Marguerite Clayton, Ray Hanford, Roy Watson, Milburn Morante, Frank Clark

Dick Bannister (Chesebro) manages a logging company in the Canadian mountains. When conflict with a competitor becomes violent, he calls upon the owner of the company he is managing to bring some order to the proceedings. He is surprised to find that a beautiful woman, Edith (Clayton), has taken over the business from her deceased father. Despite the fact that she's brought along her dutiful fiancé Dr. Horton (Hanford), Dick becomes infatuated with Edith. When a confrontation in the woods ends with Dick in danger of bleeding to death, Dr. Horton, with no willing donors upon whom to draw, transfuses blood from a wolf into Dick's body. This, improbably, saves Dick's life, but rumors circulate that the blood will transform Dick into a werewolf—and the confused young man begins to believe that such a transformation is imminent.

Wolf Blood: A Tale of the Forest is arguably one of the earliest examples of a werewolf movie. Alas, the film spends an eternity dwelling on its old-fashioned romantic scenario before even beginning to toy with the notion of a man turning into a wolf. Even more disappointing, no actual transformation ever occurs; it would take until 1935 and the release of Universal's *Werewolf of London* for audiences to see such a thing on celluloid. (Interestingly, *Wolf Blood*'s take on paranoia concerning the idea of turning into a wolf is close in tone to Curt Siodmak's original screenplay for *The Wolf Man*, 1941, though the later film wound up being much more literal.) Admittedly, *Wolf Blood* does come to life briefly during its final scenes as leading man George Chesebro wrestles with his perceived inner demons, but it doesn't take long for the film's sappy romance to come back and save the day.

Chesebro, who also co-directed the picture with B-serial veteran Bruce M. Mitchell, gives a capable performance in the lead. Yet the filmmaking is crude and antiquated, even for its time, and the overly padded first section pretty much sinks the narrative from the get-go. Genre completists will doubtless want to check it out, but taken on its cinematic merits alone, *Wolf Blood* is less than compelling. TH

Yotsuya kaidan
Toho Eiga (Kosaka); b/w; length unknown; Japan
D/S: Noro Yamagama *C:* Taisaku Takeshiro
Cast: Koichi Kuzuki, Nobuko Satsuki, Shizuko Mori, Kimiko Hara, Kan Ishii, Kenichi Miyajima

This adaptation of Tsuruya Nanboku IV's Kabuki play of the same name starred Koichi Kuzuki as the samurai Iemon, who betrays his wife Oiwa (Satsuki) for the sake of his mistress Oume (also played by Satsuki). Oiwa is disfigured and killed, but her spirit returns from the grave to drive her husband to murder Oume and commit suicide. Shizuko Mori portrayed Oiwa's innocent sister, who is drawn into her brother-in-law's quest for sex, power and money.

Toho Studios went on to become a major player in Japan's film industry, making not only domestic dramas and action/adventure films but horror and science fiction films as well. They were propelled into the international spotlight with one of the most famous monster creations of all time, *Godzilla—King of the Monsters*.

Yotsuya kaidan hit Japanese movie theaters on June 4, 1925. CW

1926

Ashridge Castle—The Monmouth Rebellion
aka **Haunted Houses and Castles of Great Britain: Ashridge Castle—The Monmouth Rebellion**; **Monmouth Rebellion**; **Haunted Castles: Ashridge Castle**
Cosmopolitan; b/w; 19 min; Great Britain
D: Charles Calvert *S/P:* George J. Banfield
Cast: Betty Faire

This is the eighth film in producer George J. Banfield's *Haunted Houses and Castles of Great Britain* series. It focuses on The Pitchfork Rebellion of 1685 in which James Scott, the Duke of Monmouth, declared himself the rightful heir to the throne of England and led a revolt against King James II. Despite the fact that James II was Catholic and the nation itself mostly Protestant, Monmouth failed and was duly executed. Many of his followers were subsequently tried and put to death in what became known as the Bloody Assizes (an "assize" was a type of British legal inquiry) presided over by so-called "Hanging Judge" George Jeffreys.

Of course, such a violent period in British history is not without its share of ghosts, and Banfield and his director Charles Calvert trotted out a few of them for this pseudo-documentary, a precursor of sorts to the type of haunted travelogues one occasionally sees on The Travel Channel. CW

Baddesley Manor—The Phantom Gambler
aka **Haunted Houses and Castles of Great Britain: Baddesley Manor—The Phantom Gambler**
Cosmopolitan; b/w; 17 min; Great Britain
D: Maurice Elvey *S/P:* George J. Banfield
Cast: John Stuart, Hugh Miller, Fred Raynham

An old English moat house built circa 1438 by the de Clinton family, Baddesley Manor is located in Warwickshire, not far from another of Britain's haunted hotspots, Warwick Castle. In 1483 Nicholas Brome inherited the manor, and he is said to have murdered a local minister after catching the man choking his wife. To this day it is claimed that a bloodstain near the library's fireplace is proof of the event and that the melancholy ghost of a woman has been seen wandering the grounds.

Strangely enough, however, producer/screenwriter George J. Banfield did not use the above tale as the basis of this two-reel episode of his *Haunted Houses and Castles of Great Britain* series, choosing instead to focus on a ghostly gambler (Miller).

Maurice Elvey, the most prolific filmmaker in Britain's history, directed this entry. Other Elvey-helmed entries in the series include *Glamis Castle, Kenilworth Castle and Amy Robsart, The Tower of London* and *Windsor Castle* (all 1926). CW

The Bat
West; b/w; 86 min; U.S.
D/Co-S/P: Roland West *S:* Julien Josephson, George Marion, Jr.
C: Arthur Edeson, Gregg Toland
Cast: Tullio Carminati, George Beranger, Emily Fitzroy, Jewel Carmen, Louise Fazenda, Charles Herzinger

A mysterious criminal known as The Bat pulls off a daring heist, then taunts the police by announcing plans to go on vacation in another country. Meanwhile, the inhabitants of an old house find themselves terrorized by the fiend, who is there to retrieve the loot from an earlier robbery.

The Bat was a popular hit on Broadway in 1920. Written by Mary Roberts Rinehart and Avery Hopwood, it mixes mystery, humor and horror in an old dark house setting. Producer/director Roland West, fresh off the success of his Lon Chaney horror/comedy *The Monster* (1925), saw *Bat* as ideal material for a follow-up. He spared no expense in bringing the story to the screen, hiring the great production designer William Cameron Menzies (*Invaders from Mars*, 1953) and gifted cinematographers Arthur Edeson (*Frankenstein*, 1931) and Gregg Toland (*Citizen Kane*, 1941) to ensure that it would be as visually dynamic as possible.

The film utilizes skillful miniatures (executed by Menzies) and Expressionist lighting to shore up the thin material. The cast performs capably, though one misses the presence of someone like Chaney to lend the film some menace. As it is, the emphasis is more on comedy, much of it flat-footed. Yet, when West emphasizes the mysterious, the film comes to life. There are some wonderfully evocative set pieces, notably a sustained long shot of a character in the foreground unaware that a hooded menace is approaching from behind. The air of impending doom is heightened when the killer turns off the lights behind him as he approaches.

The Bat was a big success, and though considered a lost title for many years, a slightly battered but still viewable print surfaced in the mid-1970s.

Four years after the production, West attempted to outdo the film's success by staging an elaborate sound remake (shot in two versions, one standard 35mm, the other an early widescreen 65mm process). That twin-adaptation—*The Bat Whispers* (1930)—remains the definitive cinematic version of the Rinehart/Hopwood play, though it was remade yet again in 1958, this time simply as *The Bat*, starring Vincent Price. TH

The Bells
Chadwick; b/w; 84 min; U.S.
D/S: James Young *P:* I.E. Chadwick *C:* L. William O'Connell
Cast: Lionel Barrymore, Caroline Frances Cooke, Gustav von Seyffertitz, Lorimer Johnston, Boris Karloff, Eddie Phillips

Mathias (Barrymore) is a generous, good-hearted innkeeper, but money woes drive him to murder. His conscience hounds him afterward, as does a mysterious mesmerist (Karloff) who knows his terrible secret.

This is the most revered of the many screen adaptations of the Alexandre Chatrain/Émile Erckmann play *Le Juif Polonais* (*The Polish Jew*). *The Bells* draws its English title from one of Edgar Allan Poe's more obscure poems, not published until after the author's death in 1849. The Poe connection is telling, for the film's theme is a variation of the far more famous short story *The Tell-Tale Heart*. Here, as in Poe's story, a man commits murder and is done in by his own guilty conscience.

Unlike the morose protagonist of Poe's tale, however, the character of Mathias is instantly likable. He is an affable family man who sacrifices greatly for his wife and daughter. His dream is to become the local burgomaster, an honor he'd be well on his way to attaining were it not for a dour moneylender (von Seyffertitz) who promises him not respect but public disgrace if he doesn't settle his mountainous debt. When Mathias finally gives in to his baser nature and murders a wealthy Jewish traveler (Warren), it's out of desperation, not cruelty or greed.

James Young was a prolific director between 1912 and the late 1920s; *The Bells* was one of his last films, and it remains his best known. He handles the material with sensitivity and a good sense of pacing. The film moves quickly but never at the expense of atmosphere. The snowy landscapes are beautifully rendered, and the main horror set piece, in which Barrymore takes an axe to his victim, is wonderfully staged—the shot of blood dripping onto fresh snow is an unexpectedly ghoulish flourish.

Lionel Barrymore does a fine job as Mathias, but if *The Bells* is remembered for anything, it's for Boris Karloff's Caligari-like mesmerist. Karloff isn't in the film much, but he's treated to a grand entrance (turning to face the camera, similar to the famous introduction afforded to him by James Whale in *Frankenstein* several years later; might the actor have suggested this touch to Whale?) and makes an indelible impression in the few scenes he's given. The make-up makes the then-39-year-old actor look much older than he really was, but his baleful smile and expressive body language are what truly bring the character to life. The film is at its best when the mesmerist is persecuting Mathias, and the two actors clearly enjoyed playing off each other.

The story got its next cinematic adaptation in the British-made *The Bells* (1931). TH

Bodiam Castle and Eric the Slender
aka Haunted Houses and Castles of Great Britain: Bodiam Castle and Eric the Slender

Cosmopolitan; b/w; 17 min; Great Britain
D: A.V. Bramble *S/P:* George J. Banfield
Cast: Madge Stuart, Gladys Jennings

According to the British film Institute, this entry in producer George J. Banfield's *Haunted Houses and Castles of Great Britain* series concerns the ruins of Bodiam Castle (which have, since the film's production, been partially restored and opened to the public) and "the ghostly legends surrounding them." It was the 12th and final entry in the series of two-reelers.

Bodiam Castle was built in 1385 in East Sussex, England by a former knight, one Sir Edward Dalyngrigge, of King Edward III. Located on a moat, the castle's main purpose was to provide defense for England from French invasion during the Hundred Years' War; it was also utilized for the same purpose during both the War of the Roses and the English Civil War, though in fact it never saw any actual action. In 1925 the building passed into the hands of the National Trust, which began the restoration referred to above.

Several ghostly tales surround the castle, including one about a lonely female who stands atop one of the castle's towers as if waiting for someone. There's another about a boy who strolls over the moat's bridge, only to disappear halfway across. And on Easter Sunday, many visitors claim to hear unearthly singing wafting from within its walls. CW

Botan dōrō

Makino; b/w; length unknown; Japan
D: Koroku Numata *S:* Rekichi Kitamoto *P:* Shozo Makino
Cast: Juzo Tanaka, Utemon Ichikawa, Tsukie Matsura, Miko Toba, Jun'ichiru Tamaki

The term *Botan dōrō* is Japanese for "peony lantern," a reference to the lamp (decorated with said flowers) carried by the story's ghost, the spirit of a spurned woman who uses the lantern to light her path to vengeance upon the lover who betrayed her.

Shozo Makino produced this adaptation and had, in 1914, directed the second known adaptation of the original *rakugo* play (a type of one-man theatrical piece) by Sanyutei Encho. Lead actor Juzo Tanaka was also a cinematographer, but it is unknown whether he shot this particular film.

The film was released to Japanese theaters on August 5, 1926. CW

Faust
aka Faust—Eine deutsch Vokssage

UFA Film; b/w; 116 (85) min; Germany
D: F.W. Murnau *S:* Hans Kyser *P:* Erich Pommer *C:* Carl Hoffman
Cast: Gosta Ekman, Emil Jannings, Camilla Horn, Frida Richard, Wilhelm Dieterle, Yvette Guilbert, Eric Barclay

The demon Mephisto (Jannings) makes a wager with an archangel (Fuetterer): If the former can corrupt the saintly academic Faust (Ekman), evil will be permitted to reign over all the Earth. To this end, Mephisto tempts Faust into calling upon him

by unleashing a plague on the elderly man's city. Faust first prays for God to intervene, but when his pleas fall on deaf ears, he calls upon the powers of darkness, thus unleashing Mephisto. The demon proposes a pact with Faust. If the mortal will sign over his soul and renounce God for a trial period of one day, Mephisto will do Faust's bidding. Faust agrees to the pact and uses Mephisto to cure the people of his village. But the people lash out at Faust when the old man flinches at the sight of someone performing the Sign of the Cross. Taking advantage of the old man's disappointment and confusion, Mephisto further tempts Faust by offering him youth and love. Faust gives in but soon becomes bored by the Earthly pleasures Mephisto provides. Things become even more complicated when Faust, using his own free will, falls in love with the virginal Gretchen (Horn).

Based on the German legend—dramatized by countless writers but most famously by Johann Wolfgang von Goethe (1749-1832)—*Faust* marked F.W. Murnau's final film produced in Germany. Conceived as a "super production" by the now-legendary UFA Studios, the film made use of every technological advancement available at the time.

Murnau gives his film the feel and texture of a genre piece. Unencumbered by the low budget and comparatively primitive resources at hand to make *Nosfertau—A Symphony of Terror* (1922),

the director allowed his vivid imagination to cut loose, resulting in a film that is a feast for the eyes. The judicious use of framing, editing, camera movement and light and shadow ensures that the film seldom appears dated on a technical level, and Murnau creates some amazing tableaux, ranging from Faust's summoning of Mephisto (a scene that had an obvious influence on Francis Ford Coppola's big-budget *Bram Stoker's Dracula*, 1992) to the nightmarish visions of the Specters of Death looming in a blackened sky.

The screenplay, while drawing freely from Goethe, is not a literal translation of the text. Rather, the script serves as a springboard for Murnau to display his technical ingenuity. But even at this, the film is not merely a showy string of bombastic set pieces; the director also shows a great sensitivity to character, especially where Faust is concerned. Introduced with a tongue-in-cheek halo effect to emphasize his saintly demeanor, Faust is an intellectual who has never really lived outside his library. Thus is Mephisto able to easily tempt him, since the old man long ago squandered his youth without ever enjoying himself on a physical level. (As Faust explores the pleasures available to him, Murnau suggests all manner of debauchery without being overly graphic about it, though the vision of a beautiful Italian woman marks a use of tasteful nudity surprising in a film of this vintage.)

Ekman was the leading Swedish stage and screen actor of his day, and he gives a remarkable performance in the title role. Whether playing Faust as a wise old man or a boyishly handsome knave, he ensures that the character is sympathetic. He never resorts to melodramatic overstatement to humanize the character, and his performance is more impressive because of it.

The great German character actor Jannings is Mephisto, who plays the role with sly wit and humor, though not so much as to reduce the character's menace. Mephisto is a cunning manipulator, and as such Jannings makes him credibly charming. Murnau allows him a few opportunities to display his gift for physical comedy as well, notably during the prolonged sequence in which Gretchen's mother (Richard) becomes hopelessly smitten with him.

The supporting cast includes Wilhelm Dieterle, who plays Gretchen's ill-fated brother; Dieterle would soon flee Germany, anglicize his first name and become a director of some repute. Among the many titles to his credit is the 1939 version of *The Hunchback of Notre Dame*.

Beautifully photographed by Carl Hoffman and utilizing some wonderful Expressionist set design, *Faust* remains one of Murnau's most deservedly revered pictures. Soon after its completion, producer William Fox, head of Fox Film Corporation, lured Murnau to Hollywood. There he went on to make *Sunrise* (1927), *4 Devils* (1928) and *City Girl* (1930). He then stepped in to direct the independent, Tahiti-lensed *Tabu* (1931). Tragically, Murnau died as the result of an automobile accident on March 11, 1931, a week before *Tabu*'s premiere.

H.B. Parkinson shot the next version of *Faust* in Great Britain in 1927. It was a filmed version of Gounod's opera with synchronized sound and was part of the *Cameo Operas* series. It starred Herbert Langley, A.B. Imeson and Margot Lees. In addition, a 1934 version was also shot, this time in Canada. It starred Serge Krizman in the title role, with cinematography by Oktavijan Miletic. Unfortunately, very little is known about the film, leaving a more exhaustive review virtually impossible to complete. It seems likely that it too, like the 1927 adaptation, focused on music rather than thrills. Also, the 1932 production *Walpurgis Night* was little more than a filmed version of a Faustian opera. TH

Glamis Castle
aka **Haunted Houses and Castles of Great Britain: Glamis Castle**
Cosmopolitan; b/w; 18 min; Great Britain
D: Maurice Elvey *S/P:* George J. Banfield
Cast: Isobel Elsom

One of the most famous castles in Scotland (an illustration of the place appears on the Royal Bank of Scotland's 10-pound notes), Glamis Castle provides the setting for William Shakespeare's *Macbeth*, though there is no true historical connection between character and structure. The castle's overall history is spotty, but a nearby creek bed is known to have provided Scotland's famed Eassie Stone. And it's also well established that, in 1034 C.E., King Malcolm II was murdered nearby and his body brought to a royal hunting lodge on the property.

Of the many legends surrounding the estate, the most famous is likely that of the Monster of Glamis, a deformed child born to a family living there. He was, the story goes, kept confined throughout his life, with his rooms bricked up after his death. The story might be based on the experience of the Ogilvies, a family who sought protection at Glamis only to be walled up in a room and murdered through starvation.

Another legend concerns Earl Beardie. Beardie was possibly modeled upon a historical personage who became so furious when others refused to play cards with him that he swore to play alone until the end of time or the devil came to play with him. Other tales include that of Janet Douglas, known as Lady Glamis, believed to be the Grey Ghost, a misty spirit that wanders the clock tower and has a special reserved seat in the chapel. Also haunting the corridors and rooms of the castle are a white lady whose identity remains unknown, a man known only as Jack the Runner and a black boy. Then there's an armored giant who watches people as they sleep and a young girl who is sometimes seen being dragged through the courtyard by an invisible spirit.

It's no wonder that producer/screenwriter George J. Banfield included Glamis Castle in his pseudo-documentary series of two-reelers, *Haunted Houses and Castles of Great Britain* (all of which were released in 1926). CW

Guy of Warwick
aka **Haunted Houses and Castles of Great Britain: Warwick Castle in Feudal Days**
Cosmopolitan; b/w; 19 min; Great Britain
D: Fred R. Paul *S/P:* George J. Banfield
Cast: Godfrey Tearle

This, the 10th episode in producer George J. Banfield's two-reeler series *Haunted Houses and Castles of Great Britain*, begins with the tale of fictional romantic hero Guy of Warwick. Guy hopes to marry Lady Felice, with whom he is in love, but because of her higher social standing, he must first prove himself by meeting a series of challenges involving dragons, giants and boars.

This narrative serves as an introduction to the famous Warwick Castle in Warwickshire, built by William the Conqueror in 1068. The castle has its share of ghosts, particularly around its Watergate Tower, which Fulke Greville (who apparently moved there after he was murdered in Holborn) is said to haunt.

New York-born Godfrey Tearle (1884-1953), the son of a British actor/manager and an American actress, portrayed Guy. Raised in England, he got his start as a thespian on the British stage and in the country's silent films before graduating to major success in Alfred Hitchcock's *The 39 Steps* (1935). He may be most famous for his portrayal of President Franklin Delano Roosevelt in MGM's *The Beginning of the End* (1946), a highly fictionalized account of the Manhattan Project. For his impressive work as a stage actor (he even conquered Broadway), he was knighted in his native country in 1951. CW

Hampton Court Palace
aka **Haunted Houses and Castles of Great Britain: Hampton Court Palace**
Cosmopolitan; b/w; 16 min; Great Britain
D: Bert Cann *S/P:* George J. Banfield
Cast: Gabrielle Morton, Eric Cowley, Shep Camp, Adeline Hayden Coffin, Annesley Healy

The Duke of Norfolk (Healy) hopes to use his niece, Catherine Howard (Morton), to gain power in King Henry VIII's court, but Catherine refuses to be used. By way of revenge, the Duke frames her for adultery, leading Henry VIII (Camp) to behead her.

As this film, an entry in the pseudo-documentary series *Haunted Houses and Castles of Great Britain*, proclaims, "[C]atherine Howard was executed on Tower Hill the 13th February 1542 in the 33rd year of the reign of King Henry VIII." It goes on to inform the audience that "about the hour of midnight the ghost of [C]atherine Howard is said to pass through the dim courtyards and cloisters of the ancient Palace." Then follows a depiction of a policeman who, while trying to set his watch by Hampton Court's clock tower at three past midnight, spies Catherine's spirit walking through the palace courtyard; she stops, sighs, lowers her head sadly and disappears. Dumbfounded, the policeman pockets his watch, rubs his eyes and departs the scene.

Catherine Howard was Henry VIII's fifth wife and first cousin to his second wife Anne Boleyn (who was also beheaded by order of her husband). Howard's marriage to the king lasted a mere two years before she was executed for treason. Specifically, she had, in the verdict of the court, been sexually unfaithful to the king. Still, she remained beloved by her subjects as "the rose without a thorn," and in fact evidence of her guilt does appear to have been largely fabricated, much of it elicited by torturing the "witnesses" in the Tower of London, a fact played up by producer George J. Banfield's script.

Hampton Court Palace's historical reenactments, including the beheading sequence, were shot on location. The episode's eeriest shot is one of a headsman leaning against his axe, which is in turn resting on the chopping block. The image of Catherine's execution is reenacted, framed and shot through a doorway. The poorest directorial move involves the "policeman and ghost" scene described above which, though set in the middle of the night, was clearly shot on a bright and sunny day! CW

Paul Wegener in *The Magician*

The Haunted Ranch
aka **The Haunted House**; **The Haunted Range**
Davis; b/w; 55 min; U.S.
D: Paul Hurst S: Frank Howard Clark P: J. Charles Davis C: Frank Cotner
Cast: Alma Rayford, Harry Moody, Al Hallett, Fred Burns, Bob Williamson

Indiana-born Ken Maynard was a professional horseman, performing for a time with Buffalo Bill's Wild West Show. After a career detour and serving in the U.S. Army during World War I, he joined Ringling Brothers. From there he moved on to stunt work at Fox, where his charm and good looks soon landed him leading roles in the movies. The film that launched his lengthy career as a Western star was J. Charles Davis' *$50,000 Reward* (1924).

Maynard had affection for scripts with weird approaches, as his early Western *The Haunted Ranch* attests. In it, he stars as Terry Baldwin, whose murdered uncle has bequeathed him a ranch. Though reputedly haunted by a specter known as the Black Rider, the movie's ghostly goings-on turn out to be a plot by a local killer to keep the heir from his inheritance.

Maynard was popular with audiences, but it was a different story behind the scenes. A raging alcoholic, he frequently mistreated co-stars and crewmembers. His short fuse and penchant for cussing out others lost him major contracts with Universal, Mascot and Columbia, among others, and his career waned in the late 1930s as his reputation sank and his weight ballooned. He managed to continue acting into the 1940s and died penniless in the early 1970s, after spending his final years in a mobile home park.

Maynard's most popular co-star (at *The Haunted Ranch* and elsewhere) was his beautiful white horse, Tarzan, which became a celebrity in its own right. Other weird Westerns in which the two starred include *Tombstone Canyon* (1932) and *Smoking Guns* (1934). CW

Kenilworth Castle and Amy Robsart
aka **Haunted Houses and Castles of Great Britain: Kenilworth Castle and Amy Robsart**; **Haunted Castles: Kenilworth Castle**
Cosmopolitan; b/w; 21 min; Great Britain
D: Maurice Elvey S/P: George J. Banfield
Cast: Gladys Jennings, John Stuart, Madge Stuart, Dick Webb

Based less on historical fact and more on Sir Walter Scott's 1821 novel *Kenilworth*, this installment in producer/writer George J. Banfield's *Haunted Houses and Castles of Great Britain* series focuses on Kenilworth Castle in Warwickshire, England. Madge Stuart stars as Amy Robsart, the wife of an Earl who keeps his marriage a secret while courting Queen Elizabeth I (Jennings). Ultimately, the queen learns of the Earl's deception, but not before Amy is murdered by her husband's servant, Varney.

Another character focused on in this episode is Robert Dudley, who in real life inherited the place after the execution of his father. The actor playing the part, John Stuart, was a Scottish thespian who found fame in British cinema both during the silent era and after working for famed director Alfred Hitchcock. Among his other horror credits were *The Mistletoe Bough* (1923), *Baddesley Manor: The Phantom Gambler* and *The Tower of London* (both 1926), *Mistress of Atlantis* and *The Hound of the Baskervilles* (both 1932), *The Black Abbot* (1934), *Old Mother Riley's Ghosts* (1941), *Candles at Nine* (1944), *House of Darkness* (1948), *Four Sided Triangle* (1953), *Quatermass 2* (1957), *The Revenge of Frankenstein* and *Blood of the Vampire* (both 1958), *The Mummy* (1959), *Village of the Damned* (1960) and *Paranoiac* (1963). His later career consisted primarily of television work, but he did land a part as an elder in Richard Donner's 1978 blockbuster *Superman—The Movie*.

Built in the early 1100s, Kenilworth Castle was partially destroyed during the English Civil War in the 1600s. It is today one of the largest castle ruins in England. Overseen by English Heritage (who works steadily at restoring it to its original splendor), the solitary ghost of a monk who wandered its grounds reputedly haunts it. CW

The Legend of Tichborne Dole
aka **Haunted Houses and Castles of Great Britain: The Legend of Tichborne Dole**
Cosmopolitan; b/w; 18 min; Great Britain
D: Hugh Croise S/P: George J. Banfield
Cast: Adeline Hayden Coffin, James Knight, Gabrielle Morton, Dorinea Shirley

Tichborne Dole is a charity festival held annually in Hampshire, England during the Feast of Annunciation. Decreed from the deathbed of Lady Mabella Tichborne circa the year 1150, the celebration originally called for a disbursement to the local poor of, among other gifts, a gallon of flour per adult and a half-gallon per child.

Legend has it that Lady Tichborne's husband Sir Roger did not approve of her planned festival and only agreed on the condition that the Dole (a British term for a distribution to the needy) consist solely of produce from the amount of land that his dying wife could encircle under her own power while carrying a flaming torch. Not to be deterred, Lady Tichborne successfully crawled around 23 acres of field before her torch was snuffed. This area is today known as the Crawls.

It's said that before she died, she placed a curse on the Dole to ensure that it was carried out as long as the land belonged to her descendants. If for any reason the Dole was abandoned, she vowed, her descendants would bear seven sons and then seven daughters, after which the family name would die out. Once, in 1796, the Dole was indeed discontinued, but when it appeared that the curse was actually coming to pass, the Tichborne family resumed the festival.

The custom continues today with some modification. Two tons of flour is divided equally to those who show up at the Tichborne Estate to claim it. A Tichborne or Cheriton parish priest usually blesses it. CW

The Magician
MGM; b/w; 71 min; U.S.
D/S/P: Rex Ingram C: John F. Seitz
Cast: Alice Terry, Paul Wegener, Ivan Petrovich, Firmin Gemier, Gladys Hamer, Hubert I. Stowitts, Michael Powell

Margaret (Terry) is seriously injured in a freak accident but is saved by the surgical prowess of Arthur Burden (Petrovich). The two fall in love, but a mysterious magician named Oliver Haddo (Wegener) interrupts their romantic idyll. Haddo believes that it's possible to create life with alchemy, and he covets Margaret as a subject on which to perform his macabre experiments. Using hypnotism, he lures her from Arthur.

W. Somerset Maugham's 1908 novel *The Magician* was something of a send-up of Aleister Crowley. Crowley, who fancied himself the wickedest man in the world, was an English writer whose passion for the occult led him to create his own religious sect after his departure from the Hermetic Order of the Golden Dawn. He was an explorer of sexual magick and other fringe disciplines and also subscribed to the notion of enlightenment through narcotics. He was an avid user of various illegal substances, and his exploits, as one might guess, drew no small measure of controversy. He openly relished his iconoclastic status, but when Maugham spoofed his image in *The Magician*, he was reportedly none too pleased. The combination of Maugham's growing repute as a writer—his most popular work, *Of Human Bondage*, came along in 1915—and Crowley's notoriety made the book a success.

Silent film pioneer Rex Ingram adapted the story for the silver screen. His only foray into the horror genre, it is a film of tremendous precision and style. His screenplay captures the gist of Maugham's novel, and his visual treatment forms a template for many a mad scientist film to follow. The scenes in which Haddo skulks about his Gothic mountainside laboratory with dwarf sidekick in tow, for example, can't help but remind one of James Whale's *Frankenstein* (1931). (And given that Whale often studied the films of others for inspiration, there can be little doubt that *The Magician* influenced him.)

The Magician also marked the American film debut (though the picture was, to be precise, shot in France for U.S. studio MGM) of Paul Wegener, the legendary actor/director responsible for *The Golem: How He Came into the World* (1920). Wegener's commanding presence is nearly enough to make one forget that he's too old for the role—the script depicts Haddo as a medical student, whereas Wegener was in his 50s when the film was shot. But that aside, the actor is in fine form; his stony expressions make Haddo legitimately menacing. And while Wegener dominates the film, Alice Terry (the wife of director Ingram) makes a likable heroine. Ivan Petrovich is credible as her frustrated suitor.

The film by necessity tones down the perversity of the Haddo/Crowley persona, but Crowley's basic worldview comes through loud and clear. Ingram's direction is fluid and imaginative. The scene in which Wegener hypnotizes Terry and transports her into a fantastic landscape teeming with fawns is particularly well realized, and the finale is staged with easy self-assurance.

Ingram's assistant was a young Michael Powell, later to become one of the most significant directors in British cinema; he would often point to his apprenticeship with Ingram as a wonderful learning experience. (Powell can be glimpsed in *Magician* as a bald, bespectacled man holding balloons during a fairground sequence.)

Ingram would direct only three more features before retiring in 1932, unhappy with, and unable to adjust to, the emergence of talking pictures. TH

Midnight Faces
Schreier; b/w; 53 min; U.S.
D/S: Bennett Cohen *P:* Otto K. Schreier *C:* King Gray
Cast: Francis X. Bushman, Jr., Jack Perrin, Kathleen McGuire, Edward Peil, Sr., Charles Belcher, Nora Cecil

Lynn Claimore (Bushman, Jr.) inherits his uncle's rambling estate in the Florida everglades. Accompanied by his trusty servant Trohelius (Turner) and his attorney Richard Mason (Perrin), he goes to take possession, but upon their arrival, strange events begin to transpire. A mysterious Chinese man (Peil, Sr.) is observed wandering the grounds, and a caped figure is seen skulking about the corridors at night, much to the consternation of the cowardly Trohelius. Tensions heighten further when Mary Bronson (McGuire) seeks shelter in the house to escape a knife-wielding murderer.

Midnight Faces is a thoroughly unmemorable entry in the run of old dark house horror comedies popularized on Broadway by the likes of *The Bat* and *The Cat and the Canary*. Bushman, Jr.—who later changed his name to Ralph, presumably to try to distance himself from his famous father, the star of the silent epic *Ben Hur: A Tale of The Christ* (1925)—is the blandly handsome hero, while Martin Turner is put upon to play the embarrassingly clichéd "fraidy-cat" black servant.

Bennett Cohen (or Ben Cohn, as he was often billed) amassed far more credits as a hack screenwriter than as a hack director. His directorial career, in fact, stalled out in the early 1930s, and *Midnight Faces* provides all the explanation one needs as to why. Cohen/Cohn handles the material with an almost intentional absence of style, atmosphere and wit. The sets are impressive enough, but they're not well utilized, and the lighting tends toward the way-too-bright.

Things do spring to life briefly at the end with a big-action set piece that seems more apropos for a B-Western serial than for a horror thriller. But the mystery's final solution is telegraphed too early on to be surprising, and even at less than an hour, the film drags interminably. TH

The Mistletoe Bough
aka **Haunted Houses and Castles of Great Britain: The Mistletoe Bough**
Cosmopolitan; b/w; 18 min; Great Britain
D: Charles Calvert *S/P:* George J. Banfield
Cast: Gladys Jennings

According to legend, somewhere in England a beautiful young bride, playing a game of hide-and-seek on the morning of her wedding breakfast, hid in an attic chest and couldn't get back out. Her friends and relatives were unable to find her and she suffocated. Her skeletal remains were discovered years later, and it is said that her spirit haunts the home in which she died.

While there is some evidence that the story (at least the part about the young bride dying in a locked chest) is true, the mishap has been ascribed to so many old British homes that its true location is difficult to pin down. It is likely, however, that for this episode of the two-reeler film series *Haunted Houses and Castles of Great Britain*, the house covered was either Marwell Hall or Bramshill House in Hampshire, England. Series producer George J. Banfield was notoriously economical and often selected shooting locations on the basis of their close proximity to one another, and the series had already covered *The Legend of Tichborne Dole* (1926), also in Hampshire.

The Mistletoe Bough story provided the plots for two other silent British horror films, both of which were titled *The Mistletoe Bough*. One was produced in 1904, the other in 1923. CW

Mummy Love
Joe Rock; b/w; 22 min; U.S.
D: Marcel Perez
Cast: Alyce Ardell, Neely Edwards, Yorke Sherwood, Gil Pratt

Trapped in an ancient Egyptian tomb, members of an archaeological group realize that their only escape is to dress as mummies.

Marcel Perez directed the two-reel short for Joe Rock's silent-era production company that specialized in comedy shorts. The company was founded by Rock, a former vaudevillian who established himself as a comedy actor in the early 1920s. He is credited with making a major star out of Stan Laurel of Laurel and Hardy fame.

Rock shouldn't be confused with the music producer of the same name, who co-wrote the Skyliners' 1958 pop classic "Since I Don't Have You," a piece covered by artists as diverse as Barbra Streisand and Guns n' Roses. Film producer Rock actually won an Oscar in 1934 for his 1933 film *Krakatoa*, a short documentary subject about the eruption of an Indonesian volcano in 1883.

Mummy Love was shot at the Egyptian Theatre in Hollywood and was released by Universal. CW

Orphan of Lowood
aka **Die Waise von Lowood**
Sternheim; b/w; length unknown; Germany
D: Curtis (Kurt) Bernhardt *S:* Hermann Kosterlitz (Henry Koster) *P:* Julius Sternheim *C:* Charles Métain, Sophus Wangöe
Cast: Evelyn Holdt, Olaf Fonss, Dina Diercks, Sybill Morel, Jenny Marba, Rosa Valetti

A dark little German drama with horror touches, Curtis Bernhardt's *Orphan of Lowood* is a claustrophobic take on Charlotte Brontë's semi-autobiographical novel *Jane Eyre: An Autobiography*, first published in 1847 under the pseudonym Currer Bell. This time around Evelyn Holdt stars as the fiery Jane Eyre, who falls in love with the mysterious Lord Edward Rochester, unaware that he has an insane wife locked away in the attic. Rochester was played by Danish star Olaf Fönss.

A major director in Germany during the silent era, Bernhardt—who was Jewish and wanted by the Gestapo—emigrated in the 1930s to the United Kingdom and then to the United States, where he had a successful career working for several major production companies, including Warner Bros., MGM, RKO and Columbia.

The next version of Brontë's tale *Jane Eyre* (1934) was the first to be filmed with synchronized sound. CW

Passion of a Woman Teacher
aka **Kyôren no Onna Shishô**; **The Love-Mad Tutoress**
Nikkatsu Kyoto; b/w; 85 min; Japan
D: Kenji Mizoguchi *S:* Kawaguchi Matsutaro *C:* Tatsuyuki Yokota
Cast: Yoneko Sakai, Eiji Nakano, Yoshiko Okada

While *Ugetsu* (1953) remains master Japanese filmmaker Kenji Mizoguchi's most critically acclaimed film, it wasn't the director's first foray into the realm of the ghostly. One of his oldest known horror films is *Passion of a Woman Teacher*. It is considered lost, along with all his other silent films and many of his early talkies.

Mizoguchi was one of three children born to a middle class carpenter. During World War I, his father invested in selling items to soldiers, but when the war ended too quickly for the investment to pay off, he sold his oldest daughter to another family. They in turn sold her as a geisha, an incident (along with his father's alleged abuse of his mother) that had a profound impact on young Mizoguchi. Mizoguchi channeled his issues into a lifelong interest in cinema, with his early films split between European literary adaptations and experimental remakes of German Expressionist movies. He eventually took up residence at Nikkatsu's Kyoto studios, where he made this early example of *kaidan eiga* (supernatural period drama). The film was reportedly critically well received in Europe upon its release there.

Passion was based on the novel *Shinkei Kasane-ga-fuchi*, written circa 1860 by Sanyutei Encho (1839-1900). Sanyutei was an early master of Japanese horror literature, writing both novels and plays. In this particular novel (and the subsequent film), the daughter (Sakai) of a samisen player loves a blind masseur (Nakano), but he is carrying on an affair with one of her students (Okada). When the young teacher learns what is happening, she kills herself in despair. But if there's one thing classical Japanese culture teaches, it's that the wrongly dead don't stay dead for long, and sure enough, the teacher's spirit returns from the grave to exact revenge on the two lovers.

The story provided the basis for several movies, including Nobuo Nakagawa's *The Ghost of Kasane Swamp* (1957). Sanyutei also wrote the classic version of *Botan dōrō* (1884), which dealt with the taboo topic of necrophilia. CW

Phantom of the Western Temple
aka **Nanbandera no kaijin**; **Nanbandera no kaijinzenpen**
Toua; b/w; length unknown; Japan
D: Shiroku Nagao
Cast: Shinpei Takagi, Aiko Hanamura, Shiko Hanayagi, Ryzaburo Mitsuoka

During the silent era, American and European horror films were hugely influential on Japanese filmmakers. *The Cabinet of Dr. Caligari* (1919) inspired Kenji Mizoguchi's *Blood and Soul* (1923), while Universal's megahit (and Lon Chaney's star-making turn) *The Hunchback of Notre Dame* (1923) may have been the reason Tomu Uchida's *The Hunchback of Enmei-in* (1924) was finally completed. When Universal's second super-jewel horror production *The Phantom of the Opera* hit it big internationally in 1925, Japanese filmmakers were quick to respond with *Phantom of the Western Temple*, their own unauthorized adaptation of Gaston Leroux's novel. It was produced by Toua and directed by Shiroku Nagao.

Nagao also directed *Kasane-ga-fuchi* (1924) and *Legend of the Nabeshima Cat Ghost* (1929). CW

Scared Stiff!
Hal Roach; b/w; 20 (25) min; U.S.
D: James W. Horne *S:* Stan Laurel *P:* Hal Roach
Cast: Clyde Cook, Eileen Percy, Stuart Holmes, James Mack, Shirley Palmer

Between 1915 and 1942, James Wesley Horne made over 200 films, many of them humorous shorts featuring Charley Chase or comedy team Laurel and Hardy. Born in 1880 in San Francisco, California, Horne was the nephew of silent-movie actress Georgia Woodthorpe (*The Four Horsemen of the Apocalypse*, 1921). In 1917, the year following his marriage to Cleo Ridgely, the couple had twins, June and James, Jr., both of whom tried their hands at acting during their lifetimes. Horne was also the uncle of both noted cinematographer Jack Stevens (*Get that Girl*, 1932) and director George Stevens (*I Remember Mama*, 1948). He died as the result of a stroke in 1942 in Los Angeles, California.

Among Horne's many films was this obscure short for Hal Roach. By all accounts it dealt with a mad scientist using an allegedly haunted house as a cover for some nefarious deed or other. Also thrown into the mix was a killer gorilla, reportedly portrayed in close-ups by Kajanja the Chimpanzee! The horror was of course tempered by the broad humor typical of the period.

Star Stuart Holmes was a popular screen actor before the sound era, mostly in period dramas (*East Lynne*, 1916; *The Scarlet Letter*, 1917), but his later career was comprised of small, un-credited bit parts. His horror-tinged films include *The Unfaithful Wife* (1915), *A Daughter of the Gods* (1916) and *Tangled Lives* (1917). Co-star Clyde Cook was a member of the original Keystone Cops; his career lasted from approximately 1920 through the 1960s. His last role was an un-credited bit part in the John Wayne classic *Donovan's Reef* (1963). The actor was popular enough early on that, in 1926, his likeness appeared on one in a British series of tobacco cards showcasing famous actors. He also directed a couple of films.

Scared Stiff! was written by Stan Laurel of the popular Laurel and Hardy duo. He did not, however, have an on-screen role in this particular production. Neither is there a connection between this film and the 1953 Jerry Lewis/Dean Martin film of the same title. CW

> ### Americans Don't Want Talking Movies; Prefer Silent Film Shows, Says Edison
>
> Special to The New York Times.
>
> ATLANTIC CITY, N. J., May 20.—Americans are not interested in talking movies; they prefer the restful quiet of the film theatre, and to reproduce the screen actor's talk would destroy the illusion.
>
> This is the way it appears to Thomas A. Edison, who led the development of both the movie and the phonograph, the instruments it is now proposed to combine.
>
> The seventy-nine-year-old inventor answered questions in the Hotel Traymore today by saying that "talking movies will not come into general commercial use as long as the American public continues to display its present attitude.
>
> "Americans require a restful quiet in the moving picture theatre," he continued; "and for them talking from the lips of the figures on the screen destroys the illusion. Devices for projecting the film actor's speech can be perfected, but the idea is not practical. The stage is the place for the spoken word. The reactions of the American public up to now indicate the movies will not supersede it."
>
> "Do your experiments lead you to believe that telephone pictures from continent to continent will soon include moving pictures, projected in London and shown in New York?" he was asked.
>
> "It is entirely possible, but only as a 'stunt.' I do not believe it would be practical for either the American or the British movie industry."
>
> Some one asked him what he thought would be happening in this world one hundred years from now. Mr. Edison smiled and said he hadn't the slightest idea; he did think the world would progress mechanically and industrially and that other men, in that future time, would answer the question.
>
> The man to whom 20,000 persons paid homage last night at the Forty-ninth National Electric Light Convention, joined his wife in telling how they have enjoyed their holiday here and Mrs. Edison spoke up.
>
> She must hurry her husband home, she said, to West Orange this afternoon. "Why," she said, "he was planning to get back to his work this morning before daylight."

From the *New York Times*, Friday May 21, 1926

Secrets of a Soul
aka **Geheimnisse einer Seele**; Secrets of a Soul: A Psychoanalytic Thriller
UFA; b/w; 75 min; Germany
D: G.W. Pabst *Co-S:* Karl Abraham, *Co-S/P:* Hans Neumann *C:* Robert Lach, Curt Oertel, Guido Seeber
Cast: Werner Krauss, Ruth Weyher, Jack Trevor, Pavel Pavlov, Ilka Gruning, Hertha Von Walther

A mild-mannered professor (Krauss) haunted by nightmarish visions worries that he is losing his sanity. Fearing that he may kill his loving wife (Weyher), he enlists the aid of a psychiatrist (Pavlov) in hopes of resolving his delusional conflicts.

Developed by Austrian scientist Sigmund Freud (1856-1939), the theory of psychoanalysis is meant to provide a framework for the identification and management of one's inner demons. Freud's groundbreaking 1900 tome *The Interpretation of Dreams*—with its ponderings on sexual repression, childhood trauma and dream symbolism—took the world by storm, influencing countless people in countless fields and sparking decades of heated debate and controversy. Even today, Freudian thought clings to the popular consciousness, though among mental-health professionals, his viewpoints are largely regarded as faulty and shortsighted.

The burgeoning field of psychiatry proved a hotbed of artistic ideas in the teens and '20s, however, and attempts were actually made to secure Dr. Freud's personal supervision and approval for various psychiatry-tinged melodramas. Nobody came closer to such a coup than German producer Hans Neumann, who actively campaigned for Freud's involvement in what would become *Secrets of a Soul*. Though unsuccessful in snagging Freud, Neumann did manage to secure the services of Karl Abraham, a member of Freud's inner circle. Working as a team, the two labored to make the film's screenplay as psychologically resonant as possible.

G.W. Pabst directed the film with an imaginative eye, especially during the wonderfully *outré* dream sequences. Though considered by some to be a silent-era European film luminary, his work never attained the status of, say, F.W. Murnau or Fritz Lang. Born Georg Wilhelm Pabst in 1885, he first made his mark in the German film scene with the drama *Joyless Spirit* (1925), starring Greta Garbo. *Secrets* was his fourth film in a career that continued until 1956. (One of his last films, *Cose de Pazzi*, 1953, was photographed by future horror filmmaker Mario Bava.)

Pabst had a reputation as an actor's director, something *Secrets of a Soul* bears out in spades. Werner Krauss, best known for his demented title role in 1919's *The Cabinet of Dr. Caligari*, gives a remarkable lead performance. He's too old for the part, which requires the viewer to believe that he's married to a childhood sweetheart easily 20 years younger than he is, but he portrays his character with sensitivity and nuance. The supporting actors, especially Ruth Weyher as Krauss' wife and Pavel Pavlov as, yes, the analyst, are all in fine form as well.

What weaknesses the film has pop up in the final section, which belabors the deep … inner … meaning … of … every … little … symbol. Nor is the final revelation of the source of Krauss' inner conflict any great surprise. Still, for much of its running time, *Secrets of a Soul* manages to be a reasonably compelling psychological thriller. TH

Shin sarayashiki
Teikine; b/w; length unknown; Japan
D: Shuichi Yamashita
Cast: Rokuro Akashi, Kyoko Chigusa

This was one of many cinematic takes on a famous Japanese folktale, the story of a servant who is murdered by her master after breaking one of his prized dishes and declining to square things by providing sexual favors. The term *sarayashiki* translates as "dish house" or "plate mansion." It refers to the home in which the 10 plates, family heirlooms all, are housed. After the servant girl is executed for her clumsiness and refusal to put out, her spirit returns from the dead, repeatedly counting the nine remaining plates and screaming when she remembers that the tenth is broken.

Because this film is considered lost, it's difficult to know just which of the many versions of the tale it adapted. Though director Shuichi Yamashita's career in horror began here, he went

Molly (Mary Pickford), the oldest of the orphans, leads the children through the swamp to safety, in *Sparrows*.

on to direct *Kasane-ga-fuchi* (1928), *Kaidan Bunya goroshi* (1929) and *Botan dorō* (1930). CW

Shivering Spooks
Roach; b/w; 20 min; U.S.
D: Robert F. McGowan *Co-S:* H.M. Walker *Co-S/Co-P:* Hal Roach *Co-P:* F. Richard Jones
Cast: Harry Bowen, Joe Cobb, Jackie Condon, Johnny Downs, George B. French, Clara Guiol

Professor French (French) is a phony spiritualist who dupes the naïve into believing he is truly in contact with the spirit world. One of his séances is disrupted by the antics of the *Our Gang* kids, which angers the professor enough that he instructs his henchmen to scare the hell out of them.

This short subject is an entry in the once popular *Our Gang* comedy series. The gang of kids—also known as *The Little Rascals* and *Hal Roach's Rascals*—got their start in 1922 courtesy of producer Hal Roach. Roach ran the kids—replaced by younger performers as they grew older—through a series of formulaic adventures. Some of the shorts, such as this one, put the kids in danger (but not, of course, *too* much of it).

These comedies remained successful well into the sound era, then they petered out in the mid-1940s. *Shivering Spooks* is, like the series overall, mild, family-oriented entertainment.

Part of the original group was Johnny Downs, who later found minor success as a character actor. As an adult he toplined the lurid B-horror movie *The Mad Monster* (1942), awarded top billing over genre favorite George Zucco. TH

The Sorrows of Satan
Famous Players-Lasky/Paramount; b/w; 111 (90) min; U.S.
D: D.W. Griffith *S:* Forrest Halsey, Julian Johnson, George C. Hull *C:* Harry Fischbeck, Arthur De Titta
Cast: Adolphe Menjou, Ricardo Cortez, Carol Dempster, Lya De Putti, Marcia Harris, Ivan Lebedeff Amiel

Director D.W. Griffith was no stranger to the notion of melding horror with Christianity and can, in fact, take partial credit for shoring up the horror genre's reactionary/conservative credentials. Films like *The Sealed Room* (1909) and *The Avenging Conscience, or: "Thou Shalt Not Kill"* (1914) sought to scare unbelieving filmgoers into seeking salvation and to bolster the conviction of believers that no bad deed goes unpunished. It's no wonder, then, that so many of his films are morality plays—though filled with racist imagery and largely devoid of compassion—that depict the perils of straying from a righteous path. This approach, somewhat predictably, infects *The Sorrows of Satan*.

Kentucky-born Griffith's film was the second adaptation of the 1895 novel *The Sorrows of Satan, or, The Strange Experience of One Geoffrey Tempest, Millionaire* by Marie Corelli. The first version, directed by Alexander Butler and released in 1917, strayed far from its source material and was already forgotten when Paramount tasked Griffith, who reportedly wasn't all that interested, with a remake.

This time out, though, the filmed narrative is at least recognizably similar to the written. After cursing God and declaring that he would gladly trade his soul for money, Geoffrey Tempest (Cortez) meets Prince Lucio de Rimanez (Menjou). The prince leads him into a life of wealth and temptation, wherein Tempest gives up his previous lover (Dempster) to marry a princess (De Putti). Once wed, however, the princess rejects her husband and throws herself at the prince. When he rejects her, she kills herself. The prince then shows his true form to Tempest—that of Satan the Devil, replete with bat wings—and demands the man's soul. Chased by the Devil's shadow, Tempest flees to his former lover, whom he begs to lead him back to God. As she recites the Lord's Prayer for him, the Prince of Darkness departs empty-handed.

Whereas the 1917 film focused on a beautiful aristocrat's ardor toward a prince she has no idea is the Devil, this version puts the novel's Geoffrey Tempest front and center. Well-played by Ricardo Cortez, the character is both unlikeable and unsympathetic. (After inheriting money, he drops his ladylove like a hot potato in favor of a beautiful but vapid gold digger who is a princess.) Cortez is most famous for originating the role of Sam Spade in the first film version of *The Maltese Falcon* (1931), but he had parts in several horror films besides *Sorrows*, including *Thirteen Women* and *The Phantom of Crestwood* (both 1932), as well as *The Walking Dead* (1936). He also starred as lawyer Perry Mason in Erle Stanley Gardner's *The Case of the Black Cat* (1936).

Actress Carol Dempster, who portrays Tempest's first lover Maive, was no stranger to D.W. Griffith. She'd had the lead role of Agnes Harrington in Griffith's 1922 horror comedy *One Exciting Night*. Version number two of *The Sorrows of Satan* was her last film, though she lived until 1991. CW

The Student of Prague really impresses from a purely visual standpoint, featuring ace cinematography by Gunther Krampf.

Sparrows
aka **Scraps**; **Human Sparrows**
Pickford/United Artists; b/w; 84 (110) min; U.S.
D: William Beaudine *S:* George Marion, Jr., C. Gardner Sullivan
P: Mary Pickford *C:* Hal Mohr, Charles Rosher, Karl Struss
Cast: Mary Pickford, Gustav von Seyffertitz, Charlotte Mineau, Spec O'Donnell, Roy Stewart, Mary Louise Miller

Somewhere in the Deep South, the despicable Mr. and Mrs. Grimes (Seyffertitz, Mineau) are foster parents to a gaggle of undernourished orphans, though their own obnoxious, misbehaving son (O'Donnell) remains well fed. Their boy doesn't work much either, while every single foster child—regardless of age—is forced into hard labor, with the foster parents spending their government checks as they see fit. After kidnappers take a baby (Miller) from her wealthy father and deliver it to Grimes in the hopes that he'll hide it among his brood, Grimes instructs his son to throw her into the alligator-infested swamp and thus avoid awkward questions about where she came from. But the eldest of the orphans, Molly (Pickford), saves the babe and leads the children through the swamp to safety, while Grimes and his family are apprehended and the kidnappers killed.

Known during her heyday as "America's Sweetheart," Mary Pickford was a major star of the silent era. Born in Toronto, Canada with the unassuming name of Gladys Louise Smith, Pickford found work on Broadway while still in her teens. In 1909 D.W. Griffith discovered her; he was so captivated by her charm and innocent beauty that he paid her double the daily fee of most Biograph actors as he placed her in both supporting and starring roles in numerous films, including *The Sealed Room* (1909). From 1910 to 1912, she worked for Carl Laemmle's Independent Moving Pictures. A second tenure with Griffith followed, during which she found lasting fame.

It wasn't long before she commanded not only sizeable salaries but also a high degree of creative control over the productions in which she starred, a situation very atypical of a period in which men ruled the film-industry roost. Joining ranks with Griffith and actors Douglas Fairbanks (whom she married in 1920) and Charlie Chaplin, she co-founded United Artists in 1919 and became even more professionally autonomous. UA proved a smart move; the following decade saw her in many successful features. One such film was *Sparrows*, the only title in Pickford's catalog that can rightly be termed a horror melodrama. While its terrors are firmly grounded in reality, its notion of spirituality is entirely ethereal, a smart decision that at the time kept Christian audiences coming back for more. The film's title is a reference to Jesus' assurance that God cares for His children as He does the sparrows of the air. The none-too-subtle analogy, then, is between said sparrows and the orphans.

And *apropos* Jesus, the most undeniably striking set piece in the film is the one in which, after the death of one of the orphans, the wall of the cold wet barn in which they sleep dissolves and the Good Shepherd appears to carry the child's soul to Heaven. The special effects are seamless, and the sequence provides the film's most powerful dramatic moment. Unfortunately, it comes so early in the film that nothing afterward can measure up to it, and the remainder of the film is a letdown in comparison. But while *Sparrows* isn't an entirely successful film from an aesthetic point of view, the problem isn't ultimately one of too much religiosity or over-sentimentality; there's enough horror in the caricature of Grimes (perfectly played by Seyffertitz) and in the dangerous quicksand-filled swamp to keep the film from collapsing into schmaltz. The main snag, rather, is that the film is simply too long and, in true blockbuster fashion, continues well past its initial resolution. It's not enough that the orphans are saved from their abusive predicament, the audience must be put completely at ease concerning their welfare by having a millionaire adopt the entire group, Molly included.

Which brings up another significant sticking point with the film: Pickford is just too old to be playing an orphaned child, even one who's the oldest of the group. After all, she was already in her mid-thirties by the time the film was shot, and her cheeky girlishness was well on the wane. (As was her acting career, which wound down after *Sparrows* as cinema transitioned to sound.)

Director William Beaudine, like Griffith, began his career with American Mutoscope & Biograph in 1909; he even performed assistant director chores on *The Birth of a Nation* (1915) and *Intolerance* (1916). He worked for most of the major studios before being exported to England to boost their cinematic appeal (a couple of his films there, *Where There's a Will* and *Windbag the Sailor*, both 1936, had future Hammer horror director Terence Fisher on board as editor). Upon Beaudine's return to the United States, he was quickly shoehorned into Poverty Row productions, where he became known as a one-take director—that is, someone who refuses to do a retake however badly the first one goes. It must be said that it's unfair to stick the talented Beaudine with such a moniker, given that the studios in question didn't provide the sort of budgets that afforded a director the luxury of shooting a scene more than once.

In any case, it was during his Poverty Row period that Beaudine made some of his best-remembered pictures, including a host of Monogram cheapies starring Bela Lugosi (*The Ape Man* and *Ghosts on the Loose*, both 1943; *Voodoo Man*, 1944). Yet, when his silent films are compared to his later period work, the dissimilarities between the two groups are striking in a way that suggests Beaudine had little enthusiasm for his later work. This becomes even more understandable when one considers the scripts he had to shoot, like those for *The Living Ghost* (1942) and *Crazy Knights* (1944).

Sparrows isn't for everyone, but it contains some of Beaudine's best work, and it's surely of interest to anyone who has ever wondered what a horror film starring Mary Pickford might be like. CW

The Student of Prague
aka Der Student von Prag; The Man Who Cheated Life
Sorkal; b/w; 91 min; Germany
D/Co-S: Henrik Galeen *Co-S:* Hanns Heinz Ewers, *P:* Harry R. Sokal *C:* Gunther Krampf, Erich Nitzschmann
Cast: Conrad Veidt, Werner Krauss, Agnes Esterhazy, Fritz Alberti, Ferdinand von Alten, Elizza La Porta

In dire need of money, a student named Balduin (Veidt) makes a deal with the mysterious Scapinelli (Krauss) in which the old man tricks the student out of his mirror image. Though horrified, Balduin is unable to prevent his doppelganger from carrying out Scapinelli's criminal directions.

Director/co-writer Henrik Galeen (1881-1949) occupies an interesting place in German cinema history. As a writer, he had a hand in many of the major horror titles produced in the nation during the silent era, including *The Golem: How He Came Into the World* (1920), *Nosferatu—A Symphony of Terror* (1922) and *Waxworks* (1924). He also directed, with Paul Wegener, the original version of *The Golem* in 1915 and was responsible for two other significant genre titles: 1926's *The Student of Prague* and 1928's *Alraune*.

The Student of Prague is generally cited as his masterpiece, and it's easy to see why. This second version of Hanns Heinz Ewers' screen story is a marked improvement over the first in pretty much every way, making the 1913 version seem creaky and antiquated by comparison. The 1926 film boasts both a much higher budget and the work of expert production personnel, including ace cinematographer Gunther Krampf (*Pandora's Box*, 1929) and art director Herrmann Warm (*Destiny*, 1921).

It also benefits from a much stronger cast, headed by Conrad Veidt as the tragic protagonist. Veidt is far more credible here than Wegener is in the previous version. Though he, like Wegener, is technically too old for the part, he invests the role with such silent intensity that age becomes a moot point. He conveys the character's vacillating emotional state magnificently, starting off as cool and aloof, then also building toward abject hysteria. It's a confident and polished piece of acting that once again reminds one of what a fine performer he was.

The role of Scapinelli is also well played by Werner Krauss, again uniting with Veidt after their work together in *The Cabinet of Dr. Caligari* (1919) and *Waxworks* (1924). Krauss, though a smaller, more compact figure than Veidt, is nonetheless believable when menacing the healthier, younger man. The supporting players also, without exception, acquit themselves well.

All that being said, it's from a purely visual standpoint that this film *really* impresses. Galeen's use of imagery is obviously and strongly influenced by the best of F.W. Murnau, with the eerie nighttime exteriors particularly atmospheric. The finale, in which Balduin is forced to confront his other half, looks wonderful, seamlessly blending Expressionist imagery with then state-of-the-art effects trickery.

Anton Walbrook played the lead in the next filmed version of the story, directed by Arthur Robinson in 1935. TH

Sweeney Todd
BMPA; b/w; 15 min; Great Britain
D: George Dewhurst *S:* P.L. Mannock, Lionel Collier
Cast: G.A. Baughan

The barbershop at 186 Fleet Street in London hides a grisly secret. The man who runs the place, one Mr. Sweeney Todd, is a butcher who slits the throats of unwary customers, then flips a switch and drops their bodies, via a trapdoor hidden beneath the barber's chair, into the basement below. After robbing the bodies and slicing them up, he gives the remains to his criminal partner, Mrs. Lovett, who uses the meat for the pies she bakes in her nearby shop.

An original story titled *The String of Pearls: A Romance* was first published anonymously in serial form in *The People's Periodical and Family Library* in 1846 and 1847. It relates the strange case of Lieutenant Thornhill, last seen entering Sweeney Todd's barbershop. The fact that he had been carrying a string of pearls, an intended gift for a missing friend's lover, Johanna, raises suspicions that he may have been robbed and murdered. By way of investigation Johanna disguises herself as a boy, gets a job for Mr. Todd and, before long, discovers what happened to her lover; it turns out that he's imprisoned in the cellar beneath the barber shop, where he's forced to work as Todd's cook. Johanna also learns about the numerous people who have been murdered by her employer and sold for meat pie filling to a neighboring bakery/restaurant run by Mrs. Lovett.

British cultural references to an unnamed killer barber date back to the early part of the 1800s and can even be found in the work of Dickens. Though it's sometimes claimed that Sweeney Todd is based on an actual historical personage, there is no real evidence for this; rather, he is likely an incarnation of an urban legend that arose among the undereducated rural folk living outside of London who feared the decadent, violent metropolis and concocted the story as a way to discourage their children from moving there.

While there have been numerous plays based on Todd, the most famous is undoubtedly Stephen Sondheim's *Sweeney Todd: The Demon Barber of Fleet Street: A Musical Thriller* (1979). Itself based on a play from the early 1970s, it added new elements to the story that have since become an integral part of the legend, including a sympathetic back story involving Todd's wife and daughter.

This, the first film adaptation of the story, came in 1926 and starred G.A. Baughan as Todd. It was one of two versions made during the silent era. (The other came two years later.) Though lost, evidence suggests that it was a short film based on the theatrical adaptation *The String of Pearls* by George Dibdin Pitt. The movie reportedly focused on comedy over horror.

Although he never made much of a name for himself, director George Dewhurst (1889-1968) was also an actor, scenarist and cinematographer. CW

The Tower of London
aka **Haunted Houses and Castles of Great Britain: The Tower of London**
Cosmopolitan; b/w; 18 min; Great Britain
D: Maurice Elvey S/P: George J. Banfield
Cast: Isobel Elsom, John Stuart

Producer George J. Banfield's *The Tower of London* is the second film to revolve around Great Britain's most famous structure, though this time around it was not based on Thomas Ainsworth's historical novel of the same name. Rather, it was an entry in the *Haunted Houses and Castles of Great Britain* series of two-reelers.

Located in the outer London area, the infamous Tower is actually a group of related buildings guarded by a large wall, a moat and the River Thames. William the Conqueror constructed the oldest structure on the lot, the White Tower, in 1078 as both defense for and protection from the people of London. King Richard the Lionhearted added the moat and the wall in the 1190s.

The Tower is probably most famous for its celebrity executions, including those of William Hastings, Anne Boleyn, Catherine Howard, Lady Jane Grey and possibly George, Duke of Clarence and King Edward IV's two young sons, Edward V and Richard of Shrewsbury, who over the years have become known simply as "the princes in the Tower."

Such a brutal place as the Tower of London is not, of course, without its share of ghostly manifestations and is today considered one of the most haunted places in the world. The ghosts include the aforementioned Anne Boleyn, who reputedly haunts the chapel where she's buried, walking about with her severed head beneath one arm. Other spectral inhabitants are said to include Henry VIII, Lady Jane Grey and the two princes. CW

Unknown Treasures
aka **The House Behind the Hedge**
Sterling; b/w; 63 min; U.S.
D: Archie Mayo S: Charles A. Logue C: Harry Davis
Cast: Gladys Hulette, Robert Agnew, John Miljan, Gustav von Seyffertitz, Jed Prouty

Bob Ramsey (Agnew) suspects that the uncle of the woman he loves (Hulette) has stashed a fortune in stolen bonds in the family mansion. The young man determines to find the treasure but instead uncovers a plot far more complex—and murderous—than he had bargained.

The story *The House Behind the Hedge* by Mary Spain Vigus becomes the basis for this old dark house thriller. Archie Mayo began film work as an actor but established a reputation as a reliable director by working on a variety of comedic short subjects; he eventually moved to more prestigious fare, including *The Petrified Forest* (1936), *The Story of Marco Polo* (1938) and *Angel on My Shoulder* (1946), the latter being his last directorial effort. *Unknown Treasures* was one of only two forays into horror he made, and though considered lost, it would seem that the goings-on were played straighter than the average old dark house film of the period.

The supporting cast includes cadaverous character actor Gustav von Seyffertitz, whose mellifluous voice graced several horror films of the 1930s, notably *The Bat Whispers* (1930) and *Son of Frankenstein* (1939). Here he plays a mad scientist who has trained a gorilla to commit murder. TH

While London Sleeps
Warner; b/w; 66 (52) min; U.S.
D: H.P. Bretherton S: Walter Morosco C: Frank Kessen
Cast: Rin Tin Tin, Helene Costello, Walter Merrill, John Patrick, Otto Matieson, George Kotsonaros

Found by an American G.I. in a bombed-out kennel in a Paris suburb shortly before the end of World War I, German shepherd puppy Rin Tin Tin was brought back to the United States, where he was trained to do tricks for spellbound audiences. He was spotted by filmmaker Charles Jones and brought to the big screen, where he became an immediate sensation with kids. How strange, then, that one of his early starring roles would be in this, a Warner Bros. horror film.

London Letter (Matieson), the scourge of the Limehouse district, has Scotland Yard Inspector Burke (Jennings) hot on his heels. Letter, being a bad guy, mistreats his dog Rinty (Rin Tin Tin), but Burke's daughter, Dale (Costello), rescues the dog to which she becomes devoted. Smarting from the loss of his abused pet, Burke dispatches The Monk, a vile ape-man (Kotsonaros), to abduct and kill Dale. The creature snatches her off, but before he can do her in, Rinty, who tears out the ape-man's throat, saves her.

The Monk is played by George Kotsonaros, a former wrestler who hailed from Greece. He repeated the ape-man killer role in his only other horror film, *The Wizard* (1927), before dying in an automobile accident in Alabama in 1933. Top-billed actress Helene Costello was sister to Maurice Costello, a director and actor of the silent cinema whose fame at the time far eclipsed his sister's.

After Rin Tin Tin's death in the early 1930s, his body was shipped back to France and buried in the *Cimetière des Chiens* near Paris. His death was not enough to end the Rin Tin Tin franchise, however. A series of related German Shepherds replaced him, and over the next 30 years more movies, radio programs and a TV series followed.

Some of *While London Sleeps'* more horrific aspects were cut for British audiences. Though the film is considered lost today, its sound disks survive. CW

Whispering Wires
Fox; b/w; 6 reels; U.S.
D: Albert Ray S: L.G. (Gordon) Rigby, William Conselman
C: George Schneiderman

Anita Stewart (left) stars as the intended victim of murder in *Whispering Wires*.

Cast: Anita Stewart, Edmund Burns, Charles Clary, Otto Matieson, Mack Swain, Arthur Housman

A person is murdered after receiving a strange, whispering phone call. When Doris Stockbridge (Stewart) receives a similar call, her boyfriend, Barry McGill (Burns), sets out to unmask the psycho before another tragedy occurs. With the help of bumbling detectives Casey (Housman) and McCarthy (Swain), Barry prevents Doris' murder and unmasks the would-be assassin.

Whispering Wires blends horror, melodrama, suspense and farce in a pleasing manner. The busy scenario was adapted from a novel by Henry Leverage. Little is known about the author, though he reportedly once did a stint in Sing Sing Correctional Facility for grand theft auto.

Director Albert Ray visited similar cinematic terrain in *A Thief in the Dark* (1928) and *The Intruder* (1933). Leading lady Anita Stewart was popular in the silent era, but her career took a nosedive with the coming of sound. Costar Edmund Burns was another all-purpose, silent-era performer whose career likewise went downhill in the early 1930s. His other horror/suspense credits include *One Hour Before Dawn* (1920), *Those Who Dare* (1924), *Ransom* (1928) and *The Death Kiss* (1932). TH

Windsor Castle
aka **Haunted Houses and Castles of Great Britain: Windsor Castle**
Cosmopolitan; b/w; 19 min; Great Britain
D: Maurice Elvey *S/P:* George J. Banfield
Cast: Isabel Jeans, Ian Wilson

Dating back to the days of William the Conqueror, Windsor Castle is one of several homes belonging to the royal family of England and lived in by the current Queen Elizabeth II. It shares several ghosts with the Tower of London, including those of King Henry VIII and his beheaded second wife Anne Boleyn. Other ghosts that are said to walk the castle's ramparts and corridors include Queen Elizabeth I, King Charles I, King George III and Sir George Villiers, the first Duke of Buckingham, as well as a keeper for King Richard II who was supposedly murdered by jealous fellow keepers. Everyone from tourists to royal family members has claimed sightings.

A pseudo-documentary exploring the ghosts of Windsor Castle, this film was part of a 12-episode series of two-reelers titled *Haunted Houses and Castles of Great Britain*. All the episodes were written and produced by George J. Banfield, though with a number of different directors and stars. It should also be noted that, though the series was made under the auspices of Cosmopolitan, Cricks and Martin released it to theaters. CW

Woodcroft Castle
aka **Haunted Houses and Castles of Great Britain: Woodcroft Castle**
Cosmopolitan; b/w; 15 min; Great Britain
D: Walter West *S/P:* George J. Banfield
Cast: James Knight

Located in Cambridgeshire, England, Woodcroft Castle is difficult to see from the road, shielded from view by a long thick row of trees. During the English Civil War, it was owned by Dr. Michael Hudson, chaplain to and supporter of King Charles I. Fighting Cromwell's rebel forces, Hudson and his men became cornered inside the castle walls. Hudson was chased to one of the turrets and fell over the edge, managing to hold on by his fingertips until they were severed by an enemy's sword. Upon landing in the moat below, he was hit with musket fire and dragged from the water. Then his tongue was cut out and displayed throughout the countryside as a trophy of the fight against the king. It is said by some that in the still of the night the doctor's screams of anguish and cries for mercy, as well as the sounds of fighting and gunfire, can be heard in and around the castle grounds. Thus history and mythology continue to flame supernatural fires.

This entry in producer/writer George J. Banfield's *Haunted Houses and Castles of Great Britain* series focuses on the tale of the doctor (Knight) and was filmed on the actual castle's property.

Today, Woodcroft Castle is a privately owned family residence. CW

1927

Akikusa dōrō
Shochiku; b/w; length unknown; Japan
D: Houtei Nomura
Cast: Chieko Matsui, Sakuko Yanagi, Emiko Yagumo, Sotaro Okada, Junsuke Hayama, Hideo Fujino

Details of this obscure Japanese horror film may never be known, but film historians can make a reasonable guess as to the time of year in which the movie was set, thanks to the title. *Akikusa* translates as "autumn grass," while *dōrō* translates as "lan-

tern." One can reasonably conclude that it has something to do with a vengeful ghost, probably of a woman transgressed against by her male lover, who carries a lantern.

Houtei Nomura also directed the 1932 horror feature *Shin Yotsuya kaidan* for Shochiku; it, too, starred Emiko Yagumo. CW

Banchō sarayashiki
Toa; b/w; length unknown; Japan
D: Tsukasa Kozuki
Cast unknown

This is one of many cinematic adaptations of the venerable Japanese folktale to be produced during the silent and early sound eras. Others include *Banchō sarayashika* (1914, 1922, 1927, and 1928), *Shin sarayashiki* (1924 and 1926), *Isetsu Banchō sarayashika* (1929) and *The Plate-Counting Ghost of Banchō* (1937).

All of them told the same story of a servant girl named Okiku who is lusted after by her depraved master, a samurai (or, in some tellings, a shogun's vassal) named Aoyama. Depending on the version, she breaks or is framed for breaking a family heirloom (usually a plate) belonging to Aoyama, who uses the threat of punishment to attempt to coerce her into bedding him. When she refuses, he murders her and throws her body into a well, after which she rises from the grave in search of the broken heirloom.

Several famous Japanese playwrights tried their hand at adapting the tale, including Ningyō Jōruri and Okamoto Kido. Jōruri's version depicted Okiku as a lowly servant in the castle of Hosokawa Katsumoto. When Katsumoto falls ill, one of his retainers, Asayama, plots the murder of Tomonosuke, Katsumoto's heir. He appeals to Okiku for help, trying at the same time to seduce the beautiful young woman. Okiku refuses to grant him either request and is tortured by being repeatedly lowered into a well, then beaten each time she is raised. Not surprisingly, she dies. Shortly thereafter, her voice can be heard counting the plates, which are a symbol of Tomonosuke's succession of Katsumoto. CW

Belphegor
Cineromans; b/w; 220 min; France
D: Henri Desfontaines S: Arthur Bernede P: Cineromans C: Maurice Arnou, Robert Lefebvre, Andre-Wladimir Reybas, Julien Ringel
Cast: Rene Navarre, Elmire Vautier, Lucien Dalsace, Michele Verly, Genica Messirio, Jeanne Brindeau

A lobby card shows Annabelle West (Laura La Plante) as the terrified sole inheritor of the entire estate of Cyrus West.

The Louvre Museum is terrorized by a phantom known as Belphegor (Vautier). Intrepid detective Chantecoq (Navarre), after a very long investigation, unmasks the apparition as an all-too-flesh-and-blood jewel thief.

Belphegor is a cinematic companion piece to the 1927 novel of the same name. Its screenwriter, Arthur Bernede, developed the tale simultaneously for page and screen. The plot takes inspiration from such popular French serials as *Fantomas* (1913) and *Les Vampires* (1915), as well as Fritz Lang's epic *Dr. Mabuse, The Gambler* (1922).

Though both film and novel were hits, it wasn't until decades later that additional adaptations came along. A 1965 French television version dropped the character of Chantecoq altogether. This same period also saw Belphegor's adventures serialized in comic strip form in France. More recently, the story was adapted as *Belphegor: Phantom of the Louvre* (2001), a big budget affair with the title character's gender changed to accommodate star Sophie Marceau. A French-Canadian animated series also appeared in 2001.

Director Henri Desfontaines had a knack for classic period horror fare, helming, among other films, an early version of Edgar Allan Poe's *The Pit and the Pendulum* (1909). He acted as well, most notably in 1909's *The Wild Ass's Skin*, adapted from the story by Honoré de Balzac.

Belphegor was one of Desfontaines' last credits before his death in 1931. TH

The Cat and the Canary
Universal; b/w; 80 min; U.S.
D: Paul Leni *S:* Alfred A. Cohn, Robert F. Hill *P:* Paul Kohner *C:* Gilbert Warrenton

Cast: Laura La Plante, Creighton Hale, Forrest Stanley, Tully Marshall, Arthur Edmund Carewe, Gertrude Astor

Cyrus West, an eccentric millionaire, likens himself to a canary being stalked by cat-like, greedy relatives. He stipulates that his will not be read until 20 years after his death and then he dies. Two decades pass and his relatives gather at his sinister home in the country to find out what they'll be inheriting. The will names Annabelle West (La Plante) as sole inheritor of the entire estate and fortune, causing no end of consternation among the more despicable would-be heirs. A storm, coupled with the escape of a dangerous maniac from the local asylum, makes it impossible for anyone to leave the mansion. The family lawyer (Marshall) turns up dead, and Annabelle and the others realize that they're *all* in danger—and with a mysterious figure lurking in the shadows, it does indeed seem likely that more blood will be shed before daybreak.

John Willard was a playwright of marginal interest, his major contribution to the American stage being his 1922 smash *The Cat and the Canary*. A playful mixture of humor, horror and suspense, it takes an Agatha Christie-like premise and milks it for all it's worth. The claustrophobic setting was tailored to the stage, but it didn't take filmmakers long to realize that it also had the makings of a good film. German-born head of Universal Pictures, Carl Laemmle, had managed to lure designer/director Paul Leni to Hollywood earlier in 1927 and now assigned the newcomer to direct the first film version of *The Cat and the Canary*.

The choice availed the film of Leni's Expressionist directorial style, an essential contribution given the material's stage-bound nature. Leni's visual fireworks are evident from the opening montage depicting Uncle Cyrus' descent into madness and death. As the old man imagines himself stalked by his greedy relatives, Leni superimposes images of hissing cats; it's a little on the nose, as it were, but it playfully underscores the story's theme in purely cinematic terms.

Leni's framing is imaginative throughout, and he explores the possibilities of mobile camerawork in aggressive terms. There are some superb examples of dolly and crane shots on display, as well as handheld camerawork, giving it a more modern texture than most American silent films. The potent imagery would prove a tremendous influence on later films and filmmakers, including James Whale (whose 1932 *The Old Dark House* borrows heavily from this picture) and Robert Siodmak (who imitates the eye-catching opening titles for his stylish B-horror film *Son of Dracula* in 1943).

It's a good thing Leni's imaginative use of the medium is so richly in evidence, given the film's shortcomings in other areas. The humor ranges from the mildly amusing to the totally ineffective, with Creighton Hale's portrayal as the nervous cousin, Paul, nearly sinking the film at times. It's obvious that Leni's sensibilities were more in tune with the darker humor of sideline characters such as the dour housekeeper Mammy Pleasant than they were with Hale's frantic antics. With his geeky mannerisms and thick glasses, Hale evokes silent comedian Harold Lloyd—without Lloyd's gift for comedic timing.

While it's true that it was considered clever and imaginative in its day, Willard's play (and thus the film based on it) stands today as a compendium of old dark house clichés, lacking the perverse and macabre sensibility that gives Whale's later entry a staying power that endures. Still, Leni's direction, coupled with terrific art direction by Charles "Danny" Hall and luminous cinematography by Gilbert Warrenton (who re-teamed with Leni the following year on the superior *The Man Who Laughs*), makes *The Cat and the Canary* a feast for the eyes. It may be a bit rocky in terms of content—thus placing it a notch lower than the director's best films, such as *Waxworks* (1924)—but on the whole it remains a passably engaging and entertaining piece of work.

With the exception of Hale, the cast performs admirably. Leading lady La Plante is pretty and likable, and the supporting players include familiar faces like Arthur Edmund Carewe (the Persian in *The Phantom of the Opera*, 1925) and Tully Marshall (Luis XI in *The Hunchback of Notre Dame*, 1923). The final revelation of the killer is easy to see coming, but the character's grotesque disguise still creates frisson.

Willard's play would be remade officially five more times: as *The Cat Creeps* in both English and Spanish versions in 1930, as the Bob Hope vehicle *The Cat and the Canary* in 1939, as a Swedish TV movie in 1961 and finally by Radley Metzger in 1979, again as *The Cat and the Canary*. TH

Easy Pickings
First National; b/w; 60 min; U.S.
D: George Archainbaud *S:* William A. Burton *P:* Frank Griffin *C:* Charles Van Enger
Cast: Anna Q. Nilsson, Kenneth Harlan, Philo McCullough, Billy Bevan, Jerry Miley, Charles Sellon, Zack Williams, Gertrude Howard

Mary Ryan (Nilsson) and Peter Van Horne (Harlan) are stranded in an old dark house inhabited by various unsavory characters. Also a detective (Bevan) mills about, investigating mysterious goings-on that the residents attribute to ghosts.

Based on a play by Paul A. Cruger, *Easy Pickings* fits snugly into the subgenre of old dark house comedy/mysteries popularized by the likes of *The Bat* (1926) and *The Cat and the Canary* (1927). As in those films, there's as much emphasis here on comedy—a great deal of it provided by mugging African American actor Zack Williams, stereotypically cast as a nervous servant—as on chills and mystery.

The cast includes character actor Billy Bevan in a more-serious-than-usual role as a detective; he later brought comedic relief to such titles as *Dracula's Daughter* (1936) and *The Invisible Man Returns* (1940). Leading lady Anna Q. Nilsson had emigrated from Sweden; she was popular in American silent features, but her career fell flat with the arrival of sound.

Director George Archainbaud was a prolific journeyman who wound up directing a number of popular TV shows, including *Lassie* and *The Gene Autry Show*. Cinematographer Charles Van Enger had previously photographed *The Phantom of the Opera* (1925) and went on to shoot such popular Universal offerings as *The Spider Woman* (1944) and *Abbott and Costello Meet Frankenstein* (1948). TH

The Ghost Train
aka **Der Geisterzug; Train Fantôme**
Gainsborough/F.P.S./Phoebus; b/w; 74 min; Great Britain/Germany
D: Geza Von Bolvary *S:* Benno Vigny *P:* Michael Balcon, Herrmann Fellner, Arnold Pressburger, Josef Somlo
Cast: Guy Newall, Ilse Bois, Louis Ralph, Hilde Jennings, John Manners, Sinaida Korolenko

Hungarian director Michael Curtiz—who went on to find fame with such disparate films as *Doctor X* (1932) and *Casablanca* (1943)—is rumored to have been the original director of this obscure production. If so, he left the project early. He's not credited on the prints, nor is the title attributed to him in any reputable source. *The Ghost Train*'s credited director, Geza Von Bolvary, helmed 100 titles between 1920 and 1958; among them is a 1927 version of *Number 17*, remade in England by Alfred Hitchcock in 1932. Von Bolvary's specialty appears to have been melodrama, though the consensus at the time was that he didn't bring the right touch to this film. The plot revolves around faked supernatural activity at a train station, the purpose of which is to scare people away from a smuggling operation.

The British/German co-production united Michael Balcon's Gainsboro studios with the UFA studios of Germany. In fact, the film was shot in Berlin. The story was again adapted in England under the same title in 1931. TH

The Gorilla
First National; b/w; 80 min; U.S.
D/P: Alfred Santell *S:* Alfred A. Cohn, Harry McArthur *C:* Arthur Edeson
Cast: Charlie Murray, Fred Kelsey, Walter Pidgeon, Alice Day, Tully Marshall, Brooks Benedict

A young woman (Day) is suspected of murder after her father becomes the victim of a killer wearing a gorilla costume.

Ralph Spence's play *The Gorilla* was a big moneymaker on Broadway in 1925; its success, in fact, contributed to the continuing popularity of the old dark house subgenre. It was quickly optioned for the screen by producer/director Alfred (Al) Santell, who helmed a number of comedies during the silent era, though his career lasted into the mid-1940s.

Though *The Gorilla* was a comparatively serious choice for Santell, the film did, to judge from reviews at the time, contain its share of slapstick. At any rate, contemporary critics were impressed. *Variety*, in a November 23, 1927 review, enthused:

> *The Gorilla* is box-office tonic for more reasons than one. It is an entertaining picture, the title boasts a reputation gained from the stage play and the story makes good exploitation material. Except in a few serious instances, the story is done in broad comedy. Technically the picture is distinctive in photography, being handled with an expert treatment of lighting values and perspectives. Sets are highly atmospheric. Effective direction by Santell ...

Similarly, a critic for the *New York Times* found much to admire in the film, as is evidenced in this review dated November 21, 1927:

> Excitement and amusement are linked in the screen translation of *The Gorilla*, Ralph Spence's burlesque on the mystery play. In quite a number of spots, Alfred Santell's easy and imaginative touch is apparent, but here and there this film slumps into horseplay and silly stunts. *The Gorilla* is very much as if Mack Sennett ... had turned to Edgar Allan Poe's *The Murders in the Rue Morgue* and decided to adapt it to the screen ... Mr. Santell ... makes very good use of settings in this production ...

As these commentaries make clear, it seems that the film offered the same blend of mystery, horror and comedy that made such pictures as Paul Leni's *The Cat and the Canary* (1927) so popular. The cast included a young Walter Pidgeon, who went on to receive Oscar nominations for *Mrs. Miniver* (1942) and *Madame Curie* (1943), though genre buffs will more likely remember him as Dr. Morbius in 1956's *Forbidden Planet*. On the technical side, the cinematography was by Arthur Edeson, later a favorite of director James Whale, for whom he would shoot *Frankenstein* (1931) and *The Invisible Man* (1933), among others.

The Gorilla was remade in 1930 and 1939, the latter version featuring Bela Lugosi and Lionel Atwill. Both the 1930 remake and Santell's original are today considered lost. TH

Irohagana Yotsuya kaidan
Makino; b/w; length unknown; Japan
D: Inoue Kintarou *S:* Sanjiro Akishino *P:* Shozo Makino
Cast: Ryunosuki Tsukigata, Sumiko Suzuki, Tsuyako Okajima, Kimie Kawakami, Kanjuro Arashi, Tsuki Matsura

This was Makino Studio's second adaptation of the classic Kabuki play *Yotsuya kaidan* (1825); the first appeared in 1923. Unlike most of the other adaptations, this was a two-parter, with the first installment making its theatrical bow on July 14, 1927 and the second following a week later, on July 22. The tale concerns a samurai (Tsukigata) who drives his wife (Suzuki) to her death, only to find he and his lover (Okajima) terrorized by her ghost.

Actress Sumiko Suzuki was born in 1904 in Tokyo, Japan. By 1921 she found herself in the movies and by the end of the silent era had become something of a staple. This was her first appearance as the doomed wife Oiwa but not her last; she took on the role once again a year later in Takuji Furumi's *Yotsuya kaidan* (where she also played the character's younger sister Osode), as well as in the 1931 film *Oiwa Nagaya* and the 1937 film *Irohagana Yotsuya kaidan*. One of her last horror film appearances came in 1938's *Ghost Cat's Mysterious Shamisen*, and her last film appearance appears to have come around 1940. She died at the age of 80 in January 1985. CW

Johann the Coffinmaker
aka **The Coffin Maker**
The Film Art Guild of New York; b/w; 27 min; U.S.
D/Co-S/P: Robert Florey *Co-S:* Slavko Vorkapich
Cast unknown

On Christmas Eve, old Johann the coffin maker receives an order for a child's casket. The request puts him in a pensive mood that coaxes three beings—an Apache, a soldier and a prostitute—back from the dead. He offers each a drink and inquires as to how they met their deaths. They tell their tales and return to their graves. There's a knock at the door, and Johann opens it to find Death has come calling. He invites her in, and the two climb into a casket that Johann has made for himself. They embrace as Johann lowers the lid over them.

Robert Florey may be most famous today for having had the directorial chores on *Frankenstein* (1931) yanked from him, but his career dates back to the silent era. One of his earliest productions was this *avant-garde* film, similar in style to the U.S. version of *The Fall of the House of Usher* (1928). Rumored to have cost as little as $200, it was shot at night while Florey worked by day on other productions. The story unfolds on three confined sets: a workshop, a graveyard and an apartment room.

Only a little less experimental than Florey's other surrealist films (*The Love of Zero*, 1927 and *The Life and Death of 9413–A Hollywood Extra*, 1928, both influenced by the Expressionist look of *The Cabinet of Dr. Caligari*, 1919), the director here aims for a mix of the mundane and the strange. But, though striking in its tone and imagery, *Johann* remains at its core a relic of cinema's earliest days, when fantastic stories were often built around trick photographic effects.

Born in Paris, France in the year 1900, Florey was educated in Switzerland and, while there, worked for a time as an actor and writer. In 1920 he worked briefly at Fueillade's studios in Nice, and in 1921 moved to Hollywood, California where he served as assistant director to the likes of Josef von Sternberg. He began directing his own short films in 1926 and by 1929 had worked up to major studio fare such as *The Cocoanuts*, the first feature film to star comedy team The Marx Brothers. Yet, success didn't put Florey in the big leagues. After losing out on Universal's *Frankenstein*, he directed the lower-budgeted *Murders in the Rue Morgue* (1932), which, though stylish, simply routed his career toward more of the same.

In 1950 he was made a knight in France's *Legion d'Honneur*. Soon thereafter, he entered the field of television. His last directorial job was on "Moonstone," an episode of *The Outer Limits* (1964). He died of cancer at the age of 79 in 1979.

His other horror efforts include *A Hole in the Wall* (1929), *The Florentine Dagger* (1935), *The Face Behind the Mask* (1941) and *The Beast with Five Fingers* (1946). CW

The Killer Dwarf
aka Issun-boshi

Makino; b/w; length unknown; Japan
D: Seika Shiba *S:* Sanjugo Naoki *C:* Toshio Kashiwada, Kenzo Sakai
Cast: Baku Ishii, Tamako Shirajawa, Konami Ishii, Chame Kuriyama

Born in 1894, Hirai Tarō grew up reading the detective and horror fiction of Edgar Allan Poe, which had long been available in Japanese translations. Several years after graduating from college, he published his first short story, a mystery in the mold of *The Purloined Letter*. The story was printed under the pseudonym Edogawa Rampo, which, when spoken quickly, sounds like a Japanese inflection of "Edgar Allan Poe." He continued to publish both short stories and novels and quickly become the most prolific fiction author in Japan. As his career progressed, his stories took increasingly darker turns toward eroticism and grotesquerie, touching upon themes including male homosexuality and human disfigurement brought about by war.

Much of his work was optioned for the big screen, with *The Killer Dwarf* being his first film adaptation. It was released on March 26, 1927. The story itself is based on the old folk tale of *Issun-boshi* (which was also the title of Rampo's tale) in which a childless older couple prays for a son, even if he be extremely short. They get their wish, though he's exceedingly small, and eventually he goes off to see the world, where he becomes a hero. By all accounts, Rampo's tale and this adaptation of it took a decidedly nasty turn from the folk tale, with the dwarf presented as a murderer.

After the end of World War II, Rampo spent a great deal of his time assisting his friend, anthropologist Jun'ichi Iwata, who had spent his career studying homosexuality among the Japanese. When Iwata—with whom Rampo had once had an ongoing competition to see who could discover and read the most books about erotic encounters between men—died, Rampo worked to ensure that his friend's writings on homosexuality were published. Rampo died of a brain hemorrhage in 1965.

The story of *Issun-boshi* was filmed again in 1948 and 1955. CW

The Last Performance
aka The Magician; The Last Call; Erik the Great

Universal; b/w; 59 (69, 48) min; U.S.
D: Paul Fejos *S:* James Ashmore Creelman, Tom Reed, Walter Anthony *P:* Carl Laemmle *C:* Hal Mohr
Cast: Conrad Veidt, Mary Philbin, Leslie Fenton, Fred MacKaye, Gusztav Partos, William H. Turner

A successful magician called Erik the Great (Veidt) is deeply in love with his pretty assistant, Julie (Philbin), who has promised to marry him when she turns 18. Though her birthday is months away, Erik's other assistant, Boffo (Fenton), who is himself smitten with Julie, is resentful of the impending nuptials. Meanwhile, when a man named Mark (MacKaye) attempts to steal from Erik, the kind-hearted magician gives the would-be burglar food and money. Julie talks Erik into hiring Mark for their act, while Boffo hatches a scheme to drive a wedge between Erik and Julie.

Director Paul Fejos certainly had a colorful background. Born in 1897, he came to acting prominence in his native Hungary before joining the army during WW1. After his discharge he took up chemistry but, even as a respected bacteriologist, continued dabbling in the arts. After associating with the likes of Max Reinhardt, he made his own debut as a director in 1920.

He came to the United States in 1927, and Universal hired him to direct *The Last Performance*. Originally planned as part of Universal's "Super Jewel" series, it was shot in 1927 and got a brief release that same year in New York City. It went into general release in 1929, just as sound films were beginning to catch on. Later release prints did actually incorporate a sound effects track, and for its Hungarian release, Conrad Veidt's part was overdubbed by Bela Lugosi.

Its belated general debut led many to conclude that *The Last Performance* was a follow-up to Paul Leni's *The Man Who Laughs* (1928), which also starred Veidt and Mary Philbin. However, Fejos' film was made first.

Performance's official running time is 69 minutes, though extant prints run at a mere 59 minutes, so it seems likely that some significant footage is lost. In any case, the rarely seen film is given merit almost solely by Veidt's skillful, controlled performance as Erik. The remainder of the cast falls short in comparison, though Mary Philbin is reasonably effective as the naïve object of Erik's affection. It has been alleged that an un-credited Walter Brennan portrays a clown in the film, but this is difficult to confirm with any degree of certainty.

The story is thin and contrived, and the finale in particular suffers because of it. Veidt's presence notwithstanding, *The Last Performance* is ultimately an exercise in style over substance.

Fejos' greatest U.S. success came with the release of the hyper-stylized *Broadway* (1929), a film renowned for its innovative and elaborate camerawork. TH

The Lodger: A Story of the London Fog
aka The Lodger; The Case of Jonathan Drew

Carlyle Blackwell Productions; b/w; 90 (83; 101; 75; 67; 98) min; Great Britain
D: Alfred Hitchcock *S:* Eliot Stannard *P:* Michael Balcon, Carlyle Blackwell *C:* Baron (Gaetano) di Ventimiglia
Cast: Ivor Novello, June Tripp, Marie Ault, Arthur Chesney, Malcolm Keen, Eve Gray

1920s London is paralyzed by a series of gruesome killings. A card left at each crime scene identifies the perpetrator as The

French poster for *The Lodger*

It was, however, *The Lodger: A Story of the London Fog* that first displayed his gifts as a cinematic storyteller. The film to a large degree proved a template for the themes, imagery and obsessions that would dominate his work for the next 50 years. The concept of a possibly innocent man wrongly suspected by a mob would color his oeuvre for decades, culminating in *Frenzy* (1972).

Renowned for his ability to milk tension from the most mundane of situations—thus earning him the title of "Master of Suspense"—Hitchcock is equally infamous for his callousness toward actors and an alleged disinterest in the screenwriting process. Yet closer analysis shows that on most occasions he chose his material wisely and that, despite his reputed indifference toward his performers, he frequently managed to draw remarkable work from them.

The merits of *The Lodger* move beyond the purely academic. While he hadn't yet begun to master the techniques that would come to infuse his best work, the film is hardly the production of an amateur. As a thriller, it's well constructed and stylishly crafted. He grabs the audience's attention from the film's first shot, a tight close-up of the Avenger's latest victim screaming in terror. There are also some striking stylistic flourishes, most notably the celebrated sequence in which the people downstairs look to the ceiling and envision the lodger nervously pacing above them. It's no surprise, really, to learn that this was the first of his films with which he was openly pleased.

A novel of the same name by Marie Adelaide Belloc Lowndes, a prolific writer who credited herself as Mrs. Belloc Lowndes, becomes the basis of the screenplay. Additional influence can be inferred from Lowndes' stage play *Who Is He?* Clearly inspired by the infamous Jack the Ripper murders, the story updates the action to the then-present day and downplays the more unsavory details of the case. Still, some genuine frisson is generated. The introductory shot of Drew standing in the doorway may well have inspired a similar image in William Friedkin's *The Exorcist* (1973), while the scene in which Drew appears to menace Daisy as she takes a bath doubtless puts today's viewer in mind of the director's later, triumphant *Psycho* (1960).

Avenger. Joe (Keen), a Scotland Yard detective, is assigned to the case. At the same time the mysterious Jonathan Drew (Novello) takes up residence at the boarding house of Mr. and Mrs. Bunting (Chesney, Ault). This catches Joe's attention, since he's wooing Bunting daughter Daisy (Tripp) and sees the handsome Drew as a potential rival. Driven in part by jealousy, Joe comes to suspect Drew of being The Avenger.

Sir Alfred Hitchcock (1899-1980) got his start in the film business in the late teens, designing title cards for British productions. After a brief stint in Germany, where he is rumored to have seen the likes of Fritz Lang at work, he returned to Great Britain and became a director.

His ascent to fame began tentatively. His first attempt at film, *Number 13* (1922), was plagued by financing difficulties and never completed. Similar misfortune weighed upon his second directorial attempt, *Always Tell Your Wife* (1923), on which Hugh Croise eventually replaced him. The British/German co-production *The Pleasure Garden* (1925) was his first completed feature, and he followed it up with another German co-production, *The Mountain Eagle* (1926).

Leading man Ivor Novello does a capable job as Jonathan Drew. One can't help but wonder if Hitchcock was referencing Novello's homosexuality with such sly bits of dialogue as "He's a bit queer!" and "Good thing he doesn't like the ladies." Though Novello's proclivities weren't public knowledge and his good looks ensured him sex symbol status during the 1920s, he didn't make many truly memorable film appearances during his career. His work is mostly unknown today except by film scholars and cinephiles. The remainder of the cast turns in decent performances but is dwarfed by Novello's magnetic presence in a role he would repeat for the 1932 version.

The film's happy ending feels contrived and was, indeed, not a part of Hitchcock's original design. It's also worth noting that only John Brahm's atmospheric 1944 version managed to outdo Hitchcock's original. TH

London After Midnight
MGM; b/w; 69 min; U.S.
D/P: Tod Browning *S:* Waldemar Young *P:* Irving G. Thalberg *C:* Merrott B. Gerstad
Cast: Lon Chaney, Marceline Day, Henry B. Walthall, Percy Williams, Conrad Nagel, Polly Moran

In 1920s London, Sir Roger Balfour (King) is found shot to death at his home. Inspector Burke (Chaney) suspects foul play but is forced to conclude—based on the note found beside the body—that it was suicide. Five years later, a pair of mysterious strangers moves into the Balfour residence, and the neighbors believe them to be vampires. Certainly their strange appearance lends credence to this. The man (also played by Chaney) wears a cloak and top hat, and his wide grin reveals a full set of razor-sharp teeth. His female companion (Tichenor) is equally ghostly and accompanies him wherever he goes. Rumors spread that the strange man is actually Balfour returned from the grave. The concerned Sir James (Walthall), executor of the Balfour estate, calls in Inspector Burke to investigate.

Of all the films that emerged from the collaborative teaming of director Tod Browning and star Lon Chaney, *London After Midnight* is the most sought after. The reason for this is simple. Despite an abundance of mouth-watering stills, the film itself is considered lost. Hollywood lore has it that the last surviving print perished in a fire in the vaults of MGM, but hope springs eternal that a print will eventually resurface.

Interestingly, the film was the most popular of the Browning/Chaney films, its box-office receipts eclipsing even those of *The Unholy Three* (1925). All of this belies the fact that its reviews were mixed; most critics who managed to see it upon its original release assured the public that it wasn't one of Browning and Chaney's more artistically successful projects.

Hitchcock's famous propensity for making cameo appearances in his own films began with *The Lodger*. He can be glimpsed from behind as he sits at a desk in a newspaper office—though at this stage it's quite probable that such cameos were done, at least in part, for the sake of expediency. In any case, it eventually became a part of the Hitchcock film experience to look for the director as each of his films unfolds.

The Lodger has been remade several times over the ensuing decades, once as *The Phantom Fiend* (1932, though it was titled *The Lodger* in its native country), twice as *The Lodger* (1944, 2009) and once as *Man in the Attic* (1953). Of the later versions,

Based on a short story by Browning titled *The Hypnotist*, it's basically a Gothic murder mystery. In the final reel, the vampires are revealed to be a hoax, a trick Browning would employ to tremendous controversy in his sound remake, *Mark of the Vampire* (1935). Given that audiences still groan over the final revelation of the later picture, it seems likely that *London* would inspire similar disdain if it ever were to re-emerge. Even so, the film gave Chaney a dual role—he

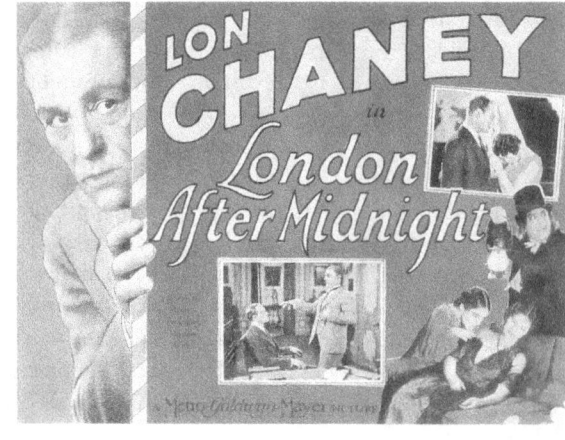

plays both square-jawed, no-nonsense Inspector Burke and the mysterious stranger with the hellish grin. The finale reveals that there really is no stranger, however; it's merely Burke indulging in some dressing-up in order to trap Balfour's murderer.

Chaney's make-up for the role of the alleged vampire is one of his most startling creations. The pale face, wide eyes and dual rows of shark-like fangs surely made a tremendous impression in 1927, no doubt accounting largely for the film's success with the public.

Given its status as one of the most sought-after lost films, it's not surprising that fans have tried to imagine what the film must be like. In 2002, producer Rick Schmidlin, in collaboration with the Turner Classic Movie network, created a reconstruction of the film using stills and a surviving continuity script. Running 45 minutes, it provides an approximation of the film, thus confirming that, while certainly not without interest, it likely remains one of the least bizarre and compelling of the Browning/Chaney collaborations. TH

The Manor House of Fear
aka **Le Manoir de la peur**; **L'Homme Noir**
Machin; b/w; 70 min; France
D: Alfred Machin, Henry Wulschleger *C:* Mario Badouaille
Cast: Romuald Joube, Gabriel de Gavrone, Lynn Arnell, Arlette Marchal, Cinq-Leon, Louis Monfils, Georges Terof, Ernest Chambery, Monsieur Schey

A mysterious "Man in Black" (Joube) terrorizes the French countryside.

The Manor House of Fear was a macabre melodrama with supernatural overtones and plenty of creepy images, many of them religious in nature (the man in black sitting at a table, a cross prominently adorning the wall behind him; a chalot towering over a graveyard in which all of the markers are crosses). Some sources state that the film was given a brief theatrical run in the United States by Universal; if so, it couldn't have found a more appropriate home. Co-director/producer Alfred Machin was a cinematic veteran by the time of the film's creation, having started out as a cameraman before transitioning to direction via documentary subjects. His early success enabled him to form Alfred Machin Film Studios in 1921. He was quite prolific in his day, though much of his work is now believed lost.

Manor appears to have been Machin's sole foray into the horror genre. It was also one of his last films before his sudden death in 1929. It is unclear why Henry Wulschleger assisted on the directorial chores; Wulschleger was a journeyman who worked sporadically throughout the 1920s and '30s.

Star Romuald Joube is best remembered today for playing the protagonist, Jean Diaz, in Abel Gance's *J'Accuse* (1919). TH

Noidan Kirot
Suomi-Filmi; 82 min; b/w; Finland
D/S: Teuvo Puro *P:* Erkki Karu *C:* Frans Ekebom
Cast: Einar Rinne, Heidi Blåfield, Irmeli Viherjuuri, Kaisu Leppänen, Hannes Närhi

A young man brings his bride and his blind sister to live with him in the Finnish wilderness. While the man is away on business, his sister tells his wife of a curse placed on the villagers by a witch. Soon the bride is having visions of the witch, but an even greater threat looms in the real world …

Väinö Kataja, born Väinö Mikael Johan Ferdinand Kataja in 1867, was a prolific writer and photographer. His love of nature stemmed from his life as a farmer; this background informed much of his writing and photography. His popularity does not seem to have extended beyond his native Finland, and only a tiny selection of his works have been adapted for the cinema.

Koskenlaskijan morsian, a straightforward drama published in 1914, was the first of his books to be brought to the screen in 1923, and it would also prove to be the last to date when it was remade in 1937. Between these two adaptations came this version of his foray into the fantastic, which was also based on a book published in 1914. *Noidan Kirot* is of note primarily as the first Finnish horror film. The genre has never really made much of a foothold in the country, truth be told. With the exception of *The Witch* and *The White Reindeer* (both 1952), it wasn't until relatively recently that Finnish filmmakers such as Tero Molin and Tommi Lepola (*The Book of Fate*, 2003; *The Skeleton Crew*, 2009) entered the horror market.

Teuvo Puro was born in Helsinki in 1884 and began working in films in the early 1900s. In addition to writing and directing, he also acted on occasion. He seems to have worked primarily in the silent era, though he racked up a few credits in the sound era as well. He died in 1956. *Noidan Kirot* was his only foray into the horror genre, and it remains a fairly tentative one at that. If anything, it's more of a domestic melodrama than a horror film proper, but its exploration of the powerful hold superstition exerts over the farming communities of Finland results in some appropriately macabre moments. TH

Odoru reikon
Makino; b/w; 60 min; Japan
D/S: Soromon Shiba *C:* Juzo Tanaka
Cast: Emiko Suda, Seiichi Arao, Reizaburo Nyaguzuma

Released in Japan on July 29, 1927, *Odoru reikon* had something to do with a dancing ghost. Whether it was humorous, horrific or both is anyone's guess, though it is frequently included in filmographies of Japanese horror films.

While modern filmographies are almost certainly incomplete, it would seem that director Soromon Shiba wrote and/or directed only a few films during his lifetime. CW

Prelude
Knight; 7 min; b/w; Great Britain
D/S/P: Castleton Knight
Cast: Castleton Knight

As he listens to Rachmoninoff's "Prelude in C Sharp Minor," a man (Knight) dreams that he is being buried alive.

Nominally based on Poe's "The Premature Burial," *Prelude* belongs to the avante-garde school of filmmaking so prevalent in the late silent era. As such, the basic story is a springboard for a series of visions that are alternately funny, disturbing and frightening. Other horror films of the era belonging to the school include *The Tell-Tale Heart* and *The Fall of the House of Usher* (both 1928).

Prelude was written, produced and directed by Castleton Knight (1894-1970). While he occasionally dipped his toe into fictional films, most of his career was spent producing documentaries; he had cut his teeth on newsreel shorts for British Gaumont. Though his career began in the silent era, it lasted through the mid-1950s. CW

Queen of Spades
aka **Pique Dame**
Phoebus; b/w; length unknown; Germany
D/Co-S: Aleksandr Razunmnyi *Co-S:* Arthur Bárdos, Charlie Roellinghoff *C:* Carl Drews, Erich Nitzschmann *M:* Willy Schmidt-Gentner
Cast: Jenny Jugo, Rudolf Forster, Alexandra Schmidt, Henry (Henri) de Vries, Walter Janssen, Alexander Murski

At a card party, army soldier Tomski (Forster) tells the group that his grandmother, the Countess Tomski (Schmidt), once learned a supernatural secret to winning at cards from an old sorcerer. Though he dismisses the veracity of the tale, his friend Hermann (Janssen) does not. Hermann plans a seduction of the Countess' ward, Lisa (Jugo), as a means to get into the Countess' orbit, but he changes his mind and instead heatedly confronts the Countess, who dies of fright. Her ghost later visits Hermann, and betrayal and madness ensue.

Queen of Spades is based on Alexander Pushkin's oft-filmed 1833 short story *Pikovaya Dama*, and it follows the yarn fairly closely. This particular film adaptation is indicative of early German cinema's obsession with horror and perversity, which had begun over a decade earlier with various adaptations of Sir Arthur Conan Doyle's classic novel *The Hound of the Baskervilles* (1901-02). After the release and subsequent international success of Robert Weine's *The Cabinet of Dr. Caligari* in 1919, the horror genre exploded, and silent German Expressionism became a major influence on filmmakers around the globe. CW

El señor Don Juan Tenorio
b/w; length unknown; Spain
D: Juan Andreu *S:* Juan Pérez del Muro *C:* Tomás Duch
Cast: José Benitez, Carmen Navarro

This was apparently a parody of José Zorillo's classic 1844 play *Don Juan Tenorio*, which is reenacted every year on November 1, the Day of the Dead—which corresponds to All Saints Day in Catholic tradition—in Mexico and Spain. The play concerns two men, Don Juan and Don Luis, who make a bet about which of them can outdo the other at seducing women and killing men. But when the father of Juan's one true love overhears their conversation, he vows never to allow the rake to marry his daughter. The result is a murderous rampage that leaves everyone but Juan dead. Years later, as he visits the graves of those he lost, he is visited by their spirits before being killed himself, with his own spirit rescued from Hell by that of his ghostly lover.

It can be assumed that José Benitez starred as Don Juan and Carmen Navarro played the part of his lover, Inés. How much true parody might have been squeezed out of the play's brutal premise is anyone's guess. CW

The Show
MGM; b/w; 65 min; U.S.
D/P: Tod Browning *S:* Waldemar Young *C:* John Arnold
Cast: John Gilbert, Renee Adoree, Lionel Barrymore, Edward Connelly, Gertrude Short, Andy MacLennan, Agostino Borgato, Betty Boyd, Edna Tichenor, Jules Cowles

"Cock" Robin (Gilbert) is a vain, egotistical performer in a traveling circus. While in Hungary, he attempts to seduce a young girl. Former conquest and current co-performer Salome (Adoree) prevents him from doing so, but when the girl's father turns up dead, Robin is immediately suspected. It turns out that the murder was actually committed by The Greek (Barrymore), another member of the troupe who is in love with Salome and looking to get Robin out of the picture by framing him. Salome hides Robin, but the Greek has further plans for all concerned.

Based on *The Day of Souls*, a 1910 novel by C.T. Jackson, *The Show* evidences Tod Browning's fascination with morbid and perverse scenarios set against a carnival backdrop. The film stars John Gilbert, then known as "The Great Lover," whose star at the time was in decline. Rumor has it that when Greta Garbo stood the actor up at the altar, producer Louis B. Mayer made a snide comment about the incident. This prompted Gilbert to attack him, and a furious Mayer retaliated by thereafter denying Gilbert the best scripts and forcing the actor into pictures he considered beneath him.

There can be little doubt that *The Show* helps make a case for the apocryphal story of Mayer's vengeance. While not a bargain basement production, any movie casting Gilbert as a proto-pedophile philanderer could hardly have been calculated to endear "The Great Lover" to audiences. Still, Gilbert dominates the film with his swaggering portrayal. He's well paired with the beautiful Renee Adoree as the woman who, though betrayed, still loves him, and Lionel Barrymore is appropriately sleazy and sinister as The Greek, a petty hoodlum who inspires loyalty through coercion.

The film enables Browning to stage one of his twisted love triangles, which would reach their pinnacle in that same year's *The Unknown*, undeniably one of the strangest and kinkiest of silent films. His direction here is efficient and breezy; the pace is snappy, and the shocks are presented with glee.

The film also manages a number of kinky visual and verbal double entendres, from the attempt to decapitate (and in so doing castrate) "Cock" Robin, to the remark a patron makes about the beautiful mermaid on display in the carnival. ("Now I know why divers go down!") It all makes for a surprisingly frank and lurid slice of melodrama, precisely the kind of material with which Browning was most at home. TH

Spooks
Bray; b/w; 20 min; U.S.
D: Robert B. Wilcox *P:* John Randolph Bray
Cast: The McDougall Kids, Bobby Newman, Hannah Washington

The McDougall Kids (also known as the McDougall Alley Kids) were John Randolph Bray's answer to Hal Roach's *Our Gang*. The McDougalls starred in more than 20 silent-era shorts, none of which are much remembered today.

Michigan-born Bray (1879-1978) was a prolific producer, making over 800 films between 1913 and 1943. *Spooks* represents the midway point in the McDougall Kids series, the last of which was produced in 1928. The film put the youngsters in a supposedly haunted house, an apparent knock-off of the previous year's successful *Our Gang* comedy *Shivering Spooks*.

Little is known about the film's players, apart from young African American actress Hannah Washington; she played "Oatmeal, a black child" (the name Buckwheat being taken) in a number of McDougal Kids movies. She is alleged to have later

Joan Crawford and Lon Chaney in *The Unknown*

had an un-credited bit part as a native child in the classic *King Kong* (1933). CW

Svengali

Terra; b/w; length unknown; Germany
D: Gennaro Righelli *S/P:* Max Glass *C:* Arpad Viragh *M:* Walter Ulfig
Cast: Paul Wegener, Anita Dorris, Andre Mattoni, Teddy Bill, Alexander Granach, Irma Green

Adaptations of George Du Maurier's three-part Gothic horror novel *Trilby* (1894) were a mainstay of silent cinema; thus it seems fitting that the final version before the advent of sound should be this Expressionist entry starring Paul Wegener, Germany's answer to Lon Chaney. Naturally, Wegener has the lead role of the sinister Svengali, a Jewish hypnotist so obsessed with the sweet but humble Trilby that he uses his supernatural powers to subjugate her. While unable to make her fall in love with him, he does hone her voice and turn her into a singing sensation. Unfortunately, doing so completely destroys her spirit, and when Svengali dies suddenly, Trilby follows shortly thereafter.

German-born Anita Doris was cast in the role of Trilby O'Farrell. Doris starred in only a handful of films between 1926 and 1931, none of which are remembered today. Italian director Gennaro Righelli made numerous films during his career, though he never achieved the sort of fame his grandson, Sergio Martino, found outside of Italy. (Martino was a mainstay writer/director of Italian horror and science fiction cinema in the 1970s and '80s.)

It's not surprising that the film should shift the focus of the story away from Trilby to the evil Jew, given that anti-Semitism was on the rise in Germany, culminating in Hitler's rise to power in the early 1930s. Shortly after taking office, Hitler began a systematic usurpation of power that led to increasingly restrictive policies aimed at individuals of Jewish decent. They were declared unclean; non-Jews kissing Jews was made illegal; Jews were forced to live in special housing units and eventually they were placed in forced labor camps, where many were gassed or burned to death.

The next version of *Trilby* was Warner's *Svengali* (1931), starring John Barrymore in the title role, which stands today as the definitive adaptation of Du Maurier's story. CW

Tokaido Yotsuya kaidan

Nippon; b/w; length unknown; Japan
D: Shiro Nakagawa
Cast: Yonosuke Toba

While all of the silent film adaptations of Tsuruya Nanboku IV's Kabuki play *Yotsuya kaidan* can justly be considered obscure (none appear to have survived), this one is less known than most, with contemporary references to it slim indeed. It appears to have been a typical rendering of the tale about a samurai who orchestrates the disfigurement and death of his impoverished wife to make room in the sack for his higher-class mistress.

Tokaido is a reference to the dirt road along which the *Ghost Story of Yotsuya* occurs. Yotsuya itself is today a district of Tokyo. CW

The Unknown

MGM; b/w; 61 min; U.S.
D: Tod Browning *S:* Waldemar Young *P:* Irving G. Thalberg *C:* Merritt Gerstad
Cast: Lon Chaney, Joan Crawford, Norman Kerry, Nick De Ruiz, John George, Frank Lanning

Alonzo (Chaney) is a fugitive masquerading as an armless knife-thrower in a traveling circus. He has trained himself to use his feet in place of his hands, in part to hide a bizarre anomaly—a double thumb on his left hand. He falls in love with a fellow performer, Nanon (Crawford), but her pathological fear of being touched makes her unattainable. A strongman, Malabar (Kerry), successfully woos Nanon, which prompts Alonzo to hatch a bizarre scheme of revenge.

Tod Browning made several strange films with Lon Chaney, but none were stranger than *The Unknown*. The director, a former carnival barker and circus performer, had an affinity for the big-top setting, and he conceived the concept for this macabre melodrama before turning script duties over to his favorite screenwriting collaborator, Waldemar Young.

The story is bizarre to the point of dark humor—a man pretending to be armless mutilates himself to win the heart of the woman he loves, only to find that she has overcome her fear of being touched and been won over by another. It's wonderfully absurd, over-baked stuff, and Browning handles it with style.

Dr. Coriolos (Gustav Von Seyfertitz) and his killer ape (George Kotsonaros) from *The Wizard*

his final role with Chaney—Norman Kerry, marginally more convincing (despite being the most unimposing circus strongman imaginable) than he was as the wooden romantic lead of both *The Hunchback of Notre Dame* (1923) and *The Phantom of the Opera* (1925). *The Unknown* climaxes with a remarkable set piece in which a vengeful Chaney attempts to rig a performance so that strongman Malobar will lose his arms. The intensity of Chaney's performance borders on camp, but somehow he keeps it believable. As with so many of his characterizations, Alonzo isn't so much a villain as a deeply flawed human being. It's hard to not feel some level of pity for him.

The Unknown is one of Browning's most compelling and original films. Its overripe scenario is handled convincingly, and Chaney impresses with yet another richly shaded characterization. Surviving prints, struck from a French source in the 1970s, are missing some material, but with such a delirious scenario, it's difficult to criticize the film for being almost incomprehensible. TH

The Wizard
Fox; b/w; 60 min; U.S.
D: Richard Rosson S: Andrew Bennison, Malcom Stuart Boylan, Harry O. Hoyt P: William Fox C: Frank Good
Cast: Edmund Lowe, Leila Hyams, Gustav Von Seyffertitz, E.H. Calvert, Barry Norton, Oscar Smith, George Kotsonaros

Viewers familiar only with the director's stagy treatment of *Dracula* (1931) really should dig deeper into his oeuvre, as much of his lesser-known work is striking in its kinky originality. It's difficult to believe that the scenario presented in *The Unknown* got the green light in 1927—and by MGM, no less, that glossiest and most high profile of studios! Clearly the Browning/Chaney team had a clout that pays off even today for fans of the macabre.

Browning's direction is assured. The pacing is steady, the camera angles are sometimes ingenious in their subterfuge and the various twists and turns artfully handled. In terms of makeup, Chaney doesn't have much room to wow the viewer the way he has elsewhere, but his almost masochistic dedication to the craft is evident in the way he tortured his physique to create the impression of a man without arms.

A long-running Hollywood legend maintains that Chaney taught himself to do various tasks (smoking cigarettes, opening doors, throwing knives) with his feet, but biographer Michael F. Blake has debunked this theory. In reality, Paul Desmuke (who *really* didn't have arms) stood in for Chaney during these shots, with Browning providing some clever sleight of hand to create the impression Chaney was doing the hard work during closer shots.

The supporting cast includes a young Joan Crawford, impressive as the neurotic apple of Chaney's eye, as well as—in

This is the second adaptation of Gaston Leroux's 1911 romantic adventure novel *Balaoo* (after 1913's *Balaoo*), though this time out the romance is downplayed in favor of comedy and the odd attempt at a shiver. It tosses out most of Leroux's original story in favor of old dark house thrills, including the usual bumbling reporters and detectives. The humanoid baboon of the novel is a very un-humanlike ape here, without the intelligence or tenderness of either his published or filmed predecessor. Dr. Coriolis has become Dr. Coriolos, and his personality has been blurred with that of Hubert the poacher, the villain of the novel. The novel's heroine Madeleine, niece of Dr. Coriolis, is named Anne here and is the daughter of a judge. (Another addition typical of films of this period is its in-your-face anti-death-penalty message.)

Dr. Coriolos' (Von Seyffertitz) son is executed for a murder he may not have committed. When an ape (Kotsonaros) comes into the doctor's possession, he trains it to kill and sends it after the men he blames for his son's death, including the prosecutor (Calvert) and judge (Trevor) in the case. When the beast threatens the judge's daughter (Hyams), the reporter hero (Lowe) comes to the rescue.

Fox granted *The Wizard* a scant release amid generally bad reviews. It bore a striking resemblance to another old dark house

thriller from the same year, aptly titled *The Gorilla*, which was released first and may have soured audiences to another film of its ilk. The last known print of *The Wizard* was allegedly destroyed in a fire at the Fox Studio vaults in the 1930s. That said, remaining stills are surprisingly tantalizing, and it can only be hoped that a complete print of the picture will one day be found.

The third, best and most well-known film version of Leroux's novel, *Dr. Renault's Secret*, was released in 1942. CW

1928

Alraune
aka **Daughter of Nature**; **Mandrake**; **Unholy Love**
Ama Film; b/w; 108 (97) min; Germany
D/S: Henrik Galeen *P:* Helmut Schreiber *C:* Franz Planer
Cast: Paul Wegener, Brigitte Helm, Ivan Petrovich, Wolfgang Zilzer, Louis Ralph, Hans Trautner

Professor Jakob ten Brinken (Wegener) makes a very comfortable living lecturing to university students on the subject of chemistry. Inspired by an ancient legend, he decides to impregnate a woman with a mandrake root, and to this end instructs his son, Franz (Petrovich), to find a prostitute on whom he can carry out his experiment. Franz, though he finds the idea revolting, agrees. A subject is found, the experiment is a success and the resulting progeny is named Alraune (Helm). As she grows, abnormally rapidly, into adulthood, she becomes sexually promiscuous and difficult to control. Her "father" develops an incestuous attraction to her as she brings him nothing but hardship, heartache and, in the end, financial ruin.

Written and directed by the talented Henrik Galeen (*The Student of Prague*, 1926), this 1928 adaptation of Hanns Heinz Ewers' oft-filmed story remains the definitive version. Whereas adaptations before and after were justly criticized for softening the story, Galeen sticks closer to the source material and in the process delivers a film with some startlingly risqué content.

Brigitte Helm is remarkable as the title character, who was renamed Mandrake for U.S. audiences. Helm is best remembered as the robotic Maria in Fritz Lang's classic *Metropolis* (1927), but her performance here is far more accomplished. Alraune could easily have been portrayed as a wanton shrew, but Helm invests her with moments of genuine humanity, hinting at the kind of creature Alraune may have become had it not been for the perverseness of her adoptive father.

Paul Wegener is also quite impressive as Professor ten Brinken. Wegener was a major star of silent German cinema, though he isn't remembered today to the extent of such contemporaries as Conrad Veidt (*The Cabinet of Dr. Caligari*, 1919) or Emil Jennings (*Faust*, 1927). Part of the reason, no doubt, is that Wegener remained in Germany during the Nazi regime, though he was a confirmed Pacifist. So while many of his countrymen fled to the United States and Great Britain and found cinematic success, Wegener's career slid into obscurity. He's best remembered for his several forays—as both actor and director—into the Golem legend, most notably *The Golem: How He Came Into the World* (1920). Though his Golem portrayal gave audiences little more than a hulking presence, his performance here shows him to be an actor of considerable nuance and ability. The sequence in which Alraune toys with Brinken's emotions, stringing him along with promises of sex, is highly charged and beautifully realized by both performers.

The kinky sexuality of Helm's performance makes the film one of the most genuinely erotic of its time, and Galeen is to be admired for approaching the material in such an adult and sophisticated manner. He would direct only a few more films, none of them horror-related, before retiring from the industry in the early 1930s; he then relocated to the United States, where he died in 1949. *Alraune* is, after *The Student of Prague*, easily his most impressive feature as director. If its pacing lags somewhat during its middle section, that can be easily forgiven.

With its silky black and white cinematography courtesy of Franz Planer—who would in time move to the U.S., anglicize his first name to Frank and shoot such prestigious films as *The Caine Mutiny* (1954) and *King of Kings* (1961)—*Alraune* is worthy of inclusion in the pantheon of standout German horrors of its period.

The next version of *Alraune* came in 1930, directed by Richard Oswald and also starring Brigitte Helm. TH

Gladys Walton, star of *The Ape*, in a studio publicity shot

The Ape
Collwyn; b/w; 55 min; U.S.
D: Beverly C. Rule
Cast: Gladys Walton, Ruth Stonehouse, Basil Wilson, Bradley Barker

A supposedly tame ape gets loose and runs amok.

The Ape's creators—for what it's worth—maintained that the film was "based on an actual police record." Whatever the case, reviews of the time reveal that this long-lost curio didn't go over very well. One of the more blistering critiques came courtesy of *Variety*'s May 2, 1928, write-up:

> Shot in the old Triangle Arts studio in Riverdale, *The Ape* is a little inferior in technique … The story, a jumbled mess of cart before the horse detail, is brought to the screen with a schoolboy's appreciation for the technicalities. Messed up with this is a cartload of the most explanatory titles. These take up half of the footage. All kinds of hands that are played upon by a baby spot and figures that shadow themselves on windowsills attempt to provide the mystery. The action confines itself to four sets with a fleeting shot of the Hudson … the thing is blah all the way.

The film marked the end of Beverly C. Rule's brief directorial career (which included the film at hand and a handful of titles from 1921) and a look at its forgotten roster of players reveals that most of them didn't work much afterward either.

The Boris Karloff B-programmer *The Ape* (1940) has no connection to this film. TH

Banchō sarayashika
aka **Banshu sarayashika**
Kako; b/w; 8 min; Japan
D: Juzo Tanaka
Cast: Sosuke Matsui, Rinosuke Shimizu, Kozaburo Kataoka, Kazuko Tsukushi, Shishou Ichikawa

This short silent film, for decades thought lost, was recently discovered in the vaults of a private collector, Abe Yoshishinge, making it something of a rarity in Japanese cinema: a silent film that's survived the ravages of time, including World War II and the subsequent occupation of Japan by the United States.

The film deals with the murder of a servant girl, Okiku, who refuses the sexual advances of her master. It was based on a famous Japanese folktale that's provided fodder for a number of filmmakers and, before that, playwrights and *ukiyo-e* block print artists. CW

The Black Pearl
Trem Carr; b/w; 58 min; U.S.
D: Scott Pembroke *S:* Arthur Hoerl *P:* Trem Carr *C:* Hap Depew
Cast: Lila Lee, Ray Hallor, Carlton Stockdale, Howard Lorenz, Thomas Curran, Sybil Grove

A priceless gem stolen from the eye of an Indian idol brings death and disaster after it falls into the hands of Silas Lathrop (Curran), who simultaneously gathers together his family for the reading of a will. The result is a series of murders in an old dark house, but in the end a detective (Stockdale) clears all this up.

Nominally based on a novel by Mrs. Wilson Woodrow, the film seems to have derived its true (though un-credited) inspiration from the Wilkie Collins novel *The Moonstone* (1868); in both the film and in Collins' book, a jewel stolen from an idol in India carries a devastating curse. Reviews from the time suggest that *The Black Pearl* was notable chiefly for offering a more straight face than usual take on the old dark house routine.

The cast included Lila Lee, a familiar presence in the genre thanks to her appearances in everything from *The Ghost Breaker* (1922) to *The Unholy Three* (1930). Director Scott Pembroke was prolific between 1920 and 1937, though he never scored a major critical or artistic success. TH

The Fall of the House of Usher
aka **La chute de la maison Usher**
Epstein; b/w; 65 min; France
D/Co-S/P: Jean Epstein *Co-S:* Luis Buñuel *C:* Georges Lucas, Jean Lucas
Cast: Jean Debucourt, Marguerite Gance, Charles Lamy, Fournez-Goffard, Luc Dartagnan, Abel Gance

Neurotic Roderick Usher (Debucourt) summons a friend (Lamy) to his crumbling mansion. Roderick is obsessed with painting a portrait of his ailing wife, Madeline (Gance). When she dies, she is buried in the family's ancestral tomb. It turns out, however, that Madeline is really only in a state of cataleptic shock, and she returns from the grave to be reunited with her husband.

This Expressionist interpretation of Edgar Allan Poe's famous short story remains one of the most renowned of experimental silent films. Interestingly, its conception and production led to a falling out between director Jean Epstein and a young Luis Buñuel. Buñuel—who directed the even more influential *Un Chien Andalou* the following year—adapted Poe's story for Epstein and was to serve as his assistant, a function he had previously performed on the director's *Mauprat* (1926). But he objected to Epstein's interpretation of the material and left the film. It's unclear how much, if any, of Buñuel's original treatment made it into the finished product, though the dreamlike tone of the picture anticipates some of his later works, including *The Exterminating Angel* (1962) and *The Discreet Charm of the Bourgeoisie* (1972).

The Polish-born Epstein (1897-1953) peaked early on; after the advent of sound, he focused primarily on short subjects and documentaries. *The Fall of the House of Usher* is his most enduring contribution to cinema, though it is for many a problematic interpretation of Poe's original text, the main bone of contention being the obliteration of the incestuous subtext in Poe's original story. Altering the relationship between Roderick and Madeline from that of brother and sister to that of husband and wife dilutes the psychological horrors with which Poe dealt.

The film's overtly experimental tone also prevents it from functioning as either a suspense film or a drama. The characters remain detached, and it's difficult to become emotionally invested in them. That said, Epstein creates a number of wonderful images. The rapid cutting, fetishistic close-ups and generally dreamy ambience bring the movie closer to the realm of filmic poetry than anything else.

James Sibley Watson and Melville Webber filmed Poe's story in the United States in 1928 as *The Fall of the House of Usher*. And though there was a British adaptation in 1948, it would take another 30 years for it to be properly realized on screen. Roger Corman's stylish *House of Usher* (1960), starring Vincent Price, remains the touchstone for both its fidelity to the source and its accomplished air of Gothic doom and gloom. TH

The experimental tone of Jean Epstein's *The Fall of the House of Usher* can be seen in this sequence with Madeline Usher (Marguerite Gance).

The Fall of the House of Usher
Film Guild; b/w; 13 min; U.S.
D/C: James Sibley Watson, Melville Webber *S:* Melville Webber *C:* Louis Siegel *FX:* Carl Gregory
Cast: Herbert Stern, Hildegarde Watson, Melville Webber, Friedrich Haak, Dorthea House

Roderick Usher (Stern) and his sister Madeline (Watson) share a gloomy existence in their crumbling country mansion. When Madeline apparently dies, a grief-stricken Roderick has her interred in the family vault, not realizing that she is actually suffering from a fit of catalepsy.

Since its first publication in 1839, *The Fall of the House of Usher* has remained one of the most popular stories ever written by Edgar Allan Poe. The tale provides a psychologically resonant portrait of an implicitly incestuous relationship, with the house's final collapse a metaphor for the siblings' final descent into madness.

1928 saw the release of two very different adaptations of Poe's tale, neither of which was faithful to its source material. This version—directed, photographed and designed by James Sibley Watson and Melville Webber—jettisons any pretense of plot and character and focuses instead on the presentation of Expressionistic visual effects. As a result, the gloomy ambience of the House of Usher is neatly established from the opening shot even as the film fails to mine the emotional resonance of the material. Still, on a purely technical level, it has its moments. The use of superimpositions, canted angles and tracking shots combine to create a sense of delirium, and the finale in which Madeline awakens in her tomb and escapes to seek vengeance is strikingly realized.

The actors have little opportunity to make much of an impression, and ultimately the film is a minor footnote in the canon of Edgar Allan Poe adaptations. TH

Thelma Todd is terrorized in this lobby card for *The Haunted House*.

Habeas Corpus
MGM/Roach; b/w; 20 min; U.S.
D/Co-S: Leo McCarey, James Parrott *Co-S:* H.M. Walker *P:* Hal Roach *C:* Len Powers
Cast: Stan Laurel, Oliver Hardy, Richard Carle, Charles A. Bachman, Charley Rogers

Technically Laurel and Hardy's first sound film, *Habeas Corpus* was shot as a silent, with sound effects and music added afterwards. But don't be fooled by that description; the film retains its intertitles and lack of spoken dialogue. The film's sound discs were thought lost for decades until they resurfaced in the 1990s, after which the film was released for home viewing. Today, it can easily be found on the Internet for free viewing.

Here we find the popular comedy duo in the employ of a mad scientist (Carle), disinterring corpses from a nearby graveyard for their boss' dubious experiments. Unknown to all, the butler (Rogers) is an undercover detective investigating the scientist's mad schemes. Once the scientist is hauled off to the loony bin, the detective follows the would-be resurrectionists to the graveyard and there, dressed in a white sheet, pretends to be a ghost in an effort to scare them off. (One sequence involving the comedy team's attempts to get over the graveyard wall takes up entirely too much running time and mires the proceedings in excessive tedium.) Comedic incidents accumulate until the film has reached the requisite running time. CW

The Haunted House
First National; b/w; 70 min; U.S.
D: Benjamin Christensen *S:* Richard Bee, Lajos Biro, William Irish *P:* Wid Gunning *C:* Sol Polito
Cast: Larry Kent, Thelma Todd, Edmund Breese, Sidney Bracy, Barbara Bedford, Flora Finch, Montagu Love

Prospective heirs to a family fortune are summoned to a sinister estate for the reading of a will. There they meet up with the inevitable mad doctor and a suspicious handyman. Sliding panels and secret rooms aside, what they initially believe to be a haunting is revealed to be nothing more than a hoax to scare them off.

With the success of *Häxan* (1922), writer/director Benjamin Christensen became established as a major talent on the European film scene. It didn't take long for Hollywood to beckon, and Christensen set up camp there in 1926. His first American film, *The Devil's Circus* (1926), was a dramatic vehicle for a young Norma Shearer, who went on to headline many a MGM tearjerker. He followed up with an atypical Lon Chaney melodrama titled *Mockery* (1927), but his next two U.S. features are considered lost: *The Hawk's Nest* and *The Haunted House* (both 1928).

The screenplay for *The Haunted House* was adapted from a 1926 stage play by Owen Davis. It seems to have been part of the run of horror comedies so popular in the late 1920s. The cast for the film included the tragic Thelma Todd, who later died under mysterious circumstances while involved in a well-publicized affair with married director Roland West (*The Bat*, 1926).

Christensen followed the film with two more comedic haunted house horrors: *Seven Footprints to Satan* (1929) and *The House of Horror* (1929). Of this trilogy of U.S.-made comedy/horror movies, only *Seven Footprints* appears to have survived. TH

The House of Terror
Pizor; b/w; 10 chapters; U.S.
D: Roland D. Reed *P:* William M. Pizor
Cast: Pat O'Brien, Dorothy Tallcot, Jack La Rue, Roy Watson, Gene Burr, Earl Gunn, Valerie Burr

Television producer Roland D. Reed's pre-TV directorial debut is something of an enigma. A lost 10-part serial, not much is known about it other than the chapter titles: *Chapter 1: Missing Men*; *Chapter 2: Tongues of Flame*; *Chapter 3: Swirling Waters*; *Chapter 4: Out of the Night*; *Chapter 5: Perilous Trails*; *Chapter 6: Secret Passage*; *Chapter 7: Division*; *Chapter 8: Revenge*; *Chapter 9: Pawns of Evil* and *Chapter 10: The Hidden Treasure*. In addition, the film was based on an obscure novel (author unknown) titled *The Haunted Hacienda*.

As with most serials of the silent and early talkie eras, *The House of Terror* was predominantly an adventure, though it does appear to have contained enough horror elements to warrant inclusion here. The original U.S. one-sheet poster for Chapter 1 details two men fighting over a woman in a dark, cobwebbed room; Chapter 2's poster shows a gruff man grabbing a startled, presumably frightened, woman's breasts from behind; Chapter 3's poster offers two men on a boat fighting over a woman who is tied up in the background and so on. The posters hint that the film tried to be all things to all people, with a little bit of every genre—from romance to action to Western—thrown in.

A publicity photo of Jacqueline Logan, who starred in *The Leopard Lady*

Reviews at the time indicate that it wasn't really thought to be satisfactory on any level. And as was often the case with movie posters of the period, the art contains a fair degree of sexual innuendo, from bondage and sadism to homoeroticism.

The film did not have anything to do with Edward Woodward's 1930 mystery novel of the same name. Nor should the lead actor, Pat O'Brien, be confused with the later Hollywood star of the same name. CW

Iemon
Bando Tsumasaburo; b/w; length unknown; Japan
D: Norikuni Yasuda *S:* Kiyoo Sasa *C:* Kiyoshi Kataoka
Cast: Reizaburo Umewaka, Mineko Komatsu, Chiyoko Azuma, Keiko Hayabashibara, Toshiko Makita, Masataro Nakamura

This is the least known of the three 1928 versions of the five-act 1825 play *Yotsuya kaidan*, the others being *New Version of the Ghost of Yotsuya* and *Yotsuya kaidan*. It takes a slightly different approach than the other two by making the relationship between the samurai Iemon (Umewaka) and his mistress Oume (Azuma) the centerpiece of the tale. Still, the ghost of his wife, who has been disfigured and driven to her death, provides the film's denouement: the death of Oume at the hands of the crazed Iemon.

The film was released in Japan on July 14, 1928. CW

Kasane-ga-fuchi
Teikine; b/w; length unknown; Japan
D: Shuichi Yamashita
Cast: Tamazo Arashi, Kyoko Chigusa

This is the second adaptation of Sanyutei Encho's classic Japanese horror novel *Shinkei Kasane-ga-fuchi* to be produced by Teikine and the third one overall. Little is known about it, causing some to conclude that it was simply a re-release of the 1924 film. However, a different cast list indicates that it was not only a separate adaptation but also possibly a sequel. The story probably didn't diverge much from that of the novel, in which the daughter of a musician falls for a blind masseur, only to discover that he is having an affair with one of her students. She kills herself, her spirit rises from the grave and the lovers who wronged her are summarily dispatched.

Kyoka Chigusa starred as the tutor-turned-ghost. Chigusa began her working career as a Geisha in the early 1900s and in 1922 became an actress for Nikkatsu. She was popular with audiences and commanded a great deal of career autonomy, moving from studio to studio as she saw fit and appearing in over 100 movies in the course of a single decade. CW

The Leopard Lady
DeMille; b/w; 70 (75) min; U.S.
D: Rupert Julian *S:* Beulah Marie Dix *P:* Bertram Millhauser *C:* John J. Mescall
Cast: Jacqueline Logan, Alan Hale, Robert Armstrong, Hedwiga Reicher, James Bradbury Sr., Charles Gemora

The ads shrieked, "A remarkable screen melodrama packed with thrills and with the most amazing climax ever shown on the screen." Maybe, maybe not—but with pedestrian hack Rupert Julian running things, it pays to remember that advertising ballyhoo is just that: ballyhoo.

The notoriously volatile and preening Julian got his big break with his assignment to direct *Merry-Go-Round* (1923) after Erich Von Stroheim was sacked for going over budget; the newcomer apparently considered himself an *enfant terrible* on par with the great German filmmaker (nor did Julian's resemblance to Kaiser Wilhelm II—which had netted him the lead in 1918's *The Kaiser, The Beast of Berlin*—inspire him to keep his ego in check). Later, as director of *The Phantom of the Opera* (1925), he strove to dominate the production in general and Lon Chaney in particular, the result being a film that fails to accommodate the brilliance of its central performance.

The Leopard Lady was one of its director's final films; he would retire after his also apparently lost *The Cat Creeps* (1930), a talkie remake of *The Cat and the Canary* (1927). Based on a play by Edward Childs Carpenter, its plot involved a series of horrific murders at a circus. An animal trainer named Paula (Logan) goes undercover to identify the murderer and learns that a gorilla (Gemora) has been trained to kill.

The cast includes a few familiar faces. Leading man Alan Hale would go on to appear in several Errol Flynn vehicles and

Conrad Veidt as Gwynplaine covers his face in this Universal lobby card from *The Man Who Laughs*.

is probably best remembered as Little John in Michael Curtiz's classic *The Adventures of Robin Hood* (1938). Robert Armstrong would put *King Kong* on display in New York City in 1933, while a third actor would become weirdly typecast: Charles Gemora played apes in a number of later films, including *Murders in the Rue Morgue* (1932; a film that bears more than a superficial resemblance to *Leopard*) and *Phantom of the Rue Morgue* (1954). TH

The Light on the Wall
Paul/Brooks; b/w; 22; Great Britain
D/Co-P: Fred Paul *S:* Patrick K. Heale *Co-P:* A.M. Brooks
Cast: Harry Agar Lyons, Fred Paul, Evelyn Arden, Wally Patch

This is the third film in the *Dr. Sin Fang Dramas* series, coming between *The Zone of Death* and *The Living Death* (both 1928). Little information about its plot exists, but one can conclude that it featured Lt. John Byrne (Paul) and his lackey Bill Riggers (Patch) in hot pursuit of the diabolical Dr. Sin Fang (Lyons), who wants to take down the British government—and the entire West with it.

Three years after the Sin Fang series, director Paul, writer Heale and actor Lyons reteamed one final time for *In a Lotus Garden* (1931), a 47-minute musical feature. Once again, Lyons was cast in the role of a "Mandarin," though one far less sinister than he was known for playing. CW

The Living Death
Paul/Brooks; b/w; 21 min; Great Britain
D/Co-P: Fred Paul *S:* Patrick K. Heale *Co-P:* A.M. Brooks
Cast: Harry Agar Lyons, Fred Paul, Evelyn Arden, Wally Patch

The Living Death is the fourth of six two-reelers comprising the *Dr. Sin Fang Dramas*, a series revolving around a nefarious British underworld kingpin named Dr. Sin Fang (a poor man's version of Sax Rohmer's extraordinary literary creation Dr. Fu Manchu). The film before this had been *The Light on the Wall* and the next would be *The Torture Cage* (both 1928).

The title evokes the horror-tinged approach that made the best of the Yellow Peril films so popular, notably in the two Fu Manchu series produced by Stoll—*The Mystery of Dr. Fu-Manchu* (15 films released in 1923) and *The Further Mysteries of Dr. Fu Manchu* (eight films released in 1924).

Other than a small role in 1926 for director Frank Borzage and Fox in the U.S.-lensed feature *The Dixie Merchant*, Evelyn Arden appears to have spent her entire career playing foil to Sin Fang and John Byrne. (She is not, by the way, actress Eve Arden, who was born Eunice M. Quedens in 1908—not, as is sometimes claimed, in 1912—and made her first screen appearance one year after this in Columbia's *Song of Love*.) CW

The Man Who Laughs
Universal; b/w; 110 min; U.S.
D: Paul Leni *S:* J. Grubb Alexander, Walter Anthony, Mary McLean, Charles E. Whittaker *P:* Paul Kohner *C:* Gilbert Warrenton
Cast: Conrad Veidt, Mary Philbin, Olga Baklanova, Brandon Hurst, Cesare Gravina, Julius Molnar Jr.

Conrad Veidt as the mutilated Gwynplaine in *The Man Who Laughs*

In 1690 England, a nobleman (Veidt) insults King George II (de Grasse). The petty monarch takes revenge by carving a permanent grin into the face of the nobleman's son Gwynplaine (Molnar), after which the child is left alone while his father is imprisoned in an Iron Maiden. Wandering aimlessly, Gwynplaine comes upon a dead woman clutching a still-breathing infant. The boy rescues the baby girl (whom he names Dea), and the two take refuge in the home of an eccentric writer, Ursus (Gravina). Ursus determines that Dea is blind from exposure and reluctantly agrees to take in the two youngsters. Years pass, and a grown Gwynplaine (Veidt again) and Dea (Philbin) make a living performing in Ursus' traveling theatrical troupe. Gwynplaine, capitalizing on his disfigurement, finds fame as "the Laughing Man." Eventually, it's discovered that he's heir to a massive estate, and his life—and potential happiness with the adoring Dea—is placed in jeopardy.

First published in 1869, Victor Hugo's *L'Homme qui rit* echoes his more famous *Hunchback of Notre Dame* with its tale of a disfigured misfit looking for love amid the splendor of royal intrigue. German-born head of Universal Studios Carl Laemmle bought the rights to the novel as a vehicle for Lon Chaney, but at the time the actor was under contract to Metro Goldwyn Mayer, who was unwilling to loan out one of their biggest box-office draws to a competing studio. Laemmle pursued the project to its eventual completion anyway.

In this, their third genre-oriented "super jewel" (A-budget) production, Universal finally got everything right—the story was intriguing, the production values lavish, the director gifted and the cast excellent. And unlike *The Hunchback of Notre Dame* (1923) and *The Phantom of the Opera* (1925), *The Man Who Laughs* was not compromised by penny-pinching. Laemmle and line producer Paul Kohner (later to supervise the studio's Spanish-language editions of *The Cat and the Canary*, 1930, and *Dracula*, 1931) obtained the services of German Expressionist director Paul Leni. Leni had been lured to the U.S. the year before to work on Universal's old dark house comedy *The Cat and the Canary*, and the film's box-office success and excellent notices convinced Laemmle to make use of him again. Leni displayed a flair for the grotesque equal to that of Tod Browning, as well as a willingness to experiment with bold visuals.

The Man Who Laughs offered Leni his biggest budget to date, and he responded by staging a film of resplendent visual beauty. The sets (by Charles D. Hall, Thomas O'Neil and Joseph Wright) surpass even those found in *Hunchback* and *Phantom*. Though Hall would go on to become one of the key architects of the aesthetic of the Universal horror film, he would never really top the best of the imaginative, opulent designs that were created for this film.

Neither does *The Man Who Laughs* fall prey to the unimaginative direction that plagued *Hunchback* and *Phantom*. Leni cuts loose, making bold use of mobile camerawork. He shoots through keyholes, incorporates rapid-fire dolly shots and even puts the camera inside a Ferris wheel to produce vertigo-inducing effects during one of the carnival sequences. His use of mobile camerawork compares favorably with the more celebrated output of his German contemporaries during this same period (F. W. Murnau's *The Last Laugh*, 1924, for example).

Leni is more than a visual stylist, however. This film, more than any other surviving work in his oeuvre, shows him to be a deeply sensitive storyteller. The tragic tale of Gwynplaine, disfigured as a child and forced as an adult to wear a macabre grin even as his heart is breaking, is firmly rooted in the tradition of melodrama. Indeed, as is the case with *Hunchback*, *The Man Who Laughs* isn't really horror at all. Hugo's story mixes intrigue with betrayal but steers clear of out-and-out shock effects. The fact that the film is considered part of the horror genre is due to the grotesque nature of Gwynplaine's appearance and some of the story's unsavory details. It's basically a variation on "Beauty and the Beast," with Leni's Expressionism nudging the film ever so subtly in the direction of terror.

The cast performs splendidly. Conrad Veidt proves yet again to be one of the most gifted performers of his generation. His portrayal of Gwynplaine is richly shaded—his ability to convey frustration and heartbreak from behind a mask of laughter is nothing short of brilliant. And while it's easy to imagine Lon Chaney, Sr. being at home in the Gwynplaine role, it seems unlikely that he would have surpassed Veidt.

Jack Pierce's make-up for the title character is simple and was an inspiration for Bob Kane's Joker in the *Batman* comic books (replicated to great effect by Heath Ledger in 2008's *The Dark Knight*). Veidt is never imprisoned by his make-up, however; Gwynplaine is recognizably human from beginning to end, and it would take a very cold heart to not be moved by the depth of his pain and torment.

Mary Philbin is top-billed as Dea, though the picture is definitely Veidt's. She performs much more effectively here than she did in *Phantom*, demonstrating the result of the sensitive direction that Leni afforded his actors. She is sweet and naïve but never unbelievably so. Her love for Gwynplaine—untainted by her inability to actually see his disfigured visage—is warmly portrayed, and she manages to hit the right emotional notes without coming across as phony.

Olga Baclanova (later to play a key role in Browning's notorious 1932 *Freaks*) is remarkable as the coquettish Duchess Josiana, who toys with Gynplaine as much out of boredom as morbid curiosity. Baclanova conveys raw sex appeal in her mannerisms, and Leni even works in a surprising (if discreet) nude view of her derriere. The way in which she manipulates Gwynplaine's emotions foreshadows her treatment of the diminutive Hercules in *Freaks*, suggesting that she may have been hired by Browning based on a screening of Leni's film.

The Man Who Laughs moves beautifully from its macabre, fairy tale beginning to its exciting, swashbuckling finale. Unfortunately, Leni would direct only one more film—*The Last Warning* (1929), also made for Universal—before his death from blood poisoning (caused by an infected tooth) on September 2, 1929. Had he lived longer, it seems likely that he would have carved an even greater niche in horror history. Universal would certainly have employed him in their early sound horror films, and there's no reason to believe that he would have shied away from such assignments. TH

Maria Marten
aka The Murder in the Red Barn; Maria Martin, or the Murder in the Red Barn

Q.T.S./Ideal; b/w; 75 min; Great Britain
D: Walter West P: Harry Rowson
Cast: Warwick Ward, Trilby Clark, James Knight, Charles Ashton, Vesta Sylva, Frank Perfitt, Dora Barton

The final silent film version of the gruesome real-life murder that shocked Great Britain in 1827, *Maria Marten* was made by the same people behind *Sweeney Todd* (also 1928). The film portrays pregnant Maria (Trilby Clark) as an angelic presence invited to the red barn by evil squire/unwilling father William Corder (Warwick Ward), who murders her in order to pursue marriage to a wealthy heiress. He buries Maria and their unborn child in the red barn but is given away when her ghost visits his victim's mother in a dream.

Of all the film versions, this one seems the least factual, though its moderate success paved the way for *Maria Marten, or The Murder in the Red Barn*, the 1935 adaptation that would make a household name of 49-year-old Tod Slaughter, British cinema's answer to Hollywood's transplanted Briton, Boris Karloff.

Director West had a fairly unremarkable career in silent cinema and retired a few years after the introduction of sound, to which he was never able to fully adapt. Leading man Ward gives the film's best performance as the murderer. Though he was English, much of his career was spent acting in films made in other European countries, until Germany's invasion and take-over turned much of the continent's film industry into a propaganda machine. Ward's most famous film may be Curt Siodmak's science fiction classic *F.P.1* (1933), which also starred Conrad Veidt.

A 35mm print of *Maria Marten* is housed in the British Film Institute's archives. CW

The Mystic Mirror
aka Der Geheimnisvolle Spiegel

UFA; b/w; 67 minutes; Germany
D/C: Carl Hoffmann, Richard Teschner S: Robert Reinert
Cast: Fritz Rasp, Felicitas Malten, Rina de Kigoure

An old castle in Bavaria houses a magical mirror, reputed to have the ability, on nights when the full moon shines brightly, to reveal the future. Various visitors to the creepy place take a look at what the future has in store for them—and no one is particularly happy with what he or she sees.

This supernatural melodrama was co-directed by distinguished cinematographer Carl Hoffmann. Hoffmann's long and varied career included collaborations with some of the leading lights of the German film industry, including Fritz Lang (for whom he shot *Dr. Mabuse, The Gambler*, 1922) and F.W. Murnau (for whom he worked on *Der Januskopf*, 1920). His work as a director was less noteworthy, commencing with *Fiesko* (1913) and ending with *Ab Mitternacht* (1938). He helmed only eight features, with several—including *The Mystic Mirror*—involving a co-director, suggesting that Hoffman was more comfortable with the technical end and preferred having others deal with the actors.

The cast of *Mystic Mirror* includes Fritz Rasp, who specialized in villainous roles on the big screen, most notably in Lang's *Metropolis* (1927). He continued to essay unsavory types well into the 1960s, including performances in such Edgar Wallace *krimis* as *The Terrible People* (1960) and *The Puzzle of the Red Orchid* (1962); he remained active in films until 1976, the year of his death.

The notion of a mirror enabling unsuspecting victims to see into the past or future later popped up in the famous Ealing Studios omnibus *Dead of Night* (1945), and a lighter take on the theme echoes throughout the Harry Potter novels and film adaptations, where a magic mirror allows one to see his or her fondest wish.

The Mystic Mirror reportedly had a "sting in the tail" ending in which the hapless hero smashes the mirror, then commits suicide—whereupon the mirror magically reassembles as if nothing has happened. TH

New Version of the Ghost of Yotsuya
aka Yotsuya Ghost story New Edition; Shinpan Yotsuya kaidan

Nikkatsu Dai-Shogun; b/w; length unknown; Japan
D: Daisuke Ito C: Hiromitsu Karasawa
Cast: Taisuke Matsumoto, Koichi Katsuragi, Naoe Fushimi, Haruko Sawamura, Midori Komatsu, Kakumatsuro Arashi

This is undoubtedly the most famous version of Tsuruya Nanboku IV's infamous ghost story/Kabuki play to be filmed during the silent era. It concerns the ghost of a spurned wife, Oiwa (Fushimi), who returns from the grave to terrorize her samurai husband Iemon (Matsumoto) and his mistress Oume (Sawamura).

Director Daisuke Ito had a long and varied career that began in the silent era and ran until the early 1970s. He was an even more prolific writer than he was a director, and it's likely that he had a hand in the script for this particular version of Nanboku's play. Cast in the lead role of Iemon was Taisuke Matsumoto, who was one of Japan's leading actors during the latter years of the silent era. He transitioned successfully from silent films to talkies and branched out into writing and directing. One of the last films on which he worked was the 1938 horror outing *Ghost Cat's Mysterious Shamisen*, directed by Kiyohiko Ushihara. (For the record, a shamisen is a long, stringed instrument.) CW

The Phantom City
aka **Phantom City**
Rogers/First National; b/w; 65 min; U.S.
D: Albert Rogell S: Adele Buffington, Fred Allen P: Harry Joe Brown C: Ted D. McCord
Cast: Ken Maynard, James Mason, Eugenia Gilbert, Jack McDonald, Blue Washington, Charles Hill Mailes

Two years after his horror/Western hybrid *The Haunted Ranch* (1926), actor Ken Maynard again mixed the two genres with *The Phantom City*. The plot concerns a killer's attempt to steal a mine from its rightful owner. Tim Kelly (Maynard), Joe Bridges (Mason) and Sally Ann (Gilbert) are summoned to Gold City, a long-deserted mining town, by a mysterious figure who knows that said mine still contains gold. A black-clad phantom warns Tim to stay away, but he ignores the warning and soon learns that he is the heir to the mine. The killer, it turns out, is Bridges, with the mysterious phantom being Tim's father. Bridges escapes with the gold but is killed when he accidentally rides over a cliff.

The Phantom City is regarded as one of Maynard's finest silent Westerns, but it dropped from circulation around the time Warner Bros. remade it as *Haunted Gold* (1932). That film starred John Wayne in the Maynard role and used a great deal of stock footage from the previous film. Both films featured African American actor Blue Washington doing the offensive "I's a-scared of ghosts" shtick foisted on him and fellow black performers by Hollywood producers and screenwriters.

Oklahoma-born Albert S. Rogell got his first taste of cinema working for the Washington Motion Picture Company in Spokane, Washington. When that company closed, he headed directly to Los Angeles to continue his career. He worked his way up the Hollywood ladder, hooking up with Sol Lesser to shoot low-budget shorts and thereafter becoming a director of feature-length (though still low-budget) programmers. In the 1950s he moved from movies into television, directing episodes of *The 20th Century Fox Hour* and *Broken Arrow*. He died of cancer on April 7, 1988 at the age of 86. CW

Ransom
aka **San Francisco**
Columbia; b/w; 58 min; U.S.
D/Co-S: George B. Seitz Co-S: Dorothy Howell, Elmer Harris, Mort Blumenstock P: Harry Cohn C: Joseph Walker
Cast: Lois Wilson, Edmund Burns, William V. Mong, Blue Washington, James B. Leong, Jackie Coombs

A government chemist named Burton Meredith (Burns) stumbles upon the formula for a new biological weapon. It isn't long before the evil madman Wu Fang (Mong), a leader in San Francisco's Chinese underground, learns of the poison gas and sets his sights on obtaining the formula by any means necessary. The arch-villain kidnaps Bobby (Coombs), the son of Meredith's fiancée Lois Webster (Wilson), then promises to release the boy in exchange for the formula. Lois pleads with Meredith to turn it over, and when he refuses, she steals a vial of what she believes is the gas and takes it to Fang. The mistake is quickly discovered, however, and Fang prepares to torture Lois. But Meredith discovers the madman's hideout and arrives with the police in time to save his future wife and stepson from harm.

Not surprisingly, the success of Sax Rohmer's Fu Manchu novels resulted in a cluster of cheap literary and cinematic imitations, *Ransom* being one of many. Whether Columbia aped the character because it was cheaper or because the rights to the original were unavailable is difficult to know. Either way, Paramount found greater success the following year with Rowland V. Lee's *The Mysterious Dr. Fu Manchu* (1929), which resulted in two sequels and an appearance by the title character in *Paramount on Parade* (1930).

George B. Seitz (1888-1944) began his Hollywood career as a screenwriter churning out cheap serials before moving on to directing. His other horror credits in either capacity include *The Shielding Shadow* (1917), *The Fatal Ring* (1917), *The Drums of Jeopardy* (1931) and *The Thirteenth Chair* (1937). CW

Rasputin, The Holy Devil
aka **Rasputins Liebesabentuer**; **Rasputin's Amorous Adventures**; **Rasputin: The Holy Sinner**
Berger; b/w; 60 min; Germany
D/P: Martin Berger S: Dosio Koffler C: Laszlo Schaffer
Cast: Nikolai Malikoff, Diana Karenne, Erwin Kalser, Alexander Murski, Nathalie Lissenko, Albert Kergy, Alfred Abel

Grigori Rasputin (Malikoff) rises from simple peasant to spiritual advisor of the Tsar (Kalser) and Tsarina (Karenne) of the Russian royal family. He seems capable of performing miracles, but his methods draw heavy criticism from skeptics. As Rasputin's control over the family and mainly the Tsarina grows, fear spreads that he is acquiring power for his own gain. Finally, Prince Yaupon (Trevor) hatches a plan to assassinate him.

Producer/director Martin Berger made a number of films in Germany during the silent era. The coming of sound derailed his career, like that of so many of his contemporaries. A look at his credits hints that *Rasputin, the Holy Devil* was one of his bigger productions, an assumption further supported by its distinguished cast. Interestingly, it seems that the director's political leanings prompted him to take here a different approach to the oft-filmed subject matter, depicting Rasputin as a man exploited by the boorish and overly pampered bourgeoisie.

Diana (Esther Ralston) is an American adrenaline junkie in *Something Always Happens*.

Russian-born lead Nikolai Malikoff received some glowing notices for his portrayal of Rasputin. Unfortunately, his career was laid low by the arrival of sound. The supporting cast includes such German film luminaries as Alfred Abel (*Dr. Mabuse, The Gambler*, 1922) and Max Schreck (*Nosferatu—A Symphony of Terror*, 1922).

Cinematographer Laszlo Schaffer also assisted Fritz Arno Wagner in lensing *The Haunted Castle* (1921) for F.W. Murnau.

Rasputin, the Holy Devil wasn't released in the United States until January 1929. TH

Rasputin, The Prince of Sinners
aka **Rasputin**; **Rasputin: Schatten der Vergangenheit**; **Rasputin, Dornenweg**; **Dornenweg einer Fürstin**
Memento Film-Fabrik/Vertrieb; b/w; 87 (66) min; Germany/ Russia
Co-D: Nikolai Larin *Co-S:* Boris Nevoli *Co-S:* Nikolai Neboli, Irvin Shapiro *C:* Emil Schünemann
Cast: Gregori Chmara, Hans Albers, Fritz Alberti, Oreste Baldini, Suzanne Delmas, Vladimir Gajdarov, Günther Hadank, Karl Platen, Ernst Rückert, Lidiya Tridenskaya, Hedwig Wangel

This little-seen film is the only known German-Russian co-production on its topic; Russia's involvement allowed much of the film to be shot in and around the historical settings where the incidents portrayed actually took place.

Unlike some early and sympathetic cinematic treatments of Rasputin, *The Prince of Sinners* did not make him out to be a misunderstood and heroic leader of the revolution. This was also no doubt due to Russia's involvement; some of the nation's ruling family (those who had allied themselves with the 1917 Bolshevik Revolution) had a vested interest in portraying Rasputin as the monster he was rather than on the specifics of his assassination at their hands. The result is a film that focuses on the vices of Rasputin's private life: his alcoholism, lack of cleanliness and sexual promiscuity. Its approach foreshadows that of Hammer Film Productions semi-classic film of 1965, *Rasputin—The Mad Monk*, which cast Christopher Lee as the nefarious peasant.

Rasputin, The Prince of Sinners appears to have been the last film directed by Nikolai Larin, a director, actor and writer whose short cinema career had begun in 1913. Conversely, Gregori Chmara, who starred as Rasputin, had a long career, acting in films from 1915 until his death in 1970. His only other horror credit was Paul Wegener's *Living Buddhas* in 1925. His last appearance, in a television adaptation of Dostoyevsky's *Crime and Punishment*, aired posthumously in 1971.

This film is often confused with another 1928 film about the mad monk, *Rasputin, the Holy Devil*. CW

The Scarred Face
Paul/Brooks; b/w; 21 min; Great Britain
D/Co-P: Fred Paul *S:* Patrick K. Heale *Co-P:* A.M. Brooks
Cast: Harry Agar Lyons, Fred Paul, Evelyn Arden, Wally Patch

Four years after Oswald Stoll's Fu Manchu films (*The Mystery of Dr. Fu-Manchu* series in 1923 and *The Further Mysteries of Dr. Fu Manchu* series in 1924), Fred Paul (who'd directed and/or written and/or starred in all 23 of the Stoll productions) joined forces with A.M. Brooks to give the world more of the same. The two were unable to afford the rights to Sax Rohmer's infamous character Fu Manchu, however. So, imitation being the sincerest form of theft, Paul and screenwriter Patrick K. Heale came up with their own nefarious Asian mastermind who was also a "doctor."

Harry Agar Lyons, who had played Fu Manchu in Stoll's two series, was cast as the sinister Dr. Sin Fang, while Paul reprised his earlier role as Nayland Smith under the moniker Lieutenant John Byrne. Evelyn Arden portrayed love interest Betty Harberry, while Wally Patch became Byrne's underling, Bill Riggers.

The Sin Fang films were, by all accounts, made on extremely low budgets, containing none of the rich location shoots found in neither the previous films nor anything approaching the impressive art direction of Walter H. Murton. The six Sin Fang films did, however, play out in two reels each just as the Fu Manchu pictures had.

It seems doubtful that any of the Sin Fang films were very successful; they were seldom reviewed at the time and all but one of them seem (along with their plot synopses) to have disappeared into oblivion. And since, unlike the Fu Manchu films, the Sin Fang movies had no literary origin, it's difficult to discern

Peeping through the window, we see Sweeney Todd (Moore Marriott), center, in front of Mrs. Lovett's meat pie shop, from *Sweeney Todd*.

what the plots might have been, apart from the usual helpings of Oriental chicanery. (If the Yellow Peril films seem xenophobic in retrospect, it's because they were.)

Still, the *Dr. Sin Fang Dramas* (released simultaneously in 1928) do seem to have made something of an impact, at least enough to warrant a decade later two more chances for Lyons to be Asian and to threaten the West: *Dr. Sin Fang* (1937) and *Chinatown Nights* (1938).

The second film in the *Dr. Sin Fang Dramas* is *The Zone of Death* (1928). CW

Shinban: Botan dōrō

b/w; length unknown; Japan
D: Tamizo Ishida
Cast: Emiko Sumiyoshi, Shuko Asama

Though the name of the film's production company is lost to time, some information survives about this obscure adaptation of Sanyutei Encho's 19th century *rakugo* play (a type of presentation in which a seated performer recites a complex narrative), *Botan dōrō*. Tamizo Ishida directed, with Emiko Sumiyoshi as a distraught lover who dies after her samurai boyfriend (Shuko Asama) leaves her, though she returns from the grave in another beautiful form to exact a terrible revenge upon him.

The film's title translates roughly as *New Version of Peony Lantern*. The film's ghost holds a peony-covered lantern while making her secret rendezvous with her doomed lover.

The next adaptation of the tale came in 1929 and was titled *Botan tou no ki*. CW

The Silent House
aka The House of Silence

Nettlefold; b/w; 95 min; Great Britain
D: Walter Forde *S:* H. Fowler Mear *P:* Archibald Nettlefold *C:* Geoffrey Faithful, Randall Terraneau
Cast: Frank Perfitt, Arthur Pusey, Mabel Poulton, Gibb McLaughlin, Arthur Stratton, Gerald Rawlinson

The writer/director team of Nettlefold's comedic *What Next?* (1928) reteamed for this more horrific outing, based on a mystery play by John G. Brandon and George Pickett. *The Silent House* features Gibb McLaughlin as a Fu Manchu-like mandarin named Chang Fu who, in a Svengali-like turn, hypnotizes a young woman into revealing the location of some very valuable bonds. As with most mysteries of the period, an old dark house was in order, as were clutching hands, hidden panels and a body count to die for.

This was director Walter Forde's first horror film. He revisited the genre many times with such films as *The Gaunt Stranger* (1931 and 1938 versions), *The Ghost Train* (1931 and 1941 versions) and *Condemned to Death* (1932). Forde, who was born Thomas Seymour in 1896, is considered an early master of the comedy thriller in his native Great Britain. Though he didn't die until 1984, he shot his last film—Columbia's *Cardboard Cavalier*—in 1949. He was a major influence on writer/director/producer Sydney Gilliat (*The Man Who Changed His Mind*, 1936; *Ask a Policeman*, 1938; *Green for Danger*, 1946), who went on to make a major name in British cinema.

A print of *The Silent House* exists in the National Film Archives in London, England. CW

Something Always Happens

Famous Players-Lasky/Paramount; b/w; 55 min; U.S.
D: Frank Tuttle *S:* Florence Ryerson, Raymond Cannon, Herman J. Mankiewicz, Frank Tuttle *P:* Jesse L. Lasky, Adolph Zukor *C:* J. Roy Hunt
Cast: Esther Ralston, Neil Hamilton, Sojin, Charles Sellon, Roscoe Karns, Lawrence Grant, Mischa Auer, Noble Johnson

Diana (Ralston) is an American adrenaline junkie engaged to quite proper Englishman Roderick (Hamilton). The husband-to-be, dismayed by Diana's thrill seeking, determines to frighten the audacity out of her with an overnighter at a haunted house. It turns out, though, that notorious Chinese criminal Chang-Tzo (Sojin) is using the place as a hideout, and by the time the couple escapes, Diana has had the time of her life.

Something Always Happens is an old dark house entry in the Yellow Peril subgenre epitomized by Sax Rohmer's Fu Manchu tales. The eventful story was penned by director Frank Tuttle, and then developed into a script by Florence Ryerson in collaboration with Raymond Cannon. Of special interest to film buffs, however, is the involvement of Herman J. Mankiewicz, who is credited with supplying the intertitles. Mankiewicz was older brother to writer/director Joseph L. Mankiewicz (*All About Eve*, 1950), but he's best remembered for co-authoring the screenplay to Orson Welles' monumental directorial debut, *Citizen Kane* (1941). *Kane* is often cited as the greatest film ever made, and though it failed to win Best Picture or Director at the Academy Awards, both Mankiewicz and Welles took home statuettes for its screenplay. Mankiewicz's career spanned from 1926 until 1952; he died in 1953.

The cast of *Something* includes a few familiar faces. Japanese character actor Sojin (real name: Mitsugu Mita) played the Chi-

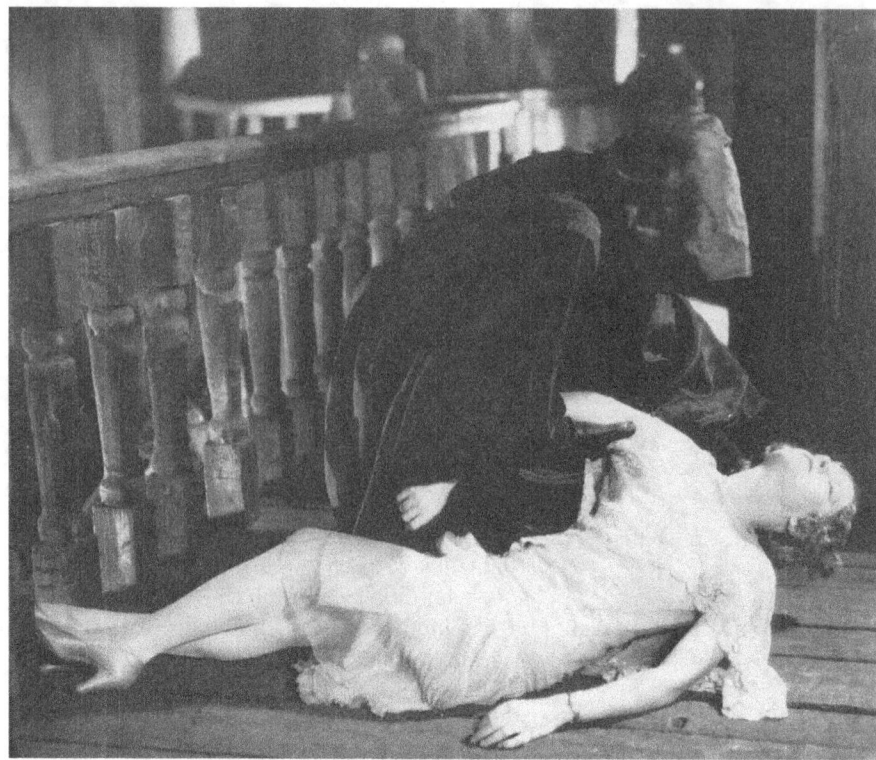

A mysterious killer, known as The Terror, wreaks havoc on the inhabitants of a spooky old house, in *The Terror*.

nese heavy Chang-Tzo, and he essayed similar ethnic types in *The Bat* (1926), *Seven Footprints to Satan* and *The Unholy Night* (both 1929). Character actors Lawrence Grant (*Son of Frankenstein*, 1939) and Mischa Auer (*Condemned to Live*, 1935) went on to appear in numerous horror and fantasy films, while African American producer/actor Noble Johnson later attained cinematic immortality as the native chieftain in *King Kong* (1933).

The film under discussion has no connection to Michael Powell's comedic *Something Always Happens* (1934). TH

Sweeney Todd
QTS/Ideal; b/w; 73 min; Great Britain
D: Walter West *S:* C. Hazelton *P:* Harry Rowson
Cast: Moore Marriott, Iris Darbyshire, Judd Green, Charles Ashton, Zoe Palmer, Philip Hewland

A barber named Sweeney Todd (Marriott) slits his customers' throats and dumps their bodies via a trapdoor into his cellar, where he cuts them up for use in meat pies sold at the shop of Mrs. Lovett (Darbyshire), his partner in crime. But in the end, it all turns out to have been a dream.

The story, based on a stage play titled *The String of Pearls: The Fiend of Fleet Street* by George Dibdin Pitt, based in turn on the anonymous story *The String of Pearls: A Romance*, was first serialized in *The People's Periodical and Family Library* in 1846-1847. Pitt's play was so successful that numerous imitations instantly sprung up, most of them just as instantly forgettable.

Moore Marriott, who plays Sweeney Todd in this version, is best known as Harbottle in Will Hays' *Oh, Mr. Porter!* (1937) and *Ask a Policeman* (1938). His other horror appearances include *The Monkey's Paw* (1923) and *Green for Danger* (1946). Having had his teeth pulled at a relatively young age, he is reputed to have had different sets of false teeth, choosing which to wear based upon the age of the character he was playing at any given time.

Director Walter West also made a film adaptation of *Maria Marten* the same year he made *Sweeney Todd*. CW

The Telltale Heart
aka **The Tell-Tale Heart**
Film Society/International Film Arts Guild; b/w; 20 min; U.S.
Co-D/S: Charles Klein *Co-D/C:* Leon Shamroy
P: Maurice Barber
Cast: Otto Matiesen, William Herford, Hans de Fuerberg, Charles Darvas

Describing itself as "A picturization of Edgar Allan Poe's immortal classic of the same name," *The Telltale Heart* utilizes the literal words of the master to tell its tale of an insane man (Matieson, made up to look like Poe) who is obsessed by his fear of the cloudy eye of the old blind man (Herford) with whom he shares an apartment. He sneaks into his roommate's bedroom at night and strangles the old man, then conceals the body beneath floorboards. When two policemen (de Fuerberg, Darvas) show up to inquire about a shriek heard by the neighbors, the insane man, tormented by the phantom beating of his victim's heart, admits his guilt, reveals the body and collapses.

Written and directed by a German playwright named Charles Klein (who should not be confused with the English playwright of the same name), the film's cinematographer, Leon Shamroy, later claimed that the original effort was so awful he had to reshoot the entire thing in a single day after Klein had departed from the set. Whether that's true or false, the film's obvious Expressionist touches betray Klein's influence. The director worked in Germany at the time Robert Weine's classic *The Cabinet of Dr. Caligari* (1919), an obvious harbinger for this film, was produced. In fact, some of the sets are so similar that one wonders why Decla-Bioscop didn't sue for royalties.

Whatever the case, the film's stilted approach—it seems intent on bringing its literary foundation to life through images of words rather than depictions of deeds—pretty much dooms it from the outset. Not that its *avant-garde* style hurt Shamroy any; the cinematographer's career lasted from 1926 to 1970. (He died in 1974.) Among his many offerings were *The Wayne Murder Case* (1932), *The Adventures of Sherlock Holmes* (1939), *A Tree Grows in Brooklyn* (1945), *Cheaper by the Dozen* (1950), *Cleopatra* (1963) and *Planet of the Apes* (1968), among many, many others. CW

The Terrible People
Pathé; b/w; 10 chapters; U.S.
D: Spencer Gordon Bennet *S:* George Arthur Gray
Cast: Allene Ray, Walter Miller, Wilfred North, Larry Steers, Al Craven, Alyce McCormick

Clay Shelton (Vroom) is condemned and executed for murder, but his ghost returns to strike down the people responsible for his execution.

The Terror
Warner; b/w; 85 min; U.S.
D: Roy Del Ruth *S:* Harvey Gates, Joseph Jackson *C:* Barney McGill *M:* Louis Silvers
Cast: May McAvoy, Louise Fazenda, Edward Everett Horton, Alec B. Francis, Matthew Betz, Holmes Herbert

A mysterious killer, known as The Terror, escapes from an asylum and wreaks havoc on the inhabitants of a spooky old house. Based on a play by Edgar Wallace, *The Terror* is of note as the first talkie horror film—indeed, it follows *The Lights of New York* (1928) as the second all-talking film ever made. (While *The Jazz Singer*, 1927, is often cited as the first talking film, it was a mostly silent picture with only a few sections utilizing sound recording.)

Seen today, most early sound films are unbearably creaky and antiquated; filmmakers and actors had not yet gotten comfortable with the new technology, making the results of their labors generally heavy going. Then-contemporary reviews hint that this was also true of *The Terror*, which is considered lost today (except for its soundtrack, which is preserved in the UCLA film and television archive). Director Roy Del Ruth was a journeyman capable of decent work—one of his last credits was 1959's deliriously goofy *The Alligator People*, featuring Lon Chaney, Jr. But it would seem that he was, at this early point in his 40-or-so-year career, still uncertain of the relationship between sound and moving images.

The cast includes some familiar faces, including popular screen fuddy-duddy Edward Everett Horton (*Arsenic and Old Lace*, 1944) and distinguished character actor Holmes Herbert (*Dr. Jekyll and Mr. Hyde*, 1931). And in a valiant but clumsy attempt to effectively utilize sound, Conrad Nagel (*London After Midnight*, 1927) appears in disguise at the opening to read aloud the titles.

A sequel, *Return of the Terror*, was lensed in 1934, and Wallace's play was later remade in Great Britain as *The Terror* (1938) and in Germany as *The Sinister Monk* (1965). TH

Edgar Wallace wrote *The Terrible People* in 1926 and, like so many of his lurid crime thrillers, it was a big hit with the public. This first cinematic adaptation, surfacing a mere two years afterward, was done in serial form—10 chapters, the first of which was titled *The Penalty*—and is now considered lost.

Director Spencer Gordon Bennet directed the 1925 Wallace serial *The Green Archer* (1925), making him something of an old hand at this kind of melodrama by the time of this production. He spent the better part of his career cranking out even more B-grade serials, including *Atom Man vs. Superman* (1950) and *Mysterious Island* (1951). *Terrible People* leading lady Allene Ray was another alumnus of *The Green Archer*. Like Bennet, she'd had plenty of experience in serials; she was regarded as the chief competitor to serial queen Pearl White.

The story was remade, also under the title *The Terrible People* (1960), as an entry in the popular series of Wallace thrillers produced by Germany's Rialto Pictures in the 1960s and '70s. TH

Terror Mountain
aka **Tom's Vacation**; Terror
FBO; b/w; 55 min; U.S.
D: Louis King *S:* Wyndham Gittens, Helen Gregg *C:* Nicholas Musuraca
Cast: Tom Tyler, Jane Reid, Al Ferguson, Frankie Darro

Sometimes erroneously referred to by the simpler title *Terror*, this film should not be confused with Warner's *The Terror* (1928), which is credited as being the first talkie horror movie. Rather, *Terror Mountain* is a silent horror Western starring Tom Tyler (*The Mummy's Hand*, 1940).

In an old dark house sitting atop a mountain, orphans Buddy Roberts (Darro, who was only 10 years old at the time) and older sister Lucille (Reid) are besieged by apparitions and letters threatening violence against them. Unknown to his sister, Buddy writes Western superstar Tom Tyler, begging for Tyler's aid. Tom, who is fortuitously about to go on vacation anyway, comes to assist his young fan and discovers that a band of thieves are using the house as a base of operations. The action hero duly brings the bad guys to justice, uncovering in the process a valuable stash that had been hidden by the siblings' deceased uncle.

This he gives to Buddy and Lucille, though not before assuring them that they'll be moving back to Hollywood, California with him.

Vincent Markowski was a weight-lifting champion when he entered the film industry in 1923 to play un-credited bit parts. He wound up signing with FBO and taking on the moniker Tom Tyler, working primarily in Westerns (though he did occasionally flirt with other genres). He also starred in *The Phantom of the Range* (1936), another horror Western, and worked with legendary horror actor John Carradine in the classic John Ford/John Wayne collaboration *Stagecoach* (1939). In 1941, Tyler starred as the eponymous comic book superhero in *The Adventures of Captain Marvel*. By the early 1950s, he had shifted his career primarily to television work. He died of a heart attack in 1954 at the too-young age of 50.

The cinematographer on *Terror Mountain* was none other than Nicholas Musuraca, who was later nominated for an Oscar for his work on *I Remember Mama* (1948). The acclaimed cameraman also shot such horror/suspense classics as *Stranger on the Third Floor* (1940), *Cat People* (1942), *The Seventh Victim* and *The Ghost Ship* (both 1943), *The Curse of the Cat People* (1944), *The Spiral Staircase* and *Bedlam* (both 1945). CW

A Thief in the Dark
Fox; b/w; 60 min; U.S.
D: Albert Ray *S:* C. Graham Baker, William Kernell *C:* Arthur Edeson
Cast: George Meeker, Doris Hill, Gwen Lee, Michael Vavitch, Marjorie Beebe, Noah Young

Professor Xeno (Vavitch) leads a group of fake psychics who travel with a carnival, carrying out robberies as time and opportunity permit. When Xeno kills an old woman for her jewelry, Ernest (Meeker), a new recruit, takes it upon himself to unmask Xeno as a murderer.

Director Albert Ray provided the story for this plagiaristic variation of Tod Browning's carnival melodramas. Most of its plot seems directly lifted from Browning's *The Unholy Three* (1925), which is not unlikely given the earlier film's success at the box office. Still, without an actor of Lon Chaney's caliber to pull it off, *Thief* failed to make an impression on much of anyone.

Ray later directed such horror/suspense films as *The Thirteenth Guest* (1932) and *The Intruder* (1933) but remained largely entrenched in B-movie fare until he retired in 1939. Leading man George Meeker specialized in portraying cads and rogues, with noteworthy turns in James Whale's *Remember Last Night?* (1936) and Robert Siodmak's *Son of Dracula* (1943). Cinematographer Arthur Edeson became a favorite of aforementioned Whale—he shot *Waterloo Bridge* (1930), *Frankenstein* (1931), *The Impatient Maiden* (1932), *The Old Dark House* (1932) and *The Invisible Man* (1933) for the director. TH

The Torture Cage
aka **The Adventure of the Torture Cage**
Paul/Brooks; b/w; 22 min; Great Britain
D/Co-P: Fred Paul *S:* Patrick K. Heale *Co-P:* A.M. Brooks
Cast: Harry Agar Lyons, Fred Paul, Evelyn Arden, Wally Patch

This is apparently the only existing film in the *Dr. Sin Fang Dramas* series, six two-reelers beginning with *The Scarred Face* and ending with *Under the Tide* (all six films, 1928). The series was an underfunded knock-off of Stoll's classier *The Mystery of Dr. Fu-Manchu* and *The Further Mysteries of Dr. Fu Manchu*, two film series released in 1923 and 1924, respectively, which starred Harry Agar Lyons as Sax Rohmer's villainous Dr. Fu Manchu and Fred Paul as Sir Nayland Smith. Here, Lyons again assumes the eponymous "Oriental" role of Dr. Sin Fang.

Bill Riggers (Patch) overhears a suspicious conversation between two men—one of them a Chinaman, the other a European—in a pub. He trails the two to the apparent hideout of the evil Dr. Sin Fang (Lyons) but is unable to follow them inside. He immediately phones his boss, Lieutenant John Byrne (Paul), who is chatting with his girlfriend Betty Harberry (Arden). Meanwhile, inside Sin Fang's hideout, the European sees first a skeleton and then a mummy case, which opens to reveal Sin Fang lying with his arms folded across his chest. Dr. Fang rises and stalks toward the European, but there's a scene change before a resolution occurs (though it's later revealed that the European is strangled after refusing to turn over a sacred seal Fang desperately wants). Off the phone now, Riggers is attacked by Fang's Chinese henchmen, dragged to the basement lair and placed in a torture cage. Lieutenant Byrne quickly joins him there, while Evelyn attempts to follow him in a taxi. Evelyn slips into the building unseen, finds the sacred seal and sticks it in her pocket. She then spots Sin Fang and follows him to the basement, where Riggers is being placed in the mummy case while Byrne is carted off in a wooden crate. Both crate and case are loaded into a van outside, and Fang gets in and drives off. Evelyn follows in the waiting taxi. Everyone arrives at a lake, where Byrne and Riggers get loose and attack Sin Fang and his men while Evelyn pulls up. Police officers, who have apparently been riding in the taxi with her, leap out and help the two men. Sin Fang is shot, and his henchmen are taken into custody.

The script, though credited to Patrick K. Heale, has more than a whiff of being made up as shooting went along. Little of it makes sense, and the last-minute surprises offer major plot holes.

The last film in the series, *Under the Tide* (1928), followed. CW

Under the Tide
Paul/Brooks; b/w; 21 min; Great Britain
D/Co-P: Fred Paul *S:* Patrick K. Heale *Co-P:* A.M. Brooks
Cast: Harry Agar Lyons, Fred Paul, Evelyn Arden, Wally Patch

This is the last of the *Dr. Sin Fang Dramas* (though they appeared to have contained more action and horror than drama), a six-film series of two-reelers released in 1928 by a distribution company named Pioneer. All were co-produced and directed by Fred Paul, who also starred, and written by Patrick K. Heale. The other titles in the series were *The Scarred Face*, *The Zone of Death*, *The Light on the Wall*, *The Living Death* and the only one about which anything important is known, *The Torture Cage*. Echoing his myriad earlier performances as Fu Manchu, Harry Agar Lyons portrays Dr. Sin Fang, while Paul plays Lieutenant John Byrne. Evelyn (not Eve) Arden is Betty Harberry, and Wally Patch is Byrne's underling Bill Riggers. Unfortunately, little else about these films is known today.

The only actor in the series to achieve lasting success was London-born Wally Patch (1888-1970). He began acting in films

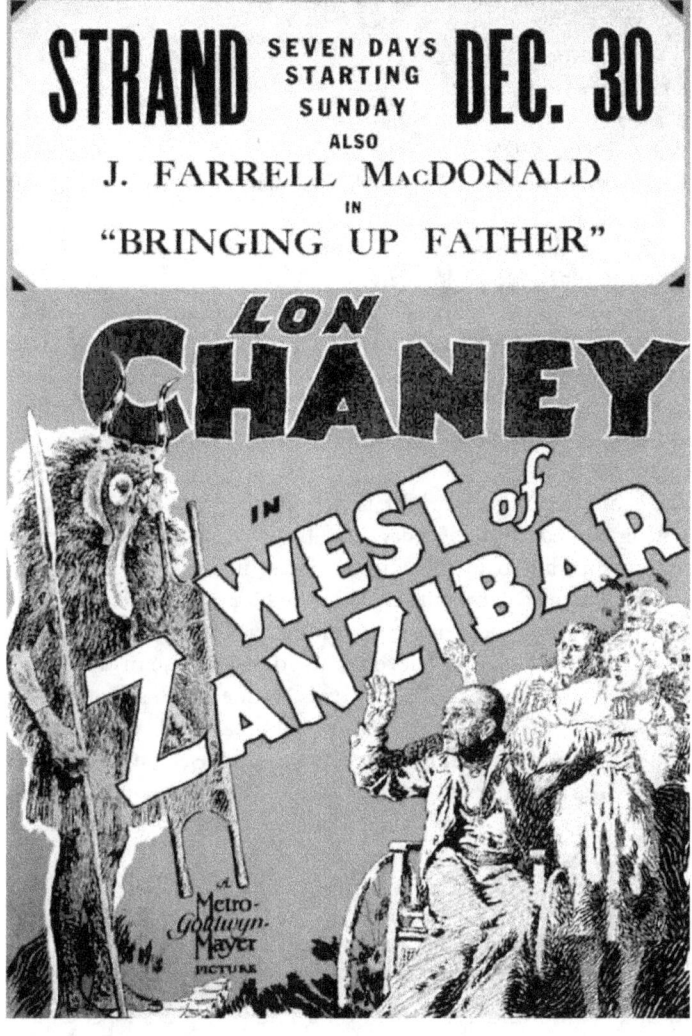

in the late 1920s and continued right up to the end of his life, with small roles on British television until just four months before his death. His other horror credits include *Castle Sinister* (1932) and *Doctor Syn* (1937), and he stars in Hammer Film Productions' first film, *The Public Life of Henry the Ninth* (1935). He also appears in such classics as *Don Quixote* and *The Private Life of Henry VIII* (both 1933), not to mention *Pygmalion* (1938).

Fu Manchu's poor cinematic relation, Dr. Sin Fang later appeared in two feature films, *Dr. Sin Fang* (1937) and *Chinatown Nights* (1938), both produced by Victory Films. Fans of Yellow Peril didn't have to wait that long for more big-screen Asian villainy, however; Paramount began their own Fu Manchu series the very next year with *The Mysterious Dr. Fu Manchu* (1929), starring Warner Oland as Sax Rohmer's criminal mastermind. CW

West of Zanzibar
MGM; b/w; 65 min; U.S.
D: Tod Browning *S:* Elliott J. Clawson *P:* Tod Browning, Irving G. Thalberg *C:* Percy Hilburn
Cast: Lon Chaney, Lionel Barrymore, Mary Nolan, Warner Baxter, Jacqueline Gadsden, Tiny Ward

Phroso Flint (Chaney) is a successful magician who is deeply in love with his wife Anna (Gadsden). When Anna confesses her love for Crane (Barrymore), Phroso confronts and attacks his rival. A struggle ensues, and Flint is paralyzed from the waist down when he falls from a balcony. Months later Anna dies, leaving behind a newborn daughter who Flint believes is Crane's. He launches a grotesque revenge, taking the baby girl to Africa and selling her to a brothel. Years later, the girl (Nolan) is a tragic shadow of what she might have been. Flint—now revered among the natives as a pseudo-king named "Dead Legs"—lures Crane to his lair to confront him one last time, hoping the girl's moral decline will unhinge his sworn enemy.

West of Zanzibar was the penultimate collaboration between director Tod Browning and star Lon Chaney. The film is pretty strong stuff for its day, but unlike their previous collaboration, *The Unknown* (1928), the lurid scenario did not originate with Browning. Rather, it is based on the stage play *Kongo*, written in 1926 by Chester De Vonde. But though the mercurial director did not conceive the strange tale of betrayal, revenge and redemption, it's easy to see why Browning and his favorite star were attracted to it.

Browning pushed the material to its limits, indulging in some wonderfully over-the-top implications of debauchery—to the point, apparently, that some of it worried the financers at Metro Goldwyn Mayer. Stills exist of Chaney wearing strange duck-man make-up, for example, but no such image is present in the film as it exists today. (While Browning would reuse this bit of grotesquerie in the notorious *Freaks*, 1932, how it might have factored into *Zanzibar* is anyone's guess.) The film's revelatory climax is suitably perverse. To delve into too much detail would ruin the surprise, but suffice it to say it pushes the proceedings even further into the realm of kinky psychodrama.

In terms of make-up, there isn't much for Chaney to do this time around. He's merely required to shave his head and pretend his legs don't work. But his wide-eyed and lovable Phroso Flint is warm and believable, and his transformation into the cruel and embittered Dead Legs is even more remarkable. Especially when compared to his broader, more dated mannerisms in such films as *Laugh Clown Laugh* (1928), Chaney's performance here is just right. The important moments are handled with sensitivity, and Chaney is able to make the character's emotional development credible.

There are also fine supporting performances from Mary Nolan and Warner Baxter, the latter as a disgraced doctor hired by Dead Legs to keep him alive long enough to execute his revenge. Lionel Barrymore's role as Chaney's rival is relatively brief, but he does a fine job with what screen time he is given. (The actor would fare better in later collaborations with Browning, most notably 1936's *The Devil Doll*.)

The director keeps the pace moving spryly and again reveals himself an assured, if hardly showy, cinema stylist. Beautifully photographed by Percy Hilburn, *West of Zanzibar* is a worthy companion-piece to such earlier Browning/Chaney collaborations as *The Unholy Three* (1925) and the previously mentioned *The Unknown*. The two would re-team one last time for *Where East is East* (1929), another jungle melodrama.

De Vonde's play was adapted again in 1932 under its original title, *Kongo*, starring Walter Huston. Ealing Studios' *West of Zanzibar* (1954), while appropriating the title and jungle setting, bears no other resemblance to Browning's macabre melodrama, being instead a straightforward action-adventure film. TH

1929

Yotsuya kaidan
Kawai; b/w; length unknown; Japan
D: Takuji Furumi *C:* Taisaku Takashiro
Cast: Goro Morino, Sumiko Suzuki, Itoji Koto, Jun'nosuke Hayama, Ichimaru Ichikawa, Somenosuke Kataoka

This is one of three versions of Tsuruya Nanboku IV's Kabuki play *Yotsuya kaidan* (the other two being *Iemon* and the creatively titled *New Version of the Ghost of Yotsuya*) to be produced in 1928. All of them told the tale of a samurai, Iemon (here, Morino), who murders his wife, Oiwa (here, Suzuki), so that he can frolic with his younger—and richer—mistress, Osumi.

Some sources cite a 1936 film of the same title, also from director Takuji Furumi, as the first sound version of the tale. It's likely, however, that said version was merely a re-release of this adaptation, though it's possible that sound was added the second time out. So little information about these films exists—some of it contradictory—that it's difficult to sort out accurately.

This was the second time that actress Sumiko Suzuki took on the role of victimized wife Oiwa; she also did double-duty on this one by portraying Oiwa's younger sister, Osode. She revisited the Oiwa character a third time in the 1931 film *Oiwa nagaya* and a fourth and final time in 1937's *Irohagana Yotsuya kaidan*. CW

The Zone of Death
Paul/Brooks; b/w; 22 min; Great Britain
D/Co-P: Fred Paul *S:* Patrick K. Heale *Co-P:* A.M. Brooks
Cast: Harry Agar Lyons, Fred Paul, Evelyn Arden, Wally Patch

After commencing with *The Scarred Face* (1928), the six-film *Dr. Sin Fang Dramas* followed it up with *The Zone of Death*. (The other titles in the series are *The Light on the Wall*, *The Living Death*, *The Torture Cage* and *Under the Tide*, all 1928).

Little is known about any of these films, apart from some cast and credits. Henry Agar Lyons portrays evil mandarin Dr. Sin Fang, a nationalistic villain intent on destroying the Occident.

Irish-born actor Lyons (commonly billed as "H. Agar Lyons") was born in 1878. By age 20, he was working in stage productions in the Drury Lane area of London. A decade after that, he began dipping his toe into the then-fledgling medium of cinema, but it wasn't until he portrayed Dr. Fu Manchu in two series of Stoll Productions that he found any degree of success.

In 1928 Lyons' friend and colleague Fred Paul (who had starred as Nayland Smith in the Stoll films) asked him to star as Fu Manchu-wannabe Dr. Sin Fang in a series of no-budget pictures. Lyons not only accepted, but he revisited the character almost a decade later for Victory Studios' *Dr. Sin Fang* (1937) and *Chinatown Nights* (1938). In the interim, he took on a number of smaller parts in various productions, often playing—you guessed it—Chinese characters.

Despite his typecasting, Lyons rarely wore make-up and never looked convincingly Asian. In some surviving stills, he does appear to have sometimes shaved his eyebrows for his roles. But the fact that he was clearly of European descent didn't stop him from gaining a sizeable fan base among Chinese immigrants in Western countries. CW

Black Waters
aka **Fog**
Wilcox; b/w; 79 (81); U.S.
D: Marshall Neilan *S:* John Willard *P:* Herbert Wilcox *C:* David Kesson
Cast: James Kirkwood, Mary Brian, John Loder, Robert Ames, Frank Reicher, Noble Johnson

A disparate group of characters is summoned to a San Francisco wharf in the dead of night and coaxed by a night watchman onto a dilapidated yacht. There, they are successively bumped off until a final pair of invitees (Loder, Brian) remains, along with a reverend (Kirkwood) that turns out to be the demented killer.

American director Marshall Neilan has the distinction of having filmed this, the very first British talking picture, even though he did so in the United States in order to access the needed sound equipment. He shot the film—with an almost entirely American cast and crew—for Herbert Wilcox, a British producer whose career had begun with the less-than-wonderful *The Wonderful Story* in 1922. Wilcox is credited with striking upon the strategy of putting American stars in British pictures, the better to make them more appealing to overseas markets. It was a ploy that began falling out of fashion in the late 1950s, with Hammer Film Productions notably rejecting the maneuver in its 1957 classic, *The Curse of Frankenstein*.

Black Waters was based on John Willard's 1927 play *Fog*, with which the author sought to repeat the triumph of his previous play, *The Cat and the Canary* (1922). By 1929 *Canary* had already been the basis of a wildly successful film adaptation (with several more to come) and a slew of rip-offs and pale imitations. Unfortunately, *Fog* itself was mostly re-tread, the major dramatic innovation being that Willard eschewed an old dark house comedy-horror formula in favor of an old dark … houseboat.

One of the film's few truly British thespians, John Loder (1898-1988), went on to become a major Hollywood star in his day. His respectable career included several horror films, notably *Alraune* (1928), *The Unholy Night* (1929), *The Man Who Changed His Mind* (1936), *Doctor Syn* (1937), *The Mysterious Doctor* (1943), *The Brighton Strangler*, *A Game of Death* and *Woman Who Came Back* (all 1945). At the same time Loder's star was rising, James Kirkwood's was descending. Kirkwood (1875-1963) had been a major star during much of the silent era, with a career that stretched back to 1909. His other horror credits include *Edgar Allen Poe* (sic) (1909) and *The Ghost* (1913). But while he wound up starring in approximately 250 films and television programs, much of his sound-era work went un-credited.

Black Waters is today considered lost. It was long thought to have received scant attention upon its initial release, though some modern film critics who have studied the original reviews suggest that it might have been more inventive than originally assumed, with dependable direction from Neilan and superior cinematography from David Kesson.

Alfred Hitchcock's *Blackmail* (1929) is often cited as the first British talking picture. While the mistake is understandable, Hitchcock's film was actually released after Wilcox's. CW

Botan tou no ki
Nikkatsu; b/w; length unknown; Japan
D: Juko Takahashi *S:* Harunosuke Nishiike *C:* Ichi Ihaya
Cast: Ijiro Kusunoki, Kyoko Sakurai

The title notwithstanding, this is yet another adaptation of Sanyutei Encho's *rakugo* (one-performer) play *Botan dōrō*, about a poor woman who falls for a handsome samurai. He professes to love her but then tires of her affection and flies the coop, leaving her to die of a broken heart. Soon thereafter he meets another beautiful woman with whom he begins an affair. A priest sees the girl for who she is—the evil spirit of a spurned woman—but does so too late to protect the samurai from her vengeance.

Botan tou no ki was released to theaters in its native country on August 23, 1929. CW

Buster's Spooks
Century; b/w; 20 min; U.S.
D: Sam Newfield *P:* Abe Stern, Julius Stern
Cast: Arthur Trimble, Doreen Turner

Ohio-born New York cartoonist Richard Felton Outcault created Buster Brown and his sidekick dog, Tige, in 1902. Brown, based on a boy in Outcault's Flushing neighborhood, was a mischievous child with long blond hair and Little Lord Fauntleroy clothes. The comic-strip character proved so popular that Outcault licensed him to a number of products, most notably the Buster Brown line of children's shoes that remains fashionable today. Outcault is widely credited as the originator of the comic strip format, despite the fact that others had previously used divided panels and word balloons to tell stories.

Buster Brown's most popular incarnation outside of comic land was in a series of short films that began in 1925 and ended in 1929. All of them starred Arthur Trimble as Brown, with Pete the dog (*Dr. Pyckle and Mr. Pride*, 1925) appearing as Tige. *Buster's Spooks*, which featured Brown in a supposedly haunted house, was the 47th entry in the series. Despite its horror slant, the film was a children's comedy, intended to compete with Hal Roach's *Our Gang* franchise. The Buster Brown character remained popular into the 1960s, making the jump from big screen to radio and television.

Though he was predominantly a comedy director during the silent era, Sam Newfield (1899-1964) made his mark in the 1930s and '40s, directing low-budget Westerns known as oaters. He was the brother of Sigmund Neufeld, who ran Producers Releasing Corporation. In the late 1950s, Newfield moved to shooting episodes of television programs, mostly Westerns. CW

Cagliostro
aka **Graf Cagliostro**; **Cagliostro – Liebe und Leben eines großen Abenteurers**
Les Films Armor/Albatros; b/w; length unknown; Germany/France/Sweden
D/Co-P: Richard Oswald *S:* Herbert Juttke, Georg C. Klaren
Co-P: Alexandre Kamenka, Wladimir Wengeroff *C:* Maurice Desfassiaux, Jules Kruger
Cast: Hans Stuwe, Renee Heribel, Rina De Liguoro, Alfred Abel, Ivan Koval-Samborsky, Charles Dullin

Italian adventurer Giuseppe Balsamo attained immortality of a kind when he changed his name to Count Alessandro di Cagliostro and became a dabbler in the occult. He claimed to be of royal lineage but was actually born into a humble and poverty-stricken family. At one point, in Paris, he became embroiled in a scandal known as "the affair of the diamond necklace," in which Queen Marie Antoinette was said to have attempted to defraud the crown jewelers of the cost of a very expensive necklace. Cagliostro was named an accomplice and jailed, but he was subsequently released for lack of evidence and ordered to leave France. Afterward, he lived for a time in England, where his exceptional ability as a forger served him well. But his interest in the occult got him into hot water when he visited Rome during the latter period of the Roman Inquisition—he was again arrested and imprisoned and, this time, put to death.

Given the exotic nature and dramatic arc of his life, it's no surprise that Cagliostro has had several filmic incarnations. Georges Méliès directed the 1899 film *Cagliostro's Mirror*, which has the distinction of being the first cinematic reference to the character. The French short subject *Cagliostro* followed in 1910, but that one owed more to George Du Maurier's horror novel *Trilby* than to anything in the life of Giuseppe Balsamo. The Russians took a crack at the story under the same title in 1918. And while the 1929 German/French/Swedish co-production under discussion appears to have been the most macabre in its presentation, it also seems to have been no more faithful to the facts than its predecessors, presenting Cagliostro as a lovable rogue.

Director Richard Oswald was no stranger to the horror genre, having helmed both *Weird Tales* (1919) and its sound remake, *Uncanny Stories* (1932). Hans Stuwe, a prolific character actor visible in German films until the late 1950s, played Cagliostro. The Cagliostro character was later interpreted by Orson Welles in *Black Magic* (1949) and also emerged in Jess Franco's bizarre blend of horror, sex and pulp comic books, *The Erotic Rites of Frankenstein* (1972), where he was played by Howard Vernon.

Universal Pictures announced its own *Cagliostro* (with Boris Karloff) in 1932, which, after heavy reworking, became *The Mummy*. TH

Chamber of Horrors
British International; b/w; 58 min; Great Britain
D/S: Walter Summers *P:* H. Bruce Woolfe
Cast: Frank Stanmore, Elizabeth Hempel, Leslie Holland, Joan Maude, Fanny Wright

This film is similar to *Conscience*, Maurice Costello's 1912 horror short, which was also released in some areas as *Chamber of Horrors*. Both films concern a person driven mad by a night in a waxworks museum. In the case of Summers' picture, that person is James Budgeforth (Stanmore), who has a terrible dream of murdering his mistress Ninette (Hempel) and, believing the nightmare real, goes insane during a night spent in Madam Tussauds' infamous wax museum. (This wasn't the only cinematic nefariousness to ever occur at Madam Tussauds' museum by the way; more came later with 1936's aptly titled *Midnight at Madam Tussauds*).

Having begun his career as a writer for Cecil Hepworth in 1917, Walter Summers graduated to directing in 1923. An unknown name to most modern buffs, he was involved in several horror films of note, including 1925's *She* (which he wrote), 1939's *The Dark Eyes of London* (which he both wrote and directed) and 1940's *At the Villa Rose* (which he directed). His son Jeremy became a television director of merit while also helming a few theatrical films, including *The Vengeance of Fu Manchu* (1967).

Many sources claim that *The Chamber of Horrors* was the last major silent film made. This is not so, although it may have been the last major silent film to come out of Great Britain. CW

The Charlatan
Universal; b/w; 68 (60) min; U.S.
D: George Melford *S:* J.G. Hawks, Robert N. Lee, Tom Reed, Jack Rollens *C:* George Robinson
Cast: Holmes Herbert, Margaret Livingston, Rockliffe Fellowes, Philo McCullough, Anita Garvin, Crauford Kent

Sideshow performer Count Merlin (Herbert) is invited to a wealthy socialite's home to perform for her guests. During the course of the evening, a secret from the Count's past is exposed, and a murder is committed.

Designed by Universal as one of their "jewel productions" for the year 1929, *The Charlatan* is prescient in its assembly of a group that came to be associated with the horror genre. The screenplay was co-written by Robert N. Lee, the brother of producer/director Rowland V. Lee, who later directed *Son of Frankenstein* (1939). (As a reward for that film's success, Rowland V. Lee was given another horror title to direct—the historical melodrama *Tower of London*, 1939, starring Basil Rathbone, Boris Karloff, and a young Vincent Price; Rowland co-wrote the film with Robert.) The director of *The Charlatan* was the talented George Melford (1877-1961), best remembered today for helming the Spanish-language version of *Dracula* (1931). Melford toiled on many low-budget assignments at Universal, bringing with him flair and style; in hindsight, it seems a pity that he wasn't awarded any of the studio's more prestigious horror pictures. The cinematographer was George Robinson (1890-1958), who later provided silky black and white images for everything from *Dracula's Daughter* (1936) to *The Scarlet Claw* (1944), the latter being the most atmospheric of the Basil Rathbone Sherlock Holmes films for Universal. Editor Maurice Pivar (1894-1982) later became supervising editor for the studio, working on such key titles as *Dracula* (1931), *Frankenstein* (1931), *The Old Dark House* (1932), *The Invisible Man* (1933) and *The Bride of Frankenstein* (1935). Last but not least, Holmes Herbert (1882-1956) became a familiar character face in genre fare over the following three decades; wherever a distinguished sort was needed to provide stiff-upper-lipped English reserve, Holmes could be counted on to fill the bill. *The Charlatan* provided the actor with a rare leading role; he spent much of his later career playing butlers, bobbies and other assorted bit parts.

Unfortunately, the film remains difficult—though not impossible—to view via a superior source, since Universal has shown no interest in promoting it on home video or screening it through syndication. TH

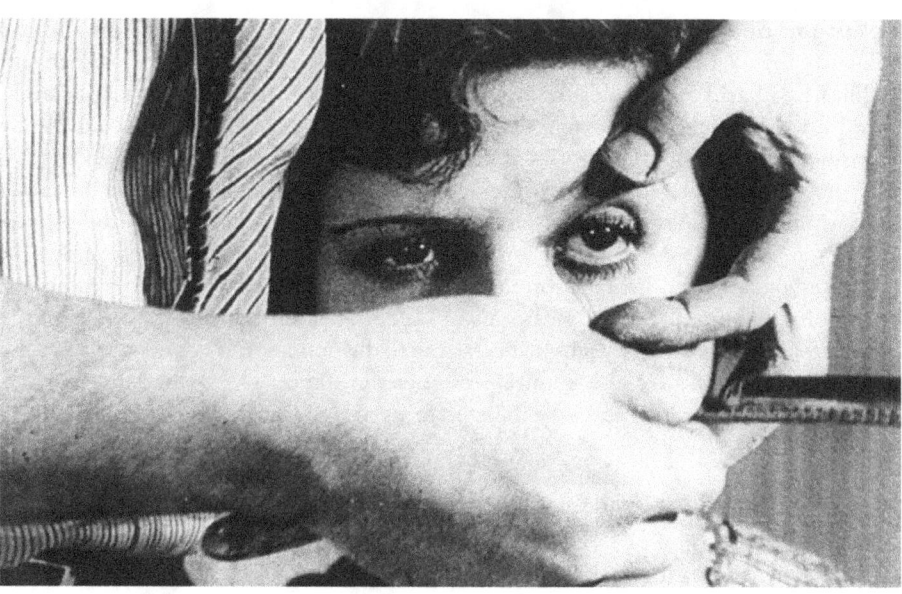

The "razorblade to the eye sequence" drives home Luis Buñuel and Salvador Dali's ultimate cinematic expression of Surrealism, from *Un Chien Andalou*.

Un Chien Andalou
aka **An Andalusian Dog**
Buñuel; b/w; 16 min; France
D/P/Co-S: Louis (Luis) Buñuel *Co-S:* Salvador Dali *C:* Albert Duverger, Jimmy Berliet
Cast: Simone Mareuil, Pierre Batcheff, Luis Buñuel, Salvador Dali, Jaime Miravilles

Un Chien Andalou is a nightmarish succession of images connected by the faintest hint of plot involving a man (Batcheff) and a woman (Mareuil) who may or may not be having an affair.

Conceived by Luis Buñuel and Salvador Dali as an ultimate cinematic expression of Surrealism, *Un Chien Andalou* remains as potent today as ever. The film marked Buñuel's debut as director after serving as assistant to noted French cineaste Jean Epstein. He built the film around a nightmare he'd had in which an eyeball was bisected by a razor blade. Not surprisingly, it's this very image that has remained the most vivid in the collective consciousness of those who have seen the picture. The director found a sympathetic collaborator in the Surrealist painter Dali, and the two deliberately made the film as off the wall and impossible to comprehend as possible.

In truth, there is no real story, though rationalists have tried to impose some order onto the proceedings. Buñuel insisted that people were wrong to do so, as he and Dali—both of whom can be spotted in the film, Buñuel as the razor-wielding man in the opening scene and Dali as a priest tied to a piano in a later scene—resisted the urge to spell things out. On the surface, the images seem pregnant with meaning, but there ultimately is no way to explain them. Rather than laboriously categorize the various images in terms of symbolism, it is far more constructive to simply accept the film for what it is: a random catalog of bizarre imagery.

Such an interpretation is entirely in sync with the Surrealist movement, which maintained that art was an assault on the senses. Despite the fact that neither Dali nor Buñuel had yet found fame at the time of the film's release—and the fact that the film lacked either star power or a storyline—*Chien* proved both a sensation and a lightning rod for controversy.

In addition to the infamous "razorblade to the eye" sequence (accomplished by using a dead calf, with Buñuel wielding the razorblade himself; perhaps not surprisingly, it left the director feeling nauseous), the film is loaded with provocative imagery: a hole in a man's hand erupts with ants; a severed hand is poked at in a town square; two dead mules are strapped to two pianos and the male lead fondles the female lead's bosom, intercut with fantasy images of him pawing her naked breasts and backside. The accumulation of these images made *Un Chien Andalou* strong stuff in 1929.

The film's success helped launch the careers of both Buñuel and Dali, though the two friends ultimately had a falling out that would last the remainder of their lives. Dali achieved major stature in the art world around the time of the film's release, but Buñuel found success harder to come by. His 1930 follow-up, *L'Age D'Or*, proved even more controversial than *Un Chien Andalou*, and he was at length obliged to leave Paris to pursue work in North America. In 1946 he relocated to Mexico, where he kicked off a prolific period with the film *Gran Casino*.

By the 1960s Buñuel had returned to France, where efforts like *Belle de Jour* (1967) would establish him as one of the most significant *auteurs* in world cinema. While none of his films can be properly categorized as horror, there is a macabre element to his masterpiece *The Discreet Charm of the Bourgeoisie* (1972) that makes it worthy of inclusion in any book dealing with the genre. The same can be said of *Un Chien Andalou*, a startling debut that defies any kind of rational categorization. TH

The spiritualism racket is exposed in the dull *Darkened Rooms*.

Darkened Rooms
Paramount; b/w; 66 min; U.S.
D: Louis J. Gasnier S: Patrick Konesky, Patrick Kearney, Melville Baker, Richard H. Digges, Jr. C: Archie Stout M: Karl Hajos
Cast: Evelyn Brent, Neil Hamilton, Doris Hill, David Newell, Gale Henry, Wallace MacDonald

Emory Jago (Hamilton) is a struggling photographer who turns to the spiritualism racket to make money. He teams up with phony medium Ellen (Brent) but begins to suspect that he may indeed possess legitimate mediumistic abilities.

Darkened Rooms sought to cash in on the interest in spiritualism generated by the likes of Harry Houdini. Like many films of its ilk, it tries to have its cake and eat it too. It spends much of its time carefully debunking the supernatural, only to then embrace it when its shady hero is revealed to possess real psychic talent.

Reviews of the day praised leading lady Evelyn Brent. Brent—a WAMPAS (Western Association of Motion Picture Advertisers) Baby Star of 1923—enjoyed a long film and television career from 1915 to 1960; among her later titles of interest are *Mr. Wong, Detective* (1938) and the Val Lewton classic *The Seventh Victim* (1943).

Like many early talkies, *Darkened Rooms* suffers from primitive staging and technique, though studio technicians managed some spooky sound effects for the séance sequences. Karl Hajos, who also scored Universal's *Werewolf of London* (1935), contributed the musical score. TH

The Hole in the Wall
Paramount; b/w; 63 min; U.S.
D: Robert Florey S: Pierre Collings C: George L. Folsey M: Gerard Carbonara, W. Franke Harling
Cast: Edward G. Robinson, Claudette Colbert, David Newell, Nellie Savage, Donald Meek, Alan Brooks

Small-time gangster The Fox (Robinson) has a phony spiritualist called Madame Mystera (Savage) on his payroll. When the ersatz medium is killed in a crash, The Fox hires fresh-faced Jean Oliver (Colbert) to replace her. Much to everybody's surprise, however, it appears that Jean actually possesses occult powers ...

French director Robert Florey is perhaps best remembered as the "almost director" of *Frankenstein* (1931). He helped develop the project for Universal as a star vehicle for Bela Lugosi, but when the studio's new golden boy, James Whale, expressed interest in the picture, Florey and Lugosi were transported to the curb. Florey spent the rest of his career helming a variety of interesting but not-quite-realized projects, though he maintains a cult following among cineastes today.

His interest in German Expressionism shows itself in many of his pictures, including *Johann the Coffinmaker* (1927). *Johann* caught the eye of studio executives in Hollywood, and Paramount picked up Florey for a time before he took his underappreciated talent to Universal. His most famous project for Paramount is the Marx Brothers vehicle *The Cocoanuts* (1929). The film pales in comparison to the comedy troupe's best films—indeed, it was their first feature, following the obscure *Humor Risk* (1921), which disappeared years ago—and it certainly didn't allow Florey room to express his stylized aesthetic.

The Hole in the Wall is an interesting amalgam of gangster melodrama and horror, one in which Edward G. Robinson steals the show. He had previously appeared in two silents—*Arms and the Woman* (1916) and *The Bright Shawl* (1923)—but *The Hole in the Wall* allowed him a chance to polish his most iconic screen persona: the gangster. It wasn't until *Little Caesar* (1931) that the actor achieved superstardom, but *Hole* can be viewed as a dry run for his eventual success.

Claudette Colbert also has one of her earliest roles—her second one, in fact—as the naïve heroine. She went on to great fame and popularity, netting an Oscar for *It Happened One Night* (1934) and getting nominated for two others besides. While her role here begins as a typical, clichéd babe-in-the-woods routine, her character becomes more complex as the picture unfolds, and the actress keeps up just fine.

Florey's direction typifies his strengths and weaknesses. The visuals are strong but the pacing and dialogue are lacking. The exaggerated set designs of the medium's den certainly betray the influence of *The Cabinet of Dr. Caligari* (1919), and if the camerawork seems static compared to some of the director's later films (notably *Murders in the Rue Morgue*, 1932), it pays to remember that this was typical of very early sound films.

Ultimately, *The Hole in the Wall* is interesting only as a curio, but its melding of horror and gangster movie conventions, combined with Florey's exaggerated visual sensibility, makes it a distinctive one. TH

The Hound of the Baskervilles
aka Der Hund von Baskerville

Erda; b/w; 87 min; Germany
D: Richard Oswald *S:* Herbert Juttke, Georg C. Klaren *P:* F.W. Kraemer, Fred Lyssa *C:* Frederik Fuglsang
Cast: Carlyle Blackwell, George Seroff, Livio Pavanelli, Betty Bird, Fritz Rasp, Alexander Murski

Dr. Mortimer (Furth) asks Sherlock Holmes (Blackwell) to protect Sir Henry Baskerville (Pavanelli). The doctor worries that Sir Henry will be killed by the ghostly Hound of the Baskervilles, a supernatural creature known to haunt the moors of County Devon. Holmes doesn't believe a supernatural agent is at work, however, and sets about unmasking the real culprit.

Shot in Berlin, this German version of Sir Arthur Conan Doyle's story boasts an unusually international roster of talent. Director Richard Oswald had already directed two 1915 episodes in a serialization of *The Hound of the Baskervilles* for producer Josef Greenbaum. This adaptation marked his final connection to the Holmes character, though he did further work in the horror genre with a 1930 remake of *Alraune* and with his best-known film, *Uncanny Stories*, a 1932 remake of his 1919 horror anthology *Weird Tales*.

New York-born character actor Carlyle Blackwell played Holmes in what would be his only crack at the role. George Seroff, an obscure performer with only a handful of titles to his credit, plays Watson. German actor Fritz Rasp, memorable for his shady character roles in everything from Fritz Lang's *Metropolis* (1927) to Edgar Wallace *krimis* in the 1960s, plays the iniquitous Stapleton.

Italian actor Livio Pavanelli portrays the endangered Sir Henry, while his perverse ancestor Sir Hugo is rendered by Russian character actor Alexander Murski. One can only imagine the cacophony of accents on parade, so it's probably just as well that the silent era lasted until just after this picture was released.

It was rumored in the 1970s that a print was stored in a Russian film archive, but to date it has not surfaced; it joins most of the silent adaptations of Doyle's most famous novel in being considered lost.

According to Phil Hardy's *The Overlook Film Encyclopedia: Horror*, the film was a "commercial disaster," ending the German cinema's fascination with Holmes until 1936—with yet another version of *The Hound of the Baskervilles*. TH

The House of Horror
aka The Haunted House

First National; b/w; 65 min; U.S.
D: Benjamin Christensen *S:* Richard Bee, William Irish, Tom Miranda *P:* Richard A. Rowland *C:* Ernest Haller, Sol Polito *M:* Louis Silvers
Cast: Louise Fazenda, Chester Conklin, James Ford, Thelma Todd, William V. Mong, Emile Chautard

Various unscrupulous characters search for a diamond in an apparently haunted mansion. "You'll Shiver With Laughter! You'll Shake With Suspense!" promises the ad, but Danish-born director Benjamin Christensen's final American feature is believed lost, making it impossible to ascertain how shudder inducing—or hysterical—it actually was.

The film used the then-impressive Vitaphone sound recording system, though only for a single dialogue sequence. (This soundtrack has been preserved, even if the visuals have not.) Reviews indicate that its horror elements were minimal, as was the case in Christensen's *Seven Footprints to Satan* (1929), with any potential supernaturalism explained away at the climax. Even so, one might assume that the director's imaginative visual sense made the most of the apparently clichéd goings-on.

Actress Thelma Todd—the victim of an apparent homicide in 1935—was a favorite of Christensen, who cast her in all three of his U.S.-lensed horror comedies. Christensen's career sputtered with the coming of sound, however, and he made only a handful of additional films before retiring in 1942. He died in 1959. Today, his reputation rests almost exclusively on his 1922 film *Häxan*. While he did contribute to MGM's lavish adaptation of Jules Verne's *Mysterious Island* (1929), his work went un-credited. That oversight, and the fact that the production stretched back to 1926—with its first director Maurice Tourneur also being given the boot—makes it unclear exactly when Christensen worked on the project, let alone how much of his material made it into the finished product.

As for *The House of Horror*, it didn't attract the enthusiastic reviews of some of Christensen's earlier pictures. *Variety*'s critic, for one, was certainly not amused, as this June 19, 1929, review indicates:

The House of Horror is one of the weakest and most boring afterbirths of pseudo-mystery-comedy ground out of Hollywood … If the thing ever had a script Christensen apparently never knew it, judging strictly from the finished product.

TH

The House of Secrets
Chesterfield; b/w; 71 min; U.S.
D: Edmund Lawrence *S:* Adeline Leitzbach *P:* George R. Batcheller *C:* Irving Browning, Lester Lang, George Peters, George Webber
Cast: Joseph Striker, Marcia Manning, Elmer Grandin, Herbert Warren, Francis V. Verdi, Richard Stevenson

Barry Wilding (Striker) goes to London to investigate mysterious goings-on at a mansion he's inherited. He and his detective friend Joe Blake (Warren) come to suspect that shadowy Chinaman Wu Chang (Roseman) is up to something, but the culprits end up being far less exotic.

The House of Secrets is a variation on the formula of a mystery surrounding a lavish inheritance. Long considered lost, it was apparently an unremarkable mystery thriller with incidental horror elements.

Sydney Horler was a popular British novelist during the 1920s and '30s. He wrote *The House of Secrets* in 1926, with this first screen adaptation following three years later. Director Edmund Lawrence was nearing the end of his lackluster directorial career when he directed the film. He died in 1931.

Horler's story got its next cinematic go-around under the same title, in 1936. TH

Isetsu Banchō sarayashika
Kawai; b/w; length unknown; Japan
D: Koji Oka
Cast: Sumiko Suzuki

Japan's First Lady of Horror, Sumiko Suzuki, stars as Okiku, a lowly maid in the mansion of a rich man who has designs on her virginity. In love with another, Okiku refuses his many advances, and he hatches a scheme to force her acquiescence. He breaks one of a set of 10 valuable plates he owns, frames Okiku for the damage and attempts to blackmail her into sexual submission.

This version of the *Banchō sarayashika* folk story is unique in that it adds to the mix the ghost of another woman named Okiku, an earlier victim of the same man who provides protection to the second Okiku. (Suzuki played both Okikus.)

The title *Isetsu Banchō sarayashika* translates roughly as "Another Story of the Banchō Dish House." This was the last film adaptation of the tale to be released in the 1920s. The next known version came in 1937, was titled *The Plate-Counting Ghost of Banchō* and was the first to be shot in sound. CW

Kaidan Bunya goroshi
Teikine; b/w; length unknown; Japan
D: Shuichi Yamashita *C:* Tei Taniguchi
Cast: Tasaburo Matsumoto, Umetaro Nakamura, Kyoko Chigusa, Sakura Yamashita

This is the second known film dealing with the Bunya murder case, known in Japan as Bunya-goroshi. Yokota Shokai made the first in 1911, but little information about that particular film survives. The title of this 1929 film translates as "Ghost Story of the Bunya Murder Case."

Lonely Bunya is blind, old and homeless. While traveling he is befriended by the much younger Jubee Itami, who offers to assist him on his way. Bunya agrees, only to be robbed of his few belongings and murdered by Itami along the Utsunoya Pass. Such a crime, of course, cannot go unpunished, and as usual in Japanese folk tradition, Bunya returns from the dead as a grudge ghost and goes after his murderer.

The story was later retold for television as *Kaidan Utsunoya-touge* (1970), which was an episode of a short-lived Japanese horror series. CW

The Last Warning

Universal; b/w; 88 min; U.S.
D: Paul Leni *S:* Alfred A. Cohn, Tom Reed, J.G. Hawks, Thomas F. Fallon *P:* Carl Laemmle *C:* Hal Mohr
Cast: Laura La Plante, John Boles, Montagu Love, Roy D'Arcy, Margaret Livingston, Burr McIntosh

An actor (Corrigan) is murdered during a stage performance, and the police, headed by Inspector McHugh (Love), are stumped. Five years elapse and the theater reopens—with a production of the same play that had been performed on the night of the murder. The murderer emerges, leaving notes warning of more mayhem should the production continue as scheduled.

Following comedy-tinged *The Cat and the Canary* (1927), the ambitious *The Man Who Laughs* (1928) and the apparently lost Charlie Chan vehicle *The Chinese Parrot* (1928), Paul Leni directed this less prestigious but no less inventive follow-up.

Carl Laemmle no doubt saw the project as a good way to get some additional mileage out of the massive, expensive sets Universal had constructed for *The Phantom of the Opera* (1925), and *The Last Warning* further confirms just how poorly *Phantom*'s director Rupert Julian had utilized the impressive designs in that bigger-budgeted bonanza. Based on the novel *The House of Fear* by Wadsworth Camp and its successful stage adaptation by Thomas F. Fallon, *The Last Warning* repackages the elements that had made both *Phantom* and *Cat* so wildly successful. An air of *déjà vu* understandably hangs over the proceedings, but Leni's imaginative staging and use of mobile camerawork are there to shore things up.

As with *Cat*, Leni was less adept with broad humor than he was at building suspense; the result is an abundance of tone-deaf comedic relief. Apart from this, however, *Warning* is mostly a sure-handed stylistic exercise. His sole collaboration with cinematographer Hal Mohr (later to win an Oscar for his color photography in the 1943 version of *The Phantom of the Opera*) displays an aggressively imaginative aesthetic sensibility. The camera dollies and cranes with willful abandon, giving the point of view of a falling piece of scenery one moment and scuttling beneath a descending curtain the next. If the whole thing proves in the final analysis to be a little too genteel, Leni nevertheless gives it everything he's got.

Laura La Plante, who'd already scored a hit with Leni in *Cat*, heads the cast. Her role isn't as well developed this time around, but she does do a convincing job. Romantic interest John Boles—later to be featured in a prominent supporting role in James Whale's 1931 *Frankenstein*—also holds his own, while Montague Love is effective as the no-nonsense police inspector.

The final revelation of the killer's identity is a genuine surprise—an indisputable way in which *Warning* outdoes *Cat*—and the use of a pair of eyes burning in the darkness makes for a memorable shock effect. On the whole, however, the humdrum setup and over-baked comedy drags the effort a level or two below Leni's earlier triumphs.

This, sadly, proved to be the director's last film. He would die at the age of 44, not long after the film's completion, from blood poisoning caused by an infected tooth. The story would be remade by another German émigré, Joe May, as *The House of Fear* in 1939.

As with numerous movies produced during the final days of silent filmmaking, *The Last Warning* was originally released with a synchronized music track that included sound effects and some dialogue. No known surviving copies retain this track. TH

Legend of the Nabeshima Cat Ghost
aka **Nabeshima kaibyô-den**

Teikine; b/w; 80 min; Japan
D: Shiroku Nagao
Cast: Dojuro Kataoka, Tsuruko Matsuda

During the mid-to-late 1920s and early 1930s, Teikine produced a number of horror films, including two versions of *Kasane-ga-fuchi* (1924, 1928), one of *Botan dōrō* (1930) and one of the *Yotsuya kaidan* legend (*Oiwa nagaya*, 1931). They are all, if not lost, at least so obscure as to be unobtainable today, and none has gained the kind of notoriety—and thus preservation of information—that has attached to similarly lost horror films of the silent era that hail from the United States and Germany. This fact is most unfortunate for students of Japanese cinema in general and Japanese horror cinema in particular.

This particular adaptation of Joko Segawa III's oft-filmed play *Hana Saga neko mata zoshi* (1853) is a variant on the tale of Naoshige Nabeshima, who, it is alleged, murdered his master in an effort to dominate the man's feudal clan. The murdered man returns as a ghost cat and seeks vengeance against his killer, who has gone on to become a great Japanese military leader. CW

Modern kaidan: 100,000,000 Yen

Shochiku; b/w; 15 min; Japan
D: Torajiro Saito *S:* Tadao Ikeda *C:* Yoshio Taketomi
Cast: Tatsuo Saito, Junko Matsui, Mitsuko Yoshikawa, Takeshi Sakamoto, Shizuko Esaka, Kaoru Futaba

This is a horror/comedy hybrid. Tomiko (Matsui) and Joji (Saito), two young people in love, run away from home because their parents (Sakamoto, Yoshikawa) don't approve of their relationship. They get lost somewhere on Mt. Akagi and there find a fortune in buried gold. The problem is that the cache is stolen loot, stashed by a long-dead gangster named Chuji Kunisada, whose ghost now protects it. The two lovers defeat the ghost and take the gold back to their parents, who do an about-face on the issue of the kids getting hitched.

Chuji Kunisada was a real-life gangster whose actual name was Chuji Nagaoka. He was born in Kunisada Village in 1810 and began a life of violent crime while still a young adult. He was arrested and executed in 1850, though not before becoming a heroic symbol of defiance to the struggling peasants of the region. Numerous films romanticizing his exploits have dotted the cinematic landscape since the birth of Japanese cinema, the most famous being *Chuji the Gambler* (1960). CW

The Mysterious Dr. Fu Manchu
Paramount; b/w; 82 min; U.S.
D: Rowland V. Lee S: Florence Ryerson, Lloyd Corrigan P: Jesse L. Lasky, Adolph Zukor C: Harry Fischbeck M: Oscar Potoker
Cast: Warner Oland, Neil Hamilton, Jean Arthur, O.P. Heggie, William Austin, Claude King, Noble Johnson

The Boxer Rebellion lasted from 1898 to 1901, a reaction to Western imperialism in China. As first-world administrators handed over more and more Chinese property to the Roman Catholic Church (while passing laws that gave missionaries more rights than the indigenous population), a secret group known as the Society of Righteous and Harmonious Fists took shape. More commonly known as Boxers due to their affinity for martial arts techniques, the Society's aim was to return China to its previous isolationist existence. China's economy was tanking under European influence, and by blaming a series of natural disasters—such as the flooding of the Yellow River in 1898 and a severe drought in 1900—on the West, the Boxers were easily able to recruit young and angry members of the Chinese population. In 1900 the country's Empress Dowager officially recognized the group, which cleared the way for their union with the Imperial Chinese Army. The result was a massacre in which thousands of Christian missionaries and their adherents were killed. Russia, Germany, the United States, France, Great Britain, Italy, Austria and Japan joined forces to suppress the uprising, and China was ultimately forced to surrender and make reparations.

It is in such a milieu that *The Mysterious Dr. Fu Manchu* begins. A kindly Christian missionary named Eltham (Dossett) fears for his life and that of his daughter Lia at the hands of the Boxers. Knowing that local scientist Fu Manchu (Oland) is supportive of the West, he places the girl in Fu's care. Eltham is then killed by Boxers holed up in the doctor's garden, after which Allied soldiers attack Fu's home and mistakenly kill the scientist's wife and son. The doctor vows revenge on the generals in charge. Years pass, and those same generals are dying mysteriously one by one. Sir Nayland Smith (Heggie) barges into the home of General Petrie (Stevenson) and warns the General that he's next on the list. Shortly thereafter Petrie is indeed killed, and Smith disappears while in pursuit of the assassin. Meanwhile, General Petrie's grandson, Dr. Jack Petrie, meets the now-adult Lia Eltham (Arthur), who introduces him to noted bacteriologist Fu Manchu. Jack seeks Fu's help in finding the missing Nayland Smith, not realizing that the madman has not only killed Jack's grandfather but hopes to kill Jack and his father, Sir John Petrie, as well.

Though he made numerous classic films in both the silent (*Alice Adams*, 1923) and talkie (*The Count of Monte Cristo*, 1934) eras, director Rowland V. Lee is best known today for his twin Universal horror films of 1939, *Son of Frankenstein* and *Tower of London*, both of which starred Basil Rathbone and Boris Karloff. But a decade earlier, Lee first stuck his toe into the horror genre by bringing Sax Rohmer's infamous criminal mastermind Dr. Fu Manchu to the big screen in the character's first feature-length adaptation.

After Stoll Studio's two series, *The Mystery of Dr. Fu-Manchu* (1923) and *The Further Mysteries of Dr. Fu Manchu* (1924), which were adaptations of individual chapters within Rohmer's early novels, the character had been banished to filmic limbo until Paramount purchased the rights for their own short-lived series. Unlike the Stoll films, however, Paramount's pictures bear little resemblance to Rohmer's plotlines. Fu Manchu's slave Karamaneh and his daughter Fah lo Suee are replaced by Caucasian slave girl Lia Eltham. Rohmer's hero, Sir Nayland Smith, is reduced to a supporting character, while Dr. Petrie, much younger and more agile on film than in print, is promoted to the role of hero. Inspector Weymouth barely appears at all.

But make no mistake: This is Fu Manchu's show all the way, with Swedish-born actor Warner Oland giving a classic portrayal. Unlike Harry Agar Lyons before him or Boris Karloff and Christopher Lee after, Oland plays the part sympathetically, helped by a script that elucidates Fu Manchu's hatred of "the white races." Yet Oland balances this depth with Fu Manchu's all-important comic book persona, prancing and preening his way through one sinister set piece after another. In fact, the actor was so convincing in the role that he made a career out of playing Asian types, from the foreign baddie in such movies as *The Drums of Jeopardy* (1931) and *Werewolf of London* (1935) to the hero of Fox-produced Charlie Chan adaptations such as *Charlie Chan in Egypt* (1935) and *Charlie Chan at the Opera* (1936).

In typical Lee fashion, The Mysterious Dr. Fu Manchu feels much bigger than its moderate budget would have one believe. It convincingly shows the audience 1900 China, jumps to mainland Britain almost 30 years later and then concludes in a dark and sinister estate. On a blustery and sinister night, Sir John Petrie and his son Jack take refuge in their castle-like home on a cliff overlooking the ocean, waves violently crashing over the rocks below. The house is full of long corridors, winding stairwells and dark shadows, with a servant (O'Brien) providing the comic relief and Lia doing the swooning. Unfortunately, cinematographer Harry Fischbeck's camerawork tends to remain locked on the frame rather than follow people and incidents with the fluid control evidenced in many other horror films of the time.

The film's horrific content isn't limited to its Yellow Peril menace or the old dark house setting of its final reel. Paramount continues the tradition of making Fu Manchu a larger-than-life figure with almost superhuman abilities. In a turn suggested by George Du Maurier's Gothic romance *Trilby* (1894), Fu exerts hypnotic control over his ward, Lia, one that is finally broken by her love for Dr. Petrie. And though the evil doctor is killed in the end, there's little doubt that he'll return from the grave…

Which he did three more times for Paramount, next in a cameo titled "Murder Will Out," shot by Lee for *Paramount on Parade* (1930), then in Lee's direct follow-up, *The Return of Dr. Fu Manchu* (also 1930) and finally in Lloyd Corrigan's *Daughter of the Dragon* (1931). When the series ended, the rights to the character were picked up by MGM for a single entry, the shockingly sadistic *The Mask of Fu Manchu* (1932), starring Boris Karloff as the Asian madman.

Though *The Mysterious Dr. Fu-Manchu* was shot in two versions—one silent and one with sound—it is the talkie version that remains accessible today. Yet it too bears the mark of the silent era as the occasional title card pops up to explain the action or a change in scenery. CW

Rasputin

Ifuk; b/w; 54 min; Germany
D: Max Neufeld
Cast: Max Neufeld, Eugen Neufeld, Renati Renee, Robert Valbar

Wild-eyed peasant monk Rasputin (Max Neufeld) gains an ever-increasing amount of influence over the Russian royal family. As his power grows, gossip runs rampant that he is running the entire government from behind the scenes. Eventually, fear and resentment prompt his assassination by aristocrats.

Rasputin was a controversial film in its day. Not only did it concern the alleged real-life exploits of the infamous mad monk and the Russian court (something that, in itself, proved enough for one of the assassins to later sue MGM over 1932's *Rasputin and the Empress*), but the film also contained orgy scenes that were cut from American prints. There was also the addition, purely for sex appeal, of an entirely fictional female secret agent (Renee). And, on top of it all, the film climaxed with a depiction of the various failed methods used in the attempt to kill Rasputin, followed at last by the one sufficient to do him in. (This was actually a reenactment of the event as related by principal assassin Prince Yusupov, though his account sometimes varied in the telling).

The story of Grigori Rasputin had inspired numerous film portrayals from many different countries before this particular effort, and it would continue to do so. This obscure German production was one of the earlier works from Austrian-born writer/producer/director Max Neufeld, who also starred as the villainous title character. Neufeld remained active until 1957, though he never made a significant name for himself in the European film scene. He died in 1967. This was not the first time Neufeld had played the part; he had previously done so in *Die Brandstifter Europas* (1926), which he likewise directed.

The director's brother Eugen Neufeld also acted in *Rasputin*. He often worked with his brother and also collaborated with other filmmakers, including Richard Oswald, before his death in 1950. TH/CW

Seven Footprints to Satan

First National/Vitaphone; b/w; 77 min; U.S.
D: Benjamin Christensen *S:* Richard Bee (Benjamin Christensen) *P:* Wid Gunning *C:* Sol Polito
Cast: Creighton Hale, Thelma Todd, Sheldon Lewis, William V. Mong, Sojin, Laska Winters, Angelo Rositto

Jim (Hale) thirsts for adventure, and one night he gets more than he bargained for. While at a party with his sweetheart Eve (Todd), the two witness an attempted burglary and go for the

The lovely Thelma Todd is menaced by the creepy Sheldon Lewis in *Seven Footprints to Satan*.

police. But before they can get there, they are whisked off to a house in the country inhabited by a Devil-worshiping cult. Jim does his best to put on a brave face, but the run of bizarre events and characters they encounter thoroughly unnerves him. He is put to a final test when he comes face to face with the mysterious Mr. Satan.

Following the success of his witchcraft epic *Häxan* (1922), studios in the United States actively courted actor/writer/director Benjamin Christensen. He directed his first Hollywood film, *The Devil's Circus* (not a horror film, despite its title), in 1926. *Seven Footprints to Satan* was the fifth of seven U.S. films he wound up making, becoming another variation on the old dark house subgenre popularized most notably by *The Bat* (1926) and *The Cat and the Canary* (1927). Christensen even casts Creighton Hale, the juvenile lead of *Cat*, in a similar role here. Hale is no more effective than he had been in the earlier picture, but the film itself is not without merit.

Christensen wonderfully evokes the shadowy atmosphere of *Häxan* and milks the various shocks for all their worth. A standout set piece involves the abduction of an implicitly naked woman by a man in a gorilla outfit; after being dragged off kicking and screaming, the woman is tied to a post and whipped by a weird group of bystanders (the S&M implications of the sect's activities are most decidedly not shied away from). The final showdown, wherein the meaning of the title is made clear, is also vividly realized.

The film is at its best when Christensen allows it to be properly eerie, yet comedy is never far from the action. And it's during the comedic moments that the film stumbles. Most regrettably, *Footprints* resorts to the old "it was all a gag" ending, a copout that threatens the air of menace even further.

As noted above, Hale's central performance is a drawback; this is, however, compensated for by the lovely Thelma Todd. Todd, whose life ended in tragedy when she died of carbon monoxide poisoning following a very public scandal involving her affair with director Roland West, was a photogenic and immensely likable performer. She makes the most of a not-very-interesting character in *Seven Footprints* and effortlessly steals the film from Hale's mugging poseur of a hero.

The supporting cast includes Sheldon Lewis—who had played the title characters in one of 1920's many versions of *Dr. Jekyll and Mr. Hyde*—and Angelo Rossitto, a diminutive character actor whose long and varied career encompassed everything from Tod Browning's notorious *Freaks* (1932), to bottom-of-the-barrel Bela Lugosi programmers like *Scared to Death* (1947), to the most lavish of George Miller's post-apocalyptic trilogy, *Mad Max Beyond Thunderdome* (1985).

Christensen finished his American career with two more films: another horror/comedy hybrid *House of Horror* (1929) and some uncredited contributions to the sci-fi epic *The Mysterious Island* (1929). TH

Seven Keys to Baldpate
RKO; b/w; 72 min; U.S.
D: Reginald Barker *S:* Jane Murfin *P:* Louis Sarecky *C:* Edward Cronjager
Cast: Richard Dix, Miriam Seegar, Margaret Livingston, Lucien Littlefield, Joseph Allen, Sr., DeWitt Jennings

William Halliwell Magee (Dix) takes a room at the secluded Baldpate Inn so that he can write his book in peace. His seclusion is disrupted by a string of bizarre visitors, all of whom are searching for a hidden fortune. His curiosity is piqued, and he abandons his book in order to get to the bottom of the mystery.

This is the first sound version of Earl Derr Biggers' 1913 novel, which had already been brought successfully to the stage by George M. Cohen and adapted for the silent-screen in 1916, 1917 and 1925. Jane Murfin's script offers a different interpretation of the material than any of the earlier renderings, no doubt due to the story's familiarity to 1929 audiences.

Leading man Richard Dix later garnered a Best Actor nomination for *Cimarron* (1931), but he found his biggest success top-lining Columbia Films' *Whistler* series in the mid-1940s. He also starred in *The Ghost Ship* (1943), a sadly neglected title from producer Val Lewton.

The supporting cast includes a number of actors familiar from earlier adaptations of the story. Crauford Kent (as Bentley) and Edith Yorke (as Mrs. Quimby) were in the 1925 version, while Carleton Macey repeats his role as Police Chief Kennedy from the 1917 adaptation. TH

Stark Mad
Warner; b/w; 70 (74) min; U.S.
D: Lloyd Bacon *S:* Harvey Gates, Francis Powers *C:* Barney McGill
Cast: H.B. Warner, Louise Fazenda, Jacqueline Logan, Henry B. Walthall, Claude Gillingwater, John Miljan, Lionel Belmore

A jarringly lurid jungle melodrama, *Stark Mad* appears to be an attempt by Warner Bros. to emulate the success of the Tod Browning and Lon Chaney jungle horrors from the same period.

After his son vanishes in the wilds of Central America (as opposed to the usual Africa), James Rutherford (Gillingwater) and a search party set sail. There's a mysterious disappearance and a threatened mutiny at sea before the crew disembarks and takes refuge in a Mayan temple. There, as night falls, they experience weird noises and lose their only lantern. The obligatory killer ape shows up, chained in the middle of a temple room. One of the party gets carried off by a hairy monster with talons, and arrows shot from the darkness bump off a couple more. It turns out that Rutherford's son was killed by a hermit who'd claimed squatter's rights in the temple and was in turn killed by the son's guide (Beranger), who then went insane due to the terrors of the jungle.

Two versions of the film—one silent, the other with sound—were made, but both are considered lost today. Director Lloyd Bacon (1889-1955) built a fairly distinguished career for himself, though his name is now largely forgotten. His films include such classics as *Moby Dick* (1930), *Gold Diggers of 1937* and *Marked Woman* (both 1937), *Knute Rockne All American* (1940), *Action in the North Atlantic* (1943), *The Fighting Sullivans* (1944), *It Happens Every Spring* (1949) and *The Fuller Brush Girl* (1950), among others.

On the other hand, scenarist Harvey Gates' career went downhill after this film, culminating in such Monogram horrors as *Black Dragons* and *The Corpse Vanishes* (both 1942). He did do some un-credited work on Universal's classic *Werewolf of London* (1935). He died in 1949, the year after writing *Racing Luck*, a cheapie romance produced by Sam Katzman and released by Columbia Pictures. CW

A Tale of the Occult
aka **Youma kitan**; **Yoma kidan**; **Tales of Monsters**
Shochiku; b/w; length unknown; Japan
D/S: Tetsuro Hoshi *C:* Eiji Tsuburaya
Cast: Junosuke Bando, Akiko Chihaya, Kokichi Takada

This is an unofficial adaptation of Oscar Wilde's classic 1890 novella *The Picture of Dorian Gray*, which tells the tale of a man who remains young in appearance while his portrait ages and is corrupted by the man's misdeeds. The story was transposed to a feudal Japanese setting, with photography and effects by none other than Eiji Tsuburaya, who went on to oversee the special effects for numerous Godzilla films. It also proved to be the last adaptation of Wilde's tale until MGM's classic 1945 film, *The Picture of Dorian Gray*.

A Tale of the Occult was released in Japan on October 25, 1929. CW

The Thirteenth Chair
MGM; b/w; 72 min; U.S.
D/P: Tod Browning *S:* Elliott J. Clawson *C:* Merritt P. Gerstad
M: William Axt
Cast: Conrad Nagel, Leila Hyams, Margaret Wycherly, Bela Lugosi, Helene Millard, Holmes Herbert

Aristocrats in colonial India gather for a séance presided over by Madame La Grange (Wycherly). Though all involved hope that the session will reveal the identity of an acquaintance's killer, it instead results in a second murder. Inspector Delzante (Lugosi) is called in to investigate.

The Thirteenth Chair is the second screen adaptation of the play by Bayard Veiller—the first was done in 1919 and is presumed lost. The plot here is typical drawing-room murder-mystery stuff, and one can only assume that director Tod Browning was drawn to the material by its occultish mood and bizarre final act.

Browning had established himself as a master of the macabre during the 1920s with a series of perverse melodramas, many of them starring Lon Chaney. With the coming of sound, however, the director began to stumble. *The Thirteenth Chair* was his first talkie picture and, like its better-known follow-up, *Dracula* (1931), suffers from a general malaise of staginess. The director's flair for evoking atmosphere is severely handicapped by the static camerawork necessitated by early sound-recording techniques. (Interestingly, the film was also shot in a silent version, now considered lost.) Browning breaks the monotony now and then with a few judicious dolly shots, but little of his peculiar imagination breaks through.

The film is nonetheless noteworthy as the first collaboration between Browning and actor Bela Lugosi. Born Bela Blasko in Hungary, Lugosi made his way to the United States in 1920. He found onstage fame in the title role of *Dracula* in 1927, and it was doubtless there that he attracted the attention of Browning.

Lugosi was a veteran of film work by this time, having appeared in dozens of movies in both Europe and the United

The ominous Bela Lugosi (left) appears in his first collaboration with director Tod Browning in *The Thirteenth Chair*.

States. Among his earliest credits is a turn as Conrad Veidt's butler in F.W. Murnau's legendary lost adaptation of *The Strange Case of Dr. Jekyll and Mr. Hyde*, *Der Januskopf* (1920). His performance in *The Thirteenth Chair* is a bit heavy-handed, though Browning's introduction of the actor is one of the film's better moments: As Lugosi slowly, compellingly turns to the audience, one gets a glimpse of the magnetic power that would lead him to superstardom in Browning's film adaptation of *Dracula*.

Leading man Conrad Nagel had already appeared in Browning's *London After Midnight* (1927), but he, like most of the cast, seems uncertain as to how to approach acting in a sound picture. Margaret Wycherly likewise overdoes it as the medium, a role she portrayed in the stage play. (Wycherly was also married to the play's writer.) In their defense, it would take some time for most silent-screen actors and directors to learn to take a low-key approach to filming. But the reliable Holmes Herbert (*Dr. Jekyll and Mr. Hyde*, 1931) is in good form in one of his larger roles.

It's a minor footnote in Browning's filmography, but *The Thirteenth Chair* does have its charms and is at least worth a look for fans of its director and/or Bela Lugosi.

The play got its final (to date) cinematic treatment in 1937. TH

The Unholy Night
aka The Green Ghost
MGM; b/w; 93 min; U.S.
D: Lionel Barrymore S: Edwin Justus Mayer, Joseph Farnham C: Ira Morgan
Cast: Roland Young, Ernest Torrence, Claude Fleming, Dorothy Sebastian, Natalie Moorhead, Sidney Jarvis, Loder, Lionel Belmore, Boris Karloff

A terrible fog grips London. On the way to his club a would-be assassin attacks Lord Montague (Coleman). He narrowly escapes and later learns that somebody is killing off the members of his old regiment. Sir James of Scotland Yard (Fleming) is determined to get to the bottom of the mystery, so he asks Lord Montague to gather the remaining members of the regiment at the lavish Montague estate.

The great stage and film actor Lionel Barrymore transitioned to directing with the short subject *His Secret* (1913). He went on to direct additional short features, along with a handful of feature films, including this one. Though based on a story by the accomplished Ben Hecht (*The Front Page*, 1934), *The Unholy Night* is a painfully creaky and melodramatic murder mystery. If the film is any indication of Barrymore's overall directing talent, it's no surprise that he eventually returned his focus exclusively to acting.

The film is more noteworthy for its cast than anything else. In his talkie debut, Roland Young (later Oscar-nominated for *Topper*, 1937) shows a flair for dry comedy but flails hopelessly when drama is called for; it's a rather embarrassing performance for so fine an actor. As awkward as Young appears, however, he gets off easy compared to an unbilled Boris Karloff who, as an enigmatic lawyer named Abdoul, gets to take advantage of his naturally dark complexion but Karloff struggles terribly with a thick Indian accent. Fine character actors John Loder (*The Man Who Changed His Mind*, 1936) and Lionel Belmore (*Frankenstein*, 1931) also come up a bit short, leading one to conclude that Barrymore simply didn't know how to guide his actors.

Barrymore also demonstrates little visual ingenuity, with much of the film unfolding in painfully static medium and long shots. There are a couple of effective moments—notably a lengthy camera pan revealing a number of dead bodies—but much of the film is deadly dull. TH

Where East Is East
MGM; b/w; 67 min; U.S.
D: Tod Browning S: Richard Schayer P: Hunt Stromberg, Irving G. Thalberg C: Henry Sharp
Cast: Lon Chaney, Lupe Velez, Estelle Taylor, Lloyd Hughes, Louis Stern, Mrs. Wong Wing

Wild animal trapper Tiger Haynes (Chaney) fears for his beloved daughter, Toyo (Velez), when she falls in love with weak-willed Bobby (Hughes), but Dad's trepidation evaporates when the prospective son-in-law rescues Toyo from an escaped tiger.

There is, it must be said, an unmistakable whiff of misogyny in the screenplay: While Tiger rightly despises his ex-wife, he never seems to feel that Bobby should be held equally accountable for his own actions. This, coupled with its depiction of "manly" men who win women with feats of strength and daring, gives the film a dated, sexist feel.

Where East is East signaled the end of the fruitful collaboration between Chaney and Browning, which had begun a decade earlier with *The Wicked Darling* (1919). TH

> Harlem Little Art Theatre to Open.
> A Harlem Little Art Theatre, located at 612 Lenox Avenue, will be opened to the public early in April. Salem Whitney and Homer Tutt, negro showmen, are to be directors of the enterprise, which, according to announcement, "will endeavor to assist the artist in all branches of art, and will act as a medium through which the amateur, artist, composer, song writer, musician or playwright will have an opportunity to present himself and his creation to the public."

The Witching Eyes
Stern; b/w; length unknown; U.S.
D/S/P: Ernest Stern
Cast: Salem Tutt Whitney, Sylvia Birdsong, Lorenzo Tucker

An early example of blaxploitation horror, *The Witching Eyes* concerns a Haitian named Val Napolo, a witch doctor with the power to cast spells. His friend Cortex convinces him to go to the United States and use his power to lead his people from their oppression. Once there, Napolo meets Sylvia Smith, the beautiful daughter of a black leader who has recently died. He falls in love with her, but since she's engaged to a kindhearted poet named Ralph Irving, Napolo puts a curse on her relationship. When Sylvia still refuses him, he abducts her. In the end Ralph rescues her and he also reveals Napolo to be the villain he really is.

Typical of the time, the film represents blacks as either evil voodoo practitioners or the gullible followers thereof. CW

The Woman in White
British & Dominions; b/w; length unknown; Great Britain
D/Co-S/P: Herbert Wilcox *Co-S:* Robert Cullen *C:* David Kesson
Cast: Blanche Sweet, Haddon Mason, Cecil Humphreys, Louise Prussing, Frank Perfitt, Minna Grey

This was the first British version of author Wilkie Collins' *The Woman in White*. There had previously been at least four official versions (two in 1912 and two in 1917) and one unofficial version (*The Twin Pawns*) in 1919.

The story concerns a ghostly woman in white who appears around the estate of a recently married heiress (Sweet), whose husband (Humphreys) is out to steal her inheritance. The heir-

After having earned the father's respect, however, Bobby jeopardizes everything by succumbing to the advances of the sultry Madame de Sylva (Taylor). Tiger informs him that de Sylva is Toyo's mother, who abandoned her family shortly after her daughter was born. He persuades Bobby to return with him to his home in Indochina, where Toyo obliviously awaits. But de Sylva, determined to steal Bobby for herself, follows.

Immediately after the delirious *West of Zanzibar* (1929), Lon Chaney and Tod Browning reteamed for this lurid jungle horror film. The scenario is pure melodrama, but Browning's propensity for dark perversity breathes a disturbed sort of life into the proceedings. And while the whole thing at times teeters dangerously close to camp, it builds to a memorably fevered and satisfying conclusion.

Chaney is in excellent form as the scarred but tender Tiger Haynes. The character of Tiger—a misfit pining for the girl of his dreams—is a change from Chaney's typical screen persona, allowing him to display a tenderness lacking in his other roles for Browning. Lupe Velez is effective as the loving and playful Toyo, while Estelle Taylor is convincingly venomous as the femme fatale.

ess' sister (Prussing) discovers the plot but falls ill and awakens to find that her sister has died. In the end, the late heiress' former lover (Mason) discovers the truth. The heiress had had a lookalike—the woman in white—an escapee from a nearby asylum. It was this woman who died and was buried in the heiress' stead, while the husband placed the heiress in the insane asylum.

Creaky stuff for sure, the plot wasn't original even when Collins wrote his novel in the mid-1800s. (Gothic romance writers had been peddling similar stories for a century.) Sources are conflicted as to whether the film was shot in England or Scotland.

Blanche Sweet (1896-1986), who played the dual role of the heiress and her lookalike, was a formidable actress during the silent era, portraying such famous heroines as *Anna Christie* (1923) and *Tess of the D'Urbervilles* (1924). She had started out as a baby star on Broadway before being discovered by fledgling director D.W. Griffith in 1909 and later working for Cecil B. DeMille. In 1922 she married director Marshal Neillan, who is mostly remembered today for his horror films. They divorced in 1929. After a few failed attempts at making a mark in the new talkie cinema, Sweet went back to Broadway.

While Herbert Wilcox directed numerous films during his career, he was better known as a producer, making well over 100 films on that front.

The next version of Collins' tale, *The Crimes at the Dark House* (1940), was by far the most horrific, while the most famous version, *The Woman in White* (1948), was perhaps the least so. CW

Right: Lon Chaney in the lurid jungle horror *Where East is East*

1895-1929 349

Bibliography/Suggested Reading List

Blake, Michael F. *The Films of Lon Chaney* (Lanham: Madison Books, 1998)
Davies, David Stuart. *Starring Sherlock Holmes* (London: Titan Books, 2001)
Eisner, Lotte H. *The Haunted Screen: Expressionism in the German Cinema and the Influence of Max Reinhardt* (Berkeley: University of California Press, 2008)
Eisner, Lotte H. *Murnau* (Berkeley: University of California Press, 1973)
Everson, William K. *Classics of the Horror Film* (New York: Citadel Press, 1990)
Everson, William K. *More Classics of the Horror Film: Fifty Years of Great Chillers* (New York: Citadel Press, 1990)
Frank, Alan. *Horror Films* (London: Hamlyn, 1977)
Griep, Maark and Margorie Mikasen. *ReAction! Chemistry in the Movies: Chemistry Movie Blog* (Oxford University Press/Alfred P. Sloan Foundation; n.d.)
Gunning, Tom. *The Films of Fritz Lang: Allegories of Vision and Modernity* (London: British Film Institute, 2000)
Hardy, Phil. *The Overlook Film Encyclopedia: Horror* (New York: Overlook Press, 1993)
Hardy, Phil. *The Overlook Film Encyclopedia: Science Fiction* (New York: Overlook Press, 1994)
Harty, Kevin J. *The Reel Middle Ages: American, Western and Eastern European, Middle Eastern and Asian Films about Medieval Europe* (Jefferson: McFarland & Company, Inc.. 2006)
Hedges, Inez. *Framing Faust: Twentieth-Century Cultural Struggles* (Carbondale: Southern Illinois University Press, 2005)
Jacobs, Stephen. *Boris Karloff: More Than a Monster* (Sheffield: Tomahawk Press, 2011)
Kalat, David. *The Strange Case of Dr. Mabuse* (Jefferson: McFarland & Company, Inc., 2005)
Kinnard, Roy. *Horror in Silent Films: A Filmography: 1896-1929* (Jefferson: McFarland & Company, Inc.. 1999)
McGilligan. *Fritz Lang: The Nature of the Beast* (New York: Faber and Faber, 1997)
Ragone, August. *Eiji Tsuburaya: Master of Monsters* (San Francisco: Chronicle Books, 2014)
Riley, Philip J. *A Blind Bargain* (Atlantic City: MagicImage, 1988)
Riley, Philip J. *The Phantom of the Opera* (Absecon: MagicImage, 1999)
Silver, Alain and James Ursini. *The Vampire Film: From Nosferatu to True Blood* (Milwaukee, Limelight Editions, 2011)
Skal, David J. and Elias Savada. *Dark Carnival: The Secret World of Tod Browning* (New York: Anchor Books, 1995)
Skal, David J. *The Monster Show: A Cultural History of Horror* (New York: W.W. Norton & Company, 1993)
Soister, John T., Henry Nicolella, Steve Joyce, and Harry H. Long. *American Silent Horror, Science Fiction and Fantasy Feature Films, 1913-1929* (Jefferson: McFarland & Company, Inc., 2010)
Soister, John T. and Pat Wilks Battle. *Conrad Veidt on Screen* (Jefferson: McFarland & Company, 2009)
Soister, John T. *Up From the Vault: Rare Thrillers of the 1920s and 1930s* (Jefferson: McFarland & Company, Inc., 2004)
Svehla, Gary J. and Susan Svehla, eds. *Midnight Marquee Actors Series: Boris Karloff* (Baltimore: Midnight Marquee, 1996)
Twitchell, James B. *Dreadful Pleasures: An Anatomy of Modern Horror* (New York: Oxford University Press, 1985)

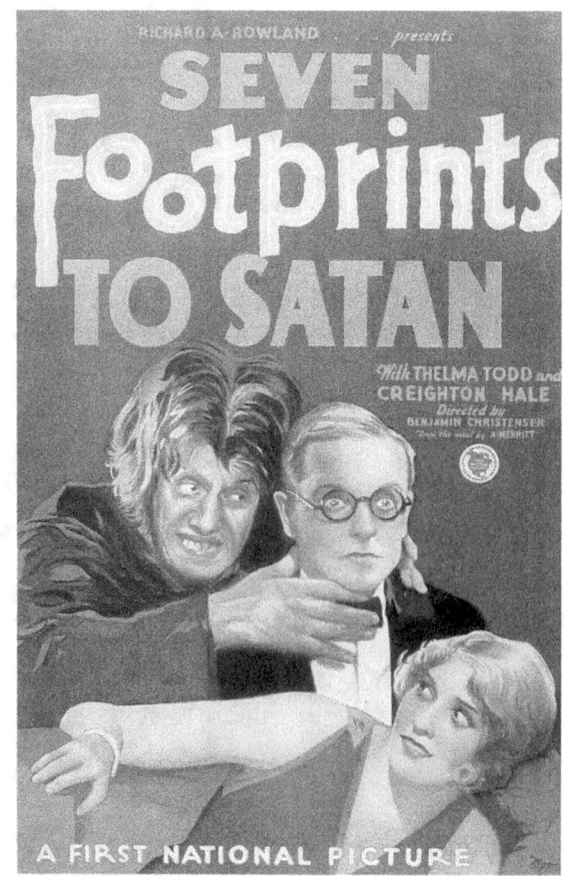

Index of Film Titles

£1000 Pound Spook, The, see *The Thousand Pound Spook*, 1907 ... 40
13 Club, The, see *The Thirteen Club*, 1905 ... 35
7 Castles of the Devil, The, see *The Seven Castles of the Devil*, 1901 ... 27
Aaron's Rod, 1923 ... 257
Accursed Cave, see *The Cave of the Demons*, 1898 ... 17
Adachihara Ubagaike yurei, 1915 ... 143
Adventure of the Torture Cage, The, see *The Torture Cage*, 1928 ... 334
Adventures of Three Knights, The, 1913 ... 105
After the Welsh Rabbit, see *After the Welsh Rarebit*, 1913 ... 105
After the Welsh Rarebit, 1913 ... 105
Agony of Fear, The, 1915 ... 143
Akakabe myojin, 1918 ... 196
Akakabe myojin, 1920 ... 212
Akikusa dōrō, 1927 ... 309
Alchemist, The, 1913 ... 105
alchemiste Parafaragaramus ou la cornue infernale, L', see *The Mysterious Retort*, 1906 ... 36
All Souls' Eve, 1921 ... 231
Alone With a Devil, see *Alone With the Devil*, 1914 ... 124
Alone With the Devil, 1914 ... 124
Alraune, 1918 ... 196
Alraune, 1918 ... 197
Alraune, 1928 ... 321
Alraune, die Henkerstochter, genannt die rote Hanne, see *Alraune*, 1918 ... 197
American Suicide Club, The, 1910 ... 64
Amore di sirena, see *The Love of a Siren*, 1911 ... 88
Ancestor's Legacy, An, 1914 ... 124
Ancient Roman, The, 1909 ... 50
Andalusian Dog, An, see *Un Chien Andalou*, 1929 ... 338
Andalusian Superstition, 1912 ... 91
Andere Ich, Das, see *The Other Self*, 1918 ... 201
Andere, Der, see *The Other*, 1913 ... 115
Anita, see *Trance*, 1920 ... 231
Another Job for the Undertaker, 1901 ... 24
Another's Ghost, 1910 ... 64
Antique Dealer, The, see *The Greater Will*, 1915 ... 151
antre infernale, L', 1905 ... 33
Antrere de la Sorciere, L', see *The Witch's Cave*, 1906 ... 37
Ape, The, 1928 ... 322
Apparitions, 1903 ... 28
Arima kaibyô-den, see *Arima no neko*, 1920 ... 212
Arima no neko sodo, 1916 ... 168
Arima no neko, 1920 ... 212
Arima no neko, 1922 ... 244
Arrow Maiden, The, 1915 ... 143
Asajigahara hitsotsuya, 1922 ... 244
Asamagatake, see *Kaidan Asamagatake*, 1914
Ashridge Castle—The Monmouth Rebellion, 1926 ... 295
Ass's Skin, The, see *The Magic Skin*, 1915 ... 157
Astronomer's Dream, The, 1898 ... 16
At The Mercy of Tiberius, see *The Price of Silence*, 1920 ... 230

At the Sign of the Jack O' Lantern, 1922 ... 245
At the Villa Rose, 1920 ... 212
Atlantide, L', see *Missing Husbands*, 1921 ... 241
atleta fantasma, L', 1919 ... 203
Au secours! 1924 ... 273
Auberge du bon repos, L', see *Inn Where No Man Rests*, 1903 ... 31
Auberge ensorcelé, L', see *The Bewitched Inn*, 1897 ... 14
Auberge rouge, L', see *The Red Inn*, 1910 ... 77
Auberge rouge, L', see *The Red Inn*, 1923 ... 267
Augen der Mumie Ma, Die, see *The Eyes of the Mummy*, 1918 ... 198
Aunt Eliza Recovers Her Pet, 1907 ... 37
Avenging Conscience, or: 'Thou Shalt Not Kill', The, 1914 ... 124
Avenging Hand, The, 1915 ... 144
aventures de baron de Münchausen, Le, see *Baron Munchausen's Dream*, 1912 ... 92
Baby's Ghost, 1911 ... 81
Baddesley Manor—The Phantom Gambler, 1926 ... 296
Bâke ginnan, 1916 ... 168
Bâke Jizo, see *Jizo the Spook*, 1898 ... 18
Bâke-ichou, see *Bâke ginnan*, 1916 ... 168
Bakejizo, see *Jizo the Spook*, 1898 ... 18
Bâke-jizo, see *Jizo the Spook*, 1898 ... 18
Bakemono yashiki, 1921 ... 232
Balaoo ou Des pas au plafond, see *Balaoo*, 1913 ... 105
Balaoo the Demon Baboon, see *Balaoo*, 1913 ... 105
Balaoo, 1913 ... 105
Ballad of a Witch, The, 1909 ... 51
Ballata di una Strega, La, see *The Ballad of a Witch*, 1909 ... 51
Banchō sarayashika, 1914 ... 126
Banchō sarayashika, 1928 ... 322
Banchō sarayashiki, 1922 ... 245
Banchō sarayashiki, 1927 ... 310
Banshū sarayashika, see *Banchō sarayashika*, 1928 ... 322
Banshū Sarayashiki, see *Banchō sarayashiki*, 1922 ... 245
Barbe-bleue, see *Blue Beard*, 1901 ... 25
Bargain with Satan, A, see *The Student of Prague*, 1913 ... 119
Baron Munchausen's Dream, 1912 ... 92
Barton Mystery, The, 1920 ... 213
Basilisk, The, 1914 ... 126
Bat, The, 1926 ... 296
Bat, The, see *The Circular Staircase*, 1915 ... 145
Batty Bill and the Suicide Club, 1914 ... 126
Bear's Marriage, The, see *The Bear's Wedding*, 1925 ... 283
Bear's Wedding, The, 1925 ... 283
beau-fils du cauchemar, Le, see *A Son-in-Law's Nightmare*, 1912 ... 102
Bébé and Spiritualism, 1912 ... 92
Bébé fait du spiritisme, see *Bébé and Spiritualism*, 1912 ... 92
Beechwood Ghost, The, 1910 ... 65
Beelzebub's Daughters, 1903 ... 29
Beelzebub's Daughters, or the Women of Fire, see *Beelzebub's Daughters*, 1903 ... 29
Beetle, The, 1919 ... 203
Behind Red Curtains, see *One Hour Before Dawn*, 1920 ... 227
Behind the Curtain, 1924 ... 273
Bei Den Teufelsanbetern, see *The Devil Worshippers*, 1920 ... 215
Bells, The, 1911 ... 81

Bells, The, 1913 ... 106
Bells, The, 1914 ... 127
Bells, The, 1918 ... 197
Bells, The, 1923 ... 258
Bells, The, 1925 ... 283
Bells, The, 1926 ... 296
Belphegor, 1927 ... 310
Beneath the Tower Ruins, 1911 ... 81
Bertie's Book of Magic, 1912 ... 92
Between Two Worlds, see *Destiny*, 1921 ... 233
Bewildering Cabinet, The, 1907 ... 37
Bewitch Inn, The, see *The Bewitched Inn*, 1897 ... 14
Bewitched Inn, The, 1897 ... 14
Bewitched Manor House, The, 1909 ... 51
Bewitched Manor, The, see *The Bewitched Manor House*, 1909 ... 51
Bewitched Matches, The, 1913 ... 107
Bewitched Messenger, The, 1910 ... 65
Bewitched Restaurant, see *Haunted Café*, 1911 ... 84
Bewitched Shepherd, see *The Witch's Cave*, 1906 ... 37
Bewitched Window, The, 1911 ... 81
Beyond the Wall, see *Destiny*, 1921 ... 233
Bildnis des Dorian Gray, Das, see *The Picture of Dorian Gray*, 1917 ... 191
Bill Taken for a Ghost, 1911 ... 82
Billy Gets Married, see *The Haunted Honeymoon*, 1925 ... 285
Billy's Séance, 1912 ... 92
Bishop of the Ozarks, The, 1923 ... 258
Black Crook, The, 1916 ... 168
Black Opal, The, 1913 ... 107
Black Orchids, 1917 ... 181
Black Pearl, The, 1928 ... 322
Black Waters, 1929 ... 336
Blade af Satans bog, see *Leaves from Satan's Book*, 1921 ... 238
Blind Bargain, A, 1922 ... 245
Blood and Soul, 1923 ... 258
Blood Seedling, The, 1915 ... 144
Blood Vengeance, 1911 ... 82
Bloodstone, The, 1908 ... 41
Blue Beard, 1901 ... 25
Bluebeard, 1909 ... 51
Bob's Nightmare, 1912 ... 92
Bobby's Nightmare, The, 1905 ... 33
Bodiam Castle and Eric the Slender, 1926 ... 297
Bogey Woman, The, 1909 ... 51
Bogus Count, The, see *The Bogus Ghost*, 1916 ... 168
Bogus Ghost, The, 1916 ... 168
bon lit, Un, see *A Midnight Episode*, 1899 ... 20
Borgias, The, see *The Power of the Borgias*, 1920 ... 229
Botan dōrō, 1914 ... 127
Botan dōrō, 1921 ... 232
Botan dōrō, 1924 ... 274
Botan dōrō, 1926 ... 297
Botan tou no ki, 1929 ... 337
Bottle Imp, The, 1917 ... 181
Bourreau turc, Le, see *The Terrible Turkish Executioner*, 1904 ... 33
Brand of Evil, The, 1913 ... 107
Brand of Satan, 1917 ... 182

Brandherd, see *Torgus, the Coffin Maker*, 1921 ... 243
Bribe, The, 1915 ... 144
Bride of the Haunted Castle, The, 1910 ... 65
Brute, The, 1912 ... 92
Bucklige und die Tänzerin, Der, see *The Hunchback and the Dancer*, 1920 ... 223
Budda's Curse, The, 1910 ... 65
Buddha's Curse, The, see *The Budda's Curse*, 1910 ... 65
Buster's Spooks, 1929 ... 337
Butcher's Dream, The, 1909 ... 52
Buu, see *The Viy*, 1909 ... 63
By the House That Jack Built, 1911 ... 82
Cabby's Dream, The, 1906 ... 35
cabinet de Mephistopheles, Le, see *The Cabinet of Mephistopheles*, 1897 ... 14
Cabinet des Dr. Caligari, Das, see *The Cabinet of Dr. Caligari*, 1919 ... 204
Cabinet of Dr. Caligari, The, 1919 ... 204
Cabinet of Mephistopheles, The, 1897 ... 14
Café L'Egypte, The, 1924 ... 274
Cagliostro, 1910 ... 65
Cagliostro, 1918 ... 197
Cagliostro, 1920 ... 213
Cagliostro, 1929 ... 337
Cagliostro, aventurier, chimiste et magician, see *Cagliostro*, 1910 ... 65
Cagliostro's Mirror, 1899 ... 19
Cagliostro—Liebe und Leben eines großen Abenteurers, see *Cagliostro*, 1929 ... 337
Call From the Dead, 1915 ... 144
Call of Siva, The, 1923 ... 258
Case of Becky, The, 1915 ... 145
Case of Becky, The, 1921 ... 232
castello di Thornfield, Il, see *The Castle of Thornfield*, 1915 ... 145
Castle Ghost, The, 1910 ... 65
Castle Ghosts, The, 1908 ... 41
Castle of Thornfield, The, 1915 ... 145
Cat and the Canary, The, 1927 ... 311
Cat That Was Changed into a Woman, The, 1909 ... 52
Cat That Was Changed into a Woman, The, 1910 ... 66
Cat's Revenge, The, 1908 ... 41
cauchemar de Rigadin, Le, see *Whiffle's Nightmare*, 1912 ... 104
Cauchemar, Le, see *A Nightmare*, 1896 ... 13
Cavalier's Dream, The, 1898 ... 17
Cave Demons, see *The Cave of the Demons*, 1898 ... 17
Cave of the Demons, The, 1898 ... 17
Cave of the Spooks, 1908 ... 41
caverne maudite, La, see *The Cave of the Demons*, 1898 ... 17
Chamber of Horrors, 1929 ... 337
Chamber of Horrors, The, see *Conscience*, 1912 ... 92
Charlatan, The, 1929 ... 338
chasse au Bois hanté, La, see *Shooting in the Haunted Woods*, 1909 ... 62
Château hanté, Le, see *The Haunted Castle*, 1897 ... 15
Chatte metamorphose en femme, La, see *The Cat That Was Changed into a Woman*, 1910 ... 66
Chaudron infernal, Le, see *The Infernal Cauldron*, 1903 ... 30
Cheval Mystery, The, 1915 ... 145

Chevalier des neiges, Le, see *The Knight of the Snows,* 1912 ... 96
Chi to rei, see *Blood and Soul,* 1923 ... 258
Chibusa enoki: Takeda genpachiro see *Kaidan chibusa enoki,* 1917 ... 190
Chibusa no enoki, 1910 ... 66
Chien Andalou, Un, 1929 ... 338
chien des Baskerville, Le, see *The Hound of the Baskervilles,* 1914 ... 132
Children of Edward IV, The, 1910 ... 66
Children of Edward, The, see *The Children of Edward IV,* 1910 ... 66
Chimes, The, 1914 ... 127
Chinese Magic, 1900 ... 22
Chirugien Americain, A, see *A Twentieth Century Surgeon,* 1897 ... 16
Chronicles of Bloom Center, The, 1915 ... 145
Chute de la maison Usher, La, see *The Fall of the House of Usher,* 1928 ... 322
Circular Staircase, The, 1915 ... 145
Cleopatra, 1899 ... 19
Cleopatra's Tomb, see *Cleopatra,* 1899 ... 19
Cléopâtre, see *Cleopatra,* 1899 ... 19
Clock-Maker's Secret, The, 1907 ... 37
Closet, The, see *The Bewildering Cabinet,* 1907 ... 37
Clown Hero, The, 1913 ... 107
Club des suicides, Le, see *The Suicide Club,* 1909 ... 63
Club Pest, The, 1915 ... 146
Clue of the Pigtail, The, 1923 ... 259
Coffin Maker, The, see *Johann the Coffinmaker,* 1927 ... 313
collier de Kali, Le, see *What the Gods Decree,* 1913 ... 123
Colonne de feu, La, see *Pillar of Fire,* 1899 ... 21
Column of Fire, The, see *Pillar of Fire,* 1899 ... 21
Conscience, 1912 ... 92
Conscience, The, 1905 ... 34
Convict Guardian's Nightmare, The, 1909 ... 52
Convicted by Hypnotism, 1912 ... 93
cottage hante, Le, 1913 ... 107
Coughing Horror, The, 1924 ... 274
Count of Cagliostro, The, see *Cagliostro,* 1920 ... 213
Countess Ankarstrom, 1910 ... 66
Cragmire Tower, 1924 ... 274
Craving, The, 1918 ... 197
Creaking Stairs, 1919 ... 205
Crime and the Penalty, 1916 ... 168
Crime de Lord Arthur Savile, Le, see *Lord Arthur Savile's Crime,* 1921 ... 239
Crimson Moth, The, 1914 ... 127
Crimson Stain Mystery, The, 1916 ... 169
Crown of Richard III, The, 1914 ... 128
Cry in the Night, A, 1915 ... 146
Cry of the Nighthawk, The, 1923 ... 259
Curse of Greed, The, see *The Twin Pawns,* 1919 ... 211
Curse of the Crimson Idol, The, 1914 ... 128
Curse of the Hindoo Pearl, The, 1912 ... 93
Curse of the Hindu Pearl, The, see *The Curse of the Hindoo Pearl,* 1912 ... 93
Curse of the Scarabee Ruby, The, 1914 ... 128
Curse of the Wandering Minstrel, The, 1910 ... 66

D.T.'s, or the Effect of Drink, 1905 ... 34
dama di picche, La, see *Queen of Spades,* 1911 ... 90
dama di Picche, La, see *The Queen of Spades,* 1913 ... 117
dame de pique, La, see *The Queen of Spades,* 1913 ... 117
damnation de Faust, Le, see *The Damnation of Faust,* 1898 ... 17
Damnation du Docteur Faust, see *Faust and Marguerite,* 1904 ... 32
Damnation of Faust, The, 1898 ... 17
Damnation of Faust, The, 1903 ... 29
Dance of Death, 1919 ... 206
Dance of Fire, The, see *Pillar of Fire,* 1899 ... 21
Dandy Dick of Bishopgate, 1911 ... 83
Dangers of Hypnosis, The, see *The Lost Soul, or: The Dangers of Hypnosis,* 1923 ... 264
danse de feu, La, see *Pillar of Fire,* 1899 ... 21
Danse Macabre, 1922 ... 245
Dante's Inferno, 1924 ... 274
Dante's Inferno, see *Inferno,* 1911 ... 86
Dante's Purgatorio, see *Purgatory,* 1911 ... 89
Dark Mirror, The, 1920 ... 213
Darkened Rooms, 1929 ... 339
Darling of Paris, The, 1917 ... 183
Daughter of Nature, see *Alraune,* 1928 ... 321
Daughter of the Gods, A, 1916 ... 169
Daughters of the Devil, The, see *Beelzebub's Daughters,* 1903 ... 29
Davy Jones' Locker, 1900 ... 22
Dead Alive, The, 1916 ... 170
Dead Secret, The, 1913 ... 107
Deal with the Devil, A, 1914 ... 128
Deal with the Devil, A, 1916 ... 170
Dearie, see *Creaking Stairs,* 1919 ... 205
Death, 1910 ... 66
Death, 1921 ... 233
Death in Real Estate, A, 1914 ... 128
Death of Dracula, The, see *Drakula halála,* 1921 ... 234
Death Stone of India, The, 1913 ... 107
Decapitation in Turkey, see *The Terrible Turkish Executioner,* 1904 ... 33
Défaite de Satan, La, see *The Defeat of Satan,* 1910 ... 67
Defeat of Satan, The, 1910 ... 67
Delirium, see *The Craving,* 1918 ... 197
Demon Barber, The, 1899 ... 19
Demon of Dunkirque, The, 1910 ... 67
Demon, The, 1911 ... 83
Demonio, see *The Demon,* 1911 ... 83
Desire, 1920 ... 214
Destiny, 1921 ... 233
Destiny's Skein, 1915 ... 146
Devil, The, 1908 ... 41
Devil, The, 1915 ... 146
Devil, The, 1921 ... 233
Devil and the Gambler, The, see *The Gambler and the Devil,* 1908 ... 43
Devil and the Statue, The, 1901 ... 25
Devil and Tom Walker, The, 1913 ... 108
Devil as a Lawyer, The, 1911 ... 83
Devil in a Convent, The, 1899 ... 20
Devil Stone, The, see *The Devil-Stone,* 1917 ... 184
Devil to Pay, The, 1915 ... 147

Devil to Pay, The, 1920 ... 214
Devil Worshippers, The, 1920 ... 215
Devil's Angel, The, see *The Sleep of Cyma Roget*, 1920 ... 230
Devil's Assistant, The, 1917 ... 184
Devil's Bondman, The, see *The Scorpion's Sting*, 1915 ... 162
Devil's Bondsman, The, see *The Scorpion's Sting*, 1915 ... 162
Devil's Bondwoman, The, 1916 ... 170
Devil's Castle, The, 1896 ... 12
Devil's Die, The, see *The Devil's Bondwoman*, 1916 ... 170
Devil's Forge, The, see *Satan's Smithy*, 1909 ... 61
Devil's Laboratory, The, see *The Cabinet of Mephistopheles*, 1897 ... 14
Devil's Locksmith, The, 1919 ... 206
Devil's Locksmiths, The, see *The Devil's Locksmith*, 1919 ... 206
Devil's Manor, The, see *The Devil's Castle*, 1896 ... 12
Devil's Money Bags, The, see *The Treasures of Satan*, 1902 ... 28
Devil's Mother-in-Law, The, 1910 ... 67
Devil's Profession, The, 1915 ... 147
Devil's Seven Castles, see *The Seven Castles of the Devil*, 1901 ... 27
Devil's Sonata, The, 1911 ... 83
Devil's Stone, The, see *The Devil-Stone*, 1917 ... 184
Devil's Toy, The, 1916 ... 170
Devil-Stone, The, 1917 ... 184
Diable au convent, Le, see *The Devil in a Convent*, 1899 ... 20
Diable géant ou le miracle de la madone, Le, see *The Devil and the Statue*, 1901 ... 25
Diabolical Box, A, 1912 ... 93
Diamond of Disaster, The, 1914 ... 129
Distilled Spirits, 1915 ... 147
Doctor Polly, 1914 ... 129
Doctor Pyckle and Mister Pride, see *Dr. Pyckle and Mr. Pride*, 1925 ... 284
Doddet Halsband, see *Necklace of the Dead*, 1910 ... 76
Doden, see *Death*, 1910 ... 66
Dodes Halsband, Den, see *Necklace of the Dead*, 1910 ... 76
Doktor Nikola III, see *The Mystery of the Lama Convent*, 1909 ... 59
Doktor Satansohn, 1916 ... 171
Doll's Revenge, The, 1907 ... 38
Dominant Will, The, see *Forces of Evil; or, The Dominant Will, The*, 1914 ... 131
Don Juan and Faust, 1922 ... 246
Don Juan et Faust, see *Don Juan and Faust*, 1922 ... 246
Don Juan Tenorio, 1898 ... 18
Don Juan Tenorio, 1908 ... 42
Don Juan Tenorio, 1909 ... 52
Don Juan Tenorio, 1922 ... 247
Doomed, 1909 ... 51
Dorfsgolem, Der, see *The Golem's Last Adventure*, 1921 ... 235
Dorian Gray Arckepe, see *The Picture of Dorian Gray*, 1918 ... 201
Dorian Gray Portrait, see *Dorian Grays Portraet*, 1910 ... 67
Dorian Gray's Portrait, see *Dorian Grays Portraet*, 1910 ... 67
Dorian Grays Portraet, 1910 ... 67
Double Life, A, see *Convicted by Hypnotism*, 1912 ... 93
Double vie, see *Convicted by Hypnotism*, 1912 ... 93
Dr. Jekyll and Mr. Hyde, 1908 ... 42
Dr. Jekyll and Mr. Hyde, 1908 ... 43
Dr. Jekyll and Mr. Hyde, 1910 ... 68
Dr. Jekyll and Mr. Hyde, 1912 ... 93
Dr. Jekyll and Mr. Hyde, 1913 ... 108
Dr. Jekyll and Mr. Hyde, 1920 ... 215
Dr. Jekyll and Mr. Hyde, 1920 ... 216
Dr. Jekyll and Mr. Hyde, 1920 ... 217
Dr. Jekyll and Mr. Hyde, Done To a Frazzle, 1914 ... 129
Dr. Jekyll and Mr. Hyde, see *Der Januskopf*, 1920 ... 224
Dr. Jekyll and Mr. Hyde; or, a Strange Case, see *Dr. Jekyll and Mr. Hyde*, 1910 ... 68
Dr. Mabuse the Gambler, 1922 ... 247
Dr. Mabuse, der Spieler, see *Dr. Mabuse the Gambler*, 1922 ... 247
Dr. Mabuse, der Spieler—Ein Bild der Zeit, see *Dr. Mabuse the Gambler*, 1922 ... 247
Dr. Mabuse, King of Crime, see *Dr. Mabuse the Gambler*, 1922 ... 247
Dr. Mesner's Fatal Prediction, see *Dr. Mesner's Fatal Prescription*, 1910 ... 68
Dr. Mesner's Fatal Prescription, 1910 ... 68
Dr. Nicola in Tibet, see *The Mystery of the Lama Convent*, 1909 ... 59
Dr. Pyckle and Mr. Pride, 1925 ... 284
Dr. Pyckle and Mr. Pryde, see *Dr. Pyckle and Mr. Pride*, 1925 ... 284
Dr. Trimball's Secret, see *Dr. Trimball's Verdict*, 1913 ... 109
Dr. Trimball's Verdict, 1913 ... 109
Dracula's Death, see *Drakula halála*, 1921 ... 234
Drakula halála, 1921 ... 234
Drama of the Castle, or Do the Dead Return?, A, 1915 ... 148
drame au chateau d'Acre, Un, see *A Drama of the Castle, or Do the Dead Return?* 1915 ... 148
drame au chateau d'Acre, Un, see *A Drama of the Castle, or Do the Dead Return?* 1915 ... 148
Dramma al castello d'Acre, Un, see *A Drama of the Castle, or Do the Dead Return?* 1915 ... 148
Dream Cheater, The, 1920 ... 218
Dream Dance, The, 1915 ... 148
Dream of an Opium Fiend, 1908 ... 43
Dream Woman, The, 1914 ... 129
Drums of Jeopardy, The, 1923 ... 259
Drunkard's Conversion, The, 1901 ... 26
Duality of Man, The, 1910 ... 68
Duel in the Dark, The, 1915 ... 148
Dungeon, The, 1922 ... 248
Dunkle Schloss, Der, see *The Hound of the Baskervilles: The Dark Castle*, 1915 ... 153
Dust of Egypt, The, 1915 ... 148
Dyavolat v Sofia, see *Satan in Sofia*, 1921 ... 242
Easy Pickings, 1927 ... 312
Edgar Allan Poe, see *Edgar Allen Poe*, 1909 ... 52
Edgar Allen Poe, 1909 ... 52
Edwin Drood, see *The Mystery of Edwin Drood*, 1914 ... 137
Eerie Tales, see *Weird Tales*, 1919 ... 211
Effects of Too Much Scotch, The, see *D.T.'s, or the Effect of Drink*, 1905 ... 34
effroi, L', 1913 ... 109
Egyptian Mystery, The, 1909 ... 53
Ek, a Fighting Soul, see *One Glorious Day*, 1922 ... 256
Ekspressens Mysterium, see *Alone With the Devil*, 1914 ... 124

Eksprestogets Mysterium, see *Alone with the Devil*, 1914 ... 124
Eleagable Kuperus, see *Nachtgestalten*, 1920 ... 226
Elet kiralya Dorian Gray, Az, see *The Picture of Dorian Gray*, 1918 ... 201
Elet kiralya, Az, see *The Picture of Dorian Gray*, 1918 ... 201
Eleventh Dimension, The, 1915 ... 148
emmuree des Balkans, L', 1910 ... 69
Enchanted Cup, The, 1903 ... 29
Enchanted Kiss, The, 1917 ... 184
Enchanted Well, The, 1903 ... 30
Enchanted Wreath, The, 1910 ... 69
Enfants d'Edouard, Les, see *The Children of Edward IV* 1910 ... 66
Enmeiin no semushi, see *The Hunchback of Enmei-in*, 1924 ... 277
Enmeiin no semushi-otoko, see *The Hunchback of Enmei-in*, 1924 ... 277
erede di Jago, L', see *The Spectre of Jago*, 1913 ... 118
eredità di Rodolfi, L', see *An Ancestor's Legacy*, 1914 ... 124
Erik the Great, see *The Last Performance*, 1927 ... 314
Esmeralda, 1905 ... 34
Esmeralda, 1922 ... 249
Esméralda, Le, see *Esmeralda*, 1905 ... 34
Eternal Penalty, The, see *The Warning*, 1915 ... 165
Eternal Sin, The, 1917 ... 185
Even As You and I, 1917 ... 185
Evil Philter, The, 1909 ... 53
Evil Power, An, 1911 ... 83
Evil Power, The, 1913 ... 109
Eyes in the Dark, see *Out of the Far East*, 1914 ... 138
Eyes of the Mummy Ma, see *The Eyes of the Mummy*, 1918 ... 198
Eyes of the Mummy, The, 1918 ... 198
Face at the Window, The, 1919 ... 206
Face at the Window, The, 1920 ... 218
Fairy Jewel, The, 1911 ... 83
Fairy of the Black Rocks, The, 1901 ... 26
Fairyland: or, the Kingdom of the Fairies, see *The Kingdom of Fairies*, 1903 ... 31
Fakier's Spell, The, see *The Fakir's Spell*, 1914 ... 129
Fakir's Spell, The, 1914 ... 129
Fall of the House of Usher, The, 1928 ... 322
Fall of the House of Usher, The, 1928 ... 323
Fall of the Romanoffs, The, 1917 ... 185
Fantasma del Castello, Il, see *The Castle Ghosts*, 1908 ... 41
Fantastical Meal, A, 1900 ... 22
fantôme d'Alger, Le, see *A Spiritualistic Meeting*, 1906 ... 36
fantôme du Moulin-Rouge, Le, see *The Phantom of the Moulin-Rouge*, 1924 ... 279
Fantôme, Le, see *The Phantom*, 1910 ... 76
Fatal Hand, The, 1907 ... 38
Fatal Invention, The, see *Dr. Jekyll and Mr. Hyde*, 1910 ... 68
Fatal Orchid, The, see *Black Orchids*, 1917 ... 181
Fatal Pact, The, 1912 ... 94
Fatal Pearl, The, 1912 ... 94
Fatal Ring, The, 1917 ... 186
Faust, 1909 ... 53
Faust, 1910 ... 69
Faust, 1910 ... 70
Faust, 1912 ... 94
Faust, 1915 ... 148
Faust, 1921 ... 234
Faust, 1922 ... 249
Faust, 1923 ... 160
Faust, 1926 ... 297
Faust, see *Faust and Mephistopheles*, 1903 ... 30
Faust and Marguerite, 1897 ... 14
Faust and Marguerite, 1900 ... 22
Faust and Marguerite, 1904 ... 32
Faust and Marguerite, 1911 ... 84
Faust and Mephistopheles, 1898 ... 18
Faust and Mephistopheles, 1903 ... 30
Faust aux enfers, see *The Damnation of Faust*, 1903 ... 29
Faust et Marguerite, see *Faust and Marguerite*, 1897 ... 14
Faust et Marguerite, see *Faust and Marguerite*, 1904 ... 32
Faust et Marguerite, see *Faust and Marguerite*, 1911 ... 84
Faust et Méphistophélès, see *Faust and Mephistopheles*, 1903 ... 30
Faust sauvé des enfers, see *The Saving of Faust*, 1911 ... 90
Faust—Eine deutsch Vokssage, see *Faust*, 1926 ... 297
Fear, 1917 ... 186
Feathertop, 1912 ... 95
Feathertop, 1913 ... 109
Feathertop, 1916 ... 171
Fée Carabosse ou le poignard fatal, La, see *The Witch*, 1906 ... 37
fée des roches noires, Le, see *The Fairy of the Black Rocks*, 1901 ... 26
femme bogey, La, see *The Bogey Woman*, 1909 ... 51
Fiaccola sotto il moggio, see *Blood Vengeance*, 1911 ... 82
Fiends of Hell, The, 1914 ... 130
Fiery Hand, The, 1923 ... 260
Fight with Sledge Hammers, A, 1902 ... 27
Figures of the Night, see *Nachtgestalten*, 1920 ... 226
fille du diable, Le, see *Beelzebub's Daughters*, 1903 ... 29
fils du diable fait la noce à Paris, Le, see *Mephisto's Son*, 1906 ... 35
Fisherman's Nightmare, The, 1911 ... 84
Five Sinister Stories, see *Weird Tales*, 1919 ... 211
Flames, 1917 ... 187
Fleur de Jeunesse, see *The Flower of Youth*, 1908 ... 43
Flower of Youth, The, 1908 ... 43
Fog, see *Black Waters*, 1929 ... 336
Foiled, 1915 ... 149
Forbidden Fruit, The, 1910 ... 70
Forbidden Room, The, 1914 ... 130
Forces of Evil, The, see *Forces of Evil; or, The Dominant Will, The*, 1914 ... 131
Forces of Evil; or, The Dominant Will, The, 1914 ... 131
Forge du Diable, La, see *Satan's Smithy*, 1909 ... 61
Fox Woman, The, 1915 ... 149
Frankenstein, 1910 ... 70
Frankenstein, see *Life Without Soul*, 1915 ... 156
Frankenstein's Monster, see *The Monster of Frankenstein*, 1920 ... 226
Freak Barber, The, 1905 ... 35
Freak of Ferndale Forest, The, 1910 ... 71
Frequentierte Mann, Der, see *The Haunted Man*, 1909 ... 54
Frilby Frilled, see *Trilby Frilled*, 1916 ... 179
From Death to Life, 1911 ... 84
From the Beyond, 1913 ... 110

From the River's Depths, see *Call From the Dead*, 1915 ... 144
fruit défendu, Le, see *The Forbidden Fruit*, 1910 ... 70
Fune yurei, 1914 ... 131
Fungi Cellars, The, 1923 ... 261
Funnicus and the Ghost, see *Gavroche and the Spirits*, 1912 ... 95
Funnicus' Ghost, see *Gavroche and the Spirits*, 1912 ... 95
Furcht, see *Fear*, 1917 ... 186
Gambler and the Devil, The, 1908 ... 43
Gavroche and the Spirits, 1912 ... 95
Gavroche et les spirits, see *Gavroche and the Spirits*, 1912 ... 95
Gefahren der Hypnose, Das, see *The Lost Soul, or: The Dangers of Hypnosis*, 1923
Geheimnisse einer Seele, see *Secrets of a Soul*, 1926 ... 304
Geheimnisvolle Klub, Der, see *The Suicide Club*, 1913 ... 120
Geheimnisvolle Spiegel, Der, see *The Mystic Mirror*, 1928 ... 328
Geisterzug, see *The Ghost Train*, 1927 ... 312
gemma solitaria, La, see *The Fairy Jewel*, 1911 ... 83
Gems of Literature #6: The Bells, see *The Bells*, 1922 ... 258
Genio del Lago, Il, see *The Spirit of the Lake*, 1910 ... 79
Genuine, die Tragödie eines seltsamen Hauses, see *Genuine: A Tale of a Vampire*, 1920 ... 218
Genuine, see *Genuine: A Tale of a Vampire*, 1920 ... 218
Genuine: A Tale of a Vampire, 1920 ... 218
Gevatter Tod, see *Death*, 1921 ... 233
Ghost Breaker, The, 1914 ... 131
Ghost Breaker, The, 1922 ... 249
Ghost Fakirs, The, 1915 ... 149
Ghost Holiday, The, 1907 ... 38
Ghost Hounds, 1917 ... 187
Ghost House, The, 1917 ... 187
Ghost in the Garret, The, 1921 ... 235
Ghost in the Oven, The, 1910 ... 71
Ghost of Mudtown, The, 1910 ... 71
Ghost of Old Morro, The, 1917 ... 188
Ghost of Sea View Manor, The, 1913 ... 110
Ghost of Seaview Manor, The, see *The Ghost of Sea View Manor*, 1913 ... 110
Ghost of Slumber Mountain, The, 1918 ... 199
Ghost of Sulphur Mountain, The, 1912 ... 95
Ghost of the Hacienda, 1913 ... 110
Ghost of the Mine, The, 1914 ... 131
Ghost of the Oven, The, see *The Ghost in the Oven*, 1910 ... 71
Ghost of the Rancho, The, 1918 ... 200
Ghost of the White Lady, The, 1913 ... 110
Ghost of Tolson Manor, The, see *A Son of Satan*, 1924 ... 280
Ghost of Tolston's Manor, The, see *A Son of Satan*, 1924 ... 280
Ghost of Twisted Oaks, 1915 ... 149
Ghost of Whispering Oaks, The, see *The Haunted Bedroom*, 1919 ... 207
Ghost Story, The, 1907 ... 38
Ghost Train, The, 1927 ... 312
Ghost, The, 1913 ... 110
Ghost's Warning, The, 1911 ... 84
Ghostly Affair, A, 1914 ... 131
Ghostly Band, The, see *The Tower of the Phantoms*, 1914 ... 141
Ghosts and Fly Paper, see *Ghosts and Flypaper*, 1915 ... 150
Ghosts and Flypaper, 1915 ... 150
Ghosts and Flypapers, see *Ghosts and Flypaper*, 1915 ... 150

Ghosts, 1912 ... 95
Ghosts, 1914 ... 132
Ghosts, The, 1913 ... 110
    Ghosts; or Who's Afraid? See *The Ghost*, 1913 ... 110
Ghosts, The, see *The Spiritist*, 1914 ... 140
Glamis Castle, 1926 ... 299
Glory of Love, The, see *While Paris Sleeps*, 1923
Go and Get It, 1920 ... 219
Golden Beetle, The, 1907 ... 39
Golden Beetle, The, 1910 ... 72
Golden Pomegranates, The, 1924 ... 275
Golem and the Dancing Girl, The, 1917 ... 188
Golem und die Tänzerin, Der, see *The Golem and the Dancing Girl*, 1917 ... 188
Golem, Der, see *The Golem*, 1915 ... 150
Golem, Der, see *The Golem: How He Came into the World*, 1920 ... 219
Golem, The, 1915 ... 150
Golem, The, see *The Golem: How He Came into the World*, 1920 ... 219
Golem: How He Came into the World, The, 1920 ... 219
Golem: Wie Er in die Welt Kam, see *The Golem: How He Came into the World*, 1920 ... 219
Golem's Last Adventure, The, 1921 ... 235
Golems Letzte Abenteuer, Des, see *The Golem's Last Adventure*, 1921 ... 235
Good Bed, A, see *A Midnight Episode*, 1899 ... 20
Gorilla, The, 1927 ... 313
Graf Cagliostro, see *Cagliostro*, 1929 ... 337
Graf von Cagliostro, Der, see *Cagliostro*, 1920 ... 213
Gräfin Ankarström, see *Countess Ankarstrom*, 1910 ... 66
Grasping Hand, The, 1916 ... 171
Gray Horror, The, 1915 ... 151
Great London Mystery, The, 1920 ... 220
Greater Will, The, 1915 ... 151
Green Archer, The, 1925 ... 284
Green Eye of the Yellow God, The, 1913 ... 111
Green Ghost, The, see *The Unholy Night*, 1929 ... 347
Green Mist, The, 1924 ... 276
Green-Eyed Monster, The, 1916 ... 171
Grey Dame, The, see *The Grey Lady*, 1909 ... 54
Grey Lady, The, 1909 ... 54
    Graa Dame, Den, see *The Grey Lady*, 1909 ... 54
Greywater Park, 1924 ... 276
Grinning Face, The, see *The Man Who Laughs*, 1921 ... 239
Grinsende Gesicht, Das, see *The Man Who Laughs*, 1921 ... 239
grotte des esprits, La, see *Cave of the Spooks*, 1908 ... 41
Guarding Britain's Secrets, see *The Fiends of Hell*, 1914 ... 130
Guy of Warwick, 1926 ... 299
Habeas Corpus, 1928 ... 324
Hachisuka no neko, 1922 ... 250
Hallucinations du Baron de Münchausen, Le, see *Baron Munchausen's Dream*, 1912 ... 92
Hallucinations pharmaceutiques ou le truc du potard, see *Pharmaceutical Hallucinations*, 1908 ... 45
Hampton Court Palace, 1926 ... 299
Hand of the Skeleton, The, 1915 ... 152
Hands Invisible, 1914 ... 132

Hands of Orlac, 1924 … 276
Hanging Lamp, The, 1908 … 43
Haunted, 1915 … 152
Haunted, 1916 … 171
Haunted Attic, The, 1915 … 152
Haunted Bedroom, The, 1907 … 39
Haunted Bedroom, The, 1913 … 111
Haunted Bedroom, The, 1919 … 207
Haunted Bell, The, 1916 … 172
Haunted by Conscience, 1910 … 72
Haunted Café, 1911 … 84
Haunted Castle, The, 1897 … 15
Haunted Castle, The, 1921 … 235
Haunted Castle, The, see *The Devil's Castle*, 1896 … 12
Haunted Castles: Ashridge Castle, see *Ashridge Castle—The Monmouth Rebellion*, 1926 … 295
Haunted Castles: Kenilworth Castle, see *Kenilworth Castle and Amy Robsart*, 1926 … 300
Haunted Chamber, The, 1913 … 111
Haunted Curiosity Shop, The, 1901 … 26
Haunted Grande, The, see *One Exciting Night*, 1922 … 255
Haunted Honeymoon, The, 1925 … 285
Haunted House, The, 1899 … 20
Haunted Hotel, The, 1907 … 39
Haunted Hotel, The, 1909 … 54
Haunted Hotel, The, 1918 … 200
Haunted Hotel: or, The Strange Adventures of a Traveler, The, see *The Haunted Hotel*, 1907 … 39
Haunted House, The, 1899 … 20
Haunted House, The, 1906 … 44
Haunted House, The, 1911 … 85
Haunted House, The, 1913 … 111
Haunted House, The, 1913 … 112
Haunted House, The, 1917 … 188
Haunted House, The, 1918 … 201
Haunted House, The, 1921 … 236
Haunted House, The, 1922 … 250
Haunted House, The, 1928 … 324
Haunted House, The, see *Au secours!* 1924 … 273
Haunted House, The, see *The Haunted Attic*, 1915 … 152
Haunted House, The, see *The Haunted Ranch*, 1926 … 300
Haunted House, The, see *The House of Horror*, 1939 … 340
Haunted Houses and Castles of Great Britain: Ashridge Castle—The Monmouth Rebellion, see *Ashridge Castle—The Monmouth Rebellion*, 1926 … 295
Haunted Houses and Castles of Great Britain: Baddesley Manor—The Phantom Gambler, see *Baddesley Manor—The Phantom Gambler*, 1926 … 296
Haunted Houses and Castles of Great Britain: Bodiam Castle and Eric the Slender, see *Bodiam Castle and Eric the Slender*, 1926 … 297
Haunted Houses and Castles of Great Britain: Glamis Castle, see *Glamis Castle*, 1926 … 299
Haunted Houses and Castles of Great Britain: Hampton Court Palace, see *Hampton Court Palace*, 1926 … 299
Haunted Houses and Castles of Great Britain: Kenilworth Castle and Amy Robsart, see *Kenilworth Castle and Amy Robsart*, 1926 … 300
Haunted Houses and Castles of Great Britain: The Legend of Tichborne Dole, see *The Legend of Tichborne Dole*, 1926 … 300
Haunted Houses and Castles of Great Britain: The Mistletoe Bough, see *The Mistletoe Bough*, 1926 … 302
Haunted Houses and Castles of Great Britain: The Tower of London, see *The Tower of London*, 1926 … 308
Haunted Houses and Castles of Great Britain: Warwick Castle in Feudal Days, see *Guy of Warwick*, 1926 … 299
Haunted Houses and Castles of Great Britain: Windsor Castle, see *Windsor Castle*, 1926 … 309
Haunted Houses and Castles of Great Britain: Woodcroft Castle, see *Woodcroft Castle*, 1926 … 309
Haunted Man, The, 1909 … 54
Haunted Ranch, The, 1926 … 300
Haunted Range, The, see *The Haunted Ranch*, 1926 … 300
Haunted Spooks, 1920 … 221
Haunting of Silas P. Gould, The, 1915 … 152
Haunting Shadows, 1920 … 222
Haunting Winds, 1915 … 152
Haunts for Hire, see *Haunts for Rent*, 1916 … 172
Haunts for Rent, 1916 … 172
Haus des Dr. Gaudeamus, Das, see *The House Without Windows*, 1920 … 223
Haus ohne Tür and Fenster, see *The House Without Windows*, 1920 … 223
Häxan, 1922 … 250
Häxan: Witchcraft Through the Ages, see *Häxan*, 1922 … 250
Head of Janus, The, see *Der Januskopf*, 1920 … 224
Headless Horseman, The, 1922 … 251
Heba the Snake Woman, 1915 … 152
Heir of Jago, see *The Spectre of Jago*, 1913 … 118
Help! See *Au secours!* 1924 … 273
Henpeck's Nightmare, 1914 … 132
Her Dolly's Revenge, 1909 … 55
Her Father's Gold, 1916 … 172
Herncrake Witch, The, 1912 … 95
Hidden Menace, The, 1925 … 285
Hilde Warren and Death, 1917 … 189
Hilde Warren und der Tod, see *Hilde Warren and Death*, 1917 … 189
Hindoo Charm, The, 1912 … 96
His Brother's Keeper, 1921 … 236
His Egyptian Affinity, 1915 … 153
His Phantom Sweetheart, 1915 … 153
His Wife's Double, see *The Dead Alive*, 1916 … 170
Hole in the Wall, The, 1929 … 339
Homme invisible, L', see *The Invisible Thief*, 1909 … 55
Homme noir, L', see *The Manor House of Fear*, 1927 … 317
Homme qui rit, L', see *The Man Who Laughs*, 1909 … 57
Homme qui vendit son ame au diable, L', see *The Man Who Sold His Soul to the Devil*, 1921 … 240
Homunculus, 1916 … 172
Hop-Frog, 1910 … 72
Horrible Hyde, 1915 … 153
Horrors of Drink, see *The Drunkard's Conversion*, 1901 … 26
Hot Water, 1924 … 277
hotel enchanté, L', see *The Haunted Hotel*, 1909 … 54
hotel hanté, L', see *The Haunted Hotel*, 1909 … 54
Hound of the Baskervilles, The, 1914 … 132
Hound of the Baskervilles, The, 1915 … 153

Hound of the Baskervilles, The, 1920 ... 222
Hound of the Baskervilles, The, 1921 ... 237
Hound of the Baskervilles, The, 1929 ... 340
Hound of the Baskervilles: The Dark Castle, The, 1915 ... 153
House Behind the Hedge, The, see *Unknown Treasures*, 1926 ... 308
House of a Thousand Candles, see *Haunting Shadows*, 1920 ... 222
House of a Thousand Candles, The, 1915 ... 154
House of Fear, The, 1914 ... 133
House of Ghosts, see *The Haunted House*, 1908 ... 44
House of Horror, The, 1929 ... 340
House of Secrets, The, 1929 ... 341
House of Silence, The, see *The Silent House*, 1928 ... 331
House of Terror, The, 1928 ... 324
House of the Devil, The, see *The Devil's Castle*, 1896 ... 12
House of the Seven Gables, The, 1910 ... 72
House of the Tolling Bell, The, 1920 ... 222
House of Whispers, The, 1920 ... 222
House with Nobody in It, The, 1915 ... 154
House Without Windows, The, 1920 ... 223
How Love Conquered Hypnotism, see *The Strange Case of Princess Khan*, 1914 ... 140
Hugo the Hunchback, 1910 ... 73
Human Sparrows, see *Sparrows*, 1926 ... 306
Humpback of Cedar Lodge, The, 1914 ... 133
Hunchback and the Dancer, The, 1920 ... 223
Hunchback of Cedar Lodge, The, see *The Humpback of Cedar Lodge*, 1914 ... 133
Hunchback of Enmei-in, The, 1924 ... 277
Hunchback of Notre Dame, The, 1911 ... 85
Hunchback of Notre Dame, The, 1923 ... 261
Hunchback of Notre Dame, The, see *Esmeralda*, 1922 ... 249
Hunchback, The, 1909 ... 55
Hunchback, The, 1911 ... 85
Hund von Baskerville, Der, see *The Hound of the Baskervilles*, 1914 ... 132
Hund von Baskerville, Der, see *The Hound of the Baskervilles*, 1915 ... 153
Hund von Baskerville, Der, see *The Hound of the Baskervilles*, 1920 ... 222
Hund von Baskerville, Der, see *The Hound of the Baskervilles*, 1929 ... 340
Hund von Baskerville: Das Dunkle Schloss, see *The Hound of the Baskervilles: The Dark Castle*, 1915 ... 153
Hunting in the Haunted Woods, see *Shooting in the Haunted Woods*, 1909 ... 62
Hypnotic Violinist, The, 1914 ... 133
Hypnotiseur, Der, see *Svengali*, 1914 ... 141
Hypnotism, 1911 ... 86
I Accuse, see *J'Accuse*, 1919 ... 207
I Believe, see *The Man Without a Soul*, 1916 ... 173
I Borgia, see *The Power of the Borgias*, 1920 ... 229
Iago's Inheritance, see *The Spectre of Jago*, 1913 ... 118
Iemon, 1928 ... 325
île d'epouvante, L', see *The Island of Terror*, 1913 ... 113
Image Maker, The, 1917 ... 189
Imp Abroad, The, 1914 ... 133

Imp of the Bottle, The, 1909 ... 55
In the Grip of a Charlatan, 1913 ... 112
In the Grip of the Vampire, 1913 ... 112
In the Power of the Hypnotist, 1913 ... 112
In the Shadow of the Sea, 1912 ... 96
In the Toils of the Devil, 1913 ... 112
Indian Legend, An, 1912 ... 96
Infernal Cauldron, The, 1903 ... 30
Inferno, 1910 ... 73
Inferno, 1911 ... 86
Inn Where No Man Rests, The, 1903 ... 31
Inner Brute, The, 1915 ... 154
Innocent Sinner, An, 1915 ... 155
Insel der Verschollenen, Die, see *The Island of the Lost*, 1921 ... 238
Inspirations of Harry Larrabee, The, 1917 ... 189
Invisible Power, The, 1914 ... 133
Invisible Thief, The, 1909 ... 55
Irohagana Yotsuya kaidan, 1927 ... 313
Isetsu Banchō sarayashika, 1929 ... 341
Island of Terror, The, 1913 ... 113
Island of the Lost, The, 1921 ... 238
Isle of the Dead, The, 1913 ... 113
Issun-boshi, see *The Killer Dwarf*, 1927 ... 314
It Is Never Too Late to Mend, 1911 ... 87
It Is Never Too Late to Mend, 1913 ... 113
It's Never Too Late to Mend, 1917 ... 190
It's Never Too Late to Mend, 1922 ... 252
Itching Palms, 1923 ... 263
Izumo kaidan, 1918 ... 201
J'Accuse, 1919 ... 207
Jane Eyre, 1910 ... 73
Jane Eyre, 1914 ... 134
Jane Eyre, 1915 ... 155
Jane Eyre, 1921 ... 238
Janus Face, The, see *Der Januskopf*, 1920 ... 224
Januskopf, Der, 1920 ... 224
Januskopf, eine Tragodie am Rande der Wirlichkeit, see *Der Januskopf*, 1920 ... 224
Japanese Mask, The, 1915 ... 155
Jericho, see *The Dark Mirror*, 1920 ... 213
Jersey Skeeter, A, 1900 ... 23
Jester, The, see *Hop-Frog*, 1910 ... 72
Jizo the Spook, 1898 ... 18
Johann the Coffinmaker, 1927 ... 313
Jones' Nightmare; or, The Lobster Still Pursued Him, 1911 ... 87
Juif Polonais, Le, see *The Bells*, 1925 ... 283
Kaidan Asamagatake, 1914 ... 134
Kaidan Bunya goroshi, 1929 ... 341
Kaidan chibusa enoki, 1917 ... 190
Kaizaka bâke ginnan, see *Bâke ginnan*, 1916
Kaliostro, see *Cagliostro*, 1918 ... 197
Karamaneh, 1924 ... 278
Karamenah, see *Karamaneh*, 1924 ... 278
Kasane-ga-fuchi, 1924 ... 278
Kasane-ga-fuchi, 1928 ... 325
Kenilworth Castle and Amy Robsart, 1926 ... 300
Key of Life, The, 1910 ... 74
Killer Dwarf, The, 1927 ... 314

Kinekature Komedies: The Haunted Hotel, see *The Haunted Hotel*, 1918 ... 200
King of Thule, The, see *Lured by a Phantom*, 1910 ... 75
King Philip the Fair and the Templars, 1910 ... 74
Kingdom of Fairies, The, 1903 ... 31
Knight Errant, A, 1907 ... 40
Knight Errant, The, see *A Knight Errant*, 1907 ... 40
Knight of the Snows, The, 1912 ... 96
Knight-Errant, 1907, see *A Knight Errant*, 1907 ... 40
Knocking on the Door, The, 1923 ... 263
Körkarlen, see *The Phantom Carriage*, 1920 ... 228
Kurfurstendamm, 1920 ... 225
Kyôren no Onna Shishô, see *Passion of a Woman Teacher*, 1926 ... 303
La main qui étreint, see *The Grasping Hand*, 1916 ... 171
Laboratory of Mephistopheles, The, see *The Cabinet of Mephistopheles*, 1897 ... 14
Laboritorio del Diablo, see *The Seven Castles of the Devil*, 1901
ladro e la testa del portinaio, Il, see *The Thief and the Porter's Head*, 1913 ... 121
Lamaklostrets Hemmelighed, see *The Mystery of the Lama Convent*, 1909 ... 59
Last Call, The, see *The Last Performance*, 1927 ... 314
Last Egyptian, The, 1914 ... 134
Last Look, The, 1909 ... 56
Last Moment, The, 1923 ... 264
Last Performance, The, 1927 ... 314
Last Warning, The, 1929 ... 342
Leaves from Satan's Book, 1921 ... 238
Leaves Out of The Book of Satan, see *Leaves from Satan's Book*, 1921 ... 238
Lebende Buddhas, see *Living Buddhas*, 1925 ... 285
Légend des Ondines, La, see *The Legend of the Undines*, 1910 ... 74
Legend of a Ghost, 1908 ... 44
Legend of Sleepy Hollow, The, 1908 ... 44
Legend of Sleepy Hollow, The, 1912 ... 97
Legend of the Bear's Marriage, The, see *The Bear's Marriage*, 1925 ... 283
Legend of the Lake, The, 1911 ... 88
Legend of the Lone Tree, The, 1915 ... 156
Legend of the Nabeshima Cat Ghost, 1929 ... 342
Legend of the Phantom Tribe, see *Legion of the Phantom Tribe*, 1914 ... 135
Legend of the Undines, The, 1910 ... 74
Legend of Tichborne Dole, The, 1926 ... 300
légende du Fantôme, La, see *Legend of a Ghost*, 1908 ... 44
leggenda del lago, La, see *The Legend of the Lake*, 1911 ... 88
Legion of the Phantom Tribe, 1914 ... 135
Leopard Lady, The, 1928 ... 325
Lidércnyomás, see *Lord Arthur Saville's Crime*, 1920 ... 225
Life of a Nun, The, 1911 ... 88
Life Without a Soul, see *Life Without Soul*, 1915 ... 156
Life Without Soul, 1915 ... 156
Light on the Wall, The, 1928 ... 326
Lilith and Ly, 1919 ... 208
Lilith und Ly, see *Lilith and Ly*, 1919 ... 208
Lille Trilby, see *Trilby*, 1908 ... 49

Little Princes in the Tower, The, 1909 ... 56
Little Trilby, see *Trilby*, 1908 ... 49
Live Mummy, The, 1915 ... 156
Live Without Soul, see *Life Without Soul*, 1915 ... 156
Living Buddhas, 1925 ... 285
Living Death, The, 1928 ... 326
Lobster Nightmare, The, 1911 ... 88
Lodger: A Story of the London Fog, The, 1927 ... 314
Lodger; The Case of Jonathan Drew, The, see *The Lodger: A Story of the London Fog*, 1927 ... 314
Lola, 1914 ... 135
London After Midnight, 1927 ... 316
London's Yellow Peril, 1915 ... 156
Lord Arthur Savile's Crime, 1921 ... 239
Lord Arthur Saville's Crime, 1920 ... 225
Lord Feathertop, 1908 ... 44
Lord John in New York, 1915 ... 157
Lord Saviles brott, 1921 ... 239
Lost Atlantis, see *Missing Husbands*, 1921 ... 241
Lost Shadow, The, 1921 ... 239
Lost Soul, or: The Dangers of Hypnosis, The, 1923 ... 264
Lost Soul, see *The Lost Soul, or: The Dangers of Hypnosis*, 1923 ... 264
Lost World, The, 1925 ... 286
Loup-Garou, Le, see *The Werewolf*, 1913 ... 122
Love from Out of the Grave, 1913 ... 114
Love of a Hunchback, The, 1910 ... 74
Love of a Siren, The, 1911 ... 88
Love Without Question, 1920 ... 225
Love's Mockery, see *Der Januskopf*, 1920 ... 224
Love-Mad Tutoress, The, see *Passion of a Woman Teacher*, 1926 ... 303
Lucrèce Borgia, 1909 ... 56
Lucretia Borgia, see *Lucrezia Borgia*, 1922 ... 252
Lucretia Borgia, see *The Eternal Sin*, 1917 ... 185
Lucrezia Borgia, 1910 ... 75
Lucrezia Borgia, 1912 ... 97
Lucrezia Borgia, 1919 ... 208
Lucrezia Borgia, 1922 ... 252
Lucrezia Borgia; Or, Playing of Power, 1923 ... 264
Luke's Double, 1916 ... 173
Lunatics in Power, 1909 ... 57
Lunatics, The, see *The System of Dr. Tarr, and Professor Fether*, 1912 ... 103
Lune à une mètre, La, see *The Astronomer's Dream*, 1898 ... 16
Lured by a Phantom, 1910 ... 75
Lured by a Phantom, or, The King of Thule, see *Lured by a Phantom*, 1910 ... 76
Luring Shadows, 1920 ... 225
Maciste all'inferno, see *Maciste in Hell*, 1925 ... 288
Maciste in Hell, 1925 ... 288
Mad Lady of Chester, The, see *Jane Eyre*, 1910 ... 73
Madman's Bride, The, 1907 ... 40
Madness, 1919 ... 208
Magia, 1917 ... 190
Magic Skin, see *Desire*, 1920 ... 214
Magic Skin, The, 1914 ... 135
Magic Skin, The, 1915 ... 157

Magic Sword, or A Medieval Mystery, The, see *The Magic Sword*, 1901 … 26
Magic Sword, The, 1901 … 26
Magician, The, 1926 … 301
Magician, The, see *The Last Performance*, 1927 … 314
Magnetic Influence, A, 1912 … 97
main du Squelette, La, see *The Hand of the Skeleton*, 1915 … 152
maison ensorcelée, Le, see *The Haunted House*, 1908 … 44
maison hantée, La, see *The Haunted House*, 1911 … 85
Man and His Bottle, The, 1908 … 44
Man in the White Cloak, The, 1913 … 114
Man Who Cheated Life, The, see *The Student of Prague*, 1926 … 307
Man Who Couldn't Beat God, The, 1915 … 157
Man Who Laughs, The, 1909 … 57
Man Who Laughs, The, 1921 … 239
Man Who Laughs, The, 1928 … 326
Man Who Sold His Soul to the Devil, The, 1921 … 240
Man with the Limp, The, 1923 … 265
Man Without a Soul, The, 1916 … 173
Mandrake, see *Alraune*, 1928 … 321
Manoir de la peur; L'Homme Noir, Le, see *The Manor House of Fear*, 1927 … 317
Manoir du diable, Le, see *The Devil's Castle*, 1896 … 12
manoir ensorcelé, Le, see *The Bewitched Manor House*, 1909 … 51
Manor House of Fear, The, 1927 … 317
Manor of the Devil, The, see *The Devil's Castle*, 1896 … 12
Maria Marten, 1928 … 328
Maria Marten, or The Murder in the Red Barn, 1913 … 114
Maria Marten: a Murder in the Red Barn, see *Maria Marten, or The Murder in the Red Barn*, 1913 …114
Maria Marten: or The Murder at the Red Barn, 1902 … 27
Maria Marten see *The Red Barn Crime*, 1908
Mark of the Phantom, The, see *Lord Arthur Saville's Crime*, 1920 … 225
Marriage Chance, The, 1922 … 253
Marvellous Pearl, The, see *The Wonderful Pearl*, 1909 … 64
maschera dell'orror, La, see *The Mask of Horror*, 1912 … 97
Mask of Horror, The, 1912 … 97
Masque of d'horreur, Le, see *The Mask of Horror*, 1912 … 97
Masque of the Red Death, The, 1911 … 88
Max 1ˢᵗ Hypnotisiert, see *Max Hypnotized*, 1910 … 75
Max and the Clutching Hand, see *The Grasping Hand*, 1916 … 171
Max et la main-qui-étreint, see *The Grasping Hand*, 1916 … 171
Max Hypnotisé, see *Max Hypnotized*, 1910 … 75
Max Hypnotized, 1910 … 75
Max victime de la Main-qui-étreint, see *The Grasping Hand*, 1916 … 171
Mechanical Man, The, 1921 … 240
Medium's Nemesis, The, 1913 … 114
Medvezhya svadha, see *The Bear's Marriage*, 1925 … 283
Melancholy Spirit, The, see *One Glorious Day*, 1922 … 256
Memoiren Des Satans, Die, see *The Memoirs of Satan*, 1917 … 190
Memoirs of Satan, The, 1917 … 190
Mephisto and the Maiden, 1909 … 57
Mephisto, 1912 … 98
Mephisto's Son, 1906 … 35
Mephistopheles' School of Magic, see *The Treasures of Satan*, 1902 … 28
Merry Frolics of Satan, The, 1906 … 36
Mesmerist, or Body and Soul, The, see *The Mesmerist*, 1898 … 19
Mesmerist, The, 1898 … 19
Mesmerist, The, 1915 … 157
Midnight, 1917 … 190
Midnight Bell, A, 1921 … 241
Midnight Episode, A, see 1899 … 20
Midnight Faces, 1926 … 302
Midnight Summons, The, 1924 … 278
Mingling Spirits, 1916 … 173
Minotaur, The, 1910 … 75
Miracle sous l'Inquisition, Une, see *A Miracle Under the Inquisition*, 1904 … 32
Miracle Under the Inquisition, A, 1904 … 32
Miracle, The, 1923 … 265
Mirakel der Liebe, see *She*, 1925 … 292
miroir de Cagliostro, Le, see *Cagliostro's Mirror*, 1899 … 19
Mirror of Cagliostro, The, see *Cagliostro's Mirror*, 1899 … 19
Miser's Doom, The, 1898 … 21
Miss Faust, 1909 … 58
Miss Jekyll and Madame Hyde, 1915 … 158
Missing Husbands, 1921 … 241
Missing Mummy, The, 1915 … 158
misteri della psiche, I, see *The Mystery of Souls*, 1912 … 99
Mistletoe Bough, The, 1904 … 33
Mistletoe Bough, The, 1923 … 265
Mistletoe Bough, The, 1926 … 302
Modern Dr. Jekyll, A, 1909 … 58
Modern kaidan: 100,000,000, 1929 … 342
Moken no himitsu, 1924 … 278
Momie du roi, La, see *The Mummy of the King Ramsees*, 1909 … 59
Money to Burn, 1922 … 253
Monkey's Paw, The, 1915 … 158
Monkey's Paw, The, 1919 … 209
Monkey's Paw, The, 1923 … 265
Monmouth Rebellion, see *Ashridge Castle—The Monmouth Rebellion*, 1926 … 295
Monster, The, 1903 … 31
Monster, The, 1925 … 289
Monster of Fate, see *The Golem*, 1915 … 150
Monster of Frankenstein, The, 1920 … 226
Monstre, Le, see *The Monster*, 1903 … 31
Monstro di Frankenstein, Il, see *The Monster of Frankenstein*, 1920 … 226
Moon to the Metre, A, see *The Astronomer's Dream*, 1898 … 16
Moonstone, The, 1909 … 58
Moonstone, The, 1911 … 89
Moonstone, The, 1915 … 158
Moonstone of Fez, The, 1914 … 136
Mortmain, 1915 … 159
Morts parlent, Le, see *Les Morts qui parlent*, 1920 … 226
Morts qui parlent, Les, 1920 … 226
morts revienent-ils?, Les, see *A Drama of the Castle, or Do the Dead Return?* 1915 … 148

Mostro di Frankenstein, Il, see *The Monster of Frankenstein*, 1920 ... 226

Mountain Devil, The, see *The Bottle Imp*, 1917 ... 181

Mr. Tvardovski, 1916 ... 174

Müde Tod, Der, see *Destiny*, 1921 ... 233

Mumie Ma, Die, see *The Eyes of the Mummy*, 1918 ... 198

Mumien Gesucht, see *Wanted—A Mummy*, 1910 ... 80

Mummy, The, 1911 ... 89

Mummy, The, 1912 ... 98

Mummy and the Cowpuncher, The, 1912 ... 98

Mummy and the King of Ramsee, The, see *The Mummy of the King Ramsees*, 1909 ... 59

Mummy and the King Rameses, see *The Mummy of the King Ramsees*, 1909 ... 59

Mummy Love, 1926 ... 302

Mummy of the King of Ramses, The, see *The Mummy of the King Ramsees*, 1909 ... 59

Mummy of the King Rameses, The, see *The Mummy of the King Ramsees*, 1909 ... 59

Mummy of the King Ramsees, The, 1909 ... 59

Murder in the Red Barn, The, see *Maria Marten*, 1928 ... 328

Murders in the Rue Morgue, 1914 ... 136

mystère de Val Boscombe, Le, see *The Speckled Band*, 1912 ... 102

Mysteries of Myra, The, 1916 ... 174

Mysteries of Souls, see *The Mystery of Souls*, 1912 ... 99

Mysterious Club, The, see *The Suicide Club*, 1913 ... 120

Mysterious Dr. Fu Manchu, The, 1929 ... 343

Mysterious Mr. Wu Chung Foo, The, 1914 ... 136

Mysterious Retort, The, 1906 ... 36

Mysterious Stranger, The, 1913 ... 115

Mystery Mind, The, 1920 ... 226

Mystery of Edwin Drood, The, 1909 ... 59

Mystery of Edwin Drood, The, 1914 ... 137

Mystery of Grayson Hall, The, 1914 ... 137

Mystery of Souls, The, 1912 ... 99

Mystery of Temple Court, The, 1910 ... 76

Mystery of the Fatal Pearl, The, 1914 ... 137

Mystery of the Lama Convent, The, 1909 ... 59

Mystic Mirror, The, 1928 ... 328

Mystic Moonstone, The, 1913 ... 115

Mystic, The, 1925 ... 289

Mystical Maid of Jamasha Pass, The, see *The Myth of Jamasha Pass*, 1912 ... 99

Mystiske Fremmede, Den, see *A Deal with the Devil*, 1914 ... 128

Myth of Jamasha Pass, The, 1912 ... 99

Nabeshima kaibyô, 1917 ... 191

Nabeshima kaibyô-den, see *Legend of the Nabeshima Cat Ghost*, 1929 ... 342

Nabeshima neko sodo, 1919 ... 209

Nabeshima neko sodo, 1921 ... 241

Nabeshima no neko, 1923 ... 266

Nächte des Grauens, see *Night of Horror*, 1916 ... 175

Nachtgestalten, 1920 ... 226

Nanbandera no kaijin, see *Phantom of the Western Temple*, 1926 ... 303

Nanbandera no kaijinzenpen, see *Phantom of the Western Temple*, 1926 ... 303

Narayana, 1920 ... 227

Nature Fakirs, 1907 ... 40

Necklace of Rameses, The, 1914 ... 137

Necklace of the Dead, 1910 ... 76

New Jonah, The, 1909 ... 59

New Lord of the Village, The, 1908 ... 45

New Version of the Ghost of Yotsuya, 1928 ... 328

Nick Carter–Le club des suicides, see *The Suicide Club*, 1909 ... 63

Night in the Chamber of Horrors, A, 1914 ... 138

Night of Horror in the Menagerie, A, see *Night of Terror*, 1916 ... 175

Night of Horror, 1916 ... 175

Night of Terror, see *Night of Horror*, 1916 ... 175

Night of Thrills, A, 1914 ... 138

Nightmare, A, 1896 ... 13

Nights of Horror, see *Night of Horror*, 1916 ... 175

Nikuzuki no men, 1922 ... 253

Noidan Kirot, 1927 ... 317

Nonnen fra Asminderod, see *The Life of a Nun*, 1911 ... 88

Nosferatu, see *Nosferatu—A Symphony of Terror*, 1922 ... 253

Nosferatu—A Symphony of Horrors, see *Nosferatu—A Symphony of Terror*, 1922 ... 253

Nosferatu—A Symphony of Terror, 1922 ... 253

Nosferatu—eine Symphonie des Grauens, see *Nosferatu—A Symphony of Terror*, 1922 ... 253

Notre Dame de Paris, see *The Hunchback of Notre Dame*, 1911 ... 85

Notre-Dame de Paris, see *The Hunchback of Notre Dame*, 1911 ... 85

Nouveau seigneur du village, Le, see *The New Lord of the Village*, 1908 ... 45

Nozze in casa Scivoloni, see *Wedding Feast and Ghosts*, 1908 ... 50

Nuit terrible, Une, see *A Terrible Night*, 1896 ... 13

Nun, The, see *The Life of a Nun*, 1911 ... 88

Nymph de Bain, La, see *The Nymph's Bath*, 1909 ... 60

Nymph's Bath, The, 1909 ... 60

O homem mechanico, L', see *The Mechanical Man*, 1921 ... 240

Occult, The, 1913 ... 115

Octave of Claudius, The, see *A Blind Bargain*, 1922 ... 245

Odoru reikon, 1927 ... 317

Oh, You Skeleton, 1910 ... 76

Okazaki kaibyô-den, 1919 ... 209

Okazaki no kaibyô-den, see *Okazaki no neko*, 1914 ... 138

Okazaki no neko, 1914 ... 138

Old Shoemaker, The, 1909 ... 60

Old Time Nightmare, An, 1911 ... 89

On Time, 1924 ... 278

Onder spiritistischen dwang, see *The Other Person*, 1921 ... 242

One Exciting Night, 1922 ... 255

One Glorious Day, 1922 ... 256

One Hour Before Dawn, 1920 ... 227

One Spooky Night, 1924 ... 279

One Terrible Night, see *A Terrible Night*, 1896 ... 13

One Too Exciting Night, 1912 ... 99

Onésime aux enfers, see *Simple Simon and the Devil*, 1912 ... 100

Onésime et la Diable, see *Simple Simon and the Devil*, 1912 ... 100

Onésime et la maison hanté, see *Simple Simon and the Haunted House*, 1913 ... 117

Only a Room-er, 1916 ... 175
oracle de Delphes, L', see *The Oracle of Delphi*, 1903 ... 32
Oracle of Delphi, The, 1903 ... 32
Oriental Mystic, The, 1909 ... 60
Orlacs Hande, see *Hands of Orlac*, 1924 ... 276
Orphan of Lowood, 1926 ... 302
Osaka-jo tenshu no kai, 1922 ... 256
Other, The, 1913 ... 115
Other Person, The, 1921 ... 242
Other Self, The, 1918 ... 201
ou, les morts revienent-ils?, see *A Drama of the Castle, or Do the Dead Return?* 1915 ... 148
Out of the Far East, 1914 ... 138
Owana, The Devil Woman, 1913 ... 115
pacte fatal, Le, see *The Fatal Pact*, 1912 ... 94
Pan Tvardovsky, see *Mr. Tvardovsky*, 1916 ... 174
Pan Twardowski, 1921 ... 242
Paradise and Purgatory, see *Purgatory*, 1912 ... 89
Paradise, 1912 ... 99
Passion of a Woman Teacher, 1926 ... 303
Patouillard fantôme, see *Bill Taken for a Ghost*, 1911 ... 82
Paul's Peril, see *The Perils of Paul*, 1920 ... 228
Peau de chagrin, La, see *The Wild Ass's Skin*, 1909 ... 64
Penalty, The, 1920 ... 228
Perils of Paul or the Duchess at Bay, see *The Perils of Paul*, 1920 ... 228
Perils of Paul, The, 1920 ... 228
perla meravigliosa, La, see *The Wonderful Pearl*, 1909 ... 64
perla sanguinosa, La, see *The Fatal Pearl*, 1912 ... 94
Pest in Florenz, Die, see *The Plague in Florence*, 1919 ... 209
Peter's Evil Spirit, 1914 ... 139
Phantom Carriage, The, 1920 ... 228
Phantom Chariot, The, see *The Phantom Carriage*, 1920 ... 228
Phantom City, The, 1928 ... 329
Phantom der Oper, Das, see *The Phantom of the Opera*, 1916 ... 175
Phantom Foe, The, 1920 ... 229
Phantom Honeymoon, The, 1919 ... 209
Phantom Light, The, 1914 ... 139
Phantom Melody, The, 1920 ... 229
Phantom of the Moulin-Rouge, The, 1924 ... 279
Phantom of the Opera, The, 1916 ... 175
Phantom of the Opera, The, 1925 ... 290
Phantom of the Violin, The, see *The Phantom Violin*, 1914 ... 139
Phantom of the Western Temple, 1926 ... 303
Phantom Signal, The, 1913 ... 116
Phantom Sirens, The, 1909 ... 60
Phantom Violin, The, 1914 ... 139
Phantom Witness, The, 1916 ... 175
Phantom, The, 1910 ... 76
Pharmaceutical Hallucinations, 1908 ... 45
Philtre Maudit, Le, see *The Evil Philter*, 1909 ... 53
Photographing a Ghost, 1898 ... 19
Picture of Dorian Gray, The, 1913 ... 116
Picture of Dorian Gray, The, 1915 ... 159
Picture of Dorian Gray, The, 1915 ... 160
Picture of Dorian Gray, The, 1916 ... 175
Picture of Dorian Gray, The, 1917 ... 191

Picture of Dorian Gray, The, 1918 ... 201
Picture of Dorian Gray, The, see *Dorian Grays Portraet*, 1910 ... 67
Pied Piper of Hamelin, The, 1918 ... 201
Pikovaya dama, see *The Queen of Spades*, 1910 ... 77
Pikovaya dama, see *The Queen of Spades*, 1916 ... 176
Pillar of Fire, 1899 ... 21
Pique Dame, see *Queen of Spades*, 1911 ... 90
Pique Dame, see *Queen of Spades*, 1922 ... 256
Pique Dame, see *Queen of Spades*, 1927 ... 318
Pit and the Pendulum, The, 1909 ... 60
Pit and the Pendulum, The, 1913 ... 116
Placard infernal, Le, see *The Bewildering Cabinet*, 1907 ... 37
Plague in Florence, The, 1919 ... 209
Plague-Stricken City, The, 1912 ... 100
Poisoned Waters, 1913 ... 117
Polidor al Club della Morte, see *Polidor at the Death Club*, 1912 ... 100
Polidor at the Death Club, 1912 ... 100
Polidor, a Member of the Death Club, see *Polidor at the Death Club*, 1912 ... 100
Polish Jew, The, see *The Bells*, 1925 ... 283
Poor Knight and the Duke's Daughter, A, 1908 ... 45
Portrait, The, 1915 ... 160
Portret Doriana Greja, see *The Picture of Dorian Gray*, 1915 ... 159
Portret Doryana Greya, see *The Picture of Dorian Gray*, 1915 ... 159
Portret, see *The Portrait*, 1915 ... 160
Power of the Borgias, The, 1920 ... 229
Prelude, 1927 ... 317
Price of Silence, The, 1920 ... 230
Prince of Darkness, The, 1902 ... 28
Princess and the Fisherman, The, 1909 ... 60
Princess in the Vase, The, 1908 ... 46
Princesse et le Pecheur, Le, see *The Princess and the Fisherman*, 1909 ... 60
Prizrak brodit po Yevrope, see *A Spectre Haunts Europe*, 1922 ... 257
Puits et le pendula, Le, see *The Pit and the Pendulum*, 1909 ... 60
Puits fantastique, Le, see *The Enchanted Well*, 1903 ... 30
Purgatorio, see *Purgatory*, 1911 ... 89
Purgatory and Paradise, see *Purgatory*, 1911 ... 89
Purgatory, 1911 ... 89
Puritan Passions, 1923 ... 266
Quatre cents farces du diable, Les, see *The Merry Frolics of Satan*, 1906 ... 36
Queen Mother, The, see *The Eternal Sin*, 1917 ... 185
Queen of Atlantis, see *Missing Husbands*, 1921 ... 241
Queen of Hearts, The, 1923 ... 266
Queen of Spades, 1911 ... 90
Queen of Spades, 1912 ... 99
Queen of Spades, 1913 ... 117
Queen of Spades, 1922 ... 256
Queen of Spades, 1927 ... 318
Queen of Spades, The, 1910 ... 77
Queen of Spades, The, 1913 ... 117
Queen of Spades, The, 1916 ... 176
Quest for the Sacred Jewel, The, 1914 ... 139
Quest of the Sacred Gem, see *The Quest for the Sacred Jewel*, 1914 ...

139

Range Rider, see *The Ghost of the Rancho*, 1918 ... 200
Ransom, 1928 ... 329
Rapsodia Satanica, see *Satanic Rhapsody*, 1915 ... 161
Rasputin, 1917 ... 191
Rasputin, 1929 ... 344
Rasputin, Das Liebesleben des Sonderbaren Heiligen, see *Rasputin, The Love Life of a Strange Holy Man*, 1925 ... 292
Rasputin, Dornenweg; Dornenweg einer Fürstin, see *Rasputin, The Prince of Sinners*, 1928 ... 330
Rasputin, see *Rasputin, The Prince of Sinners*, 1928 ... 330
Rasputin, The Black Monk, 1917 ... 192
Rasputin, The Love Life of a Strange Holy Man, 1925 ... 292
Rasputin, The Prince of Sinners, 1928 ... 330
Rasputin: Schatten der Vergangenheit, see *Rasputin, The Prince of Sinners*, 1928 ... 330
Rasputin: The Holy Devil, 1928 ... 329
Rasputin: The Holy Sinner, see *Rasputin, the Holy Devil*, 1928 ... 329
Rasputin's Amorous Adventures, see *Rasputin, the Holy Devil*, 1928 ... 329
Rasputins Liebesabentuer, see *Rasputin, the Holy Devil*, 1928 ... 329
Raven, The, 1912 ... 100
Raven, The, 1915 ... 161
Raven, The, see *Edgar Allen Poe*, 1909 ... 52
Ravengar, see *The Shielding Shadow*, 1916 ... 178
Real Thing at Last, The, 1916 ... 176
Red Barn Crime, or Maria Marten, see *The Red Barn Crime*, 1908 ... 46
Red Barn Crime, or Maria Martin, see *The Red Barn Crime*, 1908 ... 46
Red Barn Crime, The, 1908 ... 46
Red Inn, The, 1910 ... 77
Red Inn, The, 1923 ... 267
Red Lights, 1923 ... 267
Red Spectre, The, 1907 ... 40
reina de Bastos, Le, see *The Queen of Spades*, 1913 ... 117
reina de espadas, La, see *Queen of Spades*, 1911 ... 90
Reincarnation of Karma, The, 1912 ... 100
Reincarnation of Komar, The, see *The Reincarnation of Karma*, 1912 ... 100
Repas fantastique, Le, see *A Fantastical Meal*, 1900 ... 22
Resurrection of a Corpse, 1898 ... 19
Rettenfanger von Hameln, Der, see *The Pied Piper of Hamelin*, 1918 ... 201
Return of Maurice Donnelly, The, 1915 ... 161
Return of Richard Neal, The, 1915 ... 161
Rêve d'un fumeur d'opium, Le, see *Dream of an Opium Fiend*, 1908 ... 43
Revenant, Le, see *Apparitions*, 1903 ... 28
Rêver réveille, see *Andalusian Superstition*, 1912 ... 91
Rival de Satan, see *Satan's Rival*, 1910 ... 79
Rival to Satan, see *Satan's Rival*, 1910 ... 79
Rivals, see *The Pit and the Pendulum*, 1913 ... 116
Robbing Cleopatra's Tomb, see *Cleopatra*, 1899 ... 19
Robert le diable, see *Robert, The Devil: or, Freed from Satan's Power*, 1910 ... 78

Robert, The Devil: or, Freed from Satan's Power, 1910 ... 78
Roi de Thule, Le, see *Lured by a Phantom*, 1910 ... 75
roi Philippe le Bel et les templiers, Le, see *King Philip the Fair and the Templars*, 1910 ... 74
Romantic Journey, The, 1916 ... 177
Rose O'Salem Town, 1910 ... 78
Rose of O'Salem Town, see *Rose O'Salem Town*, 1910 ... 78
Royaume des fees, Le, see *The Kingdom of Fairies*, 1903 ... 31
Sacred Order, The, 1923 ... 268
Sacrifice, see *Alraune*, 1918
Saga neko sodo, 1921 ... 242
Saga no yozakura, 1917 ... 192
Saga yozakura see *Saga no yozakura*, 1917 ... 192
Saint, Devil and Woman, 1916 ... 177
Saloon Keeper's Nightmare, The, 1908 ... 46
San Francisco, see *Ransom*, 1928 ... 329
San'nô no bakeneko, 1914 ... 139
Sängers Fluch; see *The Curse of the Wandering Minstrel*, 1910 ... 66
Satan, 1912 ... 100
Satan at Play, 1907 ... 40
Satan Defeated, 1911 ... 90
Satan Finds Mischief, 1908 ... 46
Satan in Sofia, 1921 ... 242
Satan on Mischief Bent, 1911 ... 90
Satan s'amuse, see *Satan at Play*, 1907 ... 40
Satan Triumphant, 1917 ... 193
Satan Vaincu, see *Satan Defeated*, 1911 ... 90
Satan, see *Satanas*, 1919 ... 210
Satan: or, The Drama of Humanity, see *Satan*, 1912 ... 100
Satan's Pawn, see *The Devil*, 1915 ... 146
Satan's Rival, 1910 ... 79
Satan's Smithy, 1909 ... 61
Satana likuyushchiy, see *Satan Triumphant*, 1917 ... 193
Satana, see *Satan*, 1912 ... 100
Satanas, 1919 ... 210
Satanic Rhapsody, 1915 ... 161
Saving of Faust, The, 1911 ... 90
scarabee d'or, Le, see *The Golden Beetle*, 1907 ... 39
scarabée d'or, Le, see *The Golden Beetle*, 1910 ... 72
Scared Stiff! 1926 ... 303
Scarred Face, The, 1928 ... 329
Scented Envelopes, The, 1923 ... 268
Schatten des Meeres, Der, see *In the Shadow of the Sea*, 1912 ... 96
Schatten—Eine nächtliche Halluzination, see *Warning Shadows*, 1923 ... 271
Schloß Vogeloed, see *The Haunted Castle*, 1921 ... 235
Schloß Vogeloed—Die Enthüllung eines Geheimnisses, see *The Haunted Castle*, 1921 ... 235
Schrecken, see *Der Januskopf*, 1920 ... 224
Scorpion's Sting, The, 1915 ... 162
Scraps, see *Sparrows*, 1926 ... 306
Screaming Shadow, The, 1920 ... 230
Sealed Door, The, see *The Sealed Room*, 1909 ... 61
Sealed Room, The, 1909 ... 61
Séance de spiritisme, see *Spiritualistic Séance*, 1908 ... 48
Sea's Shadow, The, see *In the Shadow of the Sea*, 1912 ... 96
Sensation, see *Queen of Spades*, 1922 ... 156

Secret Club, The, see *The Suicide Club*, 1913 … 120
Secret de la Nuit, see *Ultus and the Secret of the Night*, 1916 … 180
secret horlogers, Le, see *The Clock-Maker's Secret*, 1907 … 37
Secret of the Hand, The, 1910 … 79
Secret of the Night, The, see *Ultus and the Secret of the Night*, 1916 … 180
Secret Room, The, 1915 … 162
Secrets of a Soul, 1926 … 304
Secrets of a Soul: A Psychoanalytic Thriller, see *Secrets of a Soul*, 1926 … 304
Secrets of House No. 5, The, 1912 … 100
Seltsamer Fall, Ein, 1914 … 139
Señor Don Juan Tenorio, El, 1927 … 318
sept Château du diable, Les, see *The Seven Castles of the Devil*, 1901 … 27
Serpent Man, The, see *The Snake Man*, 1910 … 79
Seven Castles of the Devil, The, 1901 … 27
Seven Footprints to Satan, 1929 … 344
Seven Keys to Baldpate, 1916 … 177
Seven Keys to Baldpate, 1917 … 193
Seven Keys to Baldpate, 1925 … 292
Seven Keys to Baldpate, 1929 … 345
Shadow of the Desert, see *The Shadow of the East*, 1924 … 279
Shadow of the East, The, 1924 … 279
Shadows—a Nocturnal Hallucination, see *Warning Shadows*, 1923 … 271
She, 1908 … 46
She, 1911 … 90
She, 1916 … 178
She, 1917 … 193
She, 1925 … 292
Sherlock Holmes and the Great Murder Mystery, see *Sherlock Holmes in the Great Murdery Mystery*, 1908 … 47
Sherlock Holmes in the Great Murder Mystery, 1908 … 47
Shielding Shadow, The, 1916 … 178
Shin sarayashiki, 1924 … 280
Shin sarayashiki, 1926 … 304
Shinban: Botan dōrō, 1928 … 331
Shinen no sosei, see *Resurrection of a Corpse*, 1898 … 19
Shinpan Yotsuya kaidan, see *New Version of the Ghost of Yotsuya*, 1928 … 328
Shivering Spooks, 1926 … 305
Shooting in the Haunted Woods, 1909 … 62
Show, The, 1927 … 318
Shrine of the Seven Lamps, The, 1923 … 269
Shunen no hebi, 1915 … 162
Sieben Schlösser Von Teufel, see *The Seven Castles of the Devil*, 1901 … 27
Sign of the Cross, The, see *The Devil in a Convent*, 1899 … 20
Silence, Le, see *The Silence*, 1920 … 230
Silence, The, 1920 … 230
Silent Command, The, 1915 … 162
Silent House, The, 1928 … 331
Silent Man, The, see *The Silent Stranger*, 1916 … 178
Silent Mystery, The, 1918 … 202
Silent Stranger, The, 1916 … 178
Silver Buddha, The, 1923 … 269
Simple Simon and the Devil, 1912 … 100

Simple Simon and the Haunted House, 1913 … 117
Simple Simon and the Suicide Club, 1913 … 118
Simple Simon Has a Fright, see *Simple Simon and the Haunted House*, 1913 … 117
Simple Simon in Hell, see *Simple Simon and the Devil*, 1912 … 100
Sinews of the Dead, 1914 … 140
The Singer's Curse, Des, see *The Curse of the Wandering Minstrel*, 1910 … 66
Skaebnesvangre Opfindelse, Den, see *Dr. Jekyll and Mr. Hyde*, 1910 … 68
Skeleton, The, 1910 … 79
Skindode, Den, see *Necklace of the Dead*, 1910 … 76
Skivvy's Ghost, The, 1912 … 102
Slave of Desire, 1923 … 269
Sleep of Cyma Roget, The, 1920 … 230
Sleeping Memory, A, 1917 … 194
Sleepy Hollow, see *The Legend of Sleepy Hollow*, 1912 … 97
Snake Man, The, 1910 … 79
Snowman, The, 1908 … 48
Soap Bubbles of Truth, The, 1910 … 79
Sogra enviado ao Diabo, see *The Devil's Mother-in-Law*, 1910 … 67
Sold to Satan, 1916 … 179
Something Always Happens, 1928 … 331
Son of Satan, A, 1924 … 280
Son of the Devil, see *Mephisto's Son*, 1906 … 35
Son-in-Law's Nightmare, A, 1912 … 102
Sorceress of the Strand, The, 1910 … 79
Sorcière de la Grève, La, see *The Sorceress of the Strand*, 1910 … 79
Sorcière des décombres, La, see *The Witch of the Ruins*, 1910 … 80
Sorrows of Satan, The, 1917 … 194
Sorrows of Satan, The, 1926 … 305
Soul of Phyra, The, 1915 … 162
Soul of the Cypress, 1921 … 242
Soul's Cycle, The, 1916 … 179
Souls Before Birth, see *One Glorious Day*, 1922 … 256
Souls Which Pass in the Night, see *Behind the Curtain*, 1924 … 273
Sparrows, 1926 … 306
Speckled Band, The, 1912 … 102
Speckled Band, The, 1923 … 269
Specter, The, 1908 … 48
Spectre de L'autre, Le, see *Another's Ghost*, 1910 … 64
Spectre Haunts Europe, A, 1922 … 257
Spectre of Jago, The, 1913 … 118
Spectre of the Vault, The, 1915 … 163
spectre rouge, Le, see *The Red Spectre*, 1907 … 40
Spectre, The, see *The Specter*, 1908 … 48
Spell of the Hypnotist, The, 1912 … 102
Spell, The, 1913 … 118
Spettro del Sotterraneo, Lo, see *The Spectre of the Vault*, 1915 … 163
Spettro di Jago, Lo, see *The Spectre of Jago*, 1913 … 118
Spirit of the Lake, The, 1910 … 79
Spirit of the Sword, The, 1910 … 80
Spirit, The, 1908 … 48
Spiritism, see *The Spiritist*, 1914 … 140
Spiritist, The, 1914 … 140
Spiritisten, see *The Spiritist*, 1914 … 140
Spirits Walk, The, see *When Spirits Walk*, 1913 … 123

Spiritualist, The, see *The Spiritist*, 1914 ... 140
Spiritualistic Meeting, A, 1906 ... 36
Spiritualistic Séance, 1908 ... 48
Spook Ranch, 1925 ... 293
Spooks Do the Moving, 1908 ... 48
Spooks, 1912 ... 102
Spooks, 1922 ... 257
Spooks, 1927 ... 318
Star of India, The, 1913 ... 118
Stark Mad, 1929 ... 345
Strange Case of Princess Khan, The, 1914 ... 140
Strange Unknown, The, 1915 ... 163
Strangers from Nowhere, 1913 ... 118
Strega de Siviglia, Le, see *The Witch of Seville*, 1908 ... 50
Stroke of Midnight, see *The Phantom Carriage*, 1920 ... 228
Student of Prague, The, 1913 ... 119
Student of Prague, The, 1926 ... 307
Student von Prag, Der, see *The Student of Prague*, 1926 ... 307
Student von Prag, Der, see *The Student of Prague*, 1913 ... 119
Suicide Club, The, 1909 ... 62
Suicide Club, The, 1913 ... 120
Suicide Club, The, 1914 ... 140
Supernatural Power, 1912 ... 102
Superstition andalouse, see *Andalusian Superstition*, 1912 ... 91
Suspension, La, see *The Hanging Lamp*, 1908 ... 43
Svengali, 1914 ... 141
Svengali, 1927 ... 319
Sweeney Todd, 1926 ... 307
Sweeney Todd, 1928 ... 332
Sword and the King, The, 1909 ... 63
System of Dr. Tarr and Professor Fether, The, 1912 ... 103
systeme du Docteur Goudron et du Professeur Plume, see *The System of Dr. Tarr and Professor Fether*, 1912 ... 103
Szenzáció, see *Queen of Spades*, 1922 ... 256
Tajemnica taksówki nr 1051, see *The Vampires of Warsaw*, 1925 ... 294
Tales of Horror, see *Weird Tales*, 1919 ... 211
Tales of Monsters, see *A Tale of the Occult*, 1929 ... 346
Tales of the Uncanny, see *Weird Tales*, 1919 ... 211
Tangled Lives, 1917 ... 194
Telltale Heart, The, 1928 ... 332
Tell-Tale Heart, The, see *The Telltale Heart*, 1928 ... 332
Temptations of Satan, The, 1914 ... 141
Tempter, The, 1913 ... 120
Tenancier de saloon's cauchemar, Le, see *The Saloon Keeper's Nightmare*, 1908 ... 46
Tenderfoot's Ghost, The, 1913 ... 121
Tense Moments with Great Authors: Trilby, see *Trilby*, 1922 ... 257
terreurs de Rigadin, Les, 1912 ... 103
terrible bourreau turk, Le, see *The Terrible Turkish Executioner*, 1904 ... 33
Terrible Night, A, 1896 ... 13
Terrible People, The, 1928 ... 332
Terrible Turkish Executioner, The, 1904 ... 33
Terrible Two in Luck, The, 1914 ... 141
Terror Mountain, 1928 ... 333
Terror, see *Terror Mountain*, 1928 ... 333

Terror, The, 1928 ... 333
Testing a Soldier's Courage, 1910 ... 80
Teufel als Rechstanwalt, Der, see *The Devil as a Lawyer*, 1911 ... 83
Teufelsanbeter, Die, see *The Devil Worshippers*, 1920 ... 215
Teufelsschlosser, Der, see *The Devil's Locksmith*, 1919 ... 206
That's the Spirit, 1924 ... 280
Theseus and the Minotaur, see *The Minotaur*, 1910 ... 75
Theseus and the Minotaurus, see *The Minotaur*, 1910 ... 75
Thesus and the Minotaur, see *The Minotaur*, 1910 ... 75
Thief and the Porter's Head, The, 1913 ... 121
Thief in the Dark, A, 1928 ... 334
Thieving Hand, The, 1908 ... 49
Thirteen Club, The, 1905 ... 35
Thirteenth Chair, The, 1919 ... 210
Thirteenth Chair, The, 1929 ... 346
Those Who Dare, 1924 ... 280
Thousand Pound Spook, The, 1907 ... 40
Three Lights, The, see *Destiny*, 1921 ... 233
Three Tales of Terror, see *Trilby*, 1912 ... 103
Three Wax Men, see *Waxworks*, 1924 ... 281
Three Wax Works, The, see *Waxworks*, 1924 ... 281
Three Wishes, The, 1915 ... 163
Through the Centuries, 1914 ... 141
Thy Soul Shall Bear Witness, see *The Phantom Carriage*, 1920 ... 228
Timely Apparition, A, 1909 ... 63
Tis Now the Very Witching Time of Night, 1909 ... 63
To Let, 1919 ... 211
To the River's Depths, see *Call From the Dead*, 1915 ... 144
Togakushi-yama no kijo, 1915 ... 163
Tokaido Yotsuya kaidan, 1927 ... 319
Tom's Vacation, see *Terror Mountain*, 1928
Too Much Champagne, 1908 ... 49
Torgus, the Coffin Maker, 1921 ... 243
Torgus; or, The Coffin Maker, see *Torgus, the Coffin Maker*, 1921 ... 243
Torre del Fantasmi, Le, see *The Tower of the Phantoms*, 1914 ... 141
Torture Cage, The, 1928 ... 334
Totentanz, see *Dance of Death*, 1919 ... 206
Tower of London, The, 1926 ... 308
Tower of the Phantoms, The, 1914 ... 141
Train Fantôme, see *The Ghost Train*, 1927 ... 312
Trance, 1920 ... 231
Treasure of Buddha, The, 1913 ... 121
Treasures of Satan, The, 1902 ... 28
Trembling Hour, The, 1919 ... 211
Trésors de Satan, Les, see *The Treasures of Satan*, 1902 ... 28
Trilby and Svengali, 1911 ... 91
Trilby Death Scene, 1895 ... 11
Trilby Frilled, 1916 ... 179
Trilby Hypnotic Scene, 1895 ... 11
Trilby, 1908 ... 49
Trilby, 1912 ... 103
Trilby, 1913 ... 121
Trilby, 1914 ... 142
Trilby, 1915 ... 164
Trilby, 1922 ... 257

Trilby, 1923 ... 270
Trilogy of Terror, see *Trilby*, 1912 ... 103
Trip to Davey Jones' Locker, A, 1910 ... 80
Trip to Davy Jones' Locker, A, see *A Trip to Davey Jones' Locker*, 1910 ... 80
Tsuchi gumo, 1914 ... 142
Tut-Tut and His Terrible Tomb, 1923 ... 271
Twentieth Century Surgeon, A, 1897 ... 16
Twin Pawns, The, 1919 ... 211
Two Strangers from Nowhere, see *Strangers from Nowhere*, 1913 ... 118
Two-Faced Man, The, see *Der Januskopf*, 1920 ... 224
Two-Soul Woman, The, 1918 ... 202
Tyrant Feudal Lord, The, 1908 ... 50
Ultus 2: The Ambassador's Diamond, see *Ultus, the Man from the Dead*, 1916 ... 180
Ultus 3: The Grey Lady, see *Ultus and the Grey Lady*, 1916 ... 179
Ultus 4: The Traitor's Fate, see *Ultus and the Grey Lady*, 1916 ... 179
Ultus 5: The Secret of the Night, see *Ultus and the Secret of the Night*, 1916 ... 180
Ultus 6: The Three-Button Mystery, see *Ultus and the Three-Button Mystery*, 1917 ... 195
Ultus 7, see *Ultus and the Three-Button Mystery*, 1917 ... 195
Ultus and the Grey Lady, 1916 ... 179
Ultus and the Secret of the Night, 1916 ... 180
Ultus and the Three-Button Mystery, 1917 ... 195
Ultus Seven, see *Ultus and the Three-Button Mystery*, 1917 ... 195
Ultus, the Man from the Dead, 1916 ... 180
 Ultus 1: The Townsend Mystery, see *Ultus, the Man from the Dead*, 1916 ... 180
Uncle Josh in a Spooky Hotel, 1900 ... 23
Uncle Josh's Nightmare, 1900 ... 24
Unconquered, 1917 ... 195
Under the Tide, 1928 ... 334
Unfaithful Wife, The, 1915 ... 164
Unfortunate Marriage, The, see *The Woman in White*, 1917 ... 196
Unheimliche Geschichten, see *Weird Tales*, 1919 ... 211
Unheimlichen Hände des Doktor Orlac, Die, see *Hands of Orlac*, 1924 ... 276
Unholy Love, see *Alraune*, 1928 ... 321
Unholy Night, The, 1929 ... 347
Unholy Three, The, 1925 ... 293
Unknown Country, The, 1914 ... 142
Unknown Treasures, 1926 ... 308
Unknown, The, 1927 ... 319
Unseen Hands, 1924 ... 281
Uomo meccanico, see *The Mechanical Man*, 1921 ... 240
Vampire of the Desert, The, 1913 ... 121
Vampire, The, 1913 ... 121
Vampires de Varsovie, Les, see *The Vampires of Warsaw*, 1925 ... 294
Vampires of Warsaw, The, 1925 ... 294
Veil of Happiness, The, 1923 ... 271
vengeance d'Edgar Poe, Une, see *The Vengeance of Edgar Poe*, 1912 ... 103
Vengeance of Edgar Poe, The, 1912 ... 103
Vengeance of Edgard Poe, The, see *The Vengeance of Edgar Poe*, 1912 ... 103
Vengeance of Egypt, The, 104 ... 104
Vengeance of the Dead, 1910 ... 80
Verlogene Moral, see *Torgus, the Coffin Maker*, 1921 ... 243
Verlorene Ich, see *The Lost Soul*, 1923 ... 264
Verlorene Schatten, Der, see *The Lost Shadow*, 1921 ... 239
Verzauberte Café, Das, see *Haunted Café*, 1911 ... 84
vieux cordonnier, Le, see *The Old Shoemaker*, 1909 ... 60
Vii, see *The Viy*, 1909 ... 63
Vij, The, 1916 ... 180
Village Golem, The, see *The Golem's Last Adventure*, 1921 ... 235
Village Scare, The, 1909 ... 63
Vivisectionist, The, 1915 ... 165
Viy, 1909 ... 63
Vogelod Castle, see *The Haunted Castle*, 1921 ... 235
Voice from the Past, A, see *The Spiritist*, 1914 ... 140
Voice on the Wire, The, 1917 ... 195
Voile du bonheur, La, see *The Veil of Happiness*, 1923 ... 271
Voleur Invisible, Le, see *The Invisible Thief*, 1909 ... 55
Voodoo Fires, 1913 ... 122
Wachsfigurenkabinett, Das, see *Waxworks*, 1924 ... 281
Wages of Sin, An Italian Tragedy, The, 1908 ... 50
Wages of Sin, The, see *The Wages of Sin, An Italian Tragedy*, 1908 ... 50
Wahnsinn, see *Madness*, 1919 ... 208
Waise von Lowood, Die, see *Orphan of Lowood*, 1926 ... 302
Wampiry Warszawa, see *The Vampires of Warsaw*, 1925 ... 294
Wampiry Warszawy, see *The Vampires of Warsaw*, 1925 ... 294
Wanted, a Mummy, see *Wanted—A Mummy*, 1910 ... 80
Wanted—A Mummy, 1910 ... 80
Warning Shadows, 1923 ... 271
Warning, The, 1915 ... 165
Water Devil, The, see *Her Father's Gold*, 1916 ... 172
Wave of Spooks, see *Cave of the Spooks*, 1908 ... 41
Waxworks, 1924 ... 281
Weary Death, The, see *Destiny*, 1921 ... 233
Web of Circumstance, The, see *The Forbidden Room*, 1914 ... 130
Wedding Feast and Ghosts, 1908 ... 50
Weird Tales, 1919 ... 211
Werewolf, The, 1913 ... 122
West Case, The, 1923 ... 272
West of Zanzibar, 1928 ... 335
What an Eye, 1924 ... 282
What the Gods Decree, 1913 ... 123
Wheel of Death, The, 1916 ... 180
When Dr. Quackel Did Hide, see *When Quackel Did Hyde*, 1920 ... 231
When Quackel Did Hide, 1920 ... 231
When Spirits Walk, 1913 ... 123
When Spirits Walked, see *When Spirits Walk*, 1913 ... 123
When the Devil Drives, 1907 ... 41
When the Spirits Moves, 1915 ... 165
Where East Is East, 1929 ... 347
Which is Witch? 1915 ... 165
Whiffle's Nightmare, 1912 ... 104
While John Bolt Slept, 1913 ... 123
While London Sleeps, 1926 ... 308
While Paris Sleeps, 1923 ... 272

Whispering Shadows, 1921 ... 243
Whispering Wires, 1926 ... 309
White Ghost, The, see *The Ghost of the White Lady*, 1913 ... 110
White Wolf, The, 1914 ... 142
Wij, see *The Vij*, 1916 ... 180
Wij, The, see *The Vij*, 1909 ... 63
Wild Ass's Skin, The, 1909 ... 64
Wild Oranges, 1924 ... 282
Willy Fantome, see *Willy the Ghost*, 1911 ... 91
Willy the Ghost, 1911 ... 91
Windsor Castle, 1926 ... 309
Witch of Abruzzi, The, 1911 ... 91
Witch of Salem Town, A, 1915 ... 166
Witch of Salem, The, 1913 ... 123
Witch of Seville, The, 1908 ... 50
Witch of the Glen, The, 1910 ... 80
Witch of the Mountains, The, 1916 ... 180
Witch of the Ruins, The, 1910 ... 80
Witch, The, 1906 ... 37
Witch, The, 1909 ... 64
Witch, The, see *Häxan*, 1922 ... 250
Witch's Ballad, The, see *The Ballad of a Witch*, 1909 ... 51
Witch's Cave, The, 1906 ... 37
Witch's Cavern, The, 1909 ... 64
Witch's Spell, The, see *The Witches' Spell*, 1910 ... 81
Witchcraft Through the Ages, see *Häxan*, 1922 ... 250
Witchcraft, 1916 ... 180
Witches, The, see *Häxan*, 1922 ... 250
Witches' Cavern, The, see *The Witch's Cavern*, 1909 ... 64
Witches' Spell, The, 1910 ... 81
Witching Eyes, The, 1929 ... 348
Witching Hour, The, 1916 ... 181
Witching Hour, The, 1921 ... 243
Without a Soul, see *Lola*, 1914 ... 135
Wizard, The, 1927 ... 320
Wolf Blood, see *Wolf Blood: A Tale of the Forest*, 1925 ... 295
Wolf Blood: A Tale of the Forest, 1925 ... 295
Woman in White, The, 1912 ... 104
Woman in White, The, 1917 ... 196
Woman in White, The, 1929 ... 348
Woman of Atlantis, A, see *Missing Husbands*, 1921 ... 241
Woman of Fire, see *Beelzebub's Daughters*, 1903 ... 29
Woman of Mystery, The, 1914 ... 143
Women of Fire, The, see *Beelzebub's Daughters*, 1903 ... 29
Wonderful Pearl, The, 1909 ... 64
Wonders of the Deep, see *The Kingdom of Fairies*, 1903 ... 31
Woodcroft Castle, 1926 ... 309
Wraith of Haddon Towers, The, 1915 ... 166
Wraith of the Tomb, The, see *The Avenging Hand*, 1915 ... 144
yazisi Portret Doryana Greya, Alt, see *The Picture of Dorian Gray*, 1915 ... 159
Yellow Claw, The, 1920 ... 231
Yellow Peril, see *Chinese Magic*, 1900 ... 22
Yoma kidan, see *A Tale of the Occult*, 1929 ... 346
Yoshiwara kaidan: Kozakura choji, 1913 ... 124
Yoshiwara kaidan: Teburi bozu, 1914 ... 143
Yotsuya Ghost Story New Edition, see *New Version of the Ghost of Yotsuya*, 1928 ... 328
Yotsuya kaidan jitsuhi kanetani goro, 1918 ... 202
Yotsuya kaidan Oiwa, 1923 ... 273
Yotsuya kaidan, 1912 ... 105
Yotsuya kaidan, 1921 ... 244
Yotsuya kaidan, 1923 ... 272
Yotsuya kaidan, 1925 ... 295
Yotsuya kaidan, 1928 ... 336
Youma kitan, see *A Tale of the Occult*, 1929 ... 346
Yurei yashiki, 1915 ... 166
Zigo, see *The Hypnotic Violinist*, 1914 ... 133
Zone of Death, The, 1928 ... 336

If you enjoyed this book, send $2.00 for a catalog of Midnight Marquee Press titles or visit our website at http://www.midmar.com

Midnight Marquee Press, Inc.
9721 Britinay Lane
Parkville, Md 21234
410-665-1198
mmarquee@aol.com

www.ingramcontent.com/pod-product-compliance
Lightning Source LLC
Chambersburg PA
CBHW081718100526

44591CB00016B/2411